Lizhu Zhou   Beng Chin Ooi
Xiaofeng Meng (Eds.)

Database Systems for Advanced Applications

10th International Conference, DASFAA 2005
Beijing, China, April 17-20, 2005
Proceedings

Volume Editors

Lizhu Zhou
Tsinghua University
Department of Computer Science
Beijing, 100084, China
E-mail: dcszlz@tsinghua.edu.cn

Beng Chin Ooi
National University of Singapore
School of Computing, Department of Computer Science
Kent Ridge, 117543, Singapore
E-mail: ooibc@comp.nus.edu.sg

Xiaofeng Meng
Renmin University
School of Information
59 Zhongguancun Road, Beijing, 100872, China
E-mail: xfmeng@ruc.edu.cn

Library of Congress Control Number: 2005923495

CR Subject Classification (1998): H.2, H.3, H.4, H.5.1, H.5.4

ISSN   0302-9743
ISBN-10   3-540-25334-3 Springer Berlin Heidelberg New York
ISBN-13   978-3-540-25334-1 Springer Berlin Heidelberg New York

This work is subject to copyright. All rights are reserved, whether the whole or part of the material is concerned, specifically the rights of translation, reprinting, re-use of illustrations, recitation, broadcasting, reproduction on microfilms or in any other way, and storage in data banks. Duplication of this publication or parts thereof is permitted only under the provisions of the German Copyright Law of September 9, 1965, in its current version, and permission for use must always be obtained from Springer. Violations are liable to prosecution under the German Copyright Law.

Springer is a part of Springer Science+Business Media

springeronline.com

© Springer-Verlag Berlin Heidelberg 2005
Printed in Germany

Typesetting: Camera-ready by author, data conversion by Scientific Publishing Services, Chennai, India
Printed on acid-free paper   SPIN: 11408079   06/3142   5 4 3 2 1 0

Lecture Notes in Computer Science 3453

Commenced Publication in 1973
Founding and Former Series Editors:
Gerhard Goos, Juris Hartmanis, and Jan van Leeuwen

Editorial Board

David Hutchison
  Lancaster University, UK
Takeo Kanade
  Carnegie Mellon University, Pittsburgh, PA, USA
Josef Kittler
  University of Surrey, Guildford, UK
Jon M. Kleinberg
  Cornell University, Ithaca, NY, USA
Friedemann Mattern
  ETH Zurich, Switzerland
John C. Mitchell
  Stanford University, CA, USA
Moni Naor
  Weizmann Institute of Science, Rehovot, Israel
Oscar Nierstrasz
  University of Bern, Switzerland
C. Pandu Rangan
  Indian Institute of Technology, Madras, India
Bernhard Steffen
  University of Dortmund, Germany
Madhu Sudan
  Massachusetts Institute of Technology, MA, USA
Demetri Terzopoulos
  New York University, NY, USA
Doug Tygar
  University of California, Berkeley, CA, USA
Moshe Y. Vardi
  Rice University, Houston, TX, USA
Gerhard Weikum
  Max-Planck Institute of Computer Science, Saarbruecken, Germany

Foreword

On behalf of the Organizing Committee, we would like to welcome you to the proceedings of the 10th International Conference on Database Systems for Advanced Applications (DASFAA 2005). This conference provides an international forum for technical discussion among researchers, developers and users of database systems from academia, business and industry. DASFAA focuses on research in database theory, and the development and applications of advanced DBMS technologies. This was the second time that this conference has been held in China, the first time was in Hong Kong in 2001. China is the third largest nation in terms of size, with the largest population in the world. The capital, Beijing, is a great metropolis, famous in Asia and throughout the world. We therefore were most privileged to host this conference in this renowned location.

This volume contains papers selected for presentation and includes the three keynote talks, by Dr. Philip Yu, Prof. Elisa Bertino and Prof. Deyi Li.

The conference also featured two tutorials: (1) Data Mining Techniques for Microarray Datasets, by Lei Liu, Jiong Yang and Anthony Tung, and (2) Pattern Management: Models, Languages, and Architectural Issues, by Barbara Catania. The technical program of the conference was selected by a distinguished Program Committee led by two PC Co-chairs, Lizhu Zhou and Beng Chin Ooi. The 89 members, half of whom reside outside Asia, made the committee a truly international one. They faced a difficult task in selecting 67 regular papers and 15 short papers from many very good contributions. This year the number of submissions, 302, was a record high for DASFAA conferences since the first conference held in 1989 in Seoul, Korea. We wish to express our thanks to the Program Committee members, external reviewers, and all authors for submitting their papers to this conference.

We would also like to thank the Honorary Conference Chair, Shan Wang; the Program Co-chairs, Lizhu Zhou and Beng Chin Ooi; the Geographic Area Chairs, Yoshifumi Masunaga, Sang Kyun Cha, Chin-Chen Chang, David Cheung, Yanchun Zhang, Vilas Wuwongse, Mukesh Mohania, Mong Li Lee, Gillian Dobbie, Stefano Spaccapietra, David Embley and Mengchi Liu; the Tutorial Co-chairs, Jayant Haritsa and Ge Yu; the Panel Co-chairs, Changjie Tang and Jeffrey Yu Xu; the Publicity Co-chairs, Liang Zhang and Katsumi Tanaka; the Publication Co-chairs, Xiaofeng Meng and Qing Li; the Finance Co-chairs, Kam-Fai Wong and Chunxiao Xing; the Local Arrangements Co-chairs, Jianhua Feng and Tengjiao Wang; the Registration Chair, Aoying Zhou; the Conference Secretary, Chao Li; and the System Administrator, Sinan Zhan.

We wish to extend our thanks to the National Natural Science Foundation of China, Microsoft Research Asia, IBM, HP, the Special Interest Group on Databases of the Korea Information Science Society (KISS SIGDB), and the Database Society of Japan (DBSJ), for their sponsorship and support.

At this juncture, we wish to remember the late Prof. Yahiko Kambayashi who passed away on February 5, 2004 at age 60. He was a founder, member, Vice Chair and Chair of the Steering Committee of the DASFAA conference. Many of us will remember him as a friend, a mentor, a leader, an educator, and our source of inspiration. We express our heartfelt condolences and our deepest sympathy to his family.

We hope that you will find the technical program of DASFAA 2005 to be interesting and beneficial to your research. We trust attendees enjoyed Beijing and visited some famous historic places, such as the Badaling section of the Great Wall, the Forbidden City, the Temple of Heaven, etc., and left with a beautiful and memorable experience.

April 2005

Tok Wang Ling
Jianzhong Li

Preface

The 10th International Conference on Database Systems for Advanced Applications (DASFAA 2005) was held in Beijing, China, from April 18 to 20, 2005. Beijing is an ancient city whose recorded history stretches back more than 3,000 years. With a landscape dotted with ancient palaces and temples in the midst of modern infrastructure and architecture, the Chinese capital city is indeed a good venue for a forum of serious academic and professional exchanges, and an ideal place for meaningful entertainment and cultural immersion on the side.

In keeping with the traditions of the conference, DASFAA 2005 provided an international forum for technical discussion among researchers, developers and users from all walks of life. The conference, which was organized by Tsinghua University and the Database Society of the China Computer Federation, aimed to promote database research and applications.

The reputation of the conference has been rising since its inception. This is apparent in the increasing number of submissions it has received over the years, and the expanding number of participants from various parts of the world. This year, the conference received 302 submissions from 20 countries/regions. The papers were rigorously reviewed by 89 Program Committee members, and 67 full papers and 15 short papers were accepted for presentation.

Being a general database conference, the areas addressed by the papers were diverse. While many papers continued to address interesting and new research issues in established areas such as XML, data mining, and spatial and temporal databases, a significant number of papers explored interesting research issues in upcoming areas such as watermarking and encryption, sensor databases, bioinformatics and Web services. The combination of papers, which had been selected solely based on reviews, not only made the conference interesting, but also provided the basis for discussion and exchange of ideas, and for future development.

The conference was privileged to have keynote speeches delivered by Philip Yu of IBM's T.J. Watson Research Center, Elisa Bertino of Purdue University, USA, and Deyi Li of the China Institute of Electronic Systems Engineering. They provided insights into various research issues such as data mining, and database security and privacy, and presented provocative challenges on related research issues. The program was made even more interesting by having panelists such as Divyakant Agrawal, Elisa Bertino and Limsoon Wong provide their views and comments on research issues in data mining on a panel chaired by Haixun Wang and Wei Wang.

The technical program was preceded by two tutorials before the conference proper. The tutorial on Pattern Management: Models, Languages, and Architectural Issues by Barbara Catania was an interesting primer for participants who might be new to the research area of knowledge management. The tutorial on Data Mining Techniques for Microarray Datasets by Lei Liu, Jiong Yang and

Anthony Tung provided a refreshing view of the research domain of data mining and bioinformatics.

In all, DASFAA 2005 lived up to the traditions of the conference as an international forum for fruitful technical discussion. And Beijing, with its vibrant blend of rich cultural heritage and dynamic modernity, was a superb background to the proceedings.

The conference would not have been a success without the help and contributions of many individuals, and our sincere thanks go to them. We would like to express our thanks to the conference General Chairs, Jianzhong Li and Tok Wang Ling; Tutorial Co-chairs, Jayant Harista and Ge Yu; Panel Co-chairs, Changjie Tang and Jeffrey Yu; Publication Co-chairs, Xiaofeng Meng and Qing Li; and others in the organizing committees for helping to put together such a great program. We would like to thank the Program Committee members and external reviewers for their rigorous and timely reviews. We would also like to thank the keynote speakers, session chairs, panelists, tutorial speakers, authors and participants who contributed to making the conference a success.

Lizhu Zhou
Beng Chin Ooi

DASFAA 2005 Conference Committee

Honorary Chair

Shan Wang   Renmin University of China, China

General Conference Co-chairs

Jianzhong Li   Harbin Institute of Technology, China
Tok Wang Ling   National University of Singapore, Singapore

Program Committee Co-chairs

Lizhu Zhou   Tsinghua University, China
Beng Chin Ooi   National University of Singapore, Singapore

Tutorial Co-chairs

Jayant Haritsa   Indian Institute of Science, India
Ge Yu   Northeastern University, China

Panel Co-chairs

Changjie Tang   Sichuan University, China
Jeffrey Yu Xu   Chinese Univ. of Hong Kong, Hong Kong, China

Publicity Co-chairs

Liang Zhang   Fudan University, China
Katsumi Tanaka   Kyoto University, Japan

Publications Co-chairs

Xiaofeng Meng   Renmin University of China, China
Qing Li   City University of Hong Kong, Hong Kong, China

Finance Co-chairs

Kam-Fai Wong Chinese Univ. of Hong Kong, Hong Kong, China
Chunxiao Xing Tsinghua University, China

Local Arrangements Co-chairs

Jianhua Feng Tsinghua University, China
Tengjiao Wang Beijing University, China

Registration Chair

Aoying Zhou Fudan University, China

Geographic Area Chairs

Japan
    Yoshifumi Masunaga Ochanomizu University, Japan
Korea
    Sang Kyun Cha Seoul National University, Korea
Taiwan
    Chin-Chen Chang National Chung Cheng University, Taiwan
Hong Kong
    David Cheung Hong Kong University, Hong Kong, China
Australia
    Yanchun Zhang Victoria University, Australia
Thailand
    Vilas Wuwongse Asian Institute of Technology, Thailand
India
    Mukesh Mohania IBM India Research Lab, India
Singapore
    Mong Li Lee National University of Singapore, Singapore
New Zealand
    Gillian Dobbie University of Auckland, New Zealand
Europe
    Stefano Spaccapietra EPFL Lausanne, Switzerland
Americas
    David W. Embley Brigham Young University, USA
Canada
    Mengchi Liu Carleton University, Canada

Conference Secretary

Chao Li   Tsinghua University, China

Conference Web Master

Sinan Zhan   Tsinghua University, China

DASFAA Steering Committee

Tok Wang Ling (Chair)	National Univ. of Singapore, Singapore
Yoshifumi Masunaga (Vice Chair)	Ochanomizu Univ., Japan
Arbee L.P. Chen	National Dong Hwa University, Taiwan
Yoshihiko Imai (Treasurer)	Matsushita Electric Industrial Co., Japan
Fred Lochovsky	HKUST, China
Seog Park	Sogang Univ., Korea
Ron Sacks-Davis	RMIT, Australia
Wang Shan	Renmin Univ., China
Katsumi Tanaka	Kyoto Univ., Japan
Kyhyun Um	Dongkuk Univ., Korea
Kyu-Young Whang (Secretary)	KAIST/AITrc, Korea

DASFAA 2005 Program Committee

Dave Abel	CSIRO, Australia
Karl Aberer	EPFL-DSC, Switzerland
Divyakant Agrawal	University of California at Santa Barbara, USA
Gustavo Alonso	ETH Zurich, Switzerland
Walid G. Aref	Purdue University, USA
Paolo Atzeni	Dipart. Informatica e Automazione Univ. Roma Tre, Italy
Elisa Bertino	Purdue University, USA
Tolga Bozkaya	Oracle, USA
Barbara Catania	University of Genoa, Italy
Sang K. Cha	Seoul National University, Korea
Arbee L.P. Chen	National Dong Hwa University, Taiwan
Ming-Syan Chen	National Taiwan University, Taiwan
David Cheung	University of Hong Kong, Hong Kong, China
Peter Dadam	University of Ulm, Germany
Wei Fan	IBM T.J. Watson Research Center, USA
Hong Gao	Harbin Institute of Technology, China
Jiawei Han	University of Illinois at Urbana-Champaign, USA
Bonghee Hong	Pusan University, Korea
Wei Hong	Intel Research Berkeley, USA
Zhiyong Huang	National University of Singapore, Singapore
Zachary Ives	University of Pennsylvania, USA
Christian S. Jensen	Aalborg University, Denmark
Kamal Karlapalem	IIIT Hyderabad, India
Norio Katayama	National Institute of Informatics, Japan
Daniel A. Keim	University of Constance, Germany
Hiroyuki Kitagawa	Tsukuba University, Japan
Wolfgang Klas	University of Vienna, Austria
George Kollios	Boston University, USA
Nick Koudas	AT&T Research, USA
Dik Lun Lee	Hong Kong Univ. of Science and Technology, Hong Kong, China
Mong Li Lee	National University of Singapore, Singapore
YoonJoon Lee	KAIST, Korea
Chen Li	University of California at Irvine, USA
Ee-Peng Lim	Nanyang Technological University, Singapore
Qiong Luo	Hong Kong Univ. of Science and Technology, Hong Kong, China
Akifumi Makinouchi	Kyushu University, Japan
Yannis Manolopoulos	Aristotle University, Greece
Alberto Mendelzon	University of Toronto, Canada

Weiyi Meng	State University of New York at Binghamton, USA
Xiaofeng Meng	Renmin University of China, China
Anirban Mondal	Tokyo University, Japan
Yunmook Nah	Dankook University, Korea
Sham Navathe	Georgia Institute of Technology, USA
Erich J. Neuhold	University of Darmstadt, Germany
Yong-Chul Oh	Korea Polytechnic University, Korea
M. Tamer Özsu	University of Waterloo, Canada
Dimitris Papadias	Hong Kong Univ. of Science and Technology, Hong Kong, China
Jignesh M. Patel	University of Michigan, USA
Marco Patella	University of Bologna, Italy
Zhiyong Peng	Wuhan University, China
Evaggelia Pitoura	University of Ioannina, Greece
Sunil Prabhakar	Purdue University, USA
Calton Pu	College of Computing, Georgia Tech, USA
Krithi Ramamritham	IIT Bombay, India
Rajeev Rastogi	Bell Labs Lucent, USA
HengTao Shen	University of Queensland, Australia
Kyuseok Shim	Seoul National University, Korea
Charles A. Shoniregun	University of East London, UK
Divesh Srivastava	AT&T Labs Research, USA
Jaideep Srivastava	University of Minnesota, USA
Jianwen Su	University of California at Santa Barbara, USA
S. Sudarshan	IIT Bombay, India
Hideaki Sugawara	National Institute of Genetics, Japan
Kian-Lee Tan	National University of Singapore, Singapore
Changjie Tang	Sichuan University, China
Yufei Tao	City University of Hong Kong, Hong Kong, China
Yannis Theodoridis	University of Athens, Greece
Anthony K.H. Tung	National University of Singapore, Singapore
Ozgur Ulusoy	Bilkent University, Turkey
Athena Vakali	Aristotle University, Greece
Guoren Wang	Northeast University, China
Xiaoling Wang	Fudan University, China
Yan Wang	Macquarie University, Australia
Kyu-Young Whang	KAIST, Korea
Peter Widmayer	ETH Zurich, Switzerland
Weili Wu	University of Texas at Dallas, USA
Dongqing Yang	Peking University, China
Jiong Yang	UIUC, USA
Jun Yang	Duke University, USA
Haruo Yokota	Tokyo Institute of Technology, Japan

Masatoshi Yoshikawa	Nagoya University, Japan
Clement Yu	University of Chicago, USA
Cui Yu	Monmouth University, USA
Ge Yu	Northeast University, China
Jeffrey Yu	Chinese Univ. of Hong Kong, Hong Kong, China
Philip S. Yu	IBM T.J. Watson Research Center, USA
Aoying Zhou	Fudan University, China
Xiaofang Zhou	University of Queensland, Australia
Justin Zobel	RMIT, Australia

DASFAA 2005 External Reviewers

Ahmed Metwally
Aixin Sun
Alexander Markowetz
Alexandros Nanopoulos
Andrew Innes
Anna Maddalena
Antonio Corral
Anwitaman Datta
Apostolos N. Papadopoulos
Avare Stewart
Bendick Mahleko
Bin Lin
Bin Wang
Bingsheng He
Cagdas Gerede
Can Lin
Chao Liu
Chen Guanhua
Chen Jidong
Chen Yan
Cheng-Enn Hsieh
Cheqing Jin
Chih-Kang Yeh
Ching Chang
Christian Thomsen
Chuan Yang
Chunnian Liu
Claudia Niederee
Depeng Dang
Ding-Ying Chiu
Dongdong Zhang
Dong-Hoon Choi
Edgar Chia-Han Lin
Evimaria Terzi
Fabius Klemm
Fang Liu
Fariborz Farahmand
Fatih Emekci
Feifei Li
Feng Yaokai
Francesca Odone

Manfred Reichert
Manish Tayal
Marco Mesiti
Maria Kontaki
Maria Luisa Damiani
Mark Cameron
Michael Vassilakopoulos
Ming Yung
Mintz Hsieh
Mohamed G. Elfeky
Mohamed Mokbel
Mourad Ouzzani
Moustafa Hammad
Na Ta
Natwar Modani
Nicholas Lester
Nikos Pelekis
Ning Zhang
Nobuto Inoguchi
Norihide Shinagawa
Norimasa Terada
Oleksandr Drutskyy
Ozgur D. Sahin
Panagiotis Papapetrou
Paolo Cappellari
Paolo Missier
Patrick Wolf
Peter Lamb
Pierluigi Del Nostro
Ralph Bobrik
Ranga Raju Vatsavai
Ravikant
Ravindranath Jampani
Reynold Cheng
Risi V. Thonangi
Roman Schmidt
Sangyong Hwang
Sarunas Girdzijauskas
Sarvjeet Singh
Satoru Miyazaki
Satyanarayana R. Valluri

Georgia Koloniari
Giansalvatore Mecca
Giuseppe Sindoni
Gleb Skobeltsyn
Guimei Liu
Guo Longjiang
Guoliang Li
Hicham Elmongui
Holger Brocks
Hong Cheng
Hong-Hoon Choi
Hongjian Fan
Huagang Li
Hua-Gang Li
Huan Huo
Hung-Chen Chen
Igor Timko
Irene Ntoutsi
Ismail Sengor Altingovde
Jaeyun Noh
Janaka Balasoorya
Jeff Riley
Jeiwei Huang
Jhansi Rani Vennam
Jiang Yu
Jie Wu
Jing Zhao
Ji-Woong Chang
Jun Gao
Junghoo Cho
Junmei Wang
Ken-Hao Liu
Kenji Hatano
Kunihiko Kaneko
Kyriakos Mouratidis
Kyuhwan Kim
Leonardo Tininini
Li Benchao
Li Juanzi
Li Zhao
Liang Zhang
Madhu Govindaraju
Magdalena Punceva

Soujanya Vadapalli
Spiridon Bakiras
Stefano Rovetta
Sungheun Wi
Sunil Prabhakar
Takashi Abe
Tengjiao Wang
Thanaa Ghanem
Toshiyuki Amagasa
Toshiyuki Shimizu
Tzu-Chiang Wu
Vincent Oria
Wai Lam
Wanhong Xu
Wanxia Xie
Wee Hyong Tok
Wei Liu
Weining Qian
Wenwei Xue
Wenyuan Cai
Wynne Hsu
Xiang Lian
Xiaochun Yang
Xiaopeng Xiong
Xiuli Ma
Xiuzhen Zhang
Yannis Karydis
Yao-Chung Fan
Yicheng Tu
Yi-Hung Wu
Yin Shaoyi
Yin Yang
Ying Feng
Ying-yi Chen
Yongsik Yoon
Yoshiharu Ishikawa
Younggoo Cho
Young-Koo Lee
Yu Wang
Yuguo Liao
Yunfeng Liu
Yuni Xia
Zhaogong Zhang

Lin Li
Linus Chang
Longxiang Zhou
M.H. Ali
M.Y. Eltabakh
Ma Xiujun

Zheng Shao
Zhi-Hong Deng
Zhiming Ding
Zhongfei Zhang
Zhongnan Shen

Table of Contents

Keynotes

Data Stream Mining and Resource Adaptive Computation
  Philip S. Yu 1

Purpose Based Access Control for Privacy Protection in Database Systems
  Elisa Bertino 2

Complex Networks and Network Data Mining
  Deyi Li 3

Bioinformatics

Indexing DNA Sequences Using q-Grams
  Xia Cao, Shuai Cheng Li, Anthony K.H. Tung 4

PADS: Protein Structure Alignment Using Directional Shape Signatures
  S. Alireza Aghili, Divyakant Agrawal, Amr El Abbadi 17

LinkageTracker: A Discriminative Pattern Tracking Approach to Linkage Disequilibrium Mapping
  Li Lin, Limsoon Wong, Tzeyun Leong, Pohsan Lai 30

Watermarking and Encryption

Query Optimization in Encrypted Database Systems
  Hakan Hacıgümüş, Bala Iyer, Sharad Mehrotra 43

Watermarking Spatial Trajectory Database
  Xiaoming Jin, Zhihao Zhang, Jianmin Wang, Deyi Li 56

Effective Approaches for Watermarking XML Data
  Wilfred Ng, Ho-Lam Lau 68

XML Query Processing

A Unifying Framework for Merging and Evaluating XML Information
  Ho-Lam Lau, Wilfred Ng 81

Efficient Evaluation of Partial Match Queries for XML Documents
Using Information Retrieval Techniques
    Young-Ho Park, Kyu-Young Whang, Byung Suk Lee,
    Wook-Shin Han... 95

PathStack¬: A Holistic Path Join Algorithm for Path Query with
Not-Predicates on XML Data
    Enhua Jiao, Tok Wang Ling, Chee-Yong Chan 113

XML Coding and Metadata Management

An Improved Prefix Labeling Scheme: A Binary String Approach for
Dynamic Ordered XML
    Changqing Li, Tok Wang Ling 125

Efficiently Coding and Indexing XML Document
    Zhongming Han, Congting Xi, Jiajin Le 138

XQuery-Based TV-Anytime Metadata Management
    Jong-Hyun Park, Byung-Kyu Kim, Yong-Hee Lee, Min-Woo Lee,
    Min-Ok Jung, Ji-Hoon Kang 151

Data Mining

Effective Database Transformation and Efficient Support Computation
for Mining Sequential Patterns
    Chung-Wen Cho, Yi-Hung Wu, Arbee L.P. Chen 163

Mining Succinct Systems of Minimal Generators of Formal Concepts
    Guozhu Dong, Chunyu Jiang, Jian Pei, Jinyan Li,
    Limsoon Wong 175

A General Approach to Mining Quality Pattern-Based Clusters from
Microarray Data
    Daxin Jiang, Jian Pei, Aidong Zhang 188

Data Generation and Understanding

Real Datasets for File-Sharing Peer-to-Peer Systems
    Shen Tat Goh, Panos Kalnis, Spiridon Bakiras,
    Kian-Lee Tan 201

SemEQUAL: Multilingual Semantic Matching in Relational Systems
    A. Kumaran, Jayant R. Haritsa 214

A Metropolis Sampling Method for Drawing Representative Samples
from Large Databases
  Hong Guo, Wen-Chi Hou, Feng Yan, Qiang Zhu 226

Panel

Stay Current and Relevant in Data Mining Research
  Haixun Wang, Wei Wang 239

Music Retrieval

An Efficient Approach to Extracting Approximate Repeating Patterns
in Music Databases
  Ning-Han Liu, Yi-Hung Wu, Arbee L.P. Chen 240

On Efficient Music Genre Classification
  Jialie Shen, John Shepherd, Anne H.H Ngu 253

Effectiveness of Note Duration Information for Music Retrieval
  Iman S.H. Suyoto, Alexandra L. Uitdenbogerd 265

Query Processing in Subscription Systems

A Self-Adaptive Model to Improve Average Response Time of
Multiple-Event Filtering for Pub/Sub System
  Botao Wang, Wang Zhang, Masaru Kitsuregawa 276

Filter Indexing: A Scalable Solution to Large Subscription Based
Systems
  Wanxia Xie, Shamkant B. Navathe, Sushil K. Prasad 288

Caching Strategies for Push-Based Broadcast Considering Consecutive
Data Accesses with Think-Time
  Wataru Uchida, Takahiro Hara, Shojiro Nishio 300

Extending XML

XDO2: A Deductive Object-Oriented Query Language for XML
  Wei Zhang, Tok Wang Ling, Zhuo Chen, Gillian Dobbie 311

Extending XML with Nonmonotonic Multiple Inheritance
  Guoren Wang, Mengchi Liu 323

Database Design with Equality-Generating Dependencies
    Junhu Wang 335

Web Services

WDEE: Web Data Extraction by Example
    Zhao Li, Wee Kong Ng 347

Concept-Based Retrieval of Alternate Web Services
    Dunlu Peng, Sheng Huang, Xiaoling Wang, Aoying Zhou 359

WSQuery: XQuery for Web Services Integration
    Zhimao Guo, Xiaoling Wang, Aoying Zhou 372

High-Dimensional Indexing

A New Indexing Method for High Dimensional Dataset
    Jiyuan An, Yi-Ping Phoebe Chen, Qinying Xu, Xiaofang Zhou 385

BM^+-Tree: A Hyperplane-Based Index Method for High-Dimensional Metric Spaces
    Xiangmin Zhou, Guoren Wang, Xiaofang Zhou, Ge Yu 398

Approaching the Efficient Frontier: Cooperative Database Retrieval Using High-Dimensional Skylines
    Wolf-Tilo Balke, Jason Xin Zheng, Ulrich Güntzer 410

Sensor and Stream Data Processing

False-Negative Frequent Items Mining from Data Streams with Bursting
    Zhihong Chong, Jeffrey Xu Yu, Hongjun Lu, Zhengjie Zhang, Aoying Zhou 422

Adaptively Detecting Aggregation Bursts in Data Streams
    Aoying Zhou, Shouke Qin, Weining Qian 435

Communication-Efficient Implementation of Join in Sensor Networks
    Vishal Chowdhary, Himanshu Gupta 447

Database Performance Issues

Zoned-RAID for Multimedia Database Servers
    Ali E. Dashti, Seon Ho Kim, Roger Zimmermann 461

Randomized Data Allocation in Scalable Streaming Architectures
  Kun Fu, Roger Zimmermann 474

Trace System of iSCSI Storage Access and Performance Improvement
  Saneyasu Yamaguchi, Masato Oguchi, Masaru Kitsuregawa 487

COCACHE: Query Processing Based on Collaborative Caching in P2P Systems
  Weining Qian, Linhao Xu, Shuigeng Zhou, Aoying Zhou 498

Clustering, Classification and Data Warehouses

Multi-represented kNN-Classification for Large Class Sets
  Hans-Peter Kriegel, Alexey Pryakhin, Matthias Schubert 511

Enhancing SNNB with Local Accuracy Estimation and Ensemble Techniques
  Zhipeng Xie, Qing Zhang, Wynne Hsu, Mong Li Lee 523

MMPClust: A Skew Prevention Algorithm for Model-Based Document Clustering
  Xiaoguang Li, Ge Yu, Daling Wang 536

Designing and Using Views to Improve Performance of Aggregate Queries
  Foto Afrati, Rada Chirkova, Shalu Gupta, Charles Loftis 548

Large Relations in Node-Partitioned Data Warehouses
  Pedro Furtado 555

Data Mining and Web Data Processing

Mining Frequent Tree-Like Patterns in Large Datasets
  Tzung-Shi Chen, Shih-Chun Hsu 561

An Efficient Approach for Mining Fault-Tolerant Frequent Patterns Based on Bit Vector Representations
  Jia-Ling Koh, Pei-Wy Yo 568

NNF: An Effective Approach in Medicine Paring Analysis of Traditional Chinese Medicine Prescriptions
  *Chuan Li, Changjie Tang, Jing Peng, Jianjun Hu,
  Yongguang Jiang, Xiaojia Yong* 576

From XML to Semantic Web
  Changqing Li, Tok Wang Ling 582

A Hybrid Approach for Refreshing Web Page Repositories
  *Mohammad Ghodsi, Oktie Hassanzadeh, Shahab Kamali,
  Morteza Monemizadeh* 588

Schema Driven and Topic Specific Web Crawling
  Qi Guo, Hang Guo, Zhiqiang Zhang, Jing Sun, Jianhua Feng 594

Moving Object Databases

Towards Optimal Utilization of Main Memory for Moving Object Indexing
  Bin Cui, Dan Lin, Kian-Lee Tan 600

Aqua: An Adaptive QUery-Aware Location Updating Scheme for Mobile Objects
  Jing Zhou, Hong Va Leong, Qin Lu, Ken C.K. Lee 612

A Spatial Index Using MBR Compression and Hashing Technique for Mobile Map Service
  Jin-Deog Kim, Sang-Ho Moon, Jin-Oh Choi 625

Temporal Databases

Indexing and Querying Constantly Evolving Data Using Time Series Analysis
  Yuni Xia, Sunil Prabhakar, Jianzhong Sun, Shan Lei 637

Mining Generalized Spatio-Temporal Patterns
  Junmei Wang, Wynne Hsu, Mong Li Lee 649

Exploiting Temporal Correlation in Temporal Data Warehouses
  Ying Feng, Hua-Gang Li, Divyakant Agrawal, Amr El Abbadi 662

Semantics

Semantic Characterization of Real World Events
  Aparna Nagargadde, Sridhar Varadarajan, Krithi Ramamritham 675

Learning Tree Augmented Naive Bayes for Ranking
  Liangxiao Jiang, Harry Zhang, Zhihua Cai, Jiang Su 688

Finding Hidden Semantics Behind Reference Linkpages: An Ontological
Approach for Scientific Digital Libraries
  Peixiang Zhao, Ming Zhang, Dongqing Yang, Shiwei Tang 699

XML Update and Query Patterns

XANDY: Detecting Changes on Large Unordered XML Documents
Using Relational Databases
  Erwin Leonardi, Sourav S. Bhowmick, Sanjay Madria 711

FASST Mining: Discovering Frequently Changing Semantic Structure
from Versions of Unordered XML Documents
  Qiankun Zhao, Sourav S. Bhowmick 724

Mining Positive and Negative Association Rules from XML Query
Patterns for Caching
  Ling Chen, Sourav S. Bhowmick, Liang-Tien Chia 736

Join Processing and View Management

Distributed Intersection Join of Complex Interval Sequences
  Hans-Peter Kriegel, Peter Kunath, Martin Pfeifle, Matthias Renz 748

Using Prefix-Trees for Efficiently Computing Set Joins
  Ravindranath Jampani, Vikram Pudi 761

Maintaining Semantics in the Design of Valid and Reversible
SemiStructured Views
  Ya Bing Chen, Tok Wang Ling, Mong Li Lee 773

Spatial Databases

DCbot: Finding Spatial Information on the Web
  *Mihály Jakob, Matthias Grossmann, Daniela Nicklas,
  Bernhard Mitschang* 779

Improving Space-Efficiency in Temporal Text-Indexing
  Kjetil Nørvåg, Albert Overskeid Nybø 791

Nearest Neighbours Search Using the PM-Tree
  Tomáš Skopal, Jaroslav Pokorný, Vášclav Snášel 803

Enhancing Database Services

Deputy Mechanism for Workflow Views
  Zhe Shan, Qing Li, Yi Luo, Zhiyong Peng 816

Automatic Data Extraction from Data-Rich Web Pages
  Dongdong Hu, Xiaofeng Meng 828

Customer Information Visualization via Customer Map
  Ji Young Woo, Sung Min Bae, Chong Un Pyon, Sang Chan Park 840

Finding and Analyzing Database User Sessions
  Qingsong Yao, Aijun An, Xiangji Huang 851

Recovery and Correctness

Time-Cognizant Recovery Processing for Embedded Real-Time
Databases
  Guoqiong Liao, Yunsheng Liu, Yingyuan Xiao 863

An Efficient Phantom Protection Method for Multi-dimensional Index
Structures
  Seok Il Song, Seok Jae Lee, Tae Ho Kang, Jae Soo Yoo 875

CMC: Combining Multiple Schema-Matching Strategies Based on
Credibility Prediction
  KeWei Tu, Yong Yu 888

XML Databases and Indexing

Translating XQuery to SQL Based on Query Forests
  Ya-Hui Chang, Greg Liu, Sue-Shain Wu 894

A New Indexing Structure to Speed Up Processing XPath Queries
  Jeong Hee Hwang, Van Trang Nguyen, Keun Ho Ryu 900

Translate Graphical XML Query Language to SQLX
  Wei Ni, Tok Wang Ling 907

GTree: An Efficient Grid-Based Index for Moving Objects
  Xiaoyuan Wang, Qing Zhang, Weiwei Sun 914

Adaptive Multi-level Hashing for Moving Objects
  Dongseop Kwon, Sangjun Lee, Wonik Choi, Sukho Lee 920

Author Index 927

Data Stream Mining and Resource Adaptive Computation

Philip S. Yu

IBM T.J. Watson Research Center,
19 Skyline Drive,
Hawthorne, NY 10532
psyu@us.ibm.com

Abstract. The problem of data streams has gained importance in recent years because of advances in hardware technology. These advances have made it easy to store and record numerous transactions and activities in everyday life in an automated way. The ubiquitous presence of data streams in a number of practical domains has generated a lot of research in this area. Example applications include trade surveillance for security fraud and money laundering, network monitoring for intrusion detection, bio-surveillance for terrorist attack, and others. Data is viewed as a continuous stream in this kind of applications. Problems such as data mining which have been widely studied for traditional data sets cannot be easily solved for the data stream domain. This is because the large volume of data arriving in a stream renders most algorithms to inefficient as most mining algorithms require multiple scans of data which is unrealistic for stream data. More importantly, the characteristics of the data stream can change over time and the evolving pattern needs to be captured. Furthermore, we need to consider the problem of resource allocation in mining data streams. Due to the large volume and the high speed of streaming data, mining algorithms must cope with the effects of system overload. Thus, how to achieve optimum results under various resource constraints becomes a challenging task. In this talk, I'll provide an overview, discuss the issues and focus on how to mine evolving data streams and perform resource adaptive computation.

Purpose Based Access Control for Privacy Protection in Database Systems

Elisa Bertino

CERIAS, CS & ECE Departments,
Purdue University
bertino@cerias.purdue.edu

Abstract. The development of privacy-preserving data management techniques has been the focus of intense research in the last few years. Such research has resulted in important notions and techniques, such as the notions of Hippocratic database systems and k-anonymity, and various privacy-preserving data mining techniques. However, much work still needs to be carried out to develop high assurance privacy-preserving database management systems. An important requirement in the development of such systems is the need of providing comprehensive and accurate privacy-related metadata, such as data usage purposes. Such metadata represent the core of access control mechanisms specifically tailored towards privacy. In this talk we address such issue. We present a comprehensive approach for privacy preserving access control based on the notion of purpose. Purpose information associated with a given data element specifies the intended use of the data element. Purpose information represents an important form of metadata, because data usage purpose is very often part of privacy policies, such as the case of policies expressed according to P3P. A key feature of our model is that it allows multiple purposes to be associated with each data element and it also supports explicit prohibitions, thus allowing privacy officers to specify that some data should not be used for certain purposes. Another important issue to be addressed is the granularity of data labeling, that is, the units of data with which purposes can be associated. We address this issue in the context of relational databases and propose four different labeling schemes, each providing a different granularity. In the paper we also propose an approach to representing purpose information, which results in very low storage overhead, and we exploit query modification techniques to support data access control based on purpose information. We conclude the talk by outlining future work that includes the application of our purpose management techniques to complex data and its integration into RBAC.

Complex Networks and Network Data Mining

Deyi Li

China Institute of Electronic System Engineering, Beijing, 100840
ziqin@public2.bta.net.cn

Abstract. We propose a new method for mapping important factors abstracted from a real complex network into the topology of nodes and links. By this method, the effect of a node is denoted with its computable quality, such as the city scale with traffic network, the node throughput of communication network, the hit rates of a web site, and the individual prestige of human relationship. By this method, the interaction between nodes is denoted by the distance or length of links, such as the geographic distance between two cities in the traffic network, the bandwidth between two communication nodes, the number of hyperlinks for a webpage, and the friendship intensity of human relationship. That is, topologically, two-factor operations with node and link are generally expanded to four-factor operations with node, link, distance, and quality. Using this four-factor method, we analyze networking data and simulate the optimization of web mining to form a mining engine by excluding those redundant and irrelevant nodes. The method can lead to the reduction of complicated messy web site structures to a new informative concise graph. In a prototype system for mining informative structure, several experiments for real networking data sets have shown encouraging results in both discovered knowledge and knowledge discovery rate.

Indexing DNA Sequences Using q-Grams

Xia Cao, Shuai Cheng Li, and Anthony K.H. Tung

Department of Computer Science, National University of Singapore
{caoxia, lisc, atung}@comp.nus.edu.sg

Abstract. We have observed in recent years a growing interest in similarity search on large collections of biological sequences. Contributing to the interest, this paper presents a method for indexing the DNA sequences efficiently based on q-grams to facilitate similarity search in a DNA database and sidestep the need for linear scan of the entire database. Two level index – hash table and c-trees – are proposed based on the q-grams of DNA sequences. The proposed data structures allow the quick detection of sequences within a certain distance to the query sequence. Experimental results show that our method is efficient in detecting similarity regions in a DNA sequence database with high sensitivity.

1 Introduction

Similarity search on DNA database is an important function in genomic research. It is useful for making new discoveries about a DNA sequence, including the location of functional sites and novel repetitive structures. It is also useful for the comparative analysis of different DNA sequences. Approximate sequence matching is preferred to exact matching in genomic databases due to evolutionary mutations in the genomic sequences and the presence of noise data in a real sequence database. Many approaches have been developed for approximate sequence matching. The most fundamental one is the Smith-Waterman alignment algorithm [14] which is a dynamic programming approach that seeks the optimal alignment between a query and the target sequence in $O(mn)$ time, m and n being the length of the two sequences.

However, these methods are not practical for long sequences in the megabases range. Effort to improve the efficiency falls into the common idea of filtering by discarding the regions with low sequence similarity. A well known approach is to scan the biological sequences and find short "seed" matches which are subsequently extended into longer alignments. This method is used in program like FASTA [13] and BLAST [1] which are the most popular tools used by biologists. An alternative approach is to build index on the data sequences and conduct the search on the index. Various index structure models [2, 4, 7, 17] have been proposed for this purpose.

Our method is based on the observation that two sequences share a certain number of q-grams if the edit distance between them is within a certain threshold. Moreover, since there are only four letters in the DNA alphabet, we know that the number of all combinations of q-grams in a DNA sequence is 4^q.

In this paper, we propose two level index to prune data sequences that are far away from the query sequence. The disjoint segments with the length ω are generated from the sequence. In the first level, the clusters (called qClusters) of similar q-grams in DNA sequence are generated; then a typical hash table is built in the segments with respect to the qClusters. In the second level index, the segments are transformed into the c-signatures based on their q-grams; then a new index called the *c-signature trees* (c-trees) is proposed to organize the c-signatures of all segments of a DNA sequence for search efficiency.

In the first level of search, the sliding segment of query sequence is generated and encoded into the key in terms of the coding function, and then the neighbors of this key will be enumerated. Thus a set of candidate segments will be extracted from the buckets pointed by the key and its neighbors, and be put into the second index structure c-trees for future filtering. In the second level of search, we only access the tree paths in c-trees that include possible similar data sequences in their leaf nodes. We also propose a similarity search algorithm based on the c-trees for query segments.

The rest of paper is organized as follows. In Section 2, we define the problem of similarity search in DNA sequence databases and briefly review related work. In Section 3, the concept of qClusters and c-signature is presented. The filter principle based on q-grams is also described. In Section 4, we propose two-level index scheme constructed on the q-grams for DNA sequences. In Section 5, an efficient similarity search algorithm is presented based on the proposed index structure. The test data and experimental results are presented in Section 6. Section 7 summarizes the contribution of this paper.

2 Problem Definition and Related Work

In this section, we formalize the similarity search problem in a DNA sequence database and describe the related existing work.

2.1 Problem Definition

The problems of approximate matching and alignment are the core issues in sequence similarity search. To process approximate matching, one common and simple approximation metric is called *edit distance*.

Definition 1. Edit Distance
The edit distance between two sequences is defined as the minimum number of edit operations (i.e., insertions, deletions and substitutions) of single characters needed to transform the first string into the second. $ed(S, P)$ is used to denote the edit distance between sequence S and P.

In general, this problem of sequence search can be described formally as follow:

Problem 1. Given the length l and edit distance ϑ, find all subsequences S in $\mathcal{D}$ which have length $|S| \geq l$ and $ed(S, Q') \leq \vartheta$ for subsequence Q' in query sequence Q.

Since with high possibility there exists a similar segment pair $(s, q), s \in S, q \in Q'$ if S is similar to Q', we instead solve the following problem.

Problem 2. Given the length ω and edit distance ε, find all the segments s_i with length ω in $\mathcal{D}$ which meet $ed(s_i, q_j) \leq \varepsilon$ for the query segments q_j with length ω in Q.

2.2 Related Work

A great amount of work has been done to improve search efficiency and effectiveness in DNA sequence databases. BLAST[1] is a heuristic method for finding similar regions between two genomic sequences. It regards the exact match of W contiguous bases as candidates which are then extended along the left side and the right side to obtain the final alignments. Unfortunately, BLAST faces the dilemma of DNA homology search: increasing the seed size W decreases sensitivity while decreasing the seed size results in too many random results. PatternHunter [8] is an improvement on BLAST both in speed and sensitivity through the use of non-consecutive k letters as model. In essence, PatternHunter's basic principles are similar to those of BLAST.

Researchers have also proposed indices for sequence databases. The suffix tree family is a well-studied category of indices to resolve string-related problems [16, 9, 2, 11, 10]. QUASAR [2] applies a modification of q-gram filtering on top of a suffix array. However, its performance deteriorates dramatically if the compared sequences are weakly similar. Also, the resulting index structure based on the suffix array and suffix tree is large compared to the size of the sequence database. Even if the suffix tree is used without links as proposed in [5], the suffix tree structure index is still nearly 10 times the size of the sequence database. Oasis [10], a novel fast search algorithm is driven by a suffix tree and it also suffers the large size of index structure.

In [15], the ed-tree is proposed to support probe-based homology search in DNA sequence databases efficiently. But the size of the tree-structure index is larger than the sequence database and also it is very time-consuming to build the ed-tree for sequences. Recently, some attempts [7, 12] have been made to transform DNA sequences into numerical vector spaces to allow the use of multi-dimensional indexing approaches for sequence similarity search. Though these methods avoid false dismissals and offer very fast filtering, their drawback is that the approximation of edit distance is not sufficiently tight, which increases the cost of refining results for final output.

SST [4] has been shown to be much faster than BLAST when searching for highly similar sequences. Unfortunately, since the distance between sequences in vector space does not correspond well with the actual edit distance, a larger number of false dismissals may occur if the similarity between the query sequence and the target sequence is not sufficiently high. Williams et al. [17] proposed a search algorithm in a research prototype system, CAFE, which uses an inverted index to select a subset of sequences that display broad similarity to the query sequence. The experiments show that CAFE is faster but also less sensitive than BLAST when searching for very similar sequences.

3 Notations

Although the edit distance is a simple but fairly accurate measure of the evolutionary proximity of two DNA sequences, the computation complexity is $O(mn)$, m and n being the length of the two sequences. To speed up approximate sequence matching, filtering is an efficient way to quickly discard parts of a sequence database, leaving the remaining part to be checked by the edit distance. Our proposed approach to sequence similarity search is based on q-grams, where the q-gram similarity is used as a filter.

3.1 Preliminaries

Before we define $qClusters$ and $c\text{-}signature$, we shall briefly review q-grams and q-gram based filter. The intuition behind the use of q-grams as a filter for approximate sequence search is that two sequences would have a large number of q-grams in common when the edit distance between them is within a certain number.

Definition 2. q-gram of Sequence
Given a sequence S, its q-grams are obtained by sliding a window of length q over the characters of S. For a sequence S, there are $|S| - q + 1$ q-grams.

Lemma 1. Filter based on q-grams (Jokinen and Ukkonen [6])
Let an occurrence of $Q[1:w]$ with at most ε edit or hamming distance end at position j in sequence database S. Then at least $w + 1 - (\varepsilon + 1)q$ of the q-grams in $Q[1:w]$ occur in the substring $S[j - w + 1 : j]$. In another word, there are at most εq q-grams in $Q[1:w]$ which do not occur in $S[j - w + 1 : j]$, and vice versa. So obviously, the number of different q-grams between $Q[1:w]$ and $S[j - w + 1 : j]$ is at most $2\varepsilon q$.

3.2 The qClusters and c-Signature

The alphabet of the DNA sequence comprises four letters: $\Sigma = \{A, C, G, T\}$. It means there are in all $|\Sigma|^q = 4^q$ kinds of q-grams, and we may arrange them according to the lexicographic order, and use r_i to denote the ith q-gram in this order. All the possible q-grams are denoted as: $\Re = \{r_0, r_1, \ldots, r_{4^q-1}\}$. The q-gram clusters(qClusters) can be defined below:

Definition 3. q-gram Clusters (qClusters)
All the possible q-grams, $\Re = \{r_0, r_1, \ldots, r_{4^q-1}\}$ are divided into λ clusters (denoted as qClusters) $\{qCluster_1, \ldots, qCluster_\lambda\}$ by a certain principle. In this paper, we simply cluster the m continuous q-grams $\{r_{(i-1)m}, \ldots, r_{im-1}\}$ together into $qCluster_i$, $1 \leq i \leq \lambda = \lceil \frac{4^q}{m} \rceil$.

The q-gram signature and c-signature of the DNA sequence are defined as follows:

Definition 4. q-gram Signature
The q-gram signature is a bitmap with 4^q bits where ith bit corresponds to the presence or absence of r_i. For a given sequence S, the ith bit is set as '1' if $r_i \in \Re$ occurs at least once in sequence S, else it is set as '0'.

Definition 5. c-signature
Let $sig^1(S) = (a_0, \ldots, a_{n-1})$ be a q-gram signature of the DNA segment S with $n=4^q$, then its c-signature is defined as: $sig^c(S) = (u_0, \ldots, u_{k-1})$ where $k = \lceil n/c \rceil$, and $u_i = \sum_{j=ic}^{(i+1)c-1} a_j$. Set $a_j = 0$ when $n \leq j < ck$. For sequence S and P, we define the distance between $sig^c(S) = (u_0, \ldots, u_{k-1})$ and $sig^c(P) = (v_0, \ldots, v_{k-1})$ as $SDist(sig^c(S), sig^c(P)) = \sum_{i=0}^{k-1} |u_i - v_i|$.

For better understanding of the definition of q-gram signature and c-signature, we consider the below example:

Example 1. For sequence P="ACGGTACT", its q-gram signature is (01 00 00 11 00 11 10 00) with 16(=4^2) dimensions when $q = 2$. In P, the q-gram 'AC' occurs twice in position 0 and 5, so we set the corresponding bit in position 1 in q-gram signature as '1'. As there is no occurrence of 'AA' in sequence P, the corresponding bit in position 0 in q-gram signature is set as '0'. For c=2, the c-signature of P is (10020210) with respect to the definition of the c-signature.

With the property $|a| + |b| \geq |a + b|$, it is not difficult to obtain the following lemma for filtering in terms of c-signature:

Lemma 2. *Filter Based on c-signatures*
Given a sequence S, there is at most ε edit or hamming distance from another sequence P with $|S| = |P|$. Let $sig^1(S) = (a_0, a_1, \ldots, a_{n-1})$ and $sig^1(P) = (b_0, b_1, \ldots, b_{n-1})$ be the q-gram signatures generated for sequence S and P respectively. Denote the c-signatures of S and P as $sig^c(S) = (u_0, u_1, \ldots, u_{k-1})$ and $sig^c(P) = (v_0, v_1, \ldots, v_{k-1})$, $c > 1$, respectively. Then $\sum_{i=0}^{k-1} |u_i - v_i| \leq \sum_{j=0}^{n-1} |a_j - b_j| \leq 2\varepsilon q$.

Proof: *In term of Lemma 1 and the definition of q-gram signature, $\sum_{i=0}^{n-1} |a_i - b_i| \leq 2\varepsilon q$ holds. According to the definition of c-signature, $u_i = \sum_{j=ic}^{(i+1)c-1} a_j$ and $v_i = \sum_{j=ic}^{(i+1)c-1} b_j$. The following formula holds: $\sum_{i=0}^{k-1} |u_i - v_i| = \sum_{i=0}^{k-1} |\sum_{j=ic}^{(i+1)c-1} a_j - \sum_{j=ic}^{(i+1)c-1} b_j| \leq \sum_{i=0}^{k-1} \sum_{j=ic}^{(i+1)c-1} |a_j - b_j| = \sum_{j=0}^{kc-1} |a_j - b_j| = \sum_{j=0}^{n-1} |a_j - b_j| \leq 2\varepsilon q$.*

4 An Indexing Scheme for DNA Sequences

A two-level indexing scheme is proposed to organize the segments in DNA sequence database and support the similarity search.

4.1 The Hash Table

In order to hash the DNA segments to a hash table with size 2^λ, it is necessary to encode the segment into a λ-bit integer. Given a segment s, we encode it into a λ bitmap $e = (e_1, e_2, \ldots, e_\lambda)$ with respect to qClusters=$\{qCluster_1, qCluster_2, \ldots, qCluster_\lambda\}$. If there exists a q-gram $gram$ in s which meets $gram \in qCluster_i$, we set $e_i = 1$, else $e_i = 0$, where $1 \leq i \leq \lambda$. Following the encoding principle, any DNA segment s can be encoded into a λ-bit integer $(e_1, \ldots, e_\lambda)$ by the coding function:

$$coding(s) = \sum_{i=1}^{\lambda} 2^{i-1} e_i$$

The hash table has totally 2^λ buckets for the qClusters $\{qCluster_1, \ldots, qCluster_\lambda\}$, and each segment s_i can be inserted into the corresponding bucket in the hash table with the use of the hash function $coding(s_i)$. Note that λ is set as 5 and 22 for q=3 and 4 respectively in the experimental studies for better performance, and we will not declare it again.

4.2 The c-Trees

The c-trees are a group of rooted dynamic trees built for indexing c-signatures. The height of the trees, ℓ is set by the users. Given the c-signature of the segment s, $sig^c(s) = (v_0, v_1, \ldots, v_{k-1})$, there are $\delta = \lceil \frac{k}{\ell} \rceil$ trees in total. We denote these trees as $T_0,\ldots,T_{\delta-1}$. Each path from the root to a leaf in T_i corresponds to the c-signature string $sig_i^c(s) = (v_{i\ell}, v_{i\ell+1}, \ldots, v_{(i+1)\ell-1})$. For ease of discussion, we shall assume without loss of generality that k is divisible by ℓ and thus $T_{\delta-1}$ also has a height of ℓ. For each internal node of the tree, there are at most $c + 1$ children. Each edge in a tree of c-trees is labeled with the respective value from 0 to c.

Algorithm 1 Tree Construction
Input: c-signatures $sig^c(s_0), \ldots, sig^c(s_{|\mathcal{D}|-\omega})$ **Output:** c-trees $(T_0, T_1, \ldots, T_{\delta-1})$

1: $T_i \leftarrow NULL, 0 \leq i < \delta$
2: **for** each c-signature $sig^c(s_j)$ **do**
3:   **for** $i \leftarrow 0 \ldots \delta - 1$ **do**
4:     TreeInsert(T_i, $sig_i^c(s_j)$, s_j)
5:   **end for**
6: **end for**
7:
8: Function TreeInsert(N_x, sig, s)
9: **if** $sig = \epsilon$ **then**
10:   insert(N_x, s, i)   /*N_x is the leaf node*/
11: **else if** there exists an edge $\langle N_x, N_y \rangle$ where $label[\langle N_x, N_y \rangle]$ is a prefix of sig **then**
12:   TreeInsert(N_y, $sig - label[\langle N_x, N_y \rangle]$, s)
13: **else if** there exists an edge $\langle N_x, N_y \rangle$ where $label[\langle N_x, N_y \rangle]$ shares a longest prefix pf with sig, $pf \neq \epsilon$ **then**
14:   split $\langle N_x, N_y \rangle$ into two parts with a new node N_z, such that $pf = label[\langle N_x, N_z \rangle]$
15:   create a new leaf $lNode$ with edge label $sig\text{-}label[\langle N_x, N_z \rangle]$ under N_z
16:   insert($lNode$, s, i)
17: **else**
18:   create a new leaf node $lNode$ under N_x with edge label $label[\langle N_x, lNode \rangle]=sig$
19:   insert($lNode$, s, i)
20: **end if**
21:
22: Function insert($lNode$, s, i)
23: **if** i=0 **then**
24:   $E_0[lNode] \leftarrow E_0[lNode] \cup \{s\}$
25: **else**
26:   build the link from c-signature of s to $lNode$ in T_i
27: **end if**

The DNA segments are transformed into the c-signatures in order to build the c-trees on them. Note that it is not necessary to store the c-signatures themselves after the trees are constructed. To further consolidate the definition of c-trees, we shall present a straightforward algorithm to build c-trees for a group of c-signatures.

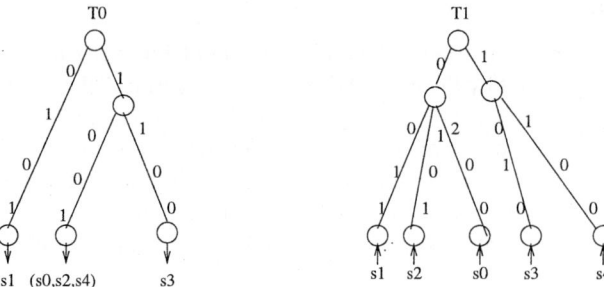

Fig. 1. The c-trees for the DNA segments

In Algorithm 1, $label[\langle N_x, N_y \rangle]$ denotes the label of edge $\langle N_x, N_y \rangle$ in the c-trees. For notation convenience, define $S - S'$ as a suffix of S, where S' is a prefix of S, and the concatenation of S' and $S - S'$ is S. ϵ is used to refer an empty string. Also $lNode$ denotes the leaf node in the c-trees, and $E_0[lNode]$ is a group of segments in $lNode$ of the first tree T_0. Note that $E_0[*]$ will be constructed only for the tree T_0. For the other trees, the link from the c-signature to the leaf node will be constructed instead.

The c-signature strings $sig_i^c(s)$ are inserted into the growing trees T_i $0 \leq i < \delta$ one by one by executing the function TreeInsert($T_i, sig_i^c(s), s$) recursively. We now demonstrate the c-trees construction for DNA segments with the following example.

Example 2. Consider the five DNA segments s_0="ACGGT", s_1="CTTAG", s_2="ACGTT", s_3="TAAGC" and s_4="GACGT". When we set q=2 and c=2, the c-signatures are: $sig^2(s_0)$=(1001 0200), $sig^2(s_1)$=(0101 0011), $sig^2(s_2)$=(1001 0101), $sig^2(s_3)$=(1100 1010), $sig^2(s_4)$=(1001 1100). If $\ell = 4$, we get $\frac{4^q}{c\ell}$=2 trees. The first tree T_0 is constructed from the c-signature strings $sig_0^2(s_i)$, $0 \leq i \leq 3$, and the tree T_1 is constructed from $sig_1^2(s_i)$, $4 \leq i \leq 7$. The c-trees (T_0, T_1) for the five DNA segments are shown in Fig. 1.

5 Query Processing

In this section, we present how to use the two-level index to get the candidates by pruning data segments that are far away from the query sequence. Then the dynamic programming is conducted to obtain the final alignments with high alignment score between the candidates and query sequence. This phase is a standard procedure, so we just skip the details about it in this paper. Before sequence similarity search begins, a hash table HT and the c-trees are built on the DNA segments. The query sequence Q is also partitioned into $|Q| - \omega + 1$ sliding query patterns $q_1, \ldots, q_{|Q|-\omega+1}$.

5.1 The First Level Filter: Hash Table Based Similarity Search

The query pattern q_i is first encoded to a hash key h_i, which is a λ bit integer. Then all the encoded neighbors $ngbr$ of the hash key h_i are enumerated, and the neighbors are those λ bit integers encoded from the segments which are within a small edit distance from q_i. In [3], an approach has been proposed to enumerate a segment's neighbors. The main idea is also applicable for our current case, but the difference is that we need to consider the impact on the q-grams to get the encoded neighbors when some edit operations are conducted on the segment. d edit operations on segment s will result in at most dq q-grams which are different from those in s, and the new neighboring key will be computed in terms of the new group of q-grams by using the coding function. In our case, d is set as 3.

Once an encoded neighbor e_{ngbr} of q_i is enumerated, the segments in the bucket $HT[e_{ngbr}]$ of the hash structure HT will be retrieved as candidates and stored into the candidate set C_{ht}.

5.2 The Second Level Filter: The c-Trees Based Similarity Search

The candidate segments C_{ht} generated from the first level filter will be further verified by the c-trees. According to the c-trees structure, the c-signature $sig^c(q)$ of query q is divided into δ c-signature strings which are $sig_i^c(q)$, $0 \le i < \delta$. Algorithm 2 shows how to retrieve the segment s which satisfies the range constraint $ed(q,s) \le \varepsilon$ for a query segment q. For clarity, threshold γ in Algorithm 2 is set as $2q\varepsilon$, where q is the q-gram length and ε is the edit distance allowed between the DNA data segment and query segment.

In Algorithm 2, $w_i[lNode]$ is used to denote the distance between $sig_i^c(q)$ and the path label $pl = label[\langle root_i, lNode \rangle]$ from the respective root $root_i$ to $lNode$ in T_i, namely $w_i[lNode] = SDist(sig_i^c(q), pl)$. We use $score[s]$ to denote the partial distance for segment s during similarity search. Also for notation simplicity, we use $sig_i^c(s)$ as its corresponding path label for a leaf node in T_i, $0 < i < \delta$, since each $sig_i^c(s)$ can only be mapped to one path or one leaf node in T_i.

During query processing, for each leaf node $lNode$ in the tree T_0, the distance $w_0[lNode]$) between the path label of $lNode$ and $sig_0^c(q)$ are computed. And the initial candidate set C includes those segments in $E_0[lNode] \cap C_{ht}$ where $w_0[lNode] \le \gamma$. For the trees $\{T_1, \ldots, T_{\delta-1}\}$, candidates will be pruned based on the partial distance gradually. For each candidate s in C, we can find its corresponding leaf node $lNode$ with label $sig_i^c(s)$ in $T_i(i \ne 0)$ in time O(1) with links constructed during tree construction, and the partial distance $score[s]$ can be computed as well.

5.3 The Space and Time Complexity Analysis

In this section, the space and time complexity are analyzed for the two-level index structure. For the space complexity of the hash table, we need $O(2^\lambda)$ for the table head. For the bucket of the table, segments will contribute space $\Theta(|\mathcal{D}|/\omega)$. Thus, the total space complexity for the hash structure will be $O(2^\lambda + |\mathcal{D}|/\omega)$. Each neighboring of the segment can be generated with time amortized complexity $O(1)$. Thus, the time complexity for the query is $O(|q|)$.

Essentially, the space complexity for the c-trees can be divided into two portions: the c-trees themselves, and space occupied by the $E_0[*]$ and links. According to the algorithm, $E_0[*]$ must be stored for the first tree; thus they require $O(|\mathcal{D}|/\omega)$ space. The height of each tree is bounded by $O(4^q/(\delta c))$, thus for each tree, the storage required

Algorithm 2 Similarity Search Algorithm
Input: The c-trees $(T_0, T_1, ..., T_{\delta-1})$ on $\mathcal{D}$, query c-signature $(sig_0^c(q), ..., sig_{\delta-1}^c(q))$, Candidate segments C_{ht}, distance γ. **Output:** Candidate set C

1: $C \leftarrow \emptyset$
2: **for** $lNode \in T_0$ **do**
3:   **if** $w_0[lNode] < \gamma$ **then**
4:     $E_0'[lNode] = E_0[lNode] \cap C_{ht}$; $C \leftarrow C \cup E_0'[lNode]$
5:     **for** each $s \in E_0'[lNode]$ **do**
6:       $score[s] \leftarrow w_0[lNode]$
7:     **end for**
8:   **end if**
9:   **return** Search($\{T_1, ..., T_{\delta-1}\}, C$)
10: **end for**
11:
12: Function: $Search(TSet, C)$
13: **if** $TSet = \emptyset$ **then**
14:   **return** C
15: **else**
16:   $T_i \leftarrow$ first entry in $TSet$
17:   **for** each $s \in C$ **do**
18:     **if** $w_i[sig_i^c(s)] + score[s] \leq \gamma$ **then**
19:       $score[s] \leftarrow w_i[sig_i^c(s)] + score[s]$
20:     **else**
21:       $C \leftarrow C - \{s\}$
22:     **end if**
23:   **end for**
24:   **return** Search($TSet$-$\{T_i\}, C$)
25: **end if**

for the edge labels is bounded by $O((c+1)^{4^q/(\delta c)} \log(c+1))$ for each tree. Besides, we also need to maintain the links for the other trees. The space required by links highly depends on the data distribution. Note there are lots of zeros in c-signatures, thus a lot of links will point to a dummy leaf (by dummy we mean that the path label is 0). So we may just compress those links. The time complexity depends on the pruning rate for each iteration. Suppose the filtering rate for each iteration is β, then the total time required to obtain the final candidate set is $O(\delta(c+1)^{4^q/(\delta c)} + (|\mathcal{D}|/\omega)\frac{(1-\beta)(1-(1-\beta)^\delta)}{\beta})$ in the worst case. Note in practice, the algorithm is much more efficient since we do not need to traverse the whole structure most of the time.

6 Experimental Studies

We evaluate the sensitivity, effectiveness and efficiency of our search method and compare it to the latest version of BLAST(NCBI BLAST2). For BLAST, we set the length of the seed as 11 in the experiment.

6.1 The Sensitivity Analysis

The key issue for the entire search approach is to find a trade-off between sensitivity and effectiveness while maintaining search efficiency. Sensitivity can be measured by the probability that a high score alignment is found by the algorithm. We define the sensitivity analysis problem as: Given a pair of genomic sequences with length L and the similarity ratio sim, compute the sensitivity or probability that they can be detected by the search model.

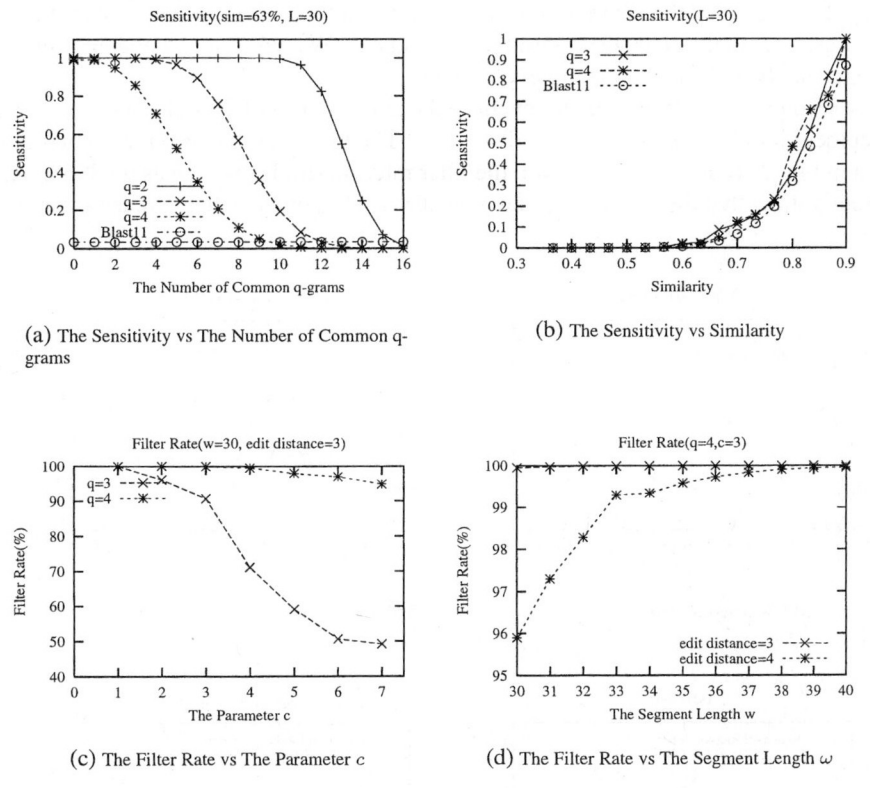

Fig. 2. Experimental Results for Sensitivity and Effectiveness

In the experiment, the sensitivity of the filter model is the probability that the two sequences S and P with length L and similarity sim can be regarded as similar sequences when the number of the common q-grams in S and P is at least ρ. Fig. 2(a) depicts how the number of common q-grams ρ affects the sensitivity of the filter model for $L=30$, $sim=63\%$ and $q = 2, 3, 4$, and compares the sensitivity to BLAST. Given $sim=63\%$, for $q=4$, it shows that our filter method can achieve higher sensitivity than BLAST as long as the number of common q-grams is no more than 9. Fig. 2(b) shows how the sensitivity of our filter model varies with the similarity sim for $L=30$. In comparison with BLAST, our filter method for $q=3,4$ achieves higher sensitivity.

6.2 The Effectiveness Analysis

Two groups of experiments were conducted to measure the effectiveness of the proposed two-level index structure by using the dataset $ecoli.nt$. The filter rate used in the experiment description is defined as the ratio of the total number of hits found to the total number of segments in data sequence.

The first group of experiments measure how the parameters c and q affect the effectiveness of filtering when we fix $\omega=30$ and $\varepsilon=3$, in the filter processing. The result in Fig. 2(c) shows that when c increasing, the filter rate drops down as the c-signature representing the segment becomes inaccurate. On the other hand, larger q results in better filter rate since the segment property can be captured more accurately by the c-signatures. The filter rate is 99.9495% for $q=4$ and $c=3$. We will use $q=4$ and $c=3$ for the efficiency analysis in the following experiment.

The second group of experiments evaluate the effectiveness of the index while varying the segment length ω as well as edit distance ε. The filter rate for different ω and ε is shown in Fig. 2(d). For $\omega=30$ and $\varepsilon=4$, the filter rate can still be as high as 95.895%. All the results show that the proposed index structure is effective for the similarity search.

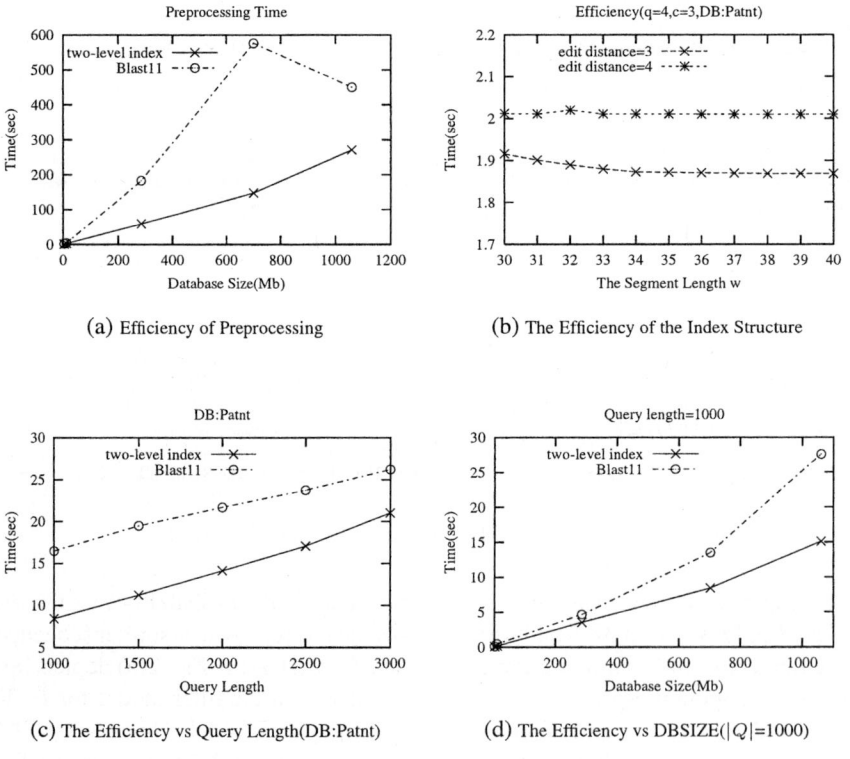

(a) Efficiency of Preprocessing

(b) The Efficiency of the Index Structure

(c) The Efficiency vs Query Length(DB:Patnt)

(d) The Efficiency vs DBSIZE($|Q|$=1000)

Fig. 3. Experimental Results for Efficiency

6.3 The Efficiency Analysis

The five DNA datasets used in the experiments are: other_genomic(1.06GB), Patnt(702.1 MB), month.gss(286.2MB), yeast.nt(12.3MB) and ecoli.nt(4.68MB). All the datasets are downloaded from NCBI website.

We first evaluate the efficiency in data sequence preprocessing before performing similarity search in terms of the proposed index structure. Fig. 3(a) shows that preprocessing with our method is much faster than that with BLAST due to the efficient algorithm for the hash table and c-trees construction.

The efficiency for searching a single segment is analyzed. The results of the efficiency of segment searching are presented in Fig. 3(b) for q=4 and c=3. We conduct the experiment by varying the segment length ω from 30 to 40, and the edit distance ε from 3 to 4 for the dataset $patnt$. The results show that better performance can be achieved for $\varepsilon = 3$ since it causes better filter rate than $\varepsilon = 4$.

An experiment is also carried out to investigate how the length of the query sequence affects the performance of our method in comparison with BLAST. To do this, we perform similarity search for query lengths of 1000, 1500, 2000, 2500 and 3000 on $patnt$. Fig.3(c) shows our search speed is about twice faster than BLAST when the query length is varied from 1000 to 3000. We performed a comparison of our search method with BLAST on the five datasets as well. We set q=4, c=3, ω=30 and ε=3. The results of the comparison are shown in Fig. 3(d) when the query length is fixed as 1000. The speed-up of the c-trees over BLAST ranges from 2 to 3 for the different size of sequence datasets.

7 Conclusion

We have devised a novel two-level index structure based on q-grams of the DNA sequences which can support efficient similarity search in DNA sequence database. The filter principle with respect to the index structure is presented and it can guarantee that we can achieve efficient sequence searching while keeping the higher sensitivity. We also carry out the experiments to evaluate the performance of our method in the sensitivity, effectiveness and efficiency, and the results show that our method can efficiently detect the regions in DNA sequence database which are similar to the query sequence with high sensitivity.

References

1. S. Altschul, W. Gish, W. Miller, E. Myers, and D. Lipman. A basic local alignment search tool. In *Journal of Molecular Biology*, 1990.
2. S. Burkhardt, A. Crauser, P. Ferragina, H. P. Lenhof, and M. Vingron. q-gram based database searching using a suffix array (quasar). In *Int. Conf. RECOMB*, Lyon, April 1999.
3. X. Cao, S.C. Li, B.C. Ooi, and A. Tung. Piers: An efficient model for similarity search in dna sequence databases. *ACM Sigmod Record*, 33, 2004.
4. E. Giladi, M. Walker, J. Wang, and W. Volkmuth. Sst: An algorithm for searching sequence databases in time proportional to the logarithm of the database size. In *Int. Conf. RECOMB*, Japan, 2000.

5. E. Hunt, M. P. Atkinson, and R. W. Irving. A database index to large biological sequences. In *International Journal on VLDB*, pages 139–148, Roma, Italy, September 2001.
6. P. Jokinen and E. Ukkonen. Two algorithm for approximate string matching in static texts. In *Proc. of the 16th Symposium on Mathematical Foundataions of Computer Science*, pages 240–248, 1991.
7. T. Kahveci and A. Singh. An efficient index structure for string databases. In *Proc. 2001 Int. Conf. Very Large Data Bases (VLDB'01)*, Roma, Italy, 2001.
8. B. Ma, J. Tromp, and M. Li. Patternhunter: faster and more sensitive homology search. *Bioinformatics*, 18:440–445, 2002.
9. U. Manber and G. Myers. Suffix arrays: a new method for on-line string search. *SIAM Journal on Computing*, 22:935–948, 1993.
10. C. Meek, J.M. Patel, and S. Kasetty. Oasis: An online and accurate technique for local-alignment searches on biological sequences. In *Proc. 2003 Int. Conf. Very Large Data Bases (VLDB'03)*, pages 910–921, Berlin, Germany, Sept. 2003.
11. S. Muthukrishnan and S.C. Sahinalp. Approximate nearest neighbors and sequence comparison with block operation. In *STOC,Portland, Or*, 2000.
12. O. Ozturk and H. Ferhatosmanoglu. Effective indexing and filtering for similarity search in large biosequence datasbases. In *Third IEEE Symposium on BioInformatics and BioEngineering (BIBE'03)*, Bethesda, Maryland, 2003.
13. W.R. Pearson and D.J. Lipman. Improved tools for biological sequence comparison. *Proceedings Natl. Acad. Sci. USA*, 85:2444–2448, 1988.
14. T.F. Smith and M.S. Waterman. Identification of common molecular subsequences. *Molecular Biology*, 147:195–197, 1981.
15. Z. Tan, X. Cao, B.C. Ooi, and A. Tung. The ed-tree: an index for large dna sequence databases. In *Proc. 15th Int. Conf. on Scientific and Statistical Database Management*, pages 151–160, 2003.
16. P. Weiner. Linear pattern matching algorithms. In *Proc. 14th IEEE Symp. On Switching and Automata Theory*, pages 1–11, 1973.
17. H.E. Williams and J.Zobel. Indexing and retrieval for genomic databases. *IEEE Transactions on Knowledge and Data Engineering*, 14:63–78, 2002.

PADS: Protein Structure Alignment Using Directional Shape Signatures*

S. Alireza Aghili, Divyakant Agrawal, and Amr El Abbadi

Department of Computer Science,
University of California-Santa Barbara,
Santa Barbara, CA 93106
{aghili, agrawal, amr}@cs.ucsb.edu

Abstract. A novel data mining approach for similarity search and knowledge discovery in protein structure databases is proposed. PADS (**P**rotein structure **A**lignment by **D**irectional shape **S**ignatures) incorporates the three dimensional coordinates of the main atoms of each amino acid and extracts a geometrical shape signature along with the direction of each amino acid. As a result, each protein structure is presented by a series of multidimensional feature vectors representing local geometry, shape, direction, and biological properties of its amino acid molecules. Furthermore, a distance matrix is calculated and is incorporated into a local alignment dynamic programming algorithm to find the similar portions of two given protein structures followed by a sequence alignment step for more efficient filtration. The optimal superimposition of the detected similar regions is used to assess the quality of the results. The proposed algorithm is fast and accurate and hence could be used for analysis and knowledge discovery in large protein structures. The method has been compared with the results from CE, DALI, and CTSS using a representative sample of PDB structures. Several new structures not detected by other methods are detected.

Keywords: Shape Similarity, Protein Structure Comparison, Biological Data Mining, Bioinformatics.

1 Introduction

Protein structure similarity has been extensively used to highlight the similarities and differences among *homologous* three dimensional protein structures. The corresponding applications include *drug discovery*, *phylogenetic analysis*, and *protein classification* which have attracted tremendous attention and have been broadly studied within the past decade. The proteins have a primary sequence, which is an ordered sequence of amino acid molecules, e.g. AALHSI-AISAJSH. However, they also appear to conform into a three dimensional shape

---

* This research was supported by the NSF grants under CNF-04-23336, IIS02-23022, IIS02-09112, and EIA00-80134.

(*fold*) which is highly conserved in the protein evolution. The fold of a protein strongly indicates its functionality and the potential interactions with other protein structures. Meanwhile, the protein sequences as well as their structures may change over time due to mutations during evolution or natural selection. High sequence similarity implies descent from a common ancestral family, and the occurrence of many topologically superimposable substructures provides suggestive evidence of evolutionary relationship [8]. This is because the genetic mechanisms rarely produce topological permutations. For two given proteins, if the sequences are similar then the evolutionary relationship is apparent. However the three dimensional structure of proteins, due to their conformational and functional restraints, are much more resilient to mutations than the protein sequences. There exist functionally similar proteins which *sequence-level* similarity search fails to accurately depict the true similarity. Such cases introduce a big challenge and the necessity of incorporating *structure-level* similarity. Meanwhile, there are two main problems in protein structure similarity:

- *Complexity*. The problem of structure comparison is NP-hard and there is no exact solution to the protein structure alignment [9]. A handful of heuristics [4, 5, 6, 8, 12, 13, 14, 15, 18] have been proposed in which, to achieve the best result the similarity might need to be evaluated using a series of techniques in conjunction. However, none of the proposed methods can guarantee optimality within any given precision! There are always cases where one heuristic fails to detect, while some of the others succeed.
- *Curse of Dimensionality*. The total number of discovered protein structures has been growing exponentially. Currently the Protein Data Bank (PDB)[1] contains 27,112 protein structures (as of September 8th, 2004.). The growth in the content of PDB demands faster and more accurate tools for structure similarity and the classification of the known structures.

We first provide the basic definitions of terms used throughout the paper in Table 1. In this paper, we consider both the sequence and structure of protein chains for more efficient similarity comparison. The main goal of protein structure similarity is to superimpose two proteins over the maximum number of residues (amino acids) with a minimal distance among their corresponding matched atoms. These methods typically employ the three dimensional coordinates of the C_α atoms of the protein backbone and sometimes, in addition, the side chain comprising C_β atoms but exclude the other amino acid atoms when making global structural comparisons. When superimposing two protein structures, side chain conformations (coordinates of O, C, C_β, N, H atoms) may vary widely between the matched residues however the C_α atoms of the backbone trace and the corresponding SSEs are usually well conserved. However, there are situations where the local comparison of the side chain atoms can be of great significance, for instance, in the comparison of residues lining an active or binding sites especially when different *ligands*[1] are bound to the same or similar structures [10].

---

[1] *ligand*: An atom, molecule, or ion that forms a complex around a central atom.

Table 1. Notations

TERM	DESCRIPTION
atom	Any of the *Nitrogen*(N), *Oxygen*(O), *Hydrogen*(H), or *Carbon*(C) atoms found in protein chains. Carbon atoms that are located on the *backbone* of the protein chains are called C_α, and those on the *side chains* of the protein are called C_β. The atoms that are located closer to the backbone are much more resilient to topological and mutational changes, compared to those atoms that are further away from the backbone. different atom combinations are approximated. For instance, the NH_3^+ and CO^- molecules may be approximated by just considering the considering the coordinates of their corresponding N and C atoms.
amino acid (*residue*)	There are 20 different amino acid molecules in nature (*Alanine, Glycine, Serine,* ...) which are the alphabets of proteins. Each amino acid is labeled by a capital letter (A, B, F, T, ...) which is made of a number of atoms. All the amino acids have the main N, O, C, and C_α atoms, however that is not true of other atoms like C_β (e.g., Glycine does not have C_β). In this paper, the terms *amino acid* and *residue* are used interchangeably.
protein	A protein is an ordered sequence of amino acids (i.e. ALFHIASUHG...). Additionally, each amino acid and as a result each protein chain takes a three-dimensional shape in nature (i.e. in solvents, reactions, ...). Given two proteins, they may be compared by just aligning their sequences or further inspecting their three-dimensional conformations. Each protein may be either represented by the sequence of its amino acid constituents or its three-dimensional conformation. The topological shape of a protein is one of the very main key factors in defining its functionalities.
SSE	Secondary Structure Element (SSE) is the ordered arrangement or conformation of amino acids in localized regions of a protein molecule. The two main secondary structures are the α-helix and β-sheets. A single protein may contain multiple secondary structures.

Distances between the atom coordinates or residual feature vectors or their corresponding biochemical properties are often used to compare protein structures. These features are considered either separately or in combination, as a basis for structural comparison. Some of these features include: *physical properties, local conformations, distance from gravity center, position in space, global/local direction in space, side chain orientation,* and *secondary structure type*. First, each amino acid of the target and query proteins are represented by a feature vector, and hence each protein is mapped into an ordered sequence of feature vectors. Comparison of the features of the query and target proteins is used as a basis to attribute the similarity. Dynamic programming [16, 20] may be used to discover the similarities between any two protein structures using any number and combination of features of individual residues or regional segments. As a result, a local alignment of the structural features may be deployed to give the best sequential alignment of the given protein structure pairs. Subsequently, the structures should be superimposed according to the results of the alignment. However, a single global alignment of the given protein structures might be meaningless while dissimilar regions (fragments) may affect the overall superimposition drastically. Hence, each fragment of the aligned protein structures should be superimposed individually and independently to explore local similarities. are superimposed on each other, independent of the other similar regions.

The rest of the paper is organized as follows: section 2, discusses the background and related work. Section 3 introduces the formulation and the proposed technique. Section 4 discusses the experimental results, and section 5 which concludes the work.

2 Background and Related Work

Given two protein chains $P = p_1 - p_2 - ... - p_m$ and $Q = q_1 - q_2 - ... - q_n$ (each p_i and q_j denote the feature vectors extracted from the ith and j^{th} amino acid molecule of P and Q, respectively), there are a variety of heuristics to find *optimal* structural similarities (global or local) among them. The techniques map the entire or the best matching regions of the given structures to each other. These algorithms may be classified into three main categories based on their choice of feature vectors and the detail level: *i*) algorithms incorporating only C_α atom coordinates as representatives of amino acid residues and inspecting their inter-atomic distances [12, 13, 18], *ii*) algorithms incorporating SSEs to find initial alignments and filter out non-desired segments [4, 13, 14, 15, 19], and *iii*) algorithms using geometric hashing as an indexing scheme to retrieve similar structural alignments [17].

The methods may also be classified based on their choice of heuristics used to align one structure against the other in order to determine the *equivalent pairs*. The term equivalent pairs is defined as the pairs of atoms (or fragments) from the given protein chains whose distance is less than a *threshold*. The threshold or cut-off value may either be a contextual characteristic of the employed method, or provided by the user, or directly learned from the input dataset. The context and the domain properties of the applied method determines the choice of the distance function and the cut-off thresholds, which explains why different structure similarity methods may return non-identical though mostly coherent results. There also exist methods[2] which employ a combination of the listed techniques, including *Dynamic programming* methods [5, 16, 18, 20], *Bipartite and Clique Detection* methods [6, 12, 13], *Match list* methods [4, 6, 12]. Different methods have different notions of similarity score or distance function. These differences make the alignment score not a tangible criterion for comparison. Some of the most frequently used indicators of the quality of a structural comparison include the Root Mean Square Deviation (RMSD) and the extent of the match which is the number of aligned residues. These factors along with the alignment score may be used to asses the quality of the alignment. PADS extends our earlier proposal [3], which considers both the sequence and structure of protein chains and constructs a rotation-invariant geometrical representation from each structure for more efficient similarity comparison. The following section introduces the theoretical aspects and formulation of the proposed protein structure similarity technique.

3 The PADS Method

PADS is a novel method for fast and accurate protein structure similarity using directional shape signatures. The algorithm not only exploits the topological properties of the amino acid and protein structures, but also incorporates the

---
[2] For a detailed survey and comparative study of these methods refer to [2].

biochemical properties (SSE assignments) of the protein chains into account. PADS starts by identifying the geometrical properties of each amino acid of the given proteins along with their directions and their SSE assignments. As a result, each protein structure is represented by a series of directional shape signature feature vectors, one for each amino acid. In the next step, a score matrix is constructed on the corresponding feature vectors. A local *structural alignment* [20] based on shape, direction and biological features detects the optimal local matching regions among the two proteins. For each of the locally matched regions (pertaining to length and score constraints), a *sequence alignment* is performed to facilitate a visualization of the sequence similarities. Thereafter, the best locally matched regions are topologically superimposed. The corresponding RMSD value, length of the aligned fragments, and sequence alignment score are reported for the assessment of the quality of the match. A *linear time* least-square solution to superimpose the ordered sets of protein feature vectors is applied (due to space limitations, the details are provided in [2]). We sort the results based on their extent(L) and RMSD value and report a list of top alignments with the best scores φ, where $\varphi = L/RMSD$.

3.1 Shape Signature Extraction

Consider a protein structure P made of an ordered set of amino acids $[a_1, ..., a_N]$, where each a_i is a vector of three-dimensional coordinates of atoms such as C_α, C, O, N, H or other side chain atoms. Hence each amino acid residue constitutes a 3D polyhedron in 3D Euclidean space. For instance, if 6 significant atoms (as in Figure 1-a) of a_i are considered, then a_i would be represented by a vector of 6 three-dimensional vectors, one for the position of each of its constituent atoms.

Definition 1 *Let $S = (v_1, \ldots, v_n)$ be a polyhedron amino acid in 3D Euclidean space. Let v_i denote an atom of S positioned at $v_i = [v_{ix}, v_{iy}, v_{iz}]$ with molar mass μ_i. The **Center of Mass**[3] of S is a multidimensional point, $C_\odot(S)$, and is defined as*

$$C_\odot(S) = [C^S_{\odot x}, C^S_{\odot y}, C^S_{\odot z}], \text{ where}$$

$$C^S_{\odot x} = \frac{\sum_{i=1}^{n} \mu_i v_{ix}}{\sum_{i=1}^{n} \mu_i}, \; C^S_{\odot y} = \frac{\sum_{i=1}^{n} \mu_i v_{iy}}{\sum_{i=1}^{n} \mu_i}, \text{ and } C^S_{\odot z} = \frac{\sum_{i=1}^{n} \mu_i v_{iz}}{\sum_{i=1}^{n} \mu_i}.$$

For instance, let $S = (N, C_\alpha)$ be an amino acid made of only two atoms, N (Nitrogen: molar mass 14.01 g/mol) and C_α (Carbon: : molar mass 12.01 g/mol) positioned at locations $[10, 4, 12]$ and $[2, 6, 1]$, respectively. The center of mass of S is a 3D point and is calculated as $C_\odot(S) = [\frac{(10 \times 12.01)+(2 \times 14.01)}{12.01+14.01}, \frac{(4 \times 12.01)+(6 \times 14.01)}{12.01+14.01}, \frac{(12 \times 12.01)+(1 \times 14.01)}{12.01+14.01}] = [5.7, 5.08, 6.08]$.

Definition 2 *Let $S = (v_1, \ldots, v_n)$ be the polyhedron amino acid with center of mass $C_\odot(S)$. **Shape Signature** of S, $\sigma(S) = (r_1, \ldots, r_n)$, is defined as the distance between each of the atoms of S to $C_\odot(S)$:*

---

[3] The notations $C_\odot(S)$ and C_M are used interchangeably to denote the center of mass.

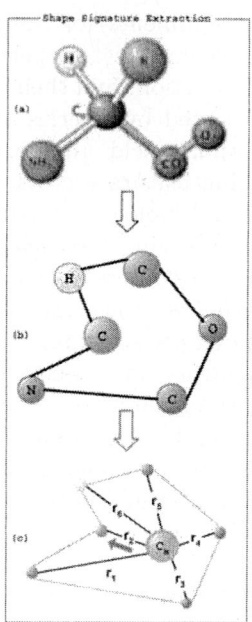

Fig. 1. Shape signature extraction process. (a) An amino acid molecule consisted of N(NH_3^+), C_α, C(CO^-), O, R(C_β), and H atoms. (b) The same amino acid visualized as a three-dimensional polyhedron with its vertices being the coordinates of the corresponding atoms, after removing the bonds. (c) Directional Shape Signature Extraction: The distances between the center of mass C_M (or $C_\odot$) and all the atoms are calculated ($r_1, r_2, \ldots$) along with the direction of the amino acid as $\overrightarrow{C_M C_\alpha}$.

$$r_i = \sqrt{(v_{ix} - C_{\odot x}^S)^2 + (v_{iy} - C_{\odot y}^S)^2 + (v_{iz} - C_{\odot z}^S)^2}.$$

For instance, let S be the same amino acid as in the previous example with $C_\odot(S) = [5.7, 5.08, 6.08]$. The shape signature of S is $\sigma(S) = (r_1, r_2)$ where

$r_1 = \sqrt{(10 - 5.7)^2 + (4 - 5.08)^2 + (12 - 6.08)^2} = 7.4$ and
$r_2 = \sqrt{(2 - 5.7)^2 + (6 - 5.08)^2 + (1 - 6.08)^2} = 6.35$.

The localized shape signature as described above captures the general shape of each amino acid and is *invariant to rotation and displacement*. The invariance property facilitates the matching of the amino acids solely based on their shape and topological properties. This is a particularly helpful summarization since most protein structures in PDB belong to different coordinate systems. Being able to capture the local and global shape of the amino acids and proteins (invariant to rotation and displacement) facilitates the initial step of protein structure similarity. also be taken into account. The next definition captures the conformational property and orientation of the amino acid structures by augmenting the direction of each amino acid molecule onto its corresponding shape signature.

Definition 3 *Let $S = (v_1, \ldots, v_n)$ be a polyhedron amino acid with the center of mass $C_\odot$. Let v_α (for some $0 < \alpha \leq n$) denote the coordinates of C_α atom of S. The **Direction** of S, $\overrightarrow{D(S)}$, is defined as the direction of the vector connecting $C_\odot$ to v_α, or in other words $\overrightarrow{D(S)} = \overrightarrow{C_\odot v_\alpha}$.*

Figure 1 depicts the steps involved in extracting the directional shape signature. We excluded C_β from the shape signature because not all amino acids possess C_β (*Glycine*, GLY) and Hydrogen(H) side chain atoms, and due to their dramatic topological variances in different amino acids. On the other hand, a good shape signature should not only capture the topological and shape properties but also biologically motivated features. As a result, PADS incorporates the secondary structure assignment of each amino acid for a more meaningful and efficient structure comparison. Let P be a protein structure with amino acids $[p_1, \ldots, p_N]$ where each p_i is a vector of the three-dimensional coordinates of atoms of the ith residue. Different amino acids have different, though unique, number of atoms. For instance, *Serine* is an amino acid residue which has only 14 atoms while *Arginine* has 27 atoms. PADS also incorporates the distances from $C_\odot$ to the coordinates of C_α, Nitrogen(N) of the *amino group*, Carbon(C) and uncharged Oxygen(O) of the *carboxyl group*, which are common among all amino acids and are topologically more resilient than other side chain atoms.

Definition 4 *Let $P = [p_1, \ldots, p_N]$ be a protein structure where each p_i represents the list of coordinates of atoms that constitute the ith amino acid of P. The **Directional shape signature** of P, P^ϑ, is defined as the feature vector $P^\vartheta = [p_1^\vartheta, \ldots, p_N^\vartheta]$ where each p_j^ϑ is a feature vector*

$$(|\overrightarrow{C_\odot N}|, |\overrightarrow{C_\odot C_\alpha}|, |\overrightarrow{C_\odot C}|, |\overrightarrow{C_\odot O}|, \overrightarrow{C_\odot C_\alpha}, SSE_j),$$

comprising the distances from the center of mass of the jth amino acid to its N, C_α, C and O atoms(Def. 2) along with its corresponding direction(Def. 3), and its secondary structure assignment.

3.2 Local Alignment Procedures

This section introduces the alignment procedures to be performed on the extracted directional shape signatures of the corresponding proteins. Structural local alignment starts by constructing a score matrix, S, on the directional shape signatures of the given proteins. This score matrix is used to structurally align the corresponding signatures in the alignment step.

Let P and Q be two protein structures with their corresponding directional shape signatures $P^\vartheta = [p_1^\vartheta, \ldots, p_N^\vartheta]$ and $Q^\vartheta = [q_1^\vartheta, \ldots, q_M^\vartheta]$, where p_i^ϑ and q_j^ϑ denote the feature vectors $[r_{i,1}^p, r_{i,2}^p, r_{i,3}^p, r_{i,4}^p, \overrightarrow{v_i^p}, SSE_i^p]$ and $[r_{j,1}^q, r_{j,2}^q, r_{j,3}^q, r_{j,4}^q, \overrightarrow{v_j^q},$

SSE_j^q], respectively. The entry $S_{i,j}$, of the score matrix S, denotes the symmetric normalized[4] score of replacing p_i^ϑ by q_j^ϑ residue and is defined

$$S_{i,j} = \sum_{k=1}^{4}(r_{i,k}^p - r_{j,k}^q)^{-2} + \cos(\vec{v_i^p}, \vec{v_j^q})^{-1} + SSE_{i,j}^{PQ},$$

where $\cos(\boldsymbol{U}, \boldsymbol{V})$ denotes the cosine of the angle between vectors $\boldsymbol{U}$ and $\boldsymbol{V}$, and

$$SSE_{i,j}^{PQ} = \begin{cases} +G & SSE_i^p = SSE_j^q \\ -G & SSE_i^p \neq SSE_j^q. \end{cases}$$

The value of the constant G is empirically chosen to be 10, which is equal to half of the range of the normalized score values. The constant G is used to favor the residue pairs that belong to similar SSEs, and to penalize those that belong to different SSEs. This constant is a tuning parameter of PADS and the user may choose to penalize the residues which have different SSE assignments with a different value for G as desired. Once the calculation of the score matrix is completed, a dynamic programming alignment algorithm is applied to align the given structures. We have deployed the local alignment algorithm [20] using the affine cost gap model with opening and extending gap penalty of -5 and -2, respectively.

Note that, PADS performs two consecutive alignment procedures, *structural alignment* and *sequence alignment*. Structural alignment aligns the corresponding proteins based on their directional shape signatures to find the best structurally-matched-regions. Thereafter, the sequence alignment [16] is performed on the amino acid sequences of the structurally-matched-regions for further refinement of the alignment. For each of the discovered locally matched regions satisfying length and score constraints[5], a *sequence alignment* is performed to facilitate the visualization of the sequence similarities and further refinement. The aligned residue coordinates passed through structural and sequence alignment steps are then passed to the superimposition stage.

Why did we need to perform the superimposition? The detected best local alignment passed from the structural alignment step is not necessarily the most optimal alignment because the directional shape signatures do not include any information on the proximity/locality of the amino acids (i.e., Center of mass ($C_\odot$) was not taken as part of the directional shape signature). Including such locality features in the shape signature would not have been very meaningful because the proteins have different coordinate frames. Should the locality information be included in the shape signature, then two very similar proteins with different coordinate frames may be reported non-similar because of their location differences. Additionally, the detected patterns may have very poor RMSD if the gaps produced by the structural alignment are in turn and twist regions of

---

[4] Scores are normalized on the range [1 ... 20] for all i, j such that $0 < S_{i,j} \leq 20$ to be similar to that of PAM [7] score matrix and CTSS [5].

[5] *Length* longer than 10 and *Score* above the 60% of the overall average score.

the protein structures. The sequence alignment step aims at eliminating those regions from affecting the superimposition process. After the local regions are passed to the superimposition step, the given proteins are translocated to a common coordinate frame. Once the structures are in a common coordinate system, they are optimally superimposed on each other (with the necessary displacements and rotations) achieving the minimal RMSD. Finally, after performing the superimposition, the RMSD values and the length of the best matched regions are reported. Figure 2 provides a summary of PADS procedure.

Input: Protein chains $P = [p_1, \ldots, p_N]$ and $Q = [q_1, \ldots, q_M]$, where each p_i and q_j represent the list of coordinates of atoms that constitute the ith and j^{th} amino acids of P and Q, respectively.

Output: Pairs of aligned/matched fragments of P and Q, reported with their corresponding RMSD and fragment length.

---

1. Directional Shape Signature Extraction:
   - Calculate the center of mass of each amino acid molecule p_i and q_j, as $C_\odot(p_i)$ and $C_\odot(q_j)$, for $1 \leq i \leq N$ and $1 \leq j \leq M$.
   - Calculate the distances between each of the atoms of p_i and q_j molecules to their corresponding center of mass $C_\odot(p_i)$ and $C_\odot(q_j)$, respectively.
   - Extract the direction of each amino acid molecule p_i and q_j.
   - Inspect and include the SSE assignment of each p_i and q_j in the shape signature.
2. Structural local alignment
   - Calculate the score matrix for P and Q protein chains as described in section 3.2.
   - Run the dynamic programming on the calculated score matrix to find the best structurally-matched (aligned) fragment pairs of P and Q.
   - Report the fragment pairs to the next step.
3. Sequence alignment
   - Run the global sequence alignment on the sequences of the structurally-matched fragment pairs
   - Remove the gapped regions of the alignment from the fragments, and report the non-gapped subfragments of the alignment to the next step.
4. Optimal Superimposition
   - Find the best rotation and translation matrix to superimpose the matched non-gapped fragment pairs.
   - Report the RMSD and the length of the matched fragment pairs in the sorted order.

Fig. 2. PADS structure similarity procedure

4 Experimental Results

We implemented our proposed technique using *Java 1.4.1* and ran our experiments on an *Intel Xeon 2.4 GHz* with *1GB* of main memory. Our experiments incorporated a representative of PDB database using the PDBSELECT[6] method [11] which does not contain any homologue protein pairs. The PDBSELECT database is an archive of 2216 *non-homologue* protein chains with a total number of 352855 residues (as of December 2003). Each of the protein pairs from the PDBSELECT protein database has less than 25% sequence identity (non-homologue). As a result, protein pairs with low sequence similarity may not be efficiently compared solely based on a sequence-level similarity procedure and

---

[6] For more information refer to *http://homepages.fh-giessen.de/ hg12640/pdbselect/*

therefore introduce a challenging problem where the combination of structure and sequence alignment is inevitable. As mentioned before, PADS incorporates a combination of structural and sequence alignment for efficient protein similarity comparison.

The performance comparison of PADS with other structural alignment methods is not always possible. One of the main challenges is the *running time* comparison of the proposed technique against current existing heuristics. This is mainly because most of the available techniques are provided as web services in which the results are notified back to the user through an e-mail. As a result, the time interval between submitting a query and obtaining the results does not truly reflect the running time of the applied method. There are many factors that may affect the running time. The servers may include pre-evaluated results for the known structures, and hence the results may be returned very fast. They may be using parallel clusters or various hardware setups for faster computation of the results. The DALI [12] interactive database search[7] may report the results back in 5 to 10 minutes or 1 to 2 hours depending on whether the query protein has a homologue in the database [5]. Meanwhile the most important obstacle is the fact that various structural alignment techniques may lead to non-identical results which makes the quality assessment an even harder problem. There are cases when the regions found very similar by one technique are not validated by other techniques[8]. Since there is no exact solution to the structural alignment problem, a combination of various techniques along with domain expert is needed to evaluate and ascertain all the similarities.

In the experiments, we discovered motifs not reported by other alignment tools such as CE [18], DALI [12], and CTSS [5]. The aligned fragment pairs are reported as a pair of fragments (r_1, r_2) where r_1 and r_2 denote the location of the matched fragments in the first and second protein chains, respectively. One such motif discovered by our technique was between 1AKT:_ (made of 147 residues and 1108 atoms) and 1CRP:_ (made of 166 residues and 2619 atoms) protein chains (having 8.9% sequence identity) with RMSD 0.58 Å. Figure 3 shows the results of structural alignments on 1AKT:_ and 1CRP:_ protein chains using CE[9] and PADS, respectively. These results are reported after finding the best similar regions (fragments) followed by the optimal superimposition of the structures of the corresponding matched fragments. However, the results are shown at the sequence level for the sake of visualization. In figure 3(b), the fragments reported by PADS are demonstrated using the output of CE as the base for better visual comparison of the results. The local fragments are identified by three numbers in the R(L,φ) format, where R, L and $\varphi = \frac{L}{R}$ denote *RMSD*, *length* and the *fragment score* of the aligned (matched) fragments, respectively. The fragment score denotes the *quality* of the matched fragments and the best aligned fragment is the one with the highest fragment score. PADS reports the aligned fragment pairs sorted by their corresponding fragment scores in decreasing order.

---

[7] http://www.embl-ebi.ac.uk/dali/
[8] Please refer to Table VI in [18]
[9] The results of CE were obtained by submitting the corresponding protein chains to CE's interactive web server at http://cl.sdsc.edu/ce.html

Table 2. Comparison of detected similar regions between 1AKT:_ and 1CRP: protein chains using PADS and DALI methods with alignment rank $\varphi = \frac{Fragment\ Length}{RMSD}$

				PADS		DALI	
Rank	φ	Fragment size	RMSD (Å)	1AKT:_	1CRP:_	1AKT:_	1CRP:_
–						[1–8]	[4–11]
2	11.66	14	1.2	[10–23]	[12–35]	[12–15] [18–23]	[12–15] [16–21]
–						[26-29]	[41–44]
5	3.7	20	5.4	[35–54]	[51–70]	[30–36] [43–58]	[53–59] [69–84]
4	6.66	28	4.2	[75–101]	[98–125]	[65–81] [83–92] [93–100]	[88–104] [107–116] [118–125]
3	7.64	13	1.7	[108–121]	[130–142]	[104–112] [121–124]	[130–138] [140–143]
–						[129–133]	[146–150]
1	29.31	17	**0.58**	[131–147]	[149–165]	[135–147]	[151–163]

Table 2 shows a detailed comparison of PADS against DALI[10] [12] on the very same pair of protein chains. Each column pair (1AKT:_ , 1CRP:_) indicates the location of the aligned fragments in the corresponding protein chains. The correspondence of the detected aligned fragments of PADS and DALI are noted in rows and labeled with φ to indicate the quality of the aligned fragments and their corresponding ranks as reported by PADS technique. There are some matched fragments reported by PADS, which do not have counterparts in the results returned by DALI. However, it is interesting to note that, the fragments matched using PADS with higher φ tend to be those fragment pairs having a higher level of similarity to their corresponding aligned fragments as reported by DALI. As a result, highly-ranked matched fragment pairs reported by PADS, have very similar counterparts in the results reported by DALI. We use DALI to validate the quality of our results, while DALI is designed with very insightful domain expertise and is expected to return biologically meaningful results. PADS results are very similar, though not identical, to that of DALI and in some cases, the fragment pairs reported by PADS are a combination of some consecutive fragment pair outputs of DALI. Meanwhile, running PADS on 1AKT:_ and 1CRP:_ protein chains takes only 0.1 CPU seconds.

Similarly, the reported results on the very same pair of protein chains were compared against the CTSS [5] algorithm. CTSS reports the best aligned fragment pair between 1AKT:_ and 1CRP:_ protein chains to be ([89–113],[140–164]) with length 24 and RMSD 2.14 Å with a fragment score of φ=11.21. On a relative note, the best aligned fragment pair reported by PADS is ([131–147],[149–165]) of length 17, though with an RMSD of 0.58 Å and the fragment score of φ=29.31. Although the best fragment pair reported by PADS has smaller length however it is aligned with a substantially better RMSD value (by a factor of 3.6) and higher quality of the alignment (by a factor of 2.6) noted by φ. The calculation

---
[10] The results of DALI were obtained by submitting the corresponding protein chains to DALI's interactive web server hosted by European Bioinformatics Institute at http://www.ebi.ac.uk/dali/

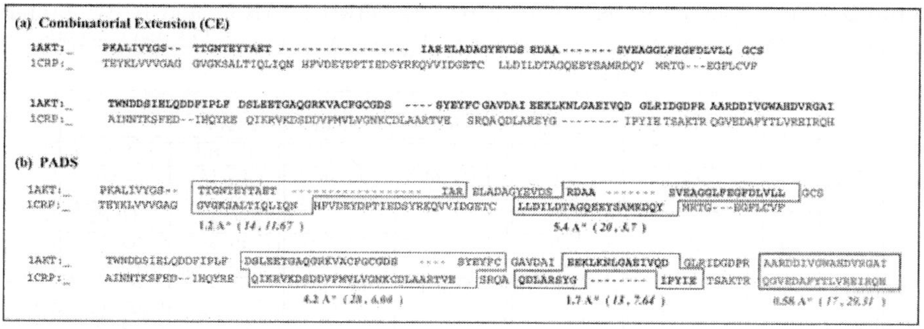

Fig. 3. (a) Structural alignment (shown at the sequence level) between 1AKT:_ and 1CRP:_ using CE. (b) The RMSD, extent and score of local fragments discovered by PADS structural alignment (shown at the sequence level) between 1AKT:_ and 1CRP:_ (The output of CE is also shown for comparison purposes)

of the value of φ in our algorithm is identical with its counterpart in the CTSS method. The intuition behind PADS finding a better fragment pair compared with CTSS, is as follows. The CTSS method approximates each protein chain by a spline (curve), however PADS represents each chain as a series of directional shape signatures (a sequence of polyhedrons in multidimensional space). To give a better visual example, suppose we would like to represent a snake, then CTSS approximates its shape with a rope while PADS approximates the shape using a chain of polyhedral beads for a more precise approximation.

5 Conclusion and Future Work

In this paper, we introduced a novel data representation technique incorporating multidimensional shape similarity and data mining techniques for the problem of structural alignment of protein structure databases. We evaluated the quality of the results of PADS on a pair of protein chains and compared the corresponding results with the other methods. The results demonstrate highly *accurate* (the reported fragments have very high score with the RMSD value much better than all other methods), *consistent* (the fragment pairs reported similar by PADS had high overlap with regions reported similar by other methods) results compared with DALI, CE, and CTSS protein structure similarity methods, while running only in fractions of a second. PADS may be used in collaboration with other protein alignment methods such as DALI and CE for providing a larger number of fragment pairs. One could potentially use PADS to get an instant feedback of the location and quality of the matched regions, and thereafter run the time-consuming DALI method to achieve the most accurate results, if desired. We intend to perform database-against-database structure similarity search for protein classification and add a 3D visualization tool to PADS for better assessment of fragment pair discovery.

References

1. Protein data bank(pdb). http://www.rcsb.org/pdb/holdings.html, 2004.
2. S. A. Aghili, D. Agrawal, and A. E. Abbadi. Pads: Protein structure alignment using directional shape signatures. Technical Report 2004-12, UCSB, May 2004.
3. S. A. Aghili, D. Agrawal, and A. E. Abbadi. Similarity search of protein structures using geometrical features. In *Proceedings of Thirteenth Conference on Information and Knowledge Management (CIKM)*, pages 148–149, 2004.
4. P. Bradley, P. Kim, and B. Berger. Trilogy: Discovery of sequence-structure patterns across diverse proteins. *Proc. Natl. Academy of Science*, 99(13):8500–5, 2002.
5. T. Can and Y. Wang. Ctss: A robust and efficient method for protein structure alignment based on local geometrical and biological features. In *IEEE Computer Society Bioinformatics Conf.*, pages 169–179, 2003.
6. O. Çamoğlu, T. Kahveci, and A. Singh. Towards index-based similarity search for protein structure databases. In *IEEE Computer Society Bioinformatics Conf.*, pages 148–158, 2003.
7. M. Dayhoff and R. Schwartz. Atlas of protein sequence and structure. *Nat. Biomed. Res. Found.*, 1978. Washington.
8. J. Gibrat, T. Madej, and S. Bryant. Surprising similarities in structure comparison. *Current Opinion Structure Biology*, 6(3):377–85, 1996.
9. A. Godzik. The structural alignment between two proteins: is there a unique answer? *Protein Sci.*, 5:1325–1338, 1996.
10. D. Higgins and W. Taylor. *Bioinformatics: Sequence, Structure and Databanks*. Oxford University Press, 2000.
11. U. Hobohm, M. Scharf, and R. Schneider. Selection of representative protein data sets. *Protein Science*, 1:409–417, 1993.
12. L. Holm and C. Sander. Protein structure comparison by alignment of distance matrices. *J. Molecular Biology*, 233(1):123–138, 1993.
13. L. Holm and C. Sander. 3-d lookup: Fast protein database structure searches at 90% reliability. In *ISMB*, pages 179–185, 1995.
14. G. Lua. Top: a new method for protein structure comparisons and similarity searches. *J. Applied Crystallography*, 33(1):176–183, 2000.
15. T. Madej, J. Gibrat, and S. Bryant. Threading a database of protein cores. *Proteins*, 23:356–369, 1995.
16. S. Needleman and C. Wunsch. General method applicable to the search for similarities in the amino acid sequence of two proteins. *J. Molecular Biology*, 48:443–453, 1970.
17. X. Pennec and N. Ayache. A geometric algorithm to find small but highly similar 3d substructures in proteins. *Bioinformatics*, 14(6):516–522, 1998.
18. I. Shindyalov and P. Bourne. Protein structure alignment by incremental combinatorial extension (ce) of the optimal path. *Protein Engineering*, 11(9):739–747, 1998.
19. A. Singh and D. Brutlag. Hierarchical protein structure superposition using both secondary structure and atomic representations. In *Proc. Int. Conf. Intelligent System Mol. Bio.*, pages 284–93, 1997.
20. R. Smith and M. Waterman. Identification of common molecular subsequences. *J. Mol. Bio.*, 147(1):195–197, 1981.

LinkageTracker: A Discriminative Pattern Tracking Approach to Linkage Disequilibrium Mapping

Li Lin[1], Limsoon Wong[2], Tzeyun Leong[3], and Pohsan Lai[4]

[1,3] School of Computing, National University of Singapore
[2] Institute for Infocomm Research, Singapore
[4] Dept of Pediatrics, National University Hospital, National University of Singapore
{linl, leongty}@comp.nus.edu.sg, limsoon@i2r.a-star.edu.sg,
paelaips@nus.edu.sg

Abstract. Linkage disequilibrium mapping is a process of inferring the disease gene location from observed associations of marker alleles in affected patients and normal controls. In reality, the presence of disease-associated chromosomes in affected population is relatively low (usually 10% or less). Hence, it is a challenge to locate these disease genes on the chromosomes. In this paper, we propose an algorithm known as LinkageTracker for linkage disequilibrium mapping. Comparing with some of the existing work, LinkageTracker is more robust and does not require any population ancestry information. Furthermore our algorithm is shown to find the disease locations more accurately than a closely related existing work, by reducing the average sum-square error by more than half (from 80.71 to 30.83) over one hundred trials. LinkageTracker was also applied to a real dataset of patients affected with haemophilia, and the disease gene locations found were consistent with several studies in genetic prediction.

1 Introduction

Linkage disequilibrium mapping has been used in the finding of disease gene locations in many recent studies [6][13]. The main idea of linkage disequilibrium mapping is to identify chromosomal regions with common molecular marker alleles[1] at a frequency significantly greater than chance. It is based on the assumption that there exists a common founding ancestor carrying the disease alleles, and is inherited by his descendents together with some other marker alleles that are very close to the disease alleles. The same set of marker alleles is detected many generations later in many unrelated individuals who are clinically affected by the same disease. In a realistic setting, the occurrence of such allele patterns is usually very low, and most often consist of errors or noise. For instance, the hereditary mutations of BRCA-1 and

---
[1] A molecular marker is an identifiable physical location on the genomic region that either tags a gene or tags a piece of DNA closely associated with the gene. An allele is any one of a series of two or more alternate forms of the marker. From the data mining aspect, we could represent markers as attributes, and alleles as attribute values that each attribute could take on.

BRCA-2 genes only account for about five to ten percent of all breast cancer patients[12]. Assuming that we know that BRCA-1 gene resides somewhere on chromosome 17, the finding of the exact location of BRCA-1 gene on chromosome 17 based on a set of sample sequence collected from breast cancer patients where at most ten percent of the sample sequence exhibit allelic association or linkage disequilibrium is a nontrivial task. To further complicate this task, the linkage disequilibrium patterns also consist of errors due to sample mishandling and contamination.

Due to errors and low occurrence of linkage disequilibrium patterns, existing data mining and artificial intelligence methods involving training and learning will not be applicable. In this paper, we propose a novel method known as *LinkageTracker* for the finding of linkage disequilibrium patterns and inference of disease gene locations. First of all, we identify the set of linkage disequilibrium patterns using a heuristic level-wise neighbourhood search and score each pattern by computing their p-values to ensure high discriminative powers of each pattern. After which, we infer the marker allele that is closest to the disease gene based on the p-value scores of the set of linkage disequilibrium patterns. *LinkageTracker* is a nonparametric method as it is not based on any assumptions about the population structure. The method is robust to cater for missing or erroneous data by allowing gaps in between marker patterns. Comparing our method with Haplotype Pattern Mining (*HPM*) which was reported by Tiovonen et. al. [16], *LinkageTracker* outperforms *HPM* by reducing the average sum-square error by more than half (from 80.71 to 30.83) over one hundred trials.

Organization of This Paper. In the next section, related work will be introduced, followed by a technical representation of the problem and a detailed description of the LinkageTracker algorithm. Next, the optimal number of gaps to set on LinkageTracker to achieve good accuracy will be discussed. We will then evaluate the performance of LinkageTracker with a recent work known as Haplotype Pattern Mining (HPM). Finally, we conclude our paper with a summary and the directions for future work.

2 Related Works

There are generally two methods used for detecting disease genes, namely, the direct and the indirect methods. Techniques used in the direct method include allele-specific oligonucleotide hybridization analysis, heteroduplex analysis, Southern blot analysis, multiplex polymerase chain reaction analysis, and direct sequencing. A detailed description of these techniques is beyond the scope of this paper but is available in [3] and [10]. Direct method requires that the gene responsible for the disease be identified and specific mutations within the gene characterized. As a result, direct method is frequently not feasible, and, the indirect method is used. The indirect methods such as [7], [14], and [16] involves the detection of marker alleles that are very close to or are within the disease gene, such that they are inherited together with the disease gene generation after generation. Such marker alleles are known as haplotypes. Alleles at these markers often display statistical dependency, a phenomenon known as linkage disequilibrium or allelic association [5]. The identification of linkage disequilibrium patterns allows us to infer the disease gene location. Most commonly, linkage disequilibrium mapping involves the comparison of marker allele frequencies between disease chromosomes and control chromosomes.

Kaplan et. al. [7] developed a maximum likelihood method for linkage disequilibrium mapping which estimates the likelihood for the recombination fraction between marker and disease loci by using a Poisson branching process. The likelihood of the haplotypes observed among a sample of disease chromosomes depends on their underlying genealogical relationships, the rates of recombination among markers, and the time since the mutation arose. Although likelihood methods have many desirable properties when used on data whose population ancestry is well understood, it is difficult to evaluate the likelihood when the data is arising from a huge number of possible ancestries.

DMLE+ proposed by Rannala & Reeve [14] uses Markov Chain Monte Carlo methods to allow Bayesian estimation of the posterior probability density of the position of a disease mutation relative to a set of markers. As similar to the maximum likelihood method, *DMLE+* has many good properties when applied to data whose population ancestry is well understood. However, *DMLE+* requires some prior information such as the fraction of the total population of present-day disease chromosome, growth rate of population and the age of the mutation, which may not be readily available. Furthermore, it is assumed that every sample sequence carries the disease mutation, although the authors claimed that this assumption can be relaxed, details on the extent that this assumption can be relaxed was not discussed.

Recently, Tiovonen et. al. [16] introduced a linkage disequilibrium mapping algorithm known as haplotype pattern mining (*HPM*). Firstly, *HPM* uses the association rule mining algorithm [1] to discover a set of highly associated patterns by setting the *Support* threshold to a certain value. Next, *HPM* uses chi-square test to discriminate disease association from control association. Finally, *HPM* computes the marker frequency for each of the markers. The frequency for each marker is computed by counting the number of associated patterns consisting of that specific marker. The marker with the largest frequency is predicted as closest to the disease gene. The main drawback of this algorithm is that it suffers from the rare item problem. As it uses association rule mining algorithm to discover highly associated patterns, and such patterns are relatively rare in the problem of linkage disequilibrium mapping. As a result the support threshold will need to be set at a very low value in order to discover those highly associated patterns.

Comparing *LinkageTracker* with the maximum likelihood method and *DMLE+*, the two methods require information about the population ancestry and assumes that the disease mutation occurs in most (or all) sample sequences, whereas *LinkageTracker* does not require any population ancestry information and allows for the disease mutation to occur in as low as 10% of the sample sequences. When compared to *HPM*, the *LinkageTracker* dose not use *Support* in the assessment of marker patterns, instead *LinkageTracker* uses a statistical method known as *odds ratio* to detect discriminating patterns that are highly associated within the patient data but not in the control data. Hence, the finding of candidate/potential linkage disequilibrium patterns and scoring their degree of associations are combined into a single step. Also as mentioned by Tamhane & Dunlop [15], chi-square test only indicate whether there exists statistically significant association, but it does not account for the magnitude of association. It is thus possible to have a significant chi-square statistics although the magnitude of association is small. The most common measure of the magnitude of association is the *odds ratio* method. *LinkageTracker* infers the marker closest to the disease gene by combining the *p*-values of association patterns consisting of that marker using a method recommended by Fisher [4], and not based on the marker frequency as in the *HPM* algorithm.

3 Technical Representation of *LinkageTracker*

The general framework of the *LinkageTracker* can be represented as a quintuple <D, Ω, L, Ψ, T> where

- D is a dataset consisting of M vectors <$x_1,..., x_M$>, where each x_i is a vector <$d_{i1},..., d_{in}$> that describes the allele values of n genes/markers in a particular biological sample.
- For each position d_{*j}, $\omega_j = \{v_1,..., v_t\}$ denotes the set of all possible expression values that d_{*j} could take on, and Ω is a collection of $\{\omega_1,..., \omega_n\}$.
- A labelling for D is a vector $L = $ <$l_1,..., l_M$>, where the label l_i associated with x_i is either *abnormal* (a biological sequence derived from an individual exhibiting abnormality) or *normal* (a biological sequence belonging to a normal control).
- Ψ is the neighbourhood definition. The neighbourhood determines the maximum allowable gap size within each pattern. The gap setting is to enable *LinkageTracker* to be robust to noise. In a very noisy environment, larger gap size is required for better accuracy by extending the search space, at the expense of computational speed.
- $T \in \Re^+$ is the threshold value for accepting a particular pattern. In statistical terms, T is the level of significance of the test. When the pattern score is less than T, the pattern is considered as significant, and will be kept for further processing.

The output P is a set of linkage disequilibrium patterns with high discriminative powers. A pattern $p=$<$d_{*i}, d_{*j},..., d_{*k}$> where $p \in P$, such that $i < j < k$. Based on the set of patterns in P, we infer the marker allele that is closest to the disease gene. For each marker allele, we combine the *p*-values of all patterns in P that consist of that marker allele. The method to combine *p*-values was first introduced by Fisher [4], and will be described in detail in the next section.

4 LinkageTracker Algorithm

There are two main steps in the *LinkageTracker* algorithm. Step 1 identifies a set of linkage disequilibrium patterns which are strong in discriminating the abnormal from the normal, and step 2 infers the marker allele that is closest to the disease gene based on the linkage disequilibrium patterns derived in step 1.

4.1 Step 1: Discovery of Linkage Disequilibrium Pattern

LinkageTracker uses a statistical method known as odds ratio to score each potential/candidate pattern. If the *p*-value of a pattern is below the threshold *T*, then it is considered as having a significant discriminative power, and will be kept for further processing. Odds ratio provides a good measure of the magnitude of association between a pattern and the binary label *L*, which is crucial in determining the discriminative power and the allelic associations of a pattern. In this section, we will first of all describe the odds ratio method; follow by the details of level-wise neighbourhood searches for potential/candidate patterns and scoring them.

Odds Ratio. Given a pattern *x*, odds ratio computes the ratio of non-association between *x* and the label *L*, to the association between *x* and *L* based on a set of data. For example, given a pattern, say (1,3), we are interested in finding out whether the marker pattern (1,3) is strongly associated with the label *abnormal*. Table 1 shows the contingency table for our example; odds ratio is defined as follows:

$$\text{Odds Ratio, } \theta = \frac{\pi_{11}\pi_{00}}{\pi_{01}\pi_{10}} \quad (1)$$

To test the significance of the magnitude of association, we compute the *p*-value of each pattern, and compare the *p*-value against *T*, if the *p*-value is less than or equals to *T*, the pattern is significant and we will use it for marker inference in the later stage. If the *p*-value is greater than *T*, the pattern is not significant, and will be discarded. The threshold *T* that we use has been adjusted using a method called Bonferroni Correction [11] in order to guarantee that the overall significance test is still at level *T* despite that we have made independent tests on each of the pattern.

Table 1. 2x2 contingency table

	Abnormal	Normal
not(1,3)	π_{00}	π_{01}
(1,3)	π_{10}	π_{11}

LinkageTracker **Algorithm.** *LinkageTracker* mines patterns of the form $<d_{*i}, d_{*j},...,d_{*k}>$, for example, (3,5,6,*,*,4) is a marker pattern of length 4. The symbol "*" represents missing or erroneous marker allele, and will not be taken into consideration when testing for significance of the pattern. Also the symbol "*" will not be considered when computing the length of a marker pattern. Therefore, marker patterns (1,*,*,3), (1,*,3), and (1,3) are all considered as having length of 2.

A gap is a "*" symbol in between two known marker alleles. For instance, the marker patterns (1,*,*,*3) has three gaps, (1,*,3) has one gap, and (1,3) has no gaps. The maximum number of gaps for this marker pattern (1,*,*,3,*,*,*,*,5) is four, as there are at most four gaps in between any two known marker alleles. The user is able to set the maximum number of gaps for the marker patterns. However, we recommend that a maximum allowable gap to be 6, giving the highest accuracy if the markers are spaced at 1 cM². The detail of such a recommendation is given in the later section.

To find linkage disequilibrium patterns using *odds ratio*, one of the way is to use the brute force method. That is, we could enumerate all possible marker patterns of length one, two, and three etc, and compute the *odds ratio* of each of the pattern and select those patterns that are significant. However, there are some practical difficulties to this approach: for n markers each with m alleles, there are $\binom{n}{k} m^k$ marker patterns of length k, which we need to test for significance. Combinatorial explosion occurs as the length of marker patterns increases.

The enumeration of all possible marker patterns is in fact unnecessary. This is because, base on studies by Long & Langley [9], allelic associations are detectable within a genomic region of 20cM, allelic associations beyond 20cM are weak and are not easily detectable. Therefore, enumerating marker patterns whose marker alleles are more than 20cM apart is unlikely to yield significant results. Based on this observation, *LinkageTracker* uses a heuristic search method which allows the user to restrict its search space by controlling the maximum allowable gap size between two marker alleles. As described in section 3, the gap size setting Ψ helps to define the search space of *LinkageTracker* as well as to enable its robustness to noise. For simplicity of illustration, all examples in this paper assume that the markers are spaced at 1cM apart, furthermore, the markers in the simulated datasets (generated by Toivonen et. al. [16]) applied by *LinkageTracker* are all spaced at 1cM apart.

LinkageTracker is a heuristic level-wise search method which allows only significant marker patterns (or linkage disequilibrium patterns) of length i-1 at level i to join with their neighbors (of length 1) whose join would satisfy the maximum gap constraint Ψ to form candidate/potential marker patterns of length i, where $1 \leq i \leq n$ and n is the number of markers. We call the procedure of joining linkage disequilibrium patterns at each level to form longer patterns the *neighborhood join*. Note that in *neighborhood join*, only the marker patterns of length i-1 need to be significant, the neighbors that they join with need not be significant and may be several markers apart.

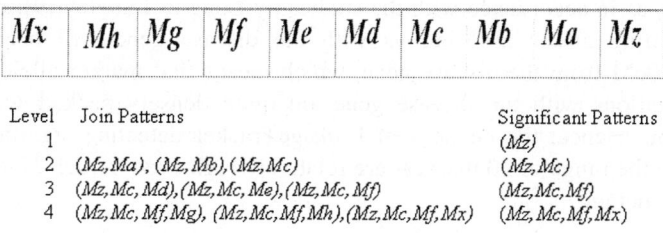

Level	Join Patterns	Significant Patterns
1		(Mz)
2	(Mz,Ma), (Mz,Mb), (Mz,Mc)	(Mz,Mc)
3	(Mz,Mc,Md), (Mz,Mc,Me), (Mz,Mc,Mf)	(Mz,Mc,Mf)
4	(Mz,Mc,Mf,Mg), (Mz,Mc,Mf,Mh), (Mz,Mc,Mf,Mx)	(Mz,Mc,Mf,Mx)

Fig. 1. Illustration of marker positions

---

² cM stands for centimorgan. It is the unit of measurement for genomic distance. In human genome, 1 centimorgan is approximately equivalent, to 1 million base pairs.

A marker allele exhibits significant allelic association with the disease gene under two conditions. Firstly, it is significant on its own when tested (i.e. at level 1). Secondly, when combine with other marker alleles that exhibit allelic associations with the disease gene, it become significant when tested.

The former condition is trivial to detect, the latter condition is concerned with a marker allele who shows significant allelic association with the disease gene when combine with other significant marker alleles but is insignificant when assessed alone. Let us denote this maker allele as *Mx*. This problem can be further divided into 2 cases. The first case is that *Mx* is close to a neighbor *Mi* that is significant when tested alone. The term "close" here means that *Mx* will be selected to join with *Mi* directly to form marker patterns for the immediate next level. For example, two markers say *Mx* and *My* are both not significant at level 1, hence they will be discarded when forming marker patterns for level 2. Now, we have *Mi* which is an immediate neighbor of *My* showing significant allelic association in level 1 (assuming that the markers are ordered as follows: *Mi*, *My* and *Mx*). Hence, in level 2, *Mi* will be made to combine with its neighbors to form marker patterns of length 2. Since *My* is the immediate neighbor of *Mi*, *My* will be selected to form pattern with *Mi*. Although *Mx* is one marker away from *Mi*, *Mx* will also be selected, because *LinkageTracker* allows joining with markers that are some gaps away as described above. Hence, in level 2, both *My* and *Mx* are included in the marker patterns.

The second case is that *Mx* is very far from a marker allele *Mz* that is significant when tested alone. The term "far" here means that *Mx* is less than 20 markers away from *Mz*, but is far enough such that *Mx* will not be selected by *Mz* to form marker pattern for the immediate next level. For example, from Figure 1, *Mx* and *Mz* is 8 markers apart. Assuming that the maximum allowable gap size is set to 2, *Mz* is made to combine with *Ma*, *Mb*, and *Mc* to form patterns of length 2. Assuming that (*Mz,Mc*) is tested significant, then (*Mz,Mc*) will combine with *Md*, *Me*, and *Mf* to form patterns of length 3. Assuming that (*Mz,Mc,Mf*) is tested significant, then (*Mz,Mc,Mf*) will combine with *Mg*, *Mh*, and *Mx* to form patterns of length 4. Hence, *Mx* will ultimately be detected to form marker patterns under the condition that there are sufficient significant "intermediate" allele markers such as *Mc* and *Mf*, to facilitate the detection of allelic associative marker alleles that are much further away (i.e. *Mx*). Nevertheless, as in accordance with the studies by Long & Langley [9], most marker alleles exhibiting allelic associations with the disease gene will occur within a distance of 20cM from the disease gene, which means that marker alleles exhibiting allelic associations with the disease gene are quite densely packed within the 20 makers region. Hence, the chances of LinkageTracker detecting significant marker alleles within the range of 20 markers are relatively high even though *LinkageTracker* is a heuristic method.

4.2 Step 2: Marker Inference

As mentioned in the earlier section, we infer the marker closest to the disease gene by combining the *p*-values of the highly associated patterns. Now, let us describe how we could combine *p*-values from *n* patterns to form a single *p*-value. R.A. Fisher's method [4] specifies that one should transform each p-value into $c = -2 * LN(P)$, where $LN(P)$ represents the natural logarithm of the p-value. The resulting n c-values are added together, and their sum, $\Sigma(c)$, represents a chi-square variable with $2n$ degree of freedom. For example, to find the marker closest to the disease gene, we compute the combine p-value and the frequency for each marker allele. In Figure 2a, Marker 2 has allele 4 occurring four times, its combined p-value is $1.4 * 10^{-6}$, which is the chi-square distribution of $\Sigma(c) = 9.4211 + 10.0719 + 11.6183 + 10.8074 = 41.9186$ with 8 degree of freedom. Figure 2b depicts the combined p-value for each of the marker alleles from Figure 2a. As we can see Marker 2 allele 4 has the lowest combined p-value, and hence we infer that Marker 2 is closest to the disease gene. If more than one marker alleles have the same lowest p-value, then the marker with the highest frequency is selected as the marker closest to the disease gene.

Marker	1 2 3 4 5 6	P-Value	$c = -2 * \ln(P)$
Pattern01	* 4 3 * * *	0.0090	9.4211
Pattern02	2 4 * * 6 1	0.0065	10.0719
Pattern03	2 4 3 5 * *	0.0030	11.6183
Pattern04	* * 3 5 * 1	0.0100	9.2103
Pattern05	2 4 * 5 6 *	0.0045	10.8074

(a)

	Freq	$\Sigma(c)$	Combine P-Value
Marker 1 allele 2	3	32.4975	1.3098E-05
Marker 2 allele 4	4	41.9186	1.4027E-06
Marker 3 allele 3	3	30.2497	3.5236E-05
Marker 4 allele 5	3	31.6390	1.9160E-05
Marker 5 allele 6	2	10.0719	0.0392
Marker 6 allele 1	2	19.2822	0.007

(b)

Fig. 2. a) Example of 5 linkage disequilibrium patterns. b) Combine p-value of each marker allele from (a)

5 Setting the Optimal Number of Gaps

To accurately find the marker closest to the disease gene, it is important to determine the optimal number of gaps to use. The marker alleles that show significant allelic associations with the disease gene (within 20 markers region) should minimize the number of joins with neighbors beyond the 20 markers region. This is because the joining of a significant marker allele with some neighbors that are beyond the 20 markers region will inevitably introduce some false positive marker patterns or noise. Such false positive marker patterns will result in the reduction in accuracy during marker inference. On the other hand, we want to be as robust as possible, that is, to maximize the total possible gaps so as to cater for erroneous marker alleles. Based on these two conditions, we compute the *Score* for each gap setting *g* as follows for patterns of length 2:

$$Score(g) = \frac{\sum_{i=0}^{g} Robustness_i}{\sum_{i=0}^{g} Noise_i} \qquad (2)$$

Figure 3 shows the *Score* values for gap settings between 0 to 20. Different gap settings will result in different values for *Noise* and *Robustness*. We shall now illustrate how the values of *Noise* and *Robustness* were computed with examples.

Noise. *Noise* is defined as the maximum possible number of patterns consisting of markers beyond the 20 markers region. Figure 4 shows a disease gene that is very close to marker *M1*, markers *M21 and M22* are in dotted boxes as they are beyond the 20 makers region from the disease gene. Assuming that marker *M2* shows significant association with the disease gene, and we set the maximum allowable gaps to 1, then *M2* can join with its neighbors *M3* and *M4* to form patterns of length 2, i.e. *(M2,M3)* and *(M2,M4)*. Recall that the joining of a significant marker with some neighbors that are beyond the 20 markers region will introduce *Noise*. In this case, if markers *M19* and *M20* are significant, they will join with *M21* and *M22* to form patterns of length 2. We can see from Figure 4 that *M19* and *M20* will join with *M21* and *M22* in three ways, as illustrated by the dotted arrows. Hence, the maximum possible number of patterns consisting of markers beyond the 20 markers region (i.e. $\sum_{i=0}^{1} Noise_i$) is 3 when the gap setting is 1. The *Noise* values for gap settings from 2 to 20 were computed similarly.

Robustness. Before computing the *Robustness* values, we need to compute the maximum possible number of patterns *p* formed within the 20 markers region when the gap setting is *g*. When the gap setting *g* is set to 1, we can have at most 18 patterns (i.e. *p* = 18) as illustrated by the arrows in Figure 5. With the values of *p* for different values of *g*, we define *Robustness* as the maximum number of patterns formed within the 20 markers region weighted by the gap setting *g* itself:

$$Robustness = p \times g. \qquad (3)$$

Recall that it is desirable to have wider gaps so as to cater for erroneous marker alleles, hence the value of *Robustness* increases as the value of *g* increases. As we can see from Figure 3 that the gap setting of 6 has the highest *Score* value, hence we recommend that for a dataset with more than 20 markers to each chromosome (i.e. more than 20 attributes to each record) and each marker is spaced at 1cM apart, the optimal allowable gap setting should be 6.

To verify our above recommendation, we evaluated the performance of *LinkageTracker* by varying the gap settings from 2 to 10 on 100 realistically simulated datasets generated by Tiovonen et. al. [16] (details in the next section). The sum-square errors were computed for different gap settings *g* when applied to the 100 datasets. We found that the gap setting of 6 has the lowest sum-square error, which means that it has the highest accuracy. This is in compliance with our above recommendation.

Num. of Gaps (g)	Noise	Num. Of patterns p form with g gaps	Robustness $= p \times g$	Score(g)
0	1	19	0	0
1	2	18	18	6
2	3	17	34	8.67
3	4	16	48	10
4	5	15	60	10.67
5	6	14	70	10.95
6	7	13	78	**11**
7	8	12	84	10.89
8	9	11	88	10.67
9	10	10	90	10.36
10	11	9	90	10
11	12	8	88	9.59
12	13	7	84	9.14
13	14	6	78	8.67
14	15	5	70	8.17
15	16	4	60	7.65
16	17	3	48	7.11
17	18	2	34	6.56
18	19	1	18	6
19	20	0	0	0
20	21	0	0	0

Fig. 3. *Score* values for 0 to 20 gaps

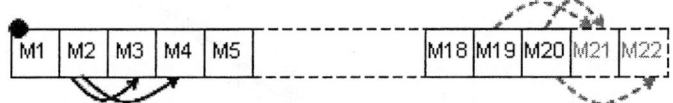

Fig. 4. The darken circle indicates the disease gene location

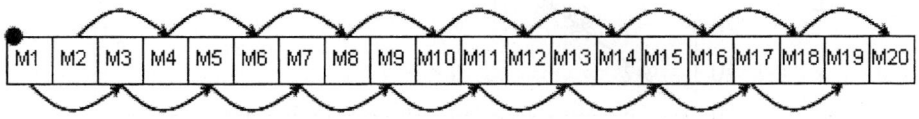

Fig. 5. Joining of markers when gap setting g is 1

6 Evaluation

6.1 Generated Datasets

The datasets used in our experiments are generated by Tiovonen et. al. [16] and are downloadable from the following URL: http://www.genome.helsinki.fi/eng/research/projects/DM/index-ajhg.html. The simulated datasets correspond with the realistic isolated founder populations which grow from 300 to about 100,000 individuals over a period of 500 years. The simulation of isolated population is suited to linkage disequilibrium studies as recommended by Wright et. al. [17].

There are altogether 100 datasets each consists of 400 biological sequences where 200 sequences were labeled *"abnormal"* and 200 labeled *"normal"*, each biological sequence consists of 101 markers. The datasets were generated such that each dataset has a different disease gene location, and our main task is to predict the marker (or attribute) that is nearest to the disease gene for each dataset.

6.2 Comparison of Performance on Generated Datasets

Figure 6 shows the performance of *HPM* (proposed by Tiovonen et. al. [16]) and *LinkageTracker* when applied to the generated datasets. Each point on the graph depicts the predicted disease gene location by *HPM* if marked "◊" and the predicted disease gene location by *LinkageTracker* if marked "+", for the 100 dataset. The straight line depicts that the predicted location is the same as the actual location, the closer the "◊" or "+" marks to the straight line the more accurate is the prediction. As we can see that the accuracy of *LinkageTracker* is reasonably good with only one significant outlier, whereas *HPM* has two significant outliers. The same outlier was encountered by *LinkageTracker* when tested on different gap settings, which means

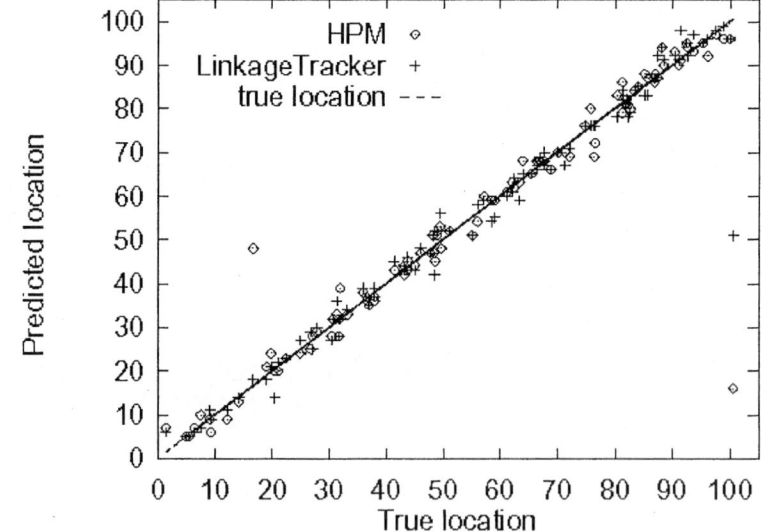

Fig. 6. Comparison of prediction accuracies between *HPM* and *LinkageTracker*

that there may exists some errors in this dataset such that a "pseudo region" occurs that differentiate itself from the normal population that is much more significant than the true region with the disease gene. The average sum-square error for *HPM* is 80.71, and the average sum square error for *LinkageTracker* is 30.83. Hence, *LinkageTracker* outperforms *HPM* in general with lower sum-square error. Even after we remove the common outlier between *LinkageTracker* and *HPM*, *LinkageTracker* continues to outperform *HPM* with an average sum-square error of 6.40, as compared to *HPM* with an average sum-square error of 15.47.

6.3 Performance on Real Dataset

We applied our algorithm on a real dataset, consisting of patients affected by hemophilia from Singapore[3], and a set of matching unaffected individuals. Hemophilia A is an X-linked recessive bleeding disorder that results from deficiency and/or abnormality of coagulation factor VIII (FVIII) [2]. The FVIII gene spans 186 kb of DNA and resides on 0.1% of the X chromosome (band Xq28).

A set of markers located on chromosome Xq28 which tags the hemophilia A disease gene were collected and analyzed from 47 patients and 47 matched normal controls. The *LinkageTracker* detected Bcl I RFLP marker as the closest to the disease susceptible gene. Our prediction results showing Bcl I association was found and confirmed through elaborate biological experiments, as Bcl I is an intragenic SNP (single nucleotide polymorphism) in intron 18 of FVII gene and is linked to hemophilia A disease phenotype [8]. *LinkageTracker* is able to guide or narrow the investigation in identifying the polymorphic markers that tag the disease genes.

7 Conclusions and Future Work

We have introduced a new method of inferring the location of disease genes based on observed associations known as *LinkageTracker*. *LinkageTracker* has shown to be highly accurate in both simulation-generated and real genetic datasets. We have also recommended the optimal number of gaps to set on *LinkageTracker* to achieve good accuracy. Comparing with the maximum likelihood method and *DMLE+*, the two methods require information about the population ancestry and assume that the disease mutation occurs in most or all sample sequences, whereas *LinkageTracker* does not require any population ancestry information and allows for the disease mutation to occur in as low as 10% of the sample sequences. Comparing the performance of *LinkageTracker* with a recent work known as *HPM*, *LinkageTracker* outperforms *HPM* with lower average sum-square error. Even after we remove the common outlier, the sum-square error of *LinkageTracker* remains significantly lower than the average sum-square error of *HPM*. In the future, we plan to extend this work to identify boundaries in which all the significant patterns can be bounded and ultimately guarantees that all significant patterns can be found.

---

[3] Data is obtained from Department of Pediatrics, National University Hospital, National University of Singapore.

Acknowledgements

This research is partially supported by a Research Grant No. R-252-000-111-112/303 from the Agency for Science, Technology, and Research (A*Star) and the Ministry of Education in Singapore.

References

[1] R. Agrawal, and R. Srikant. Fast algorithm for mining association rules. In *Proceedings of the Very Large Data Bases (VLDB) Conference*, 1994.
[2] S. Antonarakaris, H. Kazazian, E. Tuddenham. Molecular etiology of factor VIII deficiency in hemophilia A. *Human Mutation,* 5:1-22,1995.
[3] A. Beaudet, C. Scriver, W. Sly, D.Valle. Genetics, biochemistry, and molecular basis of variant human phenotypes. In: Scriver CR, Beaudet AL, Sly WS, et al, eds. *The Metabolic and Molecular Basis of Inherited Disease.* 7th ed. New York, NY: McGraw-Hill, Inc; 2351-2369, 1995.
[4] R. Fisher. *Statistical methods for research workers*, 14th edition. Hafner/MacMillan, New York, 1970.
[5] D. Goldstein, and M. Weale. Population genomics: Linkage disequilibrium holds the key. *Current Biology*, 11:R576-R579, 2001.
[6] J. Hastbacka, A. de la Chapelle, I. Kaitila, P. Sistonen, A. Weaver, and E. Lander. Linkage disequilibrium mapping in isolated founder populations: diastrophic dysplasia in Finland. *Nature Genetics,* 2:204-211, 1992.
[7] N. Kaplan, W. Hill, and B. Weir. Likelihood methods for locating disease genes in non-equilbrium populations. *American Journal of Human Genetics*, 56:18–32, 1995.
[8] S. Kogan, M. Doherty, J. Gitschier. An improved method for prenatal diagnosis of genetic diseases by analysis of amplified DNA sequences. Application to hemophilia A. *New England Journal of Medicine*, 317: 985-990, 1987.
[9] A. Long, and C. Langley. The power of association studies to detect the contribution of candidate genetic loci to variation in complex traits. *Genome Research*, 9: 720-731, 1999.
[10] S. Malcolm. Molecular methodology. In: Rimoin DL, Connor JM, Pyeritz RE, eds. Emery and Rimoin's Principles and Practice of Medical Genetics. 3rd ed. New York, NY: Churchill Livingstone; 67-86, 1997.
[11] R. Miller. *Simultaneous statistical inference* . 2nd edition. Springer Verlag, 1981.
[12] National Cancer Institute. Cancer Facts. http://cis.nci.nih.gov/fact/3_62.htm. Date reviewed: 02/06/2002.
[13] L. Ozelius, P. Kramer, D. de Leon, N. Risch, S. Bressman, D. Schuback et. al. Strong allelic association between the torsion dystonia gene (DYT1) and loci on chromosome 9q34 in Ashkenazi Jews. *American Journal Human Genetics* 50: 619–628, 1992.
[14] B. Rannala and J. Reeve. High-resolution multipoint linkage-disequilibrium mapping in the context of a human genome sequence. American Journal of Human Genetics 69:159-178, 2001.
[15] A. Tamhane, and D. Dunlop. *Statistics and data analysis: from elementary to intermediate.* Prentice Hall, 2000.
[16] H. Toivonen, P. Onkamo, K. Vasko, V. Ollikainen, P. Sevon, H. Mannila, M. Herr, and J. Kere. Data mining applied to linkage disequilibrium mapping. *American Journal of Human Genetics*, 67:133-145, 2000.
[17] A. Wright, A. Carothers, and M. Pirastu. Population choice in mapping genes for complex diseases. *Nature Genetics*, 23:397-404, 1999.

Query Optimization in Encrypted Database Systems

Hakan Hacıgümüş[1], Bala Iyer[2], and Sharad Mehrotra[3]

[1] IBM Almaden Research Center, USA
 hakanh@acm.org
[2] IBM Silicon Valley Lab., USA
 balaiyer@us.ibm.com
[3] University of California, Irvine, USA
 sharad@ics.uci.edu

Abstract. To ensure the privacy of data in the relational databases, prior work has given techniques to support data encryption and execute SQL queries over the encrypted data. However, the problem of how to put these techniques together in an optimum manner was not addressed, which is equivalent to having an RDBMS without a query optimizer. This paper models and solves that optimization problem.

1 Introduction

There is an ongoing consolidation in IT industry that results in the application-service-provider (ASP) model. Organizations outsource some or all of their core IT operations (e.g., data centers) to specialized service providers over the Internet. Many users will be storing their data and processing their applications at the remote, potentially untrusted, computers. One of the primary concerns is that of data privacy – protecting data from those who do not need to know.

There are two kinds of threats to the privacy. Outsider threats from hackers and insider threats, perhaps, disgruntled employees. Encrypting the stored data [3] is a way to address the outsider threats. The data is only decrypted on the server before computation is applied and re-encrypted thereafter. The insider threats, however, are more difficult to protect against. For example, how would one protect the privacy of data from the database system administrator who probably has the superuser access privileges? If the client is on a secure environment then one way to solve the insider threat problem is to store all the data encrypted on the server and make it impossible to decrypt on the server. In this model we assume the computation against the data stored at the server is initiated by the client. Say it is possible to transform and split the computation into two parts. The server part is sent to the server to execute directly against the encrypted data giving encrypted results, which are shipped to the client, who decrypts and performs the end user portion of the computing. This scheme, presented [1], addresses the problem of insider threats. The problem of how to perform this scheme in an optimum manner was not addressed, which is equivalent to having an RDBMS without a query optimizer. In this paper, we essentially address that problem. We will start our presentation with the description of the system model.

2 The System Model

In this paper, we follow the service-based database model. We specifically follow the system model described in [1]. In the model, the data is owned by the clients. The server exposes mechanisms for the clients to create tables, insert, update records and execute queries. The privacy challenge is to make it impossible for the server to correctly interpret the data.

The data originates from the client and the data is encrypted by the client before it is sent to the server for inclusion in a table. The data is always encrypted when it is stored on, or processed by the server. The authorized clients are given the needed encryption key(s). At no time is the encryption key given to the server, thus the data cannot be decrypted by the server. Queries against data-in-the-clear, originate from the client. The algorithms, based on client metadata, decompose the query into client and server queries. The server query is sent to the server to execute against encrypted data. The processing algorithms are designed such that the results of the original query are obtained if the client decrypts and further processes the answers of the server query using the decomposed client query.

Encrypted Data Storage Model: The encrypted storage model defines how the clients' data is stored at the server site in encrypted form. The storage model we use in this study substantially enhances the one presented in [1] and we presented essential parts of it elsewhere [4]. Hence we give the details of the storage model in Appendix A for the benefit of the reader.

3 Query Processing over Encrypted Data

Given a query Q, which is represented as an operator tree, our purpose is to define how the query can be securely evaluated in an encrypted database environment. We partition a given query tree into two parts: Q^S and Q^C, where Q^S executes at the server and Q^C at the client. Since decryption is not allowed at the server, Q^S executes over the encrypted data directly. The most obvious way to partition the query processing in this case is to store the encrypted tables at the server side and transfer them whenever they are needed for the query processing to the client. Then, the client could decrypt the tables and evaluate the rest of the query. Although this model would work, it pushes almost the whole query processing to the client and does not allow the client to exploit the resources available at the server site. In computing models we consider, the goal of the partitioning is to minimize the work done by Q^C since the clients may have limited storage and computational resources and they rely on the servers for the bulk of the computation.

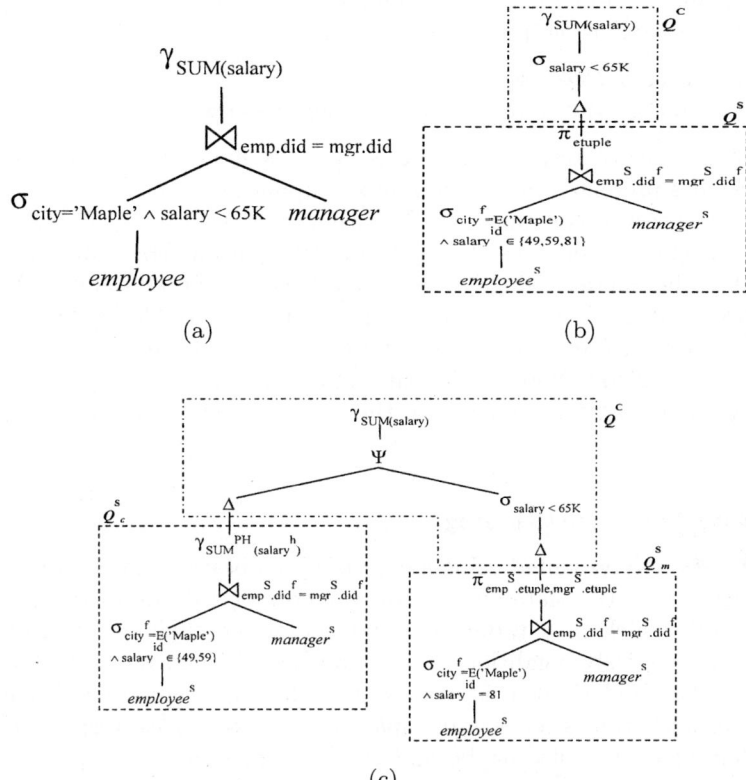

Fig. 1. Operator and Data level query partitioning

Our focus in this paper is how to partition a given query tree in a way that maximizes the benefit of the client based on system specific criteria. We formulate this concern as an optimization problem. In our system, the client is responsible to generate the partitioned query execution plans. Consequently, the client performs the optimization process based on the statistics and the metadata information maintained at the client site. Once the server side and the client side queries are identified, they are subject to the traditional query optimization at the server and at the client sites, respectively.

3.1 Operator Level Partitioning

The server query, Q^S, executes over the encrypted representation directly generating a possibly superset of the results. The results of Q^S are decrypted and further processed by the client using Q^C to generate the real answer to the original query Q. We refer to the partitioning of Q into Q^S and Q^C as the *operator-level partitioning*. Since the operator-level partitioning has been extensively studied in [1], we explain the basic idea using an example over the *employee* and *manager* tables. The sample population of *employee* table is given in Table 2 and partitioning scheme of *salary* attribute of *employee* is given in Table 3 in Appendix A. Consider the following query:

```
SELECT SUM(salary) FROM employee, manager
WHERE city='Maple' AND salary < 65K AND emp.did=mgr.did
```

The query tree corresponding to this query is shown in Figure 1(a). Based on the schemes presented in [1], the sample population given here, and the data partitions, the server side query can be formulated as shown in Figure 1(b).

Here, Δ operator denotes the decryption operation. For now, we can just assume that the operator simply decrypts all the encrypted data fed to it. We will discuss the definition and the use of Δ operator in detail later. The inequality predicate *salary* $< 65K$ over *salary* attribute is transformed into a predicate, $salary^{id} \in \{49, 59, 81\}$. Note that partition 81 may or may not include the values that satisfy the condition. Therefore, they are subject to the client side post-processing.

3.2 Data Level Partitioning

Since the data is represented using a coarse representation via partition indices, a condition in Q is translated into a corresponding condition over the partition indices in Q^S which may produce a superset of the tuples that truly satisfy Q. Tuples that satisfy conditions in Q^S can be classified into two: those that *certainly* satisfy and those that *may* satisfy the the original conditions in Q. We refer to such tuples as *certain tuples* and *maybe tuples*, respectively. This partitioning of tuples into maybe and certain tuples induces a partitioning of the server side query Q^S into two parts: Q_m^S and Q_c^S. We refer to such a data-induced partitioning of Q^S into Q_m^S and Q_c^S as the *data-level partitioning*. If the data-level partitioning is used, the results of the two server side queries must be appropriately *merged* at the client to produce the final answer to the query.

The data-level partitioning splits the server side query Q^S into two parts Q_c^S and Q_m^S, based on the records that qualify the conditions in Q^S; those that certainly satisfy the condition of the original query Q and those that may or may not, respectively.

- **Certain Query** (Q_c^S): that selects the tuples that *certainly* qualify the conditions included in Q. The results of Q_c^S can be computed at the server.
- **Maybe Query** (Q_m^S): that selects the *etuples* corresponding to the records that *may* qualify the conditions of Q but it cannot be determined for sure without decrypting.

We illustrate the data-level partitioning below using an example query over the *employee* and *manager* tables we considered earlier. Here we show the split that would result if we further considered the data level partitioning. The resulting queries, Q_c^S and Q_m^S, after the data-level partitioning are shown in Figure 1(c).

The rationale for the above split is that given the partitioning scheme shown in Table 3 (shown in Appendix A), we know that the tuples corresponding to partitions 49 and 59 certainly satisfy the condition specified in the original query

($salary < 65K$). Thus, those tuples can be collected and aggregated at the server by exploiting the PH. Q_m^S selects the tuples which may satisfy the original query condition. In our example, these correspond to the first two tuples of the $employee^S$ relation (see Table 1 in Appendix A). The query returns the corresponding $etuples$ to the client. Upon decryption, the client can figure that, the first tuple (which has $salary = 70K$) does not satisfy the query and should be eliminated. The second tuple, however, which has $salary = 60K$, satisfies the query condition and should be taken into account. The client finalizes the computation by $merging$ the answer returned by the first and second queries. This presents the data level partitioning of the query. We refer the interested readers to [4] for the details of the algorithm that derives Q_c^S and Q_m^C given Q. In the query execution tree, the Ψ operator represents the merge operation.

3.3 Multi-round Communications

There are certain cases where the server communicates with the client by sending some encrypted intermediate results, and continues the server side query processing after receiving additional information from the client. This information can be in different forms as it will be clear in the sequel. We call this process as $round\ communication$ (or round trip) and represent by a ω operator in the query execution tree. The reason we use the term of "multi-round" is that, obviously, there may be a number of such communications between the server and the client during the execution of a given query tree. In the following subsections we show the specific uses of the round communications.

Filtering the $Maybe$ Tuples. The server can communicate with the client by sending the $maybe\ tuples$ as the intermediate results for filtering, instead of "carrying" them to the later operations in a query execution tree. The server continues the server side computation after receiving back the filtered results, which include only the $certain\ tuples$ in this case. This process is the first use of the round trips between the client and the server. The output of this operator includes "only" the $certain$ records.

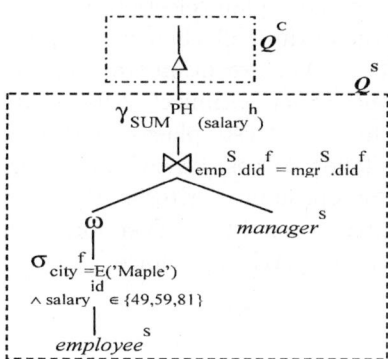

Fig. 2. Round communication for filtering the $maybe$ tuples

We illustrate the use of a round trip in Figure 2. The query execution tree represents the same query we used in Section 3.1. Differently from the previous case, the server communicates with the client after the selection operator, $\sigma_{city^f = \mathcal{E}('Maple') \wedge salary^{id} \in \{49,59,81\}}$. Recall that partition 81 produces maybe tuples as it may or may not contain records that satisfy the original query condition $salary < 65K$. Instead of carrying those maybe tuples, the server sends them to the client and receives only the ones that satisfy the original condition. Since the client can decrypt, the client performs this filtering. As the remaining operators do not produce more maybe tuples, the server is able to perform the rest of the computation over the encrypted records, including the aggregation operation. The client receives only the aggregate value and decrypts it to compute the final answer to the query.

The Use of Server-Computed Values. The second use of the round communications is for the values that are computed by the server in the encrypted form. The logical comparisons (except the equality) cannot be performed by the server over the encrypted values. This is mainly due to the security restrictions of the encryption algorithms [5, 6, 4]. We make use of the partition ids to evaluate the logical comparisons [1]. Therefore, whenever the server has to perform a logical comparison, which uses at least one value that is computed in the encrypted form, then the server needs to send the tuples that have been processed until that point to the client for the client side query processing. However, being able to make use of these values can significantly reduce the amount of work that has to be done at the client site for some cases. The aggregation queries are a typical example for that situation. Further details on the use of server-computed values could be found in [2].

4 Optimization

It is obvious that a rich set of possibilities exist in placing Δ and ω operators in a query tree and different placements indeed result in different query execution plans, which may have significantly different resource utilization and consumption. Therefore, a decision on a query execution plan should be made judiciously based on some criteria, which consider the system and application specific requirements. In this section, we study the query-plan-selection problem of this kind. We present algorithms for finding the optimal placement of Δ and ω operators in a given query execution tree. That query execution tree may be provided by any other source such as a traditional query optimizer. After that, the objective of an optimization algorithm is to find the "best" places for Δ or ω operators or both. Our optimization algorithms follow a "cost-based" approach. However, we do not assume any cost metric for optimality criteria. We only use a specific cost metric to give examples to present the ideas. Therefore, the algorithms can be integrated with any cost metric of particular choice.

4.1 Definitions and Notations

We first give necessary definitions and introduce new additional operators that are used in the query formulations.

Query Execution Tree: A query execution tree is a directed acyclic graph $G = (V, E)$, consisting of nodes V and edges $E \subset V \times V$. The internal nodes of the tree are the relational algebra operators and the leaf nodes are the base relations, $R_i : 1 \leqslant i \leqslant n$. The edges specify the flow of data. For an edge

$e = (u,v) : u,v \in V$, if the relational operator corresponding to u produces *maybe* records, then we state that, the edge "carries" *maybe* records.

Relational Algebra Operators: We consider the following relational operators: the binary operators denoted by $\odot = \{\bowtie, \rightarrow, \times\}$ ($\rightarrow$ represents left outerjoin) and the unary operators denoted by $\ominus = \{\pi, \delta, \sigma, \gamma\}$. Let $\odot_p$ denote a binary operator involving predicate p.

Renaming Base Relations: A base relation of a query tree is renamed with a unique identifier $R_i : 1 \leq i \leq n$, where n is the number of leaves (i.e., base relation) of the tree. Here, i denotes the index of the base relations. We define the set of base relation indexes as $\mathbb{I} = \{i \mid 1 \leq i \leq n$ and i is the index of base relation $R_i\}$.

Label of an Edge: A label of an edge $e = (u,v)$, $label(e)$, is the set of base relation indexes of the relations of which u is ancestor.

Δ Operator: Δ_L signifies the "last" interaction (or one way trip) case in the system. This means, if a Δ operator is placed on a path, beyond the Δ operator the execution is performed at the client site. In the process, the server sends all the intermediate results to the client and requests the needed decryptions. This concludes the server side query processing. L is a set of base relation indexes of the relations, of which the Δ_L operator is an ancestor in the query execution tree. In the most general case, a Δ_L operator implies the decryption of all of the attributes of the schema of the expression passed to the operator.

ω Operator: An ω operator represents a round trip communication between the client and the server, as it is described in Section 3.3. The server communicates with the client by sending only the *maybe* records for the intermediate processing. The client decrypts those records, and applies any needed processing, e.g., the elimination of false positives, and sends back only the records corresponding to the true positives, to the server. The output of this operator includes "only" *certain* records. The server temporarily transfers the query processing to the client and gets it back if an ω operator is used, whereas the control of query processing is totally transferred to the client and is never transferred back to the server if a Δ operator is used.

ω-Eligible Edge: ω-eligible edge is an element of E and is any edge that carries *maybe* data items or carries *server-computed* values or both.

4.2 Query Re-write Rules

To be able to generate alternate query execution plans, we have to be able to move Δ and ω operators around in the query tree. This requires the re-write rules, which defines the interaction of those operators with the relational algebra operators. ω operator does not pose any difficulty in pulling up/pushing down it above/below of a query tree node. Because, the sole purpose of ω operator is filtering out the maybe records. Eliminating false positives does not affect the

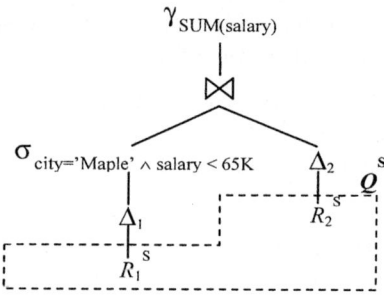

Fig. 3. Starting point for Δ optimization

correctness of the operators in the nodes above and below an ω node. However, Δ operator needs special attention.

Re-write Rules for Δ Operator: Δ operator can be pulled above of any unary and binary operator except GroupBy operator.[1] Formally, we give the re-write rules as follows:

$$\Delta_{L_1} E_1^S \odot_p \Delta_{L_2} E_2^S = \odot_{p'}^C \Delta_{L_1 \cup L_2}(E_1^S \odot_{Map_{cond}(p)}^S E_2^S)$$

$$\ominus_p \Delta_{L_1} E_1^S = \ominus_{p'}^C \Delta_{L_1} \ominus_{Map_{cond}(p)}^S E_1^S$$

where E_1^S, E_2^S are query expressions. $\odot^C$ and $\ominus^C$ represent the client site computation of the translated operators. Similarly, $\odot^S$ and $\ominus^S$ represent the server side computation of the translated operators. p' represents the client side filtering conditions for the translated operators. The details of those operator translations are fully studied in [1]. Map_{cond} function maps the query conditions into the new ones that can be evaluated over the encrypted data. The definition of Map_{cond} is fully discussed in [1] and [4].

4.3 Optimization Algorithm

In this section, we give the optimization algorithms to optimally place Δ and ω operators in a given query execution tree. We first present an algorithm, which only deals with Δ operators and then provide another algorithm, which considers both Δ and ω operators together by utilizing the first one.

Optimization for Δ Operators. The algorithm steps, which optimally places Δ operators only in a given query execution tree, is shown in Figure 4. There are pre-processing steps before the execution of the algorithm as given below.

Pre-processing over a given query execution tree:
 1) Renaming base relations: We rename the base relations as described in Section 4.1. *2) Creation of set of Δ operators:* We put a Δ_i operator as an

---

[1] The complete discussion for GroupBy operator could be found in [2].

adjacent node above each leaf node (base relation R_i) in the query tree. *3) Labeling the edges:* The labels of the edges of the query execution tree are created bottom-up fashion. The initialization of the process starts with the creation of the labels of the edges $e_i = (R_i, \Delta_i)$, where R_i is a leaf level node (a base relation) and the Δ_i is corresponding Δ operator added to the query execution tree. Then label $label(e)$ of an edge $e = (u, v) : u, v \in V$ is created as $label(e) = \bigcup label(e')$, where $e' = (w, u) : w, u \in V$.

The starting point for the algorithm is an original given query tree, for example Figure 1(a). We first rename the relations and replace them with the server-side representations of the relations. After this step, we place the Δ operators to their initial positions. Such a query tree, based on Figure 1(a), is given in Figure 3. Starting with that plan, the optimization algorithm enumerates the valid query plans by placing Δ operators using the rewrite rules. A possible outcome of the algorithm can be the plan given in Figure 1(b).

The algorithm given in Figure 4 enumerates all possible sets of edges, η, in Line 1. Those sets have two properties: 1) the labels of the edges included in the set are disjoint and 2) the labels of the edges in the set constitute the set of base relation indexes, $\mathbb{I}$, when they are combined. The first property ensures the uniqueness of the set. The second property ensures the completeness. This means, all of the tuples, which are needed to correctly finalize the query processing, from all of the encrypted tables are sent to the client.

After that step, the algorithm places Δ operators on each edge of the selected set in Line 4. This creates a unique query execution plan p augmented with Δ operators. Then the algorithm computes the cost of the plan in Line 5. The cost of a plan, $cost(p)$, is defined based on a cost metric determined for a system setup. This cost is compared with the minimum cost plan so far. At this state, the algorithm checks whether the generated query plan is realizable in line 6. To do this, the Δ operators in the generated plan are pulled up from their initial locations (right above the base encrypted relations) to the current locations determined by the plan by using the rewrite rules given in Section 4.2. If they can be pulled up in that way, this constitutes a realizable query execution plan. The algorithm returns the plan with the minimum cost after examining the enumerated plans.

Optimal Placement of ω Operators. The placement of ω operators are essentially different than that of the Δ operators. There may not be more than one Δ operator on a path in a query execution tree whereas there may be ω operators as many as the number of ω-eligible edges on a path from the root of the query execution tree to a node. As a result, the optimal placement algorithm for the ω operators considers any combination of the ω-eligible edges in a given query execution tree.

A Three-Phase Optimization Algorithm. In this section we discuss an optimization algorithm, which considers both Δ and ω operators to find the optimal query execution plan. The algorithm operates at three phases and is shown in Figure 5.

Input: A query execution tree $G = (V, E)$
Output: $bestPlan$

1. Let E' be a set of all η where $\eta \subset E$
   s.t. $\bigcap_i label(e_i) = \emptyset \wedge \bigcup_i label(e_i) = \mathbb{I} : e_i \in \eta$
2. $bestPlan =$ a dummy plan with infinite cost
3. **for all** $\eta \in E'$
4.   place Δ on each edge $e_i : e_i \in \eta$
5.   **if** $cost(p) < cost(bestPlan)$ **then**
6.   **if** p is realizable **then** $bestPlan = p$
7. **endfor**
8. **return** $bestPlan$

Fig. 4. Optimal placement for Δ operators

Input: A query execution tree $G = (V, E)$
Output: $bestPlan$

/* First Phase */
1. Let E' be a set of all η where $\eta \subset E$ s.t.
   $\bigcap_i label(e_i) = \emptyset \wedge \bigcup_i label(e_i) = \mathbb{I} : e_i \in \eta$
2. **perform** pre-processing steps on G
3. **pull** Δ operators up to highest possible locations
/* Second Phase */
4. $bestPlan =$ a dummy plan with infinite cost
5. **for all** $S \subseteq E$
6.   place ω on each ω eligible edge $s_i : s_i \in S$
7.   **if** $cost(p) < cost(bestPlan)$ **then** $bestPlan = p$
8. **endfor**
9. **define** query tree $G' = (E', V')$
/* Third Phase */
10. **perform** pre-processing steps on G'
11. Let E'' be a set of all η where $\eta \subset E'$ s.t.
    $\bigcap_i label(e_i) = \emptyset \wedge \bigcup_i label(e_i) = \mathbb{I} : e_i \in \eta$
12. **for all** $\eta \in E''$
13.   place Δ on each edge $e_i : e_i \in \eta$
14.   **if** $cost(p) < cost(bestPlan)$ **then**
15.   **if** p is realizable **then** $bestPlan = p$
16. **endfor**
17. **return** $bestPlan$

Fig. 5. Algorithm steps for three-phase optimization

The first phase, (lines 1-3), is the initial placement of Δ operators without optimization. In the pre-processing, Δ operators are placed in their initial positions, right above the encrypted base relation in the query execution tree. After this step, the Δ operators are pulled-up as high as they can be, by using the rewrite rules given in Section 4.2. Note that, here we are not interested in the optimal placement of Δ operators. Instead, we try to create a realizable query execution tree with a largest possible number of nodes included in the server side query.

The second phase (lines 4-9) starts operating on the query execution tree generated in the first phase, and it finds the optimal placements for ω operators. To do that, the algorithm enumerates the eligible subsets of E of the query execution plan G consisting of ω-eligible edges (in line 5), and places the ω operators on the ω-eligible edges of those subsets (in line 6). Then it selects the best plan with the optimal placement of the ω operators. This phase generates a query execution tree, which (possibly) includes ω operator nodes.

In the third phase (lines 10-17) the part of the query tree generated by the second phase is fed to the optimization algorithm given in Figure 4, which places the Δ operators to their final locations. Due to the space limitations we provide experimental results in [2].

5 Conclusions

We have studied the problem of query optimization in the encrypted database systems. Our system setup was a service-based database model where the client is the owner of the data and the server hosts the client's data in the encrypted form to ensure the privacy of the data. The server is not allowed to see the data in the clear at any time. The previous work studied the execution of SQL queries over the encrypted relational databases in this kind of setup. It is always desired, as the spirit of the model, to minimize the work that has to be done by the client. We formulated this concern as a cost-based query optimization problem and provided a solution.

References

1. H. Hacıgümüş, B. Iyer, C. Li, and S. Mehrotra. Executing SQL over Encrypted Data in Database Service Provider Model. In *Proc. of ACM SIGMOD*, 2002.
2. H. Hacıgümüş, B. Iyer, and S. Mehrotra. Query Optimization in Encrypted Database System. Technical Report TR-DB-05-01, Database Research Group at University of California, Irvine, 2005.
3. H. Hacıgümüş, B. Iyer, and S. Mehrotra. Providing Database as a Service. In *Proc. of ICDE*, 2002.
4. H. Hacıgümüş, B. Iyer, and S. Mehrotra. Efficient Execution of Aggregation Queries over Encrypted Relational Databases. In *Proc. of International Conference on Database Systems for Advanced Applications (DASFAA)*, 2004.

5. D. R. Menezes, P. C. van Oorschot, and S. A. Vanstone. *Handbook of Applied Cryptography*. CRC Press, 1997.
6. R. L. Rivest, L. M. Adleman, and M. Dertouzos. On Data Banks and Privacy Homomorphisms. In *Foundations of Secure Computation*, 1978.

A Encrypted Data Storage Model

The storage model is presented in [4]. The storage model includes various types of attributes to efficiently satisfy different performance and privacy requirements imposed by specific applications.

Let R be a relation with the set of attributes $\tilde{R} = \{r_1, \ldots, r_n\}$. R is represented at the server as an encrypted relation R^S that contains an attribute $etuple = \langle \mathcal{E}^t(r_1, r_2, \ldots, r_n) \rangle$, where $\mathcal{E}^t$ is the function used to encrypt a row of the relation R. R^S also (optionally) stores other attributes based on the following classification of the attributes of R:

- *Field level encrypted attributes* ($F_k \in \tilde{R} : 1 \leqslant k \leqslant k' \leqslant n$): are attributes in R on which equality selections, equijoins, and grouping might be performed. For each F_t, R^S contains an attribute $F_k^f = \mathcal{E}^f(F_k^f)$, where $\mathcal{E}^f$ is a deterministic encryption, where $A_i = A_j \Leftrightarrow \mathcal{E}_k(A_i) = \mathcal{E}_k(A_j)$, where $\mathcal{E}_k$ is a deterministic encryption algorithm with key k, used to encode the value of the field F_k.

- *Partitioning attributes* ($P_m \in \tilde{R} : 1 \leqslant m \leqslant m' \leqslant n$): are attributes of R on which general selections/joins (other than equality) might be performed. For each P_m, R^S contains an attribute P_m^{id} that stores the partition index of the base attribute values.

- *Aggregation attributes* ($A_j \in \tilde{R} : 1 \leqslant j \leqslant j' \leqslant n$): are attributes of R on which we expect to do aggregation. Specifically, we need encryption algorithms, which allow basic arithmetic operations directly over encrypted data. Privacy Homomorphisms (PHs for short) are such encryption algorithms. PHs are first introduced by Rivest et al [6]. Detailed discussion of how PHs can be used in SQL query processing including necessary extensions to PHs is found in [4]. In the storage model, for each A_j, R^S contains an attribute A_j^h that represents the encrypted form of corresponding original attribute A_j with PH, thus $A_j^h = \mathcal{E}^{PH}(A_j)$, where $\mathcal{E}^{PH}$ is a PH.

Table 1. Relation $employee^S$: encrypted version of relation $employee$

							$salary^h$	
$etuple$(encrypted tuple)	eid^{id}	$salary^{id}$	$city^{id}$	did^{id}	$city^f$	did^f	$salary_p^h$	$salary_q^h$
=*?Ew@R*((¡¡=+,-...	2	81	18	2	?Ew...	@R*...	7	27
b*((¡¡(*?Ew@=l,r...	4	81	18	3	?Ew...	=+,...	18	17
w@=W*((¡¡(*?E:,j...	7	59	22	4	¡(*...	¡(*...	2	23
¡(* @=W*((¡?E;,r...	4	49	18	3	?Ew...	E:,...	3	2
(¡(@=U(¡S?/,6...	4	49	18	2	?Ew...	@R*...	8	7
ffTi* @=U(¡?G+,a...	7	49	22	2	¡(*...	@R*...	13	12

- *Embedded attributes* ($E_\ell \in \tilde{R} : 1 \leqslant \ell \leqslant \ell' \leqslant n$): are attributes in $\tilde{R}$ that are not in any of the above four categories. These attributes are, most likely, not accessed individually by queries for either selections, group creation, or aggregation.

Given the above attribute classification, the schema for the relation R^S is as follows: $R^S(etuple, F_1^f, \ldots, F_{k'}^f, P_1^{id}, \ldots, P_{m'}^{id}, A_1^h, \ldots, A_{j'}^h)$. Table 1 shows a possible instance of the server side representation of the the *employee* relation given in Table 2.

Table 2. Relation *employee*

eid	ename	salary	city	did
23	Tom	70K	Maple	10
860	Mary	60K	Maple	55
320	John	23K	River	35
875	Jerry	45K	Maple	58
870	John	50K	Maple	10
200	Sarah	55K	River	10

Table 3. Partitions

employee.salary	
Partitions	ID
[0,25K]	59
(25K,50K]	49
(50K,75K]	81
(75K,100K]	7

Watermarking Spatial Trajectory Database

Xiaoming Jin, Zhihao Zhang, Jianmin Wang, and Deyi Li

School of software, Tsinghua University,
Beijing, 100084, China
xmjin@tsinghua.edu.cn

Abstract. Protection of digital assets from piracy has received increasing interests where sensitive, valuable data need to be released. This paper addresses the problem of watermarking spatial trajectory database. The formal definition of the problem is given and the potential attacks are analyzed. Then a novel watermarking method is proposed, which embed the watermark information by introducing a small error to the trajectory shape rather than certain data values. Experimental results justify the usefulness of the proposed method, and give some empirical conclusions on the parameter settings.

Keywords: Digital watermarks, spatial trajectory, database security.

1 Introduction

Recent advances in geographic data collection techniques have increased the production and collection of spatial trajectories of moving objects [1][2][3][4]. Generally, trajectory is a sequence of consecutive locations of a moving object in multidimensional (generally two or three dimensional) space [3]. Real world examples could be found in global positioning systems (GPS), remote sensors, mobile phones, vehicle navigation systems, animal mobility trackers, and wireless Internet clients. Recently, protection of such digital assets from piracy has become a crucial problem in both research and industrial fields, especially where sensitive, valuable data need to be released.

Digital watermarking is a promising technique to solve the issue of copyright protection. Unlike encryption techniques[5], watermarking approaches do not prevent copy or further use of the data, rather it deters illegal copying by providing a means of establishing the original owners an authorship-aware copy. This technique is based on an important assumption that database can be updated in some data items, which are such that changes in a few values do not affect the usability of the data. Accordingly, watermarking is to embed into the data a group of indelible, small errors (termed *watermark information* or simply *watermarks*) that (1) exhibit certain patterns representing the ownership of the digital assets, and (2) preserve the usability of the data [6][7][8]. For example, image data can be watermarked by introducing minor noises, which served as the watermark information, into the high frequency in transformed domain [9]. Since such modifications have little impact on the visual quality of the image from the viewpoint of human's sensitivity, the modifications are acceptable with respect to the potential use of the image. Once an illegal copy occurs, the owner of the data could therefore extract the noises that represent the watermarks from the image to verify his ownership of the data.

Due to its importance, there have been several efforts to develop effective and efficient watermarking methods for various types of data, such as multimedia data [8][9][10], software[11][12][13], relational data [14][15], and parametric curves and surfaces [16]. However, to the best of our knowledge, watermarking technique for protecting the spatial trajectories remains unexplored.

Researches on watermarking techniques are highly data-oriented, that is, they are closely related to the type and potential usage of the data. Therefore, given data objects with different characters, the respective watermarking strategies are usually of fundamental differences. Consider the trajectory data, some distinctive characters should be addressed. First, multimedia data, e.g. image, audio and video, contain large portion of redundant information, on which the modification is insensible for human being. However, consider the trajectory data in real applications, the redundancy is relatively rare. Then modifications of same "scale" on trajectory data will lead to more distinct usability decrease than that on multimedia data. Another aspect of spatial trajectory data that challenge the watermarking process is that trajectory is usually accessed as a whole data object, and the meaning of it consists in the sharp of movements, rather than any individual location value. Therefore, spatial transforms do not decrease the usability of trajectories, e.g. zoom it to another scale, or shift it to another position. Since all the data values might be completely regenerated during the spatial transform process, the watermarks that dependent on certain bits of data values are apt to be completely erased.

These particular features of trajectory data disables the application of vast previous approaches that consider precise values in a database, such as the primary key based methods for watermarking relational data [14], and the transform based methods for watermarking multimedia data [9]. A more similar effort is on watermarking vector digital maps [17]. However, the watermarks in this work is extracted by comparing the original data with the watermarked data, which is often a extremely difficult task in watermarking trajectories because the original data themselves are often hard to be validated without a proper escrow that rarely appears.

Therefore, developing a new method for watermarking trajectory data is by no means trivial. In this paper, we propose a novel watermarking method for spatial trajectory database. The main idea of our method is to embed the watermark information by introducing a small error to the shape presented by the trajectory data. Since the shape should be preserved within any migration versions and piracy versions (otherwise the data become useless), the watermarking information is also preserved within these versions.

The rest of this paper is organized as follows: Section 2 describes the problem and gives some remarks on the requirements and potential attacks. Section 3 describes our watermarking method. Section 4 presents the experimental results and some discussions. Finally, section 5 offers some concluding remarks.

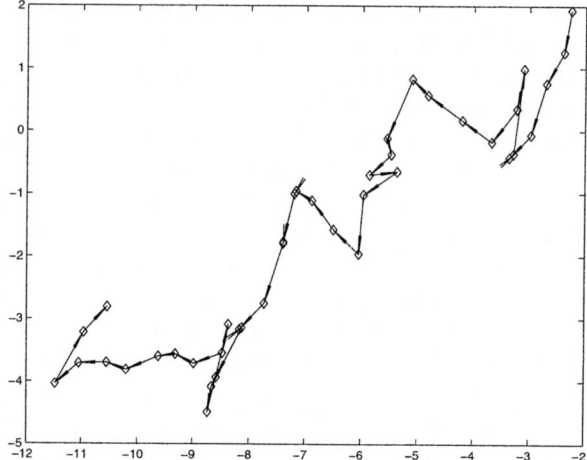

Fig. 1. An example of moving object trajectory in 2D space. Each diamond in the figure stands for a single location of the object at a certain time, and arrow represents a movement from one location to another

2 Problem Descriptions and Analysis

A spatial trajectory of a moving object is a sequence of consecutive locations in a multidimensional space. For clearness, we only consider the trajectories in 2D space in this paper without loss of generality. A trajectory is denoted as: $D = D(1), \ldots, D(N)$, where $D(n) = (T(n), A_1(n), A_2(n), \ldots)$, and $T(n) = (Tx(n), Ty(n))$ stands for the location of the moving object on the n-th sampling time, and $A_m(n)$ is the m-th none-spatial attribute collected on the n-th sampling time. Since the data we want to protect is the spatial information of the trajectory, so we use a simplified data form in this paper: $T = T(1), \ldots, T(N)$. $|T| = N$ denotes the length of T. The projection of T in x-axis and that in y-axis are represented as $Tx = Tx(1), \ldots, Tx(N)$ and $Ty = Ty(1), \ldots, Ty(N)$ respectively. Fig. 1 shows a simple example of 2D trajectory data.

Given a trajectory T, *watermarks* are a group of small errors that exhibit certain patterns representing the ownership of T. The process of watermark embedding is to generate these errors and/or their positions in the whole data set (i.e. where to embed the errors) based on a private key k known only to the owner of T, and then embed the generated errors at corresponding positions. This process can be expressed formally as:

$$T_W = \text{Embed}(T, k)$$

where $T_W = T_W(1), \ldots, T_W(N)$ is a distributable copy of T that contains watermark information.

When the copyright of a watermarked trajectory T_W need to be examined, the watermark information is extracted and then is verified to find whether it is coincident with the owner's private key, i.e.

$$\text{Deteck}(T_W, k)$$

A positive answer of the above verification means T_W was watermarked with private key k that exclusively belongs to an individual or organization, whereupon the ownership of the data is justified.

The following properties are desirable for watermarking method for trajectory data. They are similar in general to, but different in detail from, the requirements of watermarking relational data [14]. (1) Detectability: the owner of the data should be able to detect the watermarks embedded. (2) Robustness: watermarks should be robust against malicious attacks to erase them. (3) Incremental updatability: An important aspect of mobile object trajectories is that the data are usually born with streaming factor. This means the trajectories is frequently appended in the end over time. On this occasion, when the data T have been updated, incremental update on the watermarked version T_W should be enabled without destroying the watermarks. (4) Imperceptibility: The modifications caused by watermarking process should not reduce the usability of the database. That is, the important features of the data should not be significantly affected. For trajectory data, the motion shapes of the observed object need to be preserved. (5) Blind and key-based system: Watermark detection should neither require the knowledge of the original database nor the watermark. And only the private key can be regarded as unknowable for pirates, whereas the watermark embedding algorithm should remain public.

Watermark method should be able to defeat various malicious attacks. Similarly to the above requirements, the potential attacks are also data-oriented, that is, different forms of attacks may occur to different types of data objects. Consider trajectory data, malicious attacks can be inspired in the following ways:

- Scale attack: the original trajectory is zoomed to another scale, whereupon the value of each location has been changed.
- Base location attack: shift the trajectory in any direction.
- Update attack: Some selected locations are adjusted.

Consider the scale attack and base location attack, all values $T_W(n) = (Tx_W(n), Ty_W(n))$ will be completely changed. As mentioned in section 1, this disable the applications of the previous watermarking approaches that introduce small errors (generally a bit pattern) into each individual data item. The update attacks cannot be very violent, in terms of both the number of affected locations and the modification values. Otherwise the shape of the trajectory will be fundamentally changed, whereupon the usability of the data is lost. Deletion can also be a type of attack, but, for the same reason, we do not address this issue in this paper.

Table 1. Notation conversions

Notation	Explanations
T	The spatial trajectory to be watermarked
T_W	The watermarked trajectory
τ	Threshold for suspect piracy
β	The position to which the watermarking information is embedded
δ	Step in calculating new locations containing watermarks

3 Watermarking Trajectory

This section will present our watermarking approach. It is based on the notion that neither the change in the scaling factor nor that in the base location will change the trajectory shape. Then it is reasonable to embed the watermark information by introducing a small error to the features that present the trajectory shape, e.g. the length ratio of two consequence movements. Based on this property, the idea of our watermarking approach is as follows: When a trajectory needs watermarking, (1) select a set of locations to be watermarked; and (2) the watermarking information is embedded as a certain bit in the distance ratio relative to the selected locations. When a watermarked trajectory need to be examined, (1) the same set of locations are extracted; (2) distance ratios corresponding to these locations are calculated; and finally, (3) certain bit of each ratio are counted, and the result is used to verify the ownership of the data.

The algorithms for embedding and detecting watermarks will be introduced in detail in section 3.1. Section 3.2 will give some analyzing remarks. For the rest of this paper, we shall use the notational conventions showed in table 1 unless otherwise specified.

3.1 Watermarking Algorithms

The detailed watermarking algorithms are shown in Fig. 2. The embedding algorithm is first to search sequentially all the possible locations in the trajectory to select a group of locations for watermarking. Such locations are identified as *watermark locations*. Here we use a strategy similar to that in [14]: For each location $T(n)$, a message authenticated code is calculated based on the order n of the location and a private key k. Detailed calculation is $F(n, k) = H(n \circ k)$ where H is a one-way hash function, and $\circ$ stands for direct connection. Then given a parameter m indicating the percentage of watermark locations, $T(n)$ will be watermarked if and only if $F(n, k) \mod m = 0$.

For each location $T(n)$ to be watermarked, the following operation is triggered to generate the corresponding location $T_W(n)$ in the watermarked trajectory:

$$T_W(n) \leftarrow \arg\min\nolimits_{\text{BIN}_\beta \left(\frac{\max(L_2(p, T(n+1)), L_2(p, T(n-1)))}{\min(L_2(p, T(n+1)), L_2(p, T(n-1)))} \right) = 1} L_2(p, T(n))$$

where $\text{BIN}_\beta D$ stands for the bit of decimal value D with bit-wise position indicated by β (termed β bit), and $L_2(A, B)$ means the Euclidean distance between

```
Algorithm Embed
Input: trajectory T,private key k,integer m
Output: watermarked trajectory T_W

for each 0 < n ≤ |T|
    if  F(n,k) mod m=0 then
        watermark the n-th location T(n) to T_W(n)
    else
        T_W(n) = T(n)
return T_W


Algorithm Detect
Input: watermarked trajectory T_W,private key k,integer m
Output: binary decision about whether T_W was watermarked

location_count=0
watermark_count=0
for each 0 < n ≤ |T_W|
    if  F(n,k) mod m=0 then
        location_count=location_count+1
        if Verify(n)=True then
            watermark_count=watermark_count+1
If watermark_count/location_count> τ then
    return True
else
    return False
```

Fig. 2. Watermarking algorithms

location A and B. Here the location $T(n)$ is watermarked to $T_W(n)$ such that the β bit of the distance ratio relative to $T(n)$ is adjust to be 1. β controls the bit-wise position in which the watermark information is embedded. There are several ways to define the β bit. For example, a simple definition is to use the β-th bit as the β bit. Alternatively, a more meaningful definition is that the β bit of D is the last bit of the nearest integers to $10^\beta D$. We use the later definition in our experimental system.

Calculation of $T_W(n)$ seems complex, but can be simplified as follows: We expand a tentative range in a minor step until a valid location is found within that range, and then $T_W(n)$ is set approximately to be the location that is first meet. Furthermore, the range can be restricted to the four directions parallel with the axis for simpleness of computation. Given a parameter δ indicating the step of the tentative range, then only four tentative locations, $(Tx(n) - k\delta, Ty(n))$, $(Tx(n)+k\delta, Ty(n))$, $(Tx(n), Ty(n)-k\delta)$ and $(Tx(n), Ty(n)+k\delta)$, need examining in the k-th expanding step. Fig. 3 gives a example of the valid locations to which a given location is adjusted.

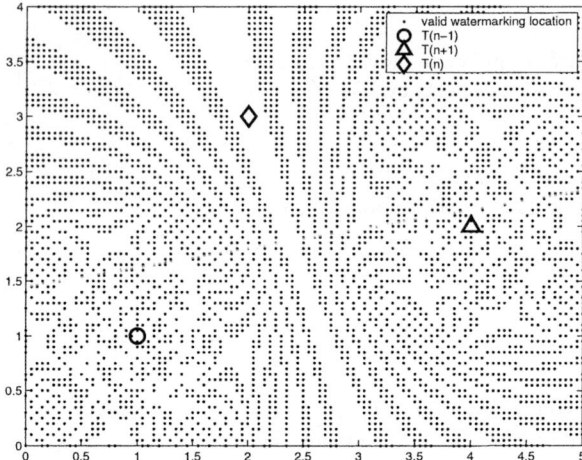

Fig. 3. A demonstration of watermarking a certain location $T(n)$

Detection of watermark is an inverse process. First, the algorithm find all locations that should have been watermarked, i.e. the *watermark locations*, based on the location order and the private key. Then each location is examined to find whether the β *bit* of the distance ratio relative to this location is (or has been set to) 1. If so, the location is marked as a *support location*. This process is formally defined as follows:

$$\text{Verify}(n) = \begin{cases} \text{True} & \text{BIN}_\beta \frac{L_2(T_W(n), T_W(n+1))}{L_2(T_W(n), T_W(n-1))} = 1 \\ \text{False} & \text{otherwise} \end{cases}$$

Finally, the *match rate*, which is the ratio of the number of *support locations* to the number of *watermark locations*, is calculated and then is compared with a user specified threshold τ to evaluate the possibility that the data are watermarked by the person who provide the key, i.e. Deteck(T_W, k) (see section 2 for its definition).

3.2 Analysis of the Proposed Approach

As discussed in section 2, the main challenge on watermarking spatial trajectory data consists in that the scaling factor and base location are apt to be modified. Our method can fill this gap since it embeds watermarks based on the relative distance of the trajectory, instead of the primitive data values. After various spatial transforms or location updates are made on the data, the overall shape of the trajectory remains unchanged, whereupon the watermark information is preserved. This make our method robust enough to serve as a counterpoise to malicious attacks.

There are several parameters that might affect the performance of our watermarking strategy. Generally, these parameters should be set based on the requirements of the application domains on data precision, time complexity, and robustness. β indicates the bit-wise position to which the watermarking information is embedded. It controls the trade-off between the error introduced and the robustness. Obviously, modifications on the first few bits will result in introducing big errors on the trajectory data. On the other hand, watermarks generated by modifying the last few bits suffer from that the watermarking bits tend to be stained by cut-off error when the trajectory are zoomed, shifted, or modified. On this occasion, the watermarking information is unstable and apt to be completely erased. δ stands for the step in calculating a new location that contains watermark information. It controls the trade-off between the complexity of the solution and the error introduced. Setting δ to relatively large value will reduce the time expense of the calculation, whereas bigger error may be introduced comparing with using a smaller δ.

From a practical point of view, β can be set around the position of the least places of decimals that are meaningful, e.g. 0 - 3 (the second definition of β bit in section 3.1); δ can be set as a/s where $a = \frac{\Sigma_n L_2(T(n), T(n-1))}{|T|-1}$ is the average distance between each two consecutive locations and s can be selected empirically around 10 - 1000 based on the discussions above; and τ can be, for example, 60% - 90% according to the requirements on decision confidence.

4 Experimental Evaluations

In this section, we give an empirical study of the proposed method. The objective is to evaluate its effectiveness and performance with respect to various parameter settings. Since watermarking trajectory database has not been considered previously, and the existing methods, which were initially designed for other data objects, are very brittle for this problem, we have not make any comparing study.

4.1 Experimental Results on Various δ and β

Given the location to be watermarked, the quality of a certain parameter setting can be directly evaluation by whether a valid location can be found efficiently and whether the error introduced (i.e. distance between the original location and the watermarked location) is small enough.

The computational processes on various δ and β are shown in Fig. 4, in which all the nearby valid watermarking locations are shown. For clearness, we show only a sub-trajectories with 3 locations. By a visual analysis, we conclude: (1) A smaller δ provided valid locations that are closer to $T(n)$. This means smaller error will be introduced. (2) When β bit is set within the first few bits, i.e. β is set to a small value, the error introduced is big. These two observations verified the discussions in section 3.2.

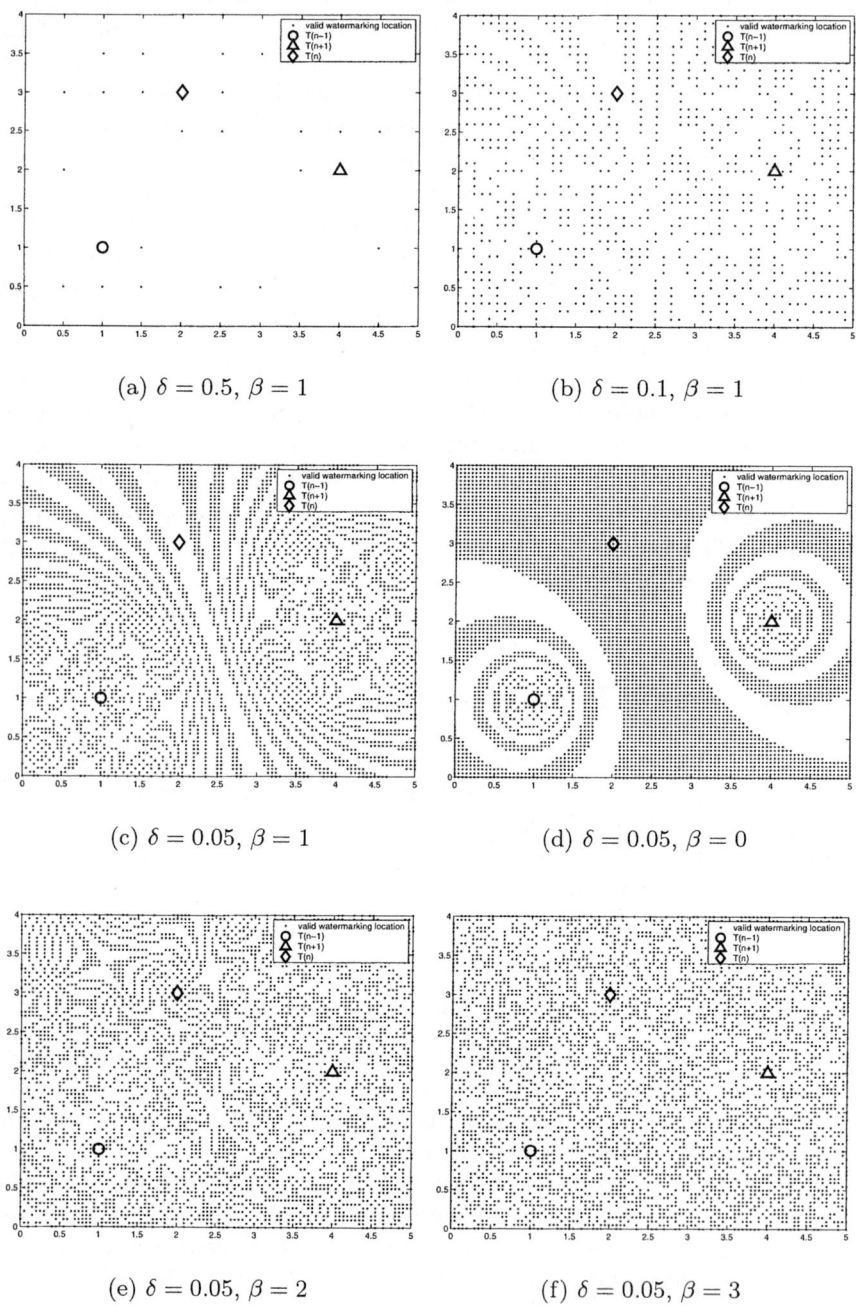

Fig. 4. Computational processes on various δ and β

4.2 Effectiveness of the Proposed Method

To evaluate our approach on data with relatively large size, we used synthetic data with 10K length. The attacks issued were combinations of the scale attacks and update attacks. Given a cut-off ratio C, the attack first transformed the watermarked trajectory T_W to T'_W where $T'_W(n) = T_W(n)/C$, then only the data values to P places of decimals were extracted in each dimension. T'_W preserved the shape on the whole, but differed from the original data in both absolute values and precisions. That is, with the increase of C, the trajectory became more compressed, and more information was lost during the cut-off process. In this part of experiments, δ was set to 0.05, β was set to 1 and 2 respectively, C varied from 1 to 50, and P was set to 3.

The resulting *match rates* (see section 3.1 for its definition) on various cut-off ratios are shown in Fig. 5. From the results, we could conclude: First, the embedded watermarks are detectable when the data are simply shifted, zoomed, or modified with a relatively small cut-off ratio. Second, the confidence of suspecting a piracy depends crucially on the amount of remained information. That is, the detectable watermarking information decreases with the increase of information that have been removed. Particularly, the watermarking bits will reduce to random selections when the cut-off ratio is too high, which means that the watermark is completely removed. However, on the other hand excessive cut-off ratio will make the shape of the trajectories changed fundamentally, whereupon the usability of the data is lost, and the attacks itself become meaningless. Therefore, the cut-off ratio is guaranteed to be small enough from a practical point of view. This justify the robustness of our approach.

In addition, these experimental results also generalized the conclusions on performance trade offs mentioned in section 4.1: the increase in β will results in both the increase in precision (i.e. less error introduced) and the decrease in robustness.

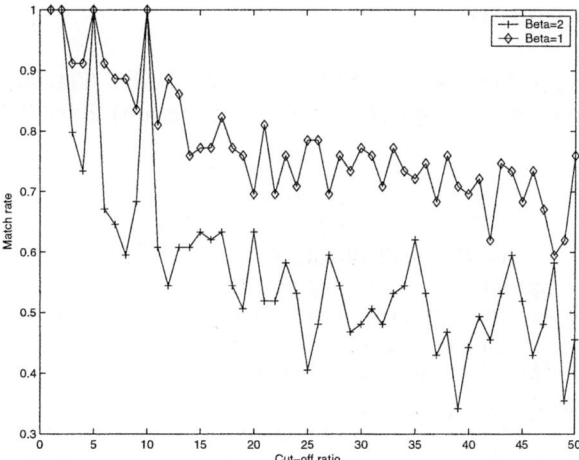

Fig. 5. Match rates of embedded watermark, on various cut-off ratios

5 Conclusion Remarks

This paper addresses the problem of watermarking spatial trajectory database. The proposed watermarking method is to embed the watermark information by introducing a small error to the trajectory shape instead of the data values. Experimental results give some empirical conclusions on the proposed method and the parameter settings, which include:

- The embedded watermarks are detectable when the trajectory data are simply shifted, zoomed, or modified with a small cut-off ratio. This justifies the usefulness of the proposed method.
- The detectable watermarking information decreases with the increase of cut-off ratio. However, since the cut-off ratio is guaranteed to be small enough from a practical point of view, our method is applicable in real applications.
- There are some trade offs in setting the parameters: Small δ help reducing the error introduced, whereas it increase the time expense of the watermarking process. Using the last few bits on watermarking can also reduce the error introduced, but such watermarking bit tends to be stained by cut-off attack, and vice versa.

The research in this paper can be extended along the following two directions: First, more sophisticated watermarking strategies can be applied to improve the efficiency and robustness of the proposed approach. Second, we believe that the underlying idea in this paper is quite general and can be used in other problems. For example, another important problem in the context of data security is trajectory authentication, which is to prevent illegal modification of the trajectories. This problem can also be solved by the ideas in this paper as follows: The trajectories can be first watermarked. And then, if major modifications have been applied, most watermark information will be destroyed, and therefore detecting algorithm will generate an alarm of insufficiency that indicates modifications.

Acknowledgements

The work was supported by the NSFC 60403021, NSFC 60473077, and the National Basic Research Program of China (973 Program) 2004CB719400.

References

1. N. Priyantha, A. Miu, H. Balakrishnan, S. Teller. The cricket compass for context-aware mobile applications. In Proc. of MOBICOM'2001, pages 1-14, 2001.
2. G. Chen, D. Kotz. Categorizing binary topological relations between regions, lines, and points in geographic databases. Technical Report TR2000-381, A Survey of Context-Aware Mobile Computing Research, Dept. of Computer Science, Dartmouth College, 2000.
3. M. Vlachos, G. Kollios, Dimitrios Gunopulos. Discovering Similar Multidimensional Trajectories. In Proc. of the 18th International Conference on Data Engineering (ICDE'02). San Jose, California, 2002.

4. Jignesh M. Patel, Yun Chen, V. Prasad Chakka. STRIPES: An Efficient Index for Predicted Trajectories. Proceedings of ACM SIGMOD 2004, pp. 635-646, 2004.
5. Rakesh Agrawal, Jerry Kiernan, Ramakrishnan Srikant, Yirong Xu. Order Preserving Encryption for Numeric Data. Proceedings of ACM SIGMOD 2004, pp. 563-574, 2004.
6. Fabien A. P. Petitcolas, Ross J. Anderson, Markus G. Kuhn. Information Hiding - A Survey. Proceedings of the IEEE, Vol.87, No.7, pp. 1062-1078, 1999.
7. S. Craver, N. Memon, B. -L. Yeo, M. M. Yeung. Resolving Rightful Ownerships with Invisible Watermarking Techniques: Limitations, Attacks, and Implications. IEEE Journal of Selected Areas in Communications, Vol.16, No.4, pp. 573-586, 1998.
8. F. Hartung, M. Kutter. Multimedia Watermarking Techniques. Proceedings of the IEEE, Vol.87, No.7, pp. 1079-1107, 1999.
9. J. J. K. Ruanaidh, W. J. Dowling, F. M. Boland. Watermarking Digital Images for Copyright Protection. IEEE Proceedings on Vision, Signal and Image Processing, Vol.143, No.4, pp. 250-256, 1996.
10. I. J. Cox, J. P. M. G. Linnartz. Some General Methods for Tampering with Watermarks. IEEE Journal of Selected Areas in Communication, Vol.16, No.4, pp. 573-586, 1998.
11. Christian Collberg, Clark Thomborson. On the Limits of Software Watermarking. Technique Reports, Department of Computer Sciences, The University of Auckland. 1998.
12. Hoi Chang, Mikhail Atallah. Protecting software code by guards. Security and Privacy in Digital Rights Management, LNCS, 2320:160-175, 2002.
13. Christian Collberg, Edward Carter, Saumya Debray, Andrew Huntwork, Cullen Linn, Mike Stepp. Dynamic path-based software watermarking. In SIGPLAN '04 Conference on Programming Language Design and Implementation. 2004.
14. Rakesh Agrawal, Jerry Kiernan. Watermarking Relational Databases. Proceedings of the 28th VLDB Conference, Hong Kong, China, 2002.
15. Radu Sion, Mikhail Atallah, Sunil Prabhakar. Rights Protection for Relational Data. Proceedings of ACM SIGMOD, pp. 98-109, 2003.
16. Ryutarou Ohbuchi, Hiroshi Masuda, Masaki Aono. A Shape-Preserving Data Embedding Algorithm for NURBS Curves and Surfaces. Computer Graphics International 1999 (CGI '99), Canmore, Canada, 1999.
17. Ryutarou Ohbuchi, Hiroo Ueda, Shuh Endoh. Robust Watermarking of Vector Digital Maps. Proceedings of the IEEE International Conference on Multimedia and Expo 2002 (ICME 2002), Lausanne, Switzerland, 2002.

Effective Approaches for Watermarking XML Data

Wilfred Ng and Ho-Lam Lau

Department of Computer Science,
The Hong Kong University of Science and Technology, Hong Kong
{wilfred, lauhl}@cs.ust.hk

Abstract. Watermarking enables provable rights over content, which has been successfully applied in multimedia applications. However, it is not trivial to apply the known effective watermarking schemes to XML data, since noisy data may not be acceptable due to its structures and node extents. In this paper, we present two different watermarking schemes on XML data: the selective approach and the compression approach. The former allows us to embed non-destructive hidden information content over XML data. The latter takes verbosity and the need in updating XML data in real life into account. We conduct experiments on the efficiency and robustness of both approaches against different forms of attack, which shows that our proposed watermarking schemes are reasonably efficient and effective.

1 Introduction

Watermarking in the contexts of image, audio or video data is well-known to be an effective technique to protect the intellectual property of electronic content. Essentially, the technique embeds a secret message into a cover message within the content in order to prove the ownership of materials. Remarkable successes in watermarking on multimedia applications have been achieved in recent years [4]. Thus, relevant business sectors are able to distribute their data while keeping the ownership and preventing the original data being resold illegally by others.

The existing watermarking technology has mostly been developed in the context of multimedia data, since such data has a high tolerance to noise and thus it is not easy to detect the watermark. Unlike multimedia data, XML data are diverse in nature: some are data-centric and numeric (e.g. regular scientific data) while some are document-centric and verbose (e.g.book chapters). It is challenging to develop an effective watermarking scheme which is invisible and is able to resist various kinds of attack.

In this paper, we attempt to develop watermarking schemes for XML data based on two different watermarking approaches. One is the *selective approach* and another is the *compression approach*. As for the selective approach, we develop a watermarking scheme for uncompressed XML data based on the database watermarking algorithm proposed by Agrawal [2]. The second approach is more interesting. It follows our advocation that in reality some XML documents are verbose and they need compression in practical applications [3]. In addition, we take into consideration that XML documents need to be updated frequently. Therefore, in the compression approach, we introduce a novel watermarking scheme based on our earlier developed XML compressor, namely XQzip, which does not require full decompression when querying. [3]. By watermarking compressed XML data, we gain the advantage of having better document security, and at the same time, higher flexibility of updating XML data.

Related Work. Agrawal presents an effective watermarking technique for the relational data [2]. This technique ensures some bit positions of certain attributes contain the watermarks. We extend their techniques on XML data by defining locators in XML in our selective approach. Sion [5] discusses the watermarking of semi-structures of multiple types of contents and represents them as graphs by characterizing the values in the structure and individual nodes. He also proposes a watermarking algorithm that makes use of the encoding capacity of different types of nodes. Gross-Amblard [1] investigates the problem of watermarking XML databases while preserving a set of parametric queries. His work mainly focuses on performing queries on different structures and pay less attention to the watermarking scheme. However, the query approaches are similar to the pre-defined queries used in the compression approach. At present, all proposed XML watermarking schemes are based on uncompressed XML data and no studies exist on watermarking compressed XML data to the best of our knowledge.

Paper Outline. After introducing our XML watermarking schemes in this section, we describe and study the selective approach, which is for uncompressed XML data, and the compression approach, which is for XQzip compressed XML data in Sections 2 and 3, respectively. Then in Section 4, we conclude our work and suggest future improvements for the watermarking schemes we developed.

2 The Selective Approach of Watermarking XML

In this section, we introduce the selective approach of XML watermarking. We also analyze the robustness of our watermarking system against the following two forms of attacks: *subtractive attack* and *additive attack*. All the experiments related to the watermarking system are conducted on a machine of the configuration as follows: P4 2.26GHz, 512MB main memory and 15GB disk space.

2.1 Watermark Insertion

In the selective approach of watermarking XML, the watermarks are randomly distributed throughout the XML document based on a secret key provided by the owner. We aim at making minor changes on XML data without causing errors during the process.

The watermark insertion algorithm and the notations we used are presented in Algorithm 1 and Table 1, respectively. Before embedding marks in XML data, we define a *locator*, which is an analogy to the primary key in relational databases, to indicate whether a particular element should be marked. Unlike watermarking relational databases [2], primary keys are not necessarily to be specified and defined in XML. We assume the owner of the watermarked data is responsible to select the elements that are suitable to be the candidates of locators. The best choice of such an element is that its value is unique, non-modifiable and has large locator space. For example, the tag "ISBN" of a book XML document could be served as a locator.

Table 1. Notation Used

v	Number of elements in the document available for marking.
ξ	Number of the least significant bits available for marking in an element.
$1/\gamma$	Fraction of marked elements in the document (the watermark ratio).
α	Significance level of the test for detecting a watermark.
N	Number of elements in the document.
τ	Minimum number of detected locators required for a successful detection.

Let E be a locator candidate and K be the secret key provided by the owner. We use the value of E in a hash function $H(E,K) = E \circ K$, which generates a hash value, h to determine whether E should be marked or not. For the sake of simplicity, we use concatenation to generate h. In fact $H(E,K)$ can be some other functions as long as it is able to generate a unique value for a given pair of E and K. After determining the marked locators, say E_m, we watermark the value of E_m according to the data type of E_m. For numerical data, we mark E_m by modifying the least significant bit specified by the control parameter, denoted as ξ. We assume that numerical data is able to tolerate small and non-detectable changes. For example, "1000.30000" can be changed to "1000.30001". For textual data, the value of E_m is replaced by a synonym function, denoted as $Synm()$, which is based on a well-known synonym database WordNet [10]. For example, "theory" can be replaced by its synonyms "concept" or "belief". Once E_m is marked, we call it the *marked element*.

2.2 Watermark Detection

To detect whether the XML data has originated from the data source, the data owner is required to supply the secret key, K, and the corresponding *setting file* to the watermark detection algorithm, which is shown in Algorithm 2. The setting file includes information such as the significance level, α, and the list of locator candidates in XPath format. The detection algorithm finds out the number of marked elements and locators in the XML data, and then evaluates the *hit rate*. We call the locator whose watermark is detected by the algorithm the *detected locator*. The detection algorithm uses a threshold function to calculate the smallest integer, denoted as t, such that if the hit rate is larger than t, the owner can claim the ownership of the document with the confidence of $(1 - \alpha)$.

Figure 1 shows the proportion of detected locators required for a successful detection with 99% confidence against different watermark ratios. It is interest-

Algorithm 1 The watermark insertion algorithm in the selective approach

1: **for each** locator candidates $r \in R$ **do**{
2:   **if** $(r.lablel() \bmod v$ equals $0)${ //mark this locator
3:     value_index $i = r.lablel() \bmod v$; //modify value A_i
4:     **if** (A_i is textual){
5:       word_index $w_i = r.lablel() \bmod$ num_of_word_in_value;
6:       $A_i = \text{markText}(r.lablel(), A_i, w_i);$} //modify the w_i^{th} word
7:     **else if** (A_i is numerical){
8:       bit_index $b_i = r.lablel() \bmod \xi$; //modify the b_i^{th} bit
9:       $A_i = \text{markNum}(r.lablel(), A_i, b_i);$}}}

10: **Procedure** markNum(secret_key sk, number v, bit_index j) **return** number
11:   $first\_hash = H(K \cdot sk)$
12:   **if**($first\_hash$ is even)
13:     set the jth least significant bit of v to 0;
14:   **else**
15:     set the jth least significant bit of v to 1;
16:   **return** v;

17: **Procedure** markText(secret_key sk, text v, word_index j) **return** text
18:   $first\_hash = H(K \cdot sk)$;
19:   **if** ($first\_hash$ is even)
20:     replace the jth word w by a synonym s where $s = \text{change}(w,0)$;
21:   **else**
22:     replace the jth word w by a synonym s where $s = \text{change}(w, 1)$;
23:   **return** v;

24: **Procedure** change(word w, value v) **return** word
25:   **if** (Symn(w) equals v)
26:     Do nothing and **return** w;
27:   **else**{
28:     syn_list = all synonyms of w from a dictionary database;
29:     randomly select a synonym s from syn_list where Synm(s) equals v;}

30: **Procedure** Synm(word w) **return** number
31:   **if** ($H(w)$ is even)
32:     **return** 0;
33:   **else**
34:     **return** 1;

ing to find that, in a small XML document ($N = 10,000$), if 1% of the records are marked, only 62% of detected locators are needed to provide 99% confidence. As the watermark ratio increases, the proportion of detected locators required decreases. The proportion tends to the constant value of 0.5 because the detection algorithm is probabilistic and needs more than 50% of detected locators to differentiate a watermark from a chance of random occurrence. In general, for an XML document with more elements, fewer detected locators are required to achieve the same level of detectability than XML documents with fewer elements.

Algorithm 2 The watermark deletion algorithm in the selective approach
1: TotalCount = 0;
2: MatchCount = 0;
3: **for each** locator $r \in R$ **do**{
4:    **if** $(r.lablel() \mod \gamma$ equals 0){// this locator is detected
5:      value_index $i = r.lablel() \mod v$; // value A_i was modified
6:      **if** (A_i is textual) {
7:         word_index $w_i = r.lablel() \mod num\_of\_word\_in\_value$; // w_i^{th} word was modified
8:         TotalCount = TotalCount+1;
9:         MatchCount = MatchCount + isMatchNum($r.lablel()$, A_i, w_i);}
10:     **else if** (A_i is numeric) {
11:        bit_index $b_i = r.lablel() \mod \xi$ // b_i^{th} bit was modified;
12:        TotalCount = TotalCount+1;
13:        MatchCount = MatchCount + isMatchWord($r.lablel()$, A_i, b_i^{th});}}}
14: t = Threshold(Totalcount, α, 0.5);
15: **if**(MatchCount $\geq t$)
16:    The document is a suspect piracy;

17: **Procedure** Threshold(number n, significance a, success probability p)
18:    $q = 1 - p$;
19:    **return** minimum integer k such that $\Sigma_{r=k}^{n} nCr \; p^r \; q^{n-r} < \alpha$;

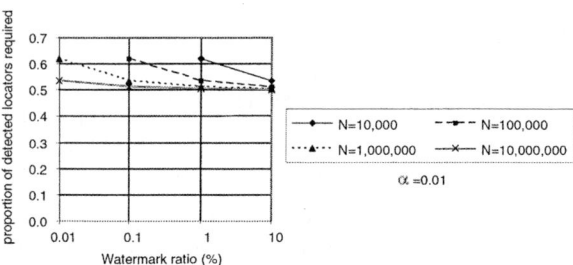

Fig. 1. Proportion of detected locators required for successful watermark detection

2.3 Experiments

Two XML data sources are used in the experiments: *1998_statistics.xml* and *weblog.xml*. Table 2 shows the features of these datasets.

Marked and Modified Records. We first examine the relationship between the fraction parameter, γ, and the marked locators. Figure 2(a) shows that the percentages of marked locators in the two XML datasets are slightly lower than our expected level (c.f. the superimposed curve representing $1/\gamma$). This is due to the fact that some locators cannot be modified by the watermark insertion algorithm, such as the synonym of a word of the locator does not exist. Figure 2(b) shows that the percentage of modified locators with different values of γ. The experimental result for "1998_statistics.xml" is fluctuating around our expected level of 50%, while that of the "weblog.xml" is usually less than 50%.

Table 2. Features of XML datasets

Documents	File size (KB)	No. of records	No. of elements available for marking (v)	No. of least significant bits for marking (ξ)
1998_statistics.xml	1227	1226	4	3
weblog.xml	89809	247024	2	3

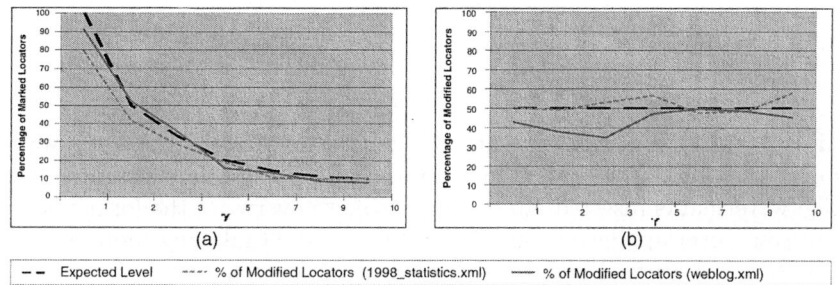

Fig. 2. Percentages of (a) marked and (b) modified locators versus γ

Table 3. Running time of watermark insertion

Watermark ratio (%)	100.00	50.00	33.33	20.00	14.29	11.11	10.00
1998_statistics.xml (sec)	0.891	0.891	0.861	0.891	0.871	0.871	0.851
weblog.xml (sec)	73.46	69.02	68.01	61.68	61.62	61.44	61.79

Running Time of Watermark Insertion. Table 3 shows the running time of applying the watermark insertion algorithm on the two XML datasets with different watermark ratios. The results show that the watermark ratios do not have a big impact on the running time of the algorithm. The I/O time is the main overhead, since the document is parsed only once, which is irrespective to the watermark ratios.

Subtractive Attack. A *subtractive attack* aims at eliminating the presence of watermarks. A successful subtractive attack reduces the watermarks created by the original owner in order to render the claim of ownership impossible. *Subset attack* is a typical form of subtractive attacks, it attempts to copy parts of the watermarked document and hence reduces the percentage of watermarks found in the document. We use the "weblog.xml" dataset to demonstrate the resistance to subset attacks in the selective approach. We randomly select elements from the watermark version of weblog.xml at different gap sizes and selectivity levels and then examine the watermark detection percentage.

In Figure 3, when the gap size is equal to 10, 90% of watermarks can be detected with only 0.02% selectivity level. When gap size increases, selectivity level also increases for detecting over 90% of watermarks. At 0.3% selectivity, watermark detection reaches 100%. For a gap size of 1000, only a small selectivity level can reach over 90% watermark detection. This result indicates that the watermarks inserted by our watermarking schemes are evenly distributed and have good resistance to the subset attack.

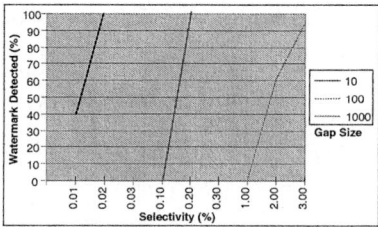

Fig. 3. Watermark detected versus selectivity level

Additive Attack. In an additive attack, illegal parties insert their own watermarks over the original document and claim the "legal" ownership of the data. Since the watermarks inserted afterwards is able to overwrite the former watermarks in some overlapping regions, it results in the illegal copy more detected elements than the original one can be found in the overlapping regions. Let M be the total number of marked element, L be the number of elements available for marking and F be the total number of watermarks added afterwards. The probability of having overlapping region is given as follows:

$$\begin{cases} 1 - \Pi_{i=0}^{F-1} \frac{(L-i)-M}{L-i}, & \text{if } M + F < L; \\ 0, & \text{if } M + F \geq L. \end{cases}$$

The mean of the overlapping region $= L \times$ Probability of collision in an element node $= L \times (M/L) \times (F/L)$.

Illegal parties may try to reduce the overlapping regions by using a low watermark ratio such as 0.1% or 0.01%. Figure 4 shows the probability and the mean of having overlapping regions when the watermark insertion algorithm is applied twice on the same XML document.

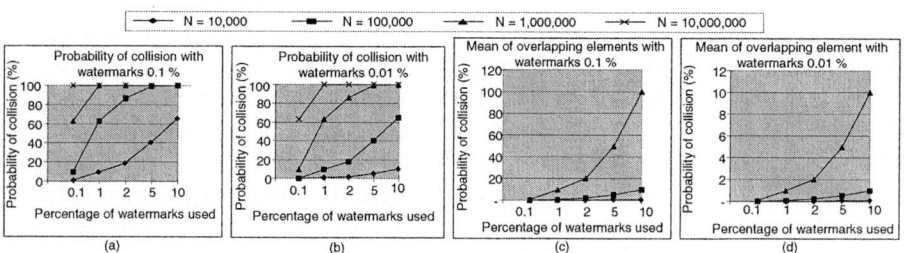

Fig. 4. Probability and mean of having overlapping region with 0.1% and 0.01% watermark ratios

Figure 4(a) shows that for a small XML document (N=10000), if the owner uses a 10% watermark ratio and the illegal party inserts watermarks with a 0.1% watermark ratio, the probability of the occurrence of overlapping regions is 65%. However, the mean of these overlapping regions is only 1 as shown in

Figure 4(c). For a large XML document ($N = 100{,}000$), if the owner uses a lower watermark ratio of 2% and the illegal party inserts watermarks with a 0.1% watermark ratio, we can achieve a higher probability of overlapping (85%) and the mean of overlapping region is 2. Figures 4(b) & (d) show the results of illegal parties using a very low watermark ratio of 0.01%. They show that the probability of an overlapping occurrence and the mean of overlapping region decrease dramatically. In this case, since the probability of overlapping region is low, in order to resist additive attacks with a very low watermark ratio, we can decrease the value of γ such that when overlapping occurs, the collisions of watermarks are large enough to make an accurate decision.

Discussions. The experimental results show that the selective approach is susceptible to subtractive and additive attacks. The performance of the approach is determined by four parameters: the size of the document (N), the watermarking ratio (γ), the number of locators (v) and the significant level of the test (α). It is worth mentioning in our finding larger documents can use a smaller watermark ratio to achieve a particular confidence of detectability (c.f. Figure 1). Computation overhead introduced by the watermark ratio to the watermark insertion algorithm is relatively small compared to the I/O time. The overhead is also directly related to the size of the documents.

Our watermark algorithm can also resists some attacks that transform the structure of the watermarked XML data conforming to DTDs or XML schemas (i.e. distortive attack). Since XML data is a tree structure, re-transformation to the original structure is possible by using the original schema, in this case we can still apply the watermark detection algorithm to examine whether the XML data belongs to the owner. In real life, some XML document is based on some well-known schema, such as the Electronic Business using eXtensible Markup Language (ebXML) [8], the distorted documents become less valuable.

3 The Compression Approach of Watermarking XML

Existing watermarking techniques are all targeted on plain XML data. The selective approach we introduced in Section 2 is efficient and effective in proving the ownerships of the owners. However, the protection on the data from access in this approach is not taken into consideration. In this section, we introduce a novel watermark approach which is based on compressed XML data which provides a prove of ownership as well as the protection of data security. The principle is that compressed XML data are unable to be retrieved directly without the correct decompression. Watermarking compressed XML data is a preventive measure for unauthorized copy or reading. Similar to the selective approach, the compression approach is also driven by the owner-selected secret key. The secret key is used to calculate the location of the watermarks, each distributed copy is watermarked by a unique secret key set by the owner. Without the secret key, the compressed data cannot be retrieved. Authorized parties are allowed to retrieve the data by using the pre-defined queries sets provided by the owner, the owner can also limit the amount of data visible to different parties by giving them different pre-defined query sets. We also consider in practice some XML data are updated frequently and thus it is inefficient to compress and watermark the XML documents again for every update activity. Therefore, we provide a facility which only requires the owner to distribute supplementary compressed files to the relevant parties when update occurs.

3.1 Architecture of the Compression System

The architecture of the compression system is shown in Figure 5. We only briefly explain the functionality of the main modules due to the space limit.

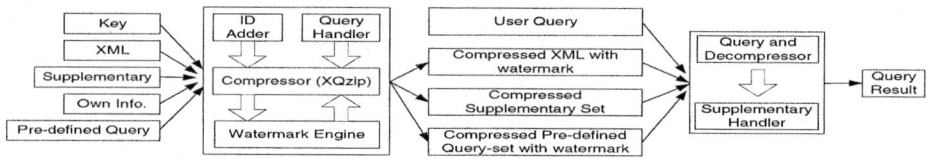

Fig. 5. An overview of the compression approach of watermarking XML

ID Adder. The ID Adder is built on a SAX parser, it parses the XML document sequentially and inserts the owner's information into the XML document. The information is stored in an "ownership node" under the root of the XML document. The label of the ownership node is simply the hash value of the owner's secret key. To support update, a unique system-assigned ID value is added for each element for easy processing when consulting the supplementary file.

Query Handler. This module is an interface that allows the owner to restrict some pre-defined queries for an authorized party. The module selects the visible parts of the XML document, then converts them into an XML document and finally passes the XML document to the compressor.

Compressor and Watermark Engine. We adopt our earlier developed XQzip [3] to carry out the XML compression. The secret key, hash function and gap value are used to determine the byte position to be marked. Roughly, a smaller gap value results in more watermarks being inserted into the compressed blocks. After all the blocks are compressed and watermarked, they are merged into a single file.

Query and Decompressor. Querying and decompressing are also executed using XQzip [3]. A compressed pre-defined queries set is first decompressed. Then, the authorized parties select and perform queries from the pre-defined query list. The system locates the position of the query solution through the index file developed in XQzip. The query solution is decompressed and passed to the supplementary handler if update is required. In the process of decompression, the query and decompressor hashes the embedded secret keys and gap values to determine the marked elements and recover them.

Supplementary Handler. There are two steps in handling the supplementary files when updating the compressed XML data. First, the handler removes the out-dated contents defined by the supplementary set. The result is then passed to the ID adder which updates the contents defined by the supplementary document. Then, the parser checks for every attributes of each element, and if an attribute is indicated as "added", the parser inserts the value to the corresponding elements and finally, the result is outputted as an XML file.

In the compressed watermark system, the number of watermarks in each compressed block is restricted. The system processes byte flipping at the locator indicated by the hash function. If one byte location is selected twice or even number of times, flipping does not occur at that byte location. To ensure that a block contains at least one watermark, the number of watermark in each compression block should be odd. The number of marks is determined by the following formula where m is the block size: $Number\ of\ mark = \begin{cases} m, & \text{when } m \text{ is odd;} \\ m+1, & \text{otherwise.} \end{cases}$

3.2 Experiments

We implement the compression watermarking system and conduct a series of experiments which are based on the same machine configuration as stated in Section 2. Four common XML datasets are used in the experiments: XMark, Shakespeare and two DBLP data sources of different size.

Effectiveness and Detectability of Compressed Watermarking System. The data of a compressed document is retrieved by using the same {key, gap} pair used in the compression. To test for the effectiveness of the system, we retrieve data from a compressed document by the query system from the following scenarios: (1) different secret keys and different gap values, (2) the same secret key but different gap values, (3) different secret keys but the same gap value, and (4) the same secret key and same gap value. Note that when a wrong {key, gap} pair is supplied, the query and decompressor cannot locate the pattern of marked element and fails to decompress the required data.

Query Response Time. We present the worst case query response time of the four datasets in the system on three different scenrios: (1) ID and update are supported, (2) ID is supported but no update and (3) ID and update are not supported. The test query we used is set to retrieve the whole document and the processing involves a full decompression.

Figure 6(a) shows the query response time of the data sources in the system which support ID and update. When the smallest gap value, i.e. gap = 1, requires roughly 30% more time to process the query than that with the largest gap value, i.e. gap = 10000. The reason for this is that the gap value controls the number of marks to be recovered, the smaller the gap value, the more the marked elements are needed to be recovered. Figure 6(b) shows the query response time of our system and XQzip which support ID but not update. It shows that when the

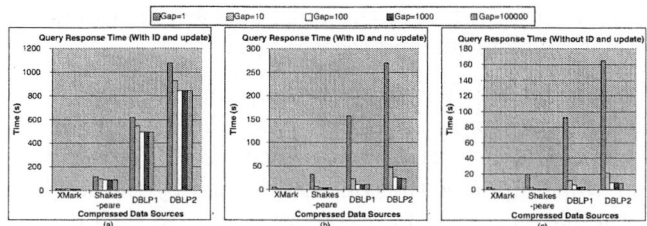

Fig. 6. Query processing time comparison (a) (support ID and update), (b) (support ID but not update) and (c) (do no support ID nor update)

gap value is smaller, the query processing time is longer; it takes 10 times longer for gap = 1 than gap = 10000.

Compared Figure 6(a) to Figure 6(b), there is a big difference in the query time between the updated case and that of not updated. The difference is obvious when the gap value is small and the file size is large, in this case handling supplementary XML documents is expensive and consumes too much time. However, when the gap value is very small, time spent on recovering the marked elements from the compressed XML data becomes critical and the time spent on handling supplementary XML document becomes less significant.

Figure 6(c) shows the query time of the system which support neither ID nor update. The result is similar to the results shown in Figure 6(b). In this case most of the time is used in recovering the marked elements from the compressed XML data. This also indicates that the time required for handling ID is linear to the size of the document, which does not introduce much overhead.

Robustness of Watermarking. We now analyze the robustness of the compression approach against various forms of attacks. An attack is assumed to be aimed at retrieving data from the compressed document without using the query system. Such attacks are classified as a *flipping attack* or an *averaging attack*.

Flipping Attack. A flipping attack attempts to destroy the watermark by flipping the value at certain byte positions. Since a compressed document is composed of many compressed blocks, an attacker attempts to attack each block and combine all the attacked blocks to form a new compressed document. If any one block is modified wrongly, the compressed document is unable to be decompressed therefore the attacker has to guess the pattern of all blocks correctly.

Suppose the attacker knows the number of marked locators, m, and the size of the data, n. If two marked elements are at the same location, they cancel the effect of each other. The probability of correctly guessing the pattern of marks is given by: $\frac{1}{\Sigma_{r=1,3,\ldots,m} nCr}$, for $0 < m \leq n$ and m is odd.

Figure 7 shows the success rate of the simulated flipping attacks. The success rate decreases upon the increase of block size at a fixed gap value. On the other hand, if the block size is fixed, a decrease in gap value decreases the success rate. For instance, a small block size ($n = 30$) and a large gap value (gap = 100000) gives a higher success rate, however, most of the success rates are within 3%, which are rather low.

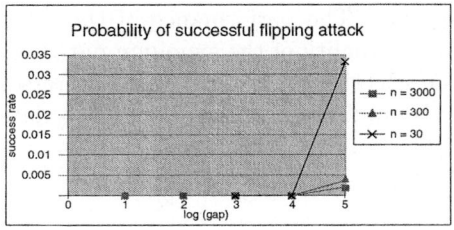

Fig. 7. Success rate for flipping attack

Averaging Attack. An averaging attack attempts to construct a watermark-free document from a number of sample watermarked documents. Similar to the flipping attacker, an averaging attacker attacks the compressed data block by block by analyzing all the compressed blocks from the available samples and uses the information to construct a new block. Let the attacker has s samples (s is supposed to be an odd number) and create a new artificial block, a. The ith byte of a is the majority value of the ith byte in all the s samples.

We carry out experiments by simulating the averaging attack by using the XMark and Shakespeare datasets. For each dataset, there are 99 samples available. We randomly generate the blocks sizes as the attack targets. To launch a successful averaging attack, all artificial blocks are required to be successfully attacked. The number of samples required is shown in Table 4 and "Fails" means the attack is fail after averaging all the samples.

Table 4. Number of samples required for averaging attack at different gap size

Gap Size	1	5	10	100	1000	10000	100000
XMark	Fails	Fails	Fails	5	3	3	3
Shakespeare	Fails	Fails	Fails	5	3	3	3

From Table 4, we find that the attack on compressed data can be easily successful if the gap values are large. This is mainly because majority of blocks being unmarked when the gap value is large. When the gap value is below 10, all attacks fail, since few byte errors are sufficient to prevent the attacker from decompressing the data. From the results, we can see that when the gap value is smaller the system is more robust against the averaging attack. Thus, there is indeed a tradeoff between the gap value and compression time.

4 Concluding Remarks

We have presented two approaches for watermarking XML for both usual XML and a compressed form, which are shown to be robust and effective. The proposed watermark algorithms are presented and various forms of attacks are studied. In the selective approach, we decide how to insert synonyms and control the synonymity level of a word. The performance of the scheme in this approach depends very much on the quality of the synonym database. In the compression approach, we rely on an effective queriable XML compressor we developed. This approach is both effective and practical for large XML datasets.

References

1. D. Gross-Amblard. *Query-preserving Watermarking of Relational Databases and XML Documents.* In Proc. of Principle of Database Systems, 2003.
2. R. Agrawal and J. Kiernan. *Watermarking Relational Databases.* In Proc. of VLDB, 2002.
3. J. Cheng and W. Ng. *XQzip: Querying Compressed XML Using Structural Indexing.* In Proc. of the EDBT, pages 219-236, 2004.
4. C. Collberg and C. Thomborson. *Software Watermarking: Models and Dynamic Embeddings.* In Proc. of Principles of Programming Languages, 1999.
5. R. Sion, M. Atallah and S. Prabhaker. *Resilient Information Hiding for Abstract Semi-Structures.* In Proc. of the IWDW, 2004
6. S. Inoue et al. *A Proposal on Information Hiding Methods using XML.* In the First NLP and XML Workshop.
7. M. Atallah, R. Sion and S. Prabhakar. *Watermarking non-media content.* In the the CERIAS Security Symposium, 2001.
8. UN/CEFACT and OASIS. *ebXML - Electronic Business using eXtensible Markup Language.* In http://www.ebxml.org/.
9. Y. Li, V. Swarup and S. Jajodia. *Constructing a Virtual Primary Key for Fingerprinting Relational Data.* In Proc. of the 2003 ACM workshop on Digital rights management, 2003.
10. C Fellbaum. *WordNet An Electronic Lexical Database.* The MIT Press, 1998.

A Unifying Framework for Merging and Evaluating XML Information

Ho-Lam Lau and Wilfred Ng

Department of Computer Science,
The Hong Kong University of Science and Technology, Hong Kong
{lauhl, wilfred}@cs.ust.hk

Abstract. With the ever increasing connection between XML information systems over the Web, users are able to obtain integrated sources of XML information in a cooperative manner, such as developing an XML mediator schema or using eXtensible Stylesheet Language Transformation (XSLT). However, it is not trivial to evaluate the quality of such merged XML data, even when we have the knowledge of the involved XML data sources. Herein, we present a unifying framework for merging XML data and study the quality issues of merged XML information. We capture the coverage of the object sources as well as the structural diversity of XML data objects, respectively, by the two metrics of Information Completeness (IC) and Data Complexity (DC) of the merged data.

1 Introduction

Information integration, a long established field in different disciplines of Computer Science such as cooperative systems and mediators, is recognized as an important database subject in a distributed environment [5, 8]. As the networking and mobile technologies advance, the related issues of information integration become even more challenging, since merged data can be easily obtained from a wide spectrum of emerging modern data applications, such as mobile computing, peer-to-peer transmission, mediators, and data warehousing.

As XML data emerges as a de-facto standard of Web information, we find it essential to address the quality issues of integrated XML information. In this paper, we attempt to establish a natural and intuitive framework for assessing the quality of merging XML data objects in a co-operative environment. We assume that there are many XML information sources which return their own relevant XML data objects (or simply XML data trees) as a consequence of searching for a required entity from the users. To gain the maximal possible information from the sources, a user should first query the available sources and then integrate all the returned results. We do not study the techniques used in the search and integration processes of the required XML data objects as discussed in [1, 2, 3]. Instead, we study the problem of how to justify the quality of merged XML information returned from the cooperative sources.

We propose a framework to perform merging and to analyze the merged information modelled as multiple XML data objects returned from a set of XML information sources. Essentially, our analysis is to convert an XML data object in an *Merged Normal Form* (MNF) and then analyze the data content of the normalized object based on a *Merged Tree Pattern* (MTP). We develop the notions of *Information Completeness* (IC) and *Data Complexity* (DC). These are the two components related to the measure of the information quality.

Intuitively, IC is defined to compute the following two features related to the completeness of those involved information sources. First, how many XML data objects (or equivalently, XML object trees) can be covered by a data source, and second, how much detail does each XML data object contain. We call the first feature of IC the *merged tree coverage* (or simply the *coverage*) and the second feature of IC the *merged tree density* (or simply the *density*).

The motivation for us to define IC is that, in reality when posing queries upon a set of XML information sources that have little overlaps in some pre-defined set of core labels $\mathcal{C}$, then the integrated information contains a large number of distinct XML data objects but with few subtrees or data values under the core labels, in this case the integrated information has comparatively high coverage but low density. On the other hand, if the sources have large overlaps in $\mathcal{C}$, the integrated information contains a small number of distinct objects with more subtrees or data elements under the core labels, in this case the integrated information has comparatively low coverage but high density.

The metric DC is defined to compute the following two features related to the complexity of the retrieved data items, resulting from merging data from those involved information sources. First, how diversified the merged elements or the data under a set of core labels are, and second, how specific those merged elements or data are. We call the first feature of DC the merged tree diversity (or simply the *diversity*) and the second feature of DC the merged tree specificity (or simply the *specificity*). In reality, when we merge the data under a label in $\mathcal{C}$ it may lead to a too wide and deep tree structure. For example, if most data of the same object from different sources disagree with each other, then we have to merge a diverse set of subtrees or data elements under the label. Furthermore, the merged tree structure under the label can be very deep, i.e. to give very specific information related to the label.

We assume a global view of data, which allows us to define a set of core labels of an entity that we search over the sources. As a core label may happen anywhere along a path of the tree corresponding to the entity instance, we propose a Merge Normal Form (MNF). Essentially, an XML object in MNF ensures that only the lowest core label along a path in the tree can contain interested subtrees or data elements. Assuming all XML objects are in MNF we aggregate them into a universal template called Merged Tree Pattern (MTP). We perform merging on the subtrees or data values associated with $\mathcal{C}$ from XML tree objects: if the two corresponding core paths (paths having a core label) from different objects are equal, then they can be unanimously merged in MTP. If the two paths are not equal, the conflict is resolved by changing the path to a general descendant path. Finally, if the two core paths do not exist then they are said to be incomplete, the missing node in MTP will be counted when computing IC.

The main contributions is that we establish a framework for evaluating the quality of integrated XML information. Our approach is based on a merged XML template called MTP, which is used to aggregate XML data objects from different sources. The framework is desirable for several reasons. First, the IC score is a simple but an effective metric to assess the quality of individual data source or a combination of data sources, which can serve as a basis for source selection optimization. The DC is a natural metric to assess the diversity and specificity of the subtrees under core labels. Second, MTP shares the benefits of traditional nested relations which are able to minimize redundancy of data. This allows a very flexible interface at the external level, since both flat and hierarchical data can be well presented to the users. The MTP provides for the explicit representation of the structure as well as the semantics of object instances. Finally, an XML data objects T can be converted into MNF in a linear time complexity, $O(k_1 + k_2)$, where k_1 is the number of nodes and k_2 is the number of edges in T.

Paper Organisation. Section 2 formalises the notion of integration for a set of XML data objects from a given source, which includes the discussion of the merged objects and the merged normal form (MNF). Section 3 introduces the concept of XML merged tree pattern (MTP) and illustrates how XML data objects can be merged under the MTP. Section 4 defines the components of measuring quality of integrated XML information. Finally, we give our concluding remarks in Section 5.

2 Merging Data from XML Information Sources

In this section, we assume a simple information model consisting of different XML sources, which can be viewed as a set of object trees. We introduce two notions of Merge Normal Form (MNF) and Merge Tree Pattern (MTP) in order to evaluate the merged results. Our assumptions of the information model of co-operative XML sources are described as follows.

Core Label Set. We assume a special label set over the information sources, denoted as $\mathcal{C} = \{l_1, \ldots, l_n\}$. $\mathcal{C}$ is a set of core tag labels (or simply core labels) related to the requested entity e. We term those paths starting from the entity node with tag label l_e leading to a core node with tag label the *core paths*. $\mathcal{C}$ also consists of a unique ID label, K, to identify an XML object instance of e. A user query $q = \langle e, \mathcal{C} \rangle$ is a selection of different information related to a core label, which should include the special K path. We assume heterogenicity of data objects to be resolved elsewhere, such as using data wrappers and mediators.

Key Label and Path. We assume an entity constraint: if two sources present an XML data object then we consider these objects represent the same entity in real world. The K label is important to merge information of identical objects from different sources. We do not consider the general case of FDs in order to simplify our discussion. The assumption of the K tag label is practical, since in reality an ID label is commonly available in XML information, which is similar to the relational setting.

Source Relationships. The information source contents *overlap* to various degrees with each others, regarding the storage of XML data objects. In an extreme case, one source can be *equal* to another source, for example mirror Web sites. In the other extreme case, one source can be *disjoint* from another, i.e. no common XML data object exists in two sources, for example one source holds ACM publications and another source holds IEEE publications. Usually, *independent* sources have different degrees of overlaps, e.g. they share information of common objects. Furthermore, if all objects in one source exist in another larger one then we say the former is *contained* in the latter.

Example 1. Figure 1 shows three publication objects T_1, T_2 and T_3, all of which have a K path, *key*, represented in different XML object trees as shown. Each object contains different subsets of the core labels $\mathcal{C} = \{key, author, title, url, year\}$.

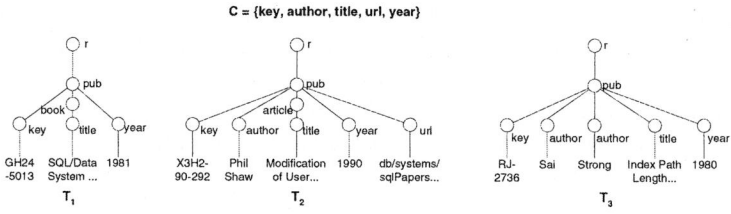

Fig. 1. A source of three XML data objects of publication records

We now consider merging the same XML data object identified by the K path. There are several scenarios arising from merging an object obtained from two different sources. (1) A core path $l \in \mathcal{C}$ of the object does not exist in either sources. (2) A core path $l \in \mathcal{C}$ of the object is provided by only one source. (3) A core path $l \in \mathcal{C}$ of the object is provided by both sources but their children under the l-node may be distinct.

The first and second cases do not impose any problems for merging, since we simply need to aggregate the existent paths in the merged result. The outcome of the merge is that there is either no information for the path l or a unique piece of information for the path l in the merged result. The last case does not bring into any problem if the children (data values or subtrees) under the core label obtained from the sources are identical. However, it poses a problem when their children disagree with each other, since conflicting information happens in the merged result. Our approach is different from the common ones which adopt either human intervention or some pre-defined resolution schemes to resolve the conflicting data. We make use of the flexibility of XML and introduce a special merge node labelled as m (m-node) as a parent node to merge the two subtrees as its children. We formalize the notion of merging in the following Definition.

Definition 1. (Merging Subtrees Under Core Labels) Let v_1 and v_2 be the roots of two subtrees, T_1 and T_2, under a core label $l \in \mathcal{C}$. Let m be the special label for merging subtrees. We construct a subtree T_3 having the children generated by T_1 and T_2, where v_3 is a m-node whose children are defined as follows. (1) T_3 has two children of T_1 and T_2 under the root v_3, if neither v_1 nor v_2 are m-nodes. (2) T_3 has the children T_1 with T_2 being added immediately under v_3, if v_1 is under a m-node but v_2 is not. (Similar for the case if v_2 is the only m-node.) (3) T_3 has the children $child(v_1)$ and $child(v_2)$ under v_3, if both v_1 and v_2 are under m-nodes.

A *merge* operator on two given subtrees having the roots, v_1 and v_2, under a given l, denoted as $merge(v_1, v_2)$, is an operation which returns T_3 as a child under the l-node, defined according to the above conditions.

Figure 2 shows the three possible results of $merge(v_1, v_2)$, on the two subtrees, T_1 and T_2, under the core node with label $\ell \in \mathcal{C}$. The three cases correspond to the cases stated in Definition 1. We can see that the resultant subtree T_3, which has the root of a m-node, is constructed from T_1 and T_2.

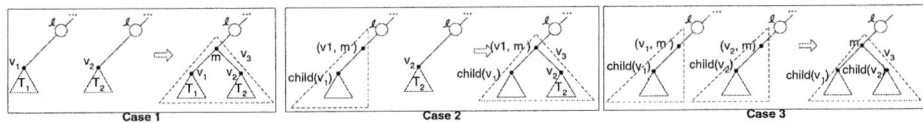

Fig. 2. The *merge* operator on two subtrees T_1 and T_2 under a core label

The *merge* operator can be naturally extended to more than two input children under a given core node with a label $l \in \mathcal{C}$. We can verify the following commutativity and associativity properties of the *merge* operator: $merge(v_1, v_2) = merge(v_2, v_1)$ and $merge(merge(v_1, v_2), v_3) = merge(v_1, merge(v_2, v_3))$. In addition, the merge operator is able to preserve the occurrences of identical data items of a core label of the same object. Our use of the merge node has the benefit that it provides the flexibility of further processing of the children under the m-node, which is independent on any pre-defined resolution schemes for conflicting data. For example, in the case of having flat data values under the m-node, we may choose an aggregate function such as min, max, sum or avg to further process the conflicting results. In the case of having tree data under the m-node, we may use a tree pattern to filter away the unwanted specific information.

One might think that it is not sufficient to define the merge operator over the same object from different sources. In fact, the merge operator has also ignored the fact that in a core path, more than one core label may occur. In order to deal with these complications, we need the concepts of Merge Normal Form (MNF) and Merge Tree Pattern (MTP) to handle general merging of XML data objects.

Definition 2. (Merge Normal Form) Let T be an XML object tree, where $\mathcal{P} \subseteq \mathcal{C}$ be the set of core labels in T and $K \in \mathcal{P}$ is the key label of T. Let us call those nodes having a core label *core nodes* and those path having a core node *core paths*. A tree T is said to be in the *Merge Normal Form* (MNF), denoted as $N(T)$, if for any core paths p in T, all the ancestor nodes of the lowest core nodes of p have one and only one child.

Intuitively, the MNF allows us to estimate how much information is associated with the core labels of an entity by simply checking the lowest core label in a path. We now present an algorithm which converts a given XML object tree, T, into an MNF. By Definition 2, we are able to view $N(T) = \{p_1, \ldots, p_n\}$ as the merged normal form of T, where p_i is the core path from the root to the lowest core node in the path. Note that any particular core label may have more than one core path in $N(T)$.

MNF Generation

Input: an XML object tree T.
Output: the MNF of the tree $T_r = N(T)$
$N(T)\{$
1.   **Let** $T_r = \phi;\ \mathcal{P} = \phi;$
2. $Normal(T.root);$
3.   **return** $N(T) := T_r;\}$
$Normal(n)\ \{$
1.   for each child node h_i of n {
2. $Normal(h_i);$
3.   if $(label(n) \in \mathcal{C})$ {
4.   if (n has non-core children) {
5.   if (there exist a path, $path(n') \in T_r$, such that $path(n') = path(n)$)
6. $child(n') = merge(child(n'), child(n));$
7.   else {
8.   if $(label(n) \notin \mathcal{P})$
9. $\mathcal{P} \cup label(n);$
10. $T_r \cup path(n);\ \}\}\}\}\}$

The underlying idea of Algorithm 2 is to visit each node in T iteratively in a depth first manner until all distinct core paths are copied as separate branches into $N(T)$. The core paths that have no non-core subtrees attached are removed. If there are two core paths ended at nodes with the same core label, we check if there exists a path, $path(n') \in N(T)$, such that $path(n') = path(n)$, their value are simply merged together, otherwise, $path(n)$ is added as a new branch. The complexity of Algorithm 2 is $O(k_1 + k_2)$, where k_1 is the number of node and k_2 is the number of edges in T. Note that the NMF of T may not be a unique $N(T)$ from Algorithm 2. However, it is easy to show that the output satisfies the requirement in Definition 2. From now on, we assume that all XML data object trees are in MNF (or else, they can be transformed to MNF by using Algorithm 2.) We now extend the merge operations on two XML data objects.

Definition 3. (Merging XML Data Object from Two Sources) Let $core(T)$ be the set of core labels in T. Given two XML object trees, $T_1 = \{p_1, \ldots, p_n\}$ and $T_2 = \{q_1, \ldots, q_m\}$, where p_i and q_j are core paths. We define $T_3 = merge(T_1, T_2)$ such that T_3 satisfies (1) $p_i \in T_3$, where $p_i \in T_1, p_i \notin T_2$. (2) $q_j \in T_3$, where $q_j \in T_2, q_j \notin T_1$. (3) $r_k \in T_3$ and $child(n_{r_k}) = merge(n_{p_i}, n_{q_j})$, where $r_k = p_i = q_j$.

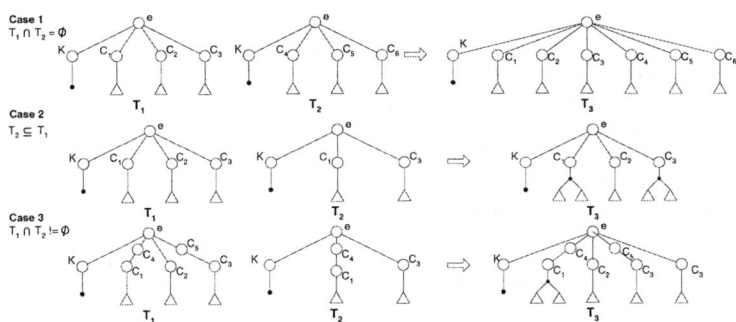

Fig. 3. Merging of MNF XML trees $N(T_1)$ and $N(T_2)$

Figure 3 shows the three possibilities of merging an XML object tree from two different sources. By Algorithm 2, we can transform an XML object tree into its MNF, which can be viewed as a set of basic core paths. We denote S as a set of XML object trees in MNF, $S = \{T_1, T_2, \ldots, T_n\}$. We further develop a template for general merging, called the *Merge Tree Pattern* (MTP), which is used to merge the information of a given set of normalized object trees obtained from different sources. Essentially, we perform merging the children of the basic core paths iteratively within MTP.

Definition 4. (Merge Tree Pattern) Let $core(T)$ denote the set of basic core labels in T. Let $\mathcal{T} = \{T_1, \ldots, T_n\}$. A Merge Tree Pattern (MTP) is a tree template obtained by combining the trees in $\mathcal{T}$. An MTP is generated according to the following algorithm. We say that two basic core paths are *mismatched*, if the two given paths both end at the same core label but they have different lists of core nodes along the basic core path. The child of each leaf of the basic core path in the MTP is a list of elements which store the data corresponding to the basic core path. We also define $desc(n)$ to be the descendant axis of the node n. For example, given $path(n) = r/a/b/c/d$, we have $desc(n) = r//d$.

Example 2. Figure 4 demonstrates the generation of MTP with three XML trees in MNF forms, T_1, T_2 and T_3. We can check that the core path for "*title*" are different in T_1, T_2 and T_3, therefore, we represent it as the descendant axis "$r//title$". The child of the core label "*author*" in T_2 is a subtree of non-core labels, in MTP, we insert a labelled pointer $(author, 1)$ to indicate it. Note that the child of the core label "*author*" subtree is a subtree having the root m-node. The list in Algorithm 4 does not store the whole tree structure, we only need to insert a labelled pointer $(m, 2)$ directed to the required subtree as shown.

MTP Generation

Let $T_i = \{path(n_{1_i}), \ldots, path(n_{p_i})\}, 1 \leq i \leq n$
and $\mathbf{T} = \{path(m_1), \ldots, path(m_q)\}$
Input: a set of trees in MNF, $\mathcal{T} = \{T_1, \ldots, T_n\}$
Output: the MTP of T
$MTPGen(\mathcal{T})\{$
1.   **Let $\mathbf{T} = T_1$;**
2.   For each T_i in $\mathcal{T}\{$
4.   For each leaf node, n, in T_i {
5.   if $(path(n_i)$ and $path(m_j)$ are $mismatched)$ {
6. $path(m_j) = desc(m_j)$;
7. $list(m_j).add(merge(value(m_j), value(n_i)));$ }
8.   else $\{\mathbf{T} \cup path(n_i);$
9. $list(n_i).add(value(n_i)); \}\}\}$
10.   **return** $MTPGen(\mathcal{T}) := \mathbf{T}; \}$

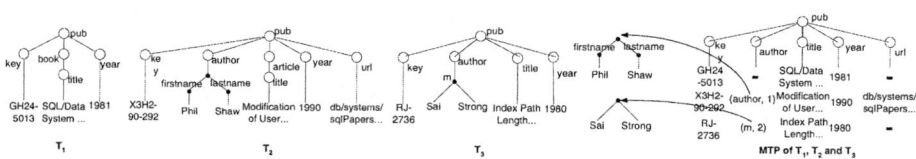

Fig. 4. Generation of MTP with three XML trees in MNF

3 Merge Operations on MTP

In order to perform merging of the entire query results from multiple sources, we define two useful merge operators on MTPs, the *join merge*, $\sqcap$, and the *union merge*, $\sqcup$.

Definition 5. (Join Merge Operator) Let P_1 and P_2 be two MTPs derived from the sources S_1 and S_2. Let $core(P_1), core(P_1) \subseteq \mathcal{C}$ be the set of core labels obtained from the sources S_1 and S_2, respectively, where $K \in core(S_1)$, and $K \in core(S_2)$. Then we define the MTP $P_3 = P_1 \sqcap P_2$, such that $\exists T_1 \in S_1$ and $\exists T_2 \in S_2$ satisfies that if $r_1//K = r_2//K$, then T_3 is constructed by:
1. $path(r_3//K) := path(r_1//K)$.
2. $path(r_3//l/v_3) := path(r_1//l/v_1)$, where $l \in (core(P_1) - core(P_1))$.
3. $path(r_3//l/v_3) := path(r_2//l/v_2)$, where $l \in (core(P_1) - core(P_1))$.
4. $path(r_3//l/v_3) := desc(v_3)$ where $child(n_{v_3}) := merge(child(n_{v_1}), child(n_{v_2}))$, where $l \in (core(P_1) \cap core(P_2))$.

The intuition behind the above definition is that in the first condition we adopt the key path as the only criterion to join the tree objects identified by K obtained from P_1 and P_2. The second and third conditions state that we choose

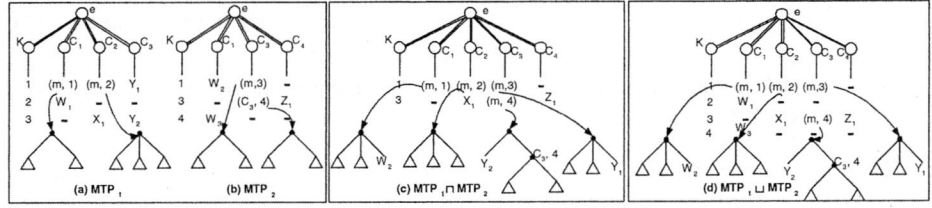

Fig. 5. The Join Merge and Join Union Operators

all the paths from the two MTPs as long as they do not overlap. The fourth condition is to resolve the conflict of having the common path in both source MTPs by using a descendant path and merging the node information.

Example 3. Figure 5(c) and 5(d) illustrates the use of the join-merge and join-union operations on P_1 and P_2.

Definition 6. (Union Merge Operator) Let P_1 and P_2 be two MTPs derived from the sources S_1 and S_2. Let $core(P_1)$, $core(P_1) \subseteq C$ be the set of core labels obtained from the sources S_1 and S_2, respectively, where $K \in core(S_1)$, and $K \in core(S_2)$. Then we define the MTP $P_3 = P_1 \sqcup P_2$, such that $\exists T_1 \in S_1$ and $\exists T_2 \in S_2$ satisfies that, if $path(r_1//K) = path(r_2//K)$, then T_3 is constructed by: (1) $path(r_3//K) := path(r_1//K)$. (2) $path(r_3//l/v_3) := path(r_1//l/v_1)$, where $l \in (core(P_1) - core(P_1))$. (3) $path(r_3//l/v_3) := path(r_2//l/v_2)$, where $l \in (core(P_1) - core(P_1))$. (4) $path(r_3//l/v_3) := desc(v_3)$ where $child(n_{v_3}) = merge(child(n_{v_1}), child(n_{v_2}))$, where $l \in (core(P_1) \cap core(P_2))$. Or else T_3 is constructed by $path(r_3//l/v_3) := path(r_1//l/v_1)$ or $path(r_3//l/v_3) := path(r_2//l/v_2)$.

Notably, the union merge operator can be viewed as a generalized from of the full-outer join in relational databases [8].

4 Quality Metrics of Merged XML Trees

We describe two measures of *information completeness* and *data complexity* to evaluate the quality of the results of the join and union merge operators.

The *merged tree coverage* (or simply the *coverage*) of an XML source relates to the number of objects that the source can potentially return. Intuitively, the notion of coverage captures the percentage of real world information covered in a search. The problem lies in the fact that XML sources mutually overlap a different extent. We need to devise an effective way to evaluate the size of coverage.

Definition 7. (Merged Tree Coverage)
Let the MTP of the source S of a set of XML data objects be P_S and n be the total number of objects related to the requested entity e specified in a query

$q = (e, \mathcal{C})$, where $\mathcal{C}$ is the set of core labels associated with e. We define the *merged tree coverage* (or the *coverage*) of P_S with respect to q as $cov(S) = \frac{|P_S|}{n}$, where $|P_S|$ is the number of XML data objects distinguished by the object key $K \in \mathcal{C}$ stored in P_S.

The coverage score of simple objects is between 0 and 1 and can be regarded as the probability that any given real world object is represented by some objects in the source. We adopt the union merge operator proposed in Definition 6 to generate the MTP for the merged objects and determine the coverage score [4].

Example 4. Assume that there are about two million electronic computer science publications over the Web (i.e. $n = 2{,}000{,}000$). About 490,000 of these are listed in the Digital Bibliography & Library Project (DBLP) and the information is available in XML format. Table 1 shows the number of electronic publications available on the Web. The coverage scores are obtained by dividing the number of publications by 2,000,000.

Table 1. The coverage score of five electronic publication sources

Electronic Publication Source	Number of Publication	Coverage Scores
CiteSeer	659,481	0.3297
The Collection of Computer Science Bibliographies	1,463,418	0.7317
DBLP	490,000	0.2450
CompuScience	412,306	0.2061
Computing Research Repository (CoRR)	75,000	0.0375

The coverage measure for the MTP from many sources can be computed in a similar way, based on the coverage scores of individual sources. In reality, we may download the source to assess the coverage or the coverage can be estimated by a domain expert. To respond to a user query, a query is sent to multiple XML information sources. The results returned by these sources are sets of relevant XML data objects. Some data objects may be returned by more than one source. We assume that there are only three different cases of overlapping data sources.

1. The two sources are *disjoint*, which means that, according to the K label, there are no common XML data objects in the two sources. Then $cov(S_i \sqcup S_j)$ is equal to $cov(S_i) + cov(S_j)$ and $cov(S_i \sqcap S_j)$ is equal to 0.

2. The two sources are *overlapping*, meaning that, according to the K label, there are some common XML data objects in the two sources. The two sources are assumed to be independent. Then $cov(S_i \sqcup S_j)$ is equal to $cov(S_i) + cov(S_j) - cov(S_i) \cdot cov(S_j)$ and $cov(S_i \sqcap S_j)$ is equal to $cov(S_i) \cdot cov(S_j)$ (if S_i is contained in S_j).

3. One source is *contained* in another, which means that, according to the K label, all the XML data objects in one source are contained in another source. Then $cov(S_i \sqcup S_j)$ is equal to $cov(S_j)$ and $cov(S_i \sqcap S_j)$ is equal to $cov(S_i)$ (if S_i is contained in S_j).

Now, we consider the general case of integrating results returned from multiple data sources. We emphasize that the extension of the two merge operations in Definitions 5 and 6 from two sources to many sources is non-trivial, since mixed kinds of overlapping may occur between different sources. We let $M = \bigsqcup(S_1, \ldots, S_n)$ be the result obtained from union-merged a set of sources $W = \{S_1, \ldots, S_n\}$. Let $S \notin W$. We define the disjoint sets of sources $D \subseteq W$ to be the maximal subset of W, such that all the sources in D are disjoint with S, the contained sets of sources $T \subseteq W$ to be the maximal subset of W, such that all the sources in T are subsets of S, and the independent sets of sources $I \subseteq W$ to be the remaining overlapping cases, i.e. $I = W - T - S$.

Theorem 1. The following statements regarding W and S are true.
1. $cov(M \sqcup S) = cov(M) + cov(S) - cov(M \sqcap S)$.
2. If $\not\exists S_i \in W$ such that $S \subseteq S_i$, then $cov(M \sqcap S) = cov(M) + cov(S) - cov(M \sqcap S)$, or else $cov(M \sqcap S) = cov(S)$.

The *merged tree density* (or simply the *density*) of an XML source relates to the ratio of core label information provided by the source. As XML objects have flexible structures, the returned object trees from a source do not necessarily have information for all the core labels. Furthermore, a basic core node may have a simple data value (i.e. a leaf value) or a subtree as its child. We now define the density of a core label in an MTP, P_S.

Definition 8. (Core Label Density) We define the *merge tree density* (or simply *density*) of a core path p_l for some $l \in \mathcal{C}$ of P_S, denoted as $den(S, l)$, by $den(S, l) = \frac{|\{T \in P_S \mid r_T//p_l/v \text{ exists in } T\}|}{|P_S|}$, where "$r_T//p_l/v$" is a basic core path and v is the corresponding core node in T. The density of the MTP P_S, denoted as $den(S)$, is the average density over all core labels and is given by $den(S) = \frac{\Sigma_{l \in \mathcal{C}} den(S, l)}{|\mathcal{C}|}$.

In particular, a core label that has a child (a leaf value of a subtree) for every data tree of the source S has a density of 1 in its P_S. The density of a core label l that is simply not provided by any object data tree has density $den(S, l) = 0$. Core labels for which a source can provide some values have a density score in between 0 and 1. By assumption $den(S, K)$ is always 1.

Table 2. The DBLP XML table from MTP(DBLP)

key	title	author	journal	volume	year	url
tr/ibm/GH24...	SQL/Data System ...	-	IBM Publication	GH24-5013	1981	-
tr/ibm/RJ...	Index Path Length...	Sai, Strong	IBM Research Report	RJ2736	1980	-
tr/sql/X3H2...	Modification of User...	Phil Shaw	ANSI X3H2	X3H2-90-292	1990	db/systems/...
tr/dec/SRC...	The 1995 SQL Reunion...	-	Digital System...	SRC1997-018	1997	-
tr/gte/TR-026..	An Evaluation of Object...	Frank Manola	GTE Laboratories...	TR-0263-08-94-165	1994	db/labs/gte/...

Example 5. Let $\mathcal{C} = (key, title, author, journal, vloumn, year, url)$ be a simplified set of core labels of an article object. Consider the DBLP table (ignoring all core paths) extracted from MTP(DBLP) as shown in Table 2. The data in the table is the information returned from the *DBLP* source for searching articles. The density of the core labels *title* and *url* are $den(S, title) = 1$ and $den(S, url) = 0.4$, respectively.

Similar to finding real coverage scores, density scores can be assessed in many ways in practice. Information sources may give the scores for an assessment. We may also use a sampling technique to estimate the density. For large data sources, the sampling process can be continuous and then the score can be incrementally updated to a more accurate value.

Now, we consider the general case of n data sources. We use the same set of notations M, W, T, S and I as already introduced in Section 4.

Theorem 2. The following statements regarding W and S are true.
1. $(den(M \sqcup S) = den(M,l) \cdot cov(M) + den(S,l) \cdot cov(S) - den(T,l) \cdot cov(T)$
$(den(S,l)+den(I,l)-den(S,l) \cdot den(I,l)) \cdot cov(S) \cdot cov(I) + (den(I,l)+den(T,l)-den(I,l) \cdot den(T,l)) \cdot cov(I \sqcap T)) \cdot \frac{1}{cov(M \sqcup S)}$
2. $den(M \sqcap S, l) = den(M,l) + den(S,l) - den(M,l) \cdot den(S,l)$.

Example 6. Assume that $DBLP(D)$ and $CiteSeer(C)$ are independent sources. Let the density scores for the *volumn* label be 1 and 0.6 respectively. The coverage score is 0.245 and 0.3297. Thus, the density score of their merged result is given by $den(D \sqcup C) = 1 \cdot 0.245 + 0.6 \cdot 0.3297 - (1 + 0.6 - 1 \cdot 0.6) \cdot 0.245 \cdot 0.3297 \cdot \frac{1}{0.245+0.3298-0.245 \cdot 0.3297} = 0.2387$. We now add the $CompuScience(S)$ and assume it is independent of $DBLP$ and $CiteSeer$. Its density of 0.8 for the *volume* label and a coverage of 0.2061. The new density score is given by: $den(D \sqcup C \sqcup S) = 0.2387 \cdot 0.5747 + 0.8 \cdot 0.2061 - (0.2387 + 0.8 - 0.2387 \cdot 0.8) \cdot 0.5747 \cdot 0.2061 \cdot \frac{1}{0.5747+0.2061-0.5747 \cdot 0.2061} = 0.4179$.

4.1 Information Completeness and Data Complexity

The notion of *information completeness* of an information source represents the ratio of its information amount to the total information of the real world. The more complete a source is, the more information it can potentially contribute to the overall response to a user query.

Definition 9. (**Information Completeness**) The *Information Completeness* (IC) of a source S is defined by

$$comp(S) = \frac{\text{No. of data objects associated with each } l \in \mathcal{C} \text{ in } P_S}{\mid W \mid \cdot \mid \mathcal{C} \mid},$$

where W is the total number of data objects of a real world entity and P_S is the MTP of S.

The following corollary allows us to employ coverage and density to find out the IC score. This corollary can be trivially generalised to a set of information sources using the corresponding MTP. Intuitively, the notion of IC can be interpreted as the "rectangular area" formed by coverage (height) and density (width). The following example further helps to illustrate these ideas.

Corollary 1. Let S be an information source. Then $comp(S) = cov(S) \cdot den(S)$.

Example 7. Table 2 represents the entries DBLP XML source. The table provides only five tuples with varying density. The coverage of the source is thus given by $cov(DBLP) = \frac{5}{2,000,000}$. The densities for the labels are 1, 1, 0.6, 1, 1, 1, and 0.4, respectively, and it follows that the density of the source is $\frac{6}{7}$. Thus, the completeness of $DBLP$ is $\frac{5}{2,000,000} \cdot \frac{6}{7} = \frac{3}{1,400,000}$.

We define *specificity* and *diversity* of an XML source to represent the depth and breadth of data that the source can potentially return. As the subtree of a core label may contain subtrees of flexible structures, the returned data does not contain the same amount of data, it may contain something as simple as a single textual value, or a complex subtree having many levels.

Definition 10. (Specificity and Diversity) Let P_S be the MTP of a source S of a set of XML data objects. Let $avg(d_i)$ and $max(d_i)$ be the average and maximum depth of child subtrees under the core node labelled by $l_i \in \mathcal{C}$ and D be the maximum of $\{max(d_1), \ldots, max(d_n)\}$ where $|\mathcal{C}| = n$. *Specificity* is defined by $spec(S) = \frac{\Sigma avg(d_i)}{n \cdot D}$. Similarly, we define *diversity* by $div(S) = \frac{\Sigma avg(b_i)}{n \cdot B}$, where $avg(b_i)$ and $max(b_i)$ are the average number and the maximum of children of subtrees under the core node labelled by $l_i \in \mathcal{C}$. Similarly, B be the maximum of $\{max(b_1), \ldots, max(b_n)\}$.

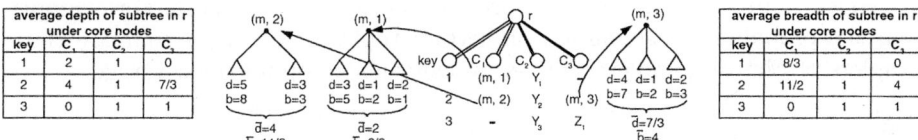

Fig. 6. Specificity and diversity of subtrees

Example 8. In Figure 6, under the core label C_1, the list contains three values: "$(m,1), (m,2), -$". The depth of core label C_1 is $d(C_1) = \frac{d((m,1))+d((m,2))+d(-)}{3} = \frac{2+4+0}{3} = 2$. Similarly, $d(C_2) = \frac{1+1+1}{3} = 1$ and $d(C_3) = \frac{0+\frac{7}{3}+1}{3} = 1.1111$. The deepest path is $(m,2)$, so we have $D = 4$. The specificity of the tree is $spec(S) = \frac{d(C_1)+d(C_2)+d(C_3)}{n \cdot D} = \frac{2+1+1.1111}{3 \cdot 4} = 0.3426$. The breadth of core label C_1, $b(C_1) = \frac{b((m,1))+b((m,2))+b(-)}{3} = \frac{\frac{8}{3}+\frac{11}{2}+0}{3} = 2.7222$. Similarly, $b(C_2) = \frac{1+1+1}{3} = 1$ and $b(C_3) = \frac{0+4+1}{3} = \frac{5}{3}$. The broadest subtree is $b((m,2))$, so we have $B = 5.5$. The diversity of the tree is $div(S) = \frac{b(C_1)+b(C_2)+b(C_3)}{n \cdot B} = \frac{2.7222+1+1.6667}{3 \cdot 5.5} = 0.3266$.

The notion of *data complexity* of an information source is employed to represent the amount of information from the source. The higher the data complexity of a source is, the richer and broader information it can potentially contribute to the overall response to a user query.

Definition 11. (Data Complexity) The *Data Complexity* (DC) of a source S is defined by $cpex(S) = spec(S) \cdot div(S)$.

Example 9. Consider the MTP in Figure 6, the data complexity, DC of the tree is $cpex(S) = spec(S) \cdot div(S) = 0.3426 \cdot 0.3266 = 0.1119$.

5 Concluding Remarks

We have proposed a framework which consists of two useful concepts, the first being information completeness (IC), which represents the coverage of data objects and the density of data related to a set of core labels, and the second being data complexity (DC), which represents the diversity and the specificity of data content for a set of core nodes associated with the search entity. The framework allows merging XML data objects obtained from different sources. We present an MNF as a standard format to unify the essential data in merged objects of an entity and an efficient algorithm to transform an XML data object into an MNF. We develop MTP as a unifying template to represent the merge of a set of XML objects. MTP serves as a basis to evaluate the IC and DC scores. We also investigated the properties of density and coverage via two merge operators in different sources that are disjoint, overlapping and independent. An important issue related to this work is how we obtain the values of various metrics of coverage, density, diversity and specificity. We suggest that this information can be derived from the data sources or from other authority corpora. For example, from the probability distribution on certain topics of CS if we compare those complete or almost complete sources we can then compute the coverage.

References

1. E. Bertino and E. Ferrari. XML and Data Integration. *IEEE Internet Computing.* 5(6):75-76, 2001.
2. V. Christophides, S. Cluet, and J. Simeon. On Wrapping Query Language and Efficient XML Integration. In *Proc. of SIGMOD Conference*, 2000.
3. Z. G. Ives et al. An Adaptive Query Execution System for Data Integration. In *Proc. of SIGMOD* , 1999.
4. D. Florescu, D. Koller, and A. Levy. Using probabilistic information in data integration. In *Proc. of VLDB*, 1997.
5. E. Lim, J. Srivastava, S. Prabhakar and J. Richardson. Entity Identification in Database Integration. In *Proc. of ICDE*, 1993.
6. A. Motro and I. Rakov. Estimating the quality of databases. In *Proc. of FQAS*, 1998.
7. F. Naumann, J. C. Freytag and U. Leser. Completeness of Information Sources. In *Proc. of DQCIS*, 2003 .
8. Elmasri and Navathe. Fundamentals of Database Systems. Addison Wesley, 3rd Edition, 1997.

Efficient Evaluation of Partial Match Queries for XML Documents Using Information Retrieval Techniques

Young-Ho Park[1], Kyu-Young Whang[1], Byung Suk Lee[2], and Wook-Shin Han[3]

[1] Department of Computer Science
and Advanced Information Technology Research Center (AITrc)**
Korea Advanced Institute of Science and Technology (KAIST), Korea
{yhpark, ywhang}@mozart.kaist.ac.kr
[2] Department of Computer Science,
University of Vermont Burlington, VT, USA
bslee@cs.uvm.edu
[3] Department of Computer Engineering,
Kyungpook National University, Korea
wshan@knu.ac.kr

Abstract. We propose XIR, a novel method for processing partial match queries on heterogeneous XML documents using information retrieval (IR) techniques. A partial match query is defined as the one having the descendent-or-self axis "//" in its path expression. In its general form, a partial match query has branch predicates forming branching paths. The objective of XIR is to efficiently support this type of queries for large-scale documents of heterogeneous schemas. XIR has its basis on the conventional schema-level methods using relational tables and significantly improves their efficiency using two techniques: an inverted index technique and a novel prefix match join. The former indexes the labels in label paths as keywords in texts, and allows for finding the label paths matching the queries more efficiently than string match used in the conventional methods. The latter supports branching path expressions, and allows for finding the result nodes more efficiently than containment joins used in the conventional methods. We compare the efficiency of XIR with those of XRel and XParent using XML documents crawled from the Internet. The results show that XIR is more efficient than both XRel and XParent by several orders of magnitude for linear path expressions, and by several factors for branching path expressions.

1 Introduction

Recently, there have been significant research on processing queries against XML documents [30]. To our knowledge, however, most of them considered only a limited number of documents with a fixed schema, and thus are not suitable for large-scale applications dealing with heterogeneous schemas–such as an Internet search engine [20] [29]. A novel method is needed for these applications, and we address it in this paper.

** This work was supported by the Korea Science and Engineering Foundation (KOSEF) through the Advanced Information Technology Research Center (AITrc).

Partial match queries in XPath [7] can be particularly useful for searching XML documents when their schemas are heterogeneous while only partial schema information is known to the user. Here, a partial match query is defined as the one having the descendent-or-self axis "//" in its path expression. A full match query [18] can be considered a special case of a partial match query.

Partial match queries can be classified into *linear path expressions (LPEs)* and *branching path expressions (BPEs)*. An LPE is defined as a path expression consisting of a sequence of labels having a parent-child relationship or an ancestor-descendent relationship between labels; a BPE is defined as a path expression having branching conditions for one or more labels in the LPE.

Existing methods for providing partial match queries can be classified into two types: schema-level methods [24] [14] [15] [8] and instance-level methods [17] [26] [4] [6] [16] [5] [9] [10] [12]. The ones of the first type are usable for both partial match queries and BPEs, but they are not designed for use in large-scale documents of heterogeneous schemas [24] [14] [15] or have only limited support for partial match queries and do not explicitly handle BPEs [8]. The ones of the second type can support both, but can not be best used in a large-scale database because of inefficiency. Between these two classes of methods, the schema level methods are much more feasible than the instance level methods for large-scale XML documents because of their abilities to "filter out" document instances at the schema level. We thus adopt the schema-level methods as the basis of our method.

We particularly base our method on the schema-level methods using *relational tables*, such as XRel [24] and XParent [14] [15]. There are two reasons for this. First, those methods can utilize well-established techniques on relational DBMSs instead of a few native XML storages. Second, those methods can also utilize SQLs to query XML documents. For the query processing, they store the schema information and instance information of XML documents in relational tables, and process partial match queries in two phases: first, find the XML documents whose schemas match a query's path expression, and second, among the documents, find those that satisfy selection conditions (if there are any) specified on the path expression.

However, query processing efficiencies of the two existing methods, XRel and XParent, are too limited for large-scale applications, as we will show in our experiments in Section 6. The hurdle in the first phase is the large amount of schema information, and the hurdle in the second phase is the large number of document instances.

The objective of our method (we name it *XIR*) is to improve the efficiencies in both phases. Specifically, for the first phase, we present a method that adopts the *inverted index* [22] technique, used traditionally in the Information retrieval (IR) field, for searching a very large amount of schema information. IR techniques have been successfully used for searching large-scale documents with only a few keywords (constituting partial schema information). If we treat the schema of an XML document as a text document and convert partial match queries to keyword-based text search queries, we can effectively search against heterogeneous XML documents using partial match queries. For the second phase, we present a novel method called, *prefix match join*, for searching a large amount of instance information.

In this paper, we first describe the relational table structures for storing the XML document schema and instance information, and then, describe the structure of the inverted index. We then present the algorithms for processing queries. We also present the prefix match join operator, which plays an essential role in the evaluation of BPEs, and present an algorithm for finding the nodes matching the BPE. Then, we discuss the performance of XIR in comparison with that of XRel and XParent, and verify our comparison through experiments using real XML document sets collected by crawlers from the Internet. The results show that XIR outperforms both XRel and XParent by several orders of magnitude for LPEs and by several factors for BPEs.

This paper makes the following novel contributions toward large-scale query processing on heterogeneous XML documents:

- In XIR, we apply the IR technology to the schema-level information rather than to the instance-level information of the XML documents. In a large-scale heterogeneous environment, schema-level information as well as instance-level information would be extremely large. By applying the IR technique to the schema-level information, we can improve performance significantly by achieving schema-level filtering. i.e., restricting the instances to be searched to those whose schema matches the query's path expression.
- XIR also presents a novel instance-level join called the prefix match join for efficiently processing queries involving BPEs. The prefix match join improves performance significantly by minimizing the number of joins for finding instance nodes satisfying branching predicates.

2   Preliminaries

2.1   XML Document Model

Our XML document model is based on the one proposed by Bruno et al. [6]. In this model, an XML document is represented as a rooted, ordered, labeled tree. A *node* in the tree represents an element, an attribute, or a value; an *edge* in the tree represents an element-subelement relationship, element-attribute relationship, element-value relationship, or attribute-value relationship. Element and attribute nodes collectively define the document structure, and we assign labels (i.e., names) and unique identifiers to them. Figure 1 shows an example XML tree of a document. In this figure, all leaf nodes except those numbered 15 and 27 (representing the two attribute values "R" and "T") represent values and all non-leaf nodes except those numbered 14 and 26 (representing the attribute @category) represent elements. Note that attributes are distinguished from elements using a prefix '@' in the labels.

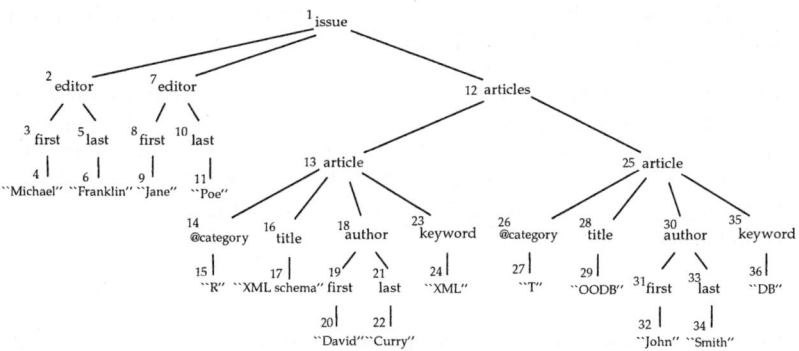

Fig. 1. An example XML tree of a document

We modify this model so that a node represents either an element or an attribute but not a value. We also extend the model with the notions of label paths and node paths as defined below.

Definition 1. A *label path* in an XML tree is defined as a sequence of node labels $l_1, l_2, ..., l_p$ ($p \geq 1$) from the root to a node p in the tree, and is denoted as $l_1.l_2.\cdots.l_p$. □

Definition 2. A *node path* in an XML tree is defined as a sequence of node identifiers $n_1, n_2, ..., n_p$ ($p \geq 1$) from the root to a node p in the tree, and is denoted as $n_1.n_2.\cdots.n_p$. □

Label paths represent XML document structures and are said to be *schema-level* information. In contrast, node paths represent XML document instances and are said to be *instance-level* information. We say a label path *matches* a path expression, a node path *belongs to* a label path, and a node path *is obtained from* a path expression. For example, in Figure 1, issue.editor.first is a label path matching a path expression //editor//first, and 1.2.3, 1.7.8 are node paths belonging to the label path. Note that there may be more than one node path belonging to the same label path because there may be more than one instance with the same structure.

2.2 XML Query Model

Our query language belongs to the tree pattern query (TPQ) class [2]. The query language supports two kinds of path expressions: 1) linear path expressions (LPEs) and 2) branching path expressions (BPEs).

An LPE is expressed as a sequence of labels connected with '/' or '//' as in Definition 3.

Definition 3. A *linear path expression* is defined as $l_0 o_1 l_1 o_2 l_2 \cdots o_n l_n$, where l_i ($i = 0, 1, \cdots, n$) is the i-th label in the path, and o_j ($j = 1, 2, \cdots, n$) is either '/' or '//' which, respectively, denotes a parent-child relationship or an ancestor-descendant relationship between l_{j-1} and l_j. Here, l_0 is the root of the XML tree denoting the set of all XML documents (i.e., document("*")) and may be omitted. □

A BPE is expressed as an LPE augmented with 'branch predicate expressions' $[C_i]$ for some labels l_i ($i \in \{1, 2, \cdots, n\}$) [7] as in Definition 5. As in some work in the literature [1] [21], for simplicity, we consider only simple selection predicates[1] for the branch predicate expressions as in Definition 4.

Definition 4. A *branch predicate expression* C_k is defined as an expression L or $L\,\theta\,v$, where L is a linear path subexpression $o_{k1}l_{k1}o_{k2}l_{k2}\cdots o_{kp}l_{kp}$ ($p \geq 1$), v is a constant value, and θ is a comparison operator ($\theta \in \{=, \neq, >, \geq, <, \leq\}$). L specifies the existence of a node path $n_1.n_2.\cdots.n_p$ that belongs to the label path matching the LPE $l_0 o_1 l_1 o_2 \cdots o_k l_k o_{k1} l_{k1} o_{k2} l_{k2} \cdots o_{kp} l_{kp}$, and $L\,\theta\,v$ further specifies the node path to satisfy the selection condition on n_p. □

---

[1] This can be easily extended to consider compound (e.g., conjunctive) predicates as supported in other work in the literature [4] [6]. However, we omit this issue since it is not the focus of this paper.

Definition 5. A *branching path expression* is defined as $l_0 o_1 l_1[C_1] o_2 l_2[C_2] \cdots o_n l_n[C_n]$ where (1) $l_0 o_1 l_1 o_2 l_2 \cdots o_n l_n$ is an LPE defined in Definition 3 and (2) C_k ($k = 1, 2, \cdots, n$) is a *branch predicate expression* as defined in Definition 4, where some (not all) of them may be omitted. □

The following query is an example BPE for retrieving the title elements that are children of the article elements that contain at least one keyword element and that are descendants of an issue element having a descendant author element whose child last element has the value "Curry".

Q1::/issue[//author/last="Curry"]//article[/keyword]/-title

Note that this BPE on the element issue has a selection condition on the label last in the LPE //issue//author/last and an existential condition on the label keyword in the LPE //issue//article/keyword.

2.3 XML Query Patterns

In this paper, we model a path expression as a *query pattern* defined in Definition 6. We modify the definition of the twig pattern originally used in the Holistic Twig Join [6] to formally represent the notions that we use in this paper. The definition is based on the BPE, as defined in Definition 5.

Definition 6. Given a path expression $o_1 l_1[C_1] o_2 l_2[C_2] \cdots o_n l_n[C_n]$ defined in Definition 5 (with l_0 omitted), we represent it as a *query pattern* that consists of a binary tree and a dangling edge connected to its root and that has the following properties:

- An edge represents o_j ($j \in \{1, 2, \cdots, n\}$) in the path expression. The edge is shown as a single line if o_j is '/' and as a double line if o_j is '//'. The dangling edge represents o_1.
- A node represents a label l_k ($k \in \{1, 2, \cdots, n\}$) in the path expression. The root node represents the label l_1.
- The left child of a node representing l_k ($k \in \{1, 2, \cdots, n-1\}$) represents l_{k+1}.
- The right subtree of a node representing l_k ($k \in \{1, 2, \cdots, n\}$) is the query pattern representing the branching predicate expression $C_k \equiv o_{k1} l_{k1} o_{k2} l_{k2} \cdots o_{kp} l_{kp}$ ($p \geq 1$).
- If the label represented by a node has a selection condition ("$\theta\, v$") on it, then the node is earmarked with "$\theta\, v$". □

The twig pattern [6] does not distinguish between the subtree whose root is also the root of the XML tree and the one whose root is not, if both match the same pattern. In contrast, the query pattern does distinguish between them by showing the dangling edge using a single line in the former case and a double line in the latter case.

Related to the query pattern, we use the following terms in this paper.

- One of the nodes in a query pattern is retrieved as the query result. This node corresponds to the label l_n in the LPE defined in Definition 3 or the BPE defined in Definition 5. We call this node the *result node* and distinguish it from the other nodes by shading it gray.
- Some of the nodes in a query pattern have a right subtree. We call such a node a *branching node*. Any node corresponding to a label l_k followed by $[C_k]$ as in $l_k[C_k]$ shown in Definition 5 is a branching node.

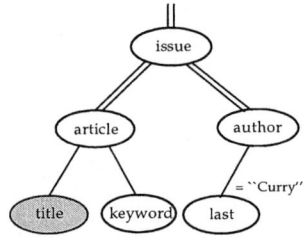

Fig. 2. Query pattern of the query Q1

Figure 2 shows the query pattern of the query Q1 in Section 2.2. The node `title` is the result node, and the nodes `issue` and `article` are branching nodes.

As a special case of the query pattern, we define the *linear query pattern* as follows.

Definition 7. The query pattern of a linear path expression is called the *linear query pattern*. Compared with the query pattern defined in Definition 6, a linear query pattern has no branching node. □

In this paper, we use the terms *root label, leaf label, result label*, and *branching label* in a path expression interchangeably with the *root node, leaf node, result node*, and *branching node* in a query pattern. For example, in Figure 2, `issue` is the root label of the query Q1; `title`, `keyword`, and `last` are leaf labels; `title` is the result label; and `issue` and `article` are branching labels.

3 Related Work

As mentioned in Introduction, there are two kinds of methods for evaluating path expressions: schema-level methods and instance-level methods. A schema-level method uses structural information like the label paths to find nodes matching a path expression [14] [15] [24] [8], whereas an instance-level method uses only node identification information like the start and end positions of a node [4] [6] [16]. In this section, we briefly discuss instance-level methods, and then, focus on schema-level methods.

3.1 Instance-Level Methods

There have been three different approaches for the instance-level method. The first uses XML tree navigation [3] [13] [19]. It converts a path expression to a "state machine"[2], and then evaluates the path expression by navigating the XML tree guided by the state machine. The second uses node instance information stored for each node in an XML tree [4] [6] [16] [17] [23] [26]. It converts a path expression to a (structural) join query, and then evaluates the join query using the node instance information. The query evaluation in this approach, however, involves comparing the node instance information, and therefore, tends to be more expensive than in the schema-level methods, which can filter out node instances significantly by using the schema information. The third uses information

---

[2] A representation of the sequence of labels in the path expression as a sequence of states in finite state automata.

retrieval (IR) technique, particularly an inverted index created on XML documents [5] [9] [10] [12]. Although using inverted indexes, however, they are fundamentally different from XIR, which creates an inverted index on the *label paths*, which are schema-level information.

3.2 Schema-Level Methods

Schema-level methods are categorized into those using special purpose indexes [8] [11] and those using relational tables [24] [14] [15] depending on where and how label paths are stored. In the former case, label paths are stored dynamically as they are used in the queries. In the latter case, all label paths in the documents are stored in the tables of a relational DBMS a priori.

Index Fabric [8] is considered the representative method in the schema-level methods using special purpose indexes. Index Fabric uses the Patricia trie to index the label paths and values that have occurred in the queries occurring frequently. However, Index Fabric is not meant to support partial match queries. Furthermore, the method is not designed to support BPEs, which are very effective for searching in a heterogeneous environment. These are critical drawbacks that render the method inapplicable in a large-scale, heterogeneous environment. Thus, in this section, we primarily focus on the schema-level methods using relational tables.

XRel [24] and XParent [14] [15], which are the two representative ones among the schema-level methods using relational tables, provide a basis for our XIR method. We describe each method in this subsection. We use the term *node* interchangeably with *element* or *attribute* as these are represented as nodes in the XML document model and the query pattern.

XRel. In XRel, the XML tree structure information is stored in the following four tables [24]:

```
Path(label_path_id, label_path)
Element(document_id, label_path_id, start_position,
   end_position, sibling_order)
Text(document_id, label_path_id, start_position,
   end_position, value)
Attribute(document_id, label_path_id, start_position,
   end_position, value)
```

XRel uses two techniques for evaluating LPEs and BPEs: *string match* and *containment join*. The former belongs to the schema-level method and is used to handle LPEs; the latter belongs to the instance-level method and is used to handle BPEs.

In the case of an LPE, XRel first finds the label paths matching the query's path expression from the Path table. The matching is done using the SQL string match operator LIKE. All label paths in the Path table must be scanned in this case because an index like the B+-tree cannot be used to search for a partially matching label path. Then, XRel joins the set of matching label paths with the table Element via the column label_path_id to obtain the result nodes.

For the case of a BPE, we use the query pattern defined in Section 2.3. XRel first decomposes a BPE into multiple LPEs consisting of one LPE from the root to each branching node and one LPE from the root to each leaf node. For example, a BPE $/l_1[/l_2/l_3 = v_2]/l_4$ is decomposed into three LPEs $/l_1$, $/l_1/l_2/l_3$, and $/l_1/l_4$. Then, for each LPE, XRel finds the set of nodes (we call it a *node set*) obtained from the LPE in the same manner described above and reduces the set to those satisfying a selection condition (e.g., $/l_1/l_2/l_3 = v_2$). Then, it compares the node set obtained from an LPE ending at a branching node (e.g., $/l_1$) with the node set obtained from the LPEs ending at the leaf nodes (e.g., $/l_1/l_2/l_3$, $/l_1/l_4$) and, among the nodes obtained from the latter LPEs, retains only those that are descendants of the nodes in the former node set. This is done using the *containment join* which is implemented as a θ-join comparing the start positions and end positions of nodes.

XParent. XParent [14] [15] is similar to XRel, but uses a different table schema so that it can implement the containment join operator using equi-joins instead of θ-joins. The schema is as follows [14].

```
LabelPath(label_path_id, length, label_path)
Element(document_id, label_path_id, node_id, sibling_order)
Data(document_id, label_path_id, node_id, sibling_order, value)
Ancestor(node_id, ancestor_node_id, offset_to_ancestor)
DataPath(parent_node_id, child_node_id)
```

In query processing, XParent evaluates an LPE in the same way as XRel. In the case of a BPE, however, XParent generates a smaller number of LPEs than XRel because it generates only those from the root to each leaf node of a query pattern. Then, after retrieving the node set in the same manner as in XRel, the node set obtained from the LPE containing the result node is reduced through joins with those obtained from the other LPEs. Here, the join is performed as an equi-join through the table `Ancestor`, thereby finding the node idenfitier of the common ancestor.

4 XIR Storage Structures

In this section, we present the storage structures used in our XIR method. XIR stores information needed for query processing at two levels – the schema level and the instance level. The schema-level information consists of the label paths occurring in the XML tree and the inverted index on these label paths; the instance-level information consists of all the node paths in the XML tree.

XIR uses two tables and an inverted index to store information about XML document structure:

```
LabelPath(pid, label_path)
NodePath(pid, docid, nodepath, value)
Inverted index on label_path of the table LabelPath.
```

4.1 Schema-Level Information

The table `LabelPath` represents the *schema-level information* and stores all the distinct label paths occurring in XML documents and their path identifiers (`pid`s). Figure 3 shows the `LabelPath` table and the inverted index for the example XML tree in Figure 1. The labels prefixed with '$' and '&' are added to denote the first label and the

(a) LabelPath table.

pid	labelpath
1	$issue.issue.&issue
2	$issue.issue.editor.&editor
3	$issue.issue.editor.first.&first
4	$issue.issue.editor.last.&last
5	$issue.issue.articles.&articles
6	$issue.issue.articles.article.&article
7	$issue.issue.articles.article.@category.&@category
8	$issue.issue.articles.article.title.&title
9	$issue.issue.articles.article.author.&author
10	$issue.issue.articles.article.author.first.&first
11	$issue.issue.articles.article.author.last.&last
12	$issue.issue.articles.article.keyword.&keyword

(b) LabelPath Inverted Index.

keyword	posting list
$issue	: <1, 1, {1}, 3> <2, 1, {1}, 4> <3, 1, {1}, 5> ...
issue	: <1, 1, {2}, 3> <2, 1, {2}, 4> <3, 1, {2}, 5> ...
&issue	: <1, 1, {3}, 3>
article	: <6, 1, {4}, 5> <7, 1, {4}, 6> <8, 1, {4}, 6> ...
&article	: <6, 1, {5}, 5>
articles	: <5, 1, {3}, 4> <6, 1, {3}, 5> <7, 1, {3}, 6> ...
&articles	: <5, 1, {4}, 4>
editor	: <2, 1, {3}, 4> <3, 1, {3}, 5> <4, 1, {3}, 5>
&editor	: <2, 1, {4}, 4>
author	: <9, 1, {5}, 6> <10, 1, {5}, 7> <11, 1, {5}, 7>
&author	: <9, 1, {6}, 6>
first	: <3, 1, {4}, 5> <10, 1, {6}, 7>
&first	: <10, 1, {7}, 7>
last	: <4, 1, {4}, 5> <11, 1, {6}, 7>
&last	: <11, 1, {7}, 7>
title	: <8, 1, {5}, 6>
&title	: <8, 1, {6}, 6>
keyword	: <12, 1, {5}, 6>
&keyword	: <12, 1, {6}, 6>
@category	: <7, 1, {5}, 6>
&@category	: <7, 1, {6}, 6>

Fig. 3. An example LabelPath table and inverted index

pid	docid	nodepath	value
1	1	1	Null
2	1	1.2	Null
3	1	1.2.3	Michael
4	1	1.2.5	Franklin
2	1	1.7	Null
3	1	1.7.8	Jane
4	1	1.7.10	Poe
5	1	1.12	Null
6	1	1.12.13	Null
7	1	1.12.13.14	R
8	1	1.12.13.16	XML schema
9	1	1.12.13.18	Null
10	1	1.12.13.18.19	David
11	1	1.12.13.18.21	Curry
12.	1.	1.12.13.23	XML
6	1	1.12.25	Null
...	...	...	...
12	1	1.12.25.35	DB

Fig. 4. An example NodePath table

last label of each label path. The first label is to match the root label of the document, and the last label is to match the leaf label of a path expression.

The `LabelPath` inverted index is created on the `labelpath` field in the `LabelPath` table. Here, we consider label paths as text documents and labels in these label paths as keywords. Like the traditional inverted index [22], the `LabelPath` inverted index is made of the pairs of a keyword (i.e., a label) and a posting list. Each posting in a posting list has the following fields: `pid`, `occurrence_count`, `offsets`, `label_path_length`, where `pid` is the identifier of the label path in which the label occurs, `occurrence_count` is the number of occurrences of the label within the label path, `offsets` is the set of the positions of the label from the beginning of the label path, and `label_path_length` is the number of labels in the label path. For instance, in the posting of the label `section` in a label path `$chapter.chapter.section.section.section.paragraph.&paragraph`, the `occurrence_count` of `section` is 3, the `offsets` of `section` is { 3, 4, 5}, and the `label_path_length` is 7.

4.2 Instance-Level Information

The table NodePath represents the *instance-level information* and stores the node paths to uniquely identify all the nodes in the XML documents. Figure 4 shows an example of the NodePath table for the XML tree in Figure 1.

The NodePath table stores all the node paths in the column nodepath. If the leaf node of a node path has a value, then the value is stored in the column value. The column pid stores label path identifiers, and is used for join with the LabelPath table to find all the node paths belonging to the same label path. The column docid stores the XML document identifiers.

5 XIR Query Processing Algorithms

In this section we present the algorithms for evaluating LPEs and BPEs based on the XIR storage structures described in the previous section, and analytically compare XRel, XParent, and XIR with a focus on their performance-related features.

5.1 LPE Evaluation Algorithm

Figure 5 shows the algorithm for evaluating an LPE. In this algorithm, XIR first finds matching label paths in the LabelPath table using the LabelPath inverted index, and then, performs an equi-join between the set of the label paths found and the NodePath table via the column pid. It then returns the matching node paths as the query result.

```
Algorithm XIR_LPE_evaluation
Input: LPE P, LabelPath inverted index, NodePath table
Output: set of node paths NPset matching the LPE
begin
  1. Convert the input LPE P to an IR expression E using the syntactic
     mapping rule LPE-to-IRExp (Rule 1).
  2. Find the set of pids (pidSet) using the LabelPath inverted index
     given the IR expression E.
  3. Find the set of node paths (NPset) through an equi-join between
     pidSet and the NodePath table.
  4. Return NPset.
end
```

Fig. 5. XIR LPE evaluation algorithm

Formally, an LPE is evaluated as

$$\Pi_{nodepath}(\sigma_{MATCH(labelpath, LPE)} LabelPath \bowtie_{pid=pid} NodePath) \tag{1}$$

Since the selection $\sigma_{MATCH(labelpath, LPE)} LabelPath$ is implemented as a text search on the labelpath column, XIR should first convert an LPE to a keyword-based text search condition (we call it *information retrieval expression(IRExp)*). The following rule specifies how the conversion is done.

Rule 1 *[LPE-to-IRExp]* An LPE $o_1 l_1 o_2 l_2 \cdots o_p l_p$, where $o_i \in \{\text{'/'}, \text{'//'}\}$ for $i = 1, 2, \cdots, p$, is mapped to an IRExp using the following rule:

$$o_1 l_1 \Rightarrow \begin{cases} l_1 & \text{if } o_1 = \text{'//'} \\ \$l_1 \text{ near}(1)\ l_1 & \text{if } o_1 = \text{'/'} \end{cases}$$

$$l_i o_{i+1} l_{i+1} \Rightarrow \begin{cases} l_i \text{ near}(\infty)\ l_{i+1} & \text{if } o_{i+1} = \text{'//'} \\ l_i \text{ near}(1)\ l_{i+1} & \text{if } o_{i+1} = \text{'/'} \end{cases}$$

$$\text{for } i = 1, 2, \cdots, p-1$$

$$l_p \Rightarrow l_p \text{ near}(1)\ \&l_p$$

where *near(w)* is the proximity operator, which retrieves the documents in which the two operand keywords appear within w words apart. □

Note that l_1 and l_p are respectively the root (i.e., first) node and the leaf (i.e., last) node of the linear query pattern representing the LPE. For example, an LPE //article//author/last is converted to an IRExp article near(∞) author near(1) last near(1) &last; an LPE /issue/articles// author is converted to an IRExp $issue near(1) issue near(1) articles near(∞) author near(1) &author. Note $issue indicates that issue is the root of the document.

5.2 BPE Evaluation Algorithm

Figure 6 shows the algorithm for evaluating a BPE. In this algorithm, XIR first decomposes a BPE into LPEs in the same way as XParent does, that is, one LPE from the root to each leaf node. It then evaluates each LPE to obtain a set of node path sets(*NPsets*).

This evaluation is done in the same manner as in Equation 1, with a slight modification to handle a branch predicate expression as

$$\Pi_{nodepath}(\sigma_{MATCH(labelpath, LPE)} \\ LabelPath \bowtie_{pid=pid} \sigma_{value\ \theta\ v} NodePath) \quad (2)$$

where "*value θ v*" is a selection condition on the leaf label of the branch predicate expression (see Definition 4) included in the LPE being evaluated.

Only one of the LPEs includes the result node (defined in Section 2.3). Let us call such an LPE the *result LPE* (P_0 in Figure 6). Then, XIR reduces the *result_NPset* obtained from the result LPE through *prefix match join* with each of the other LPEs ($P_1, P_2, \cdots, P_{r-1}$ in Figure 6). Definition 8 shows a formal definition of the prefix match join.

Definition 8. Given two relations having the schemas $R(A_1 A_2 \cdots A_c B_1 \cdots B_m)$ and $S(A_1 A_2 \cdots A_c C_1 \cdots C_k)$ that share the attributes $A_1 A_2 \cdots A_c$, the *prefix match join* between R and S, denoted by $R \triangleright S$, is defined as

$$R \triangleright S = \sigma_{R.A_1 = S.A_1 \text{ and } \cdots \text{ and } R.A_c = S.A_c}(R \times S) \quad \square$$

In Definition 8, the relational schema refers to a label path and the relation instance refers to a node path set. According to this definition, given two LPEs, the prefix match join between the two NPsets obtained from them is performed as follows: (1) find the longest

```
Algorithm XIR_BPE_evaluation
Input: BPE P, LabelPath inverted index, NodePath table
Output: set of node paths result_NPset matching the BPE
begin
      { Assume the BPE P has r leaf labels l₀, l₁, l₂, ..., lᵣ₋₁ and that l₀ is
      the result label. }
1.    Set P₀ as the LPE from the root to l₀.
2.    Obtain result_NPset by evaluating the LPE P₀.
3.    for each of the remaining leaf nodes lᵢ (i=1,2, ..., r-1)
4.    begin
5.         Set Pᵢ as the LPE from the root to lᵢ.
6.         Obtain NPsetᵢ by evaluating the LPE Pᵢ.
7.         Reduce result_NPset through a prefix match join
           with NPsetᵢ.
8.    end.
9     return result_NPset.
end.
```

Fig. 6. XIR BPE evaluation algorithm

common prefix label subpath $l_1 l_2 \cdots l_c (\equiv A_1 A_2 \cdots A_c$ in Definition 8) matching both LPEs; (2) find the set of common prefix node subpaths, $\{n_1 n_2 \cdots n_c\}$, belonging to the label subpath $l_1 l_2 \cdots l_c$; and (3) for each node subpath $n_1 n_2 \cdots n_c$ in the set, select all node paths that have the subpath in common.

Example 1. Consider the BPE //article[/keyword="XML"]//author[/last="Curry"]/first. The following three LPEs are generated: (1) //article/keyword, (2) //article//author/last, and (3) //article//author/first. Among these, LPE 3 is the result LPE. XIR retrieves the following three node path sets from these LPEs and the selection conditions on the leaf labels of LPE 1 and LPE 3: NPset$_1$ {1.12.13.23} from LPE 1 and keyword = "XML", NPset$_2$ {1.12.13.18.21} from LPE 2 and last="Curry", and NPset$_3$ {1.12.13.18.19, 1.12.25.30.31} from LPE 3. Then, the prefix match join with NPset$_2$ reduces NPset$_3$ to {1.12.13.18.19} based on the common prefix label subpath /issue/articles/article/author, and a further join with NPset$_1$ keeps NPset$_3$ to be {1.12.13.18.19} based on the common prefix label subpath /issue/articles/article.

Figure 7 shows the SQL statement generated for this BPE. It implements the prefix match join of node sets shown in Algorithm XIR_BPE_evaluation by performing tuple-by-tuple prefix matches. The function Prefix_matching performs a prefix match between two node paths provided as the first two input arguments (e.g., n1.nodepath and n2.nodepath) by comparing only the prefix characters whose length is returned from the function getCommonPrefixLength. This function takes as inputs two LPEs and two label paths matching them and calculates the prefix length in the following steps: (1) identify the longest common prefix subexpression of the two input LPEs (e.g., //article common to //article/keyword and //article/author/last in Figure 3), (2) for each of the two input label paths (e.g., p1.labelpath and p2.labelpath), count the number of prefix labels matching the common prefix subexpression (e.g., count 3 for a label path $issue.issue.articles.article.keyword.&keyword in Figure 3, excluding $issue, which is an extra addition to the label path), and (3) if the two counts are equal then return the count and otherwise return -1.   □

The query processing algorithms of XRel, XParent, and XIR share the same outline, but have some different implementations leading to their performance differences. In the

```
SELECT   DISTINCT n3.docid, n3.nodepath
FROM     LabelPath p1, LabelPath p2, LabelPath p3,
         NodePath n1, NodePath n2, NodePath n3
WHERE    p1.pid = n1.pid
AND      p2.pid = n2.pid
AND      p3.pid = n3.pid
AND      n1.value = ``XML''
AND      n2.value = ``Curry''
AND      MATCH(p1.labelpath, 'article' NEAR(1) 'keyword')
AND      MATCH(p2.labelpath, 'article' NEAR(MAXINT) 'author'
                             NEAR(1) 'last')
AND      MATCH(p3.labelpath, 'article' NEAR(MAXINT) 'author'
                             NEAR(1) 'first' NEAR(1) '&first')
AND      Prefix_matching (n1.nodepath, n2.nodepath,
         getCommonPrefixLength(p1.labelpath, p2.labelpath,
             ``//article/keyword'', ``//article//author/last''))
AND      Prefix_matching (n2.nodepath, n3.nodepath,
         getCommonPrefixLength(p2.labelpath, p3.labelpath,
             ``//article//author/last'', ``//article//author/first''));
```

Fig. 7. XIR SQL statement for the BPE in Example 1

case of LPEs, XIR's performance advantage over both XRel and XParent comes from using inverted index search instead of string match for finding label paths matching the LPE. In the case of BPEs, XIR has the performance advantage over XRel in that it generates a smaller number of LPEs for the same BPE. Another major performance advantage of XIR for BPEs over both XRel and XParent comes from the number of joins performed and the cardinalities of node sets joined to determine the node (or node path) set returned as the query result. XIR requires a far less number of joins compared with XRel and XParent. Besides, the cardinalities of node sets joined in XIR or XRel are smaller than those in XParent. Details of the analysis can be found in the reference [25].

6 Performance Evaluation

We compare the query processing performance of XIR with those of XRel and XParent. The results show that XIR is far more efficient than both XRel and XParent.

6.1 Experimental Setup

Databases. We have collected 10008 real-world XML documents from the Internet using two web crawlers: Teleport Pro Version 1.29.1959 [28] and ReGet Deluxe 3.3 Beta (build 173) [27]. For crawling XML documents, we first start with base URLs, and then, crawl all XML documents reachable from the base URLs. The base URLs include web sites of major universities, companies, and publishers in several countries. Note that about 91% of the XML documents are 4 Kbytes or less.

Using the collected XML documents, we have constructed five sets of data files of different sizes. Each set contains approximately 5000, 10000, 20000, 40000, and 80000 distinct label paths. The last set has 1460000 node paths. A larger set contains all label paths in a smaller set, i.e., is a superset of smaller sets. Documents in each set are then parsed, and the parsed results are loaded into three databases, each containing tables used by XRel, XParent, and XIR methods. The total number of databases thus generated is fifteen.

For XRel and XParent, we have used the database schema and indexes as they were used in the original designs [14,24]. For XIR, we have loaded the data files into the LabelPath and NodePath tables, created B+-tree indexes on the columns pid, docid of each table as in XRel or XParent, and created an inverted index on the labelpath column of the Labelpath table.

The resulting database size for XIR is 454 Mbytes for 79943 distinct label paths and is 10% - 29% smaller than those of XRel or XParent. Details of the analysis can be found in the reference [25].

Queries. Table 1 shows three groups of tree pattern queries: a group of LPEs, a group of BPEs whose branch predicate expressions do not contain selection conditions, and a group of BPEs whose branch predicate expressions do contain selection conditions. Each group has two sets of queries: one is on issue documents; the other on movie documents. The former has far more document instances than the latter.

Table 1. Queries

Group	Label	Tree Pattern Query
Group 1 (LPEs)	LPE1	//issue//author/first
	LPE2	//issue//article//author/first
	LPE3	//movie//actor//first
	LPE4	//movie/cast//actor//first
Group 2 (BPEs without selection conditions)	BPE1	//issue[//keyword]//author[/last]/first
	BPE2	//issue[//keyword]//article[/summary]//author[/last]/first
	BPE3	//movie[/director]//actor[/award]//first
	BPE4	//movie[/director]//cast[/actress]//actor[/award]//first
Group 3 (BPEs with selection conditions)	BPS1	//issue[//keyword=``XML"]//article[/summary]//author[/last]/first
	BPS2	//issue[//keyword=``XML"]//article[/summary]//author[/last=``Smith"]/first
	BPS3	//movie[/director/last=``Mendes"]//actor[/award]//first
	BPS4	//movie[/director/last=``Mendes"]//actor[/award=``Oscar"]//first

Computing Environment. We have conducted the experiments using the Odysseus object-relational database management system[3] on SUN Ultra 60 workstation with 512 Mbyte RAM. In order to eliminate the unpredictable buffering effect in the operating system, we have used a raw disk device to bypass the OS buffer. We have also flushed the DBMS buffer after each query execution so that the execution does not affect later ones. The cost metrics used are the elapsed time and the number of disk I/O's.

6.2 Experimental Results

Since the crawlers collect *arbitrary* documents from the Internet, new label paths are added as new documents are added by crawling. We have extracted the number of distinct label paths from the XML documents collected. We crawled a total of 10009 XML documents extracting 79943 distinct label paths.

Figure 8 shows the costs of the query LPE4 in Table 1 for the three methods as the number of distinct label paths increases. Figures 9 and 10 show those for BPE2 and BPS1 in Table 1. The buffer size has been set to 200 4Kbyte-pages to eliminate extra disk I/O's caused by an insufficient buffer size. Due to space limit, we omit the figures of the other queries; their costs show similar trends with typical curves.

---

[3] Odysseus has been developed at the KAIST Advanced Information Technology Research Center, and provides the key operations needed by a text search engine.

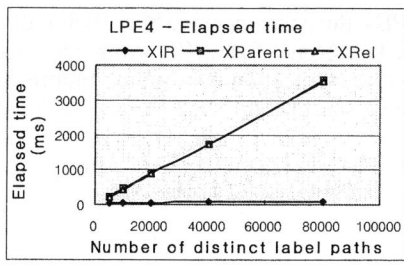 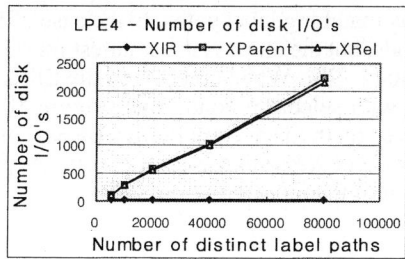

Fig. 8. Query costs of XRel, XParent, XIR for LPE4 (buffer size = 200 pages)

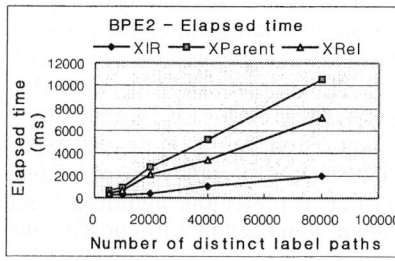 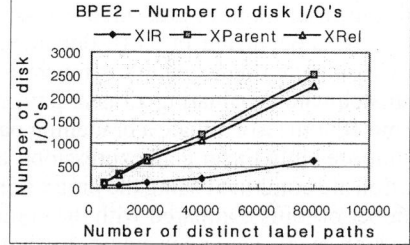

Fig. 9. Query costs of XRel, XParent, XIR for BPE2 (buffer size = 200 pages)

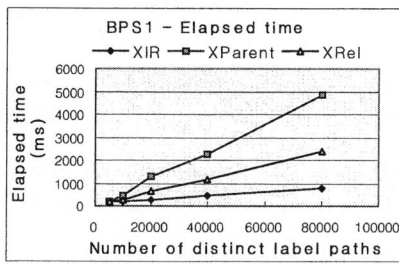 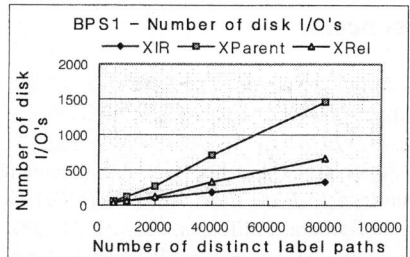

Fig. 10. Query costs of XRel, XParent, XIR for BPS1 (buffer size = 200 pages)

In Figures 8 through 10, we see that XIR is more efficient than both XRel and Xparent[4]. The performance gap varies from several orders of magnitude in the case of LPEs to several factors in the case of BPEs. In particular, the costs of LPEs increase nearly linearly for XRel and XParent while sublinearly – nearly constant – for XIR. This amounts to the difference between the string match and inverted index search for

---

[4] As mentioned in Section 3.2, we use the table Ancestor to be able to support partial match queries in XParent [14], [15]. This causes XParent to show poorer performance than XRel due to the cardinality of the Ancestor table that is heavily involved in joins. This is in contrast with the results shown in the XParent papers [14], [15], where the performances of only full match queries using the DataPath table were presented.

finding matching label paths. In the case of BPEs, the costs increase linearly for all three methods, but the slope is the smallest for XIR. This comes from XIR's join performance advantage [25]. When comparing the BPEs without selection conditions (Figure 9) and those with selection conditions (Figure 10), we see that the gaps among the costs of the three methods are smaller for BPEs *with* selection conditions. The reason for this is that XRel or XParent can take advantage of the B+-tree index created on the 'value' column of the table Text or Data.

7 Conclusions

We have proposed a novel approach called XIR to processing partial match queries on a large number of heterogeneous XML documents typical in the Internet environment. For this purpose, we have presented two key techniques. In the first technique, we treat the label paths occurring in XML documents as texts and create an inverted index on them. This inverted index supports much faster partial match than XRel's or XParent's string match when evaluating a linear path expression. In the second technique, we use prefix match joins to evaluate a branching path expression. A branching path expression is decomposed into linear path expressions, and the results of evaluating each linear path expression are combined using the prefix join. Using the prefix join significantly reduces the number of joins compared with the containment join used in XRel or XParent.

Through extensive experiments, we have compared the performance of XIR with those of XRel and XParent using real XML documents crawled from the Internet. The results show that XIR is significantly more efficient than XRel or XParent.

References

1. A. Aboulnaga, A. R. Alameldeen, and J. Naughton, "Estimating the Selectivity of XML Path Expressions for Internet Scale Applications," In *Proc. the 27th Int'l Conf. on Very Large Data Bases (VLDB)*, pp. 591-600, Rome, Italy, Sept. 11-14, 2001.
2. S. Amer-Yahia, S. Cho, L. V. S. Lakshmanan, D. Srivastava, "Minimization of Tree Pattern Queries," In *Proc. 2001 ACM SIGMOD Int'l Conf. on Management of Data*, pp. 497-508, Santa Barbara, California, May 21-24, 2001.
3. M. Altinel, M. J. Franklin, "Efficient Filtering of XML Documents for Selective Dissemination of Information," In *Proc. the 26th Int'l Conf. on Very Large Data Bases (VLDB)*, pp. 53-64, Cairo, Egypt, Sept. 10-14, 2000.
4. S. Al-Khalifa, H. V. Jagadish, N. Koudas, and J. M. Patel, "Structural Joins: A Primitive for Efficient XML Query Pattern Matching," In *Proc. the 18th Int'l Conf. on Data Engineering (ICDE)*, pp. 141-152, San Jose, California, Feb. 26 - Mar. 1, 2002.
5. Jan-Marco Bremer and Michael Gertz, "XQuery/IR: Integrating XML Document and Data Retrieval," In *Proc. the Fifth Int'l Workshop on the Web and Databases (WebDB 2002)*, pp. 1-6, Madison, Wisconsin, 2002.
6. N. Bruno, N. Koudas, and D. Srivastava, "Holistic Twig Joins: Optimal XML Pattern Matching," In *Proc. 2002 ACM SIGMOD Int'l Conf. on Management of Data*, pp. 310-321, Madison, Wisconsin, June 3-6, 2002.
7. J. Clark and S. DeRose, XML Path Language (XPath), W3C Recommendation, *http://www.w3.org/TR/xpath*, Nov. 1999.
8. B. F. Cooper, N. Sample, M. J. Franklin, G. R. Hjaltason, and M. Shadmon, "A Fast Index for Semistructured Data," In *Proc. the 27th Int'l Conf. on Very Large Data Bases (VLDB)*, pp. 341-350, Rome, Italy, Sept. 11-14, 2001.

9. Daniela Florescu, Donald Kossmann, and Ioana Manolescu,"Integrating Keyword Search into XML Query Processing ," In *Proc. the 9th WWW Conference/Computer Networks*, pp. 119-135, Amsterdam, NL, May 2000.
10. Lin Guo, Feng Shao, Chavdar Botev, and Jayavel Shanmugasundaram, "XRANK: Ranked Keyword Search over XML Documents," In *Proc. 2003 ACM SIGMOD Int'l Conf. on Management of Data*, pp. 16-27, San Diego, California, June 9-12, 2003.
11. R. Goldman and J. Widom, "DataGuides: Enabling Query Formulation and Optimization in Semistructured Databases," In *Proc. the 23th Int'l Conf. on Very Large Data Bases (VLDB)*, pp. 436-445, Athens, Greece, Aug. 26-29, 1997.
12. A. Halverson, J. Burger, L. Galanis, A. Kini, R. Krishnamurthy, A. N. Rao, F. Tian, S. Viglas, Y. Wang, J. F. Naughton, and D. J. DeWitt, "Mixed Mode XML Query Processing," In *Proc. the 29th Int'l Conf. on Very Large Data Bases (VLDB)*, pp. 225-236, Berlin, Germany, Sept. 9-12, 2003.
13. Z. Ives, A. Levy, and D. Weld, Efficient Evaluation of Regular Path Expressions on Streaming XML Data, Technical Report UW-CSE-2000-05-02, University of Washington, 2000.
14. H. Jiang, H. Lu, W. Wang, and J. Xu Yu, "Path Materialization Revisited: An Efficient Storage Model for XML Data," In *Proc. the 13th Australasian Database Conference (ADC)*, pp. 85-94, Melbourne, Australia, Jan. 28 - Feb. 1, 2002.
15. H. Jiang, H. Lu, W. Wang, and J. Xu Yu, "XParent: An Efficient RDBMS-Based XML Database System," In *Proc. the 18th Int'l Conf. on Data Engineering (ICDE)*, pp. 335-336, San Jose, California, Feb. 26 - Mar. 1, 2002.
16. H. Jiang, W. Wang, H. Lu, and J. X. Yu, "Holistic Twig Joins on Indexed XML Documents," In *Proc. the 29th Int'l Conf. on Very Large Data Bases (VLDB)*, pp. 273-284, Berlin, Germany, Sept. 9-12, 2003.
17. Q. Li and B. Moon, "Indexing and Querying XML Data for Regular Path Expressions," In *Proc. the 27th Int'l Conf. on Very Large Data Bases (VLDB)*, pp. 361-370, Rome, Italy, Sept. 11-14, 2001.
18. F. Mandreoli, R. Martoglia, P. Tiberio, "Searching Similar (Sub)Sentences for Example-Based Machine Translation," In *Proc. 2002 Italian Symposium on Sistemi Evoluti per Basi di Dati (SEBD'02)*, Isola d'Elba, Italy, June 2002.
19. J. McHugh, J. Widom, "Query Optimization for XML," In *Proc. the 25th Int'l Conf. on Very Large Data Bases (VLDB)*, pp. 315-326, Edinburgh, Scotland, UK, Sept. 7-10, 1999.
20. J. Naughton et al., "The Niagara Internet Query System," *IEEE Data Engineering Bulletin*, pp. 27-33, Vol. 24, No. 2, June, 2001.
21. N. Polyzotis and M. Garofalakis, "Statistical Synopses for Graph-structured XML Databases," In *Proc. 2002 ACM SIGMOD Int'l Conf. on Management of Data*, pp. 358-369, Madison, Wisconsin, June 3-6, 2002.
22. G. Salton and M. McGill, *Introduction to Modern Information Retrieval*, McGraw-Hill, New York 1983.
23. I. Tatarinov, S. Viglas, K. S. Beyer, J. Shanmugasundaram, E. J. Shekita, and C. Zhang, "Storing and Querying Ordered XML Using a Relational Database System," In *Proc. 2002 ACM SIGMOD Int'l Conf. on Management of Data*, pp. 204-215, Madison, Wisconsin, June 3-6, 2002.
24. M. Yoshikawa, T. Amagasa, T. Shimura, and S. Uemura, "XRel: A Path-based Approach to Storage and Retrieval of XML Documents using Relational Databases," *ACM Trans. on Internet Technology(TOIT)*, pp. 110-141, Vol. 1, No. 1, 2001.
25. Y. Park, K. -Y. Whang, B. Lee, W. Han, "Efficient Evaluation of Partial Match Queries for XML Documents Using Information Retrieval Techniques," Technical Report CS-TR-2004-212, Department of Computer Science, KAIST, Dec., 2004. Also, available on AITrc Technical Report No. 04-11-048, *http://aitrc.kaist.ac.kr/util_tr.htm*, Dec. 28, 2004.

26. C. Zhang, J. F. Naughton, D. J. DeWitt, Q. Luo, and G. M. Lohmann, "On Supporting Containment Queries in Relational Database Management Systems," In *Proc. 2001 ACM SIGMOD Int'l Conf. on Management of Data*, pp. 425-436, Santa Barbara, California, May 21-24, 2001.
27. ReGet Deluxe 3.3 Beta (build 173), *http://deluxe.reget.com/en/*.
28. Teleport Pro Version 1.29, *http://www.tenmax.com/teleport/pro/home.htm*.
29. Xyleme, *http://www.xyleme.com*.
30. eXtensible Markup Language(XML), *http://www.w3.org/XML/*.

PathStack¬: A Holistic Path Join Algorithm for Path Query with Not-Predicates on XML Data

Enhua Jiao, Tok Wang Ling, and Chee-Yong Chan

School of Computing, National University of Singapore
{jiaoenhu, lingtw, chancy}@comp.nus.edu.sg

Abstract. The evaluation of path queries forms the basis of complex XML query processing which has attracted a lot of research attention. However, none of these works have examined the processing of more complex queries that contain not-predicates. In this paper, we present the first study on evaluating path queries with not-predicates. We propose an efficient holistic path join algorithm, PathStack¬, which has the following advantages: (1) it requires only one scan of the relevant data to evaluate path queries with not-predicates; (2) it does not generate any intermediate results; and (3) its memory space requirement is bounded by the longest path in the input XML document. We also present an improved variant of PathStack¬ that further minimizes unnecessary computations.

1 Introduction

Finding all root-to-leaf paths in tree-structured XML documents that satisfy certain selection predicates is the basis of complex XML query processing. Such selection predicates are called path queries (i.e., twig queries without branches), and there has been a lot of research on the efficient evaluation of path queries (as well as the more general twig queries) [1, 4, 7, 9, 10, 11]. However, none of these works have considered the processing of more general queries that involved *not-predicates*, which are very common and useful in many applications.

As an example of a path query with a not-predicate, consider the XPath query: //supplier[not(./part/color='red')], which finds suppliers who do not supply any red color parts. A naïve approach to evaluate such path queries is to decompose it into multiple simple path queries (without not-predicates) and evaluate each of the decomposed path queries individually using an existing approach (e.g., **PathStack** [1]); the final result is then derived by combining the individual results. Thus, the example query can be computed by the set difference of two simple path queries: p1 − p2, where p1 = //supplier and p2 = //supplier[./part/color='red']. Clearly, this approach can be extended to process complex path queries with nested not-predicates by applying the decomposition recursively. However, such a naïve approach is obviously inefficient as it not only incurs high I/O cost for the repetitive scans of the data and the generation of intermediate results, but also incurs computational overhead to combine the intermediate results to derive the final result.

In this paper, we study the problem of evaluating path queries with not-predicates and make the following contributions:

1. We define both the representation of path queries with not-predicates as well as the semantics of matching such queries.
2. We develop two novel algorithms, PathStack¬ and imp-PathStack¬, to efficiently evaluate path queries with not-predicates. Our approach is a generalization of the PathStack algorithm [1], which is based on using a collection of stacks to store partial/complete matching answers.
3. We demonstrate the effectiveness of the proposed algorithms over a naïve approach with an experimental performance study.

To the best of our knowledge, this is the first paper that addresses this problem.

The rest of the paper is organized as follows. Section 2 defines the representation and semantics of path queries with not-predicates. In Section 3, we present our first algorithm for evaluating path queries with not-predicates called PathStack¬. In Section 4, we present an improved variant of PathStack¬ called imp-PathStack¬ that incorporates two optimizations to reduce unnecessary computations. We present a performance study in Section 5. Section 6 discusses related work. Finally, we conclude our paper in section 7 with some future research plans. Due to space constraint, proofs of correctness and other details are given in [6].

2 Preliminaries

2.1 Data Model

For simplicity and without loss of generality, we model an XML document as a rooted, ordered labeled tree, where each node corresponds to an element and each edge represents a (direct) element-subelement. As an example, Fig.1 (b) shows the tree representation for the simple XML document in Fig.1 (a).

Similar to [1], our work does not impose any specific physical organization on the document nodes, and it suffices that there is some efficient access method that returns a stream of document nodes (sorted in document order) for each distinct document element. We also further assume that each stream of returned nodes can be filtered to support any value predicate matching in the path queries; thus, for simplicity, we ignore value predicates in our path queries.

Finally, our work also assumes an efficient method to determine the structural relationship between a given pair of document nodes (e.g., determine whether one node is an ancestor or a parent of another node). Several positional encoding schemes for document nodes have been proposed for this purpose (e.g., [1]), and our proposed algorithms can work with any of these schemes.

2.2 Representation of Path Queries with Not-Predicates

A path query with not-predicates is represented as a labeled path $<n_1, n_2,..., n_m>$, where each node n_i (with level number i) is assigned a label, denoted by label(n_i), that

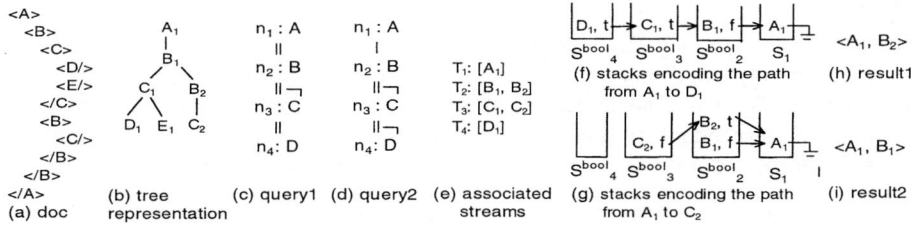

Fig. 1. (a) An XML document consisting of elements only; (b) the tree representation of the document in (a) (integer subscript here is for easy reference to nodes with the same element name); (c) representation of path query: //A//B[not(.//C//D)]; (d) representation of path query: //A/B[not(.//C[not(.//D)])]; (e) the associated streams used in PathStack¬ algorithm; (f) and (g) two examples of stack encoding for root-to-leaf paths in doc tree; (h) result for (c) on (b); (i) result for (d) on (b)

is an element name. Each pair of adjacent nodes n_i and n_{i+1} is connected by an edge, denoted by edge(n_i, n_{i+1}), which is classified into one of the following four types: (1) ancestor/descendant edge, represented as "||"; (2) parent/child edge, represented as "|"; (3) negative ancestor/descendant edge, represented as "||¬"; (4) negative parent/child ed*ge, represented as "|¬". A negative edge corresponds to a not-predicate in XPath expression. Two examples of path queries are shown in Fig.1 (c) and (d), where each node is depicted as n_i:label(n_i).

For convenience, we abbreviate the terms parent/child and ancestor/descendant by P/C and A/D, respectively. Given a node n_i, we use parentEdge(n_i) to denote edge(n_{i-1}, n_i) if $i > 1$, and use childEdge(n_i) to denote edge(n_i, n_{i+1}) if $i < m$.

2.3 Matching of Path Queries with Not-Predicates

Definition 1. (output node, non-output node, output leaf node, leaf node) A node n_i in a path query is classified as an output node if n_i does not appear below any negative edge; otherwise, it is a non-output node. The output node with the maximum level number is also called the output leaf node. The last node n_m in a path query is also referred to as the leaf node.

For example, {n_1, n_2} and {n_3, n_4} are the sets of output nodes and non-output nodes in Fig.1 (c) and (d), respectively. Note that n_2 is the output leaf node and n_4 is the leaf node.

We use subquery(n_i, n_j) ($1 \le i \le j \le m$) to refer to a sub-path of a path query that starts from node n_i to node n_j. For example, subquery(n_2, n_4) in Fig.1 (c) refers to the sub-path consisting of the set of nodes {n_2, n_3, n_4} and the two edges edge(n_2, n_3) and edge(n_3, n_4).

Definition 2. (Satisfaction of subquery(n_i, n_j)) Given a subquery(n_i, n_j) and a node e_i in an XML document D, we say that e_i satisfies subquery(n_i, n_j) if (1) the element name of e_i is label(n_i); and (2) exactly one of the following three conditions holds:

(a) $i = j$; or
(b) edge(n_i, n_{i+1}) is an A/D (respectively, P/C) edge, and there exists a descendant (respectively, child) node e_{i+1} of e_i in D that satisfies subquery(n_{i+1}, n_j) ; or
(c) edge(n_i, n_{i+1}) is a negative A/D (respectively, P/C) edge, and there does not exist a descendant (respectively, child) node e_{i+1} of e_i in D that satisfies subquery(n_{i+1}, n_j).

We say that e_i fails subquery(n_i, n_j) if e_i does not satisfy subquery(n_i, n_j). For notional convenience, we use the notation e_i to represent a document node that has an element name equal to label(n_i).

Example 1. Consider the XML document and query in Figs.1 (b) and (c), respectively. Observe that (1) D_1 satisfies subquery(n_4, n_4) (condition a); (2) C_1 satisfies subquery(n_3, n_4) because of (1) and D_1 is a descendant of C_1 (condition b); and (3) B_1 fails subquery(n_2, n_4) because of (2) and C_1 is a descendant of B_1 (condition c).

Definition 3. (Matching of Path Queries with Not-predicates) Given an XML document D and a path query $<n_1, n_2, ..., n_m>$ with n_k as the output leaf node, a tuple $<e_1, ..., e_k>$ is defined to be a matching answer for the query iff (1) for each adjacent pair of nodes e_i and e_{i+1} in the tuple, e_{i+1} is a child (respectively, descendant) node of e_i in D if edge(n_i, n_{i+1}) is a P/C (respectively, A/D) edge; and (2) e_k satisfies subquery(n_k, n_m). We refer to a prefix of a matching answer $<e_1, ..., e_k>$ as a partial matching answer.

Example 2. Consider the document in Fig.1 (b). For query1 in Fig.1 (c), $<A_1, B_1>$ is not a matching answer for it since C_1 satisfies subquery(n_3, n_4) and therefore B_1 fails subquery(n_2, n_4); hence $<A_1, B_1>$ fails condition (2) of Definition 3. However, $<A_1, B_2>$ is a matching answer for it because there does not exist a C_i node in Fig.1 (b) which is a descendant of B_2 and satisfies subquery(n_3, n_4); therefore B_2 satisfies subquery(n_2, n_4). Clearly, $<A_1, B_2>$ satisfies condition (2) of Definition 3. Similarly, for query2 in Fig.1 (d), $<A_1, B_1>$ is a matching answer for it since B_1 satisfies subquery(n_2, n_4) and $<A_1, B_1>$ satisfies condition (2) in Definition 3. However, $<A_1, B_2>$ is not a matching answer for query2 because B_2 fails subquery(n_2, n_4).

3 PathStack¬ Algorithm

In this section, we describe our first algorithm, called PathStack¬, for evaluating path queries that contain not-predicates. As the name implies, our approach is based on the stack encoding technique of the PathStack approach [1] for evaluating path queries without not-predicates.

3.1 Notations and Data Structures

Each query node n_i is associated with a data stream T_i, where each T_i contains all document nodes for element label(n_i) sorted in document order. Each stream T_i maintains a pointer that points to the next node in T_i to be returned. The following operations are supported for each stream: (1) eof(T_i) tests if the end of the stream T_i is reached; (2) advance(T_i) advances the pointer of T_i; and (3) next(T_i) returns the node pointed to by the pointer of T_i.

Each query node n_i is also associated with a stack S_i which is either a regular stack or a boolean stack. In a *regular stack*, each item in S_i consists of a pair <e_i, pointer to an item in S_{i-1}>, where e_i is a document node with the element name of e_i equal to label(n_i). In a *boolean stack*, each item in S_i consists of a triple <e_i, pointer to an item in S_{i-1}, satisfy>, where satisfy is a boolean variable indicating whether e_i satisfies subquery(n_i, n_m) w.r.t. all the nodes in the data streams that have been visited so far during the evaluation. Note that the pointer to an item in S_{i-1} is null iff i=1. The stack S_i associated with n_i is a boolean stack if n_i is a non-output node or the output leaf node; otherwise, S_i is a regular stack. If S_i is a boolean stack, we can also denote it explicitly by S^{bool}_i. Note that only regular stacks are used in the PathStack algorithm [1].

The following operations are defined for stacks: (1) empty(S_i) tests if S_i is empty; (2) pop(S_i)/ top(S_i) pops/returns the top item in S_i; and (3) push(S_i, item) pushes item into S_i. For an input XML document D, the stacks are maintained such that they satisfy the following three stack properties:

1. At every point during the evaluation, the nodes stored in the set of stacks must lie on a root-to-leaf path in the input XML document D.
2. If e_i and e'_i are two nodes in S_i, then e_i appears below e'_i in S_i iff e_i is an ancestor of e'_i in D.
3. Let m_i=<e_i, $pointer_i$> and m_{i-1}=<e_{i-1}, $pointer_{i-1}$> be two items in stacks S_i and S_{i-1}, respectively. If $pointer_i$=m_{i-1} (i.e., e_i is linked to e_{i-1}), then e_{i-1} must be an ancestor of e_i in D such that there is no other node (with the same element name as e_{i-1}) in D that lies along the path from e_{i-1} to e_i in D.

3.2 Algorithm

The main algorithm of PathStack¬ (shown in Fig.2) evaluates an input path query q by iteratively accessing the data nodes from the streams in sorted document order, and extending partial matching answers stored in the stacks. Each iteration consists of three main parts. The first part (step 2) calls the function getMinSource to determine the next node from the data streams to be processed in document order. Before using the selected next node to extend existing partial matching answers, the algorithm first needs to pop off nodes from the stacks that will not form a partial matching with the next node (i.e., preserve stack property1). This "stack cleaning" operation is done by the second part (steps 3 to 9). Each time an item <e_i, $pointer_i$, satisfy> is popped from a boolean stack S^{bool}_i, the algorithm will output all the matching answers that end with e_i (by calling showSolutions) if n_i is the output leaf node and *satisfy* is true. Otherwise, if n_i is a non-output node, then S_{i-1} must necessarily be a boolean stack, and updateSatisfy is called to update the *satisfy* values of the appropriate nodes in S_{i-1}. Finally, the third part (step 11) calls the function moveStreamToStack to extend the partial answer currently stored in stacks by pushing the next node into the stack S_{min}.

```
Algorithm PathStack¬(q)
01 while (¬end(q))
02   n_min = getMinSource(q)   // find the next node
03   for query node n_i of q in descending i order // clean stack
04     while((¬empty(S_i)) ∧ (top(S_i) is not an ancestor of next(T_min)))
05       e_i = pop(S_i)
06       if (n_i is the output leaf node ∧ e_i.satisfy=true)
07         showSolutions(e_i)   // output solution
08       else if (n_i is a non-output node)
09         updateSatisfy(n_i, e_i)
10   //push the next node
11   moveStreamToStack(n_min, T_min, S_min, pointer to top(S_min-1))
12 repeat steps 03 to 09 for the remaining nodes in the stacks

Function getMinSource(q)
  Return query node n_i of q such that next(T_i) has the minimal document
  order among all unvisited nodes.

Function end(q)
  Return ∀ n_i in q ⇒ eof(T_i) is true.
```

Fig. 2. PathStack¬ Main Algorithm

```
Procedure moveStreamToStack(n_i, T_i, S_i, pointer)
01 if S_i is a regular stack // regular stack, no Boolean value
02   push(S_i, <next(T_i), pointer>)
03 else if n_i is the leaf node
04   push(S_i, <next(T_i), pointer, true>)
05 else if childEdge(n_i) is negative
06   push(S_i, <next(T_i), pointer, true>)
07 else if childEdge(n_i) is positive
08   push(S_i, <next(T_i), pointer, false>)
09 advance(T_i)

Procedure updateSatisfy(n_i, e_i)
01 if e_i.satisfy = true
02   e_{i-1} = e_i.pointer
03   if parentEdge(n_i) is a negative edge
04     newvalue = false
05   else
06     newvalue = true
07   if parentEdge(n_i) is an A/D edge
08     for all e'_{i-1} in S^{bool}_{i-1} that are below e_{i-1} (inclusive of e_{i-1})
09       e'_{i-1}.satisfy = newvalue
10   else // parentEdge(n_i) is an P/C edge
11     if e_{i-1} is a parent of e_i
12       e_{i-1}.satisfy = newvalue
```

Fig. 3. Procedures moveStreamToStack and updateSatisfy

The details of the procedures moveStreamToStack and updateSatisfy are shown in Fig.3. In moveStreamToStack, if the input stack S_i is a boolean stack, then the *satisfy* value of the data node e_i to be pushed into S_i is initialized as follows. If n_i is the leaf node in the query (step 3), then e_i trivially satisfies subquery(n_i, n_m) and *satisfy* is set to true. Otherwise, *satisfy* is set to false (respectively, true) if childEdge(n_i) is a positive (respectively, negative) edge since e_i satisfies (respectively, fails) subquery(n_i, n_m) w.r.t. all the nodes that have been accessed so far.

Procedure updateSatisfy maintains the satisfy values of stack entries such that when a data node e_i is eventually popped from its stack S_i, its satisfy value is true iff e_i satisfies subquery(n_i, n_m), i.e, w.r.t. the whole input XML document. The correctness of updateSatisfy is based on the property that once an initialized *satisfy* value is complemented by an update, its value will not be complemented back to the initialized value again.

The details of procedure showSolutions can be found in [1].

Example 3. This example illustrates the evaluation of query1 in Fig.1 (c) on the XML document in Fig.1 (b) using algorithm PathStack⌐.

(1) The nodes A_1, B_1, C_1, and D_1 are accessed and pushed into their corresponding stacks; the resultant stack encoding is shown in Fig.1 (f).
(2) B_2 is the next node to be accessed (E_1 is not accessed as it is irrelevant to the query), and nodes C_1 and D_1 need to be first popped off from their stacks to preserve the stack properties. When node D_1 is popped, it is detected to satisfy subquery(n_4, n_4), and therefore C_1.satisfy is updated to *true*. When C_1 is popped, it is determined to satisfy subquery(n_3, n_4). Consequently, B_1.satisfy is updated to *false*.
(3) B_2 is accessed and pushed into S^{bool}_2.
(4) C_2 is accessed and pushed into S^{bool}_3; the resultant stack encoding is shown in Fig.1 (g).
(5) Since all the relevant data nodes have been accessed, the algorithm now pops off the remaining nodes in the stacks in the order of C_2, B_2, B_1, and A_1. When C_2 is popped, it is detected to fail subquery(n_3, n_4) and so no update takes place. When B_2 is popped, it is detected to satisfy subquery(n_2, n_4). Since B_2 is a leaf output node, the matching answer <A_1, B_2> is generated. When B_1 is popped, it is detected to fail subquery(n_2, n_4) and so no matching answer is produced. Finally, A_1 is popped without triggering any operations.
(6) Since all the stacks are empty, the algorithm terminates with exactly one matching answer <A_1, B_2>.

3.3 Performance Analysis

In this section, we present an analysis of the time and space complexity of algorithm PathStack⌐. Let $Size_i$ denote the total number of nodes in the accessed data streams, $Size_\ell$ denote the length of the longest path in the input XML document, and $Size_o$ denote the size of the matching answers.

Since the number of iterations in the outer while loop (steps 1 to 11) is bounded by the number of nodes in the input streams, and both the inner for loop (steps 3 to 9) and step 12 are bounded by the longest path in the input XML document, the CPU complexity of PathStack⌐ is given by $O(Size_i * Size_\ell + Size_\ell)$. The I/O complexity is $O(Size_i + Size_o)$ since the input data streams are scanned once only and the only outputs are the matching answers. The space complexity is given by $O(Size_\ell)$ since at any point during the evaluation, the data nodes that are stored in the stacks must lie on a root-to-leaf path in the input XML document.

4 Improved PathStack¬ Algorithm

In this section, we present an improved variant of PathStack¬, denoted by imp-PathStack¬, that is based on two optimizations to reduce unnecessary computations. Due to space constraint, the details of the optimizations are omitted in this paper but can be found in [6].

4.1 Reducing the Number of Boolean Stacks

One key extension introduced by our PathStack¬ algorithm to handle not-predicates is the use of boolean stacks for output leaf and non-output query nodes. Boolean stacks are, however, more costly to maintain than regular stacks due to the additional *satisfy* variable in each stack entry. In this section, we present an optimization to minimize the number of boolean stacks used in the algorithm.

Our optimization is based on the observation that boolean stacks are actually only necessary for query nodes that have negative child edges. To understand this optimization, note that a non-output node n_i can be classified into one of three cases: (1) n_i is also the leaf node; or (2) n_i has a positive child edge; or (3) n_i has a negative child edge. For case (1), since each data node e_i in S_i trivially satisfies subquery(n_i, n_m), e_i.satisfy is always true and therefore S_i can be simplified to a regular stack (i.e., S_i can be viewed as a virtual boolean stack). For case (2), the satisfy value of each node in S_i can effectively be determined from the nodes in S_j, where n_j is the nearest descendant query node of n_i that is associated with a (real or virtual) boolean stack. Details of this are given in [6]. Thus, S_i again can be simplified to a regular stack. Consequently, only non-output nodes belonging to case (3) need to be associated with boolean stacks.

4.2 Nodes Skipping

Our second optimization aims to exploit the semantics of not-predicates to minimize the pushing of "useless" data nodes into stacks that do not affect the input query's result. In the following, we explain and illustrate the intuition for this optimization; more details are given in [6].

Consider a stack S^{bool}_i that corresponds to a query node n_i with a negative child edge. Suppose e_i, the topmost node in S^{bool}_i, has a *false* value for *satisfy*. Then there are two cases to consider for the optimization depending on whether childEdge(n_i) is an A/D or P/C edge.

Case 1: If childEdge(n_i) is an A/D edge, then it follows that every data node below e_i in S^{bool}_i also has a *false* value for *satisfy*. Therefore, for each $j > i$, the nodes in T_j that precede next(T_i) in document order can be skipped as they will not contribute to any matching answers. For example, consider the query query1 on document doc1 in Fig.4. Note that after the path of nodes from A_1 to C_1 have been accessed, the satisfy values for both A_1 and A_2 are determined to be *false*. Thus, the stream of nodes $\{B_2,...,B_5\}$ and $\{C_2,...,C_4\}$ can be skipped as they will not affect the *satisfy* value of A_3.

Case 2: If childEdge(n_i) is a P/C edge, then let e'_i be the lowest node in S^{bool}_i with a *false* value for *satisfy*. It follows that for each $j > i$, the data nodes in T_j that are descendants of e'_i and precede next(T_i) in document order will not contribute to any matching answers and can therefore be skipped. For example, consider the query query2 on document doc2 in Fig.4. Note that after the path of nodes from A_1 to C_1 have been accessed, the *satisfy* values for both A_1 and A_2 are determined to be *false*, and the stream of nodes $\{B_3, B_4\}$ and $\{C_2,...,C_4\}$ can be skipped. As another example, consider query query2 on document doc1 in Fig.4. After the path of nodes from A_1 to C_1 have been accessed, the *satisfy* value for A_2 is determined to be *false*, the stream of nodes $\{B_2, B_3\}$ and $\{C_2\}$ can be skipped. Note that B_4 and C_3 can not be skipped in this case as they will affect A_1's *satisfy* value which is yet to be determined.

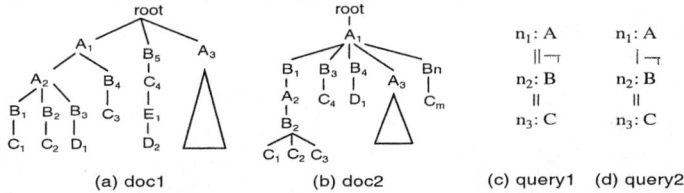

Fig. 4. XML documents and path queries

The node skipping optimization becomes even more effective when combined with the boolean stack reduction optimization since it enables the nodes' **satisfy** values to be updated earlier and a more aggressive node skipping. For example, consider the query query1 on document doc2 in Fig.4. When the boolean stack optimization is used, there is only one boolean stack S^{bool}_2, and the **satisfy** values of A_1 and A_2 are both determined to be *false* once the path of nodes from A_1 to C_1 have been accessed. In contrast, without the first optimization, all the stacks are boolean, and the **satisfy** values of A_1 and A_2 are determined to be *false* only after B_2 is popped off from its stack when B_3 is accessed; consequently, the nodes C_2 and C_3 can not be skipped.

5 Experimental Evaluation

This section presents experimental results to compare the performance of our proposed algorithms, PathStack¬ and imp-PathStack¬, as well as the decomposition-based naïve approach described in Section 1 (referred to as Naïve).

We used the synthetic data set Treebank.xml [14] with about half a million of nodes, an average path length of 8 levels, and a maximum path length of 35 levels. We generated three sets of path queries (denoted by Q1, Q2, and Q3), where each query in Qi contains exactly i number of not-predicates and has 7 levels. About 30% of the data nodes are accessed for each query, and the matching answers are formed from about 0.4% of the data nodes. For each query and approach, we measured both the total execution time as well as the disk I/O (in terms of the total number of data nodes that are read/written to disk). Our experiments were conducted on a 750MHz Ultra Sparc III machine with 512MB of main memory.

5.1 Naïve Versus PathStack¬

Fig.5 compares the execution time of Naïve and PathStack¬, and the results show that PathStack¬ is much more efficient than Naïve. In particular, observe that while the execution time of Naïve increases almost linearly as the number of not-predicates increases, the execution time of PathStack¬ remains constant. This can be explained by the results in Fig.6 (which compares their I/O performance) and Fig.7 (which gives the detailed breakdown).

Fig.6 shows that the I/O cost of PathStack¬ is independent of the number of not-predicates since each data stream is scanned exactly once (without any intermediate results generated), and the final matching answers written to disk have about the same size. On the other hand, Fig.7 reveals that as the number of not-predicates increases, Naïve incurs more disk I/O as it needs to access the data streams multiple times and output intermediate results to disk.

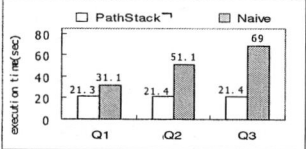 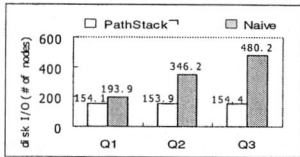

Fig. 5. Execution time comparison between PathStack¬ and Naïve

Fig. 6. Disk I/O comparison between PathStack¬ and Naïve

		Streams		Intermediate Result		Final Results		Total
		# of nodes	% of total	# of nodes	% of total	# of nodes	% of total	# of nodes
Q1	PathStack¬	152.1 k	98.7%	0 k	0%	2 k	1.3%	154.1 k
	Naïve	185.7 k	95.8%	6.2 k	3.2%	2 k	1%	193.9 k
Q2	PathStack¬	152.0 k	98.8%	0 k	0%	1.9 k	1.2%	153.9 k
	Naïve	337.1 k	97.4%	7.2 k	2.1%	1.9 k	0.5%	346.2 k
Q3	PathStack¬	152.3 k	98.6%	0 k	0%	2.1 k	1.4%	154.4 k
	Naïve	466.8 k	97.2%	11.3 k	2.4%	2.1 k	0.4%	480.2 k

Fig. 7. Breakdowns of disk I/O in PathStack¬ and Naïve

5.2 PathStack¬ Versus imp-PathStack

Fig.8 compares the execution time of PathStack¬ and imp-PathStack¬; the amount of time spent only on scanning the accessed data streams is also shown (labeled as "sequential scan") for comparison. Our results show that imp-PathStack¬ is only slightly faster than PathStack¬, with about 90% of the total execution time being dominated by the scanning of the data streams. Note that our implementation of imp-PathStack¬ did not utilize any indexes for accessing the data streams. We expect that if the data streams were indexed, the performance improvement of imp-PathStack¬ over PathStack¬ (due to the additional reduction of I/O cost in node skipping) would become more significant.

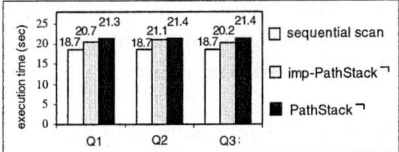

	Stream Size (# of nodes)	Nodes Skipped (# of nodes)	% of skipping
Q1	152.1 k	10.2 k	6.7 %
Q2	152.0 k	3.6 k	2.4 %
Q3	152.3 k	28.1 k	18.5 %

Fig. 8. Execution time comparison between Sequential Scan, imp-PathStack¬ and PathStack¬

Fig. 9. Percentage (%) of nodes skipped for each query set in imp-PathStack¬

Fig.9 compares the number of skipped nodes for various queries using imp-PathStack¬. Our results did not reveal any interesting relationship between the number of not-predicates and the percentage of skipped nodes (which is between 2.4% and 18.5%); we expect this percentage to be higher for an XML document that has a higher fan-out (note that the fan-out of treebank.xml is only around 2-3). More analysis can be found in [6].

6 Related Work

XML query processing and optimization for XML databases have attracted a lot of research interests. Particularly, path query matching has been identified as a core operation in querying XML data. While there is a lot of work on path and twig query matching, none of these works addressed the evaluation of queries with not-predicates. Below, we review the existing work on path/twig query evaluation, all of which do not address not-predicates.

Earlier works [3, 5, 9, 10, 12, 13, 14] have focused on a decomposition-based approach in which a path query is decomposed into a set of binary (parent-child and ancestor-descendant) relationships between pairs of query nodes. The query is then matched by (1) matching each of the binary structural relationships against the XML data, and (2) "stitching" together these basic matches. The major problem with the decomposition-based approach is that the intermediate results can get very large even when the inputs and final results are small.

The work in [1, 2] are more closely related to ours. The algorithms PathStack and PathMPMJ were proposed to evaluate path queries without not-predicates. These algorithms process a path query in a holistic manner, which do not generate large intermediate results and also avoid costly binary structural joins. PathStack has been shown to more efficient than PathMPMJ as it does not require repetitive data scans.

7 Conclusions and Future Work

In this paper, we have proposed two novel algorithms PathStack¬ and imp-PathStack¬ (which is an improved variant of PathStack¬ to further minimize unnecessary computation) for the efficient processing of path queries with not-predicates. We have defined the representation and matching of path queries with not-predicates, and proposed the simple but effective idea of using boolean stacks to support efficient query evaluation. Our proposed algorithms require only a single scan of each data stream associated with the input query without generating any intermediate results. To the best of our knowledge, this is the first work that addresses the evaluation of path queries with not-predicates.

While our proposed algorithms can be easily extended to handle twig queries with at most one path containing not-predicates, we are currently extending our work to process more general twig queries that have not-predicates in multiple branches.

References

1. N. Bruno, N. Koudas, and D. Srivastava. Holistic Twig Joins: Optimal XML pattern matching. In *Proc. of the SIGMOD, 2002*.
2. N. Bruno, N. Koudas, D. Srivastava. Holistic Twig Joins: Optimal XML Pattern Matching. *Technical Report. Columbia University. March 2002*.
3. D. Florescu and D. Kossman. Storing and querying XML data using an RDMBS. IEEE Data Engineering Bulletin, 22(3): 27-34, 1999.
4. H. Jiang, H. Lu, W. Wang, Efficient Processing of XML Twig Queries with OR-Predicates, In *Proc. of the SIGMOD 2004*.
5. H. Jiang, W. Wang, H. Lu, and J. X. Yu. Holistic twig joins on indexed XML documents. In *Proc. of the VLDB, pages 273-284, 2003*.
6. E. Jiao, Efficient processing of XML path queries with not-predicates, M.Sc. Thesis, National University of Singapore, 2004.
7. Q. Li and B. Moon. Indexing and querying XML data for regular path expressions. In *Proc. of the VLDB, pages 361-370, 2001*.
8. R. Riebig and G.Moerkotte. Evaluating queries on structure with access support relations. In *Proc. of the WebDB'00, 2000*.
9. J. Shanmugasundaram, K. Tufte, C. Zhang, G. He, D. J. DeWitt, and J. F. Naughton. Relational databases for querying XML documents: Limitations and opportunities. *In Proc. of VLDB, 1999*.
10. D. Srivastava, S. Al-Khalifa, H. V. Jagadish, N. Koudas, J. M. Patel, and Y. Wu. Structural joins: A primitive for efficient XML query pattern matching. In *Proc. of the ICDE, pages 141-152, 2002*.
11. H. Wang, S. Park, W. Fan, and P. S. Yu. Vist: A dynamic index method for querying XML data by tree structures. In *Proc. of the SIGMOD, pages 110-121, 2003*.
12. Y. Wu, J. M. Patel, and H. V. Jagadish. Structural join order selection for XML query optimization. In *Proc. of the ICDE, pages 443-454, 2003*.
13. C. Zhang, J. Naughton, D. Dewitt, Q. Luo, and G. Lohman. On supporting containment queries in relational database management systems. In *Proc. of the SIGMOD, 2001*.
14. Treebank.xml: http://www.cis.upenn.edu/~treebank/.

An Improved Prefix Labeling Scheme: A Binary String Approach for Dynamic Ordered XML

Changqing Li and Tok Wang Ling

Department of Computer Science, National University of Singapore
{lichangq, lingtw}@comp.nus.edu.sg

Abstract. A number of labeling schemes have been designed to facilitate the query of XML, based on which the ancestor-descendant relationship between any two nodes can be determined quickly. Another important feature of XML is that the elements in XML are intrinsically ordered. However the label update cost is high based on the present labeling schemes. They have to re-label the existing nodes or re-calculate some values when inserting an order-sensitive element. Thus it is important to design a scheme that supports order-sensitive queries, yet it has low label update cost. In this paper, we design a binary string prefix scheme which supports order-sensitive update without any re-labeling or re-calculation. Theoretical analysis and experimental results also show that this scheme is compact compared to the existing dynamic labeling schemes, and it provides efficient support to both ordered and un-ordered queries.

1 Introduction

The growing number of XML [7] documents on the Web has motivated the development of systems which can store and query XML data efficiently. XPath [5] and XQuery [6] are two main XML query languages.

There are two main techniques to facilitate the XML queries, viz. structural index and labeling (numbering) scheme. The structural index approaches, such as dataguide [9] in the Lore system [11] and representative objects [13], can help to traverse through the hierarchy of XML, but this traverse is costly. The labeling scheme approaches, such as containment scheme [2, 10 16, 17], prefix scheme [1, 8, 11, 14] and prime scheme [15], require smaller storage space, yet they can efficiently determine the ancestor-descendant and parent-child relationships between any two elements of the XML. In this paper, we focus on the labeling schemes.

One salient feature of XML is that the elements in XML are intrinsically ordered. This implicit ordering is referred to as document order (the element sequence in the XML). The labeling scheme should also have the ability to determine the order-sensitive relationship.

The main contributions of this paper are summarized as follows:

- This scheme need not re-label any existing nodes and need not re-calculate any values when inserting an order-sensitive node into the XML tree.
- The theoretical analysis and experimental results both show that this scheme has smaller storage requirement.

The rest of the paper is organized as follows. Section 2 reviews the related work and gives the motivation of this paper. We propose our improved binary string prefix scheme in Section 3. The most important part of this paper is Section 4, in which we show that the scheme proposed in this paper need not re-label any existing nodes and need not re-calculate any values when updating an ordered node. The experimental results are illustrated in Section 5, and we conclude in Section 6.

2 Related Work and Motivation

In this section, we present three families of labeling schemes, namely containment [2, 10 16, 17], prefix [1, 8, 11, 14] and prime [15].

Containment Scheme. Agrawal et al [2] use a numbering scheme in which every node is assigned two variables: "start" and "end". These two variables represent an interval [start, end]. For any two nodes u and v, u is an ancestor of v iff label(u.start) < label(v.start) < label(v.end) < label(u.end). In other words, the interval of v is contained in the interval of u.

Although the containment scheme can determine the ancestor-descendant relationship quickly, it does not work well when inserting a node into the XML tree. The insertion of a node may lead to a re-labeling of all the nodes of the tree. This problem may be alleviated if we increase the interval size with some values unused. However, it is not so easy to decide how large the interval size should be. Small interval size is easy to lead to re-labeling, while large interval size wastes a lot of values which causes the increase of storage.

[3] uses real (float-point) values for the "start" and "end" of the intervals. It seems that this approach solve the re-labeling problem. But in practice, the float-point is represented in computer with a fixed number of bits which is similar to the representation of integer. As a result, there are a finite number of values between any two real values [14].

Prefix Scheme. In the prefix labeling scheme, the label of a node is its parent's label (prefix) concatenates the delimiter and its own label. For any two nodes u and v, u is an ancestor of v iff label(u) is a prefix of label(v). There are two main prefix schemes, the integer based and the binary string based.

DeweyID [14] is an integer based prefix scheme. It labels the nth child of a node with an integer n, and this n should be concatenated to the prefix (its parent's label) to form the complete label of this child node.

On the other hand, Cohen et al use Binary strings to label the nodes (*Binary*) [8]. Each character of a binary string is stored using 1 bit. The root of the tree is labeled with an empty string. The first child of the root is labeled with "0", the second child with "10", the third with "110", and the fourth with "1110", etc. Similarly for any node u, the first child of u is labeled with label(u)."0", the second child of u is labeled with label(u)."10", and the ith child with label(u)."$1^{i-1}0$".

Compared to the containment scheme, the prefix scheme only needs to re-label the sibling nodes after this inserted node and the descendants of these siblings, which is more dynamic in updating.

Prime Number Scheme. Wu et al [15] proposed a novel approach to label XML trees with prime numbers (*Prime*). The label of a node is the product of its parent_label and its own self_label (the next available prime number). For any two nodes u and v, u is an ancestor of v iff label(v) *mod* label(u) = 0.

Furthermore, Prime utilizes the Chinese Remainder Theorem (CRT) [4, 15] for the document order. When using the Simultaneous Congruence (SC) value in CRT to mod the self_label of each node, the document order for each node can be calculated. When new nodes are inserted into the XML tree, Prime only needs to re-calculate the SC value for the new ordering of the nodes instead of re-labeling.

In addition, Prime uses multiple SC values rather than a single SC value to prevent the SC value to become a very very larger number.

The prefix and prime schemes are called *dynamic* labeling schemes, and we only compare the performance of *dynamic* labeling schemes in this paper.

Motivation. The Binary and DeweyID prefix schemes both need to re-label the existing nodes when inserting an order-sensitive node.

Although Prime is a scheme which supports order-sensitive updates without any re-labeling of the existing nodes, it needs to re-calculate the SC values based on the new ordering of nodes. The SC values are very large numbers and the re-calculation is very time consuming.

In addition, the Prime scheme skips a lot of integers to get the prime number, and the label of a child is the preoduct of the next available prime number and its parent's label, which both make the storage space for Prime labels large.

Thus the objective of this paper is to design a scheme 1) which need not re-label any existing nodes and need not re-calculate any values when inserting an order-sensitive node (Section 4.1 and 5.3), and 2) which requires less storage space for the labels (Section 3.2 and 5.1).

3 Improved Binary String Prefix Scheme

In this section, we elaborate our Improved Binary string prefix scheme (ImprovedBinary). Firstly we use an example to illustrate how to label the nodes based on our ImprovedBinary. Then we describe the formal labeling algorithm of this scheme. Also we analyze the size requirements of different labeling schemes.

In prefix schemes, the string before the last delimiter is called a prefix_label, the string after the last delimiter is called a self_label, and the string before the first delimiter, between two neighbor delimiters or after the last delimiter is called a component.

Example 3.1. Figure 1 shows our ImprovedBinary scheme. The root node is labeled with an empty string. Then we label the five child nodes of the root. The prefix_labels of these five child nodes are all empty strings, thus the self_labels are exactly the complete labels for these five child nodes. The self_label of the first (left) child node is "01", and the self_label of the last (right) child node is "011". We use "01" and "011" as the first and last sibling self_labels because in this way, we can insert nodes before the first sibling and after the last sibling without any re-labeling of existing nodes. See Section 4.1.

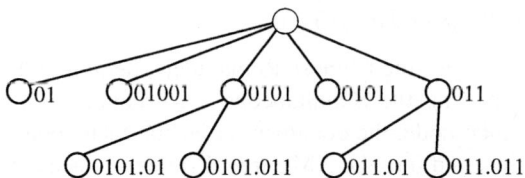

Fig. 1. ImprovedBinary scheme

When we know the left and right self_labels, we can label the middle self_label and 2 cases will be encountered: *Case (a) left self_label size ≤ right self_label size, and Case (b): left self_label size > right self_label size.* For Case (a), the middle self_label is that we change the last character of the right self_label to "0" and concatenate one more "1". For Case (b), the middle self_label is that we directly concatenate one more "1" after the left self_label.

Now we label the middle child node, which is the third child, i.e. $\lfloor (1+5)/2 \rfloor = 3$. The size of the 1st (left) self_label ("01") is 2 and the size of the 5th (right) self_label ("011") is 3 which satisfies Case (a), thus the self_label of the third child node is "0101" ("011" → "010" → "0101").

Next we label the two middle child nodes between "01" and "0101", and between "0101" and "011". For the middle node between "01" (left self_label) and "0101" (right self_label), i.e. the second child node ($\lfloor (1+3)/2 \rfloor = 2$), the left self_label size 2 is smaller than the right self_label size 4 which satisfies Case (a), thus the self_label of the second child is "01001" ("0101" → "0100" → "01001"). For the middle node between "0101" (left self_label) and "011" (right self_label), i.e. the fourth child ($\lfloor (3+5)/2 \rfloor = 4$), the left self_label size 4 is larger than the right self_label size 3 which satisfies Case (b), thus the self_label of the fourth child is "01011" ("0101" ⊕ "1" → "01011").

Theorem 3.1. The sibling self_labels of ImprovedBinary are lexically ordered.

Theorem 3.2. The labels (prefix_label ⊕ delimiter ⊕ self_label) of ImprovedBinary are lexically ordered when comparing the labels component by component.

Example 3.2. The self_labels of the five child nodes of the root in Figure 1 are lexically ordered, i.e. "01" ≺ "01001" ≺ "0101" ≺ "01011" ≺ "011" lexically. Furthermore, "0101.011" ≺ "011.01" lexically.

3.1 The Formal Labeling Algorithm

We firstly discuss the AssignMiddleSelfLabel algorithm (Figure 2) which inserts the middle self_label when we know the left self_label and the right self_label. If the size of the left self_label is smaller than or equal to the size of the right self_label, the self_label of the middle node is that we change the last character of the *right* self_label to "0" and concatenate one more "1". Otherwise, the self_label of the middle node is the *left* self_label concatenates "1".

Algorithm 1: AssignMiddleSelfLabel
Input: left self label *self_label_L*, and right self label *self_label_R*
Output: middle self label *self_label_M*, such that
$$self\_label\_L \prec self\_label\_M \prec self\_label\_R \text{ lexically.}$$
begin
1: calculate the size of *self_label_L* and the size of *self_label_R*
2: **if** size(*self_label_L*) ≤ size(*self_label_R*)
  then *self_label_M* = change the last character of *self_label_R* to "0",
       and concatenate ($\oplus$) one more "1"
3: **else if** size(*self_label_L*) > size(*self_label_R*)
  then *self_label_M* = *self_label_L* $\oplus$ "1"
end

Fig. 2. AssignMiddleSelfLabel algorithm.

Algorithm 2: Labeling
Input: XML document
Output: Label of each node
begin
1: for all the sibling child nodes of each node of the XML document
2: for the first sibling child node, *self_label[1]*="01" //self_label is an array
3: **if** the Number of Sibling nodes $SN > 1$
  then *self_label[SN]*="011"
       self_label=SubLabeling(*self_label*, 1, SN)
4: label = prefix_label $\oplus$ delimiter $\oplus$ each element of *self_label* array
end

SubLabeling
Input: *self_label* array, left element index of self_label array *L*, and right element index of self_label array *R*
Output: *self_label* array
begin
1: $M = \text{floor}((L+R)/2)$ //M refers to the Mth element of *self_label* array
2: **if** $L+1<R$
  then *self_label[M]*=AssignMiddleSelfLabel(*self_label[L]*, *self_label[R]*)
       SubLabeling(*self_label*, L, M)
       SubLabeling(*self_label*, M, R)
end

Fig. 3. Labeling algorithm.

Next we discuss how to label the whole XML tree. Figure 3 shows the Labeling algorithm. We firstly get all the sibling child nodes of a node. If there is only one sibling, the self_label of this node is "01". Otherwise, the self_label of the first sibling node is "01" and the self_label of the last sibling node is "011". We use the SubLabeling function to get all the self_labels of the rest sibling nodes.

SubLabeling is a recursive function, the input of which is a self_label *array*, the left element index of self_label "L" and the right element index of self_label "R". This function assigns the middle self_label (self_label[M]) using the AssignMiddleSelfLabel algorithm (Figure 2), then it uses the new left and right self_label positions to call the SubLabeling function itself, until each element of the self_label array has a value.

Finally the label of each sibling node is the prefix_label concatenates the self_label.

3.2 Size Analysis[1]

In this section, we analyze the size required by the DeweyID, Binary, Prime and our ImprovedBinary. The "D", "F" and "N" are respectively used to denote the maximal depth, maximal fan-out and number of nodes of an XML tree.

DeweyID. The maximal size to store a single self_label is $\log(F)$ (all the self_labels of DeweyID use this size). When considering the prefix, the maximal size to store a complete label (prefix_label $\oplus$ self_label) is $D \times \log(F)$ since the maximal depth is D and there are at most (D-1) delimiters in the prefix_label. Thus the maximal size required by DeweyID to store all the nodes in the XML tree is

$$N \times D \times \log(F) \qquad (1)$$

Binary. The size of the first sibling self_label is only 1, the second is 2, ···, and the Fth is F. Thus the actual total sibling self_label size is $1+2+\cdots+F = (1+F) \times F/2 = F^2/2 + F/2$, and the average size for a single self_label is $F/2 + 1/2$. Thus the maximal size to store all the nodes in the XML tree is

$$N \times D \times (F/2 + 1/2) \qquad (2)$$

From formulas (1) and (2), we can see that the size of Binary is larger than the size of DeweyID.

Prime. According to the size analysis of Prime in [15], the maximal size required to store all the nodes in the XML tree is

$$N \times D \times \log(N \times \log(N)) \qquad (3)$$

Comparing formulas (1) and (3), F is definitely less than $N \times \log(N)$, thus DeweyID requires smaller label size than Prime when considering the worst case.

---

[1] The size in this paper refers to bits and the log in this paper is used as the logarithm to base 2.

This is intuitive when we notice that Prime skips many integers to get the prime number and uses the product of two numbers.

ImprovedBinary. Finally we consider the size required by our ImprovedBinary.

Example 3.3. For the 5 sibling self_labels of the child nodes of the root in Figure 1, the first and last sibling self_labels are "01" and "011" with size 2 and 3 bits respectively. The middle self_label between "01" and "011" is "0101" with size 4 bits. Then for the two middle nodes "01001" and "01011" (between "01" and "0101", and between "0101" and "011"), their sef_label sizes are both 5, and so on.

Table 1 shows the relationship between the size of a label and the number of labels with this size. There is one label with size 2, one label with size 3, 2^0 label with size 4, 2^1 labels with size 5, 2^2 labels with size 6, 2^3 labels with size 7, $\cdots$, and 2^n labels with size n+4. The number of sibling nodes F is equal to $1+1+2^0+2^1+2^2+2^3+\cdots+2^n=2^{n+1}+1$. Therefore $2^n = (F-1)/2$, and $n+4 = \log(F-1)+3$. Thus the total sibling self_label size is

$$2+3+1\times 4+2^1\times 5+2^2\times 6+2^3\times 7+\cdots 2^n\times(n+4)$$
$$= 2+3+1\times 4+2^1\times 5+2^2\times 6+2^3\times 7+\cdots (F-1)/2\times(\log(F-1)+3)$$
$$= F\log(F-1)+2F-\log(F-1)+1$$

Hence the average size for a single self_label is
$$= \log(F-1)+2-\log(F-1)/F+1/F$$

Accordingly the maximal size required to store all the nodes in the XML tree is

$$N\times D\times(\log(F-1)+2-\log(F-1)/F+1/F) \tag{4}$$

Table 1. Number of sibling nodes and single sibling self_label size of ImprovedBinary

Number of labels with this size	Size (bits)
1	2
1	3
1 (2^0)	4
2 (2^1)	5
4 (2^2)	6
8 (2^3)	7
...	...
2^n	n+4

It can be seen from formulas (1) and (4) that the size required by ImprovedBinary is as small as the size required by DeweyID. In addition, DeweyID uses fixed length for all the self_labels. On the other hand, our ImprovedBinary uses variable length, therefore the self_label size of our ImprovedBinary will not always employs the maximal fan-out F. As a result, the actual total label size of our ImprovedBinary should be smaller than the actual total label size of DeweyID. Consequently the size required by our ImprovedBinary is smaller than the size required by Binary and Prime. This will be confirmed in Section 5.1 by the experimental results.

4 Order-Sensitive Update and Query

The most important part of this paper is Section 4.1, in which we show that our ImprovedBinary scheme need not re-label any existing nodes and need not re-calculate any values when inserting an order-sensitive node. In Section 4.2, we briefly introduce how to answer order-sensitive queries based on different schemes.

4.1 Order-Sensitive Update

The deletion of a node will not affect the ordering of the nodes in the XML tree. Therefore in this section, we discuss the following three order-sensitive insertion cases.

Case (1): Insert a Node Before the First Sibling Node. The self_label of the inserted node is that the last character of the first self_label is changed to "0" and is concatenated with one more "1". After insertion, the order is still kept.

Case (2): Insert a Node at any Position Between the First and Last Sibling Node. We use the AssignMiddleSelfLabel algorithm introduced in Section 3.1 to assign the self_label of the new inserted node. After insertion, the order is still kept.

Case (3): Insert a Node After the Last Sibling Node. The self_label of the inserted node is that the last self_label concatenates one more "1". After insertion, the order is still kept.

In the above three cases, the prefix_labels of the inserted nodes are the same as the prefix_labels of the sibling nodes.

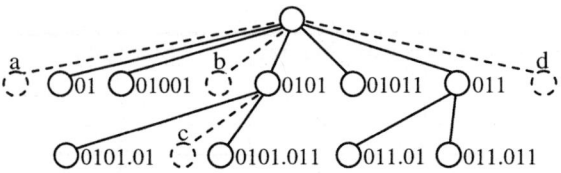

Fig. 4. Order-sensitive update for ImprovedBinary

Example 4.1. When inserting the node "*a*" (see Figure 4), it is Case (1), thus the self_label (label) of "a" is "*001*" ("01" → "00" → "001"). When inserting the node "*b*", it is case (2) and we use the AssignMiddleSelfLabel algorithm to assign the self_label of "b". The left self_label of "b" is "01001" with size 5 and the right self_label of "b" is "0101" with size 4, therefore we directly concatenate one more "1" after the left self_label ("01001" ⊕ "1" → "010011"), then the self_label of "b" is "*010011*". When inserting the node "*c*", it is still case (2), but the left self_label ("01") size < the right self_label ("011") size, therefore the self_label of "c" is "0101" ("011" → "010" → "0101"), and the complete label of "c" is "*0101.0101*". When inserting the node "*d*", it is case (3), thus the self_label of "d" is "*0111*"

("011" ⊕ "1" → "0111"). After insertion, the orders are still kept, i.e. label(a) ≺ "01", "01001" ≺ label(b) ≺ "0101", "0101.01" ≺ label(c) ≺ "0101.011", and "011" ≺ label(d) lexically.

It can be seen that for all the above three cases, ImprovedBinary need not re-label any existing nodes and need not re-calculate any values.

On the other hand, DeweyID and Binary need to re-label all the sibling nodes following the inserted node and all the descendant nodes of the following sibling nodes for Case (1) and (2). Prime needs to re-calculate the SC values for the new ordering.

4.2 Order-Sensitive Query

Besides the ancestor-descendant and parent-child relationship determinations, there are the following order-sensitive queries.

1) position = i:
Selects the ith node within a context node set. For example, the query "/play/act[2]" will retrieve the second act of the play.

2) preceding-sibling or following-sibling:
Selects all the preceding (following) sibling nodes of the context node. For example, the query "/play/act[2]/preceding-sibling::act" will retrieve all the *acts ("::act")* which are sibling nodes of act[2] and are before act[2].

3) preceding or following:
Selects all the nodes before (after) (in document order) the context node excluding any ancestors (descendants). For example, the query "/play/act[2]/following::*" will retrieve all the *nodes ("::*")* after act[2] in document order and these nodes should not be the descendants of act[2].

The Prime scheme uses the SC value and the self_label to calculate the order of each node, then it can fulfill these three types of order-sensitive queries.

From the labels only, the prefix schemes (including DeweyID, Binary and ImprovedBinary) can determine the sequence of nodes, hence they can fulfill these three order-sensitive queries.

It should be noted when inserting a node, DeweyID and Binary need to re-label the existing nodes and Prime needs to re-calculate the SC values before they can process the order-sensitive queries.

5 Performance Study

We conduct three sets of experiments (storage, query and update) to evaluate and compare the performance of the four dynamic labeling schemes, namely DeweyID, Binary, Prime and ImprovedBinary. All the four schemes are implemented in Java and all the experiments are carried out on a 2.6GHz Pentium 4 processor with 1 GB RAM running Windows XP Professional. We use the real-world XML data available in [18] to test the four schemes. Characteristics of these datasets are shown in Table 2 which shows the depths of real XMLs are usually not too high (confirmed by [12]).

Table 2. Test datasets

Datasets	Topics	# of files	Max fan-out for a file	Max depth for a file	Total # of nodes for each dataset
D1	Bib	18	25	4	2111
D2	Club	12	47	3	2928
D3	Movie	490	38	4	26044
D4	Sigmod Record	988	26	6	39058
D5	Department	19	257	3	48542
D6	Actor	480	368	4	56769
D7	Company	24	529	4	161576
D8	Shakespeare's play	37	434	5	179689
D9	NASA	1882	1188	6	370292

5.1 Storage Requirement

The label size in Figure 5 refers to the total label size for all the nodes in each dataset. As expected, ImprovedBinary has the smallest label size for each of the nine datasets. Furthermore, the total label sizes of all the nine datasets for Binary, Prime and our ImprovedBinary are 3.97, 2.00 and 0.78 times of that of DeweyID.

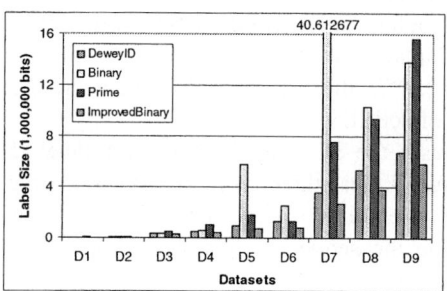

Fig. 5. Storage space for each dataset

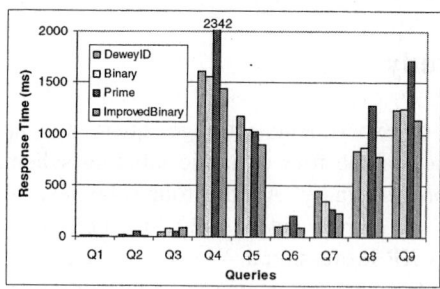

Fig. 6. Processing time of the nine queries

5.2 Query Performance[2]

In this experiment, we test the query performance of the four schemes based on all the XML files in the Shakespeare's play dataset (D8). In order to make a more sizeable data workload, we scale up (replicate) D8 10 times as described in [14]. The ordered and un-ordered queries and the number of nodes returned from this scaled dataset are shown in Table 3. Except Q3, ImprovedBinary works the fastest for the rest 8 ordered and un-ordered queries (see Figure 6).

Table 3. Test queries on the scaled D8

	Queries	# of nodes returned
Q1	/play/act[4]	370
Q2	/play/act[5]//preceding::scene	6110
Q3	/play/act/scene/speech[2]	7300
Q4	/play/*/*	19380
Q5	/play/act//speech[3]/preceding-sibling::*	30930
Q6	/play//act[2]/following::speaker	184060
Q7	/play//scene/speech[6]/following-sibling::speech	267050
Q8	/play/act/scene/speech	309330
Q9	/play/*//line	1078330

5.3 Order-Sensitive Update Performance

The elements in the Shakespeare's plays (D8) are order-sensitive. Here we study the update performance of the Hamlet XML file in D8. The update performance of other XML files is similar. Hamlet has 5 acts, and we test the following six cases: inserting an act before act[1], inserting an act between act[1] and act[2], ···, inserting an act between act[4] and act[5], and inserting an act after act[5]. Figure 7 shows the number of nodes for re-labeling when applying different schemes.

DeweyID and Binary have the same number of nodes to re-label in all the six cases. The Hamlet XML file has totally 6636 nodes, but DeweyID and Binary need to re-label 6595 nodes when inserting an act before act[1].

For Prime, the number of SC values that are required to be re-calculated is counted in Figure 7. Because we use each SC value for every three[3] labels, the number of SC values required to be re-calculated is 1/3 of the number of nodes required to be re-labeled by DeweyID and Binary. (Note that all the act nodes are the child nodes of the root play.)

In all the six cases, ImprovedBinary need not re-label any existing nodes and need not re-calculate any values.

---

[2] The query time and re-labeling (re-calculation) time in this paper refer to the processing time only without including the I/O time.
[3] The SC values for every 4 or more nodes will be very large numbers which can not be stored using 64 bits in Java for calculation, for every 1 or 2 nodes will cause more SC values to be re-calculated.

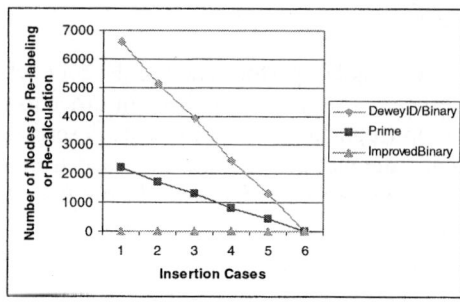

Fig. 7. Number of nodes or values for re-labeling or re-calculation

Next we study the time required to re-label nodes or re-calculate SC values. The time in Figure 8 shows that the time required by Prime to re-calculate the SC values is at least 337 times larger than the time required by DeweyID and Binary to re-label the nodes. In contrast, our ImprovedBinary needs 0 milliseconds (ms) for the insertion in all the six cases.

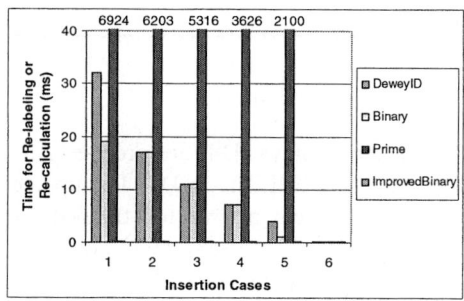

Fig. 8. Processing time for re-labeling or re-calculation

6 Conclusion and Future Work

When an order-sensitive node is inserted into the XML tree, the present node labeling schemes need to re-label the existing nodes or re-calculate some values to keep the document order which is costly in considering either the number of nodes for re-labeling (re-calculation) or the time for re-labeling (re-calculation). To address this problem, we propose a node labeling scheme called ImprovedBinary in this paper, which need not re-label any existing nodes and need not re-calculate any values when inserting order-sensitive nodes into the XML tree.

In the future, we will further study how to efficiently process the delimiters of the prefix schemes and decrease the label size, as well keep the low label update cost.

References

1. Serge Abiteboul, Haim Kaplan, Tova Milo: Compact labeling schemes for ancestor queries. SODA 2001: 547-556
2. Rakesh Agrawal, Alexander Borgida, H. V. Jagadish: Efficient Management of Transitive Relationships in Large Data and Knowledge Bases. SIGMOD Conference 1989: 253-262
3. Toshiyuki Amagasa, Masatoshi Yoshikawa, Shunsuke Uemura: QRS: A Robust Numbering Scheme for XML Documents. ICDE 2003: 705-707
4. James A. Anderson and James M. Bell, Number Theory with Application, Prentice-Hall, New Jersey, 1997.
5. Anders Berglund, Scott Boag, Don Chamberlin, Mary F. Fernandez, Michael Kay, Jonathan Robie, and Jerome Simon. XML path language (XPath) 2.0 W3C working draft 16. Technical Report WD-xpath20-20020816, World Wide Web Consortium, Aug. 2002.
6. Scott Boag, Don Chamberlin, Mary F. Fernandez, Daniela Florescu, Jonathan Robie, and Jerome Simon. XQuery 1.0: An XML Query LanguageW3C working draft 16. Technical Report WD-xquery-20020816, World Wide Web Consortium, Aug. 2002.
7. Tim Bray, Jean Paoli, C. M. Sperberg-McQueen, Eve Maler, and Francois Yergeau. Extensible markup language (XML) 1.0 third edition W3C recommendation. Technical Report REC-xml-20001006, World Wide Web Consortium, Oct. 2000.
8. Edith Cohen, Haim Kaplan, Tova Milo: Labeling Dynamic XML Trees. PODS 2002: 271-281
9. Roy Goldman, Jennifer Widom: DataGuides: Enabling Query Formulation and Optimization in Semistructured Databases. VLDB 1997: 436-445
10. Quanzhong Li, Bongki Moon: Indexing and Querying XML Data for Regular Path Expressions. VLDB 2001: 361-370
11. Jason McHugh, Serge Abiteboul, Roy Goldman, Dallan Quass, Jennifer Widom: Lore: A Database Management System for Semistructured Data. SIGMOD Record 26(3): 54-66 (1997)
12. Laurent Mignet, Denilson Barbosa, Pierangelo Veltri: The XML web: a first study. WWW 2003: 500-510
13. Svetlozar Nestorov, Jeffrey D. Ullman, Janet L. Wiener, Sudarshan S. Chawathe: Representative Objects: Concise Representations of Semistructured, Hierarchial Data. ICDE 1997: 79-90
14. Igor Tatarinov, Stratis Viglas, Kevin S. Beyer, Jayavel Shanmugasundaram, Eugene J. Shekita, Chun Zhang: Storing and querying ordered XML using a relational database system. SIGMOD Conference 2002: 204-215
15. Xiaodong Wu, Mong-Li Lee, Wynne Hsu: A Prime Number Labeling Scheme for Dynamic Ordered XML Trees. ICDE 2004: 66-78
16. Masatoshi Yoshikawa, Toshiyuki Amagasa, Takeyuki Shimura, Shunsuke Uemura: XRel: a path-based approach to storage and retrieval of XML documents using relational databases. ACM Trans. Internet Techn. 1(1): 110-141 (2001)
17. Chun Zhang, Jeffrey F. Naughton, David J. DeWitt, Qiong Luo, Guy M. Lohman: On Supporting Containment Queries in Relational Database Management Systems. SIGMOD Conference 2001
18. The Niagara Project Experimental Data. Available at: http://www.cs.wisc.edu/niagara/data.html

Efficiently Coding and Indexing XML Document

Zhongming Han[1], Congting Xi[2], and Jiajin Le[1]

[1] College of Computer Science and Technology of Donghua University,
1882 Yananxi Road Shanghai (200051), P.R. China
[2] Taiyuan University of Technology Taiyuan Shanxi P.R. China
hx_zm@mail.dhu.edu.cn, ct_xi@163.com, lejiajin@dhu.edu.cn

Abstract. In this paper, a novel and efficient numbering scheme is presented, which combines the label path information and data path information, and it can efficiently support all kinds of queries. A compact index structure, named HiD, is also proposed in this paper. Query algorithms based this index structure are introduced. At last, the comprehensive experiments are conducted to assess all the technologies in question.

1 Introduction

The Extensible Markup Language (XML) is rapidly emerging on the World Wide Web as a standard for representing and exchanging data. Several query languages, including XPath [16], Quilt [15], and XQuery [14], have been proposed for semi-structured XML data. The ability to express complex structure or efficient index structure is one of the major focuses in XML query language design. Furthermore, an efficient numbering scheme provides the foundation for an efficient index structure. A numbering scheme is to encode nodes and produce the node identification.

Nowadays, researchers have proposed many kinds of query and index technologies, such as EF-Join, EA-Join, KC-join [5], MPMCJN [6], tree-merge, XPATH Accelerator, Containment Join etc, which are based on the structure join. Other approaches, like RiST and ViST [13], use tree structures as the basic unit of query to avoid expensive join operations. All of these query approaches are constructed on some numbering scheme on XML documents. Among these numbering schemes, two types of numbering methods stand out, one is the region-based numbering scheme and the other is DataGuide.

There are some problems with the region-based numbering schemes. Firstly, they lack of flexibility. It is very difficult to support dynamic nodes inserting, deleting and modifying operations although researchers proposed some mechanisms to enlarge the range of region. Meanwhile, maintenance of numbers of nodes needs a lot of time. Moreover, region-based numbering schemes do not contain path information of nodes. Finally, region numbering schemes do not support queries in the form of document order, which is the relative ordering existing among nodes within a single document.

DataGuide provides another numbering scheme, in which the path information and node position are combined. In this numbering scheme, more information is provided. However, in this numbering scheme, nodes are also represented by the starting number of pre-order traversing XML document, and thus it is still very difficult to support dynamic nodes inserting, deleting and modifying operations.

In order to improve support dynamic operation and performance, in this paper, we propose a new novel node numbering scheme. We distinguish the label path information from the data path information for a node. This numbering scheme provides solutions to a wide range of challenges and shows a better performance. The following is the main contributions.

- A novel and efficient node numbering scheme is proposed in this paper. This node identification contains the label path information and data information.
- A compact index structure is proposed, which combine the structural index and value index. Query algorithms based this index structure are introduced.
- The comprehensive experiments are conducted to evaluate the node numbering scheme, index structure and query algorithm.

The rest of the paper is structured as follows. In Section 2, we review related work. In Section 3, basic concepts are introduced. In Section 4, the index structure is proposed. In Section 5, the focus is on query algorithms. In Section 6, through some experimental results, we analyse the presented algorithms and compare them with other existing ones. Finally we make some concluding remarks in Section 7.

2 Related Work

Node numbering scheme is the foundation for an efficient index structure. There are a lot of researches on this subject. In [1], region based numbering scheme is firstly introduced. In [4,6,10,23] researchers use this type of numbering schemes. Later, the extended preorder numbering scheme [5] is put forward which improves the region based numbering scheme. The results in [8,5,18] have demonstrated that assigning a start number, end number, and level to each element suffices. In essence, they are still region based numbering schemes.

Because the region based numbering scheme does not support dynamic node inserting or deleting operation, some researchers tried to use statistic technologies to solve this problem. This type of methods [13,17] is based on estimations of the number of attribute values, and other statistical information of the XML document.

To our knowledge, the most efficiently structural join algorithm is the twig join algorithm, including those in [5,8,9,24,25]. These stack-based approaches process the input streams of nodes whose tag appears in the query twig and they speed up join processing by skipping some nodes. The problem with these approaches is that the effectiveness depends on the distribution of the matches in the input list.

The DataGuide is proposed in [2, 11]. In the DataGuide, a number is assigned to each node; these node numbers uniquely identify the rooted label path, which is the advantage of the method. However DataGuide cannot answer the query with branching path expressions without accessing the original XML data. In [12], based on DataGuide, a new node identification is proposed.

Another query technology, sequence matching that transforms documents and queries into structured encoded sequences and evaluate queries based on the sequence matching, is recently proposed in [13, 22]. These approaches support flexible queries in query without join operations. But they still have some drawbacks. Firstly, they need a lot of post-processing to guarantee the result accuracy; otherwise they may have false alarms in the query results. The second drawback is that usually these approaches need a lot of storage spaces. Although they eliminate expensive join operations, they need more IO exchange and may lead to declining performance.

There are some other researchers concentrating on node coding and index structure. For example, a tagged perfect binary tree is employed to represent an XML document and pre-order traverse binary tree to get the node identification in [7].

3 Node Identification

We assume that a single document D is a node labeled acyclic tree with the set V of nodes and the set E of edges, and labels are taken from the set L of strings. Furthermore, text values come from a set T of text strings and can be attached to any type of nodes, not just leaf nodes. The following definitions introduce some fundamental notions used in the rest of the paper.

Definition 1. An XML document D is a tree (V, root, *label*, *children*, *text*), where
- V is a finite set of nodes;
- root $\in V$ is the root of D;
- *label* is a mapping: $V \rightarrow L$;
- *children* is a mapping from nodes to a partially ordered sequence of child nodes and induces the set of E of edges;
- *text*: $V \rightarrow T$.

Definition 2. Let $n_1, n_2 \in V$ be two nodes in an XML document. The unique label path from n_1 to n_2, denoted by *lpath*(n_1, n_2), is the label path ($l_1, l_2, \cdots l_k$) where l_1=*label* (n_1) and l_k= *label* (n_2), l_i ($i = 2, \cdots, k-1$) correspond to the sequence of labels on the path in D connecting the two nodes. If there is no such connecting path, then *lpath*(n_1, n_2)=e (the empty path). The rooted label path of a node $n \in V$, *lpath*(n), is the label path from the root node to the node n.

Definition 3. Let n_1 and n_2 be two nodes in an XML document. If n_2 is a child node of n_1, i.e. $n_2 \in$ *children* (n_1), then *position*(n_2) is the position of node n_2 in *children* (n_1) with respect to nodes that have the same label *label*(n_2). The arity of node n_2, *arity*(n_2), is the number of nodes with label *label*(n_2) in the n_1's list of children.

Definition 4. The data path from the node n_1 to n_k in an XML document D, *dpath*(n_1, n_k), is the sequence of positions of nodes along the label path from n_1 to n_k in D. That is, if ($n_1, n_2, \cdots, n_k$) $n_i \in V$ (i=1,2…k), is the path from $_1$ to n_k, then the sequence of positions is (*position*(n_1), *position*(n_2), $\cdots$, *position*(n_k)).

If n_1 is the root node, then *position*(n_1)=1. The rooted data path of n_k, *dpath*(n_k), is the data path *dpath*(root, n_k). The alternative representation of data path is *position*(n_1), *position*(n_2),. … , *position*(n_k).

3.1 Node Label Path Number

A tree always can be transformed to a binary tree without ambiguity. Thus we transform an XML label path tree to a binary tree.

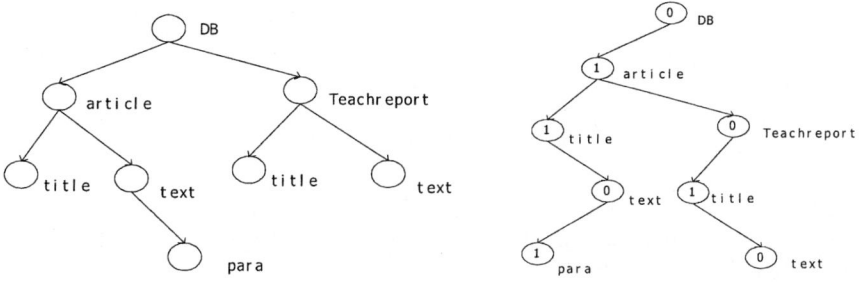

Fig. 1. An XML Label Path Tree   **Fig. 2.** The Binary Tree with Figure 1

Fig 1 shows an XML document label path tree, which consists of all label paths and reflects the structural information in the XML document. A node of the tree corresponds to a label of the document. It is easy to know all the label paths of nodes from this tree. Then we transform this tree into a binary tree shown in **Fig 2**.

Fig 2 shows the binary tree. There are many methods to code a binary tree. However we seek a coding method that can reflect path information from the number of nodes, so we choose Haveman's code. The number labelled with each node is produced according to Haveman's code. In Table 1, Haveman's code of nodes can be found. Thus, the label path of a node in a document would be expressed by Haveman's code of the node in the label path tree.

Table 1. Node Numbering

Node	Code	Arity	Data Path	Data path Number	Node identification
DB	0	1	0	0	(0,0)
article	01	2	1,2	0,1	(1,0) (1,1)
Teachreport	010	2	1	0	(2,0)
title	011	1	1	0	(3,0)
text	0110	1	1.1	01	(6,1)
para	01101	3	1.1,1.2,1.3	000,001,010	(13,0),(13,1), (13,2)
title	0101	1			
text	01010	1	1.1	00	(10,0)

Definition 5. Let n be a node in an XML document, and the bit string S be the Haveman's code of the node of the label path tree. Then the label path number of n is the decimal number to which the bit string is transformed.

3.2 Data Path Number

We use a binary number to represent a position in a data path. As a result, the data path can be represented by a binary number sequence. **Fig 3** shows a data path number.

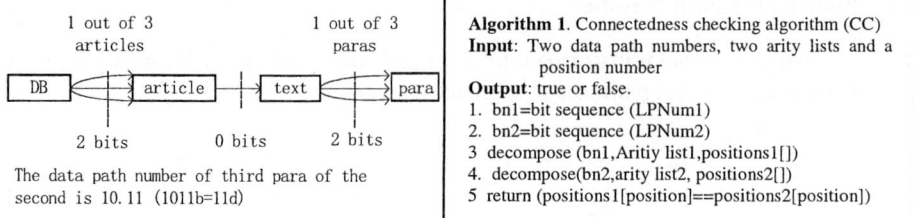

Fig. 3. One Data Path Number

Definition 6. Let n be a node in an XML document, and bit sequence S be the data path of node n. The data path number of n is defined as the decimal number to which the bit sequence is transformed.

To reduce the length of data path, a node is eliminated if the arity of the node is 1. In Fig. 3, considering that the data path of the third para. of the second article is 0.10.0.11, the node root and text are eliminated since their arity is 1. The resulting data path becomes 10.11 and the corresponding decimal number is 11. The length of the bit string in encoding a node can be determined by the arity of the node, which is shown in Table 1.

An important and extensive application for data path number query is connectedness checking, i.e. given two data path numbers and a node position, we need to check whether or not these two data paths are connected at this position. Algorithm 1 is an algorithm to check connectedness. In this algorithm, there is a function, named decompose, which has three parameters. This function decomposes the bit sequence of a data path number into a position list according to arities.

3.3 Node Identification

To identify a node in an XML document, we need two types of information, one is the structure information of the node, and the other is the data instance of the node. We combine the two types of information to identify a node in an XML document. A

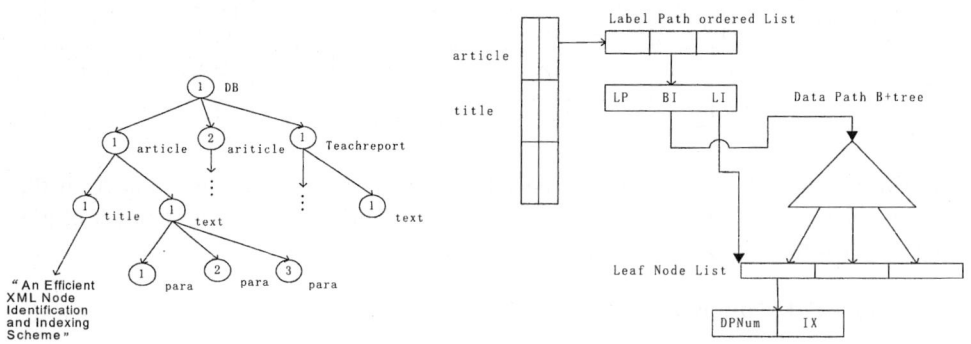

Fig. 4. An XML Document   **Fig. 5.** Structure Index

node n in an XML document can be uniquely represented by (*ln*, *dn*), where *ln* and *dn* are the label path number and data path number of n respectively.

Fig. 4 shows an XML document whose label path tree is shown in **Fig. 1**. In order to encode the article, we need 2 bits. The maximum number of the node para is 3, and thus 2 bits can represent the data path of the node para.

Table 1 shows the data path and data path number represented by binary numbers of nodes. From Table 1, we know that a node identification is represented by a pair of number (label path number, data path number). Based on this representation, we create a HiD index for an XML document.

4 Index Structure

The index structure in this paper is hybrid index structure, named HiD, and is composed of structure index and value index. The structure index is for document structure and the value index is for node values. The structure index is created based on node identification. The structure index is investigated in detail in Section 4.1 and the value index is simply introduced in Section 4.2.

4.1 Structure Index

Usually, in a large XML document, there are few label path numbers and a lot of data path numbers. So we firstly construct a Hash table for labels. A label could have more than one label path and label path number. For a complex XML schema, we create an ordered list for the label path numbers with the same label. For data path numbers of a label path number, we construct a B+Tree to index them. Fig. 5 shows a framework of the structure index.

In Fig. 5, the index framework contains 3 layers, the first layer is a Hash table, the second layer contains ordered lists, and the last layer contains B+trees. With the Hash table, a label is mapped into an address pointer. Each address pointer points to an ordered list to store all label path numbers of the label. The key of the ordered list is the label path number. Using data path numbers as keys, we create B+trees which are for data path numbers. To handle some traversing problems rapidly, we build a bi-direction list for leaf nodes of each B+Tree. The list will be called leaf node list.

Each element of the label path ordered list is composed of label path number (LP), B+Tree pointer (BI) that points to the root of the B+Tree and leaf nodes list pointer (LI) that points to the leaf node list of the B+Tree. Each leaf node of B+Tree consists of data path number (DPNum) and value index (IX), where IX is the virtual ID of the node in the value index. It is used to connect structure index with value index.

4.2 Values Index

For an XML document, the value of a node is represented by a string. With the development of XML schema, more and more data types are supported in XML documents. Consequently, index that is suitable for different data types needs to be adopted. In addition, information retrieval is widely applied. So the principle of creating a value index is (1) it is easily combined with the structure index; (2) support different data types; (3) implement a uniform interface search function for different value indices.

Now we propose two types of value indices: *Invert List* and *Number*. We implement a uniform search function: ValueSearch(VID, predication), where VID is a pointer that points to a group of value indices, and predication is a value predication. The function returns a list of elements that satisfy the value predication. Besides ValueSearch function, we implement another function, named VIValidate, with two input parameters IX and VID. IX is the virtual ID of a node. This function returns the value to that IX points. This function can efficiently support queries, in which data path numbers need to be computed so that IXs are obtained.

Invert list type: For this type, a string is treated as a bag of tokens and a mapping is created from each token to a list of absolute element references whose values contain this token.

Number type: Numerical values are indexed by a Number type, which sorts numerical values of a label path number in an ascending order. Number type supports the numerical range search. More specifically, given a range of numbers (a, b), it returns a list of node references whose values are greater than a and less than b.

Towards the end of this section, we mention the process of construct process of structure index. The process can be simply divided into two phases. In the first phase, we generate label paths and data paths of nodes. Meanwhile we collect statistical information of nodes and related values information including strings, numbers etc. to create values index. We create an invert list of all strings. In the second phase, two tasks need to be fulfilled. One task is to generate node identification based on label paths, data paths and their statistics. In the same time, we start with the other task, i.e. construct the structure index.

5 Query Handling

Our intuition is that it is necessary to reduce and eliminate expensive join operations to accelerate query process. Noticing that the numbering scheme contains path information, it is possible to compute label path numbers of related nodes to get the query results. By doing so, join operations can be significantly reduced.

Usually, there are two kinds of queries, path pattern query and tree pattern query. We firstly discuss path pattern query and how to handle wildcard // and *in Section 5.1 and tree pattern query in Section 5.2.

5.1 Path Pattern Query

Path pattern query is the simplest type of queries. Meanwhile it is the base of tree pattern query. We divide path pattern queries into two categories. The first category is the simple path pattern query that does not contain any node position. Firstly, assume that the query does not contain wildcard."//" and "*". This class of query can be simply handled. Find the label path numbers of leaf node "author" by means of Hash table. Because a label path number is directly related to a rooted label path, we can follow a bottom-up checking of parent-child relation to validate whether or not the parent node is "proceedings". It is easy to discover all label path numbers that match the given query. Then we avoid expensive join operations produced by structural join algorithms. After getting the true label path numbers, we can return the query results by traversing the leaf node list if the query does not contain a value predication.

The second category is the path pattern query based on node positions. For example, /Authors/Author [1] /AuthorInfo[2]/ AuthorURL is a path pattern query based on node positions. This class of query cannot be handled by the previous region-based numbering approaches. We can efficiently handle this type of queries by node numbering.

Now we briefly analyze the querying process in this example to illustrate Algorithm 2. Like the path pattern query without wildcard, we firstly determine the label path number of node AuthorURL. In the process of bottom-up checking of parent-child relation, arities of ancestors such as Authors, Author, AuthorInfo and AuthorURL can be available. For example, if the resulting arities list is 1.100.6.1, then the root has one sub-element Authors and AuthorInfo has one sub-element AuthorURL. Hence we can compute the data path number of node AuthorURL. In the last step, search the B+Tree pointed by BI and the given data path numbers and return IX. Algorithm 2 shows the query process for the path pattern query based on positions.

Algorithm 2. Algorithm for path pattern query based on position
Input: A path pattern query and position list.
Output: The target element list, represented by (LPNum, DPNum ,IX).
1. n=hash(leaf node)
2. Fetch each label path number in the label path ordered list pointed by n.pointer
3.   check(label path number, list of labels)
4.   GetArity(label path number)
5. DPNum=computeDP(position list, arities list)
6. BtreeSearch(DPNum, BI)
7. Return   (LPNum, DPNum ,IX)

Towards the end of this section, we briefly discuss how to handle the wildcard "//" and "*". We discuss the two cases: a//b and a*b, and others can be similarly dealt with. a//b means that a is an ancestor of b. Firstly obtain the label path number n and m of a and b respectively. We can judge whether or not n is an ancestor label path number of m. Then we can find all the label path numbers of b that satisfy a//b. As for a*b, the handling process is as follows. Firstly get the label path numbers of b. Next, compute label path numbers of the parent node. Finally, find this number in the set of label path numbers of a to validate a*b.

5.2 Tree Pattern Query

The existing structural join approaches to handle tree pattern query break up a complete tree pattern query into simple paths and then merge all these simple query results. Our method is to get one branch label path number and, based on branching point and related information, compute other branch label path number and then get final query results.

Algorithm 3 can handle tree pattern queries with two branches. As for more complex tree pattern queries, such as the query with more than 3 branches, we can extend this algorithm to support them.

Algorithm 3. Algorithm for tree pattern query
Input: A tree pattern query Q.
Output: The target element list, represented by (LPNum, DPNum ,IX).
1. If (Q has not value prediction) then
2.   Get $LPNum_1$
3.   Get $LPNum_2$
4.   Get $[DPNum_1]$
5.   Get $[DPNum_2]$
6.   fetch each ($DPNum_1$, $DPNum_2$) from $[DPNum_1]$ and $[DPNum_2]$
7.   If CC($DPNum_1$, $DPNum_2$) then output
8. else
9.   Select path with value predication
10.   Get $LPNum_1$
11.   Get $LPNum_2$
12.   Get $[DPNum_1]$
13.   Compute $[DPNum_2, DPNum_2']$
14.   Fetch each ($DPNum_1$, $DPNum_2$) from $[DPNum_1]$ and $[DPNum_2]$
15.   If VIValidate ($DPNum_2$) then output
16. end if

In Algorithm 3, with Row 2 and 3, we get the label path numbers by Hash table. The following step is to get a list of data path numbers. Because the query has no value indices, all the elements in the list are likely valid. Two lists are obtained after Row 4 and 5 are implemented. The last job is to merge the two lists. At this point, most of structural merging algorithms can be adopted. However because a data path number encodes the information of a rooted data path, we choose the semi-join algorithm to accelerate the merging process. From Row 9 to Row 15, we handle the tree pattern query with value predictions. In Row 9, a branch is selected from the query, and the selecting process is as follows:

- If only one of two branches has value prediction, then this branch is selected;
- If both of two branches have value prediction, and then the longer path is selected.

Now we have label path numbers of leaf node of this branch. The coming row 12 is different from Row 4. After executing Row 4, all data path numbers pointed by LPNum1 will be returned whereas only those numbers satisfying the value predications are returned after executing Row 12. This can avoid a lot of unnecessary path join operations. Furthermore, unlike the previous algorithm, we can compute data path numbers of the leaf node of other branch instead of joining all data path numbers pointer by $LPNum_2$. The principle of computing data path number is that if two data path numbers are connected by the branch point, then two data path numbers must possess the same prefix which the data path number of the node of the branch point. If both of two branches have value predications, then we need another value index checking process, which is the main job of the last step from Row 14 and 15.

6 Experiments

We implemented our index structure and query algorithm in C++. The XML parser is the Xerces SAX2 parser [26]. The B+Tree API is provided by the Berkeley DB library [19]. Experiments were run on a P4 1.8 GHz CPU PC with 256M main memories, running Windows 2000 Server. We also implemented a node index method similar to XISS [5], but with TwigStack [24] query algorithm on this node index. In addition, we ran ViST [13] on this PC machine for the purpose of comparison.

The data sets in experiments have public XML databases DBLP [20] and the XML benchmark database XMARK [21].

Table 4. Characteristics

Document	Nodes	Characters	Spaces	Size (M)
DBLP	1906219	11660704	61485	46.6
DBLP	5920583	95266119	5384135	197
DBLP	6391621	103717843	5817551	209
XMark	2048193	81286567	0	117
XMark	9621573	398304178	0	

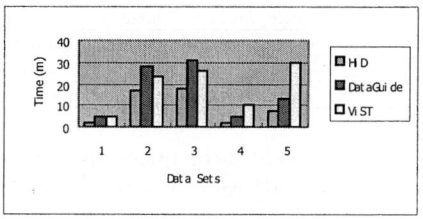

Fig. 6. Index Constructing Time

We firstly look at index constructing time of different approaches and storage requirement of index structure. The Fig 6 shows the index constructing time of different approaches.

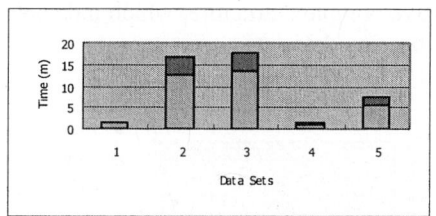

Fig. 7. Time of Different Phase

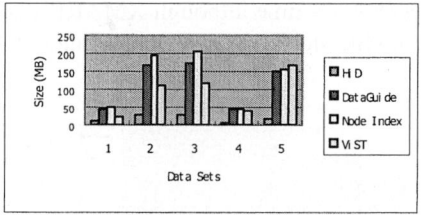

Fig. 8. Storage Requirements

As can be seen in Fig. 6, index constructing time required with our approach is the least. For large documents, we still can construct our index structure in less time. The index constructing time of node index is absent in Fig. 6 since some tasks of construct process are done by manual.

We also compare time needed for our index constructing process in two phases. The result is shown in Fig. 7. The blue bars indicate time consumed in the first phase. The red parts at the top of blue bars show time consumed in the second phase. It is obvious that we need much more time in the first phase.

The storage requirement of different approaches is shown in Fig. 8. From this figure, we can know that the occupied space for our index structure is the least among the mentioned approaches. Especially for large documents, storage requirement of our index structure is very litter.

Table 5. Queries

Queries	Data Sets
Q1: /inproceedings/title	DBLP
Q2: /*/author="David"	DBLP
Q3://item/description/keyword="attries"	XMARK
Q4:/site/person/city="New Work"	XMARK
Q5:/ariticle[./author="David"][./year=1996]	DBLP
Q6:/proceedings[./title="XML"][.//author="David"]	DBLP
Q7:/site/item[./location="USA"][./mail]	XMARK
Q8://closed auction[./seller/person="person1"][./date="12/12/2002"]	XMARK

Now we analyze the query performance. Table 5 lists 8 queries. These queries are significantly different in terms of complexity, presence of values and structure. We choose four of these queries to run on DBLP data set with size 197MB. Other 4 queries are run on XMARK data set with size 117MB. Because DataGuide cannot answer tree pattern query directly, we do not run query5-query8 by DataGuide.

Fig. 9 shows the elapsed time for query 1 to query 4 running by different approaches. From this figure, we know that HiD and TwigStack yield comparable performance. The most significant performance difference is between query 3 and 4. For path pattern query, most of time for our approach is spent on merging output lists. At this point, TwigStack costs as much time as HiD. HiD and TwigStack need not much extra time although XMARK data sets have complex structure, which indicates that HiD and TwigStack can efficiently query complex data sets.

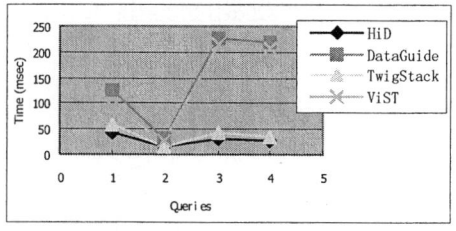
Fig. 9. Elapsed time for Query1- 4

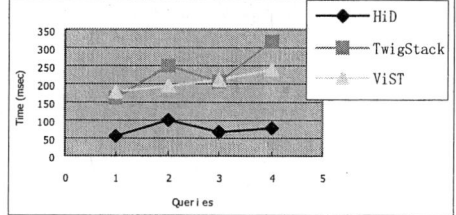
Fig. 10. Elapsed time for Query5 –8

The performances of query 5 to query 8 are shown in Fig. 10. It is obvious that HiD performs much better than TwigStack and ViST for all tree pattern queries. For complex queries, we can find necessary nodes by computing label path and data path numbers. In this way, we reduce many unnecessary nodes.

7 Conclusions and Future Work

In this paper, we present a new efficient node identification approach and construct an index structure based on this kind of identification called HiD. We also discuss some properties related to our method. For the path pattern query, our querying algorithm avoids join operations. We provide some experimental results to demonstrate the efficiency of our approach.

Actually, the node identification can be used not only to construct HiD index structure and query approach, but also to construct other query approaches such as the sequence matching approach. We are going to develop a sequence matching approach based on our node identification. We also would like to optimize our query algorithms and analyze the time and space complexity in the future.

Acknowledgement

We thank Dr. Haixun Wang in IBM Thomas J. Watson Research Center, for providing the ViST system.

References

[1] Paul F. Dietz. Maintaining order in a linked list. In Proceedings of the Fourteenth Annual ACM Symposium on Theory of Computing, pages 122-127, San Francisco, California, 5-7 May 1982.
[2] R.Sacks-Davis, T.Dao, J.A. Thom, J.Zobel. Indexing Documents for Queries on Structure, Content and Attributes. Proc. of International Symposium on Digital Media Information Base (DMIB), Nara, Japan, pages 236–245, 1997.
[3] C. L. A. Clarke, G. V. Cormack, and F. J. Burkowski. An algebra for structured text search and a framework for its implementation. The Computer Journal, 38(1):43-56 1995.
[4] D. D. Kha, M. Yoshikawa, S. Uemura. An XML Indexing Structure with Relative Region Coordinate.In Proceedings of the 17th ICDE, pages 313-320. Heidelberg, Germany, April, 2001.
[5] Q. Li and B. Moon. Indexing and querying XML data for regular path expressions. In Proceedings of the 27th VLDB, pages 361-370. Roma, Italy, September 2001.
[6] C. Zhang, J. F. Naughton, D. J. DeWitt, Q. Luo, and G. M. Lohman. On supporting containment queries in relational database management systems. In Proceedings of the 27th ACM SIGMOD, pages 425-436. Santa Barbara, California, USA, May 2001.
[7] W. Wang. H. Jiang, H. Lu and J. X. Yu. PbiTree Coding and Efficient Processing of Containment Join. In Proceedings of 19th ICDE, pages 391-402. 2003.
[8] Al-Khalifa et al. Structural Joins: A Primitive for Efficient XML Query Pattern Matching. In Proc. of ICDE, San Jose, Feb. 2002.
[9] S.-Y. Chien, Z. Vagena, D. Zhang, V. J. Tsotras, and C. Zaniolo. Efficient structural joins on indexed XML documents. In Proceedings of the 28th VLDB Conference, Hong Kog, China, August 2002.
[10] Alan Halverson, Josef Burger, etc. Mixed Mode XML Query Processing. In Proceedings of the 29th VLDB, pages 361-370. Berlin, Germany, 2003.

[11] Roy Goldman, Jennifer Widom. DataGuides: Enabling Query Formulation and Optimization in Semistructured Databases. In Proceedings of the 23rd VLDB Conference Athens, Greece, 1997
[12] Jan Marco Bremer and Michael Gertz. An Efficient XML Node Identification and Indexing Scheme. Teach report. Department of Computer Science University of California, Davis. Jan.27 2003.
[13] Haixun Wang 1Sanghyun Park Wei Fan Philip S. Yu. ViST: A Dynamic Index Method for Querying XML Data by Tree Structures. In SIGMOD 2003.
[14] D. Chamberlin, D. Florescu, J. Robie, J. Simon, and M. Stefanescu. XQuery: A query language for XML. W3C working draft. Technical Report WD-xquery-20010215, World Wide Web Consortium, 2001.
[15] D. Chamberlin, J. Robie, and D. Florescu. Quilt: An XML query language for heterogeneous data sources. In WebDB, May 2000.
[16] J. Clark and S. DeRose. XML path language (XPath) version 1.0 w3c recommendation. Technical Report REC-xpath-19991116, World Wide Web Consortium, 1999.
[17] Edith Cohen, Haim Kaplan, and Tova Milo. Labeling dynamic XML trees. In PODS, pages 271-281, 2002.
[18] Zhang et al. On Supporting Containment Queries in Relational Database Management Systems, SIGMOD Conference, 2001.
[19] Sleepycat Software, http://www.sleepycat.com. The Berkeley Database (Berkeley DB).
[20] Michael Ley. DBLP database web site. http://www.informatik.uni-trier.de/ ley/db.
[21] XMARK: The XML-benchmark project. http://monetdb.cwi.nl/ xml.
[22] Praveen Rao and Bongki Moon PRIX: Indexing And Querying XML Using Prufer Sequences. In ICDE'2004 March 2004.
[23] H.Jiang, H.Lu, W.Wang and B.C.Ooi. XR-Tree:indexing XML Data for Efficent Structural Joins. In ICDE, 2003.
[24] N.Bruno, N.Koudas, D.Srivastava. Holistic Twig Joins: Optimal XML Pattern Matching. In SIGMOD 2002.
[25] H.Jiang, W.Wang, H.Lu. Holistic Twig Joins on Indexed XML Documents. In VLDB 2003.
[26] SAX (Simple API for XML). http://sax.sourceforge.net.

XQuery-Based TV-Anytime Metadata Management

Jong-Hyun Park[1], Byung-Kyu Kim[2], Yong-Hee Lee[3],
Min-Woo Lee[4], Min-Ok Jung[1], and Ji-Hoon Kang[1,*]

[1] Dept. of Computer Science, Chung Nam National University,
Gung-Dong, Yuseong-Gu, Daejeon, 305-764, South Korea
{jhpark, ultra999, jhkang}@cs.cnu.ac.kr
[2] Korea institute of Science and Technology Information,
Eoun-Dong, Yuseong-Gu, Daejeon, 305-806, South Korea
yourovin@kisti.re.kr
[3] Electronics and Telecommunications Research Institute,
Gajeong-Dong, Yuseong-Gu, Daejeon, 305-350, South Korea
lyhcool@etri.re.kr
[4] Power Plant S/W Business Team, Korea Electric Power Data Network Co. Ltd.
Seocho2-Dong, Seocho-Gu, Seoul, 137-072, South Korea
cslmw@hanmir.com

Abstract. Digital broadcasting is a novel paradigm for the next generation broadcasting. It can offer a new opportunity for interactive services such as content-based browsing, non-linear navigation, usage of user preference, and history, etc. On the other hand, one of the important factors for this new broadcasting environment is the interoperability among providers and consumers since the environment is distributed. Therefore a standard metadata for digital broadcasting is required and TV-Anytime metadata is one of the metadata standards for digital broadcasting. It is defined using XML schema, so its instances are XML data. In order to fulfill interoperability, a standard query language is also required and XQuery, which is a forthcoming standard query language for XML data, is a natural choice. In this paper we propose an efficient XML data management system that supports TV-Anytime metadata, especially using XQuery as a query language. Since the volume of metadata would be very large in real situation, our system considers a relational database system as storage. We implement a prototype system and test performance for various typical queries by comparing our system with other general-purpose systems.

1 Introduction

Digital broadcasting is a novel paradigm for the next generation broadcasting. Its goal is to provide not only better quality of pictures but also a variety of services which are impossible in traditional airwaves broadcasting. In order to support new services such as content-based browsing, non-linear navigation, usage of user preference, and history, on-demand service, etc. [1], we need a metadata description for these information and should support management of the metadata. On the other hand, one of the

---

* He is a corresponding author.

important factors for this new broadcasting environment is the interoperability among providers and consumers since the environment is distributed. Therefore a standard metadata for digital broadcasting is required and TV-Anytime metadata [2] that is proposed by the TV-Anytime Forum is one of the metadata standards for digital broadcasting [3]. The TV-Anytime metadata is technically defined using a single XML schema, so its instances are XML data. In order to fulfill interoperability, a standard query language is also required and XQuery [4], which is a forthcoming standard query language for accessing XML data, is a natural choice.

In this paper we propose an efficient metadata management system that supports TV-Anytime metadata, especially using XQuery as a query language. Since the volume of metadata for digital broadcasting would be very large in real situation, we consider a relational database system as storage. There are some issues for managing XML data using relational databases efficiently:

- *How to store XML data into a relational database system?* XML data are semi-structured but relational databases are structured. A mapping from semi-structured data into a structured data is required for supporting efficient storage and retrieval. We also need to have a labeling mechanism in order to preserve the original document order. The label information is useful for searching and required for publishing query results.

- *How to reduce join cost when processing queries?* When a query has a long path for identifying nodes over XML instances, its processing can require many joins. For efficient processing, we need to reduce overall join cost.

- *How to transform the SQL query answers into the answesr of the original XQuery queries for returning the final results back to users?* The time for reconstructing answers depends on quires, but this job is quite time-consuming. Therefore we need a method that is less dependent on query types.

For each issue, there have been several previous work [5, 6, 7, 8, 9, 10, 11, 12, 13, 14, 15, 16, 17, 18]. In this paper, however, we try to show what the best strategy is for each issue when the strategies are integrated into a single system altogether. In order to identify whether our choice of the strategies for the issues is relevant, we compare our prototype system with other general-purpose systems and test their performance for various typical queries.

The remainder of this paper is organized as follows. Section 2 describes the architecture of the Metadata Management System for digital broadcasting. Section 3 describes our approach for managing TV-Anytime metadata. Section 4 shows the result of the performance evaluation for our system. Section 5 explains how our system has been applied to a digital broadcasting environment. Finally, Section 6 provides concluding remarks.

2 TV-Anytime Metadata Management System

The TV-Anytime Metadata Management system keeps the metadata in large-volume storage and processes queries for searching the metadata. Figure 1 shows the architecture of the TV-Anytime Metadata Management system.

We assume three user interface modules for our system, Metadata Generator, Metadata Editor, and Metadata Finder. They are generic and can be replaced by appropriate modules in real situation. Metadata Generator generates TV-Anytime metadata instances and stores them in the storage. Metadata Editor can retrieve, update, and delete a metadata instance. Metadata Finder gives a query into the system for searching the TV-Anytime metadata and gets back the query result from the system.

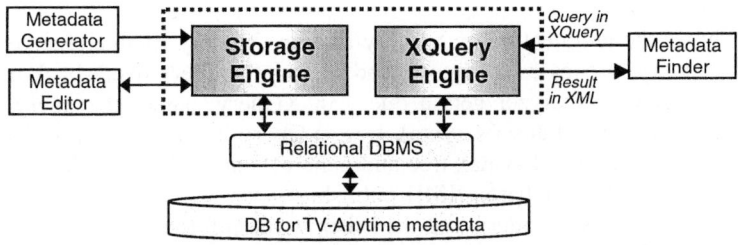

Fig. 1. TV-Anytime Metadata Management System

There are two important modules in the system, Storage Engine and XQuery Engine. Storage Engine interacts with Metadata Generator and Metadata Editor for storing and managing metadata. XQuery Engine interacts with Metadata Finder for processing queries. As we have already mentioned in Section 1, we use the XQuery as a standard query language in order to guarantee interoperability.

2.1 Storage Engine

As shown in Figure 2, Storage Engine provides basically four interfaces: InsertDoc, DeleteDoc, UpdateDoc, and GetDoc for inserting, deleting, updating, and retrieving a metadata instance, respectively.

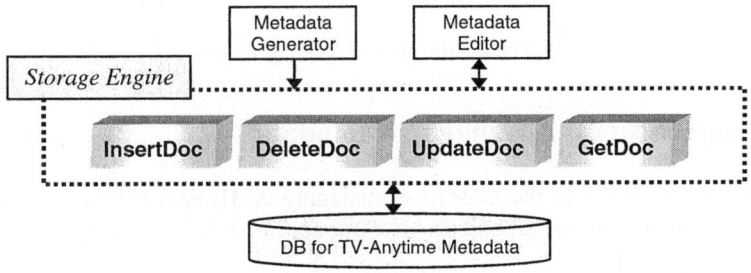

Fig. 2. The architecture of Storage Engine

When receiving a metadata instance from Metadata Generator or Metadata Editor, InsertDoc parses it and generates a DOM Tree. InsertDoc extracts both the content and structural information from the DOM Tree and stores the extracted information to the database. For identifying TV-Anytime metadata instances, we use CRID (Content

Reference ID). A unique CRID is given to each instance. DeleteDoc gets a CRID as an input and deletes the metadata instance with the given CRID. UpdateDoc gets a new metadata instance as an input. It replaces the old instance with the new one. That is, it deletes the old one with the given CRID and then inserts the new one. GetDoc gets the metadata instance with the CRID received from Metadata Editor.

2.2 XQuery Engine

Figure 3 shows the architecture of XQuery Engine. XQuery Engine receives a query written in XQuery, processes the query, and returns the query result back into Metadata Finder. XQuery Analyzer gets a query in XQuery, parses the query using an XQuery parser and generates its syntax tree. XQuery Translator extracts necessary information from the parsed syntax tree and generates an SQL query for querying the metadata stored in the database. XML publisher gets two inputs from the XQuery translator. One is the SQL query and the other is the information for reconstruction the result in XML format. Actually XQuery Translator obtains the information for reconstructing from the RETURN clause of the original XQuery query. Then the XQuery Publisher accesses the TV-Anytime metadata database to get the SQL result set and reconstructs an XML instance that satisfies the return structure described in the RETURN clause. Finally, Metadata Finder receives the reconstructed XML instance.

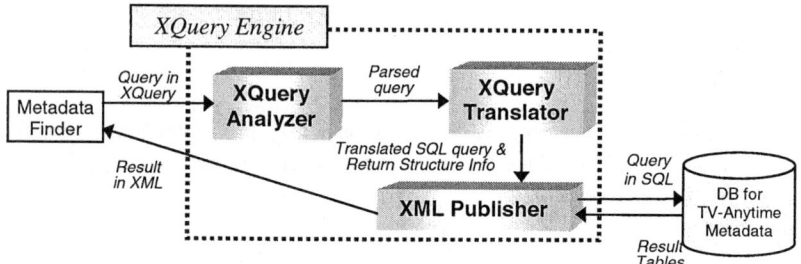

Fig 3. The architecture of XQuery Engine

3 The Approaches for Managing Metadata

In Section 1, we referred to the issues for managing XML data efficiently. Now we discuss each issue in more detail and propose our approach for solving them.

3.1 How to Store XML Data into a Relational Database System

In order to accommodate a large volume of metadata, we use a relational database system. There could be some other choices. For example, file systems, XML-native systems, XML-enabled systems, and Object-oriented database systems, etc. File systems are not appropriate for large-volume data. XML-native systems support only XML data and can be efficient for managing XML data itself. However, they cannot support other data types and thus cannot accommodate legacy non-XML data. XML-enabled systems are basically the existing database systems that support XML data additionally. They are general-purpose systems and are less efficient in performance. This can also be shown from our performance test in Section 4. Object-oriented database systems are not mature enough to process complex queries on large databases efficiently so far [7].

The problem for storing XML data into relational databases is how to map the tree structures into relational tables. There are several methods for resolving this problem [5, 6, 7, 10, 13, 15]. For our system, we take the binary approach [7]. The binary approach groups all the element nodes with the same label into one table.

The Binary approach has several merits for our system. First, we can easily map the tree structures into relational tables since every element type is mapped into its corresponding table. Moreover our system considers only one XML schema, TV-Anytime metadata schema, so that the system knows the entire tables in advance before storing data. Second, the binary approach can reduce data redundancy against other approaches [7]. Of course we could consider the edge approach, which stores all the elements and attributes into one relational table. The edge approach does not need to consider XML schemas so that it can be useful when a system should consider XML data from many schemas or even well-formed XML data with no schema.

Another thing to be considered is how to preserve the original document order when an XML document is stored into relational tables. This is important since we need to reconstruct original document from the databases. The basic idea is to give a unique label to each node in a document. There have been several labeling methods for this purpose [10, 15, 17, 18]. We adopt the Dewey order labeling [10].

The Dewey order labeling represents the path from the document's root to the element node by using the Dewey Decimal Classification. The root has the label '1'. Its first child has the label '1.1', its second child '1.2', and so on. The first child of the node labeled with '1.2' has the label '1.2.1', the second child '1.2.2', and so on. The element table in Figure 4 shows the labels in the fields 'ID_TITLE' and 'ID_PROGEAMINFORMATION'.

When a node is inserted or deleted, the Dewey order labeling requires re-labeling for all the descendents of the node and for the subtrees of its right siblings. For our system, however, the main jobs are searching so that the metadata is assumed not be modified so frequently. Moreover, the Dewey order labeling generally shows better searching performance than other labeling methods [10].

3.2 How to Reduce Join Cost

One of the main problems when processing queries in XQuery is how to reduce the number of joins, especially when queries have many long XPath expressions. The binary approach itself does not give any benefit to reduce number of joins. If the length of a path expression for specifying a set of nodes is N, we need $N-1$ joins. For our system, we adopt the path table concept [15] for reducing the number of joins.

The path table stores all the full paths from the root element to all the element nodes in every XML instances. Our path table has two fields. One is the path id. The other is the path itself. Every element table has a field for the reference to the path id. If we want to find nodes from the element E specified by a path expression, we search the path table to get a path id p for the given path expression. Then we access the table for the element *E* and select the rows with the path id *p*. Each row becomes a candidate that satisfies the path expression. Consequently we do not need any join between any two element tables to get the candidate rows. Therefore we can avoid many joins.

Figure 4 shows 'Path' table, 'Doc' table, and two Element tables. 'Doc' table stores the metadata XML instances as CLOB. Each entry represents one instance. Each of the two element tables stores the information for 'ProgramInformation' element and 'Title' element, respectively. Note that the former is an internal node in TV-Anytime metadata, ant the latter is a leaf node.

Figure 5 shows a query written in XQuery (line 1 to 9) and its translated SQL query (line 10 to 22). The XPath expressions from line 15 to 18 are constructed from

ID_Path	PathExp
1	TVAMain
2	TVAMain/ProgramDescription
...	...
6	TVAMain/ProgramDescription/ProgramInformationTable/ProgramInformation
7	TVAMain/ProgramDescription/ProgramInformationTable/ProgramInformation/BasicDescription
8	TVAMain/ProgramDescription/ProgramInformationTable/ProgramInformation/BasicDescription/Title
9	TVAMain/ProgramDescription/ProgramInformationTable/ProgramInformation/BasicDescription/Synopsis

'Path' Table

ID_DOC	CRID	CONTENT
1	Crid://...1	...
2	Crid://...2	...

'Doc' Table

ID_DOC	ID_TITLE	ID_Path	TITLE
1	1.1.1.1.1	8	navy
1	1.1.1.2.1	8	love story
2	1.1.1.1.1	8	navy

'TITLE' Element Table

ID_DOC	ID_PROGRAMINFORMATION	ID_Path	POSITION
1	1.1.1.1	6	789, 650
2	1.1.1.1	6	870, 690

'PROGRAMINFORMATION' Element Table

Fig. 4. The relationship of element, Doc and Path table

```
1: <Results>{ for $d in input("TVAnyTime") return <Result>{
2: distinct-values(
3:   for $p1 in $d0/TVAMain/ProgramDescription/..../ProgramInformation
4:   for $p2 in $p1/BasicDescription
5:   for $p3 in $p2/Title
6:   for $p4 in $p2/Synopsis
7:   where contains(string($p3), "navy") and contains(string($p4), "fight")
8:   return $p1 )
9: }</Result> }</Results>
10: SELECT DISTINCT ProgramInformation.id_ProgramInformation,
11: ProgramInformation.Position
12: FROM Title, Synopsis, BasicDescription, Path Path0, Path Path1, ProgramInformation
13: WHERE Title.Title like '%navy%'
14:   AND Title.id_Path = Path0.id_Path
15:   AND Path0.Pathexp = '/TVAMain/ProgramDescription/..../BasicDescription/Title'
16:   AND Synopsis.Synopsis like '%fight%'
17:   AND Synopsis.id_Path = Path1.id_Path
18:   AND Path1.Pathexp ='/TVAMain/ProgramDescription/./BasicDescription/Synopsis'
19:   AND Title.id_Title like BasicDescription.id_BasicDescription || '%'
20:   AND Synopsis.id_Synopsis like BasicDescription.id_BasicDescription || '%'
21:   AND BasicDescription.id_BasicDescription like  ProgramInformation.id_ProgramInformation || '%'
```

Fig. 5. An XQuery query and its translated SQL query

the FOR clauses in the line 3 to 6 of the XQuery query. If there is an abbreviated XPath expression in an XQuery query, the XPath expression for the translated SQL query will be expressed using the 'like' operator. The conditions for searching the same ancestors in the SQL query (line 19 to 21) are expressed as the comparisons between Dewey order labels so that no direct comparison between XPath expressions is required. The table names in the FROM clause of the SQL query come from the leaf node names of the XPath expressions in the XQuery query, which are Synopsis, Title, BasicDescription, and ProgramInformation. The SELECT clause (line 10) of the SQL query is generated from the RETURN clause (line 8) of the XQuery query.

3.3 How to Reconstruct the Answer of the Original XQuery Query

A new structure for the query result is described in the RETURN clause of an XQuery query. The reconstruction of XML data as a query result yields another performance issue for XQuery processing. The query result will become subtrees of the original data stored in the databases or a combination of subtrees. The problem is that we need join operations to get a subtree from the database. If the result subtree is larger, we need more number of joins. If the subtree is a leaf node, it can be obtained directly from the table for that node without any join. If the subtree is a whole document, many joins can be required. Note that the path table is not helpful for reducing joins during reconstruction although it can be helpful for searching.

In order to resolve this problem, we store every metadata instance as a CLOB. For each element node, we get both the starting and ending position from its corresponding CLOB instance, and store the pair of these position values into the corresponding row of the corresponding table. By doing so, when a subtree is required for reconstruction we can obtain the subtree from CLOB instance using the position pair without any join. Note that if the node is a leaf we do not store the position pair since the node can be obtained directly from the corresponding table.

Storing CLOB instances requires more storage volume. This problem can be ignored since the storage can be considered not so expensive. Another problem is the integrity since we store the same data twice. If an update occurs in the database, we should delete the old CLOB instance and insert the new one. Note that our approach puts an emphasis on search and retrieval.

Figure 4 shows that 'content' field in Doc table stores CLOB instances. Also 'ProgramInformation' Table for internal element node shows the 'position' field. 'Title' table has no the 'position' field since this table is for leaf nodes.

4 Performance Evaluation

In order to evaluate whether our choice of the strategies for the issues is relevant, we compare our prototype system with other general-purpose systems and test their performance for various typical queries. We select two popular general-purpose database systems. One, which is a XML-native system, is eXcelon DXE Manager Version 3.1 SP2. The other, which is an XML-enabled system, is Oracle9i. There are two ways for storing XML data in the Oracle9i system [16]. The first way is to register XML schema and then to store XML data. The second way is to store XML data just by using XML type with no schema. In this test, we only compare the result evaluated by the second way since the result from the first way is similar to the one from the eXcelon system. The experimental setup is as follows: the CPU is Intel Pentium 4 Processor 2.8 GHz, the memory size is 1024 MB, and the OS is Windows XP.

Table 1. XPath expression for experiment

Query	XPath condition / Return value
	XPath Expression
Q1	One full path expression, One string comparison / One leaf element
	/TVAMain/ProgramDescription/ProgramInformationTable/ProgramInformation[@programId='crid://www.arirang.co.kr/BBCWorldNews103040600117']/BasicDescription/Title
Q2	One full path expression, One string comparison / One internal element
	/TVAMain/ProgramDescription/ProgramInformationTable/ProgramInformation[@programId='crid://www.arirang.co.kr/BBCWorldNews103040600117']
Q3	One full path expression, One string comparison / Multiple root elements
	/TVAMain[ProgramDescription/ProgramInformationTable/ProgramInformation/BasicDescription/Title[contains(text(),'bbc')]]
Q4	Six abbreviated path expressions, Three string comparisons / One leaf element
	/TVAMain//ProgramInformation[.//BasicDescription//Name[contains(text(), 'news')] and .//Synopsis[contains(text(), 'bbc')] and .//Language[contains(text(), 'ko')]]//Title
Q5	Six abbreviated path expressions, Three string comparisons / Multiple internal elements
	//ProgramDescription//ProgramInformation[.//BasicDescription//Name[contains(text(),'news')] and .//Synopsis[contains(text(), 'bbc')] and .//Language[contains(text(), 'ko')]]
Q6	Seven abbreviated path expressions, Five string comparisons / Multiple root elements
	/TVAMain[.//ProgramInformation//DayAndYear[contains(text(),'2003')] and .//ProgramInformationTable[.//BasicDescription/Synopsis[contains(text(), 'bbc')] and .//Language[contains(text(),'ko')] and .//Name[contains(text(),'news')] and .//ProductionLocation[contains(text(), 'ko')]]]
Q7	One full path expression, One string comparison / Multiple root elements (Large volume)
	/TVAMain[ProgramDescription/ProgramInformationTable/ProgramInformation/BasicDescription/Genre/Name[contains(text(), 'drama')]]

Our system uses XQuery, which is a super set of XPath. However, eXcelon and Oracle9i do not support XQuery yet. They support only XPath. By this reason, we select the testing queries written only in XPath. Oracle9i uses XPath expressions embedded within SQL statement. We have written the queries for Oracle9i carefully so that the semantic meaning is the same as the queries for the other systems. From the previous work [6, 7, 10, 13, 15], we have found that the query processing performance can depend on the XPath expression, number of predicates, and result size. By considering these factors, we use the XPath expressions in Table 1 as sample queries for our experiment.

The characteristics of the sample queries in Table 1 are as follows. The queries Q1, Q2 and Q3 use the same XPath expression and the same predicate condition. However, the result data sizes are expected different because the result of each query is a leaf node, an internal node, and root nodes together with their descendent nodes, respectively. Q4, Q5 and Q6 use different abbreviated XPath expressions and predicates. The return value of each query is a leaf node, internal nodes, and root nodes, respectively. Q7 returns the large volume metadata instances.

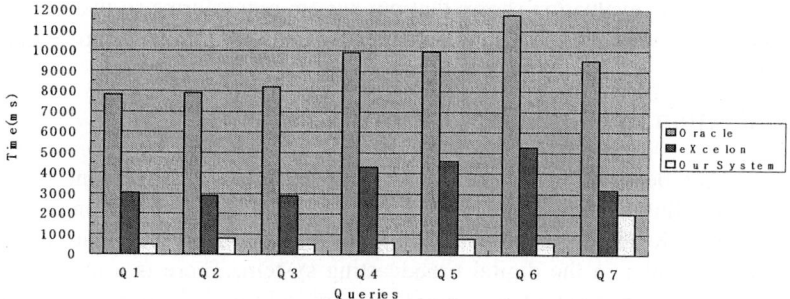

Fig. 6. Comparison of query processing times

Figure 6 summarizes the performance. The size of the test metadata is 10MB. The result shows that our system outperforms other methods for any queries except Q7. In case of eXcelon and Oracle9i, the complex queries Q4, Q5, and Q6, takes more execution time than the simple query Q1, Q2, and Q3. However, our system does not so depend on the queries. In case of our system, Q7 takes more execution time than the other queries since we need more time to get CLOB instances from the databases and to convert CLOB type into string type.

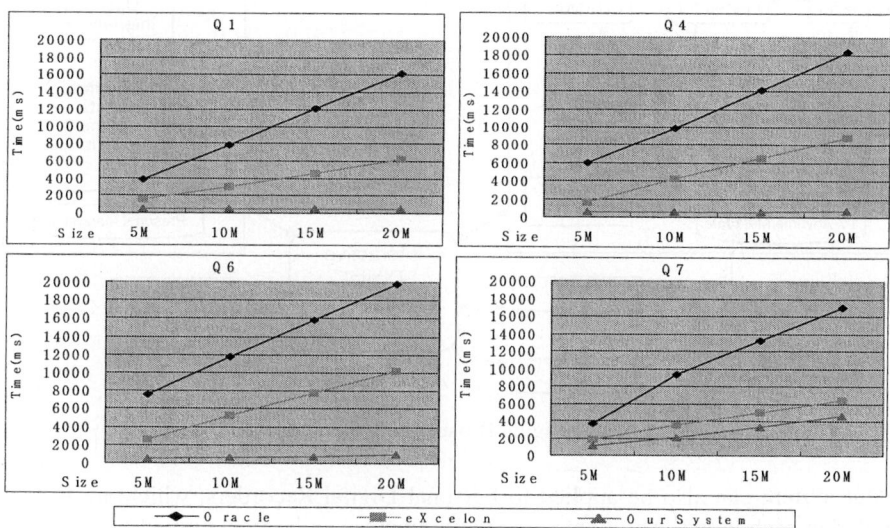

Fig. 7. Performance evaluation for scalability property

Figure 7 shows the scalability property of the systems. The size of the test data is 5M Bytes(about 400 documents), 10M (about 800), 15M (about 1500) and 20M (about 2000), respectively. In case of eXcelon and Oracle9i, the processing time increases linearly as the size of data increases. However, the processing time of our system is independent of the data size for searching.

The result of the evaluation shows that our system outperforms so that our approach is believed to be one of the efficient approaches for managing TV-Anytime metadata.

5 Application to Digital Broadcasting Systems

Our system has been applied as a TV-Anytime metadata management system to a digital broadcasting system which has been developed by the Electronics and Telecommunications Research Institute [19]. Figure 8 shows the architecture of the Content Service Provider in the digital broadcasting system. There is a user interface to access TV-Anytime metadata and content. It seems a little difficult for any user to use XQuery language directly for searching. To overcome this problem, we have designed an easy-to-use interface component which transforms the user search requirements into XQuery queries automatically. Since we are adopting a standard metadata and a standard query, we are able to send any query to other Content Service Providers and to get query results from them if the Content Service Providers support both the TV-Anytime Metadata and the XQuery language.

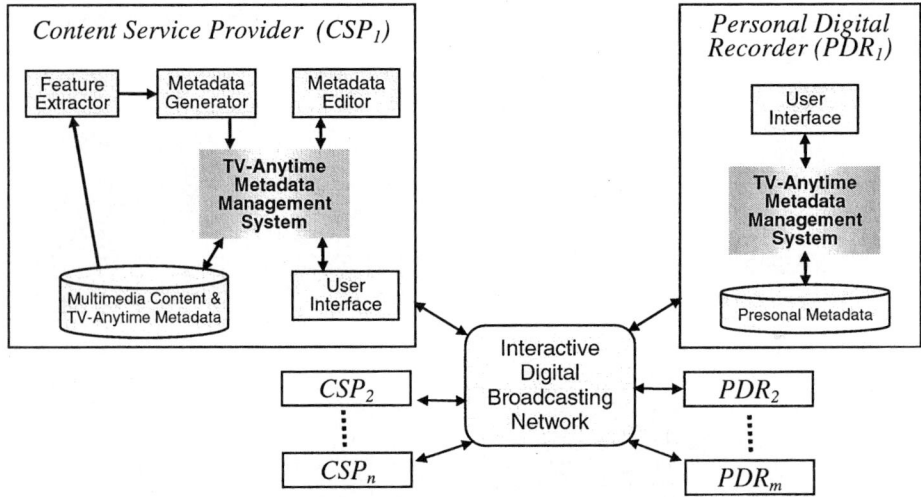

Fig. 8. Digital Broadcasting Sysstem

Our system can also be applied to Personal Digital Recorders, which are usually installed at each home. Any home user requirements can be transformed into XQuery queries and sent for searching over the broadcasting environment including Content Service Providers. Of course, each Personal Digital Recorder will manage its own local TV-Anytime metadata.

6 Conclusion

In this paper, we have proposed an efficient system for managing TV-Anytime metadata. We have identified some important issues regarding performance and have proposed our approach, which seems important since our prototype system outperforms the other compared systems. We have also shown that our system has been applied to a digital broadcasting environment. Of course, our result can be applied to any XML management systems that focus on the performance of search and retrieval. Current other existing systems do not support XQuery language. We need more evaluation after some systems are available.

Acknowledgement

This work was partly supported by BK21 Human Resource Development Consortium for Information Technology and by Software Research Center of Chungnam National University.

References

1. S. Pfeiffer & U. Srinivasan: TV Anytime as an application scenario for MPEG-7. In Proc. ACM Multimedia 2000, Los Angeles, October (2000).
2. TV Anytime Specification Series, August 2001. (http://www.tv-anytime.org/)
3. Advanced Television Systems Committee(ATSC) Standards. (http://www.atsc.org).
4. W3C, XQuery 1.0: An XML Query Language, Working Draft, November (2003). (http://www.w3.org/TR/2003/WD-xquery-20031112/)
5. A. Deutsch, M. Fernandez, & D. Suciu: Storing Semistructured Data with STORED. In Proc. ACM SIGMOD, Philadelphia, Pennsylvania, USA, June (1999).
6. A. Schmidt, M. Kersten, M. Windhouwer, & F. Waas: Efficient Relational Storage and Retrieval of XML Documents. In Proc. WEBDB 2000, Dallas, May (2000).
7. D. Florescu & D. Kossmann: Storing and Querying XML Data Using an RDBMS. IEEE Data Engineering Bulletin, Vol. 22, No. 3, (1999).
8. D. Scheffner & J.-C. Freytag: The XML Query Execution Engine (XEE). In Proc. BalticDB&IS 2002, Tallinn, Estonia, June (2002).
9. I. Manolescu, D Florescu, & D. Kossmann: Pushing XML Queries inside Relational Databases. INRIA Technical Report, INRIA, No. 4112, January (2001).
10. I. Tatarinov, S.D.Viglas, K.Beyer, J.Shanmugasundaram, E.Shekita & C.Zhang: Storing and Querying Ordered XML Using a Relational Database System. In Proc. ACM SIGMOD, Madison, Wisconsin, June (2002).
11. J. McHugh, S. Abiteboul, R. Goldman, D. Quass & J. Widon: Lore: A Database Management System for Semi-structured Data. ACM SIGMOD Record Vol. 26, No.3, September (1997).
12. J. Shanmugasundaram, J. Kiernan, E. Shekita, C. Fan & J. Funderburk: Querying XML Views of Relational Data. In Proc. 27th VLDB, Roma, Italy, September (2001).
13. J.Shanmugasundaram, K.Tufte, G.He, C.Zhang, D.DeWitt & J.Naughton: Relational Databases for Querying XML Documents: Limitations and Opportunities. In Proc. 25th VLDB, Edinburg, Scotland, September (1999).
14. M. Carey, J. Kiernan, J. Shanmugasundaram, E. Shekita & S. Subramanian: XPERANTO: Middleware for Publishing Object-Relational Data as XML Documents. In Proc. VLDB 2000, September (2000).

15. M.Yoshikawa, T.Amagasa, T.Shimura, & S.Uemura: XRel: a path-based approach to storage and retrieval of XML documents using relational databases. ACM Transactions on Internet Technology, Vol. 1, Issue 1, pp. 110~141, August. (2001).
16. S. Banerjee, V. Krishnamurthy, M. Krishnaprasad & R. Murthy: Oracle8i - The XML Enabled Data Management System. In Proc. ICDE 2000, San Diego, California, USA, March (2000).
17. Q. Li & B. Moon: Indexing and Querying XML data for Regular Path Expressions. In Proc. VLDB 2001, Roma, Italy. September (2001).
18. X. Wu, M. L. Lee & W. Hsu: A Prime Number Labeling Scheme for Dynamic Ordered XML Trees. In Proc. ICDE 2004, Boston, USA. March (2004).
19. K. Kang, J. G. Kim, H. K. Lee, H. S. Chang, S. J. Yang, Y. T. Kim, H. K. Lee & J. W. Kim: Metadata Broadcasting for Personalized Service: a Practical Solution. ETRI Journal, Vol.26, No.5, pp.452-466, October (2004).

Effective Database Transformation and Efficient Support Computation for Mining Sequential Patterns

Chung-Wen Cho[1], Yi-Hung Wu[1], and Arbee L.P. Chen[2]

[1] Department of Computer Science, National Tsing Hua University,
Hsinchu, Taiwan
[2] Department of Computer Science, National Chengchi University,
Taipei, Taiwan
alpchen@cs.nccu.edu.tw

Abstract. In this paper, we introduce a novel algorithm for mining sequential patterns from transaction databases. Since the FP-tree based approach is efficient in mining frequent itemsets, we adapt it to find frequent 1-sequences. For efficient frequent k-sequence mining, every frequent 1-sequence is encoded as a unique symbol and the database is transformed into one in the symbolic form. We observe that it is unnecessary to encode all the frequent 1-seqences, and make full use of the discovered frequent 1-sequences to transform the database into one with a smallest size. To discover the frequent k-sequences, we design a tree structure to store the candidates. Each customer sequence is then scanned to decide whether the candidates are frequent k-sequences. We propose a technique to avoid redundantly enumerating the identical k-subsequences from a customer sequence to speed up the process. Moreover, the tree structure is designed in a way such that the supports of the candidates can be incremented for a customer sequence by a single sequential traversal of the tree. The experiment results show that our approach outperforms the previous works in various aspects including the scalability and the execution time.

Keywords: Data mining, Sequential patterns, Database transformation, Frequent k-sequences.

1 Introduction

Sequential pattern mining [2][3][4][5][6][8], which discovers interesting patterns from transaction databases, is an essential problem in the data mining field. This problem was first introduced in [2]. A transaction database has three fields, i.e. customer id, transaction-time, and the items purchased. An itemset is a non-empty set of items and a sequence is an ordered list of itemsets. In this way, each transaction corresponds to an itemset. Each customer with a unique customer id may have more than one transaction with different transaction-times. All the transactions from a customer are ordered by increasing transaction-times to form a sequence, called the *customer sequence*.

The *size* of an itemset is the number of items in it. A *k-itemset* is an itemset with size k. The *length* of a sequence is the number of itemsets in it. A *k-sequence* is a sequence with length k. Moreover, the *size* of a sequence is also defined as the number of items in it. Given sequences $X=<X_1X_2...X_n>$ and $Y=<Y_1Y_2...Y_m>$ where all X_i's and Y_j's are itemsets and $n \leq m$, X is a *subsequence* of Y, i.e., *contained* in Y, if there exist n integers $1 \leq i_1 < i_2 < ... < i_n \leq m$ such that $X_1 \subseteq Y_{i_1}$, ..., $X_n \subseteq Y_{i_n}$. The *support* of a sequence is the number of customer sequences containing it in the entire database. Given a minimum support threshold *minsup*, a sequence is *frequent* if its support is not lower than minsup. We call the database composed of customer sequences the *sequence database*. The problem of sequential pattern mining is to efficiently find all the frequent sequences from a sequence database.

In the remainder of this paper, for brevity, we will use frequent itemsets and frequent sequences to mean frequent 1-sequences and frequent k-sequences for k>1, respectively, unless explicitly specified otherwise. To our knowledge, AprioriAll is the first algorithm [2] that mines frequent sequences in two phases. That is, in the first phase, only frequent itemsets are found and then frequent sequences are mined in the second phase. In both phases, patterns are mined in the bottom-up fashion, i.e., frequent k-itemsets/sequences first, then frequent (k+1)-itemsets/sequences, and so on. The stage of mining frequent k-itemsets/sequences is called pass k. Between two consecutive passes, the anti-monotonic property, that all subsets/subsequences of a frequent itemset/sequence must be frequent, is utilized for *candidate* pruning, where a candidate is a sequence whose support has not been computed yet. AprioriAll applies the Apriori algorithm [1], which is proposed to mine association rules, to Phase 1 for mining frequent itemsets from the sequence database. At the beginning of Phase 2, AprioriAll maps every frequent itemset to a unique symbol and then transforms each transaction into a set composed of all the symbols whose patterns are contained in the transaction. For example, given the sequence database in Table 1 and the minsup 2, the frequent itemsets and the corresponding symbols are listed in Table 2. Note that in our notation an itemset is enclosed with parentheses while a sequence is enclosed with angle brackets. Based on Table 2, Table 1 is transformed into Table 3. In this way, all the frequent itemsets are retained and the subsequences of customer sequence containing a non-frequent itemset will not be considered as candidates for the frequent sequences.

Table 1. A sequence database

CID	Cus. Seq.
C1	<(abc)(bc)>
C2	<(b)(abc)(ad)>
C3	<(bd)(bc)>

Table 2. Mappings

F.I.	S.	F.I.	S.
a	A	ab	E
b	B	ac	F
c	C	bc	G
d	D	abc	H

Table 3. The transformed database

CID	Customer Sequence
C1	<(ABCEFGH)(BCG)>
C2	<(B)(ABCEFGH)(AD)>
C3	<(BD)(BCG)>

In Phase 2, we call a sequence *singular* if each set in it has only one symbol. Consider a set having two symbols X and Y, where x and y are the corresponding frequent itemsets, respectively. On one hand, if x is a subset of y, a sequence containing (XY) can be replaced with the corresponding one containing (Y). On the other hand, let z be the union of x and y. If z is frequent, again a sequence containing (XY) can be replaced with the corresponding one containing (Z), where Z is the symbol corresponding to z. Therefore, after the transformation, only the singular sequences should be considered as the candidates for the frequent sequences in Phase 2.

During the support computation, AprioriAll enumerates the subsequences of each customer sequence and accumulates the support of each candidate in a *candidate tree*, where each path from the root to a leaf in it corresponds to a candidate. Two or more subsequences enumerated from a customer sequence might be identical and therefore the corresponding path in the candidate tree will be traversed and counted more than once. However, by the problem definition, no matter how many times a subsequence appears in the customer sequence, its support can be increased at most by one. Therefore, it is unnecessary to repeatedly enumerate identical subsequences from a customer sequence. In the applications, this problem is usual, e.g., a customer often buys the same items more than once. Owing to the large number of enumerated subsequences, the counting on the candidate tree can be time-consuming.

In addition to AprioriAll, SPAM [4], and Pseudo-Projection [6] find frequent sequences based on the *lattice* concept as follows. Given a set of items, a lattice is a layered graph where each node stands for a distinct sequence and each link indicates the parent-child relationship between one sequence with size k and another with size k+1. To find all the frequent k-sequences, all the two approaches recursively select a set of nodes as candidates and scan the database to compute their supports. The number of database scans in each of them is directly proportional to the total number of frequent k-sequences.

To sum up, AprioriAll retains all the frequent itemsets in the transformed database in Phase 2 to avoid enumerating the subsequences containing non-frequent itemsets. Given n distinct frequent items, if the maximal length of a frequent sequence is k, there can be in the worse case $(2^n-1)+(2^n-1)^2+...+(2^n-1)^k$ frequent sequences to be discovered. Since the 2^n-1 frequent itemsets are in the minority, mining frequent sequences is relatively important in sequential pattern mining. The two-phase architecture that finds two kinds of patterns separately should enable the mining tasks for different types of patterns improved. However, previous works [4][5][6][8] have noted that the bottom-up approach suffers from the huge amount of candidates generated at one pass. Recently, as the price-to-capacity ratio of main memory shrinks, the pain of too many candidates in AprioriAll has been alleviated. However, AprioriAll still suffers from the transformed database that can be much larger than the original one and the high execution time for support computation. Accordingly, in this paper, we develop a new two-phase approach for mining sequential patterns, equipped with the facilities for effective database transformation and efficient support computation.

Finding frequent itemsets in Phase 1 is relevant to the problem of association rule mining, which have been extensively discussed, such as [1][7]. Among them, the FP-tree based approach [7] takes advantage of the common items among itemsets to reduce the cost of subset enumeration. This inspires us to adapt the same idea to the sequence database. A straightforward way that adopts the FP-tree to find frequent itemsets from a sequence database does not work because the support of an itemset may be overestimated. In this paper, we propose the concept of *transaction intersection* to compute the correct support of each itemset.

In Phase 2, we aim at effective database transformation and efficient support computation. First, from the anti-monotonic property, it is not necessary to retain all the frequent itemsets in the transformed database. Take Table 3 as an example. Since combining A with any other symbol cannot form a frequent sequence, it guarantees that E and F (two supersets of A) cannot form any frequent sequence, either. Our approach skips this kind of symbols during the database transformation to have two advantages: no need to examine the sequences containing a symbol that cannot form any frequent sequence and the transformed database with a smaller size.

To speed up the support computation, we propose a technique to avoid redundantly enumerating the identical subsequences from a customer sequence. Moreover, the nodes in the candidate tree are sorted such that the supports of the candidates can be incremented for a customer sequence by a single traversal of the tree. In the experiments, our approach outperforms the previous works in both the execution time and database scalability. Moreover, the results also show that the main advantages of our approach lie in minimizing the number of symbols encoded and computing the supports of candidates in Phase 2 efficiently.

The rest of this paper is organized as follows. In Section 2, we present the method for mining frequent itemsets from the sequence database. In Section 3, we describe the method for mining frequent sequences. The performance evaluation and experiment results are shown in Section 4. Finally, we conclude this paper in Section 5.

2 Frequent Itemset Discovery

In Phase 1, we adapt the FP-tree based approach to finding frequent itemsets from the sequence database. The FP-tree based approach first constructs a compact data structure called *FP-tree* to keep all the transactions in the transaction database and then performs a mining algorithm on it to find all the frequent itemsets. In this paper, we adopt the mining algorithm named TD-FP-Growth. For lack of space, readers please refer to [7] for the detail.

The FP-tree based approach cannot be directly applied to finding frequent itemsets in the sequence database because the transactions in a customer sequence may contain identical itemset. In that case, the support of the itemset will be overestimated. For example, given a customer sequence <(abc)(bcd)>, as the two transactions are inserted into the FP-tree, this customer sequence will contribute 2 to the support of (bc). An intuitive response to this problem is to combine (abc) and (bcd) into a single transaction (abcd), which correctly provides the support of (bc). However, in this way the support of (ad) will be miscounted. In our approach, we introduce the concept of *transaction intersection* that can correctly compute the support of each itemset as we insert all the transactions in each customer sequence into the FP-tree.

Consider an itemset I and a customer sequence $S=<T_1T_2...T_n>$, where each T_i is a transaction. Our goal is to insert all T_i's into the FP-tree such that the correct support of I from S, i.e., 0 or 1, can be obtained from the FP-tree. This process is similar to the enumeration of I from S. If the intersection O_{ij} between T_i and T_j is I, I will be enumerated twice and its support from the FP-tree is overestimated as 2. Therefore, for every two transactions T_i and T_j in S, we consider their intersection O_{ij} as an extra transaction, called a *negative transaction intersection*, which is also inserted into the FP-tree with a negative support -1. Moreover, if the intersection O_{ijk} between T_i, T_j

and T_k is I, I will be enumerated from S thrice but decreased by the three negative instance intersections O_{ij}, O_{ik}, and O_{jk}. In that case, the support of I from the FP-tree is underestimated as 0. Therefore, for every three transactions T_i, T_j and T_k in S, we further consider their intersection O_{ijk} as a *positive transaction intersection*, which is also inserted into the FP-tree to increase the support of I by one. In this way, the two kinds of transaction intersections (abbreviated as TI) are alternatively derived from the intersections among transactions in S. The transaction intersection that is the intersection between L transactions in S is called the *L-TI*. Without loss of generality, each transaction in S is treated as a positive 1-TI.

For example, given a customer sequence S = <(abc)(bcd)(abd)(ac)>, for every two transactions, we have the 2-TIs {(bc), (ab), (ac), (bd), (c), (a)}. Moreover, for every three transactions, we have the 3-TIs {(b), (c), (a), ∅}. Finally, the 4-TI is ∅. From the 4 transactions in S, i.e., 1-TIs, the support of (a) is overestimated as 3. Since (a) appears in three 2-TIs, its support will be decreased to 0. Finally, (a) appears in only one 3-TI and therefore its support will be correctly computed as 1.

Our approach employs all the transaction intersections generated from each customer sequence to construct the FP-tree, in which the negative transaction intersections can decrease the supports of the corresponding itemsets contained in them. After the FP-tree is constructed, the count of a node in the FP-tree can be positive, zero, or negative. Finally, the TD-FP-Growth algorithm is directly applied to this FP-tree to find all the frequent itemsets.

3 Frequent Sequence Discovery

All the notations used in this section and their definitions are shown in Table 4.

The two main components of Phase 2 in our approach are *database transformation* and *frequent sequence discovery*, respectively. In the database transformation, unlike AprioriAll that encodes all the frequent itemsets at once, our approach divides the frequent itemsets into groups based on their size and encodes them at different rounds in pass 2. The groups of frequent itemsets having smaller sizes are encoded earlier, i.e., frequent 1-itemsets, frequent 2-itemsets, and so on.

In our approach, frequent k-sequences are discovered at pass k, where k≥2. In pass 2, at the first round, all the frequent 1-itemsets are encoded as symbols and the frequent 2-sequences that contain at least one of them are discovered. These frequent 2-sequences are immediately used to check the frequent 2-itemsets to see whether

Table 4. Notations and their definitions

Notations	Definitions
FE_r	The set of the frequent r-itemsets encoded in round r
$FE_{1..r}$	The set of all the frequent itemsets encoded in rounds 1…r
FS_r	The set of the symbols corresponding to FE_r
$FS_{1..r}$	The set of all the symbols generated in rounds 1…r
TD_r	The database after the transformation in round r
F_2^r	The set of the frequent 2-sequences found in round r

they should be encoded in the next round. This process repeats until there is no frequent itemset to be encoded. In pass k (k≥3), candidate k-sequences are generated according to the frequent (k-1)-sequences found in pass k-1, and then the transformed database is scanned to compute their supports. Note that, although main memory space is getting larger nowadays, it is still possible to generate too many candidates in one pass. Therefore, in each pass, our approach monitors the number of candidate sequences currently generated. If this number reaches a predefined threshold, the supports of these candidate sequences are computed via one database scan. In this way, during the support computation, all the candidate sequences involved can fit in the main memory. In the following, our procedure of database transformation is introduced first. After that, the main stages, candidate generation and support computation, for frequent sequence discovery are presented, respectively.

3.1 Database Transformation

In the first round of pass 2, each frequent 1-itemset is put into FE_1 and encoded as a distinct symbol in FS_1. Moreover, each transaction in a customer sequence that contains the frequent 1-itemsets in FE_1 is replaced with a set of the corresponding symbols in FS_1 to produce TD_1. After that, all the frequent 2-sequences in TD_1, i.e., F_2^1, are discovered. Finally, we determine whether a frequent 2-itemset should be encoded for the second round according to the following property.

Property 1. Given a frequent (r+1)-itemset X, let the r-itemsets contained in X be denoted as X_1, X_2 ... and X_{r+1}. For any frequent itemset Y, the following two rules always hold:

1. If <XY> is frequent in round r+1 $\Rightarrow$ <X_iY>$\in F_2^r$ $\forall 1 \leq i \leq r+1$.
2. If <YX> is frequent in round r+1 $\Rightarrow$ <YX_i>$\in F_2^r$ $\forall 1 \leq i \leq r+1$.

According to the anti-monotone property, the above property can be easily observed. As a result, only the frequent 2-itemsets should be encoded in round 2, if there exists a frequent itemset Y in $FE_{1..2}$ such that one of the rules in Property 1 holds. In round r (r≥2), the database TD_{r-1} is transformed into TD_r by adding the symbols in FS_r to the transactions that contain the corresponding frequent itemsets in FE_r. After that, to avoid the frequent 2-sequences that have been generated in previous rounds, only the 2-sequences that contain at least one symbol in FS_r are considered as candidates and enumerated from TD_r. Finally, the frequent (r+1)-itemsets satisfying Property 1 are encoded for round r+1. When no more frequent itemset is encoded, the database transformation is terminated in pass 2.

For example, consider the sequence database in Table 1. and the symbols in Table 2. In the first round, all the frequent 1-itemsets are encoded (A, B, and C) and TD_1 is shown in Table 5. The frequent 2-sequences composed of these symbols are <BB> and <BC>. In the second round, only (bc) has to be encoded because (ab) and (ac) do not satisfy the rules in Property 1. Symbol F is appended to each transaction containing both B and C, and the result is shown in Table 6. In this round, only <BF> is a frequent 2-sequence. Finally, pass 2 is terminated because no frequent 3-itemset should be encoded.

Table 5. TD_1

CID	Customer Sequence
1	<(ABC)(BC)>
2	<(B)(ABC)(A)>
3	<(B)(BC)>

Table 6. TD_2

CID	Customer Sequence
1	<(ABC)(BCF)>
2	<(B)(ABCF)(A)>
3	<(B)(BCF)>

Distributing the database transformation task into rounds has two advantages. First, the transformed database generated in each round is much smaller than the one generated by AprioriAll. Second, in AprioriAll, every frequent itemset is encoded at the beginning of Phase 2 and therefore the number of candidates can be huge. By contrast, in our approach, the sequences containing the frequent itemset that is not encoded are not generated as candidates. Moreover, our approach will not enumerate such kind of sequences from the customer sequences for support computation.

3.2 Candidate Generation

We describe the procedure of candidate generation in two cases, i.e., pass = 2 and pass = k for k ≥ 3. In round r of pass 2, for each symbol α in FS_r, α is combined with each β in $FS_{1...r}$ to generate the candidate sequences <$\alpha\beta$> and <$\beta\alpha$>. Since only the 2-sequences that contain at least one symbol encoded in round r are considered as candidates, our algorithm will not generate redundant candidates in different rounds.

We adopt the same method as described in [2] to generate candidates in pass k for k≥3. Each frequent (k-1)-sequence <$\alpha_1...\alpha_{k-2}\alpha_{k-1}$> is combined with each frequent (k-1)-sequence <$\beta_1...\beta_{k-2}\beta_{k-1}$>, where $\alpha_1=\beta_1$, ..., and $\alpha_{k-2}=\beta_{k-2}$, to generate the candidate sequence <$\alpha_1...\alpha_{k-1}\beta_{k-1}$>. Based on the anti-monotonic property, we further check whether any subsequence with length k-1 of <$\alpha_1...\alpha_{k-1}\beta_{k-1}$> is non-frequent. If there exists such a subsequences, <$\alpha_1...\alpha_{k-1}\beta_{k-1}$> cannot be frequent and therefore will be pruned.

In each pass, the generated candidates are stored into the candidate tree, where the support of each candidate is kept at the leaf node of the corresponding path. For each non-leaf node, all its children are stored in lexicographic order as an ordered list. This ordering of nodes in the candidate tree is used to reduce the cost on support computation, which will be detailed in the next section.

3.3 Support Computation

In pass k, for each customer sequence, all the subsequences with length k are enumerated by combining the symbols in different transactions. Given a subsequence α=<$\alpha_1\alpha_2...\alpha_k$> enumerated from a customer sequence, where α_i is a symbol, we say α *matches* a path p=$n_1n_2...n_k$ in the candidate tree if $n_i=\alpha_i$ for 1≤i≤k. For each subsequence enumerated, the candidate tree is traversed to find its match. As described in Section 1, repeated enumeration of identical subsequences from a customer sequence is unnecessary and time-consuming. Therefore, in this section, we introduce a novel method to avoid it such that only a single traversal of the candidate tree is required for counting all the subsequences enumerated from a customer sequence.

The rationale of our approach is as follows. First, since a subsequence may have multiple occurrences in a customer sequence, we need a particular representation of the customer sequence such that each distinct subsequence is enumerated exactly once from that representation. Second, the symbols in that representation should be ordered such that the subsequences enumerated from it are in the same order as the sequential traversal on the candidate tree. In the following, we first define the proposed representation and then describe the subsequence enumeration algorithm on it.

Consider a customer sequence $S=<T_1T_2...T_n>$, where T_i is the ith transaction. If a symbol α appears in T_i, this occurrence of α is denoted as α^i. For example, $<(BDE)(A)(B)(BC)>$ can be denoted as $<B^1D^1E^1A^2B^2B^3B^4C^4>$. Let i-suffix$_S$ denote the subsequence $<T_iT_{i+1}...T_n>$ of S. If α appears in T_{j_1}, T_{j_2} ... T_{j_m}, where $i \leq j_1 < j_2...j_m \leq n$, we call α^{j_k} the kth *instance* of α in i-suffix$_S$.

Definition 1. Given k occurrences of symbols $\beta_1^{i_1}$, $\beta_2^{i_2}$ ... $\beta_k^{i_k}$ in S, where $1 \leq i_1 \leq i_2... \leq i_k \leq n$, $<\beta_1^{i_1}\beta_2^{i_2}...\beta_k^{i_k}>$ is called a *necessary subsequence* of S if $\beta_1^{i_1}$ is the 1st instance of β_1 in the 1-suffix$_S$ and for $2 \leq j \leq k$, $\beta_j^{i_j}$ is the 1st instance of β_j in the $(i_{j-1}+1)$-suffix$_S$.

For example, in $<B^1D^1E^1A^2B^2B^3B^4C^4>$, $<B^1A^2C^4>$ is a necessary subsequence because B^1 is the 1st instance of B in 1-suffix$_S$, A^2 is the 1st instance of A in 2-suffix$_S$, and C^4 is the 1st instance of C in 3-suffix$_S$. On the contrary, $<B^1A^2B^4>$ is not a necessary subsequence because B^4 is not the 1st instance of B in 3-suffix$_S$. Obviously, each subsequence enumerated from S must have exact one occurrence in S, which is a necessary subsequence. As a result, only the necessary subsequences instead of all the subsequences in a customer sequence should be enumerated.

Definition 2. For each i-suffix$_S$ S', if we remove each occurrence of a symbol that is not the 1st instance of that symbol in S', the resultant subsequence is called a *pivot* and denoted as *i-pivot*.

For example, the 4 pivots of $<B^1D^1E^1A^2B^2B^3B^4C^4>$ are 1-pivot: $<B^1D^1E^1A^2C^4>$, 2-pivot: $<A^2B^2C^4>$, 3-pivot: $<B^3C^4>$, and 4-pivot: $<B^4C^4>$, respectively. For ease of presentation, we denote the jth element of the i-pivot as *i-pivot[j]* and the total number of elements in the i-pivot as |*i-pivot*|. The following lemma shows the relationships between the pivots and a necessary subsequence.

Lemma 1. If $<\beta_1^{i_1}\beta_2^{i_2}...\beta_k^{i_k}>$ is a necessary subsequence of S, it must be in the form of $<$1-pivot[j_1], (i_1+1)-pivot[j_2], ...(i_{k-1}+1)-pivot[j_k]$>$, where $j_1 \leq |$1-pivot$|$ and $j_h \leq |(i_{h-1})$-pivot$|$ for $2 \leq h \leq k$.

From Lemma 1, each necessary subsequence of a customer sequence S can be formed by the elements in the pivots of S. Therefore, our approach first derives all the pivots from S and then generates all the necessary subsequences from the pivots. Since the pivots derived from S can be much larger than S, we derive and keep the pivots of S only when S is scanned for support counting. For each customer sequence with size n, we *sort* its elements in the form of $<\beta_1^{i_1}\beta_2^{i_2}...\beta_n^{i_n}>$ such that for $1 \leq j < n$, $\beta_j < \beta_{j+1}$ or ($\beta_j = \beta_{j+1}$ and $i_j < i_{j+1}$). For instance, the sorted form of $<B^1D^1E^1A^2B^2B^3B^4C^4>$ is $<A^2B^1B^2B^3B^4C^4D^1E^1>$. Given the sorted form of a customer sequence $<\beta_1^{i_1}\beta_2^{i_2}...\beta_n^{i_n}>$, our algorithm named *Pivot Derivation* with two nested for-loops is proposed as follows.

Initially, all the pivots are set empty. Each entry of an array Index[k] is used to keep the number of elements in the k-pivot. For each symbol $\beta_j^{i_j}$ (in the i_j^{th} transaction), we check whether β_j has been stored in i_j-pivot, (i_j-1)-pivot, ... or 1-pivot. If the k-pivot does not have β_j, $\beta_j^{i_j}$ is immediately stored into it. The idea of this algorithm comes from two observations. First, the input is the sorted form of S. If k-pivot[Index[k]] does not equal β_j, this implies that $\beta_j^{i_j}$ must be the 1st instance in k-suffix$_S$ and also an element in the k-pivot according to Definition 2. On the contrary, if the k-pivot has β_j, there must exist an occurrence of β_j that is the 1st instances of β_j in h-suffix$_S$ for h=1...k. In this case, $\beta_j^{i_j}$ cannot be an element in the h-pivot for h=1...k and therefore will be skipped.

For example, consider the sorted form of $<A^2B^1B^2B^3B^4C^4D^1E^1>$ as the input. First, after A^2 is processed, both the 2-pivot and 1-pivot are $<A^2>$. Second, after B^1, B^2, B^3, and B^4 are processed, we have 1-pivot=$<A^2B^1>$, 2-pivot=$<A^2B^2>$, 3-pivot=$<B^3>$, and 4-pivot=$<B^4>$, respectively. Third, after C^4 is processed, all the 4 pivots are appended with C^4. Finally, after D^1 and E^1 are processed, only the 1-pivot is changed to $<A^2B^1C^4D^1E^1>$.

In our approach, sorting each customer sequence is done during database transformation. During the support counting, the above algorithm is invoked to derive all the pivots from a customer sequence. In the following, we will present our algorithm that can enumerate all the necessary subsequences from the pivots. Given the pivots derived from the sorted form of a customer sequence $S=<T_1T_2...T_n>$, the candidate tree, and pass k, our algorithm named *Necessary Subsequence Enumeration* (abbreviated as NSE) is shown as below. Note that the matching and counting for the candidates on T are also included in it. Given a node x on the candidate tree, its jth child and the total number of its children are denoted as *x.children[j]* and |x.children|, respectively. In addition, the serial number of the transaction having r-pivot[i] is denoted as *r-pivot[i].no*.

```
Algorithm NSE(pivots, x, L, r)

(1)    If (|x.children| ≠ 0) do {
(2)       i = j = 1;
(3)       While (i≤|r-pivot|) and (j≤|x.children|) do {
(4)          If (r-pivot[i] == x.children[j]) {
(5)             If (L == k)
(6)                x.children[j].count++;
(7)             Else If (r-pivot[i].no<n) and (L<k)
(8)                NSE(pivots, x.children[j], L+1,
                       r-pivot[i].no+1);
(9)             i ++; j ++; }
(10)         Else If (r-pivot[i] < x.children[j]) {
(11)            i++; }
(12)         Else    j++; }
```

Initially, NSE(pivots, the root of the candidate tree, 1, 1) is invoked. The parameter L is used to keep the path length currently traversed, indicating the length of candidate sequences to be counted. The parameter r will identify the pivot currently used.

In the while-loop, each symbol α in the r-pivot is compared with the symbol β in every child y of the node x. If α matches β, three cases exist. First, if a candidate k-sequence is found, its count is increased by one. Second, if y is not a leaf node and α is not in the last transaction (i.e., T_n), a further traversal of the candidate tree is required. Notice that the parameter r passed in the recursive call is determined according to Lemma 1. If neither case holds, both the next element of r-pivot and the next child of x are considered in the next iteration. On the other hand, if α does not match β, either the next element of the r-pivot or the next child of x is considered.

4 Performance Evaluation

In this section, we compare our approach with AprioriAll, Pseudo-Projection, and SPAM under different parameter settings. We implement all the approaches and follow the standard procedure in [2] to generate the synthetic databases. The number of distinct items is fixed to 1000, and the remaining parameters unmentioned are set as the default values. In addition, we modified AprioriAll to divide the candidates generated in a pass into groups such that each group of candidates can be placed in the main memory. In the following, we show the results from three experiments. At first, we compare the four approaches on the various settings of minsup. A number of databases are tested and the results are consistent. For lack of space, we only report the results from the database D10kC10T10S10I10.

In Figure 1, each point of a curve stands for the execution time of one approach. Generally, Pseudo_Projection and SPAM perform worse than our approach when minsup gets small, because of the larger amount of frequent sequences which leads to more database scans for support computation. Moreover, SPAM reports the worst processing time due to the following reasons. The computer hardware architecture cannot fully support very large bit-maps. SPAM needs additional CPU time to do the logical operations on bit-maps. As the minsup gets small, a large number of candidates need to be processed. As a result, the load of doing bit operations becomes very heavy.

Our approach outperforms M-AprioriAll (the modified AprioriAll) lightly when minsup is high. This is because only a few frequent itemsets exist. M-AprioriAll encodes all the frequent itemsets at the beginning of Phase 2, while our approach encodes them in different rounds. As a result, our approach needs more database scans than M-AprioriAll for the encoding process. However, when considerable frequent itemsets exist, the transformed database will be very large produced in M-AprioriAll, and many non-frequent sequences are generated as candidates. Moreover, the problem of repeated enumeration of identical subsequences from a customer sequence may also become worse when more frequent itemsets exist. Therefore, M-AprioriAll is worse than Pseudo_Projection and our approach.

When the database size is getting larger, all the approaches spend more time on database scans. In the second experiment, we compare the four approaches on different numbers of customer sequences, and the results are shown in Figure 2, where minsup is fixed to 50. All the three approaches are worse than our approach because Pseudo-Projection and SPAM frequently scan the databases, and M-AprioriAll produces a large transformed database.

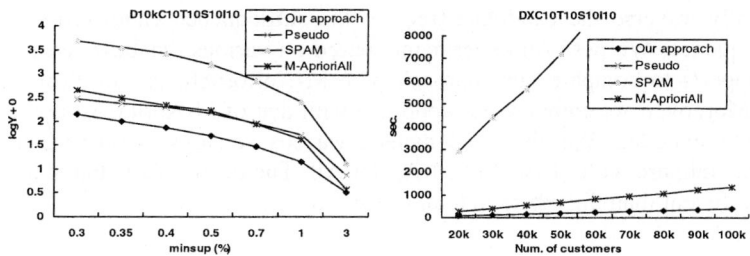

Fig. 1. Processing time for different minsup values

Fig. 2. Processing time on different database sizes

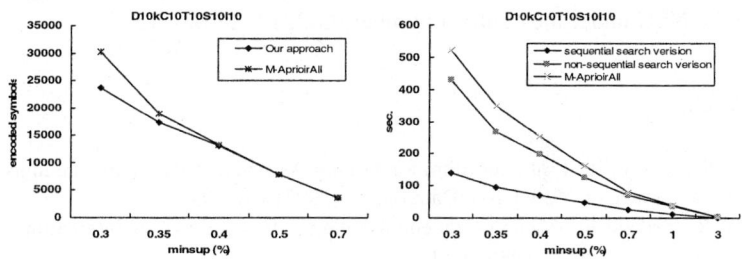

Fig. 3. The number of encoded symbols on different minsup values

Fig. 4. Processing time of Phase 2

Finally, we compare Phase 2 in our approach with that of M-AprioriAll in two aspects, i.e., the number of symbols encoded and the process time on various values of minsup. For the number of symbols encoded, in Figure 3, as the minsup gets smaller, the number of encoded symbols reduced by our approach gets larger. Figure 4 shows the detailed comparisons between our approach and M-AprioriAll. We implemented two versions of our approach. One follows the idea proposed in Section 3.3, while the other does not provide the sequential search on the candidate tree. The former is called sequential version and the latter is called non-sequential version. As a result, the sequential version of our approach has the best performance than the others and the non-sequential version still outperforms than M-AprioriAll.

5 Conclusions

In this paper, we propose a novel approach to mining frequent sequences in large sequence databases. We adopt the two-phase architecture that generates frequent itemsets and frequent sequences separately. In Phase 1, we propose the concept of transaction intersection to successfully adapt the FP-tree approach for association rules mining to the sequence database. In Phase 2, we encode the frequent itemsets in different rounds such that the size of the transformed database, the number of candidates, and the number of enumerated subsequences are reduced. In addition, we also avoid enumerating the redundant subsequences from a customer sequence and sequentially traverse the candidate tree for the subsequence enumeration of a customer sequence. We perform experiments based on various database sizes and minimum supports to compare our approach with M-AprioriAll, Pseudo-Projection, and SPAM. Moreover, we compare our approach with that of M-AprioriAll in the number of symbols encoded. We also implemented various versions of Phase 2 in our approach to compare with Phase 2 of M-AprioriAll. The results show that our approach is more efficient than the others in total processing time.

Acknowledgements

This work was partially supported by the NSC Program for Promoting Academic Excellence of Universities (Phase II) under the grant number 93-2752-E-007-004-PAE, and the NSC under the contract number 93-2213-E-004-013.

References

1. Agrawal R., Srikant R.: Fast Algorithm for Mining Association Rules. Proceedings of International Conference on Very Large Data Bases. (1994) 487-499.
2. Agrawal R., Srikant R.: Mining Sequential Patterns. Proceedings of International Conference on Data Engineering. (1995) 3-14.
3. Agrawal R., Srikant R.: Mining Sequential Patterns: Generalizations and Performance Improvements. Proceedings of the Fifth International Conference on Extending Database Technology. (1996) 3-17.
4. Ayres J., Gehrke J., Yiu T., Flannick J.: Sequential PAttern Mining using A Bitmap Representation. Proceedings of ACM SIGKDD Conference. (2002) 429-435, 2002.
5. Chiu D. Y., Wu Yi. H., Chen A. L. P.: An Efficient Algorithm for Mining Frequent Sequences by a New Strategy without Support Counting. Proceedings of International Conference on Data Engineering. (2004) 375-386.
6. Pei J., Han J., Mortazavi-Asl B., Pinto H., Chen Q., Dayal U., M. Hsu.: PrefixSpan: Mining Sequential Patterns Efficiently by Prefix-Projected Pattern Growth. Proceedings of International Conference on Data Engineering. (2001) 215-224.
7. Wang K., Tang L., Han J., Liu J.: Top Down FP-Growth for Association Rule Mining. Proceedings of Advances in Knowledge Discovery and Data Mining. (2002) 334-340.
8. Zaki M. J.: An efficient algorithm for mining frequent sequences. Machine Learning, Vol. 42(1/2). (2001) 31-60.

Mining Succinct Systems of Minimal Generators of Formal Concepts

Guozhu Dong[1], Chunyu Jiang[1], Jian Pei[2], Jinyan Li[3], and Limsoon Wong[3]

[1] Wright State University, U.S.A
{gdong, cjiang}@cs.wright.edu
[2] Simon Fraser University, Canada
jpei@cs.sfu.ca
[3] Institute for Infocomm Research, Singapore
{jinyan, limsoon}@i2r.a-star.edu.sg

Abstract. Formal concept analysis has become an active field of study for data analysis and knowledge discovery. A formal concept C is determined by its extent (the set of objects that fall under C) and its intent (the set of properties or attributes covered by C). The intent for C, also called a closed itemset, is the maximum set of attributes that characterize C. The minimal generators for C are the minimal subsets of C's intent which can similarly characterize C. This paper introduces the <u>s</u>uccinct <u>s</u>ystem of <u>m</u>inimal <u>g</u>enerators (SSMG) as a minimal representation of the minimal generators of all concepts, and gives an efficient algorithm for mining SSMGs. The SSMGs are useful for revealing the equivalence relationship among the minimal generators, which may be important for medical and other scientific discovery; and for revealing the extent-based semantic equivalence among associations. The SSMGs are also useful for losslessly reducing the size of the representation of all minimal generators, similar to the way that closed itemsets are useful for losslessly reducing the size of the representation of all frequent itemsets. The removal of redudancies will help human users to grasp the structure and information in the concepts.

Keywords: Minimal generators, formal concepts, closed itemsets, succinctness.

1 Introduction

Formal concept analysis (FCA) [7] is an important tool for data analysis and knowledge discovery. A formal concept C is determined by its extent (the set of objects or transactions that fall under C) and its intent (the set of properties, attributes, or items covered by C). Take the transaction database TDB in Figure 1 as an example. Each transaction has an identity Tid and a set of items; the set of items is written as a list of items alphabetically and the set brackets are omitted. Itemset $bcghi$ and transaction set $\{T_1, T_3, T_5\}$ form a formal concept, where itemset $bcghi$ is its intent and transaction set $\{T_1, T_3, T_5\}$ is its extent. Intuitively, $bcghi$ is the largest itemset that is contained in transactions T_1, T_3 and T_5. No other transactions contains $bcghi$. The formal concepts in the transaction database are listed in Figure 2.

In general, the intent of a formal concept C is the closure of the properties, attributes, or items that form a maximum characterization for C: Every object satisfying the intent

Tid	Items
T_1	abcdeghi
T_2	acdg
T_3	bcdghi
T_4	abdhi
T_5	bceghi

Fig. 1. A transaction database TDB

Closure	Minimal generators	Sup	SuccMinGen
ad	a	3	a
bhi	b, h, i	4	b, h, i
cg	c, g	4	c, g
d	d	4	d
bceghi	e	2	e
abdhi	ab, ah, ai	2	ab
acdg	ac, ag	2	ac
abcdeghi	ae, de, abc, abg, ach, aci, agh, agi	1	ae, de, abc
bcghi	bc, bg, ch, ci, gh, gi	3	bc
bdhi	bd, dh, di	3	bd
cdg	cd, dg	3	cd
bcdghi	bcd, bdg, cdh, cdi, dgh, dgi	2	bcd

Fig. 2. The formal concepts and their closures, minimal generators and succinct system of minimal generators in TDB of Figure 1

is in C. The closure (or a closed itemset[1]) serves as the upper bound of the attributes covered by the formal concept. Mining the intents of concepts or closed itemsets has attracted a lot of attention (e.g., [9, 10, 8, 12, 15, 14]) for their importance in knowledge discovery, and for the significant reduction in the number of necessary frequent itemsets achieved by removing redundant (recoverable) ones.

Each formal concept actually corresponds to a set of itemsets, which are all equivalent since they capture the same intent. While the closures are the maximal sets of attributes/items presenting the concept, it is often interesting to ask, "*What are the critical combinations of attributes that manifest the concept?*" That is, for a concept, we want to identify the minimal combinations of attributes—the so-called minimal generators—that distinguish the objects in this concept from the others. Such minimal generators can offer a complementary, perhaps simpler way to understand the concept, because they may contain far fewer attributes than closed itemsets.

Technically, the *minimal generators* of a formal concept C are the minimal subsets of C's intent that can characterize C, and are the lower bounds of the itemsets characterizing C [10, 12]. For the running example, itemsets bc, bg, ch, ci, gh, gi are the minimal generators of formal concept $bcghi$, since any transaction containing any of those minimal generators must also contain the other items in the closure.

Complementary to closures, minimal generators provide an important way to characterize formal concepts. However, very little has been done on understanding and mining the minimal generators. Some previous studies (e.g., [10, 15]) use minimal generators only as a means to achieve other goals such as mining closed itemsets. [12] considers the mining of *all* minimal generators, but its algorithm leaves considerable room for improvement.

Interestingly, the minimal generators still may contain a lot of redundant information. Consider the formal concepts in Figure 2. Closed itemset $bcghi$ has six minimal gener

---

[1] Since formal concepts and closed itemsets are in one-to-one correspondence, we henceforth treat a closed itemset and its corresponding formal concept as the same thing.

ators: bc, bg, ch, hg, ic and ig. From any one of them we can derive all the others, since b, h and i always appear together in transactions and are thus equivalent, and similarly for c and g. Those facts are indicated by formal concepts bhi and cg, respectively.

Can we remove the redundant information and achieve a succinct representation of the minimal generators? In this paper, we propose a novel concept of *succinct system of minimal generators* (SSMG for short). The idea is to remove the redundant information by choosing one (e.g., the lexically smallest) minimal generator of a formal concept as its representative minimal generator, and exclude non-representative minimal generators of the concept to occur as parts of minimal generators of any other concepts.

For example, we can choose b as the representative minimal generator for the formal concept bhi, and c for cg. For the concept $bcghi$ only the minimal generator bc will be included in the SSMG; all the other five (i.e. bg, ch, hg, ic and ig) are excluded and can be derived. Using SSMG there are a total of 17 minimal generators (Figure 2), compared with a total of 38 standard minimal generators. This big reduction in size causes no loss of information, as all minimal generators can be inferred from the SSMG.

Using the SSMG, the same equivalence information between the minimal generators of a concept will not occur redundantly. This helps reduce the result of mining and make it easier to browse, understand and manage, and reduce the need for the user to digest the same information multiple times and hence helps the user to concentrate on the new equivalence among minimal generators. Since the results on the equivalence among the minimal generators also reveal the minimal equivalence relation among associations and itemsets, results on SSMG are also useful for association mining.

In this paper, we give an efficient algorithm for mining SSMGs. Our algorithm is substantially more effective and efficient than the algorithm in [12], which mines all minimal generators. While the problem of mining SSMGs is computationally expensive, our experiments demonstrate that our algorithm can deal with high dimensional and large real data sets. We will also illustrate the power of our method on real data sets in terms of both effectiveness and efficiency. It should be noted that the SSMG mining is significantly more involved than the closed itemset mining, since it provides information on all the minimal generators in addition to the closed itemsets. We applied the algorithm on some real data sets and obtained some some interesting findings. But the details are omitted due to space limit.

Section 2 provides definitions of SSMG. Section 3 describes the algorithm. Section 4 reports experimental results on effectiveness and efficiency. Section 5 discusses related works and potential extensions.

2 Definition of SSMG

After revisiting the preliminaries of formal concepts, this section introduces the notion of succinct system of minimal generators (SSMG).

2.1 Preliminaries

Let $I = \{i_1, \ldots, i_n\}$ be a set of *items*. An *itemset* is a subset of I. A *transaction* is a tuple $\langle tid, X \rangle$, where tid is a transaction identity and X is an itemset. A *transaction* database TDB is a set of transactions. A transaction $\langle tid, X \rangle$ is said to *contain* itemset Y if $Y \subseteq X$. Let TDB be a given transaction database. The *support* of an itemset X, denoted as $sup(X)$, is the number of transactions in TDB that contain X. Given a minimum support threshold min_sup, X is *frequent* if $sup(X) \geq min\_sup$.

The *transaction set* of an itemset X, denoted as $\mathcal{T}(X)$, is the set of all transactions in TDB that contain X. For our running example (Figure 1), $\mathcal{T}(bc) = \{T_1, T_3, T_5\}$. Two itemsets X and Y are called *equivalent*, denoted as $X \sim Y$, if $\mathcal{T}(X) = \mathcal{T}(Y)$. The *equivalence class* of an itemset X is the set of all itemsets that are equivalent to X. For Figure 1, itemsets bc and gi are equivalent since $\mathcal{T}(bc) = \{T_1, T_3, T_5\} = \mathcal{T}(gi)$; the equivalence class of b is $\{b, h, i, bh, bi, hi, bhi\}$. Symmetrically, the *itemset* of a set of transactions $D \subseteq TDB$, denoted as $\mathcal{I}(D)$, is the set of items that appear in every transaction in D, i.e., $\mathcal{I}(D) = \cap_{(tid,X)\in D} X$. In Figure 1, $\mathcal{I}(\{T_1, T_3, T_5\}) = bcghi$.

An itemset X is call *closed* if there exists no proper superset $X' \supset X$ such that $sup(X) = sup(X')$. Easily, we can show that an itemset X is closed iff $\mathcal{I}(\mathcal{T}(X)) = X$. Symmetrically, a set of transaction D is *closed* if and only if $\mathcal{T}(\mathcal{I}(D)) = D$.

Definition 1. A *formal concept* is a pair $C = (X, D)$ where X and D are a closed itemset and a closed transaction set, respectively, such that $D = \mathcal{T}(X)$ and $X = \mathcal{I}(D)$. Given two concepts $C = (X, D)$ and $C' = (X', D')$, C is said to be *more general* than C' if $X \subset X'$.

Under the set containment order, the itemsets form a lattice $\mathcal{L}$. Moreover, under the same order on the closed itemsets, the formal concepts form a lattice $\mathcal{L}_\mathcal{C}$, which is a *Galois lattice* (see Figure 3). Apparently, the lattice of the formal concepts is a quotient lattice with respect to $\mathcal{L}$, i.e., $\mathcal{L}_\mathcal{C} = \mathcal{L}/\sim$.

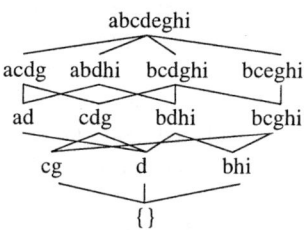

Fig. 3. Galois lattice for TDB of Figure 1

Observe that each equivalence class of itemsets contains a unique closed itemset, which serves as the upper bound for the equivalence class. Also, each class contains one or more lower bounds, which are the minimal generators. For example in Figure 1, b, h and i are the minimal generators of formal concept $(bhi, \{T_1, T_3, T_4, T_5\})$ (Figure 2).

Definition 2. An itemset Y is called a *minimal generator* for a formal concept (X, D) if $\mathcal{T}(Y) = D$ but for every proper subset $Y' \subset Y$, $\mathcal{T}(Y') \neq D$.

2.2 Succinct System of Minimal Generators

As discussed earlier, the minimal generators may still contain a lot of redundant information. Consider again the formal concept $C = (bcghi, \{T_1, T_3, T_5\})$ in our running example. In the same database, there is another concept $C_1 = (cg, \{T_1, T_2, T_3, T_5\})$. C_1 is more general than C, and C_1 has c and g as minimal generators. We can observe the following: If itemset cX is a minimal generator for C such that $g \notin X$, then gX is also be a minimal generator for C. This can be verified from Figure 2. Since we have bc, ch and ci as the minimal generators containing c but no g, we also have minimal generators bg, gh and gi. So, we only need to keep either the minimal generators containing c or those containing g, but not both; the rest can be inferred.

Can we have a *non-redundant* representation of the minimal generators? The answer is yes. The idea is intuitive though not straightforward. To illustrate the general idea, suppose a user wishes to browse the minimal generators of the formal concepts in the coarse-to-fine (or general-to-specific) order[2]. For each new concept C to be browsed, we would like to present to the user a minimal but complete set of all *new* minimal generators that cannot be inferred from the others for this concept C and from the minimal generators of the more general formal concepts already browsed.

Formally, for each formal concept C, we need to define a new equivalence relation: Two itemsets X and Y are C-*equivalent*, denoted $X \approx_C Y$ if (i) both X and Y are minimal generators of formal concept C' such that C' is more general than C, or (ii) X can be obtained from Y by replacing a subset $Z \subset X$ with $Z' \subset Y$ such that $Z \approx_C Z'$.

In our running example, if C is the formal concept whose closed itemset is $bcghi$, then $b \approx_C h$, $b \approx_C i$, $c \approx_C g$, $bc \approx_C bg$, $bc \approx_C hg$, etc. (Note that C has two more general formal concepts.) If C is the formal concept whose closed itemset is bhi, then $X \approx_C Y$ if and only if $X = Y$ since there are no concept more general than C.

The $\approx_C$ equivalence relation partitions C's minimal generators into equivalence classes. We can achieve the goal of deriving a minimal non-redundant subset of minimal generators by presenting one minimal generator for each of the equivalence classes. For example, if C is the formal concept whose closed itemset is $bcghi$, then all of its six minimal generators, namely bc, bg, ch, ci, gh, gi, belong to one equivalence class; if C is the formal concept whose closed itemset is $abcdeghi$, then its minimal generators can be partitioned into three equivalence classes: $\{ae\}$, $\{de\}$, $\{abc, abg, ach, aci, agh, agi\}$. Then, we can choose one representative for each class of minimal generators.

Which member of an equivalence class should be shown to the user, in order to minimize the overall overhead on the user? We choose one minimal generator of each formal concept as its *representative* minimal generator. This can be done freely for most basic formal concepts such as bhi, cg and d in Figure 3. To be succinct, for other concepts, we should choose one of those *canonical* minimal generators X such that X does not contain any non-representative minimal generators of more general formal concepts. For example, if C is the formal concept whose closed itemset is $bcghi$, if b and c are respectively the representative minimal generators for the concepts for bhi and cg, then bc should be the representative of C.

Definition 3. A *succinct system of minimal generators*, or SSMG for short, consists of, for each formal concept $C = (X, D)$, a representative minimal generator and a set of canonical minimal generators.

---

[2] In fact, our definitions can deal with any order of browsing.

An SSMG will remove the redundancy of minimal generators, give the users a consistent handle on each class using the representative minimal generators, and also can be used to derive all the minimal generators. The last column of Figure 2 gives an SSMG for our running example TDB, where the first minimal generators are the representatives for the concepts of the corresponding rows. Given an SSMG, clearly we can reconstruct all of the minimal generators. Also, the SSMG is not unique, even though different SSMGs have the same number of minimal generators.

Problem Definition. Given a transaction database TDB and a support threshold min_sup, the problem of *mining the succinct system of minimal generators* is to find a succinct system of minimal generators for all formal concepts $C = (X, D)$ that $sup(X) \geq min\_sup$.

3 The SSMG-Miner Algorithm

This section introduces our algorithm for mining SSMGs. It includes several novel techniques for computing local minimal generators and closed itemsets in a depth-first manner, and for using them to derive the SSMGs. While the high-level structure of the algorithm is similar to many existing DFS based algorithms, the new algorithmic contributions lie with the efficient techniques for producing representative minimal generators and removing the non-representative ones.

3.1 Depth-First Search Framework

The SSMG-Miner algorithm follows the general depth-first search framework that can be described using a depth-first search tree (e.g. *set-enumeration tree* (or SE-tree) [13]). The SE-tree enumerates all possible itemsets for a given set of items, with a global order on the items. For each node v in the tree we have a head H (consisting of items considered so far), and a tail T (consisting of items to be considered among descendant nodes). The search space associated with v consists of all itemsets of the form $Z = H \cup T'$, where T' is a nonempty subset of T. For the node labelled by ab in the SE-tree for $\{a, b, c, d\}$, we have $H = ab$ and $T = cd$, and its search space consists of abc, abd, and $abcd$. The algorithm will remove useless branches of the SE-tree, as discussed later.

3.2 Computing Local Minimals/Closures

The SSMG-Miner will efficiently compute "local minimal generators and closed itemsets" for each visited node in the depth-first search. Later we will show that some local minimal generators and closed itemsets may not be true minimal generators and closed itemsets for formal concepts, and consider efficient techniques to remove such itemsets.

In our DFS computation, for each node v with head H and tail T, those items x in T such that $T(Hx) = T(H)$ (or equivalently, $sup(Hx) = sup(H)$, in other words, item x appears in every transaction that contains H) are in the local closed itemsets, and are removed from T. Let the *local closure* of H be $LC(H) = \{x \in H \cup T \mid T(H) = T(Hx)\}$. The removal of items from T as described above will ensure that, for all ancestor nodes v' of v with head H' and tail T', $LC(H')$ is a proper subset of $LC(H)$. Hence H is considered as the *local minimal generator* for $LC(H)$.

We now illustrate the local minimal generators and closures computed for 6 nodes, using our running example (Figure 1). (1) At the root node, $H = \emptyset$, $T = abcdeghi$,

$LC(H) = \emptyset$. (2) For the first child of the root, $H = a$ and $T = bcdeghi$; since $T(a) = T(ad)$, we remove d from T (so T becomes $bceghi$; this node now has 6 children instead of the original 7); $LC(H) = ad$; a is the local minimal generator for ad and ad is the local closure for a. (3) For the node with $(H,T) = (ab, ceghi)$, $LC(ab) = abdhi$ with $sup(ab) = 2$. (4) For $(H,T) = (abc, eg)$, $LC(abc) = abcdeghi$ with $sup(abc) = 1$. (5) For $(H,T) = (abe, g)$, $LC(abe) = abdeghi$ with $sup(abe) = 1$. (6) For $(H,T) = (ae, \emptyset)$, $LC(ae) = aeghi$ with $sup(ae) = 1$.

The SSMG-Miner algorithm keeps a tuple of the form $(MinList : Max, Count)$ for each formal concept, where $MinList$ is the list of minimal generators, Max is the closed itemset, and $Count$ is the support count. The first minimal generator in $MinList$ is the representative minimal generator. For Figures 1 and 2, the tuple $(b, h, i : bhi, 4)$ is for the formal concept $(bhi, \{T_1, T_3, T_4, T_5\})$.

3.3 Determining Equivalence

The local minimal generators and closures computed at different nodes may belong to the same formal concept. The SSMG-Miner will check on this and remove any redundancy.

Lemma 1. *Let v be a node with head H and tail T. Then $LC(H)$ belongs to an existing formal concept at the time v is visited if and only if there is a node v' visited before, with head H' and tail T', such that $LC(H) \subset LC(H')$ and $sup(H) = sup(H')$.*

If one does the equivalence check based on the above lemma, the check will be inefficient. The reason is that, for each new node v with head H and tail T, we will need to go through all existing formal concepts and conduct the subset checking based on the support equivalence. In general, checking whether an itemset is a subset of another itemset in collection of itemset is very expensive.

Lemma 2. *Let v be a node with head H and tail T. Then $LC(H)$ belongs to an existing formal concept at the time v is visited if and only if there is a node v' with head H' and tail T' such that v' is visited before v and v' satisfies the following three conditions: (1) $sup(LC(H)) = sup(LC(H'))$; (2) $LC(H)$ and $LC(H')$ share a common suffix starting from x, where x is the last item of H; (3) the prefix of $LC(H))$ before x is a subset of the prefix of $LC(H')$ before x, where x is as above. Here, the values of T and T' are those when the nodes are created.*

Rationale. Clearly the "if" holds, since conditions (1–3) imply that $LC(H) \subset LC(H')$ and $sup(H) = sup(H')$, which in turn imply that $LC(H)$ and $LC(H')$ are subsets of some common closed itemset. "Only if": Suppose $LC(H)$ belongs to an existing formal concept at the time v is visited. Let v' be the node when $LC(H)$'s formal concept is first inserted; let H' be its head and T' its tail. Since $LC(H)$ and $LC(H')$ belong to the same concept, condition (1) holds. Since v' is the first node when $LC(H)$'s formal concept is inserted, by the nature of DFS computation, we have $\{y \mid y \in H \text{ and } y \text{ is before } x\} \subseteq \{y \mid y \in H' \text{ and } y \text{ is before } x\}$, and so (3) holds. This implies (2) holds.

This lemma allows us to efficiently implement the check using some comparison on the support counts, and certain suffixes and prefixes of itemsets and the local closure.

Example 1. We illustrate by considering these three formal concepts for example in Figures 1 and 2: $(a : ad, 3)$, $(ab : abdhi, 2)$ and $(abc : abcdeghi, 1)$. For the node with

$H = abe$ and $T = g$, $LC(abe) = abdeghi$ and $sup(abe) = 1$. We need to decide if this is a new formal concept and, if not new, which existing concept is that of abe. We do this as follows: We look for (1) concepts with the same support count as abe, and we compare their closed itemsets against $LC(abe) = abdeghi$. The concept C of abc is the only such concept. We note the following: (2) The closed itemset of C, namely $abcdeghi$, and $LC(abe) = abdeghi$ share the common suffix of $eghi$, starting at the item e (the last item of abe). (3) The prefix of $LC(abe) = abdeghi$ before e, namely abd, is a subset of the prefix of $abcdeghi$ before e. Lemma 2 ensures that, when this happens, abe is not generating a new formal concept, but abe is another potential generator for the concept of C.

On the other hand, if there is no concept C satisfying the conditions, then the new local minimal generator and closure form a new formal concept. Consider the formal concept $(bd : bdhi, 3)$ and we compute $LC(cd) = cdg$ and $sup(cd) = 3$ at the node with $H = cd$. We conclude that cd and bd do not belong to any previously found formal concept, since $LC(cd)$ is not a subset of any closed itemsets of existing concepts with the same support.

More specifically, Lemma 2 implies that equivalence checking can be accomplished efficiently by using a search tree structure. In such a tree, the items are ordered under the *reverse of the original order* on the items. We have one such tree for each support count. The trees will be built in a lazy manner. For each formal concept C, we use the closed itemset for C to search and insert. This is done similarly for local closures computed at nodes. For example, if the original order of items is the alphabetical order, for the closed itemset $abcdeghi$, we have a branch of $i \to h \to g \to e \to ...$ For the search involving $LC(abe) = abdeghi$, we follow the branch $i \to h \to g \to e$. Then we go through the formal concepts stored below this branch to check for containment of the prefixes. Since the search of the suffix only needs to continue if exact match is found and can be terminated as soon as a mismatch is found, it is very efficient.

3.4 Removing Non-minimal Generators and Clutters

Some local minimal generators computed in the DFS process may turn out to be not minimal generators for their formal concepts. Also, the clutters caused by redundant minimal generators need to be removed. We now discuss how SSMG-Miner handles these issues.

To show the removal of non-minimal generators, let us examine the running example again (Figures 1 and 2). For node $H = ae$, we have four formal concepts computed: $(a : ad, 3)$, $(ab : abdhi, 2)$, $(abc, abe, abg, ace, ach, aci : abcdeghi, 1)$, $(ac : acdg, 2)$. We find that ae is a new minimal generator for the concept of $abcdeghi$. Since abe and ace are supersets of ae, they are not true minimal generators for their formal concept, and should be removed. So the third formal concept becomes $(abc, abg, ach, aci : abcdeghi, 1)$, before ae is inserted. Since ae is earlier than abc in the "cognitive-order", we select ae to replace abc as the representative minimal generator.

To exemplify the removal of clutters, let us consider the running example (Figures 1 and 2). Suppose our current set of formal concepts are as given above, and we next consider the node $H = ag$. We find that $LC(ag) = adg$. We see that adg and $acdg$ are equivalent, hence ag is the second minimal generator of $acdg$. We then remove all minimal generators of other concepts which contain ag (the redundant generators). For example, abg is removed from the set of minimal generators of $abcdeghi$. So we get the following formal concepts: $(a : ad, 3)$, $(ab : abdhi, 2)$, $(ae, ach, aci, abc : abcdeghi, 1)$, $(ac, ag : acdg, 2)$.

Regarding implementation, for each formal concept we have a concept identifier CID. For each item x, we have an inverted list consisting of all those formal concepts that have one or more minimal generators containing x. These inverted lists will be used to locate formal concepts that may contain a given itemset (minimal generator).

3.5 The Pseudo-Code of SSMG-Miner

The SSMG-Miner (Figure 4) calls the DFS function for the root node, with these three arguments: $H = \emptyset, T = I - LC$, and $LC = \emptyset$, where I is the set of all items.

ALGORITHM SSMG_MINER:
INPUT: *A transaction database TDB, support threshold* min_sup.
OUTPUT: *Succinct system of minimal generators for formal concepts in TDB.*
METHOD:
let $SSMG = \emptyset$; // *SSMG is a global variable*;
let LC = {*items occurring in all transactions*};
call $DFS(H = \emptyset, T = I - LC, LC)$;
return $SSMG$;

Function DFS(H,T,LC) // *H: head, T: tail*
// *LC: local closure, with value of parent node initially*
if $sup(H) <$ min_sup *return*;
for each $x \in T$
  if $sup(H \cup \{x\}) = sup(H)$
    let $T = T - \{x\}, LC = LC \cup \{x\}$;
if $(H : LC, sup(H))$ *is a new concept*
  add $(H : LC, sup(H))$ *to SSMG*;
else add H *as minimal generator for LC and remove clutter*
for each x in T
  let $H_x = H \cup \{x\}$ and $T_x = \{y \in T \mid y > x\}$;
  call $DFS(H_x, T_x, LC)$;

Fig. 4. Algorithm SSMG-Miner

The DFS function first determines if H meets the minimal support threshold. If the answer is yes, it will move all those items x such that $sup(H) = sup(H \cup \{x\})$ from T to LC. At this time, $(H, LC, sup(H))$ becomes a candidate new concept. If LC is not equivalent to any current concept, then it inserts $(H, LC, sup(H))$ as a new concept. Otherwise it inserts H as a new minimal generator of its concept, and removes the clutters. The check regarding equivalence, the insertion of new minimal generators and the removal of clutters are discussed in the previous subsections. Limited by space, their pseudo-code is omitted. DFS calls itself for each child node of the current node.

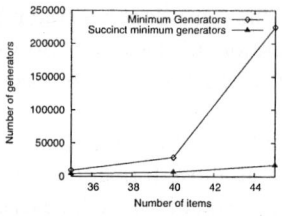 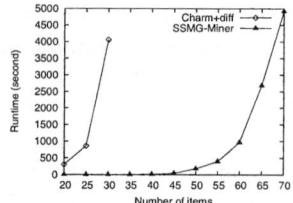 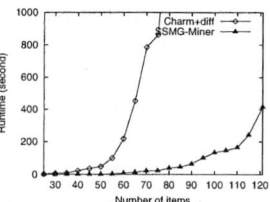

Fig. 5. Reduction of # of generators on Colon Cancer data set (support threshold = 1%)

Fig. 6. Scalability on number of items: Colon Cancer data set (support threshold=1%)

Fig. 7. Scalability on number of items: Mushroom data set (support threshold=1%)

4 Performance Study

We now report experiments on the performance of the SSMG-Miner algorithm and its effect in reducing the amount of redundant information. Experiments show that the algorithm can deal with fairly high dimensional data sets within a short time. We also provide comparison with previous work as much as we could, and with a post-processing approach. All experiments (unless indicated otherwise) were performed on a PC with P4 2.4G CPU and 512M main memory, running on Windows XP.

We used two data sets in our efficiency experiments. (1) The Mushroom data set has been frequently used for evaluating data mining algorithms and is obtained from the UCI Machine Learning Repository. It includes 22 attributes and 8,124 tuples. There are a total of 121 attribute-value pairs (items). (2) The Colon tumor gene expression data set is from [2]. It consists of micro-array gene expression data for 62 sample tissues, with 22 being normal tissues and 40 colon tumor tissues. Microarrays are a technology for simultaneously profiling the expression levels of tens of thousands of genes in a patient sample. It is increasingly clear that better diagnosis methods and better understanding of disease mechanisms can be derived from a careful analysis of microarray measurements of gene expression profiles. As with most association-type data mining, we discretized each gene into two intervals: low and high. We also used the entropy method to select the top 45 most "relevant" genes from total of 2000 genes. These data sets are typical examples of data that might be used in scientific discovery process by data mining techniques. Please also note that these two data sets are quite dense and thus challenging to mine, as indicated by many previous studies.

4.1 Redundant Information Reduction

Figure 5 shows the succinct minimal generator concept leads to a huge reduction in the number of minimal generators in the result of mining. The Colon data set is used. For the case of 40 items, 76% of the minimal generators are redundant, and for 45 items 93% of the minimal generators are redundant. The reduction on Mushroom is similar (the details are omitted due to space).

4.2 Comparison with Postprocessing Approach

Post processing seems to be much worse than the SSMG-Miner, even though we do not ask the postprocessing algorithm to remove the redundant minimal generators. For example, we compared with the postprocessing approach which combines the Charm algorithm [15] for closed itemset mining, and the Border-Diff algorithm [6] for mining the minimal generators from the closed itemsets. First, the Charm algorithm is used to compute the closed itemsets satisfying given support threshold. (We used our own implementation of the Charm algorithm.) Then, for each closed itemset X, let $S_X = \{Y \mid Y \subset X$ and Y is a closed itemset$\}$; then the Border-Diff algorithm is called to mine the minimal itemsets which occur in X but not in any itemset in S_X. Let $M_1, ..., M_k$ be the result of this operation. It can be verified that $M_1, ..., M_k$ are the minimal generators for the class represented by X. It turns out that this algorithm is very expensive: On the Colon data, on 20, 25 and 30 projected columns of the data, SSMG-Miner used 1, 1 and 2 seconds respectively, whereas post-processing used 305, 964, and 4090 seconds respectively. The main cost of the Charm+Border-Diff algorithm is due to the large number of calls fo Border-Diff.

4.3 Comparison with a Previous Algorithm

No previous work has considered the mining of succinct minimal generators. Some prior work considered the mining of all minimal generators [12]. (Several papers considered the mining of closed itemsets, and perhaps with one minimal generator for each closed itemset.) We contacted the authors of [12], but we cannot obtain either executable or source code. We are able to provide a rough comparison as follows: For the Mushroom data when all attributes are considered and the minimal support is set at 1 (so that all itemsets are frequent), our algorithm finished in about 2 hours on our machine. On the other hand, the algorithm of [12] used about one day and a half. Although the configuration of the test platform is not given in [12], we believe that our method is substantially faster. We should also note that the algorithm of [12] does not remove clutters.

4.4 Scalability on Number of Items

Figures 6 and 7 show the computation time of SSMG **as the number of items varies**. The minimum support is set at 1% and the different number of items is obtained by projecting the original data set over the first k items. Although the processing time increases exponentially with the number of items, it is encouraging to know that our algorithm finishes in a reasonable amount of time. We use random subsets of the Mushroom data to test the **scalability on size of database**. Figure 8 shows the computation time vs. the number of instances for the Mushroom data. The computation time is roughly linear as the number of instances (tuples) increases. Figure 9 shows how computation time varies **as the support threshold varies** on the Mushroom data. As the support threshold decreases, the number of minimal generators increases, leading to increased computation time.

Summary. From the extensive experiments on the two real data sets, the effectiveness and efficiency of SSMG-Miner are verified. Our results show that SSMG-Miner is feasible for mining real data sets.

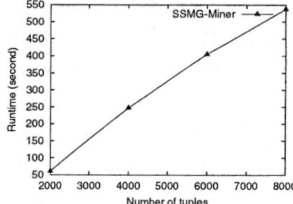 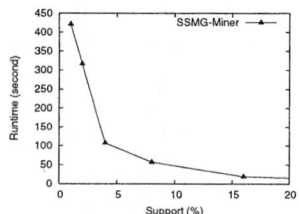

Fig. 8. Scalability on database size: Mushroom data set (support threshold=1%)

Fig. 9. Scalability on support threshold: Mushroom data set

5 Related Work and Discussion

5.1 Related Work

Formal Concept Analysis (FCA) was first pioneered by Wille in 1982 [7], and has grown into an active field for data analysis and knowledge discovery. Other previous research most related to our work can be divided into two categories: mining closed itemsets and mining minimal generators.

Closed itemset mining is one of the major classes of research addressing the frequent itemset mining problem [1]. This class of research aims at mining a concise subset of the frequent itemsets that can be used to derive all other frequent itemsets and their support counts. A major approach considers the closed itemset mining problem, initially proposed in [10], where one mines only those frequent itemsets having no proper superset with the same support. Mining closed itemsets can lead to orders of magnitude smaller result set [16] (than mining all frequent itemsets) while retaining the completeness, i.e., the concise result set can be used to generate all the frequent itemsets with correct support counts in a straightforward manner. In the last several years, extensive studies have proposed fast algorithms for mining frequent closed itemsets, such as Aclose [10], CLOSET [11], MAFIA [4], CHARM [15], and CLOSET+ [14].

While prior research considered closed itemsets, they paid little or no attention to **mining minimal generators**. Minimal generators were only used as a means to achieve other goals if they were considered. The algorithm of [10] focused on the mining of closed itemsets, but in the computation process it produces one minimal generator as a by-product. The non-derivable and free itemsets [5, 3] are related to minimal generators.

Reference [12] gave an algorithm to compute the closed itemsets and their minimal generators incrementally (by inserting tuples one at a time). However, it does not consider the removal of the redundant minimal generators.

5.2 Further Extensions

Our method can be extended in several aspects, including these three: (1) We can analyze the SSMGs and their relationship with their corresponding closed itemsets. We can also analyze the SSMGs for data with multiple classes, such as normal tissues and cancer tissues for colon cancer discussed above. (2) We can consider SSMGs for approximate formal concepts, as a generalization of "exact" equivalent classes. We can view itemsets as approximately equivalent if their transaction sets are approximately equal. This will help reduce the number of formal concepts significantly. We can also analyze the SSMGs of approximately identical formal concepts. (3) We conjecture that the following numbers can be used as indicators of the structure of the data set under consideration: the number of formal concepts, the number of formal concepts with multiple minimal generators, and the reduction ratio from number of minimal generators to succinct minimal generators.

Acknowledgement: We thank Ravi Janga who helped with the coding of the Charm-BDiff algorithm, and the reviewers of a previous version of this paper.

References

1. R. Agrawal, et al. Mining association rules between sets of items in large databases. In *SIGMOD'93*.
2. U. Alon, et al. Broad patterns of gene expression revealed by clustering analysis of tumor and normal colon tissue s probed by oligonucleotide arrays. *Proc. Nat. Academy of Sciences of the United States of American*, 96:6745.-675, 1999.
3. J-F. Boulicaut, et al. Free-sets: A condensed representation of boolean data for the approximation of frequency queries. *Data Mininig and Knowledge Discovery*, 7(1):5–22, 2003.
4. D. Burdick, et al. MAFIA: A maximal frequent itemset algorithm for transactional databases. In *ICDE'01*.
5. T. Calders and B. Goethals. Mining all non-derivable frequent itemsets. In *PKDD'02*.
6. G. Dong and J. Li. Efficient mining of emerging patterns: Discovering trends and differences. In *KDD'99*.
7. B. Ganter and R. Wille. *Formal Concept Analysis: Mathematical Foundations*. Springer, Heidelberg, 1999.
8. J. Hereth, et al. Conceptual knowledge discovery and data analysis. In *Int. Conf. on Conceptual Structures*, pages 421–437, 2000.
9. G. Mineau and B. Ganter, editors. *Proc. Int. Conf. on Conceptual Structures*. LNCS 1867, Springer, 2000.
10. N. Pasquier, et al. Discovering frequent closed itemsets for association rules. In *ICDT'99*.
11. J. Pei, et al. CLOSET: An efficient algorithm for mining frequent closed itemsets. In *ACM SIGMOD DMKD'00*.
12. J.L. Pfaltz and C.M. Taylor. Closed set mining of biological data. In *BIOKDD'02*.
13. R. Rymon. Search through systematic set enumeration. In *Proc. of Int'l Conf. on Principles of Knowledge Representation and Reasoning, Cambridge MA*, pages 539–550, 1992.
14. J. Wang, et al. Closet+: Searching for the best strategies for mining frequent closed itemsets. In *KDD'03*.
15. M. Zaki and C. Hsiao. CHARM: An efficient algorithm for closed itemset mining. In *SDM'02*.
16. M. J. Zaki. Generating non-redundant association rules. In *KDD'00*.

A General Approach to Mining Quality Pattern-Based Clusters from Microarray Data*

Daxin Jiang[1], Jian Pei[2], and Aidong Zhang[1]

[1] State University of New York at Buffalo, USA
{djiang3, azhang}@cse.buffalo.edu
[2] Simon Fraser University, Canada
jpei@cs.sfu.ca

Abstract. Pattern-based clustering has broad applications in microarray data analysis, customer segmentation, e-business data analysis, etc. However, pattern-based clustering often returns a large number of highly-overlapping clusters, which makes it hard for users to identify interesting patterns from the mining results. Moreover, there lacks of a general model for pattern-based clustering. Different kinds of patterns or different measures on the pattern coherence may require different algorithms. In this paper, we address the above two problems by proposing a general quality-driven approach to mining top-k quality pattern-based clusters. We examine our quality-driven approach using real world microarray data sets. The experimental results show that our method is general, effective and efficient.

1 Introduction

Clustering is an important data mining problem. For a set of objects, a clustering algorithm partitions the objects into a set of *clusters*, such that objects within a cluster are similar to each other, and objects in different clusters are dissimilar. While many traditional clustering methods often assume that the clusters are mutually exclusive and rely on metric distance between objects, some recently emerging applications, such as those in bio-informatics and e-business, post the challenges of mining non-exclusive, non-distance-based clusters in various subspaces from large databases.

As a typical application, a microarray data set can be modelled as a numerical data matrix recording the expression levels of genes on samples. An important task of analyzing microarray data is to find co-expressed genes and phenotypes. A group of *co-expressed genes* are the ones that demonstrate similar expression

---

* This research is partly supported by NSF grants DBI-0234895 and IIS-0308001, NIH grant 1 P20 GM067650-01A1, the Endowed Research Fellowship and the President Research Grant from Simon Fraser University. All opinions, findings, conclusions and recommendations in this paper are those of the authors and do not necessarily reflect the views of the funding agencies.

patterns over a substantial subset of samples, and the subset of samples may correspond to some *phenotype*.

Moreover, given a microarray data set, a gene can belong to more than one co-expressed gene group, since it may correlate to more than one phenotype; and a sample can manifest more than one phenotype, such as tumor vs. normal tissues and male vs. female samples. To address the novel requirements, recently, a new theme of *pattern-based clustering*, is being developed [1, 5, 6, 9, 10] (Please see Section 2 for a brief review).

As indicated by the previous studies, pattern-based clustering is effective for mining non-exclusive, non-distance-based clusters. However, the state-of-the-art methods for pattern-based clustering are still facing the following two serious challenges, which will be addressed in this paper.

Challenge 1: Pattern-based clustering may return a large number of highly-overlapping clusters.
To filter out trivial clusters, most of the pattern-based clustering methods adopt some thresholds, such as the minimum number of objects in a cluster, the minimum number of attributes in a cluster, and the minimum degree of coherence of a cluster. Since too tight threshold values may prune out most of the clusters, including those bearing interesting patterns, loose threshold values are usually preferred.

However, pattern-based clustering will return the complete set of possible combinations of objects and attributes that pass the thresholds. When loose threshold values are specified, thousands or tens of thousands of clusters will be reported. Moreover, since the microarray data are typically highly-connected [3], the reported clusters may be often highly overlapping. For example, our empirical study has shown that the average overlap among the clusters returned by a representative pattern-based clustering algorithm may be as high as 79% (Please see Section 5 for details). Clearly, it is hard for users to identify useful patterns from such voluminous and redundant mining results.

Can we develop an effective method that can automatically focus on finding a small set of representative clusters with respect to loose threshold values?

Our Contribution. In this paper, we propose a theme of *mining top-k quality pattern-based clusters*, based on a user specified quality/utilization function. In particular, the top-k clusters are sorted according to their quality, and the clusters with higher quality are reported before those with lower quality. We show that, by intuitive quality functions, highly overlapping clusters can be avoided.

Challenge 2: There are numerous pattern-based clustering models due to various definitions of patterns and coherence measures.
For example, Cheng and Church [1] measured the coherence of clusters by the *mean squared residue score*. Wang et al. [9] introduced the notion of *pScore* to measure the similarity between the objects in clusters. Liu and Wang [5] defined patterns by ordering attributes in value ascending order. Jiang et al. [4] constrained the coherence within groups of samples by the *minimum coherence threshold*. Different algorithms are proposed to handle specific models. Even

with a minor change to the specific pattern-based clustering model, such as the definition of coherence function, we may have to write a new algorithm.

Given that pattern-based clustering methods share essential intuitions and principles, can we have a general approach such that many different pattern-based clustering models can be handled consistently?

Our Contribution. In this paper, we develop a general model for pattern-based clustering to address the above challenge. Our new pattern-base clustering model is a generalization of several previous models, including *bi-Cluster* [1], δ-*pCluster* [9], *OP-Cluster* [5] and *coherent gene cluster* [4]. We study how to mine top-k quality pattern-based clusters under the general model, and give a general and efficient algorithm.

The remainder of the paper is organized as follows. In Section 2, we review the related work, and also clarify the novel progress that we make in this paper comparing to our previous studies on mining microarray data. A general quality-driven model is introduced in Section 3. A general approach to mining top-k quality pattern-based clusters is presented in Section 4. We report the experimental results in Section 5. Finally, we conclude this paper in Section 6.

2   Related Work

Our research is highly related to pattern-based clustering. Cheng and Church [1] introduced *bi-cluster* model. Given a subset of objects I and a subset of attributes J, the coherence of the submatrix (I, J) is measured by the *mean squared residue score*.

$$r_{IJ} = \frac{1}{|I||J|} \sum_{i \in I, j \in J} (a_{ij} - a_{iJ} - a_{Ij} + a_{IJ})^2, \tag{1}$$

where a_{ij} is the value of object i on j, a_{iJ} is the average value of row i, a_{Ij} is the average value of column j, and a_{IJ} is the average value of the submatrix (I, J). The problem of *bi-clustering* is to mine submatrices with low mean squared residue scores. Yang et al. [10] proposed a move-based algorithm to find biclusters more efficiently. The algorithms in [1] and [10] adopt heuristic search strategies, and thus cannot guarantee to find the optimal biclusters in a data set.

In [9], Wang et al. proposed the model of δ-*pCluster*. A subset of objects O and a subset of attributes A form a pattern-based cluster if for any pair of objects $x, y \in O$, and any pair of attributes $a, b \in A$, the difference of change of values on attributes a and b between objects x and y is smaller than a threshold δ, i.e., $|(x.a - y.a) - (x.b - y.b)| \leq \delta$. In a recent study [6], Pei et al. developed *MaPle*, an efficient algorithm to mine the complete set of maximal pattern-based clusters (i.e., non-redundant pattern-based clusters).

In [5], Liu and Wang presented the model of *OP-Cluster*. Under this model, two objects g_i, g_j are similar on a subset of attributes S if the values of these two objects induce the same relative order of those attributes. An efficient algorithm, *OPC-Tree*, was developed.

2.1 New Progress in This Paper

Since 2002, we have been systematically developing pattern-based clustering methods for mining microarray data, e.g., [6, 4, 3]. For example, we proposed a model for coherent clusters, a specific type of pattern-based clusters, in the novel gene-sample-time series microarray data sets, and developed algorithms *Sample-Gene Search* and *Gene-Sample Search* [4]. *Sample-Gene Search* was shown more efficient.

This paper is critically different from [4] and other previous studies on pattern-based clustering in the following perspectives. First, the methods discussed in [4] enumerate *all* pattern-based clusters. As discussed before, although *MaPle*, *OPC-Tree*, *Gene-Sample Search* and *Sample-Gene Search* can find the complete set of the pattern-based clusters in a data set, they may not be effective to handle the two challenges discussed in Section 1. In this paper, we address the challenges by proposing a general quality-driven pattern-based clustering framework. Instead of enumerating all the pattern-based clusters, we mine only the *top-k clusters* here according to a quality/utilization function specified by users. All existing methods cannot mine such top-k clusters.

Second, [4] studies a specific type of microarray data stes. In this paper, we do not focus on a specific model. Instead, we generalize several previously proposed pattern-based clustering models and propose a general approach.

Last, [4] and this paper share the framework of pattern-growth approaches, i.e., both methods conduct depth-first search. However, due to the quality-driven mining requirements, in this paper, we develop techniques to prune futile search subspaces using the quality criteria (e.g., Section 4.1 and Rule 3). The algorithm developed in this paper inherits and generalizes the technical merits from [4, 6].

3 Mining Quality Pattern-Based Clusters

For a set of n genes $G\text{-}Set = \{g_1, \ldots, g_n\}$ and a set of m samples $S\text{-}Set = \{s_1, \ldots, s_m\}$, the expression levels of the genes on the samples form a matrix $M = \{m_{i,j}\}$, where $m_{i,j}$ is the expression level of gene g_i ($1 \leq i \leq n$) on sample s_j ($1 \leq j \leq m$). A *cluster* is a submatrix $C = (G, S)$ of M, i.e., $G \subseteq G\text{-}Set$ and $S \subseteq S\text{-}Set$, such that C is coherent. Here, the coherence of C describes how coherently the genes in G exhibit expression patterns on the set of samples S.

The measure of coherence varies in different specific pattern-based clustering models. In this paper, we are interested in constructing a general model instead of proposing another measure of coherence. Thus, we assume that the coherence of a submatrix is given by a function $cScore$ such that (1) $cScore(C) \geq 0$ for any submatrix C; and (2) for submatrices C_1 and C_2, if $cScore(C_1) > cScore(C_2)$, then C_1 is more coherent than C_2.

For a specific model, it is easy to revise the coherence measure to satisfy the above two requirements. For example, the *bi-Cluster* model [1] minimizes the *mean squared residue score* r_{IJ} (Equation 1). Since the score is always greater than or equals to 0, minimizing r_{IJ} is equivalent to maximizing $\frac{1}{r_{IJ}}$. Thus, we can use the following $cScore()$ function.

$$cScore(C) = \frac{1}{\sum_{i \in I, j \in J}(a_{ij} - a_{iJ} - a_{Ij} + a_{IJ})^2} \qquad (2)$$

For δ-$pCluster$, we can use the following function.

$$cScore(C) = \begin{cases} 1 & \text{if } pScore(X) \leq \delta \text{ for any } 2 \times 2 \text{ sumbmatrix } X \text{ of } C \\ 0 & \text{otherwise} \end{cases} \qquad (3)$$

For OP-$Cluster$, we have

$$cScore(C) = \begin{cases} 1 & \text{if patterns in } C \text{ follow the same ordering} \\ 0 & \text{otherwise} \end{cases} \qquad (4)$$

Moreover, for *coherent gene cluster* [4], we can specify the *cScore* function as follows.

$$cScore(C) = \begin{cases} 1 & \text{if in } C \text{ each gene is coherent across the samples} \\ 0 & \text{otherwise} \end{cases} \qquad (5)$$

In real applications, users often have a preference among the clusters. For example, in mining gene expression data, clusters with a high coherence score and a large number of genes and samples are strongly preferred. Accordingly, we define the quality measure of clusters as follows.

Definition 1 (Quality of a cluster). Let $C = (G, S)$ be a submatrix of a microarray data set M, the *quality* of C is defined as $quality(C) = size(C) \cdot cScore(C)$, where $size(C) = |G| \cdot |S|$ and *cScore* is the coherence function. ∎

For a set of clusters that have no overlap, the quality of the set of clusters is simply the sum of the quality of each cluster. However, when there exist some overlaps, we have to make sure that each overlapping cell contributes to the total quality only once, and the contribution goes to the most quality cluster that contains the overlap.

Definition 2 (Quality of a set of clusters). Let Ω be a set of submatrices. The *quality* of Ω is defined as $quality(\Omega) = \sum_{m_{i,j} \in \cup_{C \in \Omega} C} Q(m_{i,j})$, where $Q(m_{i,j}) = \max\{cScore(C) | (C \in \Omega) \wedge (m_{i,j} \in C)\}$. ∎

Suppose a user wants a set of k clusters that have the best quality, the problem can be formulated as to compute a set $\Omega = \{C_1, \ldots, C_k\}$ of k submatrices such that $quality(\Omega)$ is globally maximized. However, given different numbers of clusters k and k' such that $k < k'$, the corresponding optimized sets of clusters Ω and Ω' may not be consistent. In other words, since we maximize the quality function on a global level, a quality cluster $C \in \Omega$ may not necessarily appear in Ω'. The inconsistency among the mining results with respect to different numbers of clusters is undesirable, since the number of clusters k is usually unknown a priori.

To address this problem, we turn to a greedy framework. The main idea is that we compute a series of k clusters $\Omega = \{C_1, \ldots, C_k\}$ such that (1) C_1 is the cluster with the highest quality; and (2) for C_i ($i \geq 2$), C_i is a cluster maximizing the "quality improvement" with respect to $C_1, \ldots, C_{i-1}$. In this way, for any two numbers of clusters $k < k'$, we have $\Omega \subset \Omega'$. Then the user can choose the number of clusters in an incremental manner. At first, the user can choose a small value of k, if all the clusters reported are with high quality, the user can ask for more clusters until the quality of the latest reported cluster is not satisfactory. We formulate the idea as follows.

Definition 3 (Quality gain). Let $C = (G, S)$ be a submatrix of a gene expression matrix M, and $cScore$ be a coherence function. For a set of submatrices $\Omega = \{C_1, \ldots, C_k\}$, the *quality gain* of C (against Ω) is defined as $quality(C|\Omega) = |C - overlap(C, \Omega)| \cdot cScore(C)$, where function $overlap(C, \Omega) = \{m_{i,j} | (m_{i,j} \in C) \wedge (\exists C' \in \Omega : m_{i,j} \in C')\}$ returns the set of cells in C that overlap with some clusters in Ω. ∎

Problem of Mining Top-k Quality Clusters. Given a gene expression matrix M, a coherence function $cScore(\cdot)$ and a positive integer k. The *problem of mining top-k quality pattern based clusters* is to compute a series of k submatrices $C_1, \ldots, C_k$ such that (1) $quality(C_1)$ is the maximum; and (2) for $i \geq 2$, $quality(C_i|\{C_1, \ldots, C_{i-1}\})$ is the maximum. ∎

Our general model of mining quality pattern-based clusters has the following distinct features. First, *our model can generate a list of clusters in quality descending order*. Many previous approaches such as [4, 5, 6, 9] report all the pattern-based clusters without any indication of the significance of the clusters. It is often tedious to select the interesting clusters from those trivial ones. Second, *our model is a generalization of* bi-cluster, δ-pCluster, OP-Cluster, *and* coherent gene cluster. As shown before, we can easily assign coherence functions to those specific models.

In many applications, a user has several basic constraints to avoid trivial clusters. The constraints can be specified using the following three thresholds. (1) *Minimum number of genes min_g*; (2) *Minimum number of samples min_s*; and (3) *Minimum coherence δ*. A submatrix $C = (G, S)$ will be reported as a cluster only if it satisfies the constraints: $|G| \geq min_g$, $|S| \geq min_s$ and $cScore(C) \geq \delta$.

Moreover, in some pattern-based clustering models, such as δ-*pCluster*, *OP-Cluster*, and *coherent gene cluster*, an anti-monotonicity holds: a coherence function $cScore()$ is *anti-monotonic* if for any two clusters $C_1 = (G_1, S_1)$ and $C_2 = (G_2, S_2)$ such that $G_1 \subseteq G_2$ and $S_1 \subseteq S_2$, $cScore(C_1) \geq cScore(C_2)$. The anti-monotonicity captures a natural assumption: the coherence of a submatrix monotonically decreases as more genes and/or more samples are included. In our general model, we also assume that the anti-monotonicity holds for the coherence function.

4 The Mining Algorithm

In this section, we will present a general approach to mine top-k quality clusters that satisfy the thresholds. Basically, we find the top-k clusters iteratively, one at a time. We will address the following two issues.

- In the i-th iteration ($1 \leq i \leq k$), how can we find cluster C_i that maximizes the quality gain against the set of clusters $\{C_1, \ldots, C_{i-1}\}$?
- How to search the huge space of all possible submatrices efficiently and prune unpromising subspace sharply?

4.1 Mining a Cluster Maximizing Quality Gain

A naïve method to find a cluster that has the maximum quality gain is to test every possible submatrix and its quality gain. A submatirx can be viewed as a combination of genes and samples. Therefore, the problem can be reduced to enumerating all possible combinations of genes and samples.

A systematic way to tackle an enumeration problem is to use enumeration tree [7]. Figure 1 shows the enumeration tree of a four-element set $\{a, b, c, d\}$. It provides a conceptual tool to enumerate all the subsets of $\{a, b, c, d\}$ systematically.

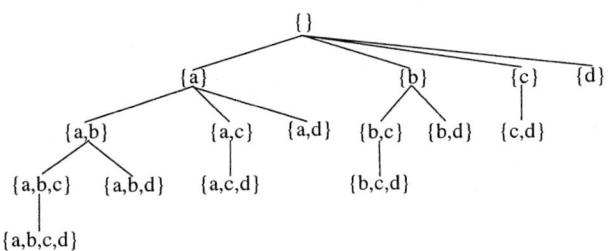

Fig. 1. Enumeration of combinations of samples

Basically, we can enumerate all the subsets of samples first. For each subset of samples S, we enumerate all subsets of genes G, and test the quality gain of (G, S). We only need to keep the submatrix $C = (G, S)$ that satisfies the thresholds and achieves the best quality gain in the current iteration. This method is called the *Sample-Gene Search*.[1]

Why do we enumerate subsets of samples first and then subsets of genes later, but not in the reverse way?

In gene expression data, the number of genes is typically by far larger than the number of samples. In other words, the number of combinations of genes

---

[1] The initial idea of enumerating samples instead of genes in microarray data sets to find pattern-based clusters was firstly proposed by Wang et al. [9], and further systematically developed in [6].

is often dramatically larger than the number of combinations of samples. With our pruning rules in Section 4.2, if the Sample-Gene Search is adopted, once a subset of samples and its descendants are pruned, all searches of related subsets of genes are pruned as well. Heuristically, the Sample-Gene Search may bring a better chance to prune a more bushy search sub-tree than the Gene-Sample Search for gene expression data.

When we enumerate the subsets of samples or genes, we can conduct a *recursive, depth-first search* of the set enumeration tree. Given a data set of m samples and n genes, the set enumeration tree has 2^{m+n} nodes. However, we never need to materialize such a tree. Instead, we only need to keep a path from the root of the tree to the node we are searching as a working set, which contains at most $m + n + 1$ nodes. Besides, proper pruning techniques will be developed to prune unpromising branches as early as possible.

4.2 The Rules for Pruning

In this subsection, we develop efficient rules to prune unpromising subspaces using the thresholds and/or the anti-monotonicity of the coherence function.

For the Sample-Gene Search, each node on the set enumeration tree contains a unique submatrix. Thus we will use the submatrix to refer to the node. At node $C = (G, S)$ of the set enumeration tree, where $G = \{g_{i_1}, \ldots, g_{i_k}\}$ ($1 \leq i_1 < \cdots < i_k \leq n$), we keep a list $gTail$ of genes. A gene $g_j \in G$-Set is included in list $gTail$ if (1) $j \geq i_k$ and (2) the coherence score of $C' = (G \cup \{g_j\}, S)$ is no less than minimum coherence threshold δ. We have the following result, which generalized some of the pruning techniques in the existing pattern-based clustering methods (e.g., [6, 4]).

Rule 1 (Pruning irrelevant genes). *For a node C in the set enumeration tree, only the genes in list $gTail$ should be used to construct super clusters of C.*

Rationale. Suppose gene $g_j \notin gTail$ of $C = (G, S)$, where $G = \{g_{i_1}, \ldots, g_{i_k}\}$ ($1 \leq i_1 < \cdots < i_k \leq n$). Two situations may happen. First, $j \leq i_k$. Second, $C' = (G \cup \{g_j\}, S)$ violates the coherence constraint. For the first situation, g_j cannot be used to expand C according to the structure of the set enumeration tree. For the second situation, since any descendant C'' of C' is a submatrix of C', according to the anti-monotonic property, C'' also violates the coherence constraint. Therefore, we can prune the genes not in the $gTail$ list. ∎

Similarly, we can maintain a list $sTail$ of samples for node C, and prune the samples not in $sTail$ when we search the subtree of C. Due to the limit of space, we omit the details here. Moreover, for any descendant node C' of C, the $gTail$ and $sTail$ lists of C' are subsets of those lists of C, respectively.

Since the $gTail$ and $sTail$ lists of the current node C tell us which genes and samples can be used to further expand the subtree of C, they actually provide us the a priori information about the subtree of C. Based on such information, we can prune the unpromising descendants of C early.

Rule 2 (Pruning small submatrices). *For a node $C = (G, S)$, the subtree of C can be pruned if $(|G| + |gTail|) < min_g$ or $(|S| + |sTail|) < min_s$.*

Rationale. Since we only use the genes and samples in $gTail$ and $sTail$ lists to expand the subtree of C, for any descendant node $C' = (G', S')$ of C, we have $|G'| \leq (|G| + |gTail|)$ and $|S'| \leq (|S| + |sTail|)$. If for node C, $(|G| + |gTail|) < min_g$ or $(|S| + |sTail|) < min_s$, then none of the descendants of C will satisfy the size constraint. Therefore, the subtree of C can be pruned. ∎

Rules 1 and 2 are essential for pattern-based clustering (as well as frequent itemset mining). The similar idea has been studied before extensively (e.g., [4, 6]). The quality mining inherits them. To push the quality requirement into the mining, the following lemma gives the upper bound of the quality gain that can be achieved in a subtree.

Input: the gene expression data set M
Output: the top-k clusters Ω
Method:
    let $\Omega = \emptyset$ // the set of top clusters already found
    for $num = 1$ to k do
        let $maxQ = -1$, $maxCluster = null$
        for each subset of samples S
            if $|S| < min_s$ continue
            for $i = 1$ to $(|G\text{-}Set| - min_g)$ do
                let $G = \{g_i\}$, $C = (G, S)$; compute $gTail$
                call recursive-search(C, $gTail$)
            end for // end the enumeration of genes
        end for // end the enumerate of samples
        let $\Omega = \Omega \cup \{maxCluster\}$
    end for
Procedure: recursive-search(C, $gTail$)
    if $(|G| + |gTail|) < min_g$ then return
    calculate the quality upper bound of C's descendants according to Lemma 1
    if C can be pruned by Pruning Rule 3 then return
    while $(gTail \neq \emptyset)$ do
        let $i = min\{j|\ g_j \in gTail\}$
        let $C' = (G \cup \{g_i\} \times S)$; compute $gTail'$
        call recursive-search(C', $gTail'$)
    end while
    if $((|G| \geq min_g)\ \&\&\ (|S| \geq min_s))$ then
        if $(quality(C|\Omega)) > maxQ$
        then let $maxQ = quality(C|\Omega)$, let $maxCluster = C$
        end if
    end if

Fig. 2. Algorithm *Q-Clustering* for mining top-k quality clusters

Lemma 1. *Let Ω be a set of clusters. For any descendant C' of node $C = (G, S)$ in the set enumeration tree, a tight upper bound of $quality(C'|\Omega)$ is given by $[(|G|+|gTail|)(|S+|sTail|) - |overlap(((G \cup gTail), (S \cup sTail)), \Omega)|] \cdot cScore(C)$.*

Proof sketch. $[(|G| + |gTail|) * (|S| + |sTail|) - overlap(((G \cup gTail), (S \cup sTail)), \Omega_{k-1})]$ is the upper bound of the non-overlapping size of the descendants of C. Given the anti-monotonicity of the coherence measure, $cScore(C)$ is the upper bound of the coherence score of the descendants of C. Therefore, Lemma 1 gives an upper bound of the quality of the descendants of C. The bound can be shown tight. Limited by space, we omit the details here. ∎

Based on Lemma 1, we have the following rule immediately.

Rule 3 (Pruning low quality submatrices). *The subtree of C can be pruned if the upper bound of the quality gain given by Lemma 1 is smaller than the best quality gain that has got so far in the current iteration.* ∎

In summary, Figure 2 shows algorithm *Q-Clustering* to mine the top-k quality clusters. Limited by space, we omit the details of pruning techniques using the $sTail$ list, which is basically symmetric to the case of $gTail$ list.

5 Experimental Results

We tested algorithm *Q-Clustering* on both synthetic data sets and real gene expression data sets. The system is implemented in Java. The tests are conducted on a Sun Ultra 10 work station with a 440MHz CPU and 256 MB main memory. The results are consistent. Limited by space, we only report the results on a real data set here.

Spellman et al. [8] reported the genome-wide 6,220 mRNA transcript levels during the cell cycle of the budding yeast *S. cerevisiae*. The complete data set consists of 3 independent time-series, namely, the $\alpha factor$ (18 time points), the *elutriation* (14 time points) and the $cdc15$ (24 time points). We choose the $cdc15$ data set since it contains the longest time-series. Out of the 6,220 monitored genes, only 800 genes are found cell-cycle-dependent. We call this subset of data cdc_800. To test the performance of our algorithm extensively, we sample the complete data set (6,220 genes and 56 time points) with various sizes.

To test the effectiveness of our general quality-driven approach, we chose a representative pattern-based clustering model, the δ-$pCluster$ [9], and compare the mining results reported by our approach with those by a representative pattern-based clustering algorithm, MaPle [6]. Given the cdc_800 data set, both *Q-Clustering* and MaPle were invoked when $min_s = 5$ and $min_g = 5$, while the δ value ranges from 0.3 to 0.4. For *Q-Clustering*, we only return the clusters with a quality gain beyond $min_s * min_g$. According to Definition 3 and the semantic meaning of min_s and min_g, such clusters may carry interesting patterns.

Figure 3(a) shows the number of clusters reported by the two algorithms. Since MaPle finds the complete set of maximal δ-pClusters, we can see the number of clusters increases dramatically when the threshold value increases. However, *Q-Clustering* only returns the quality δ-pClusters, and the number of clusters is much more stable.

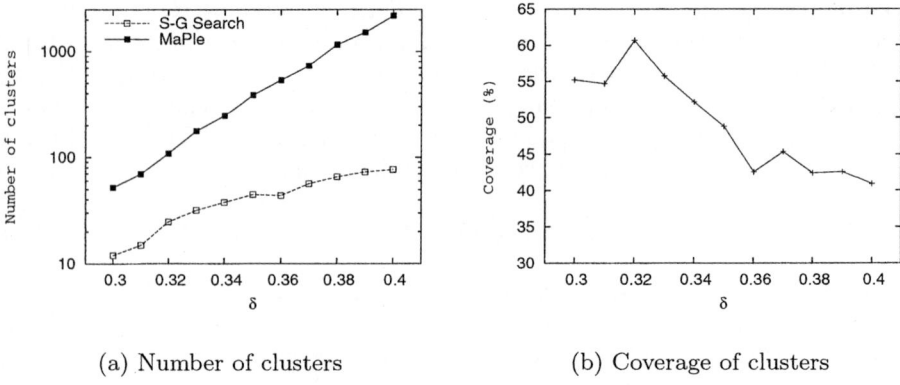

(a) Number of clusters (b) Coverage of clusters

Fig. 3. Clusters reported by MaPle and Gene-Sample Search

δ	quality clusters	all maximal clusters
3.0	0.0%	69.4%
3.2	1.2%	70.0%
3.4	1.5%	73.8%
3.6	1.6%	75.5%
3.8	2.6%	77.6%
4.0	5.8%	79.3%

Fig. 4. Overlap between clusters

We then evaluate the correlation between the clusters reported by Q-Clustering and MaPle. That is, we want to measure to which extent the quality clusters cover the set of δ-pClusters. We represent a cluster C by $\{(g_i, s_j)\}$, where g_i and s_j are the gene and sample in C, respectively. Given two sets of clusters $\Omega = \{C_1, \ldots, C_m\}$ and $\Omega' = \{C'_1, \ldots, C'_n\}$, the coverage of Ω on Ω' is defined by $\frac{(C_1 \cup \ldots \cup C_m) \cap (C'_1 \cup \ldots \cup C'_n)}{C'_1 \cup \ldots \cup C'_n}$. Figure 3 (b) illustrates the coverage of the quality clusters on the complete set of clusters. We can see that when $\delta = 0.4$, although the number of quality clusters is only 3% of the total number of clusters, the coverage of quality clusters is over 40%. That is, our quality-driven approach focuses on finding a small set of clusters which can effectively represent the underlying patterns in the data set. Please note that, to increase the coverage, users can always ask more clusters from the system until no more interesting patterns are identified.

Why the number of clusters reported by our quality-driven approach is much smaller than that by MaPle?

The rationale is that, due to the high-connectivity of microarray data, the pattern-based clusters usually highly overlap with each other. Figure 4 demonstrates the average overlap among the clusters by MaPle and Sample-Gene Sample, respectively. Given a set of clusters Ω, the average overlap of Ω is

$\frac{\sum_{C_i \in \Omega} overlap(C_i)}{|\Omega|}$, where the overlap of a cluster C_i is measured by $overlap(C_i) = max\{\frac{C_i \cap C_j}{C_i} | C_j \in \Omega, i \neq j\}$. We can see that the average overlap among the complete set of clusters is usually higher than 70%, while the average overlap among the quality clusters is less than 6%. In practice, a gene may participate in multiple cellular processes or correlate to several phenotypes. Consequently, it may belong to more than one cluster. However, such situation is not common and a ratio of about 6% overlap is biologically plausible.

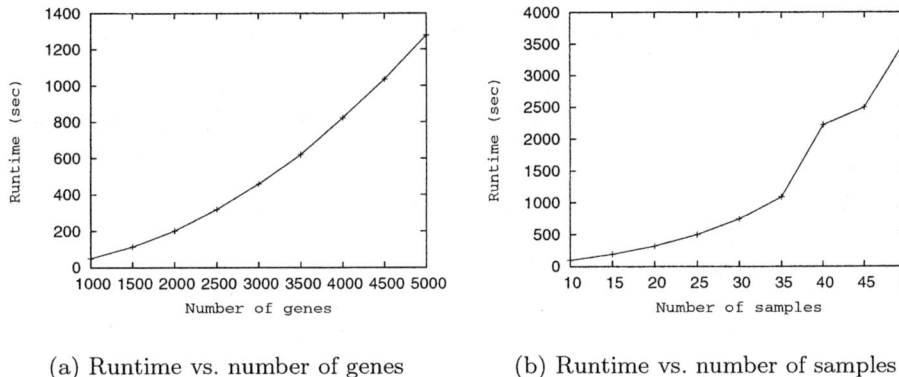

(a) Runtime vs. number of genes (b) Runtime vs. number of samples

Fig. 5. Scalability with respect to the sizes of the data sets

Finally, we test the scalability of our algorithm. We set $min_s = 6, min_g = 10$ and $\delta = 0.2$. We sample the $cdc15$ time-series (24 time points) when we test the scalability with respect to the number of genes. To test the scalability with respect the number of samples, we fix the number of genes to 3,000 and sample the time points from the complete data set. The results are shown in Figure 5(a) and (b). We can see that our algorithm scales well with respect to both the number of genes and the number of samples.

6 Discussion and Conclusions

In this paper, we proposed a general approach to mining top-k quality pattern-based clusters. The experimental results on gene expression data show that our method is general, effective and efficient. Several interesting and important problems still remain open, such as how to find multiple quality clusters during a single iteration, and how to handle non-anti-monotonic coherence functions.

Acknowledgements. We thank the reviewers for their comments and suggestions which help to improve the presentation of the paper.

References

1. Cheng, Y. and Church, G.M. Biclustering of expression data. *ISMB'00*.
2. Jain, A.K., Murty, M.N. and Flynn, P.J. Data clustering: a review. *ACM Computing Surveys*, 31:264–323, 1999.
3. Jiang, D., Pei, J. and Zhang, A. Interactive Exploration of Coherent Patterns in Time-Series Gene Expression Data. In *KDD'03*.
4. Jiang, D., Pei, J., Ramanathan, M., et al. Mining Coherent Gene Clusters from Gene-Sample-Time Microarray Data. In *KDD'04*.
5. Liu, J., Wang, W. OP-Cluster: Clustering by Tendency in High Dimensional Space. In *ICDM'03*.
6. Pei, J., Zhang, X., Cho, M., et al. MaPle: A Fast Algorithm for Maximal Pattern-based Clustering. *ICDM'03*.
7. Rymon, R. Search through systematic set enumeration. In *KR'92*.
8. Spellman, P.T., Sherlock, G., Zhang, M.Q., et al. Comprehensive identification of cell cycle-regulated genes of the yeast Saccharomyces cerevisiae by microarray hybridization. *Mol. Biol. Cell*, 9:3272–3297, 1998.
9. Wang, H., Wang, W., Yang, J. et al. Clustering by Pattern Similarity in Large Data Sets. In *SIGMOD'02*.
10. Yang, J., Wang, W., Wang, H. et al. δ-cluster: Capturing Subspace Correlation in a Large Data Set. In *ICDE'02*.

Real Datasets for File-Sharing Peer-to-Peer Systems

Shen Tat Goh[1], Panos Kalnis[1], Spiridon Bakiras[2], and Kian-Lee Tan[1]

[1] Department of Computer Science,
National University of Singapore,
3 Science Drive 2, Singapore
{gohst, kalnis, tanlk}@comp.nus.edu.sg
[2] Department of Computer Science,
Hong Kong University of Science and Technology,
Clear Water Bay, Hong Kong
sbakiras@cs.ust.hk

Abstract. The fundamental drawback of unstructured peer-to-peer (P2P) networks is the flooding-based query processing protocol that seriously limits their scalability. As a result, a significant amount of research work has focused on designing efficient search protocols that reduce the overall communication cost. What is lacking, however, is the availability of real data, regarding the exact content of users' libraries and the queries that these users ask. Using trace-driven simulations will clearly generate more meaningful results and further illustrate the efficiency of a generic query processing protocol under a real-life scenario.

Motivated by this fact, we developed a Gnutella-style probe and collected detailed data over a period of two months. They involve around 4,500 users and contain the exact files shared by each user, together with any available metadata (e.g., artist for songs) and information about the nodes (e.g., connection speed). We also collected the queries initiated by these users. After filtering, the data were organized in XML format and are available to researchers. Here, we analyze this dataset and present its statistical characteristics. Additionally, as a case study, we employ it to evaluate two recently proposed P2P searching techniques.

1 Introduction

Distributed peer-to-peer (P2P) systems provide an alternative architecture to the traditional client/server model and their initial success has captured the attention of the research community during the past few years. P2P nodes are both clients and servers and do not depend on centralized infrastructure.Participation is ad-hoc and dynamic, since nodes may independently join or leave the network.

P2P networks are classified into two main categories: unstructured (e.g., Gnutella [1]) and structured (e.g., CAN [9] and Chord [13]). Unstructured broadcast-based P2P networks are the most widely used systems today for information exchange among end-users, and provide the basis on which many popular file-sharing applications are built. Their popularity emerges primarily from their inherent simplicity; nodes that wish to exchange information, join randomly the overlay topology and are only responsible for their own data. The result is an inexpensive, easy-to-use system, which does not require any form of central administration. One major drawback, though, is the query processing protocol; whenever a node receives a query message, it broadcasts it to all of its neighbors. This is done recursively until a maximum number of hops is reached. This algorithm does not scale well to a large population size, since the whole network is overwhelmed with query messages.

As a result, research has focused on designing efficient search protocols that reduce the overall communication cost. Most of the reported results, however, are based on ad-hoc synthetic data. Clearly, the availability of real data regarding the content of users' libraries and the exact queries that these users ask, would generate more meaningful and realistic results. Motivated by this fact, we developed a Gnutella-based probe and gathered detailed data from a large and diverse user population.

In this paper, we present the data that we collected from around 4,500 Gnutella users over an extended time period. Our dataset contains information about each node (e.g., its connection speed and the software it uses) together with the index of the entire users' libraries, which is around 850,000 files in total. Additionally, we capture the exact queries initiated by each node. These data were filtered, organized in XML format and are now available to the public [3]. Moreover, since music sharing is very common in P2P networks, we processed separately a subset of the data consisting only of music files. There are around 2,000 nodes sharing almost 200,000 songs which we further organized based on the title, artist and genre (e.g., pop, rock, etc). We analyzed these data and present here some useful statistics and distribution graphs. Finally, as a case study, we investigate the performance of two recently proposed P2P searching techniques, namely Dynamic Reconfiguration [4] and Interest-based Locality [12], using the collected workload. To the best of our knowledge, our work is the first one to deal with the exact contents of the users' libraries and correlate them with the observed query patterns.

The rest of the paper is organized as follows. Section 2 reviews the related work. Section 3 describes the data collection methodology and presents an analysis of the dataset. Section 4 gives a brief overview of two case studies on which the generated workload was applied, followed by the detailed results of the trace-driven simulations. Finally, Section 5 concludes our work.

2 Related Work

Research in the P2P area was triggered by the apparent success of systems like Napster [2] and Gnutella [1]. Napster is a hybrid system, since it maintains a centralized index which is used for searching. Gnutella, on the other hand, is a pure P2P system and performs searching by Breadth-First-Traversal (BFT). Each peer that receives a query propagates it to all of its neighbors up to a maximum of d hops. The advantage of BFT is that by exploring a significant part of the network, it increases the probability of satisfying the query. The disadvantage is the overloading of the network with unnecessary messages. Yang and Garcia-Molina [14] observed that the Gnutella protocol could be modified in order to reduce the number of nodes that receive a query, without compromising the quality of the results. They proposed three techniques: *Iterative Deeping*, *Directed BFT*, and *Local Indices*. A technique similar to Local Indices is used in Ref. [15], the only difference being that indices are kept only in a subset of powerful nodes called *super-peers*.

Several studies have performed measurements in a wide range of P2P systems. Saroiu et al. [10] studied the characteristics of peer-to-peer users in the Gnutella and Napster file-sharing systems. In particular, the authors measured several parameters, including bandwidth, delay, availability (i.e., the fraction of time a user is active), and sharing patterns. Sen and Wang [11] measured flow-level information at multiple border routers of a large ISP network. They collected data from three popular P2P systems over a period of three months. The reported results illustrate a large skew in the distribution of traffic across the network, at different levels of spatial aggregation.

Contrary to the above studies that focus on P2P traffic characterization, the work by Gummadi et al. [7] provides some useful insight regarding the nature of file-sharing workloads. The authors analyzed a 200-day trace from the Kazaa network, and showed that P2P workloads are substantially different from their Web counterparts. Specifically, object popularity changes over time (with new objects being more popular), and the aggregate popularity distribution does not follow a Zipf curve. In addition, the authors observed a considerable locality in the P2P workload, which may be exploited by object caching.

In contrast to our work, none of the above papers provides the exact contents of the users' libraries together with the actual user queries.

3 Data Analysis

We implemented our probe by modifying a Limewire client [8], which connects to Gnutella networks. Limewire is implemented in Java and the source code is publicly available and well-documented. We forced our client to be promoted to an ultra-peer. In this way, we were able to observe all the queries submitted by leaf nodes connected directly to the probe. For each query, we captured the IP address[1] and port number of the initiating leaf node, a time-stamp and the query string (i.e., a set of keywords). We used the *Browse Host* operation to retrieve the contents of the leaf peers' libraries. Notice that the peers respond to this operation since our probe is an ultra-peer. The information of each peer includes its address, the type of the connection as reported by the client (e.g., Modem, Cable, etc.) and the index of its library. Index entries are composed by the filename, the filetype and the size of the file in bytes. The resulting dataset

---

[1] To preserve anonymity, we replaced the IP by a randomly generated unique key.

Table 1. Statistics for the generic and the music files dataset

	Generic Dataset	Music files Dataset
Number of Users	4,447	2,000
Number of queries	11,075	5,462
Total number of files	845,454	195,023
Number of distinct files	505,818	58,848
Number of artists	n.a.	15,499
Number of Genres	n.a.	245

relates the library of each user with the queries he asked. Except from requests originating from leaf nodes connected to the probe, many queries arrive through other ultra-peers. In such case, we cannot always retrieve the peer's index, since some users restrict the *Browse Host* operation for remote peers.

Peers may enter and leave the network frequently. Ideally, we want to record all the queries issued by a specific user, irrespectively of how often he reconnects. Unfortunately, due to dynamic IP, it is not easy to distinguish the identity of a peer. To minimize the problem, we do not rely on the IP address but we compare the contents of the libraries. If at least 90% of the contents of a peer (also considering the order) are the same as the contents of another, we assume that the two peers are identical. We allow a 10% difference, since a user might add or delete some files while he is off-line. Nevertheless, we cannot guarantee that all the queries are captured; a peer may reconnect to a different ultra-peer and its subsequent queries are not necessarily routed through our probe.

Data were collected over a two months' period. We employed two probes, one in Singapore and the other in Hong Kong[2], hoping to capture a geographically diverse population. Additionally, during the collection period the probes were disconnected and reconnected to the network several times, ensuring that our data are independent of any specific network configuration.

3.1 Generic Dataset

Here we analyze our generic dataset consisting of a set of almost 4,500 users, the indexes of their libraries (around 850,000 files of various types) and they queries they asked. Table 1 presents summarized statistics of the data. The dataset is available online [3] in XML format.

Figure 1 shows the relation between users and files; observe that both axis are logarithmic. In Figure 1(a) we show the number of files per user, after sorting the users in descending order according to the number of files they have. It is clear that most of the users have a significant number of files, although there exist some users with many files and others with only a few; this is similar to the results of Saroiu et al. [10]. In Figure 1(b) we present the popularity of each file (i.e., the number of users that have a particular file). As expected, the graph resembles a Zipf distribution.

---

[2] The domains of the captured clients where not restricted to these areas.

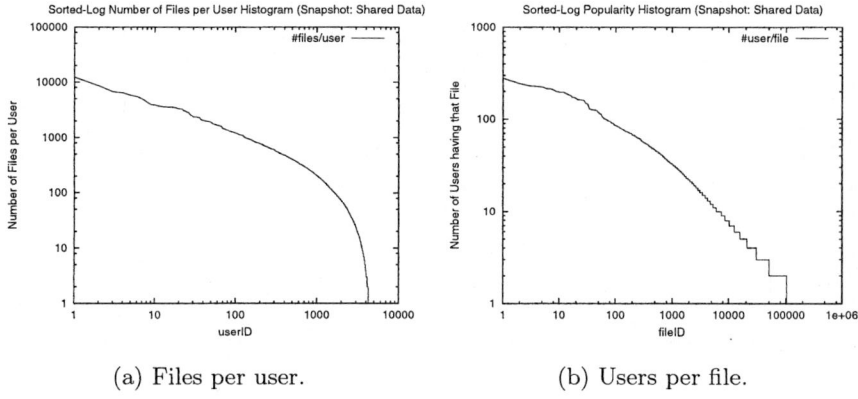

(a) Files per user. (b) Users per file.

Fig. 1. Distribution of files

In Figure 2 we present statistics related to the connection speed of the peers. Figure 2(a) shows the number of peers for each connection speed category. It is obvious that the slow connections dominate the network. Notice that these are the speeds reported by the peers themselves. Many users, however, deliberately report low bandwidth to discourage other peers from downloading files [10]. In the next graph (Figure 2(b)) we draw the average number of files shared by nodes belonging to a specific connection speed category. Although we observe some variations, it seems that the size of a user's library does not depend significantly on the connection speed.

In Figure 3(a) we present the number of queries initiated by each user. Both axis in this graph are logarithmic. The graph resembles a Zipf-like distribution, indicating that some users ask a lot of queries, while most others ask only a few. We also investigate the relationship between the number of queries asked by user and their connection speed. In contrast to our intuition, the connection speed seems to be irrelevant.

Finally, Figure 3(b) combines the queries with the contents of the users' libraries. It shows, for an average user, the cumulative value of the answers returned by other users, as a percentage of the total answers. For example, during the process of answering a specific query, if a node contacts 50 other peers it can retrieve around 62% of the available answers in the entire network. From the graph it is obvious that for any query a node needs to contact at most 120 out of the 4,500 peers, in order to find all the qualifying answers in the network. This fact indicates that it is possible to develop algorithms which answer queries efficiently in large P2P systems.

3.2 A Special Case: Music Files

A substantial percentage of the traffic in P2P systems is due to the exchange of music files among the users. To facilitate experimentation in this domain, we extracted from the original data a subset consisting only of music files. There were

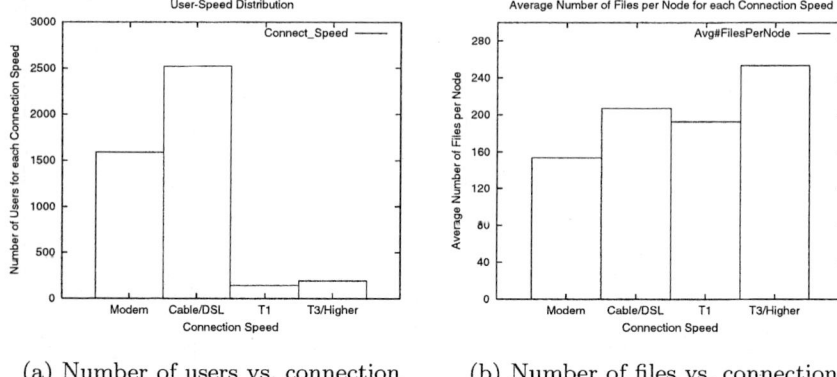

(a) Number of users vs. connection (b) Number of files vs. connection

Fig. 2. Group by connection speed

2,000 nodes containing at least one music file, while we captured approximately 200,000 such files in total; detailed statistics are presented in Table 1. Due to the restricted domain, we were able to capture additional attributes for each file. From the filename itself, we extracted the song title and the artist. Then, by consulting song databases available in the Web, we categorized each song by its genre (e.g., pop, rock, etc.) In total, 245 different genres were identified. The music file dataset is also available online [3] in XML format.

In general, we observed that the distribution of songs among users is similar to the distribution of general files presented in Figure 1. Moreover, the song popularity within a genre also follows a Zipf distribution. Due to lack of space, we do not present the corresponding graphs. The interested user should refer to the long version of this paper [3].

Figure 4(a) shows the number of songs per category. Interestingly, here the distribution does not follow Zipf's law, since many categories have a lot of songs while many others have only a few. In the next graph (Figure 4(b)) we investigate whether the queries asked by users are similar to the contents of their libraries. For instance, we want to know whether a user who owns mostly rock songs is likely to search for another rock song. To verify this, we first generated a histogram for each user's library based on the songs' genre. Then, we evaluated all the queries of each user against our entire song dataset and generated a histogram based on the genre that included all the qualifying songs. Finally, for each user, we calculated the overlap between the histogram of his library and the histogram of his queries. The graph shows that for many users their queries exhibit substantial similarity with their libraries. This fact could be exploited by an algorithm to generate an enhanced network topology based on the users' interests as reflected by their shared libraries. Other groupings are are possible (e.g., a query about a rock ballad is compatible with pop songs). Such an in-depth analysis is outside the scope of this paper.

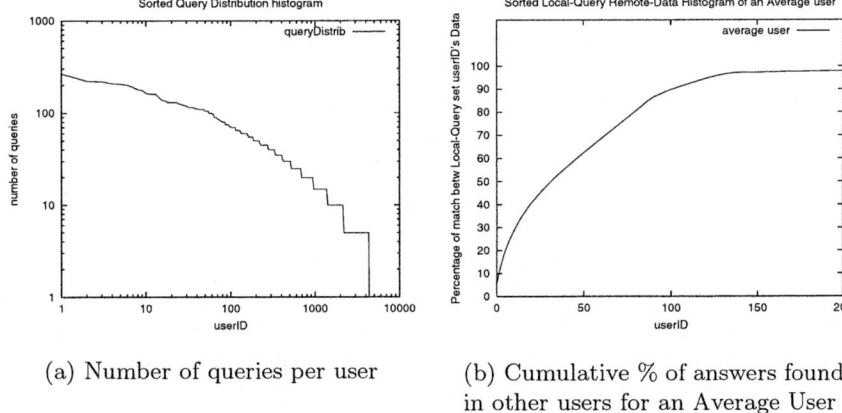

(a) Number of queries per user

(b) Cumulative % of answers found in other users for an Average User

Fig. 3. Distribution of queries and answers

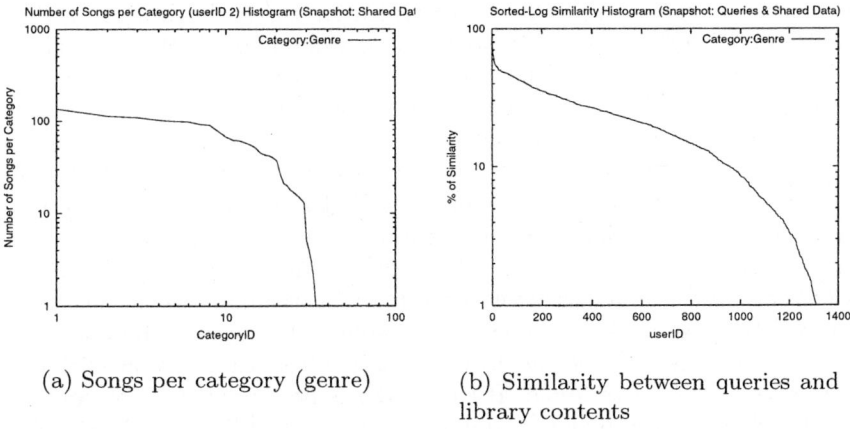

(a) Songs per category (genre)

(b) Similarity between queries and library contents

Fig. 4. Statistics for the music files

4 Case Study

As a case study, in this section we evaluate two recently proposed methods, namely the Dynamic Reconfiguration [4] and the Interest-based locality [12]. Both attempt to minimize the network traffic by identifying nodes which are beneficial in terms of content.

The intuition behind *Dynamic Reconfiguration* [4] is that there are groups of users in the network that share common interests. The method attempts to identify groups of compatible nodes and dynamically reconfigure the network to bring such nodes close to each other; thus, consequent queries will be answered with fewer hops.

When a node initiates a query, multiple peers may reply and statistics are gathered for all of them. All search results are not equally beneficial. A user will prefer to download a song from a node with high bandwidth. Moreover, the larger the results list, the lesser its significance for the reconfiguration process, since it cannot differentiate the compatible from the incompatible peers.

Based on these observations, the network reconfiguration process is implemented as follows. (i) Each obtained result accounts for a benefit of c/TRN, where c is the bandwidth of the answering link and TRN is the total number of results. Notice that the Gnutella Ping-Pong protocol, which performs exploration, specifies that information concerning bandwidth capacity is propagated together with the query reply. (ii) Periodically, each node checks the cumulative benefit of all nodes for which it keeps statistics, and includes in the new neighborhood the most beneficial ones. (iii) When a new node needs to be added, an invitation message is sent. (iv) The invited node always accepts an invitation evicting the least beneficial neighbor if necessary. (v) Neighbor log-offs trigger the update process. Note that in order to avoid frequent reconfigurations, when a node is evicted it does not attempt to replace the evicting neighbor immediately. Such a node will obtain a new neighbor if: (a) it receives an invitation from another node or, (b) reaches a reorganization threshold. In Ref. [4] the Dynamic Reconfiguration method is shown to be around 50% better than Gnutella in terms of message overhead, for a synthetic dataset.

Interest-based locality [12] is trying to improve the scalability of Gnutella-type search protocols, by introducing the concept of interest-based shortcuts. Shortcut lists are maintained at each node inside the network, which contain information (e.g., IP addresses) about other nodes that have answered a query in the past. Assuming that P2P users exhibit interest similarities, these nodes might be able to answer subsequent queries from the same user. The basic idea is to create a new overlay structure on top of the existing P2P network (based on these lists), and perform the content search in two steps. The nodes in the shortcut list are queried first (one by one, starting from the most beneficial node) until the requested file is found. If the search is not successful, the underlying P2P network is utilized by employing the standard flooding-based protocol.

In the basic algorithm, shortcuts are discovered through the Gnutella-type flooding protocol. Anytime a query is not resolved via the shortcut list, new candidate nodes are discovered following the flooding process. Then, a new node is selected and added to the shortcut list, possibly replacing a less beneficial shortcut. The size of the list is limited to ten entries, while its content is continuously updated due to the dynamic nature of the network (i.e., nodes entering or leaving the network). The importance of each shortcut (which also reflects its position in the sorted list) is determined by its success rate, i.e., the percentage of requests that it was able to answer successfully. Several enhancements to the basic algorithm were evaluated in Ref. [12] but the performance gain was relatively small compared to the increased complexity.

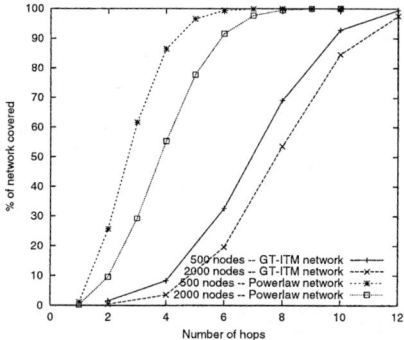

Fig. 5. Number of hops to cover the network

4.1 Experimental Setup

We developed a discrete event simulator in order to measure the query response time in addition to the number of messages which are exchanged. We split the users into three categories, according to their connection bandwidth; each user may be connected through a 56K modem, a cable modem or a LAN. The mean value of the one-way delay between two users is governed by the slowest user, and is equal to 300ms, 150ms and 70ms, respectively. The standard deviation is set to 20ms for all cases, and values are restricted in the interval $\mu \pm 3\sigma$. We experimented with various query rates. When the query rate is too high, the nodes are overloaded and all methods suffer. In the graphs we present here the query rate is slow enough to avoid this problem.

We used two network topologies for our experiments: (i) power-law [6] networks comprising of 500 and 2000 nodes, where the average number of neighbors per node was set to 3.2, and (ii) stub networks with 500 and 2000 nodes, produced with the GT-ITM [5] generator. In Figure 5 we show the percentage of the nodes that can be reached within 1 to 12 hops for each of the network topologies. Notice, that we did not keep the client population constant within the duration of each experiment. Instead, we properly set the arrival and departure rate of nodes in the system, in order to maintain the desired average population size.

In what follows, we compare the normal Gnutella protocol (denoted as *Gnutella* in the graphs) with Dynamic Reconfiguration (denoted as *Dynamic-Gnutella*) and the Interest-based Locality method (denoted as *Direct-Gnutella*).

4.2 Performance Evaluation

First, we consider a GT-ITM network with 2000 nodes. We measure the response time from the moment that a user submits a query, until the moment when the first result arrives. In the experiment of Figure 6(a) we allow the message to propagate for up to six hops and present the cumulative response time. The graph, for example, shows that after 6000 msec Dynamic-Gnutella was able to find answers for a little less than 30% of the submitted queries, while this percentage grows to almost 35% for Direct-Gnutella. The important observation

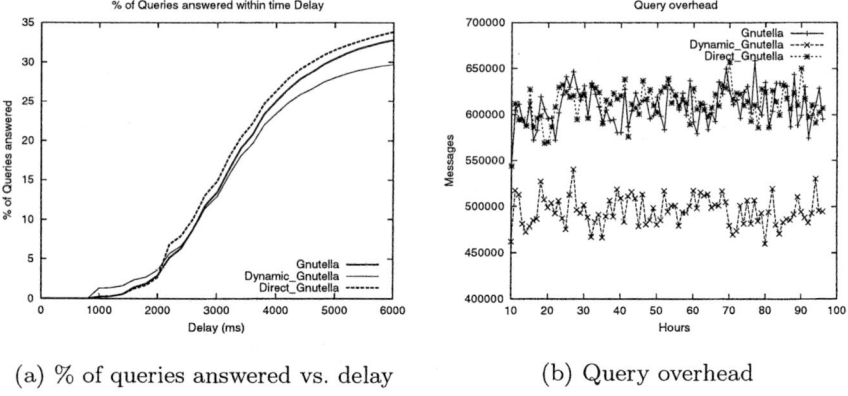

(a) % of queries answered vs. delay (b) Query overhead

Fig. 6. GT-ITM network, 2000 nodes, 6 hops

here is that the Dynamic method can be worse than plain Gnutella in terms of response time due to the reorganization overhead. Moreover, the performance improvements of Direct-Gnutella are not significant.

Figure 6(b) shows the number of messages transferred in the network per hour, for a simulated period of 100 hours. The Dynamic method needs less messages because a node does not propagate the query further as soon as a result is found. Because of the reconfiguration process, compatible nodes are gathered closer so query propagation stops earlier. The Direct method, however, needs to perform a Gnutella-style search if the results are not found by following the shortcuts. Since this is usually the case, it needs as many messages as the plain Gnutella protocol.

Figure 7(a) and Figure 7(b) present the respective results when the number of hops is increased to eight. Since all methods can reach more peers, the absolute number of the answered queries increases. However, the differences among the algorithms diminish, since the additional results are further away.

Figures 8(a) and 8(b) present similar results for a power-law network of 500 nodes. Here, we allow a smaller number of hops, because the connectivity of the network is much higher (see Figure 5). The results are similar to the previous ones. The only difference is that the number of transmitted messages is almost the same for all methods. This is due to the higher connectivity of the network: no matter how the network is reconfigured it is very likely that a query will reach a highly connected peer which will generate many messages for the Dynamic method as well as for Gnutella.

The conclusion from the above experiments is that the Dynamic and Direct variations of Gnutella can outperform the naïve protocol if the connectivity of the network is low and the allowed number of hops is limited. Then, the advanced methods can reach directly parts of the network which would take Gnutella several hops. On the other hand, if the network is well connected (e.g., power-law)

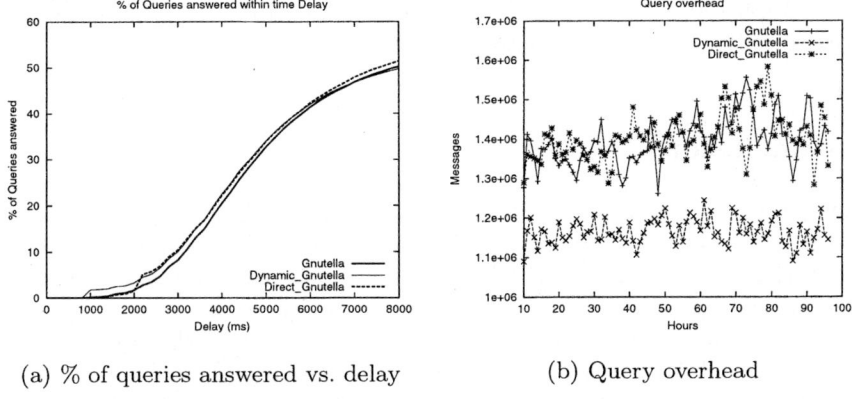

Fig. 7. GT-ITM network, 2000 nodes, 8 hops

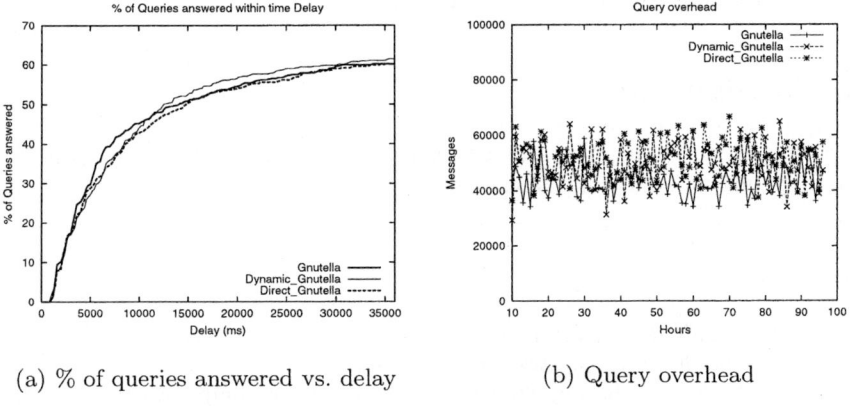

Fig. 8. Power-law network, 500 nodes, 4 hops

the performance difference diminishes since Gnutella can reach remote nodes easily.

The inherent drawbacks of the advanced methods are the assumptions that (i) during its online period each peer initiates enough queries to locate beneficial nodes, (ii) subsequent queries are relevant to the previous ones, and (iii) there is similarity among the contents of each peer. Our dataset reveals that in practice these conditions are unlikely to be met, therefore the performance of the advanced methods is not impressive. In particular, the first assumption seems to be the major factor behind these results. A peer that does not ask many queries will not able to discover many beneficial nodes. Furthermore, even when some beneficial nodes are discovered, there is no guarantee that they will stay on-line for a long period of time. Regarding assumptions (ii) and (iii), our dataset shows some degree of similarity both among peer libraries and among the content of a peer's library and the queries that this peer asks. However, this behavior was limited to only a fraction of the total population.

5 Conclusions

In this paper we presented the characteristics of a large real dataset collected from the peers in the Gnutella network. We believe that this dataset will benefit all researchers in the P2P area because (i) it can become a standard benchmark to test various algorithms, and (ii) it provides realistic results since it is the only one to include not only queries but also the exact index of the peers' libraries. Initial analysis of the dataset revealed that real systems exhibit interesting characteristics that can be used to improve searching in P2P networks. For instance, we showed that in the music sharing domain, many users search for songs similar to their own libraries. Moreover, we used the dataset to evaluate existing P2P systems which attempt to identify beneficial peers. We found that in practice these systems may not perform as well as expected.

Acknowledgments

We would like to thank Yip Jun Kwan (Elton) for the implementation of the Gnutella probe and the collection of the data.

References

1. Gnutella home page. http://gnutella.wego.com.
2. Napster home page. http://www.napster.com.
3. Real dataset for file-sharing p2p systems. http://www.comp.nus.edu.sg/~p2p.
4. S. Bakiras, P. Kalnis, T. Loukopoulos, and W. S. Ng. A general framework for searching in distributed data repositories. In *Proc. IEEE IPDPS*, pages 34–41, 2003.
5. K. Calvert, M. Doar, and E. W. Zegura. Modeling internet topology. *IEEE Communications Magazine*, 35:160–163, June 1997.
6. M. Faloutsos, P. Faloutsos, and C. Faloutsos. On power-law relationships of the internet topology. In *Proc. ACM SIGCOMM*, pages 251–262, 1999.
7. K. P. Gummadi, R. J. Dunn, S. Saroiu, S. D. Gribble, H. M. Levy, and J. Zahorjan. Measurement, modeling, and analysis of a peer-to-peer file-sharing workload. In *Proc. ACM SOSP*, pages 314–329, 2003.
8. Limewire Home Page. *http://www.limewire.com/*.
9. S. Ratnasamy, P. Francis, M. Handley, R. Karp, and S. Schenker. A scalable content-addressable network. In *Proc. ACM SIGCOMM*, pages 161–172, 2001.
10. S. Saroiu, K. P. Gummadi, and S. D. Gribble. A measurement study of peer-to-peer file sharing systems. In *Proc. Multimedia Computing and Networking*, 2002.
11. S. Sen and J. Wang. Analyzing peer-to-peer traffic across large networks. In *Proc. Internet Measurement Workshop (IMW)*, pages 137–150, 2002.

12. K. Sripanidkulchai, B. Maggs, and H. Zhang. Efficient content location using interest-based locality in peer-to-peer systems. In *Proc. IEEE INFOCOM*, pages 2166–2176, 2003.
13. I. Stoica, R. Morris, D. Karger, M. F. Kaashoek, and H. Balakrishnan. Chord: A scalable peer-to-peer lookup service for internet applications. In *Proc. ACM SIGCOMM*, pages 149–160, 2001.
14. B. Yang and H. Garcia-Molina. Efficient search in peer-to-peer networks. In *Proc. IEEE ICDCS*, pages 5–14, 2002.
15. B. Yang and H. Garcia-Molina. Designing a super-peer network. In *Proc. ICDE*, pages 49–60, 2003.

SemEQUAL: Multilingual Semantic Matching in Relational Systems

A. Kumaran and Jayant R. Haritsa

Database Systems Laboratory, SERC/CSA,
Indian Institute of Science, Bangalore 560012, INDIA
{kumaran, haritsa}@dsl.serc.iisc.ernet.in

Abstract. In an increasingly multilingual world, it is critical that information management tools organically support the simultaneous use of multiple *natural languages*. A pre-requisite for efficiently achieving this goal is that the underlying database engines must provide seamless matching of text data across languages. We propose here SemEQUAL, a new SQL functionality for semantic matching of multilingual attribute data. Our current implementation defines matches based on the standard WordNet linguistic ontologies. A performance evaluation of SemEQUAL, implemented using standard SQL:1999 features on a suite of commercial database systems indicates unacceptably slow response times. However, by tuning the schema and index choices to match typical linguistic features, we show that the performance can be improved to a level commensurate with online user interaction.

1 Introduction

Internet demographics are changing dramatically: about two-thirds of current Internet users are non-native English speakers [18] and it is predicted that the majority of web-pages will be multilingual by 2010 [22]. In such an increasingly multilingual digital world, it is critical that information management tools, *e-Commerce* portals and *e-Governance* applications, support the simultaneous use of multiple natural languages. A pre-requisite is that the underlying database engines (typically relational), provide similar functionality and efficiency for multi-lingual data as that associated with processing uni-lingual data, for which they are well-known.

From the efficiency perspective, we recently profiled in [14] the performance of standard relational operators on multilingual data and proposed efficient storage formats to make the operators *natural-language-neutral*. Subsequently, from the functionality perspective, we introduced a new SQL operator called LexEQUAL [15], for *phonetic* matching of specific types of attribute data across languages, optimized for supporting e-Commerce environments. In this paper, we take the next logical step, by proposing SemEQUAL, a *semantic* functionality for matching text attribute data across languages based on *meaning*. For example, to automatically and transparently match the English noun *mathematics*, with *mathématiques* in French or கணிதம் (transliterated as *kanitham*, meaning *mathematics*) in Tamil.

1.1 The SemEQUAL Operator

The proposed semantic matching functionality is illustrated on a hypothetical *Books.com*, with a sample multilingual product catalog, as shown in Figure 1, where the *Category* attribute stores the classification of the book in the original language of publication. In today's database systems, a query with (**Category** = 'History') selection condition, would return *only* those books that have *Category* as History in English, although the catalog also contains history books in French, Hindi and Tamil. A multilingual user may be better served, however, if all the history books in all the languages (or more likely, in a set of languages specified by her) are returned. A query using the proposed SemEQUAL and a result set, as given in Figure 2, would therefore be desirable.

Author	Author_FN	Title	Price	Category
Descartes	René	Les Méditations Metaphysiques	€ 49.00	Philosophie
நேரு	ஜவஹர்லால்	ஆதிய ஜோதி	INR 250	சரித்திரம்
無門	慧開	無門關	¥ 475.00	禅
Lebrun	François	L'Histoire De La France	€ 19.95	Histoire
Durant	Will/Ariel	History of Civilization	$ 149.95	History
नेहरू	जवाहरलाल	भारत एक खोज	INR 175	इतिहास
Franklin	Benjamin	Un Américain Autobiographie	€ 25.00	Autobiographie
Gilderhus	Mark T.	History and Historians	$ 49.95	Historiography
காந்தி	மோகன்தாஸ்	சத்திய சோதனை	INR 250	சுயசரிதம்

Fig. 1. A Multilingual Books.com

```
SELECT Author,Title,Category FROM Books
WHERE Category SemEQUAL ALL 'History'
InLanguages {English, French, Tamil}
```

Author	Title	Category
Durant	History of Civilization	History
Lebrun	L'Histoire De La France	Histoire
நேரு	ஆதிய ஜோதி	சரித்திரம்
Franklin	Un Américain Autobiographie	Autobiographie
Gilderhus	History and Historians	Historiography
காந்தி	சத்திய சோதனை	சுயசரிதம்

Fig. 2. Multilingual Semantic Selection

It should be noted that the SemEQUAL operator shown here is generalized to return not just the tuples that are equivalent in meaning, but also with respect to *semantic generalizations* and *specializations*, as in the last three tuples that are reported in the output[1]. Without the optional ALL directive, only the first three records that are directly equivalent to History would be reported.

---

[1] Historiography *(the science of history making)* and Autobiography are specialized branches of History. The third record in the result has a category value of சரித்திரம் (transliterated as *Charitram*) in Tamil, meaning History, and the last record has a category value of சுயசரிதம் (transliterated as *Suyacharitam*) in Tamil, meaning Autobiography.

To determine semantic equivalence of word-forms across languages and to characterize the **SemEQUAL** functionality, we take recourse to WordNet [23], a standard linguistic resource that is available in multiple languages and, very importantly from our perspective, features *inter-lingual* semantic linkages. After integrating WordNet with the database platform, two alternatives arise with regard to the **SemEQUAL** implementation: a *derived-operator* approach using the standard SQL features, or a *core-operator* implementation that is internally visible to the database engine. While the latter approach may prove more efficient in the long-term, we investigate the derived-operator approach here since it can be implemented immediately on existing commercial database systems using their current SQL capabilities. Specifically, we first analyse the performance of **SemEQUAL**, expressed using recursive SQL features of the SQL:1999 standard, in relational database systems. A direct implementation on three commercial database systems indicates that supporting multilingual semantic processing is unacceptably slow. However, by applying a few simple optimizations that tune the schema and access structures to match WordNet characteristics, the response times are brought down to *a few milliseconds*, which we expect to be sufficient for current practical deployments. Further, though this paper focuses only on multilingual domain, a functionality defined along the same lines may be generalized for matching in any domain with a well-specified taxonomic hierarchy.

1.2 Our Contributions

To summarize, our main contributions in this paper are:

- Motivating the need for, and formulating the notion of, multilingual semantic equality at the granularity of database attributes.
- Integration of WordNet linguistic resources with relational database systems and a *derived-operator* implementation of **SemEQUAL**, using standard SQL features.
- Optimizing the performance of **SemEQUAL**, based on WordNet linguistic features, to a level that appears sufficient for current e-Commerce deployments.

2 Multilingual Semantic Matching

In this section, we provide a brief background on the WordNet linguistic resources, on which the semantics of our current implementation of the **SemEQUAL** operator is based. Subsequently, we describe our strategy for implementing **SemEQUAL** as a *derived-operator*, using standard SQL:1999 features that are available in all commercial database systems.

2.1 Overview of WordNet

A word may be thought of as a lexicalized concept; simply, it is the written form of a mental concept that may be an object, action, description, relationship, etc. Formally, it is referred to as a *Word-form*. The concept that it stands for is referred to as *Word-sense*, or in WordNet parlance, *Synset*. The defining philosophy in the design of WordNet is that a synset is sufficient to identify a concept for the user. A short description, similar to the dictionary meaning, called the *Gloss* is provided with synsets, for human understanding. Two words are said to be synonymous, *or semantically the same*, if they have the same synset and hence map to the same mental concept. WordNet organizes all relationships between the concepts of a language as a semantic network between synsets. A lexical matrix that maps word forms to word senses constitutes the basis for mapping a word-form to synsets. For example, the word-form bird corresponds to several different synsets, two of which are {*a vertebrate animal that can typically fly*} and {*an aircraft*}; each of these two synsets is denoted differently with subscripts, in Figure 3. The synsets are divided into five distinct categories and we explore below only the *Nouns* category, as *about a fifth of normal text corpora and majority of query strings are noun-form words* [17].

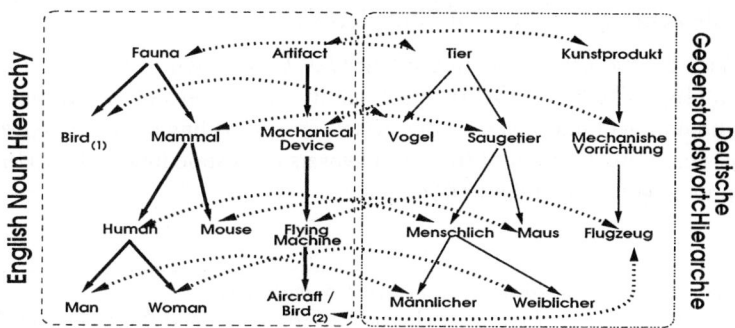

Fig. 3. Sample Inter-linked *WordNet* Noun Hierarchy

Noun Taxonomical Hierarchy. The nouns in English WordNet are grouped under approximately twenty-five distinct *Semantic Primes* [7], covering distinct conceptual domains, such as *Animal, Artifact*, etc. Under each of the semantic primes, the nouns are organized in a taxonomic hierarchy, as shown in Figure 3, with *Hyponyms* links signifying the is-a relationships (shown in solid arrows).

Several efforts are underway – such as the *European WordNet* (EWN) [6] that includes all major European languages and the *Indo-WordNet* (IWN) [13, 2] that include all 15 of the official Indian languages – to link up WordNet taxonomic hierarchies of different languages. A Chinese WordNet (CWN) initiative, along the lines of English WordNet, is outlined in [3]. A common feature among such initiatives is that they keep the basic taxonomic hierarchies nearly the same as that of English and provide mapping from their synsets to that of English. Further, inter-linking of semantically equivalent synsets between WordNets of different languages (shown as dotted arrows) is available for some languages currently [6], and is planned for others [13]. Figure 3 shows a simplified interlinked hierarchy in English and German. Such interlinked hierarchy is used for defining semantic matching in the following section.

2.2 Semantic Matching Functionality Using Interlinked WordNet

Using the lexical matrix function that is a part of the WordNet linguistic resources, the operands (i.e., the the multilingual word-forms), may be mapped on to distinct set of synsets associated with the languages of the respective operands. Further, the set of synsets corresponding to the RHS operand is augmented with synsets that are reachable using Inter-Lingual-Index (ILI) links, to the target languages. Once augmented, the semantic equality may be defined as follows: A `equivalent` match is `true`, if there is a non-empty intersection between the LHS and RHS sets of synsets. A `generalized` match is `true`, if there is a non-empty intersection between LHS set of synsets and the transitive closure of the RHS set of synsets in the above taxonomic hierarchy. Such a definition ensures that in *at least one word-sense*, the operands may be matched. For example, only in a `generalized` match, the query (*Is* `bird` SemEQUAL `Artifact`?) and (*Is* `bird` SemEQUAL `Fauna`?), both would be `true`.

2.3 Implementing Multilingual SemEQUAL

The summary function implementing SemEQUAL is shown in Figure 4 (details are available in [16]). The SemEQUAL functionality needs two significant steps (both in line 3): computation of the closure of the synsets corresponding to the RHS operand and testing non-empty intersection of the set of synsets corresponding to the LHS operand and the computed closure of the RHS operand.

SemEQUAL ($String_{Data}$, $String_{Query}$, L_D, L_Q, *match*, $T_\mathcal{L}$)
Input: $String_{Data}$ and $String_{Query}$ in languages L_D and L_Q, *match* flag, Target Languages $T_\mathcal{L}$
Output: TRUE or FALSE, [*Optional*] Gloss of Matched Synset

1. ($\mathcal{W}_D$, $\mathcal{W}_Q$) ← WordNet Of (L_D, L_Q);
2. ($\mathcal{S}_D$, $\mathcal{S}_Q$) ← Synsets of ($String_{Data}$ in $\mathcal{W}_D$, $String_{Query}$ in $\mathcal{W}_Q$);
3. **if** $Match$ **is** EQUIVALENT **then if** $\mathcal{S}_D \cap \mathcal{S}_Q \neq \phi$ **return** true **else return** false;
   else if $Match$ **is** GENERALIZED **then**
   TC_Q ← TransitiveClosure($\mathcal{S}_Q$, $\mathcal{W}_Q$, $T_\mathcal{L}$);
   if $\mathcal{S}_D \cap TC_Q \neq \phi$ **return** true **else ret urn** false;
4. [Optional.] **return** Gloss of the Matched Synset;

Fig. 4. Semantic Matching Algorithm

In the following discussions, we focus on the `generalized` matching that requires a closure computation, which is inefficient in relational systems. The transitive closure is computed using the (intra-language) Is-A relationships and the (inter-language) ILI relationships stored in the database. In our derived operator approach, the transitive closure of the $String_{Query}$ on WordNet taxonomic hierarchy is computed using the standard SQL:1999 recursive SQL constructs. After computing the transitive closure of the RHS operand, each record is checked for intersection of the synsets corresponding to the LHS operand and the computed closure, returning all records for which the intersection is non-empty. While the closure computation may be optimized by generating the closure only up to the point to determine set membership in the second step, such optimizations are not possible in the derived operator approach. Also, we restricted the closure computation only to the target languages, thus keeping the complexity linear in the number of target languages. Testing the set membership in the second step may be implemented efficiently using well-known hash-table techniques.

2.4 Semantic Matching Example

We present an example to illustrate the *derived-operator* implementation of the SemEQUAL function. The WordNet resource is stored in the $\mathcal{W_L}$ table. The user query,

```
SELECT Author, Title FROM Books
WHERE Category SemEQUAL ALL 'History'
InLanguages {English, French, Tamil}
```

is mapped to the following query, where the transitive closure on $\mathcal{W_L}$ is computed using the recursive SQL constructs and the set membership is tested by the SQL IN predicate:

```
WITH Descendants (child, lang)
    (SELECT 𝒲ℒ.sub, 𝒲ℒ.lang FROM WordNet 𝒲ℒ WHERE
    𝒲ℒ.super = 'History' AND 𝒲ℒ.lang IN ('ENGLISH','FRENCH','TAMIL')
UNION ALL
    SELECT 𝒲ℒ.sub, 𝒲ℒ.lang FROM WordNet 𝒲ℒ, Descendants Dec WHERE
    𝒲ℒ.parent = Dec.child AND 𝒲ℒ.lang = Dec.lang)
SELECT Author, Title FROM Books
WHERE Category IN (SELECT child FROM Descendants)
```

Thus, the user query effectively translates to the following SQL query:

```
SELECT Author,Title from Books
WHERE Category IN {'History','Memoir','Autobiography', ...
'Histoire','Mémoire', ... 'சரித்திரம்','சுயசரிதம்'...}
```

Here, the values in the IN clause are a few of the subclasses of `History`, in English WordNet, and their equivalents in French and Tamil WordNets. Note that any conjunction (disjunction, respectively) of SemEQUAL predicates can be handled by computing the intersection (union, respectively) of closures for the IN predicate.

3 Experimental Study

In this section, we describe our experimental setup to measure the performance of the SemEQUAL derived operator, on a suite of commercial database systems.

3.1 System Setup

A standard Pentium IV workstation with 512 MB memory running Windows NT operating system, was used as the experimental platform. Three database systems, IBM DB2 Universal Server (Ver. 7.1.0), Microsoft SQL Server (Ver. 8.00.194), and Oracle 9i

(Ver. 9.0.1), were installed with default configurations. Of these three, DB2 and Oracle support recursive SQL natively, while the functionality is simulated through scripts in SQL Server. In subsequent sections, the systems are identified randomly as A, B and C, to conceal their identities.

3.2 WordNet Storage

The entire set of noun taxonomic hierarchies of WordNet (Version 1.5), totaling about 110,000 *word forms*, 80,000 *synsets* and about 140,000 relationships between them, was loaded into each of the database systems, in a simple hierarchy table (as Parent-Child relationships). We calculate the storage space requirements of each WordNet to be about 4 MB (including index storage), based on the profile of English Wordnet (shown in Table 1). Assuming that the WordNet of each language will be similar to that of English when fully developed, the storage needed to store WordNet in non-Latin script, is about 8 MB, due to the need for Unicode format.

Table 1. Statistical Profile of WordNets [2, 6]

Characteristic	English	French	German	Spanish	Hindi
Word Forms (Words)	114,648	32,809	20,453	50,526	22,522
Word Sense (Synsets)	80,000	22,745	15,132	23,378	7,868
Average Synsets per Word Form	2.236	2.176	2.301	2.360	3.889
Average Word Forms per Synset	1.985	1.442	1.352	2.162	2.286
Equivalence Relations per Synset(to English)	1.000	0.999	1.080	0.908	Not Available

3.3 Query Workload

For profiling the performance of the SemEQUAL operator, we used queries that compute closures of varying sizes, from a few hundreds to a few thousands, on the above taxonomic hierarchy. Queries based on SQL:1999 recursive SQL constructs (as shown in Section 2.4) were used, with appropriate query terms to compute closures of the necessary sizes.

To establish the *likely* closure size (*i.e.*, the average closure size for likely query strings), we selected the top-hundred most used nouns in English [1] and the top-fifty nouns that are used in popular web-search engines [24] and computed the average of *their* closure-sizes in English WordNet, which turned out to be around 625 [16]. Hence, it is realistic to use a figure of around 2,000 for a representative closure size, assuming that a multilingual user would typically want answers in at most three languages.

3.4 Metrics Measured

In all the experiments, we measured the wall-clock runtime of a given query on the given data set. The queries were run in an SQL or a programming language environment, as appropriate. The test machine was quiesced except for the database system under study and the queries were run cold. The average runtime from several identical runs was taken as the runtime of a specific query (the graphs show mean values with relative half-widths about the mean of less than 5% at the 90% confidence interval).

It should be noted here that the *quality* of the retrieval is determined solely by the coverage (for *recall*) and the resolution power (for *precision*) of the WordNet taxonomic hierarchy. Measurement of such quality is in the domain of behavioral and linguistic experts, and beyond the scope of our research, which focuses solely on optimizing the database performance, given the linguistic hierarchies.

4 Results and Analysis

In this section, we report on the performance of a suite of commercial database systems in computing the SemEQUAL operator, as per the SQL queries described in Section 2. To profile the performance of **SemEQUAL** working with *fully developed* linguistic resources, we used the following strategy: We first profiled the structural characteristics of WordNets, as they exist now, and the results are given in Table 1.

The statistics of the individual taxonomic hierarchies indicate a very close match between the WordNets. In addition, since both Euro and Indo WordNets have conformance to English WordNet as their stated design goal, it is reasonable to expect their structures to be similar to that of English WordNet, when fully developed. Since the English WordNet is the most developed at this point of time, we replicated English WordNet in Unicode format and created ILI links between every English synset and its corresponding synset in Unicode. The resulting taxonomic hierarchy is used in the performance experiments.

4.1   Closure Computation – Baseline

For the baseline performance experiments, the interlinked WordNet taxonomic hierarchy (in Unicode format to simulate multilingual environments, as discussed earlier) was stored and queried, as specified in Section 3. The query strings for the experiment were chosen so as to result in the computation of closures of varying sizes. The *SQL-Baseline* performance (in seconds) for the basic closure computation in the three database systems (with out and with B+ tree index) is given in Figure 5 (shown in *log-log* scale). As can be observed here, the closure computations for all the systems take up to hundreds of seconds without index support and up to a few seconds even with an index. Though the variations in performance may be attributed to the respective algorithms and optimization techniques – details in [16], the net result is that the performance is unsuitable for *e-Commerce* deployments, if the size of the closure exceeds a few hundred items.

In the following sections, we outline two different (and mutually exclusive) optimization techniques that improve the performance in *System B*, which exhibits the worst indexed performance.

4.2   Optimization #1: Precomputed Closure

First, we used a standard optimization technique – *pre-computing* the closures of every element in WordNet and *storing* them explicitly as the immediate children of the corresponding element; thus, the closures could be found with a simple scan of the enhanced table. We also explored the possibility of further reducing the cost of computation by building an index on the parent attribute of the pre-computed table.

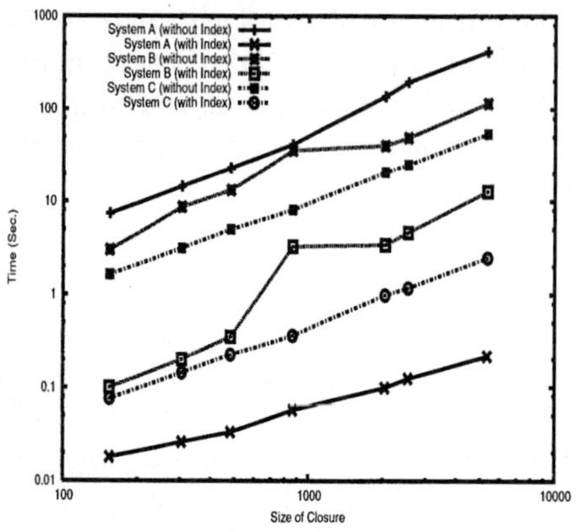

Fig. 5. Baseline Performance

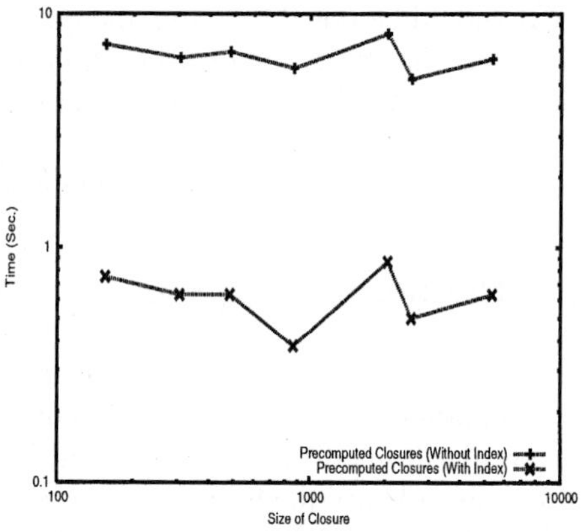

Fig. 6. Baseline Performance

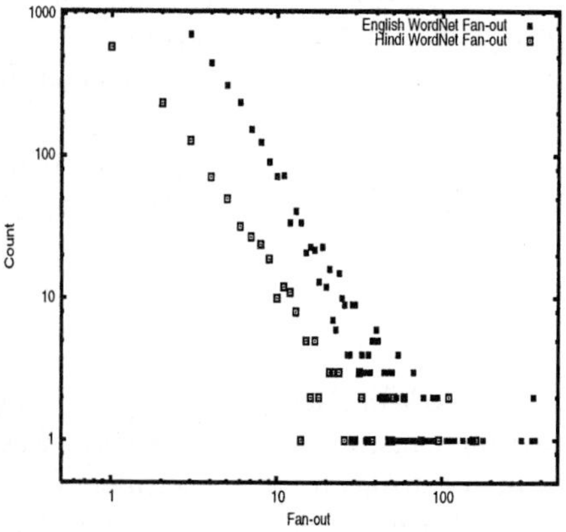

Fig. 7. WordNet Fan-out Plot

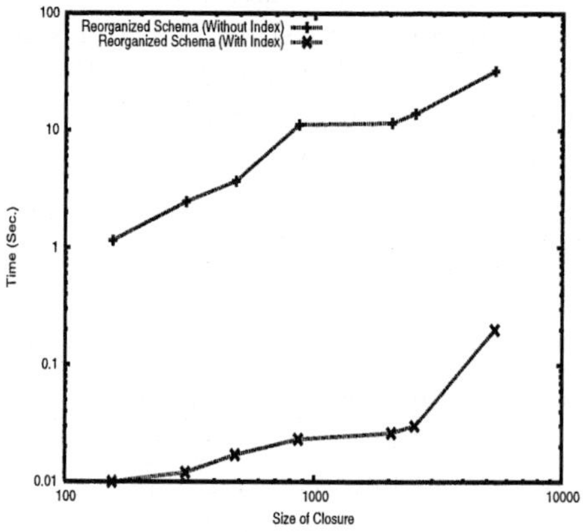

Fig. 8. WordNet Fan-out Plot

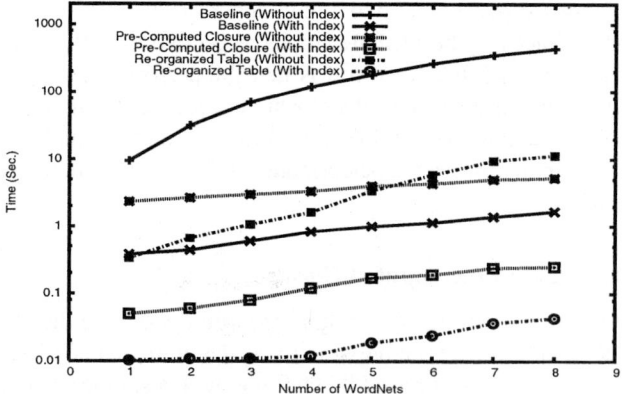

Fig. 9. Scaling of Computing Closure

We ran the transitive closure query on the resulting data set, and the performance, with and without the index, is presented in Figure 6 (the graph is shown in *log-log* scale). We observe here an improvement in performance, to about 7 seconds (without index) for the Unicode WordNet. Understandably, the closure computation takes approximately the same time for all sizes of the closure, since only a table scan is needed. With the index, as expected, the runtime is reduced by an order of magnitude from the baseline index performance, to just under one second. However, this gain comes with the penalty of enormous storage costs: the space requirements of the taxonomic tables are increased by about 20 times, to roughly 120 MB (and an additional 45 MB for index).

4.3 Optimization #2: Reorganizing Schema

We now move on to an alternative performance optimization strategy with much smaller space overheads. This strategy is based on leveraging the *distribution* of synsets in the WordNet hierarchy to reduce the calls to the expensive recursive SQL statements. We first computed and plotted the fan-out of subclasses for every parent node in English WordNet, as shown in Figure 7. The plot of the fan-out exhibits a characteristic *power-law* distribution with an exponent of -2.75. Further analysis indicated that only a small number of synsets (*less than* 10%) have a large number of children (*more than* 16), with the large majority having only a few children[2]. This distribution suggests a new, more efficient organization of WordNet hierarchy, where a certain number of sub-classes may be *inlined*. We chose to inline those synsets with upto 16 subclasses in a new taxonomy table, reducing the number of records in the new taxonomy table to about a tenth of that of the original table. All synsets with greater than 16 subclasses remained in the original table. The closure computation algorithm is modified to access the inlined table for all synsets with less than 16 children, or the original table, otherwise. The overall size of the table (in terms of number of tuples) reduces by about 90%, though the storage size remains about the same as the Baseline (about 8 MB for Unicode WordNets).

For the above schema, the performance of the closure queries – with and without indexes – are shown in Figure 8 (the graph is drawn to a *log-log* scale). As can be observed from the figure, the performance with reorganized schema is speeded up by 2 orders of magnitude on the plain table, and by 3 orders of magnitude on the indexed table, with *no perceptible increase in storage requirements from the baseline*.

4.4 Scaling of Performance with Languages

Finally, we explore how the performance behaves as function of the number of languages being considered for query processing. The runtimes for the typical query, computing a transitive closure of approximately ≈ 600 is shown in Figure 9. We observe a near-linear increase in both *pre-computed closure* and *re-organized tables* methodologies, with the number of languages. Further, even with about 8 languages, the index-based runtimes for the typical query remained within a few tens of milliseconds, which appears sufficiently small to support online interaction for a multilingual user.

---

[2] The fan-outs in Hindi and English WordNets (in Figure 7) exhibit a very similar profile differing only in scale, suggesting the applicability of power-laws in linguistic domains as well.

Thus, we show that a new semantic multilingual matching functionality may be added to current relational database systems by integrating standard linguistic resources, and leveraging only on existing SQL features. Further, we show the performance of this matching may be sufficiently optimized to support online-user interactions for multilingual e-commerce applications.

5 Related Research

To the best of our knowledge, multilingual semantic matching of attribute data – by integrating standard linguistic resources with the database engine, has not been discussed, previously in the literature. With respect to **Semantic Query Processing**, no standards have been specified in SQL and hence there is no uniformity among systems in such support. All systems support some level of semantic querying, based on NLP techniques, but are un-suitable for for attribute level matching. The WordNet based approach was used for semantic information retrieval in [19], where the emphasis was on *quality* of the results and not performance; our work on performance of such retrievals is complementary to this research. There are vast amounts of literature in the **Information Retrieval** Research community in the areas of Knowledge-based and Natural-language based retrieval. The techniques employed are diverse, ranging from syntactic and morphological analysis [8] to Machine Translation [5], statistical techniques [9], and Latent Semantic Indexing [4] for semantic querying in a single language, and to paired dictionaries [20] techniques for handling cross-language querying. We refer to the Multilingual Information Retrieval Track of the ACM SIGIR conference for a survey of current techniques. Such techniques do not perform well on attribute level data in OLTP type environments. Initiatives, such as the **Semantic Web** [21] are appropriate for meta-data management in the web domain, but not for database query processing. Finally, the existence of several **International WordNet** initiatives [3, 6, 13], with a stated objective of following similar taxonomical structures, is an enabling resource, for realizing our proposal.

6 Conclusions

In this paper, we proposed a new SQL functionality – SemEQUAL – to support seamless multilingual text data matching, based on semantics, to cater to increasingly multilingual user requirements in e-commerce deployments. Our proposal outlines a light-weight approach for implementing this feature by adopting and integrating the WordNet linguistic resource in the database system. Multilingual text attribute data are matched after transforming them to a canonical semantic form, leveraging on the rich cross-linked taxonomic hierarchies in WordNets. As a side effect, such a methodology provides a repeatable and consistent result set for a given data set across different database systems.

We outlined a *derived-operator* approach for implementing the SemEQUAL operator, using standard SQL:1999 constructs. Our performance experiments with real WordNet data on three popular commercial database systems, underscored the inefficiencies in computing transitive closure, an essential component for semantic matching. The runtimes are in the order of a few seconds, unsuitable for practical deployments. We proposed optimization techniques, by tuning the storage and access structures to match the characteristics of linguistic resources, and demonstrated that the closure computation may be speeded up by nearly 3 orders of magnitude – to *a few milliseconds* – to make the operator efficient enough for supporting online user query processing. These results underscore the viability of the **SemEQUAL** functionality for immediate practical use. Finally, we expect that for specific applications, semantic matching using domain-specific ontological hierarchies, may also benefit from a similar approach to those outlined in this paper.

Acknowledgements. We thank Dr. P. Bhattacharyya, Coordinator of Center for Indian Language Technology at IIT-Bombay, for providing us with details on Hindi WordNet.

References

1. The British National Corpus, Oxford University Press. *http://www.comp.lancs.ac.uk*.
2. Centre for Indian Language Technology, IIT-Bombay. *http://www.cfilt.iitb.ac.in*.
3. H. Chen, C. Lin and W. Lin. Building a Chinese-English WordNet for Translingual Applications. *ACM Transactions on Asian Languages Information Processing*, 2002.
4. S. Deerwester, S. T. Dumais and W. C. Ogden. Indexing by Latent Semantic Analysis. *Jour. of American Soc. of Information Sciences*, September 1990.
5. The EuroSpider. *http://www.eurospider.ch*.
6. The Euro-WordNet. *http://www.illc.uva.nl/EuroWordNet*.
7. C. Fellbaum and G. A. Miller. WordNet: An electronic lexical database (language, speech and communication). *MIT Press*, 1998.
8. C. Fluhr et al. Multilingual Database and Crosslingual Interrogation in a Real Internet Application. *AAAI Sym. on Crosslanguage Text and Speech Retrieval*, 1997.
9. F. Gey, A. Chen, M. Buckland and R. Larson. Translingual Vocabulary Mapping for Multilingual Information Access. *Proc. of 25th ACM SIGIR Conf.*, 2002.
10. The Global WordNet Association. *http://www.globalwordnet.org*.
11. J. Han et al. Some Performance Results on Recursive Query Processing in Relational Database Systems. *Proc. of 2nd ICDE Conf.*, 1986.
12. Y. Ioannidis. On the Computation of TC of Relational Operators. *Proc. of 12th VLDB Conf.*, 1986.
13. B. D. Jayaram and P. Bhattacharyya. Report on Indo-WordNet Workshop. *Central Institute of Indian Languages*, January 1999.
14. A. Kumaran and J. R. Haritsa. On Multilingual Performance of Database Systems. *Proc. of 29th VLDB Conf.*, 2003.
15. A. Kumaran and J. R. Haritsa. Supporting Multiscript Matching in Database Systems. *Proc. of 9th EDBT Conf.*, 2004.
16. A. Kumaran and J. R. Haritsa. Multilingual Semantic Operator in SQL. *Technical Report TR-2004-03, DSL/SERC, Indian Institute of Science*, 2004.
17. M. Liberman and K. Church. Text Analysis and Word Pronunciation in TTS Synthesis. *Advances in Speech Processing*, 1992.
18. The Computer Scope Ltd. *http://www.NUA.ie/Surveys*.
19. R. Richardson and A. F. Smeaton. Using WordNet in a Knowledge-based Approach to Information Retrieval. *Working Paper CA-0395, Dublin City University*, 1999.
20. D. Soergel. Multilingual thesauri in cross-language text and speech retrieval. *AAAI Sym. on Cross-Language Text and Speech Retrieval*, March 1997.
21. The Semantic Web. *http://www.w3.org/2001/sw*.
22. The WebFountain. *http://www.almaden.ibm.com/WebFountain*.
23. The WordNet. *http://www.cogsci.princeton.edu/w̃n*.
24. Word Discover. *http://www.worddiscover.com*.

A Metropolis Sampling Method for Drawing Representative Samples from Large Databases

Hong Guo[1], Wen-Chi Hou[1], Feng Yan[1], and Qiang Zhu[2]

[1] Department of Computer Science, Southern Illinois University, Carbondale IL, 62901
hou@cs.siu.edu
[2] Dept. of Computer & Info. Science, Michigan University-Dearborn, Dearborn, MI 48128
qzhu@umich.edu

Abstract. In this paper, a sampling method based on the Metropolis algorithm is proposed. It is able to draw samples that have the same distribution as the underlying probability distribution. It is a simple, efficient, and powerful method suitable for all distributions. We have performed experiments to examine the qualities of the samples by comparing their statistical properties with the underlying population. The experimental results show that the samples selected by our method are bona fide representative.

1 Introduction

While modern computers become more and more powerful, many databases in social, economical, engineering, scientific, and statistical applications may still be too large to handle. Sampling, therefore, becomes a necessity for analyses in such applications. Sampling has also been used in areas like selectivity estimation [2, 3, 5], clustering [1, 10], and spatial data mining [8]. For applications in OLAP and data mining where fast responses are required, sampling is also a viable approach for constructing in-core representations of the data [8, 10]. Due to its wide applications and importance, sampling is becoming an integral part of modern database systems, e.g., the Oracle 8i.

Uniform random sampling, in which all objects in the data set are treated equally, has been used in all sorts of applications. However, it is also criticized for its uniform treatment of objects because there are many applications where objects have non-uniform probability distributions. Strictly speaking, a uniform sampling method works only if the data has a uniform probability distribution; otherwise, the selected sample may not be representative.

To illustrate the issue, let us consider the Gallup poll for a Federal election [7]. The current dominant method for selecting a sample is by randomly picking residences' telephone numbers. A careful examination of this method reveals that the sample selected is not truly representative of the actual voters of the election. A major reason, among others, is that statistics have shown that most voters between ages 18 and 24 do not cast their ballots, while most senior citizens go to the poll-booths on Election Day. Since Gallup's sample does not take this into account, the survey could deviate substantially from the actual election results. To conduct the poll more accurately, we ought to assign a different probability to each age group based on the chance that people in that age group will cast a vote on the Election Day.

Knowing that a uniform sampling method fails to find representative samples for populations with non-uniform probability distributions, some remedies, such as the density biased sampling [10] and the Acceptance/Rejection (AR) sampling [9], have been proposed. The density-biased sampling is specifically designed for applications where the probability of a group (of similar objects) is inversely proportional to its size. The AR sampling is based on the "acceptance /rejection" (or "hit and miss") approach [11, 12]. It aims at all probability distributions and is probably the most general approach discussed in the database literature so far.

We are interested in finding a general, efficient, and accurate sampling method applicable to all probability distributions. In this paper, we develop a Monte Carlo sampling method based on the Metropolis algorithm [6] to produce representative samples. As it will be clear in the subsequent sections, the sample generated by this method is bona fide representative and is better than the samples produced by other existing methods.

The rest of the paper is organized as follows. In Section 2, we provide some background on statistical testing. Section 3 presents our Metropolis sampling. We will also make a brief comparison with the Acceptance/Rejection (AR) sampling, which is the most relevant work to our approach. In Section 4, we empirically examine the qualities of the samples drawn by our Metropolis sampling and the AR sampling. Finally, we present the conclusions in Section 5.

2 Background

Being a representative sample, it must satisfy some criteria. First, the sample mean and variance must be good estimates of the population mean and variance, respectively, and converge to the latter when the sample size increases. In addition, a selected sample must have a distribution similar to the underlying population. In the following, we briefly describe these properties.

2.1 Mean and Variance Estimation

Let $\vec{x}$ be a d-dimensional vector representing a set of d attributes that characterizes an object in a population, and $\rho(\vec{x})$ the value of $\vec{x}$. Our task is to calculate the mean and variance of ρ of the population. Let $w(\vec{x}) \geq 0$ be the probability distribution of $\vec{x}$, often called a weight function. The population mean of $\rho(\vec{x})$, denoted $\overline{\rho}$, is

$$\overline{\rho} = \sum_{all\ \vec{x}} \rho(\vec{x}) w(\vec{x}) \tag{1}$$

The probability distribution is required to satisfy

$$\sum_{all\ \vec{x}} w(\vec{x}) = 1 \tag{2}$$

Another useful quantity is the population variance, which is defined as

$$\Delta^2 = \sum_{all\ \vec{x}} (\rho(\vec{x}) - \overline{\rho})^2 w(\vec{x}). \tag{3}$$

The variance specifies the variability of the $\rho(\vec{x})$ values relative to $\overline{\rho}$.

2.2 Chi-square Test

To compare the distributions of a sample and its population, we perform the Chi-square test [11] by computing

$$\chi^2 = \sum_{i=1}^{k}(r_i - Nw_i)^2/(Nw_i), \qquad (4)$$

where r_i is the number of objects drawn from the ith bin, w_i the probability of the ith bin of the population, $\sum_{i=1}^{k} r_i = N$ the sample size, and Nw_i is the expected number of sample objects of that bin. A bin here refers to a group or range of values, e.g., an age group. The larger the χ^2 value, the greater is the discrepancy between the sample and the population distributions. Usually, a level of significance α is specified as the uncertainty of the test. If the value of χ^2 is less than $\chi^2_{1-\alpha}$, we are about $1-\alpha$ confident that the sample and population have similar distributions. Customarily, $\alpha = 0.05$. The value of $\chi^2_{1-\alpha}$ is determined by the degree of freedom involved (i.e., k -1).

3 The Metropolis Sampling

In 1953, Metropolis proposed an algorithm, known as the Metropolis algorithm [6], for studying statistical physics. Since then, it has become the most successful and influential Monte Carlo Method. Here, we shall use it for constructing representative samples. In addition, we will also incorporate techniques for finding the best start sampling point into the algorithm to improve its efficiency. Hereafter, we shall use the Metropolis algorithm and Monte Carlo method interchangeably.

3.1 Probability Distribution

The probability distribution $w(\bar{x})$ plays an important role in the Metropolis algorithm. Unfortunately, such information is usually unknown or difficult to obtain due to the infiniteness, incompleteness, or large size of a population. However, the relative probability distribution or non-normalized probability distribution, denoted by $W(\bar{x})$, can often be obtained from, for example, preliminary analysis, past experience, knowledge, statistics, etc. Take the Gallup poll for example. While it may be difficult or impossible to assign a weight (i.e., $w(\bar{x})$) to each individual voter, recalling that it has to satisfy the condition $\sum_{all\ \bar{x}} w(\bar{x}) = 1$, it can be easily known from published statistics or other resources that the relative probabilities $W(\bar{x})$ of people to vote on the Election Day are 18.5%, 38.7%, 56.5%, and 61.5% for groups whose ages fall in 18-24, 25-44, 45-65, and 65+, respectively. Fortunately, the relative probability distribution $W(\bar{x})$ would suffice to construct a representative sample [4].

3.2 Sampling Procedure

Similar to the simple random sampling, objects are drawn one after another to form the sample. Here, we shall address the issues of selecting the first sample element and accepting or rejecting a drawn element in each step, called the Monte Carlo step.

3.2.1 Selecting the Starting Point

For numerical calculations, finding the best start point may not be an important issue. For sampling, the situation may be quite different, especially when the relative probability distribution $W(\bar{x})$ is highly non-uniform. Note that objects with higher weight are more important than others. If a method does not start with these objects, we could miss them in the process or take very long time to incorporate them into the sample, which is formidable in cost and detrimental to accuracy. Selecting a good starting point is very crucial to the efficiency of sampling and quality of the sample. In the following, we propose a general approach to selecting a starting point.

We begin with searching for an object that has the maximum value of $W(\bar{x})$. If there are several objects with the same maximum value, we could just pick any of them as the "best starting host" $\bar{x}_1$. For many applications, such as the Gallup example, finding the maximal value of $W(\bar{x})$ is straightforward, e.g., using the already-known maximum, by examining the statistics, performing preliminary analysis, etc. For others, there are several useful methods, such as Golden Section search, Downhill Simplex method, Conjugate Gradient method [11], for searching for the maximum of a function. With these methods, we can easily locate the peak of $W(\bar{x})$ and use it as the starting point for our sample. Here, we implement the Downhill Simplex method because this method requires only simple computations on $W(\bar{x})$; it does not require complex derivative computations, and is among the best for multidimensional functions. The method starts with a simplex, which is a geometrical figure consisting of $d+1$ points, where d is the number of dimensions. For example, in a two dimensional space, a simplex is a triangle. Through function evaluations, the method makes the simplex roll downhill and contract in the function's minimum. Since the maximum of function f is the minimum of function -f, this method works for searching for a maximum as well. Interested readers please refer to [11] for more details.

3.2.2 Incorporating Objects into the Sample: The Monte Carlo Step

Let the object last added to the sample be $\bar{x}_i$. Now, we pick a trial object $\bar{y}$ from the population randomly. For example, one can just randomly select it from the neighbors of $\bar{x}_i$ or through the Fourier transformation such as in the quantum Monte Carlo [4]. In general, there is no restriction on how to select $\bar{y}$. The only requirement is that the random selection method must provide a chance for every element in the entire data space to be picked.

We now decide if the trial object $\bar{y}$ should be incorporated into the sample. We calculate the ratio $\theta = W(\bar{y})/W(\bar{x}_i)$. If $\theta \geq 1$, we accept $\bar{y}$ into the sample and let

$\vec{x}_{i+1} = \vec{y}$. That is, $\vec{y}$ becomes the last object added to the sample. If $\theta < 1$, we generate a random number R, which has an equal probability to lie between 0 and 1. If $R \leq \theta$, the trial object $\vec{y}$ is accepted into the sample and we let $\vec{x}_{i+1} = \vec{y}$. Otherwise, the trial object $\vec{y}$ is rejected and we let $\vec{x}_{i+1} = \vec{x}_i$. It is noted that in the latter situation, we incorporate the just selected object $\vec{x}_i$ into the sample again (i.e. $\vec{x}_{i+1} = \vec{x}_i$). Therefore, an object with a high probability may appear more than once in our sample. The above step is called a Monte Carlo step.

After each Monte Carlo step, we add one more object into the sample. The above Monte Carlo step is repeated to incorporate more objects into the sample until a predefined sample size N is reached. It is expected that the sample average converges very fast as N increases and the fluctuation decreases in the order of $1/\sqrt{N}$ [6].

The complete sampling procedure, which includes selecting the starting point and the Metropolis algorithm, is summarized as follows.

---

(1) locate an object with the maximum weight $W(\vec{x})$ as the first object $\vec{x}_1$ of the sample.
(2) **for i from 1 to N-1 do**
(3)   randomly select an object $\vec{y}$;
(4)   compute $\theta = W(\vec{y})/W(\vec{x}_i)$;
(5)   **if** $\theta \geq 1$ **then** $\vec{x}_{i+1} = \vec{y}$;
(6)   **else** generate a random number R;
(7)   **if** $R \leq \theta$ **then** $\vec{x}_{i+1} = \vec{y}$;
(8)   **else** $\vec{x}_{i+1} = \vec{x}_i$;
(9)   **end if**;
(10)   **end if**;
(11) **end for**.

Fig. 1. The Monte Carlo / Metropolis Sampling

3.2.3 A Gallup Poll Example

Let us use the Gallup poll as an example to illustrate our Monte Carlo/Metropolis sampling. From the statistics published by the Federal Election Commission [14], we obtain the turnout rate for each age group on the Election Day as shown in Table 1.

Table 1. Turnout rate in 1998 federal election

Age	18-24	25-44	45-66	65+
% voted	18.5	38.7	56.5	61.3

The process may start off by randomly picking a senior citizen (from the 65+ group) as the first element of the sample. Then, the pollster picks another registered voter, as a trial object. Assume the trial voter is in the 18-24 age group. Then, the ratio θ of the probability of the 18-24 group to that of 65+ group is 0.3018 (= 18.5 / 61.3). Since $\theta < 1$, the pollster generates a random number R, which lies between 0 and 1. If $R \leq 0.3018$, the trial voter is accepted as an element of the sample. If $R > 0.3018$, the trial voter is rejected and the last included sample element is recorded again. The pollster repeats the above procedure to incorporate more voters into the sample. The sample can be used throughout the election by the pollsters. Similar to SRSWR, voters may appear more than once in the sample. This happens because their age groups have high turnout rates. The selected voters are representatives for their age groups.

3.3 Properties of a Metropolis Sample

A Monte Carlo/Metropolis sample has several important properties. First, since the selection starts with an object having the maximum weight $W(\bar{x})$, it ensures that the sample always includes the most important objects. Second, it is known that the Monte Carlo sample has a distribution close to that of the population when sample size is large enough [4]. That is, the expected number of occurrences of object r_i in the sample is proportional to its weight in the population. Finally, it should be pointed out that when all objects have an equal weight, the Monte Carlo sampling degenerates to a simple random sampling.

3.4 Estimation of Mean and Variance

Once a sample is formed, we can easily calculate the following quantities as estimates to the population mean and variance, respectively,

$$<\bar{\rho}> = \sum_{i=1}^{N} \rho(\bar{y}_i)/N, \tag{5}$$

$$<\Delta^2> = \sum_{i=1}^{N} (\rho(\bar{y}_i) - <\bar{\rho}>)^2 / N \tag{6}$$

where $y_1, y_2, ..., y_N$ denote all objects in the sample.

Note that the sample variance $<\Delta^2>$ is computed relative to the sample mean $<\bar{\rho}>$, as shown in Eq. (4). However, if the sample mean itself is biased, the sample variance would not be able to show how different the estimates are from the true population mean. Therefore, instead of comparing the sample variance, the second moment of ρ, denoted $<\overline{\rho^2}>$, is often compared. $<\overline{\rho^2}>$ is defined as

$$<\overline{\rho^2}> = \sum_{i=1}^{N} \rho(\bar{y}_i)^2 / N = <\Delta^2> + <\bar{\rho}>^2. \tag{7}$$

3.5 Comparisons and Discussions

Our sampling and Olken's AR sampling [9] have some similarities, that is, both are Monte Carlo methods. However, the AR sampling uses the simple "hit and miss" or "rejection" technique [11], while ours is based on the more powerful and sophisticated Metropolis algorithm.

In the AR sampling, objects are picked randomly and the probability of a picked object, say A, being accepted into the sample is W(A)/W$_{max}$, where W$_{max}$ is the maximum weight of the objects. Like our approach, W(A) is compared with a randomly generated number (between 0 and 1) to determine its acceptance or rejection. While the AR sampling is very simple, efficiency can be a weakness. Indeed, it has been shown that the average number of trials for each success (i.e., an acceptance of an object) is W$_{max}$/W$_{avg}$, where W$_{avg}$ is the average weight of objects [9]. Therefore, the more "skewed" the population (i.e., fewer objects having larger weights, while more objects having smaller weights), the more trial objects need to be drawn in this process. The quality of the samples selected by the AR method is certainly of great interest. In Section 4, we will empirically evaluate the quality of the samples produced by both methods.

4 Experiments

In this section, we report the results of empirical evaluations of our Metropolis sampling and the AR sampling. We compare the efficiency of the methods and the quality of the samples generated.

4.1 Criteria and Data

From a statistical point of view, being representative requires the sample not only yields accurate estimates of the mean and variance of the population, but also has a distribution similar to the population. We shall use these criteria to measure the quality of the samples drawn. We opt to choose a family of synthetic data sets for our experiments because some subtleties may be best illustrated quantitatively and qualitatively in a more controlled environment. Here, we have chosen the Gaussian model $w(\vec{x}) = (1/\pi)^{d/2} e^{(-\vec{x}^2)}$, where d is the dimension and $\rho(\vec{x}) = \vec{x}^2$. The mean, the second moment, and variance are:

$$\overline{\rho} = \int \vec{x}^2 w(\vec{x}) d\vec{x} = d/2 , \qquad (8)$$

$$\overline{\rho^2} = \int (\vec{x}^2)^2 w(\vec{x}) d\vec{x} = (d^2 + 2d)/4 , \qquad (9)$$

$$\Delta^2 = \overline{\rho^2} - (\overline{\rho})^2 = d/2 \qquad (10)$$

Figure 2 is a 2-d Gaussian distribution. It has a high peak at the center. Only a small region near the center makes significant contributions to the integrations of Eqs. (8) and (9). As the dimension increases, the peak becomes higher and narrower, and the distribution becomes more "skewed".

4.2 Sampling Efficiency

First, let us compare the cost of sampling. As shown in Fig. 3, the AR method roughly needs 5, 10, 75, and 1,750 trials to accept just one object into the sample in 1, 3, 10, and 20-dimensional cases, respectively. It is noted that the higher the dimension, the more "skewed" the Gaussian distribution and the greater the W_{max}/W_{avg} value. This explains why the AR sampling requires more trials as the dimension increases. In comparison, our Monte Carlo sampling method accepts one object in every trial.

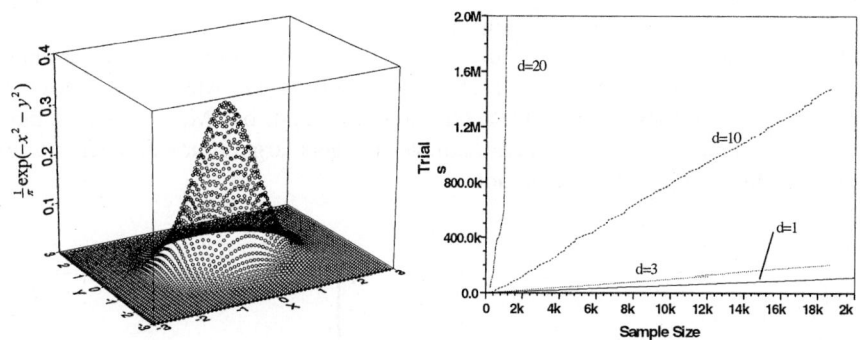

Fig. 2. A Gaussian distribution: d=2   **Fig. 3.** Cost of AR sampling

4.3 Quality of the Samples

To examine the quality of a sample, we shall examine its mean, variance, and distribution.

4.3.1 Sample Mean and Variance

We show the second moment of ρ, $<\overline{\rho^2}>$, which tells how different the estimates are from the actual values, especially when the estimate is biased.

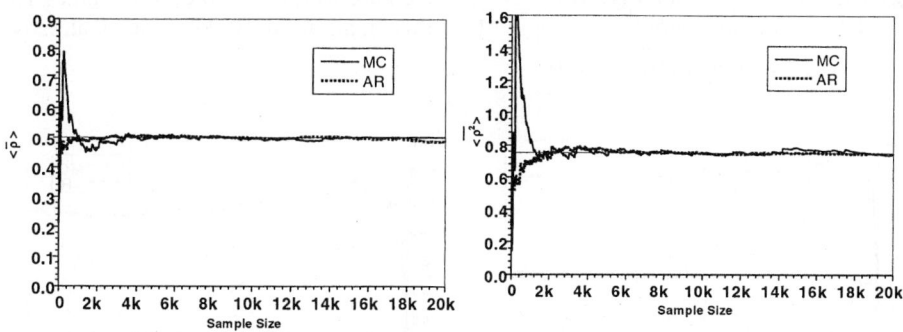

Fig. 4. Sample means for d=1. $<\overline{\rho}>$=0.5   **Fig. 5.** $<\overline{\rho^2}>$=0.75 for d=1

As shown in Figures 4 and 5, both methods yield pretty accurate estimates of the population mean (=0.5) and second moment (=0.75) in one-dimensional case. Consequently, from Eq. (10), they also give good estimates of the variance. Note that

AR sampling, however, requires 5 times more trials than our method to form a sample of the same size. While the AR sampling may seem to generate excellent estimates, a careful examination of the results reveals that, most of the time, it slightly underestimates $<\overline{\rho}>$ and $<\overline{\rho^2}>$, unlike our estimates which fluctuate around the exact values. While the underestimates may be too small to be worth any attentions, the frequency of underestimation signals a subtle problem of the AR sampling that will become more evident when the dimension increases.

As shown in Figures 6 and 7 for d=3, the AR sampling yields estimates around 1.0 and 1.7 for the mean and second moment, respectively, which are below their respective exact values 3/2 and 15/4. On the other hand, our Monte Carlo sampling yields quite accurate estimates. As the sample size gets larger, our estimates get closer to the analytic values, but AR's do not.

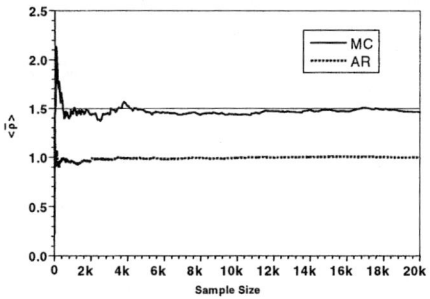

Fig. 6. Sample means $<\overline{\rho}>$ =1.5 for d=3   **Fig. 7.** $<\overline{\rho^2}>$ =15/4 for d=3

Similar results are also observed for higher dimensional cases. As shown in Figures 8 and 9, when d=20, the AR sampling yields estimates around 5.1 and 29 for the mean and second moment, respectively, which are well below the exact values 10 and 110. As for our method, a sample of size as small as of 10,000 objects already gives $<\overline{\rho}> \approx 10$ and $<\overline{\rho^2}> \approx 110$.

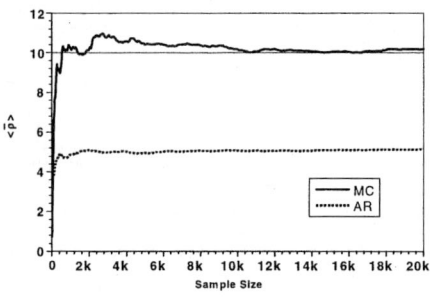
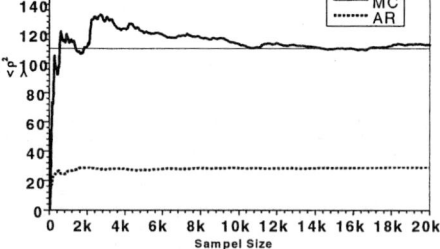

Fig. 8. Sample means $<\overline{\rho}>$ =10 for d=20   **Fig. 9.** $<\overline{\rho^2}>$ =110 for d=20

The underestimation of the AR sampling was attributed to two factors: the acceptance/rejection criterion $W(\bar{x})/W_{max}$ of the AR sampling and the random number generator. In the Gaussian model described earlier, W_{max} appears at the center (i.e., $\bar{x} = 0$), and the weight $W(\bar{x})$ diminishes quickly as we move away from the center. Indeed, the majority of the points have very small weights and thus small $W(\bar{x})/W_{max} = e^{(-\bar{x}^2)}$ ratios, especially when the dimension is high. The low $W(\bar{x})/W_{max}$ values could make the respective points not selectable when compared with the random numbers generated in the process.

The random number generators on most computers are based on the *linear congruent method,* which first generates a sequence of integers by the recurrence relation $I_{j+1} = aI_j + c$ (mod m), where m is the modulus, and a and c are positive integers [11]. The final random numbers generated have are I_1/m, I_2/m, I_3/m, ... Since a random number generator generally simulates a probability distribution, it does not generate 0. Thus the smallest numbers generated is $1/m$. As a result, a trial point in the AR sampling, whose $W(\bar{x})/W_{max}$ is smaller than $1/m$, can never be accepted. Since these "remote" points have larger values than the points near the center, recalling that $\rho(\bar{x}) = \bar{x}^2$, underestimation sets in. The higher the dimension, the more "skewed" the distribution, the more of this type of "remote" points, and the more serious the underestimation. Increasing sample size would not help because those points just will not be accepted.

While it is possible to use a larger m, it raises another issue of the generator - the randomness. Here, we use the most widely used random generator in the Monte Carlo simulation community, which is also the one of the best available random number generators [11]. This random number generator is fast and agile. Therefore, it is at least probably fair to say that while the AR sampling is theoretically sound, it may face some difficulty practically when dealing with "skewed" distributions.

On the other hand, our Monte Carlo sampling uses the weight ratio of the trial and the last accepted objects. As points away from the center are accepted, the chances of remote points being accepted increase. Therefore, it is immune from the difficulty associated with the AR sampling method.

Based on our experiments with the Gaussian distribution, a sufficient minimum size should be in the neighborhood of 500d to 1,000d, where d is the number of dimensions for the population (space). For smoother distributions, the results can be even better.

4.3.2 Distribution

To examine whether a sample has a similar distribution to the underlying population, a Chi-square test, as defined by Equation (4), is generally performed. Since the Chi-square test is designed for discrete data, we need to convert the Gaussian Model, which is a continuous model, into binned data. For one-dimensional case, we limit the data space to the range $-3.5 \leq x \leq 3.5$ because points falling outside the range carry a negligible weight $1 - \int_{-3.5}^{3.5} \frac{1}{\sqrt{\pi}} e^{(-x^2)} dx < 10^{-6}$. We divide the space into 2b+1 bins, labeled as −b, −b+1,..., b. Each bin has a length D=7/ (2b+1). The jth bin covers a region from $(j-0.5)D$ to $(j+0.5)D$ and

$$w_j = \int_{(j-0.5)D}^{(j+0.5)D} \frac{1}{\sqrt{\pi}} e^{(-x^2)} dx \tag{11}$$

With 2b+1 bins for our test, the degree of freedom v is 2b, which will be used to compute the threshold $\chi^2_{1-\alpha}$ for a given significance level α [13]. Since we convert continuous data to discrete data, Yates' correction to the Chi-square test should be considered [13]. Therefore, Eq.(4) is rewritten as

$$\chi^2 = \sum_{i=1}^{k} (|n_i - Nw_i| - 0.5)^2 / (Nw_i) \tag{12}$$

Figure 10 shows the χ^2-test results of AR's and our samples. In the test, the data space is divided into 7 bins and thus the degree of freedom v is 6. We have chosen the commonly used significance level α =0.05 in the test.

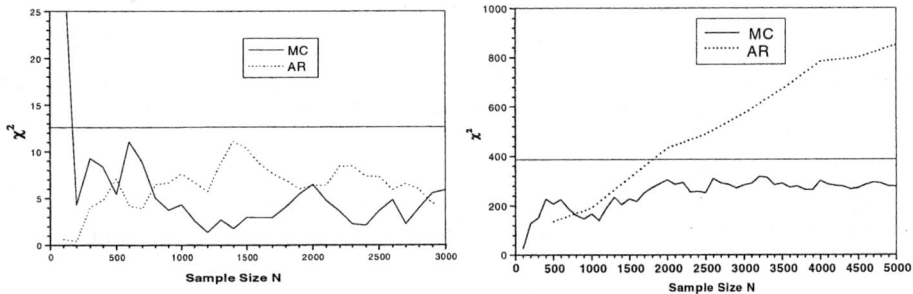

Fig. 10. $\chi^2_{0.95} = 12.6$, $v = 6$ for d=1   **Fig. 11.** $\chi^2_{0.95} = 386$, $v = 343$ for d=3

It is observed that when sample size N > 200, our χ^2 is below $\chi^2_{1-\alpha} = \chi^2_{0.95} = 12.6$ with $v = 6$. This indicates agreement between sample and population distributions. The χ^2 value stabilizes as N gets larger. We have also performed tests on other bin values and the results are similar, all verifying the agreement of the sample distribution with the population distribution. As for the AR sampling, it also performs very well, showing a strong agreement of the sample distribution with the underlying population distribution.

Expanding this test to the three-dimensional Gaussian model, we concentrate on the cubic space, $|x_i| \leq 3.5$ (i=1, 2, 3) and divide it into $7^3 = 343$ bins. As observed from Fig. 11, our χ^2 values are always less than $\chi^2_{0.95}$ (≈ 386 with $v = 342$), indicating a good agreement with the population distribution. As for the AR sampling, it is observed that for samples of any reasonable sizes, their χ^2 values well exceed $\chi^2_{0.95} \approx 386$ for $v = 342$, which indicates that the samples have different distributions from the population. As explained earlier, this is because the AR sampling could not include points with very low weights and thus as more points are included (or as the sample size increases) the more different the sample distribution is from the population distribution. The results are consistent with the evaluations of means and variances discussed in the previous sections. For higher dimensions, the results are similar and we shall not present them here.

As a short summary, the AR sampling may work well when the probability distribution is not very skewed, but our approach works for all distributions. In addition, our approach is also more efficient.

5 Conclusions

The Metropolis sampling presented in this paper is a useful and powerful tool for studying large databases. It can be applied to any probability distribution. We propose to start the sampling by taking an object from where the probability distribution has its maximum. This guarantees that the sample always includes the most important objects and it improves the efficiency of the process. Our experiments also indicate a strong agreement between the selected sample and the population distributions. The selected sample is bona fide representative, better than the samples produced by other existing methods. From our experiments with the Gaussian distribution, we estimate that the minimum sample size N is about 500d to 1,000d. For smoother distributions, the results are expected to be much better.

References

1. C. Aggarwal, P. Yu, "Finding generalized projected clusters in high dimensional spaces", Proc. ACM SIGMOD Conf., 2000, pp. 70-81.
2. P. Haas and A. Swami, "Sequential sampling procedures for query size estimation", Proc. of the ACM SIGMOD Conference, 1992, pp. 341-350.
3. W-C. Hou and G. Ozsoyoglu, "Statistical Estimators for Aggregate Relational Algebra Queries", ACM Transactions on Database Systems, Vol. 16, No. 4, 1991, pp. 600 - 654.
4. M. H. Kalos and P. A. Whilock, Monte Carlo Methods, Vol 1., Basic, John Wiley & Sons, 1986.
5. R. Lipton and J. Naughton, "Query size estimation by adaptive sampling", Proc. of the 9th ACM SIGACT-SIGMOD-SIGACT Symposium on Principles of Database Systems, 1990, pp. 40-46.
6. N. Metropolis, A. W. Rosenbluth, M. N. Rosenbluth, A. H. Teller and E. Teller, "Equation of State Calculations by Fast Computing Machines", J. of Chem. Phys., Vol. 21, No. 6, 1953, pp.1087-1092.
7. F. Newport, L. Saad and D. Moor, Where America Stands, John Wiley, 1997.
8. R. T. Ng and J. Han, "Efficient and Effective Clustering Methods for Spatial Data Mining", Proc. of the VLDB Conference, 1994, pp. 144-155.
9. F. Olken, "Random Sampling from Databases", Ph.D dissertation, U. of California, April 1993.

10. C. R. Palmer and C. Faloutsos, "Density biased sampling: An improved method for data mining and clustering", Proc. of the ACM SIGMOD Conference, Vol.29, No. 2, 2000, pp.82-92.
11. W. Press, S. Teukolsky, W. Vetterling and B. Flannery, Numerical Recipes in C, Cambridge University Press, 1994.
12. R. Rubinstein, Simulation and the Monte Carlo Method, John Wiley & Sons, 1981.
13. M. R. Spiegel, Probability and Statistics, McGraw-Hill, Inc., New York,1991.
14. Website of Federal Election Commission, http://www.fec.gov/.

Stay Current and Relevant in Data Mining Research

Haixun Wang[1] and Wei Wang[2]

[1] IBM T. J. Watson Research Center, U.S.A
[2] Fudan University, China
haixun@us.ibm.com, weiwang1@fudan.edu.cn

In a recent editorial of the Bioinformatics journal, Dr. Pavel Pevzner, a pioneering researcher in the field of bioinformatics, made the following statement [1]: *For many years algorithms were taught exclusively to computer scientists, with relatively few students from other disciplines attending algorithms courses. A biology student in an algorithms class would be a surprising and unlikely (though not entirely unwelcome) guest in the 1990s. Things change; some biology students now take some sort of Algorithms 101. At the same time, curious computer science students often take Genetics 101.*

Looking back on a decade of progress in database and data mining research, we find ourselves constantly searching for killer applications through which academic research can make bigger impacts. Yet it seems that we have not been very successful. Years ago, in a VLDB Endowment meeting (New York, 1998), concerns were expressed that the area of database research may lose the pivotal role it now plays among information system technologies. Although the outcome is still not very clear, it was agreed that database researchers should maintain a watch on trends and future directions in the general area of information management to ensure that database research remain current and relevant.

We have invited the following panelists to share with us their view toward future directions of database and data mining research. As Dr. Pevzner emphasizes the necessity for biology scientists to learn more of computer science, our panel promotes application awareness and the necessity for database and data mining researchers to start taking Genetics 101, or other initiatives that will enable our research work to make real life impact.

- **Divyakant Agrawal**, Professor and Chair of Department of Computer Science, University of California, Santa Barbara, USA.
- **Elisa Bertino**, Professor of Department of Computer Science, Purdue University, Research Director of CERIAS, USA.
- **Jinyan Li**, Lead Scientist, Knowledge Discovery Dept. Institute for Infocomm Research, Singapore.
- **Limsoon Wong**, Deputy Executive Director of Institute for Infocomm Research, Senior Scientist of Institute of Molecular & Cell Biology, Singapore.

Reference

1. Pavel A. Pevzner: Educating biologists in the 21st century: bioinformatics scientists versus bioinformatics technicians. Bioinformatics **20** (2004): 2159-2161

An Efficient Approach to Extracting Approximate Repeating Patterns in Music Databases

Ning-Han Liu[1], Yi-Hung Wu[1], and Arbee L.P. Chen[2,*]

[1] Department of Computer Science, National Tsing Hua University,
Hsinchu,Taiwan
[2] Department of Computer Science, National Chengchi University,
Taipei, Taiwan
alpchen@cs.nccu.edu.tw

Abstract. Pattern extraction from music strings is an important problem. The patterns extracted from music strings can be used as features for music retrieval or analysis. Previous works on music pattern extraction only focus on exact repeating patterns. However, music segments with minor differences may sound similar. The concept of the prototypical melody has therefore been proposed to represent these similar music segments. In musicology, the number of music segments that are similar to a prototypical melody implies the importance degree of the prototypical melody to the music work. In this paper, a novel approach is developed to extract all the prototypical melodies in a music work. Our approach considers each music segment as a candidate for the prototypical melody and uses the edit distance to determine the set of music segments that are similar to this candidate. A lower bounding mechanism, which estimates the number of similar music segments for each candidate and prunes the impossible candidates is designed to speed up the process. Experiments are performed on a real data set and the results show a significant improvement of our approach over the existing approaches in the average response time.

1 Introduction

For content-based music retrieval and music style analysis, a fundamental requirement is to extract music features from the raw data of music works. One significant feature of the music work is the *structural feature*, which is described as follows. Consider the classical music works. Most of them are composed according to a particular structure named *musical form* in which there is a basic rule: *repetition rule* [5]. The repetition rule says that there exist specific sequences of notes, known as *motives*, repeating in a movement. For example, the well-known *motive* "G-G-G-E" repeatedly appears in Beethoven's Symphony No. 5. In the previous work [4], a sequence of notes appearing more than once in the music work is regarded as the structural feature and called the *repeating pattern*. Most of the researchers in the musicology agree that repetition is a universal characteristic in music structure and style analysis [5]. Moreover, the length

---

* Corresponding author

of a repeating pattern is much shorter than that of a music work. Therefore, using repeating patterns as music features meets both efficiency and effectiveness requirements for content-based music retrieval.

The problem of finding all the repeating patterns from a music work has been discussed in [2] with suffix-tree based solutions. Each of these approaches first builds a suffix-tree, where each path represents a pattern and each leaf node keeps all the positions of the corresponding pattern located in the music work. After traversing the suffix-tree, all the repeating patterns can be extracted. These approaches consider the patterns represented by different paths to be different. As a result, they only find exact repeating patterns instead of the repeating patterns composed of strings with minor differences. In [4], a repeating pattern that is not contained in any other repeating pattern with the same count is called *non-trivial*. Two approaches based on *correlative-matrix* and *string-join*, are proposed to extract non-trivial repeating patterns. The former approach lines up the notes of a music piece along the x-axis and y-axis respectively to form a correlative matrix and uses it to find all the non-trivial repeating patterns in the music piece. The latter approach joins shorter repeating patterns into longer ones and prunes the impossible candidates in between. Similarly, both of them only focus on finding exact repeating patterns. Shih et al. [11] also propose an algorithm for extracting repeating patterns from music databases. They segment a music score into bars, which are further encoded for efficiency. As a result, the computation cost for segment matching is reduced. Except for the encoding mechanism, this approach adopts the same concept as string-join.

One the other hand, a pattern may repeatedly appear in a music work with some variations. One popular concept to coordinate such variations is the *prototypical melody*, which is a kind of abstraction of the music work to which the corresponding music segments are similar [10]. The prototypical melody has a great impact on the way the actual melody is memorized by human. The main goal of this paper is to extract all the prototypical melodies called *approximate repeating patterns* from a music work. Pienimäki [8] considers the music transposition and adopts the algorithm on text mining to extract all the longest repeating patterns, i.e., the ones that are not contained in any others. This approach allows the extracted patterns to be discontinuous in the music piece. In this approach, shorter candidates are first generated with unqualified ones removed and then combined into longer ones. Experiments show that the execution time of this approach is considerable due to the huge number of candidates to be examined. Rolland [9] proposes a flexible similarity measure of music segments and a dynamic-programming method for extracting approximate repeating patterns. First, a music segment is regarded as a point in a graph and then the similarity between every two points in the graph is computed. After that, all the prototypical melodies are found by counting the number of similar music segments for each point in the graph. This approach costs a lot on computing the similarities among music segments. For example, given a music work with 200 notes, if the user restricts the length of a repeating pattern to the range from 10 to 100, the number of music segments involved will be (101+191)*91/2=13286. In this case, the number of similarity computations will be C_2^{13286}, which is close to 10^8. Moreover, the similarity computation for every two music segments is also time consuming since its time complexity is $O(|m|*|n|)$, where $|m|$ and $|n|$ denote the lengths of music segments m and n, respectively.

In this paper, we consider each music segment as a candidate *ARP* (namely, an approximate repeating pattern or a prototypical melody). Two constraints, the maximum and minimum pattern lengths, are set to filter out the candidates that are not interesting to the user. After that, for each candidate, we use the edit distance and a threshold to identify all the music segments that are similar to it. Finally, based on the number of similar music segments and how they overlap each other, we determine whether a candidate ARP is qualified to be an ARP. For efficiency, we design a modified R*-tree to prune impossible candidates before the computations of edit distances. We propose a novel distance measure to approximate the edit distance, by which we can reduce the number of similar segments for each candidate ARP. In addition, since it is difficult to set the above constraints and thresholds perfectly at the first time, enabling the user to tune them without rerunning the entire process is necessary. We call it the *interactive environment*. Our modified R*-tree can work in the interactive environment and avoid rerunning the entire algorithm. According to the experiment results, especially on the average response time, our approach outperforms Rolland's approach [9] in both the normal and interactive environments.

The remainder of this paper is organized as follows. In Section 2, we define the approximate repeating pattern and formulate the ARP extraction problem. Section 3 presents our approach to the ARP extraction problem. Section 4 shows the experiment results with discussions. Finally, Section 5 concludes this paper with future research directions exposed.

2 Problem Formulation

The problem of prototypical melody extraction has been defined in Rolland's work [9], where the pattern composed of music segments is called the *star-type pattern*. In a star-type pattern, one music segment is its origin called the *pivot* and the others are music segments similar to the pivot over a predefined threshold. In this paper, we regard a pivot as the prototypical melody if it is the origin of a star-type pattern. In the following, we formulate our problem, where more constraints are specified.

2.1 Data Representation

There are several symbolic representations in digital music. We choose the MIDI [7] representation because of its popularity. The melody of a music work includes two kinds of basic information, i.e., pitch and duration. Each note in a MIDI file can be represented as a triple (p,s,e) where p is the pitch value, s means the starting time of playing (i.e., *note on*) and e is the ending time of playing (i.e., *note off*). As a result, a MIDI file is an ordered list of triples sorted by the note on time, e.g., (p_1,s_1,e_1), (p_2,s_2,e_2), ...,(p_n,s_n,e_n) where $s_1 \leq s_2 \leq ... \leq s_n$. Two music pieces whose notes have the same pitches is often considered the same even though their notes have different durations. Therefore, in our approach, the order instead of the exact time is retained. Moreover, since two melodies with the same contour are considered the same, we use intervals as our representation, which is defined as follows.

Definition 2.1. Pitch String:

A *pitch string* $P=(p_1, p_2, \ldots p_m)$ is the ordered list of pitch values p_i retrieved from a MIDI file, where m is the string length denoted as $|P|=m$.

Definition 2.2. Interval String:

An *interval string* of a pitch string $P=(p_1, p_2, \ldots p_m)$ is defined as $D=(d_1, d_2, \ldots d_{m-1})$, where $d_i = p_{i+1} - p_i$, $1 \leq i < m$ and d_i is called an *interval*.

The set of all the distinct interval values in D is denoted as $\sum_D$, whose size is denoted as $|\sum_D|$. Fig. 1 shows the examples of a pitch string and an interval string.

Definition 2.3. Interval Segment:

An *interval segment* $S[i:j]$ is a substring of an interval string $D=(d_1, d_2, \ldots d_n)$ from i to j, i.e., $S[i:j]=(d_i, d_{i+1}, \ldots, d_j)$.

For the simplicity of presentation, in the remainder of this paper, we use *string* and *segment* to mean *interval string* and *interval segment*, respectively.

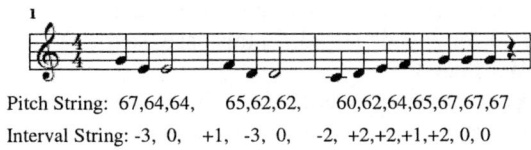

Pitch String: 67,64,64, 65,62,62, 60,62,64,65,67,67,67
Interval String: -3, 0, +1, -3, 0, -2, +2,+2,+1,+2, 0, 0

Fig. 1. A pitch string and an interval string

2.2 Approximate Repeating Patterns

If there is no constraint on the music patterns, too many patterns will be extracted and some of them can be uninteresting to user, e.g., too short and too long patterns. Therefore, we define five constraints that can filter out unimportant music patterns as follows.

In a music work, too long segments tend to contain duplicate information, while too short segments often have little information about the music semantics. Therefore, allowing users to specify constraints on the pattern length will reduce the unnecessary costs on duplicate information and a large amount of very short segments. In this paper, we use two constraints on the pattern length, called the *maximum length* (*max_len*) and the *minimum length* (*min_len*), respectively. As a result, segments are generated from the given string by using sliding widows whose sizes are from *min_len* to *max_len*. For example, given a string (a, b, c, d), the qualified segments are $(a, b), (b, c), (c, d), (a, b, c), (b, c, d)$ when *min_len*=2 and *max_len*=3. Furthermore, we adopt the *edit distance* to measure the similarity degree between two segments.

Definition 2.4. Edit Distance:

Based on the definition in [2], three types of *edit operations* that transform segment P (denoted as $p_1 \ldots p_m$) into segment Q (denoted as $q_1 \ldots q_n$) are insertion, deletion and replacement. The edit distance between segments P and Q denoted as $edit(P,Q)$, is the minimum number of edit operations required to transform P into Q.

To determine whether one segment is similar to another segment, a distance threshold (denoted as δ) is needed. Considering the prototypical melody, the difference between the pivot and a segment S can be compensated by changing a number of notes on the pivot into those on S. Owing to the definition of edit distance, for a given segment, the pivot with a long length has more chances to satisfy the distance threshold than a shorter one even when the numbers of note changes are the same. Therefore, the similarity measure should take the segment length into consideration. Instead of a constant value, we use a variable value depending on the segment length to be the distance threshold.

Definition 2.5. Distance Threshold:
A *distance threshold* for a pivot P is $\delta_P = |P| * \gamma$, where $|P|$ is the segment length of the pivot and γ is the *distance threshold ratio*, $0 \leq \gamma < 1$.

Definition 2.6. Similar Segment:
Given two segments P and Q, satisfying *max_len* and *min_len*, Q is a *similar segment* of P if $edit(P,Q) \leq \delta_P$. In this case, the segment length of Q must be at least $(|P| - \delta_P)$. Note that P is always a similar segment of P since $edit(P,P)=0$.

For example, if the distance threshold ratio is 50% and the segment length of P is 6, the distance threshold for P is 6* 0.5=3. In this case, segment Q is similar to P only if $edit(P,Q)$ is not larger than 3.

When two similar segments overlap to a high degree, they are treated as one segment. We define a measure called *overlapping degree* as follows.

Definition 2.7. Overlapping Degree:
Given two similar segments $S[a:b]$ and $S[c:d]$ where $a \leq c \leq b$, the overlapping degree of them is $(b-c+1)/min(b-a+1,d-c+1)$ if $b<d$. Otherwise it equals 1.

Since the overlapping degree also depends on the segment length, we use a variable value to restrict the maximum overlapping degree among the similar segments.

Definition 2.8. Overlapping Threshold:
An *overlapping threshold* for two similar segments I and J of a pivot is $O_{IJ} = min(|I|,|J|) * \rho$, where $|I|$ and $|J|$ are the segment lengths and ρ is the *overlapping threshold ratio*, $0 \leq \rho \leq 1$.

When ρ is zero, all the similar segments of P should not overlap any others. Another way to estimate the overlapping degree is to ignore the segment length. For instance, in Definition 2.7, the overlapping degree can be simplified to $(b-c+1)$. In this paper, we adopt the measure as Definition 2.7 states.

Definition 2.9. Extension:
Given a pivot P and the set of all its similar segments S, an *extension* of P (denoted as $Ext(P)$) is a subset of S, where every two segments in it satisfy the overlapping threshold. The number of segments in an extension is called the *support* and denoted as $|Ext(P)|$.

In the application of music classification [6], a constraint on the minimum number of occurrences for a repeating pattern in a music work makes the discovered patterns significant. In this paper, the constraint on the support of an extension is called the *support threshold (min_sup)*.

Definition 2.10. Approximate Repeating Pattern:
A pivot P is called an *approximate repeating pattern* (abbreviated as ARP) if there exists at least one $Ext(P)$ satisfying the support threshold, i.e., $|Ext(P)| \geq min\_sup$.

Definition 2.11. Problem of ARP Extraction:
Given a string S and *min_len*, *max_len*, γ, ρ, and *min_sup*, extract all the ARPs in S.

3 Our Approach

3.1 Lower-Bounding Distance

Using the dynamic-programming based approach to compute the edit distance between two strings often costs a lot of time. To reduce it, we define a novel distance measure that can be efficiently computed. The rationale of the proposed measure is as follows. From Definition 2.4, we observed that the order of values in segments has great influence on the edit distance and its computation. Therefore, we ignore the order but count the number of occurrences of each distinct value in a segment instead. The differences between such counts computed from two segments can be combined to approximate the edit distance. Moreover, the distance estimated by our measure is proved to be lower than the edit distance. In this way, we can build a lower-bounding mechanism on the index tree to prune the segments with too large distances. At first, we represent each segment as follows:

Definition 3.1. Histogram Vector:
Let D be a string with $\Sigma_D = \{a_1, a_2, \ldots a_n\}$, S be a segment of D, and h_k^S be the count of a_k in S. The *histogram vector* (abbreviated as *Hvector*) is defined as follows:

$$HV(S) = <h_1^S, h_2^S, \ldots, h_n^S>$$

All the segments are represented as their Hvectors and the Hvectors form a multidimensional space called the *histogram space*, where each dimension refers to a distinct value in the string and the total number of dimensions is $|\Sigma_D|$. Fig. 2 shows an example, where each bin in the histogram indicates the count of a distinct value in the segment. Note that different segments may be represented as the same Hvector. Moreover, the segments represented by the same Hvector must have the same length. From this property, given a Hvector V_p, we can compute the length of the corresponding segments which is denoted as $|V_p|$.

String: $D=(0,1,1,-2,0,1,1,-2,2,1,1,-1)$
$\Sigma_D = \{-2,-1,0,1,2\}$
$S=(1,1,-2,0,1,1,-2,2,1,1)$
$HV(S)=<2,0,1,6,1>$
$|HV(S)|=10$

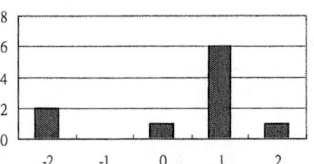

Fig. 2. Representing a segment as the Hvector

Definition 3.2. Histogram Distance:
We define *an insertion* to a dimension in the Hvector as increasing that dimension by one. For two segments S_1 and S_2 of a string D, the minimum number of insertions required to make each dimension in $HV(S_1)$ not smaller than the corresponding one in $HV(S_2)$, is calculated as follows:

$$ins(HV(S_1), HV(S_2)) = \sum_{i=1}^{|\Sigma_D|} d_i, \text{ where } \quad d_i = \begin{cases} h_i^{S_2} - h_i^{S_1} & \text{if } h_i^{S_2} > h_i^{S_1} \\ 0 & \text{otherwise} \end{cases} \quad (1)$$

The distance between the two Hvectors of segments S_1 and S_2, called the *histogram distance* (abbreviated as *Hdistance*) is formulated as follows:

$$HD(S_1,S_2)=max(ins(HV(S_1), HV(S_2)), ins(HV(S_2),HV(S_1))) \quad (2)$$

The Hdistance is guaranteed to be lower than edit distance. The time complexity of edit distance computation is $O(m*n)$, where m and n denote the two segment lengths. By contrast, the time complexity of Hdistance computation is $O(|\Sigma_D|)$, which is independent of the segment lengths. Even if the transformation cost is included, the time complexity is only $O(max(|\Sigma_D|,m,n))$. In general, $m*n$ is larger than $|\Sigma_D|$. As a result, the Hdistance computation is more efficient than the edit distance computation.

3.2 Indexing Tree

To speed up the retrieval of similar segments for each pivot, we built an R*-tree in the same way as proposed in [1] to index all the Hvectors. Each leaf node in the R*-tree is in the form of $(I, p\text{-}id)$, where I denotes a minimal bounding rectangle (MBR) and $p\text{-}id$ refers to the Hvectors contained in I. Moreover, each non-leaf node in the R*-tree is in the form of $(I, child\text{-}p)$, where $child\text{-}p$ are pointers of all the child nodes and I is an MBR that covers all the MBRs of the child nodes. Furthermore, we add entries to each node in the R*-tree such that more nodes can be pruned during the tree traversal for ARP extraction. The modified R*-tree is called the *parametric R*-tree*, where the entries added are as follows:

Definition 3.3. RM Pairs:

A range in string D is denoted as $a:b$, where a and b are two positions in D and $a < b$. Two segments with ranges $a:b$ and $c:d$ are called non-overlapping if $b < c$ or $d < a$; otherwise, overlapping. A set of overlapping segments can then be represented as (R,M), called *the RM pair*, where R is the union of all their ranges and M is the minimum of their lengths.

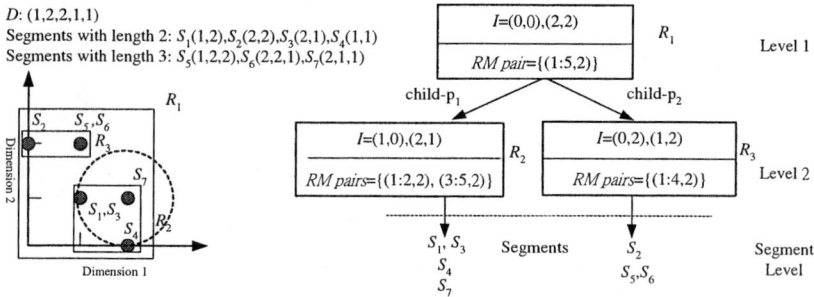

Fig. 3. An example of the histogram space and a parametric R*-tree

For example, S_2 ($D[2,3]$), S_5 ($D[1,3]$), and S_6 ($D[2,4]$) in Fig. 3 are represented as the RM pair (1:4,2). In the parametric R*-tree, for each node, the segments corresponding to the Hvectors contained by its MBR are distributed into RM pairs such that the overlapping ones fall in the same RM pair. Fig. 3 shows a parametric R* tree with two leaf nodes and only one non-leaf node. $|\sum_D|$ is 2, i.e., the number of dimensions in the histogram space. We construct the parametric R*-tree by sliding windows on D, where min_len and max_len are set to 2 and 3 respectively. As a result, only two leaf nodes are built to keep all the segments at the bottom level, called the *segment level*. For instance, in node R_2, the RM pair is computed as follows. Since S_7 overlaps S_3 and S_4, they form the RM pair (3:5, 2). On the other hand, S_1 does not overlap any other segment in R_2 and therefore a RM pair (1:2, 2) is generated.

3.3 Extraction Procedure

In this subsection, our approach to ARP extraction on a music work is introduced. In our algorithm, there are three main stages. The first stage constructs the parametric R*-tree as the index tree for subsequent processing. Second, we regard each Hvector in the index tree as a range query and execute them to generate the candidate ARPs. The candidate ARPs are recorded as a linked list named CandidateList, which is put into the last stage. As a result, ARPs satisfying all the constraints are outputted. The last two stages are repeated until the outputted ARPs fulfill user's information need.

3.3.1 Index Construction
An interval string is cut into segments by sliding windows according to the two constraints on segment lengths. After that, each segment is mapped to a Hvector and then inserted into the parametric R*-tree. The mapping is recorded in a *mapping table*. Note that the parametric R*-tree is constructed at the beginning and then updated when new segments are inserted due to a smaller min_len or a larger max_len.

3.3.2 Candidate Generation
After index construction, we regard each segment in it as a pivot and use its Hvector as a range query on the parameter R*-tree. The segments that are possible to be the similar segments of the pivot are returned and called the *candidate segments*. During the query processing, some pivots that cannot be ARP are pruned. A pivot that survives after query processing is called a *candidate ARP*. For each candidate ARP, we will further check its candidate segments to determine whether it is an ARP or not.

Given a Hvector of pivot p (denoted as V_p), we retrieval its candidate segments from the index tree in four steps:

Step 1: Range Query Formulation
V_p triggers a range query in the form of (V_p, δ_p), where V_p is the center and δ_p is the radius of a sphere in the histogram space.

Step 2: MBR Retrieval
When traversing a level of the index tree, all the MBRs overlapping with (V_p, δ_p) are retrieved and denoted as *overlapping MBRs*. Referring to the histogram space in Fig. 3 as an example, the overlapping MBRs of (<2,1>,1) are R_1 and R_2, which are located at level 1 and level 2, respectively.

Step 3: Estimation for the Maximal Number of Similar Segments

The number of similar segments in an overlapping MBR is estimated in three steps as follows. First, for each RM pair (R_X, M_X) in the MBR, the minimal length of similar segments covered by the range R_X is denoted as ML_X and computed as follows. From Definition 2.6, the length of a similar segment of p must be at least $|p|-\delta_p$. Since M_X records the actual minimal length of segments covered by R_X, we set ML_X to be the maximum of these two values, i.e., $max(|p|-\delta_p, M_X)$.

Second, for each RM pair (R_X, M_X) in the MBR, our goal is to estimate the maximal number of similar segments that can be fitted in R_X, such that any two of them satisfy their overlapping thresholds. This is similar to the following problem.

Refer to the period from a to b on the axis in Fig. 4, we draw a line with the fixed length L starting from position a. Next, we draw a line with the same length starting from the position on the right of position a such that the length of its overlap with the previous line is m. This process is repeating until a line covers position b. The total number of lines drawn in this period is $\lfloor (n - L) / (L - m) \rfloor + 1$, where $n = b - a + 1$. We denote this number as num_X.

Referring to our goal, the above formula can be used to compute the number of segments with the same length ML_X to be fitted into the range R_X for $m = \rho * ML_X$, which m indicates the overlapping threshold.

At last, all the num_X estimated for RM pairs X in an MBR R are summed up to represent the maximum number of similar segments that can be retrieved from R (denoted as num_R).

We continue using the example in Fig. 3 for illustration. Suppose that the pivot is S_7, ρ is set to 0.5, and the range query (<2,1>,1) is performed on R_2. There are two RM pairs (1:2, 2) and (3:5, 2) in R_2. For the 1st RM pair, minimal length $ML_1 = max(3-1, 2) = 2$, $\rho * ML_1 = 0.5 * 2 = 1$ and $num_1 = \lfloor (2-2)/(2-1) \rfloor + 1 = 1$. Using the same formula, num_2 of second RM pair is 1. The num_{R2} computed from the example of Fig. 3 is 1+1=2.

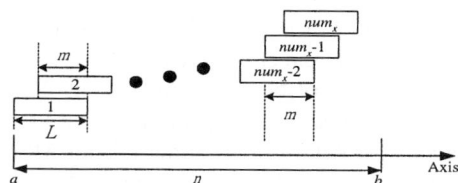

Fig. 4. Maximum number of segments fitted into a range

Step 4: Candidate Pruning Before *HD* Computations

When the range query is processed at the level above the segment level, the num_R of each overlapping MBR R is computed and their sum is denoted as max_num. To the pivot corresponding to the Hvector V_p, when max_num for the range query (V_p, δ_p) is less than min_sup, the computations for the edit distances between it and the other segments are unnecessary. If max_num is less than min_sup, we terminate the processing of this query and execute the next range query. Otherwise, this query is recursively propagated to the lower levels.

We continue the example in Fig. 3 and assume the *min_sup* is set to 3. Segment S_7 can be pruned because its *max_num* at level 2 is only 2 (according to the Step 3).

Step 5: Candidate Pruning After *HD* Computations
When the range query V_p is processed at the segment level, we compute the Hdistances between the pivot *p* and the segments covered by the overlapping MBRs. All the segments whose Hdistances satisfy δ_p are permutated to compute the *max_num* as mentioned in Step 3 and 4. Similarly, if *max_num* is less than *min_sup*, the pivot will be pruned. Otherwise, the segments are regarded as candidate segments. As a result, the CandidateList records the candidate ARP and its candidate segments.

After all the range queries have been performed, we will obtain a set of candidate ARPs and their candidate segments associated in CandidateList, which need to be processed further in the last stage.

3.3.3 ARP Extraction

The output of our approach includes each ARP and its extensions, which can be used to verify whether the ARP is a prototypical melody or not by musicians. Given a candidate ARP and its candidate segments, we first compute the edit distance between the candidate ARP and each of the candidate segments and then remove the candidate segments violating the distance threshold to obtain the set of similar segments.

After that, we generate all the extensions of the candidate ARP by considering the overlapping threshold. Then, if the support of an extension is less than the *min_sup*, the extension is not an answer. As a result, by the Definition 2.10, a candidate ARP is an answer if one of its extensions satisfies the *min_sup* threshold.

3.4 Dimensions Reduction

In a music work, the large number of distinct intervals leads to a high dimensional histogram space. Using the R*-tree to index high dimensional data can be time-consuming. Several methods have been proposed to reduce the dimensions but most of them spend a lot of time on computing the optimal number of dimensions for static data [3]. By the contrast, the parametric R*-tree in our approach is constructed dynamically and the construction time is a part of response time. Therefore, it is not allowable to spend too much time on optimization of dimension reduction. In our approach, we use a simple hashing function to reduce the dimensions of histogram space. In our approach, each interval is divided by a predefined number and the remainder is regarded as the hash value. In this way, different intervals may have the same hash value and their counts in a music work are summed up as a result. The Hdistance after the dimension reduction, denoted as the *Hdistance'*, is still guaranteed to be the lower bound of edit distance. For example, given S_1 = (1,2,3,1,1,2,3,1,3,4,5,3,4,5) and S_2 = (1,3,1,2,3,1,4,5,2,4,4), $HD(S_1,S_2)$ and $edit(S_1,S_2)$ are 4 and 5, respectively. We mod each value by 3 to transform into (1,2,0,1,1,2,0,1,0,1,2,0,1,2) and (1,0,1,2,0,1,1,2,2,1,1), respectively. The number of dimensions is reduced from five to three. Moreover, the *Hdistance'* between S_1 and S_2 is 3, which is smaller than Hdistance. Because the new lower bound provided by the *Hdistance'* is looser, more MBRs will be visited during query processing over the parametric R*-tree. Such a trade-off depends on the hashing function and data distribution.

4 Performance Evaluation

4.1 Experiment Set-Up

We compare our approach with a modified version of the dynamic-programming approach named FIExPat [9], which is a famous approach in this field. Four important factors which have great impacts on ARP extraction are investigated, i.e., maximum length, minimum length, distance threshold and support threshold. In Rolland's experiment [9], the segments are not allowed to overlap, for fair comparison, we did not consider the performance comparison on the overlapping threshold and set it to zero in all the experiments. For our approach, the number of reduced dimensions in histogram space is set to 11, which has the best performance in all the experiments. The experiment scenario is set up as follows. The user initially sets the constraints and then the system extracts the ARPs. We name one process of ARP extraction for the user-specified constraints as one *iteration*. In each iteration, one of the constraints is varied such that the influence of that constraint on the elapsed time at different iteration can be observed.

4.2 Experiment Results

Fig. 5(a) shows the result for the various values of *max_len*, where the parameters *min_len*, *min_sup* and γ are set to 4, 5 and 25%, respectively. At the first iteration, both approaches spend more time than the other iterations, which is because ARP has to build a parametric R*-tree and FIExPat has to construct a graph structure. Our approach performs better than FIExPat for all iterations. In addition, the elapsed time of our approach decreases as the *max_len* increases. The reason is because the segment with a larger length gets less chance to form a similar segment of the others and can be pruned by our approach.

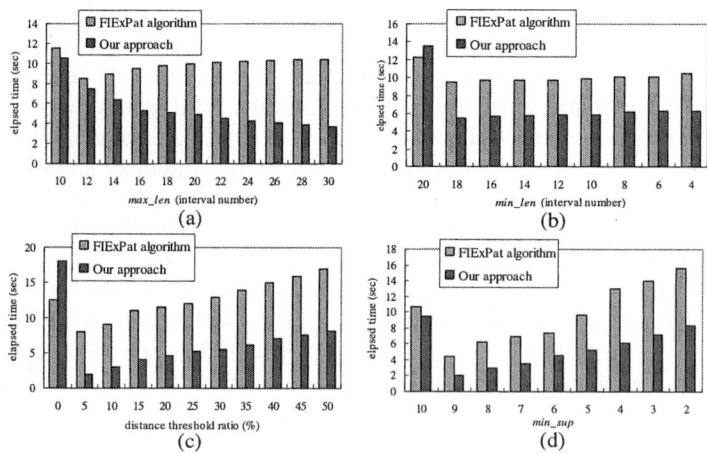

Fig. 5. Experiment results

Fig. 5(b) shows the result for various values of *min_len*, where the parameters *max_len*, *min_sup*, and γ are set to 30, 5 and 25%, respectively. Our approach also performs better than FIExPat except for the first iteration. The elapsed times of both approaches are increased as the *min_len* is decreased, because the number of smaller *min_len* produces more patterns. If we accumulate the elapsed time of first iteration and the one of second iteration for both approaches, our approach costs less than FIExPat. This means our approach is more suitable than FIExPat in the iterative environment.

Fig. 5(c) shows the result for various values of γ, where the parameters *max_len*, *min_len* and *min_sup* are set to 30, 4 and 5, respectively. This setting means that the user releases the distance threshold ratio in order to find more ARPs. Our approach spends more time at the first iteration but less time at the subsequent iterations. The reason for the observation is that our approach builds the parametric R*-tree only at the first iteration, but does not modify the index tree at subsequent iterations since the *max_len* and *min_len* are not changed.

Fig. 5(d) shows the result for various values of *min_sup*, where the parameters *max_len*, *min_len* and γ are set to 30, 4 and 25%, respectively. From the result, our approach also performs better than FIExPat.

5 Conclusion

Since the approximate repeating pattern can be found in both classical and pop music, it plays an important role in the representation of music database and the music style analysis. In this paper, we develop a novel approach to extract the approximate repeating pattern from the music work. This approach adopts the technique of the range query processing on the multidimensional data to reduce the execution time. In the performance study, the execution time of our approach is reduced dramatically when comparing with the FIExPat approach. Our approach not only can be used in the music field, but also can be applied in other fields such as patterns extraction on web click strings or DNA strings.

Some research directions can be considered further. First, improving Hdistance measure such that we can prune more impossible candidates before the computation of edit distance, it can make the ARP extraction more efficient. Second, the dimension reduction sophisticated strategy should be studied to reduce the processing time of range query. Third, the applications base on the approximate repeating patterns will be investigated in the future, e.g., the music classification, the music analysis and the music content-based retrieval.

Acknowledgement

This work was partially supported by the NSC Program for Promoting Academic Excellence of Universities (Phase II) under the grant number 93-2752-E-007-004 -PAE, and the NSC under the contract number 93-2213-E-004-012.

References

[1] Beckmann, N., H. P. Kriegel, R. Schneider, and B. Seeger, "The R*-tree: An efficient and robust access method for points and rectangles," in *Proceedings of ACM SIGMOD Int'l. Conf. on Management of Data*, 1990.
[2] Gusfield, D., *Algorithms on Strings, Trees, and Sequences*, Cambridge University Press, 1997.
[3] Han J., and M. Kamber, "Data Mining Concepts and Techniques," Morgan Kaufmann Publishers, 2001.
[4] Hsu, J. L., C. C. Liu, and A. L.P. Chen, "Discovering Non-trivial Repeating Patterns in Music Data," *IEEE Transactions on Multimedia*, Vol. 3, No. 3, 2001.
[5] Krumhansl, C. L., *Cognitive Foundations of Musical Pitch*, Oxford University Press, New York, 1990.
[6] Lin, C. R., N. H. Liu, Y. H. Wu and A. L.P. Chen "Music Classification Using Significant Repeating Patterns," in *Proceedings of International Conference on Database Systems for Advanced Applications (DASFAA'04)*, 2004.
[7] MIDI Manufacturers Association (MMA), *MIDI 1.0 Specification*, http://www.midi.org/.
[8] Pienimäk, A. "Indexing Music Databases Using Automatic Extraction of Frequent Phrases," in Proceedings of the 3rd International Symposium on Music Information Retrieval (ISMIR'02), 2002.
[9] Rolland, P. Y., "FIExPat: Flexible Extraction of Sequential Patterns," in *Proceedings of the IEEE International Conference on Data Mining (ICDM'01)*, 2001.
[10] Selfridge-Field, E., "Conceptual and Representational Issues in Melodic Comparison," in Hewlett, W. B. and E. Selfridge-Field (eds.), *Melodic Similarity: Concepts, Procedures, and Applications (Computing in Musicology: 11)*, The MIT Press, 1998.
[11] Shih, H. H., S. S. Narayanan, and C. C. Jay Kuo, "Automatic Main Melody Extraction From MIDI Files with a Modified Lempel-Ziv Algorithm," in *Proceedings of International Symposium on Intelligent Multimedia, Video and Speech Processing*, 2001.

On Efficient Music Genre Classification

Jialie Shen[1], John Shepherd[1], and Anne H.H. Ngu[2]

[1] School of Computer Sci. and Eng., University of New South Wales,
2052 Sydney NSW, Australia
{jls, jas}@cse.unsw.edu.au
[2] Department of Computer Sci., Texas State University,
601 University Drive, San Marcos, Texas, USA
angu@txstate.edu

Abstract. Automatic music genre classification has long been an important problem. However, there is a paucity of literature that addresses the issue, and in addition, reported accuracy is fairly low. In this paper, we present empirical study of a novel music descriptor generation method for efficient content based music genre classification. Analysis and empirical evidence demonstrate that our approach outperforms state-of-the-art approaches in the areas including accuracy of genre classification with various machine learning algorithms, efficiency on training process. Furthermore, its effectiveness is robust against various kinds of audio alternation.

Keywords: Music Classification, Genre, Human Factor.

1 Introduction

As a fundamental and effective tool for exploring, organising and managing the vast universe of online music, automatic music genre classification has long been an important research problem. However, current classification process is mainly relied on manual labelling, which is very time-consuming and expensive. Moreover, although various systems have been developed for content-based speech/speaker identification and music-speech discrimination, there is a paucity of literature that addresses the issue of automatic genre music classification, and in addition, reported accuracy is fairly low.

The process of automatic music genre classification can be divided into two main steps: feature extraction and multi-class categorisation. In first step, descriptive information is extracted from raw signal via special music analysis schemes. Then, genre classification can be treated as a multi-class classification problem and we might apply a classifier, which could be an algorithm or a statistic model, to identify labels of music based on their computable parameter [4]. Thus, feature extraction is crucial for whole classification process. In fact, while the extraction of acoustic features from digital music has a relatively long history, it has so far proved extremely difficult to determine how to use such features to represent high-level semantic concepts (such as genre) effectively. The reasons are as follows. First, there exists a large gap between high-level semantic musical concepts and low-level physical representation [1]. Secondly, there is a wide variety of features within a music signal (e.g. timbre texture, harmony, rhythm structure and pitch). Using a single kind of acoustic feature may not represent characteristic of music properly. Besides all above difficulties, it is worth to notice that human beings have an amazing and unique capability to percept music which should be taken into account for developing effective music information processing (classification and retrieval, in particular). Unfortunately, few research that addresses the issue of how to effectively integrate human perception.

In this paper, we present an empirical performance study of a novel feature extraction method, called *InMAF*[1] [19], on automatic music genre classification. Unlike traditional approaches which mainly rely on spectrum characteristic of raw music signal, our method integrates various acoustic feature and human musical perception into the compact (small size) feature vector to enhance genre categorisation process. Analysis and empirical evidence suggest that our proposed method outperforms state-of-the-art approaches in the areas including accuracy of classification with various machine learning algorithms, efficiency on training process and robustness against audio distortions.

The rest of the paper is organised as follows: Section 2 gives some coverage of related work and background knowledge. Section 3 presents an overview of the architecture of one feature extraction method for music data. Section 4 describes the evaluation techniques and gives a detailed analysis of results from a suite of comprehensive experiments over two large music databases. Finally, section 5 draws some conclusions and indicates future directions for this research.

2 Related Work

There are various kinds of features which can be used for content management of large music collections. Those include text labels for the title and performer(s)/composer, acoustic features, and symbolic representations of melody (e.g. MIDIs and digital music scores). In this paper, we primarily focus on content-based acoustic features.

Though various systems exist for content-based speech recognition and music-speech discrimination, much less work has focused on developing compact and comprehensive music data descriptors for effective categorisation and retrieval. Most of the existing work is based on spectral features of the raw music signal adapted from earlier work in speech recognition including Mel-Frequency Cepstral Coefficients (MFCCs), spectral centroid, linear prediction coefficients, spectral flux, and so on [11]. A typical example using this approach is the work carried out by Nam and Berger [7], who used three low-level acoustic features (spectral centroid, short time energy, and zero crossing rate) for automatic music genre classification. In [4], Logan investigated the effectiveness of MFCCs for music/speech classification. Li and Khokhar [3] proposed nearest feature line methods for content based audio retrieval and classification. *MARSYAS* which was developed by Tzanetakis et al [2] is the most advanced infrastructure framework for modelling music signal. In this framework, a set of feature is specifically developed to characterise different acoustic properties of music signals. They include timbral texture, pitch content and rhythm. Using a linear concatenation of these features, they achieved 61% classification accuracy for a ten genre sound-data set. More recently, Li et al. [5]

---

[1] *InMAF* stands for **I**ntegrating **M**utiple **A**coustic **F**eatures.

proposed using Daubechies wavelet histogram technique(*DWCHs*) to capture local and global temporal information inside music signal. It used wavelet to decompose music signal into different subband at first. Then, histogram for each subband is constructed. Finally, the first three moments of each histogram and energy for each subband are calculated to form *DWCHs* [2]. Due to its effective estimation of probability distribution over time and frequency via wavelets, *DWCHs* performs better than MARSYAS's approach, and is currently the state-of-the-art in content-based music retrieval. The problem of above traditional techniques which rely on either single type of physical feature or composite feature, is that they can not provide a "perceptually accurate" representation to describe music signal. This is because interpreting and processing of music in human perceptual system involve various kind of acoustic characteristic under complex context. Thus, single type of physical feature may not provide information which is rich enough to represent music objects comprehensively. Also, it assumes that linear combination of different low-level physical feature types can best reflect how human perceive music as similar. There is lack of evidence for this assumption so far.

3 System Overview

In following section, we present a new approach to extract descriptive information from music data to support efficient automatic genre classification. Before describing the system architecture, we firstly present a brief overview of the acoustic features that our system deals with.

3.1 Feature Extraction

Based on [2], content-based acoustic features for music can be classified into timbral texture, rhythmic content, and pitch. We use MARSYAS framework as the basis of implementation to extract different acoustic features and their information are shown below,

- **Timbre:** Timbral texture is a global statistical music property used to differentiate a mixture of sounds. To extract timberal texture, we first divide each music signal into many short time-frames. Then, different components (mainly spectral characteristics) for each frame are calculated using the Short Time Fourier Transform. These components include spectral centroid, spectral flux, time domain zero crossings, low energy, spectral roll-off and Mel-frequency cesptral coefficients (MFCCs). Our timbral texture features are presented as 33-dimensional vectors which contain: means and variance of spectral centroid, spectral flux, time domain zero crossings and 13 MFCC coefficients (32) plus low energy(1).
- **Rhythm:** Rhythmic content can be represented as beat strength and its temporal pattern. We use the beat histogram (BH) proposed by Tzanetakis et al. [2] to represent rhythmic content features. The 18-dimensional beat feature vector contains: relative amplitude of the first six histogram peaks (divided by the sum of amplitudes), ratio

---
[2] It means Daubechies Wavelet Coefficient Histograms.

of the amplitude of five histogram peaks (from second to sixth) divided by the amplitude of the first one, period of the first six histogram peaks, and overall sum of the histogram.
- **Pitch:** Pitch can be used to characterise melody and harmony information inside music. We use the multi-pitch detection algorithm proposed by Tolonen et al. [6] to extract pitch histogram which is used for describing pitch features. The signal is first divided into two frequency bands (below and above 1000Hz). Then, amplitude envelopes are extracted for each frequency and summed to construct a pitch histogram. The 18-dimensional pitch histogram includes: the amplitude and periods of the maximum six peaks in the histogram, pitch interval between the six most prominent peaks, and the overall sums of the histograms.

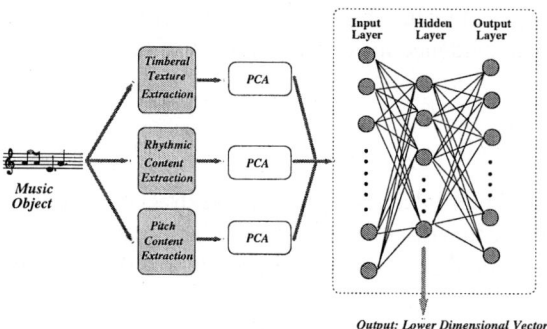

Fig. 1. The architecture of a hybrid musical feature dimensions reduction scheme. Output of the scheme is lower dimensional vectors appearing in the hidden layer of neural network

3.2 The System Architecture

The system utilises a two-tier hybrid architecture: dimension reduction via Principal Component Analysis followed by a nonlinear neural network using the Quick-prop learning algorithm [10]. Fig. 1 shows the overall architecture of the system. Feature vectors for timbre (33 dimension), rhythm (18 dimension) and pitch (18 dimension) are first extracted from the music data. Each acoustic feature is then analysed by a single PCA module in the first tier separately. The output of each PCA module are then concatenated to form a single 25-dimensional feature vector as input to the three-layer perceptron feed-forward neural network which is the second tier of *InMAF*. It is equally valid to first combine the feature vectors into a high-dimensional composite feature vector and then apply PCA to this composite feature vector to get a reduced vector which are then used for the neural network. We have tested using this configuration and similar experimental result has been obtained[3].

Principal Component Analysis(PCA). Principal Component Analysis (PCA) is one of the most widely used dimensionality reduction methods. The advantage of the PCA

---

[3] For detail, please refer to our technical report [17].

transformation is that it is linear and that any linear correlations presented in the data are automatically detected. It has been employed to reduce the dimensions of individual feature vectors so that an efficient index can be constructed for retrieval in image databases. It has also been applied to image coding (e.g. for removing correlation from highly correlated data such as face images). In our system, PCA is used as a "pre-processing" component in a NLDR method where it provides small but information-rich feature vectors for the three-layer neural network, and thus speeds up the NLDR training time in the posterior step.

Neural Network(NN). The advantage of using a neural network for NLDR is that the network can be *trained* to produce an effective solution based on pre-selected samples. In this work, a three-layer perceptron neural network with a Quick-prop learning algorithm is used to perform dimensionality reduction on music features. The network acts as an non-linear dimensionality reducer. The units in the input layer accept the feature vector preprocessed by PCA analysis. Hidden layer plays an important role in the process. It is configured to have fewer units. An *encoded* and *compressed* version of the input data, is produced as the output of hidden layer. The number of units in the output layer corresponds to the total number of classes in target data collection.

When the network has been successfully trained, the weights that connect the input and the hidden layers can be treated as entries of a transformation that maps the "raw" feature vectors **v** to smaller dimensional vectors. Thus, when a high-dimensional feature vector is passed through the network, its activation values in the hidden units form a lower-dimensional vector. Each lower-dimensional feature vector preserves only the most discriminating information from the original feature vectors.

3.3   Human Musical Perception Integration

The training process in our system consists of two stages: (1) construct a training set incorporating human musical perception information, and (2) use the training examples to generate an extractor for music descriptors.

Training Sample Selection. The first stage in using our system is to obtain a training set of music data items which includes human perceptual information. To do this, we need to first determine which high-level semantic concept is to be used to classify the data set. Note that each classification scheme needs its own feature extractor, thus needs its own training set. In our experiments we used genre based classification. Then, we select a training set of music pieces from the entire collection which covers all of the different sub-categories for the classification criterion. This requires us to ask help from domain expert. In our work, we made use of the classification from music-related online service providing professional review of a large number of western mainstream music[4], augmented by manual classification for any data items which were not classified on www.allmusic.com. Manual classification was achieved by using 10 subjects with an interest in music to classify each item according to the classification scheme, based on similarity in timbre, pitch and rhythm. If more than 5 people placed a given item in the same subclass, it was deemed to be a member of that subclass. If not, it was deemed to be

---

[4] In this project, we use service from http://www.allmusic.com

"unclassified". The size of training set is 10% of target collection and they are randomly chosen from each of the sub-categories.

Training. To train the system, we first set up a PCA dimension reducer for each type of the raw feature vectors. Note that we use the entire data set, and not just the training set, in order to determine the principle components. This has the advantage that the covariance matrix for each type of feature vector contains the global variance of music in the database. The number of principal components is determined by the cut-off value ψ. In this study, ψ is set to 99. Thus, the minimum variance retained after the PCA dimension reduction is at least 99%. Note that based on our experimental result, the cut-off value ψ can influence performance in classification. Due to space limitation, we refer the interested reader to our technical report [17] for details.

The neural network is initialised by setting the weight of each link, connecting two units in the network, to a random small value. The training then proceeds by iterating over the music data items in the training set, choosing one item from each subclass in turn. For each item, we construct a composite feature vector using a linear concatenation of the PCA-reduced timbre, pitch and rhythm feature vectors. The composite feature vector and the class number is then presented to the neural network and the weights in the network then stabilise. Finally, we test the convergence of the network. If the convergence condition is satisfied, the training process halts. Otherwise, we continue to present training examples, one at a time. The problem about the convergence of a neural network system is still an open one and is outside the scope of this paper.

4 Experimental Study

In this section, we demonstrate the superiority of our method by comparing it with the current best approaches (*DWCHs* and MARSYAS) in the areas including classification effectiveness, efficiency on training and robustness against different kinds of audio distortion. The study considers a range of possible methods for generating music descriptors, including our proposed method, *DWCHs*, and MARSYAS (denoted by MAR)[5]. For each of these (except *DWCHs*), we consider four different combinations of low-level features (Rhythm+Timbre+Pitch denoted by RTP; Timbre+Rhythm denoted by TR; Timbre+Pitch denoted by TP; Pitch+Rhythm denoted by PR). In our results, a system configuration denoted by "xxxx-yy" contains feature extraction method "xxxx" with feature combination "yy". For example, "InMAF-RTP" denotes a configuration using the our proposed method with Rhythm, Timbre and Pitch features. The size of feature vector generated by pure neural network(NN) and *InMAF* is 10, which equals to neuron number in hidden layer of multilayer perceptron. All of the experiments are conducted on a Pentium III machine with 750 MHz CPU, 256MB RAM and running Linux.

---

[5] Note that in MARSYAS, linear concatenation is used to construct composite feature vector as input to different machine-learning based classifiers.

4.1 Datasets

Two separate music databases were used in this performance study. The first one, called Dataset I, contains 1000 music data items covering ten genres with 100 songs per genre. This dataset was used in [5][2]. To ensure variety of recording quality, the excerpts of this dataset were taken from radio, compact disks, and MP3 compressed audio files. Each item in this collection belongs to exactly one of ten music genre categories: Classical, Country, Dance, Hip-hop, Jazz, Reggae, Metal, Blues and Pop.

The second dataset, called Dataset II, includes 2500 music data items. Each item in this collection belongs to exactly one of nine music genre categories: classical, country, dance, hip-hop, jazz, reggae, metal, blues and pop. The classical items are further partitioned among the sub-classes: choir, orchestra, piano, string quartet, Spanish guitar. Similarly, the jazz items are further partitioned among the sub-classes: swing, piano, Latin, bebop. Note that this is a multi-level hierarchy, whereas the classifiers we use are typically designed for single-level classification problems. We deal with this by defining three separate classifiers, one for the top-level and the others for the two sub-hierarchies. There is no overlapping between two datasets. The length of each music item in the two datasets is 30 seconds and each item in those two dataset is stored as a 22050Hz, 16 bit, mono audio file.

4.2 Classification Methods and Evaluation Metrics

Music classification can be treated as a multi-class classification problem using music descriptors as the input. In this study, we carry out the experiments using the following classifiers: Support Vector Machines (SVMs), K-Nearest Neighbour(KNN), Gaussian Mixture Models(GMM) and Decision tree. Also, in this study, the metrics for performance measures of a classification method is the *precision*. Its formula is given as below:

$$precision = \frac{true\ positive}{true\ positive + false\ positive} \times 100$$

4.3 Effectiveness

Table 1 [6] shows the results of our experiment to test the accuracy of genre classification using a variety of music descriptors as input. The classification problems were carried out on different data sets (the ones described in Section 4.1). For each of the classifiers, we used ten-fold cross validation to calculate classification accuracy [15]. This means whole dataset is divided into ten disjoint subsets of (approximately) equal size. For testing, we trained classifiers on nine of these ten disjoint subsets and then tested on the one left out, each time leaving out a different one. The above was repeated for each approach to generate music descriptors, including our *InMAF* approach (with four different combinations of acoustic features), the *DWCHs* method and MARSYAS with linear concatenation.

The bottom three rows of the Table 1 indicate how the different classifiers performed if only individual raw acoustic features were used in the descriptor. The poor accuracy

---

[6] SVM1 and SVM2 denote Support Vector Machine with one-versus-the-rest and pairwise approach. Dec. tree denotes decision tree.

Table 1. Classification accuracy of the difference learning methods with various features extraction method. I and II denote accuracy of genre classification on dataset I and dataset II. For bottom three rows, results are obtained using raw feature

Feature Extraction	Classification Methods									
	SVM1(%)		SVM2(%)		GMM(%)		KNN(%)		Dec. tree(%)	
	I	II	I	II	I	II	I	II	I	II
InMAF-RTP	89.7	91.7	90.2	91.6	81.4	82.3	85.3	86.2	81.7	83.4
InMAF-TR	80.1	81.6	82.6	79.6	70.6	70.3	73.4	75.4	70.8	73.6
InMAF-TP	79.5	80.6	80.5	78.3	71.7	72.7	73.8	72.5	71.2	70.9
InMAF-PR	77.2	75.1	78.5	78.9	71.5	68.1	70.2	69.2	70.3	70.6
DWCHs	75.5	74.7	75.2	75.5	68.2	69.4	68.3	68.6	71.2	72.5
MAR-RTP	68.7	69.7	70.1	69.5	61.7	62.4	59.5	60.8	68.1	69.5
MAR-TR	65.1	64.7	65.7	65.1	60.5	59.8	61.7	61.4	67.3	68.1
MAR-TP	68.2	69.7	68.2	71.2	60.7	61.2	61.3	58.9	68.4	68.9
MAR-RP	65.7	63.9	64.8	62.5	51.2	52.1	54.5	53.7	60.5	62.8
Beat	30.5	30.7	32.1	31.1	36.6	37.6	31.3	32.9	37.8	38.5
Timbral	49.9	50.7	50.7	51.1	45.1	47.6	47.2	49.9	49.5	48.5
Pitch	33.8	35.7	35.7	36.1	38.2	37.3	32.1	33.9	37.2	38.5

observed in this experiment (between 30% and 50% for all classifiers) verifies the claim that effective music classification cannot be achieved by considering only a single low-level acoustic feature. The same approach was investigated in [2], where they also reached the same conclusion.

Some improvement in accuracy can be observed by considering a combination of low-level features. We considered all different linear concatenations of combinations of the timbre, pitch and rhythm vectors. The best linear combination (MAR-RTP) uses all three low-level features and achieves accuracy rates of 68.7% for dataset I and 69.7% for dataset II with the best classifier (SVMs). The performance with *DWCHs* is better than any linear concatenation of acoustic features. This is because *DWCHs* provides a good estimation of probability distribution over time and frequency which leads to a better feature representation.

Using the *InMAF* for extracting music descriptors results in a significant improvement in classification effectiveness for all of the different classifiers. For dataset I, the range of this improvement over *DWCHs* is from 18% to 24%, depending on the learning method used. For dataset II, the improvement range is from 15% to 26%. Among all classification methods, the best classifier is SVMs. The accuracy achieved with the one-versus-the-rest SVMs for dataset I and dataset II is 89.7% and 91.7% respectively. In fact, based on Table 1, SVMs is the best classifier, whatever kind of music descriptor is used. It also shows that the descriptors produced by our proposed method lead to significantly better accuracy, no matter which classification method is used.

4.4 Efficiency

High dimensionality of input feature vector can make learning process of any classifiers very inefficient in terms of training time. The small but well discriminative feature vector generated by our approach not only provides superior classification accuracy but also

Table 2. Training time of the difference learning methods with various feature combination. I and II denotes genre classification for dataset I and dataset II

Feature Extraction	Classification Methods							
	SVMs		GMM		KNN		Dec. tree	
	I	II	I	II	I	II	I	II
InMAF-RTP	2.91s	2.93s	2.44s	2.45s	2.43s	2.51s	0.41s	0.46s
InMAF-TR	2.92s	2.94s	2.52s	2.51s	2.42s	2.53s	0.42s	0.38s
InMAF-TP	2.85s	2.86s	2.61s	2.67s	2.34s	2.37s	0.42s	0.42s
InMAF-PR	2.84s	2.88s	2.57s	2.57s	2.41s	2.34s	0.44s	0.41s
DWCHs	4.22s	4.21s	4.43s	4.83s	4.68s	4.97s	0.98s	0.91s
MAR-RTP	4.76s	4.75s	5.15s	5.05s	5.12s	5.07s	1.49s	1.38s
MAR-TR	4.41s	4.51s	4.31s	4.61s	4.16s	4.68s	1.18s	1.31s
MAR-TP	4.42s	4.46s	4.37s	4.87s	4.21s	4.70s	1.21s	1.26s
MAR-PR	3.22s	3.12s	3.81s	3.83s	3.57s	3.38s	1.24s	1.23s
Rhythm	3.21s	3.11s	2.54s	2.53s	2.25s	2.17s	0.67s	0.57s
Timbral	3.86s	3.86s	4.82s	4.83s	3.07s	3.09s	1.21s	1.35s
Pitch	3.23s	3.21s	2.26s	2.16s	2.14s	2.49s	0.67s	0.73s

save a large amount of training time. To further illustrate the performance advantage of using *InMAF*, we computed the actual training time for different learning methods with various feature extraction methods via a thorough experiment. Based on the result presented in Table 2, the speedup due to hybrid method is remarkable. For example, training the SVMs with *MARSYAS* [7] and *DWCHs* required 4.76s and 4.22s for dataset I, respectively, to finish. In constract, our proposed approach just needed 2.91s, nearly 38% and 31% saving.

On the other hand, although it can be seen that superior classification accuracy can be achieved using pure neural network from Table 1, the approach suffers from very long learning time. This is because time required for typical learning algorithm, such as back-propagation(BP), grows at super-linear rates with number of input. Thus, compression of data through certain kind of transformation obtain a great advantage in term of time complexity. Based on this principle, *InMAF* uses PCA as first layer of the hybrid architecture for preprocessing raw music feature vector. Results from Table 1 and Table 3 show that this approach does not lose significant classification accuracy but substantially improves the network learning cost: training neural network to achieve 91.9% with SVMs on dataset I required 6830 epochs to finish. In contrast, our *InMAF* approach required 4830 epochs to complete learning process and results in 89.7% classification accuracy. There is up to 29.3% saving on training time. From above, we can see the *InMAF* is a highly *effective* and *efficient* technique of musical feature extraction for automatic music genre classification.

4.5 Robustness

Humans have an amazing capability to classify sound or music in the presence of moderate amounts of distortion. This property is potentially useful in real world music database

---

[7] *MARSYAS* uses linear concatenation of three acoustic features to construct input feature vector.

Table 3. Training Cost of Dimension Reduction Methods. I and II denote dataset I and dataset II

Dataset	Training Cost of Dimension Reduction Methods(epoch)							
	InMAF-RTP	InMAF-TR	InMAF-TP	InMAF-PR	NN-RTP	NN-TR	NN-TP	NN-PR
I	4830	3512	3670	3490	6830	5780	5640	4567
II	3200	2372	2471	2390	4525	3829	3787	3918

applications, where the sound may have its origins in a process like low-quality live recording. Since the *InMAF* is being trained to reduce the dimensionality of raw acoustic feature vectors, this suggests that we can enhance robustness of the framework by training it using not only the original music, but also a copy of the music item which has been altered with noise or distortion.

We modified music data items with different kinds of distortion as learning examples for training purpose and carried out a series of experiments to test the performance of our system in the presence of moderate amounts of noise and other kinds of distortion. During this test, we randomly chose 20% music items from each category in the training data, applied a number of effects to each item, and included all of the distorted versions of the item, as well as the original item, in the training data. The neural network was then trained using all of this data; the aim was to train it recognise not only exact versions of the original music data, but to allow it to be robust to distortions.

In order to evaluate the effect of this on classification performance, we ran the same set of tests as described in Section 4.1 for both datasets. However, each music item was distorted before using it in the classification and the results were compared against the results obtained from using a non-distorted item. This was repeated for varying levels of distortion. Figure 2 summarises the genre classification accuracy for the different descriptor generators under various distortions using SVM with one-versus-the-rest approach[8]. It clearly demonstrates that comparing with other approach, *InMAF* emerges as the most robust technique performing well on all distortion cases. For example, using dataset I and SVM with one-versus-the-rest approach, *InMAF* is robust to echo with 8sec delay time, 6s cropping, 60% volume amplification, 75% volume deamplification, 35dB SNR white background noise and 40dB SNR pink background noise[9]. In contrast, *DWCHs* only can tolerate echo with 11sec delay time, 8s cropping, 30% volume amplification, 84% volume deamplification, 60dB SNR white background noise and pink background noise with SNR 65dB.

5 Conclusion

This paper presents a novel feature extraction method to support efficient content-based music genre classification. Distinguished from previous approaches, which were

---

[8] Due to space limitation, we only show result for SVMs with dataset I. Similar phenomena can be observation for other classifiers on different datasets. For detail, please refer to [17].

[9] We use equation $SNR_{dB} = 10 log_{10} \frac{S}{N}$ to calculate signal-to-noise ratio, where S is signal power, N is noise power and its unit is dB.

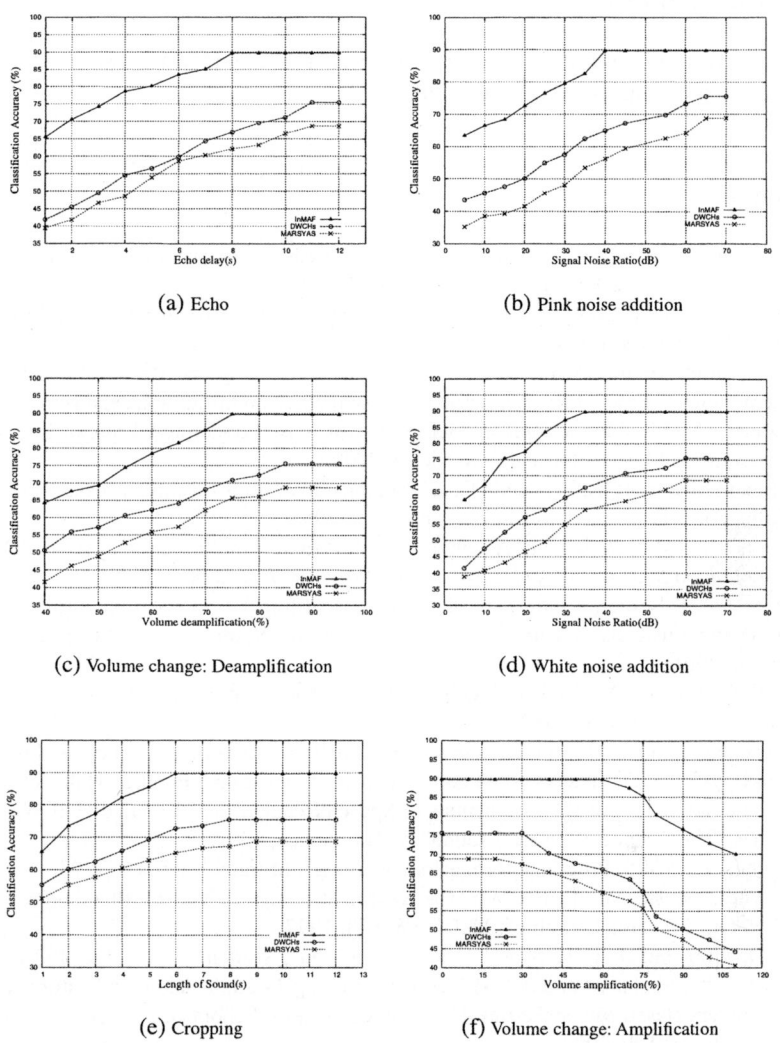

Fig. 2. Robustness of different feature extraction methods for dateset I using SVMs with one-versus-the-rest approach

based solely on automatically-derived acoustic features, our approach can easily incorporates human music perception to generate descriptors that are both efficient (low-dimensionality) and effective (good discrimination). We are not aware of any other work that considers semantic classification criteria to enhance categorisation process like our method. The approach is fully implemented and a series of comprehensive experiments have been carried out to demonstrate its superiority over state-of-art approaches has been demonstrated in the areas including effectiveness of genre classification, efficiency of classification and robustness against audio distortions.

Acknowledgements

The authors would like to thank Professor George Tzanetakis in University of Victoria, Canada for kindly sharing his dataset with us.

References

1. D. Byrd and T. Crawford, "Problems of music information retrieval in the real world", *Information Processing & Management*, 33(2):249-272, 2001.
2. G. Tzanetakis and P. Cook, "Musical genre classification of audio signals.", *IEEE Transaction on Speech and Audio Processing*, 10(5):293-302, 2002.
3. Guohui Li and Ashfaq A. Khokhar, "Content-based Indexing and Retrieval of Audio Data using Wavelets", Proc. of IEEE International Conference on Multimedia and Expo(II), 2000.
4. B. Logan, "Mel frequency cepstral coefficients for music modeling", Proc. of International Symposium on Music Information Retrieval, 2000.
5. Tao Li and Mitsunori Ogihara and Qi Li, "A comparative study on content-based music genre classification", Proc. of ACM SIGIR Conference, 2003.
6. T. Tolonen and M. Karjalainen, "A computationally efficient multipitch analysis model", *IEEE Transaction on Speech and Audio Processing*, 8(4):708-716, 2000.
7. U. Nam and J. Berger, "Addressing the Same but different - different but similar problem in automatic music classification", Proc. of International Symposium on Music Information Retrieval, 2001.
8. Gerard Salton and Michael J. McGill, "Introduction to modern information retrieval", McGraw-Hill, New York, 1983.
9. Keinosuke Fukunaga, "Introduction to statistical pattern recognition", Academic Press, 1990
10. Simon Haykin, "Neural networks: a comprehensive foundation", Prentice-Hall, NJ, 1999.
11. L. Rabiner and B. Juang, "Fundamentals of Speech Recognition", Prentice-Hall, NJ, 1993.
12. J. Pierce, "The science of musical sound", W.H.Freeman, 1992.
13. J. R. Quinlan, "C4.5: Programs for machine learning", Morgan Kaufman. 1993.
14. M. Clynes, "Music, Mind and Brain: The Neuropsychology of Music", Plenum Press, 1982.
15. T. Mitchell, "Machine Learning", McGRAW-Hill, 1997.
16. W. J. Dowling and D . L. Harwood, "Music Cognition", Academic Press, Inc. 1986.
17. J. Shen and J. Shepherd and A.H.H.Ngu, "Combining Multiple Acoustic Features for Efficient Content Based Music Retrieval", Technical Report, School of Computer Science and Engineering, UNSW, 2004.
18. Chih-Chung Chang and Chih-Jen Lin, "LIBSVM: a library for support vector machines", Software available at http://www.csie.ntu.edu.tw/~cjlin/libsvm, 2001.
19. Jialie Shen, John Shepherd and Anne HH. Ngu, "Integrating Heterogeneous Features for Efficient Content Based Music Retrieval", Proc. of ACM CIKM Conference, 2004.

Effectiveness of Note Duration Information for Music Retrieval

Iman S.H. Suyoto and Alexandra L. Uitdenbogerd

School of Computer Science and Information Technology, RMIT
GPO Box 2476V, Melbourne, Victoria 3001, Australia
imsuyoto@cs.rmit.edu.au
sandrau@rmit.edu.au

Abstract. Content-based music information retrieval uses features extracted from music to answer queries. For melodic queries, the two main features are the pitch and duration of notes. The note pitch feature has been well researched whereas duration has not been fully explored. In this paper, we discuss how the note duration feature can be used to alter music retrieval effectiveness. Notes are represented by strings called standardisations. A standardisation is designed for approximate string matching and may not capture melodic information precisely. To represent pitches, we use a string of pitch differences. Our duration standardisation uses a string of five symbols representing the relative durations of adjacent notes. For both features, the Smith-Waterman alignment is used for matching. We demonstrate combining the similarity in both features using a vector model. Results of our experiments in retrieval effectiveness show that note duration similarity by itself is not useful for effective music retrieval. Combining pitch and duration similarity using the vector model does not improve retrieval effectiveness over the use of pitch on its own.

1 Introduction

The field of music information retrieval (MIR) research explores ways in which users can better find pieces of music in which they are interested. For *content-based* MIR, we attempt to find answers to queries that contain a fragment of music. This music fragment can be of two main types: an audio sample or a set of notes. The goal of the user could be to find the exact piece of music that they have heard, or to find music that is similar, such as might occur in copyright infringement or in arrangements of a piece. The latter is our main interest in this research.

Current state of the art in content-based MIR has user queries consisting of sung or symbolically created queries. The ability to extract melodies from an audio stream consisting of a single voice is at an acceptable level of precision for matching. The same cannot be said as yet of note extraction from typical commercial recordings of music. Thus for melody search we mainly work with collections of symbolically represented music, such as found in Musical Instrument Digital Interface (MIDI) files.

A technique that has been shown to work reasonably well [1] is a three-phase matching process. First, as most pieces of music are *polyphonic*, that is, have more than one note sounding at the same time, representative melodies or themes are extracted from each piece in the collection. Second, both the pieces and queries are transformed into a standardised form that retains the salient features for matching and allows straightforward matching. Third, a similarity measure is applied to determine the amount of match for each piece, resulting in a ranked set of answers. Melody matching gives quite good results when a simple string representation of the pitch of extracted melodies is compared. While there has been work previously using both pitch and rhythm (see for example Kageyama, Mochizuki, and Takashima [2], McNab et al. [3], Chen and Chen [4], Lemström, Laine, and Perttu [5], and Dannenberg et al. [6]), the relative value of these two aspects of melody for matching have not been quantified for polyphonic collections, and whether a string-matching approach is of benefit in this situation. The experiments reported in this paper show that rhythm, when expressed using an alphabet of five relative values, is quite poor in its own right for matching, even more so than a three-value alphabet representation of a melody's pitch contour. Further, when combined using a vector model, it does not improve the precision of retrieved answers to queries.

Below we discuss the different melody standardisations used in our experiments (Sec. 2), the dynamic-programming-based matching technique we applied (Sec. 3), and the experiments that show that simple pitch matching is superior to a vector-combined pitch and rhythm approach (Sec. 4).

2 Standardisations

To support approximate matching, we convert the melody into searchable representations called *standardisations*. A standardisation is designed for approximate string matching and may not capture melodic information precisely [1]. In this paper, we discuss three pitch standardisations and one duration standardisation. The three pitch standardisations are *contour*, *extended contour*, and *directed modulo-12* (see Secs. 2.1, 2.2, and 2.3). For duration, we use both the *contour* and *extended contour* standardisation (see Sec. 2.4).

2.1 Pitch Contour Standardisation

The pitch contour standardisation uses three distinct symbols to represent a note. The symbols represent the movement direction of the previous note pitch to the current note pitch [7]. We use the convention "S" for same, "U" for up, and "D" for down. The first note is not represented. For example, the melody shown in Fig. 1 is represented as "UUUDDUUDDD".

Fig. 1. "Melbourne Still Shines" by ade ishs

2.2 Pitch Extended Contour Standardisation

For finer granularity, the pitch contour standardisation is extended so that there are *small* and *big* up's (symbolised as "u" and "U", respectively) and down's ("d" and "D"). We use three or more semitones as big intervals. For example, the melody shown in Fig. 1 is represented as "UUuDDuUddd".

2.3 Pitch Directed Modulo-12 Standardisation

The directed modulo-12 standardisation uses direction information too. A note is represented as a value ρ_{12} which is the interval between a note and its previous note scaled to a maximum of one octave [7, 8]:

$$\rho_{12} \equiv d(1 + ((I-1) \bmod 12)) \qquad (1)$$

where I is the interval between a note and its previous note (absolute value) and d is 1 if the previous note is lower than the current note, -1 if higher, and 0 if otherwise. For example, the melody shown in Fig. 1 is represented as "7 4 1 -5 -5 2 3 -2 -1 -2"[1].

2.4 Duration Contour and Extended Contour Standardisations

Just as in pitch contour-based standardisations, the duration contour and extended contour standardisations also employ three and five distinct symbols respectively to represent a note. In the case of duration, we use "S", "s", "R", "l", and "L" for "much shorter", "a little shorter", "same", "a little longer", and "much longer" respectively . (Analogous to pitch contour standardisation, the duration contour standardisation does not have "s" and "l" symbols). The quantisation we use is based on the encoding in Moles [9]. Let λ_C be the current

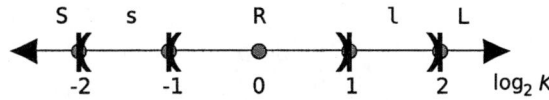

Fig. 2. Duration extended contour quantisation. $K = \lambda_C/\lambda_P$ where λ_C and λ_P are respectively the current and previous note durations

---

[1] Note that a figure is treated as a symbol. Therefore, it is a 10-symbol string.

note, λ_P be the previous one, and $K = \lambda_C/\lambda_P$. A note is represented based on the ranges of $\log_2 K$ as illustrated in Fig. 2. For example, the melody shown in Fig. 1 is represented as "LSRLSR1RRR".

3 Retrieval

The use of duration information along with dynamic programming was suggested by Kageyama, Mochizuki, and Takasima [2]. They suggest that note durations be used as penalty scores for insertion and deletion operations. How the scores are calculated is however not formally defined. In this work, we also use a dynamic programming approach. In particular, we use the Smith–Waterman alignment [10] (also known as *local alignment* [11]) which is useful to find a substring with highest similarity. Because query tunes typically translate to short strings while tunes in the collection typically to long strings, the alignment is more suitable than global alignment [1].

To calculate the local alignment between two strings s and q, we perform the following steps:

1. Prepare the data structure.
   (a) Construct a matrix of which dimension is $(|s|+1) \times (|q|+1)$. We use 0 as the base index, i.e. the column indices are $0, 1, 2, \ldots, |q|$, the row indices are $0, 1, 2, \ldots, |s|$, and the symbol indices for s and q are respectively $0, 1, 2, \ldots, |s|-1$ and $0, 1, 2, \ldots, |q|-1$.
   (b) Initialise the 0-th row and column with 0.
2. Calculate the score.
   (a) For i in $\langle 1 \ldots |s| \rangle$:
      i. For j in $\langle 1 \ldots |q| \rangle$:
         A. $D_{i,j} \leftarrow \max(0, D_{i-1,j} + I, D_{i,j-1} + I, D_{i-1,j-1} + M(s_{i-1}, q_{j-1}))$
         where I is the insertion/deletion score (commonly non-positive) and M is the match/mismatch function. The values for M and I that we use in our experiments are detailed in Sec. 4.

The local alignment score is $\max(D_{i,j}); i \in \{1 \ldots |s|\}, j \in \{1 \ldots |q|\}$. For example, suppose $s =$ UUDS, $q =$ SSDUU, $M(x,x) = 2$ (a match), $M(x,y)|_{x \neq y} = -2$ (a mismatch), and $I = -1$. The matrix looks like the one shown in Fig. 3. The local alignment score is the maximum score in the matrix, i.e. 4.

		S	S	D	U	U
	0	0	0	0	0	0
U	0	0	0	0	2	2
U	0	0	0	0	1	4
D	0	0	0	2	1	3
S	0	2	2	1	1	2

Fig. 3. Local alignment between "UUDS" and "SSDUU"

We are experimenting with a vector model to combine similarity evidences from both pitch and duration matching. The pitches and durations are symbolised by the respective standardisations. As vectors, they are modelled as being perpendicular to each other. The overall similarity is indicated by the resultant similarity vector. The following formula is based on one in our previous work [12], except that now we also assign weights for both pitch and duration components:

$$\Sigma \equiv w_\pi \varsigma_\pi \hat{\pi} + w_\delta \varsigma_\delta \hat{\delta} \qquad (2)$$

where Σ is the resultant similarity vector, ς_π is the pitch similarity, ς_δ is the duration similarity, w_π and w_δ are both weight constants, and $\hat{\pi}$ and $\hat{\delta}$ are respectively pitch and duration unit vectors. Ranking is then based on the magnitude of resultant similarity vector, $|\Sigma| = \sqrt{w_\pi^2 \varsigma_\pi^2 + w_\delta^2 \varsigma_\delta^2}$. Therefore, the value of w_π is not meaningful on its own, and neither is w_δ. However, the ratio w_π/w_δ (or reciprocally, w_δ/w_π) is.

4 Experiments

Our aim with these experiments was to determine how effective rhythm information is for melody retrieval using our experimental framework of a polyphonic MIDI file collection, manual queries, and two sets of relevance judgements [13].

The collection consists of 14,193 MIDI files, which are a superset of those used in our earlier experiments (such as Uitdenbogerd and Zobel [1, 14], and Uitdenbogerd, Chattaraj, and Zobel [13]). The query set used here is the set of 28 manual melody queries created by a musician upon listening to a set of rendered polyphonic pieces. We used two sets of relevance judgements. The first, known as *automatic*, was created by Uitdenbogerd by identifying likely matches by file-name, and verifying by listening. The second, called *manual*, was the result of pooling top answers from several matching techniques, and asking users to decide upon listening whether the pieces were similar. More detail is found in Uitdenbogerd, Chattaraj, and Zobel [13].

As a baseline of our experiment, for pitch matching, we use $M(x,x) = 1$ for a match, $M(x,y)|_{x \neq y} = -1$ for a mismatch, and $I = -2$ for an insertion/deletion (see Sec. 3) as used in Uitdenbogerd and Zobel [1]. For duration matching, we use 39 scoring matrices. The scoring matrices are obtained by varying the variables $a, b, c, \ldots, i$ shown in Fig. 4 as detailed in Table 1. The matrix means if there is

	S	s	R	1	L
S	c	d	f	i	h
s	d	b	e	g	i
R	f	e	a	e	f
1	i	g	e	b	d
L	h	i	f	d	c

Fig. 4. Scoring matrix for duration extended contour standardisation. "S", "s", "R", "1", and "L" respectively indicate a "much shorter", an "a little shorter", a "same", an "a little longer", and a "much longer"

Table 1. Scoring schemes for duration extended contour standardisation. For all scoring schemes, $a \geq b \geq c \geq d \geq e \geq f \geq g \geq i \geq h$

Scoring scheme	a	b	c	d	e	f	g	h	i
1	1	1	1	1	−1	−1	−1	−1	−1
2	2	1	1	1	−1	−1	−1	−1	−1
3	3	1	1	1	−1	−1	−1	−1	−1
4	3	2	1	1	−1	−1	−1	−1	−1
5	3	3	1	1	−1	−1	1	−1	−1
6	3	3	2	1	−1	−1	−1	−1	−1
7	3	3	3	1	−1	−1	−1	−1	−1
8	3	3	3	3	−1	−1	−1	−1	−1
9	3	3	3	2	−1	−1	−1	−1	−1
10	3	3	3	1	−1	−1	−1	−1	−1
11	3	3	3	0	−1	−1	−1	−1	−1
12	3	3	3	−1	−1	−1	−1	−1	−1
13	3	2	1	0	−2	−3	−3	−3	−3
14	3	2	1	0	−3	−3	−3	−3	−3
15	3	2	1	0	−1	−2	−3	−3	−3
17	3	2	1	0	−1	−1	−3	−3	−3
17	3	2	1	0	−1	−1	−2	−3	−3
18	3	2	1	0	−1	−1	−1	−3	−3
19	3	2	1	0	−1	−1	−1	−3	−2
20	3	2	1	0	−1	−1	−1	−3	−1
21	3	2	1	0	−1	−1	−1	−2	−1
22	3	2	1	0	−1	−1	−1	−1	−1

a match "S"-"S", $M(\text{S},\text{S}) = c$; a mismatch "S"-"s", $M(\text{S},\text{s}) = d$; etc. At any time, $a \geq b \geq c \geq d \geq e \geq f \geq g \geq i \geq h$.

5 Retrieval Performance Evaluation

The queries in our experiments are topic-oriented, i.e. for one query there can be more than one relevant answer.

To evaluate the effectiveness of every matching method, we use a standard measurement technique for such a task, i.e. using *precision* and *recall*:

$$P \equiv \frac{|\mathbf{Rel} \cap \mathbf{Ret}|}{|\mathbf{Ret}|} \qquad (3)$$

$$R \equiv \frac{|\mathbf{Rel} \cap \mathbf{Ret}|}{|\mathbf{Rel}|} \qquad (4)$$

where P is precision, R is recall, **Rel** is the set of relevant tunes and **Ret** is the set of retrieved tunes. Precision can be averaged at 11 recall levels, $0.0, 0.1, 0.2, \ldots, 1.0$, to obtain the *11-point recall-precision average* [15]:

$$\langle \overline{P}(r) \rangle_{r=0.0,0.1,0.2,\ldots,1.0} = \frac{\sum_{r=0}^{10} \sum_{i=1}^{N_q} \frac{P_i(0.1r)}{N_q}}{11} \quad (5)$$

which is the measure we use to compare the effectiveness of the techniques in our experiments. However, since some queries have less than 11 relevant answers, we use *interpolated precision* values, which can be calculated using the following formula [15]:

$$P(j) = \max_{j \le r \le j+0.1} P(r) \quad (6)$$

where $j \in \{0.0, 0.1, 0.2, \ldots, 0.9\}$. Higher 11-point recall-precision average means more effective retrieval technique.

6 Results and Analysis

In our experiment, queries were matched against all tunes in our collection 23 times, once for pitch matching using the directed modulo-12 standardisation and 22 times for duration matching using the 22 scoring schemes.

Table 2. 11-point recall-precision percentage values for automatic relevance judgments

Baseline performance = 52.15.

Scoring scheme	w_π/w_δ				
	0	1	3	5	7
1	0.87	26.40	49.73	51.32	51.32
2	2.81	18.86	47.92	50.89	51.49
3	1.71	12.67	42.41	51.40	51.41
4	2.22	8.93	38.49	51.23	51.06
5	2.57	5.46	36.00	47.63	49.72
6	2.87	4.18	37.45	46.19	49.72
7	2.47	3.59	36.78	48.39	49.41
8	4.08	7.38	37.56	45.51	50.20
9	3.27	4.36	35.52	46.16	49.50
10	2.47	3.59	36.78	48.39	49.41
11	3.84	2.16	33.48	49.50	50.70
12	3.57	2.07	34.98	50.95	50.86
13	1.35	4.74	36.61	50.23	50.14
14	1.84	4.80	36.51	50.53	50.42
15	1.34	4.09	36.58	51.24	51.07
16	1.16	4.66	34.98	51.95	51.27
17	1.16	4.66	34.98	51.95	51.27
18	1.16	4.66	34.98	51.95	51.27
19	1.16	4.66	34.98	51.95	51.27
20	1.16	4.66	34.94	51.93	51.27
21	1.16	4.66	34.94	51.93	51.27
22	1.04	4.55	34.93	51.93	51.27

To combine pitch and duration similarities using Eq. 2, We used six different w_π/w_δ values: 0, 1, 3, 5, 7, and ∞. The last one is the baseline performance, i.e. duration information is ignored ($w_\delta = 0$), whereas the first one means pitch information is ignored ($w_\pi = 0$).

For automatic relevance judgments, the baseline performance is an 11-point recall-precision value of 52.15%. The results of using other w_π/w_δ values are shown in Tables 2. For manual relevance judgments, the baseline performance is an 11-point recall-precision value of 51.84%. The results of using other w_π/w_δ values are shown in Tables 3.

Taking the best results from each w_π/w_δ value, we obtain the graph shown in Fig. 5. It shows that the peak performance is obtained when $w_\pi/w_\delta = 5$.

From both relevance judgments, duration information by itself is shown to be not useful for retrieval. In our experiments with automatic relevant judgments, duration information does not improve retrieval performance over that using pitch information per se, whereas with manual relevance judgments using $w_\pi/w_\delta = 5$ and scoring schemes 16, 17, 18, and 19, slightly better performance is obtained. We analyse further whether duration matching improves retrieval effectiveness using Wilcoxon signed-rank test with one-sided confidence level (α)

Table 3. 11-point recall-precision percentage values for manual relevance judgments

Baseline performance = 51.84.

Scoring scheme	\multicolumn{5}{c}{w_π/w_δ}				
	0	1	3	5	7
1	0.94	25.24	50.52	52.14	52.14
2	2.60	20.38	48.81	52.04	52.65
3	1.18	13.67	42.87	52.60	52.96
4	1.05	7.83	39.83	52.91	53.13
5	0.67	3.73	36.45	47.23	51.49
6	1.05	3.89	35.95	49.10	51.61
7	0.79	3.84	33.95	48.70	49.81
8	3.57	7.65	36.90	45.49	50.96
9	1.64	4.52	33.71	47.21	50.54
10	0.79	3.84	33.95	48.70	49.81
11	0.40	2.72	31.04	48.30	51.36
12	0.00	2.22	33.62	50.19	52.45
13	0.48	5.40	37.93	52.09	51.54
14	0.49	5.40	37.57	52.03	51.65
15	0.89	4.93	38.30	52.96	53.14
16	0.71	5.71	36.72	53.72	53.42
17	0.71	5.71	36.72	53.72	53.42
18	0.71	5.71	36.72	53.72	53.42
19	0.71	5.71	36.72	53.72	53.42
20	0.71	5.70	36.68	53.70	53.41
21	0.71	5.70	36.68	53.70	53.41
22	0.60	5.57	36.65	53.70	53.41

Table 4. Compressed standardised string sizes

Standardisation	Compressed size (megabytes)	Compression ratio (%)
Pitch directed modulo-12	8.15	22.74
Pitch extended contour	6.75	18.83
Pitch contour	3.95	11.02
Duration extended contour	3.83	10.69

Uncompressed size = 35.85 megabytes.

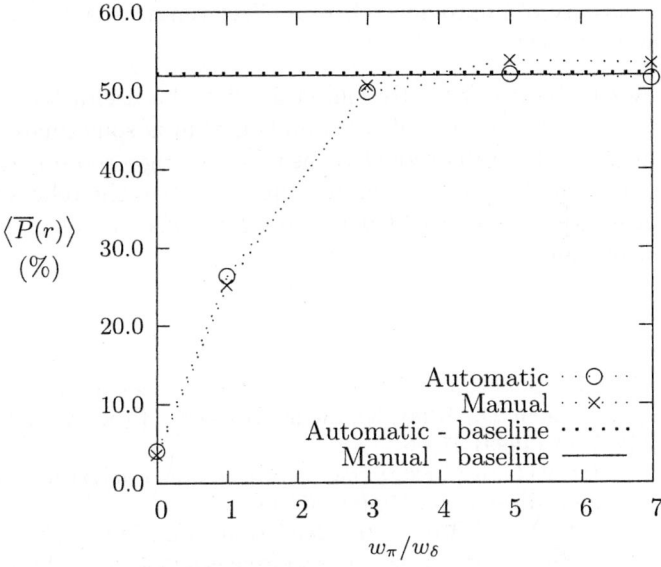

Fig. 5. Best 11-point recall-precision values

of 0.05. The null hypothesis is that duration information does not improve retrieval effectiveness; with alternative hyptothesis that duration information does improve retrieval effectivenes. It is found that incorporating duration information using the vector model does *not* imply significant performance gain.

To see how much information is actually contained in the standardised strings of the tunes in our collection, we compress the strings. The rationale behind this is that strings that contain more information (thus having higher entropy) are less compressible than those containing less information. We compress the strings using the bzip2 program[2]. In uncompressed state, pitch information occupies 35.85 megabytes and so does duration information. The compressed standardised string sizes are shown in Table 4. That duration extended contour strings are more compressible than pitch contour strings reflects that not much information

---

[2] see http://sources.redhat.com/bzip2/

is contained if tunes are represented only by their note durations despite the larger alphabet size.

7 Conclusion and Future Work

This paper inspects the performance of combining pitch and duration similarities using a vector model. The results of our experiment show that:

1. Duration information on its own is not useful for music retrieval.
2. The vector model is not appropriate to combine pitch and duration similarities for the purpose of improving retrieval effectiveness over the use of pitch information on its own.

Rhythm seems to be insufficiently varied for it to be useful for melody retrieval. However, the combination of pitch and rhythm is sometimes needed in order for humans to distinguish or identify melodies. Using a representation that combines the pitch and rhythm in a manner that preserves the relative position of the match in each case may yield better results. This should be subject to further experimentation.

References

1. Uitdenbogerd, A.L., Zobel, J.: Melodic matching techniques for large music databases. In Bulterman, D., Jeffay, K., Zhang, H.J., eds.: Proc. ACM Multimedia Conf., Orlando, USA (1999) 57–66
2. Kageyama, T., Mochizuki, K., Takashima, Y.: Melody retrieval with humming. In: Proc. Int. Computer Music Conf. (1993) 349–351
3. McNab, R.J., Smith, L.A., Witten, I.H., Henderson, C.L., Cunningham, S.J.: Towards the digital music library: Tune retrieval from acoustic input. In: Proc. ACM Digital Libraries. (1996)
4. Chen, J.C.C., Chen, A.L.P.: Query by rhythm: An approach for song retrieval in music databases. In: Proc. IEEE Int. Workshop on Research Issues in Data Engineering. (1998) 139–146
5. Lemström, K., Laine, P., Perttu, S.: Using relative interval slope in music information retrieval. In: Proc. Int. Computer Music Conf., Beijing, China (1999) 317–320
6. Dannenberg, R.B., Birmingham, W.P., Tzanetakis, G., Meek, C., Hu, N., Pardo, B.: The MUSART testbed for query-by-humming evaluation. In Hoos, H.H., Bainbridge, D., eds.: Proc. Inf. Conf. Music Inf. Retrieval, Baltimore, USA (2003) 41–47
7. Uitdenbogerd, A.L.: Music Information Retrieval Technology. PhD thesis, School of Computer Science and Information Technology, RMIT, Melbourne, Australia (2002)
8. Suyoto, I.S.H.: Microtonal music information retrieval. Master's thesis, School of Computer Science and Information Technology, RMIT, Melbourne, Australia (2003)
9. Moles, A.: Information Theory and Esthetic Perception. University of Illinois Press, Urbana, US (1966)

10. Smith, T.F., Waterman, M.S.: Identification of common molecular subsequences. J. Mol. Biol. **147** (1981) 195–197
11. Gusfield, D.: Algorithms on Strings, Trees, and Sequences: Computer Science and Computational Biology. Cambridge University Press, Cambridge, UK (1997)
12. Suyoto, I.S.H., Uitdenbogerd, A.L.: Exploring microtonal matching. In Buyoli, C.L., Loureiro, R., eds.: Proc. Inf. Conf. Music Inf. Retrieval, Barcelona, Spain (2004) 224–231
13. Uitdenbogerd, A.L., Chattaraj, A., Zobel, J.: Methodologies for evaluation of music retrieval systems. (INFORMS J. Computing) Originally presented at ISMIR 2000; to appear.
14. Uitdenbogerd, A.L., Zobel, J.: Music ranking techniques evaluated. In: Proc. Australasian Computer Sci. Conf., Melbourne, Australia (2002) 275–283
15. Baeza-Yates, R., Ribeiro-Neto, B.: Modern Information Retrieval. ACM Press, New York, USA (1999)

A Self-Adaptive Model to Improve Average Response Time of Multiple-Event Filtering for Pub/Sub System

Botao Wang, Wang Zhang, and Masaru Kitsuregawa

Institute of Industrial Science, The University of Tokyo,
Komaba 4-6-1, Meguro Ku, Tokyo, 153-8505 Japan
{botaow, zhangw, kitsure}@tkl.iis.u-tokyo.ac.jp

Abstract. Publish/subscribe system captures the dynamic aspect of the specified information by notifying users of interesting events as soon as possible. Fast response time is important for event filtering which requires multiple step processing and is also one of important factors to provide good service for subscribers.

Generally the event arrival rate is time varying and unpredictable. It is very possible that no event arrives in one unit time and multiple events arrive in another unit time. When multiple events with different workloads arrive at the same time, the average response time of multiple-event filtering depends on the sequence of event by event filtering.

As far as we know, significant research efforts have been dedicated to the techniques of single event filtering, they can not efficiently filter multiple events in fast response time. In this paper, we first propose a multiple-event filtering algorithm based on R-tree. By calculating relative workload of each event, event by event filtering can be executed with short-job first policy so as to improve average response time of multiple-event filtering. Furthermore, a self-adaptive model is proposed to filter multiple events in dynamically changing environment.

The multiple-event filtering algorithm and the self-adaptive model are evaluated in a simulated environment. The results show that the average response time can be improved maximum up to nearly 50%. With the self-adaptive model, multiple events can be filtered with average response time always same as or close to the possible best time in the dynamically changing environment.

1 Introduction

Publish/subscribe system provides subscribers with the ability to express their interests in an event in order to be notified afterwards of any event fired by a publisher, matching their registered interests [7]. It captures the dynamic aspect of the specified information. Fast response time is very important for the event filtering which requires multiple-step processing, there the events need to be filtered out first as the inputs of operator like join in continuos query, and is also one of important factors to provide good service for subscribers.

Generally the event arrival rate is time varying and unpredicatable. For example, traffic monitoring, ticket reservation, internet access, stock price, weather reports, etc.. In contrast to stable arrival rate, it's very possible that multiple events arrive in one unit time and no event arrives in another unit time.[1]

In the context of event filtering, even many index techniques such as event filtering algorithms based on multiple one-dimensional indexes [5] [8] [11] [18] [21] and event filtering algorithms based on multidimensional index [19][22], have been proposed, all these techniques are designed to filter single event instead of multiple events at one time. They can not filter multiple events directly in fast average response time if those events arrive at the same time with different workloads. Meanwhile, we found that event filtering based on multidimensional index [19] [22] is more efficient and flexible than that based on multiple one-dimensional indexes.

In order to improve average response time of multiple-event filtering, we first propose a R-tree [4] [9] based multiple-event filtering algorithm. Furthermore a self-adaptive model is proposed to filter multiple events in a dynamically changing environment with average response time always same as or close to the best possible time.

The rest of this paper is organized as follows. Section 2 introduces the background of this paper. Section 3 describes the algorithm to improve average response time. Section 4 proposes the self-adaptive model. In Section 5, the event filtering algorithm and the self-adaptive model are evaluated in a simulated environment. Section 6 discusses the related work. Finally, conclusions and future work are given out in Section 7.

2 Background

In this section, we first explain the reason why R-tree [4] [9] is chosen, and then introduce the event filtering based on R-tree briefly. We assume that readers have enough knowledge about R-tree.

- The reasons to choose R-tree
  There are two reasons to choose R-tree here. One is performance; another is space partition strategy.
  As introduced in [19] [22], event filtering based on multidimensional index (UB-tree [2] [3] or R-tree [4] [9]) is feasible, and is much efficient and flexible than that based on Count algorithm [21], which is one representative event filtering algorithm based on multiple one-dimensional indexes. Fig.1 shows a snapshot of performance differences with two examples.[2] That's the first reason to choose R-tree.
  Further UB-tree and R-tree have different partition strategies. Generally, the search algorithms (except point query) of both index structures traverse multiple paths from root node to leaf nodes. UB-tree partitions space with space filling curve. UB-tree's search algorithm is depth-first and it is not easy to calculate the number of multiple search paths at one specified middle level.

---

[1] Even logically for most of the events, there exist absolutely different arriving times, in this paper, we regard the events arriving in the same unit time as the events arriving at the same time. For example, positions reported every 30 seconds or the stock prices sampled every second.

[2] For details, please refer to [19] [22].

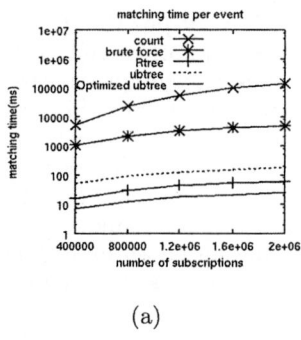 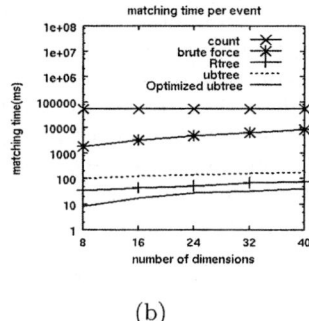

(a)　　　　　　　　　　　　　　(b)

Fig. 1. Performance Examples of Event Filtering Based on Different Index Techniques

Contrary to UB-tree, R-tree decomposes the space in a hierarchical manner. Its search algorithm does not have to be depth-first, so it is easy to calculate the number of multiple search paths at one specified middle level. Because the number of multiple search paths will be used to estimate workload of event filtering in our proposal, we choose R-tree here.

- Event Filtering based on R-tree
  The event filtering based on R-tree is executed as a point enclosed query. Subscriptions are hypercubes and events are points here. The dimension number means the number of attributes used in pub/sub system.

By the way, even the other multidimensional indexes, for example, multilevel grid file [20], are applicable, as the purpose of this paper is concerned, we will conentrate on the main idea to filter multiple events with unstable arrival rate in fast response time.

3 Algorithms to Improve Average Response Time

3.1 Motivation and Main Algorithm

Short-Job First(SJF) is one well-known policy used to improve average response time while scheduling multiple jobs. The critical thing is to estimate workloads properly. Meanwhile, the search algorithm of R-tree traverses multiple paths from root to leaf nodes. Apparently, the number of the multiple search paths reflects workload relatively.

Our motivation is that, in order to improve average response time of multiple-event filtering, first estimate workloads of multiple events relatively according to their numbers of search paths, and then filter these multiple events sequentially with SJF policy.

```
Begin BatchSearch(Root, EventArray, Level)
//Root. Root of R-tree
//EventArray. Multiple events arrived at the same time
//Level. Depth to estimate workload starting from the Root

1    Estimate Workloads of events in EventArray into WorkloadTable;
2    For each item in WorkloadTable;
3        Read the corresponding event and nodes located on the search paths at the input Level;
4        Search R-tree starting from the nodes obtained at line 3;
5        Output results of current event obtained at line 3;
6    ENDForLoop
End BatchSearch
```

Fig. 2. Main Algorithm BatchSearch

Fig.2 shows the pseudo codes of main algorithm. The algorithm is called **BatchSearch**. It is an algorithm to filter multiple events, one of whose inputs is one array of events (**EventArray**) instead of one event. The parameter **Level** controls the depth to estimate workloads starting from root node **Root**. In WorkloadTable (to be introduced later), the events will be sorted in ascending order of the number of search paths stopped at **Level**. Line 1 corresponds to workload estimation. Line 2-6 correspond to event by event filtering with SJF policy.

Line 4 filters one event with an algorithm similar to the original R-tree point enclosed query. The differences are that it starts from the nodes obtained at line 3 instead of **Root** in original point enclosed query, and the point enclosed query is executed many times (same as the number of nodes corresponding to the search paths) instead of one time. For this reason, in the following, we only describe the data structures and algorithms newly defined for workloads estimation which corresponds to Line 1 of Fig.2.

3.2 Data Structures Used to Estimate Workloads

Two data structures called WorkloadTable and IntersectBuffer, are newly defined for workloads estimation.

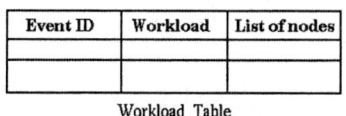

(a) WorkloadTable   (b) IntersectBuffer

Fig. 3. Data Structures Used to Estimate Workloads

WorkloadTable is an array of items with structure shown in Fig.3-a. Each item corresponds to one event. The workload is the number of search paths(nodes) stopped at the specified **Level**. "List of nodes" are pointers of the corresponding nodes. Only one WorkloadTable is used while estimating workloads.

IntersectBuffer (Fig.3-b) is used to record events whose Minimum Bounding Rectangles (MBR) intersect with those of the items inside one R-tree node. Each level uses one intersectBuffer while estimating workloads. The items in one intersect buffer correspond to those of one R-tree node.

3.3 Algorithms to Estimate Workloads

The algorithm (corresponding to line 1 of Fig.2) to fill WorkloadTable is shown in Fig.4. In function **EstimateWorkload**, line 1 initializes the IntersectBuffer of level 0, there is only one item with one pointer pointing to the root node and all events are assumed to intersect with the MBR of this item, because the item is root. Line 2 calls a recursive procedure named **BatchIntersect** to fill the WorkloadTable. Line 3 sorts the WorkloadTable according to the workloads in ascending order.

In the procedure **BatchIntersect**, line 1-2 read the parent item of current node from the IntersectBuffer of last level (the level near to root) and get all event IDs kept in the item. Line 3 checks the ending condition of the recursive search and line 4 fills the WorkloadTable with the event IDs obtained at line 1-2 and **CurrentNode**. Line 7-16 fill the IntersectBuffer of **CurrentLevel**. Line 18-20 check next level by accessing children nodes of **CurrentNode**.

```
Begin EstimateWorkload(Root, EventArray, Level)
// Root. Root of R-tree
// EventArray. Array of events arrived at the same time
// Level. Depth to eastimate workload starting from the Root

1    Set IntersectBuffer of level 0;  // intialize intersectbuffer with all events
2    BatchIntersect(Root, EventArray, 1, Level); // Estimate from the Root
3    Sort WorkloadTable by the workload in ascending order;
End EstimateWorload

Begin BatchIntersect(CurrentNode, EventArray, CurrentLevel, Level)
//CurrentNode. The node which will be processed
// EventArray. Array of events arrtive at the same time
// CurrentLevel. The level where CurrentNode is located
// Level. Level where recursive BatchIntersect stops

1      Get parent item of CurrentNode from IntersectBuffer of CurrentLevel-1
2      Read all eventIDs into EventList from the parent item obtained at line 1;
3      IF CurrentNode is leaf node or CurrentLevel >= Level
4          Add WorkloadTable with CurrentNode and the EventList;
5          //The recursive ends here
6      ELSE
7          Reset IntersectBuffer of CurrentLevel;
8          For each item in CurrentNode // beginning of checking item
9              For each event in the EventList // beginning of checking event
10                 Check MBR intersection of current item with the current event
11                 If intersection is true
12                     Insert eventID of the event into the corresponding item in
13                                  IntersectBuffer of CurrentLevel;
14                 ENDIf
15             ENDForLoop // end of checking event
16         ENDForLoop // end of checking item
17
18         For each subnode of CurrentNode
19             BatchIntersect(subnode, EventArray, CurrentLevel+1, Level);
20         ENDForLoop // End of checking subnodes
21     ENDIf
End BatchIntersect
```

Fig. 4. Algorithms to Estimate Workload

4 Self-Adaptive Model

While filtering multiple events with **BatchSearch**, for the same multiple events, the average response time depends on the value of **Level** which controls the depth to estimate workloads. The number of multiple events arriving at the same time is not fixed, and the size and data distribution of index change dynamically also. In this section, we will propose a self-adaptive model to filter multiple events in the dynamically changing environment.

4.1 Relationship Between Average Response Time and Level

Fig.5-a and Fig.5-b show two examples which reflect the relationship between average response time and **Level**. For the details of experiment environment, please refer to Section 5.1. In order to avoid overlap of results, the time here is the sum of average response times obtained with different numbers of times(loop). "Same events" means same **EventArray**s are used for different **Levels**. "Different events" means different **EventArray**s are used. The height of the index tree is 7 with 1.5 million subscriptions. The difference of two examples is the number of multiple events (size of **EventArray**).

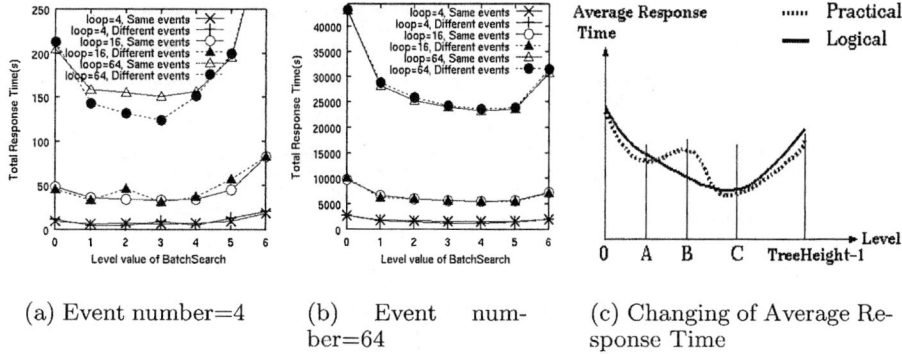

(a) Event number=4 (b) Event number=64 (c) Changing of Average Response Time

Fig. 5. Relationship between Average Response Time and Level

The point to observe is that, with same **EventArray**s, the average response time changes in the shape of concave while level changes from root to leaf. It's reasonable considering the two main steps of **BatchSearch**: estimating workloads and event by event filtering with SJF policy. While filtering multiple events arriving at the same time, time cost to estimate workloads is overhead compared to the event filtering without workloads estimation. The overhead becomes larger with value increment of **Level**. At the same time, because the higher the **Level** is, the more accurate of the workloads estimation is. Consequently the efficiency of SJF becomes more and more higher with value increment of the **Level**. That is the reason why the average response time changes in the shape of concave.

Based on the concave, we can say that the best level exits for multiple-event filtering with **BatchSearch** if the number of events is fixed. The best level is the level to get the shortest average response time while using **BatchSearch**.

On the basis of the above observations (Fig.5-a and Fig.5-b) and analyses. The logical relationship between average response time and **Level** is expressed in Fig.5-c by the line marked **Logical**. As shown in Fig.5-a and Fig.5-b, the best level changes with different event numbers. It also depends on the size of index as shown in the evaluation (Fig.7-a).

In order to get possible best average response time, the **BatchSearch** should run with **Level** valued best in the dynamically changing environment.

4.2 Adjust Best Level Dynamically According to Statistic Information

The self-adaptive model is shown in Fig.6. The function of the self-adaptive model is to adjust the best level dynamically for multiple-event filtering in the dynamically changing environment. It is built for filtering multiple events with same event number. For multiple events with different event numbers, their statuses (current best level, numbers of updates, etc.) will be kept in different buffers.

If the current level is best, we call system is stable. In stable status, **BatchSearch** is executed with **Level** valued best. As shown in the right of Fig.6, for arriving **EventArray**s (with same event number), same level **CurrentLevel** is used. In stable status, the average response time is the possible best time because **CurrentLevel** is best level. The number of update operations (insert and

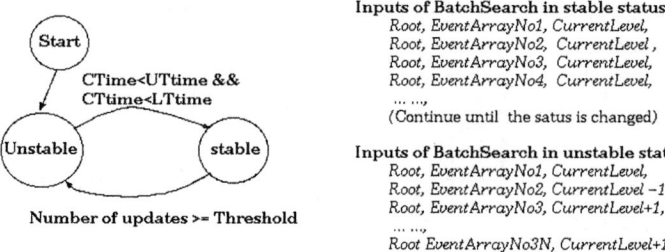

Fig. 6. Self-Adaptive Model

delete) is monitored and counted in stable status. After a lot of update operations, the height of the index tree or its data distribution might be changed, it is necessary to check the best level or adjust it if it changed. The system becomes unstable then. The **Threshold** shown in Fig.6 is the number to determine the time when the system enters unstable status from stable status.

Unstable status is the status in which the best level should be checked. In unstable status, the best level can be checked and gotten by trying all levels with same **EventArray**s naively, but it's not acceptable for a dynamic system in practice. The overhead is not neglected for a higher index tree or **EventArray**s with larger size.

Our solution is that, check the average response times of current level and its upper level and its lower level (totally 3 levels), based on the "**Logical**" concave line in Fig.5-c. There, **BatchSearch** filters different **EventArray**s (same size) with **Level** values changed in a loop of round-robin way as shown in the right of Fig.6. N is the loop counter. In unstable status, multiple events are filtered with **Level** valued same as or close to the best level.

The average response times of three different levels are summed up (called CTime, UTime, LTime in Fig.6 which correspond to current level, upper level and lower level) and checked after the loop ends. Note that, the **EventArray**s are different each time and one **EventArray** is filtered just one time. If

$$CTime < UTime \ \&\& \ CTime < Dtime$$

is true, the system will enter stable status, because the current level is the best according to the concave changes of average response time against level value. Otherwise, adjust the current level towards to the direction of to best level (bottom of the concave line marked "**logical**", Fig.5-c) according to the concave shape and restart a new loop.

Because the contents of **EventArray**s are different, so it is possible that the average response times obtained at different levels do not change logically when the loop counter N is very small, for example, the lines marked by "Different events" with loop counter valued 4 and 16 in Fig.5-a . In this case, as expressed by the line of "**Practical**" in Fig.5-c, it is possible for system to enter stable status even the current level (A) is not best level (C). It is also possible that

$$CTime > UTime \ \&\& \ CTime > LTime$$

is true as shown at level (B). The self-adaptive model can not work well in these cases. But, if the value of loop counter N is larger enough, for example 64, the "**Practical**" line will change in the same concave shape or close up to "**Logical**" line statistically as shown in Fig.5-a and Fig.5-b. The loop counter is manageable for a long time running pub/sub system.

5 Results of Evaluation

5.1 Environment

The algorithm is evaluated in main memory structure. Both subscriptions and events are created randomly. The index size (number of subscriptions) changes from 0.5 million to 3.0 millions. The number of events arriving at the same time changes from 2 to 128. The **BatchSearch** algorithm is implemented on R-tree[3] with index node capacity 10 and leaf node capacity 20 in a 12D space.[4] The

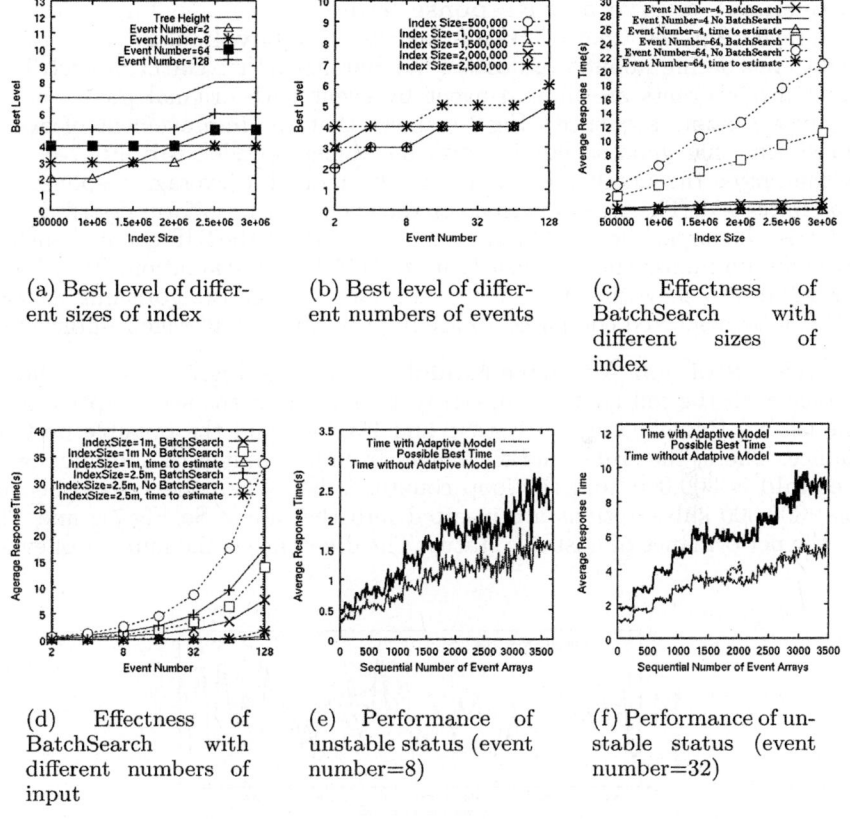

(a) Best level of different sizes of index

(b) Best level of different numbers of events

(c) Effectness of BatchSearch with different sizes of index

(d) Effectness of BatchSearch with different numbers of input

(e) Performance of unstable status (event number=8)

(f) Performance of unstable status (event number=32)

Fig. 7. Evaluation Results of **BatchSearch** and Adaptive Model

---

[3] Version 0.62b. http://www.cs.ucr.edu/ marioh/spatialindex
[4] The performance doesn't change drastically if the dimension number is located in a reasonable range as shown in Fig.1. Dimension number and node capabilities influence the performance of R-tree itself but do not influence the improvement of average response time and effectiveness of the self-adaptive model which are mainly concerned in this paper.

hardware platform is Sun Fire 4800 with 4 900MHz CPUs and 16G memory. The OS is Solaris 8.

5.2 Evaluation of BatchSearch Algorithm

Changing of Best Level. Fig.7-a shows that the best level changes slowly with increment of index size. It means the **Threshold** in Fig.6 can be set larger, for example 100,000, if the insert operation is more frequent than delete operation. For pub/sub system with balanced insert and delete operations, the value of **Threshold** is implementation-dependent. Generally, the update operations are much less than filtering operation. So in most of time, system can run in stable status. Fig.7-b shows that the smaller the number of events is, the lower the best level is.

Improvement of Average Response Time. Fig.7-c and Fig.7-d compare the average response time of **BatchSearch** with **Level** valued best to that without considering about workloads ("no BatchSearch". **BatchSearch** is not used, multiple events are filtered event by event with original point enclosed query in a random sequence). Fig.7-c shows that the improvement of average response time has good scalability with increment of index size. Fig.7-d shows that the larger the number of events is, the more the average response time can be improved. The reason is that for the events with uniform distribution of workloads, the larger the number of events is, the more the SJF can be benefited. The maximum improvement is nearly up to 50% in our evaluation. Both Fig.7-c and Fig.7-d also show that the cost to estimate workload (algorithms shown in Fig.4) can be neglected compared to the improvement of average response time.

Effectiveness of Self-Adaptive Model. Fig.7-e and Fig.7-f compare the performance with the self-adaptive model to that without the self-adaptive model (same as "no BatchSearch" in Fig.7-c and Fig.7-d) and the possible best performance. There, the size of index changes from 0.5 million to 2.6 millions, the **Threshold** is 300,000, and the loop counter is 64. When the system becomes stable, 300,000 subscriptions are inserted into the index. So Fig.7-e and Fig.7 show the performance of unstable status. The difference is the number of events.

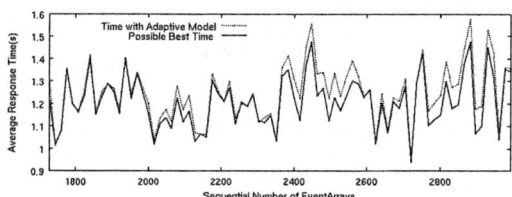

Fig. 8. One Piece of Unstable Status Performance (event number=8, index size=2,000,000)

We can find that the average response time with the self-adaptive model is much better than that without the self-adaptive model (**BatchSearch** is not used), the time differences are almost at the same level as those shown in Fig.7-c and Fig.7-d which are obtained with best level. Even in unstable status, the time obtained by using self-adaptive model is very close to the possible best time as shown in Fig.7-e and Fig.7-f. The time difference compared to the possible best time is so small that is hard to make difference in Fig.7-e and Fig.7-f. Fig.8 shows a piece of details of Fig.7-e where index size is 2 millions (the range of sequential number is about 1550-3000).

We can say that with the self-adaptive model, multiple events can be filtered with average response time same as or close to the possible best time.

6 Related Work

A lot of algorithms related to event filtering have been proposed. They are proposed for publish/subscribe systems [1] [8] [12] [18] [19] [21] [22], for continuous queries [5] [6] [15] and for active database [10] [11].

Predicate indexing techniques have been widely applied. There, a set of one-dimensional index structures are used to index the predicates in the subscriptions. Mainly, there are two kinds of multiple one-dimensional indexs based algorithms: Count algorithm [21] and Hanson algorithm [10] [11]. The performances of Count algorithm and Hanson algorithm have same complexity order, they differ from each other by whether or not all predicates in subscriptions are placed in the index structures. Meanwhile in [19] [22], event filtering based on multidimensional index is proved to be feasible and efficient compared to the popular Count algorithm. The conclusions of [19] [22] are the basis of this paper.

The testing networking based techniques [1] [12] initially preprocess the subscriptions into a matching tree. Different from predicate index, [1] and [12] built subscription trees based on subscription schema. They suffer from the problem of space and maintenance.

Event filtering is one critical step of continuous queries. In [5], predicate index is built based on Red-Black tree, there algorithm is similar to bruteforce which scans the total Red-Black tree every time when event arrives. In [6], Count algorithm is used. Adaptivity is applied in [15], it implements routing policies to let faster operators filter out some tuples before they reach the slower operators. In [17], queries are optimized based on rate of input to minimize response time by introducing event arrival rates into the optimizer cost model.

As far as we know, the problem of adaptively improving average response time for multiple events arriving at the same time has not been addressed yet.

7 Conclusions and Future Work

In this paper, in order to improve the average response time of pub/sub system with unstable event arrival rate, we first proposed a multiple-event filtering algorithm based on R-tree. The relative workload of each event is estimated according to the number of search paths so as to utilize short-job first policy. Further a self-adaptive model is designed to filter multiple events in dynamically changing environment.

According to the evaluation results, the improvement of average response time has good scalability with index size and the larger the number of events is, the more the average response time can be improved. The average response time can be improved maximum up to nearly 50%. The results also show that the overhead derived from workloads estimation can be neglected compared to the improvement of average response time. With the self-adaptive model, multiple events can be filtered with average response time always same as or close to the possible best time.

Because the proposed idea and self-adaptive model can be applied to other multidimensional index structure also, for example, multilevel grid file [20], in the future, we will try other applicable multidimensional indexs in different update scenarios and real data.

References

[1] M. K. Aguilera, R. E. Strom, D. C. Sturman, M. Astley, T. D. Chandra. Matching Events in a Content-based Subscription System. Eighteenth ACM Symposium on Principles of Distributed Computing(PODC), 1999:53-61
[2] R. Bayer. The Universal B-Tree for multidimensional Indexing. Technical Report TUM-I9637, November 1996
[3] R. Bayer, V. Markl. The UB-Tree: Performance of Multidiemnsional Range Queries. Technical Report TUM-I9814, June 1998
[4] N. Beckmann, H.-P. Kriegel, Ralf Schneidar, Berhhard Seeger. The R*-Tree: An Efficient and Robust Access Method for Points and Rectangles. SIGMOD 1990:322-331
[5] S. Chandrasekaran, M. J. Franklin. Streaming Queries over Streaming Data. Proceedings of the 28th VLDB Conference, Hong Kong, 2002:203-214
[6] J. Chen, D. J. DeWitt, F. Tian, Y. Wang. NiagaraCQ: A Scalable Continuous Query System for Internet Databases. ACM SIGMOD 2000:379-390
[7] P. T. Eugster, P. Felber, R. Guerraoui and A.-M. Kermarrec. The Many Faces of Publish/Subscribe. Technical Report 200104, Swiss Federal Institute of Technology
[8] F. Fabret, H. A. Jacobsen, F. Llirbat, J. Pereira, K. A. Ross, D. Shasha. Filtering Algorithms and Implementation for Very Fast Publish/Subscribe Systems. ACM SIGMOD 2001:115-126
[9] A. Guttman. R-Trees: A Dynamic Index Structure for Spatial Searching. ACM SIGMOD 1984:47-57
[10] E. N. Hanson, M. Chaaboun, C.-H., Y.-W. Wang. A Predicate Matching Algorithm for Database Rule Systems. ACM SIGMOD 1990:271-280
[11] E. N. Hanson, C. Carnes, L. Huang, M. Konyala, L. Noronha. Scalable Trigger Processing. ICDE 1999:266-275
[12] A. Hinze, S. Bittner. Efficient Distribution-Based Event Filtering. International Workshop on Distributed Event Based Systems. Austrai July 2002:525-532
[13] H. A. Jacobsen, F. Fabret. Publish and Subscribe Systems. Tutorial. ICDE 2001
[14] V. Markl. MISTRAL:Processing Relational Queries using a Multidimensional Access Tecnnique. Ph.D. Thesis, TU Munchen, 1999, published by infix Verlag, St.Augustin. DISDBIS 59, ISBN 3-89601-459-5, 1999
[15] S. Madden, M. Shah, J. Hellerstein, V. Raman. Continuously Adaptive Continuous Queries(CACA) over Streams. ACM SIGMOD 2002:49-60
[16] F. Ramsak, V. Markl, R. Fenk, M. Zirkel, K. Elhardt, R. Bayer. Intergrating the UB-tree into a Database System Kernel. VLDB 2000:253-272
[17] S. D. Viglas, J. F. Naughton. Rate-based query optimization for streaming information sources. SIGMOD Conference 2002: 37-48
[18] B. Wang, W. Zhang, M. Kitsuregawa. Design of B+Tree-Based Predicate Index for Efficient Event Matching. APWeb 2003: 548-559
[19] B. Wang, W. Zhang, M. Kitsuregawa. UB-Tree Based Efficient Predicate Index with Dimension Transform for Pub/Sub System. DASFAA 2004: 63-74

[20] K.Y. Whang, R. Krishnamurthy. The Multilevel Grid File - A Dynamic Hierarchical Multidimensional File Structure. DASFAA 1991:449-458
[21] T. W. Yan, H. Garcia-Molina. The SIFT Information Dissemination System. In ACM TODS 24(4):529-565 1999
[22] W. Zhang. PERFORMANCE ANALYSIS OF UB-TREE INDEXED PUBLISH/SUBSCRIBE SYSTEM. Master Thesis. Department of Information and Communication Engineering, The University of Tokyo. March 2004

Filter Indexing: A Scalable Solution to Large Subscription Based Systems

Wanxia Xie[1], Shamkant B. Navathe[1], and Sushil K. Prasad[2]

[1] College of Computing, Georgia Institute of Technology,
801 Atlantic Drive, Atlanta, GA, USA
{wanxia.xie, sham}@cc.gatech.edu
[2] Dept. of Computer Science, Georgia State University
34 Peachtree Street, Atlanta, GA, USA
sprasad@gsu.edu

Abstract. Filtering is a popular approach to reduce information traffic in subscription-based systems, especially if most subscribers are located on mobile devices. The filters are placed between the subscribers and the subscription server. With increasing number of filters from subscribers, filtering may become a bottleneck and challenge the scalability of such systems. In this paper, we propose to use filter indexing to solve this problem. We propose and study four filter-indexing schemes: Ad-Hoc Indexing Scheme (AIS), Group Indexing Scheme (GIS), Group-Sort Indexing Scheme (GSIS) and B' Tree Indexing Scheme (BTIS). We evaluate the performance of these four indexing schemes with respect to scalability and other factors. Among the proposed schemes, we find that GSIS is the most efficient indexing scheme for searching and BTIS has the best performance for updating and inserting filters.

1 Introduction

Currently subscription-based systems are widely used in many application areas. Filtering is a popular approach to reduce information traffic in these subscription-based systems. Usually a subscriber[1] sends its customized filter to the subscription management system and the system will filter the information being sent to the subscriber. Different subscribers have different filter requirements. The same subscriber may have different filter requirements under different conditions. Filtering is especially important when the subscriber is located in a mobile device as it reduces the information traffic and hence reduces the energy consumption of the mobile device. On the other hand, it is difficult to develop a scalable subscription based system, as filtering may become the bottleneck.

In [1] and [2], authors propose query grouping and [4] proposes trigger grouping for continuous queries. However, queries and triggers are applied before the information is sent to the subscription-based system. Authors in [2] and [3] also

---

[1] A subscriber can be considered an application without any loss of generality.

consider filters but their filters are either placed in the data sources (publishers) or as part of the queries. The filters that we discuss in this paper are applied to the information received at subscription-management systems.

We envision an environment where distributed publishers continuously push updates of resource objects to a centralized subscription management system that manages many resource objects. Based on the filter of a subscriber, the subscription management system will decide whether the update of the resource object should be sent to the subscriber. Our motivation comes from the experience of implementing a hybrid directory server [6] which employs both pull and push interfaces for information querying and information monitoring respectively. Here, we have extended the directory service into a general information/resource monitoring system.

With the increasing number of filters in the system, the filtering process becomes the bottleneck of the system. The system ends up repeating the same process for similar filters. The goal is to improve filter management and thereby to enhance the overall performance of the publish/subscribe system by reducing the duplicate effort in the filtering process for similar filters in the system. Given an update, the problem that we want to address is to rapidly determine the list of subscribers who are in the set to receive this update. To focus on this problem, we make a reasonable assumption that the network is reliable so that the delivery of data is guaranteed.

As there are frequent updates to the resource objects in a system, we need to schedule the updates being sent to subscribers. It takes a long time to find the real interests (the number of subscribers who need the update) of each update and this makes scheduling so difficult that most systems just send the updates in a random order.

Our solution to the problem outlined above can be presented as a combination of two-pronged techniques: (1) Filter indexing: To speed up the filter process and remove the duplicate work from processing similar filters, we group and index filters from different subscribers for each resource object; (2) Scheduling based on filter index schemes. In this paper, our emphasis will be on the analysis of the first technique - indexing of filters. We will only outline some important issues related to the scheduling of the updates.

This paper is organized as follows. Section 2 introduces the system architecture and filter design. Section 3 describes four filter-indexing schemes. Section 4 presents the performance evaluation. Section 5 describes the related work. Section 6 contains a summary and future work.

2 Adaptive Filters

2.1 System Architecture

The overall architecture is described as Fig. 1. Fig. 1 (a) shows a subscription-based system without filters. All subscribers of the same channel will receive the same information. Fig. 1 (b) demonstrates a subscription-based system with filters. A subscriber can define a filter for the information it is interested in. Usually a filter is installed in the subscription server since only the updates that the subscriber is interested in will be pushed to the subscriber in this way. Moreover, a subscriber may be located in a resource-poor device such as a PDA. Moving filter processing away from such subscribers will reduce resource contention and preserve the energy for battery-powered devices.

The detailed architecture is described as Fig. 2. A subscription server acts as the coordinator among resource publishers and subscribers. Publishers constantly push updates of resource objects to the subscription server. Subscribers need the latest updates of resource objects from the subscription server to make the best decisions. The subscription server can also aggregate the updates from different publishers so that publishers are transparent to subscribers.

When the subscription server receives an update from a publisher, it scans the filters associated with the channel to find the list of subscribers that are interested in the update. This list forms a derived channel. As the list changes with updates of resources and filters of subscribers, the derived channel dynamically adapts. In order to reduce the overhead of scanning filters, we propose an indexing of filters according to the indexing schemes discussed in Section 3.

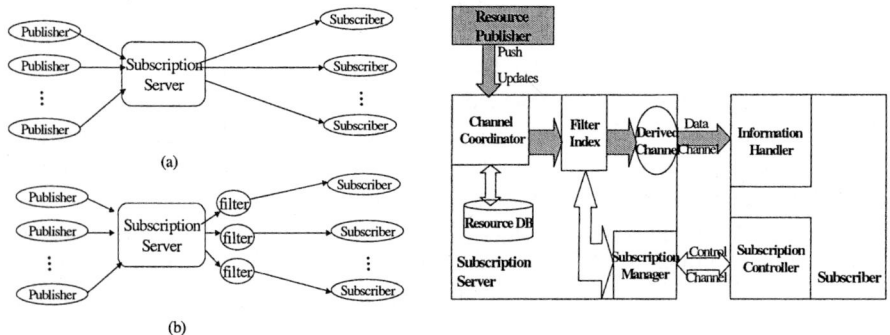

Fig. 1. (a) A subscription-based system without filters **Fig. 2.** Details of the system architecture
(b) A subscription-based system with filters

2.2 Filter Design

A filter is an XML document that is generated in a subscriber and sent to the subscription server. There are two kinds of filters. One is called **simple filter** that only needs to compare with the latest value of the attributes of resource objects. The other is called **historic filter** that needs to compare with the past values of the attributes of resource objects. The most common historic filter is one where the updated value increases by a constant value or a certain percentage compared with the old value. Some historic filters may need to apply statistics over a few past values such as the average or summary of 5 past values. In this paper, we focus on simple filters - those involving equality and inequality conditions on single attribute values. When we mention the word "filter", it will mean a simple filter unless otherwise specified.

A channel filter is composed of three parts. The first part is **Type,** which describes the filter type. The second part is **FromSource**, which describes the resource objects that the filter is related to. The last part is **WhereCondition**, which describes the requirement the update of resource objects should meet. So updates of resource objects will be tested against the WhereCondition to see whether they should be pushed to the owners of the filter.

To simplify the discussion, we only consider three basic data operators: Greater (>), Equal (=) and Less (<). Other numerical comparison operators could be built from these three operators. We consider three logical operators: AND, OR and NO. Operator 'NO' means there is only one condition and hence no logical operations are needed.

3 Filter Indexing Techniques

The system model could be simplified as follows. There are N resource objects O_i (0<=i<N), M_i subscribers and L_i filters for the resource object O_i. That means each update of resource object O_i needs to be compared with L_i filters before it is sent to subscribers.

3.1 Filter Indexing for a Single Attribute of a Resource Object

3.1.1 Ad-Hoc Indexing Scheme (AIS)
In the ad-hoc indexing scheme, filters are grouped by their associated resource objects. When an update of the resource object arrives, it will be compared with all filters associated with the resource object, even if some filters may be the same. The scheme is illustrated in Fig. 3. Let us assume that Filter 1 is the same as Filter 2 and Filter 3 is the same as Filter 4. To find whether subscriber 1 and 2 should be included in the derived channel, an update has to be compared with both Filter 1 and Filter 2. This is a waste of computation as the number of subscribers who have the same filter increases when the subscribers grow. So we introduce a Group Indexing Scheme in next section.

3.1.2 Group Indexing Scheme (GIS)
As we discussed in the AIS above, the same filters should be compared only once by an update of the resource object. All subscribers with the same filter will be added into the subscriber list of the filter. We call this as a Group Indexing Scheme and it is illustrated in Fig. 4. Since Filter 1 is the same as Filter 2 and Filter 3 is the same as Filter 4, they are grouped into two groups instead of four groups.

A variant of this scheme is to use a hash table. Since we need to compare whether the whole filter is the same, we could use the hash value of the filter to build a hash table. When a filter arrives at the subscription server, a hash function is applied to the filter. The hashed value will be used to find the entry of matching filters. The variant of Figure 5 is illustrated in Table 1.

However, in both situations, when an update of the resource object arrives, it still needs to be compared with all groups to find all subscribers who are interested in this update.

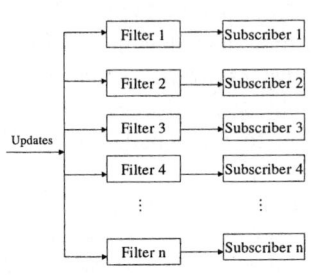
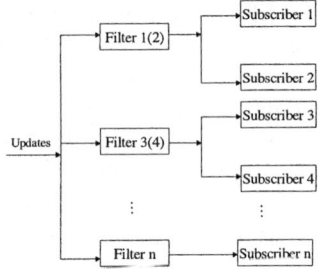

Fig. 3. Ad-hoc filter indexing scheme   **Fig. 4.** Group Filter Indexing Scheme

Table 1. Group Filter Indexing with Hash Table

Filter	Hashed Value	Subscriber List
1, 2	HashFunction(Filter 1)	1, 2
2, 3	HashFunction(Filter 3)	3, 4
...	...	...
n	HashFunction(Filter n)	N

3.1.3 Group-Sort Indexing Scheme (GSIS)

Group-Sort Indexing Scheme is designed to avoid comparing with all groups of filters. In this scheme, filters are grouped by every operator on each attribute of each resource object. At the same time, filters are also sorted by the value of the attribute of the resource object, which is set in the filter. This creates linear indices.

As we discussed in Section 2.2, we only consider three basic data operators (>, <, =). So we have three indexing possibilities for each attribute of the resource object: greater group-sort index, less group-sort index and equal group-sort index. For greater group-sort index and equal group-sort index, the values of the attribute are sorted in *increasing* order. For less group-sort index, the values of the attribute are sorted by *decreasing* order. Every value in the index is associated with a list of subscribers that have the same filters with this value.

Fig. 5 illustrates greater group-sort index and less group-sort index for value V of attribute A of the resource object O. G_i (0<i<=n) stands for the filter A>G_i (and G_i > G_{i-1}). P_i stands for the pointer to the subscriber list i. L_i (0<i<=n) stands for the filter A<L_i, (and L_{i-1} > L_i). When we scan greater group-sort index for the updated value V' of A, we will include subscriber list 1 to subscriber list i where G_{i+1} > V' (or i corresponds to the end of greater group-sort index) into the matching subscriber list. Similarly we will include subscriber list 1 to subscriber list i where L_{i+1} < V' (or we reach the end of less group-sort index) into the matching subscriber list.

In addition, equal group-sort index can also use hash functions instead of sorting. It is similar to Table 1, but we apply a hash function to the value of the attribute in the filter instead of the whole filter. When the updated value A' arrives, we apply hash function to A' to get the hashed value of A'. Then we look for the hashed value in the hash table. We return the associated subscriber list with the hashed value if we find the matching key in the hash table. Otherwise, the subscriber list will be empty.

When an update of the resource object arrives, three operator group-sort indices of each attribute should be searched. For equal group-sort index, we search for the updated value of the attribute in the index. If we find it, the associated subscriber list with this value will be returned. For greater group-sort index, we scan the index from the beginning until we find the updated value of the attribute or meet the key that is greater than the updated value. All subscriber lists associated with every value we scan before the end should be added into the returning subscriber list. Searching in less group-sort index is similar to greater group-sort index.

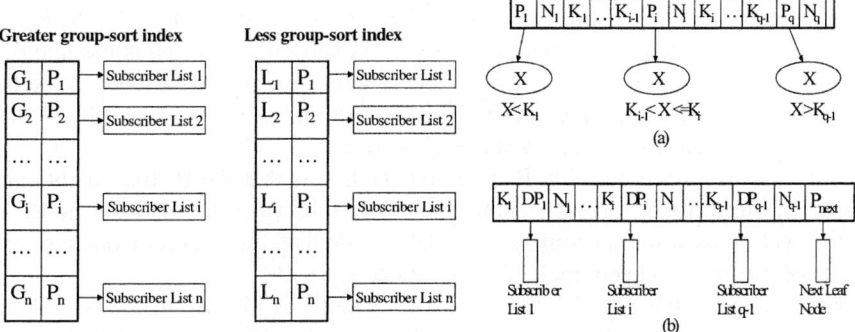

Fig. 5. Greater group-sort index and less group-sort index

Fig. 6. (a) Internal node of B' tree (b) Leaf node of B' tree

Now, we merge three subscriber lists from three operator group indices of this attribute into the subscriber list for this attribute. Then we merge subscriber lists of all attributes into the final subscriber list. This final subscriber list includes all subscribers that may be interested in this update of the resource object.

3.1.4 B' Tree Indexing Scheme (BTIS)

When the number of the filters increases, the overhead of searching the key in the group-sort indexing scheme also increases dramatically. We propose below a slight variation of B^+ tree called B' tree (pronounced B-prime tree) and use an indexing scheme based on utilizing the B' tree. Similar to the group-sort indexing scheme (which uses linear tabular indexes), we build a B' tree for each operator for each attribute of the resource object.

B' tree is a variant of B+ tree [5]. B' tree includes two kinds of nodes: internal node and leaf node. Data pointers are only stored in the leaf nodes. A data pointer points to the subscriber list associated with the key and the operator. The leaf nodes have an entry for every value of the attribute that is used with the operator in the filters, along with a data pointer to the subscriber list associated with the value of the attribute. The leaf nodes of B' tree are linked together to provide ordered access on the attribute to the subscriber lists. The leaf nodes linked list is almost the same as the index built in the group-sort indexing scheme. The main *difference* is that the leaf node linked list in less B' tree index is sorted in *increasing* order, but the less group indexing scheme sorts the linked list by *decreasing* order.

The internal nodes of the B' tree are the second level indices used to search the leaf node linked list. The structure of the internal nodes of a B' tree of degree p is illustrated in Fig. 6 (a). Every internal node is of the form $<P_1, N_1, K_1, ..., P_{q-1}, N_{q-1}, K_{q-1}, P_q, N_q>$ in which P_i is the subtree pointer that points to the subtree i, N_i is the number of subscribers in the subtree i, K_i is the i_{th} key value of the attribute in the node, q<=p and $K_1<K_2< ...< K_{q-1}$. With the exception of root node, q >= Ceiling (p/2) in every internal node.

The structure of the leaf nodes of a B' tree of degree p is illustrated in Fig. 6 (b). Every internal node is of the form $< <K_1, DP_1, N_1>, ..., <K_{q-1}, P_{q-1}, N_{q-1}>, P_{next}>$ in which DP_i is the data pointer that points to the i_{th} subscriber list, N_i is the number of subscribers in the i_{th} subscriber list, K_i is the i_{th} key value of the attribute in the node, P_{next} points to the next leaf node of the B' tree, Ceiling(p/2)<=q<=p and $K_1<K_2< ...< K_{q-1}$. In addition, all leaf nodes are at the same level.

The main difference between B' tree and B+ tree is that the B' tree maintains the number of subscribers for each subtree or each subscriber list in each node. This number will be used for scheduling of updates from different resource objects. At the same time, we need to keep track of the leftmost leaf node.

The filter processing of B' tree indexing scheme is similar to GSIS. When an update of the resource object arrives, three operator B' tree indexes of each attribute of the resource object are potential candidates to be searched. For equal B' tree index, we try to search the updated value of the attribute in the B' tree starting from the root node. If we find it, the associated subscriber list with this value will be returned. For greater B' tree index, we search the B' tree index from the root node until we find the updated value of the attribute or meet the key of the largest value that is less than the updated value in the leaf node. We identify this key as K_A. Then we traverse the leaf node link list. We start from the leftmost leaf node until we reach Key K_A. All subscriber lists associated with every value we traverse in the leaf node linked list should be added into the returning subscriber list. Searching in less B' tree index is similar as greater B' tree index.

After searching these B' tree indexes, we merge three subscriber lists from three operator- based B' tree indices of this attribute into the subscriber list for this attribute. Then we merge subscriber lists of all attributes into the final subscriber list. This final subscriber list includes all subscribers that may be interested in this update.

3.2 Filter Indexing for Multiple Conditions/Attributes of a Resource Object

Now we look at indexing the filters associated with multiple attributes of a resource object. Usually such a filter has multiple conditions connected by logical operators 'AND' and 'OR'. As we notice, multiple conditions/attributes in a filter will not affect AIS and GIS. So we mainly focus the discussion on GSIS and BTIS.

'OR' among conditions can be easily satisfied as the union of the subscriber lists from each condition forms the final subscriber list. 'AND' among conditions can be easily satisfied as the intersection of the subscriber lists from each condition forms the final subscriber list. However, since 'OR' and 'AND' coexist among conditions, we could not simply union or intersect the subscriber lists returned from each condition into the final subscriber list.

As we can see, if a filter satisfies one condition of 'OR', the owners of the filter should be included in the subscriber list. However, if a filter satisfies one condition of 'AND', it does not necessarily mean that the owners of the filter should be included in the final subscriber list.

Based on this observation, we design the following scheme. First of all, we set a flag for all filters including 'AND' operator. When an update of the resource object arrives at the subscription server, we search the operator indices of all attributes of the resource object. For each search in an operator index, a subscriber list will be returned. All subscriber lists returned from above searches are merged into two subscriber lists: the first list with subscribers without flags and the second list with subscribers with flags. For the second list, we need to check the filters of these subscribers to make sure all conditions of the filters are satisfied. In this process, some subscribers in the second list may be thrown out from the list. After this, we merge these two lists into the final subscriber list.

3.3 Filter Indexing for Multiple Resource Objects

Usually a filter concerns one resource object. When a filter involves multiple resource objects, there usually are multiple conditions connected by logical operators 'OR'. If each 'OR' condition concerns a different resource object, we could break down the filter into multiple separate filters such that each filter concerns only one resource object. Then we could use the techniques in section 3.1 and 3.2 for each filter.

If a filter does have the conditions related to multiple resource objects, we can use a similar technique used in section 3.2. At first, we union the subscriber lists returned by each condition, then we need to double-check the subscribers that have filters related to multiple resource objects. After this, we can get the final subscriber list.

4 Performance Evaluation

Experiments and simulations were done to study four indexing schemes. We implemented our prototype in Java SDK 1.4.1. We also built a simulator to simulate a large number of subscribers and filters to evaluate these indexing schemes.

The experiments are set up in two Dell Precision 360 desktops with Intel Pentium 4 2.8 GHz and 1GB Memory size. A subscription server is located in one desktop and a publisher is located in the other desktop. The two machines are connected by a 100Mbps Ethernet network.

The publisher sends updates to the subscription server. Then the server will check the filter indices to find the list of matching filters. We use exponential distribution to control the frequencies of updates. Frequency $f = \log(r)/\lambda$, in which r is a normal random variable and λ is the variable to control the frequency of updates. Normal distribution is used to generate values of updates. Value $V = u + \sigma * r$, in which u is mean variable, σ is the variance variable and r is the normal random variable. The values of parameters are listed as Table 2 unless specified otherwise. Impact of Frequencies of Updates is omitted for the sake of space. (Please refer to [14] for more details.)

Table 2. Experiment Parameters

Parameter	Value	Description
λ	5	Variable to control the frequency of updates
U1	100	Mean variable to generate values in filters
$\sigma 1$	40	Variance variable to generate values in filters
U2	90	Mean variable to generate values in updates
$\sigma 2$	50	Variance variable to generate values in updates
Sample size	150	The sample size to compute average search time

At first, we study the cost of building the index. In order to build indices for 200,000 filters, AIS needs 1,652ms, GIS needs 450,789ms, GSIS needs 407,916ms and BTIS needs 5,207ms. When the number of filters increases, the index building costs of GIS, GSIS and BTIS increases and the building cost of AIS keeps flat. As the indices can be built when the subscription server starts, this cost is not the main issue of our concern.

4.1 Scalability

We study the scalability of four indexing schemes in this section. Experiments are run for four indexing schemes from 10,000 filters to 900,000 filters. Group sizes are not controlled. The values of filters are randomly generated so that the number of groups depends on randomness of the values in filters as is the case in real world. The group size is not uniform. *The search time measures the duration in which the subscription server finds the matching filters given an update.* The average search time is the mean of results from 150 updates. As we can see from Fig. 7, the four indexing schemes are keeping the same bar in terms of performance until 600,000 filters are added. At the 900,000 filters, the performance of AIS dramatically drops, GSIS is slightly better

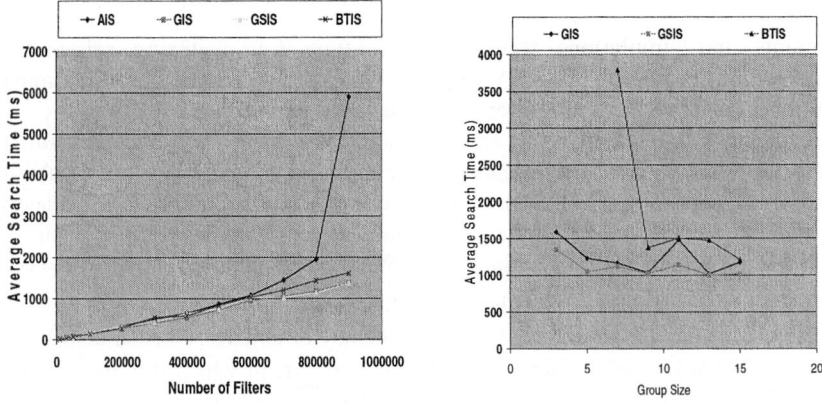

Fig. 7. Scalability comparison of four schemes   **Fig. 8.** Impact of group size

Filter Indexing: A Scalable Solution to Large Subscription Based Systems   297

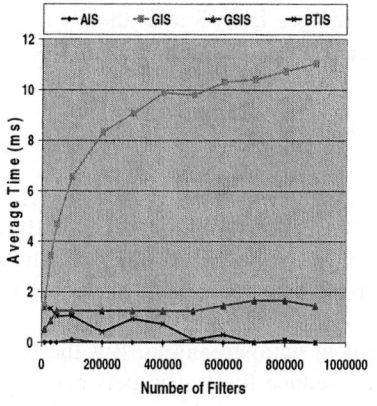
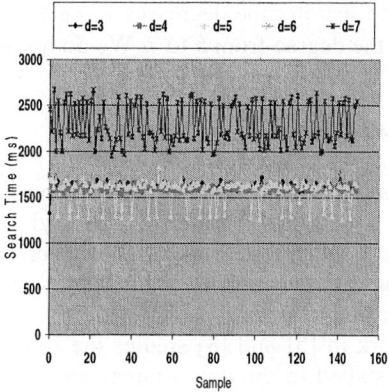

Fig. 9. Performance comparison of adding a filter   **Fig. 10.** Impact of Degree of B' Tree

than GIS and BTIS. Surprisingly, BTIS does not outperform GSIS and GIS at 900,000 filters. The reason would be that only 65,000 groups are formed from 900,000 filters. So the impact of number of groups is the issue we want to address in the next section.

4.2 Impact of Group Size

To investigate the impact of group size and the number of groups, we set up the experiment with 800,000 filters. As we know, the number of groups * group size = 800,000. In Fig. 8, we generate (800,000 / group_size) unique filters, then make as many copies as the group_size. As BTIS ran out of memory when the group size is 6, we only have the performance data from GIS and GSIS when group_size is less than 7. Surprisingly, GSIS always outperforms other two indexing schemes. BTIS's dramatic increase in average search time may come from memory contention when the group size is set as 7 and too many groups are generated.

4.3 Performance Comparison of Adding a New Filter

We also study the performance of adding a new filter. We sampled 100 times of adding a new filter when the number of total filters range from 10,000 to 900,000. Fig. 9 shows that GIS needs a much higher overhead to insert a new filter when the number of filters is more than 50,000. The time for GSIS to insert a new filter is pretty stable at 1.5ms. The overhead of inserting a new filter in BTIS is very small and is insignificant when the number of filters exceeds 500,000.

4.4 Impact of Degree of B' Tree

We also study the impact of degree of B' tree (block size in B' tree). The total number of filters is 900,000. In Fig. 10, we show that the search time of 150 samples for degrees ranging from 3 to 7. (It is out of memory when the degree is 8.) As we can see, the search time decreases when the degree changes from 3 to 5, then it increases when the degree from 5 to 7. We do not see a clear pattern as our data is limited.

5 Related Work

The proposed indexing of filters is the extension of the push interface of PeerDS [6] in the System on Mobile Devices (SyD) ([7], [13]). SyD is a middleware platform to develop collaborative application over mobile and heterogeneous devices. The push interface is the proactive directory service to push the updates of resources to the subscribing clients.

Work in [3] and [8] studies the filters applied in data streaming. But these filters are installed in the data sources and they mainly reduce the traffic between the data sources and the subscription server. Our filters are designed to reduce the traffic between the subscription server and the subscribers. Authors of [9] and [10] study the event filters between the subscription server and sinks. So their filters are similar to our filters. However, they did not try to do any optimizations for filter processing.

Query grouping ([1], [2]) and trigger grouping [4] group similar queries between the subscription server and data sources, remove the duplicate effort in the subscription server, and reduce the information traffic between the subscription server and data sources. However, in most subscription systems such as PeerDS, the subscriber cannot define its own query for a specific data source since there are too many data sources, or the subscription server wants to keep the data sources transparent to the subscribers. In this situation, the best way to reduce the information traffic between the subscription server and subscribers is to install filters customized by the subscribers. Filters between the subscription server and subscribers can also be combined with query grouping and trigger grouping to further reduce the information traffic.

There is also work [2] that tries to use grouped filters to reduce the computation for each data source. Authors in [11] focused on schema based clustering for filters. Authors in [12] discuss index structures under Boolean Model. Our work focuses on using filter indexing to reduce the overhead of finding out the list of subscribers for each update.

6 Conclusion and Future Work

In this paper, we extend the push interface of PeerDS into a general subscription system. We show that filters could greatly reduce the information traffic between the subscription server and subscribers. However, the increasing number of filters may endanger the scalability of the subscription server. So we propose and investigate four filter indexing schemes: AIS, GIS, GSIS and BTIS. B' tree is proposed as a minor variation of the B+ tree. The experiment results show that GSIS is the most efficient indexing scheme for searching among the proposed schemes and BTIS has the best performance for updating and inserting filters. BTIS can also help improving the scheduling of updates. Our future work will investigate scheduling of the updates based on different policies and experimenting with filters with multiple resource objects. We also plan to further investigate indexing of historic filters.

References

[1] J. Chen, D. J. Dewitt, F. Tian and Y. Wang, "NiagaraCQ: A Scalable Continuous Query System for Internet Databases". In ACM SIGMOD, 2000.

[2] S. Madden, M. Shah, J. M. Hellerstein and V. Raman, "Continuously Adaptive Continuous Queries over Streams". In ACM SIGMOD, 2002.

[3] C. Olston, J. Jiang and J. Widom, "Adaptive Filters for Continuous Queries over Distributed Data Streams". In ACM SIGMOD, 2003.

[4] W. Tang, L. Liu and C. Pu, "Trigger Grouping: A Scalable Approach to large Scale Information Monitoring", In NCA 2003.

[5] R. Elmasri and S.B. Navathe, "Fundamentals of Database Systems", 4th Ed, Chap. 14, Addison Wesley, 2004.

[6] W. Xie, S.B. Navathe and S. K. Prasad, "PeerDS: a scalable directory service", in submission.

[7] S. K. Prasad, V. Madisetti, S.B. Navathe, W. Xie, et al., "SyD: A Middleware Testbed for Collaborative Applications over Small Heterogeneous Devices and Data Stores", in Proc. of ACM/IFIP/USENIX 5th International Middleware Conf. (MW-04), Oct. 2004.

[8] V. Kumar, B. F. Cooper, S. B. Navathe, "Predictive Filtering: A Learning-Based Approach to Data Stream Filtering", Proc. Workshop of Data Manag. for Sensor Networks with VLDB 2004.

[9] G. Eisenhauer, F. Bustamente and K. Schwan, "A Middleware Toolkit for Client-Initiated Service Specialization", Proceedings of the PODC Middleware Symposium, 2000.

[10] Greg Eisenhauer. "The ECho Event Delivery System." Technical Report GIT-CC-99-08, College of Computing, Georgia Inst. of Tech..

[11] F. Fabret etl., "Flistering Algorithms and Implemention for Very Fast Publish/Subscribe Systems", in ACM SIGMOD,. 2001.

[12] T. W. Yan and H. Garcia-Molina, "Index Structures for Selective Dissemination of Information Under the Boolean Model", in ACM Transactions on Database Systems, VOl 19 N0.2 June 1994.

[13] W. Xie, S. B. Navathe and S. K. Prasad, "Supporting QoS-Aware Transactions in a System on Mobile Devices (SyD)" in Proc. Mobile Distributed Computing, ICDCS 2003.

[14] W. Xie, S.B. Navathe and S. K. Prasad, "Filter Indexing: a Scalable Solution to Large Subscription Based Systems", Technical Report, College of Computing, Georgia Inst. of Tech.

Caching Strategies for Push-Based Broadcast Considering Consecutive Data Accesses with Think-Time

Wataru Uchida[1], Takahiro Hara[2], and Shojiro Nishio[2]

[1] Network Laboratories, NTT DoCoMo Inc.,
3-5 Hikarino-oka, Yokosuka-shi, Kanagawa, Japan
uchida@netlab.nttdocomo.co.jp
[2] Dept. of Multimedia Eng., Grad. Sch. of Information Science and Tech.,
Osaka Univ. 2-1 Yamadaoka, Suita, Osaka, Japan
{hara, nishio}@ist.osaka-u.ac.jp

Abstract. Recently, there has been increasing interest in research on push-based information systems that deliver data by broadcast in both wired and wireless environments. This paper proposes new caching strategies to reduce the response time of data access by assuming an environment where clients consecutively issue access requests for multiple data items with think time. The proposed strategies take into account each client's access characteristics, such as correlation among data items and think-time between a data access and the next access request, and reduce the average response time by caching data items with long expected response time. Moreover, we evaluate the effectiveness of the proposed strategies by simulation experiments.

Keywords: broadcast disk, data correlation, caching strategy, think-time, push-based broadcast.

1 Introduction

Recently, along with the growth of wired and wireless environments, there has been increasing interest in research on push-based information systems that deliver data by broadcast (push-based systems, for short). Figure 1 shows a typical push-based system. Contrary to pull-based broadcast systems [3, 12], in which a server determines the data to be broadcast according to clients' access requests sent to the server, in push-based information systems each client that wants to access certain data does not send a request to the server but accesses the data by waiting for its broadcast time. Due to the absence of communication contention among clients requesting data, a key advantage of "push-based" mechanisms is the higher throughput for data access in a system with many clients.

To shorten the response time for data access in push-based systems, several strategies have been proposed. These strategies are categorized into the following research fields: strategies to schedule an effective broadcast order of data items in the server side[1, 9], caching strategies in the client side[2], and combinations of push-based and pull-based strategies[4]. In this paper, we focus on caching strategies in the client side.

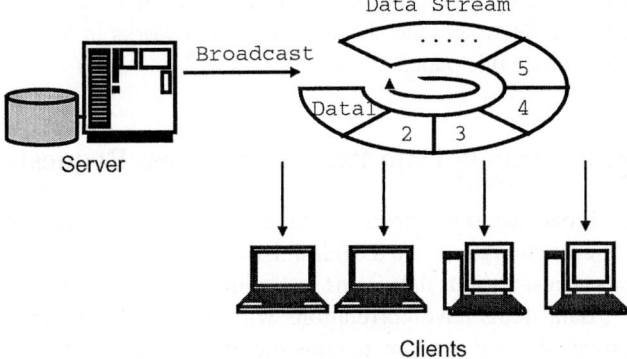

Fig. 1. Push-based system

Meanwhile, in a real environment, clients often access a certain set of data collectively. That is, correlation exists among data. When clients frequently access a set of correlated data, scheduling and caching strategies that consider the correlation among these data can reduce the response time for data access. There are two typical ways in which clients issue access requests for a set of correlated data: *simultaneously* and *with some time intervals*.

In our previous works[8, 10, 11], we proposed scheduling strategies and a caching strategy to shorten the average response time by assuming an environment where clients access multiple correlated data simultaneously. We also proposed scheduling strategies that assume an environment where clients access multiple correlated data with time intervals[10]. In this paper, we propose caching strategies that consider each client's access characteristics by assuming an environment where clients issue multiple access requests for a set of correlated data consecutively with time intervals.

In this paper, the following system environment is assumed:

– The system has a single server.
– Data are handled in clusters called data items. For simplicity, all data items are of the same size.
– The server creates a broadcast schedule consisting of M kinds of data items (ID:1, ..., M). It takes one time slot to broadcast one data item.
– No client sends access requests to the server, i.e., pure push.
– Clients have their own caches. The response time for requesting a data item in the cache is 0 and that for requesting a data item not in the cache is the time remaining until the item is broadcast next.
– Clients know the broadcast program. This is realized in several ways, e.g., disseminating information on the broadcast program periodically.
– Each client has unique access characteristics, and each client knows its own access characteristics.
– Data items are not updated.

The reminder of the paper is organized as follows. We describe assumptions on the correlation among data items and access request in Section 2. We discuss the conventional caching strategies in Section 3 and propose new strategies in Section 4. We evaluate the proposed strategies in Section 5 and show some related works in Section 6. Finally, in Section 7, we summarize this paper.

2   Correlation Among Data Items and Access Requests

In a push-based broadcast environment, data are clustered in data items considering characteristics of each data to reduce the administrative costs for scheduling or caching. Generally, clients access various data items by issuing multiple access requests for them collectively, i.e., data items have correlations with each other. Which data items are accessed collectively depends on how to construct data items.

Let us suppose a situation where the server pushes various WWW pages through a digital broadcast channel. In this case, although clients actively access WWW pages, they do not send access requests to the server but wait for their broadcast times. If all files that construct a WWW page (ex. HTML files and image files) are broadcast together as a data item, a user who accesses a WWW site first requests a data item for the top page of the WWW site. If the request is satisfied, the user browses it for a moment and then requests another page that is linked from the top page. Thus, there exists correlation between a WWW page and its linked pages, and access requests for these linked pages are issued with time intervals.

If each data item only includes each of the HTML files and image files that construct a WWW page, a user who accesses the WWW page simultaneously issues access requests for the data items that are components of the WWW page. When the client completes to get all of the requested data items, it consecutively issues access requests for data items that construct a WWW page which is linked by the previously accessed page with a time interval.

Based on the above discussion, there are three cases where clients issue access requests for a set of correlated data items: the requests are issued simultaneously, with some time intervals, and their combined case. In this paper, we assume the second case, where every time interval between a data access and the next access request is longer than one time slot. In the following, this time interval is referred to as "think-time". For the sake of simplicity, it is assumed that each client issues at most one access request at the same time.

The strength of the correlation between items i and j is defined as the probability that the client requests data item j after accessing data item i. The think-time between a previous data access and the next access request is determined by the probability density function based on the elapsed time until the previous data access.

We also assume an environment where a client issues an access request for the first data item with a constant probability and then issues multiple access requests successively for data items correlated with the previously accessed data items. We call a set of such successive data accesses a *process* and the item accessed first in a process the *top item*.

In a real environment, the access characteristics of each client, such as correlations between data items and probability density functions of think-time, are determined by logging each client's own access requests. Moreover, depending on the contents, there are some cases where the access characteristics of each client can be determined analytically (ex. in the case where WWW pages are broadcast).

3 Conventional Caching Strategy

The *PT strategy* proposed in [2] is the most famous prefetch-based caching strategy. The PT strategy assumes that every access request is issued independently of previous accesses, i.e., data correlation does not exist among data items. The PT strategy replaces cache as follows:

1. When each data item is broadcast, a client calculates *PT values* of the broadcast item and items stored in the cache. The PT value of data item i, L_i, is calculated by the following equation:
$$L_i = p_i \cdot (u_i(t) - t). \qquad (1)$$
Here, p_i is the probability that the client accesses data item i. t is the current time and $u_i(t)$ is the time when data item i is broadcast next after time t.
2. Data item j with the minimum PT value is selected among all cached data items. Then, if the PT value of broadcast data item b, L_b, is larger than the PT value of data item j, L_j, data item j is replaced with data item b.

The PT strategy replaces the cache to maximize the total benefit of response time at the moment when each item is broadcast. However, cache replacement by the PT strategy is not always optimal in the long term.

4 Caching Strategies Considering Think-Time of Access Request

In this paper, we propose caching strategies by assuming an environment where clients issue multiple access requests for correlated data items with think-time between one data access and the next access request.

4.1 RIB-PT (Request Interval Based PT) Strategy

Let c_{ij} denote the probability that a client accesses data item j after accessing i ($\sum_{j=1}^{M} c_{ij} = 1$). $f_{ij}(t)$ denotes the probability density function that the client issues an access request for data item j with think-time t, under the condition that the client requests data item j after accessing i ($\int_0^\infty f_{ij}(t)dt = 1$, $f_{ij}(t) = 0$ $(t < 0)$). Moreover, let τ denotes the current time and ζ denotes the access time of data item i for which the client issued the latest request.

Let us suppose that the latest access request for i has already been satisfied ($\zeta \leq \tau$) and that the client has not issued any access request after that. Under the condition that data item j is requested after accessing i, the probability density function that an access request for data item j is issued at time t is represented by the following equation:

$$\frac{1}{1 - \int_\zeta^\tau f_{ij}(t-\zeta)dt} f_{ij}(t-\zeta). \qquad (2)$$

Let $u_j(\tau)$ be the next broadcast time of data item j. The response time of access request for data item j issued at time t ($\tau \leq t \leq u_j(\tau)$) is $u_j(\tau) - t$ if j is not in the cache. Therefore, the expected increase in response time for the next access request caused by not caching j is expressed by the following equation:

$$R_j = S_j \cdot \int_\tau^{u_j(\tau)} f_{ij}(t-\zeta) \cdot (u_j(\tau) - t) dt. \tag{3}$$

Here,

$$S_j = \begin{cases} c_{ij} & (\tau < \zeta) \\ \dfrac{c_{ij}}{1 - \int_\zeta^\tau f_{ij}(t-\zeta)dt} & (\zeta \leq \tau) \end{cases}. \tag{4}$$

We call R_j in equation (3) the *RIB-PT value*. We can also define RIB-PT values for data items in the cache.

The RIB-PT strategy replace the cache as follows.

1. When each data item is broadcast, a client calculates the RIB-PT values of the broadcast data item and data items stored in the cache by using equation (3).
2. Data item j with the minimum RIB-PT value is selected among all cached data items. If the RIB-PT value of the broadcast item b, R_b, is larger than R_j, data item j is replaced with data item b.

In this way, the RIB-PT strategy replaces the cache to minimize the response time for the next access request issued for a data item correlated with the target item of the latest access request.

4.2 Extensions of RIB-PT Strategy

When think-time is short, to improve the cache hit rate, cache replacement has to take into account not only the next access request but also the one issued after that.

In this subsection, we extend the RIB-PT strategy to consider the response time of the access request issued after the next one. In the following, we call the response time of the next access request the *first response time* and the response time of the access request issued after that the *second response time*.

Response Time of Access Request After Next. Let us suppose a situation where the latest access request was issued for i, i was (will be) accessed at time ζ, and x ($x \neq i, j$) will be accessed next. The expected response time of the access request issued for j by the client that accesses x is expressed by the following formula:

$$\int_r^{u_j(\tau)} c_{xj} \cdot f_{xj}(t-r) \cdot (u_j(\tau) - t) dt. \tag{5}$$

Here, r is the access time of x.

When the next access request is issued for x in the cache, the probability density function that defines r is expressed by the following formula:

$$S_x \cdot f_{ix}(r - \zeta). \tag{6}$$

Consequently, the expected response time of the access request for j issued after accessing x in the cache is expressed by the following equation:

$$E_{jx} = S_x \cdot \int_\tau^{u_j(\tau)} f_{ix}(r-\zeta) \cdot \int_r^{u_j(\tau)} c_{xj} \cdot f_{xj}(t-r) \cdot (u_j(\tau)-t) dt dr. \quad (7)$$

On the other hand, let us suppose that data item x is not in the cache when it is requested, the access time, r, of x is its first broadcast time after issuing the request. Let $max(\tau, \zeta)$ denote the larger value between τ and ζ, A denote a set of broadcast times of x between $max(\tau, \zeta)$ and $u_j(\tau)$, and $v_x(t)$ denotes the previous broadcast times of x at time t. Accordingly, the probability that x is accessed at x's broadcast time, r ($r \in A$), is expressed by the following formula:

$$S_x \cdot \int_{max(\tau,\zeta,v_x(r))}^r f_{ix}(t-\zeta) dt. \quad (8)$$

In this case, the expected increase in response time caused by not caching j is expressed by the following equation:

$$N_{jx} = S_x \cdot \sum_{r \in A} \left\{ \int_{max(\tau,\zeta,v_x(r))}^r f_{ix}(t-\zeta) dt \right. \\ \left. \cdot \int_r^{u_j(\tau)} c_{xj} \cdot f_{xj}(t-r) \cdot (u_j(\tau)-t) dt \right\}. \quad (9)$$

According to the above discussions, if the contents of the cache at the moment when each data item x is requested are known, the expected second response time of j can be calculated by summing E_{jx} or N_{jx} for all data items. However, it is difficult to predict them. Accordingly, in this paper, we take a heuristic approach that calculates the second response times approximately and propose two caching strategies called *TR-NC* (*Two-step RIB-PT, Neglect of Cache*) and *TR-NSI* (*Two-step RIB-PT, Neglect of Second Interval*).

TR-NC Strategy. The TR-NC strategy calculates a second response time by assuming that data item x accessed next is never in the cache. The strategy determines cache replacement at each time slot as follows:

1. When each data item is broadcast, a client calculates RIB-PT values of the broadcast data item, R_i, and data items stored in the cache by using equation (3).
2. The TR-NC value of item i, W_i, is calculated by the following equation:

$$W_i = R_i + \sum_{x=1}^M N_{ix}. \quad (10)$$

3. The data item j with the minimum TR-NC value is selected among all cached data items. If the TR-NC value, W_b, of the broadcast item b is larger than W_j, data item j is replaced with data item b.

When the cache size is small, item x rarely exists in the cache and the TR-NC strategy can estimate the summation of the first and second response times fairly accurately.

TR-NSI Strategy. The TR-NSI strategy assumes that the contents of the cache do not change until x's next broadcast time. In addition, to simplify the calculation of E_{jx}, it assumes that the think-time of x is 0.

In this case, the expected response time of an access request issued after next is expressed not by equation (5) but by $c_{xj}(u_j(\tau)-r)$. Hence, the expected second response times when x is in the cache and not in the cache, E'_{jx} and N'_{jx}, are expressed by the following equations:

$$E'_{jx} = S_x \cdot \int_{\tau}^{u_j(\tau)} f_{ix}(r-\zeta) \cdot c_{xj} \cdot (u_j(\tau) - r) dr, \qquad (11)$$

$$N'_{jx} = S_x \cdot \sum_{r \in A} \left\{ \int_{max(\tau,\zeta,v_x(r))}^{r} f_{ix}(t-\zeta) dt \cdot c_{xj} \cdot (u_j(\tau) - r) \right\}. \qquad (12)$$

More specifically, this strategy determines cache replacement at each time slot as follows:

1. When each data item is broadcast, a client calculates the RIB-PT values, R_i, of the broadcast data item and data items stored in the cache by using equation (3).
2. The TR-NSI value of item i, V_i, is calculated by the following equation:

$$V_i = R_i + \sum_{x \in C} E'_{ix} + \sum_{x \notin C, 1 \le x \le M} N'_{ix}. \qquad (13)$$

3. Data item j with the minimum TR-NSI value is selected among all cached data items. If the TR-NSI value, V_b, of the broadcast data item b is larger than V_j, data item j is replaced with data item b.

The TR-NSI strategy can estimate the summation of the first and second response times fairly accurately when the think-time of the data item accessed next is short and the contents of the cache do not change much until the issue of the next access request.

5 Performance Evaluation

In this section, we evaluate the performances of the proposed strategies with simulation experiments.

It was reported in [6] that 80% of total access requests are issued for only 20% of data items in a real environment. Therefore, we set system parameters as follows. The total number of data items is set to 500, and they are divided into five groups ($G_1, G_2, ..., G_5$), each of which consists of 100 data items. c_{ij}, the strength of correlation between data items i and j, is determined randomly as follows. Correlation exists between i and j with the probability of 10% when $i, j \in G_k$ $(1 \le k \le 5)$ and 40% when $i \in G_k, j \in G_l, (1 \le k, l \le 5, k \ne l)$. In each case, for all pairs of two items i and j, they have the same c_{ij} so that $\sum_{i,j \in G_k} c_{ij} = 0.8$, $\sum_{i \in G_k \cap j \in G_l \cap k \ne l} c_{ij} = 0.2$.

Data items in group G_1 have 16 times higher q_i, the probability that data item i is the top item in a process, than those in the other groups. The probability that a new process is issued by a client at each time slot is set to 0.01, and the probability that a client finishes its process at each time slot is also set to 0.01.

The probability density function of think-time between data items i and j is set to the following equation:

$$f_{ij}(t) = \begin{cases} 30^{-2}(t-m) + 30^{-1} & (m-30 \leq t < m) \\ -30^{-2}(t-m) + 30^{-1} & (m \leq t \leq m+30) \\ 0 & (t < m-30, t > m+30) \end{cases} \quad (14)$$

This equation forms a protuberance connecting $(m-30, 0)$, $(m, 30^{-1})$, and $(m+30, 0)$ in the t-$f_{ij}(t)$. In the evaluation, m, which is the average think-time between i's access and j's request, is determined based on a uniform distribution with the range of $(\mu - 10, \mu + 10)$.

In the experiment, it is assumed that the server cyclically broadcasts the program scheduled by a "random-flat schedule", which allocates each data item once at a random position in the program. The number of data items that the client can cache is fixed to 100. For comparison, we also evaluated the performances of the PT strategy. In the PT strategy, access probability, p_i, was set to q_i.

In the system environment described above, we measured performances of the proposed strategies during $3,000,000$ time slots. In the following, we show the simulation results.

Figure 2 shows average response times of the caching strategies when changing μ, from 50 to 400. From Figure 2, as μ gets larger, the performances of the proposed strategies, RIB-PT, TR-NC, and TR-NSI, which replace the cache by considering both the correlation among data items and the think-time, gets better. This is because when the think-time is long a lot of data items are broadcast during the think-time and there are many occasions to cache effective data items.

When the average think-time is short, the TR-NC and the TR-NSI strategies, which take the second response time into consideration, give better performance than the RIB-PT strategy. Since the time interval between the next access and the access request after next is short, the RIB-PT strategy, which considers only the first response time, cannot sufficiently replace the cache and thus cannot reduce the average response time. Of the other two strategies that consider the second response time, the TR-NSI strategy gives better performance. This is because the contents of the cache do not change much until the next access request as well as the fact that the think-time is nearly 0. That is, the TR-NSI strategy can calculate the second response time fairly accurately.

On the other hand, the TR-NC strategy gives better performance than the TR-NSI strategy when the average think-time is very long. This is because the TR-NSI strategy estimates the second response time longer than the actual one because it assumes that the think-time of the next access is 0 and this error gets larger as the think-time gets longer.

The above results show that the optimal strategy must be chosen among the proposed strategies, i.e., RIB-PT, TR-NC, and TR-NSI, according to the system characteristics and the requirements of computational time or response time.

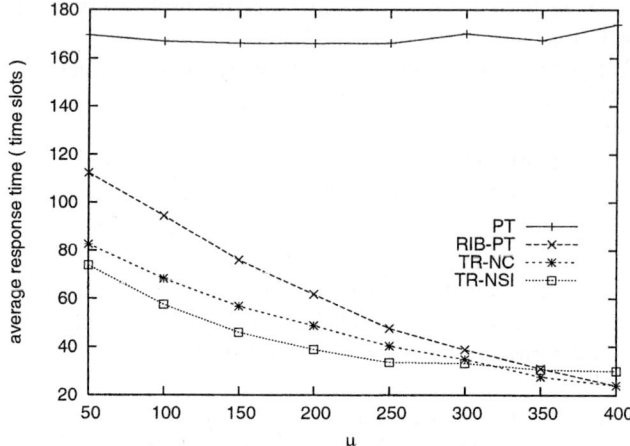

Fig. 2. μ vs. average response time

6   Related Works

There have been many works on prefetching data in various research fields such as databases and hierarchical storages[5, 7]. However, they do not consider push-based broadcast environments which we assume in this paper. In these works, it is assumed that data items are delivered in the one-to-one pull-based manner, i.e., a data item is delivered in response to an access request issued by an entity which wants to prefetch the data item.

Remarkable features of prefetch in push-based broadcast environments which differ much from those in the pull-based environments are listed below:

- Since data items are delivered by means of push-based broadcast, the server has the initiative in data delivery. Thus, if the server determine the broadcast schedule in advance, clients can know accurate broadcast time of each data item in the future.
- Since time remaining until each data item is broadcast next varies temporally, a benefit of prefetching the data item varies dynamically.
- Since access requests are not sent to the server, the cost of prefetch is only the cost of filtering and receiving the data.
- A client cannot prefetch any other data items except for the broadcast data item in each time slot.
- There is enough time to determine the behavior of caching if each data item has large size compared with the broadcast bandwidth, e.g., an image file or a movie file.

The strategies proposed in this paper are specialized for the push-based broadcast environments by considering the above features.

7 Conclusions

In this paper, we proposed caching strategies by assuming a push-based system in which a client accesses correlated data items by issuing consecutive access requests with thinktime. The proposed strategies replace the cache to maximize the total benefit of response time by estimating the response times of access requests issued next and after next.

We also evaluated the proposed strategies by simulation experiments. The simulation results show that the proposed strategies can drastically reduce response time below the levels of the conventional strategies that do not consider the think-time. The performance of each of the proposed strategies depends on system characteristics such as think-time.

We assume an environment where all of access requests are issued consecutively with think-time in this paper. However, it is more general that access requests for some correlated data items are issued simultaneously and those for the others are issued with time interval. We are also considering new caching and scheduling strategies assuming such an environment.

Acknowledgment

This research was supported in part by "The 21st Century Center of Excellence Program", by Special Coordination Funds for Promoting Science and Technology, and by Grant-in-Aid for Scientific Research on Priority Areas (16016260) of the Ministry of Education, Culture, Sports, Science and Technology of Japan.

References

[1] Acharya, S., Alonso, R., Franklin, M., Zdonik, S.: Broadcast Disks: Data Management for Asymmetric Communication Environments. Proc. ACM SIGMOD'95 (1995) 199–210
[2] Acharya, S., Franklin, M., Zdonik, S.: Prefetching from a Broadcast Disk. Proc. Int'l Conf. on Database Engineering (1996) 276–285
[3] Aksoy, D., Franklin, M.: RxW: A Scheduling Approach for Large-Scale On-Demand Data Broadcast. IEEE/ACM Transactions On Networking, Vol. 7, No. 6 (1999) 846–860
[4] Guo, Y., Das, K. D., Pinotti, C. M.: A New Hybrid Broadcast Scheduling Algorithm for Asymmetric Communication Systems: Push and Pull Data Based on Optimal Cut-off Point. Proc. Int'l Workshop on Modeling, Analysis and Simulation of Wireless and Mobile Systems (2001) 123–130
[5] Kraiss, A., Weikum, G.: Integrated Document Caching and Prefetching in Storage Hierarchies Based on Markov-Chain Predictions. VLDB Journal: The Very Large Data Bases, Vol. 7, No. 3 (1998) 141–162
[6] Lin, L., Xingming, Z.: Heuristic Multidisk Scheduling for Data Broadcasting. Proc. Int'l Workshop on Satellite-Based Information Services (1997) 1–5
[7] Palmer, M., Zdonik, S. B.: Fido: A Cache That Learns to Fetch. Proc. 17th Int'l Conf. on Very Large Data Bases (1991) 255–264
[8] Uchida, W., Hara, T., Yajima, E., Nishio, S.: Broadcast Scheduling of Correlated Data Considering Access Frequency in Push-Based Systems. Proc. IASTED Int'l Conf. on Advances in Communications (2001) 150–155
[9] Vaidya, N. H., Hameed, S.: Scheduling Data Broadcast in Asymmetric Communication Environments. ACM-Baltzer Journal of Wireless Networks, Vol. 5, No. 3 (1999) 171–182

[10] Yajima, E., Hara, T., Tsukamoto, M., Nishio, S.: Scheduling Strategies of Correlated Data in Push-Based Systems. Information Systems and Operational Research, Vol. 39, No. 2 (2001) 152-173
[11] Yajima, E., Hara, T., Tsukamoto, M., Nishio, S.: Scheduling and Caching Strategies for Correlated Data in Push-Based Information Systems. ACM Applied Computing Review, Vol. 9, No. 1 (2001) 22–78
[12] Xu, J., Hu, Q., and Lee, D. L.: SAIU: An Efficient Cache Replacement Policy for Wireless On-Demand Broadcasts. Proc. ACM Conference on Information and Knowledge Management (2000) 46–53

XDO2: A Deductive Object-Oriented Query Language for XML

Wei Zhang[1], Tok Wang Ling[1], Zhuo Chen[1], and Gillian Dobbie[2]

[1] School of Computing, National University of Singapore,
Lower Kent Ridge Road, Singapore 119260
{zhangwe2, lingtw, chenzhuo}@comp.nus.edu.sg
[2] Department of Computer Science, University of Auckland,
Private Bag 92019, Auckland, New Zealand
gill@cs.auckland.ac.nz

Abstract. In the past decade, researchers have combined deductive and object-oriented features to produce systems that are powerful and have excellent modeling capabilities. More recently, an XML query language XTree was proposed. Queries written in XTree are more compact, more convenient to write and easier to understand than queries written in XPath. In this paper, we introduce a novel XML query language XDO2 that extends *XTree*, with *deductive* features such as *deductive rules* and *negation*, and *object-oriented* features such as *inheritance* and *methods*. Our XDO2 language is more *compact*, and *convenient* to use than current query languages for XML such as XQuery and XPath because it is based on XTree, supports (recursive) deductive rules and the not-predicate. An XDO2 database example is given to motivate the usefulness of the language. The formal treatment of language syntax and semantics are presented in the appendices.

Keywords: XML query language, deductive rule, not-predicate negation, fixpoint semantics.

1 Introduction

In the past decade, a large number of deductive object-oriented database systems have been proposed, such as F-logic [6], ROL [12] and DO2 [10]. Based on these proposals and other work in the area of object-oriented data models, such as O2 [4] and Orion [7], a large number of deductive and object-oriented features have been investigated. The two most important features are deductive rules and inheritance.

XML is fast emerging as the dominant standard for data representation and exchange on the web. Many query languages have been proposed in the past few years, such as XPath [3], XQuery [1], declarative XML query languages such as [14] and XTree [2]. Although XPath has been widely adopted for XML querying, XTree has been recently proposed as a declarative XML query language which is more compact, more convenient to write and understand than XPath. However, to the best of our knowledge, there is no XML query language that can support deductive rules and object-oriented features in the XML querying community. In this paper, we introduce a novel XML query language XDO2 which extends XTree with deductive database features such as *deductive rules* and *negation*, and object-oriented features such as *inheritance* and *methods*.

In this paper, we present the language XDO2, highlighting its salient features. We present the full syntax and semantics of the language in the appendices.

The major contributions of the XDO2 query language are:

1. Negation is supported in the XDO2 language with semantics similar to the not-predicate [8] instead of the conventional logical negation symbol "∼" which is used in XQuery. A consequence of this decision is that XDO2 is able to support nested negation and negation of sub-trees.
2. Methods that deduce new properties are implemented as deductive rules. XDO2 can use the new properties directly. The presence of recursive deductive rules makes recursive querying possible.
3. Schema querying is made possible with a special term *stru : value* to explicitly distinguish the element name from the element value (or element content). *stru* binds to the element name and *value* binds to the element value. Unlike in XQuery, the name and value pair are bound to the variables together.
4. Inheritance enables a subclass object to inherit all the attributes and subelements from its superclass objects. These inherited properties can be directly used in querying.
5. Features such as the binding of multiple variables in one expression, compact return format and explicit multi-valued variables are supported in the XDO2 language naturally due to the influence of XTree [2].

The rest of this paper is organized as follows. We provide a brief introduction to XTree in section 2. We introduce an XDO2 database example in section 3. Section 4 presents and discusses the most salient features of the XDO2 query language. Section 5 compares our language with related languages. Section 6 summarizes this paper and points out some future research directions. The syntax and semantics of the XDO2 language are presented in the appendices.

2 Background

XTree [2] was recently proposed as an alternative to the XML query language XPath. The main advantages of XTree over XPath are:

1. XPath describes a linear path to the target XML node set. In the querying part of a query, one XPath expression can only bind one variable. However, XTree has a tree structure which is similar to the structure of an XML document. In the querying part of a query, one XTree expression can bind multiple variables.

2. XPath cannot be used to define the return format. However, in the result construction part of a query, one XTree expression can be used to define the result format. This effectively avoids the nested structure in the query.
3. XPath does not express multi-valued variables explicitly. However, in XTree expressions, multi-valued variables are explicitly indicated, and their values are uniquely determined. Some natural built-in functions are defined to manipulate multi-valued variables in an object-oriented fashion.

Thus, although XPath and XTree have the same expressive power (i.e., any query that can be expressed by XTree can also be expressed by several XPath expressions), XTree is more compact and convenient to use than XPath, and queries based on XTree expressions are shorter in length and easier to write and comprehend. In short, XTree takes the XML tree structure into consideration while XPath does not. For more details, please refer to XTree [2].

3 An XDO2 Database Example

In this section, using an example, we demonstrate many of the features of the XDO2 language. We show an XDO2 database, *Person_Company_Employee*, which combines features from XML, deductive databases, and object-oriented databases. Section 3.1 presents the database schema, and explains how to express deductive rules and inheritance in the database. Section 3.2 presents the XML database data, including the extensional data from XML data element facts, intensional data from deductive rules, and the class hierarchy relationships. An XDO2 query with its result is also presented. The syntax and semantics of the XDO2 language are presented in the appendices.

3.1 Schema and Rules

The ORA-SS schema model [9] is used to represent the schema, with extensions to model the deductive and inheritance features in Figure 1. In the schema

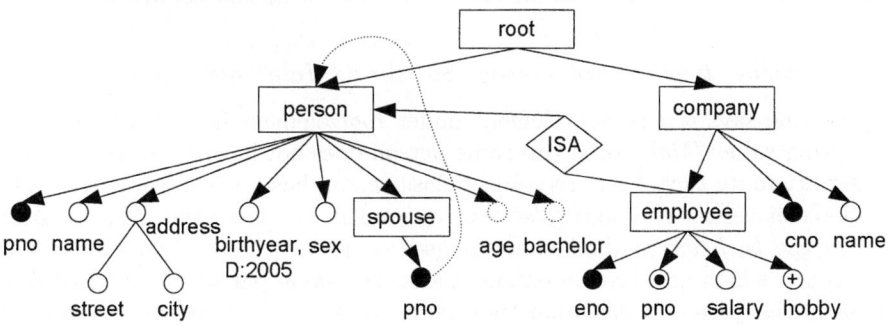

Fig. 1. Person_Company_Employee ORASS schema diagram

diagram, there are four object classes *person*, *company*, *employee* and *spouse* represented as rectangles. In the *person* class, we model the *age* as a derived attribute indicated by dashed circles. This is because *person* has an attribute *birthyear*, and *age* can be derived using *birthyear*. Another derived attribute is *bachelor* which can be derived using the person's *sex* and *spouse*. The identifier of *person* is *pno*. The *employee* class is a subclass of the *person* class, and inherits all the attributes and derived attributes from the *person* class. The inheritance relationship is denoted by the *ISA* diamond in the schema diagram. The identifier of *employee* is *eno*. The candidate identifier *pno* indicated by a filled circle inside a circle in *employee* class is from the *person* object class.

In this example, we can see the two new features that are not present in XML databases: *derived attribute* and *class inheritance*. Class inheritance is supported in XML schema [5]. We now highlight how to define the derived attributes of object classes. In object-oriented programming languages, methods are defined using functions or procedures and are encapsulated in class definitions. In deductive databases, rules are used instead of functions and procedures. By analogy, derived attributes or methods in XDO2 are defined using deductive rules and encapsulated in class definitions.

In the following, we use a deductive rule to define the method *age* encapsulated in object class *person*.

$$\$p/age : \$a :- /root/person : \$p/birthyear : \$b, \$a = 2005 - \$b.$$

This rule says if there is a *person* element under the *root* element, and the *person* has sub-element *birthyear*, then the age is equal to 2004 minus the birthyear. In the method *age* above, the notation ":-" means if a substitution of all variables to values makes the right hand side true, then the left hand side is also true. In the method, there are predicates $\$p/age : \$a$, $/root/person : \$p/birthyear : \$b$, and $\$a = 2004 - \$b$. The notation ":" binds the value of the left hand side to the right hand side. If the left hand side is an object class, then the right hand side binds to the object identifier, such as \$p binds to the person's identifier. Otherwise, it binds to the value of the left hand side. The single-valued variable is denoted by a "\$" followed by a string literal.

The below rule defines the method *bachelor* encapsulated in object class *person*.

$$\$p/bachelor : true :- /root/person : \$p/[sex : "Male", not(spouse : \$s)].$$

This rule says if a *person* element under *root* element has an attribute *sex* with string value *"Male"*, and this same person does not have a *spouse*, then the derived attribute *bachelor* of the object class *person* has boolean value *true*. The two boolean values *true* and *false* are reserved in the language. The notation "[ ]" in the *bachelor* method above is used to group the attributes, elements or methods which are directly defined under the same parent element, such as *person* in this case. The notation "not"[8] negates the predicate expression.

```
<root>
   <person pno="p1">
      <name>John</name>
      <address>
         <street>King</street>
         <city>Ottawa</city>
      </address>
      <birthyear>1975</birthyear>
      <sex>Male</sex>
   </person>
   <person pno="p2">
      <spouse pno="p3" />
      <name>Mike</name>
      <address>
         <street>Albert</street>
         <city>Ottawa</city>
      </address>
      <birthyear>1954</birthyear>
      <sex>Male</sex>
   </person>
   <person pno="p3">
      <spouse pno="p2" />
      <name>Mary</name>
      <address>
         <street>Albert</street>
         <city>Ottawa</city>
      </address>
      <birthyear>1958</birthyear>
      <sex>Female</sex>
   </person>
   <company cno="c1">
      <name>Star</name>
      <employee eno="e1" pno="p1">
         <salary>6000</salary>
         <hobby>Tennis</hobby>
         <hobby>Soccer</hobby>
      </employee>
      <employee eno="e2" pno="p2">
         <salary>4000</salary>
         <hobby>Tennis</hobby>
      </employee>
   </company>
</root>
```

(a) XML extensional database

% Rule R1 defines that the age of a
% person is 2005 minus his/her
% birthyear.

(R1) $p/age : $a :- /root/person : $p/
      birthyear : $b, $a = 2005 - $b.

% Rule R2 defines that a person is a
% bachelor if he is a male and without
% spouse.

(R2) $p/bachelor : true :- /root/
      person : $p/[sex : "Male",
      not(spouse : $s)].

(b) XML intensional database

employee ISA person
by employee.pno ISA person.pno

(c) XML class hierarchy relationships

Fig. 2. Person_Company_Employee database

3.2 Data and Query

The data or instance of the *Person_Company_Employee* database is shown in Figure 2. There are three parts to the database: the *XML extensional database*, the *XML intensional database*, and the *XML class hierarchy relationships*. The XML extensional database contains the XML data element facts with their tree structure. The XML intensional database contains the deductive rules which can be used to derive new XML data elements or attributes from the extensional database. The XML class hierarchy relationships define the object class hierarchy in the database such as *employee* is a subclass of *person*. Multiple inheritances are allowed and we can resolve the multiple inheritance conflicts using the explicit selection technique adopted from [11]. Storing the deductive rules and class hierarchy relationships in the XML database system, enables querying using deductive rules and the class hierarchy, as shown in the following example.

Example 1. This query retrieves the age and salary of all employees who are bachelors, with *age* less than 30, and *salary* larger than 5000.

$/db/youngRichBachelor : \$e/[age : \$a, payroll : \$s] \Leftarrow /root/company/$
$employee : \$e/[age : \$a, bachelor : true, salary : \$s], \$a < 30, \$s > 5000.$

Notice the query format is similar to the deductive rule used to describe methods. The notation "$\Leftarrow$" separates the return format of the query from the query and conditional part. The left hand side is used to define the XML result format, like in the *return* clause in XQuery, and the right hand side is the query and the conditional parts like the *for*, *let* and *where* clauses in XQuery. Therefore, our XDO2 query language is more simple and compact with only one line of some predicate expressions instead of the FLWR clause in XQuery. With the deductive rules and the inheritance feature defined in the XML database, the user can directly query the attributes or methods both in *employee* and its superclass *person*, such as *age* and *bachelor* in the example.

Using the XDO2 database in Figure 2, only employee '*e1*', whose *pno* is '*p1*' satisfies the conditions. The *youngRichBachelor* element and its two subelements *age* and *payroll* form the query result as follows.

```
<db>
   <youngRichBachelor eno="e1">
      <age>29</age>
      <payroll>6000</payroll>
   </youngRichBachelor>
</db>
```

Notice $e binds to the object identifier value of the employee object, i.e., eno value. The attributes of *youngRichBachelor* element, *age* and *payroll* are from the derived attribute *age* of *person* object '*p1*' inherited by '*e1*', and *salary* of *employee* object '*e1*' respectively.

4 XDO2 Language Features

In the example of section 3, we have shown how to use deductive rules to define methods so that the query language can be simplified greatly and made more compact. It also shows the advantages of the inheritance feature. In this section, we will present some other important features of the XDO2 query language. Specifically, they are multi-valued variables and aggregat function, schema querying, negation using the not-predicate [8], and querying using recursive deductive rules.

4.1 Multi-valued Variables

We use the expressions $<\$var>$ and $\{\$var\}$ to represent list-valued variables and set-valued variables respectively. Functions that are defined on lists and sets are consistently expressed in an object-oriented fashion.

Example 2. Consider the following query that returns the titles of the books that have more than one author written in XDO2.
 XDO2 query expression:
 $/result/multiAuthorBook/title : \$t \Leftarrow$
  $/bib/book/[title:\$t, author:<\$a>], <\$a>.count()>1.$

XQuery expression:
$for\ \$book\ in\ /bib/book,\ \$t\ in\ \$book/title$
$let\ \$a\ in\ \$book/author$
$where\ count(\$a) > 1$
$return\ <result><multiAuthorBook>\{\$t\}</multiAuthorBook></result>$

In the XDO2 query, the variable $<\$a>$ is bound to the list of authors for each book, and the variable $\$t$ is bound to the title of the book. The square brackets [ ] enclosing *title* and *author* specifies that these two elements are siblings, and share a common parent.

4.2 Schema Querying

We use the term *stru : value* to explicitly distinguish the element (or attribute) name from the value of the element (or attribute). It provides simple and natural facilities for exploring the structure or schema of the XML data. The user can put the variable such as $v in the left side of the : symbol to bind to the attribute name or element tag. Unlike in XQuery, both the structure and value can be bound to a variable.

Example 3. Consider the following query that finds two sibling element tags with value "King" and "Ottawa" directly or indirectly under person.
 $\Leftarrow /root/person//[\$ele1 : "King", \$ele2 : "Ottawa"].$

In this query, we omit the query result format. The square brackets enclosing $ele1 and $ele2 specifies that these two elements are siblings. The path abbreviation "//" is used to indicate they are directly or indirectly under person. The two variables $ele1 and $ele2 are used to bind the element tags that have the values as specified. Using the data from Figure 2, $ele1 = street and $ele2 = city satisfy the query.

4.3 Negation Querying

In deductive databases, negation makes the rules more powerful and queries more meaningful. However, it complicates the query's interpretation and evaluation. To represent negation in XDO2, we chose the not-predicate [8] instead of the conventional logical negation symbol "$\sim$" to express negation. It has been noted in [8] that the not-predicate is not always equivalent to "$\sim$" in negation expressions. The main difference between the not-predicate and "$\sim$" lies in the interpretation of the uninstantiable variables (i.e. variables that do not appear in any positive expression in the body of the rule or query) in the negation expression. Otherwise, they are equivalent. Using the not-predicate, the uninstantiable variables are existentially quantified while they are universally quantified using "$\sim$". For the justification, please refer to [16].

As we know, XQuery [1] provides a function *not()* which needs a boolean value as its argument and is similar to "$\sim$", and it does not support the not-predicate operator. The function *not()* is usually combined with *some* and *every* quantifiers. However, by using the not-predicate operator alone in XDO2, we can achieve the same expressive power and make our queries more simple and compact. In addition, the function *not()* in XQuery can only be applied to one XPath expression, but not to a sub-tree structure. However since we have tree-structure expressions in the XDO2 language, we can express the sub-tree structures naturally. Two examples are shown as follows.

Example 4. Consider the following query expressed in XDO2 and XQuery that retrieves the company name of companies where each employee of the company has hobby "Tennis".

XDO2 query expression:
$/db/allLikeTennisCom : \$n \Leftarrow /root/company : \$c/name : \$n,$
$\qquad \$c/not(employee/not(hobby : "Tennis")).$

XQuery expression:
for $c in /root/company
where EVERY $e IN $c/employee SATISFIES
$\qquad$ *SOME $h IN $e/hobby SATISFIES string($h)= "Tennis"*
return <db><allLikeTennisCom>{ string($c/name)}
$\qquad\qquad$ *</allLikeTennisCom></db>*

Example 5. Consider the following query that retrieves the companies which do not have employees who have sex "Male" and birthyear 1975.

XDO2 query expression:
$/db/company : \$c \Leftarrow /root/company : \$c/not(employee/$
$[sex : \text{``Male''}, birthyear : 1975])$.
XQuery expression:
for $c in /root/company
where NOT (SOME $e IN $c/employee SATISFIES
($e/sex = "Male" AND $e/birthyear = 1975))
return <db>{$c}</db>

As we can see from the two examples, our XDO2 query using the not-predicate is much more simple and compact compared with the XQuery expression which needs the key word "EVERY", "SOME", "NOT", "IN", "SATISFIES", "AND" to express the same meaning.

4.4 Recursion Querying

In deductive databases, it is natural to define a recursive query using recursive deductive rules. Similarly, in XDO2, we also support recursive deductive rules and make the recursive query possible to extend the expressive power of the XDO2 language.

Example 6. Suppose there are child sub-elements directly under the person element. The following deductive rules define descendants of a person.

(R3) $\$p/descendant : \$c$:- $/root/person : \$p/child : \$c$.
(R4) $\$p/descendant : \$d$:- $/root/person : \$p/child : \$c,$
        $\$c/descendant : \$d.$

The rule R4 says for each person bound to $p, if $c is his/her child, then $c is a descendant of $p. The rule R5 says if $c is a child of $p, and $d is a descendant of $c, then $d is also a descendant of $p. Note the rule R5 is recursively defined. Using the rules defined, we can write a recursive query to retrieve all the descendants of a person with identifier (i.e. pno) value 'p1' as follows,
    $\Leftarrow /root/person : \text{`p1'}/descendant : \$d.$

5 Comparison with Related Work

The success of *F-logic* [6] was due to the clean combination of the object-oriented and deductive paradigms. *Flora-2* [15] extended F-logic for the semantic web. However, the underlying data in F-logic and Flora-2 are objects and can not handle the current popular XML tree data structure. The XDO2 language is designed for the XML tree data while including the deductive and object-oriented features. Many languages, such as *XPath* [3], *XQuery* [1], and *XTree* [2] have been proposed for querying XML documents. However, they can not support (recursive) deductive rules which can be used to derive new properties to simplify the querying as in XDO2. The *XML_RL* [13] for XML is a language with

Table 1. Comparison between XML query languages

	XDO2	XQuery	XTree Query	F-logic	XML_RL
Underlying data	XML tree	XML tree	XML tree	Object	XML tree
Path expression	XTree	XPath	XTree	Path expression	XTree-like expression
Deductive rule	Yes	No	No	Yes	Partial
Recursion	recursive rules	recursive function	recursive query	recursive rule	recursive query
Negation	not-predicate	logical negation	logical negation	logical negation	logical negation
Quantification	No need	Yes	Yes	Yes	Yes
Multi-valued variable	Yes	No	Yes	No	Yes
Direct structure querying	Yes	No	Yes	Yes	Yes
Object-oriented features	Yes	No	No	Yes	No

the deductive features, however this query languages does not support object-oriented inheritance. Furthermore, since XDO2 is based on XTree, where queries are more compact, more convenient to write and understand than XPath queries, the XDO2 inherits these merits. Another major difference between XDO2 and other logical query languages for XML lies in the use of the not-predicate [8] for querying. As section 4.2 shows, the XDO2 query using the not-predicate is much more simple and compact compared with the XQuery expressions.

A summary of the comparison with other XML query languages is shown in table 1.

6 Conclusion

Deductive databases and object-oriented databases are two extensions of the current relational database systems. Guided by this, we propose a novel new XML query language XDO2 with deductive database features such as *deductive rules* and *negation*, and object-oriented features such as *inheritance* and *methods*. Our XDO2 language is more *compact*, and *convenient* to use than current query languages for XML such as XQuery, XPath and XML_RL[13] because it is based on XTree [2], supports (recursive) deductive rules, not-predicate negation and schema querying. An XDO2 database example is presented to motivate the usefulness of the language. In the appendices, we present a formal treatment of the XDO2 language syntax and semantics.

In the future we would like to investigate how to evaluate the queries efficiently, especially for the not-predicate and recursive queries.

References

1. D. Chamberlin, D. Florescu, J. Robie, J. Simon, and M. Stefanescu. XQuery 1.0: A query language for XML, May 2003. http://www.w3.org/TR/xquery.
2. Zhuo Chen, Tok Wang Ling, Mengchi Liu, and Gillian Dobbie. XTree for declarative XML querying. In *Proceedings of DASFAA*, pages 100–112, Korea, 2004.
3. J. Clark and S. DeRose. XML path language(XPath) version 1.0, November 2001. http://www.w3.org/TR/xpath.
4. O. Deux et al. The story of O2. *IEEE Transactions on Knowledge and Data Engineering*, 2(1):91–108, 1990.
5. D.C. Fallside. XML schema part 0: Primer, May 2001. http://www.w3.org/TR/xmlschema-0.
6. M. Kifer, G. Lausen, and J. Wu. Logical foundations of object-oriented and frame-based languages. *Journal of ACM*, 42(4):741–843, 1995.
7. W. Kim. *Introduction to object-oriented databases*. The MIT Press, Cambridge Massachusetts, 1990.
8. Tok Wang Ling. The prolog not-predicate and negation as failure rule. *New Generation Computing*, 8(1):5–31, 1990.
9. Tok Wang Ling, Mong Li Lee, and Gillian Dobbie. *Semistructured Database Design*. Springer, 2005.
10. Tok Wang Ling and W.B.T. Lee. DO2: A deductive object-oriented database system. In *Proceedings of the 9th International Conference on Database and Expert System Applications*, pages 50–59, 1998.
11. Tok Wang Ling and P.K. Teo. Inheritance conflicts in object-oriented systems. In *DEXA*, pages 189–200, 1993.
12. Mengchi Liu. The ROL deductive object base language. In *Proceedings of Database and Expert Systems Application*, pages 189–200, 1993.
13. Mengchi Liu. A logical foundation for XML. In *CAiSE*, pages 568–583, 2002.
14. Mengchi Liu and Tok Wang Ling. Towards declarative XML querying. In *Proceedings of WISE*, pages 127–138, Singapore, 2002.
15. G.Z. Yang, M. Kifer, and C. Zhao. Flora-2: A rule-based knowledge representation and inference infrastructure for the semantic web. In *CoopIS/DOA/ODBASE*, pages 671–688, 2003.
16. Wei Zhang. XDO2: An XML deductive object-oriented query language. Master's thesis, School of Computing, National University of Singapore, 2004.

A XDO2 Language Syntax

Let $\mathbb{U}$ be a set of URLs, $\mathbb{C}$ be a set of constants, and $\mathbb{V}$ be a set of variables. The set of constants $\mathbb{C}$ contain strings enclosed by " ", integers, real numbers, two boolean values and object identifiers enclosed by ' '. The set of variables $\mathbb{V}$ are partitioned into single-valued and multi-valued variables. Single-valued variables have format $S where S is a string literal. Multi-valued variables include set-valued variables with format {$S} and list-valued variables with format <$S> where S is a string literal.

Definition 1. *The* values *are defined as follows,*

1. *null is a* null *value.*
2. *if c∈ℂ then c is a* constant *value.*
3. *a set of object ids is a* set *value.*
4. *a list of constant values is a* list *value.*

Definition 2. *The* terms *are recursively defined as follows,*

1. *Let t be an XML attribute name. Then @t is an* attribute *term.*
2. *Let t be an XML element tag. Then t is an* element *term.*
3. *Let X be an attribute name or a single-valued variable, and Y a constant value, a set value, a single-valued variable or a set-valued variable. Then @X : Y is an* attribute_value *term, and Y denotes the value of the attribute X.*
4. *Let X be an element tag or a single-valued variable, and Y a constant value, a list value, a single-valued variable or a list-valued variable. Then X : Y is an* element_value *term, and Y denotes the value of the element X.*
5. *Let X be a term. Then not(X) is a* negation *term.*
6. *Let $X_1, \ldots, X_n$, ($n \geq 2$) be a set of terms. Then $[X_1, \ldots, X_n]$ is a* grouping *term.*
7. *Let $X_1, \ldots, X_n$, ($n \geq 2$) be a set of terms where $X_1, \ldots, X_{n-1}$ are either element terms or element_value terms. Then $X_1/\ldots/X_n$ is a* path *term.*

Definition 3. *The* expressions *are defined as follows,*

1. *Let $u \in \mathbb{U}$ be a URL and P be a path term. Then (u)/P is an* absolute path *expression.*
2. *Let X be a variable or an object id, and P be a term. Then X/P is a* relative path *expression. An* instantiable relative path *expression is a relative path expression X/P where either X is some object id, or the variable X has been defined in a positive term (i.e. not negation term).*
3. *Arithmetic, logical* expressions *are defined using variables, values, aggregate functions and operators in the usual way.* Instantiable arithmetic, logical *expressions are arithmetic, logical expressions such that all the variables inside have been defined in a positive term.*

Definition 4. *A* deductive rule *has the form $H :\text{-} L_1, \ldots, L_n$. where H is the head and $L_1, \ldots, L_n$ is the body of the rule. H is a positive instantiable relative path expression and $L_1, \ldots, L_n$ are either absolute path expressions or instantiable expressions.*

Definition 5. *A* query *has the form $R \Leftarrow L_1, \ldots, L_n$. where R is the result format expression and $L_1, \ldots, L_n$ are the query or conditional expressions. R is a positive absolute path expression and $L_1, \ldots, L_n$ are either absolute path expressions or instantiable expressions. If there is no result format expression specified, we use $\Leftarrow L_1, \ldots, L_n$.*

B XDO2 Language Semantics

For the language semantics, please refer to [16].

Extending XML with Nonmonotonic Multiple Inheritance

Guoren Wang[1] and Mengchi Liu[2]

[1] College of Information Science and Engineering, Northeastern University, China
[2] School of Computer Science, Carleton University, Canada

Abstract. Schema descriptions of XML documents become more and more complicated and schema documents become longer and longer as the structure of XML documents becomes more and more complex. This is mainly because they cannot take full use of object-oriented modeling abilities. In this paper, we extend XML as follows to solve this problem. (1) We extend DTD's type system to provide richer built-in types. Moreover, a user-defined type can be declared using the *ISA* mechanism in which an existing type is used as the base type and the set of values represented by the derived type is the subset of values represented by the base type. (2) We extend DTD so that element can be global as well as local. (3) We extend DTD with element hierarchy with nonmonotonic inheritance to support super-element sub-element relationship, overriding of elements or attributes inherited from super-elements, blocking of the inheritance of elements or attributes from super-elements, and conflict handling. (4) We extend XML with polymorphism, which is a fundamental feature in object-oriented data models, to support polymorphic elements, typing of references and polymorphic references. Although we extend DTD to support some key object-oriented features, there is not any syntax change of XML documents to fit for our *Extended DTD*.

Keywords: XML, XML schema languages, nonmonotonic inheritance, element hierarchy.

1 Introduction

XML is fast emerging as the dominant standard for data representation and exchange over the Internet. The database community has been paying a lot of attention to XML data management technology with a lot of research results published, such as query languages [1, 2, 3], storage management [4, 5], indexing [6, 7], query processing and optimization [8, 9, 10, 11], and others [12, 13, 14]. However, little research work has been done in the DB community to extend the modeling power of XML schema languages, using the matured object-oriented features, such as multiple inheritance, overriding, blocking, conflict handling, and polymorphism. More than ten XML schema languages have been proposed so far to constrain XML data, such as *DTD* [15], *XML Schema* [16], *SOX* [17], *XDR* [18], *Schematron* [19], *DSD* [20], *relax NG* [21]. Except for *XML Schema* and *SOX*, they do not support inheritance at all. While *XML Schema* is an ongoing effort of W3C to define and represent schemas of XML documents, *SOX* is an alternate schema language for defining structures and partial semantics of XML documents by extending *DTD* in an object-oriented way.

Because *XML Schema* provides the strongest modeling ability in terms of inheritance amongst XML schema languages, we briefly discuss its inheritance mechanisms in the following.

In *XML Schema*, a schema document may contain type definitions, element and attribute declarations. A new type can be derived by extending or restricting the base type which may be either complex or simple. A new simple type can be derived using the *restriction* mechanism and the set of values represented by the new simple type is a subset of values of the base simple type. A new complex type can be derived with the *extension* mechanism by inheriting a complex base type and appending some additional specific element and attribute declarations. Like the simple type restriction, a new complex type can also be derived using the *restriction* mechanism. Restriction of complex types is conceptually the same as restriction of simple types, and a complex type derived by restriction is very similar to a base type, except that its declarations are more limited than the corresponding declarations in the base type. The values represented by the new type are a subset of the values represented by the base type.

In *XML Schema*, there is a *substitution group*, which allows elements to be substitutable for other elements and can be used to simulate the polymorphic feature. Figure 1 declares two new elements *chineseComment* and *englishComment* and makes them substitutable for the *comment* element in the instance document. Although the *substitution* mechanism can be used to simulate the polymorphic feature, it has two shortcomings: (1) for an element hierarchy, the user has to declare an substitution group for each super-element; (2) if a new sub-element is added into the element hierarchy, then the declarations of substitution groups of its super-elements have to be modified.

```
<xsd:element name="chineseComment" type="string"
             substitutionGroup="comment"/>
<xsd:element name="englishComment" type="string"
             substitutionGroup="comment"/>
```

Fig. 1. Element substitution in *XML Schema*

XML Schema provides the *redefine* mechanism that can be used to support evolution and versioning of schemas. Unlike the *include* mechanism which enables users to use external schema components without any modification, the *redefine* mechanism allows users to incorporate external schema components with modifications. Because attribute group definitions and model group definitions may be supersets or subsets of their original definitions, the *redefine* mechanism can be used to simulate overriding and blocking of element inheritance in an element hierarchy, in a two-steps way. For example, for the element hierarchy with *person* and *student*, element *addr* is overridden with a simple type in sub-element *student*. With *XML Schema*, this can be simulated in two steps: (1) A temporary type definition *student* is derived from the base type *person* with the extension mechanism, and has the same element definitions. The derived definition is stored as a temporary schema document *student_tmp.xsd*. (2) The external schema document *student_tmp.xsd* is redefined with necessary modifications, and then the redefined schema is stored as *student.xsd*.

The main shortcoming of the two-steps way is that a temporary external schema document must be generated, because type definitions must use themselves as their base type definition in the *redefine* mechanism.

So far, we have introduced almost all the inheritance facilities in XML Schema. We can get the following conclusions: (1) XML Schema does not support the inheritance of attribute. (2) XML Schema only supports single inheritance, because only one base type is allowed to be in the *extension* construct. Since the multiple inheritance cannot be supported in XML Schema, some concept-level semantics cannot be directly mapped to XML Schema. (3) Polymorphism is not directly supported in XML Schema, it is one of the important features of inheritance. Polymorphism can be indirectly supported by using the *substitution* mechanism. (4) XML Schema does not support overriding and blocking directly. But they can be simulated via the *redefine* mechanism and a superficious external schema document has to be generated.

Nonmonotonic inheritance is a fundamental feature of object-oriented data models [22]. In object-oriented languages with multiple inheritance, a class may inherit attributes and methods from more than one superclass. One of the problems with multiple inheritance is that an ambiguity may arises when an attribute or method is defined in more than one superclass. Therefore, conflict resolution is important in object-oriented database systems with multiple inheritance and most systems use the superclass ordering to solve the conflicts [22].

In this paper, we then extend *DTD* as follows. (1) We extend DTD's type system to provide richer built-in types. Moreover, a user-defined type can be declared using the *ISA* mechanism in which an existing type is used as the base type and the set of values represented by the derived type is the subset of values represented by the base type. (2) We extend DTD so that element can be global as well as local. (3) We extend DTD with element hierarchy with nonmonotonic inheritance to support super-element sub-element relationship, overriding of elements or attributes inherited from super-elements, blocking of the inheritance of elements or attributes from super-elements, and conflict handling. (4) We extend XML with polymorphism, which is a fundamental feature in object-oriented data models, to support polymorphic elements, typing of references and polymorphic references.

The reminder of this paper is organized as follows. Section 2 extends DTD's basic type system including user-defined types. Section 3 extends DTD with inheritance, including element hierarchy, overriding, blocking, multiple inheritance and conflict handling. Section 4 extends DTD with polymorphism, including polymorphic element and polymorphic reference. Finally, Section 5 concludes this paper.

2 Extension of Basic Types

For the convenience of discussion, we first give a sample *Extended DTD* in Figure 2 and an XML instance document in Figure 3. They are used throughout the remainder of this paper. The example shows a typical university application, in which there are seven kinds of elements: *person*, *student*, *teacher*, *TA*, *course*, *underCourse* and *gradCourse*. They construct two element hierarchies, i.e., the *person* hierarchy and the *course* hierarchy. In the former hierarchy, *person* and *TA* are a super-element and a sharing sub-elements of *Student* and *Teacher*, respectively. In the latter hierarchy, *underCourse* and *gradCourse* are sub-elements of *course*.

```
<DOCTYPE univ [                                    <!ELEMENT teacher ISA person (
                                                       workphone, salary, dept, teaches)>
<!TYPE #PROVINCE ENUM {                            <!ATTLIST    teacher tno CDATA>
    Ontario, Alberta, B.C., Manitoba,...}>
<!TYPE #BIRTHDATE ISA                              <!ELEMENT phone (
    #DATE [1984-01-01..]>                              BLOCKED FROM person)>
<!TYPE #SALARY ISA                                 <!ELEMENT workphone (integer)>
    #FLOAT [1000.0..50000.0]>                      <!ELEMENT salary (#SALARY)>
                                                   <!ELEMENT dept of teacher (#PCDATA)>
<!ELEMENT univ (person*, course*)>
                                                   <!ELEMENT TA ISA
<!ELEMENT person (                                     student WITH (dept AS student-dept),
    name, birthdate, addr, homephone)>                 teacher WITH (dept AS teacher-dept)>
<!ATTLIST    person pid ID #REQUIRED>
                                                   <!ELEMENT addr OF TA (
<!ELEMENT name (#PCDATA)>                              BLOCKED FROM student)>
<!ELEMENT birthdate (#BIRTHDATE)>
<!ELEMENT addr (                                   <!ELEMENT course (
    street, city, province, postcode)>                 name, desc, takenBy, taughtBy)>
<!ELEMENT homephone (#INTEGER)>                    <!ATTLIST    course cid ID #REQUIRED>
<!ELEMENT street (#PCDATA)>
<!ELEMENT city (#PCDATA)>                          <!ELEMENT desc (#PCDATA)>
<!ELEMENT province (#PROVINCE)>
<!ELEMENT postcode (#PCDATA)>                      <!ELEMENT takenBy EMPTY>
                                                   <!ATTLIST    takenBy students
<!ELEMENT student ISA person                           IDREFS student >
    (addr, dept, takes)>
<!ATTLIST    student sno CDATA>                    <!ELEMENT taughtBy EMPTY>
                                                   <!ATTLIST    taughtBy teachers
<!ELEMENT addr OF student (#PCDATA)>                   IDREFS teacher >
<!ELEMENT dept OF student (#PCDATA)>
                                                   <!ELEMENT underCourse ISA course () >
<!ELEMENT takes EMPTY>
<!ATTLIST    takes courses IDREFS course>          <!ELEMENT gradCourse ISA course () >

<!ELEMENT teaches EMPTY>                           ]>
<!ATTLIST    teaches courses IDREFS course>
```

Fig. 2. A Sample *Extended DTD*

For element declarations, DTD supports only a basic type #PCDATA. It is obviously insufficient to model data types in the real world. Therefore, in this section we first extend the built-in types of DTD for element declarations based on the built-in types of ODMG [23] and XML Schema [24].

Besides the basic types supported by DTD such as #PCDATA, the *Extended DTD* supports new basic types for element declarations: *#INTEGER*, *#FLOAT*, *#BOOLEAN*, *#DATE*, *#TIME*, and *enum*. Values of these types are defined in the usual way. *Enum* is a type generator, which defines a named type that can take on only the values listed in the declaration. For example, in the part of type definitions of Figure 2, a new user-defined type *PROVINCE* is declared with the *enum* type generator and element *province* in *addr* is declared with the new declared type.

```
<univ>                                          <birthdate> 1976-08-29 </birthdate>
  <person pid="1000">                            <addr>
    <name> Jaonne Barbosa </name>                  <street> 440 Albert </street>
    <birthdate> 1965-04-07 </birthdate>            <city> Ottawa </city>
    <addr>                                         <province> Ontario </state>
      <street> 310 University </street>            <postcode> K1R 6P6 </postcode>
      <city> Ottawa </city>                      </addr>
      <province> Ontario </state>                <homephone> 2915318 </homephone>
      <postcode> K1S 5B6 </postcode>             <workphone> 2502600 </workphone>
    </addr>                                      <student-dept> CS </student-dept>
    <homephone> 5073322 </homephone>             <teacher-dept> SE </teacher-dept>
  </person>                                      <takes courses="CS400" />
                                                 <teaches teaches="CS300" />
  <student pid="2000" sno="S1000">             </TA>
    <name> Jones Gillmann </name>
    <birthdate> 1976-02-25 </birthdate>          <course cid="CS100" >
    <addr> 708D Somerset St </addr>                <name> Introduction to CS </name>
    <homephone> 6185708 </homephone>               <desc> Continuing Education </desc>
    <dept> Computer Science </dept>            </course>
    < takes courses="CS200 CS300" />
  </student>                                     <underCourse cid="CS200" >
                                                   <name> Introduction to DBS </name>
  <teacher pid="3000" tno="I1000">                 <desc> Basic concepts </desc>
    <name> Alley Srivastava </name>                <takenBy students="2000" />
    <birthdate> 1957-06-26 </birthdate>            <taughtBy teachers="3000" />
    <addr>                                       </underCourse>
      <street> 56 Broson </street>               <underCourse cid="CS300" >
      <city> Ottawa </city>                        <name> Introduction to SE </name>
      <province> Ontario </state>                  <desc> Basic concepts </desc>
      <postcode> K2B 6M8 </postcode>               <takenBy students="2000" />
    </addr>                                        <taughtBy teachers="3000 4000" />
    <workphone> 2314343 </workphone>           </underCourse>
    <salary> 1200.00 <salary>
    <dept> Computer Science </dept>              <gradCourse cid="CS400" >
    <teaches courses="CS200 CS300 CS400" />       <name> DBMS </name>
  </teacher>                                       <desc> Impl. Techniques </desc>
                                                   <takenBy students="4000" />
  <TA pid="4000" sno="S2000" tno="I2000">          <taughtBy teachers="3000" />
    <name> Alice Bumbulis </name>              </gradCourse>
                                               </univ>
```

Fig. 3. An XML instance document of the sample Extended DTD

Extension 1. The syntax for enum type declarations is as follows.

'<!TYPE' '#'type-name 'ENUM {' identifier + '}>'

where #*type-name* is the defined new type, *identifier* is a value of type string, + means one or more occurrences. An enum declaration defines a named type that can take on only the values listed in the declaration.

Besides the extended basic types and the *enum* type generator, users can use the ISA mechanism to derive a new simple type in the *Extended DTD*. For example, in the part of type definitions of Figure 2 two new derived types *BIRTHDATE* and *SALARY* are declared with the *ISA* mechanism, and element *birthdate* in *person* and element *salary* in *teacher* are declared with these two new derived types, respectively.

Extension 2. The syntax for a new derived simple type declaration is as follows.

'<!TYPE' '#'type-name 'ISA' '#'base-type-name
lowerBound [minVal] '..' [maxVal] upperBound '>'

where *type-name* is used to specify the name of a user-defined type, *base-type-name* is used to specify the base type from which *type-name* is derived, *lowerBound* may be either '[' or '(' and *upperBound* may be either ']' or ')', '[' and ']' are used to specify *greater than or equal*($\geq$) and *less than or equal*($\leq$) while '(' and ')' are used to specify *greater than*($>$) and *less than*($<$), the clause [$minVal$]

'..' [maxVal] is used to specify the value range of the new derived simple type. The range parameters [minVal] and [maxVal] can be optional to represent a semi-range and their expressions depends on the type of *base-type-name*.

For example, in Figure 4 statement (1) declares an enum type #WEEK, while statement (2) declares a user-defined derived type #WEEKDAY using the *ISA* mechanism. Statement (3) declares a positive integer while statement (4) declares a negative integer.

```
<!TYPE #WEEK ENUM {Sunday, Monday, Tuesday,
    Wednesday, Thursday, Friday, Saturday }>
<!TYPE #WEEKDAY ISA #WEEK [Monday..Friday]>
<!TYPE #POSITIVEINTEGER ISA INTEGER (0..)>
<!TYPE #NEGATIVEINTEGER ISA INTEGER (..0)>
```

Fig. 4. Examples of user-defined types

Compared with the *restriction* mechanism of XML Schema, the *ISA* mechanism for deriving new simple types in our *Extended DTD* has the following advantages.

(1) The *Extended DTD* uses a unified *ISA* mechanism for both derived simple and complex types, while XML Schema adopts two mechanisms, *extension* and *restriction*.
(2) The *Extended DTD* is much more concise than XML Schema. In XML Schema, more than 20 attributes may be set up for a *restriction* declaration, such as *minExclusive*, *minInclusive*, *maxExclusive*, *maxInclusive*, *totalDigits*, *fractionDigits*. These are very complicated for users to remember.

3 Extension of Elements

In this section, we extend *DTD* with element hierarchy with overriding and blocking, which are some fundamental features in OO data models. Then, we extend *DTD* to support three kinds of conflict handling mechanisms. But first, we introduce the concepts of local and global elements.

3.1 Local Element

In DTD, element declarations are global and unique. In other words, we cannot have two element declarations with the same name even the two elements are used in different places with different meanings. For example, we cannot define two name elements: one is for program name and the other is for department name with different domains. This feature greatly limits the modeling power of XML. To solve this problem, we distinguish two kinds of elements: *global elements* and *local elements*. Global elements are defined as in DTD while local elements must have unique names within the elements they appear.

Extension 3. An *element name* is either global or local. A *global* element name is just a name. A *local* element name has the form: name 'OF' name, where the first name is the name of the local element and the second name is the name of the element in which the local element appears.

3.2 Element Hierarchy

Figure 2 shows an example of the *Extended DTD* with two element hierarchies. The definition part for element *person* is similar to *DTD*. The definition part for element *student*, a sub-element of *person*, is declared by using the *ISA* construct to specify the list of its super-elements. The following gives the extension of DTD with super-element declarations.

Extension 4. The syntax for element declaration is as follows.

'<!ELEMENT' global-element-name ['ISA' super-global-element-names-list] '(' element-content-models ')>'

In the *ISA* construct ['ISA' *super-global-element-names-list*] there can be more than one super-element to be inherited. Also, an element may have no super-element declaration because the construct is optional. The syntax of *element-content-models* is the same as in *DTD*. But we focus on the sequence content model in all examples of this paper. In an element hierarchy, a sub-element inherits elements and attributes from its super-elements, and appends additional specific elements and attributes into the content model.

A specific component element or attribute in the sub-element overrides the element or attribute defined in the super-element. Overriding can be used to modify *type*, *optional vs required* and *domain constraint* for attribute inheritance, and *type* and *min & max occurence* for element inheritance. For example, in the sub-element *student* in Figure 2, the component element *addr* is local and overrides the inherited element *addr* with a new simple type. There is no special syntax extension for overriding of element and attribute.

In the definition part for element *teacher* in Figure 2, the inheritance of element *phone* is blocked from the super-element *person*. In addition, three specific elements, *workphone*, *salary* and *dept*, and one specific IDREFS *teaches* referencing to *course* are defined. The following gives the extensions of DTD for blocking the inheritance of elements and attributes.

Extension 5. The syntax for element and attribute inheritance blocking is as follows.

'<!ELEMENT' element-name '(BLOCKED FROM' super-element-names-list ') '>'

'<!ATTLIST' element-name attribute-name 'BLOCKED FROM' super-element-names-list '>'

Note that element or attribute inheritance blocking is specified using the construct *BLOCKED FROM super-element-names-list*. In [22], the return type *none* is used to specify blocking, but the superclass from which the inheritance is blocked is not specified. This way can work well in the case of single inheritance, but not in the case of multiple inheritance with *selectable blocking*, which means that subclass attributes can be blocked from some superclasses. Another advantage of the *selectable blocking* mechanism is that it can be used to resolve conflicts, described in the next subsection.

3.3 Conflict Handling

With multiple inheritance, conflicts may occur. In this subsection, we discuss conflict handling mechanisms. In Figure 2, element *TA* inherits elements and attributes from both super-elements *student* and *teacher*. There are two conflicts to be resolved, since elements *addr* and *dept* are declared on both super-elements *student* and *teacher*. In our *Extended DTD*, three ways can be used to handle conflicts. In the first way, a conflict resolution declaration is specified explicitly to indicate from which super-element an element or attribute is inherited, for example, the construct <*!ELEMENT addr (BLOCKED FROM student)*> indicates that the declaration of *addr* is inherited from the super-element *teacher* rather than from *student*. In the second way, the names of elements or attributes causing conflicts are explicitly re-named in the inheriting element declaration, for example, in the sub-element *TA* declaration, the construct *"student WITH (dept AS student-dept)"* renames element *dept* inherited from element *student* to *student-dept* while the construct *"teacher WITH (dept AS teacher-dept)"* from *teacher* to *teacher-dept*. Finally, if there is a conflict and there is no conflict resolution declaration, then the element or attribute is inherited from the super-element in the order the super-elements are listed in the element declaration in the *ISA* construct. For example, there is a conflict for element *addr*. If there is no explicit conflict resolution declared for it in the declaration of element *TA*, then element *addr* in element *student* would be inherited.

Extension 6. The *ISA* construct with the renaming clause for elements and attributes is as follows.

> 'ISA' { super-element { 'WITH ('old-element-name|old-attribute-name 'AS' new-element-name|new-attribute-name')' }* }+

where *, + mean 0 or more and 1 or more occurrences, respectively.

4 Polymorphism

In object-oriented paradigm, polymorphism is a very useful and important feature, which provides the possibility of manipulating polymorphic collections. Consider three classes *person*, *teacher* and *student*. Class *person* is the common superclass of *teacher* and *student*, and the extents of these three classes are *persons*, *teachers* and *students*, respectively. Therefore, the set *persons* contains objects of classes *person*, *teacher* and *student* due to polymorphism. Thus, the *persons* extent contains three possible classes of the elements in the collection. We think it is necessary to extend XML with the polymorphic feature.

We can simulate a polymorphic element by using *union* and * in any XML schema language. For example, Figure 5 shows a *DTD* for element *persons*, in which a *persons* instance may contain *person* instances, *student* instances, *teacher* instances, and/or *TA* instances. This design has the following disadvantages.

(1) Even though the *union* design is a possible way to simulate polymorphism, it is awkward.
(2) It is not flexible. For example, when a new sub-element is added to an element hierarchy the content models of all the super-elements of the sub-element have to be changed.
(3) Sub-elements cannot inherit elements and attributes and have to redefine them explicitly.

```
<!ELEMENT persons(person|student|teacher|TA)*>
<!ELEMENT person ....>
<!ELEMENT student ....>
<!ELEMENT teacher ....>
<!ELEMENT TA ....>
```

Fig. 5. *DTD* for element *person* to simulate polymorphic elements

4.1 Polymorphic Elements

Consider the examples described before, element *person* has three direct or indirect sub-elements, *student*, *teacher* and *TA*, and element *course* has two direct sub-elements *underCourse* and *gradCourse*. Figure 6 shows an instance document which consists of three element instances of *person* and one element instance of *course*. It is obvious that Figure 6 is a valid instance document of the schema document shown in Figure 2.

However, when polymorphism is introduced into XML, an instance of sub-element can appear in the place where an instance of super-element is expected in an instance document, and the instance document should still be valid. If an element has at least one sub-element, then the element is polymorphic. For example, *person*, *student*, *teacher* and *course* are polymorphic elements in the example. For example, in the instance document shown in Figure 6 the *person* element instances can be substituted with instances of *student*, *teacher*, or *TA*. Similarly, the instance of *course* can be substituted with an instance of *under-Course* and *gradCourse*. The substituting element instances are referred to as *polymorphic instances*. In Figure 2, we can see that element *univ* can contain a number of *person* element instances and a number of *course* element instances, because of <!ELEMENT univ (person*, course*)>. Therefore, element *univ* can

```
<univ>
  <person pid="6000">
    <name> Jaonne Barbosa </name>
    <birthdate> 1965-09-21 </birthdate>
    <addr>
      <street>515 Hast</street> <city> Ottawa </city>
      <province> Ontario </province> <postcode> V6B 5K3 </postcode>
    </addr>
    <homephone> 5073322 </homephone>
  </person>
  <person pid="7000">
    <name> Kaushik Dutta </name>
    <birthdate> 1954-10-25 </birthdate>
    <addr>
      <street> 888 Main </street> <city>Bumaby</city>
      <province> B.C. </province> <postcode> V5A 1S6 </postcode>
    </addr>
    <homephone> 2314021 </homephone>
  </person>
  <person pid="8000">
    <name> Sam Madden </name>
    <birthdate> 1948-07-08 </birthdate>
    <addr>
      <street> 2400 Bell </street> <city> Sumey </city>
      <province> B.C. </province> <postcode> V3T 2W1 </postcode>
    </addr>
    <homephone> 2389504 </homephone>
  </person>
  <course cid="CS900">
    <name> Introduction to Graphics </name>
    <desc> Course for continuing education </desc>
  </course>
</univ>
```

Fig. 6. A valid instance document of the sample extended DTD

contain seven component element instances due to polymorphism: (1) *person* instances; (2) *student* instances; (3) *teacher* instances; (4) *TA* instances; (5) *course* instances; (6) *underCourse* instances; and (7) *gradCourse* instances.

Therefore, it is necessary to incorporate polymorphism in *Extended DTD*.

Extension 7. In an instance document, the instance of an element can be substituted with an instance of its sub-elements. That is, the instance of a sub-element may occur anywhere an instance of its super-element can occur.

4.2 Polymorphic Reference

In this subsection, we extend *DTD* with polymorphic reference, which is similar to polymorphic element. A little bit complicated example for polymorphic reference is that a teacher may teach several courses including *underCourses* and *gradCourses*, see the definition of element *teacher* in Figure 2 and its instance in Figure 3. In the definition of Figure 2, *teaches* is an IDREFS to *course*. If polymorphic references are supported, that is, *teaches* can also be used to reference to either *underCourse* or *gradCourse* elements as they are sub-elements of element *course*, then the following six combinations are valid in the instance document: (1) a teacher teaches courses; (2) a teacher teaches underCourses; (3) a teacher teaches gradCourses; (4) a TA teaches courses; (5) a TA teaches underCourses; and (6) a TA teaches gradCourses.

In DTD, the target element is not specified in the IDREF(s) definitions. So we first extend the definition of IDREF and IDREFS attribute, shown in Extension 8, which specifies the reference points from *elem* to *targetElem*. Then, we introduce the concept of polymorphic reference, as shown in Extension 9.

Extension 8. An IDREF or IDREFS attribute can be constrained to a given kind of element, which is represented by the following syntax.

'<!ATTLIST' element-name attribute-name 'IDREF' '['targetElem']'···'>'
'<!ATTLIST' element-name attribute-name 'IDREFS' '['targetElem']'···'>'

For example, in the *Extended DTD* schema defined in Figure 2 the IDREFS attribute *courses* of *takes* is declared as follows.

<!ATTLIST takes courses IDREFS course #IMPLIED>

where *courses* is allowed to point to just only instances of *course*.

Extension 9. An IDREF(S) attribute pointing to an element can also point to instance(s) of its sub-elements. It is referred to as *polymorphic reference(s)*.

For the above example, *courses* can point to instances of element *course* as well as its sub-elements *underCourse* and *gradCourse*.

5 Conclusions

In this paper, we extend XML with element hierarchy to support the key fundamental object-oriented features such as nonmonotonic inheritance, overriding, blocking, conflict handling, polymophism, and typing references. Although we extend DTD to support those key object-oriented features, we do not require any change to the syntax of XML documents to fit for our *Extended DTD*.

Acknowledgment. Guoren Wang's research was supported by the National Natural Science Foundation of China (Grant No. 60273079 and 60473074), the Foundation for University Key Teacher and the Teaching and Research Award Program for Outstanding Young Teachers in High Education Institution of Chinese Ministry of Education. Mengchi Liu's research is partially supported by National Science and Engineering Research Council of Canada.

References

1. Chamberlin, D., Florescu, D., Robie, J., Siméon, J., Stefanescu: Qxuery: A query language for xml. Internet document. http://www.w3.org/TR/xquery (2001)
2. Chamberlin, D., Robie, J., Florescu, D.: Quilt: An xml query language for heterogeneous data sources. In: Proceedings of Third International Workshop WebDB. (2000) 1–25
3. Fankhauser, P.: Xquery formal semantics: State and challenges. SIGMOD Record **30** (2001) 14–19
4. D.Florescu, Kossmann, D.: A performance evaluation of alternative mapping schemes for storing xml data in a relational database. Technical report(no.3680) (1999)
5. Yoshikawa, M., Amagasa, T., Shimura, T., Uemura, S.: Xrel: A path-based approach to storage and retrieval of xml documents using relational databases. ACM Transactions on Internet Technology **1** (2001) 110–141

6. Chan, C.Y., Garofalakis, M.N., Rastogi, R.: Re-tree: An efficient index structure for regular expressions. In: Proceedings of the 28th International Conference on Very Large Data Bases. (2002)
7. Chung, C., Min, J., Shim, K.: Apex: An adaptive path index for xml data. In: Proceedings of the 2002 ACM International Conference on Management of Data SIGMOD. (2002)
8. Lv, J., Wang, G., Yu, J.X., Yu, G., Lu, H., Sun, B.: Performance evaluation of a dom-based xml database: Storage, indexing and query optimization. (In: Proceedings of the 3rd International Conference On Web-Age Information Management(WAIM2002))
9. McHugh, J., Widom, J.: Query optimization for xml. In: Proceedings of the 25th International Conference on Very Large Data Bases. (1999) 315–326
10. Wang, G., Sun, B., Lv, J., Yu, G.: Rpe query processing and optimization techniques for xml databases. Journal of Computer Science and Technology **19** (2004) 224–237
11. Wang, G., Liu, M.: Query processing and optimization for regular path expressions. In: Proceedings of the 12th International Conference on Advanced Information Systems Engineering (CAiSE2003), Klagenfurt, Austria. Lecture Notes in Computer Science 2681. (2003) 403–406
12. Li, S., Liu, M., Wang, G., Peng, Z.: Capturing semantic hierarchies to perform meaningful integration in html tables. In: Proceedings of the 6th Asia-Pacific Web Conference on Advanced Web Technologies and Applications(APWeb2004), Hangzhou, China. (2004) 899–902
13. Wang, G., Lu, H., Yu, G., Bao, Y.: Managing very large document collections using semantics. Journal of Computer Science and Technology **18** (2003) 403–406
14. Wang, G., Liu, M.: Logical foundation for updating xml. In: Proceedings of the 4th International Conference on Web-Age Information Management (WAIM2003), Chengdu, China. Lecture Notes in Computer Science 2762. (2003) 80–91
15. Bray, T., Paoli, J., Sperberg-McQueen, C.M., Maler(ed.), E.: Extensible markup language (xml) 1.0 (second edition). internet document. http://www.w3.org/TR/REC-xml (2000)
16. Fallside(ed.), D.: Xml schema part 0: Primer. Internet document. http://www.w3.org/TR/xmlschema-0/ (2001)
17. Davidson, A., Fuchs, M., Hedin, M.: Schema for object-oriented xml 2.0. Internet document. http://www.w3.org/TR/NOTE-SOX (1999)
18. Microsoft: Xml schema developer's guide. Internet document. http://msdn.microsoft.com/xml/XMLGuide/schema-overview.asp (2000)
19. Jelliffe, R.: Schematron. Internet document. http://www.ascc.net/xml/resource/schematron/ (2000)
20. Klarlund, N., Møller, A., Schwartzbach, M.I.: The dsd schema language. Automated Software Engineering **9** (2002) 285–319
21. Clark, J.: Relax ng compact syntax. Internet document. http://www.oasis-open.org/committees/relax-ng/compact-20021121.html(2002)
22. Liu, M., Dobbie, G., , Ling, T.: A logical foundation for deductive object-oriented databases. ACM Transaction on Database Systems **27** (2002) 117–151
23. Cattell, R., Barry, D., Berler, M., Eastman, J., Jordan, D., Russel, C., Schadow, O., Stanienda, T., Velez, F.: The Object Data Standard: ODMG 3.0. Morgan Kaufmann Publishers (2000)
24. Biron, P., Malhotra(ed.), A.: Xml schema part 2: Datatypes. Internet document. http://www.w3.org/TR/2001/REC-xmlschema-2-20010502/ (2001)

Database Design with Equality-Generating Dependencies

Junhu Wang

School of Information Technology,
Griffith University, Gold Coast, Australia
J.Wang@griffith.edu.au

Abstract. In relational database systems, traditional normalization techniques (eg, BCNF, 4NF) remove data redundancies from a single relation, but can not detect and remove redundancies across multiple relations. However, redundancies among multiple relations are abundant especially in integrated databases. In this paper, we first propose to detect such data redundancies using equality-generating dependencies (EGDs) and propose an extended normal form (ENF) of relational database schema with respect to EGDs. We show that a database has no potential data redundancies with respect to EGDs if and only if the schema is in ENF. For a common special class of EGDs, we provide a set of sound and complete inference rules. A normalization process is presented to losslessly transform a relational database schema to one in ENF. We then extend our EGDs and ENF to XML data, and show how similar data redundancy problems can be detected for data-centric XML documents.

Keywords: database design, relations, functional dependency, equality-generating dependency, data redundancy, normal form, normalization, XML tree.

1 Introduction

One of the primary goals of relational database design is to generate a set of relation schemas that allow us to store data without unnecessary redundancy. Data redundancies are usually caused by *dependencies* among data such as functional dependencies (FDs) and multi-valued dependencies. To prevent these data redundancies we usually require the relation to be put in some *normal form (NF)* such as BCNF and 4NF. *Normalization* is the technique that is used to transform arbitrary relation schemas to those in normal form. However, traditional normal forms are designed for a single relation schema rather than the entire database, therefore traditional normalization techniques can only remove (or reduce) data redundancies in a single relation, but not *across multiple relations*. As an example, suppose we have a university database that contains the relations

Student(sNo, sName, address)
UMember(mNo, mName, phone)

which represent students and union members, where *sNo* and *mNo* represent student number and union member number respectively, *sName* and *mName* represent student name and member name respectively. Assuming union members include both staff and students, and if a student is a union member then his/her student number is used as his/her member number. Although both relations are in BCNF, there are data redundancies across the two relations if the student information in the two relations overlap.

The data redundancies in the above example are caused by *equality-generating dependencies (EGDs)*[FV84][1]. Based on this observation, we propose a normal form (named ENF) of relational database schema, with respect to EGDs, and show ENF is necessary and sufficient to prevent potential data redundancies caused by EGDs. For a very common special case, we provide a sound and complete set of inference rules, and propose a normalization process that can be used to losslessly transform a relational database schema to one in ENF.

Native XML database, which stores data in the form of XML documents, has gained popularity in recent years. Like traditional databases, dependencies among data naturally exist in XML and these dependencies may cause data redundancies in poorly designed documents. We will define *equality-generating dependencies for XML (XEGDs)*, and propose a normal form, XENF, that prevents redundancies caused by XEGDs.

To our knowledge, little research has been done on the removal of data redundancies across multiple relations in relational databases. The only works we are aware of are [LG92] and [MR86], both of which use *inclusion dependencies*. As for XML data, we are not aware of any previous work on EGDs, although FDs have been studied by several groups of researchers, eg, [AL04], and [VLL04].

The rest of the paper is organized as follows. Section 2 provides preliminary definitions. Section 3 discusses inference rules for EGDs. Section 4 defines our new normal form (ENF) with respect to EGDs and show that ENF is necessary and sufficient to prevent potential data redundancies. Section 5 presents the normalization process. Section 6 extends our EGDs and ENF to XML data. Section 7 concludes the paper with a brief discussion of further research.

2 Preliminaries

A relation schema consists of a relation name and a list of *distinct* attributes. If R is the relation name, and $X = (x_1, x_2, \ldots, x_n)$ is the list of attributes, then the relation schema is denoted $R(x_1, x_2, \ldots, x_n)$, $R(X)$ or simply R. Often the list of attributes in R needs to be treated as a set, so that the set union, difference and intersection can apply. The *domain* of attribute x_i, denoted $dom(x_i)$, is a set (finite or infinite) of values that x_i can take. If $X = (x_1, x_2, \ldots, x_n)$ is a list of attributes, we will use $dom(X)$ to denote the set $dom(x_1) \times dom(x_2) \times \cdots \times dom(x_n)$. Following conventions in database literature, the union (concatenation) of two sets (lists) of attributes X and Y will be denoted XY. A relation instance r

---

[1] Our EGDs are not limited to a universal relation schema as the EGDs in [FV84].

of schema $R(x_1, x_2, \ldots, x_n)$ is a subset of $dom(x_1) \times dom(x_2) \times \cdots \times dom(x_n)$. Every element t in the subset r is called a *tuple* in r. If r is an instance of R, and X is a list (or subset) of the attributes in R, we will use $r[X]$ to denote the projection of r to X. Similarly if t is a tuple in r, then $t[X]$ will denote the projection of tuple t to X.

A database schema D is a set of relation schemas, and a database instance consists of a set of relation instances, one for each of the relation schemas in D.

General EGDs are special constraint-generating dependencies [BCW99] where the RHS is a conjunction of equalities. In this paper, we focus on EGDs involving up to two relations only. But the extension to multiple relations is straightforward.

Definition 1. *An* equality-generating dependency (EGD) *is an expression of the form*
$$R_1.X_1 = R_2.X_2 \rightarrow R_1.Y_1 = R_2.Y_2$$
where R_1, R_2 are relation schemas, X_i, Y_i are lists of attributes in R_i ($i = 1, 2$), $dom(X_1) \cap dom(X_2) \neq \emptyset$, and $dom(Y_1) \cap dom(Y_2) \neq \emptyset$.

A database instance containing the relation instances r_1 of R_1 and r_2 of R_2 is said to satisfy the EGD if $\forall t_1 \in r_1, t_2 \in r_2$, whenever $t_1[X_1] = t_2[X_2]$, we have $t_1[Y_1] = t_2[Y_2]$.

Example 1. In the student and union member example introduced in Section 1, we can claim there is an EGD

$Student.sNo = UMember.mNo \rightarrow Student.sName = UMember.mName$

Due to the above EGD, if there are union members who are also students, there will be redundancies across the two relations, although no redundancies exist in either relation.

In the above example, *sNo* and *mNum* happen to be keys of the two relations respectively. But in general, this may not be the case. Also, an attribute may appear more than once in an attribute list.

Example 2. Suppose we have two relations $R_1(x_1, x_2, x_3)$ and $R_2(y_1, y_2, y_3, y_4)$. Let the instances r_1 of R_1 and r_2 of R_2 be as follows:

	x_1	x_2	x_3		y_1	y_2	y_3	y_4
$r_1:$	1	1	2	$r_2:$	2	1	2	2
	1	2	2		2	3	3	0
	3	2	0		1	1	2	2

Then the following EGDs are satisfied by r_1 and r_2.

$R_1.x_2 = R_2.y_2 \rightarrow R_1.x_3 = R_2.y_3$
$R_1.x_1 = R_1.x_2 \rightarrow R_1.x_3 = R_1.x_3$
$R_2.y_1 = R_2.y_2 \rightarrow R_2.y_3 = R_2.y_4$
$R_1.x_1x_1 = R_2.y_1y_2 \rightarrow R_1.x_3x_3 = R_2.y_3y_4$

The last EGD above is often written as

$$R_1.x_1 = R_2.y_1 \wedge R_1.x_1 = R_2.y_2 \rightarrow R_1.x_3 = R_2.y_3 \wedge R_1.x_3 = R_2.y_4.$$

Note that the FD $R_1 : x_2 \rightarrow x_3$ (refer to the first EGD) does not hold.

FDs can be regarded as special EGDs where $R_1 = R_2$, $X_1 = X_2$ and $Y_1 = Y_2$.

As seen in Example 1, EGDs can cause data redundancies across relations. To counter the effects of these EGDs we need another type of constraints, called *exclusion constraints*, as defined below.

Definition 2. *Let $R_1(U)$ and $R_2(V)$ be relation schemas, $X_1 \subseteq U$ and $X_2 \subseteq V$, and $dom(X_1) \cap dom(X_2) \neq \emptyset$. An* exclusion constraint (EC) *is an expression*

$$R_1[X_1] \cap R_2[X_2] = \emptyset.$$

A database instance containing the relation instances r_1 of R_1 and r_2 of R_2 is said to satisfy *the exclusion constraint if $r_1[X_1] \cap r_2[X_2] = \emptyset$.*

3 Trivial EGDs, Closure Set, and Inference Rules

3.1 Trivial EGDs

Like FDs, an EGD can be *trivial*, that is, it is satisfied by all possible instances of R_1 and R_2. For example, every trivial FD is also a trivial EGD. The EGDs $R_1.x_1x_2 = R_2.y_1y_2 \rightarrow R_1.x_1 = R_2.y_1$ and $R_1.x_1x_2x_2 = R_2.y_1y_1y_2 \rightarrow R_1.x_1 = R_2.y_2$ are also trivial.

Generally, let λ be the EGD $R_1.X_1 = R_2.X_2 \rightarrow R_1.Y_1 = R_2.Y_2$, where $X_1 = (x_1, \ldots, x_k)$, $X_2 = (x'_1, \ldots, x'_k)$, $Y_1 = (y_1, \ldots, y_m)$, $Y_2 = (y'_1, \ldots, y'_m)$. Let

$C_1(lhs(\lambda)) = \bigwedge_{i \in [1,k]} (t.x_i = t'.x'_i),$
$C_1(rhs(\lambda)) = \bigwedge_{i \in [1,m]} (t.y_i = t'.y'_i),$
$C_2(lhs(\lambda)) = \bigwedge_{i \in [1,k]} (t.x_i = t.x'_i),$
$C_2(rhs(\lambda)) = \bigwedge_{i \in [1,m]} (t.y_i = t.y'_i).$

Treating the symbols $t.x_i$ ($t.x'_i$, $t'.y'_i$ etc) as variables from $dom(x_i)$ ($dom(x'_i)$, $dom(y'_i)$ etc), and the above conjunctions of equalities as symbolic constraints, we can identify trivial EGDs involving R_1 and R_2 (note R_1 and R_2 may be the same relation schema) using the following result.

Proposition 1. *If $R_1 \neq R_2$, then λ is trivial iff $C_1(lhs(\lambda)) \models C_1(rhs(\lambda))$. If $R_1 = R_2$, then λ is trivial iff $C_1(lhs(\lambda)) \models C_1(rhs(\lambda))$ and $C_2(lhs(\lambda)) \models C_2(rhs(\lambda))$.*

Trivial EGDs are of no use in schema design because they put no restrictions on the data.

3.2 Closure Set and Inference Rules

Given a database schema D and a set E of EGDs that hold over D, there may be other EGDs that are logically implied by E. For example, the EGD $R_1.x = R_2.x \rightarrow R_1.z = R_2.z$ is logically implied by $R_1.x = R_2.x \rightarrow R_1.y = R_2.y$ and $R_1.y = R_2.y \rightarrow R_1.z = R_2.z$. We will use $(D, E)^+$ to denote the set of all EGDs over D that are logically implied by E, and call it the *closure set* of E.

In [WTM01] we have shown that for a set of *constrained-tuple generating dependencies* (CTGD) Σ to logically imply another CTGD λ, there must be relevance mappings from the left hand side (LHS) of the CTGDs in Σ to the LHS of λ. As EGDs are special CTGDs, we can easily prove the following theorem using the above result.

Theorem 1. *Let D be a database schema containing relation schemas R_1 and R_2. Let E be a set of EGDs over D. If $R_1.X_1 = R_2.X_2 \rightarrow R_1.Y_1 = R_2.Y_2$ is logically implied by the EGDs in E, then it is also logically implied by the subset of EGDs in E which involve only R_1 or R_2 or both.*

Because of the above theorem, to find $(D, E)^+$ we can group the EGDs by the relation schemas they involve, and compute the closure sets group by group.

If $R_1 \neq R_2$, we can show that FDs over R_1 or R_2 contribute nothing towards the implication of $R_1.X_1 = R_2.X_2 \rightarrow R_1.Y_1 = R_2.Y_2$. Hence to compute the closure set of a set $E_{1,2}$ of EGDs involving R_1 and/or R_2 only, we can divide $E_{1,2}$ to disjoint sets F_1, F_2 and $E'_{1,2}$ (where F_i is the set of FDs over R_i ($i = 1, 2$), $E'_{1,2} = E_{1,2} - (F_1 \cup F_2)$), and compute the closure sets of F_1, F_2 and $E'_{1,2}$ separately. In the common special case where $R_1 \neq R_2$ and every EGD in $E'_{1,2}$ involves *both* R_1 and R_2, the closure set of $E'_{1,2}$ can be found by repeatedly applying the following inference rules.

R1 Let λ be $R_1.X_1 = R_2.X_2 \rightarrow R_1.Y_1 = R_2.Y_2$. If $C_1(lhs(\lambda)) \models C_1(rhs(\lambda))$, then λ trivially holds.

R2 If $R_1.X_1 = R_2.X_2 \rightarrow R_1.Y_1 = R_2.Y_2$, and $R_1.Y_1 = R_2.Y_2 \rightarrow R_1.Z_1 = R_2.Z_2$, then $R_1.X_1 = R_2.X_2 \rightarrow R_1.Z_1 = R_2.Z_2$.

R3 If $R_1.X_1 = R_2.X_2 \rightarrow R_1.Y_1 = R_2.Y_2$, and $R_1.X'_1 = R_2.X'_2 \rightarrow R_1.Y'_1 = R_2.Y'_2$, then $R_1.X_1X'_1 = R_2.X_2X'_2 \rightarrow R_1.Y_1Y'_1 = R_2.Y_2Y'_2$.

Using methods similar to the proof of completeness of Armstrong's inference rules [Mai83] for FDs, we can prove the following completeness result.

Theorem 2. *Suppose $R_1 \neq R_2$, and $E_{1,2}$ is a set of EGDs involving both R_1 and R_2. Then every EGD in the closure set of $E_{1,2}$ can be found by repeatedly applying the inference rules R1 – R3.*

4 Normal Form with Respect to EGDs

Before defining the normal form ENF with respect to EGDs, let us first recall BCNF, which is defined with respect to FDs. A relation schema is said to be in BCNF with respect to a set of FDs if the LHS of every non-trivial FD is a superkey. Since there can never be two distinct tuples agreeing on the superkey, what the above requirement of BCNF says is that there can never be two distinct tuples that agree on the LHS of any non-trivial FD.

ENF can be defined along the same line. The following definition of ENF is a direct extension of BCNF.

Definition 3. *A relational database schema D is said to be in* extended normal form (ENF) *with respect to a given set E of EGDs, if for every non-trivial EGD*

$$R_1.X_1 = R_2.X_2 \to R_1.Y_1 = R_2.Y_2$$

in $(D, E)^+$,

- *if $R_1 = R_2$, $X_1 = X_2$ and $Y_1 = Y_2$, then X_1 is a superkey of R_1;*
- *otherwise, there is a corresponding* exclusion constraint $R_1[X_1] \cap R_2[X_2] = \emptyset$ *over D.*

We now briefly discuss about the above definition. For the EGD in the definition, if $R_1 = R_2$, $X_1 = X_2$ and $Y_1 = Y_2$, it becomes a FD $R_1 : X_1 \to Y_1$. By requiring X_1 to be a superkey of R_1 we are demanding that R_1 be in BCNF with respect to the FD. Therefore, the first condition in our normal form is equivalent to say that all relation schema is in BCNF with respect to the FDs in $(D, E)^+$. If $R_1 \neq R_2$, or $X_1 \neq X_2$, or $Y_1 \neq Y_2$, then the EGD is not a FD, and the second condition in our normal form requires that instances of R_1 and R_2 must not overlap on the X_1 (X_2) attributes. In effect, in both cases we require that there are no distinct tuples $t_1 \in r_1$ and $t_2 \in r_2$, where r_1 and r_2 are instances of R_1 and R_2 respectively, such that $t_1[X_1] = t_2[X_2]$. In addition, if $R_1 = R_2$, but $X_1 \neq X_2$, we also require that $t[X_1] \neq t[X_2]$ for every tuple t; if $R_1 = R_2, X_1 = X_2$ but $Y_1 \neq Y_2$, we also require every instance of R_1 is empty.

For instance, the database schema in Example 1 is in ENF with respect to the given EGD if and only if $Student[sNo] \cap UMemembr[mNo] = \emptyset$ holds. That is, there are no students who are also union members.

The purpose of normal forms is to ensure all database instances are redundancy-free. For instance, it has been shown in [Vin99] that BCNF is necessary and sufficient for ensuring there is no instance of the relation which can have data redundancies with respect to FDs. Here we provide a similar result about ENF. Before that, we need to define redundancy first.

Definition 4. *Let D be a database schema and E be a set of EGDs over D. Let d be an instance of D which satisfies E. We say that there is a* value redundancy *in d if there is a tuple t in d and an attribute x, such that the value $t[x]$, if removed from t, can be recovered using E and other values in d.*

The next theorem says that ENF is a necessary and sufficient condition to ensure there are no value redundancies for every instance of D which satisfies E.

Theorem 3. *Let D be a database schema and E be a set of EGDs over D. There exists an instance of D satisfying E, which has value redundancies if and only if D is not in ENF with respect to E.*

5 Normalization

In this section, we discuss the normalization process that can be used to losslessly transform a database schema to ENF with respect to a set of EGDs. Here "lossless" means that there is a one-to-one mapping from instances of the original schema to instances of the new schema [AHV95]. Due to space limit, we will only describe the process informally for a common special case, namely the special case where the EGDs involve two *different* relation schemas $R_1(U)$ and $R_2(V)$, and the lists of attributes in the non-trivial EGDs contain *distinct* attributes.

Basically, if there is a non-trivial EGD

$$R_1.X_1 = R_2.X_2 \to R_1.Y_1 = R_2.Y_2$$

(where, $R_1 \neq R_2$, $X_1 \cap Y_1 = \emptyset$, $X_2 \cap Y_2 = \emptyset$, and every attribute occurs only once in each of the lists X_1, Y_1, X_2 and Y_2) which violates ENF, then we will replace $R_2(V)$ with $R_2'(V)$ and $R_{2,2}(X_2 Z_2)$, where $Z_2 = V - X_2 Y_2$. We also add the constraints $R_1[X_1] \cap R_2'[X_2] = \emptyset$ and $R_2'[X_2] \cap R_{2,2}[X_2] = \emptyset$.

Given instances r_1 and r_2 of R_1 and R_2 respectively, we compute instances $r_{2,2}$, r_2' of $R_{2,2}$, R_2' as follows:

$r_{2,2} = \Pi_{X_2 Z_2}((r_1[X_1 Y_1] \cap r_2[X_2 Y_2]) \bowtie_{X_1 = X_2} r_2)$,

$r_2' = r_2 - \Pi_{X_1 Y_1 Z_2}(r_1 \bowtie_{X_1 = X_2} r_{2,2})$.

One can verify that the new instances r_1, r_2' and $r_{2,2}$ satisfy the ECs mentioned above, and the original instance r_2 can be recovered from the new instances using $r_2 = r_2' \cup \Pi_{X_1 Y_1 Z_2}(r_1 \bowtie_{X_1 = X_2} r_{2,2})$.

For example, the relation schemas *Student(sNo, sName, address)* and *UMember(mNo, mName, phone)* in Example 1, if not in ENF, can be decomposed to *Student(sNo, sname, address)*, *nonstudentMember(mNo, mname, phone)*, and *StudentMember(sNo, phone)*.

If database schema D is not in ENF with respect to a set E of EGDs over D, we can transform the schema with respect to the non-trivial EGDs in $(D, E)^+$ which violates ENF one by one. However, we should note that some EGDs or ECs involving an original relation schema may be "inherited" by the new relation schemas. Therefore, after each step of decomposition, we should compute the new sets of EGDs and ECs.

We call the above schema transformation process a *specialization* process because instances of R_2 are horizontally split to two disjoint relations. A different specialization process and a generalization process for normalization are described in [Wan04].

6 EGDs for XML Data

In this section, we will define EGDs for XML data (called XEGDs), and propose a corresponding normal form XENF of XML scheme files with respect to these constraints.

342   J. Wang

Let $\mathbf{E_1}$ and $\mathbf{E_2}$ be disjoint sets of element names, $\mathbf{A}$ be a set of attribute names, $\mathbf{E} = \mathbf{E_1} \cup \mathbf{E_2}$, and $\mathbf{E}$ and $\mathbf{A}$ be disjoint. Element names and attribute names are called *labels*.

6.1   XML Trees, XML Scheme Files, and Paths

Every XML document can be represented as a labelled tree, referred to as an *XML tree*. Formally, we define an XML tree as follows.

Definition 5. *An XML tree is defined to be $T = (V, lab, ele, att, val, root)$, where (1) V is a set of nodes; (2) lab is a mapping from V to $\mathbf{E} \cup \mathbf{A}$ which assigns a label to each node in V; a node $v \in V$ is called a* complex element (node) *if $lab(v) \in \mathbf{E_1}$, a* simple element (node) *if $lab(v) \in \mathbf{E_2}$, and an* attribute (node) *if $lab(v) \in \mathbf{A}$. (3) ele and att are functions from the set of complex elements in V: for every $v \in V$, if $lab(v) \in \mathbf{E_1}$ then $ele(v)$ is a set of element nodes, and $att(v)$ is a set of attribute nodes with distinct labels; (4) val is a function that assigns a value to each attribute or simple element. (5) root is the unique root node labelled with complex element name r. (6) If $v' \in ele(v) \cup att(v)$, then we call v' a* child *of v. The parent-child relationships defined by ele and att form a tree rooted at root.*

The right side of Figure 1 shows an example XML tree that represents school students and union members in a university. In the tree, attribute names are indicated by @, simple element names are indicated by $, and string values are quoted.

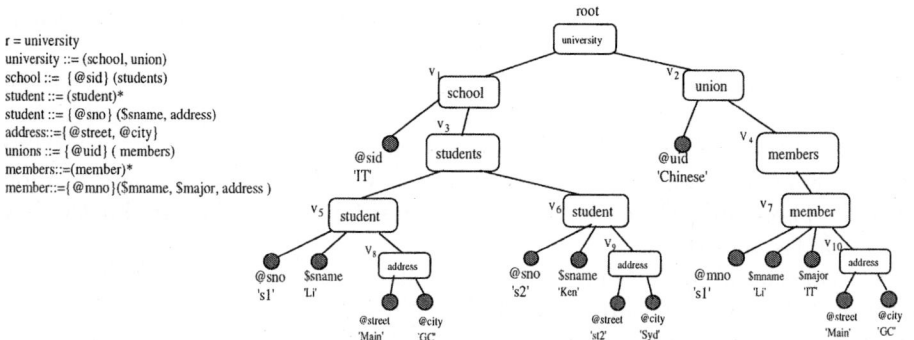

Fig. 1. The Uni-School-Union example

As well known, DTDs or XML Schema files (we call them XML scheme files) can be used to restrict the structure of the XML documents, so they play similar roles to the relational database schema. The W3C DTD and XML Schema are rather complicated languages. Therefore, rather than sticking to either of them, we will define an abstract XML scheme file similar to the DTD in [AL04].

Definition 6. *An (XML) scheme file is defined to be* $\mathcal{S} = (E_1, E_2, A, P, R, r)$ *where* $E_1 \subseteq \mathbf{E_1}$ *is a finite set of complex element names;* $E_2 \subseteq \mathbf{E_2}$ *is a finite set of simple element names;* $A \subseteq \mathbf{A}$ *is a finite set of attribute names;* P *is a mapping from* E_1 *to element type definitions:* $\forall \tau \in E_1$, $P(\tau)$ *is a regular expression*

$$\alpha = \varepsilon \mid \tau' \mid \alpha|\alpha \mid \alpha, \alpha \mid \alpha^*$$

where ε *is the empty sequence,* $\tau' \in E_1 \cup E_2$, *and* "$|$", "$,$", *and* "$*$" *denote union, concatenation, and the Kleene closure respectively;* R *is a mapping from* E_1 *to sets of attributes; for* $\tau \in E_1$, *either* $P(\tau)$ *is not* ε *or* $R(\tau)$ *is not* $\emptyset$; $r \in E_1$ *is the element name of the root, which is the only label in* E_1 *that does not appear in the alphabet of* $P(\tau)$ *for any* $\tau \in E_1$.

The upper left corner of Figure 1 shows an example XML scheme file.

An XML scheme file restricts the structure of conforming XML documents, where *conformity* is defined as below.

Definition 7. *An XML tree* $T = (V, lab, ele, att, val, root)$ *is said to* conform *to scheme file* $\mathcal{S} = (E_1, E_2, A, P, R, r)$ *if*

1 *$lab(root) = r$,*
2 *lab maps every node in V to $E_1 \cup E_2 \cup A$,*
3 *for every complex element node $v \in V$, if $ele(v) = \{v_1, \ldots, v_k\}$, then a permutation of the sequence of labels $lab(v_1) \cdots lab(v_k)$ (regarded as a string) must be in the language defined by $P(lab(v))$; if $att(v) = \{v'_1, \ldots, v'_m\}$ then the labels $lab(v'_1), \ldots, lab(v'_m)$ must be in the set $R(lab(v))$.*

For example, the XML tree in Figure 1 conforms to the scheme file in the same figure.

Next we need to define paths in a scheme file and in an XML tree.

A *path* in scheme file $\mathcal{S}$ is a string $l_1.\cdots.l_m$, where $l_i \in E_1 \cup E_2 \cup A$ for $i \in [1, m]$, l_j is in the alphabet of $P(l_{j-1})$ for $j \in [2, m-1]$, and l_m is in the alphabet of $P(l_{m-1})$ or in $R(l_{m-1})$. A path that starts from a label in $P(r)$ is called an *absolute path*. The set of all paths (absolute paths, resp.) in $\mathcal{S}$ is denoted $paths(\mathcal{S})$ ($AP(\mathcal{S})$, resp.).

A *path instance* in an XML tree T is a dot-separated sequence of nodes $v_1.\cdots.v_k$ such that v_i is a child node of v_{i-1} for $i \in [2, k]$. If $v_1.\cdots.v_k$ is a path instance in T, then $lab(v_1).\cdots.lab(v_k)$ will be called a *path* in T, and we say $v_1.\cdots.v_k$ is an *instance* of the path $lab(v_1).\cdots.lab(v_k)$. The set of all paths in T is denoted $paths(T)$, and the set of all paths in $paths(T)$ which start from the label of a child of *root* is denoted $AP(T)$. Clearly, if T conforms to a scheme file $\mathcal{S}$, then $paths(T) \subseteq paths(\mathcal{S})$, $AP(T) \subseteq AP(\mathcal{S})$, and every path instance in T is an instance of a path in $\mathcal{S}$.

Let T be an XML tree conforming to $\mathcal{S}$, and v be a node in T. Let p be a path in $\mathcal{S}$ starting with a label in $P(lab(v))$. Starting from v and following path p in T we will eventually reach a set $v[p]$ of nodes in T. We call this set the *target set* of p wrt v. Formally,

$v[p] = \{v_n \mid \exists_{v_1,\ldots,v_{n-1}}\ v_1\text{ is a child of }v,\text{ and }v_1,\ldots,v_n\text{ is an instance of }p\}$

For example, in the XML tree in Figure 1, $v_3(student.address) = \{v_8, v_9\}$.

6.2 Comparability and Value Equality

Let $\mathcal{S}$ be a scheme file, and T be a conforming XML tree. Let v_1 and v_2 be two nodes in T. If v_1 and v_2 are the same node, we will write $v_1 = v_2$. Sometimes two *different* nodes may have *equal values*. For example, the two address nodes v_9 and v_{10} in Figure 1 are considered to have the same value because they represent the same address object. To compare two nodes for value equality, the two nodes must represent the same type of things. Since the labels of nodes are used to indicate the meaning of the nodes, it has been required in previous work (such as [BDFH02]) that two nodes must have the same label if they are to be compared for value equality. However, sometimes two nodes, even if of different labels, may represent the same type of things. For instance, in Figure 1, suppose the union member number is the student number whenever the union member is a student, then a @*mno* node and a @*sno* may represent the same type of things and may have equal values. We will say the nodes labelled @*sno* and those labelled @*mno* (or simply the labels @*sno* and @*mno*) are *comparable*. In general, we will assume there is a classification $\sim$ ($\sim$ is an equivalence relation) of the labels in $\mathcal{S}$, and two nodes v_1 and v_2 in T are comparable for value equality if and only if $lab(v_1) \sim lab(v_2)$. The definition of value equality is as below.

Definition 8. *Let T be an XML tree conforming to $\mathcal{S}$, and v_1 and v_2 be two nodes in T. v_1 and v_2 are said to be* value equal, *denoted $v_1 =_v v_2$, if $lab(v_1) \sim lab(v_2)$, and*

1. *v_1 and v_2 are both attributes or simple elements, and the two nodes have the same string value, or*
2. *v_1 and v_2 are both complex elements, and for every child node a_1 of v_1, there is a child node a_2 of v_2 such that $a_1 =_v a_2$, and vice versa.*

For example, in Figure 1, suppose @*sno* $\sim$ @*mno*, and \$*sname* $\sim$ \$*mname*, then the two nodes v_8 and v_{10} are value equal, so are the @*sno* (\$*sname* resp.) node under v_5 and the @*mno* (\$*mname* resp.) node under v_7.

Note that if v_1 and v_2 are the same node, then $v_1 =_v v_2$.

6.3 XML Equality-Generating Dependencies (XEGD)

Let $\mathcal{S}$ be a scheme file, S_1 be the list of paths $p_1,\ldots,p_n$, and S_2 be the list of paths $p'_1,\ldots,p'_n$. Let v_1 and v_2 be two nodes in an conforming XML tree T. We will use $v_1.S_1 =_v v_2.S_2$ to denote the fact that $v_1[p_i] \neq \emptyset$, $v_2[p_i] \neq \emptyset$, and every node v in $v_1[p_i]$ has a corresponding node v' in $v_2[p'_i]$ such that $v' =_v v$ and vice versa, for $i \in [1, n]$.

Definition 9. *An* equality-generating dependency (XEGD) *over $\mathcal{S}$ is an expression of the form*

$$Q_1, Q_2:\ S_1 =_v S_2 \to q_1 =_v q_2$$

where Q_1 and Q_2 are paths in $AP(\mathcal{S})$, $S_1 = p_1, \ldots, p_n$ and $S_2 = p'_1, \ldots, p'_n$ are lists of paths in $paths(\mathcal{S})$, q_1 and q_2 are also paths in $paths(\mathcal{S})$. In addition, for every path p in $S_1 \cup \{q_1\}$ (in $S_2 \cup \{q_2\}$ resp.), the concatenation $Q_1.p$ ($Q_2.p$ resp.) is in $AP(\mathcal{S})$. The last labels of p_i and p'_i (also that of q_1 and q_2) are comparable.

T is said to satisfy the XEGD if for any two nodes $v_1 \in root[Q_1]$ and $v_2 \in root[Q_2]$ the following statement is true: if $v_1.S_1 =_v v_2.S_2$, then $v_1[q_1] \neq \emptyset$, $v_2[q_2] \neq \emptyset$, and $v_1.q_1 =_v v_2.q_2$.

Intuitively, Q_1 and Q_2 define two sets of nodes, and the XEGD says that for any two nodes $v_1 \in root[Q_1]$ and $v_2 \in root[Q_2]$, if the target sets of the paths in S_1 wrt v_1 agree with the target sets of the paths in S_2 wrt v_2, then the target set of q_1 wrt v_1 agrees with the target set of q_2 wrt v_2.

Example 3. The XML tree in Figure 1 satisfies the following XEGDs
$Q_1, Q_2 : @sno =_v @mno \rightarrow \$sname =_v \$mname$,
$Q_1, Q_2 : @sno =_v @mno \rightarrow address =_v address$,
where Q_1 is the path *school.students.student*,
Q_2 is the path *union.memebers.member*.

Clearly the XEGDs in the above example cause data redundancies in the XML tree.

Like EGDs in relational databases, an XEGD over $\mathcal{S}$ that is satisfied by every conforming XML document is said to be *trivial*. Also, some XEGDs may be logically implied by others, and we will use $(\mathcal{S}, \mathcal{F})^+$ to denote the set of all XEGDs that are logically implied by a set $\mathcal{F}$ of XEGDs over $\mathcal{S}$.

6.4 Normal Form of XML wrt XEGDs

Definition 10. *An XML scheme file $\mathcal{S}$ is said to be in extended normal form (XENF) with respect to a set $\mathcal{F}$ of XEGDs if for every non-trivial XEGD*

$$Q_1, Q_2 : S_1 =_v S_2 \rightarrow q_1 =_v q_2$$

in $(\mathcal{S}, \mathcal{F})^+$, the following constraint holds:

- *in every conforming XML tree, there are no distinct nodes v_1, v_2 such that $v_1 \in root[Q_1]$, $v_2 \in root[Q_2]$, and $v_1.S_1 =_v v_2.S_2$;*
- *furthermore, if $Q_1 = Q_2$, but $S_1 \neq S_2$ or $q_1 \neq q_2$, then in every conforming XML tree, there is no node $v \in root[Q_1]$, such that $v.S_1 =_v v.S_2$.*

For example, the scheme file in Figure 1 will be in XENF with respect to the XEGDs in Example 3 iff the following constraint holds: in every conforming tree, there are no student node s and member node m such that $s.@sno =_v m.@mno$.

Similar to the ENF for relational databases, we can show that XENF is sufficient and necessary to ensure no data redundancies are caused by XEGDs in any conforming XML tree.

Definition 11. *Let $\mathcal{S}$ be a scheme file, $\mathcal{F}$ be a set of XEGDs over $\mathcal{S}$, and T be an XML tree conforming to $(\mathcal{S}, \mathcal{F})$ (i.e., T conforms to $\mathcal{S}$ and satisfies $\mathcal{F}$). We say that T has data redundancies with respect to $\mathcal{F}$ if there is a node v of T such that the subtree rooted at v, if removed from T, can be fully recovered using other parts of T, $\mathcal{S}$, and the constraints in $\mathcal{F}$. That is, we can construct a tree T_1 (to be rooted at the position of v) such that v and the root of T_1 are value equal.*

Similar to Theorem 3, we can prove

Theorem 4. *Let $\mathcal{S}$ be a scheme file, $\mathcal{F}$ be a set of XEGDs over $\mathcal{S}$. There exists an XML tree conforming to $(\mathcal{S}, \mathcal{F})$ which has data redundancies wrt $\mathcal{F}$ iff $\mathcal{S}$ is not in XENF with respect to $\mathcal{F}$.*

7 Future Work

As part of our future work, we would like to investigate the implication problem for XEGDs. We would also like to investigate the normalization process of XML scheme files with respect to XEGDs.

References

[AHV95] S. Abiteboul, R. Hull, and V. Vianu. *Foundations of Databases*. Addison-Wesley, 1995.

[AL04] M. Arenas and L. Libkin. A normal form for XML documents. *ACM Transactions on Database Systems*, 29:195–232, 2004.

[BCW99] M. Baudinet, J. Chomicki, and P. Wolper. Constraint-generating dependencies. *Journal of Computer and System Sciences*, 19(1):94–115, 1999.

[BDFH02] P. Buneman, S. B. Davidson, W. Fan, and C. S. Hara. Keys for XML. *Computer Networks*, 39(5):473–487, 2002.

[FV84] R. Fagin and M. Y. Vardi. The theory of data dependencies—an overview. In *Automata, Languages and Programming, 11th Colloquium*, volume 172 of *Lecture Notes in Computer Science*, pages 1–22, 1984.

[LG92] T. W. Ling and C. H. Goh. Logical database design with inclusion dependencies. In *ICDE'92*, pages 642–649, 1992.

[Mai83] D. Maier. *The Theory of Relational Databases*. Computer Sceince Press, 1983.

[MR86] H. Mannila and K. Räihä. Inclusion dependencies in database design. In *ICDE'86*, pages 713–718, 1986.

[Vin99] M. W. Vincent. Semantic foundation of 4NF in relational database design. *Acta Informatica*, 36:1–41, 1999.

[VLL04] M. W. Vincent, J. Liu, and C. Liu. Strong functional dependencies and their applicatiopn to normal forms in XML. *ACM Transactions on Database Systems*, 29(3):445–462, 2004.

[Wan04] J. Wang. Logical database design with equality generating dependencies. Manuscript, Dec 2004.

[WTM01] J. Wang, R. W. Topor, and M. J. Maher. Reasoning with disjunctive constrained tuple generating dependencies. In *DEXA'01*, volume 2113 of *Lecture Notes in Computer Science*, pages 963–973, 2001.

WDEE: Web Data Extraction by Example

Zhao Li and Wee Keong Ng

Centre for Advanced Information Systems,
Nanyang Technological University
liz@pmail.ntu.edu.sg
awkng@ntu.edu.sg

Abstract. Web data extraction systems in use today transform semi-structured Web documents and deliver structured documents to end users. Some systems provide a visual interface to users to generate the extraction rules. However, to end users, the visual effect of Web documents is lost during the transformation process. In this paper, we propose an approach that allows a user to query extracted documents without knowledge of formal query language. We bridge the gap between visual effect of Web documents and structured documents extracted by providing a QBE-like (Query by Example) interface named WDEE. The principle component of our method is the notion of a document schema. Document *schemata* are patterns of structures embedded in documents. WDEE generates tree skeletons based on schema information and a user may execute queries by input condition in the skeltons. By maintaining the mapping relation among schemata of Web documents and extracted documents, a visual example may be presented to end users. With the example, WDEE allows a user to construct tree skeletons in a manner that resembles the browsing of Web pages.

1 Introduction

With the explosion of information on Web, the volume of Web documents has overcome the capability of human to process them manually. Many intelligent agent systems provide mediators between a user and Web documents. The principle components of those systems are Web data extraction systems that transform semi-structured Web documents and deliver structured documents to users. Figure 1 is a typical framework for Web data extraction systems. In the framework, the training set is a set of documents shareing similar structures. From the training set, an extraction rule generator constructs extraction rules. The extraction engine interprets extraction rules and extracts structured documents from Web documents. Extraction rules include information as the following:

1. *Schema* of Web documents. A schema is a pattern of structures embedded in documents. In Web documents, we assume that a class of semantic information is organized using similar structures. Thus, it is possible to induce a schema to represent these structures and corresponding information.

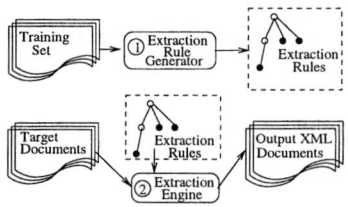

Fig. 1. Web Data Extraction Framework

2. Schema of extracted documents. Schemata of extracted documents provide an abstract layer to access extracted data. These schemata act like relational schemata in relational databases. Some Web data extraction systems extract documents with relational schemata [1]. However, a prominent property of Web documents is the hierarchical structures in them. It is more natural to store extracted data using a hierarchical format, especially XML documents.
3. Mapping relation between Web document schema and Extracted document schema. Given this relation, the extraction engine can map Web documents to extracted documents.

Some work like Elog [2,3] and WDEL [4] focuses on how to use a formal language to represent the schemata of Web documents so that the Web can be treated like a virtual database and the extraction of data from Web can be done in the manner of a database query; e.g., "select * from *DataClass*", where *DataClass* is the name of a schema and all contents in given Web documents with this schema will be returned. Lixto [5] and WICCAP [6] provide visual interfaces to generate Elog and WDEL programs semi-automatically. Much research [7,8,9] has devised approaches to detect Web document schema automatically.

Most earlier research suffers from two problems. Firstly, as the heterogeneity of Web document resources, it is difficult to efficiently execute complicated query such as *join* operation given only schemata of Web documents. Few work [1,10] stores extracted documents with explicit schemata in a database. Secondly, the most important merit of Web documents, visual effect rendered by a browser is lost in the extraction process. A user needs knowledge of formal query language to access extracted documents. In this paper, we present a new method that overcomes the two issues to query extracted documents. Our contributions are summarized as the follows:

- We propose an abstract schema layer over the Web documents and extracted documents. A schema contains descriptions and attributes of a class of fragments in documents. The schema layer provide a common foundation for complicated query operations. In particular, each document fragment corresponding to a Web document schema defined can be rendered in a Web browser with visual effect.
- A new framework for Web data extraction, so called WDEE (stands for Web Data Extraction by Example), is proposed. WDEE query language is a formal language that query documents in terms of schemata. The syntax of WDEE

language makes it suitable to generate WDEE programs using a QBE-like interface. In WDEE, the mapping relation among Web document schemata and extracted document schemata is maintained. Given a schema of extracted document, a visual Web page may be presented to a user by rendering the schema of Web documents it maps to. We shall illustrate the method to generate a WDEE program in the manner of Web browsing.

The rest of this paper is organized as follows: Section 2 introduces the concepts of data model and schema in WDEE to represent documents. In Section 3, query operations based on schema is described and compared with relational algebra. In the next section, we present a running example of how to exploit WDEE to query extracted documents in the manner of Web browsing. Section 5 compares WDEE query language with some other Web data extraction languages. After introducing some related work in Section 6, we conclude the work in future directions in the last section.

2 Notation

In this section, we present the data model we exploit to represent documents. We provide the formal definition of *schemata* that are patterns of structures embedded in documents. The concept of matching between a schema and document structures is defined. A schema itself can be treated as a query that will return all structures that match it. With the schemata, it is possible to generate WDEE programs as complicated queries using interfaces like QBE [11] and QEByE [12].

Unlike QBE and QEByE that prepares examples w.r.t. the relational query and the nested table query [12] respectively, schema defined here allows us to generate hierarchical examples. Moreover, the concepts of mapping between a schema of Web documents and a schema of extracted documents is introduced. By maintaining the mapping relationship, Web pages may be presented to a user to aid query generation.

A Web document such as HTML and XML encodes data in a tree structure and contents are stored in text labels of text nodes. We first define document tree to model Web documents as below.

Definition 1 (Document Tree). *A document tree is a rooted, labeled tree that can be defined as a 4-tuple: $t = \langle V, E, r, \gamma \rangle$, where V is the set of nodes corresponding to elements, E is the set of edges connecting these nodes, r is the root node, $\gamma : V \to L$ is a function that assigns each node a labels, where L is the label set of t. An edge e is an ordered 2-tuple (u, v) where $u, v \subseteq V$ and u is the parent node of node v. Root node r has no parent node. Each non-root node u in V has exact one parent node.*

A document tree parsed from a HTML document is a simplified DOM tree. We restrict our discussion to HTML and XML documents so that we can exploit DOM parsers to parse documents to trees. During the parsing processing, each non-text node is labeled with the name of the corresponding element in the original documents, and each text node is labeled with its value.

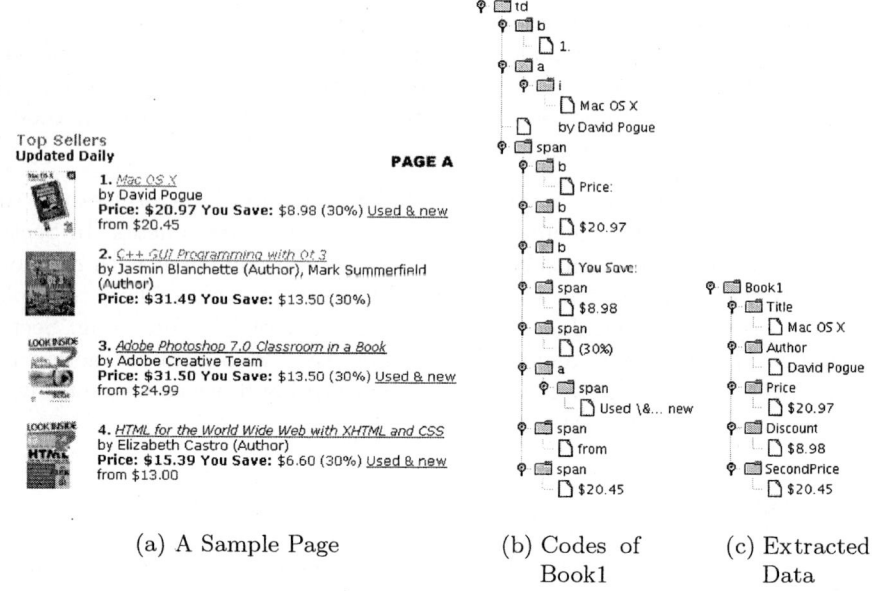

Fig. 2. Web pages and the logic view over them

As an example, Figure 2(a) is a HTML document rendered in a browser and the HTML codes corresponding to the first book is modeled as a document tree in Figure 2(b). In practice, the text nodes are what really carry data, and non-text nodes are used to organize data. Thus, given a document tree $t = \langle V, E, r, \gamma \rangle$, we say $\langle V, E, r, \gamma_s \rangle$ is the *structure* of t, where γ_s is defined on only non-text nodes and $\gamma_s(v) = \gamma(v)$. The set of labels on text nodes are *contents* of t.

The main objective of Web data extraction is to extract contents from document trees that are relevant to a user's requirements. Sometimes, structure information is also important and should be extracted. We refer to the extracted data as data instances (*DI*). We store DI in XML documents that can also modelled as document trees; e.g., Figure 2(c). If there is no confusion, we shall not distinguish Web documents and extracted documents in the following parts of this paper. While accessing a DI, it is possible to obtain the source Web document by maintaining the mapping relationship between them, as defined below:

Definition 2 (Data Instance and Mapping). *Given two document tree $t = \langle V, E, r, \gamma \rangle$ and $t_1 = \langle V_1, E_1, r_1, \gamma_1 \rangle$, if $V_1 \subseteq V$, $\gamma_1 = \gamma$, $r_1 = r$, leaf nodes in t_1 is also leaf nodes of t and $e_1 = \langle v_i, v_j \rangle \in E_1$ iff there is a path from v_i to v_j in t, then t_1 is a data instance (DI) of t (or t_1 is mapped to t), denoted as $\eta(t_1) = t$.*

In a relational database, a table stores a set of tuples with the same schema. There are relations among tables and schemata. The similar relations also exist on the Web. For instance, DIs corresponding to the first and the second books in Figure 2(a) have the same structure, with different contents. We say these DIs match the same schema, as defined below:

Definition 3 (Schema and Matching). *A schema s is a 4-tuple $\langle V, E, r, \gamma \rangle$, where $\langle V, E, r, \gamma \rangle$ is a document tree and γ labels all text nodes with "*". A DI $t = \langle V_t, E_t, r_t, \gamma_t \rangle$ match with s, denoted as $t \mapsto s$, if $\langle V, E, r \rangle = \langle V_t, E_t, r_t \rangle$ and $\gamma(v) = \gamma_t(v)$ if v is a non-text node.*

A schema describes a set of DIs. A user may write a simple query like "select * from schemaA" returns all DIs matching with schemaA. From Definition 3, as a schema is a special tree, its structure may be exploited to generate a QBE-like interface, as introduced in Section 3. With the interfaces generated, a user may submit query without knowledge of formal query language.

3   Query Operations

In this section, we introduce the query language of WDEE. The WDEE language consists of a set of schemata enhanced based on Definition 3, that has the strictly larger expressive capbility of MSO datalog [13] and may be used to represent *selection* and *projection* queries. WDEE language are augmented with set oriented features: union, join and difference.

We begin by defining matching query, followed by its extensions:

Definition 4 (Matching Query). *Given a extracted document T, a matching query $M(s) = \{t | t \mapsto s\}$, where s is a schema and $\eta(t)$ is a DI of T.*

Based on Definition 3, DIs that have the same structure as s will be returned by the matching query. This query is a bit naive and we draw ideas from [14] to improve the expressive capability of the query by augment schema with predicates, as defined below:

Definition 5 (Schema and Matching). *A schema s is a 4-tuple $\langle V, E, r, \gamma \rangle$, where $\langle V, E, r, \gamma \rangle$ is a DI and γ labels each node with a predicate formula $P(x)$. A DI $t = \langle V_t, E_t, r_t, \gamma_t \rangle$ match with s, denoted as $t \mapsto s$, if $\langle V, E, r \rangle = \langle V_t, E_t, r_t \rangle$ and $P(v)$ is true for $v \in V$.*

The predicates supported by WDEE are three types:

$x = c$ where x is the label of corresponding node in a DI, c is a constant string; e.g.,"David Progue".
$e \vdash x$ where e is a regular expressive and e can generate x. We restrict that predicates of this type appear on only leaf nodes, such that Definition 5 is equivalent to Definition 3 when e is "*", where "*" is a whildcard generating any string label.
$x = X$ where x is the label of corresonding node in a DI and X is a variable name. This predicate is important to construct join operation, as introduce in later part of this Section.

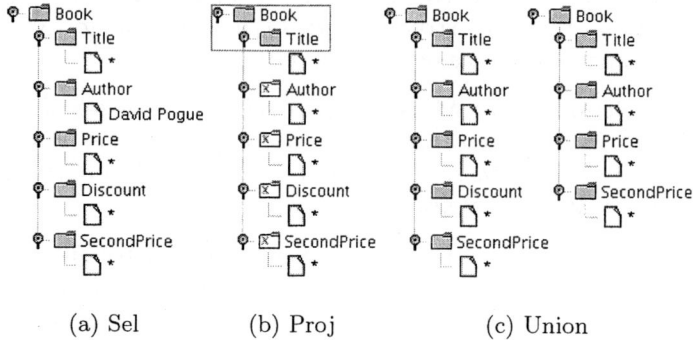

Fig. 3. Examples for Query Operations

In the following part of this section, we present how to use a matching query to represent those query operations: *selection, project, union, difference* and *join*.

Selection (σ) Selection is an unary operation on a schema, denoted as $\sigma_{condition}(s)$. It returns all DIs that match the schema and fulfill the given condition.

Suppose *Book* is a schema of the DI in Figure 2(c), a selection operation $\sigma_{author="DavidProgue"}(Book)$ returns all data of books in Figure 2(a) with author "David Progue". To represent this operation, we use a matching query with the schema in Figure 3(a). The constant string label c in the figure is the short form of $x = c$ and a regular expression label e is the short form of $e \vdash x$. This schema matchs with the first DI corresponding to the first book in Figure 2(a). Thus, the matching query will return the first DIs.

Projection (π) Projection is also an unary query operation on a schema, denoted as $\pi_{\langle fieldlist \rangle}(s)$.

The $\langle filedlist \rangle$ is a list of field with syntax of *field*:=*path*'.'*schema*, *path*:= *item*'.'...'.'*item*, *item*=*regexp*|*regexp*'['*idx*']', where *regexp* is a regular expression over node labels, *idx* is a natural number and $l[i]$ means the i-th child nodes with label l of a node.

Definition 6. *A schema $s_p = \langle V_p, E_p, r_p, \gamma_p \rangle$ is a projection schema of $s = \langle V, E, r, \gamma \rangle$, iff $\eta(s_p) = s$; i.e., s_p maps to s. A projection $\pi_{\langle path_1.s_1,...,path_n.s_n \rangle}(s)$ return a set of DIs $\{t | t \mapsto s_p\}$, where $e_p = \langle v_i, v_j \rangle \in E_p$ iff $\langle v_m, v_n \rangle \in E$, or v_m and v_n is connected by $path_i$ in E, v_m is root of s and the tree rooted from v_n match s_i.*

Suppose the schema for the book DI in Figure 2(c) is s_B and the schema for book title is s_T, a projection $\pi_{\langle Book.s_T \rangle}(s_B)$ will return DIs containing only book's titles. The schema in gray box of Figure 3 represents this query.

The selection and projection operations are both matching queries. WDEE distinguishes them by the schemata to be processed. A selection or a projection

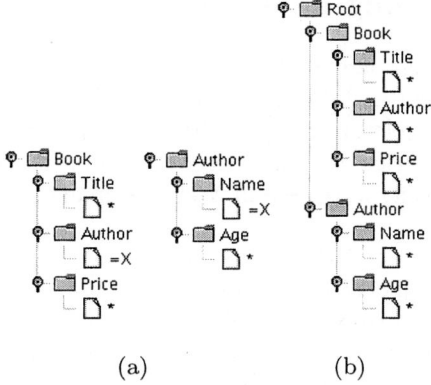

Fig. 4. Examples for Join Operations

operation returns a set of DIs matching with the given schema. We define three set-oriented operation below:

Union ($\bigcup$) Union is a binary query operation on two schema, denoted as $s_1 \bigcup s_2$.

A union operation merges two DI sets returned by $M(s_1)$ and $M(s_2)$. It may be represented as shown in Figure 3(c) and consists of two schemata corresponding to two types of DIs about book information. If s_1 and s_2 match with each other, the two sets are *union compatible*. If two DI sets are union compatible sets of DIs, the union operation need to detect overlay DIs to merge them, otherwise, the union operation simply copy two sets DIs together.

Difference (−) Difference is a binary query operation, denoted as $s_1 - s_2$.

A difference operation ask s_1 and s_2 match with each other; it simply removes overlay DIs from the DI set returned by $M(s_1)$. The difference operation and join operation introduced below may both be represented using schemata like those in Figure 3(c). As the three set operations cannot be distinguished only based on the schemta, a user need to explicitly choose the type of operation.

Join ($\bowtie_{condition}$) Join is a binary operation, denoted as $s_1 \bowtie s_2$.

To join two DI sets, s_1 and s_2 first need to be combined to s. To combin the two schemta or DIs, WDEE simply adds a root node as the parent node of both root nodes of them. For example, the two schemata in Figure 4(a) will be transformed to Figure 4(b). WDEE allows the join condition of two text nodes of two DIs share the same label. As an example in Figure 4(a), to join book DIs and author DIs sharing the same author name, a user may change the label as Figure 4(b), where $=X$ is the short form of $x=X$.

We have shown that with different schemata, we may execute various query operations on extracted documents. By parsing the schemata of extracted DIs to trees like those in Figure 3, a user can easily modify these trees and generate schemata to query extracted documents.

4 A Wdee Running Example

In this section, we present how to build examples corresponding to WDEE query operations. An example in WDEE consists of two parts: *tree skeletons* and a *browser view*. A tree skeleton is a visualized schema. To submit a query to a extracted document, a user may give some condition inside the skeleton, while the browser view presents a sample of Web documents where the document is extracted from.

The principle merit of WDEE language is that a WDEE program may be generated within a specific Web browser. When a user choose to query a certain document extracted, a corresponding Web document will be rendered in the Web browser. Given the Web page shown, a user may generate a WDEE program by select texts that are interesting to him.

Concisely, to generate a WDEE program by visual interface consists of three phases: ① Select schemata extracted documents to be queried; obtain a sample of the original Web documents to which the schemata map and generate a document tree whose text nodes can be modified by a user, so-called a tree skeleton. The Web page rendered from the sample Web document and the skeleton together is called an example. ② Generate a basic WDEE program by selecting texts in the Web browser. ③ Input conditions in text nodes of tree skelton to refine the WDEE program.

As an instance, we present how to generate a WDEE program for an example query, as described below:

QueryBook. Return book title, price and discount of the books written by "David Progue".

The detailed operations follow the 3-phase WDEE program generation procedure, as described below:

Fig. 5. A WDEE example

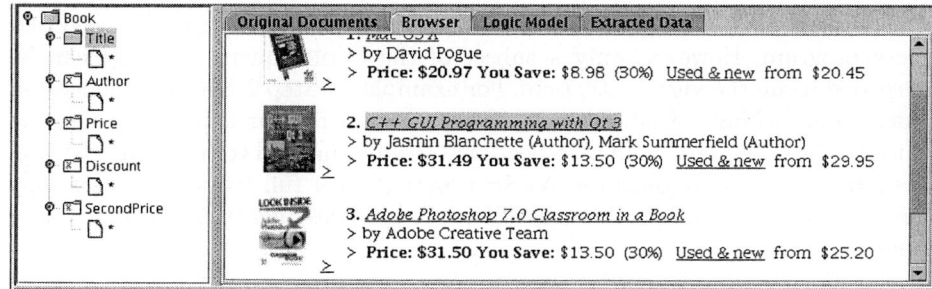

Fig. 6. A WDEE example

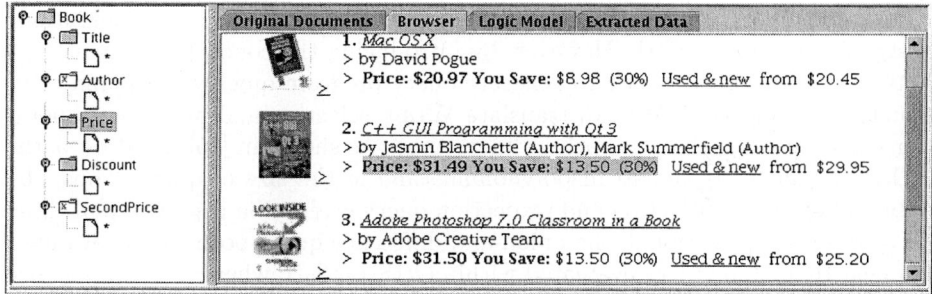

Fig. 7. A WDEE example

1. A user may select a schema using the menu. Suppose the schema *book* is selected, a tree skeleton of this schema will be shown, as the one in the left panel of Figure 5. A schema of Web documents $\eta(book)$ will be obtained by search the mapping relation. In turn, a random original Web document containing this Web schema is selected and shown in the Web browser, as shown in the right panel of Figure 5. The two panels is an example.

2. The Web page contains some books' information. A user may denote which parts should be returned by selecting texts in the page. Here, book title, price and discount are data to be returned. Initially, all nodes in the tree skeleton is unselected (denoted as white folder icons). After a user selects the book title by a mouse in the Web browser, as Figure 6, corresponding parts in the tree skeleton is selected (those gray folder icon). If the text selection cover more than one field in the give schema, as Figure 7, multiple nodes in the tree skeleton will be selected. So far, the schema corresponding to the skeleton can be used to generate a projection query.

3. After a user selects all texts that are interesting, he can give condition that must be fullfiled by the returned DIs. Here, a user may input "David Progue" in the tree skeleton, like the one in Figure 3(a). The schema corresponding to the modified skeleton can be used to generate a selection query.

The skeletons generated in the above steps may be directly saved as a WDEE query program. However, only a subset of the WDEE query language can be generated using the visual interfaces. For example, in Step 2, the fields generated contain only strings of labels and will not contain regular expression; i.e., the syntax of *item* of *field* defined in Section 3 will be changed to *item*:=*labelstring*| *labelstring*'['*idx*']'. To generate WDEE program with full features, a user may modify or exploit some techniques [8] to post-process generated WDEE query program.

5 Expressive Capability and Evaluation Complexity

The objective of WDEE is not to provide a general XML query language like XPath or XQuery. WDEE's expressiveness of selection and projection operations is strictly less than XPath. However, by introducing the concept of schema into WDEE, it is easier for a user to generate query program quickly in the majority situations of the Web. We can translate WDEE selection and projection operations to location paths of XPath in linear time. As shown in [15], location paths of XPath can be evaluated in polynomial time in the size of query. Thus, the upbound of WDEE selection and projection query evaluation is polynomial time. As introduced in Section 3, the union and difference query both can be evaluted in linear time. Join query evaluated within $O(|S_1|*|S_2|)$, where $|S_1|$ and $|S_2|$ are size of two DI sets to be joined. As the size of a DI set is less than node number, WDEE queries can be evaualted in polynomial time.

The limited form of WDEE generated by the visual interface can be translated to Monadic Datalog over the signature introduced in [3]: $\tau_r = \langle root, leaf, (child_k)_{k \leq K}, (label_a)_{a \in \sum} \rangle$ in linear time, vice versa. Thus, the evaluation complexity of a limited form WDEE query is $O(|D|*|Q|)$, where D is the size of documents to be queried and Q is the size of query.

6 Related Work

Web data extraction systems are the kernel components of agents providing mediators between users and Web data resources. In the beginning, the main purpose of Web data extraction systems is to transform semi-structured Web documents to relational databases [1] or object-oriented databases [16]. These systems need users to code by hand using formal languages to extract data from Web documents. Gottlob et al. [3] introduced an extraction language based on MSO logic.

Those formal extraction languages provide firm basis for Web data extraction. However, manually programming is always time-consuming and error-prone. The appearance of automatic extraction rule generation techniques partially solves this problem. Kushmerick [17] presents the method using grammar induction techniques to learn extraction rules. His method assumes documents to be extracted are organized like relational tables. IEPAD [8], RoadRunner [9] use various approaches to learn regular expressions as extraction rules. Those methods treats documents as flat text. Thus, it is easy to lost structural information. ExAlg [7] and Skeleton [10] can detect tree patterns, which are more intuitive and accurate. WICCAP [6] and Lixto [5] proposed supervised learning approaches based on visual interface to generate extraction program.

Although extraction efficiency can be improved obviously using these methods, extracted data are still not easy to be accessed. To exploit extracted data, a user need to program instead of browse the easy-to-read original document because of two reasons: 1. It is difficult to reverse visual effect from patterns detected by them; 2. Lack of management of documents, patterns and extracted data. Wang et al. [18] move the first step to use structured patterns in semi-structure documents to manager them. In recent years, more detailed structure-based document management techniques are devised. XRules [18] can classify semi-structured documents based on embedded subtrees very well. There are some papers discussing how to measure similarity among XML documents [19, 20]. It is easy to cluster documents based on their similarity. These approaches provide new ideas of semi-structured document management. However, the structure patterns considered by them are not easy to be rendered in Web browsers and generate examples like those in our system. Moreover, there is still no literature addressing how to exploit those techniques to help Web data extraction.

7 Conclusion

In this paper, we introduced a high level Web data extraction language — WDEE, and visual interface to generate WDEE queries. Unlike present systems that lost visual effects of Web documents during the extraction procedure, we suggest an approach to extract data instances in the manner of Web browsing. WDEE does not need a user to have knowledge about formal languages. Queries can be performed by fill up some tree skeleton such that no syntactic errors will appear in the query creation process. What this paper presents is the initial work of a high level Web data extraction language. How to improve expressive capability to efficiently query regular tree languages will be studied as part of the furture work.

References

1. Gupta, A., Harinarayan, V., Rajaraman, A.: Virtual database technology. SIGMOD Record **26** (1997) 57–61
2. Gottlob, G., Koch, C.: Monadic datalog and the expressive power of languages for web information extraction. In: Proc. of the 21th PODS. (2002) 17 – 28
3. Gottlob, G., Koch, C.: Monadic queries over tree-structured data. In: Proceedings of the 17th IEEE Symposium on Logic in Computer Science. (2002) 189 – 202
4. Li, Z., Ng, W.K.: Wiccap: From semi-structured data to structured data. In: Proc. of 11th IEEE International Conference on the ECBS. (2004)
5. Baumgartner, R., Flesca, S., Gottlob, G.: Visual web information extraction with lixto. In: Proc. of 27th International Conference on Very Large Data Bases, Roma, Italy, Morgan Kaufmann (2001) 119–128

6. Liu, Z., Li, F., Ng, W.K.: WICCAP data model: Mapping physical websites to logical views. In: Proc. of the 21st International Conference on Conceptual Modelling. (2002)
7. Arasu, A., Garcia-Molina, H.: Extracting structured data from web pages. In: Proc. of the 2003 ACM SIGMOD. (2003) 337 – 348
8. Chang, C.H., Lui, S.C.: IEPAD: information extraction based on pattern discovery. In: Proc. of the 10th WWW Conference. (2001) 681 – 688
9. Crescenzi, V., Mecca, G., Merialdo, P.: RoadRunner: Towards automatic data extraction from large web sites. In: Proc. of 27th International Conference on Very Large Data Bases. (2001) 109–118
10. Rajaraman, A., Ullman, J.D.: Querying websites using compact skeletons. In: Proc. of the 12th PODS. (2001) 16 – 27
11. Zloof, M.M.: Query-by-example: A data base language. IBM Systems Journal **16** (1977) 324–343
12. da Silva, A.S., Filha, I.M.E., Laender, A.H.F., Embley, D.W.: Representing and querying semistructured web data using nested tables with structural variants. In: Proc. of the 21st International Conference on Conceptual Modelling. (2002)
13. Neven, F.: Automata, logic, and xml. In: Proceedings of the 16th International Workshop and 11th Annual Conference of the EACSL on Computer Science Logic. (2002) 2 – 26
14. Bergholz, A.: Querying Semistructured Data Based On Schema Matching. PhD thesis, Humboldt-University Berlin (2000)
15. Gottlob, G., Koch, C., Pichler, R.: Xpath processing in a nutshell. SIGMOD Record **32** (2003) 12–19
16. May, W., Himmeröder, R., Lausen, G., Ludäscher, B.: A unified framework for wrapping, mediating and restructuring information from the web. In: Proceedings of the Workshops on Evolution and Change in Data Management, Reverse Engineering in Information Systems, and the World Wide Web and Conceptual Modeling. (1999) 307–320
17. Kushmerick, N.: Wrapper induction: Efficiency and expressiveness. Artificial Intelligence **118** (2000) 15–68
18. Wang, K., Liu, H.: Discovering structural association of semistructured data. IEEE Transactions on Knowledge and Data Engineering **12** (2000) 353–371
19. Flesca, S., Manco, G., Masciari, E., Pontieri, L., Pugliese, A.: Detecting structural similarities between xml documents. In: Proceedings of 5th International Workshop on the Web and Databases, Madison, Wisconsin, USA (2002)
20. Nierman, A., Jagadish, H.V.: Evaluating structural similarity in xml documents. In: Proceedings of 5th International Workshop on the Web and Databases. (2002)

Concept-Based Retrieval of Alternate Web Services[*]

Dunlu Peng[1,2], Sheng Huang[1], Xiaoling Wang[1], and Aoying Zhou[1]

[1] Department of Computer Science and Engineering,
Fudan University, Shanghai, 200433, P.R.China
[2] College of Computer Engineering,
University of Shanghai for Science and Technology, Shanghai, 200093, P.R.China
{dlpeng, shhuang, wxling, ayzhou}@fudan.edu.cn

Abstract. Web services have attracted much attention in recent years with the development of e-commercial technologies over the Internet. Although there are some standards and protocols for web service technologies, such as WSDL, UDDI and SOAP, the core technologies underlying Web services need further study in order to make these technologies practical and flexible. Efficient services management is the main task for services execution and services composition and there is no good solution until now. In this paper, we present a concept-based method for services management, which is efficient for services selection and alternative. Our method takes advantage of lattice and retrieves the optimal alternates for a given Web service efficiently by employing formal concept analysis and concept lattice. Compared with the former methods, this method is more efficient and accurate because the underlying semantics of Web services and users' requirements are exploited during the processing of retrieval. Experimental results also verify the efficiency and scalability of our approach.

1 Introduction

As promising e-commercial technologies over the Internet, Web services have attracted much attention in recent years. Although a set of standards and protocols, such as WSDL[4], UDDI [15] and SOAP[16], have been designed to make these technologies practical, the core technologies realizing Web services mostly rely on the traditional distributed computing techniques, such as remote procedure call (RPC) or remote method interface (RMI). In order to request a certain Web service successfully, requestors need to have complete understanding the service provider interface [1,5]. Mostly, requestors have no control over the availability of the Web services. By far, there is no related services management technology to detect whether a service is available or not and automatically select another service [2]. As a result, the applica-

---

[*] This work is supported by the National Natural Science Foundation of China under Grant No. 60228006, the National Hi-tech R&D Program of China under Grant No. 2002AA116020, and the Youth Foundation of Shanghai Education Committee for Scientific Research under Grand No. 04EC35.

tions of requestors will be unworkable because of the failure of the Web service being requested. To avoid this case, the service requestors must figure out how to choose the alternative services when the desired Web service is unavailable.

The challenge in the problem mentioned above is how to develop an efficient and accurate way to management the services and retrieve the alternates for a certain Web service from the service repositories. More precisely, it is challenging to effectively manage and search the Web services satisfying the requestors' requirements. Currently, in Web service registries the services were classified manually into different categories according to their commercial objectives described by WSDL rather than the functions provided by them [2]. This category-based service-discovery is quite informal and relies extensively on the shared common understanding of publishers and consumers. It does not provide any support for selecting competing alternate services that could potentially be reused. This paper presents a concept-based method to retrieve the optimal alternate of Web services automatically at the operation level. The main contributions are as follows:

1. Formal Concept Analysis (FCA) and concept lattice are explored to semantically group Web services by using the underlying semantics of Web services. By this method, we retrieve the alternates of a given Web service with respect to a certain requestor according to the invoked operations.
2. In order to reduce the scale of the built lattice, we minimize the number of operations which are considered as attributes in the lattice. We investigate the similarity between a pair of Web-service operations by considering the evidence drawn from different sources.
3. Since the service repositories are expanding, algorithms are proposed to maintenance the lattice dynamically for both inserting new services into and removing services from the lattice. We also develop an efficient algorithm for how to retrieve the alternate objects for the given Web service in the lattice.
4. Some experiments are conducted to show the efficiency and scalability of our approaches. The experimental results evaluated with synthetic data set and real data set. The results show our method has good performance.

This paper is organized as follows. Section 2 formally defines our problem and describes the foundation of Web services. Section 3 gives a brief overview of the main basic notations of FAC and concept lattice. We give the approach to generate the concept set and the concept lattice in section 4. We present our methods to retrieve the alternates for a given Web service in the lattice in section 5. Section 6 describes the experiments which we conducted to evaluate our approach. Finally, we introduce the related work and draw our conclusions in section 7.

2 Problem Definition

Currently, Web services are described by WSDL using four layers of abstraction [4]. The lowest layer presents the data types; the second layer represents the messages, whose structures are corresponding to the defined data types; the third layer specifies the service operations with input and output messages; the highest layer is the whole Web service description, which contains the operations defined in the third layer. According to the hierarchy, we formally define Web service as follows:

Definition 1. A **Web service** is a triple WS=(Tplist, Msglist, Oplist) where Tplist is the set of data types including all the data types used in Msglist and Msglist={Msg_1(part,type), Msg_2(Part,type) , ..., Msg_n(part,type) } is the set of messages contained in the Web service specification and defines the data types used in each message. Messages are composed of "parts" with different data types; Oplist={ $Op_1(input_1,output_1)$, Op_2($input_2,output_2$) ,...,Op_n($input_n$, $output_n$) } is the set of operations, $input_i$ /$output_i$ denote the input/output messages for executing the operation Op_i.

According to definition 1, we can describe a Web service briefly as a set of operations, WS={$Op_1,Op_2,...,Op_n$}. Each operation takes a list of input messages, finishes a certain task, and returns results in the output messages. Table 1 shows the Web services used as examples in this paper.

Table 1. Web Services and Their Operations

Service ID	Services	Operations
WS_1	TempService	getAirForecast(AF) , getDistrict(DT), getTemperature(TP), getZip(ZP)
WS_2	TravelService	getAirForecast, BookTickets(BT)
WS_3	SkatingService	getTemperature, OrderEquipment(OE)
WS_4	SportService	getAirForecast, getDistrict,
WS_5	PublicSerivice	getDistrict, getHospital(HP)
WS_6	TrainService	getTrain(TA), getHospital

The Letters in brackets following the operations are their abbreviations

Based on the definition of web service, we define the alternates of a given Web service.

Definition 2. Given two Web services WS_i ={Op_{i1}, Op_{i2},...,Op_{in} }, WS_j ={$Op_{j1},Op_{j2},...,Op_{jm}$ }, the set of operations in WS_i invoked by the requestors is R_{op}. Obviously, all elements in R_{op} are presented in WS_i, which is denoted as $R_{op} \subseteq^p WS_i$. If $R_{op} \subseteq^p WS_j$ holds, then WS_j is an **alternate** of WS_i w.r.t R_{op}, denoted as $WS_j \xrightarrow{R_{op}} WS_i$.

Another meaning of $WS_j \xrightarrow{R_{op}} WS_i$ is that WS_j can take the place of WS_i to provide same functions for the requestors whose applications invoke the operations in R_{op}. Table 2 illustrates the alternates of service TempService for different requestors. In order to distinguish the alternate services for same requestor w.r.t different operations, we use brackets and commas to partition them. For examples, in last column of the first row, {(WS_2, WS_4),(WS_4, WS_5)} means that both WS_2 and WS_4 have operation getAirForecast(AF) and both WS_4 and WS_5 contain operation getDistrict(DT).

In the Internet environment, it's quite usual for different requestors requesting the same Web service with different operations, especially for the Web service containing several operations. With the increasing of services, the Web-service repositories become larger and larger. How to retrieve the alternates of a given Web service for different requestors in the large service repositories efficiently is the problem we solve in this paper. The formalizing definition of our problem is described as follows.

Table 2. Alternates of TempService(WS_1) for Different Requestors

Requestors	Invoked Operations	Alternate Services
R_1	AF,DT	{(WS_2,WS_4),(WS_4,WS_5)}
R_2	AF, DT,TP	{(WS_2,WS_4),(WS_4,WS_5),(WS_3)}
R_3	DT	{(WS_4,WS_5)}
R_4	ZP,TP	{*Nil*, (WS_3)}

Nil: means that there is of service in the repository that holds the corresponding operations invoked by the requestor

Let $Rep=\{WS_1, WS_2, ..., WS_n\}$ be a repository of Web services, where $WS_i \in Rep$ ($1<i<n$) is a web service. The requestor is denoted as $R=\{R_1,R_2,...,R_m\}$. For each $R_j \in R$ ($1<j<m$), $R_{opj} \stackrel{p}{\subseteq} WS_k$ is the set of operations of WS_k invoked by R_j, then the alternates of WS_k w.r.t R_{opj} in Rep composes a set of A_j which satisfies $A_j \subseteq Rep$ and $\forall ws \in A_j \Rightarrow ws \xrightarrow{R_j} WS_k$. Our problem is to efficiently retrieve the alternate set A from the repository Rep of service WS_k, when WS_k is unavailable.

Our goal is to retrieve efficiently all the items listed in column named '*Alternate Services*' which are alternate Web services with respect to the certain operations invoked by the requestors in the corresponding column named '*Requestors*' in table 2. For example, each combination of (WS_2, WS_4) and (WS_4, WS_5) can be used as the alternate of *TempService* for R_1.

We take advantage of Formal Concept Analysis (FCA) to organize the Web services collection, rather than the unstructured collection of Web services [6, 10, 16]. In our approach, the concerned Web services are the services with operations similar to the invoked operations of the processing Web service rather than having high similarity at entire service. In order to implement concept structure, we borrow lattice technology, which permits efficiently and accurately retrieve of alternates for a given Web service. In section 3, we will give a brief overview of FCA and introduce some of its main notations.

3 Formal Concept Analysis (FCA)

Here we give a brief overview of the main basic concepts of theory for FCA. FCA [8, 9, 10] calculates a concept lattice, which allows queries to be processed efficient, from a binary relation of objects and attributes.

Concept-Based Retrieval of Alternate Web Services

Definition 3. A **context** is a triple $\mathcal{K}(\mathcal{W},O,\mathcal{R})$ where $\mathcal{W}$ and O are two finite sets and $\mathcal{R}$ is a relation between $\mathcal{W}$ and O, $\mathcal{R} \subseteq \mathcal{W} \times O$. $\mathcal{W}$ consists of a set of **objects** and O is the set of these objects' **attributes**.

A context can be visualized as a cross table, named a context table.

Definition 4. The **context table** T of a context $\mathcal{K}(\mathcal{W},O,\mathcal{R})$ is matrix form description of the $\mathcal{R}$ relation:

$$r_{ij} = \begin{cases} 1 & \text{if } w_i R o_j \text{ and } w_i \in w \text{ and } o_j \in O \\ 0 & \text{otherwise} \end{cases} \quad (1)$$

In a service repository, the formal context can be formed by considering services as objects, operations as attributes and the relation is the presence or absence of an operation in a Web service. Fig.2a is the context table for our examples shown in table 1.

Definition 5. For $W \subseteq \mathcal{W}$ and $O \subseteq O$ from a context $(\mathcal{W},O,\mathcal{R})$, the **common attributes** are:

$$w(o) = \{w' \in W \mid \forall o' \in O, w' R o'\} \quad (2\text{-}1)$$

and **common objects** are:

$$o(w) = \{o' \in O \mid \forall w' \in W, w' R o'\} \quad (2\text{-}2)$$

Definition 6. A **concept** $c = (W, O)$ of a context $(\mathcal{W},O,\mathcal{R})$ is a pair where $W \subseteq \mathcal{W}$, $O \subseteq O$, $w(O)=W$, $o(W)=O$. The **extent** of c is $\pi_o(c)=O$ and the **intent** of c is $I(c)=W$. The set of all concepts of $(\mathcal{W},O,\mathcal{R})$ is denoted by $C(\mathcal{W},O,\mathcal{R})$ which is the complete lattice of $(\mathcal{W},O,\mathcal{R})$.

Concepts are partially ordered and a concept's extent includes the extents of its sub-concepts and the intent of a concept includes the intents of its super-concepts.

Definition 7. Let $c_1 = (w_1, o_1)$ and $c_2 = (w_2, o_2)$ be two concepts in context $(\mathcal{W},O,\mathcal{R})$, thus, we have $w_1, w_2 \subseteq \mathcal{W}$ and $o_1, o_2 \subseteq O$, the **partial order** is:

$$c_1 \leq c_2 \Leftrightarrow o_1 \subseteq o_2 \Leftrightarrow w_2 \subseteq w_1 \quad (3)$$

R	AF	DT	TP	ZP	BT	OE	HP	TA
WS₁	1	1	1	1	0	0	0	0
WS₂	1	0	0	0	1	0	0	0
WS₃	0	0	1	0	0	1	0	0
WS₄	1	1	0	0	0	0	0	0
WS₅	0	1	0	0	0	0	1	0
WS₆	0	0	0	0	0	0	1	1

(a) An Example of Context Table   (b) Concept Lattice

Fig. 1. Context Table and Concept Lattice Representation

where c_1 is *a lower bound* of c_2 and c_2 is *a upper bound* of c_1. If there does not exist another concept c in $(\mathcal{W},O,\mathcal{R})$ satisfying $c_1 \leq c \leq c_2$, then c_2 is the *least upper bound* for c_1. Similarily, if there does not exist c in context $(\mathcal{W},O,\mathcal{R})$ satisfying $c_1 \geq c \geq c_2$, then c_1 is the *greatest lower bound* for c_2.

Fig.1b is concept lattice, which can be drawn from the context table in Fig.1a. There is an edge between c_1 and c_2 if $c_1 \leq c_2$ and there is no other concept c_3 in the lattice such as $c_1 \leq c_3 \leq c_2$. Each concept in the lattice together forms the paths and denotes an alternate of a Web service for a certain set of operations. By taking advantages of this property, it is very convenient to retrieve all the alternates among the paths. So the structure of concept lattice can be used not only to represent semantics stored in a hidden form in the underlying services, but also to show the alternate relationship among the objects. This can be used for searching purpose.

4 Generating Concept Lattice

In this section, we use the definitions and theorem described above to generate concept lattice. Before generating the concept lattice, we present the method to obtain the concept set.

4.1 Generating Concept Set

From the above introduction, we consider Web services as objects and their operations as attributes in the context area. The context table is built up according to the presence of the attributes in the Web services, so

$$W = \{WS_1, WS_2, ..., WS_n\} \\ O = \{Op_1, Op_2, ..., Op_m\} \qquad (4)$$

According to definition 1, an operation of a Web service can be expressed as *Op(input, output)*. Besides input/output messages, some other information such as operation text descriptions we can also obtain from the associated WSDL files [4]. In our approach, we determine the similarity between Web services by combining the multiple sources of evidence based on the proposal presented in [11]. The method to measure the similarity for main components considers the following factors:(1)The similarity (S_1 and S_2) of Input/output parameter name; (2)The similarity (S_3 and S_4) of Input/output concept: (3)The similarity (S_5) of Operation description; (4)The similarity (S_6) of Web service description. To evaluate the similarities, we consider the terms in every component as bags of words and use the TF/IDF (Term Frequency/Inverse Document Frequency) measure [13].

We measure the overall similarity by summing up the weighted similarities mentioned above. The weight for a given similarity is dependent on the relevance between it and the overall similarity. Thus, the overall similarity can be defined as:

$$Sim(Op_i, Op_j) = \sum_{k=1}^{6} w_k S_k \qquad (5)$$

where w_k is the weight assigned to similarity S_k. Currently, w_k is set manually based on the analysis of the results from different trial. To reduce the number of operations, we use the pruning rule that if the overall similarity between an new extracted operation Op_i and another operation Op_j existing in the attribute set O, $Sim\ (Op_i, Op_j)$, is no less than the similarity threshold s, that is, $Sim(Op_i, Op_j) \geq s$, then Op_i will not be added into the attribute set O.

4.2 Generating Concept Lattice

There exists several algorithms to compute all concepts from a context $\mathcal{K}(\mathcal{W}, O, \mathcal{R})$. For example, Ganter use an ordering relation to generate the concept lattice [8]. It is not practical by using static approaches to build the lattice because the number of Web services increases rapidly over the Internet. In our approach, we propose an optimized incremental algorithm to take account of the expanding of service repositories.

4.2.1 Basic Ideas

Building concept set in an incremental mode is based on the following rule: Every concept intent (definition 6), after inserting a new object into the context, is the result of intersecting the new objects' attribute set with some intent set already present in the concept set.

Let K be the concept lattice of the context $(\mathcal{W}, O, \mathcal{R})$. The nodes in K satisfy the partial order defined in definition 7. Given a new Web service $w(oplist)$ where w is name of the service and $oplist$ is its operation set. We use K^* representing the concept lattice generated after adding w. The basic steps about computing K^* from K are:

1. Modify the nodes (W, O) in K satisfying $O \subseteq oplist$ by adding w into W;
2. No changing the nodes (W, O) in G if $O \not\subset oplist$;
3. Create the new nodes $(W \cup w, O \wedge oplist)$ satisfying the nodes (W, O) are in K and $O \wedge oplist$ is not in K.

Thus, we conclude that the new nodes are generated from the nodes (W, O) which are called *generators* [14] in K^* such that $O \not\subset oplist$ and $O \wedge oplist$ don't appear in any node of K.

4.2.2 Algorithms for Building Concept Lattice

In this section, we describe the algorithm **Building_WSLattice** shown in Fig.2. By the algorithm we can build the concept lattice for an incremental Web-service repository. Let K be the original concept lattice corresponding to the context $(\mathcal{W}, O, \mathcal{R})$. Given a new Web service $w(oplist)$ where w is name of the service and $oplist$ is its operation set. The algorithm updates K by modifying old nodes(lines 4-11) and/or creating new nodes (line 13-16) to obtain the concept lattice K^* corresponding to the new context $(\mathcal{W} \cup \{w\}, O \cup oplist, \mathcal{R})$. The top and the bottom of the concept lattice are known and the lattice is initialized with these two nodes. The bottom is the concept with the intent O and an empty extent. The top is the concept with the smallest ele entof O, all the Web services belong to the exten of this concept. updated in the lattice.During the process of generation, the edges in the original are also updated as the new nodes joined in the lattice (in Fig.3. algorithm

UpdateEdge). The complexity of the algorithm is $O(n^2 \cdot |\mathcal{W}| \cdot |O|)$, where n is $min(|\mathcal{W}|,|O|)$, $|\mathcal{W}|$ is the number of services, and $|O|$ is the number of operations of context $(\mathcal{W},O,\mathcal{R})$.

Algorithm **Building_WSLattice** (w,oplist,K)
   Input: w-the identification of the new Web service
       oplist-the operation set of w
1. $M \leftarrow 0$ /*M contains the modified or new nodes in K^* */
2.   for each node (W_i,O_i) in K
3.   do $N \leftarrow (W_i,O_i)$
4.   if $O_i \subseteq$ oplist
5.   then $W_i \leftarrow W_i \cup \{w\}$ /* modify the node*/
6. $M \leftarrow M \cup N$
7.   if $O_i =$ oplist
8.   then return;
9.   else $O_i' \leftarrow O_i \wedge$ oplist
10.   if $\exists (W',O') \in M$
11.   then $W' \leftarrow W' \cup W_i \cup \{w\}$ /* modify node (W',O')*/
12.   else
13.   do $N_n \leftarrow (W_i \cup \{w\}, O_i')$ /* create new node N_n */
14. $M \leftarrow M \cup N_n$
15.   {create an edge between N and N_n}
16.   **UpdateEdge**(M,O_i',N,N_n)
17.   if $O_i' =$oplist
18.   then return;
19.   return

Fig. 2. Algorithm *Building_WSLattic*

Algorithm **UpdateEdge** (M,O',N,N_n)
Input:M-the set of modified or new node in K^*
   O'-the intersecting set of operations between new Web service and the generator
   N-the current node in K
   N_n-the new node in K^*
1.   for each *element* (W_1,O_1) in M
2. $N_{e1} \leftarrow (W_1,O_1)$
3.   do if $O_1 \subseteq O'$
4.   then *IsParent*$\leftarrow$true; /*N_{e1} may be a parent of N_n*/
5.   for each *element* (W_2,O_2) in Sons(N_{e1}) do
6.   if $O_2 \subseteq O'$
7.   then do *IsParent* $\leftarrow$ false
8.   break;
9.   if *IsParent*
10.   if N_{e1} is a parent of N
11.   then *remove the edge between* N_{e1} *and* N
12.   add *an edge between* N_{e1} *and* N_n
13.   return

Fig. 3. Algorithm UpdateEdge

5 Retrieving Alternate Services

In this section, we introduce how to retrieve alternate Web services for a given Web service in a concept lattice. Firstly, we will introduce some definitions about alternate services.

5.1 Optimal Alternate Set

The Web services with their operations stored in the repository form the context inducing the concept lattice. By the lattice, we perform retrieval of the alternates for a given Web service efficiently and response optimal feedback to its users. Before discussing our approach, some definitions are given.

Definition. 8. Let $WS=\{w_1(oplist_1),...,w_n(oplist_n)\}$ and $WS'=\{w_1'(oplist_1'),..., w_m'(oplist_n')\}$ be two sets of Web services. The ***correlation*** between WS and WS' is defined as:

$$Cor(WS, WS') = \frac{\bigcup_{i=1}^{n}(oplist_i) \cap \left(\bigcup_{i=1}^{m}(oplist_i')\right)}{\bigcup_{i=0}^{n}(oplist_i)} \qquad (6)$$

Definition 9. Given a Web service $ws(oplist)$, the set of operations invoked by its requestors is $o \subseteq oplist$, $o \subseteq O$ is a ***retrieval*** of lattice (W,O,R). A set $w' \subseteq W$ *satisfies* the retrieval if for each $ws'(oplist') \in w'$, $oplist' \cap o \neq \emptyset$ and $Cor(\{ws\},w')$ is maximum corresponding to context $\mathcal{K}(W,O,R)$. w' is called an ***instance*** of alternate set for ws w.r.t o in context $\mathcal{K}(W,O,R)$.

Definition 10. Let $w=\{ws_1, ws_2,...ws_n\}$ be an instance of alternate set for ws w.r.t the invoked operation set o in context $\mathcal{K}(W,O,R)$. If there does not exist $w'=(ws_1,...ws_k) \subset w$ satisfying $Cor(ws,w') = Cor(ws, w)$, then w is ***an optimal alternate set*** for ws w.r.t. o in context $\mathcal{K}(W,O,R)$

It is meaningful to response the optimal alternates to the requestors. Definition 10 shows that an alternate set with minimal size and maximum correlation to the processing Web service is an optimal alternates set. For example, in table 1 and table 2, the candidate set of alternates WS_1 w.r.t the invoked operations $\{AF,DT,TP,ZP\}$ is $WS=\{W_1=\{WS_2,WS_3,WS_5\}, W_2=\{WS_2 WS_3, WS_4\}, W_3=WS_3, WS_4, WS_5\}, W_4=\{WS_3, WS_4\}\}$. For each W_i in WS, the correlation between it and WS_1, $Cor(W_i, WS_1)$, equals to 75%. The elements in W_i are all 3 except for W_4 which are 2, so the optimal alternate set for WS_1 is W_4.

5.2 Retrieval Implementation

In Fig.4, algorithm *Retrieving_Alternates* traverse the lattice in breadth- first manner from top to bottom (lines 1-16). For example, we first process nodes {*2, 3, 4, 5*} in Fig.1b, then {*6*} and finally {*12*} if we want to search the alternates for WS_1. In order to obtain an optimal alternate set, the services are selected with a greedy method: in each step we only save the services having the largest common operations with the invoked operations of the Web service being processed, which is denoted as *ws* in the algorithm (lines 9-14). We only need to access the concepts in the upper bounds of the concept C whose intent equals to the invoked operations in *ws* (see definition 6 and 7). According to this fact, if some Web services providing the same operations with that invoked in the Web service being processed, then stop traversing the lattice (15-16). To reduce the number of services in the alternate set, we remove the services with same operations except one (lines 17-22). Finally, we return the optimal alternates in line 22. In worst case, we need to traverse all the nodes in the lattice once, so the complexity of our algorithm is $O(n^2)$, where n is the size of lattice.

Algorithm *Retrieving_Alternates(K,ws,o)*
Input: *K-the concept lattice;*
   ws-the service being processed;
   o-the invoked operations in ws
output: *the optimal alternates of ws w.r.t. o*
1. *maxlevel* ← *the longest path from top to bottom of K*;
2. for $i \leftarrow 0$ to *maxlevel*
3.   do *leve l[i]* ← {*all the concepts with level i*};/* *the longest length for top to the concept*/
4. *TMP* ← $\varnothing$; /* *TMP contains the services WS(oplist) satisfying oplist* $\cap o \neq \varnothing$*/
5. for $i \leftarrow 0$ to *maxlevel*
6.   do for each $C \leftarrow (W,O) \in leve\ l[i]$
7.   do if $ws \in W$ and $o \cap O \subseteq o$
8.   do if $W - \{ws\} \neq \varnothing$
9.   then do $O' \leftarrow o \cap O$;
10.   for each $ws' \in TMP$
11.   do *oplist* ← *the set of operations contained in ws'*;
12.   if $o \cap oplist \subseteq O'$ and $ws' \notin W$
13.   then do $TMP \leftarrow TMP - \{ws'\}$;
14. $TMP \leftarrow TMP \cup (W - \{ws\})$;
15.   if $O' = o$
16.   then goto *17*;
17.   for each pair $ws_i, ws_j \in TMP, i \neq j$;*/
18.   do *oplist $_i$* ← *the set of operations contained in ws_i*
19.   *oplist $_j$* ← *the set of operations contained in ws'*
20.   if *oplist $_i \cap o$* = *oplist$_j \cap o$*
21.   then do $TMP \leftarrow TMP - \{ws_i\}$
22.   return *TMP*;

Fig. 4. Algorithm for Retrieval of Alternate Web Service

6 Experiments

6.1 Experimental Setup

We carried out a set of experiments to evaluate the performance of our approach. All the experiments were implemented in Java and executed on a 1.4GHz Pentium III PC with 256MB memory running Windows 2000 professional. The data sets include the synthetic data generated by a WSDL generator we developed and the real data crawled from the main authoritative UDDI repositories. The synthetic data contained about 2000 Web services with 2030 operations described in 2000 WSDL files. In real data, 2000 WSDL files present 2000 Web services with 2400 operations.

The experiments we conducted to: i) measure the efficiency of our method by comparing it with a possible solution, such as keyword searching; iii) Evaluate the effects of the similarity threshold used to prune the operations on the performance of our approach, such as the lattice size and the time for building the lattice.

6.2 Experimental Results

6.2.1 Efficiency Evaluation

We first evaluate the efficiency of our approach by comparing the response time of retrieving the alternates with that of keyword searching. The response time here refers to the time from submitting a request to finishing retrieval all the alternates for the Web service in a given repository. We regard the name of each invoked operation and that of the Web service being processed as the keywords during keyword searching. In our test, the number of services varied from 1000 to 2000, and each time 200 services were added into the repositories. Because of the large difference of the response time between keyword searching and our approach, the common logarithm was exploited to represent the values when we drew the graphs (see Fig.5). The figures illustrate that keyword searching is more time consuming than our approach both in synthetic data and real data. It means that our proposal can retrieve the optimal alternates of a given Web service efficiently.

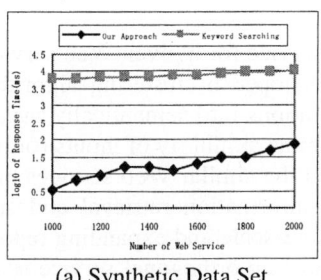   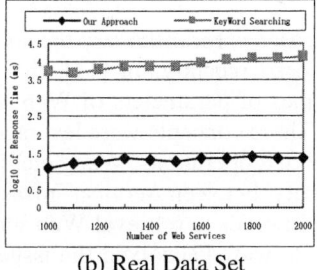

(a) Synthetic Data Set   (b) Real Data Set

Fig. 5. Eifficiency Evaluation with Different Data Set

6.2.2 Evaluating Effects of Operation Similarity Threshold on Lattice

In section 4, we have discussed that the lattice can be built in a cost effectively way by pruning the operations when we generate the concept set. According to the pruning rule given in section 4.1, we know that the most important factor influencing the size of lattice is the threshold of overall similarity between operations. We did some experiments to investigate the effects of the threshold on both the size and the time for building the lattice by varying the threshold from 0.2 to 0.9, and keeping the size of the repositories constantly. The experiments were also conducted with synthetic data (Fig.6a) and real data (Fig.6b).

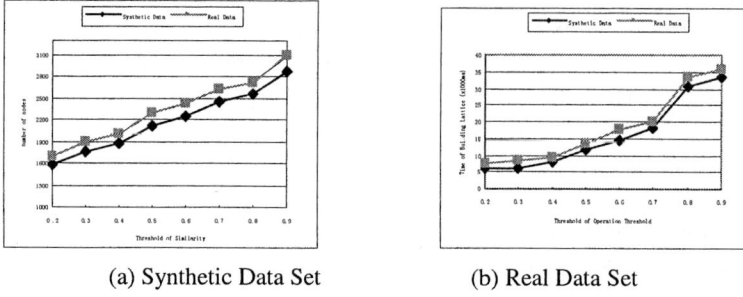

(a) Synthetic Data Set   (b) Real Data Set

Fig. 6. Effects of Operation Similarity on the Size of Lattice

The figures show that the more the threshold is, the larger the size of lattice will be and more time is needed to build the lattice. It is because as the similarity threshold growth the pruned operations become less and less, in other words, the operations added into the attribute set become more and more. As a result, the number of nodes in the concept lattice also increases and it leads to the time for building the lattice becomes longer and longer.

7 Conclusions and Related Work

Some approaches for discovery the similar Web service for a given Web service have been proposed recently. In [11], the authors developed a clustering algorithm that groups names of parameters of Web service operations into semantically meaningful concepts. These concepts were leveraged to determine similarity of inputs (or outputs) of web-service operations. Wang etc. [3] obtained the similar Web services based on the similarity between services measured with information retrieval and structure matching. In order to retrieval Web services in large-scale and expanding repositories with flexible way, [7] solved the issue by means of an orthogonal service space and establishing the multi-valued specialization relationships between services.

In this paper, we propose a novel method to retrieve all the optimal alternates of a given Web service with respect to its invoked operations. Formal Concept Analysis (FCA) and concept lattice are employed to semantically group Web services by using the underlying semantics of Web services. We also took the extension of Web services into account and proposed some algorithms for establishing and maintaining the concept lattice incrementally. Our approach can be used to retrieve the alternates in an efficient, accurate and scalable way which has been demonstrated by the experiments.In our future work, we will study an optimizer for our retrieval approach, such as clustering Web services with the domain knowledge based on our service concept lattice, since some category information can be obtained from the UDDI repositories.

References

[1] D. Booth, H. Haas, F. McCabe, E. Newcomer, M. Champion, C. Ferris and D. Orchard. *Web services Architecture*. http://www.w3.org/TR/2004/NOTE-ws-arch-20040211/, 2004.
[2] D. Chappell, T. JeWell. *Java Web service*. O'Reilly, 2002.pp:22-25.
[3] Y. Wang, E. Stroulia. Flexible Interface Matching for Web-Service Discovery. *Proceedings of the Fourth International Conference on Web Information Systems Engineering(WISE 2003)*. Alta, Canada, December 2003
[4] E. Christensen, F. Curbera, G. Meredith, and S.Weerawarana. *Web service Description Language* (WSDL). http://www.w3.org/TR/wsdl.
[5] W. Liu, W.Jia and A.PuAdd Exception Notification Mechanism to Web services. *Proceedings Fifth International Conference on Algorithms and Architectures for Parallel Processing (ICA3PP'02)*, Beijing, China , October, 2002.
[6] L. Kovics, P.Baranyi. Document clustering Based On Concept Lattice. *Proceedings of IEEE International Conference on Systems, Man and Cybernetics*, October 2002.
[7] H. Zhuge, J.Liu. Flexible retrieval of Web service. *The journal of Systems and Software*, 2004(70):106-117
[8] B. Ganter and R.Wille. *Formal Concept Analysis, Mathematical Foundation*. Spinger Verlag, 1999.
[9] [9] I.Kovacs. Efficiency Analysis of Building Concept Lattice. *Proceedings of 2nd ISHR on Computation Intelligence*, Budapest, 2001
[10] R.Wille. Concept lattice and conceptual knowledge systems. *Computers and Mathematis Applications*, 23, Number 6-9, pp. 493-515, 1992.
[11] X. Dong, A.Halevy, J. Madhavan, E. Nemes and J. Zhang. Similarity Search for Web service, *Proceedings of ^{th}e 30th VLDB conference*, Toronto, Canada, August 2004.
[12] R.Wille. Restructuring lattice theory: An approach based on hierarchies of concepts. In *Rival, editor, Ordered Sets*, pages 445-470. Reidel,1982.
[13] G. Salton, A. Wong and C.S. Yang. A Vector-space Model for Information Retrieval. *Journal of the American Society for Information Science*, 1975(18):13-620.
[14] R.Godin, R.Missaoui, and H. Alaoui. Incremental Concept Information Algorithms Based on Galois (Concept) Lattice. Computational Intelligence, 11(2):246-267, 1995.
[15] T.Bellwood,L.Clément.C.Riegen. Universal Description, Discovery & Integration (UDDI) Version 3.0. http://uddi.org/pubs/uddi_v3.htm
[16] M.Gudgin, M. Hadley, N.Mendelsohn, J.J.Moreau, H.F.Nielsen. Simple Object Access Protocol (SOAP) Version 1.2 . http://www.w3.org/TR/soap/

WSQuery: XQuery for Web Services Integration*

Zhimao Guo, Xiaoling Wang, and Aoying Zhou

Dept. of Computer Science and Engineering, Fudan University, China
{zmguo, wxling, ayzhou}@fudan.edu.cn

Abstract. Web services integration is one of key issues in many B2B applications. Yet, current approaches to this problem tend to use a general-purpose programming language, thus incur type mismatches between the type system of XML schema and the object-oriented type system. In this paper, we present a uniform method for integrating Web services. We propose an extension of XQuery, referred to as *WSQuery*, which can contain Web service calls. We first present the conceptual evaluation strategy of WSQuery programs. Then, for speeding up the evaluation, we propose to schedule Web service calls to exploit parallelism. We carry out dependency analysis to determine dependency relations among Web service calls. The *for* loops, *if* branches and unknown parameters pose particular challenges for dependency analysis and scheduling. We use unfolding techniques to deal with them.

1 Introduction

XML is the preeminent data exchange format on the Internet. Web services are becoming the standard building blocks for distributed computing over the Internet[2,3,1]. XML and Web services together provide a framework for distributed information management[7]. With the emergence of Web services, many companies are beginning to expose their business functionalities as Web services. Many applications in the context of B2B frequently demand seamless access to heterogeneous and distributed information. In this paper, we will consider the service integration problem in the Web environment. XML greatly facilitates the development as well as access and integration of Web services. However, current approaches to Web services integration tend to use an existing, general-purpose programming language. That incurs type mismatches between the type system of XML schema and the object-oriented type system[16]. In this paper, we propose a new architecture and some techniques which enable the use of XQuery as an essential tool for Web services integration.

Let us consider the following part-suppliers scenario. Assume each kind of parts has its name *p_name* and id *p_id*. The site *A* provides a Web service

---

* This work is supported in part by 863 Program 2002AA116020 and NSFC 60403019 and 60228006. Part of the work was done while the first author was visiting Hong Kong University of Science and Technology.

$\mathcal{W}_a$ which contains an operation op_a which takes a given p_name as input, and returns the corresponding p_id. The site B provides a Web service $\mathcal{W}_b$ which has an operation op_b which takes p_id as input, and produces all vendors which can offer this kind of parts. Here each vendor is indicated by the URL location of its *WSDL* file[4]. Each part supplier provides a Web service $\mathcal{W}$ such that one can ask its operations for the price of the part p_id, the supplier's name and its contact information. The prototypes of these operations are shown below:

A: $(\mathcal{W}_a, getPartID, p\_name)$
B: $(\mathcal{W}_b, getVendors, p\_id)$
Vendor: $(\mathcal{W}, getPrice, p\_id)$
Vendor: $(\mathcal{W}, getVendorInfo)$

Because each part supplier provides Web service interfaces to its business partners, the partners' application systems can directly query the price of machine parts offered by the supplier. If one wants to find out which supplier provides a certain kind of parts with the lowest price, he can compose an XQuery program Q for this purpose. Q should have a parameter $\$part\_name$, then it can also be used for other kind of machine parts. Q is shown below:

1. **let** $\$v_1 :=$ callws($\mathcal{W}_a$, *getPartID*, $\$part\_name$) **return**
2. **let** $\$v_2 :=$ callws($\mathcal{W}_b$, *getVendors*, $\$v_1$) **return**
3. **let** $\$v_3 :=$ { **for** $\$v_4$ **in** $\$v_2$ **return** callws($\$v_4$, *getPrice*, $\$v_1$) } **return**
4. **let** $\$v_5 :=$ min($\$v_3$) **return**
5. **for** $\$v_6$ **in** $\$v_2$ **return** {
6.   **let** $\$v_7 :=$ callws($\$v_6$, *getPrice*, $\$v_1$) **return**
7.   **if** ($\$v_7 = \$v_5$) **then** { $\$v_7$, { **let** $\$v_8 :=$ callws($\$v_6$, *getVendorInfo*)
8.   **return** $\$v_8$ } }
9.   **else** () }

XQuery[5] is the standard way for querying XML data. It has evolved into a fairly complex language, and is going to play a more important role in many application contexts. The future architecture of B2B platforms will take the *SOA (Services-Oriented Architecture)* approach, which is defined as a collection of software services, available to other applications across the network and accessible using a standard interface. We envision that in the future, there will be a Web portal for each industry community. An XML schema, which consists of user-defined types in this community, is kept inside the portal, and known by all members. All members of this community have agreed on this XML schema. It would be an important step towards conducting B2B over the Internet fully automatically. Via the portal, when they want to obtain the part supplier with the lowest price, users can select a program Q in the portal, and specify the part name, then submit this program. After a while, the result is returned to users, or displayed in browsers. We believe that, XQuery, originally designed for querying and constructing XML data, is well suited for this kind of applications. More precisely, we embed Web services calls into XQuery main modules, which is the basic idea of our approach. The overall system architecture of our approach is depicted in Fig. 1.

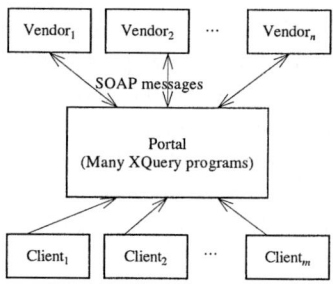

Fig. 1. The system architecture of our approach

As shown in Fig. 1, many *extended XQuery programs* are kept inside the portal. In order to evaluate an extended XQuery program Q, some parameters must be specified first. Hence, they are called *parameterized XQuery programs*, termed as *WSQuery* in this paper. There are some Web services calls embedded in Q. These services calls will invoke Web services residing in remote service providers, e.g., vendors in our example. Service calls are static concepts, while service invocations are dynamic ones. That is, service calls are embedded in programs, and these calls will be invoked during evaluation. The processing engine of the portal will send SOAP requests to service providers, and receive SOAP responses. For services integration, it is usual that Q needs to access different service providers, or invoke the same Web service with different parameter values.

Our approach is a practical one for several reasons. Ordinary users own little technical knowledge, such as that of XML, Web services and XQuery, etc. The programs in the community portal are developed and maintained by domain experts as well as experienced programmers, who know technical terms and business logic very well. Our architecture features in several distinct points: 1) if a vendor makes minor modifications to its internal system, so long as its Web service interface does not change, nothing outside of the vendor's system is required to change; 2) even if the Web service interfaces of a vendor are changed, the staff who maintain the portal can change all affected WSQuery programs accordingly, which is transparent to all users; 3) XQuery is one of declarative languages. It is not a unusual case that an XQuery program of dozens of lines can complete the same task as does a Java program of hundreds of lines. Therefore, our approach can increase the productivity of application developers.

Further, we investigate how to reduce the evaluation time of WSQuery programs. In order to achieve that, intra-query parallelism is exploited. We consider the latency between service requests and responses as one of the most important factors of the total evaluation time. Our focus will not be on the cost of XPath expressions. In the distributed environment, the unstable network condition and many other unanticipated factors affect the evaluation time much more than does the typical XPath navigation.

Related Work. [16] proposed to use XQuery to handle the messaging layer, thus give the application a more direct access to the original Web service content and semantics. Their work also provides a framework for distributed XQuery processing. We study how to reduce the total evaluation time by exploiting intra-query parallelism within a similar framework. XL[12, 11] is a platform for Web services, which provides a high-level language for Web services development, but does not provide details about how to connect to the existing Web services infrastructure. However, we focus on the service integration problem. Thus, the optimization efforts reported in [11] are aimed at totally different goals from ours. [8] developed a middle-tier Web services architecture to optimize the exchange of large XML data volumes. The authors focused on the data exchange problem. Finally, in the context of the ActiveXML project[7, 14, 15, 6], the authors study dynamic XML documents, where some of the data is given explicitly while other parts are defined only intensionally by means of embedded Web service calls. They focused on devising strategies to distribute and replicate dynamic documents in a P2P architecture, and also studied efficient evaluation of XPath queries over such documents.

Data dependency analysis is a fundamental compiler analysis tool for optimizing programs on parallel architectures. It supports many transformation strategies, and can be applied to important optimization problems such as parallelization, compiler memory hierarchy management, and instruction scheduling. For a comprehensive treatment of dependency analysis techniques and their application, one can refer to [13]. However, these techniques are mainly aimed at fully utilizing processor capabilities, and only take little consideration of network latency. Thus, they cannot be directly applied to our new problem.

Organization. The outline of the paper is as follows. In Section 2, we introduce the concepts and notions of Web services and request-response operation types. In Section 3, we give the definition of *WSQuery*, and present its conceptual evaluation strategy. In Section 4, we describe dependency analysis techniques for WSQuery expressions, and in Section 5, we discuss parallel evaluation of WSQuery expressions. Finally, our conclusion and a discussion of future work are in Section 6.

2 Preliminary

Since there exists no established and all-agreed-upon definition of Web services, we first present our definition of Web services which will be used in this paper. Intuitively, a Web service is a software module which can be invoked over the Web remotely. From a very low level, this software module takes SOAP messages as input, then produces SOAP messages as responses; from a higher and more abstract level, a Web service takes several parameters of some types, defined in the type system of XML schema, then generates a result of some pre-defined type. The parameters and results fit well together with the type system offered in XML schema. XQuery expressions also work in the same type system. Therefore, XQuery is an appropriate language for dealing with Web services integration.

Definition 1 (Web service). Given an XML schema S, there is a set T of simple, atomic or compound types defined in S. A Web service $W = (url, oplst)$, where url indicates the location of $\mathcal{W}$'s description file (i.e., its WSDL file), $oplst = (op_1, op_2, \ldots, op_n)$ is the list of *operations* provided in $\mathcal{W}$. An operation $op = (name, parlst, rst)$, where $parlst$ is the list of parameters $(para_1, para_2, \ldots)$, rst represents op's result. Each parameter $para = (v, t)$, where v is its value, and $t \in T$ is its type, and v should conform to t. The components of rst are similar to those of $para$. □

Following the definition of Web services, we define *operation types* of Web services. In this paper, we consider only the most commonly-used operation type, that is, *request-response* type. Other operation types, such as *one-way*, *solicit-response* and *notification* will be investigated in our future work. An operation of request-response type receives a request, then returns a response.

Definition 2 (Request-response operation type). Let $\mathcal{W}$ be the Web service to be invoked. More precisely, let op be the operation of $\mathcal{W}$ to be invoked. In a typical service invocation concerning op, first all real parameters are passed into op; then after the latency $lat(\mathcal{W}, op)$, the result is returned to the caller. During this process, the value of each parameter should be type-compliant, and the result conforms to the pre-defined returning type, too. □

XQuery is originally designed to query XML sources or other sources which have been exported as XML views. In this paper, however, we extend XQuery to integrate different Web services. Thus, the built-in function *fn:doc* is replaced by a new function *fn:callws*, whose prototype is of the following form

fn:callws(url as xsd:string, op as xsd:string, $para_1$, $para_2$, ...),

where url is the URL location of the WSDL file, whose purpose is to locate the Web service $\mathcal{W}$, op is the operation name of $\mathcal{W}$ to be invoked. op is followed by one or more parameters which are required by op.

In the rest of the paper, the extended XQuery is referred to as *WSQuery*, which is named after "X*Query* extended with *W*eb *S*ervice calls". The syntax and formal semantics of WSQuery are nearly the same as those of XQuery, except for the *fn:callws* construct and its corresponding semantics. Thus, we describe the semantics of *fn:wscall* here in an informal way. First, we discuss its static semantics. The input parameters' types should be compliant with the operation op of $\mathcal{W}$. The returning result should work well with other parts of the WSQuery program, with respect to their types. Then, we present the dynamic semantics of *fn:callws*. When it encounters an *fn:callws*, the evaluation procedure of a WSQuery program cannot proceed until the returning result is received. More specifically, all parameters must have obtained their value before the remote operation is invoked. After the invocation, the evaluation procedure has to wait for its returning result. In this sense, the Web service invocation in our paper is a synchronous one. We believe that it is practical in most real-world applications.

3 WSQuery

This section defines the syntax and semantics of *WSQuery*. As mentioned above, WSQuery is an extension of XQuery with embedded Web services calls. For easy discussion, we present several notations before we introduce WSQuery. First, we give the definitions of *simple paths* and *conditions*.

Definition 3. A path expression with no variables is called a *simple path*, e.g., a/b/c, a/*/c, etc. □

Definition 4. An *elementary condition* is either of the form $\$x/\pi \circ c$, exists $\$x/\pi$, or $\$x/\pi \circ \$y/\pi'$, where c is a string, an integer, a decimal, or a double, π and π' are simple paths, and $\circ \in \{=, <, >, \leq, \geq\}$. A *condition* is a boolean combination of elementary conditions using "and", "or", "not" and "true". □

For simplicity of discussion, we investigate the extension of a subset of XQuery in this paper, though the techniques proposed here can be easily extended to deal with larger subsets of XQuery.

Definition 5. Essentially, a *WSQuery program* is an *expression* e with some global parameters. An expression e is recursively defined as follows[1]:

1. e is a *literal constant*;
2. e is a *variable* $\$var$;
3. e is a *path expression* $\$var/\pi$, where π is a simple path;
4. e is an *empty sequence* ();
5. e is a *concatenation* of several expressions $e_1, e_2, \ldots, e_n$;
6. e is a *for expression*

   for $\$var$ in e_1 return e_2;

7. e is a *let expression*

   let $\$var := e_1$ return e_2;

8. e is an *if expression*

   if $(cond)$ then e_1 else e_2,

   where $cond$ is a condition;
9. Particularly, e is a *Web service call*, which is of the form

   fn:callws(url as xsd:string, op as xsd:string, $para_1, para_2, \ldots$).

As can be understood easily, all the cases but the last one are very similar to those of the standard XQuery[5]. The last case, *Web service call fn:callws*, is an extension function, with the first parameter url denoting the location of the WSDL file, op being the operation to be invoked, and a list of parameters for op. □

---
[1] We omit some cases here, e.g., $max()$, $min()$, *arithmetic expressions*, etc.

We assume that there are no two distinct variables with the same name in a WSQuery program Q. It is not a significant restriction since a variable in Q can be easily renamed without affecting the semantics of Q at all. Obviously, there are three methods to introduce a new variable: the first is via global parameters of Q; the second via *for* constructs; the third via *let* constructs. It is worth mentioning that the *for* construct also introduces an iteration, while does the *let* construct not. This is the most significant difference between *for* and *let*.

In this work, special attention is given to the last case *fn:callws*. Given a WSQuery Q, if the *url* and *op* parameters of all Web service calls are specified literally, i.e., their values are known before the running time, then Q is called *simple WSQuery*. Otherwise, Q is called *complex WSQuery*. In a complex WSQuery Q, there exists at least one Web service call *wsc*, such that one cannot decide *wsc*'s provider or the operation to be invoked during the compiling time.

Since service providers did not, or were reluctant to, offer any API interfaces to external applications for querying any statistics information, the portal itself has to maintain the latency between a service request and its response. A reasonable approach to maintaining this kind of statistics is building a hash table H. Each entry in H is a pair (wo, lat), where lat is the latency collected by the monitoring engine of the portal, and wo is itself a pair (ws, op), where ws denotes a Web service, and op is its operation. At first, since no historical data have been collected, we simply set lat to 0. After successfully requesting an operation of a Web service, this statistics information is refreshed. For figuring out the time delay of the operation op of the Web service $\mathcal{W}$, the processing engine would examine if the entry for $(\mathcal{W}, op)$ already exists in H. If the entry already exists, its lat field will be made use of; If the entry is not in H yet, a specific $latency = 0$ will be used, and a new entry for $(\mathcal{W}, op)$ is inserted into H. When the invocation is completed, the new entry will be refreshed to reflect the current system status.

Now we present the definition of *WSQuery tree*. Given an WSQuery program Q, its WSQuery tree T is its parse tree, such that

- The root node r of T corresponds to Q;
- For each non-leaf node v of T, assuming that v corresponds to the subexpression e of Q, v's children correspond to components of e. Note that v's children are ordered. For example, if e is a *for* expression, then v will have three children c_1, c_2 and c_3. c_1 corresponds to the var part, c_2 corresponds to e_1, and c_3 corresponds to e_2.
- Leaf nodes of T are either constants or Web services calls.

3.1 Conceptual Evaluation

For each expression e, there are three crucial components. The first component is a set of *free variables* $fvs = \{\$v_1, \$v_2, \ldots, \$v_n\}$. A variable v is called a *free variable* with respect to a given expression e if v's value has to be passed into e for evaluating e. In other words, the variable v is only referenced in e, instead of being defined in e. This concept of free variable is similar to that in mathematical logics. In running time, the set fvs is also called a *running context*. The second component is a directed acyclic graph (also known as *dependency graph*) which represents the dependency relations among different Web services calls inside e. The third component is e's returning value. Hence, a straightforward way for evaluating an expression e is as following: the evaluation procedure cannot begin until each free variable has obtained its concrete value; Web services calls will be invoked in a reverse topological order according to the dependency graph. The free variables of the WSQuery program Q are global parameters, which need to be specified by users before triggering Q. The dependency graph of Q consists of dependency relations among Web services calls embedded in Q. The returning result of Q is what users want.

We next present the dynamic semantics of a WSQuery program Q by describing a conceptual evaluation strategy, which is a rather straightforward one. We also call it the logical evaluation plan of Q, since we will obtain optimized evaluation plan based on this conceptual evaluation plan. And the relationship between the twos is much like that between the corresponding terms for query evaluation in database management systems. Given the global parameters of Q, Q is recursively evaluated guided by the WSQuery tree of Q:

1. If e is a *literal*, since e is a constant, it can be evaluated directly, and return the result immediately.
2. If e is a *variable* var, var must have obtained its value, therefore, the evaluation of e can return its result immediately.
3. If e is a *path expression* var/π, π has to be evaluated over var before e returns the result. As the evaluation of path expression is not our focus, in fact, this cost is trivial if compared with the invocation latency, we also deem that e can be evaluated immediately.
4. If e is (), it can return at once.
5. If e is a concatenation of $e_1, e_2, \ldots, e_n$, all e_i for $1 \leq i \leq n$ will first be evaluated in order, then the concatenation of their result forms the returning result of e.
6. If e is "for var in e_1 return e_2", first e_1 is evaluated and return a sequence s. For the first item i_1 in s, one assigns i_1 to var, and the information of var is added to the current running context to form a new running context. Then e_2 will be evaluated in this new running context. If s has the next item, the above procedure happens once again .... At last, the result in each iteration of evaluating e_2 is concatenated, then returned.
7. If e is "let $var := e_1$ return e_2", e_1 is first evaluated in the current running context. Then e_1's result is assigned to var. The running context is updated accordingly. After that, e_2 is evaluated in this new runtime context, and its evaluation result is returned also as the result of e.
8. If e is "if (*cond*) then e_1 else e_2", the branch condition *cond* is first evaluated, then according to its result, either e_1 or e_2 will be evaluated.
9. If e is a Web service call, real parameters of *fn:callws* can be calculated without or with only simple computation. They are passed to the service provider decided by the parameters *url* and *op*. The evaluation process cannot proceed until it receives the response.

There are three interesting points in the above conceptual evaluation strategy. The first is that the evaluation process is a single-threaded one. Actually, this is one of obvious drawbacks of conceptual evaluation. Going from single-threaded evaluation to multi-threaded evaluation will be a significant improvement. Only with a multi-threaded mechanism, intra-query parallelism can be fully exploited. The second is that a stack of runtime contexts should be maintained during the entire evaluation process. First, an initial context which consists of all global parameters is pushed into the stack. For evaluating *for* or *let* expressions, which introduce new variables, a new runtime context will be created based on the current one. The new context contains the information of the new variable. After accomplishing the evaluation of the *for* or *let* expression, the runtime context created just now is popped away, and the top context on the stack becomes the new current runtime context. The third is that a WSQuery program has some global parameters. Hence, it cannot be evaluated until all of its global parameters have got real values.

3.2 Cost Estimation

Here we consider three non-trivial cases, *concatenation*, *let* and *Web service call*, and defer the discussions on *for* and *if* expressions to later sections. Let $cost(e)$ denote the total evaluation time of e.

Concatenation. Let $e \leftarrow e_1, e_2, \ldots, e_n$. Since e_i's are evaluated in order, $cost(e) = \sum_{i=1}^{n} cost(e_i)$.

Let. Let $e \leftarrow$ let $\$var := e_1$ return e_2. e_1 is first evaluated, followed by the evaluation of e_2. Thus, $cost(e) = cost(e_1) + cost(e_2)$.

Web service call. Let $e \leftarrow$ fn:callws(url, op, ...). After sending out the request, the evaluation process of e cannot proceed until the response is received. Hence, $cost(e) = lat(url, op)$. As discussed above, $lat(url, op)$ is unknown at the beginning. Only after a successful invocation, during which the monitoring engine of the portal recorded its statistics information, $lat(url, op)$ will hold a concrete non-zero value, which is an estimate of $cost(e)$.

4 Dependency Analysis

The essence of the evaluation process for an WSQuery program is how to evaluate an expression. Let e be an expression with free variables $\{\$fv_1, \$fv_2, \ldots\}$. For evaluating e, the values of these free variables should be known before. In the application scenario of integrating a variety of Web services, the above requirement means that the relevant Web services must have been invoked, and the responses must have been received by the caller before evaluating e. This requirement also applies to the entire WSQuery program, whose global parameters should get values before the evaluation. Therefore, the dependency of an expression on Web service invocations is a crucial point for the analysis of WSQuery programs.

As discussed in Section 3.1, one of essential components of WSQuery programs is dependency relations. There are both control flow and data flow during the evaluation process. We construct two graphs to represent control flow and data flow, respectively. The graph for control flow is the WSQuery tree, and the one for data flow is a directed acyclic graph $G_{df} = (V, E)$. Each Web service call is represented by a vertex of G_{df}. A directed edge $e = (u, v) \in E$ indicates that the Web service call wsc_u represented by u should be invoked before the service call wsc_v represented by v. We say that wsc_v is dependent on wsc_u.

Considering a Web service invocation wsc, it requires real parameters. These parameters' value must have been determined before the invocation wsc. It is either specified by users or intermediate result. The intermediate result is obtained during the previous evaluation. Thus, wsc is dependent on other service invocations.

Web service invocation is a dynamic concept, instead of a static one. An invocation is decided by not only the Web service and the operation, but also by the value of its parameters. Different parameters would result in different invocations. Generally speaking, even if the operation and its parameters have been fixed, the result of one invocation may be different from that of another one. The reason is that the application system of the service provider can update its data or there maybe exist some Web services and operations through which users can change them. It is conceivable that there are two kinds of Web services, one of which is for querying information, the other one of which is for modifying information. In this paper, we consider only the former kind of Web services. We do not consider the *time* factor. That is, the same invocation will always return a fixed result. Since the result does not vary with time, this makes it feasible caching the result of Web service invocations.

WSQuery expressions can be composed arbitrarily. Hence, Web service invocations can occur within any subexpression and their parameters can be any previously computed result. During the evaluation of WSQuery, there are two kinds of dataflow: one is top-down, and the other is bottom-up. Let e be an expression, and e' be e's subexpression. The top-down dataflow consists of passing-by of data from e to e', while the bottom-up dataflow from e' to e. The input parameters of an WSQuery program Q specified by users would be passed to Q's subexpressions, then subexpressions of Q's subexpressions, ...

5 Parallel Evaluation

In this section, we investigate how to exploit intra-query parallelism for evaluating WSQuery programs. We begin by considering basic WSQuery programs, which do not involve *for* and *if* conditional expressions.

Considering a basic WSQuery program Q, in which the *url* and *op* parameters of each Web service call are specified. Thus, each service provider is known beforehand. We can devise its dependency graph. Then, the problem of finding a desirable evaluation plan is cast to the classical scheduling problem. Therefore, we state formally the problem as following:

Given a set of Web service invocations $S = \{s_1, s_2, \ldots, s_n\}$, and a set of service providers $P = \{p_1, p_2, \ldots, p_m\}$. Each invocation s_i for $i = 1, 2, \ldots, n$ can only be executed in certain provider p_j specified by a mapping $site : S \to P$. A dependency relation $dep \subseteq S \times S$ is also specified. If $dep(s_i, s_j)$ holds, the invocation s_i cannot be evaluated before s_j. In other words, s_i depends on s_j. There must not be cycles in the dependency relation dep because an invocation cannot directly or indirectly depend on itself. A mapping $dur : S \to \boldsymbol{R}^+$ is also given. The invocation s_i would take $dur(s_i)$ time period to complete.

Our goal is to find the optimal schedule such that the total evaluation time is the least. However, the problem of finding the optimal schedule is *NP-hard*. We can use some heuristics, e.g., similar to [10], to obtain an approximation to the optimal schedule.

Next we discuss how to deal with *for* loops and *if* conditional expressions. Our basic idea is to examine *for* and *if* nodes *level by level*. We propose two strategies.

Lazy Evaluation. Given a WSQuery program Q, its WSQuery tree T_Q is constructed. Some nodes of T_Q are *for* or *if* nodes. This strategy involves many iterations. Let n be a *for* or *if* node of T_Q. In the first iteration, we do not study the nodes below n. If n is a *for* node, assuming the corresponding expression is "for \$v in e_1 return e_2", we introduce a dummy variable \$$v_d$, whose name should not conflict with names of existing variables, and rewrite this *for* expression as "\$$v_d \leftarrow e_1$". We apply the same rewriting technique for all *for* nodes, then obtain a new WSQuery tree T'. One can derive the dependency relation of T', and obtain an approximately optimal evaluation plan. Then Q is evaluated partially. After that, all dummy variables have got their values. These intermediate results are kept in main memory.

In the second iteration, we study all the topmost *for* and *if* nodes. We do not examine the non-topmost *for* and *if* nodes which have not been examined yet. Considering a *for* expression e, because the value of the dummy variable v is known now, we can unfold it according to $|v|$. Let the loop body be denoted by e_b. In fact, the unfolding result is $|v|$ e_b's. If only considering the effect on scheduling, these $|v|$ e_b's are the same as their concatenation. Considering a *if* expression e, because the condition can be calculated easily, we pick the correct branch, and ignore the other one. Since this process is called *unfolding*, if a *for* or *if* node has been examined, we say it has been *unfolded*.

After unfolding, we obtain a forest of separate trees, whose roots are *for* or *if* nodes. It can be proved that there exists no dependency relations among different trees. Therefore, we only need to investigate dependency relations on each individual tree. Applying the same techniques as before, we derive all dependency relations, then schedule these Web service invocations. During the entire evaluation process, an approach is followed which interleaves unfolding and evaluation. This idea is similar to that adopted in [9].

Eager Evaluation. The second strategy is based on *eager evaluation*. With this strategy, we try to unfold *for* and *if* expressions as early as possible. Compared with the second strategy, the first strategy seems to be a *lazy* one. In the second strategy, once e_1 has been evaluated, the *for* expression "for $v in e_1 return e_2" is unfolded; similarly, once *cond*'s truth value is known, the branch to be evaluated can be unfolded.

Discussion. Challenges arise if the *url* or *op* parameter of any Web service invocation involves variables. If *url* contains variables, the service provider cannot be determined; if *op* contains variables, the latency cannot be decided, because we do not know which operation will be invoked. We propose to adopt the following policy similar to eager evaluation. Assume that the *url* or *op* parameter involves a variable $v. Once $v's value has been worked out, we compute the parameter. If both *url* and *op* of a Web service invocation have already been determined, this invocation is immediately added to the set of service invocations which need scheduling.

6 Conclusion

In this paper, we have presented a new paradigm for Web services integration. We extend XQuery to integrate Web services from different service providers. The extension of XQuery is called *WSQuery*. We conduct dependency analysis on WSQuery expressions. Then we try to reduce the total evaluation time by scheduling service invocations, and exploiting parallelism among providers. To deal with *for* loops, *if* conditions, lazy or eager evaluation strategy can be adopted. As part of our future work, we would like to explore a more accurate cost model which takes into consideration network latency, the size of SOAP messages, and the cardinality of results, etc.

Acknowledgments. We want to address our thanks to Qiong Luo at Hong Kong University of Science and Technology for helpful comments on previous drafts of the paper.

References

1. BEA Systems, Inc. http://www.bea.com/.
2. IONA Technologies. http://www.iona.com.
3. Ipedo, Inc. http://www.ipedo.com/.
4. Web services description language (wsdl) version 2.0 part 1: Core language. W3C Working Draft, Aug. 2004. http://www.w3.org/TR/wsdl20/.
5. XQuery 1.0: an XML query language. W3C Working Draft, July 2004. http://www.w3.org/TR/xquery/.
6. S. Abiteboul, O. Benjelloun, B. Cautis, et al. Lazy query evaluation for active XML. In *Proc. of SIGMOD*, 2004.
7. S. Abiteboul, O. Benjelloun, I. Manolescu, et al. Active XML: Peer-to-peer data and web services integration. In *Proc. of VLDB*, 2002.
8. S. Amer-Yahia and Y. Kotidis. A web-services architecture for efficient xml data exchange. In *Proc. of ICDE*, 2004.

9. M. Benedikt, C. Y. Chan, W. Fan, et al. DTD-directed publishing with attribute translation grammars. In *Proc. of VLDB*, 2002.
10. M. Benedikt, C.-Y. Chan, W. Fan, et al. Capturing both types and constraints in data integration. In *Proc. of SIGMOD*, 2003.
11. D. Florescu, A. Grünhagen, and D. Kossmann. XL: a platform for web services. In *Proc. of CIDR*, 2003.
12. D. Florescu, A. Grünhagen, D. Kossmann, and S. Rost. XL: a platform for web services. In *Proc. of SIGMOD (demo)*, 2002.
13. K. Kennedy and J. R. Allen. *Optimizing Compilers for Modern Architectures*. Morgan Kaufmann, 2001.
14. T. Milo, S. Abiteboul, B. Amann, et al. Dynamic XML documents with distribution and replication. In *Proc. of SIGMOD*, 2003.
15. T. Milo, S. Abiteboul, B. Amann, et al. Exchanging intensional XML data. In *Proc. of SIGMOD*, 2003.
16. N. Onose and J. Siméon. XQuery at your web service. In *Proc. of WWW*, 2004.

A New Indexing Method for High Dimensional Dataset

Jiyuan An[1], Yi-Ping Phoebe Chen[1], Qinying Xu[2], and Xiaofang Zhou[3]

[1] Deakin University, Australia
[2] University of Tsukuba, Japan
[3] University of Queensland, Australia
{jiyuan,phoebe}@deakin.edu.au
qinying@kslab.is.tsukuba.ac.jp
zxf@itee.uq.edu.au

Abstract. Indexing high dimensional datasets has attracted extensive attention from many researchers in the last decade. Since R-tree type of index structures are known as suffering "curse of dimensionality" problems, Pyramid-tree type of index structures, which are based on the B-tree, have been proposed to break the curse of dimensionality. However, for high dimensional data, the number of pyramids is often insufficient to discriminate data points when the number of dimensions is high. Its effectiveness degrades dramatically with the increase of dimensionality. In this paper, we focus on one particular issue of "curse of dimensionality"; that is, the surface of a hypercube in a high dimensional space approaches 100% of the total hypercube volume when the number of dimensions approaches infinite. We propose a new indexing method based on the surface of dimensionality. We prove that the Pyramid tree technology is a special case of our method. The results of our experiments demonstrate clear priority of our novel method.

1 Introduction

Multimedia objects, such as images, video and audio clips, are often mapped into a high dimensional space, such that similarity search among these multimedia objects are translated into distance-based queries in the high dimensional feature space. To facilitate efficient search in very large amount of multimedia datasets, it is necessary to use a high dimensional index mechanism that must be able to scale not with the amount of the data, but more importantly, also with the number of dimensionality. R-tree and its variations are commonly used index methods for multi-dimensional datasets [8][6]. The basic idea of R-tree and its variations can be briefly described as the following. Firstly, a multi-dimensional space is partitioned recursively into a hierarchical structure according to data distribution. Secondly, the partitioned subspaces are permitted to overlap with each other. However, the idea of permitting overlapping sibling subspaces brings a serious drawback for high dimensional spaces, as the overlapping extent of sibling R-tree nodes in the directory increases rapidly to about 90% of their entire volume when the dimensionality is increased to 5 [4][1][2]. That defeats the purpose of hierarchical indexing completely, as most nodes can not be pruned in the searching process. This type of indexes also suffers another problem.

The fan out of a node becomes very small due to the large size of coordinates for high dimensional data. Consequently, the performance of such an index structure degrades and its effectiveness is sometimes worse than linear scan. Many improvements have been proposed (e.g.[4]), but the problems mentioned above still exist for most known attempts.

If an indexing method requires keeping all coordinates of data items in the index, the size of the index structure is, of course, proportional to the dimensionality. To reduce the size of index, Bechtold *et al* proposed a method called the Pyramid-tree [5] [11][13], where high dimensional data is mapped into a linear space such that some classical index structures, such as B$^+$-tree, can be used. This results a better performance than the X-trees and other R-tree inspired multidimensional indexes. However, for one pyramid, it is known that most data items concentrate on its base. The slices in each pyramid can not make the index more discriminative, as the data points in one pyramid always have the same index value.

In a Pyramid tree, one data point is associated with one pyramid, and a data point is indexed by a base of pyramid. If the dimensionality is d, the base of pyramid is $(d-1)$-D hyperplane. In this paper, we generalize the ideal of using $(d-1)$-D hyperplane to using $(d-i)$-D hyperplane $(1 \leq i \leq d)$. The number of index values will be increased in such a way to make the index more discriminative for a better search performance. This paper, to the best of our knowledge, proposes the first solution to index high dimensional data based on surfaces. We will demonstrate its significantly improved efficiency comparing to the traditional Pyramid tree indexing. We also show that the Pyramid tree is a special case of our surface-based indexing method.

Section 2 of this paper describes the motivation of surface index structure. In Section 3, we discuss the structure of a novel surface-based spatial index method. In Section 4, we propose a method for the allocation of pyramids for the data points on the boundary. Section 5 shows the results of experiments comparing with the Pyramid-tree technique.

2 Motivation

Because of the limitation of visual, no one can see more than 3 dimensional spaces. We can only image them from 2- or 3-D space. However, we give some examples to show that high dimensional space is not imaginable from 2- or 3-D space. Throughout this paper, the data space is normalized into $(0,1]$. So our objective data space is a hypercube. Its length of edges is 1.

2.1 Non-intuition of High Dimensionality

High dimensional data can be found everywhere. Time series is a traditional high dimensional data. We can also use high dimensional data to describe an object, such as, a people can be described using his features (tall, weight, age, and etc.). If two objects are similar, we consider they are corresponded to two near data points in high dimensional space even we can no be seen. The axes of the dimensional space consist of the feature vectors. However, high dimensional data has own characters which are different with data in 2- or 3-D space. Fig. 1(A) shows a circle of r radius and its circumscribed quadrilateral. The distance from a vertex of quadrilateral to circle is denoted by a, where a holds the following inequality in 2- or 3-D space.

$$r \geq a$$

However, as the dimension increases, this inequality becomes inappropriate. For example, in the case of 16-D space, a has 3 times length of r ($a=3r$). It can easy be calculated by the following equation.

$$(r+a)^2 = \underbrace{r^2 + \cdots + r^2}_{16} \qquad (1)$$

Our visual field used to be in 3-D space. It is difficult to understand these kinds of phenomena. Many researchers try to extend spatial index method R-tree, which is originally used in 2-D dataset [8]. When these methods proved unavailable, the term "curse of dimensionality" was cited [3].

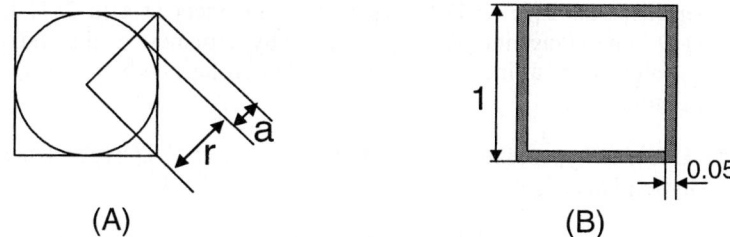

(A) (B)

Fig. 1. (a) The relation between radius and diagonal. (B) Surface and volume

2.2 Distribution of High Dimensional Dataset

To constitute the node of an index tree, the data space is partitioned. When the dimensionality increases, the exponential changes of the volume need to be considered. For example, the d-D hypercube of e edge has volume $vol = e^d$. In the case of $0 < e < 1$, the volume decreases exponentially according to d, on the other hand, when $e > 1$, the volume expands exponentially. Now we consider the distribution of data points in a hypercube. That is, how many percentage of volume is occupied by its surface? Fig. 1(B) shows a square of edge 1.

Table 1. The volume of surface

The number of dimensionality	Volume of surface
2	$1 - 0.9^2 = 0.190$
3	$1 - 0.9^3 = 0.271$
. .	
50	$1 - 0.9^{50} = 0.994846$

The volume of the margin layer has a thickness of 0.05. Table 1 shows the volume of various aspects of dimensionality. From the table, we can find that 99.5% volume is in the surface of a 50-D hypercube. In this kind of high dimensional space, if a dataset is distributed uniformly, it can be said that *most of the data points are in the surface, not in the interior of the hypercube*. This is the motivation for this paper. To cope with this "important" surface, a surface based index structure for high dimensional space is proposed.

If the number of dimensions is d, the surface of a hypercube consists of d-1, d-2, ... ,1, 0-D hyperplanes. For example, a 3-D cube consists of 6 squares (2-D), 12 edges (1-D) and 8 vertexes (0-D). These (hyper) planes anchor the index high dimensional data. The next Subsection explains this in detail.

2.3 Vertexes, Edges and Hyperplanes in Hypercube

A square (2-D) consists of 4 edges and 4 vertexes; a cube (3-D) consists of 6 squares, 12 edges and 8 vertexes. In general, the number of $(d-1)$-D hyperplanes in a d-D hypercube is $2d$. We can also say the hypercube is covered by $2d$ hyperplanes. One hyperplane is also covered by consists of $(d-2)$-D hyperplanes. Therefore, the relation of all hyperplanes is: Two $(d-1)$-D hyperplanes intersect at a $(d-2)$-D hyperplanes. Three $(d-1)$-D hyperplanes intersect at a $(d-3)$-D hyperplanes. At the end, d-1 $(d-1)$-D hyperplanes intersect at a line. The number of hyperplanes which cover a hypercube is given in Lemma 1.

LEMMA 1. A d-D hypercube is covered by 0, 1, ... , $(d-1)$-D hyperplanes, The number of i-D hyperplanes is $2^i \times C_d^i$.

Table 2. The number of hyperplanes of 20-D hypercube

The number of dimensionality of hyperplanes	Shape of hyperplanes	The number of hyperplanes
19	Hyper-plane	40
18	Hyper-plane	760
17	Hyper-plane	9,120
16	Hyper-plane	77,520
15	Hyper-plane	496,128
14	Hyper-plane	2,480,640
13	Hyper-plane	9,922,560
12	Hyper-plane	32,248,320
11	Hyper-plane	85,995,520
10	Hyper-plane	189,190,144
9	Hyper-plane	343,982,080
8	Hyper-plane	515,973,120
7	Hyper-plane	635,043,840
6	Hyper-plane	635,043,840
5	Hyper-plane	508,035,072
4	Hyper-plane	317,521,920
3	Hyper-plane	149,422,080
2	Plane	49,807,360
1	Line	10,485,760
0	Vertex	1,048,576

As dimension increases, the number of hyperplanes expands rapidly. This number is usually beyond the size of most datasets. It is therefore possible that one data point corresponds to one hyperplane of the hypercube. The hyperplane becomes the index key of a data point. Searching similar data points becomes searching near hyperplanes. We can employ pyramid tree technique to map data point to one hyperplane; that is, partitioning the data space (or hypercube) by pyramids whose tops are the centres of hypercube and whose bases are the hyperplanes. Since most data points are in the surface of data space, the data points in the pyramid can be represented with its base (a hyperplane). If the hyperplanes are ordered in a sequence, the data points within pyramids can be indexed with linear index structure B^+-tree. That is, a high dimensional data changes to linear data. When a range query is given, to search for similar data points becomes to find the pyramids overlapping with the query range.

3 Surface Based Spatial Index Structure

Data space is assumed to be normalized into a hypercube having edge 1. The bases of two opposite pyramids are perpendicular to an axis x_i. They can be expressed with $x_i = 0$ and $x_i = 1$. In a pyramid whose base is $x_i = 0$, every data point $(x_0, x_1, ..., x_{d-1})$ satisfies

$$x_i \leq \min(x_j, 1 - x_j) \quad \text{where} \quad (j = 0,1,..., i-1, i+1,..., d-1) \quad (2)$$

Based on equation (2), for a given data point, the pyramid which the data point belongs to can be determined. We use the order number of the pyramid as index key. Then B^+-tree linear index structure is used to search for similar data.

3.1 Order of Pyramid

A d-D hypercube is covered by $(d-1)$-D hyperplanes. We assume its axes are $x_0, x_1 \cdots, x_{d-1},$. The order numbers of the pyramids are assigned in Table 3. The order number of pyramid is determined by its base. Fig. 2 shows a 3-D cube. The pyramid with base $x_0 = 0$ has an order number of 0, illustrated by p_0. Its opposite pyramid is denoted by p_3.

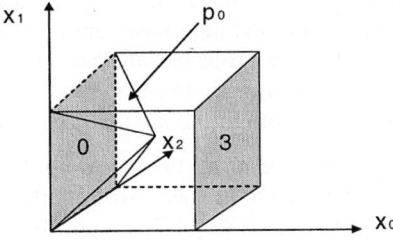

Fig. 2. The order of pyramid. A 3-D cube. The bases $x_0 = 0$ and $x_0 = 1$ are assigned the order number 0 and 3 respectively. Corresponding pyramids are denoted as p_0 and p_3

Table 3. The order of pyramids in d-D hypercube

Hyperplane	order	Order of pyramids
$x_0 = 0$	0	p_0
$x_0 = 1$	d	p_d
$x_1 = 0$	1	p_1
$x_1 = 1$	d+1	p_{d+1}
$x_{d-1} = 0$	d-1	p_{d-1}
$x_{d-1} = 1$	2d-1	p_{2d-1}

3.2 Constitution of Index Key

The index keys of all data are initialized with null. For a given data point, it must belong to one pyramid. (If the data point is on the boundary of two or more pyramids, its belongingness will be discussed in Section 4). When a hypercube is partitioned, the order number of a pyramid is appended to the index key. The process is done recursively. Fig. 3 shows how to constitute key in a 3-D cube. The given data point assumed be in the pyramid $x_1 = 0$. First, the index key is initialized with null. Second, since the data point belongs to the pyramid whose base is $x_1 = 0$, the order number "1" (refer the Table 3) is appended to the index key as shown in subfigure (A). To partition data space recursively, the data point is projected into the pyramid's base as illustrated in the subfigure (B). The base is partitioned into 4 triangles. Since the data point is in No. 3 triangle (described in Table 3), the index key becomes longer by adding "3" as shown in subfigure (C). Finally, we assume the triangle is divided into 8 slices. The slice number "2" is appended into the data key. The total index key of the given data point consists of "1", "3", "2" as shown in subfigure (D). It can easily be combined to an integer, such as (1*4+3)*8+2=58. In this formula, the coefficients "4" and "8" are total numbers of lines and slices shown in the subfigure (C), (D) respectively. The index key is easy to be decoded and find which pyramids the data points belong to. In general, the partitioning process can be described with the 2 steps below.

1. A d-D hypercube is partitioned into $2d$ pyramids, their tops are the center points of the hypercube, and their bases are $(d-1)$-D hyperplanes.
2. Within one pyramid, we projected all data into its base. Step 1 is repeated within the base of the pyramid. The base is also a hypercube. Its dimension is $(d-1)$. The base can be split into $2(d-1)$ pyramids as shown in step 1.

Along with more partition to be done, the index key becomes longer by appending the order number of its pyramid. On the last partition, the slice number which the data belongs to is appended to the index key. This algorithm is inspired by pyramid-tree technique [5]. However, pyramid-tree only partitions the hyper cube only one time.

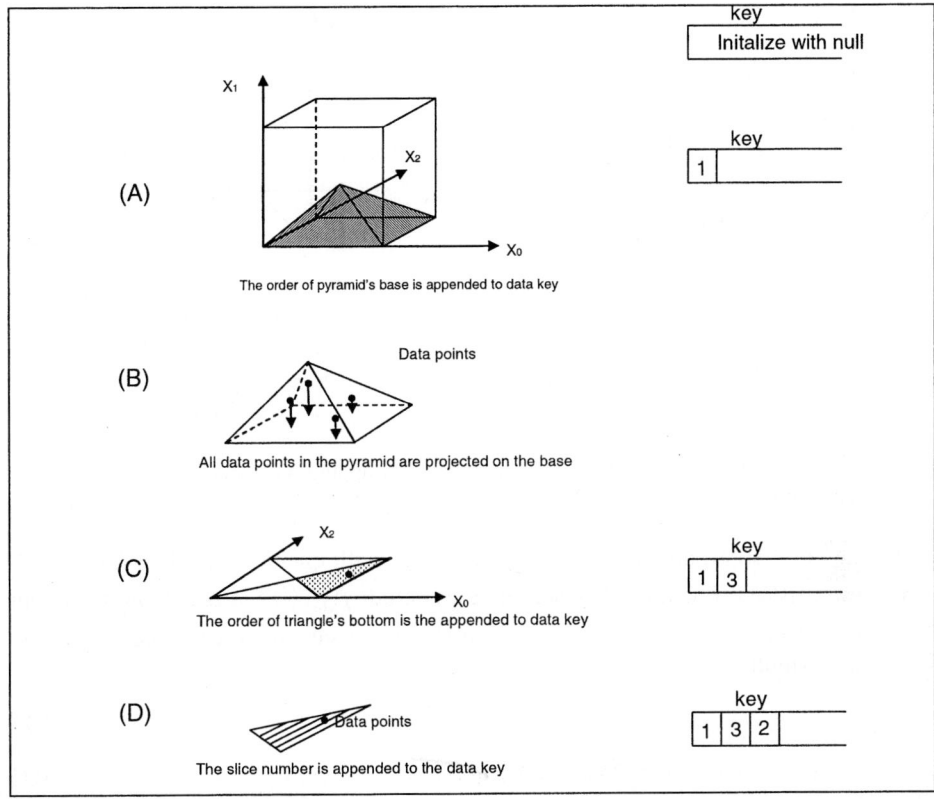

Fig. 3. Construction of key. The data space is partitioned recursively, key of a data is composed the order of bases of the pyramids which the data in

3.3 Range Search

By using the constitution of index key described in Section 3.2, the index values are lined on one sequence. We can use classical index structure B^+-tree to do range search. Given a query range, we can calculate the pyramids overlapping with the query range. If we denote a given d-D range as $[X_{0\min}, X_{0\max}], [X_{1\min}, X_{1\max}], \cdots$, the method calculating the overlapping pyramids can be described using Fig. 4 as below.

Fig. 4(A) shows the conditions of pyramid $p_i (0 \le i \le d)$ which overlap the query range. The following formula describes the conditions:

$$X_{i\min} \le X_{j\max} \tag{3}$$
$$X_{i\min} \le 1 - X_{j\min} \tag{4}$$

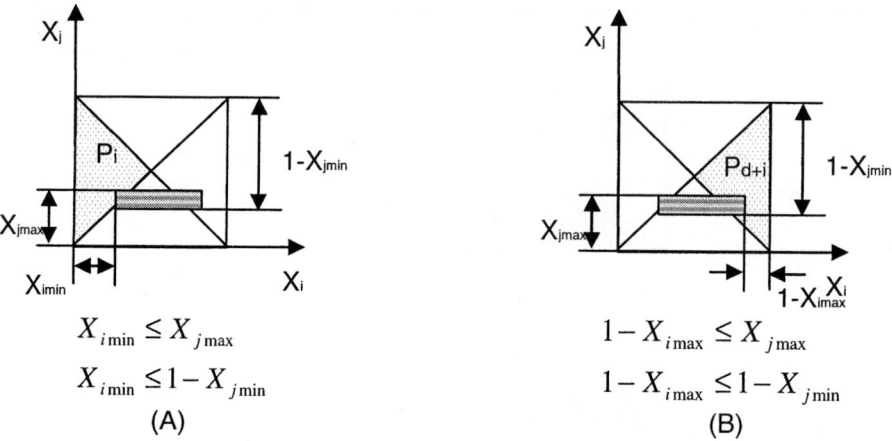

Fig. 4. Finding overlapping pyramid. The pyramids overlapping with search range can be calculated with the formula shown at below

As shown in subfigure (A) pyramid p_i overlaps with query range. The Equation 3 and 4 are satisfied. For the other side of a pyramid $p_{d+i} (0 \leq i \leq d)$, as shown in Fig. 4 (B). The condition of overlapping with query range can be explained using the following formula.

$$1 - X_{i\max} \leq X_{j\max} \qquad (5)$$

$$1 - X_{i\max} \leq 1 - X_{j\min} \qquad (6)$$

The above computing process should be done recursively just like a computing index key. All pyramids overlapping with query range will be searched by using B$^+$-tree index structure. Fig. 5 illustrates the pyramids (or index keys) translated from a given query range. The pyramids p_0 and p_2 do not overlap with query range. We can omit to check their sub pyramids. After two partitions, we find $p'_0 \cdots p'_j p''_1 \cdots p''_k$ overlap with query range. We have to make search for these index keys. The more time partition, the more index keys are needed to search. This is the reason that we can not do more partition of hypercube, although the accuracy of index keys approve, when more partition done.

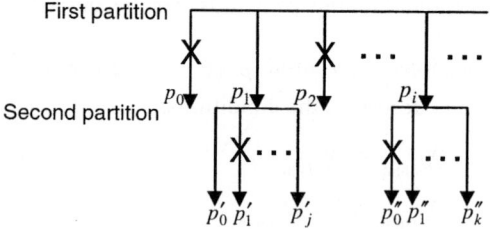

Fig. 5. Translation from query range to index keys. The mark "X" means a pyramid does not overlap with query range. In the second partition, only overlapping pyramids are checked whether their sub pyramids overlap with query range or not

4 Boundary of Pyramids Apportionment

A boundary of pyramids belongs to more than two pyramids. As an effective index structure, it is necessary to apportion one boundary to only *one* pyramid. Moreover, the boundary should be averagely apportioned. In the case of a 2-D square, there are 4 boundary lines which can be divided into 4 triangles, as shown in Fig. 6. For example, the boundary line $\overline{OA}$ is apportioned into the triangle $\triangle OAD$. $\overline{OB}, \overline{OC}, \overline{OD}$ are apportioned into $\triangle OAB, \triangle OBC, \triangle ODC$ respectively.

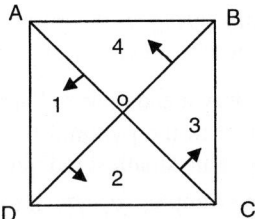

Fig. 6. Boundary lines apportion for a square

In the 3-D case, there are 6 pyramids. They intersected with 12 triangle planes as shown in Fig. 2. These 12 boundary planes can be divided into the 6 pyramids by 2. However, the problem is how to apportion line boundaries. There are 8 line boundaries which can not be equally divided into 6 pyramids. One reasonable apportion is distribute the 8 line boundaries 2, 2, 1, 1, 1, 1 into these pyramids.

When a data point is in a boundary of pyramids, a policy must be determined which pyramid the data point should be included in. Similarly, when the query range spans a boundary of pyramids, only one pyramid is considered. To solve the problem, a concept *radiant value* is introduced in this paper as a criterion how to divide a boundary to pyramids.

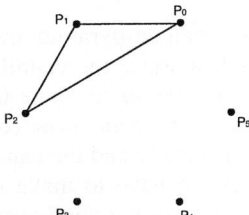

Fig. 7. Boundary graph. A boundary line in a 3-D Cube

A hyperplane (or line, vertex) boundary is the intersection of more than 2 pyramids. If a data point is on a boundary, it is simple to compute which pyramids construct the boundary by using Equation 2. A graph can be constructed for a boundary as shown in Figure 7. It illustrates 6 pyramids of a cube. Every pyramid $(p_0, p_1, ..., p_5)$ is denoted as a point in the graph. Two pyramids which are connected by a line in Fig. 7 are intersected. For example, p_1 and p_2 intersected. It is assumed that the points are put in counter clockwise order. Figure 7 shows a boundary which is constructed by three pyramids p_1, p_2, p_3. Note that a boundary is shown a complete sub-graph in the boundary graph. In principle, boundaries should be balanced distributed to pyramids. In other words, all pyramids are apportioned an average number of boundaries. The concept of radiant value defined by Definition 1 is used to determine a boundary belongs to which pyramid.

Definition 1 The radiant value of a vertex p is a binary number. It is initialized with null. All other points are traced in clockwise order and if a line is connected with p, then 1 is appended. Otherwise, 0 is appended.

Therefore, for the boundary in Fig. 7, the point p_0 has the radiant value "000111". The following steps express how to determine a pyramid for a boundary.

- The boundary graph is drawn and their radiant values of all points are computed.
- The data point is assigned to the pyramid having the least radiant value. If 2 or more pyramids have the same smallest radiant value, the point having the smaller subscript is chosen. For example, p_i, p_j have the same least radiant value, p_i is chosen, where $i \leq j$.

In Fig. 7, point p_0 has the smallest radiant value, so the boundary intersecting three pyramids is distributed to pyramid p_0.

5 Experimental Evaluation

To evaluate the effectiveness of the new surface index structure, a collection of range queries for high dimensional dataset are performed. The surface spatial index structure is implemented based on GiST C++ Package [9] on GNU/Linux (Pentium-IV, 1GHz).

5.1 The Relation Between the Size of Candidate Set and CPU Time

Surface based index technique; include pyramid–tree which is a special case of our method, filters out non-related data points for a similarity query. Smaller candidate set is desirable. It is because that we have to consume I/O and CPU costs to refine every candidate to get exact answers. If the data space (or hypercube) is partitioned more times, the index keys are more accuracy and the candidate set becomes smaller. However, as mentioned Section 3.2, we have to make more queries as shown in Fig. 5. That is a trade-off between accuracy of keys and query times.

We use a real dataset to show the trade-off. The real data is hue histogram exacted from color images. The dimension is 8 and the size of dataset is 100,000. Query data points were picked up from dataset randomly. The query range was set 1%. The more query range returns too more answers, analogically, too small query range returns only itself. The 1% query range returns about 10-100 answers which suggest meaningful for similarity search.

Fig. 8 shows the number of candidates and CPU time according to three different partitions. If we stop at the first partition, candidate set is bigger. We have to use more

CPU time to refine candidates to get real answer. If we partition hypercube by 3 times, we have a small candidate set. However, too many pyramids overlapping with query range. We must consume more CPU time in B⁺-tree. In the result, we found two time partition is the best one for the real dataset. Its CPU time is the smallest as shown in Fig. 8 (B).

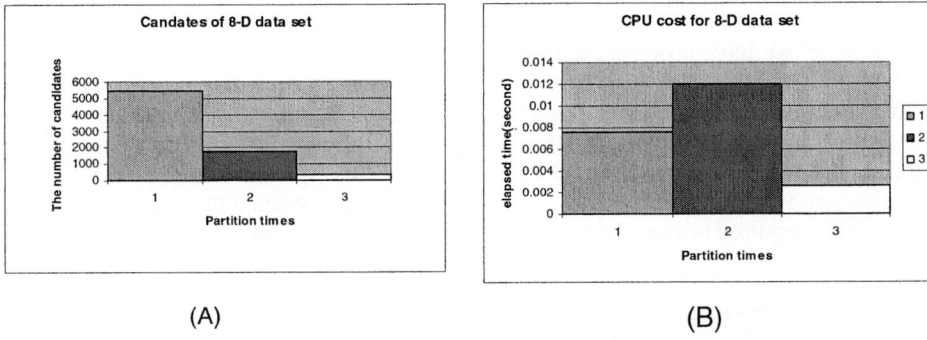

Fig. 8. The number of candidates and I/O cost for real data set

5.2 The Number of Page Access and CUP Time

To evaluate our index method on different dimensional space, we generate 15, 20, 25, .., 85-D dataset. The data is normalized into $[0,1)$. Their sizes are 100,000. The query ranges are 2% of the data space. This query range returns properly number of answer 10-50. The node size of B⁺-tree was set at 8K bytes. Similarity search range 1000 data points were randomly selected.

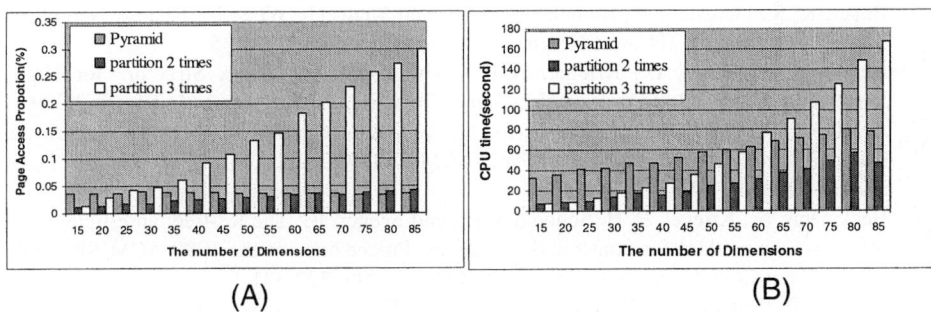

Fig. 9. (A) The number of page access. (B) Range search time

Fig. 9(A) shows the relationship between the number of page accesses and the number of dimensions. Note that the pyramid-tree index is a special case when the hypercube partition in "1 times", its pyramid's base is $(d-1)$-D hyperplane. From the number of page access, we also found "partition 2 times" is the more effective than others. Fig. 9(B) shows the search time in three spatial index structures. It is clear that, again, the patition-2-times method has the best performance, much better than "partition 1 time method" (i.e., the Pyramid trees). Fig. 9(B) shows the search time in three spatial index structures. It is clear that, again, the "partition 2 times" is the best selection, much more effective than partition 1 time (i.e., the Pyramid trees).

6 Conclusions

In this paper, we have proposed a new index structure based on recursive partitioning space. To break the curse of dimensionality, high dimensional data points are transformed to 1-dimensional values. Therefore, classical index structures such as the B^+-tree can be adapted. By partitioning the space recursively, our approach overcomes the restriction of $2d$ pyramids in the Pyramid-tree. More pyramids are partitioned and the selection of key is improved. In future work, we will estimate the optimal number of partitions required to construct an index structure considering data distribution.

Acknowledgments

The work reported in this paper was partially supported by the Australian Research Council's Discovery Project Grants DP0344488 and DP0345710.

References

1. An, J., Chen, H., Furuse, K., Ishikawa, M., and Ohbo. N.: The convex polyhedra technique: An index structure for high-dimensional space. Proc. of the 13th Australasian Database Conference (2002) 33-40.
2. An, J., Chen, H., Furuse, K., Ohbo. N.: CVA-file: An Index Structure for High-Dimensional Datasets, Journal of knowledge and Information Systems. to appear.
3. Beyer, K. S., Goldstein, J., Ramakrishnan, R. and Shaft, U.: When Is "Nearest Neighbor" Meaningful. When Is "Nearest Neighbor" Meaningful (1999) 217-235
4. Berchtold, S., Keim, D., Kriegel, H.-P. : The X-tree: An Index Structure for High-Dimensional Data. 22nd Conf. on Very Large Database, 1996. Bombay, India, pp. 28-39.
5. Berchtold, S., Keim, D., Kriegel, H.-P.: The pyramid-Technique: Towards Breaking the Curse of Dimensional Data Spaces. Proc. ACM SIGMOD Int. Conf. Managment of Data, Seattle, 1998, pp. 142-153
6. Beckmann, N., Kriegel, P. H. Schneider, R., and Seeger, B.: The R*-tree: an efficient and robust access method for points and rectangles. Proceedings of the 1990 ACM SIGMOD International Conference on Management of Data (1990) 322-331.
7. Ciaccia, P., Patella, M., Zezula, P.: M-tree:An Efficient Access Method for Similarity Seach in Metric Spaces. Proc. 23rd Int. Conf. on Very Large Data Bases, Athens, Greece, 1997, pp. 426-435.
8. Guttman, A.: R-tree: a dynamic index structure for spatial searching. Proceedings of the 1984 ACM SIGMOD International Conference on Management of Data (1984) 47-57.
9. Hellerstein, J. M., Naughton, J. F., Pfefer, A.: Generalized search trees for database systems. Proc. of the 21th VLDB conference, Zurich, Switzerland, Sept. 1995, pp. 562-573.

10. Katayama, N. and Satoh, S.: The SR-tree: An index structure for high-dimensional nearest neighbour queries. Proceedings of the 1997 ACM SIGMOD International Conference on Management of Data (1997) 369-380.
11. Ooi, B. C., Tan, K. L. Yu, C. and Bressan S.: Indexing the Edges - A Simple and Yet Efficient Approach to High-Dimensional Indexing. PODS 2000: 166-174
12. Weber, R. Schek, J. H. and Blott, S.: A quantitative analysis and performance study for similarity-search methods in high-dimensional spaces. Proceedings of 24th International Conference on Very Large Data Bases (1998) 194-205.
13. Zhang, R. Ooi, B. C. Tan, K. L.: Making the Pyramid Technique Robust to Query Types and Workloads. ICDE 2004: 313-324

BM$^+$-Tree: A Hyperplane-Based Index Method for High-Dimensional Metric Spaces

Xiangmin Zhou[1], Guoren Wang[1], Xiaofang Zhou[2], and Ge Yu[1]

[1] College of Information Science and Engineering,
Northeastern University, China
[2] School of Information Technology & Electrical Engineering,
University of Queensland, Australia

Abstract. In this paper, we propose a novel high-dimensional index method, the BM$^+$-tree, to support efficient processing of similarity search queries in high-dimensional spaces. The main idea of the proposed index is to improve data partitioning efficiency in a high-dimensional space by using a rotary binary hyperplane, which further partitions a subspace and can also take advantage of the twin node concept used in the M$^+$-tree. Compared with the key dimension concept in the M$^+$-tree, the binary hyperplane is more effective in data filtering. High space utilization is achieved by dynamically performing data reallocation between twin nodes. In addition, a post processing step is used after index building to ensure effective filtration. Experimental results using two types of real data sets illustrate a significantly improved filtering efficiency.

Keywords: Similarity search, Multidimensional index, Binary hyperplane, Range query, K-NN query.

1 Introduction

With the rapidly growth of various types of multimedia information, the need for fast processing of content-based similarity search queries in large databases has increased dramatically, and will increase at a much faster pace in the future. Since retrieving multidimensional data always incurs very high, and sometimes prohibitively high, costs for large datasets, the search for effective index structures to support high dimensional similarity query has been at the frontiers of database research in the last decade[13]. Most efficient multidimensional indexing structures originated from managing low-dimensional geographical data (such as R-tree and it variants[1, 2, 3, 4]) are not efficient in managing high dimensional data.

The approach supporting multidimensional similarity search can be classified into two categories: *position-based* indexes and *metric-based* indexes. The R-tree and its variants are representatives of the former, which deal with the relative positions in a vector space. The second type of indexes, on the other side, include the VP-tree[5], the MVP-tree[7], the M-tree[6, 8], and its optimized indexes[9, 10, 11]. These indexes manage the data based on the relative distances between objects. Among the metric-based indexes, VP-tree is the first hierarchical index structure which supports similarity search by utilizing the relative distance between objects and triangular inequality. It is of great significance for reducing the cost of similarity search. However, the query performance of VP-tree is severely suffered from a large quantity of distance calculation due to the small fanout (thus a very tall index tree). It should be pointed out that distance calculation in this type of application is typically very complex and CPU intensive. The MVP-tree is proposed to overcome these problems, by introducing multiple vantage points instead one. This idea significantly lowered its height. Both the VP-tree and the MVP-tree are constructed in a top-down way. That means they cannot support insertion and deletion of data once the index is created.

The M-tree represents a significant step forward, and is representative of metric-based indexes. It is a paged and balanced tree which adopts the bottom-up construction strategy with node promotion and split mechanisms. Therefore, it is suitable as a secondary storage index structure and can handle data updates gracefully without reconstructing the whole index when a media object is inserted or deleted. The M-tree is also the first one to recognize the high cost of distance calculation, and most distances are pre-computed and stored in the index tree, thus query-time distance calculation can be avoided. The large extent of subspace overlapping among M-tree sibling nodes, however, is a noticeable problem. Different from other high dimensional indexes, the M^+-tree has subspace overlapping minimization and tree height minimization as its aim. It improves the M-tree from the following points: (1) the concept of key dimension is proposed to eliminate the overlapping between twin nodes and to reduce the overlapping across subspaces; (2) the concept of twin nodes are introduced to lower the height of tree; (3) the idea of key dimension shift is proposed to achieve optimal space partitioning; and (4) a brand new idea of associating an index entry with twin subtrees for more efficient filtering during search.

This paper proposes a binary M^+-tree, called BM^+-tree, which improves the data partitioning method used in the M-tree. Like M-tree, BM^+-tree is a dynamically paged and balanced index tree. It inherits the node promotion mechanism, triangle inequality and the branch and bound search techniques from M-tree. BM^+-tree also fully utilizes the further filtering idea as used in M^+-tree. However, BM^+-tree uses a rotatable binary hyperplane, instead of a key dimension, to further partition the twin subspaces and to perform filtration between them. This novel idea, as we shall discuss in this paper, can improve the query processing performance significantly comparing to M-tree and M^+-tree.

The rest of the paper is organized as follows. In Section 2, we give some definitions for similarity searches. Section 3 introduces a new partition strategy. We describe BM^+-tree in Section 4, including its key techniques and algorithms. Section 5 presents performance evaluations. Section 6 concludes this paper.

2 Similarity Queries

In this section, we follow the conventions used in [8] and give basic definitions related to the BM$^+$-tree, including r-neighbor search, k-nearest neighbor search.

R-neighbor search and k-nearest neighbour search are two basic types of similarity queries. Commonly, the former is to obtain all objects within certain distance from the query object, while the latter is to find k objects which have the minimum distances to a given query object. They can be defined as follows.

Definition 1. *r-neighbor search. Given a query object $q \in O$ and a non-negative query radius r, the r-neighbor search of q is to retrieve all the objects $o \in O$ such that $d(q,o) \leq r$.*

Definition 2. *k-nearest neighbor search. Given a query object $q \in O$ and an integer $k \geq 1$, the k-NN query is to retrieve k objects from O with the shortest distances from q.*

The purpose of indexing a data space is to provide an efficient support for retrieving objects similar to a reference (query) object (for r-neighbor search or k-NN search). Here, for a given query, our main objective is to minimize the number of distance calculations, I/O operations and priority queue accesses, which are usually very expensive for many applications.

3 Data Partitioning Using Binary Hyperplane

The Strategy of data partitioning using binary hyperplanes is the main idea of BM$^+$-tree. This section will introduce this technique, including how to choose the binary hyperplanes, how to use the binary hyperplanes for data partitioning, and how to use the binary hyperplanes for filtering during the search process.

3.1 Construction of Binary Hyperplanes

Generally speaking, because of different data distributions, different dimensions carry a different weight in distance computation. Based on this fact, M$^+$-tree partitions a subspace into twin subspaces according to the selected *key dimension* which is the dimension that affects distance computation most. Different from M$^+$-tree, BM$^+$-tree uses a *binary hyperplane* to partition a subspace into twin subspaces. The binary hyperplane idea extends the (single) key dimension concept of the M$^+$-tree to make use of two key dimensions. This new data partition strategy is mainly based on the following observation.

Observation 1. *For most applications, except for the first key dimension, there is commonly another dimension which may also contains a large quantity of information. Cancelling the second dimension would cause great loss of information. Just as in the process of dimensionality reduction, we usually maintain the first few dimensions, instead of just the first one. Therefore, when performing further data partitioning, it is advisable to keep two dimensions that have maximal value variances and construct a binary hyperplane by using two dimensions.*

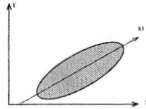

Fig. 1. A sample of data distribution

Figure 1 gives an example set of data (the shaded area). Obviously, the extent of objects along $x1$ is longer than that along x (which is in turn longer than that along y). The key dimension based data partitioning will divide data along x dimension. It is clear that much more information can be obtained if the partitioning is done using a binary hyperplane vertical to $x1$.

The selection of a hyperplane has to conform to the following rules in order to achieve optimal data partitioning, i.e., trying to keep the objects having the minimal distances in the same subspace while minimizing the overlap between twin subspaces. In the process of binary hyperplane construction, the selection of two key dimensions and the decision of the coefficients of them are the two major issues. We consider two binary hyperplane construction strategies: m-RAD-2 based strategy and max-distance based strategy. The former is based on the fact that in the M-tree the query performance of index is optimal when it adopts the m-RAD-2 partitioning strategy. This strategy ensures the maximum of the radii of the two subspaces split minimal. The latter one, on the other side, is based on our observation that the distances between objects along the max-distance dimension can usually keep maximal quantity of information.

The BM⁺-tree adopts the following steps to determine the hyperplane:

1. Choose two reference points in the following way. Use the center points of the two subspaces according to the m-RAD-2 partition strategy [8], and when these two points have the same feature value, one can compute the distances among objects in the subset, and choose two points from the subset such that the distance between the selected points is the maximal;
2. Compute the distance along each dimension between these two points; and
3. Choose two dimensions which have the biggest absolute values as the key dimensions, and consider the differences between the two center points of the two key dimensions as the coefficients of them respectively.

3.2 Binary Hyperplane Based Further Data Partition

Data partition strategy is one of the most important issues which directly affect the performance of indexes. Before introducing the binary hyperplane based data partitioning, we need to introduce another concept.

Definition 3. *Twin nodes.* In the M⁺-tree and the BM⁺-tree, an internal entry has two pointers pointing to two subtrees. These two subtrees are called twin subtrees, and the roots of the twin subtrees are called twin nodes.

In Figure 2 (a) and (b), subspaces 1 and 2 correspond to the twin nodes of the tree. Figures 2(a), (b) and (c) show the data partitioning of the BM⁺-tree,

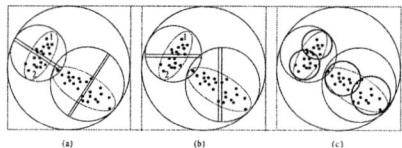

Fig. 2. Data partitioning for BM^+-tree, M^+-tree and M-tree

the M^+-tree and the M-tree respectively. The M-tree adopts distance-based data partition strategy which partitions a data space into two subspaces according to the distances between objects. Among the proposed partitioning methods in the M-tree, partitioning by m-RAD-2 is proved to be the best. The M^+-tree improves the data partition methods of the M-tree by adopting two steps data partition strategy, i.e., partitioning with m-RAD-2 way proposed in the M-tree first and then further partitioning the two subspaces into two pairs of twin nodes according to the selected key dimensions (which can be different for different subspaces). The twin nodes are expressed through two boundary values of a key dimension which are the maximal key dimension value of the left twin space and the minimal key dimension value of the right twin space.

The BM^+-tree also adopts two steps data partition strategy. Different to the M^+-tree, it uses a rotatable binary hyperplane rather than the key dimension to further partition the twin subspaces, i.e. the binary hyperplane can be different for the two data spaces and the direction of it can change according to the data distribution in the data subspace considered. The binary hyperplane construction strategy proposed in this paper ensures the binary hyperplane rotatable, deciding the key dimensions and coefficients of them according to the data distribution of a subspace. That is, the key dimensions and their coefficients are not fixed, but modifiable in the whole data space.

The data partitioning strategy in the BM^+-tree can be described as follows: (1) the twin spaces are regarded together as a whole space and then it is partitioned with the m-RAD-2 way, as in the M-tree. As a result, two new sub-spaces are produced; and (2) each subspace is further partitioned into twin sub-spaces according to the selected binary hyperplane.

Figure 2 shows that to achieve the same level of data grouping, the M-tree needs three levels of partitioning, while the BM^+-tree and the M^+-tree only need two levels. Meanwhile, it is obvious that the data partition strategy in the BM^+-tree has the better clustering effect. The distance between objects along the data partitioning direction of the BM^+-tree is much bigger than that of the M^+-tree. This figure gives the intuition that the binary hyperplane based data partitioning can keep much more distance information.

3.3 Data Filtering Using Binary Hyperplanes

The filtering using binary hyperplanes is carried out on the basis of distance from an object to a hyperplane and the triangular inequality property. Comparing the cost of calculating the distance between two points in multidimensional space, the cost of computing the distance to a binary hyperplane is quite trifling. Some inactive subtrees can be filtered out according to the hyperplanes, thus avoiding some distance calculations. The process of filtering by binary hyperplane is not complex. We sketch the process below.

Let N_l and N_r be twin nodes, k_1 and k_2 be the key dimensions of the subspace, C_1 and C_2 be the coefficients of hyperplane in k_1 and k_2 dimensions respectively. Let L_{max} and R_{min} be the maximal value of the binary hyperplane for the left node and the minimal value of that for the right node respectively. Let $C = \sqrt{C_1^2 + C_2^2}$. Then the hyperplane of this subspace is as equation (1)

$$X_{k1} * C_1 + X_{k2} * C_2 = HP \tag{1}$$

Then, for the left part, HP is equal to L_{max}. While for the right, HP is R_{min}.

Suppose that the n dimensional query object is $O(x_1 \cdots x_n)$ and the search radius is r. Then, the distance from O to the left and right binary boundary hyperplanes can be expressed as (2)(a) and (b) respectively.

$$d_L = |HP - L_{max}|/C \quad (a) \qquad d_R = |HP - R_{min}|/C \quad (b) \tag{2}$$

For the filtering process, if $HP \geq L_{max}$, the query object is outside the area of the left; thus it is possible to filter out the left. Likewise, if $HP \leq R_{min}$, the right can be filtered out. Therefore, we only consider the following case.

$$d'_L = (HP - L_{max})/C \quad (a) \qquad d'_R = (R_{min} - HP)/C \quad (b) \tag{3}$$

If $d'_L \geq r$, the left node does not contain any query results, and can be pruned. Likewise, if $d'_R \geq r$, the right can be filtered out. Obviously, the cost to compute d'_L or d'_R is much less than computing the distance in the high dimensional space. It is similar to process k-NN following the filtering discussions above.

4 BM$^+$-Tree

There are two types of node objects in a BM$^+$-tree: routing objects and leaf objects. Each leaf entry has the the same structure as that of M-tree. A routing object includes the following parts: the feature value of the routing object O_r; the covering radius of O_r, $r(O_r)$; the distance of O_r to its parent, $d(O_r, P(O_r))$; an array D_{NO} which contains two key dimension numbers; another array C containing the coefficients corresponding to the two key dimension numbers respectively; the pointers $lTwinPtr$ to the left twin sub-tree, and $rTwinPtr$ to the right twin; the maximal value of binary hyperplane in the left twin sub-tree M_{lmax} and the minimal value of binary hyperplane in the right M_{rmin}.

4.1 Building the BM$^+$-Tree

To insert an object into BM$^+$-tree, the appropriate node should be found first by performing the subtree choosing algorithm . If the node is not full, the object can be inserted directly. If one of the twin nodes is full, the entries will be reallocated between the twins. If the twins are both full, they will be considered as a whole and split by performing distance based splitting and binary hyperplane splitting.

When a new node is inserted, how to choose this appropriate node is vital for the performance of the index. The subtree selection follows the optimal principal: (1) Choosing the node of which the distance from query object to routing object is minimal if the covering radius of the subtree need not increase; (2) Choosing the subtree of which the covering radius increases most slightly, if no subtree can keep the same when an object is inserted; and (3)Trying to keep the gap between twins maximal while the subtree choosing between them are performed.

BM^+-tree grows in a bottom-up way by adopting a bottom-up split strategy. It shares the promotion strategy with M-tree and adopts a two-steps split strategy: first, splitting using the m-RAD-2 strategy; and second, splitting by the binary hyperplane. In the node splitting, the BM^+-tree adopts two strategies to choose binary hyperplane: (1) m-RAD-2 based binary hyperplane choosing strategy; and (2) Max-Distance based binary hyperplane choosing strategy.

SPLIT($entry(O_n), PEntry$)
1   Let S be a set, N_p be the parent node
2   $S \leftarrow$ entries(PEntry$\rightarrow$lTNode)$\bigcup$ entries(PEntry$\rightarrow$ rTNode)$\bigcup$ entry(O_n)
3   Reallocate a new node N'
4   $PromoteEntriesAndPartitionByDist$
5   $ChooseBHAndPartitionByHyperplane$
6   if N_p is not a root
7   then switch
8   case TwinsOf(N_p) full   : $Split$
9   case N_p is not full : $InsertIntoParentNode$
10   case $DEFAULT$: $ReallocateTheTwins$
11   else if N_p is full
12   then $SplitRootByBHyperplane$
13   else $InsertIntoParentNode$

CHOOSEBINARYHYPERPLANE($D_{1NO}, D_{2NO}, C_1, C_2$)
1   $GetTwoObjectsBymM_Rad$
2   $GetTwoMaxDiffByComputingAndSorting$
3   if $Diff[0] == Diff[1]$
4   then $GetTwoObjectsByMax_Distance$
5           $GetTwoMaxDiffByComputingAndSorting$
6   $SetMaxDimNoAndCoefToThem;$

4.2   Query Processing

BM^+−tree supports two types of similarity search: r-range search and k-NN search. The range search starts from the root of the BM^+−tree and implements the process recursively until the leaf of the tree, and keeps all matching objects.

For a certain request, in non-leaf nodes, range search needs to perform two steps filtering. First, filtering according to the distances between objects among sibling nodes; and Second, filtering according to the binary hyperplane between twin nodes. For leave nodes, a two-steps filtering operations is used. The whole process is similar to that used by M^+−tree. But it is different from the M^+−tree for filtering according to a binary hyperplane instead of a key dimension.

For k-NN search, BM^+-tree uses PR, a *priority queue* that contains pointers to active sub-trees, and NN, an array used to store the final search results. The BM^+-tree uses a heuristic criteria to select the priority node to access the priority queue and choose the next sub-tree to search. In this process, the binary hyperplane based filtering is used to reduce the I/O access and queue access of index. Due to our more effective data partitioning strategy, a binary hyperplane can be more discriminative than a key dimension.

The k-NN search using the BM^+-tree can be carried out according to the following steps: (1) keeping the root in the priority queue, PR, and the maximal distance in array NN; (2) choosing a priority node from PR; (3) searching the active subtree in the priority node. Here, the active subtree choosing follows (a) for a internal node, deciding the active subtree; (b) deciding when to update the result array NN; and (c)for a leaf node, deciding the matching objects; (4) repeating the subtree choosing process until the minimal distance of objects in PR from q is greater than NN[k-1] or PR is null. At the end of this query process, all pointers in PR will be removed and NN will be returned.

5 Performance Evaluation

This section presents an empirical study to evaluate the performance of BM^+−tree. Extensive experiments are conducted to compare the BM^+−tree with other competitors, including M-tree and M^+−tree. Our objectives of this study are:

(1) to study the scalability with number of dimensions;
(2) to evaluate the scalability with dataset sizes;
(3) to study the relative performance with the M-tree and the M^+-tree.

We use two types of real datasets: color histogram and color layout.

(1) The color histogram dataset contains vectors of Fourier coefficients of a set of images. We choose 10 sets of data with the dimensionality from 4 to 40;
(2) The color layout dataset comprises of color layout features from 20,000 images, which are 12-d data obtained by MPEG-7 feature extraction tool.

All the experiments were tested on a Pentium IV 2.5GHz PC with 256MB of memory. All data are stored in an object database system XBase [12].

5.1 Effect of the Dimensionality

We performed experiments to evaluate the impact of dimensionality and compare the performance of BM^+-tree and that of M^+-tree. The experiments were

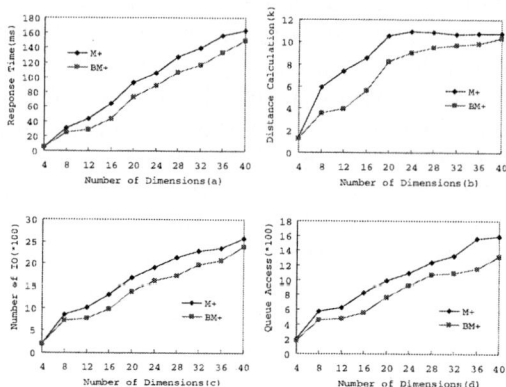

Fig. 3. The effect of dimensionality

performed on the 4 to 40-d histogram data, and the size of dataset is 20,000. As mentioned in M^+-tree[11], the number of queue accesses is also a key factor which affects the performance of k-NN search for these trees. Therefore, the performance is measured by (1) the response time of a query; (2) the average number of distance calculations required to execute the query; (3) the average number of disk accesses for the query; and (4) the average number of queue accesses. The query is to find 10 nearest neighbors of the query object.

Figure (3) shows the performance of BM^+-tree comparing with that of M^+-tree. It is obvious that BM^+-tree responses more quickly than M^+-tree irrespective of the varying of dimensionality, and BM^+-tree outperforms M^+-tree by up to 35% . While the number of I/Os, distance calculations and queue accesses for BM^+-tree and M^+-tree also increase with increasing number of dimensions, those of BM^+-tree are growing at a much slower rate. BM^+-tree outperforms M^+-tree since the rotary binary hyperplane in BM^+-tree has a stronger filtering ability comparing against the key dimension in M^+-tree; consequently, some of sub-queries can be pruned and its search space covers fewer points. Moreover, Figure(3)(b) also shows the fact that, when the dimensionality is high enough, the number of distance calculations keeps steady irrespective of further increasing of dimensionality for a query has to scan the whole index for both of them.

5.2 Effect of Data Sizes

Now we compare the performance of the M^+-tree and the BM^+-tree with varying dataset sizes. The dataset size of the 10-d color histogram data was set from 10,000 to 90,000. Figure (4) shows the results.

From Figure (4), we can see that both the BM^+-tree and the M^+-tree incurred higher I/O cost and CPU cost with increasing data set sizes. As before, the performance of the BM^+-tree degrades much slower than that of the M^+-tree, and the BM^+-tree remains superior over the M^+-tree. Noticeably, compared

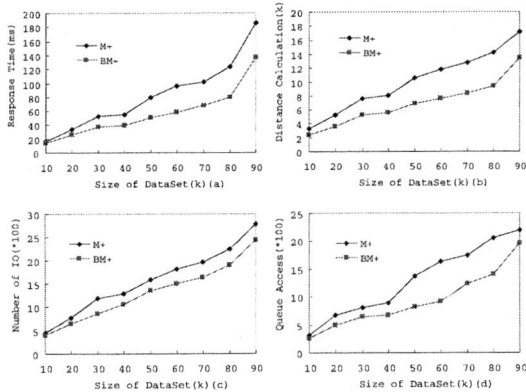

Fig. 4. The effect of dataset sizes

with the M^+-tree, The BM^+-tree saves a large number of distance calculations, I/Os and queue accesses, which combined improve the query performance. This improvement based on using the BM^+-tree originates from the stronger filtering ability of the rotary binary hyperplane, thus the number of IO can be reduced greatly. As a result, despite that, for a single operation, the comparison between binary hyperplane is a little bit slower than that of key dimension, the BM^+-tree still responses more quickly up to 40% than the M^+-tree for a k-NN search.

5.3 Comparison with M^+-Tree and M-Tree

Next we examine the experiments to compare the k-NN search and range search using the BM^+-tree, the M-tree and the M^+-tree by using a 12-d real dataset

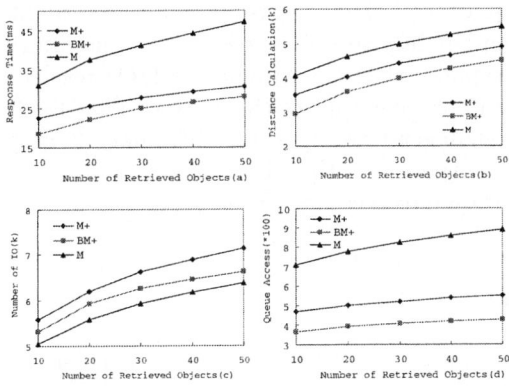

Fig. 5. k-NN search using BM^+-tree, M^+-tree and M-tree

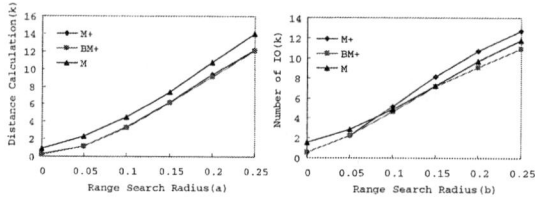

Fig. 6. Range search using BM$^+$-tree, M$^+$-tree and M-tree

which consists of the color layout information of 20,000 images. Figure (5) shows the results. First, we can see that, from the response time, for k-NN search, the BM$^+$-tree performs the best, with the M$^+$-tree following it, and the M-tree performs significantly worse than the other two. Second, from distance calculations and queue access, the BM$^+$-tree outperforms its competitors to different extent, followed by the M$^+$-tree which is superior than the M-tree remarkably. Third, we note that the BM$^+$-tree and the M$^+$-tree need more I/O than the M-tree due to the heuristic criteria used in k-NN search to select the priority node to access the priority queue and choose the next sub-tree to search. The heuristic criteria set the search radius from maximal value, which leads to inferior filtering effect for both of them. Since the filtering ability of binary hyperplane degrades to a lower extent than that of key dimension, the BM$^+$-tree needs fewer I/O when comparing against the M$^+$-tree. All factors considered, the BM$^+$-tree outperforms the M$^+$-tree. For the M-tree, although it needs fewer I/O operations, while taking other decisive factors into account, the BM$^+$-tree saves up to 30% of distance calculations and half of the queue accesses, thus have much better query performance which is shown on Figure(5)(a).

Figure (6) shows the performance of the BM$^+$-tree, the M$^+$-tree and the M-tree for range search. From this figure, we can see that, comparing with the M$^+$-tree, the BM+-tree saves about 20% of I/Os while only 5% of distance calculation. Compared with the M-tree, the BM+-tree needs much less distance calculations, even a quarter of that for M-tree, while the slight improvement of I/Os. In additon, with the increase of search radius, the filtering ability of key dimension degrades rapidly, thus the number of I/Os needed by the M$^+$-tree increases noticeably and exceeds that of the M-tree. The BM$^+$-tree remains the least of I/Os for the stronger filtering ability of binary hyperplane. Therefore, the BM$^+$-tree always outperforms the M$^+$-tree and the M-tree taking the I/O and distance computation into account. The superiority of the BM$^+$-tree is clear.

6   Conclusions

In this paper, we have proposed an improved high dimensional indexing method, the BM$^+$-tree, which is a dynamically paged and balanced metric tree. This index method partitions a subspace into two non-overlapping twin subspaces by utilizing two binary hyperplanes. An optimized method has been proposed for choosing binary hyperplanes for data partitioning. We have also given the algorithms to use the BM$^+$-tree based on rotary binary hyperplanes to perform effective filtering between twin nodes.

Experimental results obtained from using the two types of real datasets show that the BM$^+$-tree has a significantly better query processing performance. Comparing with the M-tree, the query efficiency has been improved by more than 30% on average, and up to 10 times in some cases. Comparing with the M$^+$-tree, the BM$^+$-tree reduces about 10-20% of I/O operations, about 5% distance calculations, and about 20% of queue access for K-NN search queries.

Acknowledgment. This research was supported by the National Natural Science Foundation of China (Grant No. 60273079 and 60473074), the Foundation for University Key Teacher and the Teaching and Research Award Program for Outstanding Young Teachers in High Education Institution of Chinese Ministry of Education, and the Australian Research Council (Grant No. DP0345710).

References

1. N. Berkmann, H.-P. Krigel. R. Schneider, and B. Seeger. (1990) "The R*-tree: an Efficient and Robust Access Method for Points and Rectangles" ACM SIGMOD 90, pages 322-331.
2. N. Katayama and S. Satoh. (1997) "The SR-tree: an Index Structure for High-dimensional Nearest Neighbor Queries ACM SIGMOD 97, pages 369-380.
3. D. A. White and R. Jain.(1996) "Similarity Indexing with the SS-tree" ICDE 96, pages 516-523.
4. K.-I. Lin, H. V. Jagadish, and C. Faloutsos. (1994)"The TV-tree: An Index Structure for High-Dimensional Data" VLDB Journal, Vol. 3, No. 4, pages 517-542.
5. J. K. Uhlmann.(1991) "Satisfying General Proximity/ Similarity Queries with Metric Trees", Information Processing Letters, vol 40, pages 175-179.
6. P. Zezula, P. Ciaccia, and F. Rabitteri.(1996) "M-tree: A Dynamic Index for Similarity Queries in Multimedia Databases" TR 7, HERMES ESPRIT LTR Project.
7. T. Bozkaya, M. Ozsoyoglu.(1997) "Distance-based Indexing for High-dimensional Metric Spaces" ACM SIGMOD 97, page 357-368.
8. P. Ciaccia, M. Patella, P. Zezula.(1997) "M-tree: An Efficient Access Method for Similarity Search in Metric Spaces" VLDB 97, Greece.
9. M. Ishikawa, H. chen, K. Furuse, J. X. Yu, N. Ohbo (2000) "MB$^+$tree: a Dynamically Updatable Metric Index for Similarity Search" WAIM 2000, page 356-366.
10. C. Traina Jr, A. Traina, B. Seeger, C. Faloutsos (2000) "Slim-trees: High Performance Metric Trees Minimizing Overlap Between Nodes. EDBT 2000, pages 51-65.
11. X. Zhou, G. Wang, J. X. Yu, G. Yu (2003) "M$^+$-tree: A New Dynamical Multidimensional Index for Metric Spaces" Proc of 14th Australasian Database Conference (ADC2003), pages 161-168.
12. G. Wang, H. Lu, G. Yu, Y. Bao (2003). "Managing Very Large Document Collections Using Semantics." Journal of Computer Science and Technology, 18(3): 403-406.
13. C. Böhm, S. Berchtold, D. A. Keim (2002), "High-dimensional Spaces - Index Structures for Improving the Performance of Multimedia Databases". ACM Computing Surveys, 2002.

Approaching the Efficient Frontier: Cooperative Database Retrieval Using High-Dimensional Skylines

Wolf-Tilo Balke[1], Jason Xin Zheng[1], and Ulrich Güntzer[2]

[1] Electrical Engineering & Computer Science,
University of California, Berkeley, CA 94720, USA
{balke, xzheng}@eecs.berkeley.edu
[2] Institut für Informatik,
Universität Tübingen, 72076 Tübingen, Germany
guentzer@informatik.uni-tuebingen.de

Abstract. Cooperative database retrieval is a challenging problem: top k retrieval delivers manageable results only when a suitable compensation function (e.g. a weighted mean) is explicitly given. On the other hand skyline queries offer intuitive querying to users, but result set sizes grow exponentially and hence can easily exceed manageable levels. We show how to combine the advantages of skyline queries and top k retrieval in an interactive query processing scheme using user feedback on a manageable, representative sample of the skyline set to derive most adequate weightings for subsequent focused top k retrieval. Hence, each user's information needs are conveniently and intuitively obtained, and only a limited set of best matching objects is returned. We will demonstrate our scheme's efficient performance, manageable result sizes, and representativeness of the skyline. We will also show how to effectively estimate users' compensation functions using their feedback. Our approach thus paves the way to intuitive and efficient cooperative retrieval with vague query predicates.

1 Introduction

In today's information systems instead of just retrieving all objects from databases that *exactly match* a user's query, often a set of objects *best matching* a set of query predicates has to be retrieved. To cater for this retrieval model, objects in the underlying database(s) are assigned a degree of match with respect to each 'soft' query predicate. Based on this paradigm cooperative information systems retrieve best compromises between (often mutually unsatisfiable) user needs by gradually relaxing soft constraints, where traditional SQL-based systems would just return empty result sets. Thus cooperative systems can even efficiently process overspecified queries and a tedious manual query refinement process is avoided. Consider a short example:

Example: A researcher from the Bay Area is planning a conference trip to New York. The basic 'hard' constraints for the trip are given by the dates and location of the conference. All necessary characteristics for e.g. booking a suitable flight can be evaluated relative to these constraints. For instance the flight has to arrive before the conference starts, but preferably close to the start date. Similarly the flight has to depart from a Bay Area airport and arrive in or at least close to New York. Usually the price should be minimized. Thus we have a mix of hard and soft constraints.

Retrieving best matches for such requests containing vague predicates is difficult: top k retrieval techniques efficiently answer vague queries, if adequate weightings of a compensation function (the 'utility function') are specified. However, expressing preferences by numerical weightings is neither intuitive, nor sensible without knowing the relationships between query predicates as reflected by the underlying database instance. In contrast skyline queries do offer intuitive querying by just specifying a user's basic query predicates, not exact weightings. Still, skylines guarantee to deliver *all* best objects with respect to *all* query predicates. But this advantage comes at a price: skyline sizes are known to grow exponentially with the number of query predicates and thus can exceed manageable levels already for fairly simple queries.

In this paper we propose to combine the advantages of intuitive skyline queries and manageable top k answer sets for cooperative retrieval systems by introducing an interactive feedback step presenting a representative sample of the (high-dimensional) skyline to users and evaluating their feedback to derive adequate weightings for subsequent focused top k retrieval. Hence, each user's information needs are conveniently and intuitively obtained, and only a limited set of best matching objects is retrieved. However, the huge size of skyline sets and the necessary time for their calculation remains an obstacle to efficient sampling for getting user feedback. Therefore we propose a novel sampling scheme to give users a first impression of the optimal objects in the database that is *representative* of the skyline set, *manageable* in size and *efficient* to compute, without computing the actual skyline. We will prove these characteristics and show how to subsequently estimate a user's compensation functions by evaluating feedback on objects in the sample. Our innovative approach promises to overcome the drawbacks of today's cooperative retrieval systems by utilizing the positive aspects of skyline queries in databases efficiently for the first time.

2 Intuitive Querying Versus Manageable Results

Cooperative retrieval systems generally feature a query model that allows the combination of 'hard' constraints and 'soft' constraints like shown in e.g. [14]. Since hard constraints can be quite efficiently evaluated using SQL, our sampling scheme will focus on the processing of soft constraints only. We will use a numerical query model, where each soft predicate of the query is evaluated by assigning a score in [0, 1] to each database object expressing the objects degree of match with respect to the predicate. Database objects can thus be understood as points in $[0, 1]^n$ with n as the number of soft constraints in a query. We assume that attribute values for soft predicates can always be mapped to numerical scores. For instance for our traveling researcher a flight's arrival time/date can be scored using the relative difference to the conference start, centered around the best possible arrival time. The choice of an airport in the Bay Area can similarly either be achieved by e.g. using the relative distance to our traveler's home for direct scoring, or assigning relative scores for an explicit statement of our traveler's preference as shown in [14].

2.1 Related Work in Cooperative Retrieval

The idea of extending exact-match querying frameworks by *cooperative retrieval* is generally based on the principle of query relaxation (see e.g. [13]). The idea of cooperation arises naturally due to necessary tedious query refinements in the case of empty result sets (overspecified query) or a flood of result objects (under-specified queries). Research focuses on two paradigms: Top k retrieval and skyline queries.

By aggregating all predicate scores with a single compensation function, top k retrieval (see e.g. [9], [7], and [5]) provides a simple, direct way to cooperative retrieval. Generally any monotonic function (like an average or weighted sum) to aggregate the basic scores into a single value (often called utility) can be used. The basic idea is to compensate between different aspects of objects, i.e. a good object in one predicate can afford to be worse in another. Thus objects become comparable by their respective utility to the individual user and the k best matching objects can be returned. However, expressing information needs a-priori as compensation functions is usually not very intuitive leading to a limited effectiveness of top k retrieval.

Skyline queries present a more intuitive paradigm: users only specify all important predicates for a query. The skyline then is the set of all objects that are not dominated with respect to *all* dimensions. This notion is well known in economical applications as Pareto-optimality and several basic algorithms for skylining in databases have been proposed, see e.g. [4], [421], or [1]. The exponential growth of skyline sets with the number of query predicates, however, limits the paradigm's applicability. [8] presents rough bounds for skyline sizes assuming independently distributed scores and shows that positive correlation of scores usually decreases and anti-correlation increases skyline sizes. However, no analytical model is known yet to accurately estimate skyline sizes for a given query and database instance. Moreover, post-processing skylines to get a minimum set cover with a difference of at most some fixed value ε between any skyline object and some object in the set cover has been proved NP for more than 3 dimensions [11].

Computing convex hulls over datasets (or data envelopment analysis) is a related problem, since all vertices of the convex hull over points in $[0, 1]^n$ form a subset of the respective skyline (for an efficient multi-dimensional algorithm see [3]). Thus, a convex hull could provide a coarse impression of the skyline. However, especially for anti-correlated predicates, many actual skyline objects may reside far from the convex hull, whereas desirable objects on the convex hull may not exist in the database.

2.2 Basic Query Models of Top k and Skyline Queries

Though top k retrieval is a cooperative and efficient way to answer queries, users first have to define individual utility functions. However, it is hard to guess 'correct' weightings for this function. Consider the example of our traveling researcher: usually a lot of different flights will be available, but most trade-offs are difficult to assess. What does it mean that a closer airport is 0.46 times more important than a less expensive ticket? Moreover, a really good bargain might compensate for most other inconveniences, but assigning high weightings to the price from the start might not be a good strategy, if the database only contains rather similar priced flights.

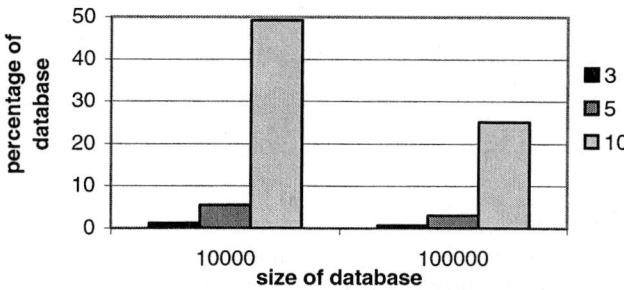

Fig. 1. Skyline sizes (in % of database retrieved) for 3, 5 and 10 soft query predicates

To overcome these problems retrieving a set of optimal objects with respect to all characteristics ('skyline' queries) has been established in query processing. However, the size of result sets generally strongly depends on the number of query predicates. Experiments in [1] show that the skyline grows exponentially and even for relatively small numbers of predicates already contains a vast portion of the entire database (cf. fig. 1 for the case of independently distributed scores). So, for practical applications the entire skylining paradigm often proves useless due to prohibitive result sizes:

Example (cont.): The query our researcher will pose to get an adequate flight will usually have to optimize several soft predicates: the flight booking will generally include predicates on the airport in the Bay Area, the departure/arrival date/time for the flight, the airport in New York, the departure date/time for the return flight, the specific airline and the respective ticket price. On all these predicates usually preferences exist (closest time for flight dates and distance for airports, specific airlines for frequent traveler programs and a minimum price). Even stating only the bare necessities we thus already are left with 6 soft predicates for the basic query rapidly increasing, if we also take class/upgrades, shortest traveling times, number of stops, etc. into account. The same applies for booking a suitable hotel, the predicates here may contain the hotel's preferred category, distance to the conference venue, amenities and price. And even if some of these characteristics (like a hotel's category and its price) are correlated limiting down the skyline size, we will nevertheless experience many independently distributed dimensions (like arrival date and choice of airports).

3 Sampling Skylines and Refining Queries with User Feedback

We have seen that even simple skyline queries may already contain many predicates. Though intuitive to ask, skylines are inefficient to compute and even if they could be computed in acceptable time, it would still not be sensible to return something like 25-50% of the entire database to the user for manual processing. Our approach aims at combining the advantages of both top k retrieval and skylining. Fig. 2 shows their respective strengths. The basic idea is to form an interactive workflow for cooperative retrieval using samples of the skyline to give users an overview of the best possible objects, evaluate their feedback and perform focused, yet meaningful top k retrieval.

	intuitive querying	manageable result set
skyline queries	✓	✗
top k retrieval	✗	✓

Fig. 2. Characteristics of top k retrieval vs. skyline queries

Bridging the gap between efficient retrieval and vague query predicates has already occurred in query processing. For instance in multimedia databases describing images for retrieval is quite a hard problem that is often dependent on inherent features like color histograms or textures used for content-based retrieval (see e.g. [6] or [16]). Whenever users are not able to directly express query needs by stating exact values for query predicates, it has proven helpful to let users pick some representative examples from the database collection and then retrieve objects similar to the chosen examples. The algorithms used are generally quite similar and rely on the idea to evaluate common characteristics of the examples to derive some abstract values for improving the retrieval. We will rely on the basic techniques for database retrieval by multiple examples as presented in [10] for the application in our cooperative querying framework. For simplicity we focus only on positive feedback, but also explicit negative feedback on disliked objects could be used and exploited in step 3:

Generic Algorithm for Query by Example:
1. Derive a suitably small set of examples (documents, images, etc.) from the database collection (randomly or given by the skyline of a first tentative query)
2. Get the user's feedback on preferred objects within the example set.
3. Derive the characteristics of a query that would have scored all positive examples most successfully (feature selection, re-weighting)
4. Re-evaluate this new query over the database collection and return the best objects to the user
5. If the user is not yet satisfied with the result set returned, take the set of step 4 as new examples and repeat the algorithm from step 2.

Please note that in contrast to e.g. query by visual example (usually starting with random images) our application in cooperative retrieval already starts with a skyline query. The feedback on subsequently retrieved examples is usually already of sufficient quality to deduce a final top k query, because users will never be offered dominated objects as examples. Hence, feedback can already be expected to be sufficiently focussed allowing to skip step 5. To demonstrate this advantage we will compare our skyline samples to randomly chosen samples from the entire set in section 4.1.

Still, one problem when using skylines to get user feedback is their prohibitive size and computation costs. Deriving a good sample of the skyline for getting feedback is therefore essential. Our work in [1] has laid the foundation to derive skyline samples without actually having to compute the entire skyline set. Since skylines tend to be still manageable in smaller dimensional problems, we propose to use the skylines of subsets of query predicates. We will now present a new algorithm for query processing and in the next section show that the sample derived is of sufficient quality. In the following we will assume that the parameter q is chosen sufficiently high to allow for each score list to be in at least one choice of subsets and that m is chosen adequately to produce low-dimensional subsets of the query predicates ($m < n$). Please note that the algorithm will output only roughly k objects depending on the numbers of regions of interest derived from the feedback. We will assume that the result set should contain at least a single object from each region of interest specified in the feedback.

Algorithm: Cooperative Querying with Reduced Dimensions Skylines Samples

0. Given a top k query with n query predicates, where each predicate can be evaluated by assigning numerical scores to all objects in the collection, and given a score list S_i ($1 \leq i \leq n$) for each such predicate ordered by descending scores. Initialize two sets P, F := $\emptyset$ to contain sample and feedback objects together with their scores, a set W of n-dimensional vectors of weightings and a counter for regions of interest as given by feedback. Initialize a counter j := 0.
1. Randomly select q subsets of score lists, each containing m different lists, such that each of the n lists occurs in at least one of the q subsets as shown in [2].
2. For each m-dimensional subset do
    2.1. Calculate the complete skyline P_i with respect to the m score lists in the subset and for all objects retrieve their missing scores from the other ($n - m$) dimensions
    2.2. Compare any two objects in P_i that have equal values with respect to all m dimensions pairwise. If an object is dominated by another, discard the dominated object from P_i.
    2.3. Union the reduced dimension skyline with the sample set P := P $\cup$ P_i (duplicates are eliminated).
3. Deliver the objects in set P as a sample of the n-dimensional skyline to the user ,and allow the user to pick a set F $\subseteq$ P of objects from the sample.
4. Calculate the difference set D between P and F, i.e. D := P\F
5. While F is not empty do
5.1. Set j := j+1
5.2. Remove an object o from F, add it to a new set F_j and calculate the minimum distance d from o to any object in D.
5.3. Remove all objects, whose Euclidian distance from o is smaller than d, from F and add them to F_j.
5.4. Calculate the n-dimensional vector w_j of weightings for the best query point having the minimum distance from the objects in F_j with respect to the generalized ellipsoid distance as shown in [10]. Add w_j to set W.
6. If k > j choose k' as closest integer number larger than k divided by j, else k':=1.
7. For all j elements in W initiate a top k' search using the arithmetical average weighted with w_j as utility function and return all results as query result.

In our experiments sampling with three-dimensional subsets ($m = 3$), values of $q = 10$ for ten score lists ($n = 10$) and $q = 15$ for 15 score lists ($n = 15$) has already provided sufficient sampling quality. Section 4.1 will deal in detail with an experimental evaluation of our sampling scheme's quality using different score distributions. Deriving optimal query weightings from feedback objects has been in deep investigated by [10] for the case of a single region of interest.

4 Theoretical Foundations and Practical Analysis

We bridge the gap between top k retrieval and skylining by providing a first impression of the database that allows for an automatic deriving of weightings from user feedback. To facilitate this, our skyline samples have to fulfil several conditions:

- **No dominated objects:** Positive feedback on already dominated objects may lead to weightings inconsistent with optimal solutions in the final result.
- **Practical runtime:** Retrieving final result sets needs user feedback, thus deriving samples in a timely manner is essential for good overall runtimes.
- **Manageable size:** Sample sizes have to be quite limited to allow for manual feedback, while staying representative enough of the actual skyline.
- **Representativeness:** To provide a good impression of the database content samples must be representative of the entire skyline set and not biased.

Let us now consider the conditions that we posed for our sampling scheme. The following theorem states that -without having to calculate the high-dimensional skyline- our sampling nevertheless always contains only actual skyline objects.

Theorem 1 (Samples contain no dominated objects):
Every object o in the sample P chosen by our retrieval algorithm in step 2 is an actual skyline object with respect to all query predicates.

Proof:
We have to show that only skyline objects are added to P in step 2.3. Assume that we have chosen an arbitrary subset of score lists and then calculate the skyline P_i of this subset like shown in step 2.1. Let us further assume that we have derived set P_i' by pairwise comparing objects with equal scores in the chosen subset of dimensions for domination and discarding all dominated objects like shown in step 2.2. Since the set P_i' is added to P after step 2.2, we have to show that it contains only objects of the higher dimensional skyline.

Now for the sake of contradiction let o be any object of P_i' and assume that o is not a skyline object with respect to all dimensions, i.e. some object p exists dominating o. Thus, for all lists S_i ($1 \leq i \leq n$) and the respective scores s_i we get $s_i(p) \geq s_i(o)$ due to the definition of domination. If, however, some index h would exist with $s_h(p) > s_h(o)$ and h would be the index of any score list within the chosen subset, p would already dominate o with respect to the chosen subset in contradiction to $o \in P_i'$. Thus o and p have to have equal scores with respect to the chosen subset and since we have compared all the objects with equal scores in the subset pairwise for domination and discarded the dominated ones from P_i', we have to conclude that p cannot exist.

Since we have shown P_i' to contain only skyline objects with respect to all query predicates independently of the specific choice of the subset, also the union of different choices of subsets contains only skyline objects. ∎

4.1 Performance Experiments and Quality Analysis

We have already proved our samples to contain no dominated objects, but guaranteeing the remaining requirements does not seem as obvious without empirical support:

- The runtime and the size of the samples can be measured directly.
- Since there is no established method of directly measuring the representativeness of samples especially in high dimensions. We will assess the quality of representation with two measures: the set coverage and a cluster analysis.
- Deducing users' preferences involves two steps: grouping user feedback into regions of interest, and then deriving a weighting vector w for each region. Quality issues of deriving weightings for a single region has often been investigated (see e.g. [10]). Therefore we will focus on how well these techniques adapt when users have more than one region of interest.

Throughout this section, our testing environment uses a database containing 100,000 objects in different synthesized score distributions for 10 or 15 query predicates. We take the union of 10 or 15 samples, each querying 3 randomly chosen dimensions. We then take averages over 50 runs with newly generated synthetic data. Real databases often contain correlated data. In our traveling researcher example, the distance of a trip will be correlated to the traveling time, and a hotel's price may be correlated to its category. Therefore we investigate different types of data distribution: independent distribution, positive correlation, and anti-correlation. In correlated databases we correlate 6 dimensions pairwise (3 pairs of correlative dimensions) with correlation factor 0.7. Similarly, the anti-correlative datasets correlate 6 dimensions pair-wise with factor -0.7. All tests were run on a single-CPU, 2.2 GHz Pentium-4 PC with 512MB of RAM under MS Windows 2000 and Sun Java VM 1.4.2.

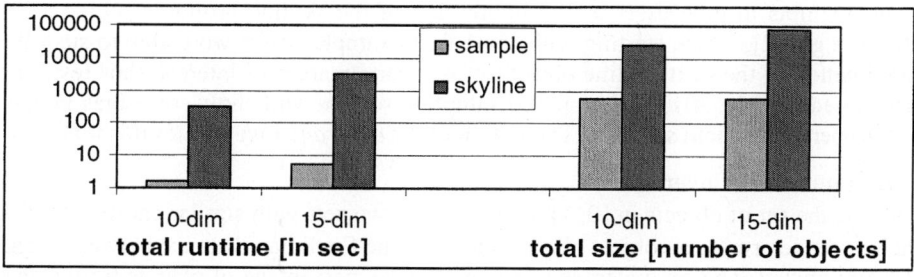

Fig. 3. Comparison for runtime for skyline computation (left) and respective skyline size (right)

Total Runtime and Sample Size
Though the actual runtime will vary depending on the hardware/software used, comparing the runtime of skyline sampling versus computing the entire skyline will give us a good idea of our sampling scheme's performance. In Figure 3 (left), we show the comparison of runtime measured in seconds on a logarithmic scale. Our sampling scheme is generally two to three orders of magnitude faster than computing the entire skyline. Note that the sampling scheme can even be parallelized for further runtime improvement, since all subsets are independent in computation and I/O.

Similar to the runtime, the manageability can be directly measured as the size of the result set. Figure 3 (right) shows the average sizes of sample sizes and the actual size of 10 and 15 dimensional skylines. Once again, we see a difference of two orders of magnitude between our sample and the actual skyline. Although a few hundred objects are much more manageable than tens of thousands of objects, going through the entire sample set may still seem challenging. Taking fewer numbers of subsets for the sample would further reduce the size of the sample set. However, it is hard to reduce the size without sacrificing the representativeness of the sample.

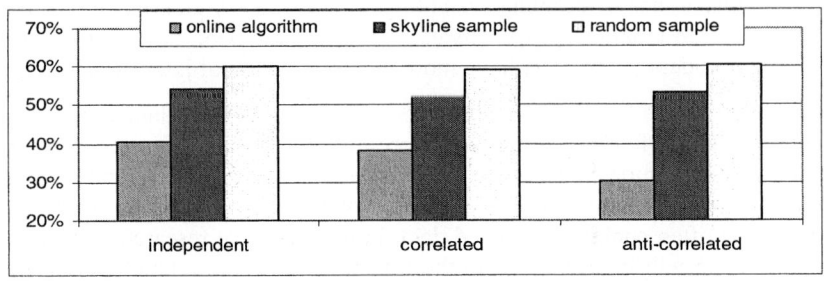

Fig. 4. Set coverage [in percent] with respect to an unbiased random sample

Representativeness of Skyline Samples: Set Coverage and Cluster Analysis

The most representative sampling method is taking random samples of the actual skyline. Here no particular region is favored, but obtaining such a random sample requires computing all skyline objects, which is prohibitive in terms of runtime. Previous attempts to give users a first impression of the skyline proposed online algorithms, e.g. [12], where starting with some first examples users were able to steer the computation of the next skyline object towards certain areas of interest, thus resulting in a biased sample. Also our proposed sampling scheme will show some bias in contrast to perfect random samples. The notion of *set coverage* investigates this bias:

Definition of Set Coverage:

Let S be the set of objects in $[0, 1]^n$ and s, s' $\subseteq$ S two sets with similar cardinality. For each o $\in$ s determine an object o' $\in$ s', such that the Euclidian distance between o and o' is minimized. The set coverage of s over s' is the percentage of objects from s' that have been assigned to objects of s.

Measuring the set coverage between independently drawn random samples of the actual skyline set gives us a good impression of the normal coverage between unbiased sets. For our experiments we considered different score distributions (independent, correlated, anti-correlated) and took averages over several runs in each instance choosing a random sample and comparing the respective set coverage of a second independent random sample, our sample and set delivered from the online algorithm in [12]. In all cases the sets were chosen with similar cardinalities, generally different runs show an insignificant variance. Figure 4 presents the results, where the y-axis is the percentage of the objects in the random sample of the actual skyline that are covered by the sample from the online algorithm, our skyline sample and a second independently drawn random sample. With very little variance in all score distributions the best set coverage between two unbiased random samples is around 60%. Clearly the set coverage for our sampling scheme is almost as good showing values around

54% with small variance, while being much better than the online algorithm's ranging between 30-40% and showing a relatively large variance with the score distributions.

Though we have seen our sample to cover randomly drawn samples quite well, we also have to focus on how the objects are distributed over the score space, i.e. if our samples closely represent the *entire* skyline and not just some portions of it. Our *cluster analysis* measures the representativeness of a sample grouped by the relative distribution of objects. Scores for each query predicate are partitioned into two buckets: [0, 0.5) and [0.5, 1] leading to e.g. 2^n different buckets in the case of n query predicates. The bucket assigned gives a rough idea where objects are located in n-dimensional space. For each sample, we count the number of objects in each bucket and compare the respective numbers using histograms. Thus we can ascertain that clusters of skyline objects are also represented by our sample. Since we cannot show such histograms (already 1024 buckets for 10 dimensions) we use the score space's symmetry and aggregate the buckets having a similar position with respect to the main diagonal. That means we aggregate all buckets with the same numbers of 'upper' score buckets, leading to n dimensional histograms for n query predicates. Figure 5 shows the histograms assessing the percentage of objects with respect to the sample size in each aggregated bucket (the connecting lines are just inserted to make the histograms more easily comparable). Focusing again on our three different score distributions, figure 5 plots the object distribution over the aggregated buckets of the actual skyline, our skyline sample and a complete random sample of the entire database (to show the normal bell-shaped object distribution under our symmetrical aggregation). We can easily see that unlike the complete sample our sample's distribution aligns smoothly with the original skyline, both showing a distinct shift to the higher buckets. This shift even becomes more pronounced for correlated score distributions (Fig. 5, right). Again our sample resembles the proportions of the actual skyline very well. The diagram for the anti-correlated case is similar, but omitted for brevity.

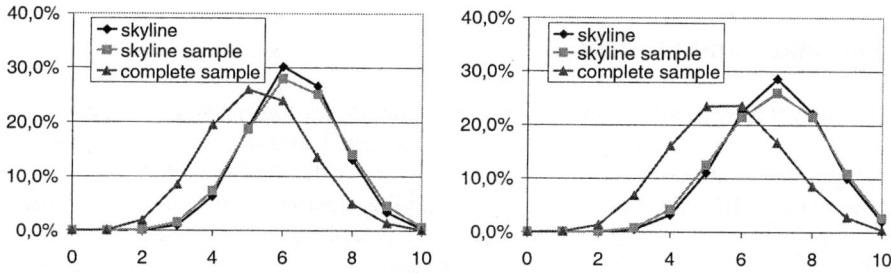

Fig. 5. Cluster analysis for independent (left) and correlated (right) score distributions

4.2 Querying Multiple Regions of Interest

Usually in query by example the user selects interesting data objects (e.g. images) and the query is reposed taking the characteristics of selected items into account. However, in skyline sets users might be interested in objects of multiple regions. Therefore we extended the MindReader re-weighting technique for single regions of interest [10] by setting a threshold for the maximum allowable distance between example objects in a single region and thus separating the selected examples into multiple regions (compare steps 4-7 in our algorithm in section 3). As threshold we chose the minimum Euclidian distance between a chosen example and any example not chosen. We then apply the MindReader algorithm with all chosen examples within this threshold as input and get the optimal weightings for a subsequent top k search. To investigate our query processing algorithm's effectiveness, we set up an experiment on a database containing 100.000 objects. Assuming the existence of three preferred objects in the actual skyline, we randomly selected three 'perfect' objects from the skyline. Ascertaining a certain maximum distance $dist$ to at least one of the 'perfect' objects we then picked all eligible objects from the sample drawn and fed these as positive feedback to our re-weighting scheme (please note that the sample may, or may not contain any 'perfect' object). After grouping the examples into regions of interest using the minimum distance to any non-picked object in the sample, we calculated the best weightings (query points) for a top k query and subsequently retrieved the best objects. We then counted how many of the initial perfect objects are in the direct vicinity (again using maximum distance $dist$) of the objects retrieved.

In our experiments for independent score distributions the samples sizes were 336.52 on average, of which an average of 13.52 objects were picked as positive feedback (at an initial value of $dist = 0.75$). These objects had an average distance of 0.579 to the closest 'perfect' object. Our algorithms on average grouped the positive feedback into 9.88 distinct groups leading to the determination of optimal query points with an average distance of 0.580 to the 'perfect' objects. The subsequent top k retrieval for each query point retrieved objects with an average 86.67% of all 'perfect' objects in the direct vicinity (within distance $dist$) of some of them. The experiments for correlated and anti-correlated data distributions show similar results, with increased numbers of positive feedback objects and even higher numbers of correctly retrieved objects in the vicinity of 'perfect' objects, on average over 90%.

5 Summary and Outlook

Cooperative retrieval with vague predicates in databases today uses two techniques: top k retrieval and skyline queries. But whereas top k result sets are well-defined, choosing appropriate compensation functions without detailed knowledge of a database instance is difficult. In contrast posing skyline queries is very simple and intuitive, but result sets grow exponentially with the number of query predicates and thus quickly become unmanageable. In this paper we focused on the efficient utilization of high-dimensional skylines to allow for intuitive querying with vague predicates in information systems, while at the same time guaranteeing manageable result sets.

Starting with a normal skyline query we designed an interactive scheme using feedback on a representative sample of the skyline for subsequent focused top k retrieval guaranteeing manageable result sets. Thus our query processing scheme combines the best of both techniques. We have proven our query processing scheme to *quickly* derive *manageable*, but *highly representative* skyline samples containing *no dominated objects*. Evaluating feedback on these samples we have then extended an efficient query by example algorithm to cater for the need in cooperative retrieval to separately investigate several regions of interest. Detailed practical experiments show that our sample can be derived up to two orders of magnitude faster than the actual skyline and is almost as representative as a similar-sized random sample of the actual skyline. Moreover, we showed our focused top k searches to deliver result sets, where over 85% of the actual objects of interest are arbitrarily close to the objects retrieved.

Applications focus on cooperative query processing in information systems for a variety of areas like E-commerce, digital libraries or service provisioning. Our future work will concentrate on further exploiting the scheme and opening up the query by example capabilities for multi-objective retrieval in databases, e.g. [1]. Moreover, we will investigate our sampling scheme's capability for interactively deriving meaningful user preferences that can be used as long-term profiles in specific domains.

References

1. W.-T. Balke, U. Güntzer. Multi-objective Query Processing for Database Systems. *Intern. Conf. on Very Large Data Bases (VLDB'04)*, Toronto, Canada, 2004.
2. W.-T. Balke, J. Zheng, U. Güntzer. Efficient Distributed Skylining for Web Information Systems. *Conf. on Extending Database Technology (EDBT'04)*, Heraklion, Greece, 2004.
3. C. Böhm, H. Kriegel. Determining the Convex Hull in Large Multidimensional Databases. *Conf. on Data Wareh. and Knowledge Discovery (DaWaK'01)*, Munich, Germany, 2001.
4. S. Börzsönyi, D. Kossmann, K. Stocker. The Skyline Operator. *Intern. Conf. on Data Engineering (ICDE'01)*, Heidelberg, Germany, 2001.
5. N. Bruno, L. Gravano, A. Marian. Evaluating Top k Queries over Web-Accessible Databases. *Intern. Conf. on Data Engineering (ICDE'02)*, San Jose, USA, 2002.
6. A. Chianese, A. Picariello, L. Sansone. A System for Query by Example in Image Databases. *Int. Workshop on Multimedia Information Systems (MIS'01)*, Capri, Italy, 2001.
7. R. Fagin, A. Lotem, M. Naor: Optimal Aggregation Algorithms for Middleware. *ACM Symp. on Principles of Database Systems (PODS'01)*, Santa Barbara, USA, 2001.
8. P. Godfrey. Skyline Cardinality for Relational Processing. *Int Symp. on Foundations of Information and Knowledge Systems (FoIKS'04)*, Wilhelminenburg Castle, Austria, 2004.
9. U. Güntzer, W.-T. Balke, W. Kießling: Optimizing Multi-Feature Queries for Image Databases. *Int. Conf. on Very Large Data Bases (VLDB'00)*, Cairo, Egypt, 2000.
10. Y. Ishikawa, R. Subramanya, C. Faloutsos. MindReader: Querying Databases through Multiple Examples. *Conf. on Very Large Data Bases (VLDB'98)*, New York, USA, 1998.
11. V. Koltun, C. Papadimitriou. Approximately Dominating Representatives. *Int. Conf. on Database Theory (ICDT'05)*, Edinburgh, UK, 2005.
12. D. Kossmann, F. Ramsak, S. Rost. Shooting Stars in the Sky: An Online Algorithm for Skyline Queries. *Conf. on Very Large Data Bases (VLDB'02)*, Hong Kong, China, 2002.
13. J. Minker. An Overview of Cooperative Answering in Databases. *Int. Conf. on Flexible Query Answering Systems (FQAS'98)*, Springer LNCS 1495, Roskilde, Denmark, 1998.
14. A. Motro. VAGUE: A User Interface to Relational Databases that Permits Vague Queries. *ACM Transactions on Information Systems*. Vol. 6(3), 1988.
15. D. Papadias, Y. Tao, G. Fu, B. Seeger. An Optimal and Progressive Algorithm for Skyline Queries. *Int. Conf. on Management of Data (SIGMOD'03)*, San Diego, USA, 2003.
16. S. Santini, R. Jain. Beyond Query by Example. *Int. ACM Conf. on Multimedia (MM'98)*, Bristol, England, 1998.

False-Negative Frequent Items Mining from Data Streams with Bursting

Zhihong Chong[1], Jeffrey Xu Yu[2], Hongjun Lu[3],
Zhengjie Zhang[1], and Aoying Zhou[1]

[1] Fudan University, China
{zhchong, zhjzhang, ayzhou}@fudan.edu.cn,
[2] Chinese University of Hong Kong, China
yu@se.cuhk.edu.hk
[3] Hong Kong University of Science and Technology, China
luhj@cs.ust.hk

Abstract. False-negative frequent items mining from a high speed transactional data stream is to find an approximate set of frequent items with respect to a minimum support threshold, s. It controls the possibility of missing frequent items using a reliability parameter δ. The importance of false-negative frequent items mining is that it can exclude false-positives and therefore significantly reduce the memory consumption for frequent itemsets mining. The key issue of false-negative frequent items mining is how to minimize the possibility of missing frequent items. In this paper, we propose a new false-negative frequent items mining algorithm, called Loss-Negative, for handling bursting in data streams. The new algorithm consumes the smallest memory in comparison with other false-negative and false-positive frequent items algorithms. We present theoretical bound of the new algorithm, and analyze the possibility of minimization of missing frequent items, in terms of two possibilities, namely, in-possibility and out-possibility. The former is about how a frequent item can possibly pass the first pruning. The latter is about how long a frequent item can stay in memory while no occurrences of the item comes in the following data stream for a certain period. The new proposed algorithm is superior to the existing false-negative frequent items mining algorithms in terms of the two possibilities. We demonstrate the effectiveness of the new algorithm in this paper.

1 Introduction

Mining frequent itemsets from transactional data streams is challenging due to the nature of the exponential explosion of itemsets and the limit memory space required for mining frequent itemsets [4, 6]. The techniques for mining frequent itemsets largely rely on the techniques for mining frequent items by scanning data once from a high speed data stream with limit memory space. The up-to-date techniques for mining frequent items can be categorized into two classes, namely, false-positive and false-negative. The former controls memory consumption with

Table 1. Bounds and Types

Algorithm	Bound	Type
Charilar et al [1]	$O(\frac{k}{\epsilon^2}\ln(n/\delta))$	false-positive
Sticky-Sampling [4]	$O(\frac{1}{\epsilon}\lg(\frac{1}{s}\frac{1}{\delta}))$	false-positive
Lossy-Counting [4]	$O(\frac{1}{\epsilon}\lg(\epsilon n))$	false-positive
Group Test [2]	$O(k\lg(k+\lg(\frac{1}{\delta}\lg(M))))$	false-positive
FDPM-1 [6]	$O(2+2\ln(2/\delta)/s)$	false-negative
LN (this paper)	$O(\frac{1}{s}\ln(s^{-1}\delta^{-1}))$	false-negative

an error parameter ϵ, and treats items with support below the specified minimum support s but above $s-\epsilon$ counted as frequent items [1, 2, 3, 4]. The latter controls the possibility of missing frequent items above the specified minimum support s using a reliability parameter δ [6]. Table 1 shows the memory bounds for false-negative algorithms is lower than the bounds for false-positive algorithms. The main advantage of false-negative approaches is that they significantly reduce the exponential explosion of itemsets, because they do not maintain any possible itemsets that include items below the minimum support s but above $s-\epsilon$, which can be very large.

In [6], we showed a false-negative algorithm FDPM-1 that is designed on top of the Chernoff bound which assumes data independent. Also, we demonstrated that FDPM-1 can handle dependent data streams in our expensive performance studies using a technique called probabilistic-inplace [3]. In the following discussions, for easy of discussions, we denote the algorithm of FDPM-1 with probabilistic-inplace as FDPM-I.

In this paper, we study a very important issue on false-negative algorithms – how to minimize the possibility of missing frequent items in the presence of bursts in high speed data streams. Here, by bursts we mean that a frequent item may repeatedly appears together in a short time and disappears for a long time. When such bursts occur in a high speed data stream, the possibility of missing frequent items can be higher. It is because that the item can be possibly pruned before its next burst comes. We show a real application below. Here, we consider finding frequent items (words) from Reuters news collection using a data archive we collected through the Reuters real-time datafeed. The dataset contains 365,288 news stories and 100,672,866 (duplicate) words. We removed all articles such as "the" and "a" and preprocessed the data collection by term stemming. Fig. 1 (a) shows the distribution of top 500 frequent words, which is a Zipf distribution with a Zipf factor of 1.5. Fig. 1 (b) shows three burst patterns for three words, represented as integers 13151, 54449 and 256421 from the 1176-th document to the 1197-th document, provided that we receive documents in order. For this dataset, FDPM-1 does not perform well because of data dependency, whereas FDPM-I performs well because it is enhanced with the technique of probabilistic-inplace. However, it is unknown theoretically how robust FDPM-I is when bursts occur.

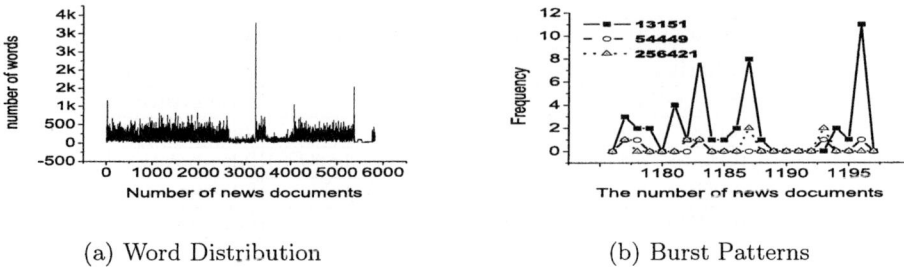

(a) Word Distribution (b) Burst Patterns

Fig. 1. A Reuters news collection

The main contribution of this paper is summarized below. We propose a new false-negative algorithm, called Loss-Negative and denoted LN, with a theoretical bound on its memory consumption. The theoretical bound of memory consumption for LN is marginally higher than that of FDPM-1 [6], but the real memory consumption, in practice, for LN is noticeably less than that of FDPM-1 (FDPM-I). Furthermore, we analyze the burst control of the new false-negative algorithm in terms of two possibilities, called in-possibility and out-possibility. The former is about how a frequent item can possibly pass the first pruning. The latter is about how long a frequent item can stay in memory while no occurrences of the item comes in the following data stream for a certain period. We show that LN is better than FDPM-1 (FDPM-I) in terms of the two possibilities. In addition, we demonstrate that LN consumes even small memory than FDPM-1 (FDPM-I) in our extensive performance study using synthetic and real data sets.

The remainder of the paper is organized as follows. Section 2 defines the problem. Section 3 introduces the proposed new false-negative frequent items mining algorithm. A performance study is given in Section 4. We conclude this paper in Section 5

2 Problem Definition

A transactional data stream, $\mathcal{D}$, is a sequence of incoming items, $(t_1, t_2, \cdots, t_n)$, where t_i is an item and n is a unknown large number. The number of occurrences of an item t_i in $\mathcal{D}$ is called the support of t_i, denoted as $sup(t_i)$. An item t_i is frequent, if and only if $sup(t_i) \geq sn$, where $s = sup(t_i)/n$ is a threshold called a minimum support such that $s \in (0, 1)$.

The problem of frequent items mining is to find an *approximate* set of frequent items in $\mathcal{D}$ with respect to a given support threshold, s. The approximation is controlled by two parameters, ϵ and δ, where ϵ ($\in (0,1)$) controls errors and δ ($\in (0,1)$) controls reliability.

In this paper, we propose a false-negative algorithm. A false-negative frequent items mining algorithm must mine frequent items from a high speed data stream with limited memory while guarantees the following two conditions: i) none of the support of the output items is less than s, and ii) each item whose support is no less than s is output with at least $1-\delta$ probability. It is worth of noting that false-negative approaches control memory using δ with $\epsilon=0$, whereas false-positive approaches mainly control memory using ϵ.

3 A New False-Negative Algorithm

We propose a new false-negative oriented algorithm, called LN, in Algorithm 1 to mine frequent items from a data stream. We first outline the main idea of the algorithm, and discuss the details later. Consider receiving data from a data stream in a unit of buckets. The width of buckets is the number of entries, where an entry is a pair of item and its count. We denote the width of buckets as ω. LN keeps only a single bucket of items in memory. The main idea of the algorithm is as follows. It expects that a frequent item will appear at least once in a unit of bucket. At the end of the b-th bucket, LN prunes those items that do not appear b times where $b = \lceil n/\omega \rceil$. If a burst of an item t appears in a bucket, then it can be kept in memory for a long time, even though it does not appear in the following buckets. LN does not prune those items, t, that appear more than b times, such as $sup(t)/n \geq b/n = \lceil n/\omega \rceil /n = 1/\omega$. As stated above, LN attempts to use ω entries to maintain frequent items, t, in memory, such as $sup(t)/n \geq 1/\omega$.

The details of Algorithm 1 are discussed below. LN takes two parameters, a minimum support s and a reliability parameter δ, and outputs frequent items in F with their recorded frequency. Each entry of F is in the format of (t, f) where t is an item and f is its count. In line 1-2, LN initializes the number of items, n, it receives from a data stream and F. In line 3, LN decides the width of the buckets, ω, using s and δ (Eq. (1)). We will explain how to determine ω later. The derived ω guarantees that LN can hold every frequent item in a bucket at least once with probability of at least $1-\delta$. The ω shows the bound of LN. In the

---

Algorithm 1 LN(s, δ)

1: $n \leftarrow 0$;
2: $F \leftarrow \emptyset$;
3: $\omega \leftarrow \lceil \frac{\ln(s^{-1}\delta^{-1})}{s} \rceil$;
4: **while** an item, t, arrives **do**
5:     $n \leftarrow n+1$;
6:     either insert a new entry for $(t, 1)$ into F or increase f of the existing entry (t, f) by 1;
7:     prune those entries from F if their support $f/n < 1/\omega$ at the end of each bucket;
8: **end while**
9: output frequent items in F on demand if their counts $\geq sn$;

---

while statement, LN creates a new entry for an item t in F if it does not appear in F and its count is initialized as 1; otherwise, LN increases the count for t by 1. In line 7, LN prunes those entries from F, if their supports are less than $1/\omega$.

On demand, LN outputs all items whose support $\geq sn$. Note: no false positives are reported. In Algorithm 1, the time complexity for inserting a new item is $O(1)$, and time complexity for pruning items at the end of a bucket is also $O(1)$ because LN only maintains w items at most.

Next, we show how to determine w below. First we have Lemma 1 as reported in [5, 6].

Lemma 1. *The number of frequent items found in a data stream is no more than $1/s$, where s is the minimum support.*

Lemma 1 is held, because if there are more than $1/s$ items and each appears at least $s \cdot n$ times, then $1/s \cdot s \cdot n > n$ which is impossible. The memory bound of LN is shown in Theorem 1.

Theorem 1. *The memory bound of LN is $w = \lceil \frac{1}{s} \ln(s^{-1}\delta^{-1}) \rceil$ to mine frequent items with probability of at least $1 - \delta$.*

We sketch our proof as follows. The width of buckets, w, is determined as to keep every frequent item in every bucket with at least $1 - \delta$ probability. LN divides the data stream into buckets of the width w, and needs the number of $b = \lceil n/w \rceil$ buckets to receive n items. Recall a frequent item should appear more than or equal to sn times. Assume the probability of a frequent item in a bucket is nearly $1/b$, the chance of a frequent item not to appear in any bucket is less than

$$(1 - \frac{1}{b})^{sn} = (1 - \frac{1}{\frac{n}{w}})^{sn} = (1 - \frac{1}{\frac{n}{w}})^{\frac{n}{w}ws} \approx (\frac{1}{e})^{ws}$$

Because there are at most $1/s$ frequent items in a data stream based on Lemma 1, the probability that none of the frequent items is located in any bucket is at most $(\frac{1}{e})^{ws}\frac{1}{s}$. Based on the notion of reliability, the probability of missing a count needs to be no more than δ, such as $(\frac{1}{e})^{ws}\frac{1}{s} \leq \delta$. Therefore,

$$w \leq \frac{\ln(s^{-1}\delta^{-1})}{s} \quad (1)$$

LN maintains items whose support is no less than $(n/w)/n = 1/w$, and needs only $1/(1/w) = w$ entries in F.

$$|F| \leq w \leq \frac{\ln(s^{-1}\delta^{-1})}{s} \quad (2)$$

Therefore, Theorem 1 holds. As shown in Theorem 1, the width of buckets, w, is determined by both the minimum support s and the reliability parameter δ. The width w becomes larger, when either s or δ becomes smaller. When w is a larger value, the probability of keeping a frequent item in a bucket becomes higher, because $1 - \delta$ becomes larger. For example, when $s = 0.1\%$ and $\delta = 0.1$, then $w = 9,210.3$; and when $s = 0.01\%$ and $\delta = 0.1$, $w = 115,129.3$. That is, if an item is frequent, it is most likely that the item will appear every w on average. Obviously, LN does not miss a frequent item, even though the frequent item may not appear in every bucket, because the frequent item may appear in some buckets more than once. Also, the probability that an item does not appear in consecutive m buckets is small, $(1/e)^m \to 0$, when m is large.

We analysis the possibility that LN misses frequent items in the following two possibilities: in-possibility and out-possibility. The in-possibility is about how a frequent item can possibly pass the first pruning. The out-possibility is about how long a frequent item can stay in memory while no occurrences of the item comes in the following data stream for a certain period. We show that LN is better than FDPM-1 in terms of the two possibilities.

3.1 In-Possibility

Suppose that an item t first appears m times in the current bucket $b = \lceil n/\omega \rceil$. It will be held in memory when LN cross the boundary of the bucket if the following condition is true.

$$m \geq \frac{n}{\omega} \qquad (3)$$

It shows that it would be more difficult for a frequent item to appear lately when i) the bucket is full and ii) n becomes larger. Still, LN is better than FDPM-1 in terms of the two issues, i) and ii). For i), the theoretical memory bound of LN is marginally larger than that of FDPM-1 as shown in Table 1. For ii), FDPM-1 allows an item t to be in memory if

$$m \geq (s - \epsilon_n)n \qquad (4)$$

When n becomes large, the running error variable ϵ_n approaches zero, and can be ignored. Therefore,

$$m \geq s \cdot n \qquad (5)$$

Compare Eq. (3) with Eq. (5), it is difficult for a frequent item to be pruned in LN than FDPM-1, if $1/\omega < s$. In other words, it means that LN requests a smaller m for a frequent item to be in memory. Based on Theorem (1), when $\omega = \frac{\ln(s^{-1}\delta^{-1})}{s}$, $1/\omega < s$ if $s \cdot \delta < 1/e$. That is, $s \cdot \delta < 0.367879$, which can be always true, for example, when $\delta = 0.1$.

3.2 Out-Possibility

Consider how long an item can be kept in memory, we define a d-robust as follows. A potential frequent item t is d-robust at a point of n, if the item t can not be pruned until $n + d$, while no occurrence of t appears from $n + 1$ to $n + d$. Without loss of generality, we consider n as the data point at the end of a bucket, because that is the time to prune items.

Consider a potential frequent item t at n. Assume that the count of the item t is c. Because the item t is still in F, it has at least $\lceil n/\omega \rceil$ occurrences until n as shown in Algorithm 1. Therefore, $c \geq \lceil n/\omega \rceil$.

$$d = (c - \lceil \frac{n}{\omega} \rceil + 1) \cdot \omega > c \cdot \omega - n = \ln(s^{-1}\delta^{-1}) \cdot \frac{c}{s} - n \qquad (6)$$

Eq. (6) shows that when $c = \lceil n/\omega \rceil$, the item t will be kept until at least the end of next bucket. The larger the count c is, the longer period the item t can be kept in memory. Because $c = \lceil n/\omega \rceil$ is the minimum count for any potential item at any bucket, therefore, LN is ω-robust.

Some comments can be made on FDPM-1. For FDPM-1, it must satisfy Eq. (7) to hold the item t in memory as shown in [6].

$$\frac{c}{n+d} \geq s - \epsilon_{n+d} \qquad (7)$$

Here, $c/(n+d)$ is $sup(t)/(n+d)$ at the point of $n+d$, and ϵ_{n+d} is the running error at the point of $n+d$. Recall $\epsilon_n \to 0$ when n becomes large. Therefore, we obtain

$$d \leq \frac{c}{s} - n \qquad (8)$$

Comparing Eq. (6) for LN with Eq. (8) for FDPM-1, LN is more robust than FDPM-1 when $\ln(s^{-1}\delta^{-1}) \geq 1$. Like the discussions on in-possibility, it implies $s \cdot \delta < 1/e$. FDPM-I is more robust than FDPM-1 based on our extensive performance studies as shown later in the paper. Because FDPM-I is a variant of FDPM-1 using probabilistic-inplace, it is difficult to analyze its d-robust.

3.3 Discussions on Bucket: False-Positive Versus False Negative

Some comments on buckets are given below. First, both false-positive and false-negative approaches can use buckets for frequent items mining. The widths of buckets have great impacts on the memory bound. Second, false-positive and false-negative approaches use different ways to determine the widths of buckets, and therefore the memory bounds. For instance, as a false-positive algorithm, Loss-Counting uses $\lceil 1/\epsilon \rceil$ to control the memory bound. As a false-negative algorithm, LN uses $\lceil \frac{\ln(s^{-1}\delta^{-1})}{s} \rceil$ to control the memory bound. Third, like FDPM-1 (Table 1), the theoretical memory bound of LN is irrelevant to the length of a data stream, n. But, the memory bound of Lossy-Counting is related to n as shown in Table 1.

4 A Performance Study

We implemented our new false-negative algorithm LN as well as the false-positive algorithms LC (Lossy-Counting) and SS (Sticky-Sampling) [4] and the best reported false-negative algorithm FDPM-1 (FDPM-I) [6], using Microsoft Visual C++ Version 6.0. We used the same data structures and subroutines in all implementations in order to minimize any performance difference caused by minor differences in implementation.

We tested above algorithms on both the synthetic data generated with various Zipfan distributions and the Reuters news collection as given in the introduction. The default length of a data stream is $1,000,000$ items.

We conducted all testings on a 1.7GHz CPU Dell PC with 1GB memory. We report our results in terms of memory consumption (the number of entries) and

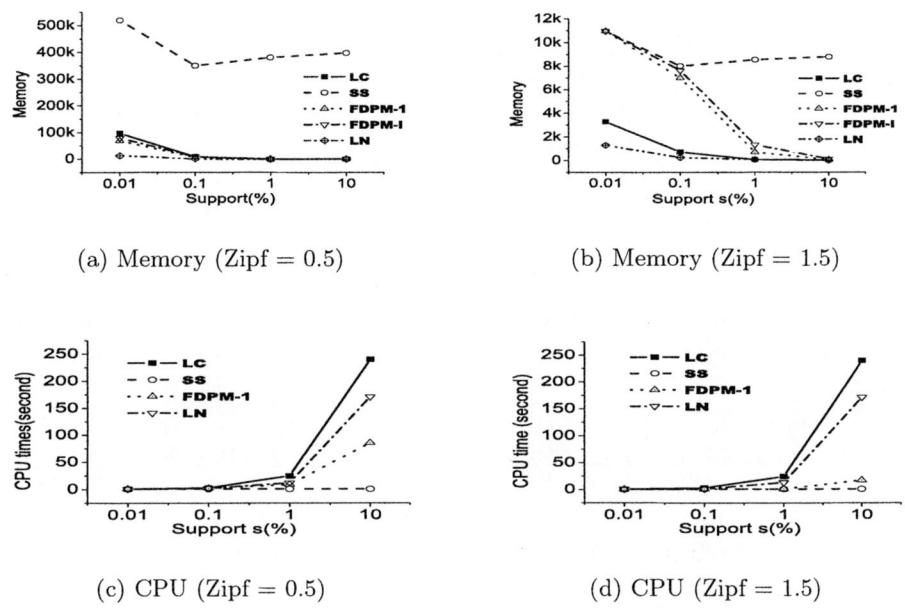

Fig. 2. Memory and CPU time

CPU time (seconds), as well as recall and precision. The recall and precision are defined as follows. Given a set of true frequent items, A, and a set of obtained frequent items B, the recall is $\frac{|A \cap B|}{|A|}$ and the precision is $\frac{|A \cap B|}{|B|}$.

4.1 Testing on Synthetic Data Sets

Varying Support. In this part, we test minimum support in a range from 0.01% to 10% with a fixed $\delta = 0.1$, using Zipf = 0.5 and Zipf = 1.5, respectively. Note that false-negative algorithms, LN and FDPM-1 (FDPM-I) do not use ϵ. We fix $\epsilon = s/10$ for LC and SS only.

The memory consumption and CPU time are shown in Fig. 2. All algorithms behave similarly over different Zipf distributions. The memory consumption is higher when data is not highly skewed (Zipf = 0.5) in comparison with that when data is rather skewed (Zipf = 1.5). SS consumes most memory with the smallest CPU time. FDPM-1 and FDPM-I perform the same in terms of CPU time.

It is important to note that LN consumes less memory than FDPM-1 (FDPM-I), as shown in Fig. 2, despite the theoretical memory bound of FDPM-1 is smaller than that of LN. The main reason is that FDPM-1 (FDPM-I) unnecessarily maintains those items whose support is above $s - \epsilon_n$, where $\epsilon_n = \sqrt{\frac{2s \ln(2/\delta)}{n}}$. Consider the case when n is rather small. Because $\epsilon_n > s$, FDPM-1 (FDPM-I) uses $s - \epsilon_n$ ($< s$) to keep infrequent items and consumes more memory than LN.

Table 2. Recall (R) and Precision (P) (Zipf = 1.5)

s(%)	LC		SS		FDPM-1(FDPM-I)		LN	
	R	P	R	P	R	P	R	P
0.01	1.00	0.91	1.00	0.91	1.00	1.00	1.00	1.00
0.1	1.00	0.96	1.00	0.96	1.00	1.00	1.00	1.00
1	1.00	0.92	1.00	0.92	1.00	1.00	1.00	1.00
10	1.00	1.00	1.00	1.00	1.00	1.00	1.00	1.00

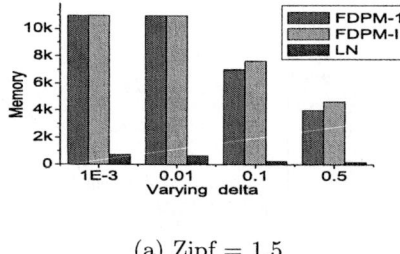
(a) Zipf = 1.5

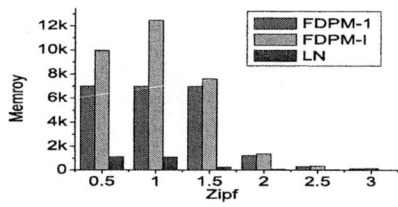
(b) Zipf Distributions ($\delta = 0.1$)

Fig. 3. The Impacts of δ on Memory Consumption ($s = 0.1\%$)

Table 2 shows the recall and precision for Zipf = 1.5. As shown in the table, false-positive algorithms, LC and SS always achieve 100% recall, while false-negative algorithms FDPM-1 (FDPM-I) and LN always achieve 100% precision. Also, all false-negative algorithms LN and FDPM-1 (FDPM-I) achieve 100% recall, whereas the false-positive algorithms LC and SS do not always 100% precision as expected.

Varying δ. The key point for false-negative algorithms is how to avoid missing frequent items, which is controlled by the reliability parameter δ. We tested the impacts of δ for the false-negative algorithms, LN and FDPM-1 (FDPM-I), while fixing the minimum support $s = 0.1\%$. Fig. 3 (a) shows that LN consumes significantly less memory than FDPM-1 (FDPM-I) with Zipf = 1.5. In this testing, all false-negative algorithms achieve both 100% recall and precision. Fig. 3 (b) shows the memory consumptions using different Zipf distributions, from Zipf = 0.5 to Zipf = 3, while $\delta = 0.1$. In a similar way, LN consumes significantly less memory than FDPM-1 (FDPM-I). LN as well as FDPM-I achieves 100% recall whereas FDPM-1 achieves at least 98% recall.

4.2 Testing on a Real Dataset

The arrival order of data item in a synthetic dataset is usually random independent and false-negative algorithms can behave well. As given in introduction, we test a real dataset using the Reuters news collection we collected through the Reuters real-time datafeed. The dataset contains 365,288 news stories and

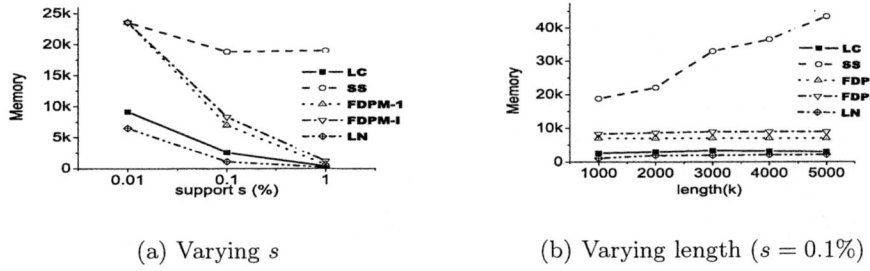

(a) Varying s (b) Varying length ($s = 0.1\%$)

Fig. 4. Memory Consumption

100,672,866 (duplicate) words (items). This dataset demonstrates burst patterns that do not show in synthetic dataset, because the words have meanings and may appear frequently in some documents but not all documents. We select 5,829 consecutive news stories to make a stream of $1,000,000$ words. The average length of a news story is 172 words. The words are converted into an integer representation in our testing beforehand.

Varying s. We first tested LN and FDPM-1 (FDPM-I) as well as SS and LC using different minimum supports s ($\delta = 0.1$). Fig. 4 (a) shows the memory consumption by varying s (0.01%, 0.1% and 1%). LN consumes the least memory in all the cases followed by LC, FDPM-1, FDPM-I and SS. Its recalls (R) and precisions (P) are shown in Table 3. The two false-positive algorithms SS and LC perform the same and reach at least 0.89 precision. The performance of false-negative algorithms perform differently. The recall of FDPM-1 can reach rather low recall 0.74, when $s = 0.1\%$, because it is designed to handle independent data. With the help of technique of probabilistic-inplace, FDPM-I improves the recall when $s = 0.1\%$ to 0.85. but it does not improve any when $s = 1\%$. The proposed LN significantly outperforms FDPM-1 (FDPM-I), and reaches at least 0.98 recall. LN is shown to be able to handle bursts in data streams.

Varying Length of Data Stream n. We also test all algorithms by varying the length of data stream from 1,000k to 5,000k, while fixing $s = 0.1\%$ and $\delta = 0.1$. SS and LC use $\epsilon = s/10$. Fig. 4 (b) shows that, except SS, the memory

Table 3. Recall (R) and Precision (P)

$s(\%)$	LC		SS		FDPM-1		FDPM-I		LN	
	R	P	R	P	R	P	R	P	R	P
0.01	1.00	0.93	1.00	0.93	1.00	1.00	1.00	1.00	1.00	1.00
0.1	1.00	0.89	1.00	0.89	0.74	1.00	0.85	1.00	0.98	1.00
1	1.00	1.00	1.00	1.00	0.75	1.00	0.75	1.00	1.00	1.00

Table 4. The effectiveness of the length of data streams (Max/Min/Avg are %)

$l(k)$	T	FDPM-1				FDPM-I				LN			
		R	Min	Max	Avg	R	Min	Max	Avg	R	Min	Max	Avg
1,000	149	0.75	0.10	0.21	0.13	0.85	0.10	0.15	0.11	0.98	0.10	0.11	0.11
2,000	171	0.52	0.10	0.24	0.15	0.79	0.10	0.18	0.12	0.92	0.10	0.18	0.13
3,000	165	0.43	0.10	0.31	0.16	0.72	0.10	0.21	0.13	0.92	0.10	0.22	0.14
4,000	165	0.39	0.10	0.37	0.16	0.63	0.10	0.27	0.14	0.93	0.11	0.25	0.16
5,000	157	0.36	0.10	0.41	0.17	0.56	0.10	0.32	0.15	0.92	0.10	0.26	0.17

Table 5. d-robust

Placement		Item 51 ($s = 0.106\%$)		
Head	Tail	FDPM-1	FDPM-I	LN
99%	1%	any	any	any
95%	5%	any	any	any
90%	10%	any	any	any
70%	30%	830,000	any	any
50%	50%	870,000	any	any
30%	70%	490,000	any	any
10%	90%	420,000	any	960,000
5%	95%	any	any	any
1%	99%	any	any	any

consumption of all algorithms does not change while the length of data varies. The memory consumption of SS increases significantly when the length of data becomes longer. LN performs the best and LC performs the second best.

We report the recall (R) of false-negative algorithms in Table 4 with the details of missed frequent items, because the precision for false-negative algorithms is 1. The column T lists the number of true frequent items. The columns of Max, Min and Avg shows the max, min and average $sup(t)/n$ (%), for the missing frequent items t.

The recall for FDPM-1 decreases significantly when the length (n) of the data stream becomes longer, because it cannot handle dependent data streams. When $n = 5,000k$, the recall of FDPM-1 is 0.36 which is very low. The max support for the missing frequent item can be high to 0.41%, which means that it may miss important frequent items. FDPM-I improves the recall of FDPM-1. When $n = 5,000k$, the recall of FDPM-I is 0.56. The max support for the missing frequent item is lower 0.32%. Even though the improvement is noticeable, it is not satisfactory. The new proposed LN significantly outperforms FDPM-I as well as FDPM-1, and reaches at least 0.92 recall. The precisions for SS and LC are the similar. They are 0.89, 0.85, 0.87, 0.92, and 0.88, for the length of data stream from 1,000k to 5,000k.

4.3 d-Robust Testing

We test d-Robust using a synthetic data set of length $n = 1,000,000$ with Zipf $= 1.5$. We choose an item 51 which appears 1,060 times (0.106%). We arrange all the occurrences of the item 51 in the head and tail of the data stream to simulate two extreme bursts, namely, head-burst and tail-burst.

Table 5 shows d-values for FDPM-1 (FDPM-I) and LN using $s = 0.1\%$ and $\delta = 0.1$. In Table 5, the column Head (Tail) indicates x% (1-x%) of 1,060 occurrences is placed at the beginning (near the end) of the data stream. The values shown in the columns of FDPM-1, FDPM-I and LN are the d values of the d-robust. A d-value is the max distance from the last occurrence of the item 51 at the end of the head burst and the first occurrence of the item in the tail burst. The larger d-value the better. The value "any" means that the corresponding algorithm can reach 100% recall no matter where the first occurrence of the tail burst is placed in the data stream of $1,000,000$ long. Table 5 shows the d-values in three cases. First, when the head burst is large consisting of at least 90% of the 1,060 occurrences, all three false-negative algorithms do not miss it, because it is heavy head burst. Second, when the head burst is very small only consisting of up to 5% of the 1,060 occurrences, all three false-negative algorithms do not miss it, because the tail burst is still large enough. Recall the minimum support used is 0.1% whereas 51's is 0.106%. Third, when the head burst is between 10% to 70%, the impacts become noticeable, because the head burst is large and cannot be ignored. When the head burst is 10%, the d value for FDPM-1 is 420,000, which means that if the first occurrence in the tail burst is any father from it, FDPM-1 will miss the frequent item 51. For the same case of 10%, the d-value of LN is more than double of that for FDPM-1. In this testing, FDPM-I outperforms LN, its d value is about 30,000 larger than that of LN, because FDPM-I does not consume all its memory. The testing confirms that LN has large d-robust than FDPM-1. As future work, we will analyze the d-robust for FDPM-I.

5 Conclusion

In this paper, we proposed a new false-negative frequent items mining algorithm LN, which is designed to handle bursts in high speed data streams. We showed that it consumes less memory than other algorithms, and can effectively handle bursts with support of analytical studies and experimental results.

References

1. M. Charikar, K. Chen, and M. Farach-Colton. Finding frequent items in data streams. In *Proc. of the 29th ICALP*, 2002.
2. G. Cormode and S.Muthukrishnan. What's hot and what's not: Tracking most frequent items dynamically. In *Proc. of PODS'03*, 2003.
3. E. Demaine, A. López-Ortiz, and J. I. Munro. Frequency estimation of internet packet streams with limited space. In *Proc. of 10th Annual European Symposium on Algorithms*, 2002.

4. G. S. Manku and R. Motwani. Approximate frequency counts over data streams. In *Proc. of VLDB'02*, 2002.
5. S. S. Richard M. Karp, Christos H. Papadimitrlou. A simple algorithm for finding frequent elements in streams and bags. In *ACM Transactions on Database Systems*, volume 28, pages 51–55, 2003.
6. J. X. Yu, Z. Chong, H. Lu, and A. Zhou. False positive or false negative: Mining frequent itemsets from high speed transactional data streams. In *Proc. of VLDB'04*, 2004.

Adaptively Detecting Aggregation Bursts in Data Streams

Aoying Zhou, Shouke Qin, and Weining Qian

Department of Computer Science and Engineering
Fudan University, 220 Handan Rd, Shanghai, China
{ayzhou, skqin, wnqian}@fudan.edu.cn

Abstract. Finding bursts in data streams is attracting much attention in research community due to its broad applications. Existing burst detection methods suffer the problems that 1) the parameters of window size and absolute burst threshold, which are hard to be determined a priori, should be given in advance. 2) Only one side bursts, i.e. either increasing or decreasing bursts, can be detected. 3) Bumps, which are changes of aggregation data caused by noises, are often reported as bursts. The disturbance of bumps causes much effort in subsequent exploration of mining results. In this paper, a general burst model is introduced for overcoming above three problems. We develop an efficient algorithm for detecting adaptive aggregation bursts in a data stream given a burst ratio. With the help of a novel inverted histogram, the statistical summary is compressed to be fit in limited main memory, so that bursts on windows of any length can be detected accurately and efficiently on-line. Theoretical analysis show the space and time complexity bound of this method is relatively good, while experimental results depict the applicability and efficiency of our algorithm in different application settings.

1 Introduction

Detecting bursts robustly and efficiently poses a challenge in many applications of online monitoring for data streams, such as telecommunication networks, traffic management, trend-related analysis, web-click streams analysis, intrusion detection, and sensor networks. Many methods have been proposed to detect bursts or changes in a time period, called a window, in E-mail [9], Gamma ray [12] and networks traffic [3, 10] data streams. However, these methods are not adaptive enough for many real-life applications, since they need fixed parameter setting for window size and absolute threshold of bursting. Furthermore, only one-side bursts can be detected by these methods.

We argue that ratio threshold for bursting measurement and adaptive window size is more suitable for data stream analysis applications. In network traffic monitoring, for example, when attacks occur, the workload of package routing to an IP address or requests to a server within a certain time period may increase remarkably compared with last certain time period. An absolute threshold may cause false report of bursts in a rush time and missing of attacks when the workload is low. Furthermore, the lasting time varies in different kinds of attacks, which are all interested by monitors. Fig.1 shows the double-side bursts with various peak height and window size.

Though, a natural solution for adaptively detecting aggregation bursts is to apply existing algorithms on different window sizes, peak heights, and both increasing and decreasing side simultaneously, apparently it may consume much storage and computation resources. Furthermore, as any other data stream mining tasks, it is required that burst detection algorithm should be accurate, while use limited storage space and scan a data stream sequentially only once. We present a novel method for adaptively detecting aggregation bursts in data streams. It relies on the efficient algorithms for construction and maintenance of a compact summary data structure, called *inverted histogram*, or IH. It is proved that the bucket error of the histogram is bounded, while the space and computation complexity for maintaining the histogram is low.

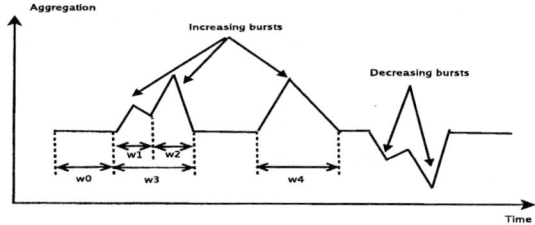

Fig. 1. Bursts with various peak height and window size. In the stream, data in window w_0 are not burst, while data in w_1 are a small burst, compared with those in w_0. Data in w_2 are another burst compared with those in w_1. Furthermore, w_3 and w_4 depict another two bursts, whose window sizes are larger than bursts w_1 and w_2

Bursts found by existing approaches at large time scales are not necessarily reflected at smaller time scales. That is because those bursts at large time scales are composed of many consecutive *bumps* which are those positions where the values are high but not high enough to be bursts. In this paper, a general burst model is introduced for overcoming the problem.

1.1 Related Work

Monitoring and mining data stream has attracted considerable attention recently [9, 12, 3, 10, 2]. An efficient work for statically detecting bursts in data stream with normal distribution based on sliding window is presented in [12]. Kleinberg focuses on modelling and extracting structure from text stream in [9]. There is also work in finding changes on data stream [3, 10, 2]. Although, they have different objectives and different application backgrounds, the same thing is that they can only monitor one window with a given size. The method in [12] can monitor multiple windows with different sizes. But, the maximum window size and window number is limited.

Some of the above approaches detect bursty behaviors of aggregate results [12, 3, 10]. The amount of streaming data is too large to maintain in main memory. This prompts a need to maintain a synopsis of the stream to all the methods. The work in [3, 10] is based on sketch. Haar wavelets can also be used to compute aggregates [7], and their error are bounded in [5]. The burst detecting method in [12] is based on wavelets. However, it can only monitor the monotonic aggregates with respect to the window size, such as *sum*. The non-monotonic ones, such as *average*, cannot be monitored with it.

Histograms have been used widely to capture data distribution, to present the data by a small number of buckets. V-optimal histograms can be maintained with dynamic programming algorithms which running in quadratic time and linear space. Over data stream model, the approximate V-optimal histograms can support the point queries, aggregate queries and range sum queries [8, 6, 11]. If the stream is ordered, namely the values of data elements are non-negative, the work of [8] has the cheapest space $O(\frac{k^2 \log n R^2}{\epsilon})$ and time $O(\frac{nk^2 \log n R^2}{\epsilon})$. It provides an $(1 + \epsilon)$ approximation for the V-optimal histogram with k levels, n is the length of stream and R is the maximum value of data elements.

1.2 Our Contributions

Our contributions can be summarized as follows:

- First, we put forward a novel definition of burst. To the best of our knowledge, this is the first work considering such adaptive burst model on data stream. This model is more general and fit for the real world applications.
- Second, we design both false positive and false negative algorithms for finding bursts accurately in high speed data streams. They can detect bursts dynamically with double side alarm domain and avoid being disturbed by bumps on overall stream.
- Third, we propose a novel histogram—IH, with relative error guaranteed in each bucket, which can answer burst queries accurately with very cheap cost of space and time. We note that IH is an interesting data structure in its own right and might find applications in other domains.
- Fourth, we complement our analytical results with an extensive experimental study. Our results indicate that the new method can indeed detect the bursts accurately within an economic space and time cost.

The remainder of this paper is organized as follows. Section 2 presents the problem and definition of the paper. Section 3 presents our algorithms for detecting bursts. Section 4 presents a novel histogram which is the base of burst detecting algorithms. Section 5 show the results and analysis of experiments. Section 6 concludes the paper.

2 Problem Statements

In this section, we present the model and definition of the problem for clarifying the objectives in this paper. As described in the introduction, bumps can induce bursts at large time scales. We can show it through a small example. In Fig.2.(a), the current stream length is 6. x_6 is a new comer and its value is 20.5. The relative threshold is denoted by β, which is a positive ratio. Here, aggregate function F is sum and $\beta = 1.1$(for detecting increasing bursts). From Fig.2.(a), x_4 and x_6 are all bumps. They cannot induce burst on the 1-length window, for $x_4 = 20.5 < \beta x_3 = 1.1 * 19 = 20.9$ and $x_6 = 20.5 < \beta x_5 = 1.1 * 19 = 20.9$. But they induce bursts on 2-length and 3-length window respectively, such as Fig.2.(b) and Fig.2.(c), for $(x_3+x_4) > \beta(x_1+x_2)$ and $(x_4+x_5+x_6) > \beta(x_1+x_2+x_3)$. In

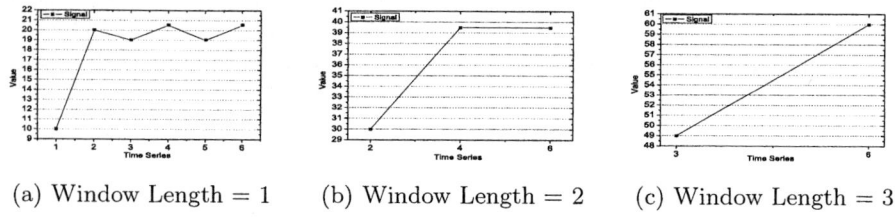

(a) Window Length = 1   (b) Window Length = 2   (c) Window Length = 3

Fig. 2. Bumps Can Induce Bursts at Large Time Scales

that, if burst does not occur in window L(window length), window $L+1$ should not be detected. Because remnant bursts, if had, are all induced by bumps.

A data stream can be considered as a sequence of points $x_1, ..., x_n$ in increasing order. Each element in stream can be a value in the range $[0..R]$. To detect bursts on overall data stream needs only caring about the latest two consecutive subsequences with the same length when each new value x_i comes. The formal definition of adaptively detecting bursts on data stream model is shown as follows. In the example of bumps above, as Definition 1, $s'_1 = x_5$, $s_1 = x_6$, $s'_2 = x_3, x_4$, $s_2 = x_5, x_6$ and $s'_3 = x_1, x_2, x_3$, $s_3 = x_4, x_5, x_6$.

Definition 1. *F is an aggregate function. s'_i and s_i are the latest two consecutive subsequences of a stream with the same length of i, $1 \leq i \leq \frac{n}{2}$. An increasing burst occurs on i-length window when x_n comes, if $\forall j \in 1..i$, $\beta > 1$, $F(s_j) \geq \beta F(s'_j)$. An decreasing burst occurs on i-length window when x_n comes, if $\forall j \in 1..i$, $0 < \beta < 1$, $F(s_j) \leq \beta F(s'_j)$.*

3 Algorithms for Detecting Bursts

We begin to present our algorithms for detecting bursts in this section. These algorithms can be based on the approximate V-optimal histogram in [8](AVOH in short) or IH. IH is a novel histogram proposed by us whose details are presented in section 4. Due to limited space allowed to detect bursts on data stream, approximate burst detecting can take two possible approaches, namely, false positive oriented and false negative oriented. The former includes some unreal bursts in the final result, whereas the latter misses some real bursts. In the real world, different application requirements need false positive oriented algorithm and false negative oriented algorithm respectively.

3.1 False Positive Algorithm

The aggregate result w_i of the latest i-length window ($1 \leq i \leq n$) can be got from AVOH or IH. In fact, $F(s_i) = w_i = f_{ss}(i)$ and $F(s'_i) = w_{2i} - w_i = f_{ss}(2i) - f_{ss}(i)$. $f_{ss}(i) = \Sigma_{j=n-i+1}^{n} x_j$, it is the suffix sum which is the sum of the last $n - i + 1$ values of stream x when x_n arrives. Therefore, the criteria of increasing burst and decreasing burst in Definition 1 can be depicted by $w_i \geq \beta(w_{2i} - w_i)$ ($\beta > 1$) and $w_i \leq \beta(w_{2i} - w_i)$ ($0 < \beta < 1$) respectively. They can also be transformed to

$$w_{2i} \geq (\beta + 1)(w_{2i} - w_i), (\beta > 1) \tag{1}$$

$$w_{2i} \leq (\beta + 1)(w_{2i} - w_i), (0 < \beta < 1) \tag{2}$$

Detecting bursts false positively is achieved by augmenting the left side of inequality (1) and the right side of inequality (2) relatively. This is fulfilled by two functions. One is IH.getLargerValue(i) which returns a value larger than real w_i from IH. The other is IH.getSmallerValue(i) which returns a value smaller than real w_i from IH. It can be seen that the accuracy of our method is only affected by these two functions. Their details and bounds are introduced in section 4.

When x_n comes and is inserted into histogram, this algorithm is called for detecting bursts induced by x_n. The algorithm has no input parameter. Its output is the alarm information. Here, we just return the number of bursts. The algorithm behaves level wise detection from level 1 to level $\frac{n}{2}$. Each level is a pair of the latest two consecutive windows with the same length on stream x. In level i, the algorithm detects burst between such two windows with length i. That is accomplished by two steps. The first step is to compute w_i and w_{2i} with the two functions above, just as the statements in Line 4 and Line 5. The second step is to detect the occurrence of a burst by inequality (1) as the statement in Line 6. The level wise detection is broken at Line 9 when inequality (1) is not met, for remnant bursts are all induced by bumps. Because of different applications oriented, there are at least three algorithms can be shown. First one is to detect increasing bursts only. Second one is to detect decreasing bursts only. Third one is to detect both two kinds of bursts. For the limitation of space, we show only the first algorithm to which the others are similar.

Algorithm 1 can catch all bursts induced by x_n on overall stream in $O(k)$ time, $k(0 \leq k \leq \frac{n}{2})$ is the number of bursts found by it. Therefore, it takes time $O(nk)$ for detecting all bursts in a stream with length n. If we just want to know whether one burst occurs or not when x_n comes instead of on which window

Algorithm 1 detectBurstsFalsePositively

1: $burstNum \leftarrow 0$;
2: $winSize \leftarrow 1$;
3: **while** $winSize \leq \frac{n}{2}$ **do**
4:   temp1=IH.getLargerValue($winSize$);
5:   temp2=IH.getSmallerValue($2 * winSize$);
6:   **if** temp2 $\geq (\beta + 1)$(temp2-temp1) **then**
7:     increase $burstNum$ and $winSize$ by 1;
8:   **else**
9:     break;
10: **end if**
11: **end while**
12: return $burstNum$;
---

burst occurs or how many bursts are induced on overall stream, the time cost can be $O(1)$. We can claim the following theorem by denoting the space cost of a B-bucket histogram with B and its updating cost for each x_i with T_B.

Theorem 1. *Algorithm 1 can detect bursts false positively on data stream in $O(n(T_B + k))$ time and $O(B)$ space.*

3.2 False Negative Algorithm

Similar to the analysis in the above section, detecting bursts false negatively is achieved by abating the left side of inequality (1) and the right side of inequality (2) relatively. Algorithm 1 can be capable of detecting bursts false negatively when given minor modification. We can just put the statements, temp1=IH.getSmallerValue($winSize$) and temp2=IH.getLargerValue($2*winSize$), instead of Line 4 and Line 5 in Algorithm 1. The analysis of its cost is same as that of Algorithm 1. We can claim the following theorem.

Theorem 2. *We can detect bursts false negatively on data stream in $O(n(T_B + k))$ time and $O(B)$ space.*

It is clear that in addition to *sum*, the two algorithms above can monitor not only monotonic aggregates with respect to the window size for example *max*, *min*, *count* and *spread*, but also non-monotonic ones such as *average*.

4 Buckets Order Inverted Histogram—IH

In this section, we begin to introduce a novel histogram, called Inverted Histogram (i.e., IH in brief). It is the base of burst detecting algorithms presented in section 3. At the beginning, a simple histogram is introduced. It is better than the existing approximate V-optimal histograms for its cheap space and time when being used to answer burst queries. But both the existing approximate V-optimal histograms and the simple histogram are facing the great challenge that the everlasting increasing of absolute error in buckets will decay the accuracy of burst detection rapidly. Later, we introduce the enhanced histogram—IH, which not only has cheap space and time, but also answers burst queries precisely.

4.1 A Simple Histogram

Each point of stream $x'_1, ..., x'_n$ we read can be thought of the prefix sum of $x_1, ..., x_n$ with $x'_i = f_{ps}(i)$. $f_{ps}(i)$ is the prefix sum of stream x when x_i comes, $f_{ps}(i) = \Sigma^i_{j=1} x_j$. Details of our idea are as follows. What we want is to partition stream x' into B intervals(buckets), $(b^a_1, b^b_1), ..., (b^a_B, b^b_B)$. b_i is the i-th bucket, $1 \le i \le B$. b^a_i and b^b_i are the minimum and maximum value within bucket b_i respectively. It's possible that $b^a_i = b^b_i$. We also want to bound the relative error δ in each bucket. The maximum relative error in b_i is $\delta = \frac{b^b_i - b^a_i}{b^a_i}$. One bucket should maintain b^a_i, b^b_i and the number of values in it, namely, its width. Furthermore, the buckets are disjoint and cover $x'_1..x'_n$. Therefore, $b^a_1 = x'_1$ and $b^b_B = x'_n$. During the processing, $b^b_i \le (1+\delta) b^a_i$ is maintained. The algorithm on seeing the n'st value x_n, will compute $x'_n = f_{ps}(n) = b^b_B + x_n$. We just have to update the last bucket, either by setting $b^b_B = x'_n$ when $x'_n \le (1+\delta) b^a_B$, or creating a new bucket when $x'_n > (1+\delta) b^a_B$, with $b^a_{B+1} = b^b_{B+1} = x'_n$. The algorithm is quite simple. It will not be shown here.

Theorem 3. *We can build the simple histogram with $O(\frac{\log n + \log R}{\log(1+\delta)})$ space in $O(n)$ time. The relative error in each bucket is at most δ.*

Although the simple histogram can be built with cheap cost of time and space, the absolute error and size of the last bucket are getting larger and larger as the increasing of stream length. Thus, the errors induced by using these buckets to compute aggregates are also increasing. When a new value x_n comes, we use the bucket from the last one to the first one to estimate w_i from 1-length window to $\frac{n}{2}$-length window. Therefore, the errors of aggregates on small windows are much larger than those on large windows. According to Definition 1, provided that the aggregate of window L is computed falsely, the bursts of windows whose sizes are larger than L may be neglected. In consequence, the greater the stream length is, the more error the detecting methods will suffer.

4.2 Enhanced Histogram—IH

To detect bursts more accurately, we want the recent bucket has higher precision, in other words, the recent bucket has smaller width. Our idea is to invert the buckets order which uses the smaller bucket to store the newer points, such as in Fig.3.(b). The oldest point x'_1 and the latest point x'_n of stream x' are in b_1 and b_B respectively. In Fig.3.(a), $x'_i = f_{ps}(i)$. In Fig.3.(b), $x'_i = f_{ss}(i)$. $f_{ss}(i)$ is the suffix sum, $f_{ss}(i) = \Sigma^n_{j=i} x_j$. Fig.3.(a) is the bucket series of our simple histogram and approximate V-optimal histogram. The size of the last bucket in Fig.3.(a) is getting larger and larger as time goes on.

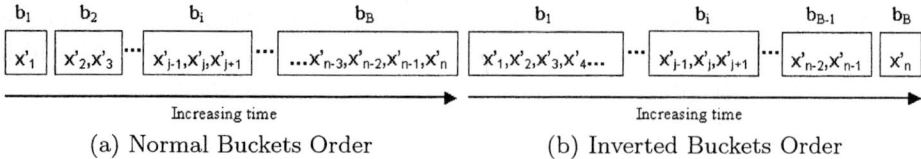

Fig. 3. Buckets Orders of Approximate V-optimal Histogram and IH

Algorithm 2 updateIH(x_n)

1: increase bucket number B by 1;
2: $j \leftarrow B$;
3: create a new bucket and put x_n into it;
4: **for** $i = B - 1$ to 1 **do**
5:     add x_n to both b_i^a and b_i^b;
6:     **if** $b_i^b \leq (1+\delta)b_j^a$ **then**
7:         $b_j^b \leftarrow b_i^b$;
8:         add width of b_i to width of b_j;
9:         delete b_i;
10:        decrease bucket number B by 1;
11:     **end if**
12:     decrease j by 1;
13: **end for**

Same as the simple histogram, we want to minimize the bucket number with relative error guaranteed in each bucket. The only difference is the stream we read can be thought of as $x_i' = f_{ss}(i)$. Details of our idea is similar to that of the simple histogram. IH can be built with Algorithm 2. It has an input parameter x_i and no output. On seeing a new value x_n, it has to update all buckets, namely, $O(\frac{\log n + \log R}{\log(1+\delta)})$ buckets by executing the statements from Line 4 to 13. First, at Line 3, it creates a new bucket for x_n and puts the bucket on the last position of buckets series. Then, at Line 5, it updates the maximum and minimum value of all the buckets by adding x_n to them from the new created one to the oldest one. In the process of updating, from Line 6 to 11, the algorithm merges consecutive buckets b_i and b_j when $b_i^b \leq (1+\delta)b_j^a$, with $b_j^b = b_i^b$. In fact, IH can also be constructed by the simple histogram algorithm fed with inverted data stream $x_n, .., x_1$. That is a very nice situation, the maximum relative error in each bucket of IH can be bounded and the space and time cost are still cheap. We claim the following theorem to guarantee these.

Theorem 4. *Algorithm 2 can build an IH with* $O(\frac{\log n + \log R}{\log(1+\delta)})$ *space in* $O(\frac{n(\log n + \log R)}{\log(1+\delta)})$ *time. The relative error in each bucket is at most* δ.

The precision of IH can be improved by considering the values within a bucket are equidistant. To guarantee false positive or false negative detection, we need to maintain $maxD$ and $minD$ within each bucket. $maxD$ is the maximum distance between two consecutive point within the bucket. $minD$ is the minimum distance between two consecutive point within the bucket. Provided that the real value of w_i is within bucket b_j, IH.getLargerValue(i) returns the value of $min(b_j^b, b_j^a + maxD(i - \Sigma_{k=1}^{i-1} Wid(b_k) - 1))$ and IH.getSmallerValue(i) returns $b_j^a + minD(i - \Sigma_{k=1}^{i-1} Wid(b_k) - 1)$. Based on Theorem 1, Theorem 2 and Theorem 4, we can get the following corollary.

Corollary 1. *We can detect bursts false positively or false negatively on data stream in* $O(n(\frac{\log n + \log R}{\log(1+\delta)} + k))$ *time and* $O(\frac{\log n + \log R}{\log(1+\delta)})$ *space.*

5 Performance Evaluation

In this section, our empirical studies show the adaptive method in this paper can efficiently give accurate alarms to bursts with just a small cost of space.

5.1 Experimental Setup

All the algorithms are implemented by using Microsoft Visual C++ Version 6.0. We conducted all testing on a 2.4GHz CPU Dell PC with 512MB main memory running Windows 2000. Due to the limitation of space, we report the results for only two representative data sets here:

- Web Site Requests (Real): This data set is obtained from the Internet Traffic Archive [1, 3]. It consists of all the requests made to the 1998 World Cup Web site between April 26, 1998 and July 26, 1998. During this 92 days period of time the site received 1,352,804,107 requests. Our basic window, namely, an item x_i is the requests number in one second. So, the stream length is $n = 92 * 24 * 3600 = 7,948,800s$. It is denoted by D1.
- Network Traffic (Synthetic): This data set is generated with the burst arrival of data stream using a pareto[4] distribution, which is often used to simulate network traffic where packets are sent according to ON OFF periods. The density function of pareto distribution is $P(x) = \frac{ab^a}{x^{a+1}}$, where $b \geq x$ and a is the shape parameter. The expected burst count, $E(x)$, is $\frac{ab}{a-1}$. The tuple arrive rate λ_1 is driven by an exponential distribution and the interval λ_2 between signals is also generated using exponential distribution. We set expect value $E(\lambda_1) = 400 tuples/s$, $E(\lambda_2) = 500 tuples$, $a = 1.5, b = 1$. The size of this time series data set is $n = 10,000,000s$. It is denoted by D2.

In the experiments, two accuracy metrics are measured: recall and precision. Recall is the ratio of true alarms raised to the total true alarms should be raised. Precision is the ratio of true alarms raised to the total alarms raised. Our aggregate function F is sum.

5.2 Performance Study

Firstly, we study the precision of detecting bursts false positively based on IH and AVOH on D1 and D2 respectively. In this experiment, we set $\delta = 0.01$. It

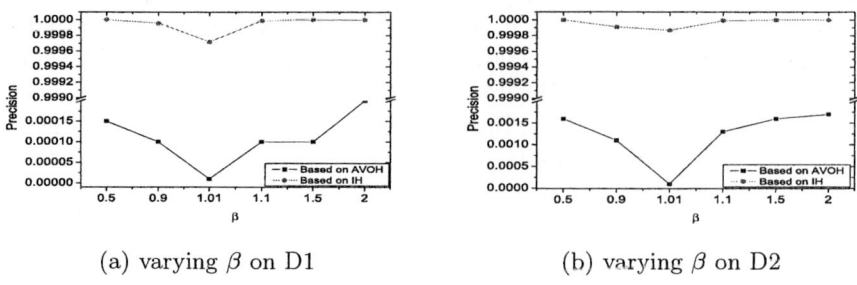

(a) varying β on D1

(b) varying β on D2

Fig. 4. Precision of burst detection based on IH and AVOH varying β ($\delta = 0.01$)

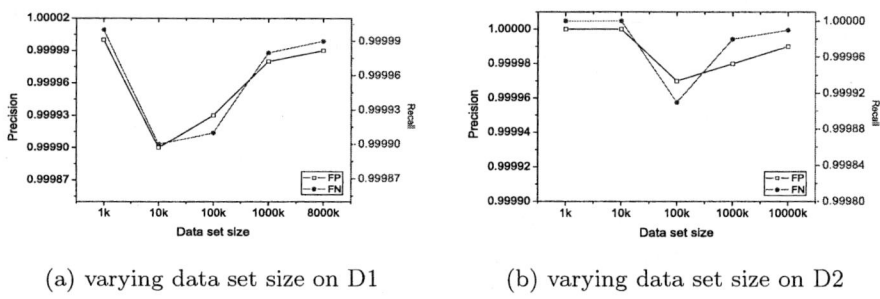

(a) varying data set size on D1

(b) varying data set size on D2

Fig. 5. Precision and Recall of FP and FN varying data set size ($\beta = 1.1, \delta = 0.01$)

can be confirmed from Fig.4 that the burst detecting method based on IH is far more accurate than that based on AVOH at any setting of threshold β.

Secondly, we test the precision and recall of both false positive algorithm(FP in short) and false negative algorithm(FN in short) on D1 and D2 respectively. We set $\beta = 1.1, \delta = 0.01$. It can be seen from Fig.5 that on both data sets the precision of FP are at least 99.99% and with recall guaranteed 1, and the recall of FN are also at least 99.99% and with precision guaranteed 1. In Fig.5.(a), we see the precision and recall of FP and FN are all 1 when stream length is 1k. When stream length is 10k, precision and recall are all 99.99% for occurring an error. Because the accuracy of burst detection does not decay with the increasing of stream length, the precision and recall are always above 99.99% and getting better as time goes on. The same result can be got from Fig.5.(b). Therefore, our method can give highly accurate answers to burst detection in data stream.

Thirdly, we discuss the setting of β and δ. From that, we can know the most appropriate setting of δ, if β have been set. It means with that setting of δ we can use the most economic space and time to find bursts accurately under relative threshold β. It can be seen from Fig.6 that the most adaptable setting of δ on each data set is $max(\frac{\beta-1}{10}, 0.01)$. The same heuristic result is also got from other experiments we have made. Fourthly, we study the space cost of IH and AVOH on condition that both of them have the same maximum relative error in their

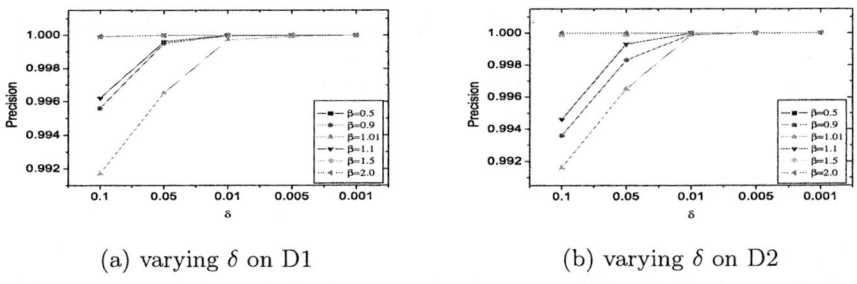

Fig. 6. Precision of detecting bursts false positively (varying δ and β, on D1 and D2)

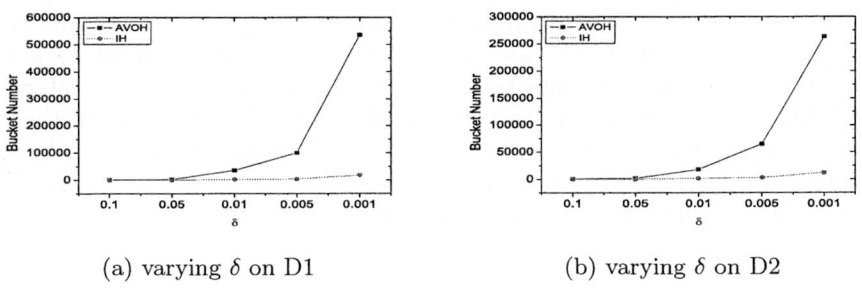

Fig. 7. Space cost of IH and AVOH (varying δ on D1 and D2)

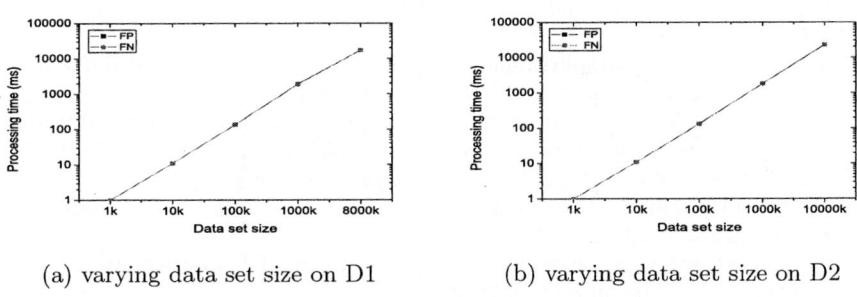

Fig. 8. Processing Time of FP and FN varying data set size ($\beta = 1.1, \delta = 0.01$)

buckets. Here, we set $k = 1$ for AVOH and vary the maximum relative error δ in each bucket of both IH and AVOH from 0.1 to 0.001. In this experiment, β has no influence on results. It can be seen from Fig.7 that IH consumes less memory than AVOH on any condition of δ. The space saved by IH is getting larger and larger as the decreasing of δ. Therefore, the IH is more adaptable to be used to detect bursts in data stream.

At last, by varying size of data sets, we study the time cost of our algorithms on D1 and D2 respectively. In this experiment, we set $\beta = 1.1, \delta = 0.01$. Our method is very efficient. This is confirmed in Fig.8, where the processing time of FP and FN are same. The method of us can process $400 * 10^7$ tuples in 20 seconds. This means that it is easily capable of processing traffic rates on 100Mbs links, and with some work then 1Gbps and higher are within reach.

6 Conclusions and Future Work

In this paper, we studied the problem of detecting bursts in data streams. A novel concept of adaptive aggregation burst is introduced for precisely modelling real-life data streams. This burst model empowers us to detect double-side relative bursts dynamically without disturbed by bumps. We propose the effective algorithms for accurately detecting such bursts under false positive and false negative constraints. The algorithms are developed based on a space and time efficient histogram, IH, which can be maintained with low overhead while being more suitable for burst detection than other popular histograms. Intensive experiments on both synthetic and real-life data sets show that our method is quite efficient on space and time for analyzing high speed data streams. Future work includes the study of extension of current IH-based burst detection method on multiple correlated data streams and burst forecasting.

References

1. Internet traffic archive. http://ita.ee.lbl.gov/.
2. S. Ben-David, J. Gehrke, and D. Kifer. Detecting change in data streams. In *Proc. of VLDB*, 2004.
3. G. Cormode and S. Muthukrishnan. Whats new: Finding significant differences in network data streams. In *Proc. of INFOCOM*, 2004.
4. M. E. Crovella, M. S. Taqqu, and A. Bestavros. Heavy-tailed probability distributions in the world wide web. *A practical guide to heavy tails: STATISTICAL TECHNIQUES AND APPLICATIONS*, pages 3–26, 1998.
5. M. Garofalakis and P. B. Gibbons. Wavelet synopses with error guarantees. In *Proc. of SIGMOD*, 2003.
6. A. C. Gilbert and et al. Fast, small-space algorithms for approximate histogram maintenance. In *Proc. of STOC*, 2002.
7. A. C. Gilbert, Y. Kotidis, S. Muthukrishnan, and M. Strauss. Surfing wavelets on streams: One-pass summaries for approximate aggregate queries. In *Proc. of VLDB*, 2001.
8. S. Guha, N. Koudas, and K. Shim. Datastreams and histograms. In *Proc. of STOC*, 2001.
9. J. Kleinberg. Bursty and hierarchical structure in streams. In *Proc. of SIGKDD*, 2002.
10. B. Krishnamurthy, S. Sen, Y. Zhang, and Y. Chen. Sketch-based change detection: Methods, evaluation, and applications. In *Proc. of IMC*, 2003.
11. S. Muthukrishnan and M. Strauss. Rangesum histograms. In *Proc. of SODA*, 2003.
12. Y. Zhu and D. Shasha. Efficient elastic burst detection in data streams. In *Proc. of SIGKDD*, 2003.

Communication-Efficient Implementation of Join in Sensor Networks

Vishal Chowdhary and Himanshu Gupta

SUNY, Stony Brook, NY 11754
{vishal, hgupta}@cs.sunysb.edu

Abstract. A sensor network is a wireless ad hoc network of resource-constrained sensor nodes. In this article, we address the problem of communication-efficient implementation of the SQL "join" operator in sensor networks. We design an optimal join-implementation algorithm that provably incurs minimum communication cost under certain reasonable assumptions. In addition, we design a much faster suboptimal heuristic that empirically delivers a near-optimal solution. We evaluate the performance of our designed algorithms through extensive simulations.

1 Introduction

A sensor network consists of sensor nodes with a short-range radio and on-board processing capability forming a multi-hop network of an irregular topology. Each sensor node can sense certain physical phenomena like light, temperature, or vibration. There are many exciting applications [3, 13, 14] of such sensor networks, including monitoring and surveillance systems in both military and civilian contexts, building smart environments and infrastructures such as intelligent transportation systems and smart homes. In a sensor network, sensor nodes generate data items that are simply readings of one or more sensing devices on the node. Thus, a sensor network can be viewed as a distributed database system where each sensor node generates a stream of data tuples. Appropriately enough, the term *sensor database* is increasingly being used in research literature. Like a database, the sensor network is queried to gather and/or process the sensed data tuples. Database queries in SQL are a very general representation of queries over data, and efficient implementation of SQL queries is of great significance because of the enormous amount of data present in a typical sensor network. Since sensor nodes have limited battery energy, the distributed implementation of SQL queries in sensor networks must minimize the communication cost incurred, which is the main consumer of battery energy [31].

In this article, we address how to efficiently execute database queries in a sensor network, when the data distributed across sensors in a sensor network is viewed as relational database tables. In particular, we address communication-efficient in-network processing of the join operator, which is essentially a cartesian product of the operand tables followed by a predicate selection. We design an optimal algorithm for a join operation that provably incurs minimum communication cost in dense sensor networks under some reasonable assumptions of communication cost and computation model. We also design a much faster suboptimal heuristic that empirically performs very close to the optimal algorithm, and results in significant savings over the naive approaches.

The rest of the paper is organized as follows. We start with modeling the sensor network as a database in Section 2. In Section 3, we present various algorithms for in-network implementation of the join operator, along with certain generalizations. We present our experiment results in Section 4. Related work is discussed in Section 5, and concluding remarks presented in Section 6.

2 Sensor Network Databases

A sensor network consists of a large number of sensors distributed randomly in a geographical region. Each sensor has limited on-board processing capability and is equipped with sensing devices. A sensor node also has a radio which is used to communicate directly with some of the sensors around it. Two sensor nodes S_1 and S_2 can directly communicate with each other if and only if the distance between them is less than the *transmission radius*. Sensor nodes may indirectly communicate with each other through other intermediate nodes – thus, forming a multi-hop network. We assume that each sensor node in the sensor network has a limited storage capacity of m units. Also, sensors have limited battery energy, which must be conserved for prolong unattended operation. Thus, we have focused on minimization of communication cost (hence, energy cost) as the key performance criteria of the join implementation strategies.

2.1 Modeling the Sensor Network as a Database

In a sensor network, the data generated by the sensor nodes is simply the readings of one or more sensing devices on the node. Thus, the data present in a sensor network can be modeled as relational database tables, wherein each sensor produces data records/tuples of a certain format and semantics. In some sense, a relational database table is a collection of similar-typed tuples from a group of sensors in the network. Due to the spatial and real-time nature of the data generated, a tuple usually has `timeStamp` and `nodeLocation` as attributes. In a sensor network, relational database tables are typically stream database tables [2] partitioned horizontally across (or generated by) a set of sensors in the network.

In-Network Implementation. A plausible implementation of a sensor network database query engine could be to have an external database system handle all the queries over the network. In such a realization, all the data from each sensor node in the network is sent to the external system that handles the execution of queries completely. Such an implementation would incur very high communication costs and congestion-related bottlenecks. Thus, prior research has proposed query engines that would execute the queries within the network with little external help. In particular, [18] shows that in-network implementation of database queries is fundamental to achieving energy-efficient communication in sensor networks. The focus of this article is communication-efficient in-network implementation of the join operator. As selection and projection are unary operators and operate on each tuple independently, they could be efficiently implemented using efficient routing and topology construction techniques. Union operation can be reduced to duplicate elimination, and the difference and intersection operations can be reduced to the join operation. Implementation of other database operators (aggregation, duplicate elimination, and outerjoins) is challenging and is the focus of our future work.

Querying and Cost Model. A query in a sensor network is initiated at a node called *query source* and the result of the query is required to be routed back to the query source for storage and/or consumption. A stream database table may be generated by a set of sensor nodes in a closed geographical region. The optimization algorithms, proposed in this article, to determine how to implement the join operation efficiently, are run at the query source. As typical sensor network queries are long running, the query source can gather all the catalogue information needed (estimated sizes and locations of the operand relations, join selectivity factor to estimate the size of the join result, density of the network) by initially sampling the operand tables. As mentioned before, we concentrate on implementations that minimize communication cost. We define the total communication cost incurred as the total data transfer between neighboring sensor nodes.

3 In-Network Implementation of Join

In this section, we develop communication-efficient algorithms for implementation of a join operation in sensor networks. We start with assuming that the operand tables are static (non-streaming). Later in the section, we describe how our algorithms can be generalized for stream database tables, as data in sensor network is better represented as data stream tables.

The SQL join operator is used to correlate data from multiple tables, and can be defined as a selection predicate over the cross-product of a pair of tables; a join of R and S tables is denoted as $R \bowtie S$. Consider a join operation, initiated by a query source node Q, involving two static (non-streaming) tables R and S distributed horizontally across some geographical regions $\mathcal{R}$ and $\mathcal{S}$ in the network. We assume that the geographic regions are disjoint and small relative to the distances between the query source and the operand table regions (see [10] for a discussion on relaxation of this assumption). If we do not make any assumptions about the join predicates involved, each data tuple of table R should be paired with every tuple of S and checked for the join condition. The joined tuple is then routed (if it passes the join selection condition) to the query source Q where all the tuples are accumulated or consumed. Given that each sensor node has limited memory resources, we need to find out appropriate regions in the network that would take the responsibility of computing the join. In particular, we may need to store and process the relations at some intermediate location before routing the result to the query source.

A simple nested-loop implementation of a join used in traditional databases is to generate the cross product (all pairs of tuples), and then extract those pairs that satisfy the selection predicate of the join. More involved implementations of a join operator widely used in database systems are merge-sort and hash-join. These classical methods are unsuitable for direct implementation in sensor networks due to the limited memory resources at each node in the network. Moreover, the traditional join algorithms focus on minimizing computation cost, while in sensor networks the primary performance criteria is communication cost. Below, we discuss various techniques for efficient implementation of the join operation in sensor networks.

Naive Approach. A simple way to compute $R \bowtie S$ could be to route the tuples of S from their original location $\mathcal{S}$ to the region $\mathcal{R}$, broadcast the S-tuples in the region $\mathcal{R}$, compute the join within the region $\mathcal{R}$, and then route the joined tuples to the query source Q. We refer to this approach as the *Naive* approach. Note that the roles of the tables R and S can be interchanged in the above approach.

Centroid Approach. Centroid approach is to compute the join operation in a circular region around some point C in the sensor network. In particular, let P_c be the smallest circular region around C such that the region P_c has at least $|R|/m$ sensor nodes to store the table R. First, we route both the operand table to C. Second, we distribute R and broadcast S in the region P_c around C. Lastly, we compute the join operation, and route the resulting tuples of $(R \bowtie S)$ to the query source Q. Since the communication cost incurred in the second step is independent of the choice of C, it is easy to see that the communication cost incurred in the above approach is minimized when the point C is the weighted centroid of the triangle formed by R, S, and Q. Here, the choice of the centroid point C is weighted by the sizes of R, S, and $(R \bowtie S)$.

3.1 Optimal Join Algorithm

In this section, we present an algorithm that constructs an optimal region for computing the join operation using minimum communication cost. We assume that the sensor network is sufficiently dense that we can find a sensor node at any point in the region. To formally prove the claim of optimality, we need to restrict ourselves to a class of join algorithms called *Distribute-Broadcast Join Algorithms* (defined below). In effect, our claim of optimality states that the proposed join algorithm incurs less communication cost than any distribute-broadcast join algorithm.

Definition 1. *A join algorithm to compute $R \bowtie S$ in a sensor network is a* distribute-broadcast join algorithm *if the join is processed by first distributing*

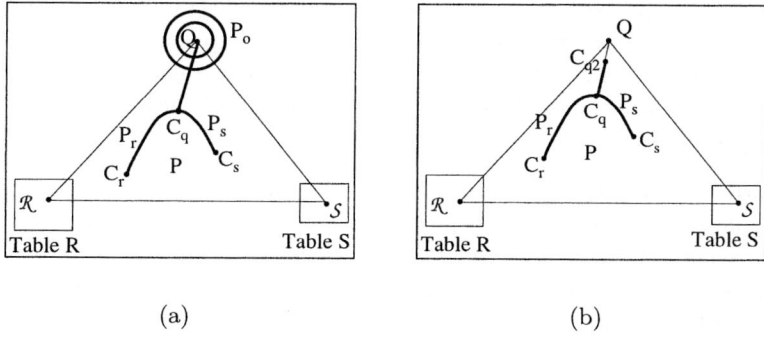

Fig. 1. Possible Shape of an Optimal Join-Region

the table R in some region P (other than the region $\mathcal{R}$ storing R)[1] of the sensor network followed by broadcasting the relation S within the region P to compute the join. The joined tuples are then routed from each sensor in the region P to the query source.

As before, consider a query source Q and regions $\mathcal{R}$ and $\mathcal{S}$ that store the static operand tables R and S in a sensor network. The key challenge in designing an optimal algorithm for implementation of a join operation is to select a region P for processing the join in such a way that the total communication cost is minimized. We use the term *join-region* to refer to a region in the sensor network that is responsible for computing the join.

Shape of an Optimal Join-Region. Theorem 1 (see [10] for proof) shows that the join-region P that incurs minimum communication cost has a shape as shown in Figure 1 (a) or (b). In particular, the optimal join-region P is formed using three point C_r, C_s, and C_q in the sensor network (typically these points will lie within the $\triangle \mathcal{RSQ}$). More precisely, given three points C_r, C_s, and C_q in the sensor network, the region P takes one of the following forms:

1. Region P is formed of the paths $P_r = (C_r, C_q)$ and $P_s = (C_s, C_q)$, the line segment $\overline{C_q Q}$, and a circular region P_O of appropriate radius around Q. See Figure 1 (a).
2. Region P is formed of the paths $P_r = (C_r, C_q)$ and $P_s = (C_s, C_q)$, and a *part* of the line segment $\overline{C_q Q}$. See Figure 1 (b).

The total number of sensors in the region P is $l = |R|/m$, where $|R|$ is the size of the table R which will be distributed over the region P, and m is the memory size of each sensor node.

Theorem 1. *The shape of the join-region P used by a distribute-broadcast join algorithm that incurs optimal communication cost is as described above or as depicted in Figure 1 (a) or (b).* ∎

---
[1] Else, the algorithm will be identical to one of the Naive Approaches.

Theorem 1 restricts the shape of an optimal join-region. However, there are still an infinite number of possible join-regions of shapes depicted in Figure 1. Below, we further restrict the shape of an optimal join-region by characterizing the equations of the paths P_r and P_s, which connect C_r and C_s respectively to Q. We start with a definition.

Definition 2. *The* sensor length *between a region $\mathcal{X}$ and a point y in a sensor network plane is denoted as $d(\mathcal{X}, y)$ and is defined as the average weighted distance, in terms of number of hops/sensors, between the region $\mathcal{X}$ and the point y. Here, the distance between a point $x \in \mathcal{X}$ and y is weighted by the amount of data residing at x.*

Optimizing Paths P_r and P_s. Consider an optimal join-region P that implements a join operation using minimum communication cost. From Theorem 1, we know that the region P is of the shape depicted in Figure 1 (a) or (b). The total communication cost T incurred in processing of a join using the region P is

$$|R|d(\mathcal{R}, C_r) + |S|d(\mathcal{S}, C_s) + |R \bowtie S|d(P, Q) + |R||P|/2 + |S||P|,$$

where the first two terms represent the cost of routing R and S to C_r and C_s respectively, the third term represents the cost of routing the result $R \bowtie S$ from P to Q, and the last two terms represent the cost of distributing R and broadcasting S in the region P. Here, we assume that lack of global knowledge about the other sensors' locations and available memory capacities preclude the possibility of distributing or broadcasting more efficiently than doing it in a simple linear manner. Now, the only component of cost T that depends on the shape of P is $|R \bowtie S|d(P, Q)$. Let $P' = P - P_r - P_s$, i.e., the region P without the paths P_r and P_s. Since the result $|R \bowtie S|$ is evenly spread along the entire region P, we have $d(P, Q) = \frac{1}{|P|}(|P'|d(P', Q) + |P_r|d(P_r, Q) + |P_s|d(P_s, Q))$, where the notation $|B|$ for a region B denotes the number of sensor nodes in the region B. For a given set of points C_r, C_s, and C_q, the total communication cost T is minimized when the path P_r is constructed such that $|P_r|d(P_r, Q)$ is minimized. Otherwise, we could reconstruct P_r with a smaller $|P_r|d(P_r, Q)$, and remove/add sensors nodes from the end[2] of the region P' to maintain $|P| = |R|/m$. Removal of sensor nodes from P' will always reduce T, and it can be shown that addition of sensor nodes to the end of the region P' will not increase the cost more than the reduction achieved by optimizing P_r. Similarly, the path P_s could be optimized independently.

We now derive the equation of the path P_r that minimizes $|P_r|d(P_r, Q)$ for a given C_r and C_q. Consider an arbitrary point $R(x, y)$ along the optimal path P_r. The length of an infinitesimally small segment of the path P_r beginning at $R(x, y)$ is $\sqrt{(dx)^2 + (dy)^2}$, and the average distance of this segment from Q is $\sqrt{x^2 + y^2}$, if the coordinates of Q are $(0, 0)$. Sum of all these distances over the

---

[2] Here, by the end of the region P', we mean either the circular part P_O or the line segment $\overline{C_q C_{q2}}$ depending on the shape.

path P_r is $F = \int_{x_1}^{x_2} \sqrt{x^2+y^2}\sqrt{(1+(y')^2}\ dx$. To get the equation for the path P_r, we would need to determine the extremals of the above function F. Using the technique of calculus of variations [15], we can show that the extremal values of F satisfy the Euler-Lagrange differential equation. The equation of the path P_r can thus be computed as (we omit the details):

$$\beta = x^2 \cos\alpha + 2xy\sin\alpha - y^2\cos\alpha$$

where the constants α and β are evaluated by substituting for coordinates of C_r and C_q in the equation.

Optimal Join Algorithm. Given points C_r, C_s, C_q, and Q, let P_r and P_s be the optimized paths connecting C_r and C_s to C_q respectively as described above. For a **given** triplet of points (C_r, C_s, C_q), the optimal join-region P is as follows. Let $l = |R|/m$ and $l_Y = |P_r| + |P_s| + |\overline{C_qQ}|$.

- When $l_Y < l, P = P_r \cup P_s \cup \overline{C_qQ} \cup P_O$, where P_O is a circular region around Q such that $|P_O| = l - (|\overline{C_q,Q}| + |P_r| + |P_s|)$. See Figure 1 (a).
- When $l_Y \geq l, P = P_r \cup P_s \cup \overline{C_qC_{q2}}$, where C_{q2} is such that $|\overline{C_qC_{q2}}| = l - (|P_r| + |P_s|)$. See Figure 1 (b).

Now, we can construct an optimal join-region to compute a join operation for tables R and S and the query source Q, by considering all possible triples of points C_r, C_s, and C_q in the sensor network, and picking the triplet (C_r, C_s, C_q) that results in a join-region P (as describe above) with minimum communication cost. The time complexity of the above algorithm is $O(n^3)$, where n is the total number of sensor nodes in the sensor network.

Suboptimal Heuristic. The high time complexity of the optimal algorithm described above makes it impractical for large sensor networks.

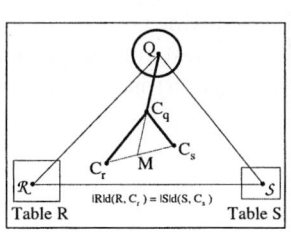

Fig. 2. Heuristic

Thus, we propose a suboptimal heuristic that runs in $O(n^{3/2})$ time, and incidentally performs very well in practice. Essentially, for a given C_r, we stipulate that C_s should be symmetrically ($|R|d(\mathcal{R}, C_r) = |S|d(\mathcal{S}, C_s)$) located in the $\triangle \mathcal{R}QS$. In addition, we approximate paths P_r and P_s to be straight line segments, and choose the point C_q on the median of the $\triangle C_rC_sQ$. See Figure 2. Thus, for each point as C_r in the sensor network, we determine C_s and search for the best C_q on the median of $\triangle C_rC_sQ$.

3.2 Join Implementation for Stream Database Tables

In the previous subsection, we discussed implementation of the join operation in a sensor network for static database tables. Since, sensor network data is better represented as stream database tables, we now generalize the algorithms to handle stream database tables. First, we start with presenting our model of stream database tables in sensor networks.

Data Streams in Sensor Networks. As for the case of static tables, a stream database table R corresponding to a data stream in a sensor network is associated with a region $\mathcal{R}$, where each node in $\mathcal{R}$ is continually generating tuples for the table R. To deal with the unbounded size of stream database tables, the tables are usually restricted to a finite set of tuples called the *sliding window* [1, 12, 27]. In effect, we expire or archive tuples from the data stream based on some criteria so that the total number of stored tuples does not exceed the bounded window size. We use W_R to denote the sliding window for a stream database table R.

Naive Approach for Stream Tables. In the Naive Approach, we use the region $\mathcal{R}$ (or $\mathcal{S}$) to store the windows W_R and W_S of the stream tables R and S.[3] Each sensor node in the region $\mathcal{R}$ uses $W_R/(|W_R|+|W_S|)$ fraction of its local memory to store tuples of W_R, and the remaining fraction of the memory to store tuples of W_S. To perform the join operation, each newly generated tuple (of R or S) is broadcast to all the nodes in the region $\mathcal{R}$, and is also stored in some node of $\mathcal{R}$ with available memory. Note that the generated data tuples of S need to be first routed from the region $\mathcal{S}$ to the region $\mathcal{R}$. The resulting joined tuples are routed from $\mathcal{R}$ to the query source Q.

Generalizing Other Approaches. The other approaches viz. Centroid Approach, Optimal Algorithm, and Suboptimal Heuristic, use a join-region that is separate from the regions $\mathcal{R}$ and $\mathcal{S}$. These algorithms are generalized to handle stream database tables as follows. First, the strategy to choose the join-region P remains the same as before for static tables, except for the size of the join-region. For stream database tables, the chosen join-region is used to store W_R as well as W_S, with each sensor node in the join-region using $W_R/|W_R|+|W_S|$ fraction of its memory to store tuples of W_R, and the rest to store tuples of W_S. Each newly generated tuple (of R or S) is routed from its source node in $\mathcal{R}$ or $\mathcal{S}$ to the join-region P, and broadcast to all the nodes in P. The resulting joined tuples are then routed to Q. As part of the broadcast process (without incurring any additional communication cost), each generated tuple of R (or S) is also stored at some node in P with available memory.

4 Performance Evaluation

In this section, we compare the performance of Naive Approach, Centroid Algorithm, Optimal Algorithm, and Suboptimal Heuristic. In our previous discussion, we have assumed dense sensor networks where we can find a sensor node at any desirable point in the region. On real sensor networks, we use our proposed algorithms in conjunction with the trajectory based forwarding (TBF) routing tech-

---

[3] If the total memory of the nodes in $\mathcal{R}$ is not sufficient to store W_R and W_S, then the region $\mathcal{R}$ is expanded to include more sensor nodes.

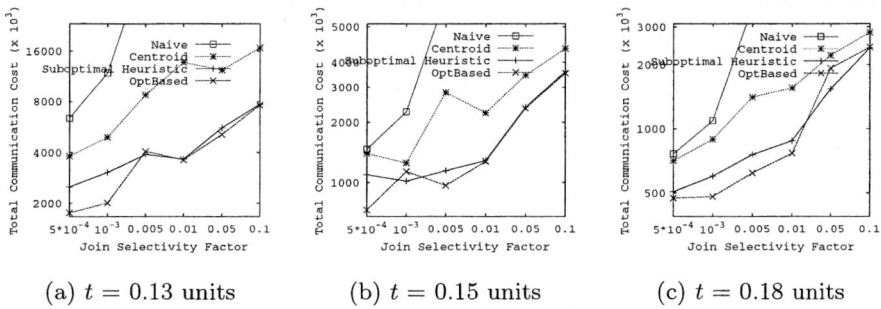

(a) $t = 0.13$ units (b) $t = 0.15$ units (c) $t = 0.18$ units

Fig. 3. Total communication cost for various transmission radii (t), and fixed $\triangle \mathcal{RSQ}$

nique [28], which works by forwarding packets to nodes closest to the intended path/trajectory. More specifically, to form the $P_r, P_s,$ and $\overline{C_q Q}$ (or $\overline{C_q C_{q2}}$) parts of the join-region, we use nodes that are closest to uniformly spaced points on the geometrically constructed paths. In addition, each algorithm is generalized for stream database tables as discussed in Section 3.2. We refer to the generalized algorithms as Naive, Centroid, *OptBased*, and Suboptimal Heuristic respectively.

Definition 3. *Given instances of relations R and S and a join predicate, the join-selectivity factor (f) is the probability that a random pair of tuples from R and S will satisfy the given join predicate. In other words, the join selectivity factor is the ratio of the size of $R \bowtie S$ to the size of the cartesian product, i.e., $f = |R \bowtie S|/(|R||S|)$.*

Parameter Values and Experiments. We generated random sensor networks by randomly placing 10,000 sensors with uniform transmission radius (t) in an area of 10×10 units. For the purposes of comparing the performance of our algorithms, varying the number of sensors is tantamount to varying the transmission radius. Thus, we fix the number of sensors to be 10,000 and measure performance for different transmission radii. Memory size of a sensor node is 300 tuples, and the size of each of the sliding windows W_R and W_S of stream tables R and S is 8,000 tuples. For simplicity, we chose uniform data generation rates for R and S streams. In each of the experiments, we measure communication cost incurred in processing 8000 newly generated tuples of R and S each, after the join-region is already filled with previously generated tuples. We use the GPSR [19] algorithm to route tuples. Catalogue information is gathered for non-Naive approaches by collecting a small sample of data streams at the query source. In the first set of experiments, we consider a fixed $\triangle \mathcal{RSQ}$ and calculate the total communication cost for various transmission radii and join-selectivity factors. Next, we fix the transmission radius and calculate the total communication cost for various join-selectivity factors and various shapes/sizes of the $\triangle \mathcal{RSQ}$.

Fixed Triangle $\mathcal{RSQ}$. In this set of experiments (Figure 3), we fix the locations of regions R, S, and query source Q and measure the performance of our algorithms for various values of transmission radii and join-selectivity factors. In particular, we choose coordinates (0,0), (5,9.5), and (9.5,0) for R, Q, and S respectively.

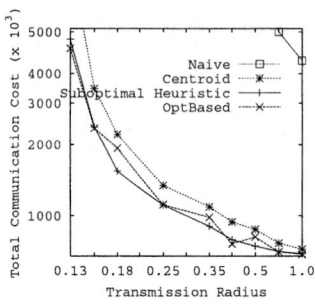

Fig. 4. Here, $f = 0.05$

We have looked at three transmission radii viz. 0.13, 0.15, and 0.18 units. Lower transmission radii left the sensor network disconnected, and the trend observed for these three transmission radii values is sufficient to infer behavior for larger transmission radii (see Figure 4). From Figure 3 (a)-(c), we can see that the Suboptimal Heuristic performs very close to the OptBased Algorithm, and significantly outperforms (upto 100%) the Naive and Centroid Approaches for most parameter values. The performance of the Naive approach worsens drastically with the increase in the join-selectivity factor, since the routing cost of the joined tuples from the join region ($\mathcal{R}$ or $\mathcal{S}$) to the query source Q becomes more dominant.

Fixed Transmission Radius (0.15 Units). We also observe the performance of various algorithms for different size and shapes of $\triangle \mathcal{RSQ}$. In particular, we fix the transmission radius of each sensor node in the network to be 0.15 units, and generate various $\triangle \mathcal{RSQ}$'s as follows. We fix locations of regions $\mathcal{R}$ and $\mathcal{S}$, and select many locations of the query source Q with the constraint that the area of the $\triangle \mathcal{RSQ}$ is between 10% to 50% of the total sensor network area. For each such generated $\triangle \mathcal{RSQ}$, we run all the four algorithms for three representative join-selectivity factor values viz. $10^{-4}, 5 * 10^{-3}$, and 10^{-2}. See Figure 5. Again we observe that the Suboptimal Heuristic performs very close to the OptBased Algorithm, and incurs much less communication cost than the Naive and Centroid Approaches for all join-selectivity factor values.

Summary. From the above experiments, we observe that the Suboptimal Heuristic performs very close to the OptBased Algorithm, but performs substantially

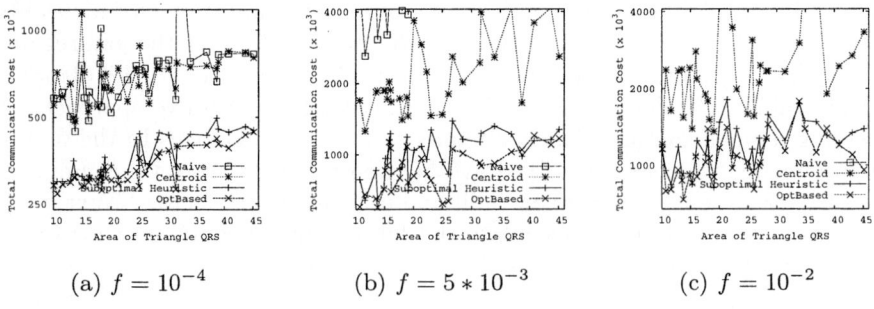

Fig. 5. Total communication cost for various $\triangle \mathcal{RSQ}$. Here, $t = 0.15$

better than the Centroid and Naive Approaches for a wide range of sensor network parameters. The savings in communication cost reduce with the increase in join-selectivity factor and/or transmission radius. We expect the join-selectivity factor to be relatively low in large sensor networks because of large sizes of operand tables and data generated having only local spatial and temporal data correlations. Moreover, since sensor nodes have the capability to adjust transmission power, effective topology control [30, 32] is used to minimize transmission radius at each node to conserve overall energy. Thus, the Suboptimal Heuristic is a natural choice for efficient implementation of join in sensor networks, and should result in substantial energy savings in practice.

5 Related Work

The vision of sensor network as a database has been proposed by many works [5, 16, 26], and simple query engines such as TinyDB [26] have been built for sensor networks. In particular, the COUGAR project [5, 33, 34] at Cornell University is one of the first attempts to model a sensor network as a database system. The TinyDB Project [26] at Berkeley also investigates query processing techniques for sensor networks. However, TinyDB implements very limited functionality [25] of the traditional database language SQL. A plausible implementation of an SQL query engine for sensor networks could be to ship all sensor nodes' data to an external server that handles the execution of queries completely [21]. Such an implementation would incur high communication costs and congestion-related bottlenecks. In particular, [18] shows that in-network implementation of database queries is fundamental to conserving energy in sensor networks. Thus, recent research has focussed on in-network implementation of database queries. However, prior research has only addressed limited SQL functionality – single queries involving simple aggregations [22, 24, 34] and/or selections [25] over single tables [23], or local joins [34]. So far, it has been considered that correlations such as median computation or joins should be computed on a single node [4, 25, 34]. In particular, [4] address the problem of operator placement for in-network query processing, assuming that each operator is executed locally and fully on a single sensor node. The problem of distributed and communication-efficient implementation of join has not been addressed yet in the context of sensor networks.

In addition, there has been a large body of work done on efficient query processing in data stream processing systems [6, 8, 9, 27]. In particular, [11] approximates sliding window joins over data streams and [17] has designed join algorithms for joining multiple data streams constrained by a sliding time window. However, a data stream processing system is not necessarily distributed and hence, minimizing communication cost is not the focus of the research. There has been a lot of work on query processing in distributed database systems [7, 20, 29], but sensor networks differ significantly from distributed database systems because of their multi-hop communication cost model and resource limitations.

6 Conclusions

Sensor networks are capable of generating large amounts of data. Hence, efficient query processing in sensor networks is of great importance. Since sensor nodes have limited battery power and memory resources, designing communication-efficient distributed implementation of database queries is a key research challenge. In this article, we have focussed on implementation of the join operator, which is one of the core operators of database query language. In particular, we have designed an Optimal Algorithm that incurs minimum communication cost for implementation of join in sensor networks under certain reasonable assumptions. Moreover, we reduced the time complexity of the Optimal Algorithm to design a Suboptimal Heuristic, and showed through extensive simulations that the Suboptimal Heuristic performs very close to the Optimal Algorithm. Techniques developed in this article are shown to result in substantial energy savings over simpler approaches for a wide range of sensor network parameters.

References

1. D. J. Abadi, D. Carney, U. Cetintemel, M. Cherniack, C. Convey, S. Lee, M. Stonebraker, N. Tatbul, and S. Zdonik. Aurora: a new model and architecture for data stream management. *The VLDB Journal*, 12(2):120–139, 2003.
2. B. Babcock, S. Babu, M. Datar, R. Motwani, and J. Widom. Models and issues in data stream systems. In *Proceedings of the ACM Symposium on Principles of Database Systems (PODS)*, 2002.
3. B. Badrinath, M. Srivastava, K. Mills, J. Scholtz, and K. Sollins, editors. *Special Issue on Smart Spaces and Environments,* IEEE Personal Communications, 2000.
4. B. Bonfils and P. Bonnet. Adaptive and decentralized operator placement for in-network query processing. In *Proceedings of the International Workshop on Information Processing in Sensor Networks (IPSN)*, 2003.
5. P. Bonnet, J. Gehrke, and P. Seshadri. Towards sensor database systems. In *Proceeding of the International Conference on Mobile Data Management*, 2001.
6. D. Carney, U. Cetintemel, M. Cherniack, C. Convey, S. Lee, G. Seidman, M. Stonebraker, N. Tatbul, and S. Zdonik. Monitoring streams - A new class of data management applications. In *Proceedings of the International Conference on Very Large Data Bases (VLDB)*, 2002.
7. S. Ceri and G. Pelagatti. *Distributed Database Design: Principles and Systems*. MacGraw-Hill (New York NY), 1984.
8. S. Chandrasekaran, O. Cooper, A. Deshpande, M. J. Franklin, J. M. Hellerstein, W. Hong, S. Krishnamurthy, S. R. Madden, F. Reiss, and M. A. Shah. TelegraphCQ: Continuous dataflow processing. In *Proceedings of the ACM SIGMOD Conference on Management of Data*, 2003.
9. J. Chen, D. J. DeWitt, F. Tian, and Y. Wang. NiagaraCQ: a scalable continuous query system for internet databases. In *Proceedings of the ACM SIGMOD Conference on Management of Data*, 2000.
10. V. Chowdhary and H. Gupta. Communication-efficient implementation of join in sensor networks. Technical report, SUNY, Stony Brook, Computer Science Department, 2004.

11. A. Das, J. Gehrke, and M. Riedewald. Approximate join processing over data streams. In *Proceedings of the ACM SIGMOD Conference on Management of Data*, 2003.
12. L. Ding, N. Mehta, E. Rundensteiner, and G. Heineman. Joining punctuated streams. In *Proceedings of the International Conference on Extending Database Technology*, 2004.
13. D. Estrin, R. Govindan, and J. Heidemann, editors. *Special Issue on Embedding the Internet*, Communications of the ACM, volume 43, 2000.
14. D. Estrin, R. Govindan, J. S. Heidemann, and S. Kumar. Next century challenges: Scalable coordination in sensor networks. In *Proceedings of the International Conference on Mobile Computing and Networking (MobiCom)*, 1999.
15. I. Gelfand and S. Fomin. *Calculus of Variations*. Dover Publications, 2000.
16. R. Govindan, J. Hellerstein, W. Hong, S. Madden, M. Franklin, and S. Shenker. The sensor network as a database. Technical report, University of Southern California, Computer Science Department, 2002.
17. M. Hammad, W. Aref, A. Catlin, M. Elfeky, and A. Elmagarmid. A stream database server for sensor applications. Technical report, Purdue University, Department of Computer Science, 2002.
18. J. S. Heidemann, F. Silva, C. Intanagonwiwat, R. Govindan, D. Estrin, and D. Ganesan. Building efficient wireless sensor networks with low-level naming. In *Symposium on Operating Systems Principles*, 2001.
19. B. Karp and H. Kung. Gpsr: greedy perimeter stateless routing for wireless networks. In *Proceedings of the International Conference on Mobile Computing and Networking (MobiCom)*, 2000.
20. D. Kossmann. The state of the art in distributed query processing. *ACM Computing Surveys*, 32(4), 2000.
21. S. Madden and M. Franklin. Fjording the stream: An architecture for queries over streaming sensor data. In *Proceedings of the International Conference on Database Engineering (ICDE)*, 2002.
22. S. Madden, M. Franklin, J. Hellerstein, and W. Hong. TAG: A tiny aggregation service for ad-hoc sensor networks. In *Proceedings of the Symposium on Operating Systems Design and Implementation (OSDI)*, 2002.
23. S. Madden and J. M. Hellerstein. Distributing queries over low-power wireless sensor networks. In *Proceedings of the ACM SIGMOD Conference on Management of Data*, 2002.
24. S. Madden, R. Szewczyk, M. Franklin, and D. Culler. Supporting aggregate queries over ad-hoc wireless sensor networks. In *Workshop on Mobile Computing and Systems Applications*, 2002.
25. S. R. Madden, M. J. Franklin, J. M. Hellerstein, and W. Hong. The design of an acquisitional query processor for sensor networks. In *Proceedings of the ACM SIGMOD Conference on Management of Data*, 2003.
26. S. R. Madden, J. M. Hellerstein, and W. Hong. TinyDB: In-network query processing in tinyos. http://telegraph.cs.berkeley.edu/tinydb, Sept. 2003.
27. R. Motwani, J. Widom, A. Arasu, B. Babcock, S. Babu, M. Datar, G. Manku, C. Olston, J. Rosenstein, and R. Varma. Query processing, approximation, and resource management in a data stream management system. In *Proceedings of the International Conference on Innovative Data Systems Research (CIDR)*, 2003.
28. B. Nath and D. Niculescu. Routing on a curve. In *Proceedings of the Workshop on Hot Topics in Networks*, 2002.
29. M. T. Ozsu and P. Valduriez. *Principles of Distributed Database Systems*. Prentice Hall, 1999.

30. J. Pan, Y. T. Hou, L. Cai, Y. Shi, and S. X. Shen. Topology control for wireless sensor networks. In *Proceedings of the International Conference on Mobile Computing and Networking (MobiCom)*, 2003.
31. G. Pottie and W. Kaiser. Wireless integrated sensor networks. *Communications of the ACM*, 43, 2000.
32. R. Ramanathan and R. Rosales-Hain. Topology control in multihop wireless networks using transmit power adjustment. In *Proceedings of the IEEE INFOCOM*, 2000.
33. Y. Yao and J. Gehrke. The cougar approach to in-network query processing in sensor networks. In *SIGMOD Record*, 2002.
34. Y. Yao and J. Gehrke. Query processing for sensor networks. In *Proceedings of the International Conference on Innovative Data Systems Research (CIDR)*, 2003.

Zoned-RAID for Multimedia Database Servers

Ali E. Dashti[1], Seon Ho Kim[2], and Roger Zimmermann[3]

[1] Electrical and Computer Engineering Department, Kuwait University, Safat, 13060, Kuwait
dashti@eng.kuniv.edu.kw
[2] Department of Computer Science, University of Denver, Denver, CO 80208, U.S.A
seonkim@cs.du.edu
[3] Department of Computer Science, University of Southern California, Los Angeles, CA 90089, U.S.A
rzimmerm@usc.edu

Abstract. This paper proposes a novel fault-tolerant disk subsystem named *Zoned-RAID* (Z-RAID). Z-RAID improves the performance of traditional RAID system by utilizing the *zoning* property of modern disks which provides multiple zones with different data transfer rates in a disk. This study proposes to optimize data transfer rate of RAID system by constraining placement of data blocks in multi-zone disks. We apply Z-RAID for multimedia database servers such as video servers that require a high data transfer rate as well as fault tolerance. Our analytical and experimental results demonstrate the superiority of Z-RAID to conventional RAID. Z-RAID provides a higher effective data transfer rate in normal mode with no disadvantage. In the presence of a disk failure, Z-RAID still performs as well as RAID.

1 Introduction

Recent years have witnessed the proliferation of multimedia databases, especially handling streaming media types such as digital audio and video, with the wide acceptance of the public and the industry. These media have become a part of everyday life including not only electronic consumer products but also online streaming media services on the Internet. Due to 1) successful standards for compression and file formats, such as MPEG (Motion Picture Expert Group), 2) increased network capacity for local area networks (LAN) and the Internet, and 3) advanced streaming protocols (e.g., Real Time Streaming Protocol, RTSP), more and more multimedia database applications, combined with the Internet, are providing streaming media services such as remote viewing of video clips.

Streaming media (SM) have two main characteristics. First, SM data must be displayed at a pre-specified rate. Any deviation from this real-time requirement may result in undesirable artifacts, disruptions, and jitters, collectively termed *hiccups*. Second, SM objects are large in size. For example, the size of a two-hour MPEG-2 encoded digital movie requiring 4 Mb/s for its display is 3.6 GBytes. Due to these characteristics, the design of SM servers has been different from that of conventional databases, file servers, and associated storage systems [5, 3] to provide a *hiccup-free display*, a higher throughput, a shorter startup latency, and a more cost-effective solution.

Magnetic disk drives have been the choice of storage devices for SM servers due to their high data transfer rate, large storage capacity, random access capability, and low price. Therefore, many studies have investigated the design of SM servers using magnetic disk drives [5, 3]. Due to the essential role of disk storage systems in SM servers, understanding recent trends in disk technologies can be helpful. First, the capacity and speed of magnetic disk drives have improved steadily over the last decade. According to [9] on the recent trends in data engineering, the storage capacity of magnetic disks has increased at the rate of about 60% per year. At the same time, the data transfer rate of magnetic disks has increased at the rate of about 40% per year. Thus, the imbalance between disk space and data transfer rate has widened. Because data transfer rate (bandwidth) is the scarce resource in the applications that intensively access disks, one wants to optimize for bandwidth rather than for space [9].

Another important physical characteristic of modern disks is *Zoned recording* (or *zoning*). This is an approach utilized by disk manufactures to increase the storage capacity of magnetic disks [12]. This technique groups adjacent disk cylinders into zones. Tracks are longer towards the outer portions of a disk platter as compared to the inner portions, hence, more data can be recorded in the outer tracks when the maximum linear density, i.e., bits per inch, is applied to all tracks. A zone is a contiguous collection of disk cylinders whose tracks have the same storage capacity, i.e., the number of sectors per track is constant in the same zone. Hence, outer tracks have more sectors per track than inner zones. Different disk models have different number of zones. Different zones in a disk provide different transfer rates because: 1) the storage capacity of the tracks for each zone is different, and 2) the disk platters rotate at a fixed number of revolutions per second. We can observe a significant difference in data transfer rates between the minimum and maximum (around 50% difference) [3, 7, 12].

Last, since disk prices are approaching tape prices and tape backup takes a far longer time, disks are replacing tapes for backup and fault tolerant systems. Thus, many applications have been using RAID (Redundant Array of Independent Disks) [14]. Out of multiple levels of RAID, especially, both RAID level 1 and level 5 have been commonly used for a fault tolerant disk system [9].

In large scale multimedia database servers in support of streaming media, it is obviously critical both to optimize disk bandwidth and to provide disk-based fault tolerance. Many studies [16, 1, 6, 17, 7] discussed data placement on multi-zone disks to maximize the effective data transfer rate. [10] provided MRS (Multi-Rate Smoothing) data placement on multi-zone disks for a smooth transmission of variable-bit-rate data over network. However, none of above studies includes reliability issue. RAID has been widely used for faut-tolerant streaming servers as well as conventional file servers. Various reliability strategies in video servers, including RAID, were surveyed and compared in [4]. However, no study considered one of the most important characteristics of disk drives, variable data transfer rates from multiple zones in a disk. Therefore, conventional techniques place data blocks without any constraints inside a disk. This may result in less optimized disk performance because the data transfer rate significantly varies depending on the location of data block in multi-zone disks.

This study proposes a novel data placement scheme to optimize the data transfer rate of RAID systems using multi-zone disks by constraining data placement, especially for streaming media server that require a high data transfer rate as well as fault tolerance. To our knowledge, combining data placement on RAID with multi-zone disks is a new approach. The main ideas of the proposed constrained data placement are 1) to store primary data blocks (for normal access) in faster zones and secondary blocks or parity blocks (for standby in case of a disk failure) in slower zones, and 2) to store frequently accessed data blocks (such as popular video clips) in faster zones and infrequently accessed blocks in slower zones. Our experimental results demonstrate a significant increase in the effective data transfer rate of RAID in normal mode with no disk failure.

2 Z-RAID

Since RAID [14] was proposed in 1988, it has been widely implemented in many systems requiring fault tolerance. Originally, RAID levels 1-5 were proposed but many variants such as level 0 and 6 have been studied and commercialized. However, level 1 (mirroring) and 5 (block-based parity encoding) received most attention in many applications due to their cost-effectiveness and implementation efficiency [9]. Thus, this study focuses on extending RAID level 1 and 5 to our proposed Zoned-RAID (Z-RAID) approach.

A multi-zone disk can be modelled as follows: A disk with total space, S, has n zones, where zone 0 is the innermost (slowest) and zone $n-1$ is the outermost (fastest). The number of cylinders in each zone is $Cyl(i)$, $0 \leq i < n$, and the total number of cylinders is Cyl. Cylinders are numbered from the innermost to the outermost. The size of a cylinder is $S(i)$ bytes, $0 \leq i < Cyl-1$. The data transfer rate of each cylinder is $R_c(j)$, $0 \leq j < Cyl$, ($R_c(0) \leq R_c(1) \leq ... \leq R_c(Cyl-1)$). Note that all cylinders in the same zone have the same data transfer rate. A rotational latency, l_{rot}, is one disk revolution time of a disk. A seek time between two locations in a disk, say x cylinders apart, can be calculated using a practical non-linear approximation, $seek(x)$ [15]. Then, an actual block retrieval time consists of a seek time, a rotational latency, and block reading time.

2.1 Z-RAID Level 1

RAID level 1 utilizes a replication of disks, called *mirroring*. When we have two disks, d_0 and d_1, then a primary copy of a block, B_i, is placed on d_0 and the secondary copy, say B'_i, is placed on d_1. Blocks are arbitrarily distributed across cylinders inside a disk. This implies the system uses the average data transfer rate of a multi-zone disk and the average seek time (one half of the worst seek which is

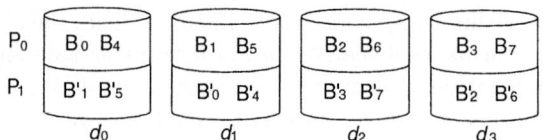

Fig. 1. Z-RAID level 1 with four disks

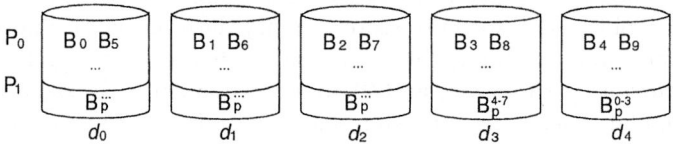

Fig. 2. Z-RAID level 5 with five disks

from the outermost cylinder to the innermost cylinder). Then, the effective data transfer rate of a disk with no overhead (no seek time, no rotational latency) is:

$$R_R = \sum_{i=0}^{Cyl-1} (R_c(i) \times \frac{S(i)}{S}) \tag{1}$$

In a streaming media server whose access unit is a block (B), each block access includes the worst seek time and rotational latency to support realtime block retrieval even in the worst case [5, 8]. Thus, the effective data transfer rate of RAID level 1 in a streaming media server is:

$$R_{RB} = \frac{B}{seek(Cyl) + l_{rot} + B/R_R} \tag{2}$$

Z-RAID level 1 also uses mirroring like RAID level 1. However, it utilizes only faster zones of disks for primary copies of blocks. All secondary copies are placed on slower zones. With Z-RAID 1, each disk is divided into two logical partitions of equal size ($P_0 = P_1 = S/2$), P_0 which occupies the faster zones ($S/2$ from the outermost cylinders) and P_1 which occupies the slower zones (remaining $S/2$). All primary blocks, B_i, are assigned to P_0 while all secondary blocks, B'_i, are stored in P_1, see Figure 1. Let us say that P_0 consists of cylinders from m to $Cyl - 1$, where m is the cylinder number that divides the disk space in half (i.e., $\sum_{i=0}^{m-1} S(i) = S/2$). Note that the value of m and Cyl should be determined using real disk characteristics because different disk models have different zone characteristics. A more general allocation of blocks is as follows: when Z-RAID consists of k disks, if B_i resides on P_0 of disk j, B'_i is stored in P_1 of disk $(j + 1) \bmod k$.

In normal mode without disk failure, blocks are retrieved from P_0s of disks. Because P_0s are located in faster zones of a disk, Z-RAID will increase the effective data transfer rate of the disk. Moreover, because the maximum cylindrical distance inside P_0 is far shorter than Cyl, Z-RAID will decrease the required seek time between two adjacent block retrievals. Both will result in a significantly enhanced effective data transfer rate:

$$R_{ZR} = \sum_{i=m}^{Cyl-1} (R_c(i) \times \frac{S(i)}{S/2}) \qquad (3)$$

$$R_{ZRB} = \frac{B}{seek(Cyl - m - 1) + lrot + B/R_{ZR}} \qquad (4)$$

2.2 Z-RAID Level 5

RAID level 5 uses a block-based parity encoding. It distributes parity blocks across disks in a parity group so that both normal blocks and parity blocks can be placed on a disk. Blocks are arbitrarily distributed in a disk. Thus, in normal mode, the effective data transfer rate of RAID level 5 is identical to RAID level 1, i.e., Equations 1 and 2.

Z-RAID level 5 follows the same way as RAID level 5 to distribute parity blocks across disks. However, the location of parity blocks inside a disk is constrained to the slower zone areas. For example, when we form a parity group with 5 disks, 4 data blocks and a parity block will be distributed across 5 disks. Thus, 20% of each disk space consisting of corresponding innermost tracks will store all parity blocks while 80% of the disk space with outer tracks stores data blocks. For example, each disk has two logical partitions, P_0 (outer 80% of disk space) and P_1 (inner 20% space). Normal data blocks are stored in P_0 and all parity blocks are in P_1, see Figure 2. The same advantages of Z-RAID level 1 in Section 2.1 are expected: higher effective data transfer rate and shorter average seek time in normal mode.

When d disks are in a parity group, $1/d$ of each disk space will be used to store parity blocks. Then, P_0 consists of cylinders from m (where $\sum_{i=0}^{m-1} S(i) = S/d$) to $Cyl - 1$. Equation 3 and 4 for Z-RAID level 1 can be used for Z-RAID level 5 with a different value of m that is a function of d.

2.3 Z-RAID for Multimedia Databases

Because Z-RAID can provide a higher effective data transfer rate with the same fault tolerant disk system compared to a conventional RAID, it can be used where ever a RAID can be used. However, some applications such as streaming applications that require a large page (block) size mostly benefit from Z-RAID because a block retrieval time depends more on data transfer time than other near constant factors such as seek time and rotational latency. Note that B/R_{ZR} becomes a dominant factor (see Equation 4) as B grows larger.

Another important observation in real streaming applications is that objects may have different popularity or access frequency. For example, in a movie-on-demand system, more than half of the total user requests might reference only a handful of recently released hot movies. It is widely understood that the popularity distribution among objects in video-on-demand systems can be well represented by the Zipf distribution [13], which is a very skewed distribution.

Z-RAID can well take advantage of this skewed popularity distribution because the distribution of data transfer rates across zones is also skewed. With n objects in the system, one can sort objects in descending order based on their popularity. Then one assigns blocks of objects from the outermost tracks in a disk which has the fastest data transfer rate towards the inner tracks, track by track. When the blocks of the first, most popular, object are all assigned, then the next object is assigned in the same way from the next track. This process is repeated until all objects are assigned.

3 Comparisons

In our experiments, we used two Seagate disk models, the Cheetah X15 and the Barracuda 7200.7 plus. The Cheetah X15 provides one of the fastest rotation speeds at 15,000 revolutions per minute (RPM), with a very short average seek time of 3.6 milliseconds. This model exemplifies a typical high performance disk and was introduced in 2000. The Barracuda 7200.7 is a typical cost-effective high capacity disks with 7,200 RPM and 8.5 milliseconds of average seek time (introduced in 2004). Table 1 and Figure 3 show the zone characteristics of Cheetah X15 and Barracuda 7200.7.

3.1 Analytical Comparison

First, we calculated and compared the effective data transfer rates of RAID and Z-RAID with the two disk drives detailed in Table 1 using equations from Sections 2.1 and 2.2. We compared our design with two conventional approaches widely used for streaming media servers. With the guaranteed approach that supports 100% hiccup-free displays, one must assume the worst case seek time and the maximum rotational latency for each data block retrieval. Many round robin data placement and retrieval schemes [5, 8] follow this guaranteed approach, hence they fall into the category of worst case analysis. To quantify the effective data transfer rates of this approach, we performed a worst case analysis assuming the maximum seek time (7.2 ms for Cheetah X15 and 17 ms for Barracuda 7200.7) and the worst rotational latency (4 ms for Cheetah X15 and 8.3 ms for Barracuda 7200.7). Second, with the statistical approach that tolerates a non-zero hiccup probability, one can take advantage of the average seek time and average rotational latency per data block retrieval. Many random data placement and retrieval schemes [11] follow this statistical approach to enhance the performance of the system at the expense of a minor degradation of display quality, i.e., occasional hiccups. For this approach, we performed an average case analysis assuming the average seek time (3.6 ms for Cheetah X15 and 8.5 ms for Barracuda 7200.7) and average rotational latency (2 ms for Cheetah X15 and 4.16 ms for Barracuda 7200.7).

It is well established that the performance of streaming media servers – especially their disk subsystems – significantly varies depending on the data

Table 1. Parameters for two Seagate disks

Model	ST336752LC	ST3200822A
Series	Cheetah X15	Barracuda 7200.7 plus
Manufacturer	Seagate Technology	Seagate Technology
Capacity S	37 GB	200 GB
Transfer rate R_c	See Table 3.a	See Table 3.b
Spindle speed	15,000 rpm	7,200 rpm
Avg. rotational latency	2 msec	4.16 msec
Worst case seek time	7.2 msec	17 msec

Zone #	Size (GB)	Read Transfer Rate (MB/s)
0	12	57.5
1	3.5	55.4
2	3.0	54.7
3	4.0	52.7
4	3.0	50.6
5	2.5	48.1
6	3.0	45.6
7	2.5	43.6
8	2.5	41.9

a. Cheetah X15

Zone #	Size (GB)	Read Transfer Rate (MB/s)
0	48	65.2
1	17	63.8
2	14	61.5
3	21	58.2
4	9	56.0
5	12	54.1
6	14	52.4
7	9	50.6
8	6	49.5
9	13	46.8
10	9	44.1
11	6	42.2
12	8	39.7
13	8	37.6
14	6	35.3

b. Barracuda 7200.7

Fig. 3. Zoning information of two Seagate disks

block size that is the unit of access to the disks. Thus, we calculated the effective data transfer rate as a function of the data block size varying from 128 Kbytes to 8 Mbytes (a reasonable range for streaming media servers).

Figure 4 shows the effective data transfer rates of RAID and Z-RAID with the Cheetah X15. RAID1 denotes the traditional RAID level 1, Z-RAID1 means the proposed Z-RAID level 1, and Z-RAID5 refers to the proposed Z-RAID level 5. Note that the effective rate of RAID5 in normal mode is identical to that of RAID1 because all data blocks are arbitrarily distributed across all zones without any constraints. In our calculation, the size of the parity group of Z-RAID5 was 5 disks so that 20% of disk space (from the slowest zone) in each disk is dedicated to store parity blocks. Figures 4.a and 4.b show the results from the worst case and the average case analysis, respectively. Compared to RAID1, Z-RAID1 demonstrates enhanced rates from 10.5% to 38.6% in the worst case analysis, and from 9.5% to 33.1% in the average case analysis. Compared to RAID5, the percentage enhancement of Z-RAID5 ranges from 4.8% to 12.7% in the worst case analysis, and from 4.5% to 11.4% in the average case analysis. Figure 5 shows the analytical results with the Barracuda 7200.7. The results and trends are similar to those of the Cheetah X15. Z-RAID1 improves over RAID1 from 18.5% to 46.8% in the worst case analysis, and from 16.5% to 43.6% in the average case analysis. Compared to RAID5, the percentage enhancement of

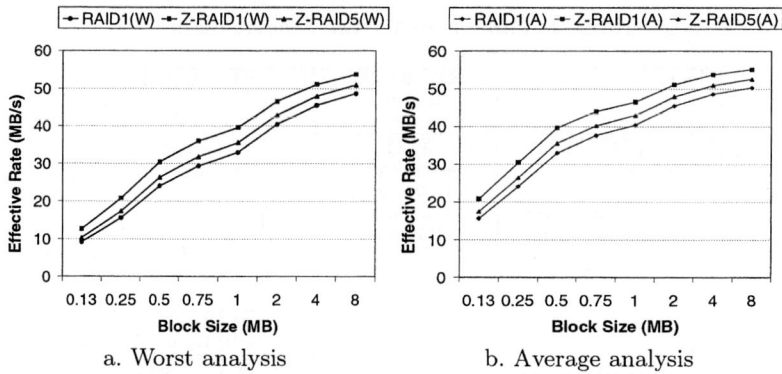

Fig. 4. Effective data rate of a Seagate X15 disk

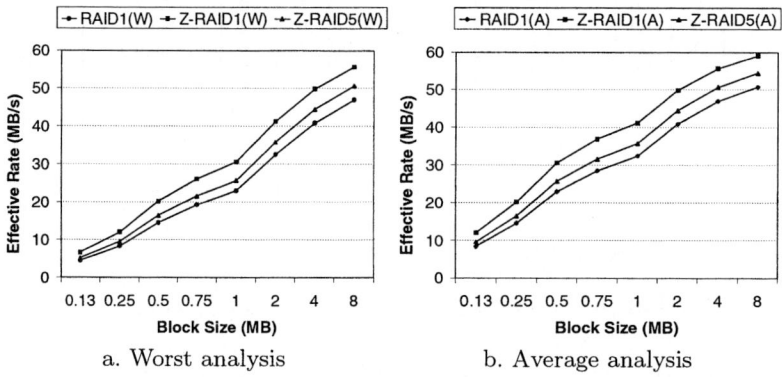

Fig. 5. Effective data rate of a Seagate 7200.7 disk

Z-RAID5 ranges from 7.9% to 14.7% in the worst case analysis, and from 7.3% to 14.1% in the average case analysis.

As shown, for all comparisons, Z-RAID outperforms RAID. The percentage improvement of the effective data transfer rate is greater for small block sizes where the reduced seek time is the dominant factor in determining the rate. The dominant factor shifts from the seek time to the actual block reading time as the block size increases, see the divisors in Equations 2 and 4. The reduced seek time is also the reason why Z-RAID1 gains a higher percentage increase than Z-RAID5. With Z-RAID5, the performance enhancement decreases as the size of the parity group increases. With a smaller group such as three disks, a higher effective rate is achieved than with larger groups.

3.2 Simulation Results

The analytical models of the previous section provide some compelling evidence that Z-RAID provides increased performance. However, they cannot encompass the full complexity of a storage system and hence are based on some arguable simplifying assumptions. Hence, to further evaluate the performance of the Z-

Table 2. Experimental parameters for the Z-RAID Level 1 simulator

Z-RAID Level 1	18 Disks (Seagate Cheetah X15)
Block size $\mathcal{B}$	0.25, 0.5, 1, 2, 4, 8 MB
Time period T_p	($\frac{\mathcal{B}}{1.5\text{Mb/s}}$) sec
Throughput $\mathcal{N}_{Tot}$	< 4800
No. of stored clips	47
Object type	MPEG-1 (1.5 Mb/s)
Object size (length)	675 MB (1 hour)
Access distribution	Zipf

RAID technique we implemented a simulator. It includes a detailed disk model that was calibrated with parameters extracted from commercially available disk drives. To model user behavior, the simulator included a module to generate synthetic workloads based on various Poisson and Zipf distributions [18].

The simulator was implemented using the C programming language on a Sun server running Solaris and it consists of the following components. The *disk emulation* module imitates the response and behavior of a magnetic disk drive. The level of detail of such a model depends largely upon the desired accuracy of the results. Our model includes mechanical positioning delays (seeks and rotational latency) as well as variable transfer rates due to the common zone-bit-recording technique. The *file system* module provides the abstraction of files on top of the disk models and is responsible for the allocation of blocks and the maintenance of the free space. Either random or constrained block allocation were selectable with our file system. The *loader* module generates a synthetic set of continuous media objects that are stored in the file system as part of the initialization phase of the simulator. The *scheduler* module translates a user request into a sequence of real-time block retrievals. It implements the concept of a time period and enables the round-robin movement of consecutive block reads on behalf of each stream. Furthermore, it ensures that all real-time deadlines are met. Finally, the *workload* generator models user behavior and produces a synthetic trace of access requests to be executed against the stored objects. Both, the distribution of the request arrivals as well as the distribution of the object access frequency can be individually specified. For the purpose of our simulations, the request inter-arrival times were Poisson distributed while the object access frequency was modeled according to Zipf's law [18].

For the evaluation of RAID1 and Z-RAID1, the simulator was configured with a total of 18 disks of the Cheetah X15, each with 37 GB of space. Table 3.2 summarizes the rest of the simulation parameters.

For regular RAID1 mirroring, the data blocks were randomly distributed across all the zones of a disk. For Z-RAID1 mirroring, the primary copies of the data were constrained to the faster half of the disk drives. We tested retrieval block sizes of 0.25, 0.5, 1, 2, 4, and 8 MB and we executed the simulation with a nominal workload of $\lambda = 2,000$ requests per hour. The simulated database consisted of video clips whose display time was one hour long and which required a constant retrieval rate of 1.5 Mb/s (e.g., MPEG-1). This resulted in a uniform

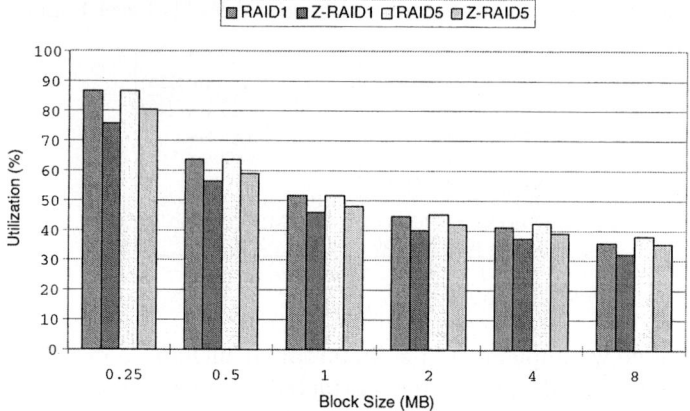

Fig. 6. Simulation results using Seagate Cheetah X15 disks

storage requirement of 675 Mbytes per clip. We also performed simulations of RAID5 and Z-RAID5 with the parity group size 5.

The frequency of access to different media clips is usually quite skewed for a video-on-demand system, i.e., a few newly released movies are very popular while most of the rest are accessed infrequently. The distribution pattern can be modeled using Zipf's law, which defines the access frequency of movie i to be $F(i) = \frac{c}{i^{1-d}}$, where c is a normalization constant and d controls how quickly the access frequency drops off. In our simulations, d was set to equal 0.271, which was chosen to approximate empirical data for rental movies [2]. For each experiment, the server had to service requests that arrived based on a Poisson distribution to simulate human behavior.

We focused on the disk utilization to compare the two techniques. A lower disk utilization – given a fixed workload – indicates a higher effective data transfer rate and a higher maximum throughput for the overall system. Because the effective bandwidth of a disk drive increases with larger block sizes, we expected to see a drop in disk utilization with increased block sizes. Figure 6 shows the results of the simulations using 18 Cheetah X15 disks, which depicts the reduction of the overall disk utilization of Z-RAID1 and 5 with a constant workload as compared with standard RAID 1 and 5. Z-RAID1 and 5 outperformed RAID1 and 5, respectively. For example, when the block size is 0.5 megabytes, the disk utilization of RAID1 was 64% while that of Z-RAID1 was 56% to service the same number of request. The percentage reduction of disk utilization between Z-RAID1 and RAID1 ranges from 11.1% (8 Mbytes of block size) to 13.6% (0.25 Mbytes of block size). Similar to the analytical comparisons, Z-RAID5 was performing lower than Z-RAID1 but still performing higher than RAID5.

We performed more simulations with different configuration using the Barracuda 7200.7. We used 33 disks and the workload was the same, $\lambda = 2{,}000$ requests per hour. Figure 7 shows similar results as the previous simulations with the Cheetah X15. The percentage reduction of disk utilization between Z-

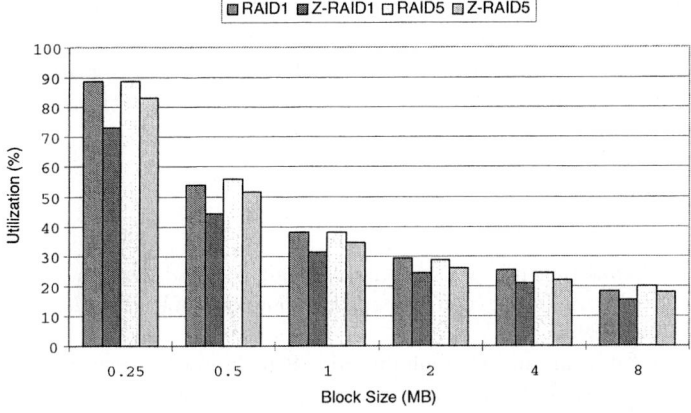

Fig. 7. Simulation results using Seagate Barracuda 7200.7 disks

RAID1 and RAID1 ranges from 16.8% (8 Mbytes of block size) to 17.9% (0.25 Mbytes of block size).

Finally, we compared the performance of two disk models using RAID1 and Z-RAID1. The configuration used 18 disks and the workload was $\lambda = 1,500$ requests per hour. With a small block size the X15 provided a lower utilization than the 7200.7, because of its exceptionally small retrieval overhead (seek time plus rotational latency). However, as the block size increases the higher transfer rate of the 7200.7 becomes the dominant factor and allows it to achieve a lower utilization than the X15.

4 Conclusion

Our proposed Z-RAID system constrains the data block placement in a RAID system utilizing the zone characteristics of multi-zone disk drives. The constrained data placement and retrieval incur a shorter seek time between two adjacent block retrievals, which results in a reduced overhead for each block retrieval. Moreover, because the blocks are retrieved from the faster zones of a disk, the effective data transfer rate is increased further. Our analytical and simulation results for a streaming media server application demonstrate that both Z-RAID level 1 and 5 outperform the traditional RAID level 1 and 5, respectively.

The practical aspect of Z-RAID can be a more cost-effective and affordable system. Typically, RAID systems have been constructed from high performance disk drives such as SCSI disks. In general, those disks provide a higher transfer rate than other inexpensive disks such as IDE models. The drawback is a higher price. For cost-effectiveness, more economical RAIDs with IDE disks (IDE-RAID) have been recently introduced. We conclude that a Z-RAID system with IDE disks can provide the same high performance as a RAID system with high-end SCSI disks, but at the lower cost of IDE-RAID. Considering the recent trend showing that the performance gap between SCSI disks and IDE disks is narrowing (while the price gap still remains very significant), Z-RAID can provide an even better solution for a disk subsystem with inexpensive disks.

References

1. Y. Birk. Track-pairing: a novel data layout for vod servers with multi-zone-recording disks. In *IEEE International Conference on Multimedia Computing and System*, June 1995.
2. A. Dan, D. Sitaram, and P. Shahabuddin. Scheduling Policies for an On-Demand Video Server with Batching. In *Proceedings of the ACM Multimedia*, pages 391–398, 1994.
3. Ali Dashti, Seon Ho Kim, Cyrus Shahabi, and Roger Zimmermann. *Streaming Media Server Design*. Prentice Hall PTR, 2004.
4. J. Gafsi and E. W. Biersack. Modeling and Performance Comparison of Reliability Strategies for Distributed Video Servers. *IEEE Transactions on Parallel and Distributed Systems*, 11(4):412–430, 2000.
5. D. J. Gemmell, H. M. Vin, D. D. Kandlur, P. V. Rangan, and L. A. Rowe. Multimedia Storage Servers: A Tutorial. *IEEE Computer*, May 1995.
6. S. Ghandeharizadeh, S. H. Kim, C. Shahabi, and R. Zimmermann. Placement of Continuous Media in Multi-Zone Disks. In Soon M. Chung, editor, *Multimedia Information Storage and Management*, chapter 2. Kluwer Academic Publishers, Boston, August 1996. ISBN: 0-7923-9764-9.
7. S. Ghandeharizadeh and S.H. Kim. A Comparison of Alternative Continuous Display Techniques with Heterogeneous Disks. In *Proceedings of the International Conference on Information and Knowledge Management*, pages 442–449, 1999.
8. S. Ghandeharizadeh, S.H. Kim, W. Shi, and R. Zimmermann. On Minimizing Startup Latency in Scalable Continuous Media Servers. In *Proceedings of Multimedia Computing and Networking*, pages 144–155. Proc. SPIE 3020, Feb. 1997.
9. Jim Gray and Prashant Shenoy. Rules of thumb in data engineering. In *Proceedings of IEEE International Conference on Database Engineering*, Feb. 2000.
10. S. Kang and H.Y. Yeom. Storing Continuous Media Objects to Multi-Zone Recording Disks Using Multi-Rate Smoothing Technique. *IEEE Transactions on Multimedia*, 5(3):473–482, 2003.
11. R. Muntz, J. Santos, and S. Berson. RIO: A Real-time Multimedia Object Server. *ACM Sigmetrics Performance Evaluation Review*, 25(2), Sep. 1997.
12. S. W. Ng. Advances in Disk Technology: Performance Issues. *IEEE Computer Magazine*, pages 75–81, May 1998.
13. J. Nussbaumer, B. Patel, F. Schaffa, and J. Sternbenz. Network Requirement for Interactive Video-on-Demand. *IEEE Transactions on Selected Areas in Communications*, 13(5):779–787, 1995.
14. D. Patterson, G. Gibson, and R. Katz. A case for Redundant Arrays of Inexpensive Disks (RAID). In *Proceedings of the ACM SIGMOD International Conference on Management of Data*, May 1988.
15. C. Ruemmler and J. Wilkes. An Introduction to Disk Drive Modeling. *IEEE Computer*, March 1994.

16. M.F. Mitoma S.R. Heltzer, J.M. Menon. Logical data tracks extending among a plurality of zones of physical tracks of one or more disk devices. In *U.S. Patent No. 5,202,799*, April 1993.
17. W.-C. Wang and et al. Fast data placement scheme for video servers with zoned-disks. In *Proceedings of Multimedia Storage and Archiving Systems II*, pages 92–102. Proc. SPIE 3229, 1997.
18. G. K. Zipf. *Human Behavior and the Principle of Least Effort.* Addison-Wesley, Reading MA, 1949.

Randomized Data Allocation in Scalable Streaming Architectures*

Kun Fu and Roger Zimmermann

Integrated Media Systems Center, University of Southern California,
Los Angeles, California 90089
{kunfu, rzimmerm}@usc.edu

Abstract. IP-networked streaming media storage has been increasingly used as a part of many applications. Random placement of data blocks has been proven to be an effective approach to balance heterogeneous workload in multi-disk steaming architectures. However, the main disadvantage of this technique is that statistical variation can still result in short term load imbalances in disk utilization. We propose a *packet level randomization* (PLR) technique to solve this challenge. We quantify the exact performance trade-off between PLR approach and the traditional *block level randomization* (BLR) technique through both theoretical analysis and extensive simulation. Our results show that the PLR technique can achieve much better load balancing in scalable streaming architectures by using more memory space.

1 Introduction

Large scale digital continuous media (CM) servers are currently being deployed for a number of different applications. Magnetic disk drives are usually the storage devices of choice for such streaming servers and they are generally aggregated into arrays to enable support for many concurrent users. Multi-disk CM server designs can largely be classified into two paradigms: (1) Data blocks are striped in a *round-robin* manner [1] across the disks and retrieved in *cycles* or *rounds* for all streams. (2) Data blocks are placed *randomly* [5] across all disks and the data retrieval is based on a *deadline* for each block. The first paradigm attempts to guarantee the retrieval or storage of all data. It is often referred to as *deterministic*. With the second paradigm, a disk may briefly be overloaded, leading to a few missed deadlines. This approach is often called *statistical*.

We focused on the statistical approach because of its many advantages. For example, a much higher resource utilization can be achieved. Moreover, the statistical approach can be implemented on widely available platforms such as Windows or Linux that do not provide hard real time guarantees. It can also naturally

---

* This research has been funded in part by NSF grants EEC-9529152 (IMSC ERC), IIS-0082826 and CMS-0219463, and unrestricted cash/equipment gifts from Intel, Hewlett-Packard, Raptor Networks Technology and the Lord Foundation.

support a variety of different media types that require different data rates (both constant (CBR) or variable (VBR)) as well as interactive functions such as pause, resume and fast-forward. Moreover, it has been shown that the performance of a system based on the statistical method is on par with that of a deterministic system [6]. Finally, it can support on-line data reorganization more efficiently [3], which is very crucial for scalable storage systems. Even though the statistical approach is very resource efficient and ensures a balanced load across all disk devices over the long term, short term load fluctuations may occur because occasionally consecutive data blocks may be assigned to the same disk drive by the random location generator. During the playback of such a media file, the block retrieval request queue may temporarily hold too many requests such that not all of them can be served by their required deadline.

In this paper we introduce a novel *packet-level randomization* (PLR) technique that significantly reduces the occurrence of deadline violations with random data placement. PLR is the focus of the remainder of this paper which is organized as follows. Section 2 reviews the related work. Section 3 presents our proposed design. Performance analysis and evaluation are contained in Section 4 and 5, respectively. Finally, Section 6 outlines our future plans.

2   Related Work

Three techniques have been proposed to achieve load balancing in striped multi-disk multimedia storage systems. One approach is to use large stripes that access many consecutive blocks from all disks at a single request for each active stream [8]. It provides perfect load balancing because the number of disk I/Os is the same on all the devices. However, it results in extremely large data requests with large number of disks. Furthermore, it does not efficiently support unpredictable access patterns. The second approach uses small requests accessing just one block on a single disk, with sequential requests cycling over all the disks [1]. This technique does not support unpredictable access patterns well. The third technique randomly allocates data blocks to disks blocks [6, 7], and therefore supports unpredictable workloads efficiently. To our knowledge, no prior work has quantified the exact trade-off between the randomization at the packet and block levels when fine-grained load balancing is desired or required.

3   Design Approach

We assume a multi-disk, multi-node streaming media server cluster design similar to the one used in our previous research activities. Our first prototype *Yima* [7], was a scalable streaming architecture to support applications such as video-on-demand and distance learning on a large scale. Our current generation system, termed the *High-performance Data Recording Architecture* (HYDRA) [10] improves and extends Yima with real time recording capabilities. For load-balancing purposes, without requiring data replication, a multimedia object X is commonly striped into blocks, e.g., $X_0, X_1, \ldots, X_{n-1}$, across the disk drives that form the storage system [4, 8]. Because of its many advantages, we consider randomly allocating data to the disk drives.

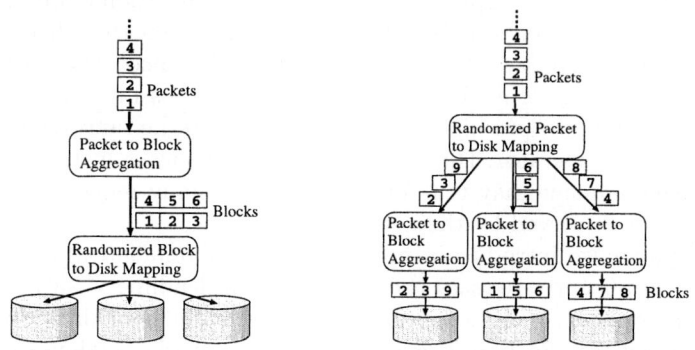

Fig. 1(a): Block Level Randomization (*BLR*)

Fig. 1(b): Packet Level Randomization (*PLR*)

Fig. 1. Two different randomization schemes that can be applied in a Recording System, e.g. HYDRA [10]. Note that in this example, each block contains 3 packets

3.1 Packets versus Blocks

Packet-switched networks such as the Internet transmit relatively small quanta of data per packet (for example 1400 bytes). On the other hand, magnetic disk drives operate very inefficiently when data is accessed in small amounts. This is due to the fact that disk drives are mechanical devices that require a transceiver head to be positioned in the correct location over a spinning platter before any data can be transferred. The seek time and rotational latency are wasteful [10]. Consequently, media packets need to be aggregated into larger data blocks for efficient storage and retrieval. Traditionally this is accomplished as follows.

Block-Level Randomization (BLR): Media packets are aggregated in sequence into blocks (see Figure 1(a)). For example, if m packets fit into one block then the data distribution algorithm will place the first m sequential packets into block X_0, the next m packets into block X_1, and so on. As a result, each block contains sequentially numbered packets. Blocks are then assigned randomly to the available disk drives. During retrieval, the deadline of the first packet in each block is essentially the retrieval deadline for the whole block. The advantage of BLR is that only one buffer *at a time* per stream needs to be available in memory across all the storage nodes. In order to allow high disk utilization while still reducing the probability of hot-spots we propose a novel technique as follows.

Packet-Level Randomization (PLR): Each media packet is randomly assigned to one of the storage nodes, where they are further collected into blocks (Figure 1(b)). One advantage is that during playback data is retrieved randomly from all storage nodes at the granularity of a packet. Therefore, load-balancing is achieved at a very small data granularity. The disadvantage is that memory buffers need to be allocated concurrently on all nodes per stream. In the next section we quantify the load-balancing properties of both BLR and PLR.

4 Performance Analysis

We evaluate *PLR* and *BLR* with three metrics: (1) the uniformity of data distribution on each disk, (2) the disk I/O imbalance across every disk during a streaming experiment, and (3) the memory size and potential caching effects.

Table 1. List of terms used repeatedly in this study and their respective definitions

Term	Definition	Units
N_D	Total number of disks	
M	Total data size	MB
S_P	Packet size	MB
S_B	Block size	MB
M_B	Total data size in blocks	
M_P	Total data size in packets	
D_{PLR}	The amount of data assigned to a disk in PLR	MB
D_{BLR}	The amount of data assigned to a disk in BLR	MB
X	The number of packets assigned to a disk in PLR	
Y	The number of blocks assigned to a disk in BLR	
R	Ratio of block size and packet size, i.e., $\frac{S_B}{S_P}$	
N_C	The number of concurrent clients supported by the storage server	
N_S	Total number of storage server nodes	
S_{mem}^{blr}	Memory size required for BLR	MB
S_{mem}^{plr}	Memory size required for PLR	MB
α	The number of disks attached to each server node [1], i.e. $\alpha = \frac{N_D}{N_S}$	

4.1 Data Placement Imbalance Analysis

With *PLR*, let the random variable X denote the number of packets assigned to a specific disk. As proposed in [3], uniformity of data distribution can be measured by the standard deviation and the coefficient of variation (CV) of X, represented by σ_X and $CV(X)$, respectively. $CV(X)$ can be derived from dividing σ_X by the mean value of X, μ_X. If we consider the random assignment of a packet to a disk as a Bernoulli trial, which has probability $p = \frac{1}{N_D}$ to be successfully allocated to a specific disk, then the total number of successful Bernoulli trials could be naturally mapped to X. Intuitively, X follows a Binomial distribution, where the number of Bernoulli trials is the total number of packets to be assigned, and denoted as M_P. Note that M_P can be computed as $M_P = \frac{M}{S_P}$, where M is the total data size and S_P is the packet size. Therefore, we can obtain

$$\mu_X = \frac{M}{S_P \times N_D}, \sigma_X = \sqrt{\frac{M \times (N_D-1)}{S_P \times N_D^2}}, CV(X) = \sqrt{\frac{(N_D-1) \times S_P}{M}} \times 100 \quad (1)$$

With *BLR*, let Y denote the number of blocks assigned to a disk. Furthermore, M_B represents the total data size in blocks. M_B can be calculated as $M_B = \frac{M}{S_B}$, where S_B denotes the block size. Similar to *PLR*, we obtain

$$\mu_Y = \frac{M}{S_B \times N_D}, \sigma_Y = \sqrt{\frac{M \times (N_D-1)}{S_B \times N_D^2}}, CV(Y) = \sqrt{\frac{(N_D-1) \times S_B}{M}} \times 100 \quad (2)$$

Let D_{PLR} and D_{BLR} denote the amount of data assigned to a disk with PLR and BLR, respectively. Then, D_{PLR} and D_{BLR} can be calculated by

$$D_{PLR} = XS_P, \quad D_{BLR} = YS_B \qquad (3)$$

Using Equations 1 and 3, we obtain the mean, standard deviation and coefficient of variation of D_{PLR} as expressed in Equation 4.

$$\mu_{D_{PLR}} = \frac{M}{N_D}, \quad \sigma_{D_{PLR}} = \sqrt{\frac{S_P^3 M(N_D-1)}{N_D^2}}, \quad CV(D_{PLR}) = \sqrt{\frac{(N_D-1) \times S_P^3}{M}} \times 100 \qquad (4)$$

Similarly, with Equation 3 and 2, we can obtain the mean, standard deviation and coefficient of variation of D_{BLR} as Equation 5.

$$\mu_{D_{BLR}} = \frac{M}{N_D}, \quad \sigma_{D_{BLR}} = \sqrt{\frac{S_B^3 M(N_D-1)}{N_D^2}}, \quad CV(D_{BLR}) = \sqrt{\frac{(N_D-1) \times S_B^3}{M}} \times 100 \qquad (5)$$

Finally, from Equations 4 and 5, we obtain:

$$\mu_{D_{BLR}} = \mu_{D_{PLR}}, \quad \frac{\sigma_{D_{BLR}}}{\sigma_{D_{PLR}}} = \frac{CV(D_{BLR})}{CV(D_{PLR})} = R^{\frac{3}{2}} \qquad (6)$$

where $R = \frac{S_B}{S_P}$. There are two important observations we obtain from Equation 6. First, the mean values of D_{BLR} and D_{PLR} are the same, which confirms that both the BLR and PLR schemes achieve the same level of load balancing in the long run as expected. Second, with respect to short term load balancing, PLR has a significant advantage over BLR.

Impact of Block to Packet Size Ratio R: Figure 2 shows the ratio of load imbalance $\frac{\sigma_{D_{BLR}}}{\sigma_{D_{PLR}}}$ as a function of the block to packet size ratio R. When R increases from 1 to 2,000, $\frac{\sigma_{D_{BLR}}}{\sigma_{D_{PLR}}}$ increases sharply from 1 to approximately 90,000. The figure clearly indicates the significant performance gain of PLR over BLR. In fact, 2,000 packets in one block is not unusual. For example, a 512 byte packet size and a 1 MB block size are a quite common configuration in streaming servers [7].

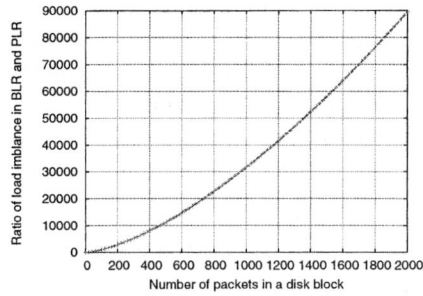

Fig. 2. Load imbalance ratio $\frac{\sigma_{D_{BLR}}}{\sigma_{D_{PLR}}}$, with different block to packet size ratio $R = \frac{S_B}{S_P}$

Table 2. Parameters for movie "Twister" used in analysis

Parameters	Configurations
Test movie "Twister"	MPEG-2 video, AC-3 audio
Average bandwidth	698,594 bytes/sec
Length	115 minutes
Throughput std. dev.	308,283.8
RTP packet size	512 bytes
Total number of RTP packets	10,740,000

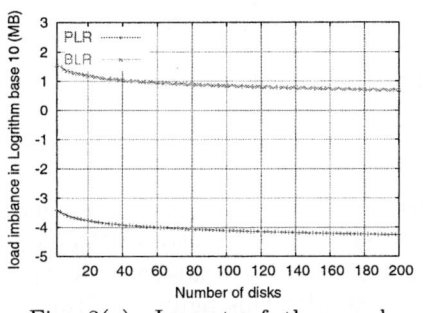
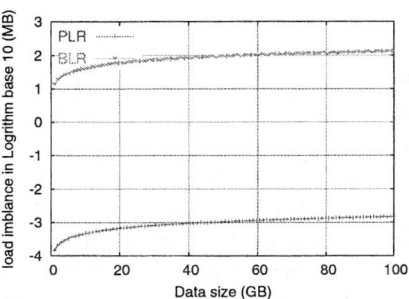

Fig. 3(a): Impact of the number of disks N_D based on DVD movie "Twister" (see Table 2).

Fig. 3(b): Impact of data size M, with $N_D = 4$, $S_P = 512$ bytes, and $R = 2,000$.

Fig. 3. Impact of the number of disks N_D and data size M on the standard deviation $\sigma_{D_{BLR}}$ and $\sigma_{D_{PLR}}$. Note that the figures are logarithmic in scale

Impact of the Number of Disks N_D: Figure 3(a) shows the standard deviation of the amount of data assigned to a disk in BLR and PLR, i.e., $\sigma_{D_{BLR}}$ and $\sigma_{D_{PLR}}$, respectively, as a function of the number of disks N_D on a logarithmic scale. Note that the data assigned is from the DVD movie "Twister" (see Table 2). As shown in the Figure 3(a), $\sigma_{D_{BLR}}$ is larger than $\sigma_{D_{PLR}}$ by several orders of magnitude, which implies that PLR allocates the movie data much more evenly across all the disks than BLR. Furthermore, when the total number of disks N_D increases from 2 to 200, $\sigma_{D_{BLR}}$ decreases from 35 MB to 5 MB. Similarly, $\sigma_{D_{PLR}}$ also follows this trend. In fact, we can formally prove that, if $N_D \geq 2$ and as N_D increases, $\sigma_{D_{BLR}}$ and $\sigma_{D_{PLR}}$ both decrease monotonically as given in Lemma 4.2.

Lemma 4.1. Let $A(n) = \frac{\sqrt{n-1}}{n}, \forall n \geq 2, A(n+1) < A(n)$.

Proof. $\forall n \geq 2, A(n) > 0$, thus, we need to prove Equation 7,

$$\frac{A(n+1)}{A(n)} < 1 \iff \sqrt{\frac{n^3}{(n+1)^2(n-1)}} < 1 \qquad (7)$$

To prove Equation 7, we need to show Equation 8.

$$n^3 - (n+1)^2(n-1) < 0 \qquad (8)$$

Equation 8 can be rewritten as $-[(n-1)^2 + (n-2)] < 0$, which is always true for all $n > 2$.

Lemma 4.2. $\forall N_D \geq 2$, if M, S_P and S_B are fixed, both $\sigma_{D_{PLR}}$ and $\sigma_{D_{BLR}}$ monotonically decrease as N_D increases.

Proof. Because S_P and M are constant, using Equation 4 and Lemma 4.1, it is straightforward to prove that, as N_D increases, $\sigma_{D_{PLR}}$ monotonically decreases. Similarly, since S_B and M are fixed, and using Equation 5 and Lemma 4.1, we can prove that, as N_D increases, $\sigma_{D_{BLR}}$ monotonically decreases.

Impact of the Data Size M: Figure 3(b) shows the load imbalance metric for both schemes as a function of the data size M. In the analysis, the total number of disks $N_D = 4$, packet size $S_P = 512$ bytes for *PLR*, and block to packet ratio $R = 2,000$ for *BLR*. As illustrated, as the data size M increases from 0 to 100 GB, the load imbalance metric of *BLR* $\sigma_{D_{BLR}}$ increases sharply from 0 to more than 120 MB. Similarly, the load imbalance metric of *PLR* $\sigma_{D_{PLR}}$ also increases, but because it is several orders of magnitude smaller than $\sigma_{D_{BLR}}$, $\sigma_{D_{PLR}}$ is still less than 2 Kbytes for $M = 100$ GB. This figure confirms that, when more data are loaded or recorded into the storage system, the imbalance of the amount of data assigned across all the disks will increase significantly, which explicitly shows the great performance gain of *PLR*. Next, we compare the disk load imbalance through the analysis of a streaming experiment.

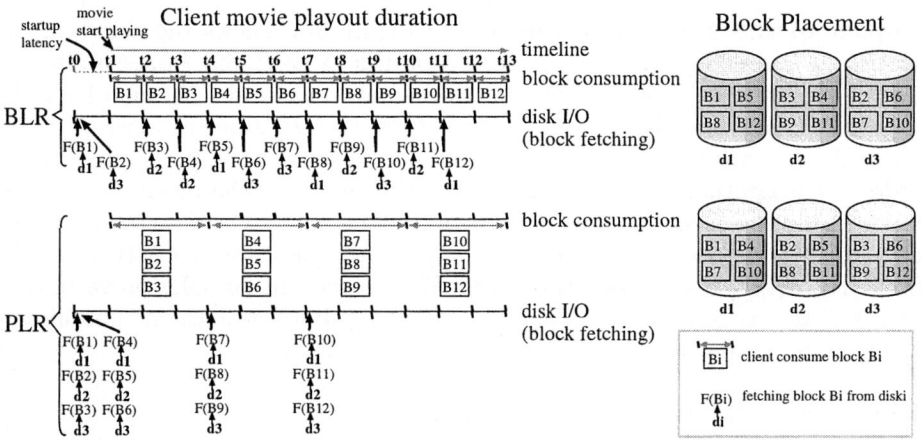

Fig. 4. Illustration of the disk I/O load imbalance during the playback of a CBR movie with $N_D = 3$ and $M_B = 12$ for both the *BLR* and *PLR* schemes

4.2 Disk I/O Imbalance Time Analysis

As suggested by [2], the disk load imbalance during a predefined measurement period is characterized by the *Global Standard Deviation* $\sigma_{B_{disk}}$, which is defined as the utilized disk I/O bandwidth of all the N_D disks [1], shown in Equations 9.

$$\sigma_{B_{disk}} = \sqrt{\frac{\sum_{i=1}^{N_D}(L_i - \mu_{B_{disk}})^2}{N_D}} \qquad (9)$$

where L_i denotes the utilized disk I/O bandwidth during the measurement period for disk i, $i \in [1, N_D]$ and $\mu_{B_{disk}}$ represents the mean value of the utilized disk I/O bandwidth and can be computed as:

$$\mu_{B_{disk}} = \frac{1}{N_D}\sum_{i=1}^{N_D} L_i \qquad (10)$$

Our experimental setup is as follows. Three disks ($N_D = 3$) are attached to a server. A client streams a constant bit rate (CBR) movie from the server, and the movie contains 12 blocks ($M_B = 12$) of size $S_B = 1$ MB. The movie consumption rate is 1 MB/s. Therefore, a block is consumed every second during the movie playback, and the movie length is 12 seconds. The server employs random data placement with deadline driven disk scheduling algorithm. Recall that the deadline of each block is set to the first packet in each block. A simple double buffering scheme is adopted for memory management.

Figure 4 shows a detailed analysis of all the disk I/O events during the playback of the movie. During the movie startup period, which is between time t0 and t1, the server prefetches some blocks. Because of double buffering, in *BLR* two blocks, $B1$ and $B2$, are prefetched, while in *PLR* six blocks are prefetched. A client starts the movie playback at time t1. With *BLR*, after every second when one block is consumed, the server fetches the next block. This process continues until the end of the movie. In *PLR*, the process is similar to *BLR* except that it takes 3 seconds from t1 to t4 for the client to consume blocks $B1$, $B2$ and $B3$. Note that because the randomness granularity is at the packet level, these three blocks are consumed almost at the same time. Subsequently, at time t4, blocks $B7$, $B8$ and $B9$ are fetched in parallel. A similar procedure is repeated at time t7 for blocks $B10$, $B11$ and $B12$. Note that *PLR* exploits the disk I/O parallelism naturally in this multi-disk environment. Table 3 summarizes the computed load imbalance for *BLR* and *PLR* based on Equations 9 and 10 for each second during the movie playback. Throughout the movie playback session, *PLR* perfectly balances the load, while *BLR* suffers from load imbalance with a global standard deviation value of 0.471 MB/s during more than 80% of the playout time. Next, we compare the impact of the memory size and its usage.

4.3 Memory Usage Analysis

Memory Size Requirement. Assuming that the same number of disks are attached to each storage server node and let N_S denote the total number of server

---

[1] We believe that in the analysis of storage systems, the absolute values are intuitively more understandable. Thus, we do not normalize the *Global Standard Deviation* by the mean value.

Table 3. Disk I/O imbalance computation results during the playback of a 12 seconds CBR movie for both *BLR* and *PLR* scheme

Parameters		Time Slots												
Scheme	Statistics (MB/s)	t0 -t1	t1 -t2	t2 -t3	t3 -t4	t4 -t5	t5 -t6	t6 -t7	t7 -t8	t8 -t9	t9 -t10	t10 -t11	t11 -t12	t12 -t13
BLR	L_1	1	0	0	0	1	0	0	1	0	0	0	1	0
	L_2	0	0	1	1	0	0	0	0	1	0	1	0	0
	L_3	1	0	0	0	0	1	1	0	0	1	0	0	0
	$\mu_{B_{disk}}$	0.67	0	0.33	0.33	0.33	0.33	0.33	0.33	0.33	0.33	0.33	0.33	0
	$\sigma_{B_{disk}}$	0.471	0	0.471	0.471	0.471	0.471	0.471	0.471	0.471	0.471	0.471	0.471	0
PLR	L_1	2	0	0	0	1	0	0	1	0	0	0	0	0
	L_2	2	0	0	0	1	0	0	1	0	0	0	0	0
	L_3	2	0	0	0	1	0	0	1	0	0	0	0	0
	$\mu_{B_{disk}}$	2	0	0	0	1	0	0	1	0	0	0	0	0
	$\sigma_{B_{disk}}$	0	0	0	0	0	0	0	0	0	0	0	0	0

nodes. Let us further assume that double buffering techniques are adopted in the system. In the *PLR*, the blocks from multiple disks within one server node can be accessed in parallel even for a single stream. Therefore, two buffers per disk are necessary for each *stream*. However, in *BLR*, because the blocks from multiple disks within one server node will be accessed sequentially for a single stream, only two buffers per server *node* are required for each stream. Accordingly, S_{mem}^{blr} and S_{mem}^{plr}, the memory size required for *BLR* and *PLR*, can be computed as

$$S_{mem}^{blr} = 2 \times S_B \times N_C \times N_S, \quad S_{mem}^{plr} = 2 \times S_B \times N_C \times N_D \qquad (11)$$

where N_C denotes the number of concurrent clients. We define α as the ratio between the total number of disks N_D and N_S, i.e, $\alpha = \frac{N_D}{N_S}$. Therefore, we obtain $\frac{S_{mem}^{plr}}{S_{mem}^{blr}} = \alpha$, which means that *PLR* requires more memory resources than *BLR* when more than one disk is attached to each server node.

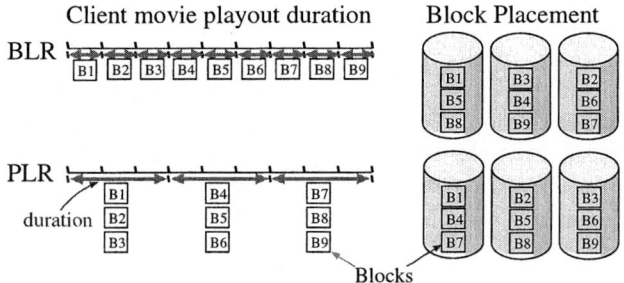

Fig. 5. Illustration of the memory access duration during the playback of a CBR (constant bit rate) movie with $N_D = 3$ and $M_B = 9$ for both the *BLR* and *PLR* techniques

Memory Access Duration. Figure 5 shows the *memory access duration* during the playback of a CBR (constant bit rate) movie with $N_D = 3$ and $M_B = 9$ for both the *BLR* and *PLR* techniques. It clearly shows that the access duration for a block in PLR is N_D times that of the BLR scheme. Intuitively, due to the finer granularity of randomness, the buffered blocks from multiple disks are used simultaneously, which naturally leads to much longer consumption time for each memory buffer. Because the memory access duration is the minimum time that the corresponding blocks must be kept in memory, we believe that PLR could potentially result in greater caching effects in the server.

5 Performance Evaluation

5.1 Experimental Setup

To evaluate the performance of PLR and BLR in a more practical environment, we integrated both the BLR and PLR methods into a simulation system. Fig. 6 illustrates the structure of our experimental setup.

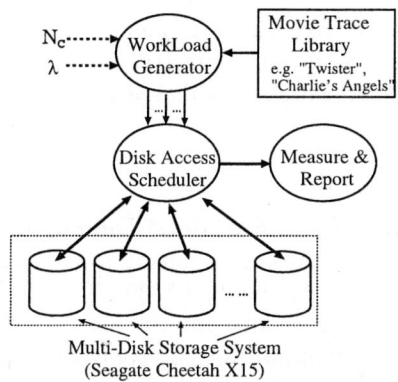

Fig. 6. Experimental system setup

Note that we did not integrate a full fledged streaming server into our simulation system to reduce the number of factors that would influence the results. The WorkLoad Generator produces stream requests based on a Poisson process with a mean inter-arrival time of $\lambda = 2$ seconds. Each stream retrieval produces data block requests based on either the PLR or BLR schemes with associated disk I/O deadlines according to movie traces from the Movie Trace Library. The movie blocks are allocated to disks in BLR or PLR schemes. The block requests are forwarded to the corresponding disk by the Disk Access Scheduler at the set times. The Measure & Report module generates the measured result. In a deadline driven streaming system, one of the most important parameters is the probability of a disk I/O request deadline miss, denoted p_{iodisk}. In the output report, both the number of requests with missed deadlines and the total number of disk block requests are collected. Furthermore, the ratio between these two numbers, which represents the fraction of the missed deadline requests, is interpreted as the probability of missed deadlines p_{iodisk}. The WorkLoad Generator has two configurable parameters: the mean inter-arrival time λ and the number

Table 4. Parameters used in the experiments

Parameters	Configurations
Test movie "Saving Private Ryan"	MPEG-2 video, AC-3 audio
Average bandwidth	757,258 bytes/sec
Length	50 minutes
Throughput std. dev.	169,743.6
Disk Model "Seagate Cheetah X15"	Model ST336752LC
Capacity	37 GB
Spindle speed	15,000 rpm
Avg. rotational latency	2 msec
Worst case seek time	$\approx$ 7 msec
Number of Zones	9
Transfer rate	See Fig.1(b) in [9]
Mean inter-arrival time λ of streaming request	2 seconds
Data Packet size S_P	0.5 KB
Disk block size S_B	1.0 MB
Number of disks N_D	4
Number of concurrent clients N_C	1, 2, 3, ..., 230

of movie streams N_C. In the experiments, we used the DVD movie "Saving Private Ryan," whose profile is shown in Fig.1(a) in [9]. Our disk system simulates four independent Seagate Cheetah X15 disk drives. Table 4 summarizes all the used parameters.

5.2 Experimental Results

Comparison Based on *Global Standard Deviation* $\sigma_{B_{disk}}$: Figure 7 shows the *global standard deviation* measured during streaming experiments with the number of concurrent clients N_C being 10, 20, 50, and 100, respectively. In all these four scenarios, *PLR* significantly improves the load balancing over *BLR* in the multi-disk system. For example, with 50 concurrent streams, *PLR* decreases the global standard deviation from 1.0721 MB/s to 0.3263 MB/s with $N_C = 50$ and from 1.4982 MB/s to 0.4593 MB/s with $N_C = 100$.

Figure 8(a) compares the general trend of the average global standard deviation during each experiment as a function of the number of concurrent streams N_C. As N_C increases, the average global standard deviation increases, which verifies our analysis results in Section 4.1. That is, as the data size M increases the imbalance also increases. Note that in all these measurement, *PLR* reduces the load imbalance significantly.

Comparison Based on the Probability of a Disk I/O Request Missed Deadline p_{iodisk}: To evaluate the performance impact of the two schemes *BLR* and *PLR* at the system level, we compared the measured results based on the probability of a disk I/O request missing its deadline. Figure 8(b) shows the measured p_{iodisk} as a function of the number of concurrent streams N_C for both *PLR* and *BLR*. With *PLR*, the system always experiences fewer disk I/O requests that missed their deadlines. For example, with 205 concurrent streams, the system reported 0% of the total I/O requests that missed their deadlines with *PLR*, compared to 37.91% with the *BLR* scheme. This implies that with the *PLR* scheme, the system can support more concurrent streams than with

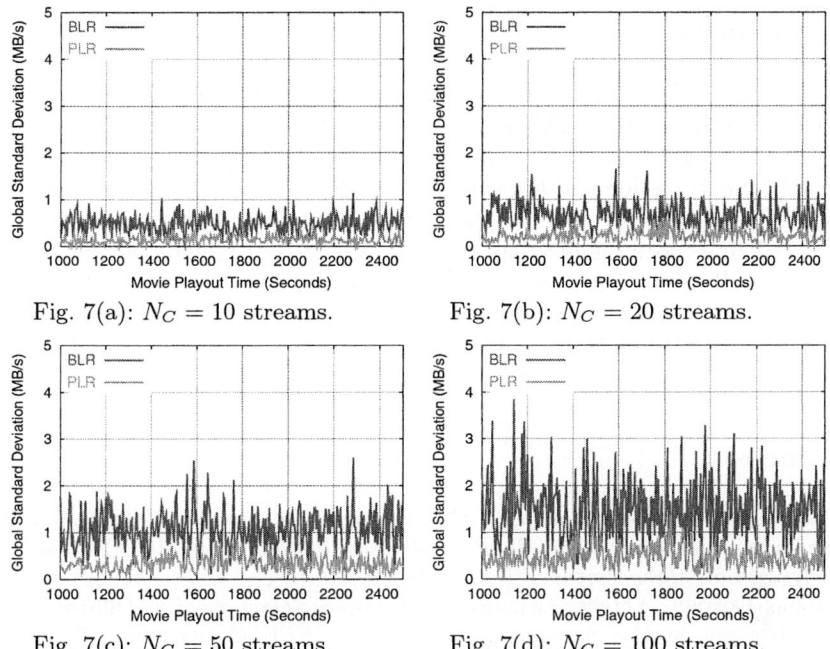

Fig. 7. Disk load imbalance across time for different number of concurrent DVD streams ("Saving Private Ryan"), where $N_C = 10$, 20, 50, and 100 respectively

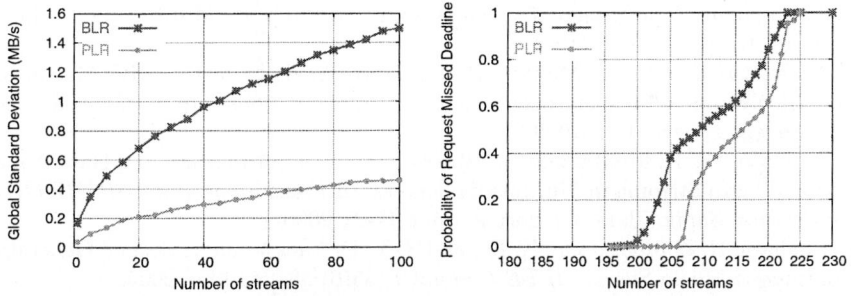

Fig. 8(a): The average disk load imbalance in terms of the global standard deviation with different number of streams.

Fig. 8(b): Probability of a request missed deadline with different number of streams.

Fig. 8. Important experimental results

the BLR scheme. Assuming that the end user can tolerate up to 1% of disk I/O request missed deadlines, then with PLR, the current experimental system setup could support 206 streams, but it can only support 199 streams with the BLR scheme, which is approximately a 3.5% improvement in terms of the number of supportable streams.

6 Conclusions

Load balancing is important to ensure overall good performance in a scalable multimedia storage system. This paper identifies and quantifies the performance trade-off of the packet level randomization (*PLR*) scheme over the traditional block level randomization (*BLR*) scheme. Both *BLR* and *PLR* ensures long term load balancing. But *PLR* achieves much better short term load balancing over *BLR* by utilizing more memory space. However, we believe the benefit of *PLR* outweighs its disadvantage since the cost of memory is continually decreasing. Therefore, *PLR* is a promising technique for high-performance media servers. Furthermore, we plan to implement the *PLR* approach into our streaming prototype, HYDRA, and evaluate its performance with real measurements.

References

1. S. Berson, S. Ghandeharizadeh, R. Muntz, and X. Ju. Staggered Striping in Multimedia Information Systems. In *Proceedings of the ACM SIGMOD International Conference on Management of Data*, 1994.
2. Antonio Corradi, Letizia Leonardi, and Franco Zambonelli. Diffusive load-balancing policies for dynamic applications. *IEEE Concurrency*, 7(1):22–31, January-March 1999.
3. A. Goel, C. Shahabi, S.-Y. D. Yao, and R. Zimmermann. SCADDAR: An Efficient Randomized Technique to Reorganize Continuous Media Blocks. In *Proceedings of the 18th International Conference on Data Engineering*, pages 473–482, February 2002.
4. V.G. Polimenis. The Design of a File System that Supports Multimedia. Technical Report TR-91-020, ICSI, 1991.
5. J. R. Santos and R. R. Muntz. Performance Analysis of the RIO Multimedia Storage System with Heterogeneous Disk Configurations. In *ACM Multimedia Conference*, Bristol, UK, 1998.
6. J. R. Santos, R. R. Muntz, and B. Ribeiro-Neto. Comparing Random Data Allocation and Data Striping in Multimedia Servers. In *Proceedings of the SIGMETRICS Conference*, Santa Clara, California, June 17-21 2000.
7. C. Shahabi, R. Zimmermann, K. Fu, and S.-Y. D. Yao. Yima: A Second Generation Continuous Media Server. *IEEE Computer*, 35(6):56–64, June 2002.
8. F.A. Tobagi, J. Pang, R. Baird, and M. Gang. Streaming RAID-A Disk Array Management System for Video Files. In *First ACM Conference on Multimedia*, August 1993.
9. Roger Zimmermann and Kun Fu. Comprehensive Statistical Admission Control for Streaming Media Servers. In *Proceedings of the 11th ACM International Multimedia Conference*, Berkeley, California, November 2-8, 2003.
10. Roger Zimmermann, Kun Fu, and Wei-Shinn Ku. Design of a large scale data stream recorder. In *The 5th International Conference on Enterprise Information Systems (ICEIS 2003), Angers - France*, April 23-26 2003.

Trace System of iSCSI Storage Access and Performance Improvement

Saneyasu Yamaguchi[1], Masato Oguchi[2], and Masaru Kitsuregawa[1]

[1] IIS, The University of Tokyo
{sane, kitsure}@tkl.iis.u-tokyo.ac.jp
[2] Ochanomizu University
oguchi@computer.org

Abstract. In this paper, an IP-SAN access trace method is proposed and its evaluation is presented. IP-SAN and iSCSI are expected to remedy problems of Fibre Channel (FC)-based SAN. Servers and storage cooperatively work with communications through TCP/IP in IP-SAN system, thus an integrated analysis of both sides is considered to be significant for achieving better performance.

Our system can precisely point out the cause of performance degradation when IP-SAN is used for a remote storage access. In experiment of parallel iSCSI access in a high-latency network, the total performance is limited by a parameter in an implementation of the SCSI layer in the iSCSI protocol stack. Based on the result obtained with our IP-SAN access trace system, the parameter in the layer is modified. As a result, more than 30 times performance improvement is achieved compared with the default value case. Thus it is effective to monitor all the layers in the iSCSI protocol stack and execute an integrated analysis, using our system.

1 Introduction

Recently, storage management cost is one of the most important issues of computer systems [1, 2]. Since periodical backup is required for management of storage, if the storage is distributed among many servers, its management cost is extremely high. Storage Area Network (SAN), a high speed network for storage, is introduced to resolve this issue. Each server is connected to consolidated storage devices through SAN. Management cost can be significantly decreased by the consolidation of storage, thus SAN has already become an important tool in the business field. However, current generation SAN based on FC has some demerits; for example, (1) the number of FC engineers is small, (2) installation cost of FC-SAN is high, (3) FC has distance limitation, (4) the interoperability of FC is not necessarily high.

The next generation SAN based on IP (IP-SAN) is expected to remedy these defects. IP-SAN employs commodity technologies for a network infrastructure, including Ethernet and TCP/IP. One of the promising standard data transfer protocol of IP-SAN is iSCSI [3], which was approved by IETF [4] in February

2003. IP-SAN has following advantages over FC-SAN [5, 6, 7]: (1) the number of IP engineers is large, (2) initial cost of IP-SAN is low, (3) IP has no distance limitation, (4) Ethernet and IP have no interoperability problem. However, the problem of low performance and high CPU utilization is pointed out as demerits of IP-SAN [6, 7, 8]. Thus improving its performance and keeping CPU utilization at low rate [6, 9] are critical issues for IP-SAN.

We clarify the performance issue of iSCSI in this paper. As an instance of evaluation, an iSCSI access in a high-latency network environment is investigated. This is because performance decline caused by network latency is pointed out in IP-SAN [2, 10], although iSCSI achieves almost comparable performance with that of FC-SAN in a LAN environment [5, 11]. A SCSI access over a high-latency network is an important in practice, since iSCSI has no distance limit. However, this issue has not been discussed enough, as far as we know.

An iSCSI storage access in IP-SAN is composed of many protocols, that is "SCSI over iSCSI over TCP/IP over Ethernet". The protocol stack of iSCSI is complicated and the storage access is executed through all these layers, so that any layers can be a performance bottleneck of end-to-end performance. Consequently, all these layers should be observed for improving iSCSI storage access performance. In addition, integrated analysis of the behavior of both server computers and storage appliances is important because iSCSI is composed of the protocol stack in both sides. In IP-SAN system, server computers and storage appliances work cooperatively via iSCSI protocol. However, they are monitored separately in general, because they have their own OSs. It is difficult to understand the whole system's behavior by monitoring only one side, thus the integrated analysis is inevitable.

In this paper, we propose an "IP-SAN trace system", which can monitor all the layers in IP-SAN protocol stack and show the integrated analysis of the whole IP-SAN system. Next, we apply the system to be proposed to parallel iSCSI accesses in a high-latency network, and demonstrate the system can point out the cause of performance decline. In our experiment, significant iSCSI performance improvement is achieved using the system.

Studies for CPU utilization during communications can be found in the literatures [6, 7, 9, 12, 13]. We do not discuss hardware-supported TCP processing in this paper, because literatures [5, 6, 7] concluded that although such hardware is effective for reducing CPU utilization, it does not achieve better performance than that of the software-based approach. We also evaluated the hardware-supported TCP processing by ourselves and obtained a similar result: In our experiments, TCP/IP communication throughput and CPU utilization with software TCP/IP implementation are 70.4 [MB/sec] and 27.5 %, respectively. Throughput and CPU utilization with TCP/IP offload engine (TOE) are 63.1 [MB/sec] and 10.4%, respectively.

The rest of this paper is organized as follows. We propose "IP-SAN Trace System" in Section 3, and present its evaluation by an actual adaptation of the system in Section 4. Section 2 introduces the related work. In Section 5, we conclude this paper.

2 Related Work

Some studies present performance evaluation of IP-SAN using iSCSI [2, 5, 6, 7, 10, 11]. These evaluations and discussions are significantly important for understanding IP-SAN performance and impact of each factor on performance. However, these studies are obtained by executing various workloads outside the IP-SAN system. Consequently, these studies do not reveal accurate behaviors inside IP-SAN systems. Our work presents very exact behaviors inside the IP-SAN system including those in kernel space, for example process scheduler, the SCSI layer, iSCSI layer and the TCP/IP layer. This monitoring is the novelty of our work. In addition, our work can point out the cause of performance decline by applying the proposed system while existing studies give experimental results. This is another novel point of our work. Our work analyses IP-SAN from broad perspective to focused perspective. In broad perspective, the system can trace from issuing system call at an initiator host to a storage access in a target host, and it can visualize a whole access. In focused perspective, the system can trace a behavior at kernel source code level. Thus, very detailed behaviors can be monitored. These are also characteristic points of our work.

Fujita et al. [8] presented an analysis of iSCSI targets. The work gave out not only performance evaluations but also discussions including the iSCSI target implementation and kernel implementation. This discussion also mentions behaviors inside IP-SAN system, but the objective of their work and that of our work are different. Their work highlights the analysis of an iSCSI target while our objective is constructing an integrated trace system including both an initiator and a target.

3 IP-SAN Trace System

In this section, we will introduce the proposed "IP-SAN Trace System" in detail.

We have implemented a monitoring system which monitors behaviors of all the layers in IP-SAN. We have also constructed an integrated trace system which comprehensively analyzes logs recorded in both server computes and storage appliances. In our experiments, open source codes of an OS implementation and an iSCSI driver are used. We inserted monitoring codes into these implementations for recording IP-SAN system's behavior. Linux (kernel version 2.4.18) is adopted as an OS implementation and iSCSI reference implementation (version 1.5.02) [14] developed by University of New Hampshire's InterOperability Lab [15] (we call this implementation "UNH") is used as an iSCSI driver.

Figure 1 shows an example of a visualized iSCSI trace obtained by the trace system. In the figure, Y-Axis stands for the state transition of iSCSI storage access. Each label beside Y-Axis indicates each layer in the iSCSI protocol stack. Meanings of these labels (Init_syscall, Init_raw_dev and so on) are; 1) system calls issued by applications, 2) the raw device layer, 3) the SCSI layer, 4) the iSCSI layer, 5) the TCP/IP layer, 6) Packet transmission by the Ethernet layer, 7) the TCP/IP layer, 8) the iSCSI layer, 9) the SCSI layer, 10) HDD device

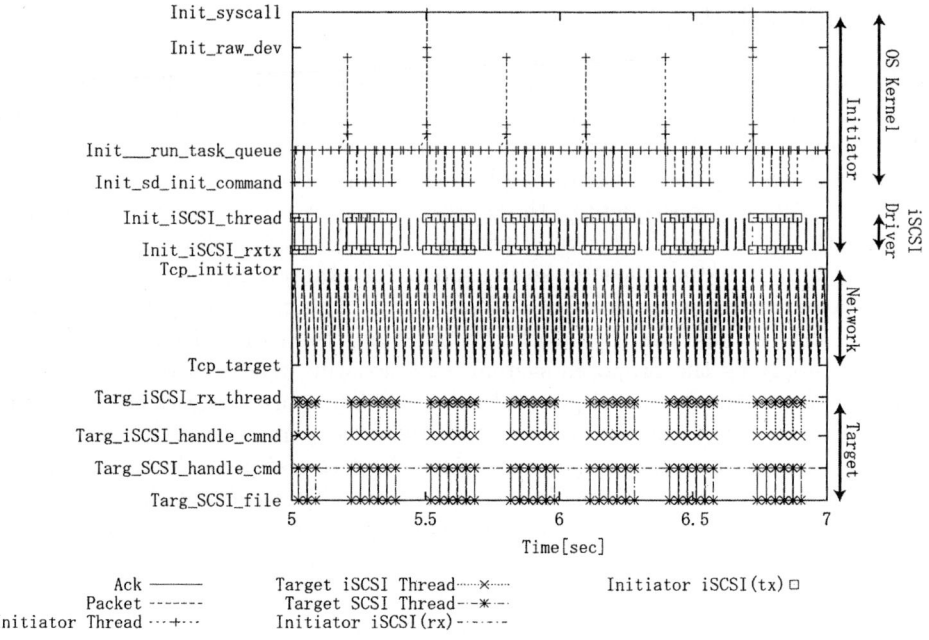

Fig. 1. iSCSI Access Trace

access from the top to the bottom respectively. The labels from 1) to 5) belong to processes in server computers (iSCSI initiator) and the labels from 7) to 10) belong to processes in storage appliance (iSCSI target). In this case, we have used raw device mode instead of file system mode in the iSCSI initiator. The iSCSI target works with "File Mode" of UNH implementation[1], thus the trace in the lowest layer is not that of HDD device access but that of file access in the target OS's file system. X-Axis stands for the time of each trace.

Figure 1 helps to understand IP-SAN's behavior. For example, Figure 1 indicates which process in iSCSI protocol stack dominantly consumes time, in which layer processes are waiting for I/O responses, and a block of the issued I/O requests are divided into small blocks by some layers. In the case of this figure, an application issues a system call read() with 2MB block size. The raw device layer divides it into 4 blocks of 512KB, then issues 512KB I/O requests one by one to the lower layer (the SCSI layer), finally it returns I/O responses to the upper layer (the system call layer) after completing 4 requests. After the SCSI layer receives 512KB I/O requests, it divides the requests into multiple 32KB SCSI read commands and transfers them to the lower layer (the iSCSI layer). iSCSI tx_thread is activated when requests are sent from the SCSI layer, and the iSCSI layer transfers the requests to the TCP/IP layer. The TCP layer sends data segments to the Ethernet layer, and the Ethernet layer sends them to the storage appliance (target computer).

---

[1] UNH implementation can export a local file to initiator as a storage image.

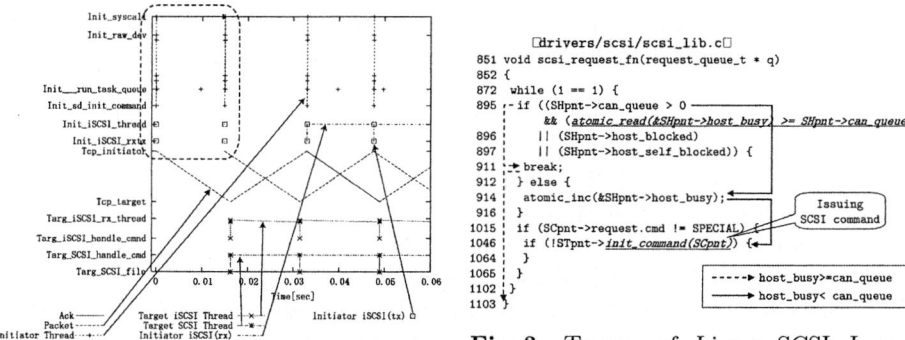

Fig. 2. Visualized Trace of Parallel iSCSI Access: (A)

Fig. 3. Trance of Linux SCSI Layer: "drivers/scsi/scsi_lib.c"

Figure 2 shows an example of a visualized traces in the case of parallel iSCSI accesses (the area surrounded by the dotted line will be mentioned in Section 4.3). According to the figure, each system call issued at the initiator is received at the target and processed on it. Cooperation of the initiator and the target can be understood easily with this figure.

The proposed system monitors the IP-SAN's behavior by insertion of monitor codes into the source codes, thus the system can observe the behavior of the kernel and the iSCSI driver at source code level. For example, this system records which way is selected in a branch like Figure 3. These figures will be mentioned in Section 4.3 again.

As shown above, the whole IP-SAN's behavior can be easily understood with the trace system.

4 Evaluation

In this section, we evaluate the proposed system by actually applying it to IP-SAN. In addition, we show that the proposed system can point out the cause of performance decline.

4.1 Experimental Setup

The proposed system is applied to a short block of parallel iSCSI accesses in a high-latency network environment. We have constructed a high-latency IP-SAN environment by inserting a network delay emulator between an iSCSI initiator (server computer) and an iSCSI target (storage appliance). The network delay emulator is constructed with FreeBSD Dummynet [16]. The initiator and the target establish TCP connection over the delay emulator and an iSCSI connection is established over this TCP connection.

The connections between the initiator and the delay emulator, and between the delay emulator and the target, are established with Gigabit Ethernet. The UNH iSCSI implementation (refer to Section 3) is employed as iSCSI initiator and target implementation. Since the iSCSI target works with "File Mode", the following experiments do not include actual HDD device accesses. One way delay time is 16 ms.

The initiator, the Dummynet and the target are built with PCs. The detailed specifications of the initiator and the target PC are as follows: CPU Pentium4 2.80GHz, Main Memory 1GB, OS Linux 2.4.18-3, NIC Gigabit Ethernet Card Intel PRO/1000 XT Server Adapter. The detailed specifications of Dummynet PC are as follows: CPU Pentium4 1.5GHz, Main Memory 128MB, OS FreeBSD 4.5-RELEASE, NIC Intel PRO/1000 XT Server Adapter×2.

We have executed the following benchmark in this experimental environment. The benchmark software iterates issuing system call read() to raw device which is established with an iSCSI connection. The block size of the read requests is 512 Bytes. The addresses to be read do not have an impact on experimental performance because of file system cache on target side (which will be mentioned later in this section). We executed multiple processes simultaneously and measured total performance of all processes. Each benchmark process iterates 2048 times system call read(). In this environment, the issued system calls are always transmitted to the SCSI layer in the target side without any cache hit in the initiator side, because the benchmark processes issue system calls to the raw device. These experiments are executed when target storage image in file (the iSCSI target is executed with "File Mode") is stored in file system's cache on the target (worm cache). Consequently, all read requests issued from the initiator reach the SCSI layer in the target side and hit file system cache on the target side, thus it does not include HDD device access. We have employed the file mode iSCSI target in order to separate the efficiency of the behavior of IP-SAN system from that of the HDD device. Although behavior of HDD device is also important in IP-SAN performance study, it strongly depends on implementation of the product and it is not the dominant factor in a high-latency network environment.

Experiments in Section 4.2 and Section 4.4 are executed without the monitoring system, thus the performances shown in Fig. 4 and Fig. 8 are not effected by the monitoring system.

4.2 Experimental Results

The experimental results with default setup, which does not have any tuning, are shown as "can_queue = 2 (default)" in Fig. 4. The other line (can_queue=30) is explained later in Section 4.4. X-Axis in the figure stands for the number of processes executed simultaneously. Y-Axis stands for the number of total transactions of all processes per second. The number of transactions means the number of 512 Bytes system calls read().

The result shows that performance improvement with increasing number of processes stops when the number of processes is two. It indicates that a layer in the protocol stack restricts number of simultaneous process to two in parallel access.

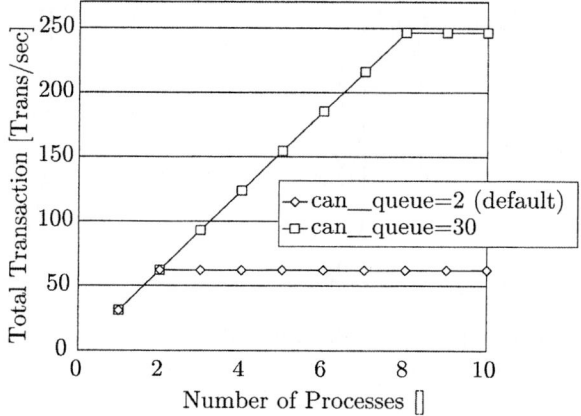

Fig. 4. Experimental Result A: Total performance of parallel I/O, 16ms (default setup)

4.3 Trace Analysis of Parallel iSCSI Access

In this subsection, we present an analysis of the trace to determine a cause of the restriction for parallel processing and demonstrate that the proposed system can point out the cause of performance decline.

Analysis of the Trace Across Multiple Layers. The trace is analyzed across multiple layers of iSCSI at first. Figure 2 is obtained by analyzing traced logs of the experiment in Section 4.1 and Section 4.2. The number of processes is three. The trace lines of "Initiator Thread" are drawn discontinuously in the figure. This is because context switches are issued by OS's process scheduler, and the processes are suspended and resumed on these lines. Plots at 0.010 [sec] and 0.040 [sec] also indicate context switches by the process scheduler. Although the scheduler allocates CPU resources to the processes at these points, the processes are waiting for I/O response at that time, thus they immediately invoke context switches and release CPU resources. According to the figure, only two I/O requests are sent from the initiator to the target within RTT (32ms). This indicates the number of I/O requests processed concurrently is restricted in the initiator side.

Figure 5 is obtained by magnifying the area surrounded by the dotted line in Fig. 2. Figure 6 shows the magnified view of the area surrounded by the dotted line in Fig. 5. In these figures, three processes running concurrently are drawn, labeled as "I/O(A)", "I/O(B)", and "I/O(C)". Traced lines are shown discontinuously like Fig. 2. The lines terminate when context switch occurs and processes resume. Figure 5 shows that I/O(A), (B), and (C) issue a system call at 0.000 [sec], 0.015 [sec] and 0.015[sec] respectively. According to the figure, three system calls can be issued within one RTT, without receiving any response from the target.

The trace of "I/O(A)" shows that the request by "I/O(A)" is transferred through the raw device layer, the SCSI layer, and the iSCSI layer, then the

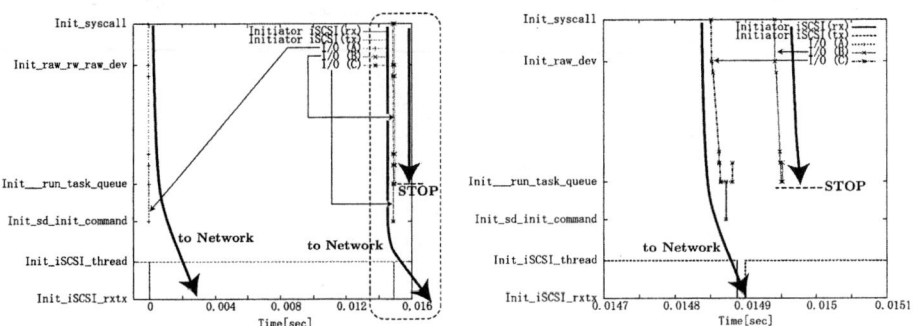

Fig. 5. Visualized Trace of Parallel iSCSI Access: (B)

Fig. 6. Visualized Trace of Parallel iSCSI Access: (C)

iSCSI layer issues a request to the TCP/IP layer. Figure 6 shows that "I/O(C)" issues a system call at 0.01485 [sec], and the request is transferred up to the iSCSI layer and sent to the network.

On the other hand, in the case of "I/O(B)", the issued request is not sent to the iSCSI layer. A system call is issued by "I/O(B)" at 0.01494 [sec], and the raw device layer also issues the I/O request to the lower layer (the SCSI layer) after the issue of the system call. However, the SCSI layer returns without issuing a SCSI command even though the layer has received the request. This result indicates that the maximum number of SCSI commands issued simultaneously is restricted to two in the SCSI layer, which is considered to be the cause of the upper limit of total performance.

Analysis of the Trace Inside a Layer. The trace is analyzed more precisely, focusing on a particular layer, which is determined in the previous analysis. The proposed system can trace the behavior inside an IP-SAN system in source code level.

The branch point of the first two requests (I/O(A) and (C)) and the third request (I/O(B)) is in "drivers/scsi/scsi_lib.c" in the implementation of Linux SCSI layer, as shown in Fig. 3. This part in Linux SCSI implementation compares "host_busy" [2], the number of active commands, and "can_queue" [3], the maximum number of SCSI commands the lower layer (iSCSI driver implementation in our case) can receive simultaneously. The default value of "can_queue" in the UNH iSCSI implementation is 2.

At the beginning, "host_busy" is 0. In the cases of the first two I/O requests (I/O(A) and (C)), "host_busy" are 0 and 1 respectively, thus the route labeled as "host_busy<can_queue" in the figure is traced. In this route, incrementing

---

[2] "host_busy" is explained as "commands actually active on low-level" in Linux SCSI implementation "drivers/scsi/hosts.h".

[3] "can_queue" is explained as "max no. of simultaneously active SCSI commands driver can accept" in the UNH iSCSI implementation "initiator/iscsi_initiator.c".

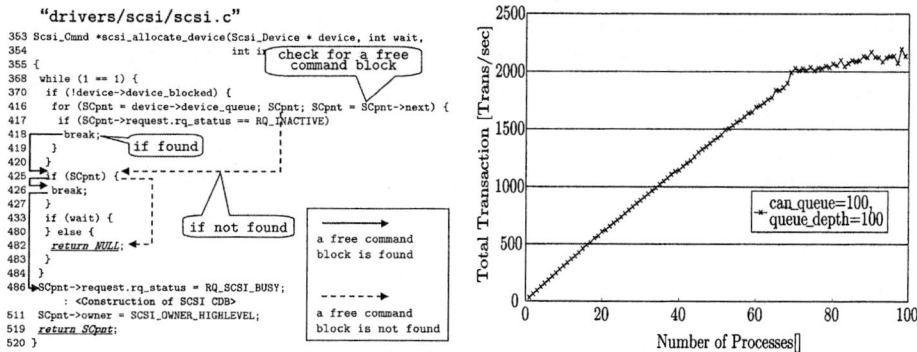

Fig. 7. Trance of Linux SCSI Layer: "drivers/scsi/scsi.c"

Fig. 8. Experimental Result C: Total performance of parallel I/O, 16ms

"host_busy" at line 914 and issuing a SCSI command at line 1046 are recorded. In the case of the third I/O request (I/O(B)), "host_busy" is 2, thus the route labeled as "host_busy>=can_queue" in the figure is traced. In this route, a SCSI command is not issued as shown in the figure.

These analyses of the SCSI layer, which are determined in the proposed analysis system, point out that the upper limit of the total performance of parallel I/O requests is decided by the iSCSI implementation's default value of "can_queue".

4.4 Resolving the Pointed Out Issue

We measure the total performance of concurrent iSCSI accesses with "can_queue" = 30 and obtained "can_queue = 30" in Fig. 4. The total performance of all processes increases linearly from single process to eight processes. Four times performance improvement is achieved when the number of processes is greater than 8 by resolving the cause (problem) of the performance decline pointed out by the proposed analysis system.

4.5 Analysis After Resolving the Issue

The restriction of number of simultaneous processing can reach eight. We adopt the proposed system again for resolving the next restriction. It can be found that the next restriction also exists in the SCSI layer by analysis of the trace across multiple layers. Analysis of the trace inside a layer shows that the branch point is in "scsi_allocate_devide" in "drivers/scsi/scsi.c" in the Linux SCSI layer implementation (refer to Fig. 7).

This part of the implementation works for finding a free SCSI command block from a block queue and creating a SCSI command block. In the cases of the previous eight requests, the routes labeled with "a free command block is found" are recorded. A free block is found at line 417 (SCpnt is not NULL) and a

SCSI command block is created. On the other hand, in the cases of after the ninth request, The routes labeled with "a free command block is not found" is recorded. Although a free block is searched at line 416, no free block is found and NULL is returned. In other words, creating a new SCSI command block fails. These trace analysis indicates that the restriction to eight is caused by the length of a queue for command blocks. The queue length is called "queue_depth" in Linux implementation and it is specified by the lower layer implementation (the UNH iSCSI implementation in this case). The default value of "queue_depth" is eight.

4.6 Resolving the Pointed Out Issue

We got the result shown in Fig. 8 with "can_queue"=100 and "queue_depth" = 100. The total performance improves almost linearly to 69 simultaneous processes by resolving the pointed out issue. The total performance with 69 processes and 98 processes are 1992.9 [Trans/sec] and 2195.0 [Trans/sec], respectively. The performance before adopting the proposed system is 61.9 [Trans/sec], then 32.2 times and 35.3 times performance up were gained, respectively.

As we have shown, the integrated analysis of both server computers and storage appliances, monitoring all layers from application's system calls to HDD device access in the iSCSI protocol stack, is an effective method for improving iSCSI performance. We have demonstrated it by applying the system to an actual IP-SAN system so that the proposed system can properly point out the cause of performance limit, and the performance is significantly improved by resolving the pointed out issue.

5 Conclusion

In this paper, we proposed an integrated IP-SAN trace method, implemented a system based on the idea, and demonstrated that the system could precisely point out the cause of performance decline. It has been proved that iSCSI performance can be significantly increased by resolving the pointed out issue. In the case of our experiments, more than 30 times performance improvement has been obtained in the case of simultaneous read calls. Thus we can say that monitoring all the layers in the iSCSI protocol stack and executing an integrated analysis including both server computers and storage appliances are effective for improving iSCSI performance.

We plan to explore the following matters as a future work. In this paper, we selected raw device as an upper layer of the SCSI layer. The iSCSI target driver worked with "File Mode". We plan to analyze IP-SAN's behavior using a file system and actual HDD devices. We also plan to evaluate an overhead of the proposed analysis system.

References

1. Neema, F., Waid, D.: Data Storage Trend. In: UNIX Review, 17(7). (1999)
2. Ng, W.T., Shriver, B.H.E., Gabber, E., Ozden, B.: Obtaining High Performance for Storage Outsourcing. In: Proc. FAST 2002, USENIX Conference on File and Storage Technologies. (2002) 145–158
3. Satran, J., et al.: Internet Small Computer Systems Interface (iSCSI), http://www.ietf.org/rfc/rfc3720.txt (2004)
4. : IETF Home Page, http://www.ietf.org/ (2004)
5. Aiken, S., Grunwald, D., Pleszkun, A.: A Performance Analysis of the iSCSI Protocol. In: IEEE/NASA MSST2003 Twentieth IEEE/Eleventh NASA Goddard Conference on Mass Storage Systems and Technologies. (2003)
6. Sarkar, P., Uttamchandani, S., Voruganti, K.: Storage over IP: When Does Hardware Support help? In: Proc. FAST 2003, USENIX Conference on File and Storage Technologies. (2003)
7. Sarkar, P., Voruganti, K.: IP Storage: The Challenge Ahead. In: Proc. of Tenth NASA Goddard Conference on Mass Storage Systems and Technologies. (2002)
8. Tomonori, F., Masanori, O.: Analisys fo iSCSI Target Software. In: SACSIS (Symposium on Advanced Computing Systems and Infrastructures) 2004. (2004) (in Japanese).
9. Mogul, J.C.: Tcp offload is a dumb idea whose time has come. In: 9th Workshop on Hot Topics in Operating Systems (HotOS IX). (2003)
10. Radkov, P., Yin, L., Goyal, P., Sarkar, P., Shenoy, P.: A performance Comparison of NFS and iSCSI for IP-Networked Storage. In: Proc. FAST 2004, USENIX Conference on File and Storage Technologies. (2004)
11. Lu, Y., Du, D.H.C.: Performance Study of iSCSI-Based Storage Subsystems. IEEE Communications Magazine (2003)
12. Clark, D.D., Jacobson, V., Romkey, J., Salwen, H.: An Analysis of TCP Processing Overhead. IEEE Communications Magazine **27(6)** (1989) 94–101
13. Shivam, P., Chase, J.S.: On the Elusive Benefits of Protocol Offload. In: Proceedings of the ACM SIGCOMM workshop on Network-I/O convergence: Experience, Lessons, Implications. (2003) 179–184
14. : iSCSI reference implementation, http://www.iol.unh.edu/consortiums/iscsi/downloads.html (2004)
15. : University of new hampshire interoperability lab, http://www.iol.unh.edu/ (2004)
16. Rizzo, L.: dummynet, http://info.iet.unipi.it/~luigi/ip_dummynet/ (2004)

CoCache: Query Processing Based on Collaborative Caching in P2P Systems

Weining Qian, Linhao Xu, Shuigeng Zhou, and Aoying Zhou

Department of Computer Science and Engineering, Fudan University
{wnqian, xulh, sgzhou, ayzhou}@fudan.edu.cn

Abstract. In this paper, we propose CoCache, a P2P query processing architecture that enables sophisticated optimization techniques. CoCache is different from existing P2P query processing systems in three ways. First, a coordinator overlay network (CON) maintaining the summary of the whole system is constructed by applying DHT technique to query plan trees. CON protocol ensures the efficiency for handling dynamic environments. Second, a preliminary cost-based optimization technique for retrieving appropriate cached copies of data is studied. With the help of CON, we show the possibility of fine optimization in even large scale and dynamic environments. Third, the collaborative caching strategy is presented, with which even small portion of cache storage on each peer may result in great improvement on query processing performance. Extensive experiments over real-world and synthetic settings show the effectiveness and efficiency of CoCache.

1 Introduction

Enabling query processing is a natural extension of key and keyword based search in existing P2P systems [2, 8, 1, 5, 12]. There are several challenges to implement complex query answering functionalities in P2P systems. First of all, as in any P2P system, peers can join and leave the system anytime, anywhere and anyhow, which results in a purely dynamic and ad hoc network environment. Thus, the underlying protocol should be robust enough to handle peer and network failure. Secondly, a full decentralized process must be adopted for query processing. In a dynamic P2P environment, due to the lack of global knowledge, both query execution and optimization become difficult. At last, the collaboration of autonomous peers is essential to fully take advantage of the resources in the system. This usually involves more optimization issues, such as coordination, locality-aware peer clustering, and load balancing. In summary, P2P query processing should be effective and efficient for handling a large scale of *autonomous* peers in *dynamic* and *distributed* networks.

In this paper, we present CoCache, a query processing system with collaborative cache. Caching or replication is widely adopted in centralized and distributed systems, which has several advantages. First, data is available even when the source is temporarily inaccessible. Second, since the retrieval of cached data is usually much cheaper than that of the source, caching is often used as an optimization technique for decreasing latency. Finally, in distributed systems, cached objects become partial copies of source that can serve different requests from different machines at different time. Hence, caching is also employed in many P2P systems and studied intensively [4, 14, 3, 12].

CoCache is different from existing P2P systems using cache. First, each peer collaborates with other ones to determine what to be cached. Intuitively, a peer tends to the cache data complementary to cached data in nearby peers. Furthermore, both the caching process and query processing, i.e. the process to find cached or source data, are fully decentralized based on a distributed hash table (DHT) scheme, called CON, for Coordinator Overlay Network. The third difference is the cost-based optimization employed in dynamic environments. Query answering performance is improved greatly with low overhead for maintaining CON. In summary, our contributions are as follows:

- A P2P query processing framework, CoCache, is designed with a DHT-based subnet, CON, which is used to index both data sources and caches.
- A cost-based optimization scheme is introduced to CoCache. With low overhead of statistics exchanging, query performance can be improved greatly.
- An implementation of the collaborative caching strategy and experimental results show that even a small portion of storage devoted for caching on each peer can improve the performance of query processing greatly.

The rest of the paper is organized as follows. Section 2 introduces the architecture and protocol of CoCache. Section 3 presents both query processing and optimization scheme. Section 4 describes the details of implementation for collaborative caching. Section 5 shows the experimental evaluation of CoCache. Section 6 reviews the related work and Section 7 concludes the paper.

2 The Architecture of CoCache

2.1 The CoCache and CON Networks

A peer may take different roles in CoCache network: a *requester* is a peer who issues one or more queries. A *source peer* is a peer whose database is accessible by other ones. A *caching peer* is a requester who caches result(s) of its queries or subqueries. Both source peers and caching peers are called *providers*. A *coordinator* is a peer in charge of maintaining information about a specific query expression. The information includes the providers that can provide data to answer the query, the locality information of the providers, and the coordinators corresponding to the sub- and super-expressions. The coordinators are also responsible to coordinate the requesters to determine which part of data to be cached by which peer.

Figure 1 (a) illustrates the architecture of a CoCache network. A CoCache network can be an arbitrary peer-to-peer network[1]. Each peer may share its data

---
[1] Currently, CoCache is developed based on BestPeer[7].

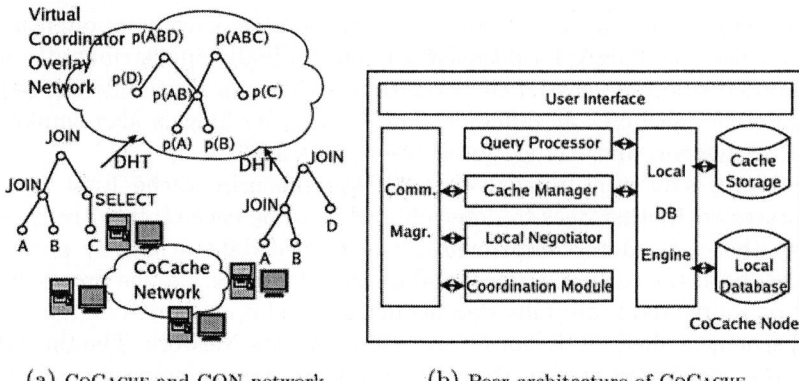

Fig. 1. Archiecture of CoCache network and nodes

with other peers and pose queries. Each node in the query plans is mapped to a specific node via distributed hash table (DHT), who will become the coordinator of the query expression. A coordinator maintains a finger table in which each entry points to the coordinator of a super- or sub-query expression. The coordinators form a *virtual* coordinator overlay network (CON), that is embedded in CoCache. The architecture of a node in CoCache network is shown in Figure 1 (b). Different from other peer data management systems, each node is equipped with two modules called *Local Negotiator* and *Coordination Module*. The former module takes the responsibility of negotiating with coordinators to determine what data should be cached, while the later is in charge of the coordination among the requesters for collaborative caching when the node becomes a coordinator.

A query is represented by a relational calculus expression[2], which can be transformed to a query tree. The peer identifier $p(v)$ of the coordinator corresponding to a node v in the tree is determined by using the following rules:

1. If v is a leaf node, $p(v) = h(v)$, in which $h()$ is a general purpose hash function, such as MD5 or SHA.
2. For node v corresponding to a unitary operator, such as σ or π, $p(v) = p(v')$ in which v' is the child of v.
3. For node v corresponding to a binary operator, i.e. $\bowtie$, $p(v) = p(v_1)|p(v_2)$, in which v_1 and v_2 are the children of v, and $|$ means bitwise OR of two bit strings.

Thus, given a query, the coordinator of each sub-query can be determined by using consistent hashing $h()$. Coordinator $p(v)$ is also called the *host* of node v.

Each coordinator maintains a finger table, in which entries are coordinators corresponding to parent and children nodes in the query tree. Formally,

---

[2] In this paper, we do not consider the equivalence of two query expressions.

given a query q, v is a node in the query tree, while v', v_1 and v_2 are parent, children nodes of v respectively. Then, $< v', v, p(v') >$, $< v, v_1, p(v_1) >$ and $< v, v_2, p(v_2) >$ are three entries in peer $p(v)$'s finger table. Note that for coordinators corresponding to more than one query expressions, the hosts of parent and children nodes in each query should be included in the finger table. The peers in the finger table are called its *neighboring coordinators*.

The coordinators are logical peers. In a P2P network, it is possible that there is no peer whose identifier is the same as the identifier of a specific coordinator. Different P2P platforms use different ways for handling this kind of problems. Chord, for example, uses the peer whose peer-id is the first one follows a specific identifier in the identifier space to be responsible for the tasks assigned to that specific identifier [13]. Another popular P2P platform CAN uses the closest peer in the torus-like identifier space to take over the tasks for a specific identifier [10]. COCACHE is implemented on top of a hybrid P2P system, BestPeer [7], in which superpeers, called LIGLO servers, are responsible for this physical-logical identifier mapping task. It should be noted that although BestPeer is chosen as the bottom platform, COCACHE is independant of underground layer. It can be moved to other P2P platforms with few modifications.

Peer Join. When joining a COCACHE network, a requester first determines the coordinators corresponding to its queries. Then, the queries along with the peer information, such as peer identifier, locality information and other statistics about the peer, is sent to the coordinators. The requester also collects information about the cached data from the coordinators. Thus, a query plan is generated, and evaluated by retrieving data from providers in the query plan[3]. If a requester agrees to cache data, it informs the coordinators of the cache. The coordinators updates their local index when new caching peer's notification is received. When a coordinator has collected a set of updates of caching peers, it initiates a re-caching process, which is introduced in Section 4.

It is possible that a new arrival peer's identifier is more suitable for a logical coordinator than the current one's. The new peer takes over the information of the old coordinator including the finger table. Then, it sends update information to all neighboring coordinators, so that they can update their finger tables.

Peer Leave. For the leave of a requester or provider, or the drop of a query by a requester, the leaving peer informs the coordinators to update their indexed information. If the leaving peer is a coordinator, it contacts the next suitable peer in the system to take over the coordination information. It also informs its neighboring coordinators to update their finger tables to point to the new one.

Failure Handling. A peer may leave the system due to power, hardware or network failure. In such cases, a peer may not be able to inform other peers or coordinators. A failure may be detected by various ways. The failure of a coordinator may be found due to a connection failure of a neighboring coordinator

---

[3] The details of query processing are introduced in the next section.

or a requester, while the failure of a provider may be detected when a requester tries to retrieve data from the failed peer. In CoCache, each requester sends the information about its queries to the coordinators periodically. When a coordinator fails, the information is routed to the new coordinator, which takes over the work of failed one automatically. When a peer notices the failure of a provider, it informs the corresponding coordinators to update the index. The coordinator then forward this message to all requesters that are registered to retrieve data from the failed peer[4].

3 Query Processing in CoCache

A cache is a binary tuple (v, N), in which v is the logical expression, and N is a multiset of peers, which is called the *container* of the cache. For each occurance $p \in N$, peer p contributes fixed size of storage space to caching data of logical expression v. Note that a source peer can be treated as a special cache, whose v is the data source, and N is the set only having the peer itself.

A *query plan* of a query q is a set of caches $P\{(v_i, N_i)\}$ satisfied that $\bigcup_i R(v_i) \supseteq R(q)$, in which $R(v_i)$ and $R(q)$ mean the relations with logical expressions v_i and q respectively. The cost of a query plan is defined as

$$cost_q(q|P) = \sum_{i, v_i \in P} c(v_i \to p_q) + C(\{v_i\}, q) \qquad (1)$$

in which $c(v_i \to p_q)$ is the cost for transmitting cache (v_i, N_i) to requester p_q, while $C(\{v_i\}, q)$ is the computation cost to evaluate query q given cached data.

Algorithm 1 Query processing in CoCache

Input: query Q, cost threshold t **Output:** query plan P
1: send($p(Q), Q$); $C \leftarrow \{< Q, p(Q) >\}$; $V \leftarrow Q$; {Send query q to coordinator $p(q)$}
2: $R \leftarrow$ retrieve($p(Q)$, "SELECT $C(v_i, N_i)$ FROM CACHE WHERE $v_i = Q$");
3: $best \leftarrow$ choose(R);
4: **while** $cost_q(best) > t$ **do**
5:   **for all** $< v_0, c > \in C$ **do**
6:     $C' \leftarrow C' \bigcup$retrieve(c, "SELECT $< v', p >$ FROM FT(v, v', p) WHERE $v = v_0$");
7:   **end for**
8:   $C \leftarrow C'$;
9:   **for all** $< v', c' > \in C$ **do**
10:     $R \leftarrow R \bigcup$retrieve(c', "SELECT $C(v_i, N_i)$ FROM CACHE WHERE $v_i = v'$");
11:   **end for**
12:   $best \leftarrow$ choose(R);
13: **end while**
14: **returen** $best$;

In implementation, $c(v_i \to p_q)$ is estimated using $|R(v_i)| \times b_{v_i, p_q}$, where $|R(v_i)|$ is the size of the relation, and b_{v_i, p_q} is the cost to transfer one unit of data from peers in the container to the requester. Assuming that peers in a container is close to each other in a subnet, b_{v_i, p_q} can be approximated by using b_{p_j, p_q}, in

---
[4] The details about cache selection and registration is introduced in the next section.

which p_j is an arbitrary peer in the container. Ping-pang protocol can be used for estimating b_{p_j,p_q}.

Having received a query, after the host of the query is determined, a requester sends the query along with the peer information to the coordinator, and retrieves the part of index about available caches. In case the caches cannot satisfy the query processing request, the neighboring coordinators corresponding to the sub-queries are contacted, and more information of caches is collected. This process is iterated until a query plan satisfying the cost request is found (Algorithm 1).

4 Collaborative Caching

A *cache plan* is a set of valid caches, $P\{(v_i, N_i\}$. Its cost is defined as

$$cost_c(P) = \sum_{v_i \in P} cost_q(v_i|P_{v_i}) \qquad (2)$$

in which P_{v_i} is the query plan to answer query (cache) v_i satisfying that $P_{v_i} \in P$. The aim of collaborative caching is to minimize the cost of the cache plan. Note that the purpose of query processing is different from that of caching in that the former aims at optimizing a specific query on a specific peer, while the later tries to coordinate different peers to achieve a globally optimized caching solution.

The caching process is driven by the coordinators. When a coordinator has collected a set of updates about the requesters, it starts a re-caching process. Otherwise, when detecting a new requester that agrees to cache some data, the coordinator assigns it to the cache in the query plan whose $c(v_i \rightarrow p_q)$ is the maximum. The main process of caching can be roughly divided into three phases: cache plan initialization by CON, negotiation, and construction of cache.

4.1 Cache Plan Initialization by CON

A coordinator partitions requesters with common sub-query v, and being willing to cache, into k groups based on their locality information. Thus, peers within the same group can communicate to each other via high-bandwidth connections. Then, the small groups N that are not capable enough to cache the subquery, i.e. (v, N) is not a valide cache, are assigned to nearby groups of peers.

The partitions of requesters are populated in CON with K levels, which is called *coordination level*. Thus, each coordinator has collected a set of candidate caches $P'\{(v_i, N_i)\}$, in which each v_i is a logical expression and N_i is a group of peers. Each coordinator greedily choose caches with maximum cost gain per unit of storage for queries $\{v_i\}$. Here, cost gain of a cache c for a specific query q is defined as $\Delta_q(c) = cost_q(q|P) - cost_q(q|P \cup \{c\})$. Thus, the cost gain is evaluated using $\Delta(c) = \sum_{v_i \in P'} \Delta_{v_i}(c)$. The chosen caches are put into the candidate cache plan P, and the record of free space on a requester is decreased. This process is iterated until no requester has free space or no valid cache remained.

The caches (v_i, N_i) in the candidate cache plan whose logical expression v_i is the same as that of the coordinator are chosen as initial caches. This process is conducted in the spare time of the coordinators.

4.2 Negotiation for Caching

A coordinator informs the peers in the containers of initial caches. A requester may receive several notifications from different coordinators. It chooses the caches with logical expressions closest to that of the query of the requester to cache, until no free space is left. The requester sends the feedback to the coordinators. The coordinator removes the peers do not agree to cache from the containers, and checks if the cache is still a valid one. The requesters in the valid caches are informed, so that they retrieve the data for caching. For those invalid caches, a coordinator informs the requesters in the containers, so that the requesters can reassign the spaces left for the invalid cache for other caches.

4.3 Cache Construction

When a requester receives is notified for caching by a coordinator, it begins the cache construction process. If the free storage space is large enough for caching all result of the logical expression, the requester evaluates the query corresponding to the expression, and caches the result. Otherwise, the requester chooses the portion of result that are not cached by other peers in the container. In CoCache implementation, data are partitioned into chunks with identifiers. The identifiers are assigned to the peers in the container via hashing. Furthermore, each caching peer multicast its cached chunks to those peers in the same container. Each peer in the container is responsible for maintaining the cache, and serve other requesters. Since only nearby peers are put into the same container in cache plan initialization process, the peers in the container may serve each other efficiently.

4.4 Query Processing Implementation

Each CoCache peer is equiped with a query engine[5]. Queries are written in standard SELECT-FROM-WHERE form without aggregation. Some peers may share the common schema of data. Each requester knows the schema of data to be queried. We believe that this setting is common in many applications, such as information management in large enterprises. The problem of schema discovery can be solved using information retrieval style method introduced by PeerDB[8].

The logical query expressions are translated to SQL queries for query processing. For retrieval of data in caches, a query is transformed to a set of SQL queries for chunks respectively, and then sent to the caching peers in the container. In case that a caching peer fails, the corresponding subquery is sent to data source to retrieve the missing chunks. The caches are retrieved simultaneously. After obtaining all the data cached (or from data sources), the query is evaluated, and

---

[5] Current implementation of CoCache uses IBM DB2 UDB 7.1 as query engine.

the result is returned to users. Cache construction is similar to query processing. A requester or caching peer periodically re-evaluate its query. The problem of ensures consistency of query result in P2P systems is left as open problems for further study.

5 Empirical Study of CoCache

5.1 Simulation Experiments

For synthetic data, we generate a table with 32 columns and 128 rows blocks, in which each block is in the same size, and is marked with coordinate (rid, cid). Thus, given a quadruple $(top, left, bottom, right)$, the blocks whose coordinate satisifies $left \leq cid \leq right$ and $top \leq rid \leq bottom$ are determined. Each peer generates such a quadruple to determine the data to be stored, while each query is also a quadruple. The data overlapped by a query is the answer to the query. If any blocks on any single peer only overlaps part of the blocks of a query, the data on different peers must be joined together. The query with maximum number of joins involves data on sixteen peers to be joined. The synthetic data set is tested in a P2P system simulator with 1,000 peers[6]. In addition to CoCache, PeerDB [8] without caching (PDB-NC) is used as baseline, while PeerDB with caching (PDB-C) is compared with CoCache. Note that in the later case, each peer devotes the same size of storage space for caching.

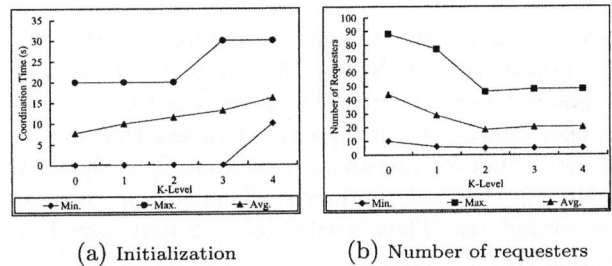

(a) Initialization   (b) Number of requesters

Fig. 2. Workload on coordinators with different coordination levels

In Figure 2 (a), the minimum, average and maximum runtime of cache plan intialization is shown. It is obvious that the runtime is ascendant with the increasing of coordination level K. For some coordinators with few corresponding requesters, the process may be very fast. Furthermore, it is shown that even K is set to 3, the average runtime of coordinators does not increase much. Since in worst case, the candidate cache plans collected by a coordinator is explosive to K, the performance goes bad when K is larger than 4. However, the average

---

[6] The topology is generated by the program downloaded from http://www.cc.gatech.edu/fac/Ellen.Zegura/gt-itm/gt-itm.tar.gz.

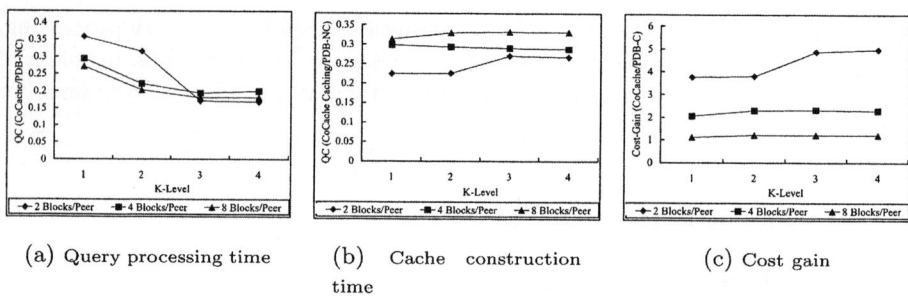

(a) Query processing time (b) Cache construction time (c) Cost gain

Fig. 3. The cost of query processing, view construction compared with PDB-NC and PDB-C, with different settings of caching space and coordination level

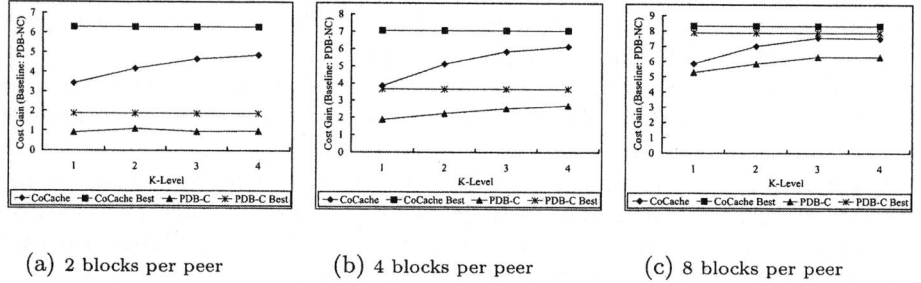

(a) 2 blocks per peer (b) 4 blocks per peer (c) 8 blocks per peer

Fig. 4. Cost gain comparison of COCACHE and PDB-C, divided by that of PDB-NC

runtime is linear to K in our experiments. In Figure 2 (b), the requesters a coordinator should negotiate with is shown. The larger K is used, the less requesters a coordinator should negotiate with. The reason is that by exchanging candidates caches, a coordinator may drop a lot of caches that are not preferred for their limited contribution for increasing cost gain. It is shown that when K is equal or larger than 2, the view candidate refinement process eliminates a large amount of view candidates. Thus, setting $K = 2$ may save both computation and communication cost.

Figure 3 (a) shows the query processing cost comparison between COCACHE and PDB-NC, in the condition that caches are constructed, while the cache construction cost is shown in Figure 3 (b). It is shown that both query processing and cache construction cost is quite small when compared with the query processing cost of PDB-NC. In Figure 3 (c), COCACHE is compared with PDB-C on query processing cost. COCACHE outperforms PDB-C when each peer contributes limited storage for caching (2 blocks/peer). Even when the storage for caching is large enough for the whole query result (8 blocks/peer), COCACHE is slightly better than PDB-C on average. If collaborative caching is less frequent

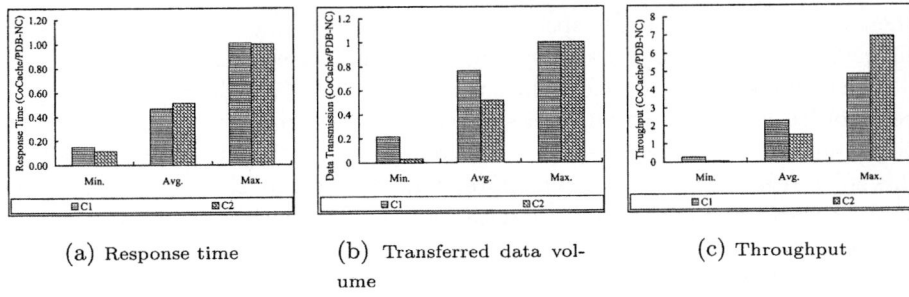

(a) Response time (b) Transferred data volume (c) Throughput

Fig. 5. Experiments in a real P2P environment: CoCache vs. PDB-NC

than query processing, such as applications of continuous query processing, CoCache is more efficient than PDB-NC and PDB-C, and its advantage is much more obvious when cache space is limited.

The cost gains under different K's and different block-size settings are shown in Figure 4. Here, CoCache-Best means the cost gain obtained when each coordinator knows the status of the whole system, which is an ideal condition and is impossible to be reached in applications, while PDB-C Best means the cost gain obtained for all the peers while PDB-C means the cost gain obtained only for those peers participating in collaborative caching. The figures show that the cost gain increases along with K. In any cases, the cost gain of CoCache is at least half of that obtained under ideal environment. When it is impossible to store the required data locally, CoCache always outperforms PDB-C. Even all query results can be cached, CoCache is still a little better than PDB-C, since only raw data are cached in PeerDB.

5.2 Experiments in a Real P2P Environment

DBLP data set is transformed from DBLP XML records[7], in which the total number of tuples are more than 600,000, and the corresponding storage space is more than 200MB. The data set is partitioned and assigned to the peers. Furthermore, the quries are generated by a generator. Totally 144 queries are generated to be used in experiments, in which the number of joins varies from zero to five. The details of the data set partition and query generation are introduced in [9].

The DBLP data set is tested in a LAN environment with 40 peers, each of which is a PC with Pentium 1.4 GHz processor and 128MB RAM. The peers are divided into four groups. Within each group, ten peers are connected with one hub, and the hubs are connected by campus network with each other. CoCache is developed using Java, and running under Microsoft Windows 2000 Workstation. IBM DB2 UDB 7.1 is used as database engine. In experiments on DBLP data set, two schemes of block sizes are tested. In C1 scheme, each peer contributes a large storage space for caching (512KB per query), while in C2

---

[7] http://dblp.uni-trier.de/xml/

scheme, only a small storage space is devoted for caching on each peer (128KB per query). Furthermore, the scheme of PDB-NC is used as baseline.

The response time, volume of data transfered, and throughput for 144 queries are recorded and shown with their summaries in Figure 5. It is interesting that the volume of data transfered in C1 scheme is more than that in C2 scheme. This is because that in C1 scheme, more cachess are established, which presumes more overhead and cache-to-cache data transfer. However, it is shown that the response time of C1 is better than C2, since cache-to-cache data transmission is usually cheap. Even in C2 scheme, the performance is not far worse than that in C1 scheme. The result is quite consistent with that obtained in simulation. It can be concluded that by collaborating, few contribution on each peer can gain much improvement on performance. The throughput of C2 scheme does not win PDB-NC scheme much. Since only part of data with maximum cost can be stored in caches, requesters still need to obtain data from some data sources that are not very far away.

6 Related Work

There are several popular P2P platforms that support key-based search, such as Chord [13], CAN [10], Pastry [11] and BestPeer [7]. Caching is supported by some such platforms [13, 10]. However, the key-based caching scheme is usually too coarse to support complex query processing.

Query processing in P2P systems is a hot research topic and some prototype systems have been developed with different purposes, such as, interactive query processing (PeerDB [8]), DHT-based query execution (PIER [2]), schema mapping based query rewriting and processing (PIAZZA [1]), and data mapping based query processing (Hyperion [6]). In PIER, authors assume that schema information can be obtained in advance by requesters [2]. However, COCACHE employs a different method to facilitate query processing with partial results obtained from nearby peers with common subqueries.

Caching in P2P systems is extensively studied for its advantages for performance improvement. SQUIRREL [3] and BuddyWeb [14] are two prototype systems that allow peers to share their Web caches with one another in the same community. PeerOLAP [4] is designed for online analytical query processing, where data are partitioned into aligned chunks for caching. Different caching strategies are studied, and the efficiency is shown under the setting of a self-configurable P2P network. The work closest to our research is range query result caching [12]. The ranges in a one-dimensional space are mapped to a two-dimensional CAN. Efficient search algorithm is developed to find the cached ranges. However, the methods above suffer from the disadvantage of each peer caching data blindly with other peers, while COCACHE uses collaborative caching based on information collected via CON. Furthermore, CON indexes combinations of both dimensionality and peers.

7 Conclusions

In this paper, a query processing framework called COCACHE is designed to utilize the limited storage devoted by various peers. The collaborative caching scheme adopted is a natural extension of key-based caching. With the help of DHT-based coordinator overlay network, peers can obtain summary information of the related queries and providers' information. Thus, collaborative caching can serve the queries more efficiently than existing caching schemes in P2P systems. Furthermore, the coordinator overlay network enables the cost-based optimization with low maintenance overhead. Experimental results show that COCACHE is especially effective when each peer has limited storage for caching, which is a great challenge in real-life applications.

Acknowledgement

This work is supported by Infocomm Development Authority of Singapore (IDA). The authors would like to thank Jianfeng Yin, Wenyuan Cai and Tian Xia for their help in implementing the previous version of COCACHE, called PeerView, and Dr. Wee Siong Ng for providing the source code of PeerDB.

References

1. A. Halevy, Z. Ives, P. Monk, and I. Tatarinov. Piazza: Data management infrastructure for semantic web applications. In *Proceedings of the 12th World-Wide Web Conference (WWW'2003)*, 2003.
2. R. Huebsch, J. M. Hellerstein, N. Lanham, B. T. Loo, S. Shenker, and I. Stoica. Querying the internet with pier. In *Proceedings of the 29th International Conference on Very Large Databases (VLDB'2003)*, 2003.
3. S. Iyera, A. Rowstron, and P. Druschel. Squirrel: A decentralized, peer-to-peer web cache. In *Proceedings of the 21st ACM Symposium on Principles of Distributed Computing (PODC'2002)*, 2002.
4. P. Kalnis, W. S. Ng, B. C. Ooi, D. Papadias, and K.-L. Tan. An adaptive peer-to-peer network for distributed caching of olap results. In *Proceedings of ACM SIGMOD 2002 International Conference on Management of Data (SIGMOD'2002)*, 2002.
5. A. Kementsietsidis, M. Arenas, and R. J. Miller. Managing data mappings in the hyperion project. In *Proceeding of IEEE Conference on Data Engineering (ICDE'2003)*, 2003.
6. A. Kementsietsidis, M. Arenas, and R. J. Miller. Mapping data in peer-to-peer systems: Semantics and algorithmic issues. In *Proceedings of ACM SIGMOD 2003 International Conference on Management of Data (SIGMOD'2003)*, 2003.
7. W. S. Ng, B. C. Ooi, and K.-L. Tan. Bestpeer: A self-configurable peer-to-peer system. In *Proceedings of IEEE Conference on Data Engineering (ICDE'2001)*. IEEE Press, 2002.
8. W. S. Ng, B. C. Ooi, K.-L. Tan, and A. Zhou. Peerdb: A p2p-based system for distributed data sharing. In *Proceedings of IEEE Conference on Data Engineering (ICDE'2003)*. IEEE Press, 2003.

9. W. Qian, L. Xu, S. Zhou, and A. Zhou. Peerview: View selection for query processing in p2p systems. Technical report, Dept. of Computer Science and Engineering, Fudan Univeristy, Available at http://www.cs.fudan.edu.cn/wpl/memeber/wnqian/, 2004.
10. S. Ratnasamy, P. Francis, K. Handley, R. Karp, and S. Shenker. A scalable content-addressable network. In *Proceedings of the ACM SIGCOMM 2002 Conference on Applications, Technologies, Architectures, and Protocols for Computer Communication (SIGCOMM'2001)*, 2001.
11. A. Rowstron and P. Druschel. Pastry: Scalable, distributed object location and routing for large-scale peer-to-peer systems. In *Proceedings of the IFIP/ACM International Conference on Distributed Systems Platforms (Middleware'2001)*, pages 329–350, 2001.
12. O. Sahin, A. Gupta, D. Agrawal, and A. E. Abbadi. A peer-to-peer framework for caching range queries. In *Proceedings of the 20th IEEE International Conference on Data Engineering (ICDE'2004)*, 2004.
13. I. Stoica, R. Morris, D. Karger, M. F. Kaashoek, and H. Balakrishnan. Chord: a scalable peer-to-peer lookup service for internet applications. In *Proceedings of the ACM SIGCOMM 2001 Conference on Applications, Technologies, Architectures, and Protocols for Computer Communication (SIGCOMM'2001)*, pages 149–160. ACM Press, 2001.
14. X. Wang, W. S. Ng, B. C. Ooi, K.-L. Tan, and A. Zhou. Buddyweb: A p2p-based collaborative web caching system. In *Proceedings of Peer-to-Peer Computing Workshop (Networking 2002)*. IEEE Press, 2002.

Multi-represented kNN-Classification for Large Class Sets*

Hans-Peter Kriegel, Alexey Pryakhin, and Matthias Schubert

Institute for Computer Science, University of Munich,
Oettingenstr. 67, 80538 Munich, Germany
{kriegel, pryakhin, schubert}@dbs.ifi.lmu.de

Abstract. The amount of stored information in modern database applications increased tremendously in recent years. Besides their sheer amount, the stored data objects are also more and more complex. Therefore, classification of these complex objects is an important data mining task that yields several new challenges. In many applications, the data objects provide multiple representations. E.g. proteins can be described by text, amino acid sequences or 3D structures. Additionally, many real-world applications need to distinguish thousands of classes. Last but not least, many complex objects are not directly expressible by feature vectors. To cope with all these requirements, we introduce a novel approach to classification of multi-represented objects that is capable to distinguish large numbers of classes. Our method is based on k nearest neighbor classification and employs density-based clustering as a new approach to reduce the training instances for instance-based classification. To predict the most likely class, our classifier employs a new method to use several object representations for making accurate class predictions. The introduced method is evaluated by classifying proteins according to the classes of Gene Ontology, one of the most established class systems for biomolecules that comprises several thousand classes.

Keywords: Multi-represented objects, classification, instance based learning, k nearest neighbor classifier.

1 Introduction

Modern information systems are collecting enormous amounts of data every day. In addition to the sheer amount of data, the complexity of data objects increases as well. Companies store more detailed information about their costumers, satellites take pictures with additional frequency spectra, and HTML-documents provide embedded multimedia content which makes them much more complicated

---

* Supported by the German Ministery for Education, Science, Research and Technology (BMBF) under grant no. 031U212 within the BFAM (Bioinformatics for the Functional Analysis of Mammalian Genomes) project which is part of the German Genome Analysis Network (NGFN).

than ordinary text documents. The analysis of large collections of complex objects yields several new challenges to data mining algorithms.

One of the most important tasks of data mining is classification. Classification learns a function $Cl : O \to C$ that maps each object $o \in O$ to the class $c \in C$ that it most likely belongs to. The class set C is a predefined set of categories. In order to make a class prediction, a classifier has to be trained. For the classification of complex objects, there are various important applications, e.g. the classification of proteins into functional catalogues or secure personal identification using several biometric characteristics. These applications yield interesting challenges to novel classification techniques.

First of all, the more complex a data object is, the more feature transformations exist that can be used to map the object to a representation suitable for data mining. Furthermore, many objects are describable by different aspects, e.g. proteins can be described by text annotations and amino acid sequences. This yields a problem for data mining in general because it is not clear which of these aspects is most suited to fulfill the given task. Therefore, it would be beneficial if a classification algorithm could employ all of the given representations of an object to make accurate class predictions. Another important aspect is that many classification algorithms rely on an object representation providing feature vectors. However, complex objects are often represented in a better way by treating them as sequences, trees or graphs. Last but not least, the number of classes in the given example applications can be exceptionally high. Gene Ontology [1], one of the most established class systems for proteins, currently has more then 14,000 classes and biometric databases will have to identify one special person among thousands of people. Though this problem is not directly connected to the complexity of the given data objects, it often co-occurs in the same application and should therefore be considered when selecting the classification method.

To cope with these challenges, we introduce a new classification technique based one k nearest neighbor (kNN) classification [2]. A kNN classifier decides the class of an object by analyzing its k nearest neighbors within the training objects. kNN classifiers are well-suited to solve the given problem because they do not have to spend additional effort for distinguishing additional classes. The new training objects are simply added to the training database and are only considered for classification if they are among the nearest neighbors of the object to be classified. Additionally, kNN classifiers can be applied to any type of object representation as long as a distance measure is available. Unfortunately, kNN classification has a major drawback as well. The efficiency of classification is rapidly decreasing with the number of training objects. Though the use of index structures such as the M-tree [3] or the IQ-Tree [4] might help to reduce query times in some cases, it does not provide a general solution. Another approach to limit the problem is the reduction of the training objects to some basic examples as proposed in [5]. However, these approaches are aimed at limited training data and are therefore very inefficient when applied to large training sets.

Thus, to apply kNN classification to the described classification scenario, we introduce a more efficient method to speed up kNN classification by employing density-based clustering to reduce the necessary training instances. Afterwards, we introduce a new method for the classification of multi-represented (MR) objects. The idea of the method is to determine the k nearest neighbors in a database for each representation. Then, the class prediction is derived by considering the normalized distances within each result. To demonstrate the good performance, we apply our new method to four scenarios of protein classification. Each protein is represented by an amino acid sequence and a text annotation. Our results demonstrate that density-based clustering outperforms other methods of reducing the training set for kNN classification. Furthermore, the achieved results indicate that our new decision rule for multi-represented kNN classification yields better accuracy than other classification methods that are suitable for large class sets.

The rest of the paper is organized as follows. In section 2, we discuss related work on speeding up kNN classification and classification of multi-represented objects. Section 3 describes the use of density-based clustering to reduce the number of training instances without losing essential concepts. Additionally, our new approach to combine multi-represented classification is introduced. Section 4 provides an experimental evaluation based on protein data that consists of sequential and text representations. The last section sums up the introduced solutions and gives some directions for future work.

2 Related Work

k Nearest Neighbor Classifier. The k nearest neighbor (kNN) classification [2] mentioned above classifies a new data object o by finding its k nearest neighbors with respect to a suitable distance function. In its basic form, kNN classification predicts the class that provides the most training objects within the k-nearest neighbors. To the best of our knowledge, there exists no form of kNN classification that is directly applicable to multi-represented data objects. The common approach to apply kNN classification to this kind of data is to build a joint distance measure on the complete MR object. However, we argue that this method is not suitable to derive good results because it is not capable to weight the different representations on the basis of the given object.

Instance Reduction. In the last decades, the research community introduced several methods for instance reduction [5, 6, 7, 8, 9]. All approaches try to reduce the number of instances in the training set in a way that the classifier provides comparable or even better accuracy and demands less processing time. In [8] the authors discuss several reduction techniques and [10] illustrates an experimental evaluation of these algorithms on 31 data sets. This evaluation demonstrates that the RT3 algorithm [8] outperforms other techniques of instance reduction for many data sets. Another approach to instance reduction is called iterative case filtering (ICF)[5]. This novel and effective approach to data reduction employs two steps. The first step performs so-called "Wilson editing". It detects all instances that are classified incorrectly by the kNN classifier. These instances are afterwards removed. The second step calculates for each remaining object the so-called *reachability* and *coverage* [5]. Every object o with $|reachable(o)| < |coverage(o)|$ is removed. The second step is iterated until no removable object exists. A broad experimental evaluation [11] on 30 databases compares ICF with the reduction technique RT3 [8]. Both algorithms achieve the highest degree of instance reduction while maintaining classification accuracy.

GDBSCAN. GDBSCAN [12] is a density-based clustering algorithm. Clusters are considered as dense areas that are separated by sparse areas. Based on two input parameters (ε and $MINPTS$), GDBSCAN defines dense regions by means of core objects. An object $o \in DB$ is called *core object*, if its ε-neighborhood contains at least $MINPTS$ objects. Usually clusters contain several core objects located inside a cluster and border objects located at the border of the cluster. In addition, the objects within a cluster must be "density-connected". GDBSCAN is able to detect clusters by one single pass over the data. The algorithm uses the fact, that a density-connected cluster can be detected by finding one of its core-objects o and computing all objects which are density-reachable from o. To determine the input parameters, a simple and effective method is described in [13]. This method can be generalized and used for GDBSCAN as well.

Classifier Fusion. The task of learning from objects, when more than a single classifier has beeen trained, has recently drawn some attention in the pattern recognition community [14, 15, 16]. In [15], the author describes the method of classifier fusion to combine the results from multiple classifiers for one and the same object. Furthermore, [15] surveys the four basic combination methods and introduces a combined learner to achieve combination rules offering better accuracy. In [17], a method for the hierarchical classification of MR objects was introduced. Though this method provides superior accuracy to the compared methods, it is not suitable for our described scenario because the efficiency of the method relies on the existence of a class hierarchy that can be exploited. Furthermore, the proposed classifier is based on Support Vector Machines that are not as generally applicable as kNN classification.

3 kNN Classification of Complex Objects

As mentioned in the introduction, classification of complex objects into large class sets yields the following challenges. First of all, the selected classification approach has to cope with the large number of classes without losing performance. Second, complex objects might be described by multiple representations. Furthermore, these representations might consist of varying object types, e.g. vectors, sequences and graphs. A good approach to handle these problems is kNN classification which does not need to spend additional efforts for distinguishing additional classes. Another benefit of kNN classifiers is that they do not rely on a special data type but can cope with any object type as long as there is a distance function. A drawback of kNN classification is that the classification time strongly depends on the number of training objects. Therefore, the number of training objects should be kept as low as possible to ensure efficient classification. In this paper, we discuss a method to reduce training instances based on density-based clustering. Furthermore, we introduce a new method for the classification of multi-represented objects that is capable of achieving significantly better accuracy than the classification based on only one representation or related methods of classification.

In the following, we present a brief problem description. Afterwards, we introduce an approach to reduce the given training data with the help of density-based clustering. Finally, we use multiple object representations to derive accurate class predictions.

3.1 Problem Definition

In our given application scenario, we want to find a classifier $Cl : O \to C$ that maps each data object $o \in O$ to its correct class $c \in C$. The data space O is given by the cartesian product of m representations $R_1 \times \ldots \times R_m$. Each representation R_i consists of a feature space $F_i \cup \{-\}$. A feature space F_i may consist of varying data types. For comparing two objects $u, v \in F_i$, there exists a distance measure $dist_i : F_i \times F_i \to \mathbb{R}_0^+$. To apply our method, it is necessary that $dist_i$ is symmetric and reflexive. The symbol $\{-\}$ denotes that a particular object representation is missing. However, for a usable class prediction a tuple should provide at least one instance $r_i \in F_i$. To conclude, the task of multi-represented classification is to find a function $Cl_{mr} : (R_1 \times \ldots \times R_m) \to C$ that maps as many objects o to their correct class $c \in C$ as possible. For training, a set T of tuples (o, c) of objects $o = (r_1, \ldots, r_m)$ and their correct classes c are given to the classifier, the so-called training set. We denote in further sections the correct class of an object o by $c(o)$ and the class detected by multi-represented classification as $Cl_{mr}(o)$.

3.2 Density-Based Instance Reduction

The performance of kNN classification depends on the number of objects in the training set. Though a lot of methods that reduce the training data for kNN classification have been proposed so far, most of these techniques perform poorly for large amounts of training data. In order to reduce the number of available training objects more efficiently, we suggest a novel approach – density-based instance reduction (DBIR).

The DBIR-algorithm works as follows. For each representation and each class, the training data is clustered by using the algorithm GDBSCAN. Let us note that the input parameters can be chosen as described in [13]. GDBSCAN provides a set of clusters $Clust = \{Clust_1, \ldots, Clust_j, \ldots, Clust_l\}$, where $j = 1, \ldots, l$ is the index of the cluster, and additionally a set of objects N that are noise, i.e. objects that cannot be associated with any clusters. An important characteristic of GDBSCAN for our problem is that the number of found clusters l is not predefined, but a result of the clustering algorithm. Thus, the number of important concepts is determined by the algorithm and not manually. Another important advantage of GDBSCAN is that it is capable to cluster any data type as long as there is a reflexive and symmetric distance measure to compare the objects. After clustering, DBIR iterates through the set $Clust$ and determines

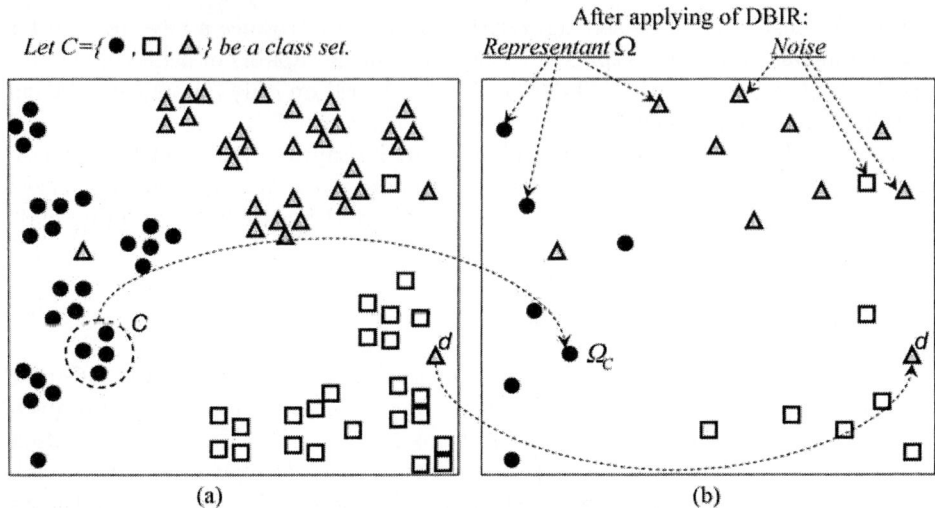

Fig. 1. (a) Objects before data reduction, (b) Objects after reduction by using of DBIR. The density-based cluster C can be reduced to a representant Ω_C. The noise object d is not removed. However, it can not change the decision of a kNN classifier with $k > 2$

for each cluster $Clust_j$ a representant Ω_j. The representant Ω_j is the centroid of the cluster $Clust_j$ in the case of a representation given by a vector space and the medoid of the cluster $Clust_j$ otherwise. Afterwards, all objects belonging to the set $Clust_j \setminus \Omega_j$ are removed from the data set.

Like most other instance reduction methods, we assume that the training data for each class contains all important examples to specify a given class. To reduce the number of training objects without losing accuracy, we have to discard the training objects that are likely to represent a concept that is not typical for the given class. Furthermore, if a typical concept is described by several training objects, we reduce the representatives of this concept to a single one to save classification time. We argue that a density-based clustering of the training objects for a given class is sufficient to decide both cases. Objects that are not typical for a given class do not have any close neighbors and are usually separated from the rest of the training set. Thus, the noise objects in a density-based clustering are likely to correspond to these objects. Of course, it is possible that a noise object alone is an important concept. However, a single object is not likely to change the decision of a kNN classifier and the decision would most likely be wrong even without the deletion. Important concepts that are represented by several training objects are usually located very closely to each other in the feature space. Thus, these concepts are likely to correspond to a density-connected cluster in our density-based clustering. For each of these clusters it is sufficient that the training set contains a single object to represent it. Figure 1 displays both effects in a two dimensional example.

Our method has a runtime complexity of $O(\sum_{c_j \in C} |\{o \in O \mid c(o) = c_j\}|^2)$ for the case that it is not supported by index structures. ICF has a runtime complexity of $O(2 \times (\#Iteration) \times |DB|^2)$ where $\#Iteration$ is the number of iterations (in our experiments it was between 9 and 12) and $|DB|$ is the size of the database. Thus, our method is considerably faster than other state of the art feature reduction techniques.

As described above, we apply the DBIR-algorithm separately to the training objects in one representation and for one class. Afterwards we integrate all instances of a representation i into one training database DB_i. Let us note that it is possible to speed up k nearest neighbor queries in each of these training databases as long as there are suitable index structures for the given object type. For example, if the distance function is metric it might be beneficial to further increase the classification time by employing a metric tree like the M-Tree [3].

3.3 kNN-Classification of Multi-represented Objects

Based on the training databases for each representation, we apply the following method of kNN-based classification. To classify a new data object $o = (r_i, \ldots, r_m)$, the kNN sphere $sphere_i(o, k)$ in each representation with $r_i \neq " - "$ is determined. Formally, the $sphere_i(o, k)$ can be described as follows:

$$sphere_i(o, k) = \{o_1, \ldots, o_k \mid o_1, \ldots, o_k \in DB_i \wedge \nexists o' \in DB_i \setminus \{o_1, \ldots, o_k\}$$
$$\wedge \nexists \xi, 1 \leq \xi \leq k : dist_i(o', r_i) \leq dist_i(o_\xi, r_i)\}$$

To combine these kNN spheres and achieve accurate classification, we first of all derive a confidence vector $cv_i(o)$ from each available $sphere_i(o, k)$. Let $c(o)$ denote the correct class of object o and let $d_i^{norm}(u, v)$ be a normalized distance function. Then the confidence vector for an object o with respect to its kNN sphere $sphere_i(o, k)$ for the representation i is defined as follows:

$$cv_i(o) = (cv_{i,1}(o), \ldots, cv_{i,|C|}(o)), \quad (1)$$

$$\forall j, 1 \leq j \leq |C| : cv_{i,j}(o) = \frac{\sum_{u \in sphere_i(o,k) \wedge c(u) = c_j} \frac{1}{d_i^{norm}(o,u)^2}}{\sum_{k=1}^{|C|} cv_{i,k}(o)} \quad (2)$$

To normalize our distance function for each representation, we apply the following modification:

$$d_i^{norm}(o, u) = \frac{dist_i(o, u)}{\max_{v \in sphere_i(o,k)} dist_i(o, v)} \quad (3)$$

where $dist_i$ is the distance function between two objects in the i-th representation. The normalization in formula 3 maps the distance values for each representation to the range $[0, 1]$ with respect to the radius of $sphere_i(o, k)$. Thus, the confidence vector of the i-th representation at the j-th position (cf. formula 2) is a normalized sum of the inverse quadratic distances.

After we have determined the confidence vectors $cv_i(o)$ for each representation i, we use a weighted linear combination for combining them. Let us note that

Table 1. Details of the test environments

	Set 1	Set 2	Set 3	Set 4
Name	Enzyme Activity	Metabolism	Transferase	Cell Growth
Number of Goal Classes	267	251	62	37
References to proteins	16815	19639	4086	4401

the combination of confidence vectors to achieve multi-represented classification has been proposed in [15]. However, the used weights in the former approaches do not adjust to the individual classification object. We argue that in order to use each representation in a best possible way, a multi-represented decision rule must weight the influence of all available representations individually for each object.

To achieve this individual weighting, our classification rule is built as follows:

$$Cl_{mr}(o) = \max_{j=1,\ldots,|C|} \sum_{i=1}^{m} w_i \cdot cv_{i,j}(o) \qquad (4)$$

where m is the number of representations and

$$w_i = \begin{cases} 0 & \text{, if } r_i = "-" \\ \frac{1+\sum_{j=1}^{|C|}(cv_{i,j}(o)\cdot\log_{|C|}cv_{i,j}(o))}{\sum_{k=1}^{m}(1+\sum_{j=1}^{|C|}(cv_{k,j}(o)\cdot\log_{|C|}cv_{k,j}(o)))} & \text{, otherwise} \end{cases} \qquad (5)$$

The idea of our method is that a kNN sphere containing only a small number of classes and several objects of one special class is "purer" than a kNN sphere containing one or two objects for each of the classes. Thus, the "purer" a kNN-sphere for a representation is, the better is the quality of the class prediction that can be derived from this representation. To measure this effect, we employ the entropy with respect to all possible classes. The weight is now calculated by normalizing the entropy of its kNN sphere with respect to the entropy of the kNN spheres in all representations. As a result the weights of all representations add up to one. In conclusion, our decision rule for multi-represented objects measures the contribution of each available representation by the entropy in the local kNN spheres of all available representations.

4 Experimental Evaluation

4.1 Test Bed

In order to demonstrate the advantages of our approach, we carried out a versatile experimental evaluation. All algorithms are implemented in Java and were tested on a work station that is equipped with a 1.8 GHz Opteron processor

Table 2. Experimental results Classification accuracy (in %) of kNN classifier on: unreduced data, data reduced by DBIR and ICF. Rune time (in sec.) and reduction rate (in %) reached by DBIR and ICF. (Using two representations Rep. 1 and Rep. 2.)

	Classification Accuracy (in %)							
	Set 1, Rep. 1	Set 2, Rep. 1	Set 3, Rep. 1	Set 4, Rep. 1	Set 1, Rep. 2	Set 2, Rep. 2	Set 3, Rep. 2	Set 4, Rep. 2
kNN	64.43	61.41	72.01	76.2	46.6	43.9	47.48	62.92
kNN DBIR	61.95	60.29	72.56	73.91	44.5	45.5	48.97	56.58
kNN ICF	46.44	35.56	47.92	40.72	37.85	33.21	31.37	34.58
	Runtime of Instance Reduction (in sec.)							
DBIR	163.0	253.9	8.0	27.5	275.9	1069.6	36.6	119.9
ICF	12,809.1	15,616.7	590.0	632.0	93,416.8	112,248.2	4,258.0	3,772.0
	Reduction Rate (in %)							
DBIR	26.1	27.4	33.1	32.0	28.1	22.9	33.8	35.0
ICF	57.0	64.3	71.8	77.7	37.8	46.5	64.0	65.5

and 8 GB main memory. We used the classification accuracy to measure the effectiveness of algorithms and 5-fold cross-validation to avoid overfitting.

The properties of each test bed are shown in table 1. The 4 test beds consist of 37 to 267 Gene Ontology[1] classes. The corresponding objects were taken from the SWISS-PROT [18] protein database and consist of a text annotation and an amino acid sequence of a protein. In order to obtain a flat class-system with sufficient training objects per class, the original environment was pruned.

We employed the approach described in [19] to extract features from the amino acid sequences. The basic idea is to use local (20 amino acids) and global (6 exchange groups) characteristics of a protein sequence. To construct a meaningful feature space, we formed all possible 2-grams for each kind of characteristic, which generated us the 436 dimensions of our sequence feature space. For text descriptions, we employed a TFIDF [20] vector for each description that was built of 100 extracted terms. We used the cosine distance function as distance measure for both representations.

4.2 Experimental Results

To demonstrate that DBIR is suitable for large data sets w.r.t. efficiency, we compared the run time needed for data reduction by using DBIR and ICF on single-represented data. As presented in table 2, the DBIR outperforms ICF in terms of efficiency, e.g. on the 1st representation of data set 1, DBIR needed only 163 sec. whereas ICF spends 12,809.1 sec. for the data reduction.

To show the effectiveness of DBIR, we compared the classification accuracy achieved by the kNN classifier on unreduced data, data reduced by DBIR and data reduced by ICF (cf. table 2). All these experiments were performed on

Table 3. Classification accuracy (in %) and average classification time per object (in msec.) of our approach (MR-kNN DBIR) compared to: kNN on single representations reduced by DBIR; Naive Bayes (NB) on single representations and on multiple representations combined by sum rule [15]; kNN classifiers combined by sum rule

	Set 1	Set 2	Set 3	Set 4
Classification accuracy (in %)				
1st Representation, kNN DBIR	61.95	60.29	72.56	73.91
2nd Representation, kNN DBIR	44.5	45.5	48.97	56.58
1st and 2nd Representations, MR-kNN DBIR	**67.65**	**65.17**	**75.52**	**76.8**
1st Representation, NB	43.45	39.95	58.41	41.08
2nd Representation, NB	28.44	22.36	32.87	31.35
1st and 2nd Rep., NB with sum rule fusion	39.64	35.47	51.15	36.03
1st and 2nd Rep., kNN classifier fusion by sum rule	62.1	63.18	64.14	74.67
Average classification time per object (in msec.)				
1st Representation, kNN DBIR	196.1	198.87	38.22	39.86
2nd Representation, kNN DBIR	740.5	907.78	160.42	161.88
1st and 2nd Rep., MR-kNN DBIR	1,005.4	1,105.4	198.3	201.6
1st Representation, NB	45.06	43.54	15.4	9.04
2nd Representation, NB	155,91	150,75	48,34	29,62
1st and 2nd Rep., NB with sum rule fusion	206.37	198.3	61.54	36.73
1st and 2nd Rep., kNN classifier fusion by sum rule	1,251.3	1,456.2	295.6	316.8

single-represented data. The accuracy achieved by the kNN classifier on data reduced by using DBIR was for all of the data sets comparable to the unreduced data set. In contrast to these results, the classification accuracy achieved while using ICF was considerably lower. E.g. on the 1st representation of data set 1, the kNN classification on the data reduced by DBIR reaches 61.95% accuracy, whereas the kNN classification on the data reduced by ICF reaches only 46.44% accuracy. Though the reduction rate achieved by ICF is higher than that of DBIR, the clearly superior accuracy that is achieved by using DBIR indicates that ICF removed important information from the training data set.

In order to demonstrate the effectiveness of the proposed multi-represented kNN classifier (MR-kNN DBIR), we compared it to the kNN classifier on single representations, naive Bayes (NB) on unreduced single-represented data, NB classification combined by the sum rule and kNN classification combined by the sum rule. The sum rule described in [15] adds up the confidence vectors delivered by classifiers responsible for single representations. Table 3 illustrates the experimental results of this comparison. Our method showed the highest classification accuracy on all data sets and achieved a significant increase of accuracy in comparison to single-represented classification, e.g. on the first set the kNN classifier delivered 61.95% accuracy on the first and 44.5% accuracy on the second representation whereas our approach achieved a significantly higher accuracy of 67.65%. NB showed in our experiments low accuracy both on single representations and when combining single NB classifiers employing the sum rule. Our method outperforms also the combination of kNN classifiers using the sum rule in all test environments (cf. table 3).

5 Conclusions

In this paper, we proposed a novel approach for classifying multi-represented data objects into flat class-systems with many classes. Our method aims at a common application scenario that can be described by the following characteristics: First, objects in modern applications often provide multiple representations which are derived from multiple views of the same data object. Second, complex objects might be described by representations that are not necessarily in feature vector form. Thus, a classifier should cope with a variety of data types. Last but not least, novel applications often provide large class sets that distinguish huge amounts of classes. Therefore, classifiers should be able to distinguish additional classes with a minimum of additional training and classification effort. To cope with these requirements, our new method for classification of multi-represented objects employs kNN classification because this approach is naturally able to handle the last two requirements. An important contribution of our method is a new way of instance reduction to limit the number of employed training objects and thus to speed up classification time without significantly loosing accuracy. To integrate the information of several representations, we present a new decision rule that employs a weighted combination of confidence values to derive a class prediction. The idea of the used weighting is to measure the entropy of each kNN sphere and thus representations are weighed in a different way for different data objects. In our experimental evaluation, we compared our new instance reduction technique called DBIR to one of the best performing instance reduction techniques so far, ICF. Our results indicate that DBIR is capable to reduce the training database faster and provides better accuracy than ICF. To demonstrate the effectiveness of our multi-represented kNN classifier, we compared the classification accuracy using related methods and employing classification based on single representations. The results demonstrate that our new method is capable of outperforming the compared approaches and significantly increases the accuracy by integrating all representations.

For future work, we plan to examine the use of various index structures to speed up classification. Furthermore, we plan to apply our method on the second application area mentioned in the introduction, biometric identification. This area yields several individual challenges like the combination of different classification methods. For example, facial features can be checked by kNN classification. However, in order to recognize a person by its speech pattern other ways like hidden Markov models are reported to provide better accuracy. Thus, a flexible model should support different classification algorithms. Another interesting direction is to further speed up classification by employing only some of the representations. For example, it might be unnecessary to query the sequence database if the text database provides sufficient confidence.

References

1. Consortium, T.G.O.: "Gene Ontology: Tool for the Unification of Biology". Nature Genetics **25** (2000) 25–29
2. Cover, T., Hart, P.: Nearest neighbor pattern classification. IEEE Transactions on information Theory **IT-13** (1967) 21–27
3. Ciaccia, P., Patella, M., Zezula, P.: "M-tree: An Efficient Access Method for Similarity Search in Metric Spaces". In: Proc. of the 23rd Int. Conf. on Very Large Data Bases, Morgan Kaufmann, San Francisco, CA, USA (1997) 426 – 435
4. Berchtold, S., Böhm, C., Jagadish, H., Kriegel, H.P., Sander, J.: "Independent Quantization: An Index Compression Technique for High-Dimensional Spaces". In: Int. Conf. on Data Engineering, ICDE 2000. (2000)
5. Brighton, H., Mellish, C.: On the consistency of information filters for lazy learning algorithms. In: PKDD. (1999) 283–288
6. Gates, G.: The reduced nearest neighbour rule. IEEE Transactions on Information Theory **18** (1972) 431–433
7. Ritter, G., Woodruff, H., Lowry, S.R. Isenhour, T.: An algorithm for the selective nearest neighbor decision rule. IEEE Transactions on Information Theory **21** (1975) 665–669
8. Wilson, H., Martinez, T.: Instance pruning techniques. In: Proc. 14th Int. Conf. on Machine Learning, Morgan Kaufmann Publishers (1997) 403–411
9. Aha, D.: Tolerating noisy, irrelevant and novel attributes in in instance-based learning algorithms. Int. Jurnal of Man-Machine Studies **36** (1992) 267–287
10. Wilson, H., Martinez, T.: Machine Learning, 38-3. Reduction Techniques for Instance-Based Learning Algorithms. Kluwer Academic Publishers, Boston. (2000)
11. Brighton, H., Mellish, C.: Data Mining and Knowledge Discavery, 6. Advances in Instance Selection for Instance-Based Learning Algorithms. Kluwer Academic Publishers. (2002)
12. Sander, J., Ester, M., Kriegel, H.P., Xu, X.: "Density-Based Clustering in Spatial Databases: The Algorithm GDBSCAN and its Applications". In: Data Mining and Knowledge Discovery, Kluwer Academic Publishers (1998) 169–194
13. Ester, M., Kriegel, H.P., Sander, J., Xu, X.: "A Density-Based Algorithm for Discovering Clusters in Large Spatial Databases with Noise". In: Proc. KDD'96, Portland, OR, AAAI Press (1996) 291–316
14. Kittler, J., Hatef, M., Duin, R., Matas, J.: "On Combining Classifiers". IEEE Transactions on Pattern Analysis and Machine Intelligence **20** (1998) 226–239
15. Duin, R.: "The Combining Classifier: To Train Or Not To Train?". In: Proc. 16th Int. Conf. on Pattern Recognition, Quebec City, Canada). (2002) 765–770
16. Kuncheva, L., Bezdek, J., Duin, R.: "Decision Templates for Multiple Classifier Fusion: an Experimental Comparison". Pattern Recognition **34** (2001) 299–314
17. Kriegel, H.P., Kröger, P., Pryakhin, A., Schubert, M.: Using support vector machines for classifying large sets of multi-represented objects. In: Proc. SIAM Int. Conf. on Data Mining, Lake Buena Vista, Florida, USA. (2004) 102–114
18. Boeckmann, B., Bairoch, A., Apweiler, R., Blatter, M.C., Estreicher, A., Gasteiger, E., Martin, M., Michoud, K., O'Donovan, C., Phan, I., Pilbout, S., Schneider, M.: "The SWISS-PROT Protein Knowledgebase and its Supplement TrEMBL in 2003". Nucleic Acid Research **31** (2003) 365–370
19. Deshpande, M., Karypis, G.: "Evaluation of Techniques for Classifying Biological Sequences". In: Proc. of PAKDD'02. (2002) 417–431
20. Salton, G.: Automatic Text Processing: The Transformation, Analysis, and Retrieval of Information by Computer. Addison-Wesley (1989)

Enhancing SNNB with Local Accuracy Estimation and Ensemble Techniques

Zhipeng Xie[1], Qing Zhang[1], Wynne Hsu[2], and Mong Li Lee[2]

[1] Department of Computing and Information Technology,
Fudan University, Shanghai, P. R. China, 200433
`xiezp@fudan.edu.cn`
[2] School of Computing, National University of Singapore,
3 Science Drive 2, Singapore, 119260
`{whsu, leeml}@comp.nus.edu.sg`

Abstract. Naïve Bayes, the simplest Bayesian classifier, has shown excellent performance given its unrealistic independence assumption. This paper studies the selective neighborhood-based naïve Bayes (SNNB) for lazy classification, and develops three variant algorithms, SNNB-G, SNNB-L, and SNNB-LV, all with linear computational complexity. The SNNB algorithms use local learning strategy for alleviating the independence assumption. The underlying idea is, for a test example, first to construct multiple classifiers on its multiple neighborhoods with different radius, and then to select out the classifier with the highest estimated accuracy to make decision. Empirical results show that both SNNB-L and SNNB-LV generate more accurate classifiers than naïve Bayes and several other state-of-the-art classification algorithms including C4.5, Naïve Bayes Tree, and Lazy Bayesian Rule. The SNNB-L and SNNB-LV algorithms are also computationally more efficient than the Lazy Bayesian Rule algorithm, especially on the domains with high dimensionality.

1 Introduction

Naïve Bayes [6] is a probability-based classification method, which assumes that attributes are conditionally mutually independent given the class label. Despite this clearly unrealistic assumption, naïve Bayes has surprisingly good performance in a wide variety of domains. In addition, naïve Bayes is robust to noise and irrelevant attributes and the learnt theories are easy for domain experts to understand. Due to all the advantages, naïve Bayes is widely employed for classification.

No doubt naïve Bayes succeeds in some domains with violations of the attribute independence assumption, but it fails in many. Recently, a lot of researchers have attempted to alleviate this unrealistic assumption. Their research work can be broadly divided into three main categories.

The first category aims to improve naïve Bayes by transforming the feature space through the techniques such as feature subset selection and constructive feature generation. Kononenko's semi-naïve Bayesian classifier [11] performed exhaustive search by iteratively joining pairs of attribute values to generate constructive features based on statistical tests for independence. The constructive Bayesian classifier [13] employed a wrapper model to find the best Cartesian product attributes from existing nominal attributes, and possible deletion of existing attributes. Langley and Sage [12] used the Forward Sequential Selection (FSS) method to select a subset of the available attributes, with which to build a naïve Bayes classifier. It is shown that such attribute selection can improve upon the performance of the naïve Bayes classifier when attributes are inter-dependent, especially when some attributes are redundant.

The second category of research extends naïve Bayes by relaxing the attribute independence assumption explicitly. This covers many classification methods based on Bayesian network. Friedman and Goldszmidt [9] explored the Tree Augmented Naïve Bayes (TAN) model for classifier learning, which belongs to a restricted sub-class of Bayesian network by inducing a tree-structure network.

The third category employs the principle of local learning to naïve Bayes. It does not intend to break this assumption, but expect it to (approximately) come true in local areas (or subspaces). It is well-established that large, complex databases are not always amenable to a unique global approach to generalization. This is because different models may exist specific to different data points. A typical example in this category is the naïve Bayes tree, NBTREE [10], which used decision tree techniques to partition the whole instance space (root node) into several subspaces (leaf nodes), and then trains a naïve Bayes classifier for each leaf node. Zheng Zijian, et al [18] presented the Lazy Bayesian Rule (LBR) classification method to construct a Bayesian rule for each specific target example in order to solve the small disjunct problem of NBTREE. Another more recent work is the algorithm LWL [8], which is a locally weighted version of naïve Bayes.

Besides the work described above, a lot of other research still exists. For example, Zheng [17] presented a method to generate naïve Bayes Classifier Committees by building individual naïve Bayes classifiers using different attribute subsets in sequential trials. Majority vote of the committees was applied in the classification stage.

On the other hand, we can divide classification methods into two types: eager learning and lazy learning, depending on when the major computation occurs [1]. Lazy learning is distinguished by spending little or no effort during training and delaying computation until classification time, while eager learning replaces the training inputs with an abstraction expression, such as rule set, decision tree, or neural network, and uses it to process queries. The majority of the methods to extend naïve Bayes are eager, except for LBR and LWL. We also observe that most existing techniques for improving the performance of the naïve Bayesian classifier require complex induction processes.

LBR can construct highly accurate classifier, competitive to other methods, such as TAN and NBTREE. However, the computational complexity is quadratic to the number of attributes. Similarly to LBR, Xie et al [16] designed a new lazy learning strategy, (SNNB) belonging to the third category above, motivated by Nearest Neighbor algorithm. The underpinning is to construct multiple naïve Bayes classifiers on multiple neighborhoods by using different radius values for a target test example, and then to select the most accurate one to classify the test example. In the framework of SNNB, three variants of algorithm will be developed here. The first called the Selective Neighborhood naïve Bayes with Global Accuracy Estimation (SNNB-G). The second is an enhanced version, SNNB with local accuracy estimation (SNNB-L). And the third one, SNNB-LV, improves SNNB-L with majority vote strategy. All the algorithms have the linear complexity to the size of training set for lazily classifying a test example. Experimental results show that all the three algorithms have achieved rather satisfactory accuracy.

The rest of the paper is organized as follows. Section 2 briefly reviews the framework of selective neighborhood-based naïve bayes and then presents two accuracy estimation techniques to materialize the framework of SNNB. In section 3, we describe a specifically designed ensemble technique for SNNB. In section 4, we evaluate the algorithms on datasets from the UCI Repository for accuracy and computational complexity, and follow it by conclusions and future work in Section 5.

2 Selective Neighborhood-Based Naïve Bayes

Consider a domain where instances are represented as instantiations of a vector $A=\{a_1, a_2, ..., a_m\}$ of m nominal variables. Here, each instance x takes a value $a_i(x)$ from *domain*(a_i) on each a_i. Further, an example (or instance) x is also described by a class label $c(x)$ from *domain*(c). Let $D=\{(x_i, c(x_i)) \mid 1 \leq i \leq n\}$ denote the training dataset of size n. The task of classification is to construct a model (or classifier) from the training set D, which is a function that assigns a class label to a new unlabelled example.

The classifier constructed from the training set D using the naïve Bayes method is denoted by NB(D). This classifier, also represented by NB(x, D), assigns a value from *domain*(c) to an example x.

To alleviate the independence assumption and expect it to come true in a local area (or neighborhood), the <u>S</u>elective <u>N</u>eighborhood based <u>n</u>aïve <u>B</u>ayes (SNNB) was first developed in [16]. The underlying idea is, for a test example, first to construct multiple classifiers on its multiple neighborhoods with different radius, and then to select out the classifier with the highest estimated accuracy to make decision.

For any two examples x and y, the distance between them is normally defined as the number of the attributes on which x and y take on the different values, that is,

$$distance(x, y) = |\{a_i \in A \mid a_i(x) \neq a_i(y)\}|. \tag{1}$$

For an input test example x, its k-neighborhood consists of all the examples in training set D with the distance to x not larger than k, denoted as

$$NH_k(x) = \{x_i \in D \mid distance(x_i, x) \leq k\} \tag{2}$$

We call the naïve Bayes classifier k-NB_x=NB$(NH_k(x))$, trained on $NH_k(x)$, as the k-th local naïve Bayes classifier of x. Clearly, for any input example x, m-NB_x is trained on the whole training set $NH_m(x)=D$, so it is also called the global naïve Bayes classifier.

Due to the fact that naïve Bayes is quite stable, and insensitive to the small change in the training set, not all the $(m+1)$ local naïve Bayes classifiers are necessary and informative enough to construct, for the consideration of efficiency. In other words, we are only interested in a restricted subset of the $(m+1)$ possible neighborhoods, with each neighborhood of interest called a candidate neighborhood. For Simplicity, we use the subscripts in descending order, $S=\{S[1]=m, S[2], ..., S[p]\}$ with $S[i] > S[i+1]$ for $1 \leq i < p$, to denote the subset of neighborhoods $\{NH_{S[1]}, NH_{S[2]}, ..., NH_{S[p]}\}$. We speak of the subset as restricted because it must satisfy two constraints that follow. On the one hand, due to the stability of naïve Bayes, $S[i+1]$ is the maximal number satisfying $|NH_{S[i+1]}| \leq \theta \times |NH_{S[i]}|$, where θ is the support difference threshold (0.5 as the default value) controlling the difference degree of two adjacent candidate neighborhood. This is the support difference constraint. On the other hand, for a small value of k, the k-neighborhood of x may consist of too few examples, making the corresponding k-th local naïve Bayes lack of generalization ability. Therefore, we request that the neighborhood $NH_{S[p]}$ have enough training examples, that is, $|NH_{S[p]}| \geq \varphi$. Here, φ is the support threshold (30 as the default value), and this kind of constraint is called the support constraint.

```
Input: Training set D and target example x;
Output: Predicted classes label of x;
Step 1. Calculate all the candidate neighborhoods
for the test example x.
Step 2. For each candidate neighborhood, learn the
corresponding local naïve Bayes classifier and cal-
culate its estimated accuracy.
Step 3. Choose the local naïve Bayes classifier
with the highest estimated accuracy to make the
decision.
```

Fig. 1. The framework of selective neighborhood-based naïve Bayes

The skeleton of selective neighborhood-based naïve Bayes is shown in figure 1. To instantiate the skeleton, we will use two different accuracy estimation techniques, namely, global accuracy estimation and local accuracy estimation, in this paper. Two variant algorithms, SNNB-G and SNNB-L, are generated as a result.

2.1 Global Accuracy Estimation

Given a data set D_1 and the classifier $NB(D_1)$, the global accuracy is the accuracy estimated with the leave-out-one technique, that is,

$$ACC_G(NB(D_1)) = |\{x \in D_1 | NB(x, D_1-\{x\}) = c(x)\}|/|D_1| \quad (3)$$

To check whether $NB(x, D_1-\{x\}) = c(x)$ holds, we must first leave the example x out of D_1 to get $NB(D_1-\{x\})$ in time $O(m)$, then use $NB(D_1-\{x\})$ to predict the class label of x in time $O(m)$, and finally put x back to restore $NB(D_1)$ in time $O(m)$. Thereby, the complexity of global accuracy estimation is $O(|D_1| \times m)$.

It is evident but seldom stated that a classifier performs quite differently in different regions (or subspaces) of the instance space. The global accuracy estimation takes it for granted that a classifier performs equally well everywhere. This measure expresses the overall "goodness" of a classifier. But for a specific point in the instance space, what we need is a domain expert, namely, a classifier doing best in the local region of the instance. To further justify the local accuracy estimation, let us consider the Nearest Neighbor algorithm (NN) in traditional machine learning. NN algorithm has been widely adopted to make classification with the philosophy that if two examples look similar, they are probably of the same class label. Analogously in this paper, we extend this philosophy to that if a classifier can correctly make the decision for the examples that are most similar to the example x, then we think it can also make the correct decision for x. Such an idea leads to the local accuracy estimation employed in the algorithm SNNB-L as follows.

2.2 Local Accuracy Estimation and Point Accuracy Estimation

Similarly, for a subset $D_2 \subseteq D_1$, the local accuracy of $NB(D_1)$ on D_2 is

$$ACC_L(NB(D_1), D_2) = |\{x \in D_2 | NB(x, D_1 - \{x\}) = c(x)\}| / |D_2| \tag{4}$$

Point accuracy estimation is defined based on local accuracy estimation. For a test example x, let $S = \{S[1] = m, S[2], ..., S[p]\}$ be the set of candidate neighborhoods. We define the point accuracy of $S[i]$-th local naïve Bayes on x as the local accuracy of $S[i]$-th local naïve Bayes on the $S[p]$-th neighborhood of x, that is

$$\begin{aligned} ACC_P(NB(NH_{S[i]}(x)), x) &= ACC_L(NB(NH_{S[i]}(x)), NH_{S[p]}(x)) \\ &= |\{y \in NH_{S[p]}(x) | NB(y, NH_{S[i]}(x) - \{y\}) = c(y)\} \cap NH_{S[p]}(x)| \end{aligned} \tag{5}$$

Evidently, the complexity of point accuracy estimation is $O(|NH_{S[p]}(x)| \times m) = O(\varphi \times m)$, where φ is the support threshold.

2.3 Complexity Analysis

We now begin to analyze the complexity of the algorithms. Let m be the number of attributes and n be the number of objects. The SNNB framework consists of three main steps, as listed in figure 1.

The first step calculates the candidate neighborhoods, $S = \{S[1] = m, S[2], ..., S[p]\}$. Most computation occurs in computing the distance between the input test example x and each training example y in training set D, and storing all the training examples according to their distances to x. So the complexity is $O(m \times n)$.

After step 1, let us assume that all the examples of distance *dist* to x have been stored in $OWD[dist]$. Therefore, we have

$$NH_{S[i]}(x) = NH_{S[i+1]}(x) \cup \bigcup_{j=S[i+1]+1}^{S[i]} OWD[j].$$

The work in step 2 consists of two parts. The first part is to learn a local naïve Bayes classifier for each candidate neighborhood. The complexity is $O(m \times n)$, because we can construct the $S[i]$-th local classifier from $S[i+1]$-th local classifier by incrementally adding the examples in $\bigcup_{j=S[i+1]+1}^{S[i]} OWD[j]$. The second part is to estimate the accuracy of each local classifier. When global accuracy estimation is used, the computation involved is

$$\sum_{i=1}^{p} (|NH_{S[i]}(x)| \times m) \leq m \times n \times \sum_{i=0}^{p-1} \theta^i \leq m \times n \times \frac{1}{1-\theta}.$$

With point accuracy estimation applied, the involved computation is $\varphi \times m \times p \leq \varphi \times m \times \log_2 n$. As a result, the complexity of step 2 is $O(m \times n \times \frac{1}{1-\theta})$ for SNNB-G, while $O(m \times \varphi \times \log_2 n + m \times n))$ for SNNB-L.

The last step uses the local classifier with the highest estimated accuracy to make the decision for x. It can be done in $O(m)$.

From the analysis above, conclusion can be drawn that:

Because θ and φ are preset and remain constant during running, both SNNB-G and SNNB-L have the same computational complexity, $O(m \times n)$.

3 Improving SNNB-L with Ensemble

A large body of research work revealed that ensemble techniques are very effective for improving accuracy. However, the results in [4] and [2] both suggested that ensemble techniques that involve any significant degree of resampling or replication of training examples (for example, Bagging or Boosting) will not work with the nearest neighbor classifier or naïve Bayes classifier. SNNB-L, as a hybrid algorithm of naïve Bayes and nearest neighbor, is likely to bear this characteristic. Our experiments in section 4 will show that Bagging technique does not work for SNNB-L too. This section is to present an effective ensemble method for improving SNNB, which leads to a new algorithm SNNB-LV when applied to SNNB-L. It is based on manipulating the attribute of attribute set.

```
    (1)  Firstly, randomly generate s different attribute
subsets, {B_1, B_2, ..., B_s}. Each subset is generated with
the following method: Randomly select one feature a_i in
A and mark it. Repeat the selection |A| times and set B
as the set of all the marked attributes in A.
    (2) For each B_i, 0≤i≤s,
        (2.1) Calculating all the B_i-candidate neighborhoods
        (2.2)  For each candidate neighborhood, learning the
corresponding local naïve Bayes classifier with the
whole attribute A, and calculating its estimated accu-
racy.
        (2.3)  Voting on the class label predicted by the
local classifier with the highest estimated point accu-
racy. This estimated accuracy is the confidence of the
vote.
    (3)  Return the class label with the maximum votes. The
vote with the highest confidence is used to break the
tie.
```

Fig. 2. The algorithm SNNB-LV

In previous sections, the definitions of distance and neighborhood are both defined with the whole attribute set A. Here, for an attribute subset $B \subseteq A$, we define the B-

distance function: $distance_B(x, y)=|\{b \in B: b(x) \neq b(y)\}|$, and (B, k)-neighborhood of x: $NH_{B, k}(x)=\{x_i \in T | distance_B(x_i, x) \leq k\}$. Accordingly, we can also define B-candidate neighborhoods with the support difference threshold and support threshold.

With s as the size of ensemble, the algorithm SNNB-LV goes as follows.

4 Experimental Evaluations

With the constraint that each dataset should contain at least 300 examples, we selected 22 datasets from UCI machine learning repository [3] to evaluate the algorithms in this paper. Table 1 lists all the datasets used and the related characteristics. Three-fold cross validation was executed on each dataset to obtain the results. For comparison of these algorithms, we made sure that the same cross-validation folds were used for all the different learning algorithms involved in the comparison. All the algorithms were coded in Visual C++ 6.0 with the help of standard template library.

Table 1. Datasets Information

DATA SET	#EXMP	#ATT	#ATT2	#CLS	DATA SET	#EXMP	#ATT	#ATT2	#CLS
ADULT	48842	14	13	2	PIMA	768	8	5.33	2
ANNEAL	898	38	37.33	5	SATIMAGE	6435	36	36	6
AUSTRALIAN	690	14	13.33	2	SEGMENT	2310	19	17	7
CHESS	3196	36	36	2	SHUTTLE-SMALL	5800	9	7	6
GERMAN	1000	20	14.67	2	SICK	2800	29	26	2
HYPO	3163	25	22.67	2	SOLAR	323	12	9	6
LED7	3200	7	7	10	SOYBEAN-LARGE	683	35	35	19
LETTER	20000	16	15	26	TIC-TAC-TOE	958	9	9	2
MUSHROOM	8124	22	22	2	VEHICLE	846	18	18	4
NURSERY	12960	8	8	5	VOTE	435	16	16	2
PENDIGITS	10992	16	16	10	WAVEFORM	5000	21	19	3

#EXMP: the total number of examples;
#ATT: The number of conditional attributes before preprocessing;
#ATT2: The averaged number of conditional attributes after preprocessing over the three folds;
#CLS: the number of class labels.

The algorithms evaluated here include:

- SNNB-G, SNNB-L, SNNB-LV: The algorithms described in this paper.
- SNNBLBAG: The bagging version of SNNB-L.
- C4.5: the well-known decision tree algorithm [14], which has been studied most widely.
- NB: the naïve Bayes algorithm used in this paper, which serves as baseline.
- NBTREE: our implementation of the naïve Bayes Tree algorithm in [10].

- LBR: the Lazy Bayesian Rule algorithm. We ported the implementation version in Weka suite [15] from Java language to C++, in order to make the running time comparison more meaningful.

Since the current implementation of our algorithms can only deal with nominal attributes, the entropy-based discretization algorithm [7] were employed to discretize the numeric attributes in the training set for a given fold, as pre-processing.

4.1 Error Rate Comparison

The detailed error rates on individual datasets are presented in Figure 3. Table 2 lists the mean error rates across the experimental domains.

Table 2. Mean error rates across all the experimental domains

NB	C4.5	NBTREE	LBR	SNNB-G	SNNB-L	SNNBLBAG	SNNB-LV
15.25%	13.66%	11.81%	12.04%	12.59%	11.72%	11.76%	11.01%

The following facts have been observed during the experiments, which follow:

(1) Of the seven learning algorithms, SNNB-LV achieves the lowest average error rate across the 22 domains, and SNNB-L gets the second. The ensemble technique employed has successfully improved the mean error rate of SNNB-L from to 11.72% to 11.01%. At the same time, SNNB-L with the local accuracy estimation performs much better than SNNB-G with the global accuracy estimation.

(2) Compared with NB for error rate, SNNB-L wins in 18 out of the 22 domains, and loses only in 3; while SNNB-LV wins also in 18, and loses in 4. Compared with LBR, SNNB-LV gets 16 wins and 4 loses; while SNNB-L gets 14 wins and 6 loses. Compared with NBTREE, SNNB-L wins in 13 and loses in 9; while SNNB-LV wins in 14 and loses in 7.

(3) Bagging does not work for SNNB-L, while SNNB-LV works well. there is almost no difference in error rate between the SNNB-L and its bagged version SNNBLBAG. On the other hand, SNNB-LV has successfully improve the averaged error rate of SNNB-L from 11.72% to 11.01%

(4) LBR is less accurate than NBTREE, which is contrary to the results in [18]. This is possibly because that Zheng & Webb [18] did the experiments with 10-fold cross validation, while we do with 3-fold. We conjecture that LBR's accuracy improves faster than NBTREE, with the increasing size of training set. In order to support this conjecture, we apply 10-fold cross validation on TIC-TAC-TOE domain. The Accuracy of LBR is 87.16% compared with 81.11% for 3-fold cross validation; while the accuracy of NBTREE is 80.58%, even a little lower than 81.52% for 3-fold cross validation. Further justification is beyond the scope of this paper, and we will do deeper research in the future.

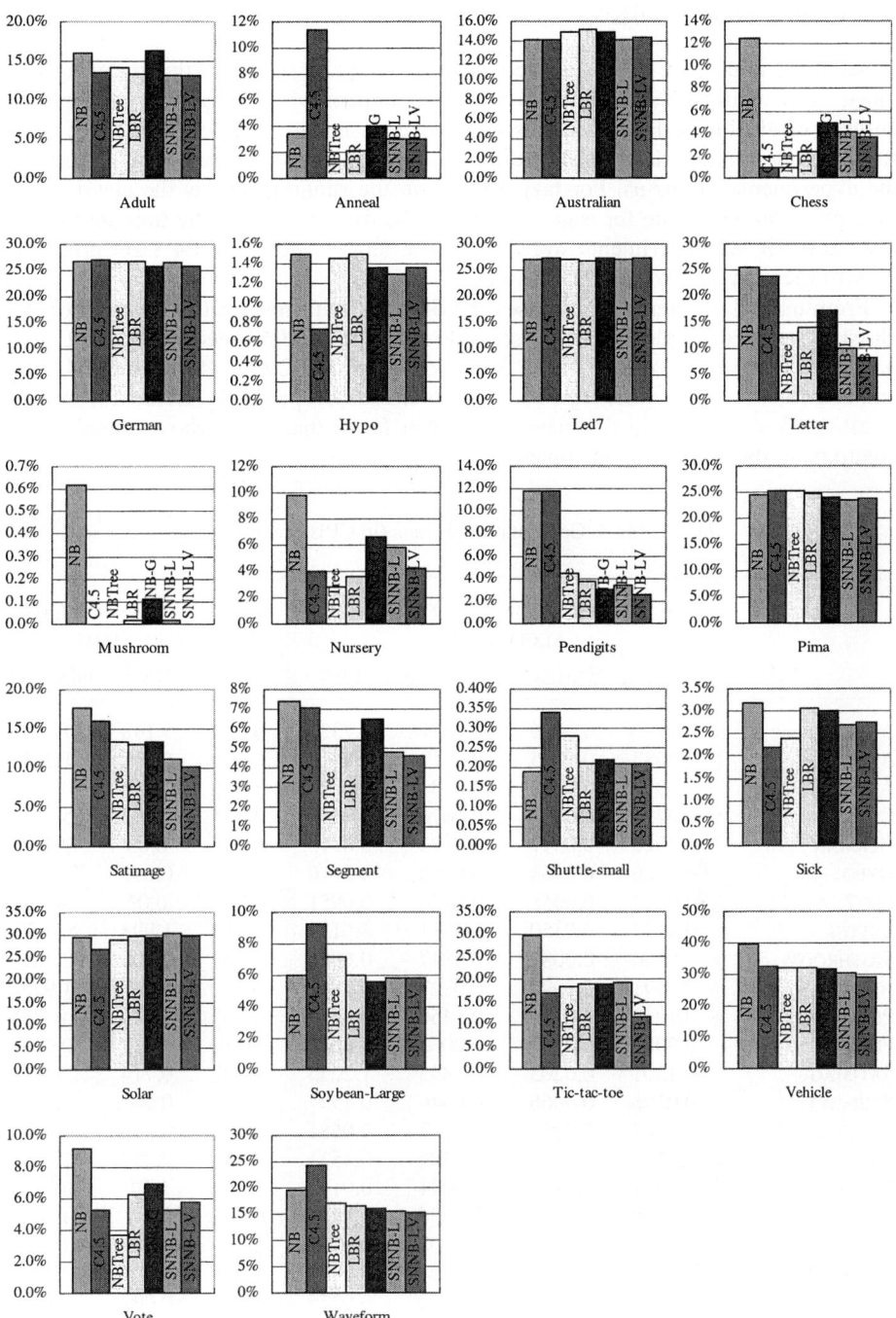

Fig. 3. Error rate comparison on individual datasets

4.2 Computational Costs

In section 2 and 3, we have analyzed that the three algorithms of this paper all have linear computational complexity to both the number of training examples and the number of attributes. However, this analysis does not give any indication of actual running times on real datasets. Therefore in table 3 we list the actual running times on the experimental domains. For lazy algorithm, the running time is the classification time per example; while for eager algorithm, the running time is the training time for one trial. All the experiments were done on a laptop with Intel P4 1.2G processor, 256Mb Memory and WinXP platform.

From table 3, the three worst cases for SNNB-L (with respect to execution time of classifying one example) are 0.035 seconds in LETTER, 0.030 seconds in ADULT, and 0.020 seconds in SATIMAGE. These three domains have 20000, 48842 and 6435 examples; 16, 14 and 36 attributes; 26, 2 and 6 classes; respectively. Evident from table 3, all the 3 algorithms in this paper run much faster than LBR whose complexity is quadratic to the number of attributes.

Table 3. Computational costs (in CPU seconds)

	CLASSIFICATION TIME FOR LAZY ALGORITHM				TRAINING TIME FOR EAGER ALGORITHM		
	SNNB-G	SNNB-L	SNNB-LV	LBR	NB	C4.5	NBTREE
ADULT	0.1190	0.0296	0.2677	1.7325	0.020	3.148	7.344
ANNEAL	0.0083	0.0055	0.0519	0.3413	0.003	0.047	1.816
AUSTRALIAN	0.0017	0.0013	0.0131	0.0224	0.00	0.013	0.060
CHESS	0.0227	0.0071	0.0676	2.0130	0.003	0.097	5.368
GERMAN	0.0026	0.0017	0.0170	0.0315	0.003	0.03	0.074
HYPO	0.0106	0.0063	0.0680	0.3410	0.007	0.043	0.854
LED7	0.0113	0.0058	0.0720	0.0951	0.000	0.02	0.18
LETTER	0.4372	0.0350	0.3581	3.6175	0.013	1.993	55.957
MUSHROOM	0.0364	0.0087	0.0847	0.6984	0.003	0.100	2.781
NURSERY	0.0491	0.0093	0.0727	0.1866	0.00	0.117	1.923
PENDIGITS	0.1059	0.0147	0.1450	0.6664	0.007	0.514	10.699
PIMA	0.0007	0.0007	0.0063	0.0047	0.00	0.00	0.017
SATIMAGE	0.1201	0.0203	0.1895	1.2235	0.007	0.714	25.063
SEGMENT	0.0196	0.0066	0.0646	0.1557	0.007	0.047	1.599
SHUTTLE-SMALL	0.0164	0.0048	0.0522	0.0681	0.003	0.017	0.658
SICK	0.0116	0.0052	0.0569	0.4531	0.00	0.057	1.578
SOLAR	0.0011	0.0015	0.0094	0.0119	0.00	0.01	0.043
SOYBEAN-LARGE	0.0307	0.0197	0.1956	0.7961	0.003	0.08	4.363
TIC-TAC-TOE	0.0018	0.0011	0.0108	0.0115	0.00	0.01	0.07
VEHICLE	0.0052	0.0031	0.0304	0.0977	0.00	0.037	0.474
VOTE	0.0015	0.0014	0.0132	0.0275	0.00	0.003	0.113
WAVEFORM	0.0253	0.0063	0.0597	0.2299	0.0033	0.217	1.799

SNNB-L runs much faster than LBR. The best case is in the CHESS domain with 36 attributes, where SNNB-L is about 284 times faster than LBR. The worst case is in the PIMA domain with 5.33 attributes after discretization, with SNNB-L around 6.8 times faster than LBR. The number of attributes is an important factor in influencing the running time ratio, due to their computational complexity. Another factor is the average size of the antecedents of Bayesian rules for LBR, for the computational complexity of LBR is also linear to the average size.

Table 4. How many examples can be lazily classified with SNNB-L during the time of training a NBTREE classifier

ADULT	248.2	PIMA	24.6
ANNEAL	332.4	SATIMAGE	1233.6
AUSTRALIAN	45.4	SEGMENT	242.2
CHESS	758.3	SHUTTLE-SMALL	137.3
GERMAN	42.7	SICK	305.8
HYPO	136.2	SOLAR	28.9
LED7	31.1	SOYBEAN-LARGE	221.1
LETTER	1598.5	TIC-TAC-TOE	65.0
MUSHROOM	319.0	VEHICLE	150.5
NURSERY	207.0	VOTE	81.9
PENDIGITS	729.9	WAVEFORM	286.5

In addition, we also compared the SNNB-L algorithm with NBTREE by measuring how many examples can be lazily classified with SNNB-L during the time of training an NBTREE classifier, namely, the ratio between the training time of NBTREE and the classification time of SNNB-L. Such information is listed in table 4. SNNB-L is more advisable for the domain with higher ratio. And we also find that the domains with a large number of attributes often have big ratio values, such as the CHESS and SATIMAGE domains. Such phenomenon is because the computational complexity of NBTREE is quadratic to the number of attributes.

Let us consider the problem of choosing between a lazy algorithm and a non-lazy one without regard to accuracy. In practical application domain, new data are generated from time to time, and training data needs to be updated regularly. The updating frequency is normally determined by changing speed of pattern buried in the data. If only a few (or precisely, no more than the ratio in table 4) classifications are performed between two updates, then the lazy algorithm may have an advantage.

5 Stability in Computational Costs

The involved computation in SNNB-L has been analyzed detailedly in section 2. Here, one more factor, the number of classes, is introduced to help model the computational cost of SNNB-L. Let q be the number of classes and t be the time used to classify a test example. The computational complexity of point accuracy estimation is also linear to the number of classes. Since the number of candidate neighborhoods is at most

$\log_2(n)$, we have the formula: $\dfrac{t}{m \times n} = k_1 + k_2 \times \dfrac{q \times \log_2 n}{n}$, where k_1 and k_2 are two coefficients fixed for a given computer.

Next in the figure 4, we draw a graph to describe the relationship of running time of SNNB-L with the characteristics of the experimented dataset. Each dot in the graph represents a dataset. The y-coordinate represents the value of $\dfrac{t}{m \times n}$ in seconds, while the x-coordinate represents the value of $q \times \dfrac{\log_2 n}{n}$. Evidently, this graph manifests that the empirical running time of SNNB-L fits the formula very well.

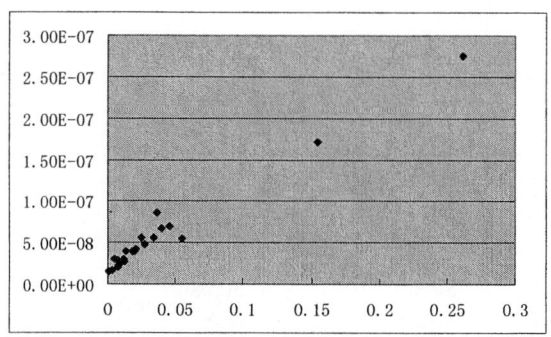

Fig. 4. Relationship between the running time of SNNB-L

6 Conclusions and Future Work

We introduced SNNB, a framework for improving naïve Bayes. In SNNB, multiple local classifiers are trained on multiple neighborhoods with different radius with respect to the target test example, and the local classifier with the highest estimated accuracy is then used to make decision.

Two variant algorithms SNNB-G and SNNB-L, in the framework of SNNB, are instantiated with two accuracy estimation techniques. We also investigated an ensemble technique, and got the algorithm SNNB-LV by applying it to SNNB-L. Those algorithms incorporate some desirable properties of the nearest neighbor classifier and naïve Bayes classifier. Empirical results show that the SNNB algorithms are effective in improving the accuracy and efficient in computational cost.

Future work includes:

(1) *New metrics for accuracy estimation.* One possible way, motivated by [8], is locally weighted accuracy estimation.

(2) *Internal vote strategy.* It seems promising to integrate statistical significance test [5] into the comparison of different local classifiers, and then to use the vote strategy of multiple local classifiers to make decision.

(3) *Application to other classification algorithms.* Beside the naïve Bayes algorithm in this paper, how about applying the idea of SNNB to other classification methods, such as decision tree and neural network, and will it still work well?

Acknowledgments. Thanks are given to Professor Geoffrey Webb in Monash University, who kindly provided the LBR software to the author. This work was funded in part by the Science & Technology Commission of Shanghai Municipality under grant number 03ZR14014, and by the project sponsored by SRF for ROCS, SEM.

References

[1] Aha, D. W.: Lazy learning. Kluwer Academic Publishers (1997)
[2] Bauer, E., & Kohavi, R.: An empirical comparison of voting classification algorithms: Bagging, boosting, and variants. Machine Learning, 36 (1999) 105-142.
[3] Blake, C. L., & Merz, C. J.: UCI repository of machine learning databases. University of California, Irvine, CA (1998) http://www.ics.uci.edu/~mlearn/MLRepository.html
[4] Breiman, L.: Bagging predictors. Machine Learning, 24 (1996) 123-140.
[5] Dietterich, T. G.: Approximate statistical tests for comparing supervised classification learning algorithms. Neural Computation, 10 (1998) 1895-1924.
[6] Duda, R. O., & Hart, P. E.: Pattern classification and scene analysis. New York: John Wiley (1973)
[7] Fayyad, U. M., & Irani, K. B.: Multi-interval discretization of continuous-valued attributes for classification learning. Proceedings of the Thirteenth International Joint Conference on Artificial Intelligence, Morgan Kaufmann (1993) 1022-1027
[8] Frank, E., Hall, M., & Pfahringer, B.: Locally weighted naive Bayes. Proceedings of the 19th Conference on Uncertainty in Artificial Intelligence, Morgan Kaufmann (2003) 249-256
[9] Friedman, N., & Goldszmidt, M.: Building classifiers using Bayesian networks. Proceedings of the Thirteenth National Conference on Artificial Intelligence, AAAI Press/ MIT Press (1996) 1277-1284
[10] Kohavi, R.: Scaling up the accuracy of naïve-Bayes classifiers: a decision-tree hybrid. Proceedings of the Second International Conference on Knowledge Discovery & Data Mining, Cambridge/Menlo Park: AAAI Press/MIT press (1996) 202-207
[11] Kononenko, I.: Semi-naïve Bayesian classifier. Proceedings of the Sixth European Working Session on Learning, Berlin: Springer-Verlag (1991) 206-219
[12] Langley, P., & Sage, S.: Induction of selective Bayesian classifiers. Proceedings of the Tenth Conference on Uncertainty in Artificial Intelligence, Morgan Kaufmann (1994) 339-406
[13] Pazzani, M.: Constructive induction of Cartesian product attributes. Proceedings of the Conference ISIS96: Information, Statistics and Induction in Science, Singapore: World Scientific (1996) 66-77
[14] Quinlan, J. R.: C4.5: Programs for machine learning. Morgan Kaufmann (1993)
[15] Witten, I. H., & Frank, E.: Data Mining: Practical machine learning tools with Java implementations. San Francisco: Morgan Kaufmann (2000)
[16] Xie, Z., Hsu, W., Liu, Z., & Lee, M.-L.: SNNB: a selective neighborhood-based naïve Bayes for lazy classification. Lecture Notes in Computer Science 2336, Springer-Verlag (2002) 104-114
[17] Zheng, Z.: Naïve Bayesian classifier committees. Proceedings of the Tenth European Conference on Machine Learning, Berlin: Springer-Verlag (1998) 196-207
[18] Zheng, Z., & Webb, G. I.: Lazy learning of Bayesian rules. Machine Learning, 41 (2000) 53-84

MMPClust: A Skew Prevention Algorithm for Model-Based Document Clustering*

Xiaoguang Li, Ge Yu, and Daling Wang

School of Information Science and Engineering, Northeastern University,
Shenyang 110004, P.R.China
yuge@mail.neu.edu.cn

Abstract. To support very high dimensionality, model-based clustering is an intuitive choice for document clustering. However, the current model-based algorithms are prone to generating the skewed clusters, which influence the quality of clustering seriously. In this paper, the reasons of skew are examined and determined as the inappropriate initial model, the unfitness of cluster model and the interaction between the decentralization of estimation samples and the over-generalized cluster model. This paper proposes a skew prevention document-clustering algorithm (MMPClust), which has two features: (1) a content-based cluster model is used to model the cluster better; (2) at the re-estimation step, a part of documents most relevant to its corresponding class are selected automatically for each cluster as the estimation samples to break this interaction. MMPClust has less restrictions and more applicability in document clustering than the previous methods.

1 Introduction

In recent years, high-quality document clustering plays more and more important role in the applications such as information retrieval, Web data mining, and Web data management. In general, document clustering can be divided into the similarity-based approach and the model-based approach. Due to the very high dimensionality and the sparsity of document features, the former met with a great challenge. Strehl [1] has proved that the traditional similarity functions are not adaptable to high-dimensional space. Moreover, a cluster in the similarity-based approach is represented by a medoid or mean commonly, which is almost meaningless for document clustering. In contrast, probabilistic model-based clustering is a natural choice for very high-dimensional data and has shown the promising results [2~15]. In model-based clustering, a cluster is described by a representative probabilistic model, which provides a probabilistic interpretation. Typically, model-based clustering can be divided into the partitioning approach and the hierarchical approach. In this paper, we focus on the latter.

In practice, model-based clustering, as well as similarity-based clustering, quite often generates some skewed clusters that are empty or extremely small, especially

---

* Supported by the National Natural Science Foundation of China under Grant No.60173051 and the Teaching and Research Award Program for Outstanding Young Teachers in Higher Education Institution of the Ministry of Education, China

when data is in high dimensional (>100) space [15]. The skewed clusters influence the quality of clustering seriously. Even though feature selection technique applied, a document has approximately ten thousands dimensions so that it is prone to generating the skewed clusters for document clustering. To prevent the skewed clusters, the balanced clustering methods [2, 14, 15, 16, 17] were proposed in the past. Generally, their idea is to set the proportion of each cluster to the whole data as the algorithm's constraint, and they are applied mostly into the situations where the clusters have the comparable size. Actually it is difficult to set this constraint in most cases, and the previous works do not study further why the skewed clusters generate, and just consider it as a constraint-based optimization problem.

Our basic idea is to design a clustering algorithm that can group the documents into the clusters of inherent size without any balancing constraint. With the analysis, we consider that there are three factors to the occurrence of skewed clusters: the inappropriate initial model, the unfitness of cluster model and the interaction between the decentralization of estimation samples and the over-generalized cluster model. Our solution focuses on the last two factors and propose a content-based partial re-estimating document-clustering algorithm (MMPClust), which has two features: firstly, to solve the unfitness problem, MMPClust applies a two-component mixture model (topic-based model and general model), which can model document content more accurately and shows a goodness of fit with the experiments. Secondly, to solve the over-generation problem, for each cluster, in stead of all the documents, but a part of documents that most relevant to the corresponding class, are selected automatically as the samples to re-estimate the cluster model. It reduces the decentralization of estimation samples, and then prevents the model to be estimated over-generally. Compared with the previous works, MMPClust doesn't need the prior knowledge about the proportion of each cluster, and is more feasible in the practical applications. The experiments show that MMPClust prevents the skewed clusters in a great degree, and its Macro-F1 measure outperforms the previous' methods.

The rest of the paper is organized as follows. Section 2 introduces briefly probabilistic model-based partitioning clustering. Section 3 gives some definitions and conception, and examines how the skewed clusters generate. Section 4 proposes the MMPClust algorithm. The experiments to evaluate its performance are provided in section 5. Section 6 discusses the related works. Section 7 gives the conclusions and our future works.

2 Overview of Probabilistic Model-Based Partitioning Clustering

In this section, we introduce briefly model-based partitioning clustering. Given data collection $X = \{x_1, x_2...x_n\}$, for model-based clustering, the data $x_i \in X$ is considered to be a sample independently drawn from a mixture model [18] $\theta = \{\theta_1, \theta_2,..., \theta_k\}$. The main assumption is that data points are generated by, first, randomly picking a model θ_j with probability $P(\theta_j)$, and second, by drawing a data x_i from a corresponding distribution. Each cluster j is associated with the corresponding distribution model θ_j, called *cluster model*, and each data point carries not only its observable attributes, but also a hidden cluster. The overall likelihood of the data collection X is its probability to be drawn from a given mixture model θ, and then model-based clustering boils down to finding the maximum likelihood estimation of θ.

In general, the partitioning clustering can be divided into three categories: hard clustering, soft clustering and stochastic clustering [2]. Due to its simplicity, hard clustering has been applied widely into document clustering [2, 10, 11, 12]. The most popular probabilistic models in document clustering are the multivariate Bernoulli model [2], the multinomial model [2, 12] and the von Mises-Fisher (vMF) model [10, 11]. Of the three types of models, the vMF leads to the best performance and the multivariate Bernoulli the worst, and the multinomial model is a bit worse than the vMF. However, the parameter estimation of the vMF model is computationally much more expensive, multinomial distribution is used widely as the underlying cluster model for document clustering. In this paper, the multinomial model-based partitioning hard clustering, denoted by multiK-means, is selected as the baseline algorithm [2].

3 Analysis of Clustering Skew

Given a document collection X and a inherent criteria R for X to evaluate the relevance between documents, suppose that there are k inherent classes in X with respect to R. Let l_i, $i = 1\sim k$ be a class and $L=\{l_1, l_2 \ldots l_k\}$ be the class set. For the model-based clustering, each class $l_i \in L$ is associated with a class model θ_i, and let θ be a class model set. A partitioning clustering constructs k partitions of X, where each partition represents a cluster, denoted as c_i, $i = 1\sim k$. Let $C = \{c_1, c_2 \ldots c_k\}$ be a cluster set. The documents assigned to cluster c_i construct the ***sample set*** X_i, which satisfies $\cup X_i = X \wedge X_i \cap X_j = \Phi$, $i = 1\sim k$, $I \neq j$. Each $c_i \in C$ is associated with a cluster model θ'_i obtained by a clustering algorithm, and let θ' be a cluster model set. Without the loss of generality, let each $c_i \in C$ be associated with $l_i \in L$ correspondingly.

Definition 1. (*Estimation sample*) For a cluster, the *estimation sample* is the data used to re-estimate the cluster model's parameters.

Definition 2. (*Decentralization of estimation sample*) For a *cluster* c_i, if its estimation samples contain many documents $x \in l_j$, $j \neq i$, we call it the decentralization of estimation sample.

Definition 3. (*Over-generalization of cluster model*) If a cluster model θ'_j reflects not only the characteristic of l_j, but also that of other l_i, $i \neq j$, especially when $P(x|\theta'_j) > P(x|\theta'_i)$, $x \in l_i$, it is called over-generalization of cluster model θ'_j.

Definition 4. (*Clustering skew*) Given X, L and C, if there is a subset $C' \subset C$, where the cluster $c_i \in C'$ contains so many documents satisfying $x \in X_i \wedge x \notin l_i$ as to generate empty or extremely small cluster $c_j \notin C' \wedge c_j \in C$, called *Clustering skew*.

In general, there exists the "winner-take-all" behavior for high dimensional space. For similarity-based clustering, it has been argued in [19, 20] that given two targets, one target is prone to winning most of data and few of data are assigned to the other, since the contrast between the distances of different data points does not exist. This behavior also appears in model-based clustering so that if an inappropriate model applied, most of data are prone to being grouped into a few wrong clusters. An appropriate model here has two points:

(1) The model initialization. Since clustering is an unsupervised learning process, there is not enough prior knowledge to select a perfect initial model. There are many initialization techniques proposed in the past, but none of them perform well [12].

(2) The fitness of cluster model. The task of document clustering is to group the documents with respect to the content-based relevance, so the model should reveal the characteristic of content. The more fitness to content characteristic a cluster model is, the more documents can be grouped into correct clusters, and the less the decentralization occurs. Generally, the current cluster model assumes that the document is generated by one and only one component, but it is well-known that the content of document is determined by the multiple factors such as topic, background, general knowledge of writing, styles, context etc. It is more appropriate to using multi-component to model the cluster.

Ideally, the model θ'_j of cluster c_j will approach gradually to the distributional characteristic of class l_j. However, because of the inappropriate cluster model mentioned above, at the assignment stage, especially the first assignment stage, most of data are prone to being assigned to a few wrong clusters, denoted by C', and then it results in the decentralized samples X_c for each cluster $c \in C'$. If all the decentralized samples X_c are used as the estimation samples, as the current model-based methods do, the cluster model θ'_c is most likely to be estimated over-generally, and then with this θ'_c, the more data $x \notin l_c$ are assigned to c at the next assignment step. With the interaction between the decentralization of estimation samples and the over-generalization of cluster model, the skewed clusters are generated ultimately.

4 MMPClust Algorithm

Naturally, to prevent the skewed clusters, in addition to select an appropriate initial model, there are two more works to do. One is to model the cluster properly to reveal the content-based characteristic so as to make the samples more centralized at the assignment stage. The other is that at the model re-estimation stage a part of documents that are the most relevant to the corresponding class for each cluster, are selected as the estimation samples to break the interaction between the decentralization and the over-generalization. Actually, even though the decentralized samples occur in some clusters on account of the inappropriate initial model, with the estimation samples selection, this influence will not expand further.

4.1 Content-Based Cluster Model

In this paper, suppose that the document feature is the word independent with each other. On selecting a word to describe the content, only topic and general knowledge are taken into account. General knowledge is referred to as the knowledge irrelevant to topic but helpful to describe the content, e.g. how to choose an adjunct. We assume that the content of each cluster and document is related to only one topic. The cluster model is mixture model combined the topic model with the general model, whose parameters are denoted by θ_T and θ_G respectively. Certainly, in addition to these two factors, there are many factors to determine the document characteristic, yet the two-component mixture model is easy to implement, and still achieves the significant performance much better than the single-component model. Here, we assume both the topic model and the general model are multinomial distribution. Note that other probabilistic distributions, such as Bernoulli, vMF, etc., also can be applied. The multinomial distribution is selected in this paper just for its good performance in document clustering [2].

We define the latent variable z that takes two values: T and G, representing the topic model and the general model respectively. Given document x and cluster c_j, the probability that c_j generate x is:

$$P(x|c_j;\theta_j') = \prod_{t \in x} P(t|c_j;\theta_j') = \prod_{t \in x} \sum_{z=\{T,G\}} P(t|c_j,z;\theta_z^j) P(z) \qquad (1)$$

Because the latent variable exists, the EM algorithm is applied to estimate θ_T and θ_G. However, EM algorithm exhibits slow convergence and is costly, so some simplifications are made as follow: $P(t|c_j,z=T;\theta_T^j)$ and $P(t|c_j,z=G;\theta_G^j)$ are estimated with the maximum likelihood $P_{ML}(t|c_j,z=T;\theta_T^j) = \dfrac{c(t,X_j)}{\sum_{t'} c(t',X_j)}$

and $P_{ML}(t|c_j,z=G;\theta_G^j) = \dfrac{\sum_{x \in X} c(t,x)}{\sum_{x' \in X}\sum_{t' \in x'} c(t',x')}$, where $c(t, X_j)$ is the counts of word t occurring in X_j. After this simplification, only $P(z)$ is required to be estimated. The detailed algorithm is as follow. Note that in algorithm 1, $\theta_{tc_j,T} \equiv P_{ML}(t|c_j,z=T;\theta_T^j)$ and $\theta_{tc_j,G} \equiv P_{ML}(t|c_j,z=G;\theta_G^j)$.

Algorithm 1: Cluster model estimation
Input: X_j for cluster c_j.
Output: $P(z)$ for c_j
1. Initialize $P^0(z=T)$ and $P^0(z=G)$
2. Do until convergence {
   //E-step

   $\hat{P}^{(i)}(z=T|t) = \dfrac{\theta_{tc_j,T} P^{(i-1)}(z=T)}{\sum_{z'} \theta_{tc_j,z'} P^{(i-1)}(z')}$; $\hat{P}^{(i)}(z=G|t) = \dfrac{\theta_{tc_j,G} P^{(i-1)}(z=G)}{\sum_{z'} \theta_{tc_j,z'} P^{(i-1)}(z')}$;

   //M-step:

   $P^{(i)}(z=T) = \dfrac{1}{N}\sum_{t'} n(t') \hat{P}^{(i)}(z=T|t')$; $P^{(i)}(z=G) = \dfrac{1}{N}\sum_{t'} n(t') \hat{P}^{(i)}(z=G|t')$;}
3. Return $P(z=T)$ and $P(z=G)$;

4.2 Estimation Samples Selection

This subsection will show how to select the most relevant part of documents as the estimation samples to prevent the model from being estimated over-generally.

Definition 5. For a cluster c_j and the corresponding document set X_j, if a document $x \in X_j$ belongs to class l_j, we call it as that x *matches* the cluster c_j, otherwise, x *mismatches* c_j and is called a *noise* data of cluster c_j.

We define the *matching function* $\Delta: X \to R^+$ as: Given the cluster set $C = \{c_1, c_2 \ldots c_k\}$, for $x \in X$,

$$\Delta(x) = Max\{P(x|c_i) | i = 1 \sim k\} - \frac{1}{k}\sum_{i=1\sim k} P(x|c_i) \qquad (2)$$

Given c_j and X_j, the function $\Delta(x)$ measures the matching degree between $x \in X_j$ and c_j. In general, given $x_1, x_2 \in X_j$, if x_1 belongs to l_j, but x_2 not, then $\Delta(x_1) > \Delta(x_2)$. If the Δ of document is near to zero, it is difficult to judge which cluster it belongs to. Note that, it is not true for all cases, i.e. given $x_1, x_2 \in X_j$ and $x_1 \in l_j$, $x_2 \notin l_j$, $\Delta(x_1)$ may be smaller than $\Delta(x_2)$, but as discussed as follow, according to the matching degree we could select the estimation samples where the probability of matching the cluster is higher than that of mismatching.

We define the variable z that takes two values: r and $\bar{r}$, which represent "match" and "mismatch" respectively. From a lot of experiments we found that for each cluster c_j, the Δ distribution of the documents that match c_j can be modeled as a normal distribution (Formula 3), while the Δ distribution of the documents that mismatch c_j can be modeled as an exponential distribution (Formula 4). The Fig. 1 illustrates the Δ distribution in one of our experiments.

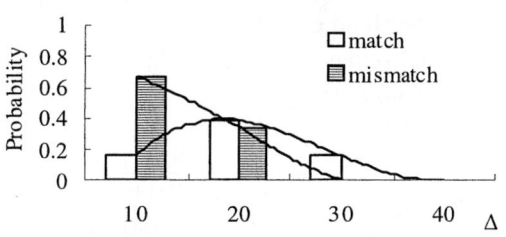

Fig. 1. Δ distribution of matching and mismatching

$$P(\Delta|z=r;c_j) = \frac{1}{\sqrt{2\pi}\delta_j}\exp\left(-\frac{(\Delta-\mu_j)^2}{2\delta_j^2}\right) \qquad (3)$$

$$P(\Delta|z=\bar{r};c_j) = \lambda_j \exp(-\lambda_j \Delta) \qquad (4)$$

The EM algorithm is used to estimate the parameters $\hat{\mu}_j$, $\hat{\delta}_j$ and $\hat{\lambda}_j$.

Theorem 1. Given $\hat{\mu}_j$, $\hat{\delta}_j$, $\hat{\lambda}_j$, $P_j(r)$ and $P_j(\bar{r})$, for $x \in X_j$, if $\frac{1}{2}(a - \sqrt{a^2 - 4b}) < \Delta(x) < \frac{1}{2}(a + \sqrt{a^2 - 4b})$, then $P(r|\Delta(x);c_j) > P(\bar{r}|\Delta(x);c_j)$, where $a = 2(\hat{\mu}_j + \hat{\lambda}_j\hat{\delta}_j^2)$, $b = \hat{\mu}_j^2 + 2\hat{\delta}_j^2 \ln \sqrt{2\pi}\hat{\lambda}_j\hat{\delta}_j P_j(\bar{r}) / P_j(r)$.

Proof:

$$P(r|\Delta(x);c_j) > P(\bar{r}|\Delta(x);c_j) \stackrel{(1)}{\Rightarrow} P(\Delta(x)|r)P_j(r) > P(\Delta(x)|\bar{r})P_j(\bar{r})$$

$$\Rightarrow \frac{1}{\sqrt{2\pi}\hat{\delta}_j}\exp\left(-\frac{(\Delta(x)-\hat{\mu}_j)^2}{2\hat{\delta}_j^2}\right)P_j(r) > \hat{\lambda}_j \exp(-\hat{\lambda}_j\Delta(x))P_j(\bar{r}) \stackrel{(2)}{\Rightarrow} \Delta(x)^2 - a\Delta(x) + b < 0 \qquad (5)$$

where (1) applies the Bayes rule; (2) takes the logarithm for both sides of the inequation, and then $a = 2(\hat{\mu}_j + \hat{\lambda}_j \hat{\delta}_j^2)$, $b = \hat{\mu}_j^2 + 2\hat{\delta}_j^2 \ln \sqrt{2\pi} \hat{\lambda}_j \hat{\delta}_j P_j(\bar{r})/P_j(r)$. The inequation 5 is a one variable quadratic inequation, its solution is $\frac{1}{2}(a - \sqrt{a^2 - 4b}) < \Delta(x) < \frac{1}{2}(a + \sqrt{a^2 - 4b})$. ∎

When $\Delta(x) > \frac{1}{2}(a + \sqrt{a^2 - 4b})$, though it doesn't satisfy Theorem 1, $P(\bar{r}|\Delta;c_j)$ is usually so small as to be close to zero, we can ignore it and set the threshold for the cluster c_j as

$$\varepsilon_j = \frac{1}{2}(a - \sqrt{a^2 - 4b}) \qquad (6)$$

The algorithm of computing the selection threshold is given as follows. Note that in the step 1, all $\Delta(x)$, $x \in X_j$ are sorted descending, and the 2/3 highest Δ in X_j are used to compute the mean and variance as the initial value of μ_j and δ_j. The initial value of λ_j is the mean over X_j and $P^0(r) = 0.5$ empirically. In the step 2, $N = |X_j|$.

Algorithm 2: Compute the selection threshold
Input: cluster model $\theta = \{\theta_1, \theta_2, \ldots, \theta_k\}$ and X_j for cluster c_j
Output: threshold ε for X_j
1. Initialize the μ^0, δ^0 and λ^0;
2. Do until convergence {
    //E-step
$$\hat{P}^i(r|\Delta) = \frac{P^{i-1}(\Delta|r)P^{i-1}(r)}{P^{i-1}(\Delta|r)P^{i-1}(r) + P^{i-1}(\Delta|\bar{r})P^{i-1}(\bar{r})};$$

$$\hat{P}^i(\bar{r}|\Delta) = \frac{P^{i-1}(\Delta|\bar{r})P^{i-1}(\bar{r})}{P^{i-1}(\Delta|r)P^{i-1}(r) + P^{i-1}(\Delta|\bar{r})P^{i-1}(\bar{r})};$$

  //M-step
$$\mu^i = \frac{\sum_\Delta \hat{P}^i(r|\Delta)\Delta}{\sum_{\Delta'} \hat{P}^i(r|\Delta')}; \quad \delta^i = \frac{\sum_\Delta \hat{P}^i(r|\Delta)(\Delta - \mu^i)^2}{\sum_{\Delta'} \hat{P}^i(r|\Delta')}; \quad \lambda^i = \frac{\sum_\Delta \hat{P}^i(\bar{r}|\Delta)}{\sum_{\Delta'} \hat{P}^i(\bar{r}|\Delta')\Delta'};$$

$$P^i(r) = \frac{1}{N}\sum_\Delta P^i(r|\Delta); \quad P^i(\bar{r}) = 1 - P^i(r);\}$$
3. Compute ε by Formula 6;
4. Return ε;

4.3 MMPClust Algorithm

Like other model-based partitioning algorithms, the MMPClust algorithm mainly consists of document assignment step and cluster model re-estimation step. Unlike the previous algorithms, MMPClust adopt content-based cluster model and the estimation samples selection.

Algorithm 3: MMPClust
Input: $X = \{x_1, x_2 \ldots x_n\}$.
Output: Trained cluster model $\theta = \{\theta_1, \theta_2 \ldots \theta_k\}$, and a partition of X given by the cluster identity vector $Y = \{y_1, y_2 \ldots y_n\}$, $y_i \in \{1, \ldots, k\}$.

1. Initialize θ^0, P_t^0 and $m = 0$;
2. For each $t \in V$, $V = \{t' | t' \in x,$ for all $x \in X\}$
3. Compute $P_{ML}(t|G) = \dfrac{\sum_{x \in X} c(t,x)}{\sum_{x' \in X} \sum_{t' \in x'} c(t',x')}$;
4. Do until convergence {
    //Assignment step
5.   Compute Pt_j^m, $j = 1 \sim k$ by the algorithm 1;
6.   For each $x_i \in X$, $i = 1 \sim n$,
7. $y_i = \arg\max_j \sum_{t \in x_i} \log\left(P^m{}_{ML}(t|c_j,T)Pt_j^m + P^m{}_{ML}(t|G)(1 - Pt_j^m)\right)$;
    //Re-estimation step
8.   For $j = 1 \sim k$, do {
9.   Let $X_j = \{x_i | y_i = j\}$;
10.   Compute ε_j by the algorithm 2;
11.   Let $X_j' = \{x_i | y_i = j \wedge \Delta(x_i) > \varepsilon_j\}$;
12. $P^{m+1}{}_{ML}(t|c_j,T) = \dfrac{c(t,X_j')}{\sum_{t'} c(t',X_j')}$;}
13. m++;}
14. Return θ and Y;

Note that in the step 5, when training the $P(T)$, its initial value is set to 0.9 empirically, and then $P(G)$ is 0.1. Moreover, in the step 7, for the word t appears in x but not in cj, i.e. $t \notin V_j \wedge t \in x$, $P_{ML}(t|c_j,T)$ is usually estimated by a small value, e.g. $1/|V|$, $V = V_1 \cup \ldots \cup V_k$, or zero. The paper adopts the latter.

5 Performance Experiment

In this section, we first introduce the experiment method, and then give our experiment results and make analysis.

5.1 Experiment Method

20NG [21] and BINGLE [22] are selected as testing corpus. In order to evaluate the algorithm's performance on the different datasets, 7 datasets are constructed from these two corpuses. All the words are stemmed, and then the stop words are removed according to an artificial dictionary. The summary of datasets is shown in the Table 1.

Because of the constraints on the cluster size, the results obtained by the balanced methods aren't skewed certainly. So MMPClust is not compared with the balanced methods, but with multiK-means. In order to evaluate the performance of the content-based cluster model and the estimation samples selection respectively, we design another algorithm using the content-based model only, called mmK-means, and compare the mmK-means, MMPClust with multiK-means on the 7 datasets. These three algorithms are initialized with the same models selected at random.

In this paper we use the confusion matrix and Macro-F1 as evaluation criteria. The confusion matrix can reflect intuitively whether the clustering skew or not, and Macro-F1 can evaluate the overall quality of clustering.

Table 1. Summary of datasets

Dataset	K	Number of documents	Number of words
20NG4C4000	4	3995	14077
TALK4C4000	4	3997	12186
SCI4C4000	4	4000	13427
BG2C1000	2	987	14256
BG3C600	3	585	10380
BG6C120	6	120	2559
BG10C1000	10	1000	17142

5.2 Result and Analysis

Due to the space limitation, only the confusion matrix of the three algorithms in BG3C600 is given, as shown in Fig. 2. In the 1st-iteration, of all three algorithms, the cluster #3 appears the decentralization, while with the content-based cluster model the decentralization is reduced greatly, as shown in Fig. 2(b) and Fig. 2(c). In the 3rd-iteration, no further improvements are achieved by multiK-means and mmK-means, but with the estimation sample selection the decentralization in the cluster #3 are reduced further by MMPClust. At last, MMPClust avoids the skew clusters, much better than mmK-means does.

Table 2 summarizes the Macro-F1 measure of three algorithms. For the multiK-means algorithm, the clustering skew appears in 20NG4C4000, TALK4C4000, SCI4C4000, BG3C600, BG6C120 and BG10C1000, but not in BG2C1000. BG2C1000 dataset includes two classes: art and networks with high inter-similarity and low intra-similarity, so multiK-means performs better in the BG2C1000 dataset than on the others. The average Macro-F1 of multiK-means is 0.447, which is much lower than that of mmK-means and MMPClust.

Both mmK-means and MMPClust prevent the clustering skew in a great degree. The average Macro-F1 of mmK-means is 0.589, 31.77% higher than that of multiK-means. On the whole, mmK-means reduces the clustering skew, especially in the 20NG4C4000 dataset, where the Macro-F1 of mmK-means is 118.09% higher than that of multiK-means. But in SCI4C4000, it also generates the clustering skew. The reason is that there are multi-topics in each class, which doesn't satisfy our assumption that each cluster only focuses on one topic. MMPClust performs best among the three algorithms. It prevents the clustering skew in all the 7 datasets. The average Macro-F1 of MMPClust is 0.732, 24.28% higher than that of mmK-means, furthermore 63.76% higher than that of multiK-means. Especially in the SCI4C4000 dataset, MMPClust prevents the clustering skew and achieves significant performance improvement, 101.2% and 253.8% higher than those of mmK-means and multiK-means respectively.

6 Related Work

Although the clustering skew often occurs in high-dimensional data clustering and influences the quality of clustering seriously, it is surprising that there are few studies

(a) mulitK-means

	<1>	<2>	<3>
#1	75	15	22
#2	17	121	12
#3	104	56	163

1st-iteration

	<1>	<2>	<3>
#1	38	2	4
#2	10	126	6
#3	148	64	187

3rd-iteration

	<1>	<2>	<3>
#1	17	2	3
#2	8	122	6
#3	171	68	188

Clustering results

(b) mmK-means

	<1>	<2>	<3>
#1	92	20	21
#2	17	126	12
#3	87	46	164

1st-iteration

	<1>	<2>	<3>
#1	99	17	21
#2	16	132	12
#3	81	43	164

3rd-iteration

	<1>	<2>	<3>
#1	99	14	21
#2	16	135	12
#3	81	43	164

Clustering results

(c) MMPClust

	<1>	<2>	<3>
#1	92	20	21
#2	17	126	12
#3	87	46	164

1st-iteration

	<1>	<2>	<3>
#1	126	18	14
#2	3	139	2
#3	67	35	181

3rd-iteration

	<1>	<2>	<3>
#1	162	5	13
#2	4	155	3
#3	30	32	181

Clustering results

Fig.2. Clustering process of three algorithms in BG3C600

Table 2. Summary of Macro-F1

dataset	multiK-means	mmK-means	MMPClust	mmK-means vs. multiK-means	MMPClust vs. mmK-means	MMPClust vs. multiK-means
20NG4C4000	0.293	0.639	0.785	+118.09%	+22.8%	+167.9%
SCI4C4000	0.145	0.255	0.513	+75.86%	+101.2%	+253.8%
TALK4C4000	0.383	0.509	0.607	+32.9%	+19.3%	+58.5%
BG2C1000	0.92	0.93	0.94	+1.09%	+1.08%	+2.17%
BG3C600	0.502	0.68	0.853	+35.46%	+25.4%	+69.9%
BG6C120	0.477	0.617	0.721	+29.35%	+16.86%	+51.15%
BG10C1000	0.411	0.49	0.703	+19.22%	+43.47%	+71.05%
Avg.	0.447	0.589	0.732	+31.77%	+24.28%	+63.76%

focusing on it in the past. To prevent the clustering skew, current solutions is to set the size constraints on each cluster and to consider the clustering as constraint-based optimization problem.

In [15] a balanced clustering method assumes that the data points satisfy the balancing constraint. Reference [14] also constrains each cluster to be assigned at least a minimum number m ($<N/k$) of data points. The data assignment problem is formulated as a minimum cost flow problem. Zhong [2] proposes a balanced model-based hard clustering framework that is applied to any distribution. They [16] also propose a soft balancing strategy built on a general soft model-based clustering framework. Instead of constraining the actual number of data objects in each cluster to be equal, they constrain the expected number of data objects in each cluster to be equal.

In [17] the approach to obtain balanced clusters is to convert the clustering problem into a graph-partitioning problem, and proposed the "min-cut" algorithms that incorporate a balancing constraint.

These algorithms focus on the efficiency and scalability, and are only applicable for some applications where the constraints can be obtained in advance, such as segmenting customers into the groups of rough equal size in market analysis. Differed from above methods, MMPClust need not the prior knowledge about the proportion of each cluster, but with the content-based cluster model and the automatic selection of samples, to prevent the skewed clusters. These features make it more feasible in the practical usages.

7 Conclusion and Future Work

In this paper we analyze the reason of skew generating in document clustering, and propose the MMPClust algorithm to prevent the clustering skew. Different from the current cluster model, our model is derived from the viewpoint of document content, and both the topical content and the general content are taken into account. It has been proved to be effective in our experiments. In order to avoid the influence of estimation samples decentralization we automatically select samples within a cluster to re-estimate model, which needn't set the parameters manually and achieves a further improvement on the clustering results. Compared with the balanced methods in previous work, MMPClust has less restrictions and more applicability for document clustering.

In next step, we will further develop the MMPClust method in three aspects: (1) the efficiency can be further improved, e.g. the estimation samples selection needn't be done at every iteration whenever the skew disappears; (2) the multi-topic situation will be supported, while the current algorithm supports only one topic; (3) the performance of the algorithm will be validated by applying it into text mining applications.

References

1. A. Strehl, J. Ghosh, and Mooney, R., Impact of Similarity Measures on Web Page Clustering, In Proc. 17th National Conf. On artificial Intelligence: Workshop of Artificial Intelligence for Web Search, 2000.
2. S. Zhong, Probabilistic Model-Based Clustering of Complex Data, PhD thesis, The University of Texas at Austin, 2003.
3. S. Zhong and J. Ghosh, A Unified Framework for Model-based Clustering, Machine Learning Research, 2003.
4. S. Kamvar, D. Klein, and C. Manning, Interpreting and Extending Classical Agglomerative Clustering Algorithms Using A Model-based Approach. In Proc. 19th Int. Conf. Machine Learning, 2002.
5. J. D. Banfield and A. E. Raftery, Model-based Gaussian and non-Gaussian Clustering, Biometrics, 1993.
6. C. Fraley, Algorithms for Model-based Gaussian Hierarchical Clustering, SIAM Journal on Scientific Computing, 1999.

7. S. Vaithyanathan and B. Dom, Model-based Hierarchical Clustering, In Proc. 16th Conf. Uncertainty in Artificial Intelligence, 2000.
8. M. Ramoni, P. Sebastiani, and P. Cohen, Bayesian Clustering by Dynamics, Machine Learning, 2002.
9. I. V. Cadez, S. Ganey, and P. Smyth, A General Probabilistic Framework for Clustering Individuals and Objects. In Proc. 6th ACM SIGKDD, 2000.
10. I. S. Dhillon and D. S. Modha, Concept Decompositions for Large Sparse Text Data Using Clustering, Machine Learning, 2001.
11. A. Banerjee and J. Ghosh, Frequency Sensitive Competitive Learning for Clustering on High-Dimensional Hyperspheres, In Proc. IEEE Int. Joint Conf. Neural Networks, 2002.
12. M. Meila and D. Heckerman, An Experimental Comparison of Model-Based Clustering Methods. Machine Learning, 2001.
13. A. K. Jain, M. N. Murty, and P. J. Flynn, Data Clustering: A Review, ACM Computing Surveys, 1999
14. P. S. Bradley, K. P. Bennett, and A. Demiriz, Constrained k-means Clustering, Technical Report MSR-TR-2000-65, Microsoft Research, Redmond, WA, 2000.
15. A. Banerjee and J. Ghosh, On Scaling Up Balanced Clustering Algorithms, In Proc.2nd SIAM Int. Conf. Data Mining, 2002.
16. S. Zhong and J. Ghosh, Model-based Clustering with Soft Balancing, ICDM 2003.
17. G. Karypis and V. Kumar, A fast and high quality multilevel scheme for partitioning irregular graphs, SIAM Journal on Scientific Computing, 1998.
18. G. McLachlan and D. Peel, Finite Mixture Models, John Wiley & Sons, 2000.
19. Beyer K., Goldstein J., Ramakrishnan R., Shaft U., When is Nearest Neighbors Meaningful? ICDT, 1999.
20. Charu C. Aggarwal, Alexander Hinneburg, Daniel A. Keim, On the Surprising Behavior of Distance Metrics in High Dimensional Spaces. ICDT 2001.
21. http://kdd.ics.uci.edu/databases/20newsgroups/20newsgroups.html
22. http://net.pku.edu.cn/~yanqiong/

Designing and Using Views to Improve Performance of Aggregate Queries (Extended Abstract)

Foto Afrati[1], Rada Chirkova[2,*], Shalu Gupta[2], and Charles Loftis[2]

[1] Computer Science Division, National Technical University of Athens,
157 73 Athens, Greece
afrati@cs.ece.ntua.gr
[2] Computer Science Department, North Carolina State University,
Raleigh, NC 27695, USA
{chirkova, sgupta5, celoftis}@csc.ncsu.edu

Abstract. Data-intensive systems routinely use derived data (e.g., indexes or materialized views) to improve query-evaluation performance. We present a system architecture for Query-Performance Enhancement by Tuning (QPET), which combines design and use of derived data in an end-to-end approach to automated query-performance tuning. Our focus is on a tradeoff between (1) the amount of system resources spent on designing derived data and on keeping the data up to date, and (2) the degree of the resulting improvement in query performance. From the technical point of view, the novelty that we introduce is that we combine aggregate query rewriting techniques [1, 2] and view selection techniques [3] to achieve our goal.

1 Introduction

Derived data, such as materialized views or indexes, are routinely used in data-intensive systems to improve query-evaluation performance. In this context, the problem of *designing derived data* can be stated as follows: Given a set of queries, a database, and a set of constraints on derived data (e.g., view-maintenance costs), return definitions of derived data that, when materialized in the database, would satisfy the constraints and reduce the evaluation costs of the queries. Automated design of materialized views and indexes to answer queries is an important component of *automated query-performance tuning*, where a system addresses the performance requirements of *current* important queries by periodically redesigning the stored derived data. For this reason, developing techniques for designing derived data to improve query-answering performance is a recognized research direction in self-administering data-intensive systems [4, 5, 6]. In

---

* This author's work on this material has been supported by the National Science Foundation under Grant No. 0307072.

this extended abstract[1] we outline our approach and an implementation and preliminary evaluation of it on the extensible system architecture for Query-Performance Enhancement by Tuning (QPET) [8].

Generally, spending more time on designing derived data tends to pay off, as greater query-evaluation performance improvement can thereby be achieved. At the same time, often it is not practical to obtain sets of derived data that would *globally minimize* the evaluation costs of the input queries [9, 10, 3]. Several approaches (see, e.g., [10, 3, 11, 12]) have been proposed to design good-quality sets of derived data for SQL queries. Unfortunately, it is not always possible to use algorithms in the literature in automated query-performance tuning. The reason is, in many practical scenarios limited system resources are available for (1) designing derived data, and for (2) keeping the stored derived data up to date.

We study design and use of materialized views and indexes in automated query-performance tuning in relational data-management systems. Our objective is to minimize the evaluation costs of a given query workload by designing and using derived data, subject to given restrictions on design time and on the maintenance time for the stored derived data. To address the tradeoff between these time constraints and the quality of the resulting views or indexes, our approach is to develop specialized algorithms for specific practically important query types. In this paper we present techniques for designing and using materialized views; the techniques are applicable to a practically important class of range-aggregate queries on star-schema data warehouses.

We give an example to show how aggregate query rewriting techniques can contribute to a better view design.

Example 1. Consider a data warehouse with three stored relations:

```
Sales(CustID,DateID,ProductID,SalespersonID,QtySold,Discount)
Customer(CustID,CustName,Address,City,State,RegistrDateID)
Time(DateID,Month,Year)
```

Sales is the fact table, and Customer and Time are dimension tables.

Let the query workload of interest have two star-schema queries, Q1 and Q2. Query Q1 asks for the total quantity of products sold per customer in the second quarter of the year 2004. Q2 asks for the total product quantity sold per year for all years after 1997 to customers in North Carolina.

```
Q1: SELECT c.CustID, SUM(QtySold)      Q2: SELECT t.Year, SUM(QtySold)
    FROM Sales s, Time t, Customer c       FROM Sales s, Time t, Customer c
    WHERE s.DateID=t.DateID                WHERE s.DateID=t.DateID
    AND s.CustID=c.CustID AND Year=2004    AND s.CustID=c.CustID
    AND Month >= 4 AND Month <= 6          AND Year > 1997 AND State = 'NC'
    GROUP BY c.CustID;                     GROUP BY t.Year;
```

We can use techniques from [1] to find that the following view V1 can be used to answer both queries.

---

[1] A full version [7] of this paper is available online.

V1: SELECT CustID,DateID,State,SUM(QtySold) AS SumQS FROM Sales
    GROUP BY CustID,DateID,State;

A rewriting R1 of the query Q1 uses a join of V1 with Customer and Time:

R1: SELECT c.CustID, sum(SumQS) FROM V1, Time t, Customer c
    WHERE V1.DateID = t.DateID AND V1.CustID = c.CustID AND Year = 2004
    AND Month >= 4 AND Month <= 6 GROUP BY c.CustID;

Moreover, techniques from [1] can handle query workloads which do not have the same relation in the FROM clause. Earlier algorithms (e.g., [3]) focused on the datacube and did not consider this more general setting. Note that our approach is also applicable to aggregate queries of a more general type than star-schema queries [7].

Contributions. Our contributions are as follows. (1) We propose a system architecture for automated query-performance tuning in data-management systems, by periodically designing derived data that reduce the evaluation costs of current prevalent queries. (2) We present a theoretical study of the problem of designing materialized views subject to input restrictions on design time. (3) We present a parameterized algorithm for designing and using materialized views subject to input restrictions on design time. Our algorithm uses algorithms such as BPUS [3] as a subroutine and is applicable to a more general class of aggregate queries than just queries on star-schema data warehouses. (Our approach can be easily extended to designing materialized views *and indexes*, by using, instead of BPUS, its extension described in [11]. In addition, the approach can be used to design derived data that satisfy view maintenance-cost requirements.) (4) We experimentally validate the approach using our QPET implementation [8] of the proposed system architecture.

Related Work

Designing and using derived data to improve query-evaluation performance has long been a direction of research and practical efforts. Over time, a wealth of theoretical results (see [13] for a survey) and practical solutions (e.g., [14, 10]) have been accumulated on using derived data in query answering. The problem of answering aggregate queries using views has been considered in relation to data warehouses and data cubes [15, 16, 17, 18]; some results are presented in [19, 20].

Considerable work has been done on efficiently selecting views and indexes for general SQL queries [10] and for aggregate queries (e.g., [3, 11, 12, 1]). [10] has introduced an end-to-end approach for designing and using derived data to answer queries. In our framework we extend the architecture of [10]; to the best of our knowledge, we are the first to address architectural issues in periodic redesign of derived data. In addition, we show that to design derived data under constraints, one has to consider the design and use (i.e., rewriting) problems together. In the next subsection we discuss further this issue.

Discussion of the Technical Content of Our Contribution

Recent work [1, 2] has considered the problem of rewriting aggregate queries using multiple views and has provided sound and complete algorithms for obtaining natural rewritings of aggregate queries using views. Moreover, in [1], the problem of view selection has been considered as closely related to the problem of query rewriting using views. Therein, algorithms have been provided for selecting a compact set of views which can be used to rewrite all queries in a given workload. The set is compact in the sense that the algorithm is based on techniques that search for views that can be used to answer as many queries as possible from the workload under certain template constraints. In addition, these techniques make use of common subexpressions among the queries in the workload.

2 Using QPET to Design and Use Derived Data

In this section we outline our system architecture, QPET.[2] We use the architecture of [10] to implement and validate our work in designing and using derived data to improve the evaluation performance of frequent and important queries. Our concentration and contributions in the system architecture are threefold. First, we use *specialized* algorithms for defining and using views and indexes for specific practically important classes of queries, such as the star-schema queries we discuss in this paper. Thus, our framework for designing and using derived data is *extensible*. We argue that specialized algorithms are required to ensure a guaranteed degree of improvement in query-evaluation performance, with respect to the *best possible* performance for the queries. In addition, different specialized algorithms are needed under different constraints on derived data materialized in the system, such as a storage limit on materialized views.

Second, we look in particular into developing a system architecture for periodic *online* (re)design of materialized views and other derived data in data-management systems. In that context, it is imperative that algorithms for designing and using derived data be lightweight, efficient, and scalable. Moreover, we argue the need to consider the interaction and interdependence of techniques for *generating* derived data with techniques for *rewriting* the given queries using the data that end up being materialized. For instance, while simple rewriting techniques can be used for star-schema query workloads, they would not be sufficient for more general aggregate queries [1].

The third contribution of our approach is a component of the system architecture that determines the "format" of views that should be materialized, based on the rewriting types considered for the given queries. This component of QPET, *view-format manager*, is used at the stage of designing derived data to determine the search space of derived data considered for materialization.

---

[2] For details please see the full version of the paper [7].

3 Complexity and Parameterized Algorithm

We now outline an approach we use within our QPET framework to improve the efficiency of evaluating aggregate queries without self-joins, using specially designed aggregate views. Using the results in [1], we generalize the approach of [3] into an approach that uses one *or more* views to answer each query and that applies to a *more general class* of queries that aggregate the same table. In this framework, when looking for views that are potentially usable in computing given queries, we take into account (unlike [3]) that it might be more efficient to use two or more views to answer a query. This is done by considering rewritings of the queries using views [1, 2].

The idea of our approach is to extract, from a workload of aggregate queries, *view templates*, which serve as input queries to the view-selection algorithm that we use as a subroutine. (In our current implementation of QPET, this subroutine is the BPUS algorithm of [3].) The views returned by the subroutine are then materialized and used to automatically construct rewritings of the workload queries; the rewritings have one or more relations in their FROM clause and may or may not be aggregate queries [1]. This approach can be tuned to explore different subspaces of the search space of views, depending on the constraints such as the amount of system resources available for designing derived data. See full version of the paper [7] for the complexity results and our parameterized algorithm for designing materialized views.

4 Implementation and Experimental Evaluation

Our implementation of the QPET framework [8] is based on an open-source relational data-management system PostgreSQL [21]. Using the TPC-H database benchmark [22], we have conducted preliminary experiments to evaluate the system architecture and techniques. Due to space constraints, we give here just a brief summary of the experiments; a detailed ac-

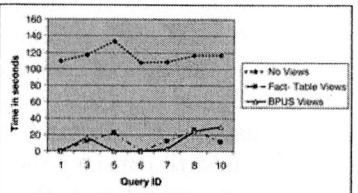

Fig. 1. Query runtimes

count of the experimental setup and results can be found in the full version of the paper [7]. The preliminary experimental results show the following. (1) Using materialized views designed by our *fact-table* approach, see Figure 1, results in query runtimes comparable to runtimes of the queries using views output by the BPUS algorithm, which we used for comparison purposes. (2) Disk-space requirements for storing materialized views in our approach are acceptable. (3) Finally, the time required to *design* views in our approach can be, in certain cases, drastically lower than the time required to design BPUS views for the same queries — e.g., in cases where the queries in the workload can be rewritten using only a few views. We are currently working on a full-scale implementation and further theoretical exploration to precisely quantify the advantages of our approach and provide a complete characterization of specific query types where our approach outperforms earlier approaches.

References

1. Afrati, F., Chirkova, R. Selecting and using views to compute aggregate queries. In: Proceedings of ICDT (2005)
2. Cohen, S., Nutt, W., Serebrenik, A. Rewriting aggregate queries using views. In: Proceedings of PODS (1999) 155–166
3. Harinarayan, V., Rajaraman, A., Ullman, J. Implementing data cubes efficiently. In: Proc. SIGMOD (1996) 205–216
4. Shasha, D., Bonnet, P. Database Tuning: Principles, Experiments, and Troubleshooting Techniques. Morgan Kaufmann (2002) http://www.distlab.dk/dbtune/.
5. Microsoft Research AutoAdmin Project: Self-Tuning and Self-Administering Databases. (http://research.microsoft.com/dmx/autoadmin/default.asp)
6. IBM Autonomic Computing. (http://www.research.ibm.com/autonomic/)
7. Afrati, F., Chirkova, R., Gupta, S., Loftis, C. Designing and Using Views to Improve Performance of Aggregate Queries. Technical Report NCSU CSC TR-2004-26, http://www4.ncsu.edu/~rychirko/Papers/techReport090904.pdf (2004)
8. Chirkova, R., Gupta, S., Kim, K.H., Sandhu, S. Extensible framework for query-performance enhancement by tuning. Code downloads and documentation are available from http://research.csc.ncsu.edu/selftune/ (2004)
9. Chirkova, R., Halevy, A., Suciu, D. A formal perspective on the view selection problem. VLDB Journal **11** (2002) 216–237
10. Agrawal, S., Chaudhuri, S., Narasayya, V. Automated selection of materialized views and indexes in SQL databases. In: Proceedings of VLDB (2000) 496–505
11. Gupta, H., Harinarayan, V., Rajaraman, A., Ullman, J. Index selection for OLAP. In: Proceedings of ICDE (1997) 208–219
12. Shukla, A., Deshpande, P., Naughton, J. Materialized view selection for multidimensional datasets. In: Proceedings of VLDB (1998) 488–499
13. Halevy, A.Y. Answering queries using views: A survey. VLDB Journal **10** (2001) 270–294
14. Chaudhuri, S., Krishnamurthy, R., Potamianos, S., Shim, K. Optimizing queries with materialized views. In: Proceedings of the Eleventh International Conference on Data Engineering (ICDE) (1995) 190–200
15. Widom, J. Research problems in data warehousing. In: Proceedings of CIKM (1995)
16. Gray, J., Chaudhuri, S., Bosworth, A., Layman, A., Reichart, D., Venkatrao, M. Data cube: A relational aggregation operator generalizing Group-by, Cross-Tab, and Sub Totals. Data Mining and Knowledge Discovery **1** (1997) 29–53
17. Chaudhuri, S., Dayal, U. An overview of data warehousing and OLAP technology. SIGMOD Record **26** (1997) 65–74
18. Agarwal, S., Agrawal, R., Deshpande, P., Gupta, A., Naughton, J., Ramakrishnan, R., Sarawagi, S. On the computation of multidimensional aggregates. In: Proceedings of VLDB (1996) 506–521

19. Gupta, A., Harinarayan, V., Quass, D. Aggregate-query processing in data warehousing environments. In: Proceedings of VLDB (1995) 358–369
20. Srivastava, D., Dar, S., Jagadish, H., Levy, A. Answering queries with aggregation using views. In: Proc. VLDB (1996) 318–329
21. PostgreSQL (Open source database-management system) http://www.postgresql.org/.
22. TPC-H: TPC Benchmark H (Decision Support). (Available from http://www.tpc.org/tpch/spec/tpch2.1.0.pdf)

Large Relations in Node-Partitioned Data Warehouses

Pedro Furtado

DEI /CISUC, Universidade de Coimbra, Portugal
pnf@dei.uc.pt
http://eden.dei.uc.pt/~pnf

Abstract. A cheap shared-nothing context can be used to provide significant speedup on large data warehouses, but partitioning and placement decisions are important in such systems as repartitioning requirements can result in much less-than-linear speedup. This problem can be minimized if query workload and schemas are inputs to placement decisions. In this paper we analyze the problem of handling large relations in a node partitioned data warehouse (NPDW) with a basic placement strategy that partitions facts horizontally and replicates dimensions, with the help of a cost model. Then we propose a strategy to improve performance and show both analytical and TPC-H results.

1 Introduction

Clusters of low-cost nodes can be used to process efficiently large databases, provided good data allocation, query processing and load balancing algorithms are used. However, some access patterns do not benefit linearly (linear speedup) from parallel architectures, requiring expensive massively parallel hardware to be fast. The basic partitioning problem is simply stated as follows: consider relations R_1 and R_2 to be joined as part of the query processing: $R_1 \bowtie_A R_2$. Consider also that R_1 is fully horizontally partitioned into nodes and each node or processor out of N should process only 1/N of the total work in order to take full advantage of parallel execution. If both relations are partitioned by the same equi-join key, the join can be processed locally and this is the fastest alternative. The expression $R_1 \bowtie_A R_2$ is processed as $(R_{11} \bowtie_A R_{21})$ U ... U $(R_{1n} \bowtie_A R_{2n})$, each part of this expression in a different node/processor. This is because the join between two fragments in different nodes is an empty set (e.g. $R_{11} \bowtie_A R_{22} = \emptyset$). But if they are not equi-partitioned, at least one of the relations must be moved. If relation R_1 is partitioned on the join key, we can dynamically partition the other relation on the same key and proceed with the parallel equi-join. This repartitioning is accounted as an extra overhead, increasing total work and response time. Alternatively, relation R_2 can be fully replicated into all nodes. This strategy adds processing costs to each node, as it must deal with one full relation while processing the join. Finally, if neither relation is partitioned by the equi-join key, it is necessary to repartition both relations. Workload-based placement algorithms aim at determining the best partitioning key to favor local joins. We analyze the problem of handling large relations in a node partitioned data warehouse with a basic placement strategy that partitions facts horizontally and replicates dimensions, with the help of a simple cost model. We also show how a better partitioning can be used to improve performance. For lack of space, we briefly review only some related work. Related work on query processing in parallel and distributed databases includes [1,2,4,6]. Issues are raised concerning mainly join processing and communication overheads [4,6]. Parallel Hash Join [1,4] and Placement Dependency [2] improve on these problems. Data placement is discussed in [3, 8] and also reviewed in [7].

2 Schema Placement

Data warehouse schemas can frequently be described as star schemas with large central facts (F) and small dimensions (D), for which a simple partitioning can be based on replicating dimensions and randomly partitioning the fact, as in Figure 1a. A good example of a more complex schema (not a pure star schema at all) and query set is the one illustrated in Figure 1b. (TPC-H [5]), which represents ordering and selling activity (LI-lineitem, O-orders, PS-partsupp, P-part, S-supplier, C-customer).

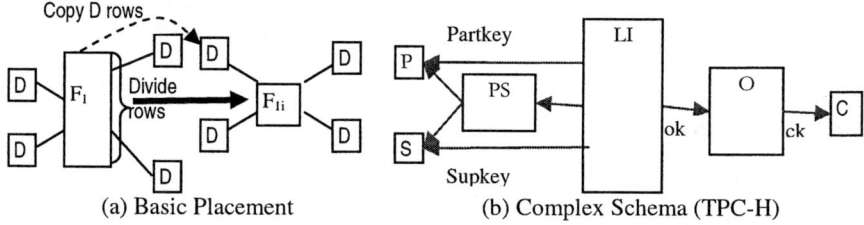

(a) Basic Placement (b) Complex Schema (TPC-H)

Fig. 1. Basic Placement

The objective of the basic placement of Figure 1a is to allow nodes to process their part of the query independently to achieve a speedup expected to be near to linear with the number of nodes. Each node applies exactly the same initial query on its partial data and the results are merged by applying the same query again at the merging node with the partial results coming from the processing nodes.

That basic placement does not work well for Figure 1b. The TPC-H query set includes frequent joins between two or more large relations. The basic node partitioning strategy defines that P, S and C be copied into each node. On the other hand, relations LI, PS and O can be horizontally partitioned into the nodes using round-robin or random partitioning. Although joins involving a single partitioned relation and any number of replicated relations require no data exchange, the frequent join (at least half TPC-H queries) between very large relations (LI, O, PS) requires extensive repartitioning overhead. Even if two facts are co-located, queries involving a third one must incur repartitioning. This issue must be dealt with by the placement algorithm if possible.

3 Cost Model

Cost models for analyzing part of these matters in shared-nothing environments were given in [4] and [6]. They typically include a partitioning or repartitioning cost (PC, RC), needed for data re-organization during query processing. It is associated with retrieving the relation or partition from secondary memory, dividing it into fragments by applying a hash function to a join attribute and assigning buffers for the data to send to other nodes. We assume the (re)partition cost to be monotonically increasing on the relation size. The local processing cost (LC) is also assumed monotonically increasing with the size of the relations involved. As in [4] and [6] we also define weighting parameters: α, for local processing cost and β, for repartitioning cost. The smaller the value of β, the smaller the repartitioning cost relative to the local processing cost. The total cost expression is: **TC** $= \beta \times$ **PC** $+ \alpha \times$ **LC**. Parameter β must account not only for the network speed but also for queuing, messaging, buffering the data that is exchanged between nodes. In [4] the value β=2α was obtained experimentally. This simplified cost model is useful for analysis purposes and does not dispense a more complete cost model of the optimizer taking into account other costs such as CPU instructions for I/O, processing and network, network delays.

Multiple Facts: consider NPDW with fact size F, N nodes and the linear cost model. The fact fragment size is F/N. The join-processing cost for queries requiring the join between equi-partitioned facts with sizes Fi and dimensions d_i is:

$$\text{Cost}_{\text{equipart}} = \alpha \times \left(\frac{F}{N} + d_1 + \ldots + d_l \right) \approx \alpha \times \left(\frac{F}{N} \right), \text{ where F is the sum of facts} \quad (1)$$

In this expression we are assuming the dimensions have insignificant size, so they can be ignored in the cost expression. The cost when facts are not equi-partitioned considering a switched network is:

$$\text{Cost}_{\text{repart}} = \left(\frac{IR}{N} - \frac{IR}{N^2} \right) \times \beta + \alpha \times \left(\frac{F}{N} \right) \approx \left(\frac{IR}{N} \right) \times \beta + \alpha \times \left(\frac{F}{N} \right) \text{ if N large.} \quad (2)$$

This expression accounts for local processing cost of 1/N of the fact (assuming small dimensions), and repartitioning overhead of an intermediate result IR. IR_i can be a fact or more frequently the result of locally computed joins and restrictions with replicated dimensions. Considering many joins, the total repartitioning cost is based on the sum of intermediate results. The increase in cost if (2) is required instead of (1) is therefore $\left(\frac{IR}{N} \right) \times \beta$, which depends on intermediate result selectivity and should be minimized.

Large Dimensions: large dimensions cause large performance degradation in the basic partitioning scheme. If they are fully-partitioned instead, the fact or intermediate results will typically need to be repartitioned before being joined with the partitioned dimension (d_L is the sum of sizes of dimensions with significant size):

$$\left(\frac{IR}{N} - \frac{IR}{N^2} \right) \times \beta + \alpha \times \left(\frac{d_L}{N} + \frac{F}{N} \right) \approx \left(\frac{IR}{N} \right) \times \beta + \alpha \times \left(\frac{d_L}{N} + \frac{F}{N} \right) \text{ if N large.} \quad (3)$$

This expression accounts for repartitioning overhead of an intermediate result IR and the local processing cost of fact and large dimension fragments. If we compute when it is better to replicate from (1) (3):

$$\frac{\beta}{\alpha} > d_L / \frac{IR}{N} \quad (5)$$

This simple result shows that if the ratio between repartitioning and local processing cost parameters is larger than the size ratio between the large dimension(s) and the intermediate result(s), it is better to have replicated dimensions. Otherwise it is better to have partitioned dimensions while repartitioning intermediate results. The size of IR depends on each query and the best execution path for the query.

4 Improved Placement in NPDW

The inputs to an improved strategy are the set of facts and dimensions from a generic schema and a query workload. Dimensions with size dj<dsmall are replicated into all nodes. Above this threshold, dimensions are partitioned into all nodes. If a dimension size is not too big dj<dvery_large, it can simultaneously be replicated into all nodes to allow different processing alternatives. The different combinations of equi-join keys from facts and partitioned dimensions are the input to a partitioning key decision algorithm (partitioning by hashing the keys):

FOR EACH Dimension d_i IF size d_j<d_{small}, dimension is to be **replicated**;
ELSE   IF size d_i>d_{very_large}, dimension is to be **partitioned** by its key;
ELSE   Assume **Redundant replicate and partition;**

FOR EACH fact that is to be partitioned
    Determine its equi-join attributes with other relations from the workload (or given metadata) A_i

FOR EACH possible placement PA_j = combination of partitioning attributes between relations
    FOR EACH query in the workload
        Estimate best execution path and cost C_i (consider alternative paths for redundant dimensions)
        END FOR
    Increment sum of costs PA_i+=C_i

Choose PA_i with the minimum cost;

5 Experimental Analysis

For the cost model experiments, we consider one or two 50GB facts and 5 to 10 small (up to 150MB), medium (500MB) or large (2.5GB) dimensions, depending on the features we wanted to test, $\beta = 2\alpha$, the selectivity of IRs=10% and also tested variations of β from 0.5α to 2α and variations of selectivity between 1% and 50%.

Figure 6 shows speedup for varying number of nodes and dimension sizes (5-100 MB), considering a single fact and replicated dimensions.

These results show that the speedup deteriorates significantly as the number of nodes and dimension size increases. This is because replicated dimensions become almost as large as fact fragments. The next results concern IR selectivity and partitioned medium-sized dimensions (D is for dimension replication instead).

These results show that replicated medium-sized dimensions (D) prevent acceptable speedup to be achieved and the importance of IR selectivity. If selective conditions are applied locally before repartitioning, the speedup will be nearer to linear. The unfilled dots in Figure 3(a) show when the partitioned dimension is slower than the replicated one. Repartitioning dimensions is very effective with many nodes.

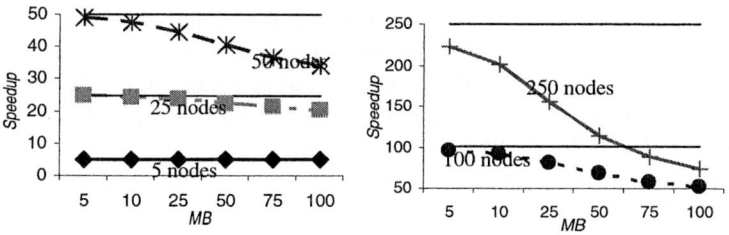

Fig. 2. Speedup with Dimension Sizes - Replicated

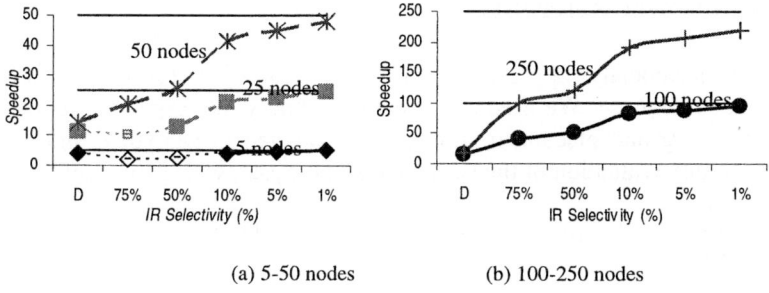

(a) 5-50 nodes (b) 100-250 nodes

Fig. 3. Speedup for IR (medium-sized dimensions)

Our next experiments were based on a 50GB TPC-H [5] run. We partitioned the relations using the algorithm described in this paper and obtained near-to-linear speedup for queries accessing a single fact, shown in Figure 4b.

	LI	O	PS	P	S	C	nodes	Q1	Q6	Q11	Q15
Type, Size	F, 35	F, 8.7	F,4.6	D,1	D,0.05	D,0.75	10	9.4	9.2	9.7	9.1
Partition	Okey	Ckey	Pkey	Pkey	Replicated	Redundant	25	24.7	28.3	29.1	29.4

(a) Partitioning Keys <(F-fact, D-dimension), size>   (b) Speedup, single fact

Fig. 4. Experimental Setup and Speedup on Single-fact Queries

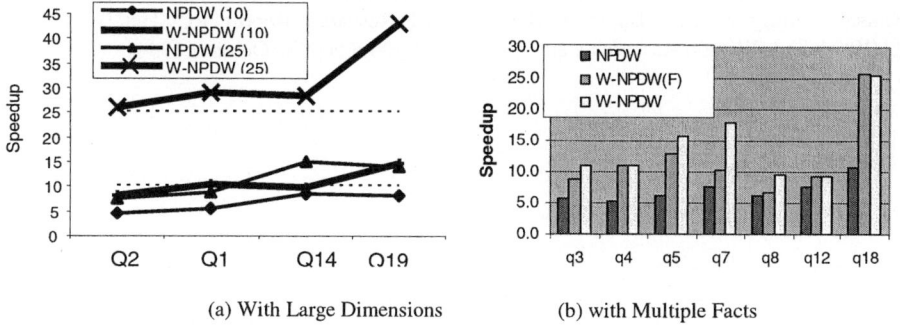

(a) With Large Dimensions   (b) with Multiple Facts

Fig. 5. Speedup Large Dimensions / Multiple Facts

Figure 5a shows the speedup when a single fact and at least one large dimension was also accessed. The advantage of partitioning the dimension (W-NPDW) versus replicating it (NPDW) is large, as replicated dimensions hurt speedup. Figure 5b shows the speedup for multiple facts in TPC-H. NPDW stands for the basic strategy with random partitioning of facts (L, O, PS) and replication of dimensions (P, C, S); W-NPDW is the improved partitioning. W-NPDW(F) uses the improved strategy for facts but replicates dimensions. W-NPDW had much better results than NPDW again, which incurred higher repartitioning costs. and W-NPDW(F) reveals the contribution of fact partitioning to that.

6 Conclusions and References

In this paper we have analyzed placement factors influencing performance in a node-partitioned data warehouse. We used a cost model to study the problem, proposed an effective partitioning and placement strategy and engaged in analytical and experimental (TPC-H run) evaluation of the issue and the proposal, with good results.

References

1. Kitsuregawa M., H. Tanaka, and T. Motooka. Application of hash to database machine and its architecture. New Generation Computing, 1(1):66-74, 1983.
2. Liu, Chengwen, Hao Chen, Warren Krueger, "A Distributed Query Processing Strategy Using Placement Dependency", Proc. 12th Int'l Conf. on Data Eng, pp. 477-484, Feb. 1996.
3. Rao, Jun., Chun Zhang, Nimrod Megiddo, Guy M. Lohman: Automating physical database design in a parallel database. SIGMOD Conference 2002: 558-569.
4. Shasha, D.,Wang, T.-Li: Optimizing Equijoin Queries (...) where Relations are Hash-Partitioned. ACM Transactions on Database Systems, V.16, No.2, pp. 279-308, June 1991.
5. Transaction Processing Council Benchmarks, www.tpc.org.
6. Yu, Clement T., Keh-Chang Guh, Weining Zhang, Marjorie Templeton, David Brill, Arbee L. P. Chen: Algorithms to Process Distributed Queries in Fast Local Networks. IEEE Transactions on Computers 36(10): 1153-1164 (1987).
7. Zhou S., M.H. Williams, "Data Placement in Parallel Database Systems," Parallel Database Techniques, IEEE Computer Society Press, 1997.
8. Zilio, Daniel C., Anant Jhingran, Sriram Padmanabhan, Partitioning Key Selection for a Shared-Nothing Parallel Database System IBM Research Report RC 19820 (87739) 11/10/94 ,T. J. Watson Research Center, Yorktown Heights, NY, October 1994.

Mining Frequent Tree-Like Patterns in Large Datasets*

Tzung-Shi Chen and Shih-Chun Hsu

Department of Information and Learning Technology,
National University of Tainan,
Tainan 700, Taiwan
chents@mail.nutn.edu.tw

Abstract. In this paper, we propose a novel data mining scheme to explore the frequent hierarchical structure patterns, named tree-like patterns, with the relationship of each item on a sequence. By tree-like patterns, we are clear to find out the relation of items between the cause and effect. Finally, we discuss the different characteristics to our mined patterns with others. As a consequence, we can find out that our addressed tree-like patterns can be widely used to explore a variety of different applications.

Keywords: Data mining, frequent patterns, sequential patterns, tree-like patterns, World Wide Web.

1 Introduction

Over the past decade, many research are contributed to mining the sequential patterns or frequent patterns in time-related dataset [1][4][5][7][8]. Most of schemes are to exploit association rules or market-basket analysis in terms of extracting the frequent patterns. Web mining [2][3] is of a typical case for mining the sequential patterns. By these explored frequent patterns, we can discover the users' traversal behaviors on the Internet. Furthermore, more complex structures, such as tree and graph structures, in a dataset are discussed. In [6][8], they proposed the mining schemes to discover the tree-type patterns on a given dataset.

Tree type of structure is a special hierarchical structure widely applied to many domains. Sequential patterns are a list of subsequences. In this paper, we concentrate the mined pattern on a tree-like form which is conceptualized from a sequence. We employ the particular hierarchical form to represent the relation between cause and effect of items. In addition, based on the tree-like form, we intend to extract the potential partial order relationships from the tree-like form. As our knowledge, this kind of structures is first to discuss and exploit.

The main contribution of this paper is to present a novel data mining scheme for mining the frequent tree-like patterns on a sequence database. We exploit the structure to represent

---

*This work is supported by National Science Council under the grants NSC-93-2213-E-024-005 and NSC-93-2524-S-156-001, Taiwan.

relationship of items. There are not only full ordered but partial ordered on the tree-like patterns. In support values counting, we propose an efficient scheme to count the support value. Moreover, we count the weighted support values efficiently by dynamic programming approach. Due to limitation of paper length, we omit to address these approaches here.

The rest of this paper is organized as follows. In Section 2, we illustrate basic concepts and terminology definitions. The mining algorithm and the mined pattern are proposed in Section 3. In Section 4, we compare our proposed scheme with others. Finally, we conclude in Section 5.

2 Basic Concepts and Terminologies

Let I be a set of m distinct items composed of the alphabet. A sequence has k items belonging to I. $D_T = \{S_l | S_l = <i_1,...,i_k>, i_j \in I, 1 \leq j \leq k, 1 \leq l \leq N\}$ is defined as a collected database with sequences, where N is the size of database, denoted by $|D_T| = N$. For example, we suppose that $I=\{A, B, C, D, E, F, G\}$. Five sequences as in Table 1 are in database D_T. The size of database D_T is $|D_T|=5$.

Table 1. An example of database

Sequence ID	Item (Sequence)
S_1	<A, B, D, B, C, A, B, A, B, D>
S_2	<A, B, C, B, A, B, C>
S_3	<A, B, D, B, C>
S_4	<A, E, G, H, A, B>
S_5	<A, E, G, E, F, E, G, H>

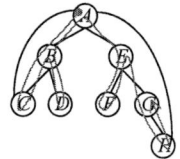

Fig. 1. Examples of a structure of a web site as well as the traversal path

The sequential patterns mining is applied widely to many kinds of applications and datasets collected. Here, we only take the application on a web structure into consideration. For example, there is a web site with 8 pages as in Figure 1. When users surf the web site, they probably are visited many different traversal paths. For example, the traversal path from A to G is as shown in Fig. 1. The traversal sequence is S=<A, B, C, B, D, B, A, E, F, E, G, H, G>. We exploit the front-and-rear relationships of items on the sequence. According to the support value, we probably discover different tree-like patterns from a database.

There is a non-contiguous subsequence $<t_1, t_2,...,t_k>$, called tree-like pattern with k vertices, from given a sequence, $t_i \in I$, $1 \leq i \leq k$; however, t_1 is a root, t_i has a parent between t_1 and t_{i-1}, where $1 < i \leq k$, as well as t_i has children or non between t_{i+1} and t_k, where $1 \leq i < k$. Here, a k-tree is denoted as T^k. Additionally, there are many different kinds of k-tree patterns in the same sequences, when $k \geq 3$. There are two main relationships. One is for the parent-child; another is for the siblings. For example, a sequence <A, B, C> implies the sequence with two kinds of 3-tree, T^3, patterns as in Figs. 2(a) and 2(b), respectively.

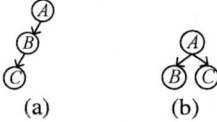

Fig. 2. Examples of different relationships from sequence <A, B, C>

3 Mining Frequent Patterns

We will address how to mine the frequent tree-like patterns from a database in this section. Consider the database in Table 1 as a running example. We use C_k to present the set of k-tree pattern candidates. Each k-tree candidate is of length k, $1 \leq k \leq l$, where the value of l is the maximum number of the nodes. In addition, we use F_k to present the set of large k-trees, each with the number of occurrences appeared in database D_T being equal to or larger than the given minimum support value. Throughout this paper, we suppose the *min_sup* $\sigma = 60\%$, i.e., each of frequent patterns is appeared more than 3 times in all sequences because $|D_T|=5$. The formal mining algorithm is described in below.

Algorithm: Mining a set of frequent k-tree patterns
Input: Database D_T and *min-sup* σ
Output: All of frequent k-tree patterns
1. $F_1 \leftarrow$ detect all of frequent 1-trees in D_T
2. $k \leftarrow 2$
3. **while** $F_{k-1} \neq \emptyset$ **do**
4. $C_k \leftarrow$ generate_candidate(F_{k-1})
5.   **for each** candidate $T^k \in C_k$ **do**
6. $F_k \leftarrow \{T^k \in C_k | \sup(T^k) \geq \sigma |D_T|\}$
7. $k \leftarrow k+1$
8. **return** $F_1, F_2, ..., F_l$

At first, we scan the database D_T to generate the set of frequent 1-tree patterns. Next, we employ join method to generate 2-tree candidate. After that, we count the support of each candidate and prune down the infrequent patterns. When we generate 3-tree pattern candidates, we enumerate all the relational patterns (including the parent-child and siblings) by join method. We repeatedly generate (k+1)-tree pattern candidates, until the set of frequent k-trees was empty or produce the empty set of next larger candidates.

For example as depicted in Table 1, we obtain the frequent 1-trees (i.e. *A*, *B*, and *C*) as shown in Fig. 3. Next, we join 1-tree with each other to generate candidates and then to get the frequent 2-trees as shown in Fig. 4. In generating 3-tree candidates, we consider the relationships for items, parent-child and siblings. Finally, we explore the frequent 3-trees as shown in Fig. 5. No more next step exists.

In what follows, we will discuss how to generate the candidates automatically. We use join operation to produce the larger tree-like patterns increasingly. Here we have the set of candidates $C_k = F_{k-1} \times F_{k-1}$, $1 \leq k \leq l$. Thus, it is important for us how to generate the next larger candidates, k-trees, from the frequent (k-1)-trees.

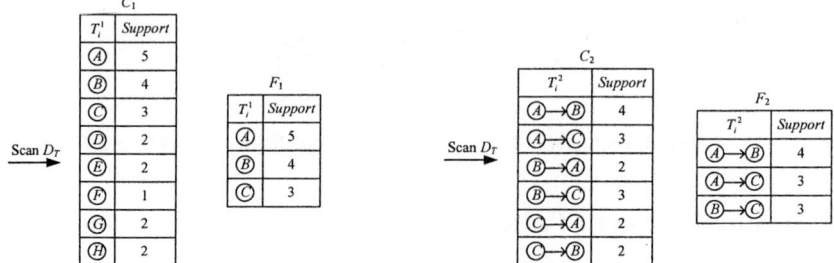

Fig. 3. Scanning D_T to produce the sets of C_1 and F_1

Fig. 4. Scanning D_T to produce the sets of C_2 and F_2

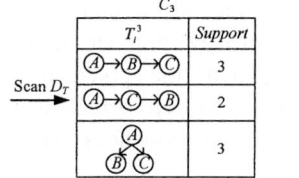

Fig. 5. Scanning D_T to produce the sets of C_3 and F_3

Before describing how to join F_{k-1} by itself, we define how two patterns can be joined together. According to the order and type of both patterns, two kinds of relationship between two subtrees are defined, one for equivalent subtrees and the other for strongly ordered subtrees. Note that the k-tree, T^k, is qualified as a frequent tree if all of (k-1)-subtrees of T^k are frequent.

Suppose that we have two different k-trees T_i^k and T_j^k, where $i \neq j$. T_i^k and T_j^k remove a node to form (k-1)-subtrees patterns T_n^{k-1} and T_m^{k-1}, respectively, where $1 \leq n \leq k, 1 \leq m \leq k$. If all of nodes and relationships of T_n^{k-1} are the same as those of T_m^{k-1}, T_n^{k-1} and T_m^{k-1} are called the equivalent subtrees, denoted by $T_n^{k-1} \equiv_R T_m^{k-1}$.

For example, the equivalent subtrees are shown as in Fig. 6(a). T_i^4 and T_j^4 are removed the different nodes B and E, from themselves, respectively. We got T_n^3 and T_m^3, called the equivalent subtrees, $T_n^3 \equiv_R T_m^3$.

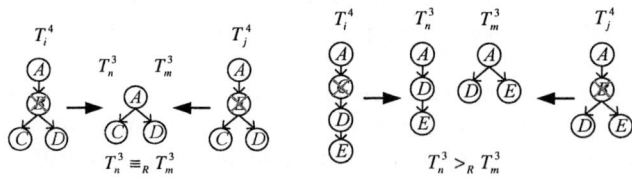

Fig. 6. (a) An example of equivalent subtrees; (b) an example of strongly ordered subtree

Suppose that we have two different k-trees T_i^k and T_j^k, where $i \neq j$. T_i^k and T_j^k are removed a node, maybe different, from themselves to produce (k-1)-subtrees T_n^{k-1} and T_m^{k-1}, respectively, where $1 \leq n \leq k, 1 \leq m \leq k$. Suppose that all of items in T_n^{k-1} are the same as those in T_m^{k-1}, but relationships are slightly different. It means that these exists all nodes of relationship of T_n^{k-1} being parent-child (strongly ordering) and the relationship of T_m^{k-1} being siblings (partially ordering). We can know that the strongly ordered, parent-child relationship, is more stronger than that of siblings. Therefore, we can find out the relationship of T_n^{k-1} is more strongly ordered than that of T_m^{k-1}, denoted by $T_n^{k-1} >_R T_m^{k-1}$. For example, suppose that T_i^4 and T_j^4 are removed the only one different nodes C and B from themselves, respectively. The order of T_n^3 is stronger than the order of T_m^3 as in Fig. 6(b).

Below we will discuss how to perform the join operation between two k-tree patterns. The symbol ⊗ is denoted as the joining operator. At first, we compare any pair of two k-trees, T_i^k and T_j^k. Suppose that k-1 nodes are the same in the two k-trees except one node. Next, we remove the different nodes from their corresponding k-trees to produce the $(k-1)$-trees, denoted as T_n^{k-1} and T_m^{k-1}, respectively. If the two $(k-1)$-tree patterns conform to one of the situations mentioned above, we try to join two k-trees to generate $(k+1)$-tree candidates. If we have $T_n^{k-1} >_R T_m^{k-1}$ with the strongly ordered subtrees, we let T_n^{k-1}, which is the stronger ordered, be as the key k-tree pattern. If we have $T_n^{k-1} \equiv_R T_m^{k-1}$ with the equivalent subtrees, we will let them be as the key tree with each other. Here we have different a pair of join patterns to be created to k-trees since the positions of the different nodes would be existed either in leaf node or in internal node. Thus, we have four types for the positions of the different nodes to discuss, i.e., leaf-leaf (L-L for short), internal-leaf (I-L for short), leaf-internal (L-I for short), and internal-internal (I-I for short). Since the two kinds of types I-L and L-I for the equivalent subtrees to generate candidates are the same, we only discuss one for the type of I-L.

In the following, we only discuss how to generate the candidates for the case of two equivalent subtrees with type L-L due to the limitation of paper length. For two k-trees, we remove the different nodes to form two equivalent subtrees, $T_n^{k-1} \equiv_R T_m^{k-1}$ as in Figs. 7(a) and 7(b), respectively. First of all, we attach these two different nodes to the parent B to generate a candidate as in Fig. 7(c). In addition, we know that X may be either in the front of or back of Y; however, B is definitely as the parent or grandparent of X and Y. Thus, we have to generate these two situations. We attach one of the different nodes to the other, i.e., either X is the parent of Y or Y is the parent of X shown in Figs. 7(d) and 7(e), respectively. But, if the different nodes be connected to different parents, there exists only one candidate, i.e., the different nodes are attached to their corresponding parents.

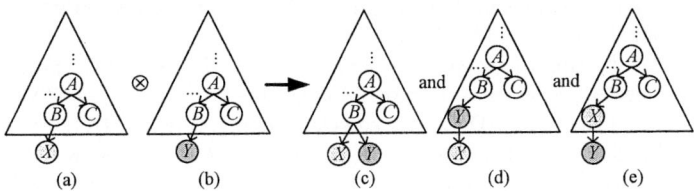

Fig. 7. L-L and $T_n^{k-1} \equiv_R T_m^{k-1}$

4 Discussions

We will compare our method with other more related work about mining the tree structure [8] and traversal patterns [2][3]. To sum up, we compare these schemes in terms of the scopes of characteristics as depicted in Table 2.

Table 2. Comparisons to different patterns

Mined patterns / Characteristics	Tree-like (ours)	Tree [10]	Path [2]	Trip [3]
Non-contiguous subsequence allowed	O	×	×	O
Partial order	O	×	×	O
Repeated occurrences of an item	O	O	×	O
Significance of sequences	O	×	×	×
Applications	Web mining, e-learning, purchase behaviors, etc.	Web mining, bioinformatics, XML documents	Web mining, e-learning	Web mining, e-learning

5 Conclusions

In this paper, we proposed a novel data mining scheme for mining the large k-tree patterns. Finally, we addressed the different characteristics to our mined patterns with others. As a result, we can find out that our proposed k-tree patterns can be widely used to explore a variety of applications.

References

1. Agrawal, R., Srikant, R.: Mining Sequential Patterns. In Proceedings of the 1995 International Conference on Data Engineering, Taipei, Taiwan (1995) 3-14
2. Chen, M.-S., Park, J.-S., Yu, P.-S.: Efficient Data Mining for Path Traversal Patterns. in IEEE Transactions on Knowledge and Data Engineering, Vol. 10, No. 2 (1998) 209-221
3. Chen, T.-S.: Mining Traversal Patterns on the Internet. In IEICE Transactions on Information and Systems. Vol. E86-D, No. 12 (2003) 2722-2730
4. Cheng, H., Yan, X., Han, J.: IncSpan: Incremental Mining of Sequential Patterns in Large Database. In Proceedings of 2004 International Conference on Knowledge Discovery and Data Mining, Seattle, WA (2004) 527-532
5. Han, J., Pei, J., Mortazavi-Asl, B., Chen, Q., Dayal, U., Hsu, M-C.: FreeSpan: Frequent Pattern-Projected Sequential Pattern Mining. In Proceedings of 2000 International Conference on Knowledge Discovery and Data Mining, Boston, MA (2000) 355-359
6. Kubat, M., Hafez, A., Raghavan, V. V., Lekkala, J. R., Chen, W.-K.: Itemset Trees for Targeted Association Querying. In IEEE Transactions on Knowledge and Data Engineering, Vol. 15, No. 6 (2003) 1522-1534
7. Lin, X., Liu, C., Zhang, Y., Zhou, X.: Efficiently Computing Frequent Tree-like Topology Patterns in a Web Environment. In Proceedings of the 31st International Conference on Technology of Object-Oriented Languages and Systems, Nanjing, China (1999) 440-447

8. Pei, J., Han, J., Mortazavi-Asl, B., Wang, J., Pinto, H., Chen, Q., Dayal, U., Hsu, M.-C.: Mining Sequential Patterns by Pattern-Growth: The PrefixSpan Approach. In IEEE Transactions on Knowledge and Data Engineering, Vol. 16, No. 10 (2004) 1424-1440
9. Yang, J., Wang, W., Yu, P. S.: STAMP: On Discovery of Statistically Important Pattern Repeats in Long Sequential Data. In Proceedings of the 3rd SIAM International Conference on Data Mining, San Francisco, CA, USA (2003) 224-238
10. Zaki, M. J.: Efficiently Mining Frequent Trees in a Forest. In Proceedings of the 8th ACM SIGKDD International Conference on Knowledge Discovery and Data Mining, Edmonton, Alberta, Canada (2002) 71-80

An Efficient Approach for Mining Fault-Tolerant Frequent Patterns Based on Bit Vector Representations

Jia-Ling Koh and Pei-Wy Yo

Department of Information and Computer Education
National Taiwan Normal University, Taipei, Taiwan
jlkoh@ice.ntnu.edu.tw

Abstract. In this paper, an algorithm, called VB-FT-Mine (Vectors-Based Fault–Tolerant frequent patterns **Mining**), is proposed for mining fault-tolerant frequent patterns efficiently. In this approach, fault–tolerant appearing vectors are designed to represent the distribution that the candidate patterns contained in data sets with fault-tolerance. VB-FT-Mine algorithm applies depth-first pattern growing method to generate candidate patterns. The fault-tolerant appearing vectors of candidates are obtained systematically, and the algorithm decides whether a candidate is a fault-tolerant frequent pattern quickly by performing vector operations on bit vectors. The experimental results show that VB-FT-Mine algorithm has better performance on execution time significantly than FT-Apriori algorithm proposed previously.

1 Introduction

Among the various data mining applications, mining association rules is an important one [1]. Several efficient algorithms have been proposed for finding frequent patterns and association rules are derived from the frequent patterns, such as the Apriori[1], DHP[3], and FP-growth[2]. When mining frequent patterns, an expected minimum support may cause only few frequent patterns are discovered because real-world data tends to be dirty. Although much more specific frequent patterns could be obtained by lowering the minimum supports, no general information about the representative frequent patterns is returned. The problem of mining fault-tolerant frequent patterns (itemsets) was defined and solved in [5] by proposing FT-Apriori algorithm. FT-Apriori algorithm was extended from Apriori Approach, in which downward closure property is applicable for mining fault-tolerant frequent patterns. Similar to Apriori-like[1] algorithms, FT-Apriori algorithm suffered from generating a large number of candidates and repeatedly scanning database. Moreover, fault toleration usually introduces much huge number of candidates when increasing the fault tolerance or decreasing the support thresholds.

In this paper, an algorithm, called VB-FT-Mine (Vector-Based Fault–Tolerant frequent patterns **Mining**), is proposed for speeding up the process of mining fault-tolerant frequent patterns. In this approach, fault–tolerant appearing vectors are designed to represent the distribution that the candidate patterns contained in data sets with fault-tolerance. VB-FT-Mine algorithm applies depth-first pattern growing method to generate candidate patterns. The fault-tolerant appearing vectors of candidate patterns are obtained systematically, and the algorithm decides whether a candidate is a fault-tolerant frequent pattern quickly by performing vector operations on bit vectors. The experimental results show that VB-FT-Mine algorithm has better performance significantly on execution time than FT-Apriori algorithm[5] proposed previously.

The remaining of this paper is organized as follows. The problem of fault-tolerant frequent pattern mining is defined in Section 2. In Section 3, the bit vector representation is introduced and applied to develop the proposed VB-FT-Mine Algorithm. The performance study of VB-FT-Mine is reported in Section 4, which shows the efficiency comparison with FT-Apriori. Finally, Section 5 concludes this paper.

2 Preliminaries

The following definitions refer to [1]. Let $I = \{i_1, i_2, \ldots, i_m\}$ be a set of literals, called *items*. A set of items is called an *itemset*. Itemsets containing k items are called *k-itemsets*. Let *DB* be a database of transactions, where each transaction T in *DB* is an itemset such that $T \subseteq I$. For a given itemset $X \subseteq I$, we say that a transaction T *contains* itemset X if and only if $X \subseteq T$. The *support count* of an itemset X in *DB*, denoted as Sup_X, is the number of transactions in *DB* containing X. Given a *minimum support threshold* s, an itemset X is called a *frequent* pattern in *DB* if $Sup_X \geq s$. Otherwise, X is named an *infrequent* pattern.

Transaction ID	Items
T1	BDEF
T2	ACDE
T3	BEFG
T4	CFG
T5	ABDEG

(a)

Item	Appearing Vector
A	<0,1,0,0,1>
B	<1,0,1,0,1>
C	<0,1,0,1,0>
D	<1,1,0,0,1>
E	<1,1,1,0,1>
F	<1,0,1,1,0>
G	<0,0,1,1,1>

(b)

Fig. 1. Sample database TDB and its appearing vector table

Example 1. In the transaction database TDB shown in Figure 1(a), if the minimum support threshold is set to 4, E is the only one frequent pattern. Although lowering the minimum support threshold to 3 will get 7 frequent patterns (B, D, E, F, G, BD, and DE), the result still consists of short patterns and which is less representative (with lower support). However, observe the transactions in database TDB closely, three transactions T1, T3, and T5 contain four out of the five items: B, D, E, F, and G. Therefore, when checking whether a transaction containing a pattern with fault-tolerance(contain 4 out of 5 items), a longer "approximate" pattern (BDEFG) with support count 4 is obtained. This problem of mining *fault-tolerant frequent patterns* was defined in [5].

Definition 1 (Fault-tolerant support): Given a **fault tolerance** δ ($\delta > 0$) and an itemset P. A transaction T = (tid, S) is said to **FT-contain** itemset P under fault tolerance δ iff there exists $P' \subseteq P$ such that $P' \subseteq S$ and $|P'| \geq (|P| - \delta)$. The number of transactions in a database DB which FT-contain itemset P is called the FT-support of P under fault tolerance δ, denoted as **FT-sup$^\delta$ (P)**. The set of transactions FT-containing P is called the **FT-body** of P, denoted as **FT-body$^\delta$(P)**. For each item p in itemset P, the number of transactions in FT-body$^\delta$(P) containing item x is called the **item support** of x in FT-body$^\delta$(P), denoted as **Item-Sup$_P^\delta$ (x)**.

Definition 2 (Fault-tolerant frequent pattern): Given a fault tolerance δ, a FT-support threshold min-sup^{FT}, and a frequent-item support threshold min-sup^{item}. An itemset P is called a fault-tolerant frequent pattern iff

1) FT-sup$^\delta$ (P) $\geq$ min-sup^{FT}; and
2) For each item x $\in$ P, Item-Sup$_P^\delta$ (x) $\geq$ min-sup^{item}.

3 Bit Vector Representations

3.1 Appearing Vectors

Let |DB| denote the number of transactions in database. For each item x, the *appearing vector* of x, denoted as Appear$_x$, is a binary vector of |DB| dimensions. If x is contained in the ith transaction, the ith dimension in its appearing vector is set to be 1; otherwise, the dimension is set to be 0. Then, an *appearing vector table*, which consists of appearing vectors of various items, is constructed to represent the distribution of items in a transaction database.

Consider the sample database TDB shown in Table 1. There are 7 various items and 5 transactions in the database. Item A is contained in transactions T2 and T5, thus the appearing vector of A, denoted as Appear$_A$, is <0,1,0,0,1>. Similarly, the appearing vectors of B, C, D, E, F, and G are obtained to construct the appearing vector table of TDB, as shown in Table 2.

For each item x, the number of dimensions with value 1 in Appear$_x$ implies its support count in the database. This value could be obtained by performing a support counting function, Count(), which computes an inner product operation on Appear$_x$ and a |DB|-dimensional vector with 1s in all the dimensions (denoted as $I_{|DB|}$).

An appearing vector is also applied to represent the distribution of an itemset P in transactions of a database. Suppose itemset P consists of k items: $i_1, i_2 ..., $ and i_k. The appearing vector of P is obtained by performing AND operations on appearing vectors of its k elements. Similarly, support count of P could be obtained quickly by performing the same support counting function.

3.2 FT_Appearing Vectors

Given a fault tolerance δ, the *FT-appearing vector* of an itemset P is denoted as FT-Appear$_P(\delta)$. If the ith transaction FT-contains itemset P, the ith dimension in FT-Appear$_P(\delta)$ is set to be 1; otherwise, the dimension is set to be 0. The appearing vector of itemset P is regarded the FT-appearing vector of P under fault tolerance 0.

The dimensions in FT-Appear$_P(\delta)$ with 1s imply the corresponding transactions in FT-body$^\delta$(P). Thus, the FT-support of an itemset P under fault tolerance δ could be obtained by inputting FT-Appear$_P(\delta)$ to the support counting function, Count(), introduced in section 3.1. In addition, for each item x in P, Item-Sup$_P^\delta$ (x) equals to the number of dimensions with 1s after performing AND operation on FT-Appear$_P(\delta)$ and Appear$_x$. That is, Item-Sup$_P^\delta$ (x) could be obtained by performing an inner product operation on FT-Appear$_P(\delta)$ and Appear$_x$.

3.3 Generation of FT-Appearing Vectors

Given a fault tolerance δ, a transaction T FT-contains an itemset P means T contains at least |P|- δ items in P. The cost is significant to compute the appearing vectors of these $C_{|P|-\delta}^{|P|}$ subsets and perform ($C_{|P|-\delta}^{|P|}$ -1) OR operations among these vectors when the number of elements in P is large. For solving this problem, the following theorem provides a property for generating FT_appearing vectors recurrently.

[Theorem 1] Let P denote a nonempty itemset and P´=P∪{x}, where x is an item not in P. A transaction T FT-contains P´ under fault tolerance δ iff

1) T FT-contains P under fault tolerance (δ -1), or
2) T contains x and FT-contains P under fault tolerance δ.

Suppose itemset P´ is obtained by inserting an item x into a nonempty itemset P. According to theorem 1, the FT-appearing vector FT-Appear$_{P´}$ could be computed from FT-Appear$_P$ and Appear$_x$ according to the following definition of recurrent function.

Recurrent Function for FP-Appearing Vectors:
Input: Itemset P, item x(x∉P), FT_appearing vectors of P, Appear $_x$, and fault tolerance δ.
Output: the appearing vectors of P´, where P´=P∪{x}.

P´=P∪{x};
If | P´|≤δ, FT-Appear$_{P´}(\delta)$ = I$_{|DB|}$;
If δ=0, FT-Appear$_{P´}(\delta)$=Appear$_{P´}$=FT-Appear$_P(0)$∧Appear$_x$;
Otherwise, FT-Appear $_{P´}(\delta)$=FT-Appear$_P(\delta$-1)∨(FT-Appear$_P(\delta)$∧Appear$_x$).

That is, for any given pattern P and an item x, where x is not in P, FT-appearing vectors of the pattern P´=P∪{x} with various fault tolerances could be obtained when all the FT-appearing vectors of P with fault tolerance from 0 to δ are known.

3.4 VB-FT-Mine Algorithm

VB-FT-Mine algorithm is designed based on the FT-appearing vectors representation and the recurrent relation introduced in Section 3.3. First, the transactions in database are read in one by one to construct an appearing vector table. Then the candidates are generated by performing depth-first pattern growing method. For each newly generated candidate pattern, the recurrent function defined in Section 3.3 is performed to obtain its FT-appearing vectors with various tolerances. The FT-support and item-supports of a pattern are thus checked efficiently by performing inner product operations on appearing vectors as introduced in Section 3.2. The VB-FT-Mine algorithm is shown as follows.

Algorithm VB-FT-Mine

Input: Transaction database DB, min-sup^{item}, min-sup^{FT}, and fault tolerance δ.
  Output: the complete set of FT-patterns.
1. Scan DB once to construct the appearing vector table.
2. Compute the support count for each item x. An item x is global frequent iff $Sup_x^{DB} \geq$ min-sup^{item}. Let the global frequent items be denoted as $x_1, x_2, ..., x_n$.
3. For i=1 to n {
   (a) Initialization: Set P = {x_i}; FT-Appear$_P(0)$ =Appear$_{xi}$;
              Set j= i+1; Push (P, FT-appearing vectors of P, j) into stack;
   (b) While (stack is not empty){
      (b-1) Generate a candidate pattern P´= P ∪ {x_j};
        FT-Appear$_{P'}(0)$ = FT-Appear$_P(0) \wedge$ Appear$_x$;
        For (k = 1 to δ)
        { If |P´|≤k, FT-Appear$_{P'}(k)$ = $I_{|DB|}$;
           else FT-Appear$_{P'}(k)$ =FT-Appear$_P(k-1) \vee$ (FT-Appear$_P(k) \wedge$ Appear$_{xj}$)}
      (b-2) Compute FT-sup$^\delta$(P´) = FT-Appear$_C(\delta) \cdot I_{|DB|}$;
      (b-3) If FT-sup$^\delta$(P´)≥min-sup^{FT},
           for (each item x in P´) performs FT-Appear$_{P'}(\delta) \cdot$ Appear$_X$ to obtain Item-Sup$_{P'}^\delta$(x);
      (b-4) If Item-Sup$_{P'}^\delta$(x)≥min-sup^{Item}
           for (each x in P´) { Output P´ as a result;
             Set P = P´ and j=j+1;
             If j≤n Push(P, FT-appearing vectors of P, j) into stack;}
             else Repeat
             { Pop(P, P's FT-appearing vectors, j) from stack; j=j+1;}
           until ((j≤n) or (stack is empty))
   } /* end while
} /* end for

4 Performance Evaluation

In order to show the efficiency and effectiveness of our approach by comparing with FT-Apriori[5] algorithm, both algorithms are implemented using Microsoft Visual C++ 6.0. The experiments are performed in a PC with an Intel Pentium4 2.4GHz CPU and 256MB main memory, running Microsoft Windows XP Professional. The experiments were performed on synthetic data generated by the IBM synthetic market-basket data generator.

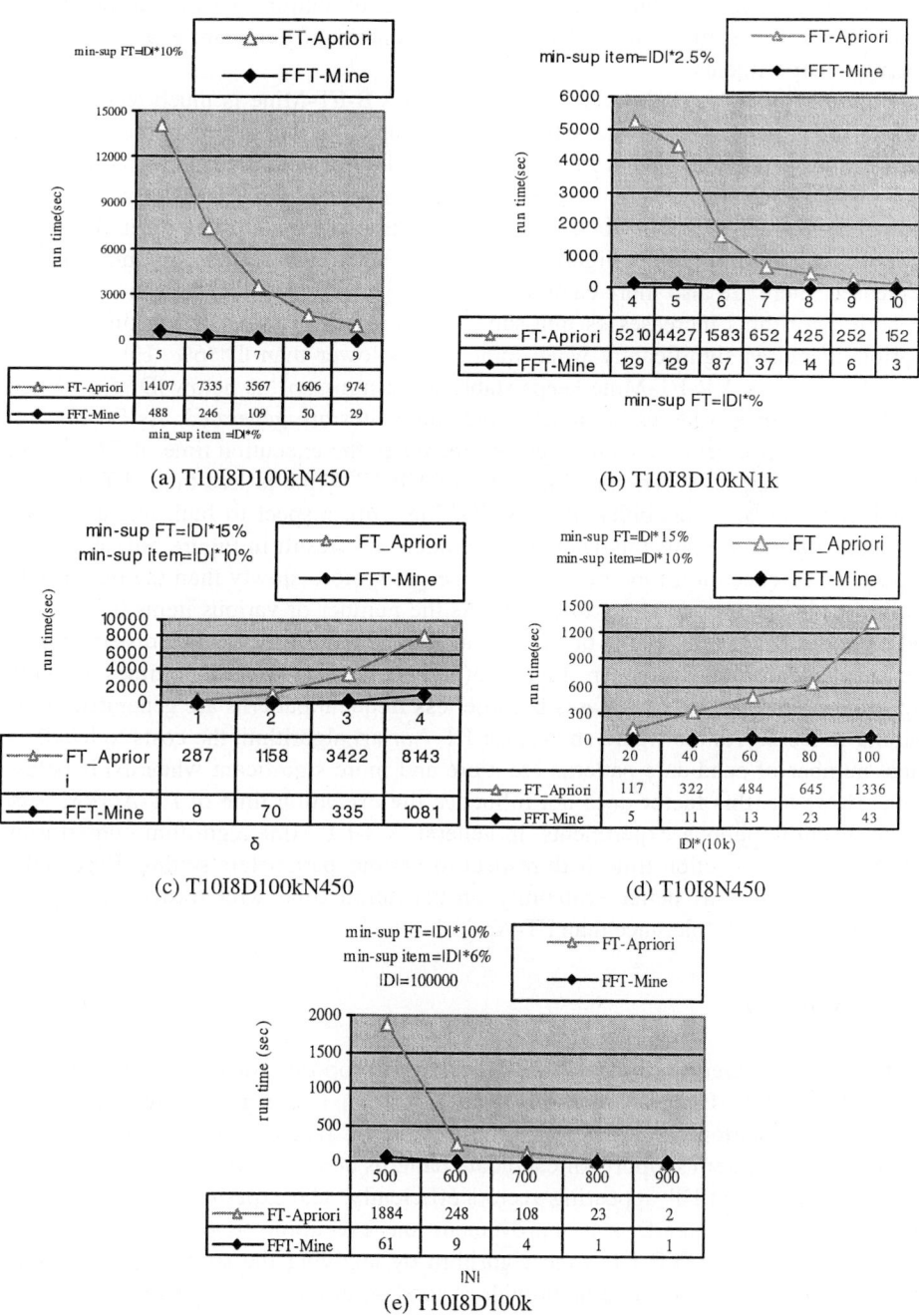

Fig. 5. Experimental Results

In the following experiments, the three run-time parameters (min-sup^{item}, min-sup^{FT}, and δ) are controlled individually for observing their effects on execution time of the two mining algorithms. In addition, the execution times on different data sets with various setting on database size and number of items are evaluated in the other two experiments.

Figure 5(a) shows that the execution time of VB-FT-Mine is much less than the time of FT-Apriori. When the setting on min-sup^{item} is decreased, more candidate itemsets are generated. Therefore, the execution time of both algorithms increases as min-sup^{item} is decreased. Moreover, the increasing rates of both algorithms are similar. However, VB-FT-Mine is about 30 times faster than FT-Apriori with the same support threshold settings. Figure 5(b) shows, when the setting on min-sup^{FT} is decreased, there are also more candidate itemsets generated. Thus, the execution time of both algorithms increases as min-sup^{FT} is decreased. The execution time of FT-Apriori increases significantly when min-sup^{FT} is lower than |D|*6%. However, the execution time of VB-FT-Mine keeps stable when min-sup^{FT} is below |D|*5%. When the fault tolerance δ increases, much more candidates are generated. As Figure 5(c) shows, a minor increase of fault tolerance increases the execution time of FT-Apriori algorithm dramatically. The growing ratio of VB-FT-Mine is less than FT-Apriori, which indicates the scalability of VB-FT-Mine with respect to fault tolerance. VB-FT-Mine algorithm scans the database only once. The result in Figure 5(d) shows, as expected, the execution time of VB-FT-Mine glow more slowly than the one of FT-Apriori as the size of database increases. As the number of various items in database |N| increases, the average size of the transactions remains 10, the data distribution in the database becomes sparser. Figure 5(e) shows that, execution times of both algorithms decrease as N increases because less frequent patterns are generated in the mining process. As the figure shows, for FT-Apriori algorithm, the costs to handle a huge number of candidate patterns are more and more significant when |N| is below 600. However, this factor does not influence the execution time of FT-Apriori very much. From the above experiments, in general, VB-FT-Mine algorithm outperforms FT-Apriori on execution time with respect to various parameters setting. Especially, the VB-FT-Mine has better scalability on execution time with respect to support thresholds and fault tolerance than FT-Apriori.

5 Conclusion

In this paper, an algorithm named VB-FT-Mine is proposed for mining fault-tolerant frequent patterns efficiently. VB-FT-Mine algorithm is designed based on the bit vector representations. According to the depth-first pattern growing strategy, the FT_supports and item supports of candidate patterns could be obtained by performing vector operations on FT_appearing vectors efficiently. The experimental results show our approach has significant improvement on execution time than FT-Apriori algorithm. To extend VB-FT-Mine algorithm by applying the strategies for mining frequent patterns in data streams provide a good solution for this problem, which is under our study currently.

References

[1] R. Agrawal and R. Srikant, "Fast Algorithms for Mining Association Rules," in Proc. of Int. Conf. on Very Large Data Bases, 1994.
[2] J. Han, J. Pei, Y. Yin and R. Mao, "Mining Frequent Patterns without Candidate Generation: A Frequent-Pattern Tree Approach", Data Mining and Knowledge Discovery, 8(1):53-87, 2004.
[3] J.S. Park, M.S. Chen, and P.S. Yu, "An Effective Hash-based Algorithm for Mining Association Rules," in Proc. of the ACM SIGMOD International Conference on Management of Data (SIGMOD'95), May, pages 175-186, 1995.
[4] J. Pei, A.K.H. Tung, and J. Han, "Fault-Tolerant Frequent Pattern Mining: Problems and Challenges," in Proc. of ACM-SIGMOD Int. Workshop on Research Issues on Data Mining and Knowledge Discovery (DMKD'01), 2001.
[5] S.-S. Wang and S.-Y. Lee, "Mining Fault-Tolerant Frequent Patterns in Large Database," in Proc. of Workshop on Software Engineering and Database Systems, International Computer Symposium, Taiwan, 2002.

NNF: An Effective Approach in Medicine Paring Analysis of Traditional Chinese Medicine Prescriptions[1]

Li Chuan[1], Tang Changjie[1], Peng Jing[1], Hu Jianjun[1]
Jiang Yongguang[2], and Yong Xiaojia[2]

[1] The Data Base and Knowledge Engineering Lab (DBKE),
Computer School of Sichuan University,
{lichuan, tangchangjie}@cs.scu.edu.cn
[2] Chengdu University of Traditional Chinese Medicine
{cdtcm, rainjia}@163.com

Abstract. Medicine Paring Analysis is one of the most important tasks in the research of Traditional Chinese Medicine Prescriptions. The most essential and difficult step is to mine associations between different medicine items. This paper proposes an effective approach in solving this problem. The main contributions include: (1) proposing a novel data structure called indexed frequent pattern tree (IFPT) to maintain the mined frequent patterns (2) presenting an efficient algorithm called Nearest Neighbor First (NNF) to mine association rules from IFPT (3) designing and implementing two optimization strategies that avoid the examinations of a lot of subsets of Y that can't be the left part of any association rule of the form $X \Rightarrow Y - X$ and thus achieving a wonderful performance and (4) conducting extensive experiments which show that NNF runs far faster than Apriori algorithm and has better scalability. And finally we demonstrate the effectiveness of this method in Medicine Paring Analysis.

Keywords: New Application, Data Mining and Knowledge Discovery, Traditional Chinese Medicine, Medicine Paring Analysis

1 Introduction

Traditional Chinese Medicine (TCM) has a long therapeutic history of thousands of years and the therapeutic value of which, especially on chronic diseases, has been winning wider and wider acknowledgement in the World [1]. However, despite its existence and continued use over many centuries, and its popularity and extensive use during the last decades, its chemical background and formula synergic effects are still

---

[1] This work was supported by Grant from National Science Foundation of China (60473071), Specialized Research Fund for Doctoral Program by the Ministry of Education (SRFDP 20020610007), and the grant from the State Administration of Traditional Chinese Medicine (SATCM 2003JP40). LI Chuan, PENG Jing, HU Jianjun are Ph. D Candidates at DB&KE Lab, Sichuan University. Jiang Yongguang is a Professor at Chengdu University of Traditional Chinese Medicine. And TANG Changjie is the associate author.

a mystery at least in theoretical sense because of its complex physiochemical [2]. In this study, we propose an effective approach in solving this problem. Our performance study shows that the NNF algorithm is by far faster than other methods such as Traverse, Linear, Apriori etc. and has better scalability. And we also present results of applying this algorithm to spleen-stomach prescriptions as is an important part of the whole TCM Dictionary, which shows the effectiveness of our method. Interested readers are referred to references [3]-[11] for related studies. Due to space limitation, the experimental part has to appear elsewhere [12].

The remaining of the paper is organized as follows. Section 2 presents the IFPT structure. Section 3 details the design and implementation of NNF. Section 4 exhibits the applications of NNF in Medicine Paring Analysis of Traditional Chinese Medicine. And Section 5 concludes the paper.

2 Indexed Frequent Patterns Tree

2.1 A Different Frequent Patterns Tree

Definition 2.1 Frequent Patterns Tree (FPT) is a tree structure that satisfies the following properties:

1. FPT consists of a root node and a set of sub-trees. Each node in the sub-trees contains the item and the item's support count (frequency of occurrences).
2. FPT is an ordered tree in that: (a) if $N1$ is a child of non-root node N, $N1.item \prec N.item$ (b) if $N1$ and $N2$ are both children of non-leaf node N and $N1$ is the left sibling of $N2$, $N2.item \prec N1.item$.
3. Each frequent pattern X corresponds to a single node N and hence the single path from root to that node: if $X = \{a_1, a_2, ..., a_k\}$ is a frequent pattern, there exists one and only one node N in FPT such that the items of the path starting from root to node N (not including the root node) are $a_1, a_2, ..., a_k$ respectively and the support count of N, $N.count$ is equal to the support count of frequent pattern X and vice versa.

It's notable that the FPT is rather different from the FP-Tree proposed in paper [4] by Han. Traditional FP-Tree is constructed directly from transaction database and each node, factually the path from root to that node, represents an existing transaction. But there's no correspondence between theses paths and frequent patterns. However, in FPT each node is the one and only one representative of a frequent pattern and vice versa. Therefore, FPT is a truly frequent pattern tree whereas FP-Tree is merely a transaction tree.

2.2 Indexed Frequent Patterns Tree (IFPT)

FPT has the following valuable property that for any frequent pattern Y, nodes of all of its sub-patterns can't be found to its left. Formally, we have the following definition and lemma.

Definition 2.2 Suppose N_1 and N_2 are two different nodes in FPT. **Node N_1 positions to the left of N_2** if and only if at least one of the following criteria holds:

(1) Both N_1 and N_2 are children of the same parent node and $N2.item < N1.item$ (namely, N_1 is the left sibling of N_2)
(2) There exist nodes $N1'$ and $N2'$ that are ascendants of N_1 and N_2 respectively such that $N1'$ and $N2'$ have the same parent node and $N2.item < N1.item$.

Lemma 2.1 Suppose X and Y are both frequent patterns with corresponding paths in FPT to be P_1 and P_2, if $X \subset Y$, $P1$ can't position to the left of $P2$.

So as to take better advantage of FPT, we introduce indexes onto FPT, and put forward the concept of IFPT.

Definition 2.3 IFPT is an indexed FPT with the following links:

1. **Node-link**: node link is formed by linking all the nodes of the same item from left to right
2. **Leaf-link**: leaf-link links all the leaves from right to left
3. **Sub-pattern-link**: Suppose N to be a non-leaf node, with corresponding pattern to be Y. M (suppose its corresponding pattern to be X) lies in the sub-pattern-link if and only if:
   a) X is a sub-pattern of Y,
   b) N positions to the left of M,
   c) $M.item = N.item$, and
   d) $N.count/M.count \geq min\_conf$

3 Nearest Neighbor First

3.1 Optimization Strategies

Lemma 3.1 Suppose Y to be a frequent pattern, $X \subset Z$, $X \neq \emptyset$. If $X \Rightarrow Z - X$ is not a strong rule, for any Y, $Y \supset Z$, $X \Rightarrow Y - X$ is not strong.

Lemma 3.1 shows an interesting anti-tonal that if X can't pass the confidence test against Z (i.e. $X \Rightarrow Z - X$ is not a strong association rule), for any super-pattern of Z, denoted as Y, X can't pass the confidence test against Y either. And by further deepening from lemma 3.1, we get the following optimization strategy:

Optimization 3.1. When investigating the supper-patterns of Z, all the sub-patterns X that can't be the left part of $X => Z-X$ should be ignored.

Lemma 3.2 Suppose Y to be a frequent pattern, $X \subset Y$, $X \neq \emptyset$. If $X \Rightarrow Y - X$ is not strong, for any $X' \subset X$, $X' \Rightarrow Y - X'$ is not strong.

Lemma 3.2 proves another interesting anti-tonal different from that of lemma 3.2 that if X can't pass confidence testing against Y, for any sub-patterns of X, denoted as Z, Z can't pass the confidence test against Y either. Lemma 3.2 tells us the following optimization strategy:

Optimization 3.2 When investigating frequent pattern Y, if frequent pattern X can't be the left part of the rule $X \Rightarrow Y-X$, any sub-pattern of X should be ignored.

3.2 NNF Algorithm

The main idea of NNF algorithm is sketched as follows:

NNF (Nearest Node First) algorithm processes every branch one by one from right to left across IFPT. Since every path of length m (there are m nodes in the path from root to that node) has $m-1$ sub-paths from root to that node with length no less than 2, NNF investigates the nodes nearest to root first (i.e. suppose the frequent pattern represented by that node to be Y and produce all possible association rules in the following steps by judging if any sub-pattern of Y, namely, X can pass the confidence test against Y) in order to better utilize optimization strategy 1 and when considering the sub-patterns of Y, investigate the longest sub-patterns first in order to make full use of optimization 3.2.

Algorithm NNF: Mining the complete set of strong association rules with minimum confidence *min_conf* in a transaction database.

Input: IFPT
Output: The complete set of strong association rules
Procedure:
(1) **for** (each unprocessed node *M* in the IFPT)
(2)   RuleGen(*N*);

Function RuleGen(*N*) {

(3) Suppose node *N* correspond to pattern Y, with its support count to be c;
(4) **for** (each node *Q* in the node-link of *N*) {
(5)   Suppose node *Q* corresponds to pattern X, with its support count to be $c1$;
(6)   **if** (X passes test with *min_conf*) {
(7)   Output an association rule: $X \Rightarrow Y-X$, its support $c/|D|$ and confidence $c/c1$;
(8)   **if**(*N* is a non-leaf node) link *Q* into the sub-pattern link of node *N*;
(9) }}
(10) Let *p* point to the parent node of *N*;
(11) **while** (*p* != *root*) {
(12) Suppose the node pointed by *p* is *P*; *P* corresponds to frequent pattern Z with support count to be $c1$;
(13) **if** (Z passes test with *min_conf*) {
(14)   Output an association rule: $Z \Rightarrow Y-Z$ together with its support $c/|D|$ and confidence $c/c1$;
(15)   **for** (each node *Q* in the sub-pattern-link of *P*) {
(16)   Suppose *Q* corresponds to frequent pattern X, with its support to be $c1$;
(17)   **if** (X passes test with *min_conf*)
(18)   Output an association rule $X \Rightarrow Y-X$ its support $c/|D|$ and confidence $c/c1$;
(19)   }
(20)   *p* points to the parent of *P*;

(21)   } else break;
(22) }}

Theorem 3.1 Given minimum confidence threshold, *min_conf*, algorithm NNF can generate the complete set of association rules correctly.

4 Applications in Medicine Paring Analysis

By introduction of dual-direction association NNF can be used to mine and get closely related medicine pairs and groups. E.g. by mining a subset of Spleen-stomach prescriptions database we got the result shown as below, where support is set to 7% (for too high support will vacate the analysis result) and the confidence is set to 30%.

ginseng<-> atractylodes rhozome   (12%, 75%/66%)
atractylodes rhozome<-> cork-tree bark (25%, 40%/44%)
chrysanthemum, amur<-> cork-tree bark (8%, 56%/39%)
coptis root, fresh rehmannia root <-> lotus seed (9%, 54%/43%)
tangerine peel <->nandina fruit (7%, 54%/52%)

It's notable that a quite large portion of the result is meaningful and interpretable by TCM theory. E.g. ginseng and atractylodes rhizome are the major ingredients of a Spleen stomach prescription which clears up heat and excretes damp and suitable for patients with yellowish and slimy tongue coating, soggy and rapid pulse.

5 Conclusion

Medicine Paring Analysis is one of the most important tasks in research of Traditional Chinese Medicine Prescriptions. In this study, we propose an effective approach in solving this problem. The main contributions are as follows: (1) we propose a novel data structure called indexed frequent pattern tree (IFPT) to maintain the mined frequent patterns (2) we present an efficient algorithm called Nearest Neighbor First (NNF) to mine association rules from IFPT (3) we design and implement two optimization strategies that avoid the examinations of a lot of subsets of Y that can't be the left part of any association rule of the form $X \Rightarrow Y - X$ and thus achieve a good performance (4) we conduct extensive experiments to test the efficiency and effectiveness of NNF. And finally we present results of applying this algorithm to spleen-stomach prescriptions as is an important part of the whole TCM Dictionary, which shows the effectiveness of our method.

References

1. General Guidelines for Methodologies on Research and Evaluation of Traditional Medicine, http://www.who.int/medicines/library/trm/who-edm-trm-2000-1/who-edm-trm-2000-1.pdf
2. Guste Editors' Notes on the special issue, http://www.sinica.edu.tw/~jds/preface.pdf
3. FAN Ming, LI Chuan, Mining Frequent Patterns in an FP-tree Without Conditional FP-tree Generation, Journal of Computer Research and Development, 40th Vol. 2004
4. J. Han, J. Pei and Y. Yin. Mining frequent patterns without candidate generation. Proc. 2000 ACM-SIGMOD Intl. Conf. on Management of Data, pages 1-12. May 2000.
5. LI Chuan, FAN Ming, A NEW ALGORITHM ON MULTI-DIMENSIONAL ASSOCIATION RULES MINING, Journal of Computer Science, Aug. 29th Vol. A Complement, page 1-4, 2002
6. LI Chuan, FAN Ming, GENERATING ASSOCIATION RULES BASED ON THREADED FREQUENT PATTERN TREE, Journal of Computer Engineering and Application, 4th Vol., 2004
7. FAN Ming, LI Chuan, A Fast Algorithm for Mining Frequent Closed ItemSets, submitted to ICDM'04
8. LI Chuan, FAN Ming Research on Single-dimensional Association Mining, Full Paper Data Base of Wanfang Network
9. R. Agrawal and R. Srikant. Fast algorithms for Mining association rules. Proc. 1994 Int'l Conf. on Very Large Data Bases, pages 487-499, Sept. 1994.
10. Jian Pei, Jiawei Han, and Runying Mao. CLOSET: An Efficient Algorithm for Mining Frequent Closed Itemsets. Proc. 2000 ACM-SIGMOD Int. 2000 ACM SIGMOD Intl. Conference on Management of Data. page 8-10.
11. http://www.ics.uci.edu/~mlearn/MLRepository.html
12. http://teacher.scu.edu.cn/~chjtang/buf/download/test/lichuan.zip

From XML to Semantic Web

Changqing Li and Tok Wang Ling

Department of Computer Science, National University of Singapore
{lichangq, lingtw}@comp.nus.edu.sg

Abstract. The present web is existing in the HTML and XML formats for persons to browse. Recently there is a trend towards the semantic web where the information can be can be processed and understood by agents. Most of the present research works focus on the translation from HTML to semantic web, but seldom on XML. In this paper, we design a method to translate XML to semantic web. It is known that ontologies play an important role in the semantic web, therefore firstly, we propose a genetic model to organize ontologies, and based on this model, we use three steps, viz. semantic translation, structural translation and schematic translation, to translate XML to semantic web. The aim of the paper is to facilitate the wide use of semantic web.

1 Introduction

Today, the web is increasingly moving to the semantic web [13], where the web information is annotated with concepts from sharing ontologies [10], thus the semantics of information can be understood and consumed by agents. Researchers [5, 7] have focused on how to annotate the HTML information. XML is another important format to store the current web information, but seldom researches are about how to translate XML to semantic web.

The rest of the paper is organized as follows. Section 2 reviews the related work, and Section 3 describes the preliminary and motivation of this paper. In Section 4, we propose a genetic model for ontology organization. Section 5 discusses the three steps of translations. The conclusion to this research is in Section 6.

2 Related Work

Resource Description Framework (RDF) [8] organizes information in a Subject-Verb-Object (SVO) (or Resource-Property-Resource triples) form, thus the RDF files can be processed semantically.

Some primitives are defined in RDF Schema (RDFS) [1] and the successors of RDFS: viz. DARPA Agent Markup Language (DAML) [11], Ontology Inference Layer (OIL) [6], DAML+OIL [4] and Web Ontology Language (OWL) [3]. OWL has three increasingly-expressive sublanguages: OWL Lite, OWL DL (Description Logic) and OWL Full. These languages all follow the RDF structure.

When the ontology languages are ready, the ontologies for different domains can be created. And based on the ontologies, the web information can be annotated for agents to process, which is today's semantic web. Most of the current techniques focus on the annotations of the information in HTML. SHOE Knowledge Annotator [5] and AeroDAML [7] are two tools to annotate HTML.

SHOE Knowledge Annotator is a manual tool. The user needs to manually select ontologies and concepts to annotate the HTML information, which is tedious. On the other hand, AeroDAML annotates HTML information based on the using frequency of an ontology concept and it is an automatic tool without any human interference. This tool uses a single predefined ontology to include all the concepts for different domains in. Therefore, when searching ontologies for annotations of HTML, all the concepts in this predefined ontology have to be traversed.

Another important format for the current web is XML. OntoParser [2] is a tool which only translates the structure of XML to satisfy the RDF structure.

3 Preliminaries

If an XML file confirms to an XML schema, it is said to be a valid XML file, otherwise it is an invalid XML file. For valid XML files, we can firstly translate their schemas to satisfy the semantic web requirement, then the valid XML files can be easily translated when confirming to the new translated schema, i.e. keep the changes of the XML schemas and update them into the XML files. For invalid XML files, we have to translate them individually.

3.1 ORA-SS Model

The XML Schema and DTD are two main schema definition languages for XML data. But they lack semantics. We employ the semantic rich model ORA-SS (Object-Relationship-Attribute Model for Semi-structured Data) [9] which distinguishes whether the relationship among the elements is binary or n-ary, and whether an attribute belongs to an element object class or to the relationship type among elements.

In Figure 1, student, course and part_time are treated as object classes. The id, name, contact_no, grade and position are treated as attributes. The filled circles are the object identifiers. The label "sc, 2, 3:8, 4:n" means: there is a binary relationship type named "sc", where one student may take 3 to 8 courses and one course should be taken by at least 4 students.

The "sc" label near the edge from course to grade indicates that the grade is an attribute belonging to the relationship type "sc" rather than the object class course.

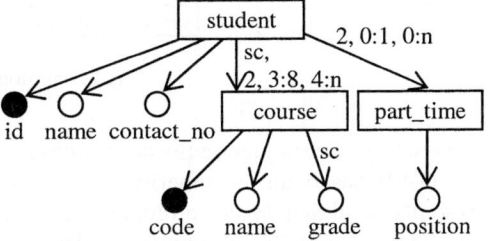

Fig. 1. The ORA-SS schema diagram

3.2 Motivating Example

Figure 1 shows that both the "student" and "course" have the "name" attribute, but they are different in semantics. It is easy for a person to distinguish the semantics of the two "name"s, but the agent will identify them as the same string if there is no semantic processing to the two "name"s.

The "part_time" and "position" show that the "student" may also be a part time employee, thus the semantics of "student_employee" is clearer than "student".

There is a relationship type "sc" between "student" and "course", but the semantics of "sc" is not clear. We do not know whether the student takes a course or drops a course. And the ORA-SS schema does not require the relationship to be an element name in the XML file, for example, the relationship type "sc" does not necessarily appear in a student XML file. That is to say, the semantics of the relationship between "student" and "course" is not clear.

We will address these problems in this paper.

4 A Genetic Model for Ontology Organization

We propose a genetic model to organize ontologies. This genetic model includes the following operators, viz. inheritance, block, atavism and mutation.

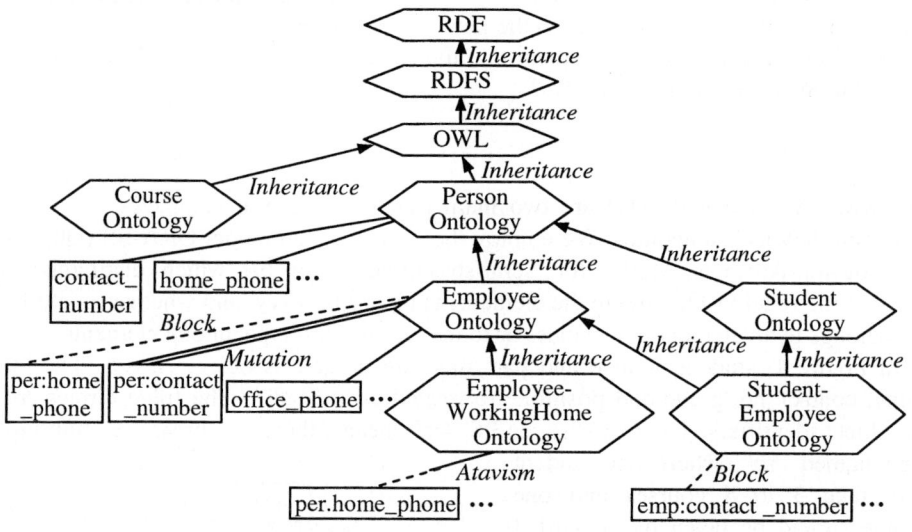

Fig. 2. Ontology hierarchy

In Figure 2, Ontologies reuse the primitives of ontology languages e.g. RDF, RDFS and OWL based on the inheritance operator. And lower level ontologies reuse the concepts of higher level ontologies, e.g. Employee Ontology inherits Person Ontology. The concept "home_phone" of Person Ontology is blocked by Employee Ontology because the home phone of an employee should not be public. The "contact_number" in Employee Ontology (refers to "office_phone") is a mutation of the "contact_number" in Person Ontology (refers to "home_phone").

The atavism operator is used to show that the "home_phone" of grandparent (Person) ontology blocked by parent (Employee) ontology is reused in the grandchild

(EmployeeWorkingHome) ontology. The *atavism* operator in this model is absent in other inheritance mechanisms.

Furthermore, StudentEmployee ontology inherits both Student and Employee ontologies. StudentEmplyee Ontology blocks the "emp:contact_number" and inherits the "contact_number" from Student Ontology in the multiple inheritance. For the multiple inheritance, we assume that the concept from only one parent ontology is inherited, and the conflict concepts from all the other parent ontologies are blocked. Course Ontology does not inherit Person Ontology etc., but directly inherits OWL.

The "per", "emp" etc. in Figure 2 are namespaces [12] referring to Person and Employee ontologies etc.

5 The Translations

5.1 Semantic Translation

The *Semantic Translation (SemT)* from an XML file or schema to a semantic web file or schema in this paper means that the XML elements, attributes and values are replaced with concepts from ontologies.

Rule SemT 1 (Rule for that only one matched concept is returned from ontologies). The XML element, attribute or value is replaced with this only returned concept.

Rule SemT 2 to 4 are used for that more than one matched concepts are returned.

Rule SemT 2 (Rule for Multiple Inheritance and Block). If the child ontology inherits several parent ontologies, the concept from that unblocked parent ontology is selected for the replacement.

Rule SemT 3 (Rule for Atavism). If the concept of the grandparent or ancestor ontology is an atavism in the grandchild or descendant ontology, the concepts in the grandchild or descendant ontology are used for the replacement.

Rule SemT 4 (Rule for Mutation). If a concept in the parent ontology is a mutation in the child ontology, the concept in the child ontology is used for the replacement.

Example 1. If an XML is about student employee, the StudentEmplyee ontology is specified for search, and the ancestor ontologies of this specified ontology will be searched also. The "contact_number" from Student Ontology is used for replacement.

Rule SemT 5 (Rule for that no matched concept are returned from ontologies). If the element, attribute or value cannot be found in the ontologies, our system suggests adding new concepts into the ontologies (adding new concepts needs the confirmation from the domain expert).

Rule SemT 1 to 5 can be applied to the XML values also. The next two rules are for some special values.

Rule Sem 6 (Rule for Numbers). If the values in the XML are numbers, such as the contact_no "9876543", they need not be searched in ontologies.

Rule Sem 7 (Rule for Person Names). If the values in the XML are person names (or company names etc.), such as "John", they need not be searched in ontologies.

Since we use a top-down method for the replacement, the student "name" element will be replaced to "per:name" firstly ("per" is the namespace [12]), then later we know the value ("John") of element "per:name" is a person name. We do NOT need a person name dictionary for this case.

5.2 Structural Translation

Structural Translation (StrT) in this paper refers to the translation of an XML file or schema to a file or schema complying with the RDF structure, i.e. SVO format.

Rule StrT 1 (Rule for checking structure). For any path of the XML from the root to the leaf, if the nesting is not resource, property, resource, property, resource etc. interleaved, this XML does not satisfy the RDF structure.

Rule StrT 2 (Rule for modifying structure). If resources or properties are required to be inserted in the XML to satisfy the RDF structure, the resources or properties are searched in the ontology hierarchy based on the domain and range of properties (not based on name).

5.3 Schematic Translation

Schematic Translation (SchT) in this paper means that some features of the XML schema are translated to follow the RDF, RDFS and OWL languages.

Rule SchT 1 (Rule for ID and ID reference). For the object identifier of ORA-SS or the ID attribute of DTD, it will be translated to the "rdf:ID" (an identification primitive of RDF) and the value for the object identifier will be kept unchanged. We use the "rdf:resource" to refer to the referenced object.

Rule SchT 2 (Rule for default and fixed values). If the value of an attribute is a default or fixed value, it is kept unchanged.

Rule SchT 3 (Rule for order sensitive, composite and disjunctive attributes). The order sensitive attribute is translated to the "rdf:Seq", the composite attribute to the "rdf:Bag", and the disjunctive attribute to the "rdf:Alt".

Rule SchT 4 (Rule for cardinality). The cardinality to constraint the objects and attributes is kept unchanged after translation. Thus the structure information of the original XML schema can be kept.

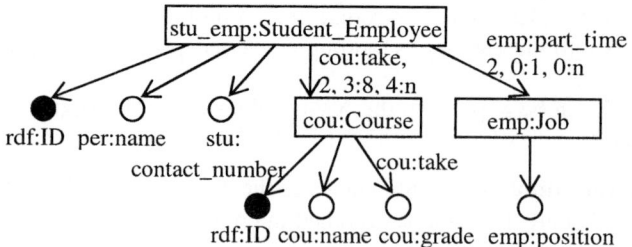

Fig. 3. The ORA-SS schema diagram after the three-step translations

After the semantic, structural and schematic translations, the ORA-SS schema in Figure 1 becomes the schema in Figure 3 where "stu_emp", "per", "cou" and "emp" are namespaces to refer to Student_Employee, Person, Course and Employee ontologies, and "rdf" is the namespace to refer to the RDF ontology language. The "take", "Job" etc. are concepts defined in Course, Employee ontologies etc.

6 Conclusion

In this paper, we use three steps, viz. semantic translation, structural translation and schematic translation, to translate XML to semantic web. For a valid XML, their schemas are translated firstly, then the XML files confirming to the schemas can be translated easily, which improves the efficiency of translation. More important, we organize ontologies based on the genetic model. The searching to ontologies is only at several related paths of the genetic model, thus less concepts need to be traversed and less confused concepts will be returned, and the rules introduced in this paper make the semantics of the returned concepts clearer.

References

1. Dan Brickley and R.V. Guha. Resource Description Framework (RDF) Schema Specification 1.0, W3C Candidate Recommendation 27 March 2000.
2. Avigdor Gal , Ami Eyal, Haggai Roitman, Hasan Jamil, Ateret Anaby-Tavor, and Giovanni Modica. OntoParser: an XML2RDF translator of OntoBuilder ontologies, OntoBuilder project. 2004.
3. Frank van Harmelen, Jim Hendler, Ian Horrocks, Deborah L. McGuinness, Peter F. Patel-Schneider and Lynn Andrea Stein. OWL Web Ontology Language Reference.
4. Frank van Harmelen, Peter F. Patel-Schneider, and Ian Horrocks. Reference description of the DAML+OIL (March 2001) ontology markup language
5. Jeff Heflin and James Hendler. A Portrait of the Semantic Web in Action. IEEE Intelligent Systems, 16(2), 2001.
6. I. Horrocks, D. Fensel, J. Broekstra, S. Decker, M. Erdmann, C. Goble, F. van Harmelen, M. Klein, S. Staab, R. Studer, and E. Motta. The Ontology Inference Layer OIL.
7. Paul Kogut, and William Holmes. AeroDAML: Applying Information Extraction to Generate DAML Annotations from Web Pages. K-CAP 2001 Workshop, October 21, 2001.
8. Ora Lassila and Ralph R. Swick: Resource description framework (RDF). 1999.
9. Tok Wang Ling, Mong Li Lee, Gillian Dobbie. Semistructured Database Design, Springer, 2005
10. Robert Neches, Richard Fikes, Timothy W. Finin, Thomas R. Gruber, Ramesh Patil, Ted E. Senator, William R. Swartout: Enabling Technology for Knowledge Sharing. AI Magazine 12(3): 36-56 (1991)
11. Lynn Andrea Stein, Dan Connolly, and Deborah McGuinness. DAML Ontology language specification. October 2000
12. Namespaces in XML, World Wide Web Consortium 14-January-1999.
13. http://www.w3.org/TR/REC-xml-names/
14. The SemanticWeb Homepage. http://www.semanticweb.org

A Hybrid Approach for Refreshing Web Page Repositories

M. Ghodsi, O. Hassanzadeh, Sh. Kamali, and M. Monemizadeh

{ghodsi, hassanzadeh, kamali, monemi}@ce.sharif.edu

Computer Engineering Department
Sharif University of Technology, Tehran, Iran

Abstract. Web pages change frequently and thus crawlers have to download them often. Various policies have been proposed for refreshing local copies of web pages. In this paper, we introduce a new sampling method that excels over other change detection methods in experiment. Change Frequency (CF) is a method that predicts the change frequency of the pages and, in the long run, achieves an optimal efficiency in comparison with the sampling method. Here, we propose a new hybrid method that is a combination of our new sampling approach and CF and show how our hybrid method improves the efficiency of change detection.

Keywords: web crawling, change detection, sampling, change frequency, hybrid algorithm

1 Introduction

Crawlers and spiders download and accumulate web pages to be categorized and ranked fast by search engines in response to users' queries. On the other side, web pages are updated frequently; new pages appear and old pages disappear quite often. To refresh web repositories, crawlers have to download new pages, clean the page archive from disappeared pages and update it with the new ones.

In [4] *Change Frequency (CF) method* was introduced for estimating the frequency of changes in web pages. Based on the past change history of the pages, this method estimates how often a page changes and decides on how often it must be revisited.

Sampling method is another approach for downloading web pages [5]. In this method, a small number of pages from each web site is sampled and the number of changed pages is then estimated. Based on the estimates, the download resource for each web site is allocated accordingly.

In this paper, we propose a hybrid model that commences to sampling, in the beginning, based on an improved sampling algorithm. With the passage of time, when the sampling resources reduce and when it gains a complete history of the page changes, our algorithm switches to CF and allocates more resources to this method.

In the remainder of the paper, in Section 2, we present our new sampling algorithm. Section 2 describes the CF method followed by the overall hybrid method which is proposed in Section 3. Our experimental results are presented in Section 5.

2 Improved Sampling Method

We suppose that all pages are equal in size and the resource available for crawling is counted based on the maximum number of pages we can download. We also assume that there are L web sites each having the same number of pages, denoted by M. The problem is to decide how we can best refresh the repository. Our measure for the optimality of an algorithm is its *efficiency* which is measured by the fraction of total number of downloaded items that have been changed.

Our iterative sampling method proceeds as follows. In each iteration, a fraction R pages (called the *sampling size*) of each site is downloaded uniformly at random. We estimate ρ_i, the percentage of the downloaded pages of site i that have been changed.

Let $P(\rho_i)$ be the probability of downloading another R pages from each site i. We continue the above iteration and download further R pages from site i with this probability.

We propose the following estimate for $P(\rho_i)$ to be calculated in each iteration.

$$P(\rho_i) = \frac{tanh(10(\rho_i - \rho_0) + 1)}{2} \quad (1)$$

where ρ_0 is the point of inflection. Reducing the resources available for sampling is done by increasing the value of ρ_0.

Here we justify the choice of equation 1. We would like to choose values for $P(\rho_i)$ that maximizes the number of detected changed pages in site i and considering our limited resource. For this, we calculate N_i, the average number of detected changed pages in site i, as follows.

We first assume that ρ_i is equal in all iteration. In other words, we assume the estimation of ρ_i is without error; we relax this assumption later. N_i is then computed as follows:

$$N_i = R\rho_i + R\rho_i \sum_{t=2}^{k} tP^{t-1}(\rho_i)(1 - P(\rho_i))$$

$$= R\rho_i * [1 - P^k(\rho_i) + \frac{P(\rho_i)}{1 - P(\rho_i)}(P^{k-1}(\rho_i) - 1) - (k-1)P^k(\rho_i) + P(\rho_i)]$$

where k is the maximum number of iterations which is equal to $\frac{M}{R}$.

Let N be the total number of detected changed pages. Then,

$$N = R * \sum_{i=1}^{L} \rho_i * [1 - P^k(\rho_i) + \frac{P(\rho_i)}{1 - P(\rho_i)}(P^{k-1}(\rho_i) - 1) - (k-1)P^k(\rho_i) + P(\rho_i)] \quad (2)$$

The best choice for $P(\rho)$ that maximizes the expression in equation 2, taking into account the limited number of pages we can download, is a pulse function (Figure 1.1).

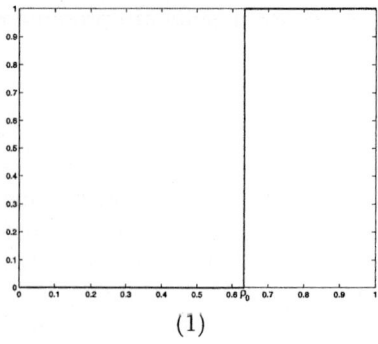 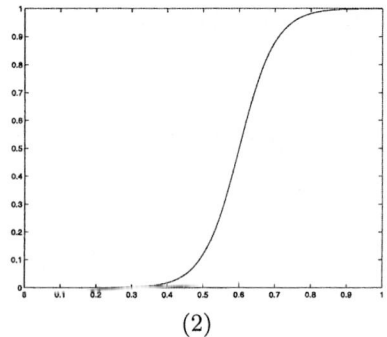

(1)   (2)

Fig. 1. (1) Diagram of $P(\rho)$ if ρ is estimated without error, (2) Diagram of $P(\rho)$.

The pulse function is the best choice when we can estimate the percentage of changed pages in the site without error. But in practice, this estimation is not exact and contains error. This error can affect the efficiency of our algorithm specially near ρ_0. To remedy this effect we can smooth the diagram of $P(\rho_i)$ near this point. The result is shown in figure 1.2. The diagram of figure 1.2 is very similar to the diagram of equation 2. This justifies why we choose tanh function to represent $P(\rho_i)$.

3 Change Frequency Method

Here, we briefly describe the CF phase. To help our discussion, we first borrow some notation from [4]. We assume n is the number of accesses to the page in interval I and X is the total number of changes detected within these accesses. Let f be the frequency at which we access the element and its value is $f = \frac{1}{I}$. λ, the change frequency of a page, is the number of times that the page was changed during a specific time. Now we can define the *frequency ratio* $r = \frac{\lambda}{f}$, the ratio of the change frequency to the access frequency. We can estimate frequency ratio $r = \frac{\lambda}{f}$ first and estimate λ indirectly from r. We use the estimator $\hat{r} = -\log(\frac{\bar{X}+0.5}{n+0.5})$, where $\bar{X} = n - X$ is the number of accesses that the element did not change, because it is more useful as shown in [4]. Consider two queues and call them *Normal* and *Slow*. Slow queue contains all pages that change rarely and we guarantee to crawl them in every one month, i.e., $I = 30$. The other pages are placed in Normal queue which are guaranteed to be crawled twice per month, i.e., $I = 15$. Over time, pages commute between Normal and Slow queues based on their estimated change frequency.

After creation of Normal and Slow queues, the algorithm works as follows: We crawl pages approximately twice per month in Normal queue and once per month in Slow queue. For each page p in each queue, we download p and compare p with the local copy to determine if it has changed, then calculate the new change frequency for it. If the new change frequency of page was still greater than some adaptive threshold, we append the page to the end of Normal queue, otherwise the page falls down into Slow queue.

4 The Hybrid Algorithm: An Overall View

4.1 Definitions

We denote a *cycle* to be an interval consisting of a *sampling phase* and a *CF phase*. For each site in a sampling phase a sequence of *steps* are defined where a step is an interval that the algorithm samples a specified number of pages from the site.

4.2 Towards Change Frequency

Sampling performs well without knowing the change history of pages. In contrast, frequency-based policy suffers from poor performance with insufficient knowledge of change history. This happens at the beginning which we have a poor estimation of change frequencies. But as time passes on, its performance improves over the sampling, as the history of changes converges to its more accurate values. So, it seems that we can gain more efficiency if we allocate more resources to CF as our crawling progresses. The migration towards CF should be done slowly. This is an important part of our algorithm whose overall view is described in the following algorithm.

Algorithm: HYBRIDALGORITHM()
    Input:
    ρ_0: The inflection point that takes its value from $[0..1]$.

1   Crawl all pages in the beginning and store them in repository REP
2   **while** True
3   **do** Increase ρ_0 one step
4   Call SAMPLINGPHASE
5   Call CHANGEFREQUENCYPHASE

Above algorithm is based on allocating resources between its two phases. We define a function that shows the used resource in the sampling phase. By adjusting the value of this function we can migrate from sampling to CF. For this purpose, we adjust the value of parameter ρ_0. As we increase it, the diagram of P shifts to the right. Let $U(\rho_k)$ be the average number of sampling phases in a cycle that we download from site k.

$$U(\rho_k) = \sum_{i=2}^{\frac{M}{R}} i P(\rho_k)^{i-1}(1 - P(\rho_k)) + 1 \qquad (3)$$

The total number of resources that will be used in sampling phase is $\sum_{i=1}^{L} RU(\rho_i)$. Thus, by reducing the probability $P(\rho_i)$, the value of $U(\rho_i)$ will be dwindled and eventually tends to one.

5 Experimental Results

For evaluating the various strategies as discussed above, we conducted a number of experiments. In this section, we first describe the distribution of our data-set and then compare various algorithms from the perspective of efficiency.

5.1 Our Data-Set

We collected over 100,000 pages (1000 web pages in 100 web sites) and kept track of their changes over two months. We crawled every site twice per month. It seems that 4 cycles for tracing the changes is relatively small, but based on the previous works [4, 5], we extend our cycles up to 500 cycles (i.e., we repeated the 4 cycles 125 times without actual downloading). We then simulated adaptive sampling, our new sampling, and hybrid algorithms on our data-set.

5.2 Comparison of Algorithms

As you see in figure 2, adaptive sampling has an efficiency of around 75 percent. Our new sampling, the first algorithm presented in this paper, has efficiency of approximately 81 percent. The other algorithm is hybrid algorithm which is a combination of improved sampling and CF and has the average efficiency of about 87 percent over time. As we observe in the figure, still there is a narrow fluctuation in the diagram of CF.

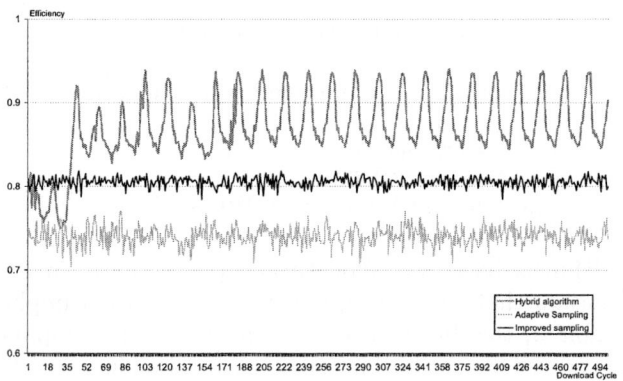

Fig. 2. Comparison of the various download policies over time

6 Conclusion

In this paper, we studied how we can detect changes effectively using a hybrid policy. We introduced a new sampling method that excels over other change detection methods in experiments and suggested improvements to Change

Frequency(CF) in order to increase its efficiency. We also proposed a new hybrid method that is a combination of our new sampling and CF and finally showed how the new method improves efficiency of change detection.

References

1. S. Brin and L. Page. The anatomy of a large-scale hypertextual web search engine. In Proc. WWW conf., April 1998.
2. J. Cho and H. Garcia-Molina. The evolution of the web and implications for an incremental crawler. In Proc. 26th VLDB Conf. , September 2000.
3. J. Cho and H. Garcia-Molina. Synchronizing a database to improve freshness. In Proc. SIGMOD Conf., May 2000.
4. J. Cho. Crawling the web: Discovery and maintenance of a large-scale web data. PhD. Thesis, Stanford University, 2001.
5. A. Ntoulas and J. Cho. Effective change detection using sampling. In Proc. 28th VLDB Conf., Hong Kong, China, 2002.

Schema Driven and Topic Specific Web Crawling[1]

Qi Guo, Hang Guo, Zhiqiang Zhang, Jing Sun, and Jianhua Feng

Tsinghua University, Beijing, China
{guoqi00, guohang02, jing-sun00}@mails.tsinghua.edu.cn
{zqzhang, fengjh}@tsinghua.edu.cn

Abstract. We propose a new approach to discover and extract topic-specific hypertext resources from the WWW. The method, called schema driven and topical crawling, allows a user to define schema and extracting rules for a specific domain of interests. It supports automatically search and extract schema-relevant web pages from the web. Different from common approaches that surf solely on web pages, our approach supports crawler to surf on a virtual network composed by concept instances and relationships. To achieve such a goal, we design an architecture that integrates several techniques including web extractor, meta-search engine and query expansion, and provide a toolkit to support it.

1 Introduction

The traditional web search engines treat the World Wide Web as a huge documents collection, and process queries by keyword matching. Due to the properties of large size, dynamic nature and diversity of the web, the keyword-based query usually returns hundreds of web pages. Hence, it is rather difficult to find the required information for a user from such a data mountain.

Based on above observation, we propose a novel approach to build powerful search engines for a specified topic. In this approach, user interested data from the web form a topic which is modelled by a schema, and queries are expressed on the schema and processed against the data extracted from topic-relevant web pages. The key part of the approach is to find the data relevant to the schema from the web. To achieve this goal, we build a system, called Schema Driven and Topic Specific Web Crawler, to allow a user to give schema definition and extracting rules for a topic. The crawler can then selectively seek out web pages relevant to the schema, and extract the data automatically. The extracted data is stored in a database, so can be queried through a structural query language.

Different from the common crawler that surfs the web graph composed by HTML pages and hyperlinks, our approach supports the crawler to surf on a virtual network formed by concept instances and relationships. The system uses web extractors to find the concept instances from fetched web pages, and uses meta-search engine and query

---

[1] This research work is part of the ALVIS project of EU's 6th Framework Programme and funded by the Ministry of Science and Technology of China.

expansion techniques to search the schema relevant web pages that contain at least one concept instance defined by the schema.

In the remaining part of this paper, first we introduce the method to represent a topic by a data schema, and then briefly describe the architecture of the crawler, followed by technical discussions on information extracting and searching of relevant web sources. Finally, we conclude the paper and indicate future works.

2 Related Works

Many different solutions have been proposed in the recent years. One popular approach, called focused crawling [1], collects domain-specific documents from the web selectively. The approach cares a narrow fragment of the web that is likely to be relevant to the specific domain, and avoids irrelevant regions of the web. The method leads to significant savings in resources, and the search results are considered to be more relevant to users who are interested in the specific domain. The pioneer focused crawler introduced by Chakrabarti [1] used a topical taxonomy, learning from examples, and use graph distillation to track topical hubs. Later works focused on the web search algorithms to increase the efficiency and quality [1,2,3,4,6]. To overcome the lower recall and less diverse caused by the existence of web communities [3,7], Bergmark proposed to use tunneling technology[7] to address the problem. Qin and Zhou proposed a meta-search enhanced focused crawler [6] to achieve both high precision and high recall.

There are many other approaches to encapsulate the heterogeneity by information extractor, through which the meaningful data are fetched from the documents of various format. One kind of these approaches restructure the original HTML into an intern representation, and provide a specific wrapper generation language for users, for instances, WebOQL[8], FLORID[9], WebL [10], etc. To reduce manual efforts, XWrap [11], Lixto [12], and NoDoSE[13] use an interactive tool to determine the document structure by users' hierarchical actions. The work of the Data Extraction Group[14] at BYU built a domain ontology to describe the data of interest, including relationships, lexical appears, and content keywords. But their approach focused on extracting semi-structured data from unstructured documents which are rich in data and narrow in ontological breath.

3 The Proposed Techniques

3.1 The Concept Schema

Because of the dynamic nature of the web, it is difficult to define an exact schema for a domain. In our previous work, we adopted a simple and flexible method using concept schema at a logical level to describe user interested data on the web. Figure 1 illustrates a concept schema example. To see the detail for concept schema, please refer to [15].

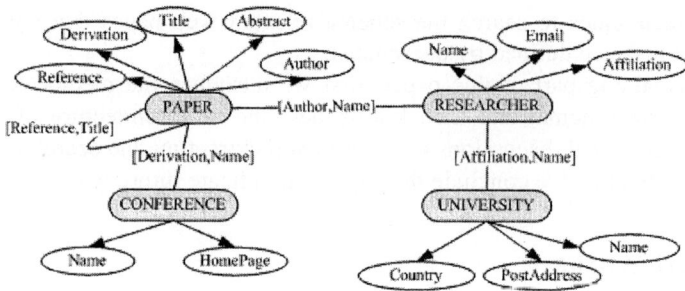

Fig. 1. The Concept Schema Example

3.2 System Architecture

The next figure shows the architecture of the crawler.

The core component of the system is the Schema Manager. It provides an interface for managing data schema of specific topic and rules to search and extract relevant pages. The Concept Queue Manager maintains a queue of concept instances for finding and extracting. The task of Concept Selector is to select a concept instance from web pages obeying defined rules. The Concept Seeker searches the web pages that possibly contain the data of concept instances. The Page Fetcher downloads schema-relevant pages to temporary storage, and the Page Extractor locates concept instances and extracts them from web pages.

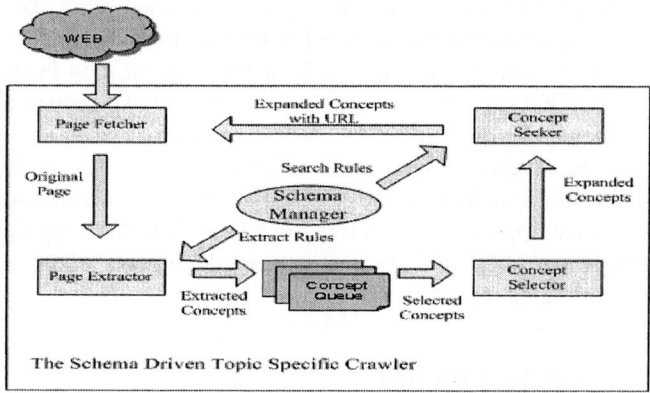

Fig. 2. System Architecture

3.3 Concept Seeking

We use the concept schema in Figure 1 to show this process. At the very beginning, the crawler is given some seeding web pages that contain concepts of the schema, say PAPER. Starting from these seeding pages, the seeking of other concepts, RESEACHER for example, will be proceeded by the crawler in following way.

1) The Page Extractor analyzes the seeding page and finds the attribute values of PAPER instance. For the attribute Author which forms the relationship between PAPER and RESEACHER, the extractor locates the text region of the attribute and annotates it as potentially relevant page to the RESEARCHER concept. These relevant pages will be put in the Concept Queue for further exploring. In same way, the crawler can use the attribute Derivation of PAPER, the attribute Affiliation of RESEARCHER to find the concepts of CONFERENCE and UNIVERSITY of the schema in Figure 1.

2) The crawler uses the meta-search method to find new instances and get data for concept instances from relevant pages. For example, given an author's name, the crawler can use Google or Yahoo to get a publication list from the author's home page. This list gives the crawler more PAPER instances to be included in the CONCEPT QUEUE. In finding the data of a paper, the crawler posts the text, such as a paper's title, to Google or Yahoo, and picks up relevant URLs from the results.

3) To improve the efficiency, we adapt query expansion technique to reduce irrelevant pages returned by the general search engines. For example, when searching a PERSON concept, the system will merge the person's name with some string such as "Home Page", "Email", etc, to refine the result set. In practice, the crawler may try several times with differently expanding strings to reduce more irrelevant results.

3.4 Concept Extracting

The major task of concept extracting is to discover the schema defined data from HTML pages, including concept instances, attribute values and relationships. In our approach, the system needs to acquire data from diverse data sources distributed on the web, so it is not acceptable to build individual extractors for each web site. We need adaptable extractors for the concepts of the schema rather than for each web site. In our previous works, we built highly adaptable wrappers for solving this problem. For the detail, please refer to [16][17].

4 Experiments

We conducted a set of experiments to test the performance of Page Extractor, Concept Selector, and Concept Seeker of the crawler. The metrics for this performance testing are commonly used concept of recall and precision from IR area. For these experiments, a simple topic composed of two concepts PAPER, and RESEARCHER was created as the schema. Because of the space limitation, in this section, we only give the performance testing result of Concept Seeker. The test shows when given the value of key attribute of a concept instance, how many relevant pages the Concept Seeker can find from the web..

We created 2 sets of test cases, one containing 1000 Paper titles and the other containing 1000 Researcher names. Firstly, we posted the text of the paper title and researcher name to Google directly, and selected the top 5 result for each query, and sent to Page Extractor to determine whether it is relevant or not. The concept PAPER got a recall of 77.2%, and the concept RESEARCHER got a recall of 64.3%. Next, we expanded each query by appending the strings "Home Page" and "Abstract" respectively. The recall of concept PAPER increased to 81.1%, and the recall of concept RESEARCHER increased to 73.0%. The result seems to be acceptable. It also shows that the query expansion doesn't improve the effect significantly in this experiment. After analysis on the results, we found that some cases got a better result after query expansion, but some cases did not because more noises were introduced. To see the detail, please refer to [16] [17].

5 Conclusion and Future Work

In this paper, we describe the architecture and discuss some technical issues of our schema driven and topic specific crawling approach and the crawler. The major contributions of this work are:

1) Unlike common crawlers that usually travel on the hyperlinks between web pages, the proposed approach uses data schema to model the topic, and navigate in the virtual network composed by concepts and relationships. The fetched data is the structural data extracted from web pages, so the structural query could be supported.

2) We propose the concept extension model, and design an architecture that closely integrates a number of techniques including information extracting, meta-search engine and query expansion to implement the model.

3) We introduce a concept seeking method enhanced with meta-search engine and query expansion.

Our ultimate goal is to provide a database view for the web, thus, query the web just like query a database. The next steps of our work include:

1) To improve the precision and coverage of concept seeking through error feedback mechanism.

2) To develop a user friendly interface to facilitate the configuration and management of the crawler.

References

[1] Chakrabarti, S., van den Berg, M. and Dom, B. Focused crawling: a new approach to topic-specific Web resource discovery," in Proc. of the 8th International World Wide Web Conference, Toronto, Canada, 1999.

[2] Flake, G. W., Lawrence, S. and Giles, C. Efficient Identification of Web Communities. in Proc. of the 6th ACM SIGKDD International Conference on Knowledge Discovery and Data Mining, Boston, Massachusetts, USA. 2000

[3] Flake, G. W., Lawrence, S. and Giles, C. Efficient Identification of Web Communities. in Proc. of the 6th ACM SIGKDD International Conference on Knowledge Discovery and Data Mining, Boston, Massachusetts, USA. 2000

[4] McCallum, A., Nigam, K., Rennie, J. and Seymore, K. Building Domain-Specific Search Engines with Machine Learning Techniques. in Proc. AAAI-99 Spring Symposium on Intelligent Agents in Cyberspace.

[5] Jialun.Qin, Yilu Zhou, Michael Chau: Building domain-specific web collections for scientific digital libraries: a meta-search enhanced focused crawling method. International Conference on Digital Libraries, Proceedings of the 2004 joint ACM/IEEE conference on Digital libraries

[6] Chau, M. and Chen, H. Comparison of Three Vertical Search Spiders, IEEE Computer, 36(5), 56-62. 2003
[7] Bergmark, D., Lagoze, C. and Sbityakov, A. Focused Crawls, Tunneling, and Digital Libraries. in Proc. of the 6th European Conference on Digital Libraries, Rome, Italy, 2002
[8] G. O. Arocena, A. O. Mendelzon. WEBOQL: Restructuring Documents, Databases, and Webs. In proceedings of the 14th IEEE International Conference on Data Engineering. pp. 24-33.
[9] Wolfgang May, Rainer Himmeröder, Georg Lausen, Bertram Ludäscher. A Unified Framework for Wrapping, Mediating and Restructuring Information from the Web. International Workshop on International Workshop on the World-Wide Web and Conceptual Modeling (WWWCM'99), pp. 307-320.
[10] T. Kistler and H. Marais. WebL - A programming language for the Web, in: Proceedings of WWW7, pages 259-270, 1998
[11] L. Liu, C. Pu, W. Han. XWrap – An XML-enabled Wrapper Construction System for Web Information Sources, Proceedings of the 16th International Conference on Data Engi-neering (ICDE'2000)
[12] R. Baumgartner, S. Flesca, G. Gottlob. Visual Web Information Extraction with Lixto, Paper for the 27th International Conference on Very Large Data Bases (VLDB 2001)
[13] B.Adelberg. Nodose – a tool for semi-automatically extraction structured and semi-structured data from text documents. ACM SIGMOD, 1998
[14] D.W. Embley, D. M. Campbell, Y.S. Jiang, S.W.Liddle, Y. Kaing, D.Quass, R.D.Smith. Conceptual-Model-Based Data Extraction from Multiple-Record Web Pages. Data and Knowledge Engineering 31, 3(1999), 227-251
[15] Zhiqiang Zhang, Cunxiao Xing, Lizhu Zhou and Jianhua Feng, "A New Query Processing Scheme in a Web Data Engine", 2nd International Workshop on Databases in Networked Information Systems (DNIS 2002), LNCS 2544, pp 74-87, Japan December 16-18, 2002.
[16] Qi Guo, Lizhu Zhou, Zhiqiang Zhang and Jianhua Feng, "A Highly Adaptive Web Extractor." Proc. of the 6th Asia Pacific Web Conference. 2004
[17] Qi Guo. Technique Report of GQML. http://dbroup.cs.tsinghua.edu.cn/sesq/

Towards Optimal Utilization of Main Memory for Moving Object Indexing

Bin Cui, Dan Lin, and Kian-Lee Tan

School of Computing & Singapore-MIT Alliance,
National University of Singapore
{cuibin, lindan, tankl}@comp.nus.edu.sg

Abstract. In moving object databases, existing disk-based indexes are unable to keep up with the high update rate while providing speedy retrieval at the same time. However, efficient management of moving-object database can be achieved through aggressive use of main memory. In this paper, we propose an *Integrated Memory Partitioning and Activity Conscious Twin-index* (IMPACT) framework where the moving object database is indexed by a pair of indexes based on the properties of the objects' movement - a main-memory structure manages *active* objects while a disk-based index handles *inactive* objects. As objects become active (or inactive), they dynamically migrate from one structure to the other. Moreover, the main memory is also organized into two partitions - one for the main memory index, and the other as buffers for the frequently accessed nodes of the disk-based index. Our experimental study shows that the IMPACT framework provides superior performance.

1 Introduction

Over the years, many data structures have been proposed for moving object indexing [4, 6, 8, 10, 12, 13]. Most of these indexing techniques are disk-based and tend to leave memory exploitation to independent buffering strategies. Main memory is much faster than disk and becomes increasingly voluminous and inexpensive. However, it remains a scarce resource with increasingly sophisticated software and the rapid buildup of huge datasets. Buffer management is effective in gaining faster access to the main memory, and tends to result in the better memory utilization by loading popular paths of the index into memory. Nevertheless, most buffering strategies do not guarantee that the main memory is being utilized in an optimal fashion. Capturing continuous locations of moving objects would entail either performing very frequent updates or recording outdated, inaccurate data. Therefore, the traditional buffering scheme may not work efficiently for the moving object index structures.

To better manage moving object databases, we need to improve the utilization of the main memory. Our solution is based on three observations. First, the moving objects can be classified into two groups, *active* objects and *inactive* objects. Typically, active objects tend to have relatively higher speed and change velocity frequently, and trigger relatively more updates. Second, we observe that most of the moving objects are inactive. Our analysis of the dataset generated by the City Simulator [5] reveals that only a small portion of users are active at a time, while the majority of the users are inactive. Third, although the active objects constitute a small fraction of the dataset, they incur the fast enlargements of MBRs (minimum bounding rectangle) in the TPR-tree like indexes [10, 12], which results in severe overlaps and degenerates the index performance.

Now, the first and third observations suggest that we should consider active and inactive objects separately. The second observation suggests that active objects can potentially be kept in the main memory. Thus, in this paper, we propose a novel framework, called *Integrated Memory Partitioning and Activity Conscious Twin-indexing* (IMPACT), that combines two mechanisms to make aggressive use of the main memory. First, a pair of indexes manages the moving object database based on the objects' activities - *active* objects are managed by a main memory index, while *inactive* objects are stored in a disk-based structure. As objects become active or inactive, they *dynamically* migrate from one structure to another. Second, the main memory is split into two partitions – one for the main memory index, and the other as buffers for the frequently accessed nodes of the disk-based index. In this way, active objects can be processed efficiently in memory, while there will be less activities occurring on the disk.

To realize the framework, we employ a grid structure for the main memory index and the TPR*-tree [12] as the disk-based structure. We also use an OLRU buffering strategy [9] to cache frequently accessed nodes of the TPR*-tree. For memory partitioning, we devise a scheme to optimally allocate space for the main memory index and buffers. We implemented the proposed framework, and evaluated its performance. Our experimental study shows that the proposed IMPACT framework significantly outperforms the TPR*-tree.

The rest of the paper is organized as follows: in Section 2, we review some related work, including buffering algorithms and existing moving object index structures. In Section 3, we present our proposed IMPACT framework and its realization. Section 4 reports the experimental results. Finally, we concludes our work in Section 5.

2 Related Work

In this section, we shall first review buffering algorithms, and then look at some index structures for moving objects.

Buffer management for indexes has been reported in the literature [3, 9]. ILRU (Inverse LRU) and OLRU (Optimal LRU) are studied in [9], and are shown to be better than the classic LRU. We shall briefly describe the OLRU strategy which we adapted in our work. In the OLRU strategy, the index pages are logically partitioned into L independent regions. Whenever an index page at level i is accessed, it is kept in region i of the buffer, or in the single free buffer in the case of *coalesced* regions. In general, the OLRU scheme allocates the available buffer according to reference frequency of nodes. Therefore this strategy can guarantee that top-level pages of a tree have higher priority compared to those further from the root. As reported in [9], OLRU shows near optimal performance for both uniform and skew data.

According to the type of data being stored, the indexes [1, 6, 7, 10, 11, 12, 13] for moving objects can be classified into two categories: indexing the past positions of objects (i.e. trajectories) and indexing the current and anticipated future positions of objects. We focus on related works in the latter category because our methods belong to it. To index the current and near-future positions of moving objects, most existing approaches describe each object's location as a simple linear function, and update the database only when the predicted position deviates from the actual position larger than a threshold. One representative indexing is the time-parameterized R-tree (TPR-tree) [10]. The bounding rectangles in the TPR-tree are functions of time, as are the moving objects being indexed. Intuitively, the bounding rectangles are capable of continuously following the enclosed data points or other rectangles as these move. Most recently, the TPR*-tree [12] is proposed in order to optimize the TPR-tree. Next, Patel et al. [8] propose an indexing method, called STRIPES, which indexes predicted trajectories in a dual transformed space. The Q+R-tree makes use of the topography and the patterns of object movement and handles different types of moving objects separately [13]. In the Q+R tree, quasi-static objects are stored in an R*-tree and fast-moving objects are stored in a Quad-tree. Another recent index is the B^x-tree [4] which enables B^+-tree to manage moving objects efficiently. The performance of the above index structures are all largely influenced by active objects which dominate the enlargements of MBRs or query windows.

3 The IMPACT Framework

This section presents the IMPACT (Integrated Memory Partitioning and Activity Conscious Twin-index) framework and the specific data structures and algorithms that we have employed to realize its implementation.

3.1 The Basic Framework

As observed in the introduction, a small portion of active moving objects have high speed and incur frequent updates. This prompted us to design the proposed IMPACT framework which comprises the following components:

1. A twin-index structure to dynamically manage the moving objects. One of the indexes is a main memory structure used to index active objects. Another index structure is a disk-based structure to index the inactive objects. Separating the active and inactive objects is expected to improve the overall system performance: (a) Active objects contribute to both high update cost and degrade query performance, and so keeping them away from the main bulk of the database can reduce the load on the database. (b) Managing active objects in main memory can further facilitate their processing, while

managing the inactive objects on disk also leads to less activities on the disk portion.
2. A buffering scheme for the disk-based structure to cache frequently and recently accessed paths or nodes. This is necessary as accesses to the disk-based structure would be costly if frequently accessed paths or nodes are not buffered.
3. A memory partitioning mechanism to optimally allocate the main memory to the memory-resident index and the buffer. Clearly, from the above point, allocating all the space to the main memory index is not likely to lead to good performance. Similarly, ignoring the main memory index reduces the problem to traditional buffering of a single disk-based index which, as we have argued, is not optimal either.

The IMPACT framework is generic. Any index structure can be used as the main memory index and/or disk-based index. In fact, the two structures can be different. Similarly, any existing index buffering strategies can also be employed. Moreover, we note that the memory partitioning mechanism is dependent on the structures used.

In this work, we employ a grid structure as the main memory index. Grid structure is preferred to be stored in the memory since (a) grid structure works well with hashing techniques to provide random and direct access; (b) each grid in memory only needs to store pointers to objects instead of storing full information of objects when residing in disk; (c) grid structure requires duplicating an object across all grids that it intersects, which speeds up query processing while results in poor update performance if it is disk-based.

For the disk-resident index, we employ the TPR*-tree. The TPR*-tree is built on the ideas of the TPR-tree, and has been shown to be a near-optimal structure for large moving object databases. To keep the commonly traversed index nodes in the cache, we adapted the OLRU scheme for our purpose. OLRU is chosen because it gives greater priority to the nodes of the tree nearer to the root. Furthermore, it is simpler and is reported to yield good performance.

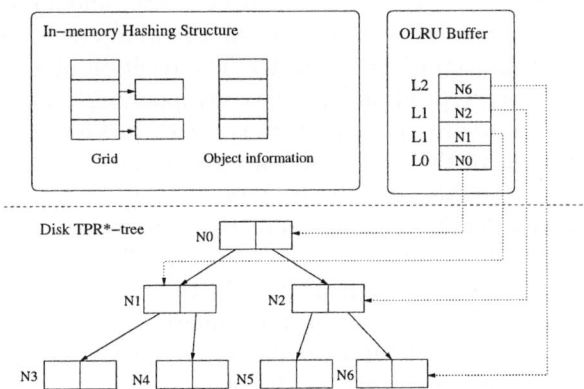

Fig. 1. The IMPACT structure

Figure 1 provides a pictorial representation of how the different data structures are related to one another. The figure contains two parts: the top portion shows that the available main memory space is split into two regions, one for the grid structure and the other for the OLRU; the bottom portion shows the disk-based TPR*-tree. Both the TPR*-tree and grid structure store the moving objects with different velocities, while the OLRU buffer manages frequent accessed nodes of the disk-based TPR*-tree. We note that as objects' activities change, they may be migrated from one structure to the next.

For the rest of this section, we shall first present the grid structure for active objects. Then we present the query and update algorithms on the twin-index structure. Finally, we will describe how we determine the memory allocation between the grid structure and the buffer for the TPR*-tree.

3.2 In-Memory Grid Structure

To manage the active moving objects in main memory, we employ a grid structure to capture these objects' current and future positions. Basically, we partition the two-dimensional domain space into a regular grid structure where each cell is a bucket. To support queries on future positions, we calculate the future trajectories of objects in a given time length and store the objects in the buckets their trajectories intersect. To define how far the trajectories need to be indexed, we use three time parameters as in [10], i.e. *query interval* (I), *index usage time* (U) and *time horizon* (H). Thus we can see that H represents how far into the future the index may reach and it is the upper limit of the index valid period. The grid structure must support queries that reach up to H time units into the future.

Each object may be hashed into several cells in the grid because of the existence of the trajectory. The entire grid is implemented as an array of cells, which efficiently supports random accesses to individual cells. To efficiently utilize the memory space, we do not store the detail information of moving objects in each corresponding bucket, but only keep the object identifier ID in the grid which can reduce memory consumption. A separate hash table with the key ID is used for the storage of objects, which supports fast random access to the detail information of moving objects. In case of a system crash, we backup these objects information to the disk periodically. The position of a moving object is represented by a reference position (x, y), a corresponding velocity vector v, and reference time t. The overall grid structure is shown in Figure 2.

We present two algorithms to deal with the insert and query in the grid structure, i.e. *Insert_hash()* and *RangeQuery_hash()*. To insert a new object O, we first store the details of object into the hash table. Then we map the object into the cell and save its ID in the mapped cell. After that, we compute the trajectory of the object movement within time horizon H, and insert its ID into each intersected cells. When a range query is issued at time t, we hash the lower bound and upper bound points of the query rectangle to the cells in the grid, and retrieve the objects in the buckets overlapping with the query rectangle.

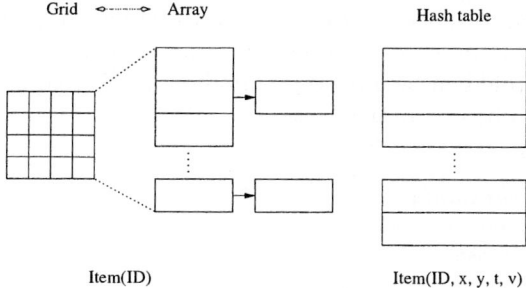

Fig. 2. The in-memory grid structure

3.3 Managing Moving Objects with the Twin-Index

We are now ready to look at how the twin-index is used to support moving objects. We shall address the primitive operations for construction, update and search. Delete operation is very simple: locate the object (either in memory or on disk), then delete the object accordingly, and so we omit the details here. In this discussion, we shall assume that certain amount of memory has been allocated to the grid structure. We defer how this amount is determined to the next subsection.

Building the Twin-Index. To build the twin-index, we first need to determine what constitutes an active object. We introduce a self-adaptive *velocity threshold* (V) for this purpose: those objects moving with velocities larger than the threshold will be stored in main memory, and those moving with lower speed are indexed on disk. Using speed as a splitting metric is effective because (a) no matter how frequently they change directions, fast objects may lead to huge expansion of MBRs; (b) slow moving objects which change directions frequently do not affect the TPR*-tree's performance but only introduce a few update numbers.

If we underestimate V, then the memory can be filled up. In this case, we will raise the threshold V. If we overestimate V, the memory will be under-utilized, and hence we have to decrease the value of V. Initially, we can estimate V as follows. We first get a sample from the dataset and store the statistic information of the speed with a histogram. The histogram partitions the speed domain into several sub-domains (called buckets) and counts the number of objects that fall into each bucket. According to the velocity distribution and available memory space, we get the initial V. We update the histogram for each object insertion, and V can be adjusted during the construction.

As shown in Figure 3, to construct the twin-index, the first step is to initiate the threshold V. As the V is self-adaptive, we can randomly select an initial value for it. However, to predict the V more precisely, we apply a sampling mechanism and calculate the initial value via the velocity histogram. For each object, we check whether the moving object is active. If the object is active and there is free space in memory, we insert the object into the in-memory grid structure; otherwise the new object has to be inserted into the TPR*-tree on disk. During this process, we maintain a speed histogram in memory, and the velocity threshold can be adjusted periodically. Therefore, we can index the majority of active objects in memory.

Algorithm Construction()
Input: the moving object dataset
1.   get a sample dataset;
2.   initialize velocity histogram and V;
3.   for each object O in dataset
4.   if $(O_v > V)$
5.   if (Memory has free space)
6.   invoke Insert_hash(O);
7.   else
8.   insert O to the TPR*-tree;
9.   update the velocity histogram;
10. adjust V if necessary;

Fig. 3. Construction algorithm

Range Query. The search operation consists of three steps: search the grid structure (which we have already described in the previous subsection), search the TPR*-tree (see [12]), and finally combine the answers. We expect the algorithm to be efficient because (a) the search in memory is much faster, (b) the search on the TPR*-tree is also faster (compared to a pure TPR*-tree that indexes all moving objects) since our structure only indexes inactive objects.

Moving Object Update. Whenever an update occurs, we need to determine whether to migrate the object that changes its activity status. Because the velocities of the moving objects may change from time to time, sometimes we need to switch the objects between the grid structure and the TPR*-tree to improve the efficiency. We deal with the objects in the main memory and disk using different policy since moving objects with high velocities tend to change the speed more frequently. To avoid oscillating between memory and disk too frequently, a moving object is allowed to reside in the memory even if its speed is less than the threshold. However, we tag these objects as inactive objects and store their IDs in an inactive object queue. Since we only store IDs in the queue, the space overhead is low. Whenever the speed of an object on disk exceeds the threshold and the main memory has no free space, these tagged objects will be replaced. In this way, we can fully utilize the memory space, and reduce the frequency of switch between memory and disk. The update algorithm is shown in Figure 4.

To update an object, we first locate the object to be updated. If the object is in memory, we update the object, and tag it as inactive (put its ID in the inactive object queue) if the new speed is less than the velocity threshold. If the object is on disk and still inactive, we just update the object in the TPR*-tree.

Algorithm Update(O)
Input: O is the object to be updated
1.   locate the object O;
2.   if (O is in memory)
3.   update O in hash structure;
4.   if ($O_v <$ velocity threshold V)
5.   tag O as inactive object;
6.   insert O to the inactive object queue;
7.   else
8.   if $(O_v < V)$
9.   update O in the TPR*-tree;
10.   else
11.   if (memory has free space)
12.   delete O from the TPR*-tree;
13.   invoke Insert_hash(O);
14.   else
15.   if ($\exists\ O'$ tagged as inactive)
16.   switch(O, O');
17.   else
18.   update O in the TPR*-tree;
19.   update the velocity histogram;
20.   adjust V if necessary;

Fig. 4. Update algorithm

Otherwise, if there is free memory space, we move the object into memory. If there is no more memory space but there are inactive objects in memory, we replace the inactive objects with the new ones. In the last case, we have to update the object in the TPR*-tree even if the object becomes active. For each update, we adjust the counter of corresponding bucket in the velocity histogram and update the velocity threshold V if necessary.

Our algorithm is flexible even if the speed distribution is not constant. For example, the average speed of vehicles during the rush hour may be lower than that during the off-peak period. To reflect the variation of the speed distribution, the twin-index can automatically adjust the velocity threshold with respect to the objects' movements. This is done during the update operations with the aid of the speed histogram. According to the counter of V, when there are too many fast objects, we increase the value of V; otherwise, we decrease it.

3.4 The Memory Partitioning Strategy

In this subsection, we present how the main memory can be allocated optimally to the main memory grid structure and the buffer for the TPR*-tree. We note that there is a relationship between the space allocated for buffering the TPR*-tree and that allocated for the main memory grid structure. Clearly, more space allocated to the buffer implies less space is left for the grid structure (i.e. fewer fast objects can be stored in memory). While this contributes to reduced I/O cost to retrieve data from the TPR*-tree, it also means that the TPR*-tree is larger (since fewer objects can be retained in the main memory structure). Therefore, our goal is to solve this dilemma and achieve optimal memory utilization.

We analyze the performance of the twin-index and reveals the factors that determine the query cost, and then give the optimal memory allocation ratio between the grid structure and the OLRU buffer[1]. Based on the cost analysis, we found that it is more beneficial to buffer the top two levels of the TPR*-tree but use the remainder memory space to index active objects for uniformly distributed data. Note that, the optimal memory allocation, i.e. buffering top two levels, may not be optimal for data with different distribution. However, this result suggests that a buffering strategy that gives priority to higher levels of index structure is preferred.

4 An Experimental Study

In this section, we report results of an experimental study to evaluate the IMPACT framework. As reference, we compare the IMPACT scheme against the TPR*-tree). For the TPR*-tree, all the available memory is used to buffer the index nodes/paths according to OLRU buffering scheme. We run 200 Range queries (4% of the space), and use the average I/O cost as the performance metrics. All the experiments are conducted on a 1.6G Hz P4 machine with 256M of main memory. Page size is set to 4KB and the default memory size is 8M bytes. Our evaluation comprises both uniform and skew datasets with 1M points. The default values of H (time horizon) and I (query interval) are 120 and 60 respectively.

4.1 Performance on Uniform Dataset

In this set of experiments, we use randomly distributed uniform dataset as in [10], i.e., the objects are uniformly distributed in the space 1000×1000, and also the velocities of moving objects are uniformly distributed between 0 and 3.

Effect of Memory Allocation. Given a fixed amount of memory space available for the processing of moving objects, we would like to study how the twin-index's performance is affected by the allocation of memory space between the grid structure and the OLRU buffer under varying amount of main memory. We fix the total memory to 8M. The results are shown in Figure 5 (a).

As expected, the results show that the twin-index yields better performance as more memory is allocated to the grid structure. When all the memory is used for the OLRU buffer, the twin-index behaves like the TPR*-tree. The active objects introduce heavy overlap in the disk index structure which degrades the query performance. As more memory is allocated to the grid structure, more active objects are kept in memory. This in turn significantly reduces the activities

---

[1] For the details of cost analysis, interested readers are referred to [2].

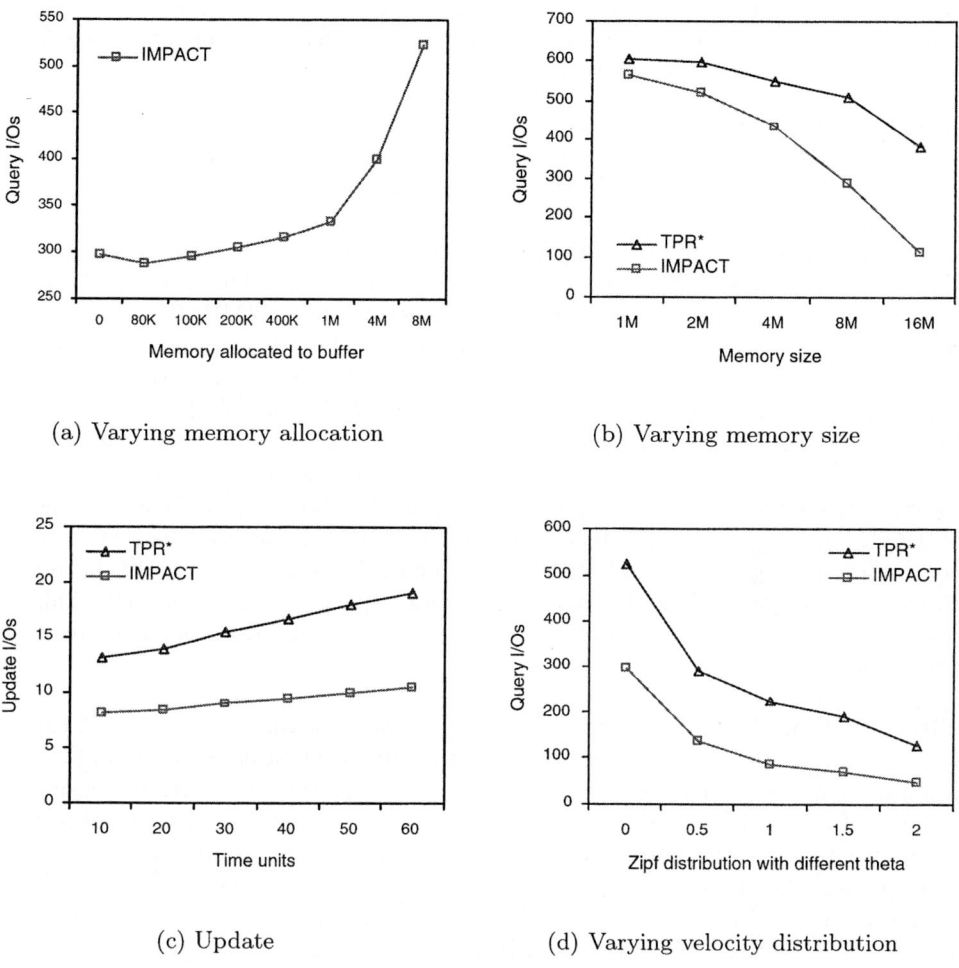

Fig. 5. The experimental results

on the disk structure. Moreover, query processing on the grid structure is fast. We also observe that the difference in performance can be more than 40% between the two extreme memory allocations (either all for the OLRU buffer or all for the grid structure). The results suggest that even traditional buffering schemes that perform well (such as OLRU) may not cope well in moving object databases.

We also note that the best performance appears when we use around 80K memory space for OLRU buffer which is sufficient to keep the top two level nodes of the disk-based TPR*-tree in the buffer. From the view of buffer, buffering the top two levels is very effective. It does not cost much memory space, but is very helpful to improve the disk-based index performance, because most of these nodes have to be accessed by queries. Additionally, this OLRU buffer size is small compared to the overall memory available. The gain on the buffer surpasses the loss on the disk-based TPR*-tree, because the TPR*-tree has to index a bit more objects whose space is occupied by the buffer. Therefore the optimal memory allocation is a compromise of these factors.

Effect of Memory Size. In this experiment, we compare the IMPACT against the TPR*-tree as we vary the total available memory size from 1M to 16M. We only show the performance of IMPACT with optimal memory allocation.

As shown in Figure 5 (b), both the schemes' performances improve with the increasingly lager memory size. When the available memory size is small ($< 1M$), the IMPACT is only marginally better than the TPR*-tree. This is because the small main memory allocated to the grid structure in the IMPACT does not hold enough active objects to result in significant workload reduction on the disk-based structure (as a large portion of the objects are still disk-based). However, as the memory size reaches beyond a certain point ($> 2M$), the IMPACT performs better than the TPR*-tree. The performance difference widens as the memory space increases. Indexing the active objects in main memory can significantly improve the efficiency of the disk portion (i.e. disk-based TPR*-tree) of the IMPACT. Additionally, the OLRU portion of IMPACT can still benefit from the buffering despite its small buffer size. The IMPACT can be 100% better than the TPR*-tree when the available memory space is larger than 8M. This study again confirms that traditional buffering techniques does not effectively utilize the main memory.

Effect of Update. In this experiment, we investigate the update cost of the two schemes. Figure 5 (c) compares the average update cost as a function of the number of updates. The performance of these methods decreases with increasing number of updates. Each update needs to conduct a query to retrieve the object to be updated, and this query cost increases with the number of updates because the updates will degenerate the efficiency of the index. However, the IMPACT outperforms the TPR*-tree and yields better scalability. It has two advantages over the TPR*-tree. First, since the IMPACT indexes the active objects in memory, most of the updates are restricted in memory and can be performed quickly. Second, the IMPACT can locate the inactive objects faster on disk, because the inactive objects introduce less overlap and slower MBR enlargement.

4.2 Performance on Skew Dataset

In the previous experiments, the objects and their velocities are uniformly distributed. However, most of the objects do not move at high speeds most of the time, i.e., a large portion of objects are in inactive state most of the time. We first test the effect of speed distribution on the query performance, shown in Figure 5 (d). The skew data is generated by varying the θ of the Zipf distribution, e.g. $\theta = 2$ means 80% of the objects fall in the 20% low velocity of the domain. The active objects are the main culprits for the heavy overlap in the index structure, and hence the range query has to search more nodes. When the data is skewed, all the indexes yield better performance, however the gain (in terms of percentage) between the IMPACT and the TPR*-tree is widened. As the skew dataset has fewer active objects, it is possible to index a larger proportion of the active objects in the main memory. Thus, the IMPACT can benefit more from the velocity skewness.

5 Conclusion

In this paper, we have revisited the problem of moving object indexing. We propose a framework, called IMPACT, that integrates efficient memory allocation and a twin-index structure to manage moving objects. The IMPACT partitions the dataset into active objects and inactive objects and then processes the moving objects respectively. To efficiently support the query in memory, we apply a grid structure to index the active objects. To reduce the disk I/O, the remainder memory space is used as an OLRU buffer that allows frequently accessed nodes of the disk index to remain in main memory. We also conducted a series of experiments which shows convincingly that the proposed framework can lead to better performance.

References

1. H. D. Chon, D. Agrawal, and A. El Abbadi. Query processing for moving objects with space-time grid storage model. In *Proc. MDM*, pages 121–128, 2002.
2. B. Cui, D. Lin, and K.L. Tan. Towards optimal utilization of memory for moving object indexing. In *Technical Report, National University of Singapore*, 2004.
3. C. H. Goh, B. C. Ooi, D. Sim, and K. L. Tan. GHOST: Fine granularity buffering of index. In *Proc. VLDB*, pages 339–350, 1999.
4. C. S. Jensen, D. Lin, and B. C. Ooi. Query and update efficient B+-Tree based indexing of moving objects. In *Proc. VLDB*, 2004.
5. J. Kaufman, J. Myllymaki, and J. Jackson. *City Simulator spatial data generator*. http://alphaworks.ibm.com/tech/citysimulator, 2001.
6. D. Kwon, S. J. Lee, and S. H. Lee. Index the current positions of moving objects using the lazy update R-tree. In *MDM*, pages 113–120, 2002.
7. M. L. Lee, W. Hsu, C. S. Jensen, B. Cui, and K. L. Teo. Supporting frequent updates in R-Trees: A bottom-up approach. In *Proc. VLDB*, pages 608–619, 2003.
8. J. M. Patel, Y. Chen, and V. P. Chakka. Stripes: An efficient index for predicted trajectories. In *Proc. ACM SIGMOD*, pages 637–646, 2004.
9. G. M. Sacco. Index access with a finite buffer. In *Proc. VLDB*, pages 301–309, 1987.
10. S. Saltenis, C. S. Jensen, S. T. Leutenegger, and M. A. lopez. Indexing the positions of continuouslu moving objects. In *Proc. ACM SIGMOD*, pages 331–342, 2000.
11. Z. Song and N. Roussopoulos. Hashing moving objects. In *Proc. MDM*, pages 161–172, 2001.
12. Y. Tao, D. Papadias, and Jimeng Sun. The TPR*-Tree: An optimized spatio-temporal access method for predictive queries. In *Proc. VLDB*, pages 790–801, 2003.
13. Y. Xia and S. Prabhakar. Q+Rtree: Efficient indexing for moving object databases. In *Proc. DASFAA*, pages 175–182, 2003.

Aqua: An Adaptive QUery-Aware Location Updating Scheme for Mobile Objects

Jing Zhou[1], Hong Va Leong[1], Qin Lu[1], and Ken C.K. Lee[2]

[1] Department of Computing, Hong Kong Polytechnic University, Hong Kong
{csjgzhou, cshleong, csluqin}@comp.polyu.edu.hk
[2] Penn State University, Pennsylvania, USA

Abstract. Conventionally, the problem of location updates for moving objects has been addressed by adjusting the location reporting frequency or setting the uncertainty bound, according to object mobility patterns. This induces an obvious tradeoff between the communication cost and the uncertainty bound in querying moving object locations. Most existing works are focused on the object mobility pattern, without exploring the interdependency between queries and location updates. Furthermore, they take the precision of query results for granted as a result of a negotiated deviation threshold for reporting. The Aqua (**A**daptive **QU**ery-**A**ware) location updating scheme proposed in this paper exploits the interdependency between queries and updates. In particular, our scheme is adaptive to changes in both object mobility patterns and query characteristics, thereby resulting in significant performance improvement in terms of communication cost and query processing precision. We performed simulation studies and demonstrated that Aqua can produce desirable performance in most situations.

1 Introduction

To furnish a class of innovative context-aware services (e.g., location-aware advertising, proactive tourist services), there is a fundamental need to develop a comprehensive infrastructure, in which the locations of moving objects are to be managed effectively. For example, to process a typical spatial query on moving objects like *"Report all taxicabs which are within 500m of my current position"*, the positions of both the moving query issuer and all taxicabs should be made available to the service system.

In a mobile environment, moving object locations are maintained by a location server, which supports location-aware query processing and is assumed to be based on a moving-object database (i.e., MOD). Moving objects may be passively tracked by the communication infrastructure or actively reporting their locations to the server. To reduce extensive resource consumption, object movement modeling [8] and threshold techniques [13] have been proposed.

There is a tradeoff between location update frequency and uncertainty bound. Extensive research work in location management has been focused on addressing the tradeoff between the accuracy of the maintained location records in MOD and the update frequency from a large moving object population. Compared with traditional location updating approach such as distance-based update scheme in personal communication network [1], *deviation-based policy* [13] could attain dramatic resource saving while maintaining the same level of location uncertainty bound.

Despite recent research efforts, there are two issues remaining unaddressed. First, none of the existing methods address the combined effect of object movement patterns and query characteristics to the location updating schemes, though the two inter-related factors have been investigated separately. Second, the issue on improving the precision of the query results returned to the requesting user with respect to the tradeoff has largely been ignored. Existing updating schemes merely establish an agreement with the user for a service of reporting the object position within a certain deviation.

To address these limitations, we propose an efficient *adaptive* location updating scheme for moving object location updating and query processing. Our work is motivated by the observation that query processing on moving objects is the major subscriber to moving object location tracking. We are more interested in the positions of moving objects returned for these queries. Frequent location updates to objects which are seldomly included in a result set are unnecessary. Appropriately reducing the deviation threshold for objects which are frequently returned in a result set can yield better query precision with only slight increase in updating traffic. As a result, an integrative framework of location updating strategy and query processing could lead to reduced resource consumption and improved query precision.

In this paper, we realize our observation by specializing on the location updating scheme for moving objects, into the *Aqua* (**A**daptive **QU**ery-**A**ware) location updating scheme. The goal is to achieve improvement in not only reducing communication cost, but also enhancing query processing precision. We then study Aqua via simulated experiments and uncover its huge potential in performance improvement. The remainder of this paper is organized as follows. Section 2 gives a survey on related research in location management. Section 3 describes our research problem, with a formulation of our Aqua scheme. We propose the concept of **QU**ery-**A**djustable moving **SA**fe **R**egion (*quasar*) and define mathematically the size of the quasar. The system model on which Aqua is realized through the use of quasar is defined in Section 4. We then evaluate the performance of Aqua with extensive experiments in Section 5. Finally, we conclude this paper briefly with our future research directions.

2 Related Work

The research issue of how to accurately maintain the current location of a large number of moving objects while minimizing the number of updates is not trivial, given that the location of a moving object changes continuously but the database cannot be updated continuously. Different update strategies were proposed for MOD [12]. To reduce the update cost, a linear function $f(t)$ is used for expressing object movement and position estimation at different moment. The database is updated only when the function parameters change. This scheme avoids excessive location updates because no explicit update is required unless the parameters in $f(t)$ change [12]. In real applications, however, it is difficult to define a good function to describe the object movement. If the simple linear function cannot describe the complex movement, a lot of updates are generated with parameter changes. To better fit for practical systems, threshold techniques are adopted in the update scheme of moving objects. An alternative deviation-based policy for location updating in MOD was proposed [10], based on the MOST data model for moving objects [9]. As with [12], it represents and records the position of a moving object as a function of time and updates the location record in database whenever the distance between the current location and the stored location exceeds a given threshold. However, the stored location is no longer a static value, but a timely changing one computed by an appropriate location function.

With threshold techniques, the actual position of a moving object can deviate from its position computed by the server. There always exists a tradeoff between update communication cost and position error bound in the sense that the more update messages sent, the lower the position error bound is. Bearing this in mind, much research work has been conducted in determining the appropriate update frequency to balance the update communication cost and positioning error cost in query answering. An information cost model that captures uncertainty, deviation and communication is proposed in [11], based on which a set of dead-reckoning policies is designed. Performance of those dead-reckoning policies is studied [5]. The performance of deviation-based policy with a predefined threshold setting has also been studied, under the assumption that the threshold setting in most practical systems is up to the choice of users [13]. The work targets at reducing the communication cost as much as possible while living with the agreed level of location uncertainty. The deviation-based policy is shown via simulated experiments to be up to 43% more efficient than the commonly used distance-based policy in terms of messaging cost. However, query precision issues were not addressed.

There are a range of update techniques to process individual updates more efficiently [3]. Moving objects can also be clustered into groups so that the group leader will send location update on behalf of the whole group, thereby reducing the expensive uplink updates from the objects to the location server [4].

3 The Adaptive Location Management Problem

The adaptive location management problem that Aqua is designed to solve is related to two interdependent issues: location updating and query processing. It is focused on reducing the communication cost while maintaining a *similar* service level in terms of positioning error bound and query precision. Our motto is to invest the resource (update) wisely. Note that this differs from existing work that ensures the *same* error bound [11].

Consider an Intelligent Transportation Systems launched in a city for answering queries from drivers, passengers, police and other interested parties. Typical queries include *"What is the congestion level on I-10 near downtown Los Angeles?"* and *"What are the nearest taxicabs to me when I am at the junction of State Street and Second Street?"*. It can be expected that the querying pattern exhibits a strong temporal and spatial property, namely, more queries would be issued during the peak hours in early morning or late afternoon and against downtown area. In this example, the downtown area is a hot-spot for queries. One should distinguish moving objects that are seldomly queried (like those far away from downtown) from those frequently queried (residing in downtown area). Intuitively, in the former case, it is not necessary to update the object location since almost no one is interested. Very infrequent update or paging technique can be adopted to return the object location. In the latter case, a higher update frequency should be made, despite the relatively slower movement of the object due to traffic jam, thereby reducing the uncertainty or error bound and hence enhancing the precision of the query result. This is the central idea behind our novel Aqua scheme. Incidentally, this observation has not been exploited in existing location management schemes.

Aqua is built upon the concept of *quasar* (**QU**ery-**A**djustable moving **SA**fe **R**egion). A *safe region* is one in which a moving object can be found located. A safe region will expand in size in the absence of location update and it shrinks with an update from the moving object. An *adaptive safe region* expands with different speed according to the speed of the moving object [6]. We extend adaptive safe region further into *quasar* by allowing the center and hence the whole safe region to move. Conceptually, *quasar* is defined as a moving circular region out of which the object should send an update message to the location server. The area or covering scope of *quasar* is defined adaptively for different moving objects and at different moment for the same object.

Formally, a *quasar* is expressed as $\langle RC, RR \rangle$, where RC and RR are the region center and region radius respectively. RC is a moving point which indicates the predicted position of a moving object, while RR bounds the maximum allowable deviation from the predicted position. RC is modeled as a function of time $f(t)$ as with previous work. The actual region center RC should be computed on-the-fly according to a specific function whenever the *quasar* is used.

The adaptive nature of *quasar* comes from the adjustable setting of RR. Location-aware services built upon the location management system often define a minimal requirement on the uncertainty bound of moving object position. Given a user-defined uncertainty threshold τ, the object is requested to issue an update to the server when its actual movement deviates by more than the required uncertainty bound τ from the server record. Similar to previous work, Aqua accepts τ as an input parameter which captures the user's primary requirement to the system performance. For every object, τ is assumed to be the same. However, RR values for different objects are set adaptively according to the query pattern. Intuitively, the more frequently an object is involved in query results, the smaller its RR value should be.

We characterize the query pattern by the *query arrival rate*, qr. For a specific moving object, the larger qr is at a specific moment, the smaller RR should be defined for its *quasar*. Whether a query arrival rate qr is large depends on the overall query arrival rate over time, $\overline{qr}$. Thus, $RR = g(\tau, \overline{qr}, qr)$, where g is a generic function to be defined properly. We pictorialize the general idea in Figure 1, and examine the relationship among the three factors more clearly. The reason of defining *maxRR* is to set a bound on the size of *quasar* for the extreme cases. For example, when the current query arrival rate qr of an object is equal to or close to 0, RR will be unreasonably large, depriving of the need of updates from that object and leading to unacceptable location precision.

Among common functions, e.g., power function, exponential function, logarithmic function, a decreasing power function ($P(x) = x^{-\beta}$ with $\beta > 0$) appears to be a most appropriate one for g, since both P and g match the general relationship among the three factors for RR, with similar function properties. We thus define RR as:

$$RR = \min(\tau(\frac{qr}{\overline{qr}})^{-\beta}, maxRR) \qquad (1)$$

β is a system parameter for performance tuning. τ and $\overline{qr}$ are known to the system.

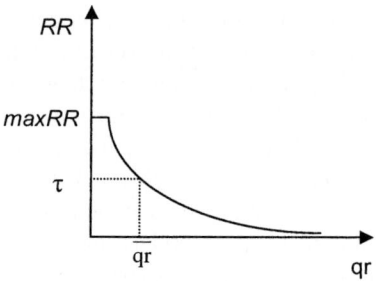

Fig. 1. General relationship among factors affecting *RR*

By setting *RR* adaptively, Aqua actually trades the communication cost of infrequently queried object for those frequently queried ones. The immediate benefit is reduction in communication cost when the query distribution is skewed with some hot objects (objects moving around hot areas). A large amount of location updating messages from less interested objects can be eliminated. Even no communication cost can be saved, reducing the *quasar* size can lead to better precision result. Despite the simple power function adopted, Aqua performs surprisingly well in delivering a satisfactory performance under the shadow of inevitable communication cost and precision tradeoff.

4 System Model

After defining the Aqua scheme with *quasar*, we now describe the system model that realizes Aqua. Figure 2 depicts a mobile computing system that supports location management of moving objects and corresponding querying processing. The location server communicates with the moving objects via a low bandwidth network and records their locations. Queries issued by users are sent to the location server which performs query processing and returns the query results to users. It is the responsibility of the moving objects to generate update reports on their locations to the server. Cooperation between the server and moving objects is needed to compute the size of the *quasar* for every update because the objects possess no up-to-date knowledge on the query pattern of the whole system. The models for moving object and server are described next.

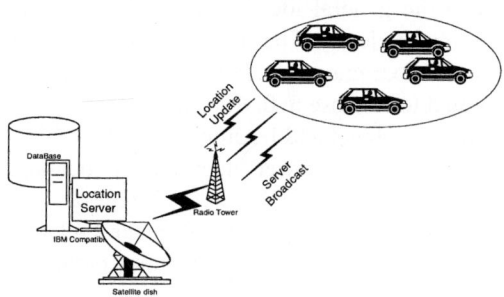

Fig. 2. System model for a mobile computing environment

4.1 Moving Object Model

In our conceptual system, we assume that moving objects make continuous movement within a two-dimensional space. They can also determine their location and velocity via devices such as GPS. Upon each update, moving object o sends a report with a quadruple: $\langle oid, p, v, RR \rangle$, where oid is the unique object identifier, p is the current position, v is the predicted velocity vector for determining RC, and RR is a value that o computes for defining its *quasar*. Besides sending the *quasar* to the server, o also stores the value of RC and RR and keeps monitoring its current position. Whenever o moves out of the boundary of its *quasar*, another update is issued.

According to Equation 1, to compute RR, o needs its qr, the overall $\overline{qr}$, and the system parameter τ. τ is defined based on user or application requirement and is known in advance. $\overline{qr}$ depends on the current system conditions and can be obtained periodically from server broadcast. qr depends on the current position of o and can be conveyed by the server via regional broadcast.

4.2 Server Model

The location server maintains a database to record the current positions of all moving objects. The database may adopt different location modeling for a moving object, e.g., an exact point-location, or an area in which the object is located. Aqua stores the *quasar* for each object which is known to lie within the *quasar*. With the *quasar* for the objects, the server can perform query processing and object filtering to answer queries.

To process a query, the server computes the current *quasar* for each moving object that overlaps with the range query and returns the result set based on this approximate position. Figure 3a illustrates an example of processing a range query. The *quasar* for o_1 does not overlap with q and can be filtered. o_2 is definitely included in the query range and is returned as a correct result. o_3 and o_4 overlap partially with the range query. The degree of overlapping reflects the probability that these objects reside in the query range and hence belong to the result set. An approximated result set is computed based on a heuristic threshold which filters the result set to achieve a higher query precision. If the threshold is small (unwilling to miss a potential object), both will be returned. If the threshold is large, both will not be returned. With a medium value, o_4 may be returned while o_3 may not be returned. In Figure 3b, both objects will be returned as correct result for a large query range but would not be returned for a small query range.

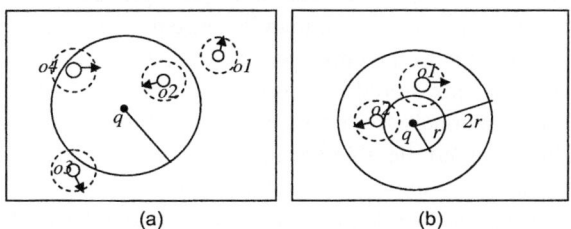

Fig. 3. Range query processing

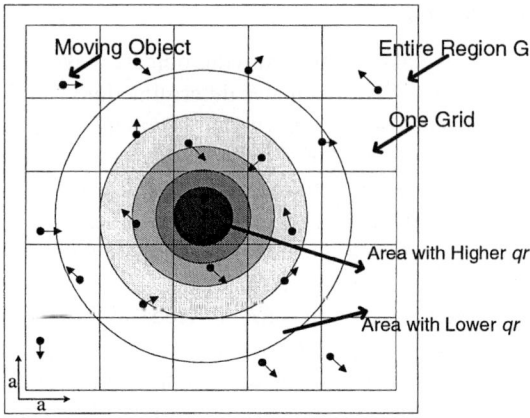

Fig. 4. Grid model of unevenly distributed queries in spatial domain G

In order to provide moving objects with proper query arrival rate information to compute their *RR*, the location server collects the query pattern information and delivers them to the moving objects accordingly. The server maintains the historical knowledge of queries and thus is able to compute the expected average query arrival rate $\overline{qr}$ based on the long-time historical data. This information should be propagated to moving objects, for example, via broadcasting.

It is more interesting for the server to propagate the query pattern to the moving objects. In fact, the definition of query pattern can vary with different query types. We consider here a most common query type, namely, range queries. Range queries are concerned with specific spatial regions and the query distribution is characterized by the spatial distribution of the query areas. Let G be the spatial domain, i.e., the entire region covered by the mobile computing environment, within which moving objects can freely move around. Certain sub-regions in G are of stronger interests (witnessing higher query arrival rates) than others, which we call "hot regions". The query rates in "hot regions" are higher and moving objects residing around these hot regions should be informed that a higher query arrival rate qr prevails.

To manage query arrival rates for different regions efficiently, the spatial domain G is conceptually fragmented into sub-regions, according to query distribution. For simplicity, we adopt a grid model to realize this space fragmentation. Figure 4 illustrates the grid model. The entire domain is divided into square grid cells of size a by a, where a is a system parameter. Each object can map its current position to the grid cell it just moves in and set its qr value to the corresponding value of the grid cell. The qr value for each grid cell is either pre-stored into moving object as default value, or obtained on-the-fly via wireless channels from the server. The former method consumes less downlink bandwidth but is not flexible because the hot and cold sub-regions are only relative and may change over time when query patterns change. The latter can adapt the "temperature" of sub-regions to changing query patterns and deliver the changes to the moving object appropriately, at the expense of higher communication cost.

5   Performance Studies

In this section, we compare Aqua with the deviation-based policy which is regarded as producing the best performance in location updating for moving objects [13]. In particular, we measure two standard metrics to demonstrate the performance improvements: the number of update messages (measuring the uplink bandwidth consumption) and the query precision rate (indicating the observed accuracy to a query). The query precision is defined as the ratio of the number of *correct objects* to the total number of objects returned in the result set, based on the corresponding *quasar* of the moving objects in the database. Here, a correct object is one which is actually residing within the scope of the query.

Table 1. Simulation parameters

Parameter	Value range	Default value
Number of moving objects	1000 to 10000	5000
Object velocity	0.2, 0.5, 1, 1.5, 2	1
Percentage of objects changing direction	75%	
Mean to query distribution, μ_q	50	
Standard derivation to query distribution, σ_q	5 to 100	10
Query range, r_q	0.5, 1, 1.5, 2	1
Deviation threshold, τ	0.1 to 1	0.5
Quasar parameter, β	0.1, 0.5, 1, 2	

The parameters adopted in our simulations are depicted in Table 1. Each experiment models the movement of the objects for 1000 time units. The spatial domain G of interest is a square-shaped region of size 100 by 100. The domain is fragmented into 5 by 5 grids. The number of moving objects ranges from 1000 to 10000. These objects are initially placed randomly in the entire domain G. The total number of queries is 50000. These parameters can basically be scaled up without much effect on our conclusions from our experiments, as long as the object density remains unchanged. We assume range queries, with circular-shaped querying region. The center of each range query is randomly distributed in G, following a 2-dimensional Gaussian distribution, with a mean $\mu_q = 50$ and standard deviation $\sigma_q \in [5, 100]$, modeling a range of highly skewed query sets to the almost uniformly distributed ones. The movement of objects is modeled similar to MobiEyes [2]. We assign randomly a velocity to each object uniformly from the list $\langle 0.2, 0.5, 1, 1.5, 2 \rangle$. The velocity of each object is constant throughout each simulation. Their initial moving directions are set randomly. In each time unit, we pick a number of objects at random and change their movement direction to a new random one. Other objects are assumed to continue with their existing motion.

We conducted four sets of experiments to evaluate the performance of our Aqua scheme (*Aqua*) with different β values against the best performing deviation-based policy (*Deviation*). The experimental parameter settings are listed in Table 2.

Table 2. Experimental parameter settings

Parameter	Number of objects	Threshold τ	Query range r_q	σ_q	β
Experiment #1	1000, 5000, 10000	0.05 to 1	1	10	0.1, 0.5, 1, 2
Experiment #2	1000 to 10000	0.1, 0.5, 1	1	10	0.1, 0.5, 1, 2
Experiment #3	5000	0.05 to 1	1	5 to 100	0.1, 0.5, 1, 2
Experiment #4	5000	0.05 to 1	0.5, 1, 1.5, 2	10	0.1, 0.5, 1, 2

5.1 Experiment #1: Effect of Threshold

We study in our first experiment the influence of different deviation thresholds. In general, it can be observed from Figure 5 that all schemes perform better in terms of number of updates but worse in terms of query precision with increasing τ. With smaller τ, update is more frequent, leading to a smaller deviation between the real location of a moving object and its predicted one in database. Query processing based on the more accurate location information leads to a better precision result. With respect to updates, *Aqua* performs much better than *Deviation* for small to medium τ. Even with very large τ, all except one *Aqua* schemes are superior. Interestingly, when query precision is concerned, all *Aqua* schemes outperform *Deviation* under all scenarios and the performance gap widens with larger τ. The key performance gain in *Aqua* lies in the adaptivity of the *quasar* size with respect to an accurate query arrival rate, so as to gain more in one metrics, while losing less in the other for each query set. In summary, *Aqua* is effective in reducing message cost without sacrificing precision with small τ and improving query precision without sacrificing message cost with large τ.

We now investigate the impact of β. It is obvious from Figure 5 that its value does not lead to much difference in the number of updates, but is much more significant with respect to query precision. Furthermore, its impact is amplified with larger value of τ, which is not surprising, since at a larger τ, the *quasar* size increases, producing a bigger impact on the observed performance. Smaller value of β leads to fewer updates but yields lower query precision and vice versa. It is apparent that a medium to large

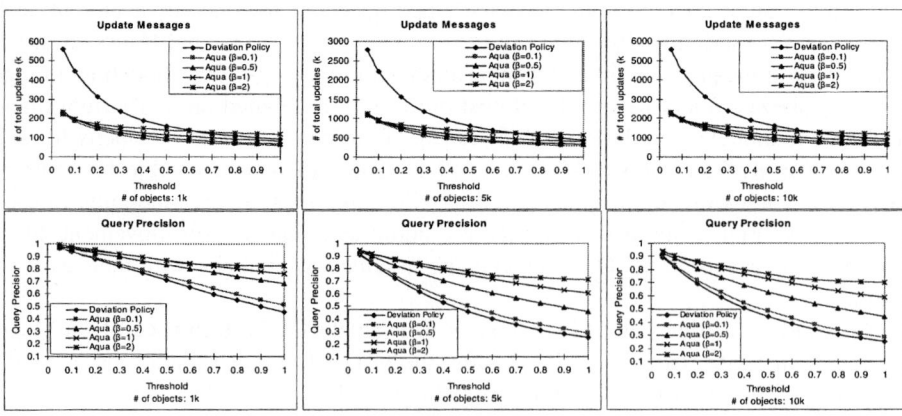

Fig. 5. Effect of threshold

value of β seems to yield a better aggregated performance. Our final observation is that the relative shapes of performance curves of *Deviation* and *Aqua* remain similar with different number of moving objects, especially from medium to large number.

5.2 Experiment #2: Effect of Number of Objects

We examine the effect of the number of objects in the second set of experiments, as depicted in Figure 6. It is understandable that the number of update messages increases linearly with the number of objects. However, there is a corresponding non-linear drop in query precision, though one would expect a relatively flat curve. The main reason behind this phenomenon on higher precision with fewer objects is due to the variation in query selectivity. With fewer objects, the chance for a range query to select zero object is higher; returning no object will lead to a 100% precision, thus boosting the overall precision metrics. The performance gap between *Deviation* and the *Aqua* schemes widens with higher threshold τ. The variation in performance with respect to β is similar to that in Experiment #1, namely, lower β leads to fewer updates but lower precision, and vice versa. Nevertheless, *Aqua* is more effective in both performance metrics than *Deviation*.

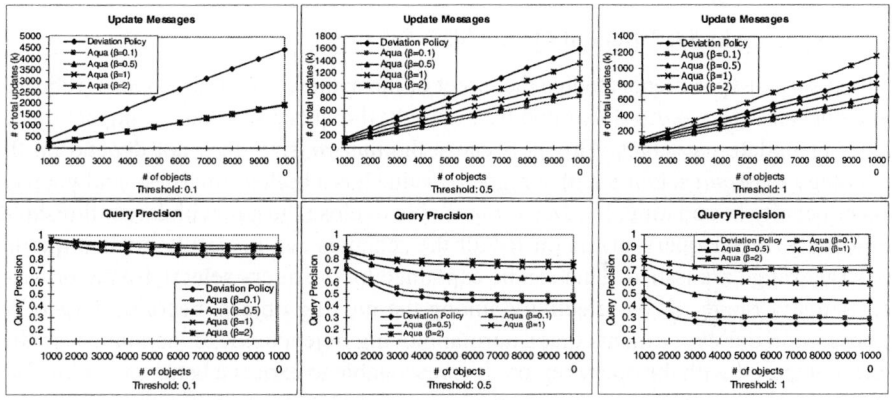

Fig. 6. Effect of number of objects

5.3 Experiment #3: Effect of Query Distribution Skewness

Aqua is designed to take advantage of query distribution. The skewness of query (affected by the standard deviation σ_q on the distribution), thus, plays an important role to its effectiveness. When σ_q is large, the behavior becomes similar to queries issued randomly and almost uniformly throughout the domain. Our third set of experiments is conducted to examine the influence of the query distribution skewness to the improvement achieved by Aqua. The results are shown in Figure 7. With larger σ_q, the improvement brought about by *Aqua* is curtailed. Under those scenarios, *Aqua* starts to exhibit the familiar behavior of tradeoff between update cost and precision at a scale close to *Deviation*. There exist different breakeven points for the performance between *Aqua* with different

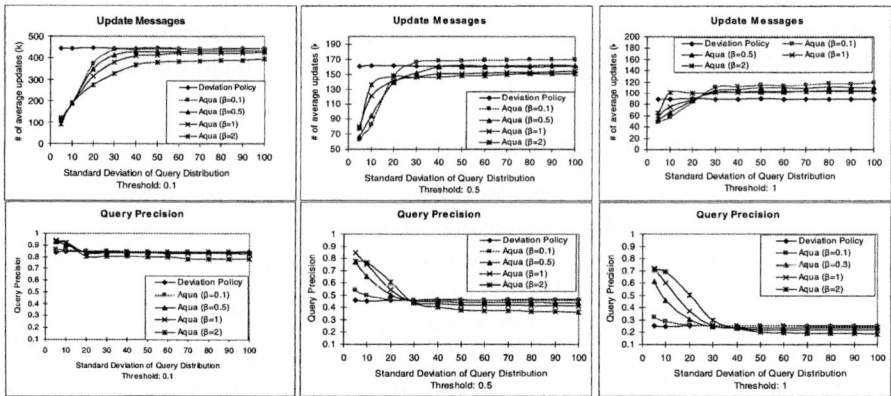

Fig. 7. Effect of skewness in query distribution

β values against *Deviation*. Among all *Aqua* schemes, those with smaller β seem to yield a closer behavior to *Deviation*. The situation for *Aqua* is worsen with higher threshold τ.

5.4 Experiment #4: Effect of Query Size

Our final set of experiments studies the effect of the scope of the range query (reflected by the query range r_q). As illustrated by Figure 8, the query size has no impact on the number of update messages. This is because the *quasar* size does not depend on the query range r_q. *Aqua* scheme with a higher β value has a higher precision, and yet pays a higher penalty in updating, but *Deviation* is able to close the gap with larger threshold. Interestingly, better query precision for all the schemes can be resulted when queries with larger range are issued. This can be explained by the query selectivity factor. With a larger query range r_q, its selectivity among the moving objects becomes larger. We can observe in our experiments that a normal moving object tends to maintain a smaller *quasar* compared with the query region. It is reasonable to expect a better precision for a query with a larger selectivity because the number of objects actually returned is larger. Taking the example in Figure 3b, an object that is deemed incorrectly returned for a small query with $r_q = r$ will be considered correctly returned for a larger query with $r_q = 2r$. Therefore, the query precision can be improved in general.

6 Conclusion and Future Work

Upon considering existing location update reporting strategies for moving objects, two unaddressed issues have been identified: 1) no existing method considers the possible interaction of query patterns to the location update schemes; 2) the issue on improving the precision of the query results returned has been ignored. To address these limitations, we propose in this paper the novel Aqua location updating scheme, which is adaptive to query distribution in the sense that it differentiates the location updating frequency for different moving objects according to their own querying characteristics. Aqua is able to

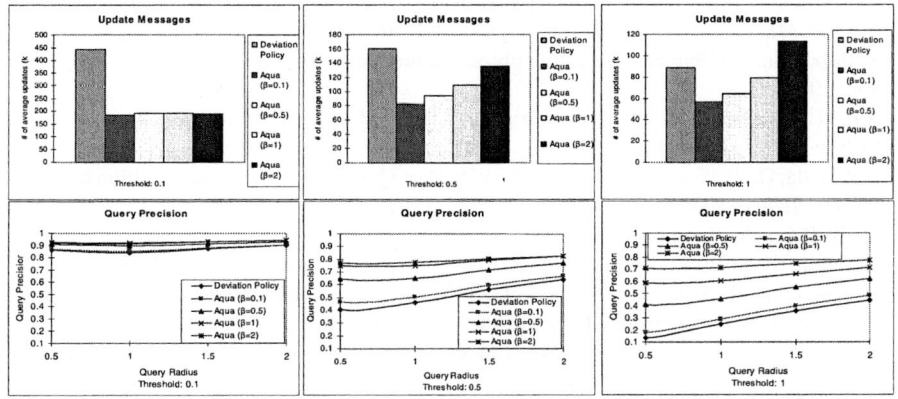

Fig. 8. Effect of query size

improve existing methods by investing on preferred objects so that the communication cost is paid for updating those who can get more precision gain. A higher precision level is maintained for location of objects interested by more queries. In other words, we follow the motto to invest our "money" wisely for maximal return.

The improvement brought about by Aqua are two-folded. First, much fewer location update messages from moving objects to the server are generated. This is particularly important in a mobile environment, where communication is expensive. Less frequent location updating also reduces the consumption of precious energy for moving objects. Second, the precision of query processing can be improved without much tradeoff. The significant improvement in this aspect can be attained when the queries display some form of skewness, as exhibited in most real practical environments.

We plan to build up a comprehensive location management model based on our adaptive location update models, including Aqua and GBL [4]. Another issue is about the extension of the Aqua framework to cater for more practical situations such as road networks in a city rather than based on the free movement assumption for objects.

References

1. A. Bar-Noy, I. Kessler and M. Sidi. Mobile users: To update or not to update? *ACM-Baltzer Journal on Wireless Networks*, 1(2):175–186, 1994.
2. B. Gedik and L. Liu. MobiEyes: Distributed processing of continuously moving queries on moving objects in a mobile system. In *Proc. EDBT*, pages 67–87, 2004.
3. C.S. Jensen and S. Saltenis. Towards increasingly update efficient moving-object indexing. *Special Issue on Indexing of Moving Objects, IEEE Data Engineering Bulletin*, 25(2):35–40, 2002.
4. G.H.K. Lam, H.V. Leong and S.C.F. Chan. GBL: Group-based location updating in mobile environment. In *Proc. DASFAA*, pages 762–774, 2004.
5. K. Lam, O. Ulusoy, T.S.H. Lee, E. Chan and G. Li. An efficient method for generating location updates for processing of location-dependent continuous queries. In *Proc. DASFAA*, pages 218–225, 2001.

6. K.C.K. Lee, H.V. Leong and A. Si. Approximating object location for moving object database. In *Proc. MDC'03 (ICDCS Workshop)*, pages 402–407, 2003.
7. E. Pitoura and G. Samaras. Locating objects in mobile computing. *IEEE TKDE*, 13(4):571–592, 2001.
8. A.P. Sistla, O. Wolfson, S. Chamberlain and S. Dao. Modeling and querying moving objects. In *Proc. ICDE*, pages 422–432, 1997.
9. A.P. Sistla, O. Wolfson, S. Chamberlain and S. Dao. Querying the uncertain position of moving objects. *Temporal Databases*, pages 310–337, 1997.
10. O. Wolfson, S. Chamberlain, S. Dao, L. Jiang and G. Mendez. Cost and imprecision in modeling the position of moving objects. In *Proc. ICDE*, pages 588–596, 1998.
11. O. Wolfson, A.P. Sistla, S. Chamberlain and Y. Yesha. Updating and querying databases that track mobile units. *Distributed and Parallel Databases*, 7(3):257–287, 1999.
12. O. Wolfson, B. Xu, S. Chamberlain and L. Jiang. Moving objects databases: Issues and solutions. In *Proc. SSDBM*, pages 111–122, 1998.
13. O. Wolfson and H. Yin. Accuracy and resource consumption in tracking moving object. In *Proc. SSTD*, pages 325–343, 2003.

A Spatial Index Using MBR Compression and Hashing Technique for Mobile Map Service

Jin-Deog Kim[1], Sang-Ho Moon[2], and Jin-Oh Choi[2]

[1] Dept. of Computer Eng., Dongeui Univ., Busanjin-gu, Busan, 614-714, Korea
jdk@deu.ac.kr
[2] Dept. of Computer Eng., Pusan University of Foreign Studies, Wooam-dong Nam-gu, Busan, 608-738, Korea
{shmoon87, jochoi}@pufs.ac.kr

Abstract. While the volumes of spatial data are tremendous and spatial operations are time-intensive, mobile devices own limited storages and low computational resources. Therefore, a spatial index for mobile map services should be small and efficiently filter out the candidate objects of a spatial operation as well. This paper proposes a spatial index called MHF(Multilevel Hashing File) for the mobile map service. The MHF has a simple structure for storage utilization and uses a hashing technique for search efficiency. This paper also designs a compression scheme of MBR(Minimum Bounding Rectangle) called HMBR. Although the HMBR scheme reduces the volume of MBR to almost a third, it still achieves a good filtering efficiency because of no information loss by quantization in case of small objects that occupy a major portion. Our experimental tests show that the proposed MHF with HMBR is appropriate for mobile devices in terms of the volume of index, the number of the MBR comparisons, the filtering efficiency and the execution time of spatial operations.

1 Introduction

The volume of spatial data and the computational cost of spatial operations are very tremendous, but on the other hand the mobile devices own a limited memory and a low computational capacity than the PC. Therefore, a spatial index for the mobile devices should be small and achieve good filtering efficiency as well. The existing spatial indices based on the PC, such as R-tree, are not applicable to the mobile devices based on memories. In the mobile device's applications, since the data transmitted from servers always reside in the memory of the mobile devices and disk accesses are not required for data retrievals, the working mechanism of an index for the mobile devices is quite different from that of the existing indices. The indices based on disks hold a node structure for paged I/O and use clustering techniques in order to reduce the number of disk seeks. On the other hand, because search operations in the indices based on the memory are irrelevant to disks accesses, the node structure and the clustering which are important factors of performance improvements of the existing indices maybe yields contrary results in the mobile devices. Also, the great volume of the existing spatial indices is not appropriate for the mobile devices.

In addition to that, the low utilization of each node of the existing indices is due to the property of dynamic update. Because the applications of the mobile devices are mostly bounded to retrieval, not update, the property of dynamic update is an obstacle of performance improvements in the mobile devices. The update is generally processed by servers in the mobile map service.

In this paper, we propose a spatial index structure for the mobile devices, which is so simple and small that shows good storage utilization and filtering efficiency as well. We take the small memory and low computing capacity of the mobile devices into consideration. We also propose a new compression scheme of MBR, which occupies about 80% of the spatial index volume in the two dimensional case, in order to maximize storage utilization. We would like to prove that the deterioration of performances has not occurred regardless of the MBR compression.

In order to evaluate the performances of the proposed spatial indexing method and the MBR compression schemes in comparison with R*-tree, several experiments are conducted on the Sequoia 2000 benchmark data [9]. The items of the performance evaluations are the volume of each spatial index, the number of MBR comparison in the filter step, filtering efficiency and the total operation time. The results of the experiments clearly show that we can decide a suitable spatial index for the mobile devices and the proposed methods are also expected to be important technology for the mobile map services to be wide used recently.

The rest of this paper is organized as follows. In section 2, we investigate the related works on spatial index based on disks and memories respectively. In section 3, we propose a spatial index structure based on memory for the sake of the mobile map services. In section 4, we also introduce MBR compression schemes to cut down the volume of a spatial index. In section 5, the results of experiments are presented and analyzed. Finally, we give conclusions in section 6.

2 Related Works

The size of spatial objects in a relation varies extremely. In order to deal with such large objects and at the same time to preserve spatial locality in pages, spatial access methods organize only approximations of objects as an index instead of the exact representation. The minimum bounding rectangle(MBR) of an object is a very common approach for an approximation. A spatial query is processed in two steps, called filter and refinement step [5]. Because the refinement step applies the exact representation to check procedures, it is very time-consuming. Therefore, it is had better cut down the number of candidate objects in the filter step if possible.

Spatial indices are used for the efficient processing of the filter step. Many researches on spatial indices have been studied so far. The index in these literatures, however, is almost based on the disks [1,2,5,8,10,15]. The R*-tree called a representative spatial index based on disks is studied in [1]. The low utilization of each node may be a fatal defect in the mobile devices with limited storages. Besides, the overlap of each node in R*-tree brings about inefficiency for the display of a given rectangle area required frequently in the applications of the mobile devices. In spite of these drawbacks, the performance of the R*-tree is derived from a paged I/O and natural clustering which reduce the number of seek operations. The A-tree [15] index structure which uses a relative approximation scheme is proposed for similarity searches in high-dimensional data. Its VBR can be quite compactly and thus affect the reduction of the number of node accesses. In spatial indices based on memory, however, there is no longer any reason for such paged I/O mechanism to exist.

There have been many works on indices of main memory database systems recently global [3,4,6,7,8]. The T-tree global [4] is the binary tree of which each node maintains several number of data and just two number of link fields in order to maximize storage utilization. It can accommodate text data, but it is impossible for T-tree as an index to hold multidimensional spatial data.

The CR-tree [3] based on main memory is the cache-conscious version of the R-tree. To pack more entries in a node, the CR-tree compresses MBRs. While the QRMBR proposed in CR-tree saves memory, it yields low filtering efficiency which is a fatal drawback in the mobile devices.

The literature [11,12] proposed a clustering-based map compression method which adapts a dictionary to a given dataset. The proposed method achieves lower error than a static dictionary compression such as the one used by the FHM algorithm[13]. This research is different from our study in that it does not treat index structures.

3 Spatial Index Based on Memory for Mobile Devices

The requirements of the spatial index for the mobile devices are as follows. : First, small volume and simple structure. Second, quick response for spatial queries. Third, easy to load all the objects of a rectangle region in order to display the map of the screen size of the mobile devices. Fourth, easy to manage non-uniformly distributed data.

We propose a new spatial index, MHF(multi-level hashing file) to obey above four requirements. This index delivers high storage utilization due to its simple structure, and it also has small number of the MBR comparison due to the hash-based indexing technique. Although it takes regular decomposition, it manages non-uniformly distributed data very well.

The MHF hashes the overall space on the basis of X and Y coordinates of each object. The hash functions are as follows. The Xmin, Ymin, Xmax and Ymax mean the extents of the overall space. The Nx and Ny are the numbers of buckets of X and Y axes respectively.

- $H_x(x) = int[(x - X_{min})/(X_{max}-X_{min})*N_x]$
- $H_y(y) = int[(y - Y_{min})/(Y_{max}-Y_{min})*N_y]$

The hash table is two dimensional structure and the second(or subsequent) hashing is executed to prevent a bucket overflows as shown in figure 1. To load all the objects located in a rectangle area for simple display is straightforward because the MHF decomposes data space regularly. Even though the data distribution is non-uniformed and skewed, therefore the reasonable response time is guaranteed without severe delay for spatial queries.

The second hash function is similar to the first hash function except for the min and max values of the extents. The min and max values in the second function are changed the extent of entire data space into the extent of the overflowed bucket. The third or more hashing is executed successively until no longer overflows. We assume that the Nx and Ny of second or more hashing are a half of those of first hashing respectively. The capacity(M) of a bucket is determined by the combinations of the whole number of the objects, the desired volume of the index and the desired search time.

The header of the MHF consists of an extent of entire map and the number of buckets of both X and Y axes as shown in figure 2. A bucket entry holds the number of objects and the pointers to indicate each object in data file. The pointer is classified by the number of objects as follows.

- [# of Obj. = 0]   Empty Bucket Condition : Pointer is NULL
- [# of Obj. 1~ M]   Normal Condition : Pointer to indicate each bucket
    Each bucket holds following information
    <MBR of Object, Pointer to Object> * # of Obj.
- [# of Obj. > M]   Overflow Condition : Pointer to sub hash table

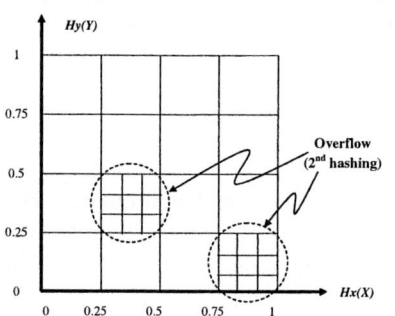

Fig. 1. Hash Table

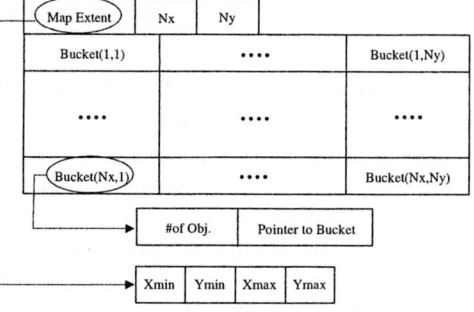

Fig. 2. Header Format

In the following, we introduce the procedures of a point query and a region query used frequently in the map service applications.

```
Procedure Point_Query( )
Input : Header, Point(query point)
Output : selected objects
Read Extent from Header
X = Hx(Point.x); Y = Hy(Point.y);    // Hash X,Y
Read Information of Bucket(X,Y)
CASE( # of Obj. )
   [0] :     "Not Found"
   [>M] :    Bucket_Header = Pointer_to_Bucket;
             Point_Query(Bucket_Header, Point)
                                        // Recursive Call
   [1~M] :  S = Pointer_to_Bucket;
            FOR( all Obj. ∈ S )    // from 1 to # of Obj.
                IF( Obj.MBR ∩ Point ≠ ∅)
                    Result += Obj.
end of Procedure
```

```
Procedure Region_Query( )
Input : Header, Region(query region)
Output : selected objects
Read Extent from Header
X_low = Hx(Region.X_min);  X_max = Hx(Region.X_max);
Y_low = Hy(Region.Y_min);  Y_max = Hy(Region.Y_max);
FOR( X = X_low ~ X_max )
    FOR( Y = Y_low ~ Y_max )
        Read Information of Bucket(X,Y)
        CASE( # of Obj. )
            [0]  : Continue
            [>M] : Bucket_Header = Pointer_to_Bucket;
                   Region_Query(Bucket_Header, Region)
                                    // Recursive Call
            [1~M] :S = Pointer_to_Bucket;
                   FOR( all Obj ∈ S )// from 1 to # of Obj.
                       IF( Obj.MBR ∩ Region ≠ ∅)
                           Result += Obj.
end of Procedure
```

4 Compression Schemes of MBR

One of the most important characteristics of GIS data in view of the mobile device is that the volume of spatial data is tremendous. To filter efficiently candidate objects, spatial indices usually use MBRs organized by the coordinates of low left corner and upper right corner as the approximation of each spatial object. The 16 byte MBR is generally used for two-dimensional key because a coordinate of each axis takes a 4 byte number. The existing spatial indices are usually too big to use in the mobile devices. The MBR keys also occupy almost 80% of their indices. Therefore, we focus on the MBR compression scheme for the sake of a small index.

We now introduce some kinds of the MBR compression schemes : The relative representation of MBR(RMBR), the quantized representation of MBR(QMBR) [3], the hybrid representation of MBR(HMBR) proposed newly in this paper.

The proposed schemes are also useful for compressing the exact geometry of spatial objects with a little modification. However, as the purpose of this paper is concerned, it is not necessary to discuss the compression of exact geometry.

4.1 Relative Representation of MBR : RMBR

A normal MBR represented by absolute coordinate system occupies 16 bytes in figure 3. On the contrary, we can save 8 bytes per MBR with relative representation because each coordinate can be represented by 2 bytes instead of 4 bytes in figure 4.

4.2 Quantized Representation of MBR : QMBR

The QMBR achieves better storage utilization than RMBR. Figure 5 shows the QMBR with quantization level 13(x axis) and 9(y axis) respectively. The quantization level means each axis is divided by a given number. If the quantization level is less than 256, each coordinate can be represented by quantized value of 1byte. It means the QMBR achieves compression effects four times in comparison to normal MBR

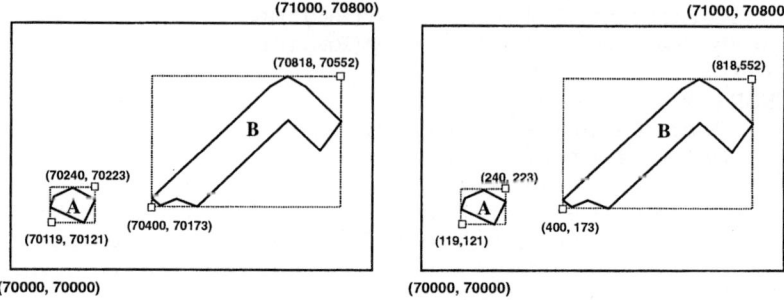

Fig. 3. Normal MBR **Fig. 4.** RMBR

On the contrary, the QMBR brings about the enlargement of MBR of each object. This enlargement causes the increase of the number of candidate objects in refinement step after filter step. Eventually, the QMBR results in the increase of the query time, particularly in the mobile devices with low computational resources. As the size of a spatial object is small, the percentage of the enlargement becomes large.

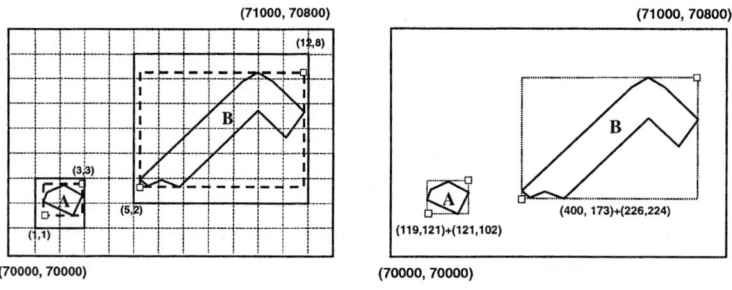

Fig. 5. QMBR **Fig. 6.** HMBR

4.3 Hybrid Representation of MBR : HMBR

The HMBR newly proposed in this paper takes the hybrid representation scheme that makes use of the merit of not only reasonable storage utilization but also good filtering efficiency. The low left corner of HMBR is identical with that of RMBR, but the upper right corner of HMBR is represented by the lengths(width, height) of MBR.

· HMBR = Xmin(2byte) + Ymin(2byte) + Width(1byte) + Height(1byte)

In order to represent the width and height of MBR by means of 1 byte respectively, a following method is introduced. If the length of MBR is smaller than threshold value(β), the length is represented by actual value just as it is. If not, the length is represented by a quantized value. The β is determined by quantization level. The β is 255-n, where n is quantization level. The procedure to generate HMBR is as follows.

```
Procedure Generate_HMBR( )
Input : normal_MBR, Ext_of_Bucket, Quant_level
Output : HMBR
   HMBR.Xmin = MBR.Xmin - Ext_Bucket.Xmin
   HMBR.Ymin = MBR.Ymin - Ext_Bucket.Ymin
   β = 255 - Quant_level
   X_Length_Obj = MBR.Xmax - MBR.Xmin
   X_quant_length = Ext_Bucket.Xmax - Ext_Bucket.Xmin
   IF ( X_Length_Obj <= β )
            HMBR.Width = X_Length_Obj
   ELSE HMBR.Width = β + X_Length_Obj / X_quant_length
   Y_Length_Obj = MBR.Ymax - MBR.Ymin
   Y_quant_length = Ext_Bucket.Ymax - Ext_Bucket.Ymin
   IF ( Y_Length_Obj <= β )
            HMBR.Height = Y_Length_Obj
   ELSE HMBR.Height = β + Y_Length_Obj / Y_quant_length
end of Procedure
```

For example, figure 6 depicts HMBR derived from normal MBR of figure 3. While the lengths of MBR of object A are represented by actual values, the lengths of MBR of object B are represented by quantized values when n is 50 in figure 6.

A HMBR can be represented by means of 6 bytes. Although the storage utilization of HMBR is slightly lower than that of QMBR, the filtering efficiency of HMBR is superior to that of QMBR. If the lengths of most spatial objects are smaller than β value, the HMBR of these objects doesn't bring about the enlargement of MBR of objects. The big objects with quantized lengths are generally infrequent. The quantized length yields the enlargement of MBR, and then deteriorates filtering efficiency. The impacts of this enlargement will be examined in chapter 5.

5 Performance Evaluation

The test data for performance evaluation are Sequoia 2000[9] which is widely used as benchmark data. The H/W platform is Compaq iPAQ with 32 Mbyte memories for data area. The point and region query are carried out 1000 times respectively.

5.1 Volume of Index

Figure 7 graphs the volumes of the two indices, R*-tree and MHF, with the proposed compression schemes. The node size of R*-tree is 512 bytes and the M of top level of MHF is 50, the capacities of second and more levels are assigned a value decreased by 5 compared with that of previous level. The quantization levels of QMBR and HMBR are 256 and 50 respectively. The Nx and Ny of MHF are both 50.

The following results are obtained from figure 7. First, the MHF outperforms the R*-tree in the storage utilization aspect when an identical MBR representation scheme is used by each index. For example, the volume of MHF with QMBR is almost 50 % of that of R^*-tree with the same MBR scheme.

Second, compared with the volume of spatial index according to the MBR compression schemes, the QMBR outperforms the others as might have been expected. However, the filtering efficiency of spatial index with QMBR is not good at all. You will see this problem in section 5.3. Additionally, figure 7 tells us that HMBR also achieves a good compression effect which is placed after QMBR.

5.2 Number of MBR Comparison in Filter Step

Figure 8 depicts the number of the MBR comparison operations which means search performance in the filter step of point query. First, the MHF generally outperforms the R^*-tree. More precisely, the MHF with either HMBR or QMBR requires almost 50% of MBR comparison of R^*-tree.

Second, the QMBR requires more MBR comparison than the others. It was found from the experimental results that the enlargement of MBR is strongly related to deterioration of the performance of filter step. Particularly, the R^*-tree with QMBR may be worst case because the enlargement of MBR of R^*-tree occurred from high level to leaf node brings about excessive overlapped regions.

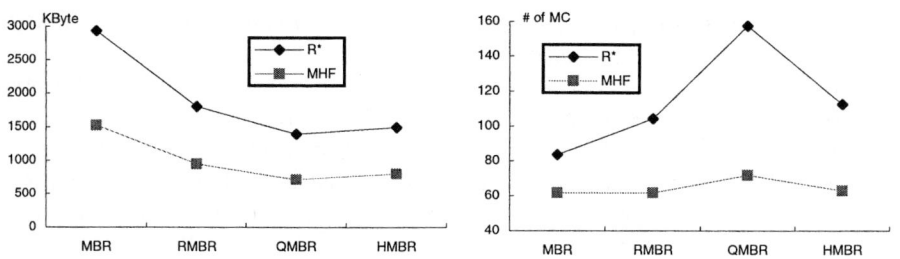

Fig. 7. Size of Spatial Indices　　**Fig. 8.** Number of MBR Comparison Operations

Consequently, the MHF usually outperforms the R^*-tree in the aspect of MBR comparison of filter step. HMBR also achieves an overwhelming performance in comparison with the others. The performance of region query is also quite similar to that of point query, so we will leave that results out of consideration.

5.3 Filtering Efficiency of MBR Compression Schemes

The aim to use spatial indices is to execute efficiently filter step as well as to minimize the candidate objects participated in the refinement step. If the low computational resource of the mobile devices is taken into consideration, the number of the candidate objects is strongly related to overall execution time of spatial operations. Table 1 summarizes the average number of candidate objects after filter step of point and region query. The areas of the query region are 0.1%, 0.4 and 1% of the whole data space respectively. The experimental results indicate that the number of candidate objects is almost irrelevant to the kind of spatial indices, but it depends on the compression schemes. The QMBR with the enlargement increases the number of candidate objects compared with the others. Particularly, in case of the point query and the region query with very small region, the performance of QMBR is more inferior to the others. On the contrary, even if HMBR uses the quantization technique like QMBR, the number of the candidate objects in HMBR is almost identical with that of normal MBR because this quantization is only used for big objects.

Table 1. Number of Candidate Objects

Query Region / MBR Rep.	PointQuery	0.1%	0.4%	1%
MBR/RMBR	3.2	187.4	521.3	1038.9
QMBR	7.3	318.5	672.5	1266.7
HMBR	3.5	201.3	553.8	1052.0

5.4 Query Execution Time

Table 2 describes the average execution time of QMBR and HMBR. Generally, HMBR improves the performance of about 40% percents in comparison with QMBR. It is for this reason that the candidate objects increased by QMBR causes long execution time in the refinement step as shown in table 1. The results obtained from experiments coincide with what was expected. Table 2 also shows that the query execution time have nothing to do with the area of query region mostly.

Table 2. Query Execution Time(unit : ms)

Query / MBR Rep.	Point Query	0.1%	0.4%	1%
R^*-tree(QMBR)	106.2	901.7	1278.3	1934.9
R^*-tree(HMBR)	69.1	543.8	881.2	1215.2
MHF(QMBR)	78.8	792.3	1159.1	1773.2
MHF(HMBR)	46.8	451.8	782.9	1103.0

5.5 Data Loading Time with Various Data Distribution

Table 3 summarizes the time to load the results of point and region queries of MHF and R^*-tree without refinement step. The region for data loading is occupied with 1% of entire data space. Each query is performed in random area and skewed area respectively. We define the skewed area as where to hash 3 or more times subsequently. The results clearly show that the MHF generally outperforms the R^*-tree for the simple display to load all the objects in a rectangle region. Far from our anticipation, the MHF carries out region queries for data loading well in case of skewed area. Moreover, the performance of point query of MHF is also superior to that of R^*-tree regardless of data distribution.

Table 3. Data Loading Time(unit : ms)

	MHF with HMBR	R*-tree with HMBR
Random Area(1%)	313.5	427.9
Skewed Area(1%)	1805.2	1814.8
Point(Random)	32.0	53.7
Point(Skewed)	44.3	56.2

5.6 HMBR : Impacts of Bucket Capacity

The Nx, Ny and M are the consideration points in MHF design. Large Nx, Ny and small M bring about low performance due to excessive subsequent hashing and the redundancy of objects caused by multiple assignment[14]. Also, small Nx, Ny and large M bring about low performance due to extended search space. That is, when the values of Nx, Ny and M are almost equal, the performance of MHF is enhanced.

The 100 percent cell utilization can be possible in the text data and uniform distributed spatial data, but it is not probable in the non-uniformly distributed spatial data due to frequent overflow and sub hashing. Therefore, we assume the cell utilization to be about 65 ~75%. The cell utilization is defined as follows. For example, in case of sequoia 2000 benchmark data and above condition, the proper numbers of Nx, Ny and M are about 50.

· Cell_Utilization ≈ #_of_Objects / [(Nx*Ny)*M] where Nx, Ny and M are equal

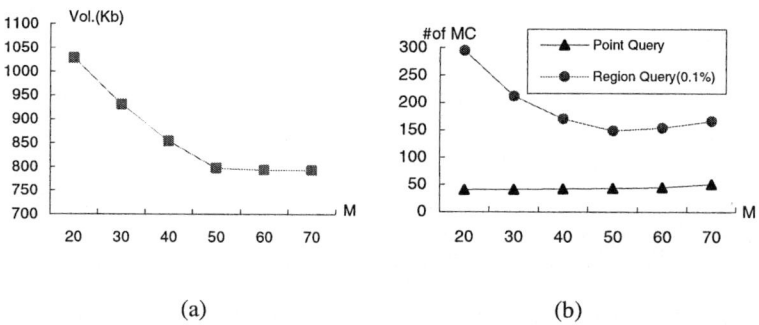

Fig. 9. Impacts of Bucket Capacity. (a) Volume of MHF, (b) Number of MBR Comparison

Figure 9 shows that this seems to be a realistic assumption. Figure 9(a) depicts the volume of MHF with various bucket capacities(M). The Nx and Ny are assumed to be 50. As M increases, the volume of MHF with HMBR decreases. Figure 9(b) depicts the number of MBR comparison in filter step with various M. When M is 50, the number of MBR comparison is minimized. Therefore, when the Nx, Ny and M are 50, the volume of index and the number of MBR comparison are improved as expected.

5.7 HMBR : Effects of Enlargement of MBR

Table 4 shows the effects of enlargements of HMBR with various quantization levels. When the quantization level is so small, the number of candidate objects increases due to large quantum. When the level is so large, the number of candidate objects also increases due to the increase of the objects with the enlarged MBR. Consequently, if the quantization level is neither too small nor large, the performance is enhanced.

Table 4. Effect of Enlargement of MBR in HMBR

n	# of enlarged Object(%)	Increment of Candidates(%) : region query(0.1%)
10	0.8	14.3
30	0.9	7.3
50	1.1	7.1
100	3.6	13.8
256	100	68

From what has been discussed above, following conclusions were obtained : 1) The MHF achieves better storage utilization than R^*-tree. The storage required by MHF is less than half of R^*-tree. 2) The HMBR outperforms the others in terms of filtering efficiency and overall execution time. Even though the storage efficiency of QMBR is slightly better than that of HMBR, the low filtering efficiency of QMBR deteriorates whole performance. To sum up the results so far achieved, the MHF with HMBR may be a reliable spatial index for the mobile devices.

Undoubtedly, the R^*-tree outperforms MHF in dynamic update operations. In the mobile applications, however, the spatial data is updated by servers, not the mobile devices. The dynamic update problems are not addressed here.

6 Conclusions

We would like to propose a reliable spatial index for the mobile map service. The requirements of this are high storage utilization, quick response time and easy simple display.

In this paper, a new spatial index called MHF is proposed. The MHF has simple structure for storage efficiency and uses a hashing technique, which is direct search method, for search efficiency. Furthermore, the newly proposed HMBR compression scheme not only saves storages but also doesn't bring out the lowing of performance caused by the enlargements of MBR at all in case of small objects.

The experimental results indicate that the R^*-tree, one of the most efficient spatial index based on disk, is possible to be inefficient in memory based mobile device system. On the contrary, the proposed MHF outperforms R^*-tree due to the MHF's high storage utilization and retrieval efficiency. The proposed HMBR compression scheme requires small storages and achieves high filtering efficiency. The MHF consumes about 50% less memory space in comparison with R^*-tree, and the number of MBR comparison in filtering step of HMBR is about 50% less than that of R^*-tree. In the

MBR compression aspects, the spatial index with HMBR requires about 50% smaller than the spatial index with normal MBR. The performance of HMBR is enhanced by as much as about 2 times over that of QMBR.

In summary, it seems reasonable to conclude that the proposed spatial index structure is appropriate for the spatial index in the mobile devices with small memory space and low processing capacity. Furthermore, the index is expected to be useful for mobile map service, ITS(Intelligent Transportation System), LBS(Location Based Service) to have been increasingly studied recently.

References

1. N. Beckmann, H.P. Kriegel, R. Schneider, B. Seeger : R^*-tree : An Efficient and Robust Access Method for Points and Rectangles : Int. Conf. on ACM SIGMOD(1990) 322-331
2. E.G. Hoel, H. Samet : A Qualitative Study of Data Structures for Large Line Segment Databases. Int. Conf. on ACM SIGMOD(1992) 205-214
3. K.H. Kim, S.K. Cha, K.J. Kwon : Optimizing multidimensional index trees for main memory access. Int. Conf. on ACM SIGMOD(2001)
4. T.J. Lehman, M.J. Carey : A Study of index structures for main memory database management system. Int. Conf. on VLDB(1986) 294-303
5. H. Lu, B.C. Ooi : Spatial Indexing : Past and Future. IEEE Data Engineering Bulletin, Vol. 16, No. 3(1993) 16-21
6. J. Rao, K.A. Ross : Cache conscious indexing for decision-support in main memory. Int. Conf. on VLDB(1999) 78-89
7. J. Rao, K.A. Ross : Making B+-trees cache conscious in main memory. Int. Conf. on ACM SIGMOD(2000) 475-486
8. A. Shatdal, C. Kant, J.F. Naughton : Cache conscious algorithms for relational query processing. Int. Conf. on VLDB(1994) 510-521
9. M. Stonebraker, J. Frew, K. Gardels, J. Meredith : The SEQUOIA 2000 Storage Benchmark. Int. Conf. on ACM SIGMOD(1993) 2-11
10. K.Y. Whang, R. Krishnamurthy : The Multilevel Grid Files – a Dynamic Hierarchical Multidimensional File Structure. Int. Conf. on Database Systems for Advanced Applications(1991) 449-459
11. S. Shekhar, Y. Huang, J. Djugash : Dictionary Design Algorithms for Vector Map Compression. Proc. of Data Compression Conf(2002) 471
12. S. Shekhar, Y. Huang, J. Djugash, C. Zhou : Vector Map Compression : A Clustering Approach. ACM Int. Symposium on Advances in GIS(2002) 74-80
13. P.W. Wong, J. Koplowitz : Chain Codes and Their Linear Reconstruction Filters. IEEE Trans. On Information Theory, Vol. 38, No. 2(1992) 268-280
14. X. Zhou, D. J. Abel, David Truffet : Data Partitioning for Parallel Spatial Join Processing. Int. Conf. on SSD(1997) 178-196
15. Y. Sakurai, M. Yoshikawa, S. Uemura, H. Kojima : Spatial indexing of high-dimensional data based on relative approximation. VLDB J. 11(2002) 93-108

Indexing and Querying Constantly Evolving Data Using Time Series Analysis*

Yuni Xia[1], Sunil Prabhakar[1], Jianzhong Sun[2], and Shan Lei[1]

[1] Computer Science Department, Purdue University
[2] Mathematics Department, Purdue University
{xia, sunil, leishan}@cs.purdue.edu, sunj@purdue.edu

Abstract. This paper introduces a new approach for efficiently indexing and querying constantly evolving data. Traditional data index structures suffer from frequent updating cost and result in unsatisfactory performance when data changes constantly. Existing approaches try to reduce index updating cost by using a simple linear or recursive function to define the data evolution, however, in many applications, the data evolution is far too complex to be accurately described by a simple function. We propose to take each constantly evolving data as a time series and use the ARIMA (Autoregressive Integrated Moving Average) methodology to analyze and model it. The model enables making effective forecasts for the data. The index is developed based on the forecasting intervals. As long as the data changes within its corresponding forecasting interval, only its current value in the leaf node needs to be updated and no further update needs to be done to the index structure. The model parameters and the index structure can be dynamically adjusted. Experiments show that the forecasting interval index (FI-Index) significantly outperforms traditional indexes in a high updating environment.

1 Introduction

Constantly evolving data arises in numerous applications, for example, a moving objects database stores the current positions for millions of moving objects and these data change frequently over the time. A stock database stores the latest quotes for a large collection of stocks and they vary by minute or even second. The constant changing nature of the data brings challenges to a wide range of issues such as data storing, indexing, querying, mining and so on. In this paper, we focus on indexing and querying constantly evolving data.

Existing dynamic index structures perform satisfactorily for traditional database applications where updates are infrequent in comparison to queries. They are designed mainly for the purpose of efficiently supporting query processing. For evolving data applications that are characterized by numerous and

---

* Portions of this work were supported by NSF CAREER grant IIS-9985019, NSF grant 0010044-CCR, NSF grant 9988339-CCR.

frequent data updates, these indexes suffer from high updating overhead and result in poor performance. In order to reduce the index updating cost, most existing approaches use a simple linear or recursive function to describe the data changing patterns. However, the changing patterns in many situations (for example the stock prices) are too complex to be described by a simple function that changes infrequently.

In this paper, we propose to use time series analysis techniques to model and forecast constantly evolving data. We choose Box-Jenkins's autoregressive integrated moving average (ARIMA) methodology to identify the models, estimate model parameters and make N-step ahead predictions for each data. The index is built based on the forecasting interval for each data. Since the ARIMA model can efficiently capture the patterns of the data evolutions, the forecasting intervals are expected to be accurate and tight. An index built based on the forecasting intervals can accommodate data evolutions and substantially reduce index updating cost.

The rest of the papers proceed as following: section 2 discusses the related work for constantly evolving data indexing. In section 3, we propose a framework to use ARIMA technique to model and forecast the data and develop index based on the predicated intervals. We also explain the index details including its construction, updating and query processing. In section 4, we propose a mathematical model to determine the optimal interval size by balancing the indexing updating and querying cost. Experimental evaluation of the proposed approach is presented in section 5 and section 6 concludes the paper.

2 Related Work

Developing efficient index structures for constantly evolving data is an important research issue of databases. Most works in this area so far focus on moving object environment, where the positions of objects keep changing. As a simple approach, multi-dimensional spatial index structures can be used for indexing the positions of moving objects, however, they are not efficient because of frequent and numerous update operations. To reduce the number of updates, many approaches describe the moving object location by a linear function. Saltenis et al. [1] proposed the time-parameterized R-tree (TPR-tree). In this scheme, the position of a moving point was represented by a reference position and a corresponding velocity vector. Later, Tao et al [2] presented TPR*, which extends the idea of TPR-trees by employing a different set of insertion and deletion algorithms in order to minimize the query cost. Recently, Tao et al [3] proposed a novel recursive motion function to support a broad class of non-linear motion patterns. They also proposed a general client-server architecture for answering typical spatio-temoral queries and STP-tree for indexing the expected trajectories. Kollios et al. [4] proposed an efficient indexing scheme using partition trees. Tayeb et al. [5] introduced the issue of indexing moving objects to query the present and future positions and proposed PMR-Quadtree for indexing moving objects. Agarwal et al.[6] proposed various schemes based on the duality and developed an efficient indexing scheme to answer approximate nearest-neighbor queries. All these techniques use linear or recursive functions to describe the data changing patterns, however, in many applications, the data evolutions are far more complicated to be defined by simple linear or recursive functions.

Other techniques have been proposed to reduce the index updating cost. In [7], Kwon propose the lazy Rtree. The index structure is updated in a lazy way that is, if the point is still within the current MBR, then just update the old position to new position and no further update is needed to be done to the index structure. Only when the new position is out of the current MBR, the old position should be deleted and the new position should be inserted into the index. In [8], a bottom-up approach is proposed to improve the updating performance. The strategy improves the robustness of R-trees by supporting different levels of index reorganization ranging from local to global during updates, thus using expensive top-down updates only when necessary.

In time series area, numerous work had been done on various issues including classification, clustering, representation, anomaly detection, similarity-based query, whole-sequence and sub-sequence matching, time sequence indexing, statistical monitoring and so on. Our work distinguishes itself from above in that we go beyond the idea of time series modeling and forecasting. We use the modeling and forecasting intervals to develop an index for the constantly evolving data and effectively reduce index updating cost and improve the index performance.

3 Indexing Constantly Evolving Data

In this section, we explain the time series modeling and forecasting process and the details of the index construction, updating and querying procedures.

Our index uses the lazy-update Rtree [7], as shown in figure 1. It consists of two components, a regular Rtree as the primary index and an secondary index mapping the data ID to its page in the primary index. With the secondary index, it takes constant I/O to find the page for each data given its ID. In practice, the secondary index is usually put in memory. When the new value Vi_{new} for data i arrives, The index is updated in a lazy way that if Vi_{new} is still within the MBR of the old value Vi_{old}, then just update Vi_{old} to Vi_{new} and no further update is need to be done to the index structure. Only when Vi_{new} is out of the MBR of Vi_{old}, Vi_{old} is deleted and Vi_{new} is inserted to the index.

We propose to take each evolving data as a time series and use time series analysis tools to identify the model for each data based on its history and make n-step ahead forecasts $(V_1, V_2, ..., V_n)$ for it. The forecasting interval (FI) is the smallest interval (I_{low}, I_{high}) that contains $(V_1, V_2, ..., V_n)$. An Rtree index is built based on the forecasting intervals for each data. We call it the Forecasting Interval Rtree (FI-Rtree). The leaf node of the FI-Rtree stores both the forecasting interval and the current value for each data. When the new value Vi_{new} for data i arrives, it is checked against its forecasting interval (I_{low}, I_{high}), if it is within (I_{low}, I_{high}), just update its old value Vi_{old} in the leaf node to Vi_{new} and no further update need to be done to the index structure. Only when Vi_{new} is out of the interval (I_{low}, I_{high}), the interval needs to be adjusted and the index should be updated.

The time series modeling tool is time or error triggered, which means it is triggered to run at certain time interval, for example, every n minutes, or when the newly arriving data values are different from the forecasted intervals by some thresholds. When the newly arriving data are quite different from the forecasted interval, it could be an indication that the data evolving patterns changes, therefore, the time series modeling process should be rerun by taking the recently history into consideration and determine if the model should be changed or the model parameters should be adjusted. The framework we propose for indexing constantly evolving data is shown in figure 2.

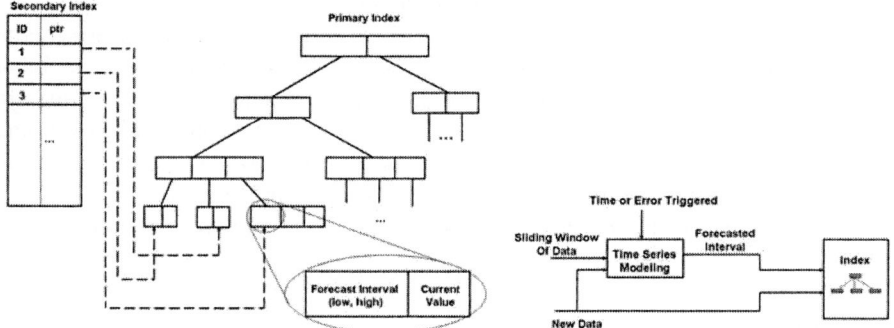

Fig. 1. Indexing Constantly Evolving Data   **Fig. 2.** FI-Rtree Index Structure

3.1 Time Series Modeling

A discrete time series is a set of time-ordered data $(x_{t_1}, x_{t_2}, ..., x_{t_n})$ obtained from observations of some phenomenon over time. An intrinsic feature of a time series is that typically, adjacent observations are dependent. We choose ARIMA for time series modeling because it covers a wide variety of patterns, including: *stationary* time series, which is in statistical equilibrium and fluctuates around a constant mean with constant variance. *non-stationary* time series, which has no natural mean, but tends to increase or decrease over time. *seasonal* time series, which repeat at regular intervals. Stationary series are described by Autoregressive Moving Average ARMA(p,q) models, non-stationary series by Autoregressive Integrated Moving Average ARIMA(p,d,q) models and seasonal series by $ARIMA(p,d,q) \times (P,D,Q)^S$ multiplicative models.

An ARMA(p,q) model captures two types of correlation via two main components, show in the following Equation:

$$X_t = \phi_0 + \phi_1 x_{(t-1)} + \phi_2 x_{(t-2)} + ... + \phi_p x_{(t-p)} + \epsilon_t + \theta_1 \epsilon_{(t-1)} + \theta_2 \epsilon_{(t-2)} + ... + \theta_q \epsilon_{(t-q)}$$

The autoregressive (AR) component describes the most p significant correlations between the current observation X(t) and the past observations x(t-1), ..., x(t-p). Here, we assume observations that are close together are more likely to be correlated than those are far apart. The moving average (MA) component describes the most q significant correlations between the current observations y(t) and the past noise terms e(t-1), ..., e(t-q).These noise represents uncertainty and are used to estimate the non-deterministic characteristics in time series. They are assumed to be normally distributed with zero mean and constant variance. $(\phi_1, \phi_2, ...\phi_p)$ and $(\theta_1, \theta_2, ...\theta_q)$ are autoregressive (AR) coefficients and moving average (MA) coefficients respectively and they express the magnitudes of correlations.

The arma(p,q) model can be extended to be the arima(p,d,q) model by inserting the number of differencing transformations d. It indicates that, after transforming the series d times, the final series will be stationary and will have p autoregressive terms and q moving average terms. Seasonal series can also be transformed via differencing to become stationary, just similar to non-stationary series. Here, the differencing interval (i.e. the gap between two differenced observations) is the season length S. To represent seasonal series, the arima(p, d, q) model can be further extended to include a seasonal component $(P, D, Q)^S$. This component specifies that after D seasonal differencing with a season length S, the correlation structure among those differenced observation pairs that are separated by S is stationary, with P autoregressive and Q moving average terms. The $ARIMA(p, d, q) \times (P, D, Q)^S$ model is also known as the general ARIMA model because it can represent all three types of series, namely stationary, non-stationary and seasonal and their combinations. Note that ARIMA(p, 0, q) X(0, 0, 0) model is simply the ARMA(p, q).

The usual approach to fit an ARIMA model to a time series includes three steps:

1. Model Identification: There are two important parameters for identifying time series, Autocorrelation Function (ACF) ρ_k and Partial Autocorrelations (PACF) ϕ_{kk}. ACF is represented as a plot of the autocorrelation as a function of lag. The autocorrelation is simply the correlation of a time series with itself at a specified lag. The partial autocorrelation (PACF) at a given lag is the autocorrelation that is not accounted for by autocorrelations at shorter lags. Details of computing ACF and PACF can be found in [9].

2. Parameter Estimation: Once a model is identified, the next step is to estimate the parameters, which are the magnitudes of the p and P autoregressive terms and the q and Q moving average terms. To find the correlation magnitude, also known as the model coefficients, common technique include maximum likelihood estimation and least squares. We choose the least square approach.

3. Forecasting: Based on the estimated parameters and the model structure, we can produce n-step ahead forecasts $(\hat{y}(t + 1), \hat{y}(t + 2), ..., \hat{y}(t + n))$ for each data. The n-step ahead forecasting interval for each data is (I_{low}, I_{high}), in which $I_{low} = min(\hat{y}(t + 1), \hat{y}(t + 2), ..., \hat{y}(t + n))$ and $I_{high} = max(\hat{y}(t + 1), \hat{y}(t + 2), ..., \hat{y}(t + n))$.

3.2 Index Construction

Assume there are m constantly evolving data $(o_1, o_2, ..., o_m)$ in the database, after the timer series modeling and forecasting, we obtain the n-step ahead predictions intervals for each data $(I_1, I_2, ..., I_m)$. The index is then built based on these intervals. The leaf nodes of the index contain both the actual values as well as the forecasting intervals for each data and the MBRs of the index are computed based on the forecasting intervals instead of the actual data values. Please note that when history data is not available, we can still make simple initial forecast for each data. Although the initial forecasting interval might be inaccurate in the beginning, as data stream in and more history data become available for modeling, the forecasting intervals will become more accurate.

As mentioned earlier, the index we propose is a lazy-update Rtree with a secondary index. Each entry in the secondary index maps a data ID to its page number in the Rtree. Therefore, for each data ID, we put in the secondary index the corresponding page number which identifies the page in the Rtree that contains that data.

3.3 Index Update

When a data changes and the new value arrives, first, the secondary index is looked up to find out its the page number in the Rtree corresponding to that data. According to the page number, we can immediately retrieve the page that contains that data and find out its old value and its forecasting interval. If the new data value is still within its forecasting interval, the old value is updated to the new value and no further update is needed to be done to the index structure. This is because that the MBRs of the FI-index is computed based on the forecasting intervals instead of the accurate data values. Thus as long as the data changes within its forecasting interval, the index structure remains correct and no need for updating.

When the new data value moves out of its forecasting interval, we will check if it deviates from the forecasting interval by a certain threshold, or if the ForecastMissCount has reached a certain threshold (ForecastMissCount is a counter that records how many times the forecasting interval fail to accommodate the data changes). All these indicate that the time series model for that data may be outdated. In that case, the time series modeling and forecasting process is triggered to rerun by taking the recent history into consideration and the new forecasting interval is obtained. If the new data value is out of the forecasting interval, but it does not deviate from it by a certain threshold; we will simply enlarge the forecasting interval to accommodate the new data value and increase the ForecastMissCount by 1, which means forecasting interval fails to enclose the data changes for one more time. The reason we keep an ForecastMissCount is that we do not hope one or two outliers or noise data trigger the time series modeling process to rerun. After the new forecasting interval is obtained, the Rtree index is updated in a lazy way, that is, if the new forecasting interval is within the MBR of the old forecasting interval, just update the old interval with the new one and no further update to the index is needed. When the new forecasting interval is out of the MBR of the old interval, the old interval together with the old data value should be deleted, and the new forecasting interval with the new data value will be inserted. The pseudo code of the index updating procedure is given in the algorithm 1. Our index is developed to for the purpose of reducing index updating cost when data changes. Since we analyze and model the data evolutions and make effective forecasts and build index based on the forecasting intervals, the data are very likely to change within the forecasting intervals and do not incur additional update to the index structure.

Algorithm 1 Index Updating Algorithm

1: Read in the new value V_{i-new} for data i
2: Look up the secondary index and find the page number Pi for data i
3: Read in Page Pi from the Primary Rtree index, find its interval $(I_{old-low}, I_{old-high}, V_{i-old})$
4: **if** $Vi - new \in (I_{old-low}, I_{old-high})$ **then**
5:    Update V_{i-old} to V_{i-new}
6:    Return;
7: **else**
8:    **if** $(V_{i-new} \leq I_{old-low} - Threshold)$ or $(V_{i-new} \geq I_{old-high} + Threshold)$ or ForecastMissCount[i]$\geq$T **then**
9:      $(I_{new-low}, I_{new-high})$=TimeSeriesModeling()
10:      ForecastMissCount[i] = 0;
11:    **else**
12:      $(I_{new-low}, I_{new-high})$=ExpandInterval($V_{i-new}$)
13:      ForecastMissCount[i]++;
14:    **end if**
15:    **if** $(I_{new-low}, I_{new-high})$ is within the MBR of $(I_{old-low}, I_{old-high})$ **then**
16:      Update $(I_{old-low}, I_{old-high}, V_{i-old})$ with $(I_{new-low}, I_{new-high}, V_{i-new})$
17:      Return;
18:    **else**
19:      Delete $(I_{old-low}, I_{old-high}, V_{i-old})$
20:      Insert $(I_{new-low}, I_{new-high}, V_{i-new})$
21:    **end if**
22: **end if**

3.4 Query Processing

In this section, we explain how the forecasting interval index (FI-Index) supports querying. We start with the range query. A range query (a, b) searches for all data items that falls within the interval (a,b). To process a range query, we first check the query (a,b) against MBRs of the nodes in this tree. A node N is pruned when it is guaranteed that no item in the subtree rooted at N can satisfy (a, b). Let $I_{low-min}$ be the minimal of the interval lower ends over all the forecasting interval in the subtree of N and $I_{high-max}$ be the maximal of all the interval high ends in the subtree. Note that the MBR for N is $[(I_{low-min}, I_{high-max})]$. if the query (a, b) does not overlap with $[(I_{low-min}, I_{high-max})]$, we can say the no data items in the subtree of N overlap with query (a,b) and the subtree of N can be safely pruned. The reason is that the forecasting interval for each data covers the its current value, therefore, if the interval does not intersect with the query, then the data can not fall in the query range (a,b) either.

The same pruning approach can be used for other queries such as point queries and nearest neighbor queries. For nodes that can not be pruned, if it is a leaf node, all the data items it contained will be compared with the query; if it is an internal node, its children nodes should be retrieved and this pruning process will run recursively.

4 Optimal Interval Size

In this section, we give an analysis to the performance of the FI-Index and give insight on how to determine the optimal interval size the index should choose. The disc I/O cost consists of two main components:

- Update: Both the current value and the old value of the data could be retrieved through the secondary index, based on the range stored in the corresponding page, we decide whether to update the tree or not. Hence the disc I/O cost is $1 + \{\text{updating cost}\}$ if we need to update the tree, otherwise just 1, where the update tree cost includes the cost to search the object in the R-tree and the cost to insert the object into the R-tree. We use the following heuristic formula to calculate the average cost of the disc I/O:

$$1 + R(x)(\{\text{average updating cost}\}),$$

where $R(x)$ is the probability that the update operation is a non-lazy one, that is, the probability that the new data value falls out of the interval. Obviously, this probability depends on the interval size x. The larger the interval size x, the smaller the probability. We assume $R(x)$ is inversely proportional to x, $R(x) = \frac{\mu}{x+\lambda}$. To make it cover the case of the traditional R-tree and the lazy updating cases, let $R(0)$ correspond to the traditional R-tree which is built based on the current value of the data with interval size 0. The disc I/O cost for one update tree operation is usually proportional to the height of the tree, hence

$$\{\text{average updating cost}\} = (C_s + C_i)\lceil \log_F N_{obj} \rceil,$$

where F is the average fan-out, C_s is a constant depending on the search performance of the R-tree, and C_i is a constant depending on the insertion performance of the R-tree, C_s and C_i can be decided by experiments.
- Query: The cost of one range query is related to the size of the query and the search of the boundary data. Assume the total number of pages covered in the average range is T, We use the following heuristic formula to bound the average cost of the range query disc I/O cost:

$$C_s Q(x)(T + \frac{T}{F} + \frac{T}{F^2} + ... + 1) = \frac{C_s Q(x) T}{1 - \frac{1}{F}}$$

where C_s is the search cost. $T, \frac{T}{F}, \frac{T}{F^2}, ...$ are the number of nodes need to be accessed in different levels. T is the number for the leaf level, $\frac{T}{F}$ for the level above the leaf, and so on, till the root level, which is 1. $Q(x)$ is an increasing function depends on the average variance of the total objects. Let $Q(0) = 1$ correspond to the traditional R-tree. Obviously, the larger the intervals are, the less precise the index is, and the less efficient the index is for supporting query processing. We assume $Q(x)$ is proportional to x and since $Q(0) = 1$, we define $Q(x) = \kappa x + 1$, where κ is a constant depending on the selectivity. { total pages covered in the average range} depends on the size of the query and the probability distribution of the objects.

To simplify the analysis, we assume the objects stay in $[0, 1]$ follow the uniform distribution, and the moving of every object follows the normal distribution $N(0, \bar{\sigma})$, The average query size is assumed to be f_q in sense of the total length of the query interval, hence

$$\{ \text{total pages covered in the average range}\} = \lceil \frac{N_{obj} f_q}{F} \rceil.$$

The sum of the updating cost and query cost in term of disc I/O is

$$I_{I/O} = N_u(1+R(x,u)(C_s+C_i)\lceil \log_F N_{obj} \rceil + N_q C_s Q(x)(\frac{N_{obj} f_q}{F} + \frac{N_{obj} f_q}{F^2} + ... + 1)$$

Since $R(x) = \frac{\mu}{x+\lambda}$ and $Q(x) = \kappa x + 1$, then

$$I_{I/O} = N_u(1+\frac{\mu}{x+\lambda}(C_s+C_i)\lceil \log_F N_{obj} \rceil + N_q C_s(\kappa x+1)(\frac{N_{obj} f_q}{F} + \frac{N_{obj} f_q}{F^2} + ... + 1)$$

To get the minimum value of $I_{I/O}$, we make $\frac{dI}{dX} = 0$, therefore

$$-N_u(C_s + C_i)\lceil \log_F N_{obj} \rceil \mu (x+\lambda)^{-2} + N_q C_s \kappa (\frac{N_{obj} f_q}{F} + \frac{N_{obj} f_q}{F^2} + ... + 1) = 0.$$

We obtain the optimal interval size for the data is:

$$x = \sqrt{\frac{N_u(C_s + C_i)\lceil \log_F N_{obj} \rceil \mu}{N_q C_s \kappa(\frac{N_{obj} f_q}{F} + \frac{N_{obj} f_q}{F^2} + ... + 1)}}$$

From the above formula, we can see that the optimal interval size is proportional to the number of updates and inversely proportional to the number of the queries. This is natural since the larger the intervals are, the less likely the data values will move out of the intervals and the less update needs to be done on the index structure, however, the query performance will be worse due to the impreciseness of the data, which leads to less pruning. Therefore, when the number of the update operations is much larger than the query, the index should take large intervals, while when queries operations are dominant, the index should take smaller intervals.

5 Experimental Evaluation

Three index structures are evaluated in our experiments: the traditional R-tree; the lazy Rtree (The traditional R-tree augmented with lazy updating using the secondary index structure) and the FI-Rtree. Our experiments are based real stock data. 25,000 stocks time series, each of which contains over 200 data points are used in the experiments. The first 100 data points of each stock are used for ARIMA modeling and forecast. Based on the forecasting intervals, we build the FI-Rtree. Once the FI-Rtree is built, the remaining data points are modeled as dynamic updates to the FI-Rtree, as well as other R-tree variants. At the same time, a number of range queries are generated and evaluated. Each range query has its central location chosen randomly and has a query size a fraction of the price range.

Since these are disk-based index structures, the number of page I/Os is the natural metric for measuring the performance of the indexes. We measure the number of page I/Os for reads and writes of both dynamic updates and queries during the simulation. The secondary index of the LazyRtree and the FI-Rtree is assumed to be in the main memory. For the time series modeling, we used the TsModeler, an automatic ARIMA Time Series Modeling Tool. [10].

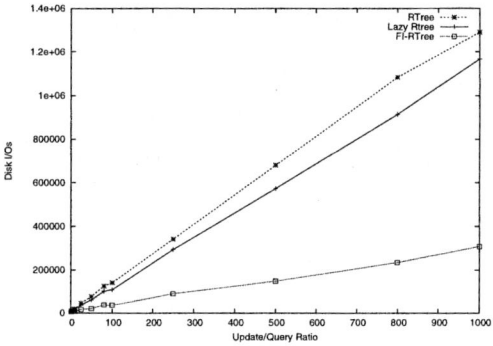

Fig. 3. Overall Disk I/Os

We study the relative performance of the various index structures as the relative number of queries and updates is varied. Figure 3 shows the total number of page I/Os performed for querying and updating the R-tree, the *lazy*-R-tree, and the FI-Rtree. The performance is measured under the same query generation rate but different update arrival rates. As the ratio of update rate over the query rate is increased from 0 to 1000, all four indexes show an increase in the number of I/Os. This is because increasing the update rate implies more demands on the index, and consequently more I/Os are needed.

When the update/query ratio is very low, the FI-Rtree takes more I/Os than the other R-tree variants. The reason is that the R-tree and the *lazy*-R-tree uses actual data values, while the FI-Rtree employs data intervals and result in a worse query performance. Towards the right end of the graph, when the update workload dominates the query workload, the FI-Rtree has a significant improvement over other R-tree variants. In fact, the number of I/Os needed by all three R-trees increases sharply, whereas the FI-Rtree gracefully handles the high update burden. When updates are much more frequent than queries, which is a typical scenario in sensor and moving object databases, the R-tree suffers from expensive updates. The distinction between the R-tree and the *lazy*-R-tree begins to show in this high update setting as the secondary index yields significant gains from cheaper updates. The FI-Rtree clearly outperforms the other indexes in this high update environment since its structure is inherently designed to maximize tolerance to changes in data values. The advantage of better update performance more than compensates for the slightly poorer query performance. As the update/query ratio increases, the improvement of the FI-Rtree over R-trees is more obvious. In particular, when the update/query ratio is 1000, the number of I/Os required by the FI-Rtree is only one-fourth that of the lazy Rtree, and one-fifth that of the R-tree.

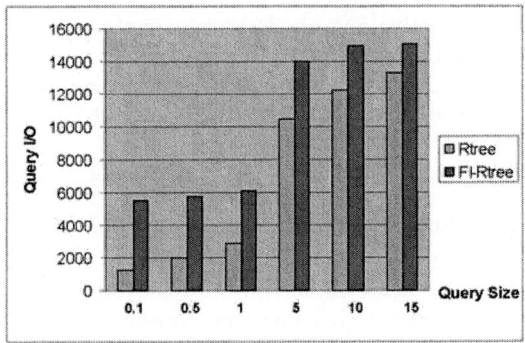

Fig. 4. Query I/Os vs. Query Size

We also studied how the query size affects the query performance of the FI-Rtree and the traditional Rtree. Note that since the *lazy*-R-tree and the traditional R-tree have almost identical query performance, here we compare the query I/Os of FI-Rtree with only the traditional Rtree. Figure 4 shows the query I/Os for FI-Rtree and traditional Rtree over different query sizes. The query size is varied from 0.1% to 15% of the domain. We find that the FI-Rtree always requires more query I/Os than the traditional R-tree. However, as the query size increases, the performance of the FI-Rtree gets closer to that of the R-tree. The reason is that with a large query area, the probability that a given region will be covered by a query increases. Thus the advantage of having a small MBR is diminished with larger queries.

6 Conclusions and Future Work

This paper proposes a new approach for efficiently indexing and querying constantly evolving data. Each data is considered as a time series and we apply the ARIMA methodology to model it. The model enables making effective forecasts for the data and the index structure is developed based on the forecasting intervals. The model parameters and the index can be dynamically adjusted. Our experiments show that the FI-index significantly outperforms traditional indexes in a high-updating environment. In ongoing work, we would explore processing time series with noise or uncertainty and developing index that support temporal and window queries.

References

1. Saltenis, S., Jensen, C., Leutenegger, S., Lopez., M.: Indexing the position of continuously moving objects. Proceedings of ACM SIGMOD Conference (2000) 261–272
2. Tao, Y., Papadias, D., Sun, J.: The TPR*-Tree: An optimized spatio-temporal access method for predictive queries. Proceedings of the 29th International Conference on Very Large Databases(VLDB) (2003) 790–802
3. Tao, Y., Faloutsos, C., Papadias, D., Liu, B.: Prediction and indexing of moving objects with unknown motion patterns. Proceedings of the SIGMOD (2004) 611–622
4. Kollios, G., Gunopulos, D., Tsotras, V.J.: On indexing mobile objects. (1999) 261–272
5. Tayeb, J., Ulusoy, O., Wolfson., O.: A Quadtree-based dynamic attribute indexing method. The Computer Journal (1998) 185–200
6. Agarwal, P.K., Arge, L., Erickson, J.: Indexing moving points. (2000) 175–186
7. Kwon, D., Lee, S.J., Lee, S.: Indexing the current positions of moving objects using the lazy update R-tree. The 3rd International Conference on Mobile Data Management (2002)
8. Lee, M.L., Hsu, W., Jensen, C.S., Cui, B., Teo, K.L.: Supporting frequent updates in R-trees: A bottom-up approach. Proceedings of the 29th International Conference on Very Large Databases(VLDB) (2003) 608–620
9. Box, G.E., Jenkins, G.M., Reinsel, G.C.: Time Series Analysis Forecasting and Control. Englewood Cliffs, N.J.: Prentice Hall (2004)
10. Tran, N., Reed, D.A.: Arima time series modeling and forecasting for adaptive I/O prefetching. Proceedings of the 2001 International Conference on Supercomputing (2001) 473–485

Mining Generalized Spatio-Temporal Patterns

Junmei Wang, Wynne Hsu, and Mong Li Lee

School of Computing,
National University of Singapore, Singapore 117543
{wangjunm, whsu, leeml}@comp.nus.edu.sg

Abstract. Spatio-temporal databases offer a rich repository and opportunities to develop techniques for discovering new types of spatio-temporal patterns. In this paper, we introduce a new class of spatio-temporal patterns, called the *generalized spatio-temporal patterns*, to describe the repeated sequences of events that occur within small neighbourhoods. Such patterns are crucial to the understanding of habitual patterns. To discover this class of patterns, we develop an algorithm GenSTMiner based on the idea of pattern growth approach, and introduce some optimization techniques that are used to reduce the number of candidates generated and minimize the size of the projected databases. Our performance study indicates that GenSTMiner is highly efficient and outperforms PrefixSpan.

1 Introduction

Spatio-temporal databases offer a rich repository of information, and opportunities to develop techniques for discovering new types of patterns that capture the multi-states (i.e. past, present and future states) information in relation to their spatial locations. In particular, repeated sequences within some small neighborhood regions typically reveal some interesting habitual patterns. For example, knowing the sequence of neighborhood places visited by terrorists allows one to understand their mindsets and habits.

Previous studies mainly focus on the discovery of *spatial patterns* [4, 8, 11] or *sequential patterns* [6, 2, 10]. Both types of patterns do not have the ability to encode a sequence of events in the context of spatial locations. Recently, [12] introduced the *flow patterns* that aim to capture the evolution of events in neighboring regions over time. While flow patterns can clearly capture the flow of events to some degree, they rely heavily on the assumption that these events will repeat themselves in exactly the same locations. However, we observe that in some applications, the absolute locations in which event e has occurred are not important. Rather, it is the relative locations of events with respect to the event e that are interesting.

In this paper, we introduce a new class of spatio-temporal patterns called *generalized spatio-temporal patterns* to summarize the sequential relationships between events that are prevalent in sharing the same topological structures. We adopt the pattern growth approach and develop an algorithm called GenSTMiner to discover the generalized spatio-temporal patterns. To increase the efficiency of the mining process, we also present two optimization techniques. One is *conditional projected databases* to prune infeasible events and sequences. The other is the *pseudo projection* to reduce the memory requirement. The performance study indicates that GenSTMiner is highly efficient, and the optimization techniques dramatically reduce many unnecessary patterns.

The paper is organized as follows. Section 2 defines some preliminary concepts. Section 3 reviews the projection based sequence mining. We present the algorithm and optimization techniques in section 4. Section 5 describes the experiments. Section 6 reviews the related work, and section 7 concludes the paper.

2 Problem Statement

Spatio-temporal databases capture events in both time and space dimensions. The space dimension can be partitioned into a set of disjoint grid cells similar to [8,9]. Each cell represents a spatial region (or location), denoted as (x, y). Let R denote a spatial neighborhood relation over the set of partitioned cells. Two cells (x_1, y_1) and (x_2, y_2) are said to be neighbours, denoted as $\langle (x_1, y_1), (x_2, y_2) \rangle \in R$, if $|x_1 - x_2| \leq n_r$ and $|y_1 - y_2| \leq n_r$ where n_r is the number of grid cells. Similarly, the time dimension can be divided into disjoint time windows or time periods of width W. Time t_1 is said to be a neighbour of t_2 if t_1 and t_2 are in the same time window, denoted as $(t_1, t_2) \in W$.

An *event*, e, occurring in the location (x, y) at time t is denoted as $e(x, y, t)$, and abbr. as $e(x, y)$ when the sequential context is clear. Two events $e_1(x_1, y_1, t_1)$ and $e_2(x_2, y_2, t_2)$ are said to be *CloseNeighbours iff* $\langle (x_1, y_1), (x_2, y_2) \rangle \in R$ and $(t_1, t_2) \in W$, denoted as $\langle e_1(x_1, y_1, t_1), e_2(x_2, y_2, t_2) \rangle \in (R, W)$.

An *eventset* is defined as a set of events occurred at the same time, denoted as $E = \langle e_1(x_1, y_1), \ldots, e_m(x_m, y_m) \rangle$. Two eventsets E_1 and E_2 are said to be CloseNeighbours *iff* each event in E_1 is a CloseNeighbour of each event in E_2.

Figure 1 shows an example of spatio-temporal databases which records the various locations where cyclones and storm occur over time. The space is partitioned into 25 disjoint locations, and the time is divided into 3 disjoint time windows. Figure 1(a) shows the events $\{a, b, c, d, etc\}$ that are observed at various locations over time.

A *flow pattern*[12] is defined as a sequence of eventsets such that any two consecutive eventsets are CloseNeighbours. Some sequences in Figure 1(a) that satisfy the *flow pattern* definition are shown in Figure 1(c). Each of the above flow patterns occurs only once and will be discarded by most mining algorithms. However, a closer examination reveals that these patterns actually convey some interesting behavior of the cyclones, i.e., "*event a in an area that has been hit by the storm always leads to event f in its north neighbours and event d in its northeast neighbours*. In other words, the absolute locations in which event a has occurred are not important. Rather, it is the relative locations of event d or f with respect to event a that are interesting.

We note that relative addresses play an important role in capturing the invariant topological relationships of a pattern. In order to incorporate the concept of relative addresses, we first select a *reference location*, denoted as $l_{ref} = (x_{ref}, y_{ref})$. For each occurring event $e_1(x_1, y_1), e_2(x_2, y_2), \ldots, e_m(x_m, y_m)$, we map them to their corresponding relative occurring locations as $e_1(x_1 - x_{ref}, y_1 - y_{ref}), e_2(x_2 - x_{ref}, y_2 - y_{ref}), \ldots, e_m(x_m - x_{ref}, y_m - y_{ref})$.

A *RelativeEventset* is a set of mapped events that occur at the same time t, denoted as $\vec{E} = E \langle e_1(x_1 - x_{ref}, y_1 - y_{ref}), e_2(x_2 - x_{ref}, y_2 - y_{ref}), \ldots, e_m(x_m - x_{ref}, y_m -$

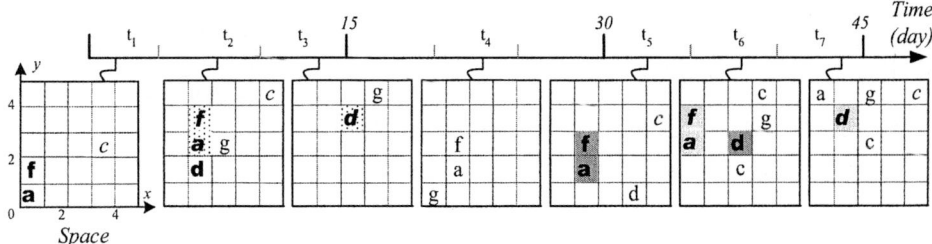

(a) Space-time view

(b) Datasets of Events

(c) flow patterns

Fig. 1. Example spatio-temporal database ($W = 15$ days, $R = 1$)

$y_{ref})\rangle$. We assume that all the events in a RelativeEventset are listed alphabetically. A RelativeEventset $\vec{E}_p$ is a *CloseNeighbour* of a RelativeEventset $\vec{E}_q$ if every event in $\vec{E}_p$ is a *CloseNeighbour* of every event in $\vec{E}_q$, denoted as $(\vec{E}_p, \vec{E}_q) \in (R, W)$.

Definition 1. *(Generalized spatio-temporal pattern)*
A generalized spatio-temporal pattern is a sequence of RelativeEventsets, *and all the RelativeEventsets are* CloseNeighbuors *of each other, denoted as*, $\vec{E}_1 \to \vec{E}_2 \to \cdots \to \vec{E}_m$, *s.t.* $\forall i, j \in (1..m), (\vec{E}_i, \vec{E}_j) \in (R, W)$.

Note that the generalized spatio-temporal patterns can be specialized to spatial patterns and sequential patterns. When the space is reduced to a single location (i.e. $S \to 0$), the spatio-temporal pattern is simply the sequential pattern. On the other hand, if we limit the time window to a snapshot (i.e. $t \to 0$), we will have the co-located events among the spatial neighbuorhoods [8].

A generalized spatio-temporal pattern is said to be frequent if there are at least t-$minsup$ (i.e. temporal support) different occurrences of the pattern over time, and in each time window, there are at least s-$minsup$ (i.e. spatial support) patterns occurring in the space. A generalized spatio-temporal pattern involving k different events is called a k-generalized spatio-temporal pattern.

Given two generalized spatio-temporal patterns, $P = \vec{E}_1 \to \ldots \to \vec{E}_m$ and $Q = \vec{E}'_1 \to \ldots \to \vec{E}'_m$. Let P' be generated by concatenating P with Q, denoted as $P' = P \cdot Q$. P is called the *prefix* of P' and Q, *suffix* of P'. Q can be concatenated with P in two ways, namely Q is an *eventset extension*, i.e. $\vec{E}_1 \to \ldots \to (\vec{E}_m \cup \vec{E}'_1) \to \vec{E}'_m$; or Q is a *sequence extension*, that is $\vec{E}_1 \to \ldots \to (\vec{E}_m \to \vec{E}'_1) \to \ldots \to \vec{E}'_m$.

sid.	Sequence
s_1	$\langle a, c, f \rangle \to \langle a, c, d, f, g \rangle \to \langle d, g \rangle$
s_2	$\langle a, f, g \rangle$
s_3	$\langle a, c, d, f \rangle \to \langle a, c, d, f, g \rangle \to \langle a, c, d, g \rangle$

sid.	Sequence
s_{1a}	$\langle \ddagger, c, f \rangle \to \langle a, c, d, f, g \rangle \to \langle d, g \rangle$
s_{2a}	$\langle \ddagger, f, g \rangle$
s_{3a}	$\langle \ddagger, c, d, f \rangle \to \langle a, c, d, f, g \rangle \to \langle a, c, d, g \rangle$

(a) Sample sequence database   (b) a-projected database

Fig. 2. Projection sequential pattern mining

Suppose there is a lexicographic ordering $\leq$ among the set of events in the spatio-temporal database. Given two events $e_1(x_1, y_1)$ and $e_2(x_2, y_2)$, $e_1(x_1, y_1) \leq e_2(x_2, y_2)$ if and only if (i) $e_1 \leq e_2$, or (ii) $e_1 = e_2, x_1 \leq x_2$, or (iii) $e_1 = e_2, x_1 = x_2, y_1 \leq y_2$.

In this work, we focus on finding the frequent generalized spatio-temporal patterns by exploiting its similarity to sequence patterns. We use the pattern growth approach because it has been shown to be one of the most effective method for frequent pattern mining and is superior to the candidate-maintenance-and-test approach, especially on the dense database or with low minimum support threshold [1, 3].

3 Projection-Based Sequential Pattern Mining

The sequential pattern mining algorithm PrefixSpan[6] provides a general framework of the pattern growth method. The basic idea is to use a set of locally frequent items to grow patterns. Figure 2(a) shows a sample sequence database. The set of frequent items $F_1 = \{a, c, d, f, g\}$ when $minsup = 2$. Figure 2(b) shows the a-projected database, where only the subsequence prefixed with the first occurrence of a is considered. By scanning a-projected database once, we get $LF_a = \{\langle \ddagger c \rangle, \langle \ddagger f \rangle, a, c, d, f, g\}$, and generate the corresponding 2-sequences with prefix a, i.e., $\langle a, c \rangle, \langle a, f \rangle, a \to a, a \to c, a \to d, a \to f$ and $a \to g$. Then, we can further partition the set of frequent patterns prefixed with a into $|LF_a| = 7$ subsets, construct their corresponding projected databases, and mine them recursively.

Let us examine how PrefixSpan can be used to discover generalized spatio-temporal patterns. First, it finds all the frequent sequential patterns that satisfy $t\text{-}minsup$. Next, it scans each time window and checks if there are $s\text{-}minsup$ spatial-sequences which are instances of the frequent sequential patterns and all eventsets in a spatial-sequence are close neighbors, and adds them into the candidate sets. Finally, all the frequent generalized spatio-temporal patterns are obtained by mapping the spatial-sequences in the candidate sets into their relative addresses, where their support is larger than or equal to $s\text{-}minsup$.

Although PrefixSpan could find all the frequent generalized spatio-temporal patterns, it is neither efficient nor scalable as it needs to generate a set of candidates before pruning the infrequent ones. This requires maintaining a large number of candidates in memory, and scanning the database more than twice.

Wid	Sid	Sequences	Prefix
1	1	$\langle \ddagger, c(3,2), f(0,1) \rangle \to \langle a(1,2), c(4,4), d(1,1), f(1,3), g(2,2) \rangle \to \langle d(2,3), g(3,4) \rangle$	$a(0,0)$
	2	$\langle \ddagger, c(4,4), d(1,1), f(1,3), g(2,2) \rangle \to \langle d(2,3), g(3,4) \rangle$	$a(1,2)$
2	1	$\langle \ddagger, f(1,2), g(0,0) \rangle$	$a(1,1)$
3	1	$\langle \ddagger, c(4,3), d(3,0), f(1,2) \rangle \to \langle a(0,2), c(2,1), c(3,4), d(2,2), f(0,3), g(3,3) \rangle$ $\to \langle a(0,4), c(2,2), c(4,4), d(1,3), g(2,4) \rangle$	$a(1,1)$
	2	$\langle \ddagger, c(2,1), c(3,4), d(2,2), f(0,3), g(3,3) \rangle \to \langle a(0,4), c(2,2), c(4,4), d(1,3), g(2,4) \rangle$	$a(0,2)$
	3	$\langle \ddagger, c(2,2), c(4,4), d(1,3), g(2,4) \rangle$	$a(0,4)$

Fig. 3. The projected database of event a

4 GenSTMiner Algorithm

In this section, we describe an efficient algorithm called GenSTMiner that follows the framework of pattern growth methods and finds the complete set of generalized spatio-temporal patterns directly without maintaining a large number of candidates. We also devise optimization techniques that will eliminate redundant candidates, and reduce the size of the projected database so that it will fit into the memory. The GenSTMiner algorithm consists of the following three steps:

1. Find the set of frequent events F_1 (1-general spatial-sequences) by scanning the database once, and sort them according to their lexicographic order.
2. Next, divide the set of frequent patterns into $|F_1|$ partitions and retrieve the projected database PDB_e of each event $e \in F_1$ from the database D. Then, for each sequence in PDB_e, choose its reference location and map events in it into their relative locations. The transformed PDB_e is called the generalized projected database, denoted as GDB_e.
3. Finally, based on GDB_e, find all the frequent k-generalized spatio-temporal patterns prefixed with e by constructing and mining the projected databases of the length-k generalized spatio-temporal patterns recursively.

The spatial support of an event e in a time window is decided by the number of different locations where it occurs, and its temporal support is equal to the number of different time windows where it is spatially frequent. Only when the temporal support of an event is larger than $t\text{-}minsup$, it is said to be frequent.

Note that in the second step, we use all the instances of an event e regardless of its location in an input sequence in the database to retrieve the projection database of the event e. For the same instances of the event e (same location), we only consider the first occurrence of it. This differs from PrefixSpan which considers only the first occurrence of the event e in an input sequence.

Consider Figure 1(c). Suppose $R = 1$, $W = 15 days$, and the input sequence $s_1 = \langle \boldsymbol{a(0,0)}, c(3,2), f(0,1) \rangle \to \langle \boldsymbol{a(1,2)}, c(4,4), d(1,1), f(1,3), g(2,2) \rangle \to \langle d(2,3), g(3,4) \rangle$. Suppose we want to retrieve the projection of s_{1a}. Since there are two instances of a in s_1, namely $a(0,0)$ and $a(1,2)$, the projection of s_{1a} consists of two subsequences: $\langle \ddagger, c(3,2), f(0,1) \rangle \to \langle a(1,2), c(3,4), d(1,1), f(1,3), g(2,2) \rangle \to \langle d(2,3), g(3,4) \rangle$ and $\langle \ddagger, c(4,4), d(1,1), f(1,3), g(2,2) \rangle \to \langle d(2,3), g(2,4) \rangle$. Figure 3 shows the a-projected database obtained from Figure 1(c).

Wid	Sid	Sequences
1	1	$\langle\ddagger, c(3,2), f(0,1)\rangle \to \langle a(1,2), c(4,4), d(1,1), f(1,3), g(2,2)\rangle \to \langle d(2,3), g(3,4)\rangle$
	2	$\langle\ddagger, c(3,2), d(0,-1), f(0,1), g(1,0)\rangle \to \langle d(1,1), g(2,2)\rangle$
2	1	$\langle\ddagger, f(0,1), g(-1,-1)\rangle$
	1	$\langle\ddagger, c(3,2), d(2,-1), f(0,1)\rangle \to \langle a(-1,1), c(1,0), c(2,3), d(1,1), f(-1,2), g(2,2)\rangle$
		$\to \langle a(-1,3), c(1,1), c(3,3), d(0,2), g(1,3)\rangle$
3	2	$\langle\ddagger, c(2,-1), c(3,2), d(2,0), f(0,1), g(3,1)\rangle \to \langle a(0,2), c(2,0), c(4,2), d(1,1), g(2,2)\rangle$
	3	$\langle\ddagger, c(2,-2), c(4,0), d(1,-1), g(2,0)\rangle$

Fig. 4. Generalized projected database of event a

Having obtained the projected database of the frequent events, we need to choose the reference locations of the sequences, and then map events in a sequence into their relative locations. However, the problem is how to choose the reference location.

4.1 Choice of Reference Location

We can either use the location of the event e or the base location of a sequence as the reference location. The base location of a sequence s is given by $\{(x,y)|\forall x_{i_j} \in s, y_{i_j} \in s, x = min(x_{i_j}), y = min(y_{i_j})\}$. If we use the base location of a sequence as the reference location, then we may change the center of the topological structure to another event since the base locations of the sequences in the projected database may not be the locations of the event e.

For example, the a-projected database consists of two sequence $s_1 = d(0,1) \to \langle a(1,2), g(2,2)\rangle$ and $s_2 = a(1,2) \to \langle f(1,3), g(2,2)\rangle$, and $base(s_1) = (0,1), base(s_2) = (1,2)$. If we choose the base locations of the sequences as the reference locations, then the center of the topological structure of s_1 is changed to the event d, instead of a.

Hence, to keep all the events in the generalized spatio-temporal patterns consistent in their topological structure, we use the location of the event e as the reference location. Figure 4 shows the generalized projected database of the event a.

4.2 Mining k-Generalized Spatio-Temporal Patterns

Having obtained the *generalized projected database* of an event e, we proceed to discover the frequent k-generalized spatio-temporal patterns ($k \geq 2$) that are prefixed with it. We first find the set of the locally frequent events LF_e. Then, for each valid event in LF_e, we generate the $(k+1)$-generalized spatio-temporal patterns, construct its projected database, and mine it recursively. Note that in the projected database of a length-k generalized spatio-temporal pattern, the spatial support of a local event at time window i is decided by the number of sequences in the projected databases that contain it, and the temporal support is up to the number of time windows where it is spatially frequent.

Figure 5 shows the GenSTMiner algorithm. It first scans the database once to find the frequent 1-generalized spatio-temporal patterns F_1(line 2), treats each $e_k \in F_1$ as a prefix, builds its projected database PDB_{e_k}, and then transforms PDB_{e_k} into GDB_{e_k} (lines 3-5). Next, it calls the subroutine Ptn-growth method (line 6). Subroutine Ptn-growth method recursively calls itself and works as follows: For prefix e, scans its projected database once to find its locally frequent events (line 9), grows e with each valid locally frequent event to get a new prefix e' and builds the projected database for the new prefix, and calls itself recursively (lines 12-16).

Algorithm GenSTMiner($\mathcal{D},R,W$,s-minsup,t-minsup)
1: $M = \emptyset$;
2: $F_1 = \{$all the frequent events$\}$;
3: **for each** $e_k \in F_1$ **do**
4: $\quad PDB_{e_k}$ = projected database(D, e_k);
5: $\quad$ Convert PDB_{e_k} into GDB_{e_k};
6: $\quad$ Call *Ptn-growth*(e_k,GDB_{e_k},s-minsup,t-minsup);
7: **return** M
Subroutine Ptn-growth(α, PDB_α,s-$minsup$,t-$minsup$)
8: $M = M \cup \alpha$;
9: Scan PDB_α once and get all frequent LF;
10: **if** LF is empty **then**
11: $\quad$ **return**;
12: **for each** $e_j \in LF$ **do**
13: $\quad$ **if** $\forall e_i \in \alpha, (e_i, e_j) \in (R, W)$ **then**
14: $\quad\quad \alpha' = \alpha \cdot e_j$;
15: $\quad\quad PDB_{\alpha'}$ = projected database (PDB_α, α');
16: $\quad\quad$ Call *Ptn-growth*(α',$PDB_{\alpha'}$,s-minsup,t-minsup);
17: **return**

Fig. 5. GenSTMiner Algorithm

Compared to PrefixSpan, GenSTMiner can find the complete set of generalized spatio-temporal patterns by generating much smaller set of candidates. The following section describes optimization techniques that are further used to reduce the number of candidates generated and to reduce the memory requirement.

4.3 Conditional Projected Database

We observe that not every event or eventset in the sequence in the database participates in a generalized spatio-temporal patterns. In order to eliminate those non-promising events or eventsets in the projected database of an event, we introduce the concept of the conditional database with respect to an event e.

Given a sequence s in the database, *the conditional spatial-sequences* w.r.t. *an event* e of s is the set of subsequences of s prefixed with e, and each of them is a spatial-sequence and every eventset in these subsequences is CloseNeighbour of the event e.

For example, given the sequence $s = \langle a(0,0), c(3,2), f(0,1)\rangle \rightarrow \langle a(1,2), c(4,4), d(1,1), f(1,3), g(2,2)\rangle \rightarrow \langle d(2,3), g(3,4)\rangle$, and $R = 1$, $W = 15 days$. We want to retrieve the conditional spatial sequence of the event a. Notice that there are only two instances of a in s, i.e. $a(0,0)$ and $a(1,2)$. First, for the instance $a(0,0)$, there are only two events $f(0,1)$ and $d(1,1)$ in s that can form a conditional spatial sequence together with $a(0,0)$; and for the instance $a(1,2)$, the events $d(1,1), f(1,3), g(2,2)$ and $d(2,3)$ are valid. Hence, the final s_a consists of two sequences $\langle a(0,0), f(0,1)\rangle \rightarrow d(1,1)$ and $\langle a(1,2), d(1,1), f(1,3), g(2,2)\rangle \rightarrow d(2,3)$.

The collection of all the conditional spatial-sequences w.r.t. an event e in the database $\mathcal{D}$ forms the *conditional database* w.r.t. *an event* e. All the conditional spatial-sequences are ordered according to their time.

GenSTMiner obtains the projected database of an event e from its conditional database, instead of database D. This effectively remove unpromising events from the projected databases of the event e. For simplicity, we call the projected databases of an event e retrieved from the conditional database as the *conditional projected databases* w.r.t the event e or *e-conditional projected databases*.

While the conditional database can be used to remove unpromising events from the event e-projected database, there are still unpromising events when we further construct the projected database of length-k ($k > 2$) generalized spatio-temporal patterns. We use the Apriori checking as in [6] to prune events during the construction of the projected databases of length-k generalized spatio-temporal patterns.

To construct the P-conditional projected database, where P is a length-l generalized spatio-temporal pattern, let E be the last element of P and P' be the prefix of P such that $P = P' \cdot E$.

If $P' \cdot x$ is not frequent, then event x can be excluded from projection. For example, if we know that $a(0,0) \rightarrow g(0,1)$ is not frequent, then event $g(0,1)$ can be excluded from construction of $a(0,0) \rightarrow d(1,1)$-conditional projected databases.

However, if $P' \cdot x$ is frequent, but there $\exists e \in P, s.t. \langle e, x \rangle \notin R$, then event x can be excluded from projection. For example, let $R = 1$ and $\langle a(0,0), g(-1,-1) \rangle$ is frequent, but since $\langle f(0,1), g(-1,-1) \rangle \notin R$, we can remove g(-1,-1) from the construction of $\langle a(0,0), f(0,1) \rangle$-conditional projected database.

Moreover, let E' be formed by substituting any item in E by x. If $P' \cdot E'$ is not frequent, then event x can be excluded from the first element of suffix of that element is a superset of e. For example, suppose $a(0,0) \rightarrow \langle b(0,1), f(1,1) \rangle$ is not frequent. To construct $a(0,0) \rightarrow \langle b(0,1), c(0,1) \rangle$-projected database, conditional spatial-sequence $a(0,0) \rightarrow \langle (b(0,1), c(0,1), f(1,1), g(1,1) \rangle \rightarrow d(0,1)$ should be projected to $\langle \ddagger, g(1,1) \rangle \rightarrow d(0,1)$.

4.4 Pseudo Projection

In general, we obtain the projected databases by scanning the sequences at each time window in the databases. However, after scanning the projected databases, we have known the time windows in which the locally frequent event e is not spatially frequent, and we can stop retrieving projection of sequences prefixed with e at those time windows. To realize this, for each locally frequent event e, we use a bitmap to record the time windows in which it is frequent. We only retrieve the projection of the sequences from the time windows where its corresponding value in the bitmap is set to 1. Moreover, we could get the frequent period of a generalized spatio-temporal pattern by scanning the bitmap once.

In addition, when we retrieve the conditional projected database of an event e, we observed that an event e_k in the sequence in the database may appear many times in the e-conditional projected database. The cost of the projection (constructing the conditional projected database recursively) becomes a major cost in GenSTMiner. We can use the pseudo projection to reduce the cost of the projection.

In PrefixSpan, the pseudo projection is used to avoid physically copying suffixes. When the database can be held in main memory, instead of constructing a physical projection by collecting all the suffixes, the pseudo-projection uses pointers referring to

$s = \langle a(0,0), c(3,2), \boldsymbol{f(0,1)} \rangle \to \langle a(1,2), c(4,4), \boldsymbol{d(1,1)}, f(1,3), g(2,2) \rangle \to \langle d(2,3), g(3,4) \rangle$		
	prefix	physical projection	pseudo projection
s_a	$a(0,0)$	$\langle \ddagger, f(0,1) \rangle \to d(1,1)$	$\langle pointer\ to\ s, 3, 10010000, (0,0) \rangle$
	$a(1,2)$	$\langle \ddagger, d(1,1), f(1,3), g(2,2) \rangle \to d(2,3)$	$\langle pointer\ to\ s, 6, 11110, (1,2) \rangle$

Fig. 6. Example of pseudo projection

the sequences in the database. Every projection consists of two pieces of information ⟨*pointer, offset*⟩, where *pointer* points to the sequence in database and *offset* indicates the start position of the suffix in the sequences. Unlike in PrefixSpan where only the first occurrence of an item is considered, GenSTMiner needs to consider the suffixes in an input sequence prefixed with different instances of the event e. Hence, the problem of pseudo projection becomes more complicated.

In GenSTMiner, every projection consists of 4 pieces of information: ⟨*pointer, offset, bitmap, refloc*⟩, where *pointer* points to the sequence in the database; *offset* indicates the start position of the suffixes in the sequence, and *bitmap* indicates the appearance of the events in the suffixes of the sequence in the event e conditional spatial sequence, and the size of $bitmap$ is equivalent to the number of events in the suffixes of the sequence; and *refloc* stores the reference location of the conditional spatial sequence. Figure 6 shows an example of the pseudo projection of the sequence in the database.

5 Performance Evaluation

We implement the algorithms in C++ and evaluate their performance on both synthetic and real-life datasets. The experiments are carried out on a Pentium 4, 1.6 GHZ processor with 256MB memory running Windows XP.

5.1 Experiments on Synthetic Dataset

We augment the IBM Quest synthetic data generator [1] to include spatial information by generating N item using F spatial features and L locations. We generate datasets by setting N=10,000, F=1,000, L=100. Other parameters include D, number of of sliding windows (= size of Database); C, average number of Eventsets per sliding window; and T, average number of events per Eventsets.

We test the performance of GenSTMiner on the dataset $C10T10D10k$ by varying the parameters R, t-$minsup$, and s-$minsup$. We evaluate the performance of GenSTMiner with and without optimization techniques and compare it with PrefixSpan. The results are shown in Figure 7. The results indicate that GenSTMiner outperforms PrefixSpan, especially when it uses optimization techniques. This is expected as the pruning techniques we use in GenSTMiner not only reduce the size of the projected databases, but also eliminate infeasible events and sequences.

Figure 7(a) examines the efficiency of the algorithms by varying the size of R from 1 to 9. It shows that the runtime of GenSTMiner grows linearly as spatial neighbour relation R increases. This is because when R is large, the number of spatial neighbourhoods of an event tends to be large, and the length of the frequent patterns becomes longer.

---

[1] http://www.almaden.ibm.com/software/quest

Figure 7(b) shows that GenSTMiner requires more time to find the frequent patterns when t-minsup tends to be small. This is due to more local frequent patterns become globally frequent when t-minsup is small. As a result, the size of the frequent patterns become larger. Similarly, Figure 7(c) indicates that GenSTMiner requires more time to find the frequent patterns when s-minsup tends to be small. Finally, Figure 7(d) shows the runtime of the GenSTMiner by varying the parameter D (i.e. number of sliding windows) from $20k$ to $100k$. From the figure, we could see that GenSTMiner grows linearly with the increase of database sizes.

5.2 Comparative Study

This set of experiments aims to show the usefulness of the generalized spatio-temporal patterns as compared to flow patterns using a real-life dataset. We obtain 3 years of standard meteorological data from 5 stations that are closely located in space from the

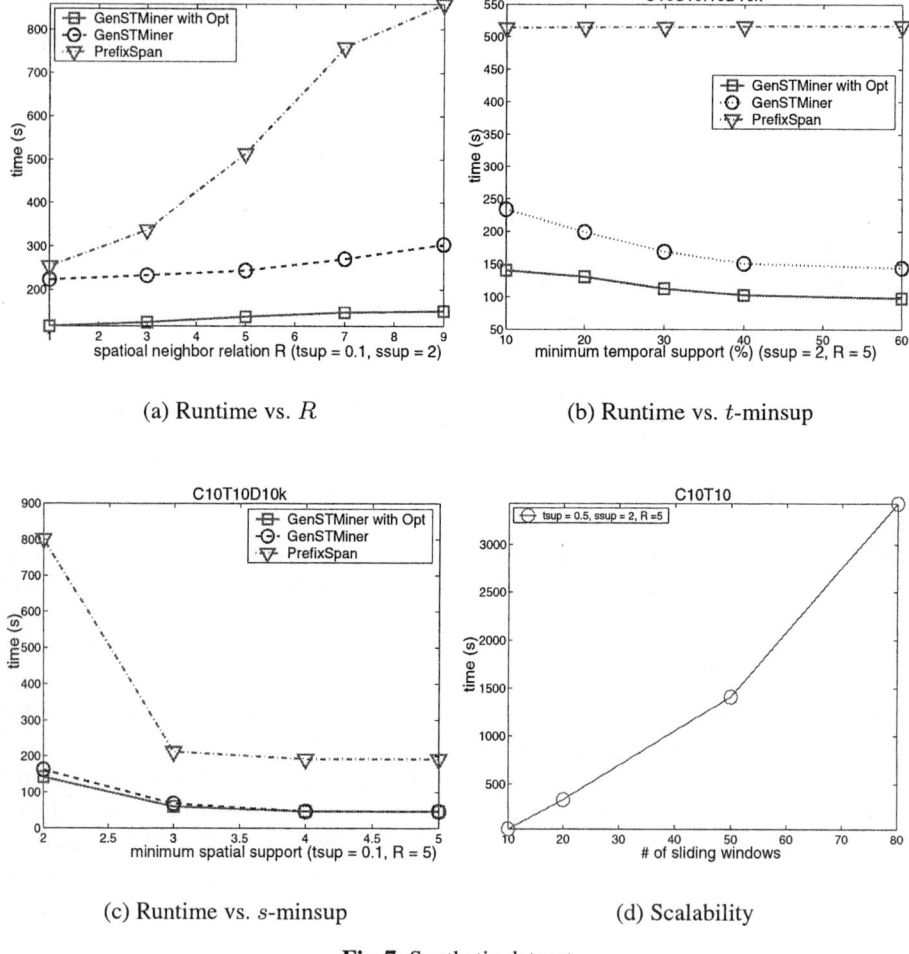

(a) Runtime vs. R

(b) Runtime vs. t-minsup

(c) Runtime vs. s-minsup

(d) Scalability

Fig. 7. Synthetic dataset

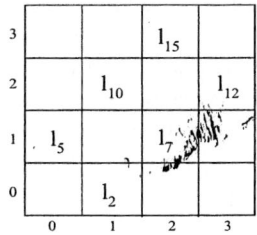
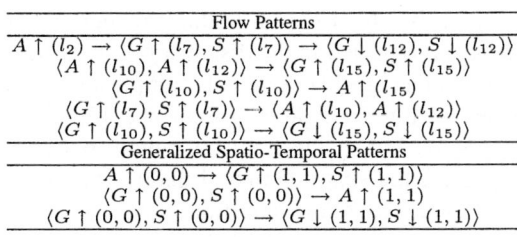

(a) Neighbour relations   (b) Interesting frequent patterns

Fig. 8. Comparison of flow patterns and generalized spatio-temporal patterns

Nation Data Buoy Center. The dataset has 10 features that are recorded hourly. After discretization, the final dataset contains 30 features. With these 30 features, we define a set of meteorological events. A sample of the events defined are as follows. $A \uparrow (l_a)$ (or $A \downarrow (l_a)$): denote the event that the air temperature at location l_a has increased (or decreased); $S \uparrow (l_a)$ (or $S \downarrow (l_a)$): denote the event that the wind speed at location l_a has increased (or decreased); and $G \uparrow (l_a)$ (or $G \downarrow (l_a)$): denote the event that the gust speed at location l_a has increased (or decreased).

We divide the whole space into 4×4 grids so that the 5 locations are distributed uniformly. Figure 8(a) shows the geographical positions of the 5 locations, namely l_2, l_7, l_{10}, l_{12} and l_{15}. FlowMiner[12] and GenSTMiner are applied on this dataset with t-minsup = 10, s-minsup = 2, $W = 6 days$ and $R = 2$. Figure 8(b) summarizes some of the interesting patterns we have found.

We observe that flow patterns are able to capture the flow of events such as: an increase of air temperature at location l_2 leads to an increase in wind speed and gust speed at location l_7; and an increase of air temperature at location l_{10} leads to an increase in wind speed and gust speed at location l_{15}. However, the usefulness of these flow patterns is rather limited as they are unable to provide a general trend. On the other hand, the generalized spatio-temporal pattern reveals the trend that whenever there is an increase of air temperature at a specific location, we can expect an increase in wind speed and gust speed at its Northeast neighbor. By knowing the general trend, the meteorologist is able to perform more accurate forecast of the weather.

6 Related Work

Spatial data mining and sequence mining have received a lot of attention. Much research has focused either on discovering spatial patterns, such as spatial association patterns [4] and co-location patterns [8], geographical features of co-location patterns [11], etc; or sequential patterns, such as mining frequent sequential patterns [2,6], mining closed sequential patterns [10] etc. Recently, with many applications of spatio-temporal data, knowledge discovery in spatio-temporal databases becomes more important.

Previous work on spatio-temporal data mining can be divided into two directions: (i) approaches focusing on finding frequent movements of objects over time, and (ii) approaches engaged in the discovery of evolution patterns of natural phenomena, such as forest coverage. In the case of multiple moving objects where trajectories are typically concatenated to a single long sequence, [7] proposed a method to optimize the mobile systems by finding the frequent motion patterns of objects. [5] studied the problem to optimize the spatio-temporal queries through the discovery of the spatio-temporal periodic patterns. At the same time, many methods proposed to find the evolution patterns of natural phenomena. [9] studied the discovery of frequent patterns related to changes of natrual phenomena in spatial regions. [12] introduced the discovery of flow patterns, which describe the change of the events over the space and time.

Our work is different from [12], because the generalized spatio-temporal patterns is locally frequent patterns, while the flow patterns are global ones. Moreover, the algorithm in [12] cannot be used to mine the generalized spatio-temporal patterns directly. While with some minor modifications, it can be used to mine the generalized spatio-temporal patterns, the complexity of its performance will be very high and it does not scale very well with respect to the number of frequent generalized spatio-temporal patterns, since it also follows the *candidate-maintenance-and-test* approach.

7 Conclusions

In this paper, we have introduced a new class of spatio-temporal patterns, called generalized spatio-temporal patterns. We have presented a framework *GenSTMiner* based on the methodology of the pattern growth method to discover the generalized spatio-temporal patterns. Some optimization techniques are presented to improve the efficiency of the GenSTMiner. Our experimental study indicates that with the optimization techniques, GenSTMiner improved its performance by an order of magnitude, and has a linear scalability in terms of the database size.

References

1. R. C. Agarwal, C. C. Aggarwal, and V. V. V. Prasad. Depth first generation of long patterns. *ACM SIGKDD*, 2001.
2. J. Ayres, J. Gehrke, T. Yiu, and J. Flannick. Sequential pattern mining using a bitmap representation. *ACM SIGKDD*, 2002.
3. J. Han, J. Pei, and Y. Yin. Mining frequent patterns by pattern-growth: Methodology and implications. *ACM SIGKDD*, 2001.
4. K. Koperski and J. Han. Discovery of spatial association rules in geographic information databases. *SSD*, 1995.
5. N. Mamoulis, H. Cao, G. Kollios, M. Hadjieleftheriou, Y. Tao, and D. Cheung. Mining, indexing, and querying historical spatiotemporal data. *ACM SIGKDD*, 2004.
6. J. Pei, J. Han, and B. Mortazavi-Asl. Prefixspan: Mining sequential patterns efficiently by prefix-projected pattern growth. *ICDE*, 2001.
7. W. Peng and M. Chen. Developing data allocation schemes by incremental mining of users moving patterns in a mobile computing system. *IEEE TKDE*, 2003.
8. S. Shekhar and Y. Huang. Discovery of spatial co-location patterns. *SSTD*, 2001.

9. I. Tsoukatos and D. Gunopulos. Efficient mining of spatiotemporal patterns. *SSTD*, 2001.
10. J. Wang and J. Han. Bide: Efficient mining of frequent closed sequences. *ICDE*, 2004.
11. J. Wang, W. Hsu, and M. L. Lee. Discovering geographical features for location-based services. *DASFAA*, 2004.
12. J. Wang, W. Hsu, M. L. Lee, and J. Wang. Flowminer: Finding flow patterns in spatio-temporal databases. *ICTAI*, 2004.

Exploiting Temporal Correlation in Temporal Data Warehouses*

Ying Feng, Hua-Gang Li, Divyakant Agrawal, and Amr El Abbadi

Department of Computer Science,
University of California, Santa Barbara
{yingf, huagang, agrawal, amr}@cs.ucsb.edu

Abstract. Data is typically incorporated in a data warehouse in increasing order of time. Furthermore, the MOLAP data cube tends to be sparse because of the large cardinality of the time dimension. We propose an approach to improve the efficiency of range aggregate queries on MOLAP data cubes in a temporal data warehouse by factoring out the time-related dimensions. These time-related dimensions are handled separately to take advantage of the monotonic trend over time. The proposed technique captures local data trends with respect to time by partitioning data points into blocks, and then uses a *perfect binary block tree* as an index structure to achieve logarithmic time complexity for both incremental updates and data retrievals. Experimental results establish the scalability and efficiency of the proposed approach on various datasets.

1 Introduction

Most applications such as environmental studies, census databases and telecommunication systems generate large amounts of temporal data. The notion of time is critically involved in such applications and its semantics has been recently discussed to make decision-making queries in data warehouses more efficient. In fact, data items often have time-related attributes, e.g., time of a sales transaction or an order and the shipping date of a product.

Temporal datasets distinguish themselves due to the existence of one or more time dimensions. First of all, these time dimensions are usually of high cardinality, which implies that the datasets are sparse when taking the time dimension into consideration. Thus if we just consider the data at one time slice, say the records at one specific date in a daily transaction summary data cube, there might be only one record. Second, there is typically a correlation between the value of time attribute and other attributes of the data items incorporated into the data collections. For example, sales transactions are recorded in a timely manner and hence the earlier a sales transaction posted, the earlier the shipping date. Another example is that the stock price may increase over a period of time and may keep on falling during another period. We refer to such datasets as

---

* This work has been supported by the NSF under grant numbers CNF-04-23336, IIS-02-23022 and EIA-00-80134.

append-only data [9] since the updates can only affect data items with the latest time coordinate. Third, time evolving data grow rapidly, thus requiring rapid integration into the data warehouses.

These characteristics of temporal datasets impose challenges to data analysis in MOLAP data cubes. The time dimension and its correlated dimensions lead to a high degree of sparsity in a traditional array-structure [14] based MOLAP data cubes, like the *prefix sum cube* [6] and *hierarchical cubes* [3]. Either the result induces huge storage costs because of the large cardinality of time-related dimensions [6], or large query overhead to answer time-parameterized range queries for a data cube is involved to retrieve all data points in the query range.

The temporal aggregation problem was studied in [12, 11, 13, 10] to address the challenges of temporal data. These works concentrate on one time-related attribute and most deal with time-interval data. In addition, Riedewald et al. [9] proposed efficient range aggregation in temporal data warehouses by exploiting the append-only property of the time-related dimension. In practice we also observe that many datasets have multiple time-related attributes and they usually have some semantic relationship. One such semantics is referred to as the Multi-Append-Only-Trend (MAOT) property in [8]. [8] studied the range aggregate queries over datasets with multiple append-only dimensions. The solution assumes some ε-bound to restrict the MAOT property in the datasets, i.e. two time-related attributes cannot deviate by more than ε from each other. In this paper, we show that such restriction is not necessary, and propose a general approach for efficiently answering range aggregate queries over several time-related dimensions in temporal data warehouses.

Multiple range aggregate queries make trend analysis possible. For instance, *"what is the total value of all orders in California which were ordered in the first half of July 2002 and shipped in August or later?"*. Our approach factors out the time-correlated dimensions to reduce the sparsity of MOLAP data cubes. For the time-related dimensions, we capture the local trend by partitioning points into blocks and index blocks with a *perfect binary block tree*. Our index structure allows efficient integration and aggregation of append-only data with logarithmic incremental update and search complexity. Moreover, they can be maintained in an online fashion, which may be used to provide real-time analysis for human analysts in massive data streaming applications [4].

The rest of the paper is organized as follows. In Section 2, a general model for MAOT datasets is presented. In Section 3, we propose data structures exploiting the semantics of time-correlated dimensions, on which the range aggregate query processing algorithm in Section 4 is based. In Section 5, we empirically evaluate our technique by using both synthetic and real datasets. Conclusions and future research work are provided in Section 6.

2 A Data Model

In this section, we propose a simplified and general data model for *Append-Only-With-Trend* datasets. Let $\mathcal{D}$ denote a data set with d dimensional attributes $\delta_1, \ldots, \delta_d$. Let (X^d, v), $X^d = (x_1, \ldots, x_d)$, refer to a data point in $\mathcal{D}$ and its measure value is v. A multi-dimensional range query $\texttt{RQuery}(L^d, U^d)$ specifies a lower-bound query point

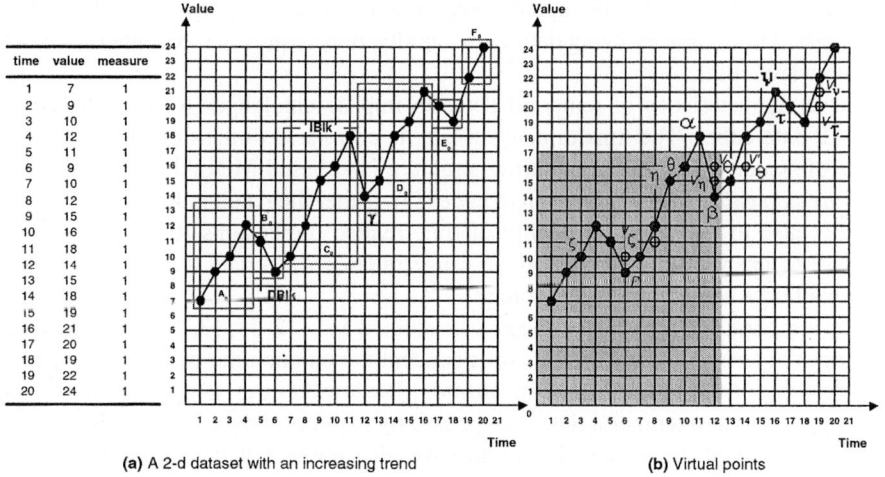

Fig. 1. Example of append-only-with-trend data sets

$L^d = (L_1, \ldots, L_d)$ and an upper-bound query point $U^d = (U_1, \ldots, U_d)$. The query selects all data points X^d that satisfy $L_i \leq x_i \leq U_i$ for all dimensions δ_i. A **range aggregate query** applies an aggregate operator (e.g. SUM) over the measure values of all the data points selected. It is called as **prefix range aggregate query** when the lower-bound query point is $(0, \ldots, 0)$. The d-dimensional dataset $\mathcal{D}$ is an **Append-Only-With-Trend** dataset if it has the following properties:

1. One of its dimensions, say δ_1, is a *temporal dimension* (T-dimension). Data points are always appended on T-dimension.
2. d_v of its dimensions, say $\delta_2, \ldots, \delta_{d_v+1}$, are *value dimensions* (V-dimensions), which are time-correlated dimensions. The V-coordinates maintain either a non-decreasing or a non-increasing trend approximately.
3. v is the measure dimension, on which the aggregate operators could apply.

The value dimension here also captures the *valid time dimension* in bitemporal databases [7]. The approximate trend implies that the probability that a data point is off the trend decreases as the distance increases.

Figure 1 shows an example of a two-dimensional append-only dataset, which exhibits an append-only trend on the `time` dimension and approximately increasing trend in the `value` dimension. RQuery$((0,0), (12.5, 17))$ is a (prefix) range aggregate query whose T-dimension range is $[0, 12.5]$ and V-dimension range is $[0, 17]$.

In the paper, we mainly discuss the case when $d_v = 1$, that is, there is one V-dimension in addition to the temporal dimension, since there is an important class of applications with two time-related dimensions, for example, the bitemporal databases [7]. To simplify the following discussion, we assume that no two data points have the same coordinate in the T-dimension. We will discuss later how to deal with two data points with the same T-coordinates. Furthermore, our discussion is based on the aggregate operator of SUM. However it can be easily extended to incorporate other invertible aggregate operators such as COUNT and AVG [9].

3 Data Structures for Range Queries

In this section we present how to store and index two dimensional append-only-with-trend datasets for efficient range aggregate query processing. The main idea is to partition the dataset into monotonic blocks and then index these blocks using a *perfect binary block tree*.

3.1 Partitioning Data Points

Range queries on a sequence of data points can be performed efficiently using binary search if the data are monotonic in all dimensions. In order to exploit this monotonic property to support efficient range queries, we partition the datasets into blocks. Each block contains a sequence of consecutive data points with a non-decreasing or non-increasing trend. Particularly in terms of a two-dimensional append-only-with-trend dataset, the monotonic trend of a block can be differentiated w.r.t. the V-coordinates of data points as the T-coordinates always follow a non-decreasing trend. Depending on the monotonicity, each block can be categorized as either IBlk or DBlk, where IBlk represents a non-decreasing block and DBlk represents a non-increasing block.

In Figure 1(a), the data points are partitioned into six blocks according to the trend of their V-dimension values. Since the dataset follows an overall non-decreasing trend approximately in this example, there are more IBlk blocks than DBlk blocks, and DBlk blocks contain fewer data points than IBlk blocks.

Partitioning an append-only-with-trend dataset can be performed in an online manner. When a new data point is appended, it is compared with the most recent data point in the current block. If it does not follow the trend of the current block, the current block is ended and the new data point starts a new block. Each block contains at least two data points, since at least two data points determine a trend.

3.2 Maintaining Aggregate Information in Blocks

In order to avoid aggregation on-the-fly when answering range aggregate queries, we maintain cumulative information for each data point so that the range aggregate query can be answered by accessing a constant number of points [6]; Therefore each data point P maintains two kinds of aggregate information: (1) the aggregates of all data points occurring until data point P, named the *prefix sum* (PSUM); (2) the aggregates of those data points occurring until data point P with V-dimension values no greater than data point P's V-dimension value, named the *partial prefix sum* (PPSUM).

Suppose there is a range sum query, whose T-dimension range is $[7, 10]$ and V-dimension range is $[11, 17]$. The range sum query falls into block C_0 shown in Figure 1. Hence the query result is the difference between the PSUM of data point $(10, 16)$ and the PSUM of data point $(8, 12)$. For another example query $((0, 0), (8, 10))$, the PPSUM of data point $(7, 10)$ in Figure 1 is the answer.

From the above, we observe that if all the data points within the T-dimension query range are also within the V-dimension query range, the query can be answered using the PSUM of the data point closest to the T-dimension boundary. Otherwise, some of the data points within the T-dimension query range might jump out of the V-dimension query range. In this case, we need to find the data point closest to both the T-dimension and V-dimension upper boundaries of a range aggregate query, so that we can use the PPSUM of that data point as an answer. However, it is possible that the data point closest to the T-dimension boundary is not closest to the V-dimension. For the query $((0,0),(12.5,17))$ in Figure 1(b), data point β is closest to T-dimension boundary 12.5. However, the earlier point θ is closer to the V-dimension boundary than β. So we introduce the notion of *virtual points* by mapping the V-coordinate of point θ at point β.

A *virtual point* at point P is the projection of an earlier data point at point P, whose V-dimension values fall in the interval between point P and its immediately previous point. For example, the virtual point V_θ at point β is the projection of point θ at point β. When the V-dimension values are monotonic w.r.t the T-dimension, no virtual points need to be kept. The smoother the data points, the less virtual points are kept. Figure 1(b) shows all the virtual points (represented by empty dots) added.

The following summarizes the aggregate information maintained for each data point and the aggregate information stored at an example block D_0 is shown in Figure 2.

- the PSUM of data point P: the aggregate information of all data points whose T-coordinates are no greater than the T-coordinate of P.
- the PPSUM of data point P: the aggregate information of all data points whose T-coordinates are no greater than the T-coordinate of P and V-coordinates are no greater than the V-coordinate of P.
- the V-coordinates of virtual points at point P: the V-coordinates of all data points which are earlier than data point P and whose V-coordinates are between the V-coordinate of P and the V-coordinate of the data point preceding P.
- the PPSUM of each virtual point at point P: the PPSUM of the virtual point whose T-coordinate is no greater than that of data point P and V-coordinate is maintained as above.

The aggregate information and virtual points above can be maintained in an online fashion. We keep a list of all V-dimension values. When a new data point arrives, we check the list to derive the virtual points and their partial prefix sums. The PSUM and PPSUM of the new data point can be computed by its own measure value and the aggregate information of its preceding point. The time complexity to maintain the information above for a new data point is bounded by $log(n) + k$, where n is the number of data points and k is the number of virtual points in the interval. In worst case, the number of virtual points for the new data point is no more than $min\{n, D\}$, where D is the cardinality of the V-dimension. If a data set follows some trend approximately, the actual virtual points are much fewer as analyzed later.

3.3 The Index Structure

We index blocks which contain data points using a *perfect binary block tree*. Each leaf node corresponds to a block with its summary information including the interval in the V-dimension and the end point, as well as a pointer to the block as shown in Figure 2. For example leaf node A_0 in Figure 2 corresponds to block A_0 in Figure 1(a).

Every two leaf nodes at level 0 are grouped together by an internal node at level 1. An internal node contains the union of V-dimension intervals of its child nodes. Every two consecutive nodes at level i are grouped together as a node at level $i+1$ recursively until reaching the root node. For example, in Figure 2, the internal node A_1 contains

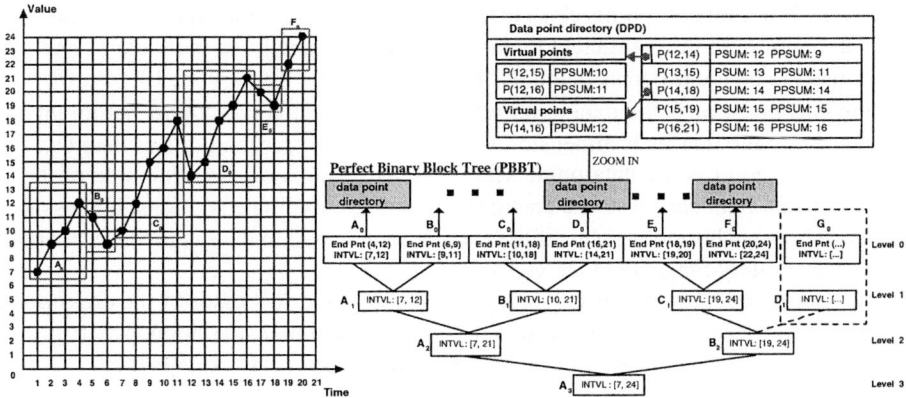

Fig. 2. Perfect binary block tree

the V-dimension intervals of data points in both block A_0 and block B_0 in Figure 1(a), which is the union of the V-dimension intervals of node A_0 and B_0 at the leaf level (level 0). It is possible that the last node at each level could be the only child node (left child) of its parent node, such as node C_1 shown in Figure 2, which is the only single left child node of node B_2.

A *perfect binary block tree* (PBBT) has some nice properties since it is based on a perfect binary tree. The level of the PBBT tree is no more than $\lceil log_2 N_B \rceil$, where N_B is the number of blocks. The total number of internal nodes is no more than N_B.

When a new block is appended as a new leaf node, the *perfect binary block tree* can be updated online as follows.

- If the last node in the leaf level is the only child of its parent, the new block is inserted as the sibling of the last node. Then the V-dimension interval of their parent node is updated accordingly to be the union of both nodes' V-dimension intervals. Then their parent node propagates the updates to their ancestor nodes level by level until the root node is reached.
- If every leaf node has a sibling, a new parent node is created in level 1 for the new block with the same V-dimension interval as that of the new block. Similarly this process is propagated level by level until the root node is reached. If a new node needs to be added to the topmost level, the number of levels is increased by one.

Since the total number of levels is $\lceil log_2 N_B \rceil$, the time complexity to append a new block is logarithmic. For the example in Figure 2, if a new leaf node, G_0, is added, a new node D_1 will be added as G_0's parent. Thus node G_0 will be the only child of node D_1 which has the same V-dimension interval as node G_0. If node D_1 is added at level 1, it is grouped with the only child node of C_1 and the V-dimension intervals of all their ancestor nodes will be updated accordingly to include node D_1's V-dimension interval.

4 Range Aggregate Query Processing

We start with prefix range aggregate queries, represented as $((0,0), (U_t, U_v))$ and extend to the general range aggregate queries later. The underlying idea of prefix query processing is to find data points close to the upper boundaries of the query such that their aggregate information is sufficient to answer the query exactly. In particular, three data points need to be identified sequentially for a prefix query $\texttt{RQuery}((0,0),(U_t,U_v))$.

- the *anchor point* is the data point whose T-coordinate is the largest but no greater than U_t. Note that its V-dimension value could be greater than or less than U_v.
- the *cross point* is the data point whose V-coordinate is on the other side of the V-dimension boundary w.r.t the anchor point and T-coordinate is closest but less than that of the anchor point. Thus if the anchor point is within the range, the cross point is out of query range and vice versa.
- the *closest point* is the virtual data point stored at the successor of the cross point, whose V-coordinate is closest to and within the V-dimension boundary. If it does not exist, it can be either the cross point or the successor as explained later.

4.1 Prefix Query Processing Algorithm

The general idea of the prefix range query algorithm is to find the closest point by finding the anchor point and its cross point. With respect to the relative position of its anchor point, prefix queries can be classified into two categories: (1) Anchor-out prefix query if the anchor point $P_a(a_t, a_v)$ is outside the V-dimension query boundary, i.e., $a_v > U_v$; (2) Anchor-in prefix query if the anchor point is below the V-dimension query upper boundary, i.e., $a_v \leq U_v$.

Anchor-Out Prefix Query Processing For this case, the cross point, P_{cross}, is the data point within the query having the greatest T-coordinate. It can be obtained by searching the prefect binary block tree as follows.

First we check if the start point of Blk_U is inside the query. If so, it means the cross point is in Blk_U and a binary search is performed to find it. Otherwise a bottom-up search process from Blk_U is performed as follows. From Blk_U in level 0, traverse the perfect binary block tree through the parent links until reaching a node which has a left sibling whose V-dimension interval covers U_v or the root node. If the root node is reached, there is *no cross point* and hence the query returns zero as the query result. Otherwise, a top-down search process is performed from the node's left sibling to identify the block Blk_C in level 0, whose V-dimension interval covers U_v. Note that in the top-down search process, the right branch of a node is always searched first as it contains points with greater T-dimension values. Once Blk_C is obtained, a binary search is performed in the data point directory of Blk_C to identify P_{cross}. The general algorithm for identifying the cross point from the anchor point is in Appendix.

If the cross point is close enough to the V-dimension boundary U_v, that is, no other point within the query range is closer to U_v, the cross point is chosen as the closest point and its PPSUM is used to answer the query. However, if there exists such data point within the range whose V-coordinate is closest to U_v, its V-coordinate must be within the V-dimension interval between the cross point and its successor and its T-coordinate must be smaller than the cross point. In this case, the data point is stored as a virtual point as described previously, and hence we choose the virtual point corresponding to the data point closest to U_v as the closest point.

Consider the prefix query $\texttt{RQuery}((0,0),(16.5,17))$ shown in Figure 3(a). Blk_U, block D_0(Figure 1) is first identified by a binary search. Then the anchor point P_{anchor}

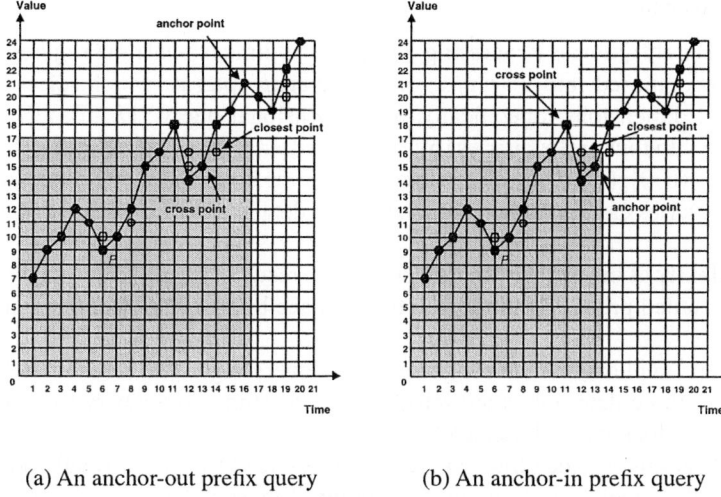

(a) An anchor-out prefix query   (b) An anchor-in prefix query

Fig. 3. Two types of prefix queries

$(16, 21)$ is identified by a binary search in the data point directory maintained in D_0. Since the V-coordinate of $P_{anchor}(16, 21)$ is greater than the upper bound of V-dimension, 17, it is an anchor-out prefix query. Now the cross point needs to be identified by traversing the perfect binary block tree (Figure 2) as described before. In this example, as the V-dimension interval of D_0 covers 17, traversing the tree is not needed. A binary search can be performed directly in the data point directory maintained in D_0 to identify the cross point, which is $P_{cross}(13, 15)$. Then virtual points at $P_{successor}$ whose V-coordinate is between the cross point and its next point are searched to identify the closest point, which results in a virtual point $P_{closest}(14, 16)$. The query returns $P_{closest}(14, 16)$.PPSUM as the result. The process is formalized in the prefix search algorithm in Appendix.

Anchor-In Prefix Query Processing Anchor-in prefix queries can be processed in a similar way to anchor-out prefix queries. The cross point is out of boundary in this case as shown in Figure 3(b) and can be found in the same way as before.

If the cross point exists, it is the data point which is outside the V-dimension range with the greatest T-coordinate. If no such cross point exists, then every data point preceding the anchor point must be within the given query range. Hence, P_{anchor}.PSUM gives the query result. The successor point of the cross point, $P_{successor}$, must have a V-coordinate less than or equal to the V-dimension upper bound. If any virtual point at $P_{successor}$, whose V-coordinate is the largest but less than the V-dimension upper bound, it is the closest point. Otherwise, $P_{successor}$ is the closest point.

As $P_{closest}$.PPSUM gives the aggregate information of all those data points preceding $P_{successor}$ (inclusive) within the query and $(P_{anchor}.\text{PSUM} - P_{successor}.\text{PSUM})$ gives the aggregate information of all those points after $P_{successor}$, the query answer is the $P_{closest}.\text{PPSUM} + (P_{anchor}.\text{PSUM} - P_{successor}.\text{PSUM})$. The processing of the example query shown in Figure 3(b) is similar to the example query in Figure 3(a). The complete prefix query algorithm is summarized in Appendix.

4.2 Discussion

Range Aggregate Queries Processing Given any d-dimensional range aggregate query, it can be decomposed into 2^d *prefix range aggregate queries* which select half-open ranges in all dimensions. Specifically, a 2-dimensional query $((L_t, L_v), (U_t, U_v))$ is decomposed into four prefix queries [6]: $((0,0), (U_t, U_v)) - ((0,0), (L_t, U_v)) - ((0,0), (U_t, L_v)) + ((0,0), (L_t, L_v))$. Since they share some boundaries, the processing of the four prefix queries can be further optimized. The details are omitted due to space limit.

The Complexity of the Algorithm We present the result of the algorithm analysis briefly here. The detailed proof is omitted due to the space limit. Let n denote the number of data points.

The time complexity of our range aggregate query algorithm is $O(log(n))$. This is because only three data points are retrieved and the time complexity to search in the perfect binary block tree is bounded by $O(log(n))$.

The perfect binary block tree, whose size is bounded by $O(n)$, usually could reside in memory. The block containing the data point of interest can be retrieved from disk. If the V-dimension follows a monotonic trend approximately, the disk space needed for the pre-computed aggregate information is $O(n)$ with high probability. Moreover, if the V-dimension values are from a finite domain, the space complexity is also $O(n)$. However, in the worst case, that is, the domain is infinite and the virtual points stored at each data point increase linearly over time, the disk space cost can be $O(n^2)$.

Data Points with Common T-coordinates The assumption that no two data points has the same T-coordinates can be relaxed as follows. Suppose k data points with the same T-coordinate T_i, and their next data point has T-coordinate T_{i+1}. If the current block at T_i is IBlk, that is, non-decreasing block, we order the k data points according to the ascending V-coordinates, otherwise, sort them in the descending order of V-coordinates. We replace the T-coordinates of ordered k data points with $T_{(i+1),1}, T_{(i+1),2}, ..., T_{(i+1),k}$ accordingly. The new T-coordinates satisfy $T_i < T_{(i+1),1} < T_{(i+1),2} < ... < T_{(i+1),k} < T_{i+1}$. Since the domain size on the T-dimension does not affect the complexity of the algorithm, the asymptotic cost is not affected by this transformation.

Limiting the Size of Each Block If a long sequence of data points follows the same trend, the block size might grow too large. The size of each block does not affect the logarithmic time bound of range aggregate query processing, but we need to load a large block into memory. In this case, we could split the block into several blocks by imposing a threshold on the number of data points in the block. Since our algorithm does not require two consecutive blocks to have different trends, the correctness of our algorithm still holds.

5 Experimental Evaluation

We perform experiments on both synthetic datasets and real datasets and compare our perfect binary block tree (PBBT) with R^* tree [1], which is the most popular multi-dimensional index structure and implemented in commercial RDBMS. Note that for a

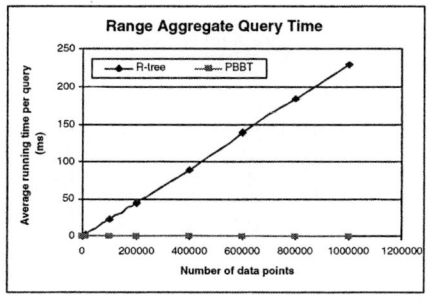 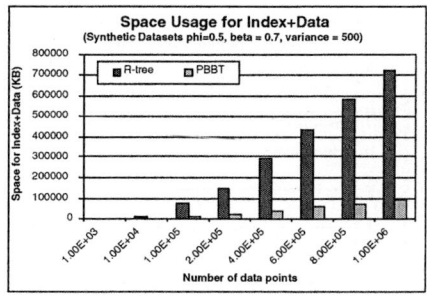

(a) per query time vs. dataset size (b) space required vs. dataset size

Fig. 4. Evaluating the impact of the dataset size

d-dimensional dataset, we assume two time-related dimensions. We measure the total space cost for both data and index structure, and the average per query time cost. We study how performance changes with varying dataset size and the degree of randomness, as explained in Section 5.1.

The implementations of both approaches are in Gnu C++. We use the R*-tree implementation by M. Hadjieleftheriou [5]. The experiments are performed on Mandrake Linux 9.0 running on AthelonXP1800 1533MHZ PC with 1G RAM and 50G disk. We assign the same amount of memory to both implementations for fair comparisons.

Two kinds of queries are used in the experiments: uniform queries and biased queries. The uniform queries are generated by choosing the T-dimension query range uniformly from t_{min} to t_{max} and the V-dimension range from v_{min} to v_{max}. The biased queries follow the distribution of data points, so that the query selectivity can be controlled. The query boundaries are generated using Gaussian distribution with the expected query range. The details of experimental setup are omitted due to space limit.

5.1 Experiments on Synthetic Datasets

We evaluate the effect of the dataset size and the degree of randomness using synthetic datasets with uniform queries, which contain queries with different levels of selectivity.

The synthetic datasets are generated from some popular time series models [2]: random walk and Auto-Regression model (AR(1)). We need to add a linear trend to the stationary AR(1) model to satisfy our append-only-with-trend data model. These two models can be captured with the equation below with different parameter settings:

$$V(t) = \phi * V(t-1) + \beta * t + \alpha_t$$

where α_t is a random variable following the normal distribution (a.k.a white noise) with mean 0. The variance of α_t represents how widely the random factor can go. When $\phi = 1$ and $\beta = 0$, it is a random walk. When ϕ is within the range $(-1, 1)$ and $\beta = 0$, it is a stationary AR(1) time series model. β represents the linear trend of the time series data. ϕ represents how the current value is correlated to the previous value. When $\phi = 1$ as in the case of a random walk, the data are smoother than the case of $|\phi| < 1$ in AR(1)

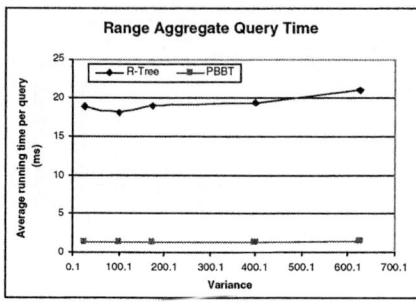 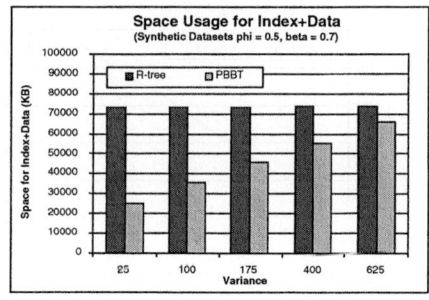

(a) per query time vs. randomness (b) space required vs. randomness

Fig. 5. Evaluating the impact of randomness

model. The experimental results on random walk data always outperform the results for AR(1) model with linear trend. Given the lack of space, we only report the experiments on the latter case.

Figure 4 demonstrates the scalability of our approach (PBBT) with increasing dataset size. The parameters in the synthetic dataset are fixed at $\phi = 0.5$ and $\beta = 0.7$ and the variance of the random variable is 500. We can see our approach is fairly scalable even when the dataset size increased from 1K to 1M, the per query time does not increase more than three times as shown in Figure 4(a). The space in Figure 4(b) increases linearly with the dataset size. This is consistent with our analysis of linear space and logarithmic time complexity. The query time grows linearly for R*-tree, since the number of nodes accessed is proportional to the dataset size in the case. Also the rate of increases in space for R*-tree is significantly larger than that of our approach.

The query time saving of our approach comes from two aspects: precomputed aggregate information and fewer disk I/Os resulting from constant number of disk accesses. We use the perfect binary block tree to decide the block of data that needs to load into memory, so the disk access time is constant per query if the binary tree can always be accommodated in memory. Since the perfect binary tree has the same number of internal nodes as blocks and each node contains only the boundary information, the total size of the index structure is actually small enough to fit in the main memory in practice.

Another factor we consider is the randomness of the data (Figure 5). We change the variance of the random variable α from 25, 100, 175, 400 to 625. More points will jump off the trend further with the increased randomness. In this case, more virtual points need to be stored and the space cost increases. However, since the query time complexity is logarithmic to the number of points as analyzed before, the query time deteriorates slightly with the increased randomness(variance of the trend).

5.2 Experiments on Real Dataset

We also evaluate the performance of the proposed approach on a real dataset: the daily industry average open price of the Dow Jones stocks for the last 74 years. It is available from http://finance.yahoo.com/. There are 18,656 data points in the dataset and the value

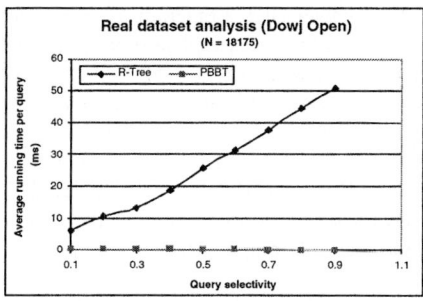

Fig. 6. per query time on stock price dataset

ranges from 41.63 to 11719.19. To maintain the precision to 0.01, we enlarge the domain size 100 times. The time-related dimensions are the date and the daily open price, while we use the stock volume as the measure dimension.

We evaluate the query performance with the selectivity using biased queries. The experiment results in Figure 6 show that our approach has fairly stable query time w.r.t query selectivity. The query time using R*-tree index increases linearly with the selectivity. The reason is that R*-tree needs to visit all data points in the range. In contrast, our approach (PBBT) only used 4M bytes disk space and R*-tree used more than 14M bytes. In summary, the experiments demonstrate the effectiveness of our approach in a variety of time series datasets.

6 Conclusion

We proposed an effective approach for range aggregate query processing in append-only datasets with two time-related dimensions. Our approach improves the MOLAP efficiency on the sparse append-only datasets by factoring out the two time-related dimensions and makes the query cost independent of the query length. A novel data structure, the perfect binary block tree, is proposed to allow logarithmic time complexity to append data and query processing. This idea can be extended to multiple time-correlated dimensions. However, this naïve extension of the two-dimensional algorithm compromises the performance efficiency. In this case, the logarithmic time complexity for query processing cannot be guaranteed. How to improve the efficiency on more time-related dimensions is one of our future works.

References

1. N. Beckmann, H. Kriegel, R. Schneider, and B. Seeger. The r* -tree: An efficient and robust access method for points and rectangles. In *Proc. Int. Conf. on Management of Data (SIGMOD)*, pages 322–331, 1900.
2. P. J. Brockwell and R. A. Davis. *Introduction to Time Series and Forecasting*. Springer, 2002.
3. C.-Y. Chan and Y.E. Ioannidis. Hierarchical cubes for range-sum queries. In *Proc. Int. Conf. on Very Large Data Bases (VLDB)*, pages 675–686, 1999.

4. Yixin Chen, Guozhu Dong, Jiawei Han, Benjamin W. Wah, and Jianyong Wang. Multi-dimensional regression analysis of time-series data streams. In *Proc. Int. Conf. on Very Large Data Bases (VLDB)*, pages 323–334, 2002.
5. Marios Hadjieleftheriou. C++/java spatial index library. http://www.cs.ucr.edu/marioh/spatialindex/index.html, 2004.
6. C. Ho, R. Agrawal, N. Megiddo, and R. Srikant. Range queries in olap data cubes. In *Proc. Int. Conf. on Management of Data (SIGMOD)*, pages 73–88, 1997.
7. C. S. Jensen and et al. *Temporal Databases - Research and Practice*, volume 1399 of *LNCS*, chapter The Consensus Glossary of Temporal Database Concepts, pages 367–405. Springer Verlag, 1998.
8. Hua-Gang Li, Divyakant Agrawal, Ami El Abbadi, and Mirek Riedewald. Exploiting the multi-append-only-trend property of historical data in data warehouses. In *Proc. Int. Symp. on Spatial and Temporal Databases (SSTD03)*, pages 179–198, 2003.
9. M. Riedewald, D. Agrawal, and A. El Abbadi. Efficient integration and aggregation of historical information. In *Proc. ACM SIGMOD Int. Conf. on Management of Data*, pages 13–24, 2002.
10. Yufei Tao, Dimitris Papadias, and Christos Faloutsos. Approximate tempral aggregation. In *Proc. Int. Conf. on Data Engineering (ICDE)*, 2004.
11. Jun Yang. *Temporal Data Warehousing*. PhD thesis, Stanford University, 2001.
12. Jun Yang and Jeniffer Widom. Incremental computation and maintenance of temporal aggregates. In *Proc. Int. Conf. on Data Engineering (ICDE)*, 2001.
13. Donghui Zhang, Alexander Markowetz, Vassilis J. Tsotras, Dimitrios Gunopulos, and Bernhard Seeger. Efficient computation of temporal aggregates with range predicates. In *Proc. Int. Conf. on Principles of Database Systems(PODS)*, 2001.
14. Y. Zhao, P. M. Deshpande, and J. F. Naughton. An array-based algorithm for simultaneous multidimensional aggregates. In *Proc. Int. Conf. on Management of Data (SIGMOD)*, pages 150–170, 1997.

Semantic Characterization of Real World Events

Aparna Nagargadde[1], Sridhar Varadarajan[1], and Krithi Ramamritham[2]

[1] Applied Research Group, Satyam Computer Services Limited,
Entrepreneurship Centre, IISc Campus, Bangalore - 560012, INDIA
{aparna_nagargadde, sridhar}@satyam.com
[2] Indian Institute of Technology-Bombay Powai, Mumbai 400 076, INDIA
krithi@cse.iitb.ac.in

Abstract. Reducing the latency of information delivery in an event driven world has always been a challenge. It is often necessary to completely capture the attributes of events and relationships between them, so that the process of retrieval of event related information is efficient. In this paper, we discuss a formal system for representing and analyzing real world events to address these issues. The event representation discussed in this paper accounts for the important event attributes, namely, time, space, and label. We introduce the notion of *sequence templates* that not only provides event related semantics but also helps in semantically analyzing user queries. Finally, we discuss the design for our Query-Event Analysis System, which is an integrated system to (a) identify a best sequence template given a user query; (b) select events based on the best sequence template; and (c) determine content related to the selected events for delivering to users.

1 Introduction

Real world events are of interest to people with diverse interests. For example, when the event 'Cricket match' is in progress, the queries from users could span a wide-range such as "What's the current run-rate?," "How many wickets are down?," "What was the highest total chased successfully on this ground?," "What is the history of matches played here?," and so on. The ability to semantically characterize the events enhances the scope and flexibility of the event management system in answering these complex queries.

There is a need to formally address the issues related to representation and analysis of real-world events. Some of these issues include (a) Characterization of event attributes (b) Identification of event relationships (c) Identification of composite and derived events (d) Derivation of additional information from a set of events (e) Closures on real world events, and (f) Processing of event related information in order to answer user queries, based on a set of events. In this paper, we describe a formal framework to clearly address these issues. In building our formal framework, we draw upon the various advances in the fields of temporal semantics, spatial semantics and event composition in distributed systems. However, though these advances address the various facets of the issue of semantics of real world events, there is no comprehensive formalization of representation of real world events. Real world events are characterized by temporal, spatial and label attributes; the lack of even one attribute would result in an incomplete characterization of the event. For example, the event "Kaif hits half-century at Lords" is incomplete without the time stamp *13th July 2002*, location *Lords* and an event tag (label) *half-century by Kaif*. The formalism presented in this paper represents a holistic approach to the analysis of the temporal, spatial and label attributes of real world events.

The main contributions of this work include a) Event representation in terms of temporal, spatial and label attributes b) The use of domain-specific hierarchies along temporal, spatial and label dimensions for enhanced semantic analysis, c) The definition of event closures in conjunction with these domain specific hierarchies in order to recognize the similarities between otherwise unrelated events d) The use of comprehensive sequence templates for semantic analysis of events and e) A system that aggregates, creates events with a view to answer diverse user queries. We also discuss the problem of event analysis in a real world scenario and present a methodology of identifying *meta events* from an event history by means of sequence templates. Most of the scenarios in this paper are drawn from the realm of international cricket, in particular from the NATWEST series in 2002 [14] A table of the various terms used in the realm of cricket is found in the technical report [3].

1.1 Related Work

Event representation and analysis has been an area of active research. In particular, the temporal nature and properties of events have been widely studied. The representation of time and temporal relationships has been addressed in several papers, notably [2]. Though the temporal and spatial attributes of events have been widely studied, there are very few event specification languages that support a unified view of both these attributes in the case of real world events. Composite event detection by means of using event templates has also been proposed in several papers [4], [5], [12]. But the proposed event templates do not consider the temporal, spatial and label event attributes holistically. Table. 1 depicts a comparison of the related work in this sphere. *Derived events* represent all those events that can be generated using the various event operators and closures. In the real world, event input is received through several loosely coupled event sensors/detectors. We employ the temporal frameworks suggested in [11], [12] to order the event input for processing. We subscribe to the use of interval-based semantics [1] for composite event detection. Two aspects are important in the case of real world events: event attributes and event content. Event attributes must be able to provide adequate cues for the automatic generation and dissemination of event contents. For example, in the case of an event *Six* by a batsman in an ODI match, it is required to automatically generate a video clip depicting the batsman hitting the ball directly outside the boundary line. We suggest that the sequence templates, introduced in this paper, can play an important role in this content generation activity. In our related papers [6],[13], we have described issues related to content generation and dissemination.

Table 1. Comparison of related work

Ref	Temporal Dimension	Spatial Dimension	Additional Event Dimensions	Derived Events	Model used to capture Derived Events
1	Interval Based Semantics	--	Event Type used to identify other attributes	Event expressions using temporal relationships	Event Graphs
9					Full power coloured petri nets
5, 8	Detection Based Semantics				Coloured petri nets
4		Considered in broader context of event attributes		--	Behavioural Models
7	Interval Based Semantics	Spatial Dimension of multiple objects in event scene are based on bounding box description	Used in description of objects within the video	Spatiotemporal relationships between objects in multiple scenes used to derive events	Specified Using Bilbvideo Query Language
Our Work		Region Semantics based on formalisms such as [9]	Value along label dimension is part of real world events. Operations are defined on label attribute to derive additional events	Events derived using closure operations and relationships along TSL dimensions	Sequence Templates defined for event expressions

2 Events and Their Representations

We describe an algebra for real world events, and in this respect, every real world happening is an event. Event related information can be categorized into two kinds: formal attributes and informational attributes. Formal attributes form the basis for formally analyzing events. On the other hand, informational attributes provide more information regarding events. An example is a video clip associated with an event. Informational attributes can also be viewed as a bag of attributes. In this paper, we consider time, space and label as part of the formal attribute set of events. Accordingly, we define an event to be characterized along three event dimensions, namely, time, space, and label dimensions. It is apparent that the event specification is complete when an event possesses attribute values along these three dimensions. Hereafter, we shall refer to the time, space and label dimensions as T, S, and L dimensions, and the respective attributes as TSL attributes of an event. We now provide an analysis of the event dimensions and event compositions, and further describe closures related to a set of events.

2.1 Event Dimensions

The three event dimensions of time, space and label are each unique and distinct in their characteristics.

The time dimension is continuous and dynamic. The temporal attribute of an event can either specify a time point of occurrence or a time-interval over which the event was observed. The granularity of a time point depends on the *event space*[1] within which the event is defined. For example, the time attributes '2004:08:03:05:xx:xx' and '2004:08:03:xx:xx:xx' can both be considered as time points, depending on whether the time granularity is in hours or days. Since events are detected by a distributed network of sensors/detectors; it would be simplistic to presuppose the existence of a global clock. In this paper, we resort to temporal modelling assuming a global reference time as proposed in [11].

We define the spatial attribute as a region that exhibits a physical contiguity and can be well defined using 2D/3D bounds. Using the lower-level representations of spatial attributes, in terms of bounding boxes as a basis [10], we can define the semantics of region bounding operators to describe 'regions'. However, we attach names to these regions for the sake of simplicity. For example, the region 'Trent-bridge' can be described using a set of 2D/3D points that satisfy its region-attributes. Similar to the temporal dimension, the granularity of space attribute is also determined by the event space. Depending on the granularity, a region could comprise of other smaller regions, with well defined spatial relations defining the orientation of the component regions with each other. A few relational operations (`touch, inside`) are described in [7]. The various spatial relationships can be automatically derived using the procedural semantics associated with these regions [10].

Event labels are used to categorize events that occur. Every domain is associated with a set of generic event labels that categorize the various events in that domain. For example, the domain of soccer is associated with event labels such as *Goal*, *Penalty*, *Match*, etc. Event labels can be represented as a hierarchical set, with the root being a generic label, and each child node being a specialization of the corresponding parent. Label hierarchies form an important tool in determining relationships between events, as well as in analyzing composite events. They can also be used to provide some additional information about events such as their frequency, location, sensitivity, and criticality. If label l_1 is a specialization of a label l_2, then $l_1 \rightarrow l_2$. $l_1 \leftrightarrow l_2$ indicates the existence of an alias. Logical operations and, or and not($\neg$) are defined on label attributes.

An event that can be detected by an event sensor is called a *basic event*. Basic events could be sensed or detected automatically, or could be provided as input by an event originator.

2.2 Event Composition and Event Sequences

A *composite event* is an event that is derived using one or more events. The two fundamental event composition operations are *disjunction* and *conjunction*. Event composition along the temporal dimension is a well researched topic. We follow the same temporal semantics as presented in [1]. These semantics follow from the 7 well known relational operators [2] along the temporal dimension namely, before, during, starts, finishes, overlaps, meets and equals. We define the spatial and label semantics for conjunction and disjunction of events. A

---

[1] An event space ψ is defined as the space encompassing a time interval T $= <T_s, T_t>$, a region $\Re$ and a set of label hierarchies $\mathcal{L}$[3].

detailed description of the semantics as well as the relationships on which these semantics are based can be found in the technical report [3]. A more generic event composition operation is the *sequence* operation.

Event Sequence : $e^3_{t_3,s_3,l_3} = e^1_{t_1,s_1,l_1} \odot_k e^2_{t_2,s_2,l_2}$
An event e^3 composed of two events e^1 and e^2 with a well defined temporal ordering forms an event sequence. By the natural definition of a sequence, $t_1 \leq t_2$ is a constraint that needs to be satisfied. The other constraints to be specified could include constraints such as $t_2 - t_1 \leq \Delta$; locations $s_1, s_2 \in \mathcal{R}$, etc. The sequence operator is $\odot$. The subscript k represents the set of constraints along the TSL dimension that must be satisfied by the two adjacent events in an event sequence. The time of occurrence of the sequence is given by the time interval $t_3 = < min(t_1,t_2), max(t_1,t_2) >^2$. The region of occurrence of the sequence is given by $s_3 = s_1 \cup s_2$), where s_3 represents the total region encompassed by the individual regions s_1 and s_2.

An event sequence π can be generalized as an ordering of events $\{e^1_{t_1,s_1,l_1} \odot_{k_1} e^2_{t_2,s_2,l_2} \odot_{k_2} e^3_{t_3,s_3,l_3}, \ldots, e^n_{t_n,s_n,l_n}\}$. The set of all events belonging to a sequence π is represented by E^π. $\kappa^\pi = \{k_1, k_2, \ldots k_n\}$ represents the set of all constraints satisfied by the events in the event sequence π. An example of a generic event-sequence is the 'run-out' event (see Fig. 1 on page 682). A generic event sequence is referred to as a *meta-event*, and the label of a meta-event is called *meta-label*. Further explanations on meta-events follow in section 3.3.

2.3 Event Closure

Various types of *event closures* can be defined on real world events so as to enable a quick retrieval of the related events based on a query. We discuss below two types of event closures, namely, *logical closure* and *sequence closure*. The logical closures help in retrieving the events that are logically related along the *TSL* dimensions. Logical closures can be used in analyzing various aspects of basic, conjunct, disjunct, and negation events. The sequence closure describes the closure rules for event sequences. Sequence closures help in determining alternate sequences that can be constructed from logical closures of events in a given sequence π. *Event closures are defined only for basic events.*

Logical Closure: We categorize logical closure into two categories: generic closure and semantic closure.

Generic closure, $C_G(e)$, of an event e is used to identify those events that are contained within an occurred basic event. The generic closure on an event $e_{t,s,l}$ is given by

$$C_G(e) = \{e_{t_1,s_1,l_1} \mid e_{t,s,l} \wedge (t_1 \in t) \wedge (s_1 \subseteq s) \wedge (l \rightarrow l_1)\}$$

Consider the event $e^a_{<2004:03:24:16:30:xx, 2004:03:24:18:30:xx>, cricket-field, rain}$. Let event e^a represent rains over the region *cricket-field* during the time interval

---

[2] $< t_1, t_2 >$ represents a continuous interval of time beginning at t_1 and ending at t_2.

16:30 to 18:30 on the 24th of March 2004. The pitch is a rectangular area of the ground between two bowling creases and is at the center of the cricket-field. The batsmen hit the balls bowled to them and run between the wickets on the pitch to score the runs. Since the location pitch is contained in the region *cricket-field*, by generic closure, we have: $e^1_{2004:03:24:16:45:xx,pitch,rain} \epsilon\ C_G(e^a)$.

Semantic closures, $C_S(e)$, are closures based on logical implication. Semantic closures have been defined in order to allow the closures related to description of time, space attributes such as *today, yesterday, this city*, and *this block*. Semantic closure also addresses the issue of alias along the label dimension. For example, on the 25th of March 2004, the semantic label *yesterday* refers to any point of time on the 24th of March 2004. Therefore, $e_{yesterday,cricket-field,rain} \epsilon\ C_S(e^a)$. The semantic closure of an event e is defined as:

$$C_S(e) = \{e_{t_1,s_1,l_1} \mid e_{t,s,l} \wedge t \to t_1 \wedge s \to s_1{}^3 \wedge l \leftrightarrow l_1\}.$$

Sequence Closure: A sequence closure C_Q is used to determine the closure of a sequence of events in terms of individual events of the sequence. In other words, a sequence closure of an event sequence π is the set of all possible sequences that can be constructed using the events present in the closures of individual events in the sequence such that the sequence constraints are not violated.

Sequence closure of an event sequence π is given by

$$C_Q(\pi) = \{\pi^1 \mid \forall\ e^1 \epsilon E^{\pi^1} \ \exists\ e \epsilon E^{\pi} \wedge (e^1 \epsilon C_G(e) \vee e^1 \epsilon C_S(e)) \wedge \kappa^{\pi} = \kappa^{\pi^1}\}$$

Let e be an event in the sequence. Then, the sequence closure is used to determine whether there exists any other event e' which can be substituted for e, while still satisfying all the sequence constraints. . It is apparent that if such an event e' exists, it must belong to the closure of event e. π, π^1 are the two event sequences. The events belonging to these sequences are represented by E^{π} and E^{π^1} respectively. Every element in the event sequence π^1, belongs to the generic or semantic closures of the events in the event sequence π. $\kappa^{\pi} = \kappa^{\pi^1}$ indicates that both π and π^1 satisfy the same set of constraints. (Refer sections 2.2 and 2.3 for the notations used.)

Note that the generic and semantic closures are defined only for basic events. As a result, every event that is generated using the closure operation is a valid event and can be derived from the event history H (see 3.2). Sequence closures represent the valid sequences that can be generated by permutations of events generated by logical closures on events of an elementary sequence.

3 Event Analysis

In the previous section, we discussed, in general, about events and event relationships from the point of view of basic events. However, while dealing with real

---

[3] Let ς denote a verbose translation of a region with respect to an observer; examples include *here, this city* etc. We have $s \to \varsigma$ if s belongs to the region $\mathcal{R}$ that is referred to by ς. A more detailed explanation of semantic closure is found in [3].

world events and trying to answer queries based on such real world events, there is a need for detailed analysis of the observed events. For example, consider the event set: $\{e^1_{2004:07:07:12:46:30, Manchester, Bowl:Vaughan}, e^2_{2004:07:07:12:46:55, Manchester, Miss:Sangakara}, e^3_{2004:07:07:12:47:15, Manchester, BallHitsPad}, e^4_{2004:07:07:12:47:50, Manchester, OutCalled:Umpire}\}$. In order to deduce that the above set of events depicts an lbw[3] event, a proper semantic analysis of the observed events needs to be carried out. The event analysis is done based on an event history H that is compiled from event sets received from one or more event detectors in different locations.

3.1 Event History

Event history H is a set of observed, basic events. Event history H is also associated with a corresponding event space ψ (Recall that event space ψ defines a bound on temporal, spatial, and label dimensions). Typically an event needs to be analyzed in the context of those events that occurred prior to the event under consideration and those that could occur after the event consideration. Such an analysis is required as observed or basic events are quite primitive and are not sufficient to answer the complex user queries. The objective of event analysis is to analyze the events contained in H to derive the interesting meta-events. Note that some of these meta-events could arise due to closure operations, some due to composition operations, and some more due to sequence operations.

3.2 Derived Events

Event history H is a set of only the observed, basic events. In order to be able to process queries, it is necessary to augment H and in this subsection, we briefly discuss this augmentation process. In the previous subsections, we discussed several operations related to a set of events and repeated application of one or more of these operations on H is one of the ways to augment H. Specifically, closure and composition operations are helpful in expanding H. The derivation rules for deriving events from H are given below:

1. $e \in H \rightarrow H \vdash e$
2. $e \in H \land e^1 \in C_G(e) \rightarrow H \vdash e_1$
3. $e \in H \land e^1 \in C_S(e) \rightarrow H \vdash e_1$
4. $H \vdash e_1 \land H \vdash e_2 \rightarrow H \vdash e_1 \; op \; e_2$, where op represents the conjunction, disjunction or sequence operator.

Note that, '$a \vdash b$' is used to denote that given a, the derivation of b is possible by using a set of inference rules.

3.3 Identification of Meta-Events in H

In order to semantically characterize H, we need some additional information about event space ψ. In this section, we propose the notion of capturing event semantics in the form of sequence templates. A sequence template is semantic characterization of a meta event that addresses the temporal and spatial relationship of a set of events from a semantic point of view. An illustrative sequence

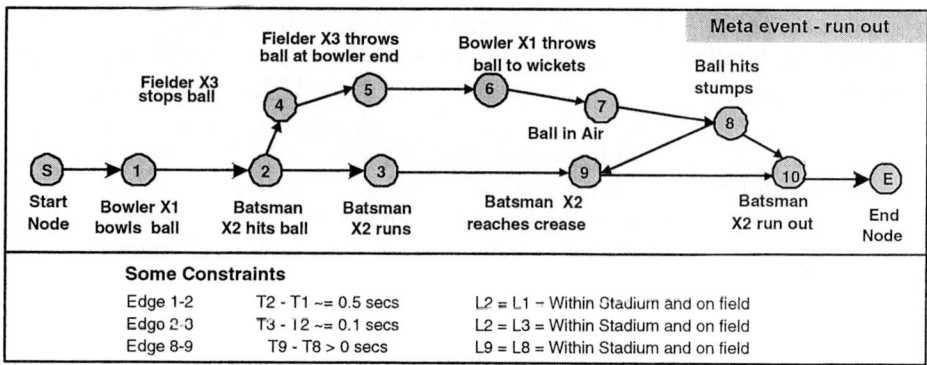

Fig. 1. Example Sequence Template

template is depicted in Fig. 1. Note that, as Fig. 1 depicts a sequence template, the actual event attributes are left unspecified. Furthermore, a sequence template defines certain important constraints on the event attributes such as temporal and spatial constraints.

Based on domain and related queries of interest, multiple sequence templates are defined and are made part of the *Sequence Template Database* (ST Database). The objective is to analyze H with respect to *ST Database* to generate the G_S, which is a semantic characterization of H. A meta event in G_S is depicted by using only the initial event(e_i) and final event(e_f) of the sequence template and a directed edge from e_i to e_f. The label of this directed edge holds the information of the instantiated sequence template corresponding to the actual meta-event that has transpired.

The event history H, the ST Database and the corresponding semantic representation G_S are used to develop a query-event analysis system.

4 Query-Event Analysis System (QEAS)

In this section we discuss a query and event processing system that is based on events contained in H. Query Event Analysis System is a formal system that generates responses to user queries using either H or G_S as input. Fig. 2 depicts the functional description of QEAS. The QEAS has two basic functions namely a) Analysis of input events and b) Analysis of user queries. Every new observed event must be made a part of the event history H. The event aggregator adds the new event e to H. It also dispatches e to ST State Machine, in order to verify whether the event e is a part of a meta-event. The ST State Machine matches the event e to the available sequence templates in ST, and suitably updates G_S. A user query Q is first analyzed with respect to the available sequence templates. If a matching template is found, the query is analyzed using G_S as input. Else, the query is analyzed by the Query Processing System using H as input. The result of a query is the set of one or more events that match the query. The appropriate content associated with these events is sent to the user.

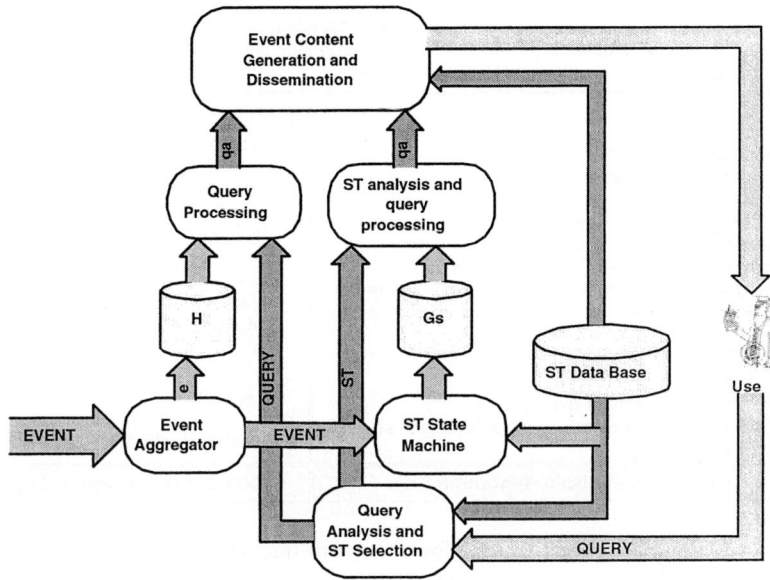

Fig. 2. Functional description of QEAS

4.1 Event Analysis

Events are analyzed by using state machines associated with the sequence templates, in order to identify the instantiated meta-events. A new state machine is instantiated when the start of a new meta event is detected. The occurrence of an event could (a) Cause one or more state machines to terminate successfully (b) Cause one or more state machines to make a legal transition (c) Invalidate one or more state machines. (d) Instantiate a new state machine m, which corresponds to a sequence template of a meta-event. Every time a state machine terminates, G_S is updated to reflect the meta events that have taken place. Lapse of time/space constraints could also cause state machine invalidation. The algorithm to generate G_S is shown in fig 3(a).

Theorem 1: With the assumption that no two events occur simultaneously, an occurred event alone is adequate to derive all consequential meta-events in G_S. A proof of the same is to be found in the technical report [3]. Note that, when two or more events can occur concurrently, the set of concurrent events has to be processed together; and all possible permutations of the concurrent events must be taken into account while deducing the possible transitions.

Corollary 1: If a sequence of events E that cause valid transitions on any state machine M appears in the event history H, then the events $e \epsilon$ E are consumed by M to recognize the corresponding meta-event.

4.2 Query Analysis

Every event query can be represented as an ordered pair (E, ψ), where E is the event expression and ψ is the event space that corresponds to the user

H - Event History ST - Set of sequence templates ei - Initial event	Gs - Event graph, depicting semantic characterisation of H M - Set of active state machines Q - User Query ef - Terminal event J, Je - Event Sets

For every new event e{
anal:
  for all m ∈ M{
    if (e can cause valid transitions on m) {
      make the transition
      if m terminates successfully {
        Identify e_i, e_f for the meta event E
        Create a graph g, using e_i and e_f as nodes
        Add directed edge from e_i to e_f, with appropriate label
        M := M-m
        Gs := Gs + g
        e := E, goto anal   } } }
  for all st ∈ ST{
    if(e can initiate new meta-event){
      initiate state machines m_{new} corresponding to st
      M = M + m_{new} } } }
	Express Q as an event expression X,
	    and associated event space
	J = ∅
	For every event e in X {
	  if (e is a basic event)
	    Je = {all instances of e in H}
	  else if (e is a meta-event)
	    Je = {all instances of e in Gs}
	  if n(Je) = 0 {
	    determine E' = {e'
		e ∈ G(e') or e ∈ C(e')}
		    Je = {all instances of (e' ∈ E') in H, Gs}
		  }
		  J = J + Je
		}
		Use J to evaluate X and generate the result

(a) Event Analysis -Algorithm	(b) Query Analysis -Algorithm

Fig. 3. Algorithms for event and query analysis

query. As depicted in Fig. 2, Query analysis begins by comparing the input query with sequence templates contained in ST database. As sequence templates capture semantics, using them in query processing enables semantic analysis of a query. The objective of comparison is to select a sequence template st that best matches with the input query. This st is used in generating the query answer (qa) using H and G_S. Finally, the content database is analyzed to extract the relevant content using st and qa to generate the most appropriate event related content that is delivered to user. The algorithm for query analysis is shown in Figure 3(b). The QEAS analyzes every user query as being equivalent to an event expression. An event expression consists of one or more events combined using the conjunction, disjunction and sequence operations along with the related constraints. The safety and liveness properties of QEAS have been proved in the technical report [3].

In general,query processing involves three distinct steps namely (a) query pre-processing (b) retrieval of event information using SQL queries and (c) post processing. The pre processing step involves identification of (a) meta event labels (b) temporal characteristics and (c) spatial characteristics of the input query, and the TSL hierarchies associated with each domain play a significant role in this process. Observe that the input events are analysed in real time to update H, G_S (refer Fig. 2, Fig. 3) which are stored in the database as the basic and meta event tables respectively. The retrieval of event information using SQL queries mainly uses these two tables. Post processing involves filtering and rearrangement of events to suit the user requirements. Such a three step query processing system would help in answering complex queries such as "Generate a 30 minute highlight of the first innings of the cricket match between England and Sri Lanka on the 27th June, 2002 at Trent-Bridge".

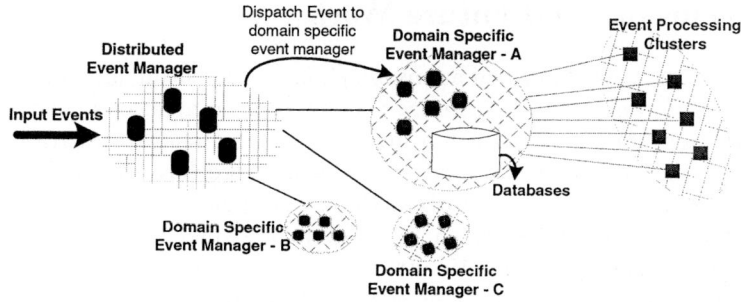

Fig. 4. Illustration of distributed event processing

As an example, consider the following query that was posed after the first innings of the match between England and SriLanka on the 27th June, 2002: "Generate the highlights of all boundaries hit by each SriLankan player today?" The query can be mapped to the event-expression:
$E = (e_{today,\ trent-bridge,\ boundary\ by\ SriLankan\ player\ X})^+$ and the corresponding event space $\psi = \{$today, trent-bridge, $\{$Set of labels in the domain 'cricket'$\}$ $\}$
The simplification of the Event expression, which gets evaluated for every Sri-Lankan player X is shown below:
$e = e_{(today, trent-bridge, boundary:X)}$
$= e_{(today,\ trent-bridge, four:X)} \mid e_{(today, trent-bridge, six:X)}$ (by generic closure)
$= e_{(<2002:06:27:10:30:xx, 2002:06:27:13:30:xx>,\ trent-bridge, four:X)} \mid$
$e_{(<2002:06:27:10:30:xx, 2002:06:27:13:30:xx>, trent-bridge, six:X)}$ (by semantic closure)
The events four:X and six:X are meta-events and are a part of G_S. The QEAS looks for the events in G_S in order to evaluate the event expression.

4.3 Distributed Event Processing

It is easy to see that the event analysis and query processing have to meet real time constraints. The processing of any event should preferably be completed before its real time successor occurs. In a scenario wherein there are a considerable number of incoming events belonging to different domains, a distributed event processing network can provide a substantial increase in processing speed. Fig. 4 shows an illustration of a hierarchical event processing system. There exist several clusters of Domain Specific Event Managers that process the events occurring within a particular domain. The Distributed Event Manager routes the incoming events to the domain specific event managers for further processing. The domain specific event Manager manages several event processing clusters and it identifies a suitable cluster to process an input event based on the attributes of the event. For example, location attribute could be used to cluster events that occur in a particular locale.

5 Conclusions and Future Work

In this paper, we have described an approach for representing and analyzing real world events. Events are characterized along three dimensions, namely, time, space, and label dimensions. Such a multidimensional characterization helps in better syntactic and semantic analysis of events. We have defined the notion of event closures and have categorized them into logical closures and semantic closures. We have also introduced the notion of sequence templates that are useful in (a) providing a semantic structure (G_S) to an otherwise a collection of events H; and (b) characterizing content related to meta events. We have described the main steps involved in the generation of G_S given H and have illustrated the use of G_S in answering queries related to real world events. The broad outline of Query Analysis System also describes an important step of event related content identification and dissemination. We have illustrated the proposed formal and query analysis system with the help of a set of real world events.

From the point of view of event related content dissemination, it is required to be able to derive the meta events that are of interest to users as soon a basic event occurs. We are focusing our efforts on how to (a) identify all such meta events; (b) identify related content; (c) identify users who are interested in the occurred and meta events; and (d) efficiently and effectively deliver content. Observe that some of the users could be mobile demanding effective caching and transcoding techniques. Our objective in event representation and analysis is to ultimately deliver content to mobile users with minimum delay. We are in the process of implementing a system for the dissemination of event related information based on the formalism presented in this paper.

References

1. R. Adaikkalavan, *Snoop Event Specification: Formalization Algorithms, And Implementation Using Interval-Based Semantics*. MS thesis, The University of Texas At Arlington, 2002.
2. J. F. Allen, "Time and time again: the many ways to represent time," *International Journal of Intelligent Systems*, vol. 6, pp. 341–355, 1991.
3. Aparna Nagargadde, Sridhar. V, Krithi Ramamritham.,"Syntactic and Semantic characterisation of real world events," *Technical Report, Satyam Computer Services Limited*, SCSL/ARG/2004/1, Sept. 2004
4. P. Bates., "Debugging heterogeneous distributed systems using event-based models of behavior," *ACM Transactions on Computer Systems*, pp. 1–31, 1995
5. Branding. H, Buchmann. A. P, Kudrass. T, Zimmermann. J., "Rules in an Open System: The REACH Rule System," in *Procs of 1st Intl. Workshop on Rules in Databases*, (Edinburgh), Sept. 1993.
6. Darshan Gujjar, Amit Thawani, Srividya Gopalan, Sridhar V., "An Efficient Web based Event Management System for Distributed Multimedia Services", *The IASTED International Conference on Internet And Multimedia Systems and Applications (EuroIMSA 2005)*, (Grindelwald, Switzerland), 2005 (to appear)

7. Dönderler. M. E, Ulusoy. Ö, Güdükbay. U., "Rule based spatiotemporal query processing for video databases," *The VLDB Journal*, vol. 12, pp. 86–103, 2004.
8. Gatziu. S, K. R. Dittrich, "SAMOS: an Active Object-Oriented Database System," *IEEE Quarterly Bulletein*, Jan 1993.
9. M. Z. Hasan, *The Management of Data, Events, and Information Presentation for Network Management*. PhD thesis, University of Waterloo, 1996
10. Kuijpers. B, Paredaens. J, Vandeurzen. L., "Semantics in Spatial Databases," *Semantics in Databases, LNCS 1358*, pp. 114–135, 1998.
11. C. Liebig, M. Cilia, A. Buchmann., "Event Composition in Time-dependent Distributed Systems," in *Procs of the 4th IFCIS (CoopIS 99)*, 1999.
12. Pietzuch. P. R, Shand. B, Bacon. J., "Composite Event Detection as a Generic Middleware Extension," *IEEE Network Magazine, Special Issue on Middleware Technologies for Future Communication Networks*, pp. 44–55, 2004.
13. A. Thawani, S. Gopalan, Sridhar. V, "Event driven semantics based ad selection," in *Procs of IEEE International Conference on Multimedia and Expo (ICME'2004)*, (Taipei, Taiwan), June 2004.
14. http://plus.cricinfo.com/link_to_database/Archive/2002/OD_Tourneys /NWS/Scorecards/ENG_SL_NWS_ODI7_07JUL2002_BBB-COMMS.html.

Learning Tree Augmented Naive Bayes for Ranking

Liangxiao Jiang[1,*], Harry Zhang[2], Zhihua Cai[1], and Jiang Su[2]

[1] Department of Computer Science, China University of Geosciences,
Wuhan, China 430074
[2] Faculty of Computer Science, University of New Brunswick,
P.O. Box 4400, Fredericton, NB, Canada E3B 5A3

Abstract. Naive Bayes has been widely used in data mining as a simple and effective classification algorithm. Since its conditional independence assumption is rarely true, numerous algorithms have been proposed to improve naive Bayes, among which tree augmented naive Bayes (TAN) [3] achieves a significant improvement in term of classification accuracy, while maintaining efficiency and model simplicity. In many real-world data mining applications, however, an accurate ranking is more desirable than a classification. Thus it is interesting whether TAN also achieves significant improvement in term of ranking, measured by AUC(the area under the Receiver Operating Characteristics curve) [8, 1]. Unfortunately, our experiments show that TAN performs even worse than naive Bayes in ranking. Responding to this fact, we present a novel learning algorithm, called forest augmented naive Bayes (FAN), by modifying the traditional TAN learning algorithm. We experimentally test our algorithm on all the 36 data sets recommended by Weka [12], and compare it to naive Bayes, SBC [6], TAN [3], and C4.4 [10], in terms of AUC. The experimental results show that our algorithm outperforms all the other algorithms significantly in yielding accurate rankings. Our work provides an effective and efficient data mining algorithm for applications in which an accurate ranking is required.

Keywords: data mining and knowledge discovery, learning algorithms, Bayesian networks, decision trees.

1 Introduction

Classification is one of the most important tasks in data mining. In classification, a classifier is built from a set of training examples with class labels. The predictive ability of a classifier is typically measured by its classification accuracy on the testing examples. In fact, most classifiers can also produce probability estimates or "confidence" of the class prediction. Unfortunately, this information is often ignored in classification.

---

* This work was done when the author was a visiting scholar at University of New Brunswick.

In many data mining applications, however, the classifier's accuracy are not enough, because they cannot express the information how "far-off" (be it 0.45 or 0.01?) is the prediction of each example from its target. For example, in direct marketing, we often need to promote the top X% of customers during gradual roll-out, or we often deploy different promotion strategies to customers with different likelihood of buying some products. To accomplish these tasks, we need more than a mere classification of buyers and non-buyers. We often need a ranking of customers in terms of their likelihood of buying. Thus, a ranking is more desirable than just a classification.

A natural question is how to evaluate a classifier in terms of its ranking performance, rather than classification accuracy. Recently, the area under the Receiver Operating Characteristics curve [8, 1], or simply AUC, has been used for this purpose and received a considerable attention. AUC compares the classifiers' performance cross the entire range of class distributions and error costs and is a good "summary" for comparing two classifiers. Hand and Till [4] show that, for binary classification, AUC is equivalent to the probability that a randomly chosen example of class − will have a smaller estimated probability of belonging to class + than a randomly chosen example of class +. They present a simple approach to calculating the AUC of a classifier G below.

$$\hat{A} = \frac{S_0 - n_0(n_0 + 1)/2}{n_0 n_1}, \tag{1}$$

where n_0 and n_1 are the numbers of negative and positive examples respectively, and $S_0 = \sum r_i$, where r_i is the rank of i_{th} positive example in the ranked list. From Equation 1, it is clear that AUC is essentially a measure of the quality of a ranking. For example, the AUC of a ranking is 1 (the maximum value of AUC) if there is no positive example preceding a negative example.

In classification, an example $E = (a_1, a_2, \cdots, a_n)$, where a_i is the value of attribute A_i, is classified into the class C with the maximum posterior class probability $P(C|E)$ (or simply, class probability), as shown below.

$$C_{pb}(E) = \arg\max_C P(C|E). \tag{2}$$

Assume that all the attributes are independent given the value of class, called conditional independence assumption and shown in Equation 3. The resulting classifier, called naive Bayes, is shown in Equation 4. Figure 1 shows an example of naive Bayes.

$$P(a_1, \cdots, a_n | C) = \prod_{i=1}^{n} P(a_i | C). \tag{3}$$

$$C_{nb}(E) = \arg\max_C P(C) \prod_{i=1}^{n} P(a_i | C). \tag{4}$$

The structure of naive Bayes can be extended to represent the dependences among attributes. Tree Augmented naive Bayes (TAN) is an extended tree-like

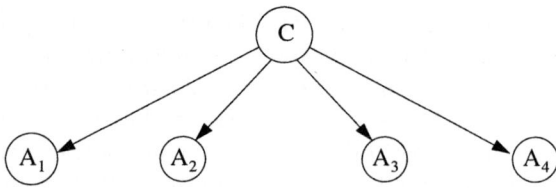

Fig. 1. An example of naive Bayes

naive Bayes [3], in which the class node directly points to all attribute nodes and an attribute node can have only one parent from another attribute node (in addition to the class node). Figure 2 shows an example of TAN. In TAN, each node has at most two parents (one is the class node). TAN outperforms naive Bayes in terms of accuracy [3] and still maintains a considerably simple structure.

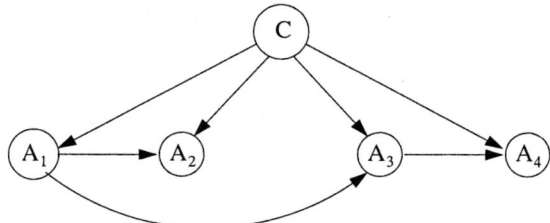

Fig. 2. An example of TAN

One interesting question is whether TAN is also a good model for ranking. In this paper, we investigate the ranking performance of TAN. Unfortunately, the traditional TAN learning algorithm does not produce high quality ranking. We propose a new TAN learning algorithm and our experiments show that our algorithm performs better not only than the traditional TAN learning algorithm, but also other popular state-of-the-art algorithms designed for yielding accurate ranking.

The rest of the paper is organized as follows. In Section 2, we introduce the related work on improving naive Bayes and on improving decision tree for ranking. In Section 3, we present our new algorithm. In Section 4, we describe the experimental setup and results in detail. In Section 5, we make a conclusion.

2 Related Work

It is obvious that the conditional independence assumption in naive Bayes is rarely true in many applications. Therefore, researchers have made a substantial amount of effort to improve naive Bayes in classification. Research work to improve the naive Bayes can be broadly divided into two approaches below.

1. Select attributes subsets in which attributes are conditionally independent. For example, Langley and Sage [6] presented an algorithm, called Selective Bayesian Classifiers (simply SBC), to improve naive Bayes. They used a forward greedy search method to select a subset of attributes.
2. Relax the conditional independence assumption by extending the structure of naive Bayes to represent the dependences among attributes. TAN is an example of this approach. TAN is a specific case of general augmented naive Bayesian networks (ANB), in which the class node also directly points to all attribute nodes, but there is no limitation on the links among attribute nodes (except that they do not form any directed cycle).

Unfortunately, learning an optimal ANB is intractable. Thus, TAN is a good trade-off between the model complexity and learnability in practice. A number of TAN learning algorithms have been proposed, among which the ChowLiu algorithm (CL-TAN) [3] and the SuperParent algorithm (SP-TAN) [5] performs significantly better than naive Bayes in classification. SP-TAN is a greedy heuristic search algorithm in which an arc of achieving the highest accuracy improvement is selected in each step. One disadvantage of SP-TAN is its time complexity of $O(mn^3)$, where m is the number of training examples and n is the number of attributes. However, CL-TAN has the time complexity of $O(mn^2)$, a considerable advantage over SP-TAN. CL-TAN is depicted below, which is the base of our work.

Algorithm CL-TAN
1. Compute $I_{\hat{P}_D}(A_i, A_j|C)$ between each pair of attributes, $i \neq j$.
2. Build a complete undirected graph in which nodes are attributes $A_1, \cdots, A_n$. Annotate the weight of an edge connecting A_i to A_j by $I_{\hat{P}_D}(A_i; A_j|C)$.
3. Build a maximum weighted spanning tree.
4. Transform the resulting undirected tree to a directed one by choosing a root attribute and setting the direction of all edges to be outward from it.
5. Construct a TAN model by adding a node labeled by C and adding an arc from C to each A_i.

In the preceding algorithm, $I_{\hat{P}_D}(A_i, A_j|C)$ is an estimate of the conditional mutual information which will be defined in Section 3.

Both SP-TAN and CL-TAN outperforms naive Bayes significantly in classification. Moreover, the ranking performance of SP-TAN has been studied [14]. Since CL-TAN is more efficient than SP-TAN, it is more practical in data mining applications. In this paper, we focus on the ranking performance of CL-TAN.

Decision tree learning algorithms are a major type of effective learning algorithms in data mining. However, traditional decision tree algorithms, such as C4.5 [11], have been observed to produce poor estimations of probabilities [10]. Aiming at this fact, Provost and Domingos [10] presented an algorithm, called C4.4, to improve C4.5's performance in ranking measured by AUC. In detail, they used two techniques to improve the AUC of C4.5: smooth probability estimates by Laplace correction and turn off pruning. Their experiments show that C4.4 performs significantly better than C4.5 in ranking. In this paper, we compare our new algorithm with C4.4.

3 Forest Augmented Naive Bayes: FAN

At first, let us introduce the definitions of mutual information and conditional mutual information used in this paper.

Definition 1. *Let X, Y are two variables, then the mutual information between X and Y is defined by the following equation [3].*

$$I_P(X;Y) = \sum_{x,y} P(x,y) \log \frac{P(x,y)}{P(x)P(y)}. \tag{5}$$

Roughly speaking, this function measures how much information Y provides about X.

Definition 2. *Let X, Y, Z are three variables, then the conditional mutual information between X and Y given Z is defined by the following equation [3].*

$$I_P(X;Y|Z) = \sum_{x,y,z} P(x,y,z) \log \frac{P(x,y,z)P(z)}{P(x,z)P(y,z)}. \tag{6}$$

Roughly speaking, this function measures the information that Y provides about X when the value of Z is known.

In a TAN, the class probability $P(C|E)$ is estimated by the following equation:

$$P(C|E) = P(C) \prod_{i=1}^{n} P(A_i|A_{ip}, C) \tag{7}$$

where A_{ip} is the parent of A_i and

$$P(A_i|A_{ip}, C) = \begin{cases} P(A_i|A_{ip}, C) & \{A_{ip}\} \neq \emptyset \\ P(A_i|C) & \{A_{ip}\} = \emptyset \end{cases} \tag{8}$$

An instance is classified into the class with the maximum class probability.

We experimentally investigate the ranking performance of CL-TAN, measured by AUC. Unfortunately, CL-TAN yields poor AUC (see Table 1 and 2, although its accuracy is higher than naive Bayes (see Table 3 and 4). By experiments, we observe that there are two factors contributing this fact:

1. The directions of edges in a TAN are crucial. In Step 4 of the CL-TAN algorithm, an attribute is randomly chosen as the root of the tree and the directions of all edges are set outward from it. Notice that the selection of the root attribute actually determines the structure of the resulting TAN, since a TAN is a directed graph. It is interesting that the directions of edges in a TAN do not affect the classification accuracy significantly. In contrast, however, AUC is quite sensitive to it. Thus the selection of the root attribute is important for building a TAN with accurate ranking.

2. Irrelevant edges may exist in a CL-TAN. In Step 3 of the CL-TAN, a maximum weighted spanning tree is built. Thus, the number of the edges is fixed to $n-1$. Sometimes, it might overfit the data, since some edges may not be necessary to exist in the TAN.

Based on the preceding observations, we modify the CL-TAN algorithm correspondingly as follows.

1. We choose the attribute A_{root} with the maximum mutual information with class, defined by Equation 1, as the root. That is,

$$A_{root} = \arg\max_{A_i} I_P(A_i; C), \qquad (9)$$

where $i = 1, \cdots, n$. It is natural to use this strategy, since intuitively the attribute which has the greatest influence on classification should be the root of the tree.

2. We filter out the edges that have a conditional mutual information less than a threshold. To our understanding, those edges have a high risk to overfit the training data, and thus undermine the probability estimation. More precisely, we use the average conditional mutual information I_{avg}, defined in Equation 10, as the threshold. All the edges with the conditional mutual information less than I_{avg} are removed.

$$I_{avg} = \frac{\sum_i \sum_{j, j \neq i} I_P(A_i; A_j | C)}{n(n-1)}, \qquad (10)$$

where n is the number of attributes.

Since the structure of the resulting model is not a strict tree, we call our algorithm forest augmented naive Bayes (FAN), depicted in detail as follows.

Algorithm FAN
1. Calculate the conditional mutual information $I_P(A_i; A_j | C), j \neq i$ between each pair of attributes, and calculate the average conditional mutual information I_{avg}, defined in Equation 10.
2. Build a complete undirected graph in which nodes are attributes $A_i, i = 1, 2, \ldots, n$. Annotate the weight of an edge connecting A_j to A_i by $I_P(A_i; A_j | C)$.
3. Search a maximum weighted spanning tree.
4. Calculate the mutual information $I_P(A_i; C)$, $i = 1, 2, \ldots, n$ between each attribute and the class, and find the attribute A_{root} that has the maximum mutual information with class, according to Equation 9.
5. Transform the resulting undirected tree to a directed one by setting A_{root} as the root and setting the directions of all edges to be outward from it.
6. Delete the directed edges with the weight of the conditional mutual information below the average conditional mutual information I_{avg}.
7. Construct a FAN model by adding a vertex labeled by C and adding an directed arc from C to each $A_i, i = 1, 2, \ldots, n$.

The time complexity and space complexity of FAN are $O(n^2 \cdot N)$ and $O(|C|(n|V|)^2)$, respectively, where n is the number of attributes, N is the number of training instances, $|C|$ is the number of classes, and $|V|$ is the average number of values for an attribute. Both of them are same as the CL-TAN algorithm. However, our experiments, described in next section (Section 4) that FAN improves the ranking performance of CL-TAN significantly.

4 Experimental Methodology and Results

We conduct our experiments on all the 36 data sets recommended by Weka [13], which come from the UCI repository [7]. We download these data sets in format of arff from main web of Weka. All the preprocessing stages of data sets were carried out by the Weka system. They mainly include the following three processes:

1. We use the filter of ReplaceMissingValues in Weka to replace the missing values of attributes.
2. We use the filter of Discretize in Weka to discretize numeric attributes.
3. It is well-known that, if the number of values of an attribute is almost equal to the number of instances in the data set, this attribute does not contribute any information to classification. So we use the filter of Remove in Weka to delete these attributes. In these 36 data sets, there only exists three this type of attributes, namely Hospital Number in data set horse-colic.ORIG, Instance Name in data set Splice and Animal in data set zoo.

We conduct experiments to compare our algorithm (FAN) with naive Bayes, SBC [6], TAN [3], and C4.4 [10] in AUC . All algorithms are implemented within the Weka framework. Multi-class AUC has been calculated by M-measure in [4]. The AUC of each classifier is measured via the ten-fold cross validation for all data sets. Runs with the various classifiers were carried out on the same training sets and evaluated on the same test sets. In particular, the cross-validation folds are the same for all the experiments on each data set. Throughout, we compare our algorithm with each other algorithm via two-tailed t-test with significantly different probability of 0.95, because we speak of two results for a data set as being "significantly different" only if the difference is statistically significant at the 0.05 level according to the corrected two-tailed t-test.

Table 1 shows the AUC and standard deviations of each classifier on the test sets of each data set, and the average AUC and deviation are summarized at the bottom of the table. Table 2 shows the results of two-tailed t-test between each pair of algorithms, and each entry $w/t/l$ means that the algorithm at the corresponding row wins in w data sets, ties in t data sets, and loses in l data sets, compared to the algorithm at the corresponding column.

The detailed results displayed in Table 1 and Table 2 show that our algorithm outperforms significantly all the other algorithms in AUC. Now, we summarize the highlights as follows:

Table 1. Experimental results on AUC. FAN: Forest Augmented naive Bayes; NB: naive Bayes; SBC: Selective Bayesian Classifiers; CL-TAN : Tree Augmented naive Bayes with smoothed parameter of 5.0; C4.4: C4.5 with Laplace correction and without tree pruning

Data set	FAN	NB	SBC	CL-TAN	C4.4
anneal	96.4±0.51	95.9±1.3	94.7±3.92	92.97±2.51	93.78±2.9
anneal.ORIG	95.1±2.93	94.49±3.67	94.35±4.31	85.42±7.04	92.69±3.15
audiology	70.92±0.59	70.96±0.73	70.98±0.67	70.16±0.55	70.58±0.63
autos	92.13±5.24	89.18±4.93	90.43±3.43	90.28±2.59	90.73±4.52
balance-scale	84.46±4.1	84.46±4.1	84.46±4.1	76.47±7.56	63.06±6.18
breast-cancer	68.04±12.43	69.71±15.21	67.67±12.63	67.4±10.4	59.3±12.03
breast-w	99.15±0.94	99.19±0.87	99.16±0.62	98.74±1.32	97.85±1.86
colic	85.25±6.16	83.71±5.5	84.86±7.13	50.6±8.29	85.02±7.03
colic.ORIG	74.91±9.77	80.67±6.98	81.82±4.9	62.89±7.73	80.56±8.94
credit-a	91.3±3.36	92.09±3.43	87±3.75	63.3±13.3	89.42±3.1
credit-g	78.25±6.42	79.27±4.74	77.41±4.67	60.18±6.84	69.62±5
diabetes	82.71±5.65	82.31±5.17	82.79±5.04	74.18±5.87	75.5±5.76
glass	79.03±7.02	80.5±6.65	80.97±8.37	84.79±4.34	82.36±4.38
heart-c	83.95±0.71	84.1±0.54	83.87±0.64	82.96±1.12	83.1±1.19
heart-h	83.66±0.8	83.8±0.7	82.83±1.38	82.69±0.72	83.04±0.85
heart-statlog	90.42±5.36	91.3±4.19	87.98±6.91	80.12±11.94	81.36±9.15
hepatitis	85.91±11.52	88.99±8.99	83.62±12.29	53.83±14.97	82.03±14.04
hypothyroid	86.69±9.61	87.37±8.52	85.25±8.16	84.03±12.22	81.58±8.8
ionosphere	98.48±1.47	93.61±3.36	92.26±5.26	72.05±7.4	93.1±3.76
iris	98.58±2.67	98.58±2.67	99±1.46	94.17±5.51	97.33±2.63
kr-vs-kp	98.12±0.9	95.17±1.29	96.41±0.78	87.21±1.49	99.95±0.06
labor	93.33±14.05	98.33±5.27	65.83±32.5	68.33±40.41	74.17±31.04
letter	98.28±0.19	96.86±0.24	97.03±0.23	94.5±0.25	95.39±0.39
lymph	89.95±1.57	89.69±1.49	88.14±3.35	85.56±6.98	87.26±3.75
mushroom	100±0	99.79±0.04	99.98±0.02	99.87±0.04	100±0
primary-tumor	78.9±1.03	78.85±1.35	78.88±1.45	76.39±1.9	75.48±2.33
segment	99.55±0.27	98.51±0.46	98.93±0.42	95.35±1.06	98.85±0.32
sick	98.22±0.77	95.91±2.35	94.5±4.28	73.25±2.73	99.07±0.35
sonar	85.96±10.19	85.48±10.82	79.89±13.1	67.4±13.83	77.01±8.59
soybean	99.61±0.64	99.53±0.6	99.08±0.74	96.73±1.59	91.43±2.6
splice	99.47±0.32	99.41±0.22	99.14±0.36	97.72±0.68	98.14±0.72
vehicle	89.05±2.99	80.81±3.51	81.31±4.02	76.86±3.8	86.5±2.28
vote	98.03±1.51	96.56±2.09	94.26±4.14	93.49±1.38	96.77±2.96
vowel	99.51±0.26	95.81±0.84	96.12±0.59	92.33±1.23	91.28±2.46
waveform-5000	94.92±0.63	95.27±0.58	95.12±0.76	78.9±2.03	80.83±1.24
zoo	89.88±4.05	89.88±4.05	89.06±4.49	89.88±4.05	88.88±4.5
Mean	89.95±3.795	89.61±3.54	87.92±4.746	80.58±5.991	85.92±4.708

1. FAN outperforms naive Bayes significantly: It wins in 9 data sets, ties in 27 data sets and loses in 0 data set. The average AUC for FAN is 89.95%, it is slightly higher than the average AUC 89.61% of naive Bayes. This fact is understandable, since the conditional independence among attributes have

Table 2. Results of two-tailed t-test on AUC. An entry $w/t/l$ means that the algorithm at the corresponding row wins in w data sets, ties in t data sets, and loses in l data sets, compared to the algorithm at the corresponding column. The significantly different probability of two-tailed t-test is **0.95**

	NB	SBC	CL-TAN	C4.4
FAN	9/27/0	11/25/0	24/12/0	13/20/3
NB	-	1/31/4	23/12/1	13/20/4
SNB	-	-	20/16/0	9/22/5
CL-TAN	-	-	-	4/20/12

been relaxed and represented in FAN. Thus, the class probability estimates of FAN are expected to be more accurate than those of naive Bayes.
2. FAN also outperforms C4.4 significantly: It wins in 13 data sets, ties in 20 data sets and loses in 3 data sets. The average AUC for C4.4 is 85.92%, lower than that of FAN. Since C4.4 is the state-of-the-art decision tree algorithm designed specifically for yielding accurate rankings, this comparison also provides evidence to support FAN.
3. FAN outperforms significantly SBC and TAN. It wins in 11 data sets, ties in 25 data sets and loses in 0 data set, compared with SBC; and it wins in 24 data sets, ties in 12 data sets and loses in 0 data set, compared with TAN. Notice that, although SBC and TAN improve naive Bayes' performance in classification, they do not improve naive Bayes' performance in ranking.

In our experiments, we also observe the classification accuracy of each algorithm, shown in Table 3, and Table 4 shows the results of two-tailed t-test with confidence level of 95% between each pair of algorithms in terms of accuracy. We can see that our experiment repeats experimental results of SBC [6] and CL-TAN [3], both of which improve the classification performance of naive Bayes. It is also interesting to notice that FAN also slightly outperforms all the algorithms in terms of accuracy.

5 Conclusions

In this paper, we investigate the ranking performance of the CL-TAN learning algorithm, and find that CL-TAN performs even worse than naive Bayes in ranking. Responding to this problem, we present a novel TAN learning algorithm FAN to build a TAN for accurate ranking. We experimentally test our algorithm measured by AUC, using all the 36 data sets recommended by Weka, and compare our algorithm FAN with naive Bayes, SBC, TAN, and C4.4. The experimental results show that our algorithm improves significantly naive Bayes' performance in ranking, and outperforms some widely used extended naive Bayes algorithms, such as SBC and CL-TAN and the state-of-the-art decision tree learning algo-

Table 3. Experimental results on accuracy. FAN: Forest Augmented naive Bayes; NB: naive Bayes; SBC: Selective Bayesian Classifiers; CL-TAN: Tree Augmented naive Bayes with smoothed parameter of 5.0; C4.4: C4.5 with Laplace correction and without post pruning

Data set	FAN	NB	SBC	CL-TAN	C4.4
anneal	97.1±1.5	94.32±2.38	96.88±2.5	96.66±2.35	99±0.98
anneal.ORIG	90.98±3.64	87.53±4.69	88.75±3.72	87.98±3.62	91.76±3.07
audiology	71.19±5.14	71.23±7.03	76.01±7.05	75.16±8.45	78.3±8
autos	77.55±8.11	64.83±11.18	67.71±11.27	76.07±10.01	81.45±7.48
balance-scale	91.36±1.38	91.36±1.38	91.36±1.38	86.08±3.18	69.3±4.25
breast-cancer	68.21±5.11	72.06±7.97	73.45±8.91	66.82±7.01	68.57±7.49
breast-w	97.13±2.03	97.28±1.84	96.42±2.26	96.71±1.79	92.99±3.66
colic	81.25±5.31	78.81±5.05	81.77±4.89	77.18±7.04	80.17±5.95
colic.ORIG	72.57±6.5	75.26±5.26	75.53±6.15	75.51±7.15	76.08±8.74
credit-a	84.49±3.99	84.78±4.28	85.51±4.16	84.64±5.03	83.19±3.5
credit-g	75.6±5.15	76.3±4.76	74.1±3.87	73.4±4.12	68.6±4.3
diabetes	75.4±6.61	75.4±5.85	75.53±5.07	75.13±4.71	69.54±5.12
glass	59.87±7.98	60.32±9.69	57.99±6.89	55.71±10.81	58.83±7.73
heart-c	81.13±7.8	84.14±4.16	82.47±7.61	77.53±7.41	74.26±11.46
heart-h	82±5.94	84.05±6.69	79±9.77	79.97±6.39	72.78±11
heart-statlog	82.59±6.77	83.7±5	79.26±9.75	81.11±3.68	75.93±8.95
hepatitis	83.17±9.66	83.79±8.79	80.63±6.8	83.83±8.05	81.25±11.52
hypothyroid	93.19±0.78	92.79±1.02	93.53±0.66	92.79±1.06	92.5±0.58
ionosphere	92.61±4.64	90.89±3.49	91.17±4.12	90.6±3.83	84.63±4.45
iris	94.67±8.2	94.67±8.2	97.33±4.66	90.67±11.42	92.67±5.84
kr-vs-kp	92.52±2.09	87.89±1.81	94.34±1.23	93.18±1.6	99.41±0.45
labor	88.33±15.81	93.33±11.65	77±11.91	88±11.46	77.67±15.64
letter	76.77±0.78	70±0.81	70.57±0.88	80.45±0.91	80.56±0.87
lymph	83.14±7.22	85.67±9.55	79±6.84	84.38±9.1	74.29±12.56
mushroom	99.4±0.27	95.57±0.45	99.67±0.23	99.77±0.12	100±0
primary-tumor	46.31±2.33	46.89±4.32	46.02±5.19	48.37±5.83	38.91±4.97
segment	94.37±1.59	88.92±1.95	90.43±1.96	86.36±2.36	92.86±1.39
sick	97.67±0.47	96.74±0.53	97.59±0.69	97±0.4	97.83±0.61
sonar	78.5±16	77.5±11.99	70.71±12.97	71.62±12.64	67.69±10.94
soybean	95.76±1.61	92.08±2.34	91.79±2.72	93.41±2.1	92.68±1.56
splice	95.3±1.48	95.36±1	94.76±1.6	95.39±1.35	91.57±1.37
vehicle	69.98±3.29	61.82±3.54	60.65±4.73	69.86±3.47	69.03±2.63
vote	92.66±4.65	90.14±4.17	95.18±3.93	93.12±4.02	94.96±3.83
vowel	92.42±2.2	67.07±4.21	68.69±3.47	83.43±3.84	75.66±5.18
waveform-5000	82±1.24	79.96±1.92	81.32±1.54	81.52±1.21	64.86±1.83
zoo	97.09±4.69	94.18±6.6	93.18±7.93	97.09±4.69	92.18±8.94

rithm C4.4. In a word, our work provides an effective and efficient data mining algorithm especially when a ranking is more desirable than just a classification.

Table 4. Results of two-tailed t-test on accuracy. the results of two-tailed t-test between each pair of algorithms, each entry $w/t/l$ means that the algorithm at the corresponding row wins in w data sets, ties in t data sets, and loses in l data sets, compared to the algorithm at the corresponding column. The significantly different probability of two-tailed t-test is **0.95**

	NB	SBC	CL-TAN	C4.4
FAN	10/26/0	5/29/2	4/30/2	12/21/3
NB	-	1/29/6	4/26/6	11/15/10
SNB	-	-	4/28/4	7/22/7
CL-TAN	-	-	-	7/15/4

References

1. Bradley, A. P.: The use of the area under the ROC curve in the evaluation of machine learning algorithms. Pattern Recognition **30** (1997) 1145-1159
2. Cohen, W. W., Schapire, R. E., Singer, Y.: Learning to order things. Journal of Artificial Intelligence Research, **10** 1997 243-270
3. Friedman, N., Greiger, D., Goldszmidt, M.: Bayesian Network Classifiers. Machine Learning **29** (1997) 103–130
4. Hand, D. J., Till, R. J.: A simple generalisation of the area under the ROC curve for multiple class classification problems. Machine Learning **45** (2001) 171-186
5. Keogh, E., Pazzani, M. : Learning augmented bayesian classifiers. Proceedings of Seventh International Workshop on AI and Statistics. (1999) Ft. Lauderdale.
6. Langley, P., Sage, S.: Induction of selective Bayesian classifiers. in Proceedings of the Tenth Conference on Uncertainty in Artificial Intelligence, 1994, pp. 339-406.
7. Merz, C., Murphy, P., Aha, D.: UCI repository of machine learning databases. Dept of ICS, University of California, Irvine (1997). http://www.ics.uci.edu/ mlearn/MLRepository.html
8. Provost, F., Fawcett, T.: Analysis and visualization of classifier performance: comparison under imprecise class and cost distribution. Proceedings of the Third International Conference on Knowledge Discovery and Data Mining. AAAI Press (1997) 43-48
9. Provost, F., Fawcett, T., Kohavi, R.: The case against accuracy estimation for comparing induction algorithms. Proceedings of the Fifteenth International Conference on Machine Learning. Morgan Kaufmann (1998) 445-453
10. Provost, F. J., Domingos, P.: Tree Induction for Probability-Based Ranking. Machine Learning **52(3)** (2003) 199-215
11. Quinlan, J. R.: C4.5: Programs for Machine Learning. Morgan Kaufmann: San Mateo, CA (1993)
12. http://prdownloads.sourceforge.net/weka/datasets-UCI.jar
13. Witten, I. H., Frank, E.: Data Mining –Practical Machine Learning Tools and Techniques with Java Implementation. Morgan Kaufmann (2000)
14. Ling, C. X., Zhang, H.: Toward Bayesian classifiers with accurate probabilities. Proceedings of the Sixth Pacific-Asia Conference on KDD. Springer (2002) 123-134

Finding Hidden Semantics Behind Reference Linkages: An Ontological Approach for Scientific Digital Libraries[*]

Peixiang Zhao[1], Ming Zhang[2], Dongqing Yang[2], and Shiwei Tang[2]

[1] Department of Systems Engineering and Engineering Management,
The Chinese University of Hong Kong,
Hong Kong SAR, China
pxzhao@se.cuhk.edu.hk

[2] Department of Computer Science and Technology, Peking University,
Beijing, China
{mzhang, ydq}@db.pku.edu.cn
tsw@pku.edu.cn

Abstract. The contents and topologies of inter-document linkages, such as citations and references among scientific literature, have received increasing research interests in recent years. Some technologies have been fully studied and utilized upon this meaningful information to improve the organization, analysis and evaluation of scientific digital libraries. In this paper, we present a CiteSeer-like system to access scientific papers in computer science discipline by reference linking technique. Moreover, implicit semantics behind reference indices are mined and organized to improve accessibility of scientific papers. In order to model scientific literature and their interlinked relationships, we develop a domain-specific ontology to analyze contents and citation anchor context of scientific papers. Compared with abstract of a specific paper written by authors themselves, we introduce an automatic summary generation algorithm to create objective descriptions from other scholars' perspectives based on the ontology. Semantic queries can also be asked to discover interesting patterns in scientific libraries in order to provide a comprehensive and meaningful guidance for users.

1 Introduction

With the rapid development of Internet and the increasing ripeness of the Web, more and more scientific papers appear on the Web in digital form instead of paper-based form. These digitized scientific documents have greatly facilitated the Web to be an efficient repository of up-to-date information. However, as the availability of scientific literature greatly improves, the inability of people to disseminate, share and profitably utilize such a large amount of information becomes more and more severe. Published scientific papers available on the Web are widely spread and are often poorly organized, neither comprehensively indexed nor interlinked in terms of logical correlations among them. People get limited supports in searching, reviewing, and

---

[*] This research is funded in part by NSFC grant 90412010 as well as grant 60221120144.

analyzing scientific literature from academic perspectives. This problem is now becoming an important research issue both in computer science and in digital libraries.

One original approach for managing such a huge volume of scientific literature is by reference linking different papers from bibliographic perspectives. Reference indices are useful for a number of purposes, such as literature dissemination, search, analysis and evaluation. Fig.1 shows main components of a reference index and a sample of reference linking. The left diagram gives a link topology among different scientific papers denoted by node *A*, *B*, *C*, *D*, *E*, *F* and *G*. The right diagram shows article *D* cites article *G*. Components of a reference index between *D* and *G* are citation anchor context in *D* and the corresponding bibliographic entry in the reference section of *D*. Through a reference link from "citing" papers to the "cited" one, users can find citation patterns and relationships among different documents. By navigating backward and forward though reference indices, users can promptly find a series of papers and perceive a thorough understanding of related research. The context of a citation in citing papers is quite illuminating in judging the motivation of reference, the contributions of the cited paper and the usefulness of a paper for a given query [11]. Reference indices are now widely used in reference linking [4], link analysis [3,7], hypertext and web mining [6], text classification [12] etc. The potential usefulness of reference indices contained in scientific literature has now been widely convinced and related services are provided in a range of applications, especially in scientific digital libraries.

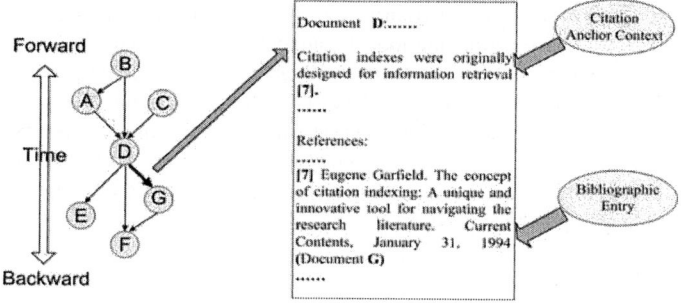

Fig. 1. A reference linking sample: from the time perspective

In resent years, several digital libraries have established large repositories of scientific literature, such as ISI SCI®, CiteSeer.IST [10], CORA [2], and ML Papers [13] etc. These projects pay much attention to interlinking different scientific papers via reference indices. However, few of them richly utilize semantic information hidden behind reference linkages. HITS [9,3] and PageRank [17] algorithms are widely applied to identify "important" web pages or papers in the web and digital libraries by analyzing link topologies of hyperlink or citation graph, but both of them neglect to analyze contents of web pages and scientific papers. In this paper we present a reference linking prototype for automatically linking scientific literature in computer science discipline. We develop a domain-specific ontology that models scientific literature and interlinked reference indices in order to identify semantics behind reference linkages. As to a specific scientific paper, we use descriptions derived from citation anchor context of citing ones to automatically generate summary which includes information of research theme and motivation, research topics, research background, research impact and applied fields etc. Compared with the abstract written by authors themselves, the summary is objective from different scholars' perspectives. Thus it is quite helpful for researchers to understand the literature better. Further reasoning upon the ontology is also provided by semantic query form in order to reveal new facts in scientific digital libraries. In this way, users can perceive a comprehensive understanding of a specific research domain, but not merely one scientific paper.

The reminder of this paper is organized as follows. Section 2 describes how to interlink scientific literature with metadata information. In section 3 there is a detailed description of the domain-specific ontology construction. Based on this ontological knowledge base, section 4 comments on how to automatically generalize summary information of a scientific paper and to provide further reasoning upon the ontological knowledge base by semantic queries. Section 5 shows experiments and evaluations of the prototype system. The final section presents conclusions of our work.

2 Reference Linking with Metadata

Reference linking means turning references within a scientific paper into "live reference" so that you can follow them in citing article to other accessible cited ones [4]. In order to facilitate reference linking in scientific literature, the first task is to extract metadata precisely and automatically from papers. Our metadata definition of scientific literature is derived form Dublin Core [5], which consists of title, author information, abstract, keywords, content of paper, bibliographic information, citation anchor context and appendix etc. Due to the inconsistency of metadata formats in scientific literature, we use information extraction techniques to improve the parsing of documents.

We use heuristic rules and regular expression matching technique to extract metadata from scientific papers. Extraction rule database is applied to accommodate various bibliographic styles appeared in scientific literature. We also use databases of author name, journal/conference name and domain name to help identify metadata. Font information and layout clues are quite helpful to determine specific metadata, such as title of a scientific paper. Different granularity strategies during metadata extraction are applied. For metadata such as title, abstract, content etc., coarse granularity strategy is used because these metadata could be extracted within one path. Metadata such as author information and bibliographic information should be extracted by fine granularity strategy in order to identify subfields of metadata. As shown in Fig.1, a reference index has two components: the detailed reference information in the bibliographic entry and citation anchor context (the sentences occurring near the citation tag) in the content of citing papers. Thus a reference index should be matched with its corresponding citation anchor context for further analysis.

After metadata extraction and reference/context matching, metadata of scientific papers are stored in citation database. Fig.2 shows the detailed metadata information of a scientific paper *"Hierarchical Clustering for Data Mining"* retrieved by a standard *SQL* query. The "Cited Paper(s)" section lists a paper *"Probabilistic Hierarchical Clustering with Labeled and Unlabeled Data"* who cites *"Hierarchical Clustering for Data mining"* and the "Context of citations to this paper" section lists corresponding citation anchor context. The "References" section lists scientific papers cited by *"Hierarchical Clustering for Data mining"*

```
Title:
Hierarchical Clustering for Data Mining

Author:
Anna Szymkowiak, Jan Larsen, Lars Kai Hansen

Abstract:
This paper presents hierarchical probabilistic clustering methods for
unsupervised learning in data mining applications. The probabilistic
clustering is on the previously suggested Generalizable Gaussian
Mixture model. A soft version Generalizable Gaussian Mixture model is
also discussed. The proposed hierarchical is agglomerative and based
on a L 2 distance metric. Unsupervised and supervised are
successfully tested on artificial data and for segmentation of emails.

Keywords:

Journal\Conference:
Proceeding 5th International Conference on Knowledge-Based
Intelligent Information Engineering Systems and Allied Technologies
KES' 2001

Publish Year: 2001

Context of Citations to this paper: Enter

Cited Paper(s):
Probabilistic Hierarchical Clustering with Labeled and Unlabeled Data

References:
A Mixture of Experts Classifier with Learning Based on both Labeled
and Unlabelled Data
Restructuring sparse high dimensional data for effective retrieval
Discriminant analysis by Gaussian Mixtures
A Unifying information-theoretical framework for independent
component analysis
Indexing by Latent Semantic Analysis
... ...
```

Fig. 2. Metadata of a scientific paper "Hierarchical Clustering for Data mining"

3 The Domain-Specific Ontology Construction

Ontology is the study of "things that exist" that began as a branch of philosophy and is now popular in the field of knowledge management [8]. We are developing an ontology that models scientific literature and their interlinked relationships toward producing an indexing and evaluation system for scientific digital libraries, as shown in Fig.3. By analyzing contents of cited paper and citation anchor context of citing ones, we automatically identify concepts with the aid of the ontological knowledge base. We also extract implicit claims concerning cited paper's motivations, contributions and relationships to corresponding research issues by analyzing citation anchor context of citing papers,. The interlinked concepts, together with semantic claims are modeled to form ontology for scientific literature in computer science discipline. This ontological knowledge base is powerful to intelligently communicate, analyze and reason over concepts and knowledge of scientific literature.

3.1 Topic Distillation by WordNet and Ontological Knowledge Base

We want to build ontology that models concepts in scientific literature and their relationships described in citation anchor context. Thus we have to extract concepts, namely topics from scientific papers. We analyze title and keywords of cited paper, together with descriptions in citation anchor context of all citing papers to distill research topics. Because title and keywords are written by authors themselves whereas citation descriptions by other scholars and researchers, a combination of analyses both from subjective perspective and from objective one is proved to be convincing.

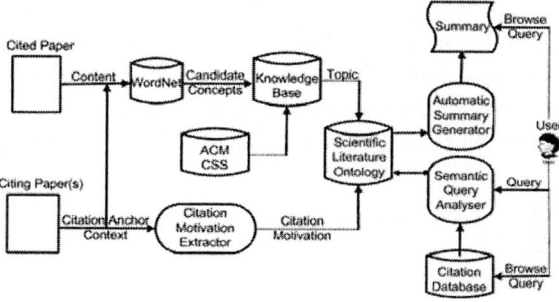

Fig. 3. The construction process of the ontological knowledge base that models scientific literature in computer science discipline

As to keywords of cited paper, we simply separate each keyword from the other. Since title and citation anchor text are always sentences describing cited paper, and the most common type of concept is a sequence of proper nouns or noun phrases, we use WordNet [14], a successful concept ontology, to parse contents of these sentences. After proper stemming and sense-tagging by WordNet, nouns and noun phrases are extracted from sentences. These nouns and noun phrases, together with the separated keywords, are candidate concepts of cited paper for further analysis.

While WordNet is a general purpose concept ontology, it can not be expected to provide exhaustive coverage of concepts in some specific domains. We develop an ontological knowledge base in computer science discipline to help distill research topics from candidate concepts. This knowledge base is a concept hierarchical tree-like ontology derived from ACM CCS (Computing Classification System) [1], an existing knowledge base in computer science discipline. Each candidate concept of paper will be mapped on the node of the knowledge base and those with a complete match are topics of related scientific papers. We calculate weights for each topic that represents its importance as a descriptor for paper. Concept weight is calculated using the metric based on TFIDF, a standard term-weighting measure from the information retrieval research community.

$$w_t = \frac{n_t}{1 + \log N_t} \qquad (1)$$

Where w_t is the weight of the concept t completely matched with corresponding node in the knowledge base. n_t is the number of times concept t appeared in title, keywords of cited paper and in citation anchor context of citing papers. N_t is the number of documents concept t appears.

3.2 Ontological Knowledge Base Construction

As mentioned in section 3.1, we develop an ontological knowledge base in computer science discipline to help extract research topics from scientific literature. Based on ACM CSS, our knowledge base has a hierarchical tree-like structure. There are two relations between concepts in knowledge base: the "*Is-a*" relation in the same categorization sub-tree and the "*Similar*" relation between different categorization sub-tree. As shown in Fig.4, the concept "*Statistical database*" has a "Is-a" relation with "*Database Management*" and has a "Similar" relation with "*Probability & Statistics*" in another categorization sub-tree. A hash table is built to facilitate concept matching process between candidate concepts and nodes in knowledge base.

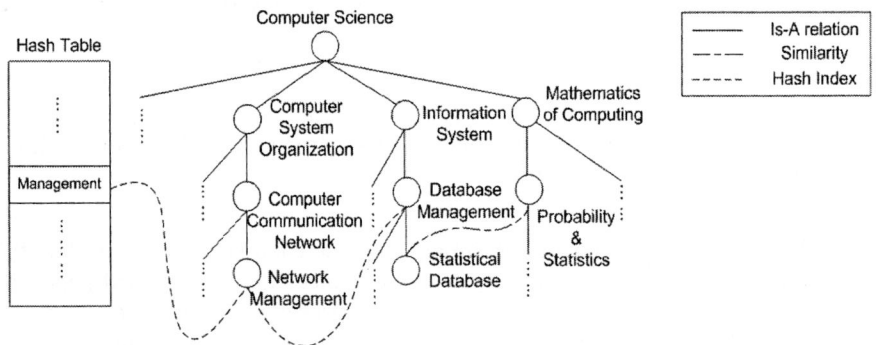

Fig. 4. The ontological knowledge base in computer science discipline

Upon the knowledge base, we define operations to identify semantic relations between different nodes. From a concept node in knowledge base, we could find more general or specific concepts by **Parent** operation or **Child** operation respectively and those similar concepts could also be retrieved by **Similar** operation. **Sim** operation provides anther approach to measure similarities of different concepts by calculating semantic distances in the knowledge base. In the following equations, X, Y and Z denote concepts of the knowledge base.

$$\textbf{\textit{Parent}} \ (\ X \ ) = \{ \ Y | \text{ where } X \text{ has a direct "Is-A" relation with } Y\} \quad (2)$$

$$\textbf{\textit{Child}} \ (\ X \ ) = \{ \ Y | \text{ where } Y \text{ has a direct "Is-A" relation with } X\} \quad (3)$$

$$\textbf{\textit{Similar}} \ (\ X \ ) = \{Y | \text{ where } Y \text{ has a direct "Similar" relation with } X\} \quad (4)$$

$$Dist\ (X, Y) = \text{number of "Is-a" relation links between } X \text{ and } Y \text{ in the same categorization sub-tree} \quad (5)$$

$$Sim\ (X, Y) = Dist\ (X, Z) + Dist\ (Y, Z), \text{ where Z is the nearest parent node of both X and Y} \quad (6)$$

Based on the ontological knowledge base mentioned above, we could conveniently extract research topics from scientific papers in computer science discipline. In the next section, we will analyze citation anchor context to find citation motivations and relationships between cited paper and citing ones.

3.3 Citation Motivation Extraction and Analysis

Citation anchor context of citing papers are "meaningful" text which can provide detailed descriptions and evaluations to the cited one. It is quite helpful to find out "why" and "how" a particular scientific paper is cited and relationships to other papers in the literature. We extract citation motivations from citation anchor context and classify them into several types in order to assign semantic meanings to interlinked reference indices in scientific literature. [18] proposed 15 categories for the reasons of citation, but we classify reference motivations into the following 5 categories:

- Providing background knowledge
- Identifying methodology
- Pointing out problems or drawbacks
- Indicating or predicting future research
- Others

Similar to [15], we make rules for each category and extract reference motivations based on cue phrases. When a cue phrase is identified in citation anchor context, we classify the citation motivation of this reference index into the category which the cur phrase belongs to. For example, if the phrases in citation anchor context such as "make use of", "present", "applied to" etc. are identified, corresponding reference indices are classified to the "Identifying methodology" category; if the phrases with "little influence", "inconsistent with", "raise problems" etc. are identified, the reference indices are classified to the "Pointing out problems or drawbacks" category. For each citation motivation, we assign an attribute to identify attitudes of authors toward the cited paper: 1 for positive attitude, -1 for negative attitude and 0 if the attitude can not be identified. By analyzing content of citation anchor context, especially those verbs mentioned above, and adjectives or adverbs, such as "extensively", "efficiently", "difficultly" etc., attributes of citation attitude could be extracted which implies inclinations of authors whether to recommend or criticize related research described in the cited paper.

After citation motivation extraction and analysis, semantic meanings are identified and assigned to reference indices in scientific literature. It offers intellectual linkage among different papers and it is helpful for users to learn more from citing papers about the cited one by descriptions and evaluations from other researchers' perspectives. It also provides us with meaningful linkage among concepts of our own ontological knowledge base. Further analysis will be applied upon the ontological knowledge base to infer interesting citation/reference patterns in scientific literature.

4 Analyses and Reasoning Upon the Ontology

4.1 Automatic Summary Generation

As shown in Fig. 3, based on research topics extracted from scientific papers and citation motivations from interlinked reference indices, we develop an ontological knowledge base to model scientific literature and their relationships. This knowledge base is efficient to communicate, analyze and reason over concepts and knowledge of scientific literature. One of the most important applications upon it is automatic summary generation.

A summary of a scientific paper is very helpful and instructive for readers to know what has been studied. As writing a summary or a survey by manual work is quite time-consuming, it is desirable to generate comprehensive summaries for scientific papers automatically. In our prototype system, summary of a scientific paper is composed of four components:

- research theme and motivation
- research topics
- research background
- research impact and applied fields

Based on the ontology of scientific literature in computer science discipline, we apply automatic summary generation algorithm to get each component of summary for scientific papers. As to the component *"research theme and motivation"*, we have got results by analyzing citation anchor context of citing papers in section 3.3. The results are grouped by different citation categories and ordered by attributes of authors' attitudes. Users could follow hyperlinks to examine detailed descriptions in citation anchor context of each citing papers. As to the component *"research topics"*, we have got results by topic distillation with the aid of WordNet and ontological knowledge base in section 3.2: Research topics are ordered by concept weight defined in equation (1). Because research topics are matched with concepts in the knowledge base, we can apply operations defined from equation (2) to (6) upon corresponding concepts of the knowledge base to get additional information for topics of scientific papers. For example, while referring to subordinate topics of *"Information Systems"*, we can get research issues such as *"Database Management"*, *"Information Retrieval"*, *"Digital Library"* etc. While referring to similar topics of *"File"*, we can get topics such as *"File Systems Management"*, *"Database Management"* etc., which may share research similarities with the topic *"File"* but are quite different issues in some other research background. As to the component *"research background"* and *"research impact and applied fields"*, we simply organize research topics of cited papers and citing ones, respectively. The topics are also grouped and ordered by concept weight. Fig. 5 presents a summary automatically generated by our algorithm. The summary consists of four components mentioned above which gives a comprehensive description for the scientific paper *"Melodic matching techniques for large music databases"*. Users can follow hyperlinks to get detailed information of related research issues and corresponding scientific papers.

```
Title:
Melodic matching techniques for large music databases  (7 citations)
Summary:
    Theme and Motivation:
        Identifying methodology              (3 papers)
        Providing background reading         (1 paper)
        Others                               (2 papers)
        Pointing out problems or drawbacks   (1 paper)
    Research Topic:
        Music database                       (3 papers)
        Information Retrieval                (2 paper)
        Searching                            (2 papers)
    Research Background:
        Music database                       (3 papers)
        Information retrieval                (3 papers)
        Pattern Recognition                  (3 papers)
        Algorithm                            (2 papers)
        Artificial Intelligence              (1 paper)
    Impact and Applied Fields:
        Music Database                       (4 papers)
        Information retrieval                (2 papers)
        Data Structure                       (1 paper)
```

Fig. 5. Summary of the paper "Melodic matching techniques for large music databases"

4.2 Reasoning by Semantic Queries Upon the Knowledge Base

In addition to automatic summary generation, the ontological knowledge base also makes it possible to infer knowledge in scientific literature. In our prototype, the ontological knowledge base enables discoveries of implicit information by semantic queries which are described as OWL QL [16] query patterns, namely a set of triples of the form (<property> <subject> <object>). Each triple is mapped to several operations of the ontological knowledge base or standard SQL statements on the citation database. Our prototype system provides limited triples describing the most common operations upon the ontology and the citation database. For example, to find scientific papers a research organization has published, we can follow:

Query: ("Scientific papers published by research organization A")
Query Pattern: {(is-author ?a ?p)(work-for ?a ?o) (equal ?o "A")}
Must-Bind Variables List: (? p)
May-Bind Variables List: ( )
Don't-Bind Variables List: (? a)

Where variables *a* stands for author names, *p* stands for scientific papers and *o* stands for research organizations. And, withal, *is-author*, *work-for* and *equal* etc. are semantic queries supported by our prototype system.

Taking advantage of the expressive power of the ontological knowledge base built upon scientific literature, the prototype system can provide structural queries, such as queries asking of super-class, subclasses and similar classes of a given concept in computer science. All these structural queries are formulated to operations upon the ontological knowledge base. We also provide complicated queries involving concepts not expressible in the ontological knowledge base such as *"Which organizations are research communities in information retrieval research domain?"* or *"Who are noted authorities on data mining?"* These complicated queries are constructed by those system-supported query triples. Users can write their own semantic queries in OWL-QL query patterns by means of combining different system-supported queries into more complicated and comprehensive ones. Heuristic rules are also provided to solve analytical queries. For example, to answer the query *"which research subfields are quite relevant to digital library research?"* We define that *"quite relevant"* subfields to *"digital library"* are those research topics with a similarity link to the node *"digital library"* in the ontological knowledge base or research topics whose similarity distances to the node *"digital library"* measured by *Sim* operation are less than or equal to 2. The number 2 represents user definable thresholds.

5 Experimental Evaluation

In our prototype system, we locate and download over 10,000 scientific papers in computer science discipline from Internet by web crawler. After preprocessing, metadata extraction and reference/context matching, metadata information is stored in citation database implemented by PostGreSQL. In order to improve the accessibility of reference linking, documents without full text that can not be parsed or those with less than 3 in-degrees are eliminated from database. There are finally 7,973 scientific papers in our citation database.

The effectiveness of reference linking in scientific literature heavily relies on precision of metadata extraction. We do several experiments to evaluate our extraction technique and final extraction results. We choose 1430 scientific papers in CiteSeer.IST. After preprocessing, 293 papers with errors are eliminated from test beds. The metadata extraction results are shown in Table 1. Our extraction precision is a litter higher than CiteSee.IST and Opcit [4].

Table 1. Metadata extraction precision results of sceintific articles

Automatic Metadata Extraction	Metadata of Scientific Papers						
	Title	Author Information	Abstract	Keywords	Content	Reference	Appendix
Extraction Precision	92.1%	87.8%	98.9%	100%	100%	83.3%	100%

While extracting topics from scientific literature described in section 3.1, one of the important steps is to distill candidate concepts with the aid of the ontological knowledge base. However, there is a possibility that some candidate concepts are not perfectly matched with those appeared in knowledge base. We do an experiment to investigate how well candidate concepts from titles, keywords and citation anchor context match with concepts in the ontological knowledge base. We choose 200 scientific articles from ML Papers, 150 for training and 50 for testing. We manually choose concepts from title, keywords and reference anchor context in the training paper set in order to train our ontological knowledge base, especially in machine learning research field. Fig.6. shows concept matching results in the test bed. Each left column shows numbers of concepts that should be extracted and corresponding right column shows numbers of concepts that are perfectly matched and extracted by the ontological knowledge base.

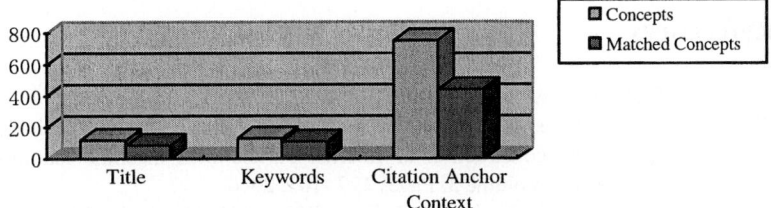

Fig. 6. Concept matching results in the test bed

As shown in Fig.6, concepts matching precisions from title, keywords and citation anchor context sections of scientific papers in the test bed are 74.8%, 82.3% and 58.5%. Compared with concept matching precisions in title and keywords section, that in citation anchor context is low. That is partially because the ontological knowledge base does not contain newly emerging concepts from citation anchor context and some of keywords fall out of machine learning classification sub-trees.

6 Conclusions

In Recent years the Web has developed to be a medium for scientific literature dissemination, retrieval and evaluation. However, experience show that hundreds of thousands of scientific papers are neither comprehensively indexed nor interlinked in terms of citation/reference semantics. In scientific digital libraries domain, reference indices are increasingly being applied to improve the ability of management, analysis and evaluation of scientific literature. In this paper we investigate the usage of a domain-specific ontology to improve semantic linking of scientific literature via reference indices among different scientific papers. The ontological knowledge base is consisted of concepts extracted from papers and reference motivations derived from citation anchor context. Moreover, we utilize automatic summary generation algorithm upon the ontological knowledge base to give an objective description for cited paper from scholars' perspectives. Further reasoning is also provided by system-supported or user-defined semantic queries upon the knowledge base in order to reveal new facts and interesting patterns in scientific libraries.

Our prototype system is implemented and some experiments are conducted. We are now encouraged to apply ontology techniques in scientific digital libraries and further research in this field is ongoing.

Acknowledgements

The authors would like to thank Prof. Jian Pei in Department of Computer Science and Engineering, University of Buffalo, the Sate University of New York for his comments on an early version of this paper.

References

[1] ACM CCS. http://www.acm.org/class/
[2] Andrew Kanchites McCallum, Kamal Nigam, Jason Rennie and Kristie Syemore. "Automating the construction of Internet portals with machine learning". *Information Retrieval Journal*. Volume 3. Pages 127 -163. 2000.
[3] Ding C., Zha H., He X., Husbands P., and Simon H. "Analysis of hubs and authorities on the web". Lawrence Berkeley Nat'l Lab Tech Report 47847(www.nersc.gov/~cding /hits.ps). 2001
[4] Donna Bergmark. "Automatic extraction of reference linking information from online documents". Technical Report TR 2000 -1821, Cornell Computer Science Department. October 2000
[5] Dublin Core Metadata Initiative http://purl.oclc.org/dc/
[6] Flake, G. W., Lawrence, S., and Giles.C.L. "Efficient identification of web communities". *Sixth ACM SIGKDD International conference on Knowledge Discovery and Data Mining*. Pages 150-159, 2000
[7] Gerard Salton. "Automatic indexing using bibliographic citations". *Journal of Documentation*, Volume 27. Pages 98-110. 1971
[8] Guarino, N. "Formal Ontology and Information Systems". in *Proc. FOIS'98 trento*. Italy. 6-8 June
[9] Jon Kleinberg. "Authoritative sources in a hyperlinked environment". In *Proceedings of the Ninth Annual ACM-SIAM Symposium on Discrete Algorithms*. 1998
[10] Kurt D. Bollacker, Steve Lawrence, C. Lee. Giles. "CiteSeer: an autonomous web agent for automatic retrieval and identification of interesting publications". *Proceedings of 2nd International Conf. on Autonomous Agents*. ACM Press. Pages 116-123. May 1998.
[11] Lempel R. and Moran S. "SALSA: stochastic approach for link-structure analysis and the TKC effect". *ACM Trans. Information Systems*. Volume 19. Pages 131-160. 2001
[12] Lu Q. and Getoor L. "Link-based classification". In *Proc of ICML-03*, 2003
[13] ML Papers. http://www.ai.mit.edu/people/ayn/cgi/vpapers
[14] Miller G.A., Beckwith R., Felbaum C. Gross D. and Miller K. "Introduction to WordNet: An On-line Lexical Database". *International Journal of Lexicography*. Volume 3. Pages 235-244. 1990
[15] Nanba, H., and Okumura M. "Towards Multi-paper Summarization Using Reference Information". *Proceedings of the 16th International Joint Conferences on Artificial Intelligence (IJCAI-99)*. Pages926-931. 1999
[16] R. Fikes, P.Hayes and I. Horrocks. "OWL-QL – a language for deductive query answering on the semantic web". Technical Report KSL-03-14, Knowledge Systems Lab, Stanford University, CA, USA. 2003
[17] Sergey Brin and Lawrence Page. The Anatomy of a Large-scale Hypertextual Web Search Engine. In *the Seventh International World Wide Web Conference*. 1998.
[18] Weinstock, N. "Citation indexes, in Kent A (Ed.)". Encyclopedia of Library and Information Science, New York. Pages 16-41. 1971.

XANDY: Detecting Changes on Large Unordered XML Documents Using Relational Databases

Erwin Leonardi[1], Sourav S. Bhowmick[1], and Sanjay Madria[2]

[1] School of Computer Engineering,
Nanyang Technological University, Singapore
{pk909134, assourav}@ntu.edu.sg
[2] Department of Computer Science,
University of Missouri-Rolla, Rolla, MO 65409
madrias@umr.edu

Abstract. Previous works in change detection on XML documents are not suitable for detecting the changes to large XML documents as it requires a lot of memory to keep the two versions of XML documents in the memory. In this paper, we take a more conservative yet novel approach of using traditional relational database engines for detecting the changes to large *unordered* XML documents. We elaborate how we detect the changes on unordered XML documents by using relational database. To this end, we have implemented a prototype system called XANDY that converts XML documents into relational tuples and detects the changes from these tuples by using SQL queries. Our experimental results show that the relational approach has better scalability compared to published algorithms like X-Diff. The result quality of our approach is comparable to the one of X-Diff.

1 Introduction

Detecting changes to XML data is an important research problem. Cobena et al. [3] proposed an algorithm, called XyDiff, for detecting changes on ordered XML documents by using the signature and weight of nodes. XMLTreeDiff [2] is also proposed for solving the problem of detecting changes for ordered XML documents by using DOMHash. In [10], the authors presented X-Diff, an algorithm for detecting the changes on unordered XML documents. In this paper, we focus on detecting the changes on the unordered XML documents.

The changes on unordered XML documents can be classified into two types: *changes to the internal nodes* and *changes to the leaf nodes*. An *internal node* does not contain textual data. For example, consider the two versions of an XML document in Figure 1. Nodes 2 and 7 in Figure 1(a) are the internal nodes. The changes that occur in the internal nodes are called as *structural changes* as they modify the structure but do not change the textual data content. There are two types of *structural changes* for unordered XML documents: *insertion of internal nodes*, and *deletion of internal nodes*. For instance, node 102 in Figure 1(b) is an example of internal nodes insertion. A *leaf node* is the node/attribute which contains textual data. For example, node 3 is a leaf node which has name

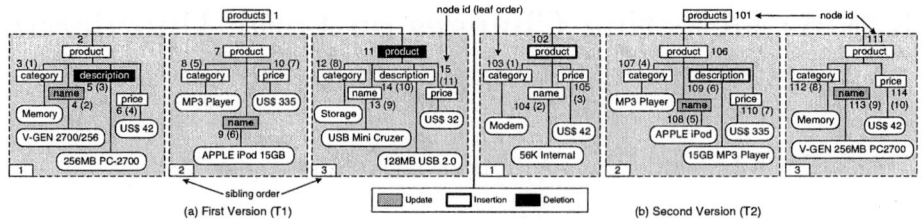

Fig. 1. Example

"category" and textual content "Memory". The changes in the leaf nodes are called *content changes* as they modify the textual data content. There are three types of *content changes* for unordered XML documents: *insertion of leaf nodes*, *deletions of leaf nodes*, and *content update of a leaf nodes*. For example, a leaf node 5 is a deleted leaf node. In this paper, we present a novel technique for detecting the *content* and *structural* changes in *unordered* XML using RDBMS.

The main-memory-based approaches have some limitations as far as change detection is concerned. First, they require the entire trees (i.e., DOM trees) of both versions of an XML document to be memory resident. This problem is exacerbated by the fact that these trees are typically much larger than their XML documents. Thus, the scheme is not scalable for very large XML documents. In fact, the scheme is inefficient. We need to parse an XML document multiple times whenever we want to compare it with more than one document at different times.

The above limitations coupled with the recent success in storing XML data in relational databases [4, 8, 7] force us to ask whether we can address these problems by using relational techniques to detect the changes on XML documents. In our preliminary effort in [5, 1], we have demonstrated that it is indeed possible to use the relational database to detect the changes to *ordered* XML data. In [5, 1], we present relational approaches for detecting the *content changes* on *ordered* XML documents. However, the underlying relational schema of [1] is simplistic and is not efficient for path expressions query processing. Ideally, a change detection system build on top of a relational database should also support efficient insertion and extraction of XML documents and efficient execution of path expression queries. Hence, our approach in [5] uses SUCXENT schema that enables us to insert, extract, and query XML data efficiently [7].

In this paper, we present a novel relational approach for detecting the changes on *unordered* XML documents called XANDY (**X**ml en**A**bled cha**N**ge **D**etection s**Y**stem). Our approach differs from our previous efforts in two ways. First, we focus on unordered XML documents. To the best of our knowledge, currently, there is no published approach for detecting the change on *unordered* XML documents by using relational database. Detecting changes on *unordered* trees are substantially harder than that on *ordered* trees [10]. Second, we detect both content and structural changes.

2 Background

In this section, we present the relational database scheme used for storing two versions of XML documents. We have extended the relational schema of our XML storage system called SUCXENT (**S**chema **U**n**C**oncious **X**ML **EN**abled Sys**T**em) [7]. We chose SUCXENT because we have shown in [7] that our approach outperforms significantly the current state-of-the-art model mapping approaches like XParent [4] as far as storage size, insertion time, extraction time, and path expression queries are concerned [1]. The SUCXENT schema is shown in Figure 2(a). We use the Document table for storing the names of the documents in the database. This allows us to store multiple versions of XML documents. The Path table is used to record the all paths from the root to the leaf nodes. It maintains the path ids and the relative path expressions as instances of the PathID and PathExp attributes respectively.

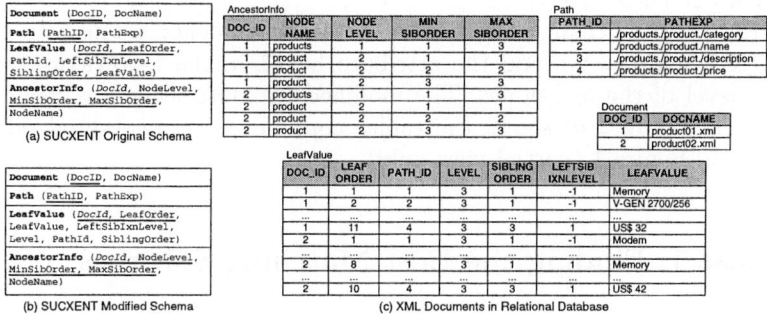

Fig. 2. XML Documents in Relational Database

The LeafValue table is used for storing the information of the leaf nodes. The DocID attribute indicates which XML document a particular leaf node belongs to. The PathID attribute maintains the id of the path of a particular leaf node stored in the Path table. The LeafOrder attribute is used to record the *node order* of the leaf nodes in an XML tree. For example, consider the XML tree in Figure 1(a). When we parse the XML document, we will find the leaf node "category" with value "Memory" as the first leaf node in the document. Hence, we assign the LeafOrder equal to "1" for this leaf node. The LeafOrder of the next leaf node (node "name" with value "V-GEN 2700/256") is equal to "2". Two leaf nodes have the same SiblingOrder if they share the same parent. For example, the leaf nodes with LeafOrder equal to "1", "2", "3", and "4" shall have the same SiblingOrder (equal to "1") since they share the same parent node (node 2). The dotted boxes in Figure 1 indicate the leaf nodes that have the same SiblingOrder. The LeftSibIxnLevel (Left Sibling Intersection Level) is the

---

[1] Jiang et al. has shown in [4] that XParent outperforms various existing model mapping approaches.

level at which the leaf nodes belonging to a particular sibling order intersect the leaf nodes belonging to the sibling order that comes immediately before. For example, consider the leaf nodes with `SiblingOrder` equal to "2" in the XML tree. These leaf nodes shall intersect with the leaf nodes having `SiblingOrder` equal to "1" at the node "products" (id=1) which is at level 1. The `LeafValue` stores the textual content of the leaf nodes. Note that the attribute `LeftSibIxnLevel` in this table is only useful for constructing the XML documents from the relational database [7]. We use the `AncestorInfo` table for storing the information of the internal nodes. The `DocID` attribute indicates which XML document a particular ancestor node belongs to. We record the names and the level of ancestor nodes in the `NodeName` and `NodeLevel` attributes respectively. The `MinSibOrder` and `MaxSibOrder` store the minimum and maximum sibling orders of the leaf nodes under a particular ancestor node respectively. For example, the node "products" (id=1) in Figure 1(a) has `MinSibOrder` and `MaxSibOrder` equal to "1" and "3" respectively. Node "product" (id=7) has `MinSibOrder` and `MaxSibOrder` equal to "2" and "2" respectively.

For detecting the changes in unordered XML documents, we need to modify the `SUCXENT` schema. We add the attribute `Level` in the `LeafValue` table to store the level of the leaf nodes. The modified `SUCXENT` schema is depicted in Figure 2(b). Figure 2(c) shows the tables containing the two shredded XML documents in Figure 1 (partial view only).

3 Phase 1: Finding the Best Matching Subtrees

Suppose we have two versions of an XML tree, T_1 and T_2. The objective of this phase is to find the most similar subtrees in T_1 and T_2. First, the algorithm determines the *matching leaf nodes* in in T_1 and T_2 by issuing a SQL query against the database. Then it starts to match the ancestor nodes of the matching leaf nodes up to the root nodes. Note that the algorithm issues several SQL queries to match the subtrees. The most similar subtrees are considered as the *best matching subtrees*. This first phase results a set of *best matching internal nodes* at which the best matching subtrees are rooted. We use the information of the best matching subtrees to determine the *minimum delta*. In this section, we shall elaborate this phase further.

Definition 1. [**Matching Leaf Nodes**] *Let $L(T_1)$ and $L(T_2)$ be two sets of the leaf nodes in T_1 and T_2 respectively. Let $name(\ell)$, $level(\ell)$, and $value(\ell)$ be the node name, node level, and textual content of a leaf node ℓ respectively. Then ℓ_1 and ℓ_2 are **matching leaf nodes** (denoted as $\ell_1 \leftrightarrow \ell_2$) if $name(\ell_1) = name(\ell_2)$, $level(\ell_1) = level(\ell_2)$, and $value(\ell_1) = value(\ell_2)$, where $\ell_1 \in L(T_1)$ and $\ell_2 \in L(T_2)$.*

Next, we define the notion of *matching sibling orders*. A set of leaf nodes that have the same parent node will have the same sibling order. The matching sibling orders can summarize the information of matching leaf nodes. Hence, the storage space needed for storing the matching information is reduced.

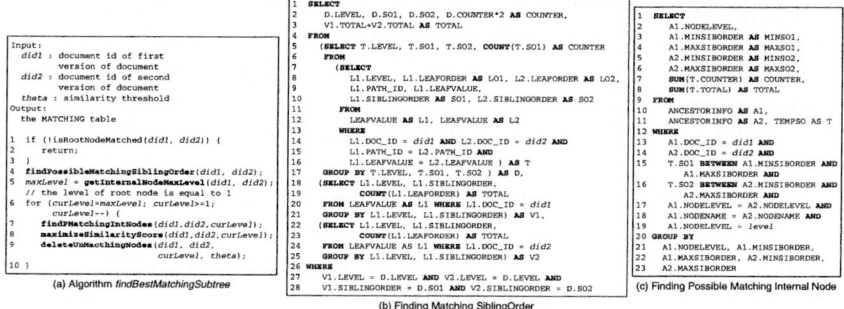

Fig. 3. Algorithm *findBestMatchingSubtree* and SQL Queries

Definition 2. [**Matching Sibling Orders**] *Let so_1 and so_2 be two sibling orders in T_1 and T_2 respectively. Let $P = \{p_1, p_2, ..., p_x\}$ and $Q = \{q_1, q_2, ..., q_y\}$ be two sets of leaf nodes, where $\forall p_i \in P$ have the same sibling order so_1, and $\forall q_j \in Q$ have the same sibling order so_2. Then so_1 and so_2 are the **matching sibling orders** (denoted by $so_1 \Leftrightarrow so_2$) if $\exists p_i\ \exists q_j$ such that $p_i \leftrightarrow q_j$ where $p_i \in P$ and $q_j \in Q$.*

After determining the matching sibling orders, we are able to find the *possible matching internal nodes* at which the *possible matching subtrees* are rooted. Informally, the *possible matching subtrees* are the subtrees in which they have at least one matching sibling orders. Note that the subtrees in T_1 are possible to be matched to more than one subtrees in T_2.

Definition 3. [**Possible Matching Subtrees**] *Let $I(T_1)$ and $I(T_2)$ be two sets of the internal nodes in T_1 and T_2 respectively. Let S_1 and S_2 be two subtrees rooted at nodes $i_1 \in I(T_1)$ and $i_2 \in I(T_2)$ respectively. Let $name(i)$ and $level(i)$ be the node name and node level of an internal node i respectively. S_1 and S_2 are the **possible matching subtrees** if the following conditions are satisfied: 1) $name(i_1) = name(i_2)$, 2) $level(i_1) = level(i_2)$, and 3) $\exists P\ \exists Q$ such that $P \Leftrightarrow Q$ where $P \in S_1$ and $Q \in S_2$.*

We only consider matching subtrees in the same level for the same reason as in [10]. Next, we determine the *best matching subtrees* from a set of possible matching subtrees. Consequently, we have to measure how similar two possible matching subtrees are. Formally, *similarity score* can be defined as follows.

Definition 4. [**Similarity Score**] *The similarity score $\Re$ of two subtrees t_1 and t_2 as follows: $\Re(t_1, t_2) = \frac{2|t_1 \cap t_2|}{|t_1 \cup t_2|}$ where $|t_1 \cup t_2|$ is the total number of nodes of subtrees t_1 and t_2, and $|t_1 \cap t_2|$ is number of matching nodes.*

The similarity score will be between 0 and 1. Based on the similarity score, we are able to classify the matching subtree into three types: 1)**Isomorphic Subtrees** ($\Re(t_1, t_2) = 1$). We say two subtrees are isomorphic if they are identical except for the orders among siblings. 2)**Unmatching Subtrees** ($\Re(t_1, t_2) = 0$). We say

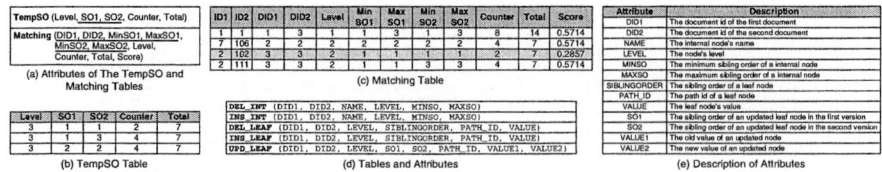

Fig. 4. The `TempSO` and `Matching` Tables, and Table Description

two subtrees are unmatching if they are totally different. 3)**Matching Subtrees** ($0 < \Re(t_1, t_2) < 1$). The matching subtrees have some parts in the trees that are corresponded each other.

After we are able to determine how similar the possible matching subtrees are, the best matching subtrees can be determined. The formal definition of the best matching subtrees is as follows.

Definition 5. [**Best Matching Subtrees**] *Let $t \in T_1$ be a subtree in T_1 and $P \subseteq T_2$ be a set of subtrees in T_2. Also t and $t_i \in P$ are possible matching subtrees $\forall\ 0 < i \leq |P|$. Then t and t_i are the **best matching subtrees** (denoted by $t \backsimeq t_i$) iff $(\Re(t, t_i) > \Re(t, t_j))\ \forall\ 0 < j \leq |P|$ and $i \neq j$.*

The algorithm for determining the best matching subtrees is depicted in Figure 3(a). Given two XML trees T_1 and T_2 shredded in a relational database as shown in Figure 2 and the similarity score threshold (say θ=0.25), the *findBestMatchingSubtree* algorithm starts finding the matching best subtrees by checking the root nodes of T_1 and T_2 (lines 1-3, Figure 3(a)). If they have different names, then both XML documents are considered as different. Consequently, the delta only consists of a deletion of T_1 and an insertion of T_2. Otherwise, the algorithm finds the *matching sibling orders* (line 4, Figure 3(a)). The SQL query for retrieving the matching sibling order is depicted in Figure 3(b). The results are stored in the `TempSO` table (Figure 4(b)) whose attributes are depicted in Figure 4(a).

Next, the *findBestMatchingSubtree* algorithm determines the deepest level *maxLevel* of the root nodes of subtrees in T_1 and T_2 (line 5, Figure 3(a)). For each level *curLevel* starting from level *maxLevel* to the level of the root nodes of the trees (level=1), the algorithm starts by finding the best matching subtrees (lines 6-10, Figure 3(a)). First, the algorithm finds the *possible matching internal nodes* (line 7, Figure 3(a)). The SQL query shown in Figure 3(c) is used to retrieve the *possible matching internal nodes*. We store the results in the `Matching` table whose attributes are depicted in Figure 4(a). The `Matching` table of T_1 and T_2 is depicted in Figure 4(c).

The next step is to maximize the similarity scores of the possible matching internal nodes at level *curLevel* at which the possible matching subtrees are rooted (line 8, Figure 3(a)) since we may have some subtrees and sibling orders at (*curLevel*+1) in T_1 that can be matched to more than one subtrees and sibling orders in T_2 respectively, and vice versa. The *maximizeSimilarityScore* algorithm is similar to the Smith-Waterman algorithm [9] for sequence alignments. Due to the space constraints, we do not present the *maximizeSimilarityScore* algorithm here. It can be found in [6]. For instance, the score of possible matching subtrees rooted at nodes 1 and 101 at level 1 is maximized if $t_2 \simeq t_{111}$ and $t_7 \simeq t_{106}$. The The corresponding tuple of the possible matching subtrees which are not used in maximizing the score are deleted (highlighted row, Figure 3(c)).

4 Phase 2: Detecting the Changes

In the second phase, first, we detect the inserted and deleted internal nodes. Then we find the inserted and deleted leaf nodes. Finally, we detect the updated leaf nodes from the inserted and deleted leaf nodes as they can be decomposed into pairs of deleted and inserted leaf nodes. The formal definitions of types of changes can be found in [6].

Insertion of Internal Nodes. Intuitively, the inserted internal nodes are the internal nodes that are in the new version, but not in the old version. Hence, they must be not the root nodes of the best matching subtrees as they are in both versions. The SQL query depicted in Figure 5(a) (*did1* and *did2* refer to the first and second versions of the document respectively) detects the set of newly inserted internal nodes. Consider the example in Figure 1. We notice that the subtree rooted at node 102 in T_2 is inserted. The inserted internal nodes are retrieved by the SQL query depicted in Figure 5(a) and are stored in the INS_INT table as shown in Figure 6(a).

Deletion of Internal Nodes. We can use the same intuition to find the deleted internal nodes that are in T_1, but not in T_2. The deleted internal nodes can be detected by slightly modifying the SQL query depicted in Figure 5(a). We replace the "*did2*" in line 6 with "*did1*". The "MINSO2" and "MAXSO2" in line 8 are replaced by "MINSO1" and "MAXSO1" respectively. In the example shown in Figure 1, we observe that the subtree rooted at node 11 in T_1 is deleted. The deleted internal nodes are retrieved by the SQL query depicted in Figure 5(a) (after some modification) and are stored in the DEL_INT table as shown in Figure 6(b).

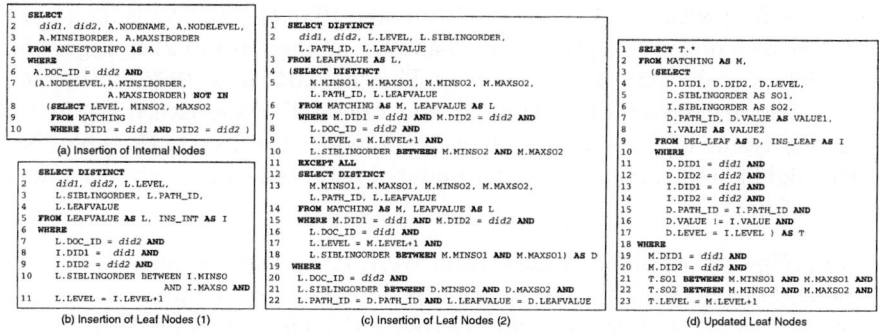

Fig. 5. SQL Queries for Detecting the Changes

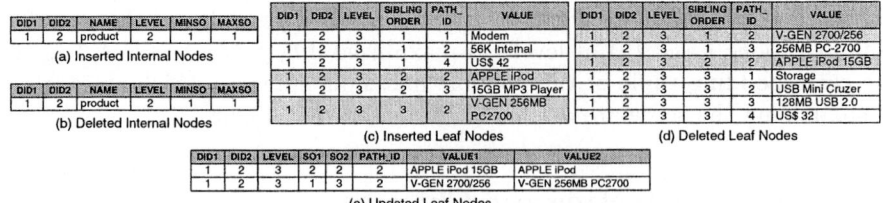

Fig. 6. Detected Delta

Insertion of Leaf Nodes. The *new* leaf nodes are only available in the second version of an XML tree. These new nodes should be either in the *best matching subtrees* or in the newly *inserted subtrees*. Consider the Figure 1. The leaf nodes 103, 104, and 105 belong to the newly *inserted subtree* rooted at node 102. The leaf node 109 is also inserted in the new version but it is contained in the best matching subtree rooted at node 106. Note that this subtree is not newly inserted one. We use two SQL queries to detect the two types of inserted leaf nodes as depicted in Figures 5(b) and (c). The SQL query shown in Figure 5(b) is used to detect the inserted leaf nodes that are in the newly inserted subtrees. The inserted leaf nodes that are in the matching subtrees are detected by using the SQL query shown in Figure 5(c). The result of the queries is stored in the INS_LEAF table as shown in Figure 6(c). Note that the highlighted tuples in Figure 6(c) are actually updated leaf nodes. However, they are detected as inserted nodes.

Deletion of Leaf Nodes. The *deleted* leaf nodes are only available in the first version of an XML tree. These deleted nodes should also be either in the *best matching subtrees* or in the *deleted subtrees*. Consider the Figure 1. The leaf nodes 12, 13, 14, and 15 belong to the *deleted subtree* rooted at node 11. The leaf node 5 is also deleted but it is contained in the best matching subtree rooted at node 2. We also use two SQL queries for detecting these two types of deleted leaf nodes. These SQL queries are generated by slightly modifying the queries in the Figures 5(b) and (c). We replace "INS_INT" in line 5 in Figure 5(b) with "DEL_INT". We also replace the "*did2*" in line 7 in Figure 5(b) and in lines 8 and 20 in Figure 5(c) with "*did1*". The "*did1*" in line 16 in Figure 5(c) is replaced by "*did2*". We also replace "MINSO2" and "MAXSO2" in lines 10 and 21 in Figure 5(c) with "MINSO1" and "MAXSO1" respectively. The "MINSO1" and "MAXSO1" in line 18 in Figure 5(c) are replaced by "MINSO2" and "MAXSO2" respectively. Figure 6(d) depicts the result of the queries which is stored in the DEL_LEAF table. Note that the highlighted rows are actually updated leaf nodes which are detected as deleted leaf nodes.

Content Update of Leaf Nodes. Intuitively, an updated node is available in the first and second versions, but its value is different. As the updated leaf nodes are detected as pairs of deleted and inserted leaf nodes, we are able to find the updated leaf nodes from two sets of leaf nodes: the *inserted leaf nodes* and the *deleted leaf nodes* respectively. In addition, we also need the information of the

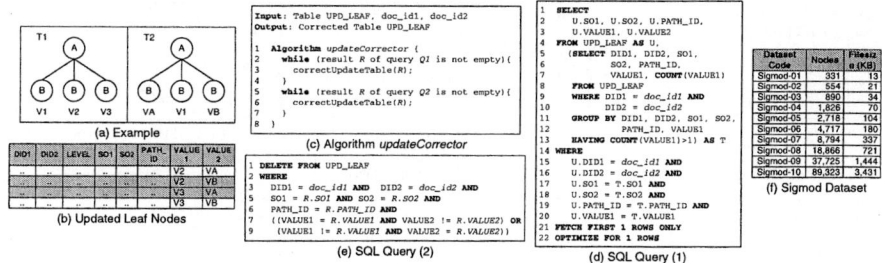

Fig. 7. Example Uncomplete Results of Update Query and Datasets

best matching subtrees in order to guarantee the updated leaf nodes are in the best matching subtrees. Note that we only consider the update of the content of the leaf nodes. Similar to [10], the modification of the name of an internal node is detected as a pair of deletion and insertion. The SQL query for detecting the updated leaf nodes is depicted in Figure 5(d) and the results are in the UPD_LEAF table. The updated leaf nodes of the example in Figure 1 are shown in Figure 6(e) (the UPD_LEAF table). We observe that the result of this SQL query may not be correct result in some cases. Let us elaborate further. Suppose we have two trees as depicted in Figure 7(a). The result of the SQL query depicted in Figure 5(f) is shown in Figure 7(b) (partial view only). We notice that nodes B with values "V2" and "V3" are detected as updated leaf nodes twice. This is because the sub query in lines 3-17 in Figure 5(d) only finds the leaf nodes which have the same paths, but different values. We use the *updateCorrector* algorithm that is depicted in Figure 7(c) to correct the result by finding the *incorrect tuples*. A tuple t is an *incorrect tuple* if one and only one of the following conditions is satisfied: 1) the VALUE1 of tuple t is equal to VALUE1 of tuple R, 2) the VALUE2 of tuple t is equal to VALUE2 of tuple R. The algorithm iteratively issues the SQL queries depicted in Figures 7(d) and (e) until no *incorrect tuple* is found.

5 Performance Study

We have implemented XANDY entirely in Java. The Java implementation and the database engine were run on a Microsoft Windows 2000 Professional machine having Pentium 4 1.7 GHz processor with 512 MB of memory. The database system was IBM DB2 UDB 8.1. Appropriate indexes on the relations are created. We used a set of synthetic XML documents based on SIGMOD DTD (Figure 7(f)). Note that we focus on the number of nodes in the datasets as the higher the number of nodes the database engine will join more number of tuples. The experimental results that support this decision are available in [6]. We generated the second version of each XML document by using our own change generator. We distributed the percentage changes equally for each type of changes. We compared the performance of XANDY to the Java version of X-Diff [2].

---

[2] downloaded from www.cs.wisc.edu/~yuanwang/xdiff.html

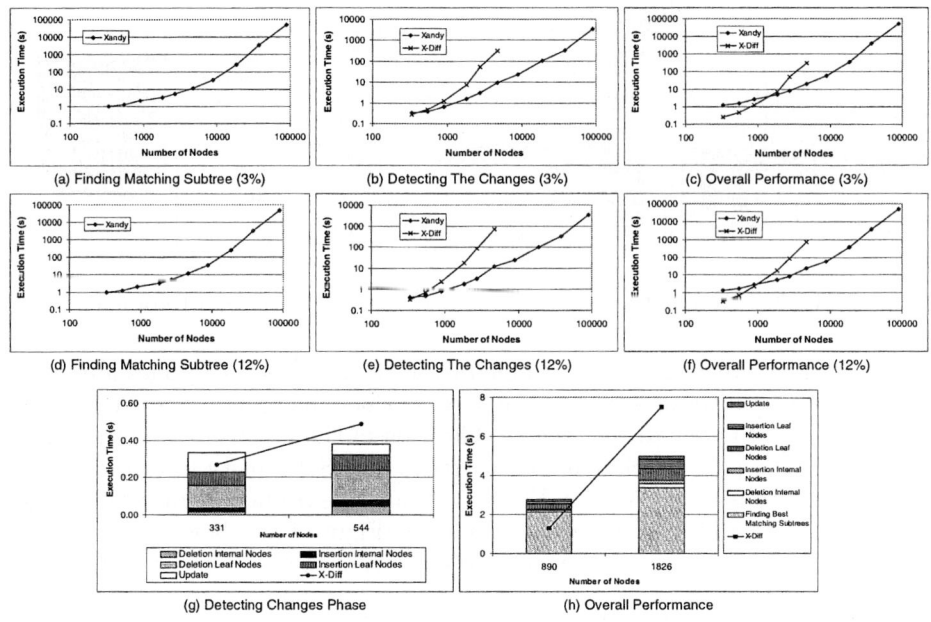

Fig. 8. Execution Time vs Number of Nodes (Logarithmic Scale)

Execution Time Versus Number of Nodes. In this set of experiments, we study the performance of XANDY for different number of nodes. The percentages of changes are set to "3%" and "12%" and the threshold θ is set to "0.0" which shall give us the upper bound of the execution time. Figures 8(a) and (d) show the performance of the first phase (*Finding Best Matching*) when we set the percentages of changes to 3% and 12% respectively. For XML documents that have less than 5000 nodes, the execution time of the first phase is less than 12 seconds. Figures 8(b) and (e) show the performance of the second phase (*Detecting the Changes*) compared to X-Diff when we set the percentage of changes to 3% and 12% respectively. We observe that XANDY performs better than X-Diff except for the smallest data set. Figure 8(g) depicts the performance comparison between X-Diff and second phase of XANDY for "Sigmod-01" and "Sigmod-02". We observe that most of the execution time of the second phase is taken by finding the updated leaf nodes, detecting the inserted leaf nodes, and detecting the deleted leaf nodes. Even then, it is faster than X-Diff (for "Sigmod-02" dataset). In this experiment, X-Diff is unable to detect the changes on the XML documents that have number of nodes over 5000 nodes due to lack of the main memory. Figures 8(c) and (f) show the overall performance of XANDY compared to X-Diff when we set the percentages of changes to 3% and 12% respectively. We notice that the difference of execution time between XANDY and X-Diff reduces as the number of nodes increases. Finally, XANDY becomes faster than X-Diff after the number of nodes is greater than 1000 nodes. This is because the

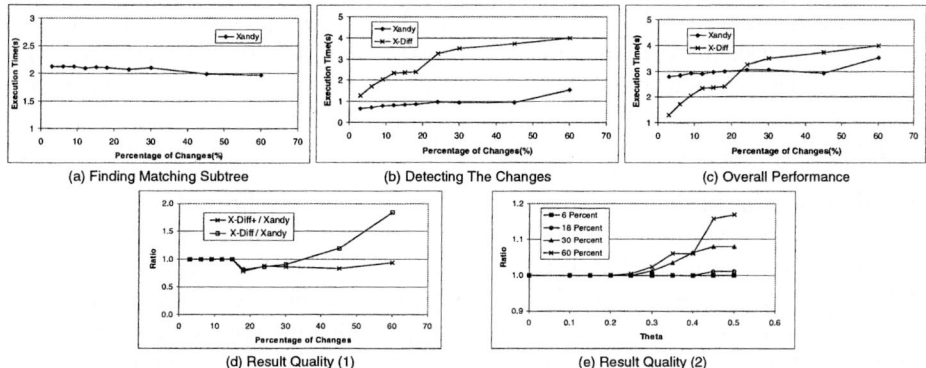

Fig. 9. Execution Time vs Percentage of Changes and Result Quality

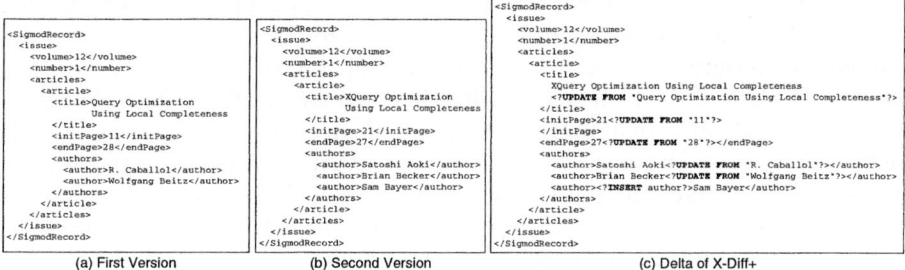

Fig. 10. Example

query engine of the relational database is still able to process the data efficiently as the increment of the size of data is not significant. Figure 8(h) depicts the comparison between X-Diff and of XANDY for the third and fourth datasets. We observe that the first phase takes up to 70% of the overall execution time in average. XANDY is able to detect the changes on XML documents with over 89,000 nodes. From these experiments, we conclude that XANDY has better scalability than X-Diff. For small datasets, XANDY has comparable performance compared to X-Diff. XANDY has better performance than X-Diff for the large datasets.

Execution Time Versus Percentage of Changes. In this set of experiments, we use the dataset "Sigmod-03" and the threshold θ is set to "0.0". We vary the percentages of changes from "3%" to "60%". Figure 9(a) depicts the execution time of the first phase in XANDY. We observe that the percentage of changes influence the execution time for finding the best matching subtrees. This is because there will be more number of matching sibling orders when the documents are changed slightly. On the other hand, when the documents are changed significantly, we will have lesser number of matching sibling orders. Figure 9(b) depicts the execution time of the second phase in XANDY. We observe that XANDY outperforms the X-Diff. We also notice that the execution times of XANDY and X-Diff are affected by the percentage changes. Figure 9(c) shows the overall performance. X-Diff is faster than XANDY for the percentage of changes less than around 20%. As the percentage of changes is larger than 20%, XANDY becomes faster than X-Diff. This is because the time for finding the best matching subtrees is reduced as the percentage of changes is increased.

Result Quality. In the first experiment, we examine the effect of the percentage of changes on the *result quality* by using "Sigmod-03" as the data set. A series of new versions are generated by varying the percentage of the changes. XANDY, X-Diff, and X-Diff+ [3] were run to detect the changes on these XML documents. The number of nodes involved in the deltas is counted for each approach. We compare the number of nodes in the deltas detected by XANDY to the one detected by X-Diff, and X-Diff+. The ratios are plotted in Figure 9(d). We observed that XANDY detects the same deltas as X-Diff+ until the percentage of the changes reaches 15%. The quality ratios of X-Diff+ and XANDY are smaller than 1 when the percentage of the changes is larger than 15%. This happens because X-Diff+ detects a deletion and insertion of subtrees as a set of update operations. For example, we have two versions of an XML document as depicted in Figures 10(a) and (b). Figure 10(c) depicts the delta detected by X-Diff+. XANDY detects as a deletion of an article and an insertion of an article. We notice that the quality ratios of X-Diff and XANDY are larger than 1 when the percentage of the changes are larger than 30%. This is because X-Diff does not calculate the minimum editing distance. Consequently, X-Diff may detect as a deletion of a subtree if it is changed significantly. Note that this does not happen on X-Diff+ as it calculates the minimum editing distance.

In the second experiment, we study the effect of the similarity threshold θ in our approach on the *result quality* by using "Sigmod-04" data set. Then a series of new versions are generated by setting the percentages of the changes to 6%, 18%, 30%, and 60%. For each percentage of changes, XANDY was run by varying threshold θ. The number of nodes involved in the deltas is counted for each threshold θ. We compare the number of nodes in the deltas detected by XANDY with $\theta = 0.0$ to the one detected by XANDY with $0.10 \leq \theta \leq 0.50$. The ratios are plotted in Figure 9(e). We observe that the threshold θ may not affect the result quality if the documents are changed slightly. On the other hand, the result quality is affected by the threshold θ if the documents are changed significantly. When the percentage of changes is set to 60%, the result quality becomes worse as the threshold $\theta \geq 0.25$. We conclude that the result quality of the deltas detected by XANDY is influenced by the percentage of changes, the distribution of the changes, and the threshold θ. The distribution of the changes influences the result quality in the following way. Suppose we have a subtree t_1 in which the changes are concentrated. t_2 is the matching subtree of t_1. The similarity score $\Re(t_1,t_2)$ will be reduced as t_1 and t_2 have less common nodes. Consequently, t_1 and t_2 may be considered as unmatching subtrees if $\Re(t_1,t_2) < \theta$.

---

[3] We activate the option "-o" of X-Diff so it calculates the minimum editing distance in finding the matchings.

6 Conclusions

The relational approach for unordered XML change detection system in this paper is motivated by the scalability problem of existing main memory-based approaches. We have shown that the relational approach is able to handle XML documents that are much larger than the ones detected by using main-memory approaches. In summary, the number of nodes and the percentage of changes influence the execution time of all approaches. XANDY is able to detect the changes on XML documents with over 89,000 nodes, while X-Diff is only able to detect the changes the XML documents with up to 5,000 nodes. We also show that the execution of XANDY is faster than X-Diff for large data sets. This shows that the powerful query engine of the relational database can be utilized for the detecting the changes. The result quality of XANDY is comparable to the one of X-Diff. In XANDY, the result quality depends on the threshold θ, the percentage of changes, and the distribution of the changes.

References

1. YAN CHEN, S. MADRIA, S. S. BHOWMICK. DiffXML: Change Detection in XML Data. *DASFAA 2004*, Jeju Island, Korea, 2004.
2. CURBERA, D. A. EPSTEIN. Fast Difference and Update of XML Documents. *XTech'99*, San Jose, 1999.
3. G. COBENA, S. ABITEBOUL, A. MARIAN. Detecting Changes in XML Documents. *ICDE 2002*, San Jose, 2002.
4. H. JIANG, H. LU, W. WANG, J. XU YU. Path Materialization Revisited: An Efficient Storage Model for XML Data. *Australasian Database Conference*, Melbourne, Australia, 2002.
5. ERWIN LEONARDI, S. S. BHOWMICK, S. MADRIA. Detecting Content Changes on Ordered XML Documents Using Relational Databases. *DEXA 2004*, Zaragoza, Spain, 2004.
6. ERWIN LEONARDI, S. S. BHOWMICK. XANDY: Detecting Changes on Large Unordered XML Documents Using Relational Database. *Technical Report, Center for Advanced Information System, Nanyang Technological University*, Singapore, 2004. http://www.cais.ntu.edu.sg/~erwin/docs/
7. S. PRAKASH, S. S. BHOWMICK, S. MARDIA. SUCXENT: An Efficient Path-based Approach to Store and Query XML Documents. *DEXA 2004*, Spain, 2004.
8. J. SHANMUGASUNDARAM, K. TUFTE, C. ZHANG, G. HE, D. J. DEWITT, AND J. F. NAUGHTON Relational Databases for Querying XML Documents: Limitations and Opportunities. *The VLDB Journal*, 1999.
9. T. F. SMITH AND M. S. WATERMAN Identification of common molecular subsequences. *Journal Molecular Biology* 147:195-197, 1981.
10. Y. WANG, D. J. DEWITT, J. CAI. X-Diff: An Effective Change Detection Algorithm for XML Documents. *ICDE 2003*, Bangalore, 2003.

FASST Mining: Discovering Frequently Changing Semantic Structure from Versions of Unordered XML Documents

Qiankun Zhao and Sourav S. Bhowmick

School of Computer Engineering, Nanyang Technological University, Singapore
{pg04327224, assourav}@ntu.edu.sg

Abstract. In this paper, we present a FASST mining approach to extract the *frequently changing semantic structures* (FASSTs), which are a subset of semantic substructures that change frequently, from versions of unordered XML documents. We propose a data structure, H-DOM$^+$, and a FASST mining algorithm, which incorporates the semantic issue and takes the advantage of the related domain knowledge. The distinct feature of this approach is that the FASST mining process is guided by the user-defined *concept hierarchy*. Rather than mining all the frequent changing structures, only these frequent changing structures that are semantically meaningful are extracted. Our experimental results show that the H-DOM$^+$ structure is compact and the FASST algorithm is efficient with good scalability. We also design a declarative FASST query language, FASSTQUEL, to make the FASST mining process interactive and flexible.

1 Introduction

Frequent substructure mining [3,5] is one of the most well researched topics in the area of XML data mining. Current research on frequent substructure mining is to extract substructures that occur frequently in individual XML document or in collections of XML documents. However, most of the existing research of frequent substructure mining focuses on snapshot data collections, while XML data is dynamic in real life applications.

The dynamic nature of XML leads to two challenging problems. First, is the maintenance of frequent substructures. For this problem, incremental data mining techniques [1] can be applied to maintain the mining results. Second, is the discovery of novel knowledge such as *association rules* and *frequent changing structures*, which are hidden behind the historical changes to XML data as described in [6]. The frequent changing structure (FCS) is defined as substructures in the XML versions that change frequently and significantly in the history. In [6], we proposed a novel approach to discover the frequently changing structures from the sequence of historical structural changes to unordered XML. The usefulness and importance of such frequently changing structures, with corresponding applications, have also been discussed. To make the structure discovering process efficient, an expressive and compact data model, Historical-Document Object Model (H-DOM), is proposed. Using this model, two basic algorithms, which can discover all the *frequently changing structures* with only two scans of the XML version sequence, were designed and implemented. We deal with unordered XML documents since the unordered model of XML is more suitable for most database applications [4]. Hereafter, whenever we say XML, we mean unordered XML.

However, discovering all the frequently changing structure is challenging due to the presence of exponential number of substructures, while the mining results of our previous approach include any arbitrary substructure that change frequently. We observed that not all the frequently changing substructures are semantically significant and meaningful. Usually, in a specific domain, users are interested in only some specified structures that corresponding to certain semantic concepts. To reduce the number of structures in the mining results and keep all the meaningful structures, we propose to incorporate the semantic constraints in the form of user-defined *concept hierarchy* into the frequently changing structure mining process.

In this paper, we defined a subset of frequently changing structures as *Frequently chAnging Semantic STructures* (FASSTs) based on the *dynamic metrics* and *concept hierarchy*. Given a sequence of XML documents (which are different versions of the same XML document), the objective of FASST mining is to discover the frequently changing structures according to the user specified semantic concepts.

2 The FASST Mining Problem

In this section, we present the preliminaries and problem statement for the FASST mining problem. First, a set of dynamic metrics is proposed to measure the changes to XML structural data. After that, the concept of semantic structure is presented. Lastly, we formulate the FASST mining problem. Details and examples of the definitions are available in [6], only a brief introduction is presented here.

2.1 Dynamic Metrics

We model the structures of XML documents as unordered, labeled, rooted trees. We denote the structure of an XML document as $S = (N, E, r)$, where N is the set of labeled nodes, E is the set of edges, $r \in N$ is the root. We do not distinguish between elements and attributes, both of them are mapped to the set of labeled nodes. Each edge, $e = (x, y)$ is an ordered pair of nodes, where x is the parent of y. The *size* of the structure S, denoted by $|S|$, is the number of nodes in N.

Definition 1 (Substructure). *A structure $s = (N', E', r')$ is a substructure of $S = (N, E, r)$, denoted as $s \preceq S$, provided i) $N' \subseteq N$, and ii) $e = (x, y) \in E'$, if and only if x is the parent of y in E.*

Definition 2 (Structural Delta). *Let S_i and S_{i+1} be the tree representations of two XML documents X_i and X_{i+1}. The structural delta from X_i to X_{i+1} is represented as Δ_i, where Δ_i is a structural edit script $\langle o_1, o_2, \cdots, o_m \rangle$ that transforms S_i into S_{i+1}, denoted as $S_1 \xrightarrow{o_1} s_1 \xrightarrow{o_2} \cdots \xrightarrow{o_m} S_{i+1}$.*

Definition 3 (Consolidate Structure). *Given two structures S_i and S_j, where $r_i = r_j$. The consolidate structure of them is $S_i \uplus S_j$, where i) $N_{s_i \uplus s_j} = N_{s_i} \cup N_{s_j}$, ii) $e = (x, y) \in E_{s_i \uplus s_j}$, if and only if x is the parent of y in $E_{s_i} \cup E_{s_j}$.*

We observed that different substructures of the XML document might change in different ways at different frequencies. To evaluate their historical behaviors, we propose a set of dynamic metrics. The first metric is called structure dynamic.

Definition 4 (Structure Dynamic). *Let $\langle S_i, S_{i+1} \rangle$ be the tree representations of XML documents $\langle X_i, X_{i+1} \rangle$. Suppose $s \preceq S_i$. The structure dynamic of s from document X_i to document X_{i+1}, denoted by $N_i(s)$, is defined as: $N_i(s) = \frac{|\Delta_{s_i}|}{|s_i \uplus s_{i+1}|}$.*

Here $N_i(s)$ is the structure dynamic of s from version i to $i + 1$. $N_i(s)$ is the percentage of nodes that have changed from X_i to X_{i+1} in s against the number of nodes in its consolidation structure. A larger value of structural dynamic implies that the more *significantly* the substructure changed.

Definition 5 (Version Dynamic). *Let $\langle S_1, S_2, \cdots, S_n \rangle$ be the tree representations of XML documents $\langle X_1, X_2, \cdots X_n \rangle$. Suppose $s \preceq S_j$. The version dynamic of s, denoted as $V(s)$, is defined as:*

$$V(s) = \frac{\sum_{i=1}^{n-1} v_i}{n-1} \text{ where } v_i = \begin{cases} 1, \text{ if } |\Delta_{s_i}| \neq 0; \\ 0, \text{ if } |\Delta_{s_i}| = 0; \end{cases}$$

Similarly, it can also be observed that the larger the value of version dynamic is, the more *frequently* the substructure changed in the history.

Definition 6 (DoD). *Let $\langle S_1, S_2, \cdots, S_n \rangle$ be the tree representations of XML documents $\langle X_1, X_2, \cdots, X_n \rangle$. Suppose $s \preceq S_j$, $N_i(s)$ and $V(s)$ are the values of structure dynamic and version dynamic of s; α is the pre-defined threshold for structure dynamic. The DoD for s is defined as:*

$$DoD(s, \alpha) = \frac{\sum_{i=1}^{n} d_i}{(n-1) * V(s)} \text{ where } d_i = \begin{cases} 1, \text{if } N_i \geq \alpha \\ 0, \text{if } N_i < \alpha \end{cases}$$

The metric DoD is defined based on the threshold of structure dynamic. It represents the fraction of versions, where the structure dynamic values for the substructure are no less than the predefined threshold α, against the total number of version the substructure has changed over the history. Extended from the structure dynamic, the value of DoD implies the overall significance of the substructure, the larger the value is, the more *significant* the changes are.

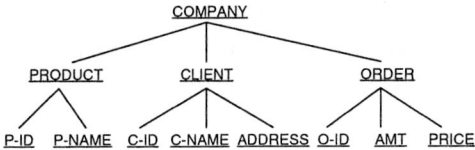

Fig. 1. An Example of Concept Hierarchy

2.2 Semantic Structure

One of the distinctive features of XML is that XML is semantic. Tags within the XML documents are self-describing. However, if we represent an XML document as a tree structure, not all the substructures are semantically significant to users. For example, users in the e-commerce domain may be more interested in the substructures corresponding to *products* and *clients* than other substructures such as *Name*. In this section, we define the *semantic structure* to represent substructures that are semantically meaningful.

Definition 7 (Semantic Structure). *Given a concept C in a specific domain, a structure s is a semantic structure of concept C, denoted as $s \simeq C$, if s provides the required information of the concept C.*

Based on the definition, it is obvious that the semantic structures are based on the underlining concepts, which is domain dependent. There are two approaches to obtain such concepts. The first approach is to extract interesting concepts from ontology in the corresponding domain. Another approach is to build the concepts based on DTDs (Document Type Definitions) used in this domain. Recently, DTDs are widely used to specify the legal building blocks in XML documents. Each legal building block corresponds to a concept in ontology.

However, users may not be interested in all the semantic concepts/ structures while the number of concepts/structures can be huge. Moreover, even in the same domain, different users may have different interests. For instance, in the e-commerce domain, the material control people may be more interested in the semantic structure *products* than others; while the marketing people may be more interested in the semantic structure *clients* than others. Given a set of semantic concepts/ structures, users can specify the concepts they are interested in.

Our research focuses on extracting the frequently changing structures that are *semantically meaningful*. The set of user-specified concepts is used to guide the FASST mining process. Similar to [2], interested concepts are represented in a hierarchy that specifies the relation among them. Nodes of the hierarchical structure can be classified as *primitive* or *nonprimitive*. The *primitive* concepts, which represent the basic elements in a domain, reside in the lowest level in the hierarchy; all *nonprimitive* concepts, which consist of a conglomeration of the primitive concepts, reside in the higher level of the hierarchy. The higher the node's level, the more complex is the concepts it represents. Figure 1 shows an example of concept hierarchy. The leaf nodes such as *P-ID*, and *P-NAME* are primitive concepts; while internal nodes and root node such as *CLIENT* and *COMPANY* are nonprimitive concepts. In our FASST mining, we assume that the specified concept hierarchy is provided by users.

2.3 Problem Statement

In our previous work [6], we have defined the frequently changing structures (FCS) based on the dynamic metrics as substructure that have version dynamic and degree of dynamic values no less than the user-defined thresholds. Similarly, here we give a formal definition of *Frequent chAnging Semantic STructure* (FASST).

Definition 8 (FASST). *Let $\langle S_1, S_2, \cdots, S_n \rangle$ be the tree representations of XML documents $\langle X_1, X_2, \cdots, X_n \rangle$; H is a concept hierarchy that contains a set of concepts $\{c_1, c_2, \cdots, c_i\}$; the thresholds for structure dynamic, version dynamic and DoD are α, β, γ respectively. A structure $s \preceq S_j$ is a **FASST** in this sequence if and only if i) $V(s) \geq \beta$, ii) $DoD(s, \alpha) \geq \gamma$, and iii) $s \simeq c_m$, where $1 \leq m \leq i$.*

The FASST is defined based on the predefined thresholds of the dynamic metrics and a set of user-defined concepts. To be a FASST, it must be a semantic structure (defined by H) and change at certain frequency (defined by β) and corresponding changes must be significantly enough (defined by α and γ). The FASST mining problem is to discover all the FASSTs from a sequence of XML documents with the user-defined concepts and thresholds for the dynamic metrics.

3 Algorithm

In this section, we present our FASST mining algorithm. First, we introduce the H-DOM+ data structure to store and represent relevant historical structural information. After that, detail of the FASST algorithm is presented.

3.1 The H-DOM+ Structure

The structure of an XML document can be represented and stored as a tree such as the DOM tree proposed by W3C. In this section, we present an H-DOM+ model to represent the history of changes to XML data. The H-DOM+ is an extension of the DOM model with some historical properties so that it can compress the history of changes to XML into a single H-DOM+ tree. Formally, we define an H-DOM+ tree as follows:

Definition 9 (H-DOM+). *An H-DOM+ tree is a 4-tuple $H = (N, A, v, r)$, where N is a set of object identifiers; A is a set of labelled, directed arcs (p, l, c) where $p, c \in N$ and l is a string; v is a function that maps each node $n \in N$ to a set of values (C_n, C_v), C_n is an integer and C_v is a set of integers; r is a distinguished node in N called the root of the tree.*

We now elaborate on the parameters C_n and C_v. The two parameters are introduced to record the historical changes for each substructure. C_n is an integer that records the number of versions that a substructure has changed significantly enough (the structure dynamic is no less the corresponding threshold). C_v is a set of integers that represents the versions where the substructure has changed in the history. For instance, a value of "i" denotes that the structure has changed from version i to version $i+1$. Differ from the H-DOM model in [6], the types of changes are specified using integers with "$+$" and "$-$" in H-DOM$^+$. Such knowledge will be used in our proposed FASST query language, FASSTQUEL, to mine different types of FASSTs. A value of "$-i$" in C_v means the structure is "deleted" in version $i+1$ while a value of "$+i$" means the structure is "inserted". In the H-DOM$^+$ tree, the C_v value for each structure is finally updated by using the formula: $C_v(s) = C_v(s_1) \cup C_v(s_2) \cup \cdots \cup C_v(s_j)$, where $s_1, s_2, \cdots, s_j$ are the substructures of s. In the updating process, insertion and deletion of a structure is determined by the majority of the changes to its substructures (if the number of insertions among its substructures is no less than deletions, then we consider it as an "insertion" in that version. Otherwise, it is considered as a "deletion").

With C_v and C_n, the values of structure dynamic, version dynamic, and DoD can be calculated based on this model as follows.

- $N_i(s) = \frac{1}{|s_i \uplus s_{i+1}|} \sum C_v(s_j)[i]$, where s_j is the list of substructures of s, $C_v(s_j)[i]$ is 1 if any of $\pm i$ is in $C_v(s_j)$, otherwise it is 0.
- $V(s) = \frac{1}{n-1} \sum_{i=1}^{n-1} C_v[i]$, where $C_v(s)[i]$ is 1 if any of $\pm i$ is in $C_v(s)$, otherwise it is 0; n is the total number of XML documents.
- $DoD(s) = C_n (\sum_{i=1}^{n-1} C_v[i])^{-1}$, where $C_v(s)[i]$ is 1 if any of $\pm i$ is in $C_v(s)$, otherwise it is 0; n is the total number of XML documents.

3.2 FASST Mining

There are three major phases in our FASST mining. The *H-DOM$^+$ construction* phase, the *FASST extraction* phase, and the *visualization* phase. Since the visualization phase is straightforward, we discuss the first two phases in turn.

The H-DOM$^+$ Construction Phase: Figure 2 (a) describes the phase of H-DOM$^+$ construction. Given a sequence of historical XML documents, the H-DOM$^+$ tree is initialized as the structure of the first version. After that, the algorithm iterates over all the other versions by extracting the structural changes and mapping them into the H-DOM$^+$ tree. The SX-Diff function is a modification of the X-Diff [4] algorithm that generates only the structural change from two different versions of a document. The structural changes are mapped into the H-DOM$^+$ tree according to mapping rules described in Figure 2 (a). The SX-Diff function and the mapping phase iterate until no more XML document is left in the sequence. Finally, the H-DOM$^+$ tree is returned as the output of this phase. Figure 2 (b) is an example of an H-DOM$^+$ tree.

Given an XML document and the corresponding DTD, according to the DTD, it is possible to know that some of the elements (attributes) cannot be changed individually. For example, in a DTD, some elements (attributes) may be defined

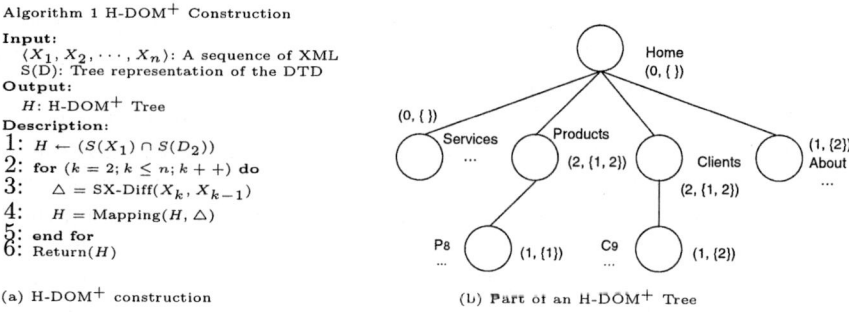

(a) H-DOM+ construction (b) Part of an H-DOM+ Tree

Fig. 2

as *required* with exactly one occurrence. Such nodes cannot be inserted or deleted individually, which means they can only change with the insertion or deletion of their parent nodes. Based on this observation, elements (attributes) in the XML documents can be classified into two groups. Elements (attributes) that cannot be inserted or deleted individually are classified into group 1, others are in group 2. In the initialize process, rather than store the entire structure of the first version, we only map nodes that belong to group 2. Nodes in group 1 are ignored.

Algorithm 2 in Figure 2 (a) describes the mapping function. Given the H-DOM+ tree and the structural changes, this function is to map the structural changes into the H-DOM+ tree and return the updated H-DOM+ tree. The idea is to update the corresponding values of the nodes in the H-DOM+ tree. The values are updated according to following rules:

i) If the node does not exist in the H-DOM+ tree, then the node is inserted. The value of $\pm i$ is inserted into C_v where i is the version number of the structural delta. In addition, the N_i value is calculated. If $N_i \geq \alpha$, then C_n is set to 1 and the C_n values of its parent nodes are incremented by 1 until N_i is less than α. Otherwise, C_n is set to 0 and the process terminates.

ii) For nodes that exist in the H-DOM+, the value of C_v is updated by inserting the value $\pm i$ into C_v if $\pm i$ is not in C_v. The value of C_n is also updated based on N_i and α. Similarly, If $N_i \geq \alpha$, then C_n is incremented by 1 and the C_n values of its parent nodes are updated based on the same rule until N_i is less than α. Otherwise, C_n does not change and the process terminates.

The FASST Extraction Phase: In this phase, given the H-DOM+ tree, the FASSTs are extracted based on the user-defined concept hierarchy. First the substructures are compared with the user-specified concept hierarchy as shown in line 3 in Figure 3 (b). If the structures are instances of the concepts in the hierarchy, then the values of the required parameters (version dynamic, and DoD) for each node are calculated and compared against the predefined thresholds as shown in lines 5 and 6. Since for a FASST, both its version dynamic and DoD should be no less than the thresholds, we first calculate only one of the parameters and determine whether it is necessary to calculate the other parameter. In our algorithm, the version dynamic for a node is checked against the correspond-

```
Algorithm 2 Mapping
Input:
    H: H-DOM+ Tree
    α: Threshold of structure dynamic
    △: Structural delta
Output:
    H: The updated H-DOM+ tree
Description:
 1: for all n_i ∈ △ do
 2:   if n_i ∉ H then
 3:     update C_n(n_i)
 4:   end if
 5:   if AAAA then
 6:     BBBB
 7:   else
 8:     if CCC then
 9:       DDD
10:     else
11:       EEE
12:     end if
13:   end if
14:   if N_i(n_i) ≥ α then
15:     update C_v(n_i)
16:     n_i = n_i.parent(H)
17:   end if
18: end for
19: Return(H)
```

(a) Mapping Algorithm

```
Algorithm 3 FASST Extraction

Input:
    H: H-DOM+ Tree
    T: User specified concept hierarchy
    β, γ: Threshold of version dynamic and DoD
Output:
    F: A set of nodes where FASSTs are rooted
Description:
 1: for all n_j=Bottom-upTrav(H)≠ null do
 2:   while T_i=Bottom-upTrav(T)≠ null
 3:     if S(n_j) ≃ T_i , then
 4:       for all s ⪯ S(n_j) do
 5:         if C_n < γ × V(s), {n_j = n_j.next, break}
 6:         if V(n_j) ≥ β & DoD(n_j) ≥ γ, {F = F ∪n_j}
 7:       end for
 8:       break; end if
 9:   end for
10: Return(F)
```

(b) FASST Extraction Algorithm

Fig. 3

ing threshold first. If it is no less than the threshold, then we check its DoD. Considering the traversal strategy of the H-DOM+ tree, we use the bottom-up method since the set of interesting concepts is represented in a hierarchical manner with primitive concepts in the lower level. Guided by the concept hierarchy, the FASST extraction phase can be more efficient.

Lemma 1. *Let S_1 and S_2 be any two structures, $S_2 \preceq S_1$. Given the threshold for DoD as γ, the necessary condition for structure S_1 to be a FASST is that $C_n(S_1) \geq \gamma \times V(S_2)$.*

From the above lemma, we observed that it is not necessary to traverse the entire H-DOM+ tree. We can skip checking some structures that cannot be FASSTs. Based on this lemma, for any nodes, rather than calculate its version dynamic value, the C_n value of the node is checked against the value of $\gamma \times V(S_i)$, where S_i is any of its substructures. If $C_n < \gamma \times V(S_i)$, then it is not necessary to calculate the version dynamic and DoD for this structure since it cannot be a FASST. This pruning technique is shown in Figure 3 (b) in lines 5 and 6.

4   FASSTQUEL: Query Language for FASST

To make the FASST mining process interactive, we design a FASST query language called *FASSTQUEL*. In this section, we discuss the syntax of the language and how it is useful.

The FASST query language consists of the specifications of four major parameters in FASST extraction from a sequence of XML documents. They are *types of FASST, relevant source, a hierarchy of concepts,* and *threshold values.* The syntax for the FASST query language is defined in a simplified BNF grammar (words in `type writer` font represents keywords) as shown in Figure 1 (i):

- "EXTRACT ⟨*structure_type*⟩" specifies that the FASSTs to be discovered are of type "⟨ *structure_type* ⟩". The following types of FASSTs are supported in our query language:
  - *Insertion-based* (Only insertions are considered as changes)
    ⟨*structure_type*⟩ :: = `Ins_FASST`
  - *Deletion-based* (Only deletions are considered as changes)
    ⟨*structure_type*⟩ :: = `Del_FASST`
  - *FASST* (Both insertions and deletions are considered as changes)
    ⟨*structure_type*⟩ :: = `All`
- "FOR ⟨*concepts*⟩" specifies that the concept hierarchy to be used to guide the FASST mining. The concept hierarchy can be stored in an XML document.
- "FROM ⟨*source*⟩" specifies on which dataset the FASST extraction should be performed. It can the entire sequence or from version i to version j, which are specified as `All` and [i, j] respectively.
- "WHERE THRESHOLD = ⟨*N, V, DoD*⟩" specifies the thresholds for structure dynamic, version dynamic, and DoD. If the any of the threshold values is not specified by the user, then a default value is used.

For example, given a hierarchy of concepts H, to extract all types of FASSTs from a sequence of n XML documents with the thresholds for structure dynamic, version dynamic and DoD are specified as $0.3, 0.4$, and 0.75 respectively. The FASST query can be formulated as shown in Figure 1(j). The FASST query language is proposed for interactive FASST mining. That is users may not be able to get their desired knowledge at the first hit. Based on the mining results, users can specify and modify their requirements explicitly using this query language. Moreover, the FASST query language makes the interactive mining process more efficient.

5 Performance Evaluation

Experiments are conducted on a P4, 1.7GHz PC with 256M RAM, running Microsoft Windows 2000 Professional. The algorithm is implemented in Java. In the following experiments, the real data, SIGMOD XML document, is downloaded from UW XML repository [1]. Based on this XML document, sequences of synthetic XML versions are generated using our synthetic XML delta generator. Similar to the experiments in [6], we vary the characteristics and the parameters for the algorithm to evaluate the performance of FASST mining. All the datasets are generated based on the basic dataset generated from the SIGMOD XML. The basic dataset, D_1 in Figure 4 (i), consists of 40 versions of XML documents, with an average number of 2500 nodes. The average percentage of changes be-

[1] http://www.cs.washington.edu/research/xmldatasets

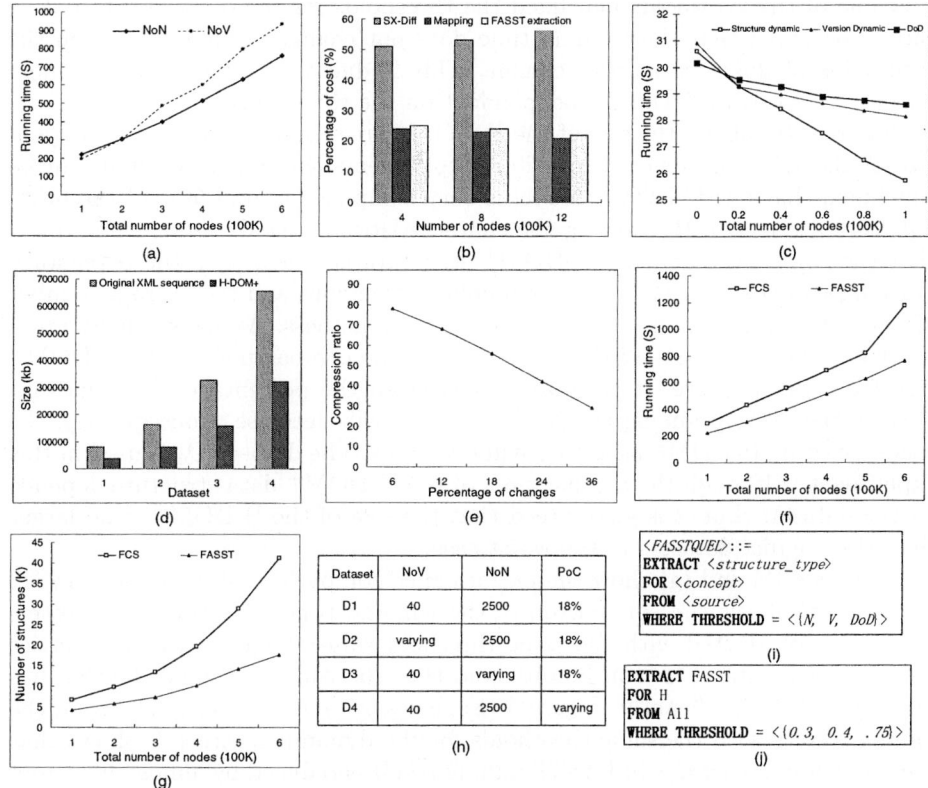

Fig. 4. Experiment Results

tween any consecutive versions is 18% in the basic dataset, which consists of 9% of insertion and 9% of deletion.

Figure 4 (a) shows how the running time changes by varying the total number of nodes in the XML sequence. There are two ways of increasing the total number of nodes in the sequence. One way is to increase the number of versions (NoV) in the XML sequence, another way is to increase the average number of nodes (NoN) in each version. Datasets D_2 and D_3 are used in the following experiments. The threshold values for *structure dynamic, version dynamic,* and *DoD* are fixed to 0.2, 0.2, and 0.2 respectively. Both results show good scalability with the total number of nodes, while the running time is more sensitive to the number of versions in the XML sequence than the average number of nodes in each version. This is due to the fact that the change detection process is the major cost for FASST mining, as we can see from Figure 4 (b). The first three datasets in Figure 4 (i) are used. As shown in Figure 4 (b), among three processes: *SX-Diff, Mapping,* and *FASST Extraction,* we observed that the SX-Diff process is the most expensive process that takes more than half of the running time.

Figure 4 (c) shows how the running time changes by varying the thresholds for the dynamic metrics. The D_1 dataset is used. In the three experiments, we vary one of the thresholds and fixed the thresholds for the other two to 0.2. It can be observed that the running time does not change significantly when the thresholds of dynamic metrics change. This is due to the fact that the most expensive process, SX-Diff, is independent on the thresholds.

Figure 4 (d) shows the size of the H-DOM$^+$ tree comparing with the original size of the XML sequence in previous experiments. From the result it can be concluded that our H-DOM$^+$ model is very compact (around 50% of the original XML sequence). By varying the characteristics of the datasets, we find out that the compactness of the H-DOM$^+$ structure is sensitive to the percentage of changes in the dataset, while the number of versions and the average number of nodes in each version do not affect the compactness. As shown in Figure 4 (e), when the percentage of changes increases the compactness of the H-DOM$^+$ structure will decrease. It is because that when the percentage of changes increases, the overlap among the XML sequence will decrease. Consequently, the space saved by H-DOM$^+$ structure will decreases. The dataset D_4 is used in this experiment. Although the compactness of the H-DOM$^+$ data structure depends on the datasets, but it is guaranteed that the size of the H-DOM$^+$ is no larger than the original datasets in the worst case.

Figures 4 (f) and (g) show the performance comparison of FCS and FASST. Figure 4 (f) shows the comparison of the running time. The two set of experiments are conducted with the same threshold values for the dynamic metrics using the D_1 dataset. It can be observed that the running time of FASST has been improved significantly. Figure 4 (g) shows the number of structures in the mining results with the same thresholds for the dynamic metrics. It shows that the number of structures in FASST mining result is reduced by almost 40% from the FCS mining result. This two results shows that the object of our FASST mining has been achieved successfully.

6 Conclusions

In this paper, we propose an approach to extract the FASSTs from a sequence of historical XML documents. We propose an H-DOM$^+$ to store and represent the historical structural information of the XML documents sequence. Using the H-DOM$^+$, an algorithm is proposed to mine the FASSTs. Experimental results show that FASST has good scalability and efficiency. We also propose a declarative FASST query language to make the mining process interactive.

References

1. V. Ganti, J. Gehrke, and R. Ramakrishnan. DEMON: Mining and monitoring evolving data. In *Proc. IEEE ICDE*, pages 439–448, 2000.
2. J. Han and Y. Fu. Dynamic generation and refinement of concept hierarchies for knowledge discovery in databases. In *Proc. KDD Workshop*, pages 157–168, 1994.
3. A. Inokuchi, T. Washio, and H. Motoda. An apriori based algorithm for mining frequent substructures from graph data. In *Proc. PKDD*, pages 13–23, 2000.

4. Y. Wang, D. J. DeWitt, and J.-Y. Cai. X-diff: An effective change detection algorithm for XML documents. In *Proc. ICDE*, pages 519–530, 2003.
5. M. J. Zaki. Efficiently mining frequent trees in a forest. In *Proc. ACM SIGKDD*, pages 71–80, 2002.
6. Q. Zhao, S. S. Bhowmick, M. Mohania, and Y. Kambayashi. Discovering frequently changing structures from historical structural deltas of unordered XML. In *Proc. ACM CIKM*, pages 188–198, 2004.

Mining Positive and Negative Association Rules from XML Query Patterns for Caching

Ling Chen, Sourav S. Bhowmick, and Liang-Tien Chia

School of Computer Engineering, Nanyang Technological University,
Singapore, 639798

Abstract. Recently, several approaches that mine frequent XML query patterns and cache their results have been proposed to improve query response time. However, frequent XML query patterns mined by these approaches ignore the temporal sequence between user queries. In this paper, we take into account the temporal features of user queries to discover association rules, which indicate that when a user inquires some information from the XML document, she/he will probably inquire some other information subsequently. We cluster XML queries according to their semantics first and then mine association rules between the clusters. Moreover, not only positive but also negative association rules are discovered to design the appropriate cache replacement strategy. The experimental results showed that our approach considerably improved the caching performance by significantly reducing the query response time.

1 Introduction

Extensible Markup Language (XML) has emerged as a standard for data representation and exchange on the World Wide Web. With the rapid growth of XML applications, there is a pressing need to swiftly retrieve information from remote XML sources. Consequently, issues related to efficient processing of XML queries have received considerable attentions.

Recently, caching XML queries has been recognized as an orthogonal approach to improve the performance of XML query engines [3] [11]. Three basic issues are involved in XML query caching: 1) *Containment Relationship*: When a new XML query is issued, decisions should be made whether it is contained by any cached queries so that answers to it can be retrieved from the local cache. 2) *Query Rewriting*: If the new XML query is contained by or overlapping with some cached queries, it should be rewritten with respect to these cached ones. 3) *Replacement Strategy*: A value function should be applied to each query region. When additional space is required in the cache, regions with the lowest values will be the victims. In this paper, we focus on the third problem.

1.1 Motivation

As the cache space is a limited resource, appropriate replacement strategy should be designed to discard data to free space for new data while keeping the cache

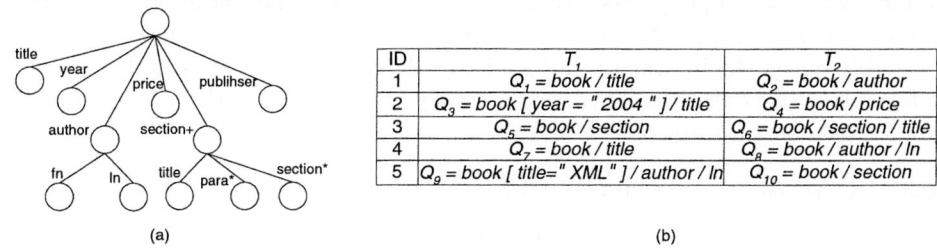

Fig. 1. DTD and Queries

performance. FastXMiner [11] mined frequent XML query patterns from the user queries. Once the cache is full, query regions of infrequent query patterns will be purged first. However, frequent query patterns may not always be reliable in predicting the subsequent queries, as the frequent query pattern-based technique in [11] ignores the temporal feature of user queries. Consider the XML DTD tree in Figure 1 (a) and two sequential queries of five users (expressed as XPath query for ease of exposition) at time points T_1 and T_2 in Figure 1 (b). Applying FastXMiner [11] here will result in the following two cases.

- If we apply FastXMiner at T_1, then we consider the queries in the second column of the table in Figure 1 (b). Suppose the *minimum support* is 0.4. We discover that *book/title* is a frequent query pattern. Unfortunately, caching answers to *book/title* cannot benefit the processing of queries at T_2, as none of the users inquires the information of *book/title*.
- If we apply FastXminer at T_2, then we consider all the queries in the second and third columns of the table in Figure 1 (b). Suppose the *minimum support* is 0.2. We discover that *book/title*, *book/author*, *book/author/ln* and *book/section* are all frequent query patterns. However, if the cache space is not enough to accommodate all these frequent queries, FastXMiner cannot break ties to improve the cache performance.

Hence, in this paper, we consider the sequence between user queries to discover association rules. We use the association rules to predict the subsequent user queries and the confidence of the rules to break ties.

However, few users issue the *exactly* same queries sequentially. For example, consider the queries in Figure 1 (b) again. If only the exactly same queries are considered, then no association rule will be discovered as no two rows are same. Hence, rather than mining association rules between exactly same queries, we mine association rules between semantically related queries. The intuition is that although users may not issue the exactly same queries sequentially, it is possible that they inquire the similar information in sequence. For example, the first and the forth rows in Figure 1 (b) are different in the queries at time T_2. One is *book/author* and the other is *book/author/ln*. Since the two queries are semantically related, we can cluster them into a group representing the queries about the information of book author. Then, an association rule between queries about book title and queries about book author may be discovered from the table in Figure 1 (b). According to this rule, we can predict that users will probably query the information of book author subsequently if they queried the information of book title. Then we can delay the eviction of the information of book author if they are cached before.

1.2 Overview and Contributions

Firstly, we cluster user queries so that queries about similar information are grouped together. Next, we mine association rules between the clusters. Particularly, we mine association rules between singular query clusters. That is, there is only one cluster on both sides of our association rules. This restriction frees us from maintaining too many historical queries of a user to predict his subsequent query, and significantly reduce the complexity of the mining process. In addition to positive association rules, we also mine negative association rules, which indicate when a user issue some query, she/he probably will not issue some other query subsequently. Finally, we design an appropriate replacement strategy based on the knowledge obtained from the discovered rules.

The main contributions of this paper are summarized as follows.

- We proposed to mine association rules from user queries for XML caching, which is the first that captures the temporal features of user queries to discover knowledge for optimizing caching strategy.
- We designed a novel method to cluster XML queries based on their semantics.
- We implemented our approach and conducted various experiments. Experimental results showed that the replacement strategy incorporated with discovered association rules had better performance than existing approaches.

The rest of the paper is organized as follows. Section 2 briefly discuss some related work of XML query caching in the literature. Sections 3 and 4 present our approach in two stages, clustering user queries based on their semantics and mining association rules. Section 5 shows the experimental results and the comparison with other algorithms. We conclude the paper and outline future directions of research in Section 6.

2 Related Work

Due to its flexibility, semantic caching was popular in XML query caching [6] [3]. Hristidis and Petropoulos [6] proposed a compact structure, *modified incomplete tree (MIT)*, to represent the semantic regions of XML queries. ACE-XQ [3] is a holistic XQuery-based semantic caching system. The authors discussed how to judge whether a new query is contained by any cached query and how to rewrite the new query with respect to the cached queries. However, this work did not consider using the knowledge mined from historical user queries to design the replacement function.

Recently, intelligence has been incorporated into Web/XML query caching by constructing predictive models of user requests with the knowledge mined from historical queries [7] [2] [11]. Lan et al. [7] mined association rules from Web user access patterns. Then they prefetched Web documents based on discovered associations and current requested documents. They focused on the placement strategy (fetching and prefetching) while we focused on the replacement strategy. Bonchi et al. [2] mined association rules from Web log data to extend the traditional LRU replacement strategy. However, their work cannot be applied in XML query caching directly because answers to XML query do not have explicit identifiers such as URL. Hence, our work is different from this one in that we mine association rules between query groups in which queries are semantically close. Furthermore, we also use negative association rules to demote the replacement values of corresponding query regions.

3 Query Clustering

Due to the intuition that few users issue the exactly same queries sequentially while many users may inquire similar information consecutively, we cluster the queries based on their semantics before mining association rules. In this section, we discuss our clustering method.

3.1 Clustering Criterion

An XML query can be represented as a node labeled tree. For example, consider the query Q_1 expressed in XQuery syntax in Figure 2 (a). The semantics of query Q_1 are composed of two essential parts: the predicate part (*for-where* clauses) and the result part (*return* clause). Both parts can be represented as a tree and the query tree can be constructed by combining the two trees. For example, the query tree of Q_1 in Figure 2 (a) is shown in Figure 2 (b).

After representing each XML query as a query tree, the semantics of the query is captured by its query tree structure. For example, the query tree of Q_1 in Figure 2 (b) indicates that Q_1 inquires the information of the *title, author, section* and *price* of the book. Hence, for the purpose of clustering queries based on their semantics, we can cluster them based on their tree structures.

Existing approaches of clustering tree structures usually employ the agglomerative clustering technique [8] [4]. They are different in defining the *similarity*

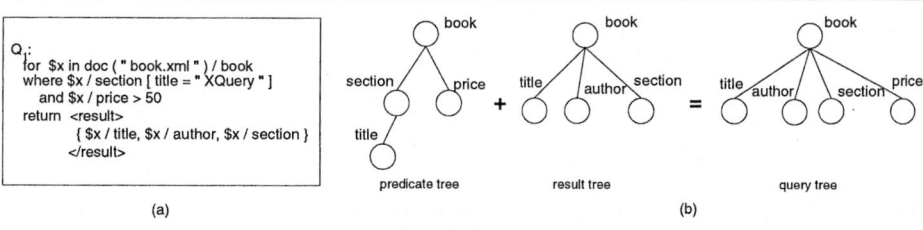

Fig. 2. XQuery Tree

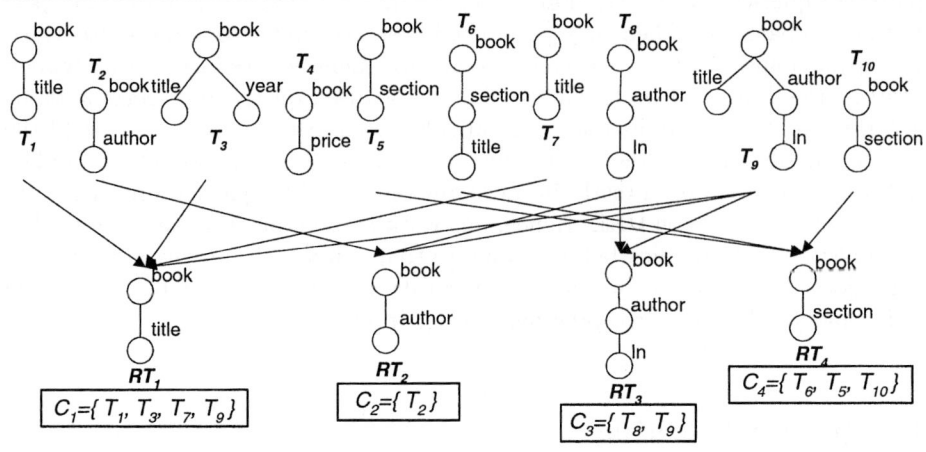

Fig. 3. Initial Clusters

between two trees or clusters. Basically, the definitions of the similarity can be divided into the following two categories: node-based [4] and edge-based [8]. In order to achieve better accuracy in clustering trees, in this paper, we base our similarity measure on considering the common rooted subtrees between XML query trees. Intuitively, query trees sharing larger common rooted subtree should be semantically closer.

3.2 Clustering Method

Now, we discuss the clustering method. Basically, we cluster query trees by using a "cluster-centered" method [9] [5] rather than an agglomerative method. We employ such a clustering strategy here as it is revealed in [5] that the "cluster-centered" method can distinguish the documents of different semantics better and achieve higher clustering accuracy.

In order to employ such a clustering method, we should discover the frequent rooted subtrees before clustering user queries. We borrow the algorithm FastXMiner [11] to discover frequent rooted subtrees from XML queries.

Example 3.1 Consider the ten queries in Figure 1 (b), whose query tree structures are redrawn in the upper part of Figure 3. Suppose the *minimum support* δ is 0.2. Four rooted subtrees, *book/title*, *book/author*, *book/author/ln* and *book/section*, are frequent as shown in the lower part of Figure 3.

After discovering frequent rooted subtrees from the collection of query trees, our method constructs clusters in the following three steps: initializing clusters, disjointing clusters and pruning clusters.

Initializing Clusters. In this step, we construct the initial clusters. We use the frequent rooted subtrees as the labels of the initial clusters. A query tree will be assigned to an initial cluster if the label of the cluster is the maximal

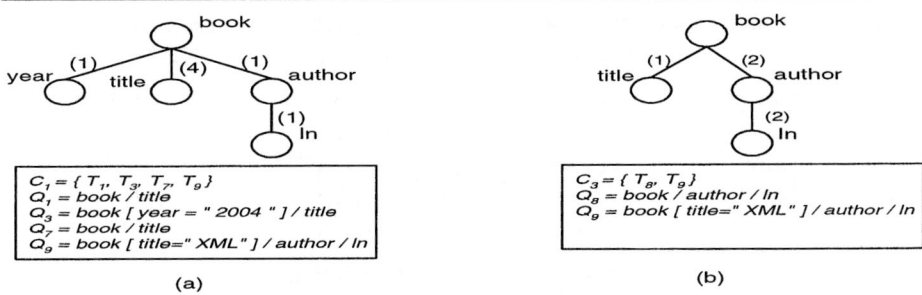

Fig. 4. Intra-cluster Dissimilarity

frequent rooted subtree included by the query tree[1]. For example, consider the query T_8 in Figure 3. Two frequent rooted subtree are included by it, RT_2 and RT_3. We assign T_8 to the initial cluster of RT_3 since RT_2 is not the maximal frequent rooted subtree included by T_8. If a query tree does not contain any frequent rooted subtree, such as T_4, the semantic of the query is not significant in the collection of queries and the query tree will be treated as an outlier. Initial clusters may not be disjoint because a query tree may contain more than one maximal frequent rooted subtrees, such as T_9. Thus, T_9 is assigned to the two corresponding initial clusters.

Disjointing Clusters. We make the initial clusters disjoint in this step. For each query tree, we identify the best initial cluster and keep the query only in the best cluster. We define the *goodness* of a cluster for a query tree based on the intra-cluster dissimilarity. We measure the intra-cluster dissimilarity based on the number of infrequent edges in the cluster. That is, we merge all query trees in a cluster into a tree structure. For the merged tree, each edge e is associated with a support, denoted as *supp(e)*, which is the fraction of query trees containing it. Given a *minimum cluster support* ξ, an edge in the merged tree is *infrequent* if its support is less than ξ. Then, we define the intra-cluster dissimilarity as follows.

$$Intra(C_i) = \frac{|\{e \in M_i | supp(e) < \xi\}|}{|\{e \in M_i\}|}$$

where M_i is the merged tree of all query trees in cluster C_i. The value of $Intra(C_i)$ ranges from 0 to 1. The higher the $Intra(C_i)$, the more dissimilar the query trees in cluster C_i. We assign a query tree to a cluster such that the *intra-cluster dissimilarities* are exacerbated least. That is, a query tree T_i is kept in cluster C_j if

$$C_j = argmin_{C_j \in C, T_i \in C_j} Intra(C_j)$$

---

[1] A frequent rooted subtree is not maximal w.r.t. a query tree if it is included by any other frequent rooted subtree included by the query tree.

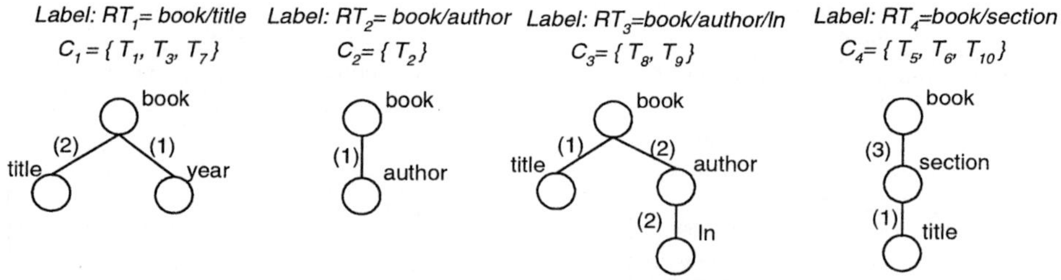

Fig. 5. Clusters after Disjointing

Example 3.2 For example, T_9 is assigned to both initial clusters C_1 and C_3. The merged trees for the two clusters are shown in Figure 4. Let the *minimum cluster support* ξ be 0.6. Grouping T_9 in C_1 generates the $Intra(C_1) = 0.75$, whereas grouping T_9 in C_3 results in the $Intra(C_3) = 0.66$. Hence, we remove T_9 from cluster C_1. After this step, the initial clusters in Figure 3 are adjusted as shown in Figure 5, where each cluster is represented as a merged tree of all query trees in it.

Pruning Clusters. If the *minimum support* δ is small, many frequent rooted subtrees will be mined from the user queries. Then there may be many clusters while only some of them are semantically close. Hence, in this step, we perform cluster pruning to merge close clusters.

We measure the inter-cluster similarity based on the number of frequent edges the clusters share. Given a *minimum cluster support* ξ, the set of frequent edges of cluster C_i, denoted as F_{C_i}, are the edges in the merged tree of C_i with their support no less than ξ. That is, $F_{C_i} = \{e | e \in M_i \land supp(e) \geq \xi\}$, where M_i is the merged tree structure of cluster C_i. Then, we define the *inter-cluster similarity* as follows.

$$Inter(C_i \to C_j) = \frac{|\{e | e \in F_{C_i}, e \in F_{C_j}\}| - |\{e | e \in F_{C_i}, e \notin F_{C_j}\}|}{|\{e | e \in F_{C_i}\}|}$$

That is, the more overlap in their frequent edges, the closer the two clusters. The value of $Inter(C_i \to C_j)$ ranges from -1 to 1. If $Inter(C_i \to C_j)$ is greater than 0, cluster C_i is semantically close to cluster C_j. We merge two clusters C_i and C_j if not only $Inter(C_i \to C_j)$ but also $Inter(C_j \to C_i)$ are greater than 0. Furthermore, we select the cluster label of C_j as the label of the merged cluster if $Inter(C_i \to C_j) > Inter(C_j \to C_i)$.

Example 3.3 Consider the clusters C_2 and C_3 in Figure 5 again. Let ξ=0.6. Then, F_{C_2} ={(book, author)} and F_{C_3} ={(book, author), (author, In)}. Thus, $Inter(C_2 \to C_3) = (1-0)/1 = 1$ because the frequent edge in C_2 is frequent as well in C_3. Whereas, $Inter(C_3 \to C_2) = (2-1)/2 = 0.5$ because the frequent edge (author, In) in C_3 is infrequent in C_2. Hence, we merge C_2 and C_3 and use book/author/In as the cluster label of the new cluster.

The final clustering result of the ten queries in Figure 1 (b) is shown in Figure 6 (a). The semantics of the queries in a cluster can be approximately represented by the cluster label.

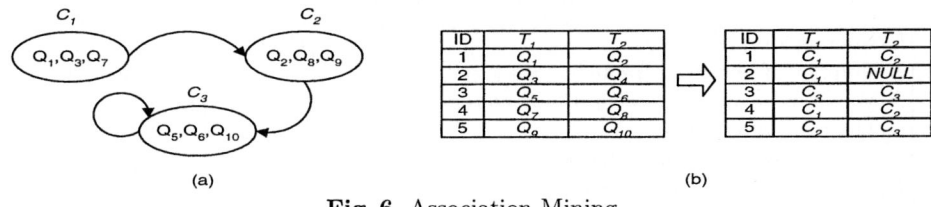

Fig. 6. Association Mining

4 Association Rule Mining

In this section, we discuss the second stage of our approach: mining positive and negative association rules between the clusters. The input of this stage is the set of 2-cluster sequences, which is generated by replacing the queries with the corresponding clusters created in the first stage. For example, using the final clustering results as in Figure 6 (a), the initial XML queries in Figure 1 (b) is transformed to a set of five 2-cluster sequences as shown in Figure 6 (b). Note that, outlier queries, such as query Q_4, are replaced with NULL.

In this paper, we employed the metric *interest* on top of the *support-confidence* framework as in [10] to define positive and negative association rules. We represent *1*-cluster sequences as $<C_i,>$ or $<,C_i>$ to distinguish the different positions of cluster C_i. A sequence of clusters $<C_i, C_j>$ supports two 1-cluster sequences $<C_i,>$ and $<,C_j>$, and one 2-cluster sequence $<C_i, C_j>$. Let D be a database of sequences of 2-cluster over $C=\{C_1, ..., C_k\}$. Let $supp(<C_i, C_j>)$ be the fraction of sequences in D that support it, $conf(<C_i, C_j>) = \frac{supp(<C_i,C_j>)}{supp(<C_i,>)}$, $interest(<C_i, C_j>) = \frac{supp(<C_i,C_j>)}{supp(<C_i,>)supp(<,C_j>)}$. Given the user defined *minimum support* α, *minimum confidence* β and *minimum interest* γ, $C_i \Rightarrow C_j$ is a positive association rule if 1) $supp(<C_i, C_j>) \not\geq \alpha$; 2) $conf(<C_i, C_j>) \geq \beta$; 3) $interest(<C_i, C_j>)) > \gamma$. A negative association rule $C_i \Rightarrow \neg C_j$ can be defined similarly. In-

---

Algorithm 1 Positive and Negative Association Rule Generation

Input: $D, min\_supp, min\_conf, min\_interest$
Output: PR: A set of positive association rules, NR: A set of negative association rules
Description:
1: scan D to find frequent 1-sequence (F_1) /*$supp(<C_i,>)$ or $supp(<,C_i>) \geq min\_supp$*/
2: $P_2 = F_1 \bowtie F_1$ /*candidate frequent 2-cluster sequence*/
3: for each $<C_i, C_j> \in P_2$ do
4:   if $supp(<C_i, C_j>) \geq min\_supp$ then
5:     if $(confidence(C_i \Rightarrow C_j) \geq min\_conf)$ && $(Interest(C_i \Rightarrow C_j) \geq min\_interest)$ then
6:       $PR = PR \cup \{C_i \Rightarrow C_j\}$
7:     end if
8:   else
9:     if $supp(<C_i, \neg C_j>) \geq min\_supp$ then
10:       if $(confidence(C_i \Rightarrow \neg C_j) \geq min\_conf)$ && $(Interest(C_i \Rightarrow \neg C_j) \geq min\_interest)$ then
11:         $NR = NR \cup \{C_i \Rightarrow \neg C_j\}$
12:       end if
13:     end if
14:   end if
15: end for

Table 1. Parameter List & Clustering Accuracy

N	Number of query trees	1K-10K
L	Number of potential frequent rooted subtrees	8
P	Maximum overlap between frequent rooted subtrees	0.5
O	The ratio of outliers	0.05
D	Average depth of query trees	4
F	Average fanout of query trees	4

N	DS	IS
1K	0.026	0.082
2K	0.022	0.080
4K	0.047	0.096
6K	0.038	0.112
8K	0.051	0.128

(a) (b)

stead of discovering frequent 2-cluster sequences first and then deriving possible rules as commonly done by traditional association rule mining algorithm, we discover positive and negative association rules directly. The algorithm is presented in Algorithm 1.

Finally, we discuss how to design the replacement strategy with discovered association rules. Without loss of generality, we assume that *"the most recent value for clusters"*, V_{top}, is incremented by one, each time a new query Q_i is issued. Suppose Q_i is semantically contained by or close to an existing cluster C_i, a positive association rule $C_i \Rightarrow C_j$ with confidence σ was discovered, and the current replacement value of C_j is V_j. Then, we calculate a new replacement value for C_j as $V_j' = V_j + (V_{top} - V_j) \times \sigma$. Since $V_j \leq V_j' \leq V_{top}$, we delayed the eviction of queries in cluster C_j based on the rule. It is similar for negative association rules. For example, with a negative rule $C_i \Rightarrow \neg C_j$, we update $V_j' = V_j + (V_j - V_{top}) \times \sigma$. As $V_j' < V_j$, we actually hasten the the purge of queries in cluster C_j.

5 Performance Study

In this section, we evaluate the performance of our approach with some preliminary experimental results. We implemented our approach in Java. Experiments are carried out on a Pentium IV 2.8GHz PC with 512 MB memory. The operating system is Windows 2000 professional.

5.1 Performance of Query Clustering

Firstly, we investigate the performance of our query clustering method. Given a DTD file, We generate synthetic query trees in the following steps: 1) A set of potential frequent rooted subtrees is generated by controlling the overlap between them. 2) We also create some infrequent rooted subtrees as outliers. 3) Finally, we generate the query trees based on the rooted subtrees produced in the first two steps. The parameters we used in the data set generation process are summarized in Table 1 (a), where the third column shows the default values.

We conducted experiments to evaluate the accuracy, efficiency and scalability of our clustering method respectively by varying different parameters.

- *Accuracy Study.* We evaluate the accuracy of our clustering method by varying the number of query trees from 1,000 to 8,000. The *minimum global*

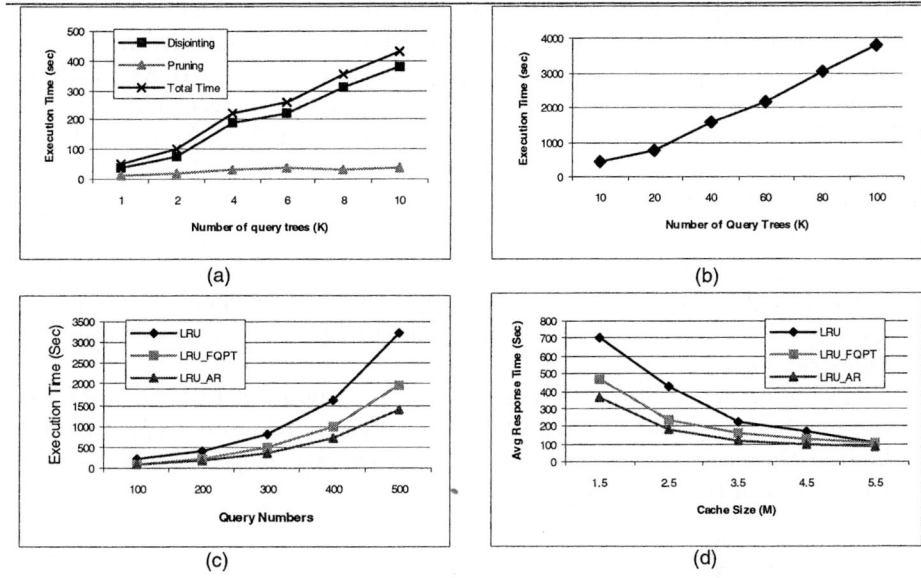

Fig. 7. Performance of Clustering

support is set as 5% and the *minimum cluster support* is set as 25%. Table 1 (b) shows the average intra-cluster dissimilarity (DS) and the average inter-cluster similarity (IS) of the resulting clusters. We observed that our clustering method can achieve small intra-cluster dissimilarity and small inter-cluster similarity.
- *Efficiency Study.* We evaluated the efficiency of the clustering method by showing the time cost of different phases in Figure 7 (a) except the cost of initialization step which is very trivial. The main cost of our clustering method is the disjointing step as it recursively optimizes the intra-cluster dissimilarity.
- *Scalability Study.* We evaluate the scalability of the clustering method by duplicating the query trees until we get 100K query trees. Figure 7 (b) shows that our clustering algorithm scales well with respect to the number of query trees.

5.2 Performance of Replacement Strategy

We then show the effectiveness of our replacement strategy with discovered association rules. We used a simple XQuery processor [1] that process queries directly from the source XML file. In our experiment, we generated a fragment of DBLP data as the source XML document. The file size is 10.5M and there are totally 248,215 nodes. We first generate a training data set of *2-cluster sequences* to discover positive and negative association rules. Then, we generate a testing data set of *2-cluster sequences* to evaluate the performance of caching.

Two sets of experiments were carried out to investigate the effect of varying the number of queries and varying the size of cache respectively. We compared our association rule based LRU replacement strategy (LRU_AR) with another two strategies, LRU and LRU with frequent query patterns mined by [11] (LRU_FQPT). We use the *Average Response Time*, which is the ratio of total execution time for answering a set of queries to the total number of queries in this set, as the metric.

- Variation of Query Numbers. Because of the limited power of the query processor, we vary the number of queries from 100 to 500 and the cache size is fixed at 2.5MB. As we can see from Figure 7 (c), when the number of queries is large, the average response time of LRU_AR surpasses the other two strategies.
- Variation of Cache Size. We vary the size of cache from 1.5M to 5.5M, and the number of queries is fixed at 300. As shown in Figure 7 (d), the more limited the cache size, the greater gap in average response time between LRU_AR and the other two competitors.

6 Conclusions

In this paper, we presented an approach that mines association rules from XML queries for caching. Since our association rules address the temporal sequence between user queries, it is more reliable in predicting future queries than the approaches that address the frequency or recency only. Due to the intuition that few users issue the exactly same queries sequentially, we cluster queries based on their semantics first and then discover the positive and negative associations between them. The knowledge obtained from the discovered rules are incorporated in designing appropriate replacement strategies. As verified by the experimental results, our approach improved the cache performance significantly.

References

1. http://www.cs.wisc.edu/ mcilwain/classwork/cs764/.
2. F. Bonchi, F. Giannotti, C. Gozzi, and G. Manco et al. Web log data warehousing and mining for intelligent web caching. In *Data and Knowledge Engineering, 39(2):165-189*, 2001.
3. L. Chen, E. A. Rundensteiner, and S. Wang. Xcache-a semantic caching system for xml queries. In *Demo in ACM SIGMOD*, 2002.
4. T. Dalamagas, T. Cheng, K. Winkel, and T. K. Sellis. Clustering xml documents by structure. In *Proc. of SETN*, 2004.
5. B. C. M. Fung, K. Wang, and M. Ester. Hierarchical document clustering using frequent itemsets. In *Proc. of SDM*, 2003.
6. V. Hristidis and M. Petropoulos. Semantic caching of xml databases. In *Proc. of the 5th WebDB*, 2002.
7. B. Lan, S. Bressan, B. C. Ooi, and K. L. Tan. Rule-assisted prefetching in web-server caching. In *Proc. of ACM CIKM*, 2000.

8. W. Lian, D. W. Cheung, N. Mamoulis, and S. Yiu. An efficient and scalable algorithm for clustering xml documents by structure. In *IEEE TKDE, vol. 16, No. 1*, 2004.
9. K. Wang, C. Xu, and B. Liu. Clustering transactions using large items. In *Proc. of ACM CIKM*, 1999.
10. X. Wu, C. Zhang, and S. Zhang. Mining both positive and negative association rules. In *Proc. of ICML*, 2002.
11. L. H. Yang, M. L. Lee, and W. Hsu. Efficient mining of xml query patterns for caching. In *Proc. of 29th VLDB*, 2003.

Distributed Intersection Join of Complex Interval Sequences

Hans-Peter Kriegel, Peter Kunath, Martin Pfeifle, and Matthias Renz

University of Munich, Germany
{kriegel, kunath, pfeifle, renz}@dbs.ifi.lmu.de

Abstract. In many different application areas, e.g. space observation systems or engineering systems of world-wide operating companies, there is a need for an efficient distributed intersection join in order to extract new and global knowledge. A solution for carrying out a global intersection join is to transmit all distributed information from the clients to a central server leading to high transfer cost. In this paper, we present a new distributed intersection join for interval sequences of high-cardinality which tries to minimize these transmission cost. Our approach is based on a suitable probability model for interval intersections which is used on the server as well as on the various clients. On the client sites, we group intervals together based on this probability model. These locally created approximations are sent to the server. The server ranks all intersecting approximations according to our probability model. As not all approximations have to be refined in order to decide whether two objects intersect, we fetch the exact information of the most promising approximations first. This strategy helps to cut down the transmission cost considerably which is proven by our experimental evaluation based on synthetic and real-world test data sets.

Keywords: Distributed intersection join, probability model, interval sequences.

1 Introduction

After two decades of temporal and spatial index research, the efficient management of one- and multi-dimensional extended objects has become an enabling technology for many novel database applications. The interval, or, more generally, the sequence of intervals, are basic datatypes for temporal and spatial data. Interval sequences are used to handle finite domain constraints [10] or to represent periods on transactions or valid time dimensions [11]. Typical applications of one-dimensional interval sequences include the temporal tracing of user activity for service providers. In general, any time series may be aggregated to an interval sequence, such as periods of "high" stock prices for technical chart analysis (cf. Figure 1).

Further examples of interval sequences residing on different, independently working computers which are connected to each other via local or wide area networks (LANs or WANs) comprise distributed mobile networks, sensor networks or vehicle manufacturers, where the development agencies are located at different places, distributed all over the world. For instance, international companies such as DaimlerChrysler have some development agencies which are located in Europe, some in Asia, and some located in the US. When applied to space-filling curves, interval sequences naturally represent spatially extended objects with even intricate shapes (cf. Figure 1). By expressing spatial region queries as interval sequence intersections, vital operations for the digital

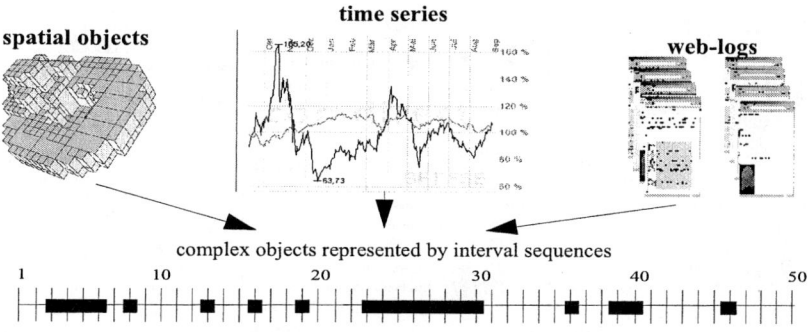

Fig. 1. Interval sequences

mock-up of vehicles and airplanes [5], haptic simulations in virtual product environments [8] or engineering data management can be supported. In these areas as well as in the areas of two-dimensional GIS and environmental information systems [7] the locally collected data can only, with great difficulty, be transmitted to a central site to be joined centrally there. Meeting the need of all these application ranges, we will present a distributed interval intersection join in this paper which extracts global knowledge while taking limited bandwidth and security aspects into account.

The remainder of this paper is organized as follows. In Section 2, we present the related work on distributed interval intersection joins. In Section 3, we shortly sketch our general idea, followed by the presentation of the basic definitions and theorems in Section 4. In Section 5, we show how to group different intervals together to coarser approximations on the client site in order to reduce the overall transmission cost. After having transmitted these approximations to the server, we present in Section 6, the server-side join algorithm trying to avoid as many as possible further client accesses for fetching the exact interval sequence objects. In Section 7, we will present convincing experimental results demonstrating the superiority w.r.t. low transmission cost of our new algorithm compared to less sophisticated algorithms. We will close this paper in Section 8 with a short summary and a few remarks on future work.

2 Related Work

Several different approaches to provide efficient interval joins already exist in the literature, especially in the field of temporal applications [3]. For instance, Seidl et al. proposed an interval intersection join based on the Relational Interval Tree which can easily be implemented on top of any relational database system [2]. Furthermore, there exist specialized index structures suitable for detecting intersecting interval sequences [6] which can be used as foundation for an index-based nested loop join.

Similarly, considerable work has been done in the area of distributed data management [9], for instance in the area of Distributed Data Mining (DDM) [4]. Generally, distributed databases constitute a very important and emerging research area which crucially depends on efficient query processing.

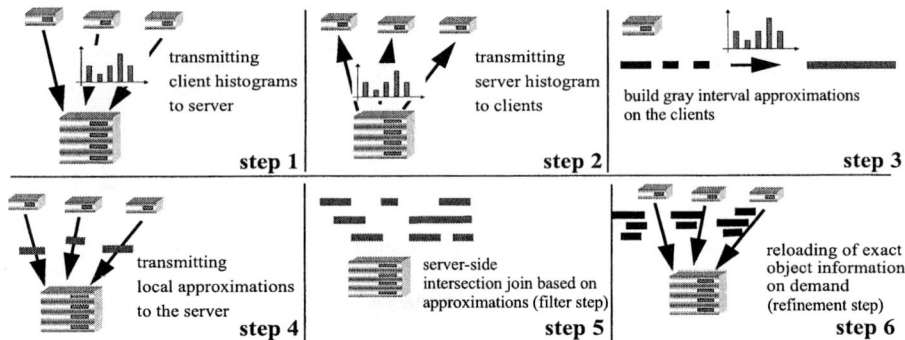

Fig. 2. Distributed Intersection Join on Interval Sequences

Unfortunately, to the best of our knowledge, there has been no work published which brings the two independent research areas of "distributed databases" and "join processing of interval sequences" together.

3 General Idea

The goal of this paper is to present a distributed algorithm which detects intersecting interval sequences residing on different local clients. Note that determining pairs of intersecting interval sequences located at the same local site is a rather straightforward task which can be handled independently by the corresponding local clients. These locally determined result sets can easily be combined with the global result set determined by the distributed intersection join presented in this paper. In this section, we shortly sketch the complete distributed intersection join process (cf. Figure 2).

At first all clients collect statistical information reflecting the interval distributions of the data residing at their own local site. Then, the clients send this statistical information to the server (step 1). At the server site the local client statistics are merged into a global statistic reflecting the interval distribution of all local clients. This global statistic is sent back to each client (step 2). Each client groups "black" intervals belonging to the same interval sequence together to coarser approximations called "gray" intervals (step 3). This grouping process is decisively based on the data distribution of the join partners residing on the other local clients which is reflected by the global statistic minus the own local client statistic. The resulting statistic is not only used for the grouping process but also for a fast filter step on the client sites. If by means of this statistic a global intersection of a gray interval cannot be ruled out, the hull of the gray interval along with additional aggregated information, i.e. the density of the gray interval and the number of bytes required for sending the corresponding (compressed) exact information, is sent to the server (step 4). The server detects all intersecting gray intervals based on their hulls (step 5). Based on the intersection length of the hulls and the density of the gray intervals the server computes a probability that not only the gray intervals intersect but also the corresponding black intervals. The pairs of gray intervals with intersecting hulls are ranked ascendingly according to a combination of the determined probability value and the transmission cost of the exact information. The server iteratively refines the top-listed pairs by fetching the exact information, i.e. the (compressed) black inter-

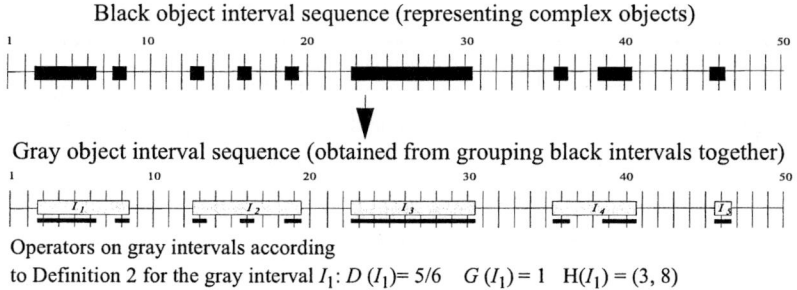

Fig. 3. Gray object interval sequence

vals, belonging to the corresponding gray intervals from the local clients (step 6). Gray interval pairs which belong to object pairs already known to intersect do not have to be refined. Thereby, we can enormously save on the overall transmission cost.

4 (Gray) Interval Sequences

In this section, we formally introduce interval sequence objects. Furthermore, we propose an intersection probability model, which is used for the client-side grouping approach (cf. Section 5) as well as for the server side join processing (cf. Section 6). We start with the definition of some notions.

4.1 Definitions

Interval sequences representing complex objects often consist of very short intervals connected by short gaps (cf. Figure 3). For instance, in the case of high resolution linearized spatial objects the interval sequences may contain several hundred thousands of small intervals per object. When the server request the objects from the clients, the huge amount of interval data would lead to high transmission cost due to a low transfer rate of the network connection. In order to overcome this obstacle, it seems promising to pass over some "small" gaps and approximate the interval sequence by much less intervals. In this paper, we confine ourselves to integer boundary values for intervals, as in all investigated domains, e.g. for time series, stock charts, or spatially extended objects linearized via space-filling curves, only integers are used due to the use of a finite resolution.

Definition 1 (*gray interval sequence objects*). Let id be an *object identifier* and $W = \{(l, u) \in IN^2, l \leq u\}$ be the domain of intervals which we call *black* intervals throughout this paper. Furthermore, let $b_1 = (l_1, u_1), \ldots, b_n = (l_n, u_n) \in W$ be a sequence of intervals with $u_i + 1 < l_{i+1}$ for all $i \in \{1, \ldots, n-1\}$. Moreover, let $m \leq n$ and let $i_0, i_1, i_2, \ldots, i_m \in IN$ such that $0 = i_0 < i_1 < i_2 < \ldots < i_m = n$ holds. Then, we call $O_{gray} = (id, \langle \langle b_{i_0+1}, \ldots, b_{i_1} \rangle, \langle b_{i_1+1}, \ldots, b_{i_2} \rangle, \ldots, \langle b_{i_{m-1}+1}, \ldots, b_{i_m} \rangle \rangle)$ a *gray interval sequence object* of cardinality m. If m equals n, we denote O_{gray} also as a *black interval sequence object* O_{black}. We call each of the $j = 1, \ldots, m$ groups $\langle b_{i_{j-1}+1}, \ldots, b_{i_j} \rangle$ of O_{gray} a *gray interval* I_{gray}. If $i_{j-1}+1$ equals i_j, we denote I_{gray} also as a *black interval* I_{black}.

In the next definition, we introduce a few useful operators on *gray intervals* which we will use frequently throughout the remainder of this paper.

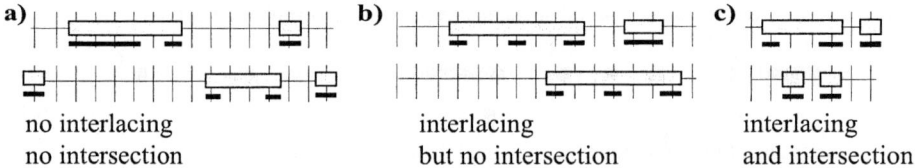

Fig. 4. Gray object interval sequences
a) non interlacing, b) interlacing but no intersection, c) intersection

Definition 2 (*operators on gray intervals*). For any gray interval $I_{gray} = \langle (l_r, u_r), \ldots, (l_s, u_s) \rangle$ we define the following operators:

Density: $\quad D(I_{gray}) \quad = \quad \sum_{i=r\ldots s}(u_i - l_i + 1)/(u_s - l_r + 1)$

Gap: $\quad G(I_{gray}) \quad = \quad \begin{cases} 0 & r = s \\ \max\{1 + l_i - u_{i-1}, i = r+1, \ldots, s\} & \text{else} \end{cases}$

Hull: $\quad H(I_{gray}) \quad = \quad (l_r, u_s)$

Figure 3 exemplarily demonstrates the values of these operators for a gray interval I_1. In the following, we define intersect predicates for *intervals, interval sequences* and *gray intervals*:

Definition 3 (object intersection). Let $W = \{(l, u) \in \mathbb{N}^2, l \leq u\}$ be the domain of intervals, and let $I = \langle b_1, \ldots, b_n \rangle$ and $I' = \langle b'_1, \ldots, b'_{n'} \rangle$ be two gray intervals. Furthermore, let $O = (id, \langle I_1, I_2, \ldots, I_m \rangle)$ and $O' = (id', \langle I'_1, I'_2, \ldots, I'_{m'} \rangle)$ be two gray interval sequence objects. Then, the notions *intersect* and *interlace* are defined in the following way (cf. Figure 4):

1a. Two intervals, $b = (l, u)$ and $b' = (l', u')$ *intersect* if $l \leq u'$ and $l' \leq u$.
1b. The intersection length $intersect_{length}((l, u), (l', u'))$ of two intervals is equal to $\max(0, \min(u, u') - \max(l, l')+1)$.
2a. Two gray intervals I and I' *intersect* if for any $i \in \{1, \ldots, n\}, j \in \{1, \ldots, n'\}$ the black intervals b_i and b'_j intersect.
2b. Two gray intervals I and I' *interlace*, if their hulls, $H(I)$ and $H(I')$ intersect.
3a. Two objects O and O' *intersect* if for any $i \in \{1, \ldots, m\}, j \in \{1, \ldots, m'\}$, the gray intervals I_i and I'_j intersect.
3b. Two objects O and O' *interlace* if for any $i \in \{1, \ldots, m\}, j \in \{1, \ldots, m'\}$, the gray intervals I_i and I'_j interlace.

4.2 Intersection Detection

In this section, we first present two rather obvious lemmas which state whether two gray intervals intersect or not, based on relatively little information. The first lemma can be used as filter for detecting intersecting interval sequence objects (cf. Figure 4a).

Lemma 1 (non-intersecting gray intervals). Let $I = \langle b_1, \ldots, b_n \rangle$ and $I' = \langle b'_1, \ldots, b'_{n'} \rangle$ be two gray intervals. Then the following statement holds:

$$\neg\, interlace(I, I') \Rightarrow \neg\, intersect(I, I')$$

Proof. First, $\neg$ *interlace*$(I, I') \Rightarrow \neg$ *intersect*(I, I') is equivalent to *intersect*$(I, I') \Rightarrow$ *interlace*(I, I'). Then, *intersect*$(I, I') \Rightarrow \exists\ (b_i, b'_j) \in \{\{b_1, .., b_n\} \times \{b'_1, .., b'_n\}\}$: *intersect*$(b_i, b'_j) = true$. Let $b_i = (l_i, u_i)$, $b'_j = (l'_j, u'_j)$, $H(I)=(l, u)$, and $H(I')=(l', u')$, then $l \leq l_i \leq u'_j \leq u'$ and $l' \leq l'_j \leq u_i \leq u$ holds which proves that I and I' interlace (cf. case 1a and 2b in Definition 3). ∎

Let us note that the we cannot pinpoint any intersecting interval sequence objects by means of Lemma 1, as *interlace*$(I, I') \Rightarrow$ *intersect*(I, I') does not hold (cf. Figure 4b). Thus, a refined evaluation of the intersect predicate is necessary when two gray intervals interlace. Only in the rare case where both gray intervals have maximum density, we can abstain from this refinement step.

Lemma 2 (*intersecting gray intervals*). Let $I = \langle b_1, ..., b_n \rangle$ and $I' = \langle b'_1, ..., b'_{n'} \rangle$ be two gray intervals. Then the following statement holds:

$$(D(I) = 1 \land D(I') = 1 \land interlace(I, I')) \Rightarrow intersect(I, I')$$

Proof. According to Definition 1 and 2: $D(I) = 1 \Rightarrow n = 1$ and $D(I') = 1 \Rightarrow n' = 1$. According to Definition 3: *interlace*$(I, I') \Rightarrow$ *intersect*$(b_1, b'_1) \Rightarrow$ *intersect*(I, I'). ∎

Lemma 2 shows that we can sometimes pinpoint whether two gray interval pairs intersect based on relatively little information. Unfortunately, as in most cases the precondition of Lemma 2 does not hold, we will not be able to apply it very often. Nevertheless, it is still helpful if we can predict how probable an intersection of interlacing gray intervals might be.

4.3 Intersection Probability

The probability model introduced in this section is easy to compute and will be applied in various different forms throughout our approach. The model is equal to the *coin-toss experiment*, i.e. it is a *Bernoulli experiment*. It assumes that the intervals and gaps covered by a gray interval are equally distributed.

Theorem 1 (*intersection probability*). Let I and I' be two gray intervals with densities $D = D(I)$ and $D' = D(I')$. Furthermore, let $L = intersect_{length}(H(I), H(I'))$. Then the probability $P(I, I')$ that the two gray intervals I and I' intersect is equal to:

$$P(I, I') = 1 - (1 - D \cdot D')^L$$

Proof. Let x be one of the points in the interlacing area. Obviously, the probability that this point is covered by an interval contained in I is equal to the density D. Subsequently, the probability that two intervals I and I' intersect at the point x is $P_x = D \cdot D'$. The probability, that either x or another point $y \neq x$ is covered by intervals from I and I' is $P_{\{x,y\}} = D \cdot D' + (1 - D \cdot D') \cdot D \cdot D'$. As we assume that the interval bounds are mapped to discrete integer values, the probability that I and I' share at least one point can be computed as follows:

$$P(I, I') = \sum_{i=0}^{L-1} D \cdot D' \cdot (1 - D \cdot D')^i = D \cdot D' \cdot \frac{1 - (1 - D \cdot D')^L}{1 - (1 - D \cdot D')} = 1 - (1 - D \cdot D')^L \ \blacksquare$$

Note that Lemma 1 and 2 can be derived from the above theorem by setting the interlacing length L to 0 (Lemma 1) or setting D and D' to 1 (Lemma 2). Similar to the above reasoning, we are going to derive the probability that one gray interval I_0 intersects at least one of n other gray intervals $I_1, .., I_n$.

Theorem 2 (*combined intersection probability*). Let I_0 be a gray interval that intersects with n other gray intervals I_i, $i \in 1..n$, with a probability $P(I_0, I_i)$. Then, the total probability $P(I_0)$ that I_0 intersects with at least one of the other gray intervals can be computed by

$$P(I_0) = 1 - \prod_{i=1}^{n}(1 - P(I_0, I_i))$$

Proof. The probability $P'(I_0)$ that none of the gray intervals $I_1, .., I_n$ intersect with I_0 is $P'(I_0) = (1 - P(I_0, I_1)) \cdot ... \cdot (1 - P(I_0, I_n))$. Consequently, the total probability $P(I_0)$ that I_0 intersects with at least one of the other gray intervals is $P(I_0) = 1 - P'(I_0)$. ∎

5 Client-Side Approximation of Interval Sequences

The central question is how to group the interval sequence of a client object into gray intervals serving as suitable object approximations. In this section, we first introduce probability histograms which are used to estimate the intersection probability of gray intervals. Secondly, we present our cost model which takes the probability histograms as well as the transmission cost into account. Finally, we present a cost-based grouping algorithm which aims at minimizing the overall transmission cost.

5.1 Estimation of the Intersection Probability

We use simple statistics of the interval sequence objects to estimate the probability $P(I_{gray})$ that any gray interval I_{gray} intersects with at least one other gray interval located on a different client. In order to cope with arbitrary interval distributions, histograms can be employed to capture the data characteristics at any desired resolution. The expected intersection probability $P(I_{gray})$ can be determined by using an appropriate intersection probability histogram which reflects aggregated information over all interval sequence objects distributed over all local clients.

Definition 4 (*intersection probability histogram*). Let $IB = [0, max \in I\!N]$ be a domain of interval bounds. Let the natural number $v \in I\!N$ denote the *resolution*, and $\beta_v = max/v$ be the corresponding *bucket size* of the histogram. Let $b_{i,v} = [1 + (i - 1) \cdot \beta_v, 1 + i \cdot \beta_v]$ denote the *span of bucket i*, $i \in \{1, ..., v\}$. Let further DB be a database of interval sequence objects and the function $\Omega(o_j, b_{i,v})$ denotes the sum $\Sigma_\iota intersect_{length}(\iota, b_{i,v})$ over all intervals ι of the interval sequence object o_j. Then, $\Psi(DB, v) = (n_1, ..., n_v) \in I\!N^v$ is called the *intersection probability histogram* on DB with resolution v, iff for all $i \in \{1,.., v\}$:

$$n_i = 1 - \prod_{\forall o_j \in DB}\left(1 - \frac{\Omega(o_j, b_{i,v})}{\beta_v}\right)$$

In the above definition, we map an interval sequence object to v gray intervals congruent to the histogram buckets each having a density $(\Omega(o_j, b_{i,v}))/\beta_v$. This density corresponds to the probability that one point $x \in b_{i,v}$ is intersected by the interval sequence object of o_j. Theorem 2 shows that the value n_i in Definiton 4 reflects the probability that $x \in b_{i,v}$ is intersected by at least one interval sequence object of the domain DB.

All local clients send their own intersection probability histogram to the server. The server computes for each client C^j a specific global intersection probability histogram Ψ^j.

Definition 5 (*global intersection probability histogram*). Let $DB_1, .., DB_m$ be the data sets of m different local clients with congruent intersection probability histograms $\Psi(DB_s, v) = (n_{1,s}, ..., n_{v,s})$, $s \in \{1,.., m\}$. Then, the global intersection probability histogram $\Psi^j(\bigcup_{\substack{s=1...m \\ s \neq j}} DB_s, v) = (n_1^j, ..., n_v^j)$ for the client C^j can be computed as follows:

$$n_i^j = 1 - \prod_{\substack{s=1 \\ s \neq j}}^{m} (1 - n_{i,s})$$

Similar to the argumentation following Definition 4, the value n_i^j of Ψ^j in Definition 5 reflects the probability that $x \in b_{i,v}$ is intersected by at least one interval sequence object located at a client C^s where $s \in \{1,.., m\}\setminus j$.

5.2 Cost Model

The approximation quality has a significant influence on the performance of the multi-step join process. If we adjust the approximation quality too low, for example by taking one-value approximations, the filter step is not very selective, thus many exact object informations have to be requested from the server. On the other hand, if we choose very accurate approximations, the initial transmission cost for sending the aggregated information of the gray intervals to the server are very high.

The overall join cost $cost_{join}$ related to a gray interval I_{gray} are composed of two parts, the filter cost $cost_{filter}$ and the refinement cost $cost_{refine}$:

$$cost_{join}(I_{gray}) = cost_{filter}(I_{gray}) + cost_{refine}(I_{gray}).$$

Filter Cost. The filter cost $cost_{filter}(I_{gray})$ related to a gray interval I_{gray} depends mainly on the cost required to transmit the aggregated information of I_{gray} to the server. Furthermore, transmission includes the necessary identifier of I_{gray}, the hull $H(I_{gray})$ and the density $D(I_{gray})$. The total size of the transmitted data is constant, thus, we penalize each transmission by a constant c_{trans} which reflects the transmission cost related to one gray interval.

Refinement Cost. The refinement cost related to I_{gray} depend on whether the server asks for the exact information of I_{gray} during the join process or not. Obviously, the probability that the server asks for the exact information depends on the probability whether I_{gray} intersects at least one gray interval or not. Thus we can estimate the refinement cost as follows:

$$cost_{refine}(I_{gray}) = \left(1 - \prod_{i=1}^{v}(1 - P(I_{gray}, I_{i,v}))\right) \cdot cost_{trans}(I_{gray}),$$

```
GroupIS ($I_{gray}$, $\Psi^j(DB,v)$) {
    interval_pair := split_at_maximum_gap($I_{gray}$);
    $I_{left}$      := interval_pair.left;    $I_{right}$ := interval_pair.right;
    $cost_{gray}$   := $cost_{join}(I_{gray})$;
    $cost_{dec}$    := $cost_{join}(I_{left}) + cost_{join}(I_{right})$;

    if $cost_{gray} > cost_{dec}$ then return GroupIS ($I_{left}$,$\Psi^j(DB,v)$) $\cup$ GroupIS($I_{right}$, $\Psi^j$ (DB,v));
    else return $I_{gray}$; }
```

Fig. 5. Grouping algorithm GroupIS

where $cost_{trans}(I_{gray})$ denotes the cost required to transmit the gray interval I_{gray} from client C^j to the server. Furthermore, $I_{i,v}$ denotes a gray interval having the extension of the histogram bucket $b_{i,v}$ and a density equal to the value n_i^j of Ψ^j (cf. Definition 5). $P(I_{gray}, I_{i,v})$ denotes the probability that I_{gray} intersects at least one gray interval in the bucket $b_{i,v}$ stored at a client C^s where $s \in \{1,..,m\}\backslash j$ (cf. Theorem 1). The probability that I_{gray} intersects at least one gray interval in any bucket can be computed by means of Theorem 2 which is reflected in the above equation for $cost_{refine}(I_{gray})$.

5.3 Grouping Algorithm

Our cost-based grouping algorithm depicted in Figure 5 is a greedy approach which is performed in top-down fashion. It starts with a one-value approximation of the input interval sequence, i.e. all intervals are grouped into one large gray interval I_{gray}. At first we search the largest gap of I_{gray} and split it at this gap into two smaller gray intervals I_{left} and I_{right}. As long as the estimated transmission cost of the resulting gray intervals are smaller than the cost according to the unsplitted interval I_{gray}, the algorithm is applied recursively to both gray intervals I_{left} and I_{right}.

6 Server-Side Join Algorithm

The server-side join algorithm is based on the multi-step query processing paradigm. First, we detect all interlacing objects (cf. Definition 3). In order to decide whether an interlacing object pair intersects, it suffices to detect one intersecting gray interval pair of this object combination. Consequently, all remaining intersection tests according to these two objects can be discarded and the corresponding transmission cost can be saved. Therefore, it is desirable to rank interlacing gray intervals according to their intersection probability and their transmission cost. Obviously, the intersection probability should be high and the transmission cost should be low for a top-ranked interlacing gray interval pair. Thus, we compute the ranking value for a pair (I, I') as follows:

$$rank(I, I') = (1 - P(I, I')) \cdot (cost_{transmit}(I) + cost_{transmit}(I'))$$

Thereby, the intersection probability $P(I, I')$ between two interlacing gray intervals is computed according to Theorem 1. Note that all transmitted information is stored on the server site. Therefore, for each gray interval I which has already been transmitted from a local client to the server $cost_{transmit}(I)$ is equal to 0.

The interlacing gray interval pairs are organized in ascending order according to their ranking value in a sorted list *SortList*. The join algorithm iteratively carries out the refinement step for the top-listed gray interval pair. After the exact information of a gray interval I was transmitted from a local client to the server, $rank(I, I_i)$ of all gray interval pairs (I, I_i) stored in *SortList* is updated. Furthermore, if an object intersection is detected during the refinement step of the top-listed gray interval pair, all gray interval pairs belonging to the corresponding object pair are deleted from *SortList*.

7 Experiments

In this section, we evaluate the performance of our approach with a special emphasis on the overall transmission cost which are measured in bytes. All experiments were performed on a Pentium 4/2600 machine with IDE hard drives.

Test Data Sets. The tests are based on a test data set *CAR* which consists of 200 high-resolution 3D CAD objects provided by our industrial partner, a German car manufacturer. These voxelized objects have been linearized via a space filling curve leading to 200 interval sequence objects. Each of these objects consists of approximately 50,000 black intervals. Furthermore, we used an artificial test data set *ART* consisting of 1,024 interval sequence objects each represented by 10,000 black intervals. The objects are equally distributed in a range $[0..2^{27}-1]$ and the gap lengths inside an object follow a normal distribution. During the experiments, the objects of both test data sets were equally distributed on the available clients.

Grouping. We used two different grouping strategies for forming the gray intervals. The *MaxGap* approach tries to minimize the number of gray intervals while not allowing that a maximum gap $G(I_{gray})$ of any gray interval I_{gray} exceeds a given *MAXGAP* parameter. By varying this *MAXGAP* parameter, we can find the optimum trade-off between the two opposing grouping goals of Section 5.2, namely accurate approximations but a small number of gray intervals. A one-value interval approximation is achieved by setting the *MAXGAP* parameter to infinite. If the parameter is set to zero, each gray intervals is identical to one black interval. Furthermore, we used the *GroupIS* approach according to Figure 5, where we set the resolution of the used histograms to 10,000 buckets by default.

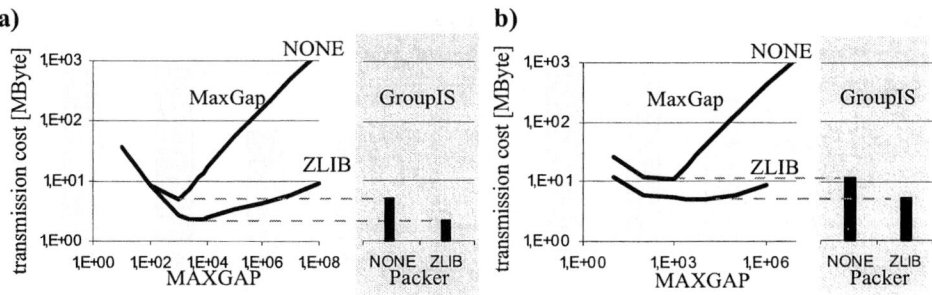

Fig. 6. Grouping strategies using (un)compressed data
(a) CAR and (b) ART which are equally distributed on 4 local clients

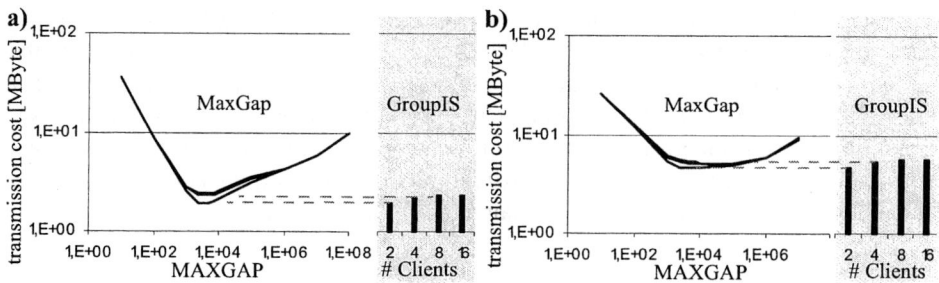

Fig. 7. Different grouping strategies on the two datasets (*ZLIB*)
(a) CAR and (b) ART which are equally distributed on 2, 4, 8 and 16 local clients

Client-Side Grouping. In a first set of experiments, we compare our different client-side grouping strategies to each other. Figure 6 shows that for the MaxGap approach we have rather high transmission cost when using too small or two large MAXGAP parameters. When the parameter is two small many hulls have to be transmitted. On the other hand, when the parameter is very high the filter selectivity is very bad leading to high transmission cost during the refinement step of the server-side join algorithm. Figure 6 shows that by applying suitable packers for compressing the exact information of the gray intervals, these cost can dramatically be reduced. Note that our GroupIS approach does not produce higher transmission cost than the "optimal" MaxGap approach independent whether a packer (*ZLIB* [1]) is used or not (*NONE*).

In another experiment, we investigated the dependency of the different grouping approaches for a varying number of clients. In this experiment, we transmitted the exact information of the gray intervals in a compressed way. Figure 7 shows that our GroupIS approach yields optimum results independent of the number of used clients. Again, for low MAXGAP values, the number of hulls sent to the server is quite large and dominates the overall transmission cost. High MAXGAP values lead to a very small number of gray intervals per object, thus, almost all join candidates have to be refined.

Server-Side Join. In Figure 8 it is shown how the ranking function influences the transmission cost of the refinement step. Thereby, we compare our cost-based ranking approach (*CBR*) with the following methods which differ in the order in which the join

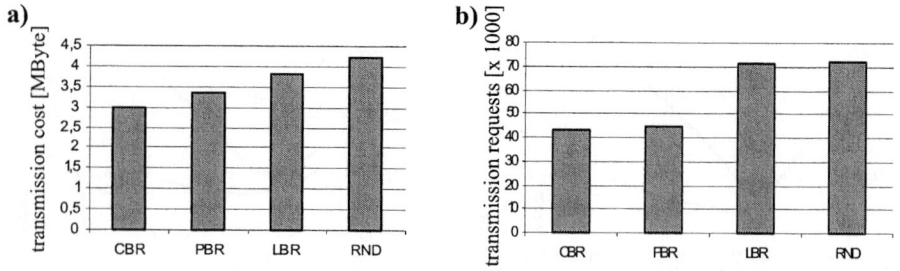

Fig. 8. Different join strategies (4 Clients, *ZLIB*, *GroupIS*, *ART*)
(a) transmission cost (b) transmission requests

candidates are refined: Ordered exclusively by the intersection probability (*PBR*), by the transmission cost (*LBR*), or in a randomized order (*RND*). This experiment shows that our approach achieves the lowest transmission cost, as well as the lowest number of transmission requests, i.e. our cost-based ranking approach produces the smallest additional communication overhead. Note that we made similar results for the CAR data set, a varying number of clients, and if we transmit the exact information uncompressed.

8 Conclusion

In this paper, we presented an intersection join for complex objects represented by interval sequences. Thereby the objects are assumed to be distributed on clients located at different sites. The intersection join is executed at a central server which is connected to all clients via local or wide area networks. The main goal of our approach is to minimize the client-server-communication cost incurred by the server side join process. Our proposed solution is based on generating approximations of the interval sequence data which are transmitted from the clients to the server site for a filter step. In contrast to existing solutions, e.g. error-bound approaches, our statistic driven proposal achieves a good trade-off between the communication cost of the filter and the refinement step. It adapts automatically to different client-server characteristics, e.g. different data sets, varying number of clients, or the used compression technique. Another contribution of this work is a cost based strategy for the refinement step. The experiments show that our approach leads to a speed-up of more than one order of magnitude compared to the use of one-value approximations or the use of no approximations at all.

In our future work, we plan to develop an even more efficient approximative distributed intersection join allowing fuzzy query responses.

References

1. Deutsch P.: RFC1951, DEFLATE Compressed Data Format Specification. ht-tp://rfc.net/rfc1951.html, 1996.
2. Enderle J., Hampel M., Seidl T.: *Joining Interval Data in Relational Databases*, Proc. ACM SIGMOD Int. Conf. on Management of Data (SIGMOD'04), Paris, France, 2004.
3. Gao D., Jensen C. S., Snodgrass R. T., Soo M. D.: *Join Operations in Temporal Databases*, A Time Center Technical Report (TR-71), 2002.
4. Kargupta H., Chan P.: *Advances in Distributed and Parallel Knowledge Discovery*, AAAI/MIT Press, 2000.
5. Kriegel H.-P., Pfeifle M., Pötke M., Seidl T.: *Spatial Query Processing for High Resolutions*, Proc. 8th Int. Conf. on Database Systems for Advanced Applications (DASFAA), Kyoto, Japan, pp. 17-26, 2003.
6. Kriegel H.-P., Pötke M., Seidl T.: *Interval Sequences: An Object-Relational Approach to Manage Spatial and Temporal Data*, Proc. 7th Int. Symposium on Spatial and Temporal Databases (SSTD), LNCS 2121: pp. 481-501, 2001.
7. Medeiros C. B., Pires F.: *Databases for GIS*, ACM SIGMOD Record, 23(1): pp. 107-115, 1994.
8. McNeely W. A., Puterbaugh K. D., Troy J. J.: *Six Degree of Freedom Haptic Rendering Using Voxel Sampling*, ACM SIGGRAPH, pp. 401-408, 1999.

9. Özsu T., Valduriez P.: *Principles of Distributed Database Systems*, Prentice Hall, ISBN 0-13-659707-6, 1999.
10. Ramaswamy S.: *Efficient Indexing for Constraint and Temporal Databases*, Proc. 6th Int. Conf. on Database Theory (ICDT), LNCS 1186, pp. 419-413, 1997.
11. Tansel A. U., Clifford J., Gadia S., Jajodia S., Segev A., Snodgrass R.: *Temporal Databases: Theory, Design and Implementation*, Redwood City, CA, 1993.

Using Prefix-Trees for Efficiently Computing Set Joins

Ravindranath Jampani and Vikram Pudi

Center for Data Engineering,
International Institute of Information Technology, Hyderabad, India
ravi@students.iiit.net, vikram@iiit.net

Abstract. Joins on set-valued attributes (set joins) have numerous database applications. In this paper we propose PRETTI (PREfix Tree based seT joIn) – a suite of set join algorithms for containment, overlap and equality join predicates. Our algorithms use prefix trees and inverted indices. These structures are constructed on-the-fly if they are not already precomputed. This feature makes our algorithms usable for relations without indices and when joining intermediate results during join queries with more than two relations. Another feature of our algorithms is that results are output continuously during their execution and not just at the end. Experiments on real life datasets show that the total execution time of our algorithms is significantly less than that of previous approaches, even when the indices required by our algorithms are not precomputed.

1 Introduction

Set-valued attributes are a natural and concise representation for many real life models. Object Oriented and Object Relational DBMS require the support of set-valued attributes. Efficient execution of queries involving these attributes is therefore an important problem [14]. Set join [11, 10, 7, 6, 13] is perhaps the most important operator on set-valued data since it is useful in several real-world problems, while at the same time being difficult to compute [2]. A set join between two relations R and S, retrieves pairs of records (t_R, t_S), $t_R \in R$ and $t_S \in S$, for which $t_R.p \; \theta \; t_S.q$ returns true, where p and q are set-valued attributes and θ can be any boolean valued function over two sets. Examples of such functions include set containment, set equality and set overlap.

As an example of a set containment join, consider the join of a relation *students* with a relation *courses*, where *students* has a set-valued attribute *coursesTaken*, and *courses* has a set-valued attribute *prerequisites*. This join finds all students eligible for taking each course when the predicate is *courses.prerequisites* $\subseteq$ *students.courses*. Overlap joins can be very useful in any match-making domain. One example is to find pairs of customers of amazon.com who purchase at least 5 books in common.

A number of partition based [11, 10] and inverted index based approaches [7, 6, 13] have been proposed for set joins. These studies were a welcome first step in addressing the problem of efficient computation of set joins. The partition based approaches do not require any precomputed index, but they are in general not as efficient as the inverted index based approaches [7]. The state-of-the-art inverted index based approaches, while being more efficient, have the drawback of requiring a precomputed index – this slows down database updates.

Our contributions in this paper are as follows:

1. We propose PRETTI (PREfix Tree based seT joIn) – a suite of novel algorithms for set containment, overlap and equality joins.
2. Our algorithms use prefix trees [4] in addition to inverted index structures. This helps utilize overlaps in records resulting in less rework.
3. Our algorithms build the required prefix trees and inverted indices "on-the-fly". This makes them usable for relations without indices and when joining intermediate results during join queries with more than two relations.
4. Computing indices on-the-fly instead of precomputing them means that there is no maintenance cost in terms of disk-space or time for updates.
5. Our algorithms can beneficially utilize precomputed indices if they are available. We note that our algorithms out-perform previous approaches even when our algorithms build the indices on-the-fly.
6. Join results are output continuously during the execution of the algorithm and not just at the end. In experiments on real life datasets where the join results are *huge* the (initial) response was almost instantaneous.
7. The output of our algorithms is organized without special effort in the following fashion: the output corresponding to records (in one of the relations) that have the same set contents are clumped together. Further, the output corresponding to "prefixes" of a record appear just before the output corresponding to that record. This organization of output helps in making sense of large join results.

We assume a nested representation of the data [11]. In this representation all the set elements are stored at the same place, facilitating efficient joins on them.

Organization. In Section 2, we formally define the set join problem. Next, in Section 3, we motivate the use of prefix tree and inverted index structures for the computation of set joins and their on-the-fly construction. In Section 4, we present the proposed set join algorithms. Related work is described in Section 5. The performance of the set join algorithms is evaluated in Section 6. Finally, in Section 7, we summarize the conclusions of our study.

2 Problem Definition

Definition 1 (Set Join). *The set join of two relations R and S is defined as $R \bowtie_{p \theta q} S$ where p and q are set-valued attributes, and θ is a join condition. A pair of records $t_R \in R$ and $t_S \in S$ will be present in the join result, if θ is satisfied for $t_R.p$ and $t_S.q$.*

For pedagogical reasons, we assume that relations R and S contain only two attributes: (1) the set-valued attribute that they are joined on, and (2) the record identifier (*rid*). Hence, each record t contains a set, which we refer to as $t.set$. For convenience, we use t_R to represent $t_R.p$ and t_S to represent $t_S.q$.

In this paper we study set *containment*, *equality* and *overlap* joins. The set containment join retrieves all pairs of records (t_R, t_S), for which $t_R \subseteq t_S$. In equality join, (t_R, t_S) is in the result iff t_R and t_S are exactly the same. Set overlap join retrieves all pairs (t_R, t_S), for which t_R and t_S has at least one common element. We also handle the more general overlap join called as ϵ-overlap, where t_R and t_S should have at least ϵ common elements.

3 Index Structures for Set Joins

In this section, we motivate the use of prefix trees [4] and inverted indices [5] for the computation of set joins. We also discuss how they can be computed efficiently on-the-fly, instead of precomputing them. As mentioned in the Introduction, this is useful because no disk-space is reserved for the index, and database updates require no extra work in keeping the index up-to-date.

3.1 Prefix Trees

Prefix trees have been used in [4] to store sets for the purpose of mining frequent itemsets. This has resulted in several elegant algorithms [4, 3] for that task. Prefix trees can similarly be used to store sets for set-join applications. Since prefix trees store (ordered) sequences and sets are unordered, an ordering is imposed upon the set-elements based on their frequency of occurrence (in a given relation).

Each node n in the tree (except root) holds a set-element (referred to as $n.element$). The node n also represents a set (referred to as $n.set$) – containing the elements stored in n and its ancestors. We also store in n, an *rid-list* containing the rids (record identifiers) of all records whose content is the same as $n.set$. We refer to this list as $n.ridlist$. The structure is *compact* because a common prefix of several sets is represented only once. Ordering the set-elements based on their frequency helps in identifying more and longer common prefixes.

In addition to saving space, a prefix tree also saves on time because tasks that need to be performed over all the sets can be performed just once for each common prefix. Thus *prefix trees help avoid redundant work*. Our algorithm to construct prefix trees (adapted from [4]) is as follows:

First the root node of the prefix tree is created. Each record t of the relation is then inserted into the tree as follows: The elements of t are first sorted in decreasing order of their frequency in the relation. Starting from the root of the tree, we follow a path P as long as the sequence of elements in the nodes of P is a *prefix* of the sorted record t. We finally reach a node n such that $n.set$ is the longest prefix of t currently represented in the tree. Then we add a path P' of nodes, as descendants of n, to hold the remaining elements of t. The last node in the entire path $P + P'$ from the root now represents the newly inserted record t. The rid of t is appended to the $ridlist$ of this node.

The above algorithm is sufficient if the entire prefix tree fits in main memory. Otherwise, we logically divide the database into *horizontal* partitions such that the prefix tree built on that partition fits in main memory. This reduces the efficiency of the above approach because common prefixes between records *across partitions* are not used.

3.2 Inverted Indices

Inverted indices were first used in [6] for the computation of set joins. A recurring task in set join computation is to find all the records that contain a given set. It is possible to do this efficiently using an inverted index, in which for each element in the domain D a list of record-identifiers (rids) of records having that element is maintained. Thus, the records containing a given set can be found by just intersecting the lists corresponding to each element in the set.

The inverted index can be constructed by making a single pass over the data. We build a list for each set-element x containing the rids of records containing x. We refer to this list as the *inverted list* of x and represent it by x_{list}. Using the inverted index, the list of records that contain a given set X (referred to as the inverted list of X, or X_{list}) can be computed by simply *intersecting* the inverted lists of each element in X.

As noted earlier, if the entire index does not fit in main memory, the database is logically divided into *horizontal* partitions such that the index constructed over that partition fits in main memory. Note that this partitioning of the database differs from the *vertical* partitioning in [7]. There, the set-elements were divided into disjoint partitions, whereas here, the records are divided into disjoint partitions.

Precomputing Indices. Building the above index structures (both prefix trees and inverted indices) on-the-fly has a cost of $\Theta(N)$, where N is the total number of elements in all records of the relation. The constant factor involved is reasonably small. For prefix trees, the constant factor would include $log(k)$ – the additional cost for sorting elements of each record of length k. A similar cost (with a still smaller constant factor) would be incurred for simply reading a precomputed index from disk. We feel that in most cases, the additional cost for building indices on-the-fly is justified by the index maintenance costs in terms of disk space and update time. However, we note that *if* a pre-computed index is available, our algorithms described in the next section can make use of it directly instead of building it on-the-fly.

4 The PRETTI Algorithms

In this section we present the PRETTI (PREfix Tree based seT joIn) suite of algorithms for set containment, overlap and equality joins between two relations R and S. These algorithms use a prefix tree on R and an inverted index on S, unless otherwise specified. For equality join we give an additional algorithm using prefix trees on both R and S.

Algorithm PRETTI: Nested Loop(R, S)

1   **for each partition** P_R **in** R
2   R_{PT} = build_prefixTree(P_R)
3   **for each partition** P_S **in** S
4   S_{IL} = build_invertedList(P_S)
5   Set Join(R_{PT}, S_{IL})

Fig. 1. Partition Nested Loop Set Join

If the main memory is insufficient, *a nested loop join* is used, as shown in Figure 1. In the nested loop join, each relation is partitioned *horizontally* so that indices constructed on each pair of partitions (P_R, P_S), $P_R \in R$ and $P_S \in S$, fit in main memory.

The required join algorithm is performed on each such pair. Therefore, without loss of generality, we assume that the relations to be joined can be processed in main memory.

4.1 Set Containment Join

A set containment join, represented by $R \bowtie_{p \subseteq q} S$, is one of the important operators among set joins. It was shown in [7] that set containment joins using inverted indices on S are more efficient than signature-based and partition-based approaches. In our approach, we retain this idea of using an inverted index on S (represented as S_{IL}) and in addition use a prefix tree on R (represented as R_{PT}).

We need to find pairs of records (t_R, t_S) from R and S such that $t_R \subseteq t_S$. That is, for each node n of R_{PT}, we need to find $n.set_{list}$ – the records in S that contain $n.set$. To do this we need to intersect the inverted lists (from S_{IL}) of all elements in $n.set$. Now, it is clear that $n.set = \{n.element\} \cup m.set$ where m is the parent of n. Therefore, $n.set_{list} = n.element_{list} \cap m.set_{list}$. It follows that for each node n, we can compute $n.set_{list}$ by processing the nodes of R_{PT} in a depth-first traversal, since in such a traversal the parent m of n is visited before n.

The pseudo-code of the above algorithm is shown in Figure 2. The function Set Containment is a recursive implementation of depth-first traversal over R_{PT}. Initially it is called separately for each child n of the root of R_{PT} with the following arguments – (1) n itself, and (2) $n.set_{list}$ (initially equal to $n.element_{list}$ from S_{IL}). It first outputs pairs of rids of records (rid_R, rid_S) such that $rid_R \in n.ridlist$ and $rid_S \in n.set_{list}$ (lines 1–3 of Figure 2). Then, for each child c of n, it computes $c.set_{list}$ by intersecting $n.set_{list}$ with $c.element_{list}$, which is obtained from S_{IL} (lines 5–7).

Algorithm PRETTI:Set Containment(n, $n.set_{list}$)

```
1      for each rid_R in n.ridlist do
2          for each rid_S in n.set_list do
3              output( rid_R, rid_S )
4
5      for each child c of n do
6          c.set_list = n.set_list ∩ c.element_list
7          Set Containment( c, c.set_list )
```

Fig. 2. Set Containment Join

4.2 Set Overlap Join

The set overlap join retrieves all pairs of records (t_R, t_S) from relations R and S, for which $|t_R \cap t_S| \geq 1$. A more general form is ϵ-overlap where $|t_R \cap t_S| \geq \epsilon$, where ϵ is a user-specified parameter. We again use a prefix tree on R and an inverted index on S. However, for pedagogical reasons, we first explain the algorithm without using a prefix tree on R.

Without Prefix Trees. For each record t_R in R, we need to determine all the records t_S in S such that t_R and t_S share ϵ elements. To do this, we build an array $Count_S$ that holds for each record in S, the number of elements it contains in common with t_R.

This array can be built by simply scanning each rid in the inverted lists (in S_{IL}) of all elements in t_R and incrementing its counter in $Count_S$. If and when the count of an rid in $Count_S$ reaches ϵ, that rid along with the rid of t_R is output because then they share ϵ elements in common.

The above approach does a lot of redundant work – if two records are identical, the above operation can be performed just once for both records. Even if the two records are not exactly equal, but share several elements in common, much of the work can be reused. Using a prefix tree on R can help identify such common elements between transactions and avoid redundant work. We now describe this approach.

With Prefix Trees. An immediate benefit that is obtained by using a prefix tree is that the above operation of building the $Count_S$ array, etc. needs to be done *only once* for all records in the $ridlist$ of each node. In addition, since the set corresponding to a node n shares all the elements of its parent node m, we can reuse the $Count_S$ array of m for processing n – this $Count_S$ array is up-to-date with respect to the inverted lists of all elements in m. We only need to update the $Count_S$ array by scanning each rid in $n.element_{list}$ and incrementing its counter. We note that partial results are output as soon as the value of a counter reaches ϵ, instead of waiting till $Count_S$ is updated completely for node n.

In the above procedure, we observe that if the $Count_S$ array for node m has an entry whose count equals or exceeds ϵ, then it would automatically equal or exceed ϵ even for n. Therefore, we maintain the rids corresponding to such entries of $Count_S$ separately in an array called Cur_{sol}. Then, while processing node n, we output the pairs of rids in Cur_{sol} and $n.ridlist$, without further processing.

The above paragraphs describe how the $Count_S$ array of a parent node can be reused at a given node. In a depth-first traversal of the prefix tree, a node n and all its children are visited before the next sibling of n is visited. In order to ensure that the $Count_S$ array is usable by the next sibling of n, we need to *undo* changes made to it while processing n (and its children). This is achieved by simply scanning each rid in $n.element_{list}$ and *decrementing* its counter, after the processing over n has been completed. Finally, if this decrement operation causes an entry in $Count_S$ to fall below ϵ, the corresponding rid needs to be removed from Cur_{sol}.

The pseudo-code of the algorithm described above is shown in Figure 3. Like the set containment join (Figure 2), the overall structure of this algorithm is a recursive implementation of a depth-first traversal over R_{PT}. It is initially called with the root of R_{PT} as the first argument. The $Count_S$ array described above is the second argument and is initialized to zeros before calling the function for the first time. The third argument to the function is Cur_{sol}, which as described above, is an array of rids corresponding to the entries of $Count_S$ whose values equal or exceed ϵ. It is initially empty.

4.3 Set Equality Join

The set equality join retrieves all pairs of records (t_R, t_S) from relations R and S, for which $t_R == t_S$. We present two different algorithms for set equality join. The first algorithm is a variant of the set containment join presented in Section 4.1 and therefore uses a prefix tree on relation R and an inverted index on S. The second algorithm uses prefix trees on both relations and no inverted index.

Algorithm Set Overlap (n, $Count_S$, Cur_{sol})

```
1      for each child c of n do
2          for each rid_S in c.element_list
3              Count_S[rid_S] + + // increment
4              if Count_S[rid_S] == ε
5                  append rid_S to Cur_sol
6          for each rid_R in c.ridlist do
7              output( rid_R, rid_S )
8
9          Set Overlap (c, Count_S, Cur_sol)
10
11         for each rid_S in c.element_list
12             Count_S[rid_S] - - // decrement
13             if Count_S[rid_S] == ε - 1
14                 delete rid_S from Cur_sol
```

Fig. 3. Set Overlap Join

Using a Prefix Tree and an Inverted Index. The set equality join can be considered to be a special case of the set containment join – we first find all pairs (t_R, t_S) from R and S such that $t_R \subseteq t_S$ and among these pairs, we output only those for which $|t_R| == |t_S|$. We can obtain $|t_R|$ from the depth of the node corresponding to t_R in the prefix-tree. The value of $|t_S|$ can be precomputed and stored while building the inverted index on S – this results in a small memory overhead.

Using Two Prefix Trees. An equality join can be computed efficiently when both relations R and S are *sorted* on the join attribute. We achieve this by constructing prefix trees R_{PT} and S_{PT} on R and S, respectively. A depth-first traversal on R_{PT} or S_{PT} yields the sets stored in it in a sorted lexicographic order, as explained below.

As mentioned in Section 3.1, the individual set elements are ordered based on their frequency in each relation. Here, we order them based on their *total* frequency in both relations. We then define the lexicographic ordering of sets with respect to this frequency-based ordering of individual set elements. Note that prefix tree construction is more efficient than generic sorting since it requires only $\Theta(N)$ time (see Section 3).

The equality join algorithm then merely consists of a simultaneous depth-first traversal over both R_{PT} and S_{PT}. Let the current nodes during the traversals be n_R and n_S in R_{PT} and S_{PT}, respectively. If $n_R.set < n_S.set$, then the traversal over S_{PT} is *suspended* until $n_R.set == n_S.set$. Similarly, if $n_R.set > n_S.set$, then the traversal over R_{PT} is *suspended*. As long as $n_R.set == n_S.set$, the pairs of rids in the ridlists of n_R and n_S are output.

Note that for each node n in a prefix tree, we do *not* store $n.set$ in the node. Instead, this is computed on the fly during the depth-first traversal by forming the union of the *element* fields stored at n and its ancestors.

5 Related Work

Set join operators received significant attention recently. In [2], the authors showed that set-joins are one of the hardest operators to optimize. Several nested loop join techniques were evaluated in [5] and *signature-hash join* was found to be the best among them. A recent work [13] studied more complex varieties of similarity joins on set valued data. Applicability of set division operator for containment join on set-data in first normal form is discussed in [12]. The Apriori algorithm [1] for mining frequent itemsets has been suggested for containment joins since it counts the occurances of "candidate itemsets" in set-data.

Several partition based approaches for set joins have been proposed such as PSJ [11], APSJ, DCJ and ADCJ [9, 10]. In these approaches, the relations are partitioned based on hash functions such that pairs of records in the output fall in the same partition. Although faster than signature based methods, their performance heavily depends on the number of partitions and the hash function used. A bad partitioning can make these approaches perform near the worst case quadratic time complexity due to false drops. Though adaptive approaches [10] have been proposed to overcome the first drawback, the problem of false drops still remains. Also, most adaptive approaches perform better than PSJ only in cases of very large average set cardinality [9].

Block Nested Loop Join (BNL) was proposed in [7]. It first constructs an inverted index S_{IL} over the relation S. Then, for all elements in each record $t_R \in R$, the corresponding inverted lists are intersected to get the records in S that contain t_R. Since the complete relation S may not fit in main memory S_{IL} is *vertically* partitioned into a number of blocks such that each block fits in main memory. Each partition has inverted lists of a subset of the total elements in the domain.

In BNL, instead of loading R record by record, a page of records is read. For each page of R all blocks of S_{IL} are loaded one by one and processed. Since all elements in a record of R need not belong to a single block of S, *temporary files* are used to store the partial results for each block.

The major drawbacks of BNL (w.r.t. PRETTI) are: (1) In BNL, overlaps between records are not taken into account. (2) Due to the vertical partitioning approach, BNL needs to maintain temporary files. The sizes of these files can be of the order of output size, which can be quadratic over the size of the relations. (3) To build a complete vertical partition, the entire database needs to be scanned. This excludes the possibility of constructing a vertical partition on-the-fly.

6 Experiments

In this section we compare our proposed algorithms with BNL [7] and partition based PSJ [11] and APSJ [10] algorithms. We mainly compare our approach with BNL since it was shown [7] to outperform partition based PSJ. In this section we always perform self-joins, i.e. $R = S$. We also assume that R is the outer relation and S is the inner relation. All the experiments are performed on a 2.6 GHz Celeron PC with 256 MB main memory, running Red Hat Linux 2.4.20-8. An illusion of limited main memory is created by limiting the buffer size and also ensuring that Linux does not cache S during nested loop joins – we made several copies of S and used a different one for each iteration of the nested loop join.

For comparison with APSJ, we used the Set Containment Join Testbed [8]. We implemented the BNL suite of algorithms as described in [7] in which we incorporated the functionalities such as compression, pipelining and pruning using set cardinalities. We study these algorithms for varying buffer and relation sizes. In experiments where we do not vary buffer sizes, we fix it to 25% of the corresponding relation size.

For the datasets used in our experiments, the output of set joins are *huge*. Writing this to disk would over-shadow the actual join processing cost. To avoid this, we only count the number of pairs in the solution, instead of writing them to screen or disk.

BMS Dataset	Dom. Size	Avg. Set Card.	Relation Card.	Max. Set Card.	Set Card. ≥ 10	Set Card. ≥ 20	Set Card. ≥ 50	Set Card. ≥ 100	Rel. Size
WebView1	497	2.5	59,602	267	2098	411	72	34	588KB
WebView2	3340	5	77,512	161	10971	2574	160	8	1.5MB
POS	1657	6.5	515,597	164	128098	29934	955	37	11MB

Fig. 4. Dataset Characteristics

For our experiments, we used the real life datasets BMS-POS, BMS-WebView1 and BMS-WebView2 from Blue Martini Software [15]. These datasets originated from a dot-com company called Gazelle.com, a leg-wear and leg-care retailer and contains several months of click-stream data. Figures 6 shows the characteristics of these datasets.

The major criteria [11] to test join algorithms are their scalability with increasing relation cardinality, domain cardinality and record length. BMS WebView1 has a small domain cardinality but some records are very long. BMS WebView2 has a large domain cardinality of 3340. Both the domain size and relation cardinality are large in BMS POS.

6.1 Set Containment Join

In this section we compare the performance of PRETTI with BNL, PSJ and APSJ for set containment joins. The first experiment, Figure 5a, tests the scalability of the algorithms w.r.t. relation cardinality. Note that the y-axis is shown in *log-scale*. The dataset R is constructed by taking random samples from BMS-POS of increasing cardinalities. The buffer size was set to 25% of the size of S. We see that the response time of PRETTI increases very slowly for larger relations. This can be attributed to the overlaps between new records and old records in R.

On the other hand, we see that the performance of BNL deteriorates significantly as the relation cardinality increases. The major reason for this is its inability to exploit overlaps between records in R. Another reason is that as the relation cardinality increases, inverted lists become longer, resulting in fewer lists loaded into memory each time, which in turn results in large temporary files.

Figure 5b shows the running times of PRETTI and BNL for increasing buffer sizes on WebView1 and WebView2 datasets. We see that PRETTI consistently outperforms BNL. The response times for WebView2 show that PRETTI is well suited for datasets

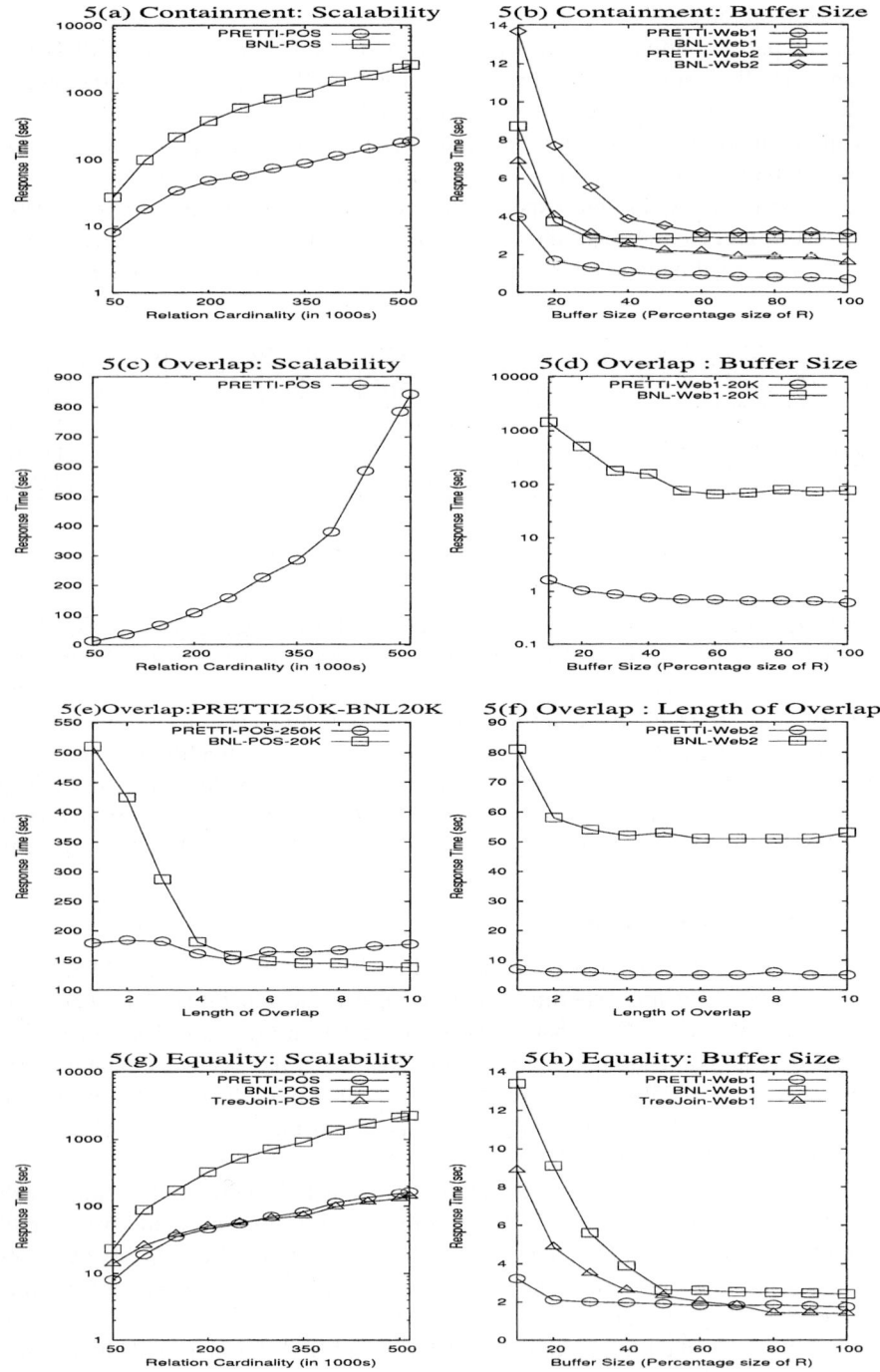

Fig. 5. Experimental Results

Table 1. Containment Join (Set Card. Vs Resp. Time)

Set Card.	10	20	40	60	80	100
PRETTI	10s	20s	39s	66s	84s	123s
APSJ	977s	812s	276s	158s	156s	172s
PSJ	479s	714s	1139s	1095s	-	-

with large domains. We also see that as the buffer size decreases, BNL performs much worse since it needs to rely more on large temporary files.

Table 1 compares PRETTI, PSJ and APSJ on a 100K record dataset generated by the testbed used in [8]. We see that PRETTI outperforms PSJ and APSJ significantly.

6.2 Set Overlap Join

Set overlap join is the most time-consuming operation among the three join types studied in this paper. Figure 5c shows the performance of PRETTI on the POS dataset. We see that PRETTI can handle large datasets even for overlaps. Due to the very large temporary files, BNL could not be run on this dataset.

Figure 5d (y-axis in *log-scale*) shows the running times of the algorithms for increasing buffer sizes on the WebView1 dataset. Figure 5e shows the running time of PRETTI for increasing values of ϵ for a relation of 250K records. We see that PRETTI is scalable for high values of ϵ. The difference in the response time is due to the varied cost in maintaining Cur_{sol} for different ϵ. To compare PRETTI and BNL, we show the response time for BNL on 20K records. Figure 5f shows the performance of the algorithms for varying overlap sizes on the WebView2 dataset.

In these graphs, PRETTI clearly outperforms BNL. For each record of R, BNL computes the union of inverted lists of all its elements. Since long records are common in real datasets, the resulting list explodes and can reach the worst case size (the relation cardinality). Further, the sizes of temporary files needed to eliminate duplicates (and hence the time to process them) can be quadratic on the relation cardinality.

6.3 Set Equality Join

For equality join, we compare the two PRETTI algorithms in Section 4.3 with BNL. We refer to the PRETTI algorithm that uses two prefix trees as "tree-join". Figure 5g (y-axis in *log-scale*) shows the algorithms' scalability with increasing relation cardinality.

As expected, we see that the response time of PRETTI and BNL is similar to their set containment join counter-parts. Surprisingly, we find that PRETTI outperforms tree-join in most cases. This is due to the maintenance of two prefix trees in main memory. Each node occupies three times space compared to that of a single element. This results in more partitions on R and S, which increases the number of iterations in the join. This experiment also shows that PRETTI outperforms BNL by a large margin.

Figure 5h shows response times of these algorithms on WebView1 for increasing buffer sizes. The rapid increase in response time of BNL as the buffer size decreases can be attributed to large temporary files.

7 Conclusions

In this paper we proposed the PRETTI suite of algorithms for set containment, overlap and equality joins. We investigated the use of prefix trees and inverted indices for performing set joins efficiently. Our algorithms do not require these structures to be stored on the disk, but instead build them on the fly. This property makes them useful in computing joins of intermediate results (which have no indices) in large join queries. Our results show that our algorithms significantly outperform previous approaches.

References

1. R. Agrawal and R. Srikant. Fast algorithms for mining association rules. In *Proc. of Intl. Conf. on Very Large Databases (VLDB)*, September 1994.
2. J. Cai, V.T. Chakaravarthy, R. Kaushik, and J.F. Naughton. On the complexity of join predicates. In *ACM SIGMOD-SIGACT-SIGART Symp. on Principles of Database Systems*, 2001.
3. G. Grahne and J. Zhu. Efficiently using prefix-trees in mining frequent itemsets. In *IEEE ICDM Workshop on Frequent Itemset Mining Implementations (FIMI)*, 2003.
4. J. Han, J. Pei, and Y. Yin. Mining frequent patterns without candidate generation. In *Proc. of ACM SIGMOD Intl. Conf. on Management of Data*, 2000.
5. S. Helmer and G. Moerkotte. Evaluation of main memory join algorithms for joins with set comparison join predicates. In *Proc. of Intl. Conf. on Very Large Databases (VLDB)*, 1997.
6. S. Helmer and G. Moerkotte. A study of four index structures for set-valued attributes of low cardinality. Technical report, University of Mannheim, 1999.
7. N. Mamoulis. Efficient processing of joins on set-valued attributes. In *Proc. of ACM SIGMOD Intl. Conf. on Management of Data*, 2003.
8. S. Melnik. Set containment joins: Testbed. http://www-db.stanford.edu/ melnik/scj.
9. S. Melnik and H. Garcia-Molina. Divide-and-conquer algorithm for computing set containment joins. In *Intl. Conf. on Extending Database Technology*, 2002.
10. S. Melnik and H. Garcia-Molina. Adaptive algorithms for set containment joins. *ACM Transactions on Database Systems (TODS)*, 28(2), 2003.
11. K. Ramasamy, J.M. Patel, J.F. Naughton, and R. Kaushik. Set containment joins: the good, the bad and the ugly. In *Proc. of Intl. Conf. on Very Large Databases (VLDB)*, 2000.
12. R. Rantzau. Processing frequent itemset discovery queries by division and set containment join operators. In *8th ACM SIGMOD DMKD Workshop*, 2003.
13. S. Sarawagi and A. Kirpal. Efficient set joins on similarity predicates. In *Proc. of ACM SIGMOD Intl. Conf. on Management of Data*, 2004.
14. M. Stonebraker. *Object-relational DBMS: The Next Great Wave*. Morgan Kaufmann, 1996.
15. Z. Zheng, R. Kohavi, and L. Mason. Real world performance of association rule algorithms. In *Intl. Conf. on Knowledge Discovery and Data Mining (KDD)*, 2001.

Maintaining Semantics in the Design of Valid and Reversible SemiStructured Views

Ya Bing Chen, Tok Wang Ling, and Mong Li Lee

School of Computing, National University of Singapore
{chenyabi, lingtw, leeml}@comp.nus.edu.sg

Abstract. Existing systems that support semistructured views do not maintain semantics during the process of designing views. Thus, there is no guarantee that the views obtained are valid and reversible views. In this paper, we propose an approach to designing valid and reversible semistructured views. We employ four types of view operators, namely, *select*, *drop*, *join* and *swap* operators, and develop a set of rules to maintain the semantics of the views when the *swap* operator is applied. We also examine the reversible view problem and develop rules to guarantee the designed views are reversible. Finally, we examine the possible changes to the participation constraints of relationship types and propose rules to keep the participation constraints correct.

1 Introduction

Existing systems [1, 2, 3, 4, 7, 9, 10, 11, 12] for semistructured views do not maintain semantics during the process of designing views. Thus, they cannot guarantee the validity and reversibility of the views. [5, 6] propose a novel approach to design valid views over semistructured data. A conceptual schema for source data is first extracted based on a semantically rich data model, the Object-Relationship-Attribute model for Semi-Structured data (ORA-SS) [8]. Semistructured views are created by applying four transformation operators on the source ORA-SS schema. The operations are *select*, *drop*, *join* and *swap*.

In this paper, we develop a complete set of rules to ensure that the designed views are meaningful and reversible back to the original source schema when the *swap* operator is applied. We also develop additional rules to keep the participation constraints correct for relationship types in the views. To the best of our knowledge, this is the first work to address the problem of maintaining semantics in the design of valid and reversible semistructured views.

The rest of the paper is organized as follows. Section 2 reviews the ORA-SS data model and highlight the semantics that are captured in ORA-SS for the design of valid and reversible semistructured views. Section 3 presents the design rules for the *swap* operator. Additional rules for the evolution of the participation constraints of object classes in relationships are given in Section 4, and we conclude in Section 5.

2 Motivating Example

The ORA-SS model comprises of three basic concepts: *object classes, relationship types* and *attributes*, and captures richer semantics compared to models such as OEM and XML DTD/Schema.

Example 1. Figure 1 depicts an ORA-SS source schema. This schema has 4 object classes: *course, student, lecturer and tutor*. Each object class has a key attribute, which is denoted by filled circle. The attribute *hobby* of *student* is a multi-valued attribute which is indicated by an asterisk inside the circle. There is a binary relationship type between object class *course* and *student*, which is labeled as "*cs, 2, 1:n, 1:n*" on the incoming edge of *student*. In the label, *cs* denotes the name of the relationship type, 2 indicates the degree of the relationship type, the first "*1:n*" indicates the parent participation constraints in the relationship type, and the second "*1:n*" indicates the child participation constraints in the relationship type. The relationship type has an attribute *grade* attached to *student* with label *cs* on the incoming edge of the attribute, which implies a functional dependency *stuNo, code → grade*. Similarly, there is a ternary relationship type "*cst, 3, 1:n, 1:n*" labeled on the

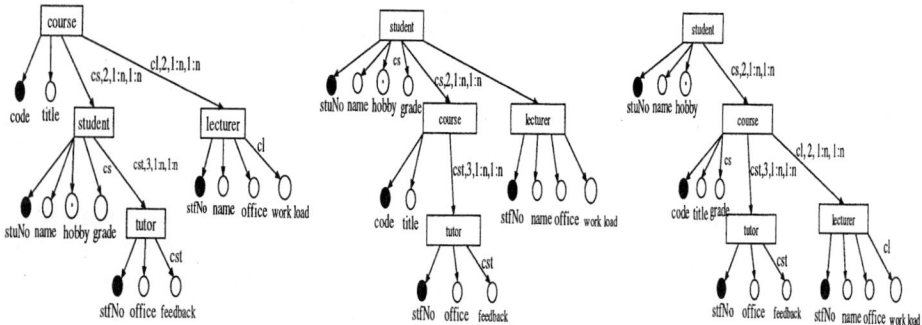

Fig. 1. ORA-SS source

Fig. 2. Invalid ORA-SS view obtained by swapping *course* and *student* in Figure 1

Fig. 3. Valid reversible ORA-SS view obtained by swapping *course* and *student* in Figure 1

incoming edge of *tutor*. The relationship type involves three object classes *course, student* and *lecturer*. In this case, the first "*1:n*" indicates the participation constraints of the relationship type *cs* in the ternary relationship type. The second "*1:n*" indicates the participation constraints of the object class *tutor* in the ternary relationship type.

Based on the ORA-SS schema in Figure 1, let us design a view by swapping *course* and *student*. The attributes of the two object classes will move with their owner object classes respectively. The attribute *grade* which belongs to the relationship type *cs* will move with *student* if we design the view based on XML DTD/Schema or OEM graph. This is because XML DTD/Schema or OEM do not differentiate between attributes of object classes and attributes of relationship types. For illustration purposes, the view in Figure 2 attaches *grade* to *student* to show such a case, which violates the functional dependency implied in the source schema, i.e., *stuNo, code* → *grade*. The view in Figure 2 is invalid since it violates the semantics in the source schema.

The above example shows that invalid views arise when important semantics are not expressed in the underlying data model. Figure 3 shows a valid ORA-SS view when the *swap* operator is applied on the same source schema in Figure 1. In Figure 3, the attribute *grade* is moved down and attached to *course* to keep the functional dependency of the relationship type *cs* intact. The object class *lecturer* also needs to move down with *course* to keep all the three participating object class of *cst* in one hierarchical path. Thus, the semantics of the relationship type *cst* is kept intact.

3 Design Rules for Swap Operator

Valid semistructured views considered in this work can be obtained by applying four view operators on an ORA-SS schema. The four operators are *select*, *join*, *drop* and *swap*. As a subset of XQuery, these operators fulfill most of the data-centered query requirements for XML. [5] develops a set of rules to guarantee the validity of semistructured views when the operators *select*, *join*, *drop* are applied, and gives an initial proposal of how the validity of views can be maintained when *swap* operator is applied. In this section, we will detail how valid semistructured views can be designed with *swap* operator. The *swap* operator restructures an ORA-SS source schema by exchanging the positions of a parent object class and its child object class.

Rule Swap_1: *If an object classes O_i and its descendant object class O_j in a source schema are swapped in designing a view; then the attributes of O_i and O_j must remain attached to O_i and O_j respectively in the view.*

Rule Swap_1 is straightforward and ensures that the attributes of two object classes O_i and O_j do not become meaningless in the view after O_i and O_j are swapped. More importantly, we observe that the relationship types in an ORA-SS source schema that involve O_i and/or O_j are also affected since the hierarchical positions of O_i and O_j have been interchanged after a *swap* operator is applied. Given two object classes O_i and O_j where O_j is a descendant of O_i in an ORA-SS schema, the relationship types that are affected after a swap of O_i and O_j can be classified into three categories.

The first category is the set of relationship types which do not involve any other object classes but O_i and/or O_j and/or the ancestors of O_i or O_j in the ORA-SS source schema. In another words, these relationship types involve object classes that occur in the straight path of O_i and O_j (see Figure 4).

The second category is the set of relationship types which involve at least both O_i and object classes in the branch paths between O_i and the parent of O_j, as shown in Figure 5. The third category is the set of relationship types which involve at least both O_j and its descendants, as shown in Figure 6. The three categories of affected relationship types are handled by the rules Swap_2, Swap_3 and Swap_4 respectively.

Rule Swap_2: *Suppose an object classes O_i and its descendant object class O_j in a source schema S are swapped in designing a view. Let S be the set of relationship types which do not involve any other object classes but O_i and/or O_j and/or the ancestors of O_i or O_j in the source schema. For each relationship type R in S, the attributes of R are attached to the lowest participating object class of R in the view.*

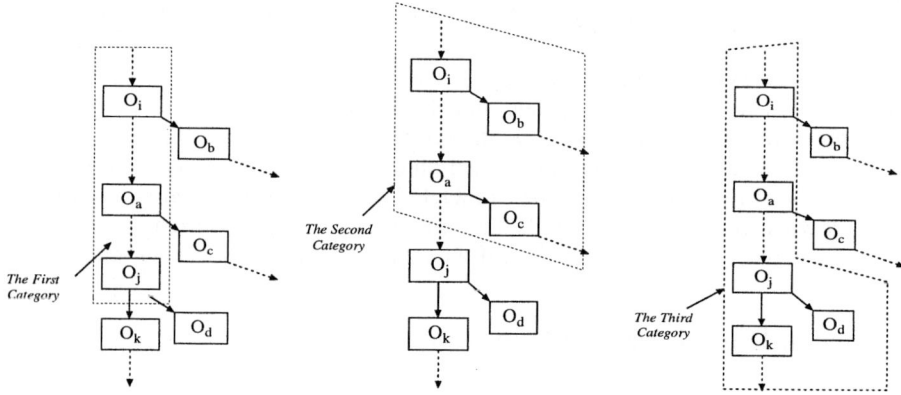

Fig. 4. *First category* of relationship types

Fig. 5. *Second category* of relationship types

Fig. 6. *Third category* of relationship types

Rule Swap_3: *Suppose an object class O_i in a source schema is swapped with its descendant object class O_j in designing a view. If there exists a relationship type which involves at least O_i and O_e, where O_c is a descendant of an object class O_a that lies in the path between O_i and O_j (including O_i) but O_c does not lie in the path between O_i and O_j in the ORA-SS source schema, then the subtree rooted at O_c is attached to O_i in the view.*

Rule Swap_4: *Suppose an object class O_i in a source schema is swapped with its descendant object class O_j in designing a view. For each child O_d of the object class O_j, let T be the subtree that is rooted at O_d. Let S be the set of relationship types which involve at least O_j and its descendants in T. If O_l is the lowest participating object class among all the relationship types in S that lie in the path between O_i and O_j after the swap, then the subtree rooted at O_d is attached to O_l in the view.*

The swap operator also introduces the issue of reversible views in semistructured data. A valid view schema V of a source schema S is called a reversible view if S can be produced back from V through applying our view operators, i.e. *select*, *drop*, *join* and *swap*. Here, we only consider *swap* operator for the issue of reversible view.

We observe that the rules Swap_3 and Swap_4 not only maintain the semantics of a semistructured view so that it is kept valid, but they also guarantee that the view is reversible. For example, let us now apply another *swap* operator to the view in Figure 3 to swap *student* and *course* again. Applying the rules Swap_1 and Swap_2, the attributes of *student* and *course* will move with their owner object classes. The relationship attribute *grade* is thus attached to the object class *student* again. Applying the rule Swap_4, the object class *lecturer* will move up with *course* as a whole since *course* is the lowest participating object class of *dcl*. On the other hand, *tutor* will be attached to *student* because *student* is the lowest participating object class of *cst*. In this way, the semantics of the two relationship types are kept intact. Furthermore, the view obtained is the same as the original source schema in Figure 1. Thus, the view in Figure 3 is a reversible view because we can produce the original source schema back by applying swap operator on it.

4 Participation Constraints in Views

During the design of semistructured views, new relationship types may be derived from existing relationship types. The view may change the order of participating object classes of an existing relationship type. Thus, we need to determine the participation constraints of the relationship type in the view. We design four rules to handle the participation constraints for relationship types in semistructured views under the four view operators.

We use p and c to denote the parent and child participation constraints of an original relationship type R respectively. Likewise, we use p' and c' to denotes the parent and child participation constraints of a derived relationship type R'.

The first rule handles the case when a *swap* operator is applied on two participating object classes of a binary relationship type. The order of the two participating object classes will be reversed in the view schema. Thus, in the new relationship type in the view, the participation constraints will also be reversed.

Rule PC_1: *If R' is derived in the view by swapping two participating object classes of an existing binary relationship type R in the source schema; then $p' = c$ and $c' = p$.*

Rule PC_2: *If R' is derived in the view by swapping two participating object classes in an existing n-ary (n>2) relationship type R in the source schema, and $O_1, O_2, ..., O_n$ is participating object classes of R' in the order from ancestor to descendant in the view schema; then*

   for p': If there exists a functional dependency $\{O_1, O_2, ... O_{n-1}\} \rightarrow O_n$, then set p' to be 1:1, otherwise set p' to be 0:n (or *).

   for c': if there exists a functional dependency: $O_n \rightarrow \{O_1, O_2 ... O_{n-1}\}$, then set c' to be 1:1, otherwise c' is set 0:n (or *).

Rule PC_3: *If R' is derived in the view by projecting an existing relationship type R in the source schema, and $O_1, O_2, ..., O_n$ is participating object classes of R' in the order from ancestor to descendant in the view schema; then*

   for p': If there exists a functional dependency $\{O_1, O_2, ... O_{n-1}\} \rightarrow O_n$, then set p' to be 1:1, otherwise set p' to be 0:n (or *).

   for c': if there exists a functional dependency: $O_n \rightarrow \{O_1, O_2 ... O_{n-1}\}$, then set c' to be 1:1, otherwise c' is set 0:n (or *).

Rule PC_4: *If R' is derived in the view by joining one relationship type $R_1 (O_{11}, O_{12}, ..., O_{1n})$ with another relationship type $R_2 (O_{21}, O_{22}, ..., O_{2m})$, where $O_{1n} = O_{21}$ is the common object class they are joined on, then*

   for p': If there exists a functional dependency $\{O_{11}, O_{12}, ..., O_{1(n-1)}, O_{22}, ..., O_{2(m-1)}\} \rightarrow O_{2m}$ or a functional dependency $\{O_{22}, O_{23}, ..., O_{2(m-1)}\} \rightarrow O_{2m}$ or the two functional dependencies $\{O_{11}, O_{12}, ..., O_{1(n-1)}\} \rightarrow O_{1n}$ and $\{O_{21}, O_{22}, ..., O_{2(m-1)}\} \rightarrow O_{2m}$; then set p' to be 1:1, otherwise, set p' to be 0:n.

   for c': If there exists a functional dependency $O_{2m} \rightarrow \{O_{11}, O_{12}, ..., O_{1(n-1)}, O_{22}, ..., O_{2(m-1)}\}$, then set c' to be 1:1, otherwise set c' to be 0:n (or *).

The second rule handles the case where the order of participating object classes of n-ary (n>2) relationship types is changed. The third rule then handles the case where new relationship types are derived by projecting existing relationship types. Finally, the last rule handles the case where new relationship types are derived by joining existing relationship types.

5 Conclusions

Existing systems for semistructured views do not maintain semantics at all in the process of designing the views. Thus, they cannot guarantee the validity and reversibility of the views. This paper proposes a novel approach to solve the two issues based on a semantically rich semistructured data model – ORA-SS. The *swap* operator is unique in semistructured data as it interchanges the positions of parent and child object classes, and raises the issue of view reversibility. In this paper, we have developed a complete set of rules for the *swap* operator and show that the proposed approach can maintain the evolution and integrity of relationships. We also examine the possible changes for participation constraints of the relationship types and propose rules to keep the participation constraints correct in the view. To the best of our knowledge, this approach is the first work to employ a semantic data model for maintaining semantics of semistructured views and solving the reversible view problem. By considering the validity and reversibility of semistructured views, this approach provides for a more robust view mechanism so that we can greatly exploit the potential of XML/semistructured data to exchange data on the Web.

References

1. Serge. Abiteboul, S. Cluet, L. Mignet, et. al., "Active views for electronic commerce", VLDB, pp.138-149, 1999.
2. Chaitanya. Baru, A. Gupta, B. Ludaescher, et. al., "XML-Based Information Mediation with MIX", ACM SIGMOD Demo, 1999.
3. Michael. Carey, J. Kiernan, J. hanmugasundaram, et. al., "XPERANTO: A Middleware for Publishing Object-Relational Data as XML Documents", VLDB, pp. 646-648, 2000.
4. Michael. Carey, D. Florescu, Z. Ives, et. al., "XPERANTO: Publishing Object-Relational Data as XML", WebDB Workshop, 2000.
5. Ya Bing. Chen, Tok Wang Ling, Mong Li Lee, "Designing Valid XML Views", ER Conference, 2002
6. Ya Bing Chen, Tok Wang Ling, Mong Li Lee, "Automatic Generation of SQLX Definitions from ORA-SS Views", DASFAA, 2004.
7. Sophie. Cluet, P. Veltri, D. Vodislav, "Views in a large scale xml repository", VLDB, pp. 271-280, 2001.
8. Gillian. Dobbie, X.Y Wu, T.W Ling, M.L Lee, "ORA-SS: An Object-Relationship-Attribute Model for SemiStructured Data", Technical Report TR21/00, School of Computing, National University of Singapore, 2000.
9. Mary. Fernandez, W. Tan, D. Suciu, "Efficient Evaluation of XML Middleware Queries", ACM SIGMOD, pp. 103-114, 2001.
10. Mary. Fernandez, W. Tan, D. Suciu, "SilkRoute: Trading Between Relations and XML", World Wide Web Conference, 1999.
11. Philip. Bohannon, H. Korth, P. Narayan, S. Ganguly, and P. Shenoy. Optimizing view queries in ROLEX to support navigable tree results. VLDB, 2002.
12. Alin. Deutsch and V. Tannen. MARS: A System for Publishing XML from Mixed and Redundant Storage. VLDB, 2003.

DCbot: Finding Spatial Information on the Web

Mihály Jakob, Matthias Grossmann, Daniela Nicklas,
and Bernhard Mitschang

University of Stuttgart, Institute of Parallel and Distributed Systems,
Universitätsstraße 38, 70569 Stuttgart, Germany
{jakobmy , grossmms , danickla , mitsch}@informatik.uni-stuttgart.de

Abstract. The WWW provides an overwhelming amount of information, which – spatially indexed – can be a valuable additional data source for location-based applications. By manually building a spatial index, only a fraction of the available resources can be covered. This paper introduces a system for the automatic mapping of web pages to geographical locations. Our web robot uses several sets of domain specific keywords, lexical context rules, that are automatically learned, and a hierarchical catalogue of geographical locations that provides exact geographical coordinates for locations. Spatially indexed web pages are used to construct Geographical Web Portals, which can be accessed by different location-based applications. In addition, we present experimental results demonstrating the quantity and the quality of automatically indexed web pages.

1 Introduction

Location-based applications adapt their behavior to the spatial context of the user, e.g. by providing local maps and navigational information. They rely on spatial data that has previously been gathered and preprocessed to fit their needs. This data is often expensive because it has to be manually collected, edited and updated. Therefore, automatic gathering of spatial information is needed to efficiently serve mobile applications.

In this paper we present a solution for providing web pages which are related to the spatial context of a user. To achieve that, an index for web pages with references to geographical locations must be generated. We use a three stage process, depicted in Figure 1, for providing location-based applications with spatially indexed web pages. First, our web robot, DCbot, crawls the web and gathers pages with references to geographical locations (❶). It analyses page content using domain specific keywords and lexical context rules. The result of this first step is a repository of spatially indexed web pages.

After this, we generate so called Geographical Web Portals (GWP), that represent web pages, which are related to a specific region (❷). GWPs can be used for location-based augmentation of maps. If a mobile user enters the visibility area of a GWP, it becomes visible on his map. Finally, GWPs have to be made available to mobile applications. We use our location-based service platform (Nexus) [9], to provide applications with spatial context information (❸). The Nexus platform federates local world models and stores virtual objects [10] on Spatial Model Servers. Location-based applications

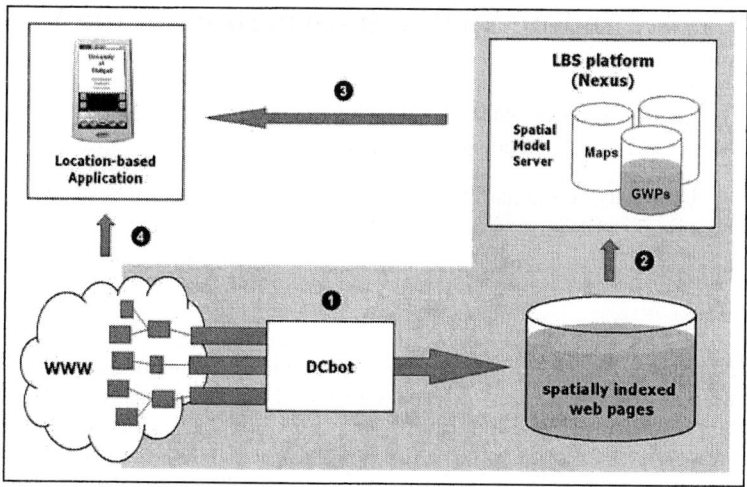

Fig. 1. Usage scenario

are served with maps and virtual objects (like GWPs) by Spatial Model Servers and can access web pages directly on the web following web references on GWPs (❹).

We describe our solution in detail in the following sections. Section 2 covers related work and projects. In Section 3, we present the architecture and analysis methods of DCbot. In Section 4 we discuss experiments and first experiences gained with these techniques and assess our approach. Section 5 presents postprocessing steps describing the selection of the best spatial reference from a web page and the generation of GWPs. Finally, Section 6 concludes the paper.

2 Related Work

The problem of linking web pages to geographical positions has already been subject to other research.

The approach presented in [3] exploits two different kinds of information: Names of locations like cities and states on a web page and the structure of links between web pages. It is based on a hierarchical location model which allows to generalize locations. Location names are weighted, a web page is considered to be more relevant to a location if a higher fraction of all location names on the page reference this location or a 'geographical child' of this location (according to the hierarchical location model) and if the location names on the page are distributed uniformly across all 'geographic children' of this location. The consequence of the latter criterion is that a page mentioning 'New York' several times (and no other location) is relevant to the location 'New York' and not to the more general location 'US'. The exploration of the link structure uses an approach similar to standard web search engines. A web page is considered relevant to a particular location if it is referenced by other pages relevant to this location. The algorithm proposed in [3] weighs links in a similar way as location names.

While the approach presented in [3] uses locations on the city and more coarse levels, we assume that the results are not precise enough for mobile users. Our experiments have shown that several thousands of pages can be found referencing a city of about 600,000 inhabitants, so that searching for finer grained location information – e.g. by parsing addresses – seems to be more promising, even if such methods usually have to be tailored to specific languages and countries. There are probably only a few cases where generalizations of location information on fine grained levels like addresses is possible. Furthermore, we assume that in general for our scenario of mobile users generalization is not desirable since we consider fine-grained location information to be more valuable.

'Google Search by Location' [6] is an extension to the Google web search engine and is currently in a test stage. It allows search results to be restricted to web pages relevant to a specified location. While an exact description of the search method is currently not available, tests suggest that searching for and parsing of addresses seem to be an important part of the algorithm. This is probably the reason why this service currently only works within the US.

The Information Extraction System RAPIER [2] searches information items by means of so-called filler patterns. A filler pattern describes a sequence of words, it can consist of an enumeration of the matching words (e.g. 'the' or 'a' followed by 'bridge'), or of part of speech (e.g. an article followed by a noun) or even semantic descriptions. The pre-filler and post-filler patterns describe the words preceding and following the information item, the filler pattern the information item itself. DCbot uses keyword and pattern-recognition methods (see Section 3.3), which work in a similar way, but are restricted to comparing words.

In [8], an architecture for mapping web pages to locations is presented. It consists of three stages. In the first stage, an initial set of possible locations for a page is determined, the second stage removes presumably wrong locations from the set and merges the remaining locations, the third stage improves the mapping by evaluating link structures. The geospatial search engine based on this architecture performs a combined keyword and location search. The page rank is calculated based on different weights for the relevance of the page for the keyword and its distance from the desired location. In this paper, we focus on detecting location information in individual pages, basically corresponding to the first stage in [8], where we propose the use of more sophisticated methods like parsing of addresses and learning lexical contexts of geographical location names. For determining the correct location (corresponding to the second stage), we rank the spatial references found on a page and select the best one.

The Semantic Web [1] is an extension to the WWW, which adds semantic information in machine-understandable form. It relies on the web page authors to describe the semantics of their pages using the Resource Description Framework (RDF) [12] or the Web Ontology Language (OWL) [13]. For the more specific problem of describing the location for which a web page is relevant, the Dublin Core Metadata Initiative [4] already provides a solution, which is less complex than an RDF or OWL description. However, our experiments show that even simple metadata tags for providing location information are rarely used, thus we believe that – at least for the near future – it is necessary to analyze web page contents.

3 DCbot

Web pages have a simple mechanism for providing meta-data about their content: meta-tags. Our initial approach for finding spatial references in web pages was to analyze the meta-data provided by web site creators in meta-tags. Besides commonly known tags such as *keywords* or *description* there are a lot of other ones, some of them even bundled into meta-data standards such as the Dublin Core Metadata Element Set [4].

We implemented a web robot, called DCbot (DC stands for Dublin Core), that searches for meta-tags and uses the Dublin Core meta-data element *DC.Coverage* to get spatial information about the corresponding web page. However, we found that only a tiny percentage of web pages use the *DC.Coverage* tag containing spatial information [11]. This is probably due to the fact that spatially aware applications aren't yet wide spread, thus there is little need for web site creators to provide spatial information for their web pages. Therefore, we decided to enhance DCbot to also analyze other page parts such as the URL, the title and the body section. We developed and implemented several analysis methods for application to different page parts. Our result was a web robot successfully locating spatial information in web pages using basic techniques of natural language processing and machine learning.

3.1 Architecture

The basic idea behind DCbot and the resulting architecture, shown in Figure 2, is simple. DCbot crawls the web and carries out a set of actions for each web page (❶). After the initial parsing, relevant page parts such as the title, meta-tags or the body are temporarily stored. Analyzed web page parts are described in Section 3.2. Hyperlinks of the page are extracted and stored on the hyperlink stack for further processing (❷). As the name hyperlink stack suggests, we don't merely store the URL but also the texts of hyperlinks allowing us to examine them. Next, the Content Handler (❸) applies DCbot's four analysis methods, which we will introduce in Section 3.3. These analysis methods use special keywords and patterns (❹) to extract geographical reference candidates from each web page. These candidates can be proper names of

- geographical sites (e.g. names of lakes or mountains).
- institutions or buildings (e.g. cultural, educational or government institutions).
- political regions (e.g. counties, cities or districts).
- administrative areas (e.g. postal code areas).

After the extraction, geographical reference candidates are cross-checked with DCbot's geographical database, called GeoBase (❺). We will introduce GeoBase in Section 3.4.

After the evaluation of a web page, meta-data extracted from the page is stored in a repository of spatially indexed web pages (❻). Such a repository can be used for many different purposes. One of them is the creation of Geographical Web Portals, that represent a set of web pages related to a region. We describe the creation and storage of GWPs in Section 5.2. After the examination of a web page DCbot continues with the next hyperlink from the hyperlink stack.

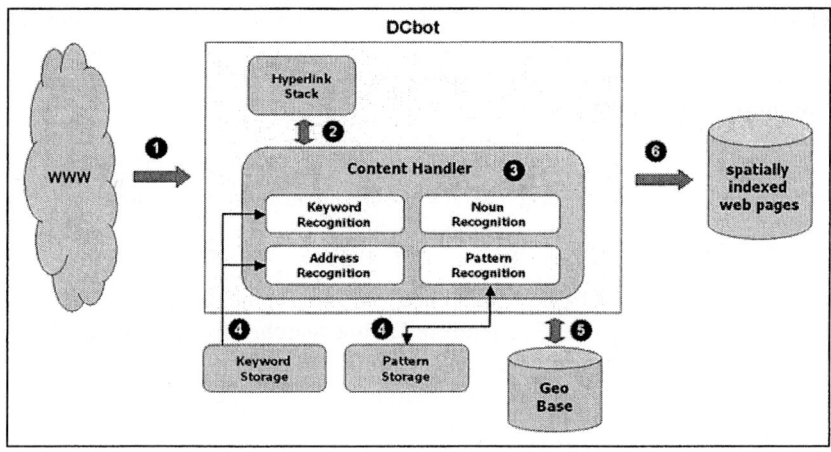

Fig. 2. DCbot architecture

3.2 Analyzed Web Page Parts

As we already mentioned, a previous version of DCbot concentrated on the analysis of web page meta-tags that explicitly specified geographical information. We analyzed web pages using the *DC.Coverage* tag from the Dublin Core Metadata Element Set. Results of several test runs have shown that only 0.07% of web pages actually provide an explicit geographical reference [11]. Therefore, we extended our analysis to the following web page parts:

Hyperlink Text. During the analysis of web pages DCbot stores not only URLs but also the hyperlink texts of each examined web page on its hyperlink stack. That gives us the opportunity to look for geographical references in the text of the hyperlink pointing to a web page and to associate the result with this particular page.

URL. Sometimes domain names give a hint about the content of a web site. An example is http://www.stuttgart.de, which leads to a web site about the capital of the federal state Baden-Württemberg in Germany.

Title. The title of a web page is one of the most important places to look for geographical references. In most cases it reflects the content of the web page at hand. For this reason search engines pay high attention to page titles. If a spatial reference is found in the title it should be treated as a rather valuable one.

Meta-Tags. As we already mentioned before there are some meta-tags that can explicitly provide geographical information. However, they are very rarely used. Nevertheless, it is reasonable to examine more common tags such as the *keywords* and *description* tags, which can provide valuable information about the page content.

Body. The text content of a web page usually contains a significant number of words and sentences. While dealing with a page part containing only a few words or phrases it is possible to cross-reference all of them using DCbot's geographical database. However we need to use more sophisticated methods for a larger page part such as the body section. Instead of treating each word or phrase as a possible geographical reference candidate, we have to identify those that are likely to be ones. For that reason DCbot uses keywords and patterns that enable it to identify possible candidates.

3.3 Methods of Analysis

As previously mentioned in Section 3.1, the first step of calculating the best geographical reference on a web page is to extract geographical reference candidates from the page. In this section we introduce methods, which DCbot uses to identify these candidates.

It is unlikely to find an explicit reference to a geographical location (i.e. geographical coordinates) on a web page. Therefore DCbot searches for proper names of locations. Examples are names of institutions, names of important landmarks or postal addresses. DCbot uses the following methods to identify such proper names:

Noun Recognition. This component concentrates on finding one word proper names on web pages. The main aspect is the identification of nouns, which is an easy task in German because of their capitalization. In other languages an appropriate grammatical tagging tool has to be used. Depending on the size of a web page part, all nouns are extracted or only the first n nouns are extracted. Additionally, most frequent nouns can be determined and added to the list of geographical reference candidates.

Keyword Recognition. The previous method concentrates on the extraction of one-word proper names. However, there are a lot of names that consist of several words. This method identifies such composed names based on a set of keywords, which indicate a possible proper name. Currently, DCbot uses three types of keywords to identify:

- natural geographical sites (e.g. lakes, mountains, ...).
- institutions or buildings (e.g. museums, universities, ...).
- postal addresses.

Examples for keywords we use are *Museum* or *Brücke* (bridge). Proper names often contain such keywords. An example of a composed proper name is *Deutsches Museum*. If a keyword is detected on a web page, then several geographical reference candidates are extracted from its lexical environment and added to the list of geographical reference candidates.

Pattern Recognition. The building of context patterns is one of the more sophisticated methods used by DCbot. It stores lexical context patterns for each successfully verified geographical reference. For example if a proper name of a geographical location was found on a web page after the term *'near to'*, then one of the patterns extracted would be *'near to <geo_ref>'*. Upcoming web pages are searched for such patterns. Thus, if the term *'near to'* is encountered again, the expression matching *<geo_ref>* is treated like a geographical reference candidate. The frequency of patterns is a quality indicator allowing DCbot to rate patterns and to use a continuously improving set of patterns. This set of patterns is persistently stored and with each analyzed web page it becomes further refined.

Address Recognition. As previously mentioned, DCbot uses a list of keywords indicating possible postal addresses. Examples for such keywords are *Straße* (street) or *Platz* (square). An example for a partial address is *Alexanderplatz*. If such keywords are encountered, then the address recognition is triggered. The address recognition algorithm tries to parse a postal address composed of a house number, the street name, the postal area code and the city name. This is achieved by cross-checking the address components with DCbot's geographical database leveraging the hierarchical structure of the database.

3.4 GeoBase

Geographical reference candidates, that were extracted from web pages have to be confirmed. To achieve that DCbot uses a geographical database containing geographical locations. This database, GeoBase, is our own hierarchically organized catalogue inspired by The Getty Thesaurus of Geographic Names [5]. It provides for each entry the name of the represented geographical location, the location type, geographical coordinates, and the spatial extent of the location. GeoBase has a hierarchical structure. For each entry a reference to the parent location is stored. The hierarchical structure of GeoBase allows the verification of complex geographical references such as postal addresses, where the different parts of the address (city, postal area code, street) stand in a spatial child-parent relationship.

At the moment the most important entries in GeoBase are entries representing states, cities, and postal code areas from Germany as well as streets, institutions and service facilities from Stuttgart. Note that the number of entries in the database is crucial for finding pages with geographical references. Only those geographical reference candidates can be confirmed, that have a corresponding entry in GeoBase.

3.5 Customizing DCbot

Currently DCbot is set up to analyze web pages in German describing german regions. However, the modular design of DCbot allows – after simple adjustments – the analysis of web pages in other languages and from other regions as well. Language-dependent parts such as the keyword lists or the names of locations in GeoBase are easily extensible. Additionally, the address recognition, that is obviously culture- and region-dependent has to be replaced.

4 Experiments

In this section, we present results of a test run, in which we let DCbot analyze 25000 web pages. As we already pointed out, DCbot can only recognize geographical references on web pages if these are in DCbot's catalogue, GeoBase. Since GeoBase is not an extensive geographical database, our experimental results should merely demonstrate, that finding web pages with geographical references using DCbot is an easy task. However, if a large percentage of web pages related to a region should be found, one has to use a geographical catalogue containing all the locations in that region.

This experiment focuses on German web pages from the region of the state capital, Stuttgart. This is reflected by the region-specific contents of GeoBase as well as by the region specific start URL for the search.

4.1 Experimental Setup

Our experiments were run on a Sun UltraSparc-60 with 640 MB RAM. GeoBase and the data, which DCbot collected, were stored in IBMs DB2 UDB V7.2 running on the same computer. The main entries in GeoBase were German geographical locations:

Nationwide Locations:	Locations in Stuttgart:
16 states	4197 streets
6345 cities	134 hotels and restaurants
8264 postal code areas	75 theatres, museums and libraries
114 colleges and universities	
74 mountains and lakes	

We set up DCbot to analyze 25000 web pages starting from a Google result page showing the first 100 web pages having *'Stuttgart'* in their title. An additional setting instructed DCbot not to go further than five hyperlinks from the start page.

4.2 Experimental Results

DCbot successfully analyzed 87.81% of the web resources behind the 25000 URLs. The remaining 12.42% of the URLs were pointing to irregular or not existent web pages or automated analysis by a robot was denied. More than half (52.13%) of the successfully analyzed web pages contained some kind of geographical reference. These pages held in average 3.65 references.

The majority of geographical references on web pages (81.73%) were city names. The second largest group were postal addresses. DCbot recognized several hundred complete addresses from Stuttgart (1.66%) and several thousand addresses from other parts of Germany (9.3%), where the street entry was missing in GeoBase and DCbot could only recognize the postal area code and the city name. The third largest group were universities and college references (6.4%). However, the majority of theses pages belonged to the University of Stuttgart, which resulted from the location specific start URL. Other groups were lakes and mountains (0.75%) and museums, theaters and libraries from Stuttgart (0.17%).

Section 3.2 describes which web page parts are analyzed by DCbot and which methods it uses to extract geographical reference candidates. Figure 3 shows the distribution of geographical references by these aspects.

The majority of geographical references were found in the body part of web pages followed by the *keywords* and *description* meta-tags (Figure 3a). The unusually high percentage of geographical references in URLs originates from the location-specific start URL. Many pages had *'Stuttgart'* in their host name.

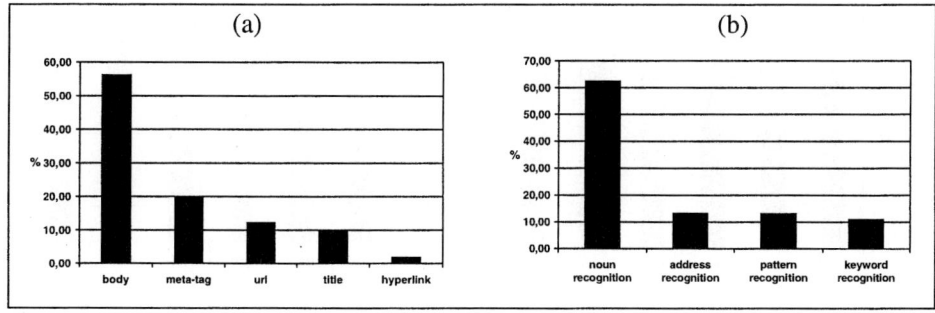

Fig. 3. Distribution of geographical references by web page parts (*a*) and by analysis methods (*b*)

Figure 3b also shows that the noun extraction method found over 60% of the geographical references. This is a result of the overwhelming majority of city names among geographical references on web pages. City names are in most cases one word references found by noun recognition.

Beside the distribution of geographical references by web page parts and extraction methods, we were interested in the quality of extracted references. We examined over nine hundred geographical references originating from over seven hundred web pages by hand in order to review DCbot's results. We selected only geographical references to locations with a small spatial extent (museums, universities, postal addresses, ...), because locations having a large extent, such as cities are not very useful for mobile applications interested in their immediate spatial context.

Quality measurements are shown in Figure 4. For the rating process we defined three categories for the quality of a geographical reference:

- good references, where the content of the web page was strongly related to the referenced location (black).
- mediocre references, where the content of the web page was somewhat related to the referenced location (dark grey).
- false references, where the content of the web page was not related to the referenced location (light grey).

Figure 4 illustrates the quality of geographical references for each web page part and for each extraction method. As Figure 4a shows, references extracted from the title, from the *keywords* meta-tags and from the *description* meta-tags are of excellent quality. Geographical references found in the first few sentences of the page body and in hyperlink texts are still in most of the cases strongly or somewhat related to the referenced location.

Figure 4b shows the quality distribution of references by the extraction method. For each method it is separately indicated if references were extracted from the first few words or sentences of the corresponding web page part or if they were found further behind. Postal addresses and references extracted by keyword recognition from the first few words and sentences of web page parts are significantly better than those extracted from further behind. The overall percentage of false geographical references is rather low.

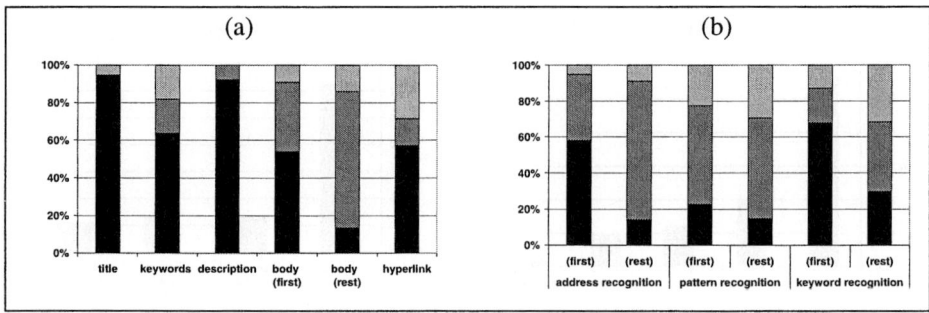

Fig. 4. Quality of geographical references by web page parts (*a*) and by analysis methods (*b*)

5 Postprocessing

In this section we describe how the best geographical reference from a web page is selected, how Geographical Web Portals (GWP) are generated and which methods can further improve the presentation of web pages to mobile users. These postprocessing steps operate on spatially indexed web pages, that were gathered and indexed by DCbot.

5.1 Selection of Geographical References

DCbot builds a repository of spatially indexed web pages. For each web page all geographical references are stored. In this manner, several strategies for the selection of the best geographical reference can be applied. Our current algorithm for rating geographical references and choosing the best reference in a web page is based on a weight matrix. The rows of the matrix correspond to extent sizes of geographical locations, the columns to web page parts. For each geographical reference, the corresponding weight from the weight matrix is selected. In the end the geographical reference candidate with the largest weight wins. One should of course set larger weights for web page parts, that are known for providing good geographical references (see Figure 4a).

5.2 Generating Geographical Web Portals

Our goal is to provide mobile users with web pages related to their local environment. In our Nexus platform we use Virtual Information Towers (VIT) [7], to augment maps with additional information. We created for the presentation of web pages to users GWPs, which are light-weight VITs having a location and a visibility area. Each GWP covers a specific region. If the best geographical reference on a web page falls into the region of a GWP, it becomes associated with the region's GWP. If there is no existing GWP for a region, a new one is created.

GWPs are virtual objects, that can be used to augment maps. If a user is within the visibility area of a GWP, then it is visible on the users electronic map. He can access the GWP and receive a list of web pages related to his current environment.

5.3 Future Methods

DCbot treats every web page as a stand alone resource. The web presence of a company or a facility like a museum, however, typically consists out of many web pages. Our experiments show that DCbot tends to find the same location information on all pages belonging to a single web presence, e.g. because it is part of the URL or of a standard page layout used by all pages. As a consequence, the search results presented to a user may be overcrowded by dozens of web pages belonging to a single company. Especially for mobile devices with small displays, it would be better just to present one summary page for the whole web presence, from which all other pages can be reached. To implement this behavior, all web pages belonging to the same location have to be analyzed. Pages, which have significant parts of their URL in common can be assumed to belong to the same web presence and are assigned to the same summary page. Two problems have to be solved: What are 'significant parts' of the URL and what is a 'summary page'.

The most simple approach to solve the first problem is to compare the host parts of the URLs, but this fails for small organizations, which may share the domain of their provider, or for large organizations, which may use more than one domain. A more advanced approach is to search common parts within the complete URL.

The most simple solution for the second problem assumes the web page with the fewest components in the path part to be the root page of the web presence and takes this page as the summary page. More advanced approaches may try to analyze the link structure between the web pages, but this can be very costly.

6 Conclusions and Future Research

Tapping the ubiquitous WWW in order to considerably enhance the information provided to applications and users is an ever lasting task. In this paper, we described an approach to achieve this for the class of spatial information. We devised a set of technologies and a system architecture to automatically map web page content to the associated spatial location. In doing so, we described how web pages related to specific locations can be found, how the best geographical reference on a web page can be selected and how a mobile application could present location-specific web pages to users and thus benefit from this additional information.

Early experiences gained from a first prototype evaluation clearly show that geographical references found in the title, in the *keywords* meta-tag or in the *description* meta-tag are of high quality. Special meta-tags, that can be used to explicitly provide a geographical reference (e.g. *DC.Coverage*), are very rarely used. While more than half of the geographical references found at the beginning of the body part have a high quality, the quality of references found in subsequent parts is significantly lower. It seems to be reasonable to restrict the search for geographical references to the beginning of the body, which also would speed up the search process, as only a fraction of the page has to be analyzed.

The evaluation of our analysis methods has shown that methods using domain specific knowledge such as the keyword recognition or the address recognition perform significantly better than the usage of domain independent lexical context patterns.

Because the gathering and the analysis of web pages are done in advance, the performance of DCbot is not crucial to system effectiveness. However, the number of indexed web pages can be easily multiplied by running several DCbot instances in parallel. We also discovered, that retrieving web pages from the WWW is the system bottleneck. Thus efficiency can be further boosted by running several instances that retrieve the web documents and fewer instances that perform the analysis.

There are still many open issues. One we are still working on is the selection of the best geographical reference on a web page. Our approach is based on the web page part, in that the reference was found, and the extent of the referenced location. However, if several references to different locations occur on a web page, then the selection of the best reference can also be based on the homogeneity or the heterogeneity of the geographical references.

Acknowledgements

The Nexus project is funded by the German Research Association (DFG) as Center of Excellence (SFB) 627.

References

[1] T. Berners-Lee, M. Fischetti: *Weaving the web*. 1. paperback ed., HarperCollins, 2000
[2] M. E. Califf, R. J. Mooney: *Relational Learning of Pattern-Match Rules for Information Extraction*. Proceedings of AAAI 1998 Spring Symposium on Applying Machine Learning to Discourse Processing, March 23-25, 1998
[3] J. Ding, L. Gravano, N. Shivakumar: *Computing Geographical Scopes of Web Resources* 26th International Conference on Very Large Databases (VLDB), September 10-14, 2000
[4] *Dublin Core Metadata Element Set:* http://www.dublincore.org/documents/dces/
[5] *The Getty Thesaurus of Geographic Names:* http://www.getty.edu/research/ conducting_research/vocabularies/tgn/
[6] *Google Search by Location:* http://labs.google.com/location
[7] A. Leonhardi, U. Kubach, K. Rothermel: *Virtual Information Towers – A metaphor for intuitive, location-aware information access in a mobile environment*. Proc. of third International Symposium on Wearable Computers, San Francisco, CA, 1999
[8] A. Markowetz, T. Brinkhoff, B. Seeger: *Geographic Information Retrieval*. 3rd International Workshop on Web Dynamics, 2004
[9] D. Nicklas, M. Großmann, T. Schwarz, S. Volz, B. Mitschang: *A Model-Based, Open Architecture for Mobile, Spatially Aware Applications*. 7th International Symposium on Spatial and Temporal Databases (SSTD), Redondo Beach, CA, USA, 2001.
[10] D. Nicklas, B. Mitschang: *On building location aware applications using an open platform based on the Nexus Augmented World Model*. Software and Systems Modeling, 3(4), 2004.
[11] M. Sütö: *Ortsbasierter Web-Zugriff*. (In German). University of Stuttgart, 2002
[12] W3C: *Resource Description Framework (RDF)*. http://w3.org/RDF/
[13] W3C: *Web Ontology Language (OWL)*. http://w3.org/2004/OWL/

Improving Space-Efficiency in Temporal Text-Indexing

Kjetil Nørvåg* and Albert Overskeid Nybø

Department of Computer and Information Science
Norwegian University of Science and Technology
7491 Trondheim, Norway

Abstract. Support for temporal text-containment queries is of interest in a number of contexts. In previous papers we have presented two approaches to temporal text-indexing, the V2X and ITTX indexes. In this paper, we first present improvements to the previous techniques. We then perform a study of the space usage of the indexing approaches based on both analytical models and results from indexing temporal text collections. These results show for what kind of document collections the different techniques should be employed. The results also show that regarding space usage, the new ITTX/VIDPI technique proposed in this paper is in most cases superior to V2X, except in the case of patterns of high number of new documents relative to number of updated documents.

1 Introduction

Temporal text indexes are used to reduce the cost of performing temporal text-containment queries, i.e., query for all versions of documents that contained one or more particular words at a particular time. The importance of such indexes will increase as the ability to manage timestamped or temporal documents becomes common. For example, an increasing amount of documents in companies and other organizations is now only available electronically, and exist in several versions updated at different times. These documents can be in a number of formats like plain text, HTML, XML, Microsoft Word, Adobe PDF, etc. Many organizations already have searchable repositories or intranet search engines that can be used to retrieve documents based on keywords search, and possibly also other searchable parameters like create or update. Another example is web warehouses which collect web pages from a number of sites at regular intervals, and whose information contents can be queried and analyzed.

We have previously proposed two text-indexing techniques for transaction-time temporal document database systems: the *V2 temporal text index* (V2X) [1] used in the V2 temporal document database system, and the *interval-based temporal text index* (ITTX) [2]. V2X is a combination of full-text indexes and time indexes for performing efficient text-containment queries, and is most suitable for documents with few versions or with a high degree of change between versions. In the ITTX, word occurrences and stored in a way that is particular space-efficient when most documents have several versions and the change between versions is relatively small.

---

* Email of contact author: Kjetil.Norvag@idi.ntnu.no

This paper is the first comparative study of temporal text-indexing techniques, and the contributions of this paper are 1) a more detailed study of the space usage of the indexing approaches, 2) improvements to the ITTX, and 3) a study for what kind of document collections the different techniques should be employed.

The organization of the rest of this paper is as follows. In Sect. 2 we give an overview of related work. In Sect. 3 we give an overview our two basic techniques for temporal text indexing, the V2X and ITTX indexes. In Sect. 4 we present several improvements to the ITTX approach. In Sect. 5 we study the space usage of the different indexing alternatives, and for what document collection types the different alternatives should be used. Finally, in Sect. 6, we conclude the paper.

2 Related Work

There has been a large amount of research on indexing temporal data in context of traditional data types, see [3] for an extensive survey. However, as explained in detail in [1], the traditional temporal indexing methods are not directly applicable to temporal text indexing.

The only research work we are aware of that directly focuses on access methods for general temporal document querying, is the proposal from Anick and Flynn [4] on how to support versioning in a full-text information retrieval system. In their proposal, the current version of documents are stored as complete versions, and backward deltas are used for historical versions. This gives efficient access to the current (and recent) versions, but costly access to older versions. They also use the timestamp as version identifier. This is not applicable for transaction-based document processing where all versions created by one transaction should have same timestamp. In order to support temporal text-containment queries, they based the full-text index on bitmaps for words in current versions, and delta change records to track incremental changes to the index backwards over time. This approach has the same advantage and problem as the delta-based version storage: efficient access to current version, but costly recreation of previous states is needed. It is also difficult to make temporal zig-zag joins (needed for multi-word temporal text-containment queries) efficient.

Related to the task of temporal full-text indexing, is indexing temporal XML documents [5]. In this case the focus is on improving path queries. It should be noted that temporal full-text indexes like the ones presented in our paper can also be used to improve performance of temporal XML queries, and this is described in more detail in [6].

The inverted file indexes used as basis in our work is based on traditional text-indexing techniques, see for example [7].

3 Basic Temporal Text-Indexing Techniques

The basic lookup operation in non-temporal text indexing is to retrieve the document identifiers of all documents that contain a particular word w. The most common access method for text indexing is the inverted file, which is also the basis of our approaches.

An inverted file index is a mapping from a term (text word) w to the documents $d_1, d_2, \ldots, d_j$ where the term appears. Inverted files are also the basis of our approaches.

In the inverted file index, a *posting list* $PL = (w, d_1, d_2, \ldots, d_m)$ is created for each index term, where w is the text word, and d_i are the document identifiers of the documents the term appears in. The tuple $P = (w, d_i)$, i.e., an index term and a document identifier, is called a *posting*.

In order to make this paper self-containing, and provide the context for the rest of this paper, we will in this section give a short overview of the V2 index (V2X) and the interval-based temporal text index (ITTX). Both the V2X and ITTX have been implemented in temporal document database prototypes built on top of Berkeley DB [8].

The V2X Temporal Text-Index. A document version stored in V2 is uniquely identified by a *version identifier* (VID). In order to support partial retrieval of documents, the document versions are chunked and stored in a B-tree-based document-version index. The VID is essentially a counter, and given the fact that each new version to be inserted is given a higher VID than the previous versions, the document-version index is append-only and always compact. A document is identified by a *document name*. Conceptually, the document name index has for each document name some metadata related to all versions of the document, followed by specific information for each particular version, including both timestamp and VID for each version. Thus, the document name index can be used to retrieve particular versions of a particular document by providing the VIDs to be used in the lookup in the document-version index.

The words in the document versions are indexed by variants of inverted lists, which essentially provides a mapping from a word to the VIDs of all document versions containing the word. In order to support efficient temporal text-containment queries, a separate index called *VIDPI* is employed. The VIDPI provides the mapping from VID to validity period (start- and end-timestamp), which is the timestamp of the document version identified by VID and the timestamp of the next version (or time of deletion) of the particular document.

Temporal text-containment queries using the VIDPI-index-based approach can be performed by the following two-step algorithm:

1. A text-index query using the text index that indexes all versions in the database. The result is a set of VIDs of all document versions containing the particular word.
2. A time-select operation selects the actual versions (from stage 1) that were valid at the particular time or time period. For this purpose the VIDPI is used. One lookup is needed for each of the VIDs returned in stage 1.

The ITTX Temporal Text-Index. One problem with the V2X is that each unique word in a document version requires a separate posting in the text index. This makes the size of the text index proportional to the size of the document version database. In a document database with several versions of each document, the size of the text index can be reduced by noting the fact that the difference between consecutive versions of a document is usually small: frequently, a word in one document version will in also occur in the next (as well as the previous) version. Thus, we can reduce the size of the text index by storing word/version-range mappings, instead of storing information about individual versions.

In order to benefit from the use of intervals, we use *document version identifiers* (DVIDs) instead of the version identifiers used in the V2X. Given a version of a document with DVID=v, then the next version of the same document has DVID=$v+1$. In contrast to a VID that uniquely identifies a document version stored in the system, different versions of different documents can have the same DVID, i.e., the DVIDs are not unique between different versions of different documents. In order to uniquely identify (and to retrieve) a particular document version, a *document identifier* (DID) is needed together with the DVID, i.e., a particular document version in the system is identified by (DID||DVID). In this way, consecutive versions of the same document that contain the same word can form a range with no holes.

Conceptually, the text index that use ranges can be viewed as a collection of (w,DID,$DVID_i$,$DVID_j$)-tuples, i.e., a word, a document identifier, and a DVID range. Note that for each document, there can be several tuples for each word w, because words can appear in one version, disappear in a later version, and then again reappear later. A good example is a page containing news headlines, where some topics are reoccurring.

When a new document version with DVID=$DVID_i$ is inserted, and it contains a word that did not occur in the previous version, a (w,DID,$DVID_i$,$DVID_j$) tuple is inserted into the index. $DVID_i$ is the DVID of the inserted version, but $DVID_j$ is set to a special value UC (until changed). In this way, if this word is also included in the next version of this document, the tuple does not have to be modified. This is an important feature (a similar technique for avoiding text index updates is also described in [4]). Only when a new version of the document that does not contain the word is inserted, the tuple has to be updated. It is important to note that using this organization, it is impossible to determine the DVIDs of the most recent versions from the index. For the [$DVID_i$,UC] intervals only the start DVID is available, and we do not know the end DVID. As will be described later, this makes query processing more complicated.

In order to save some space and increase performance of queries for current documents, a separate index is used for the entries that are still valid, i.e., where the end of the interval is UC. In this index the end value UC is implicit, so that only the start DVID needs to be stored. We denote the index for historical entries *HTxtIdx* and the index for valid entries *CTxtIdx*.

One of the main reasons why the VIDPI is very attractive in the context of V2, is that storing the time information in the VIDPI is much more space efficient than storing the timestamps replicated many places in the text index (once for each word). However, when intervals are used, one timestamp for each start- and end-point of the intervals is sufficient, and the increase in total space usage, compared with using a VIDPI index, should be less than what is the case in V2 (although, as we shall see later in this paper, this is unfortunately not always the case). It could also be more scalable, because the V2 approach is most efficient when the VIDPI index can always be resident in main memory. To summarize, our final solution for the ITTX as presented in [2] was to store (w,DID,$DVID_i$,$DVID_j$,T_S,T_E) in the HTxtIdx (where T_S and T_E are the start- and end-timestamps of the interval [$DVID_i$,$DVID_j$>), and to store (w,DID,DVID,T_S) in the CTxtIdx. In [2] we outline the algorithms to be applied when inserting, updating and deleting documents, as well as algorithms for temporal text-containment queries using the ITTX.

4   Improving the Interval-Based Temporal Text Index

After some experimenting with the ITTX we have discovered that for many types of temporal document collections the assumption that ITTX is usually more space-efficient than the V2X does not hold. As a result, we have developed several variants of ITTX where the space efficiency is improved. The ITTX improvements will now be presented together with a discussion about space usage of the variants. We start with the original ITTX, which we from now on will denote *ITTX-24/14* in order to avoid any confusion between the variants.

ITTX-24/14. In the original implementation of ITTX we used 4 bytes to represent DIDs and DVIDs, and 6 byte for each timestamp. This means a total of 24 bytes to represent a posting interval in the historical index, and 14 bytes in the current index where the end of interval is not known and therefore does not have to be stored. In V2X, on average just a little over 2 bytes where needed to represent a posting. This means that in order to be competitive, the ITTX posting intervals need to cover on average at least 12 versions in order to be competitive compared to the V2X. For many application areas this was not the case, and the space usage when using the ITTX was much higher than if V2X was used.

ITTX-16/11. One way to reduce the space usage is to use a compressed representation of the identifiers. In traditional non-temporal posting lists, the difference is often small between two consecutive document identifiers in large posting lists. This makes it possible to encode the identifiers very efficiently, for example using Elias encoding [9] or variable length encoding [10]. In the case of the intervals in ITTX this is more difficult, but one possible approach is to reduce the size of the representation of the DVIDs. Instead of using 4 bytes for each DVID, we can use 3 bytes for the start DVID, and 1 byte to represent the difference between the end DVID and start DVID. The consequences of using this representation is that we can only have $2^{24} \approx 16$ million versions of each document, and that no interval can have more than 256 versions. It is not very likely that a document in a document database should have more than 16 million versions, and intervals over 256 versions can simply be represented by two or more intervals instead. The result of this representation is 16,7% reduced space usage.

Using the same difference-based technique to reduce space usage of timestamps is not possible. The problem is that by using 1 byte to represent a difference, the technique is only useful if most differences is less than what 1 byte represents, which is only about 7 minutes. This will definitely not be the case in general. Even 2 bytes is not sufficient, as it only increases the possible difference to 18 hours. However, in the case of document databases it should be enough with a coarser granularity than the one provided by the 6 bytes for each timestamp that were used in the original ITTX. Similar to the V2X, 4-byte-timestamps with resolution of 1 second should suffice. The result is then that the space needed for storing a posting interval, i.e., DID/DVID/DVID/T/T, is $4+3+1+4+4=16$ bytes, a total reduction of 33% from the original size.

ITTX/VIDPI. The improvements proposed so far are fairly simple and give only a moderate reduction of space. In order to reduce the size more drastically, some change to the indexing architecture itself is necessary. One possibility is to make the text index itself "non-temporal" by not including the timestamps in the main index, but instead using a strategy similar to the VIDPI [1] approach used in V2. The result is that it is sufficient to store the time interval once for each version, instead of once for each interval in the text index. The text index itself still contains intervals of version identifiers, thus still has the property of not increasing proportional to the version database size which was the case of the index used in V2.

Using the ITTX/VIDPI approach, each posting interval in the index is a DID/DVID/DVID record, using $4 + 3 + 1 = 8$ bytes. The records in the new VIDPI index are DID/DVID/T/T structures, using 16 bytes each assuming 4 byte large timestamps. In order to support efficient search in this index, the records should be sorted on DID/DVID. Similar to what is done in the VIDPI index in V2, DVIDs are sequential so they do not really have to be stored. In addition, the end timestamp of one version is the start timestamp of the next, so only one timestamp for each version needs to be stored, i.e., 8 bytes is sufficient for each version.

There is one important difference between the VIDPI index used in V2 and the one proposed here: in V2 the VIDPI index was sorted on VIDs and was append-only, thus having very low update cost. In the ITTX/VIDPI approach this is not the case, so the update will have a higher cost, approximately one block to be update per version, instead of one per transaction as was the case for V2. However, compared to the cost of indexing words in documents, the VIDPI update cost is only marginal.

ITTX/ND. During a temporal text-containment query using the implemented version of ITTX (the ITTX-24/14 variant), a lookup in the text index returns for each document where the word appears, an interval of versions (DVID,DVID) and a time period (T,T). In order to determine the actual versions, a separate lookup in the document name index is necessary. The DVDIs can be used to reduce the amount of work during the lookup in the document name index, but are not strictly necessary. The reason for still including the DVIDs in the ITTX, is that they are needed to support efficient removal of individual versions from the database. If removal of intermediate versions will not occur, it is possible to omit explicit storage of the DVID interval in the index, and instead having a DID together with the time interval. In this case, only 8 byte is needed for an entry in the CTxtIdx, and 12 bytes in the HTxtIdx.

5 Evaluation of Space Usage

In this study the main focus will be on reducing space usage, instead of studying the access cost directly. When using the indexes discussed in this paper, the space usage also indirectly determines the access cost because access cost is a function of posting list/interval sizes and buffer-hit probability. We will now first describe the test data that is used in the study, then the evaluation approach will be described, and an evaluation of space usage will be performed.

5.1 Test Data

Acquiring real-world temporal document collections is difficult. In some of our previous studies in temporal document databases, we have used a document collection that is

Table 1. Space usage of different indexing alternatives. The numbers in paranthesis are the number of bytes used to represent the fields in the index. Number of historical intervals is denoted N_{IH}, intervals in CTxtIdx is denoted N_{IC}, and number of postings in total is denoted N_{P}

Index type	HTxtIdx	CTxtIdx	Space
ITTX-24/14	DID(4) DVID(4) DVID(4) T(6) T(6)	DID(4) DVID(4) T(6)	$N_{\text{IH}} * 24 + N_{\text{IC}} * 14$
ITTX-16/11	DID(4) DVID(3) DVID(1) T(4) T(4)	DID(4) DVID(3) T(4)	$N_{\text{IH}} * 16 + N_{\text{IC}} * 11$
ITTX/VIDPI	DID(4) DVID(3) DVID(1)	DID(4) DVID(3)	$N_{\text{IH}} * 8 + N_{\text{IC}} * 8$
ITTX/ND	DID(4) T(4) T(4)	DID(4) T(4)	$N_{\text{IH}} * 12 + N_{\text{IC}} * 8$
V2X	VID(2)	VID(2)	$N_{\text{P}} * 2$

based on the evolution of pages from a set of web sites. Even though that collection was sufficient for the use in our previous work, it has a number of shortcomings that makes it less satisfactory for the purpose of this paper: it has a very high number of documents that are never updated, and it only presents one application area (temporal web warehouses). When comparing different indexing approaches, it is necessary with a number of test collections with different characteristics/statistical properties, and is also an advantage if we know and can control these characteristics, in order to make it easier to explain the results. For this purpose we have developed *TDocGen*, temporal document generator.

TDocGen creates a temporal document collection whose characteristics are decided by a number of configurable parameters. For example, the probability of update, average number of new documents in each generation, etc., can be configured. One of the important properties of TDocGen is that the documents it creates have vocabulary, vocabulary size, and words distribution according to what is expected in the real world. The created documents contain real words taken from histograms based on real (but non-temporal) documents and follows empirical laws like Heaps' law and Zipf's law. In order to capture the aspect of dynamic and static documents, every new document created by TDocGen is characterized as being dynamic or relatively static. The percentage of documents in each partition and the probability of updates to each partition is configurable. In a typical configuration 20% of the documents are defined to be dynamic, and 80% of the updates are performed on dynamic documents. TDocGen is described in more detail in [11].

5.2 Evaluation Method and Validation

Our approach to comparison is to use the simple disk usage models as summarized in Tab. 1 as basis for calculating the space usage (note that the extra space needed for the VIDPI indexes in the case of the ITTX/VIDPI and V2X alternatives is very small compared to the rest of the index structure and is therefore omitted from the space usage models, the same is the case for the start-VID of each chunk in the V2X index). In order to calculate the space usage for the different indexing alternatives, the models will be instrumented with words, validity intervals, etc., based on the document collections created by TDocGen. The statistics is acquired by inserting the collections into an IDDB database and using the statistics from the ITTX index.

In order to have confidence in the result using our evaluation methods, a validation of the approach is necessary. The modeling approach is the same for all the ITTX-variants, so validation of one of them suffices. The ITTX-24/14 variant is implemented in the IDDB prototype, and we insert one of the test collections into an IDDB database and compare the actual disk space usage of the ITTX index in IDDB with the predicted values resulting from instrumentation of the model as described above.

In order to predict the actual space usage from the values described in the previous section, page utilization and page overhead has to be taken into account. Figure 1 illustrates space usage of storing a test collection in IDDB for different amounts of data. The uppermost curve shows the actual disk space used for data stored in the IDDB system (having page fill factor of 67%), the second curve shows space usage adjusted for page utilization (i.e., space usage if fill factor was 100%), and the lower curve shows the space usage as predicted by the model which assumes 100% fill factor. The discrepancy between the model and real values is the space occupied by keys (words) and overhead on each page.

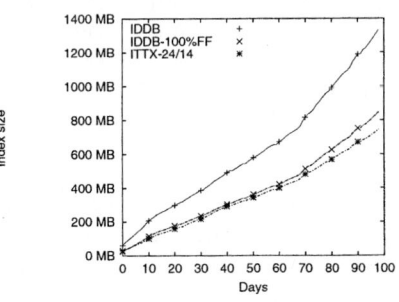

Fig. 1. Space usage of storing a test collection in IDDB for different amounts of data

The effects of page utilization and space for keys and overhead is approximately the same for the indexing alternatives, so in the rest of this study we will use the values predicted from the models. These values reflects space usage after a reorganization of the database, which would bring page utilization close to 100%. Figure 1 shows that the accuracy of the model is good, and the small difference also gives high confidence in the models for the indexing techniques that are not actually implemented (ITTX-16/11, ITTX/VIDPI, and ITTX/ND).

A similar approach is followed to validate the V2X model. With the test data we have studied, the difference between predicted and real values is approximately 3%, this is the result of omitting the start VID of each chunk in the V2X index from the model.

5.3 Space Usage

Different document database applications have different access pattern and document characteristics. A big advantage of having document collections created by a synthetic document generator is that we are able to produce collections reflecting the different applications. We will now study space usage for a number of different temporal document collections. Our application case that is behind the parameters, is a company or department involving a number of persons that each day create and update a certain number of documents. The starting point for the study is a document collection created by TDocGen using the parameters in Tab. 1. These parameters can for example reflect a group of 10 people where each of them every day on average creates 2 new documents and updates 10 documents, and once in a while delete documents. Assuming 50 lines on a page, a typical new document has 3 pages, and an update is typically addition of text equivalent to one new page, and removal of text equivalent to half a page. In addition to performing a study using the default parameters in Tab. 1, we have also changed some of the parameters to understand how these changes will affect space usage.

Table 2. Default document generator parameters

Parameter	Default value	Normal distributed Average	Std. dev.
Number of documents first that exists the first day	20		
Percentage of documents being dynamic	20		
Percent of updates applied to dynamic documents	80		
Number of words in each line in document	10		
Number of new documents created/day		20	10
Number of deleted documents/day		3	1
Number of updated documents/day		200	75
Number of lines in new document		150	50
Number of new lines when updating		50	10
Number of deleted lines when updating		20	5

The results are presented in Fig. 2. In all graphs, the space usage for the index is presented as a function of document collection size, which is given as number of days there have been actions performed on the database. In order to make it easier to see details in the graphs, we have only included the interesting part of the range (days), i.e., up to the interesting points of crossing. The actual document collection size at the end of each experiment is typically in the order of 15 times the space usage of the V2X, i.e., between 1 GB and 4 GB (depending on number of days and update/create patterns).

Figure 2(a) illustrates space usage using the default parameters as presented in Tab. 1. As can be seen in the figure, already early in the experiment it becomes obvious that using the default parameters, the interval-bases indexing techniques based on the ITTX excel.

The default parameters represent a quite aggressive update pattern in terms of amount of updated documents, although the percentage of documents that are updated decreases as the size of the database grows larger. In order to study the effect of the update rate, we have run the experiments based on the default parameters, but with number of updated documents each day reduced to 100. The results are illustrated in Fig. 2(b), and shows that the space usage of the V2X does not increase at the same very high rate as in Fig. 2(a). It also shows that it takes a longer time before the difference between V2X and the other techniques becomes significant. However, the difference increases with time, so it is obvious there are great benefits gained from using intervals-based indexes also in this case.

Figure 2(c) shows the space usage when the update rate is further reduced, to 50 updates documents per day. It illustrates well the fact that the V2X is best when most documents have few updates, because short intervals make the interval-based indexes inefficient. The same aspect can also be illustrated by increasing the number of new documents created each day, instead of reducing the update rate. This is illustrated in Fig. 2(d), which shows space usage when the number of new documents has been increased to 40. What happens is essentially that new documents are created so fast that it is not possible to update all old documents with the given update rate. For the values as shown in Fig. 2(c) and 2(d), there is not a very significant difference between ITTX/ND, ITTX/VIDPI, and V2X, and access performance can be just as important as space when

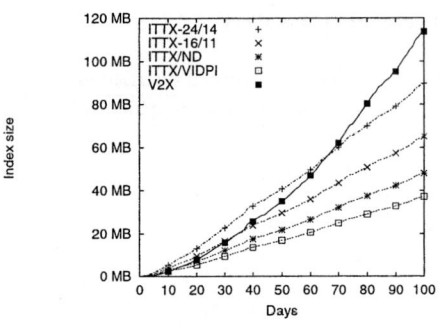

(a) Default parameters.

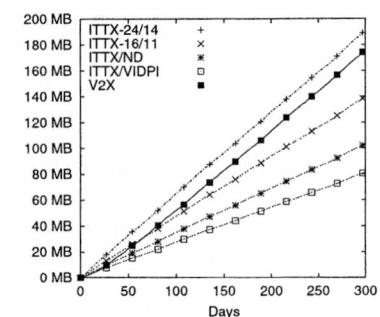

(b) Number of updated documents/day reduced to 100.

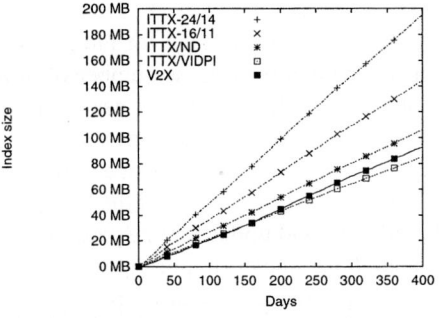

(c) Number of updated documents/day reduced to 50.

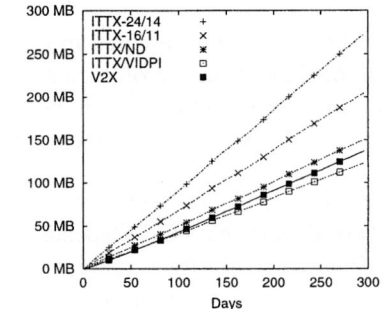

(d) Number of new documents/day increased to 40.

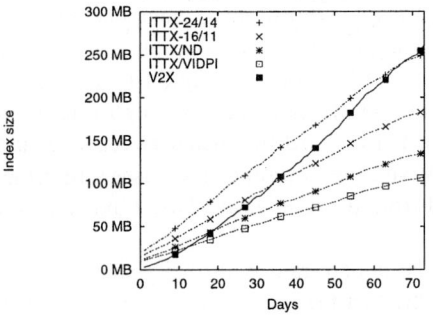

(e) Increasing intial number of document and the update rate.

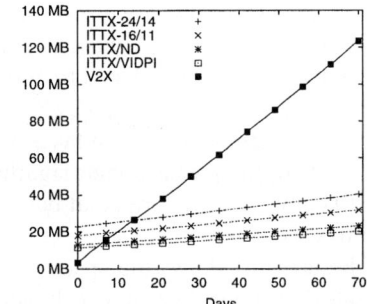

(f) Pattern consisting of mostly small updates.

Fig. 2. Space usage for different temporal document collections

choosing which index to use. However, when the number of new documents relative to number of updated documents increases even more, using the V2X will become more and more beneficial. The extreme parameters are when there are no updates, only new created documents. In that case, a new interval has to be created for each document, and space usage will increase linearly with increasing document collection size for the interval-based indexes as well. However, an interval occupies much larger space in the index than just a VID as is the case for the V2X, so V2X will in total have a much lower space usage in that case.

In order to study how the index structures scales to a larger number of documents, we increased the number of documents at the start to 1000, and the number of updated documents each day to 400. The space usage is illustrated in Fig. 2(e), and the difference between V2X and the interval-based alternatives is significant.

In addition to the experiments presented so far on basis of the parameters in Tab. 1, we have also studied the impact of varying the other parameters. One interesting case is when most updates are very small, i.e., only one line added by during each update. One possible application area where this could occur is a CV database. This is essentially a best-case for the interval-bases index, and is very obvious when we see the graphs in Fig. 2(f): very little increase in index size of the interval-based approaches, but very high increase in space usage for the V2X approach.

6 Discussion and Conclusions

Support for temporal text-containment queries is of interest in a number of contexts, both temporal document databases and temporal XML databases[6]. In this paper, we have presented improvements to the previous temporal text-indexing techniques and studied in more detail the space usage of the indexing approaches. As has been shown, regarding space usage the ITTX/VIDPI is in most cases superior to V2X, except in the case of:

- High number of new documents relative to number of updated documents. In that case, many intervals will be one-version intervals, which are expensive in terms of space usage.
- Possibility of physically deleting historical versions from the database, for example if granularity reduction [12] or vacuuming is performed (note that in the case of ordinary/logical deletions of documents, previous versions will be retained in the database). In that case, intervals will be destroyed and the relative space usage of interval-based approaches will be very high.

For both ITTX/VIDPI and V2X, a query has to be performed by a lookup in the text index followed by a lookup in the VIDPI index. As long as the VIDPI index can fit in main memory the cost of the VIDPI lookup is not significant and does not have to be taken into account. In this case, choice of index structure can be based on create/update pattern. However, if the number of document versions is very large, the VIDPI index might not fit in main memory. This can for example be the result of a very large document collection, but can also happen in the case of a small collection that contains many small documents. In this case, the extra lookups in the VIDPI index can contribute much to the overall access time, and using an index variant without the need up the extra lookup can be beneficial. The ITTX/ND normally occupies more space than an ITTX/VIDPI index, but the difference is small enough to consider it a good alternative when the VIDPI index does not fit in main memory.

The proposed indexing techniques work well even for large document collections. However, we believe there still are possible ways of improving indexing performance in the case of very large document collections, and our current work focuses on designing index structures that are truly scalable. These indexes will be needed when the document collection and indexes are of such sizes that only small parts of the index structures can be assumed to be resident in main memory.

References

1. Nørvåg, K.: Supporting temporal text-containment queries in temporal document databases. Journal of Data & Knowledge Engineering **49** (2004) 105–125
2. Nørvåg, K.: Space-efficient support for temporal text indexing in a document archive context. In: Proceedings of the 7th European Conference on Digital Libraries (ECDL'2003). (2003)
3. Salzberg, B., Tsotras, V.J.: Comparison of access methods for time-evolving data. ACM Computing Surveys **31** (1999) 158–221
4. Anick, P.G., Flynn, R.A.: Versioning a full-text information retrieval system. In: Proceedings of SIGIR'1992. (1992)
5. Mendelzon, A.O., Rizzolo, F., Vaisman, A.A.: Indexing temporal XML documents. In: Proceedings of VLDB'2004. (2004)
6. Nørvåg, K.: Algorithms for temporal query operators in XML databases. In: Workshop on XML-Based Data Management and Multimedia Engineering. (2002)
7. Witten, I.H., Moffat, A., Bell, T.C.: Managing Gigabytes: Compressing and Indexing Documents and Images. Morgan Kaufmann (1999)
8. Olson, M.A., Bostic, K., Seltzer, M.: Berkeley DB. In: Proceedings of the FREENIX Track: 1999 USENIX Annual Technical Conference. (1999)
9. Elias, P.: Universal codeword sets and representations of the integers. IEEE Transactions on Information Theory **IT-21** (1975) 194–203
10. Fraenkel, A., Klein, S.: Novel compression of sparse bit-strings — preliminary report. In: Combinatorial Algorithms on Words, NATO ASI Series Volume 12. Springer Verlag (1985)
11. Nørvåg, K., Nybø, A.O.: Creating synthetic temporal document collections. Technical Report IDI 6/2004, Norwegian University of Science and Technology. Available from http://www.idi.ntnu.no/grupper/DB-grp/ (2004)
12. Nørvåg, K.: Algorithms for granularity reduction in temporal document databases. (Accepted for publication in Information Systems)

Nearest Neighbours Search Using the PM-Tree

Tomáš Skopal[1], Jaroslav Pokorný[1], and Václav Snášel[2]

[1] Charles University in Prague, FMP, Department of Software Engineering,
Malostranské nám. 25, 118 00 Prague, Czech Republic, EU
tomas@skopal.net, jaroslav.pokorny@mff.cuni.cz
[2] VŠB–Technical University of Ostrava, FECS, Dept. of Computer Science,
tř. 17. listopadu 15, 708 33 Ostrava, Czech Republic, EU
vaclav.snasel@vsb.cz

Abstract. We introduce a method of searching the k nearest neighbours (k-NN) using PM-tree. The PM-tree is a metric access method for similarity search in large multimedia databases. As an extension of M-tree, the structure of PM-tree exploits local dynamic pivots (like M-tree does it) as well as global static pivots (used by LAESA-like methods). While in M-tree a metric region is represented by a hyper-sphere, in PM-tree the "volume" of metric region is further reduced by a set of hyper-rings. As a consequence, the shape of PM-tree's metric region bounds the indexed objects more tightly which, in turn, improves the overall search efficiency. Besides the description of PM-tree, we propose an optimal k-NN search algorithm. Finally, the efficiency of k-NN search is experimentally evaluated on large synthetic as well as real-world datasets.

1 Introduction

The volume of multimedia databases rapidly increases and the need for efficient content-based search in large multimedia databases becomes stronger. In particular, there is a need for searching for the k most similar documents (called the k nearest neighbours – k-NN) to a given query document.

Since multimedia documents are modelled by objects (usually vectors) in a feature space $\mathbb{U}$, the multimedia database can be represented by a dataset $\mathbb{S} \subset \mathbb{U}$, where $n = |\mathbb{S}|$ is size of the dataset. The search in $\mathbb{S}$ is accomplished by an access method, which retrieves objects relevant to a given similarity query. The similarity measure is often modelled by a *metric*, i.e. a distance d satisfying properties of reflexivity, positivity, symmetry, and triangular inequality. Given a metric space $\mathcal{M} = (\mathbb{U}, d)$, the *metric access methods* (MAMs) [4] organize objects in $\mathbb{S}$ such that a structure in $\mathbb{S}$ is recognized (i.e. a kind of *metric index* is constructed) and exploited for efficient (i.e. quick) search in $\mathbb{S}$. To keep the search as efficient as possible, the MAMs should minimize the *computation costs* (CC) and the *I/O costs*. The computation costs represent the number of (computationally expensive) distance computations spent by the query evaluation. The I/O costs are related to the volume of data needed to be transfered from secondary memory (also referred to as the disk access costs).

In this paper we propose a method of k-NN searching using PM-tree, which is a metric access method for similarity search in large multimedia databases.

2 M-Tree

Among the MAMs developed so far, the M-tree [5, 7] (and its modifications) is still the only dynamic MAM suitable for efficient similarity search in large multimedia databases. Like other dynamic and paged trees, the M-tree is a balanced hierarchy of nodes. Given a metric d, the data objects $O_i \in \mathbb{S}$ are organized in a hierarchy of nested clusters, called *metric regions*. The leaf nodes contain *ground entries* of the indexed data objects, while the *routing entries* (stored in the inner nodes) describe the metric regions. A ground entry is denoted as:

$$grnd(O_i) = [O_i, oid(O_i), d(O_i, \text{Par}(O_i))]$$

where $O_i \in \mathbb{S}$ is the data object, $oid(O_i)$ is identifier of the original DB object (stored externally), and $d(O_i, \text{Par}(O_i))$ is precomputed distance between O_i and the data object of its parent routing entry. A routing entry is denoted as:

$$rout(O_i) = [O_i, ptr(T(O_i)), r_{O_i}, d(O_i, \text{Par}(O_i))]$$

where $O_i \in \mathbb{S}$ is a *routing object* (local pivot), $ptr(T(O_i))$ is pointer to the covering subtree, and r_{O_i} is the covering radius. The routing entry determines a hyper-spherical metric region (O_i, r_{O_i}) in $\mathcal{M}$, for which routing object O_i is the center and r_{O_i} is the radius bounding the region. In Figure 1 see several data objects partitioned among (possibly overlapping) metric regions of M-tree.

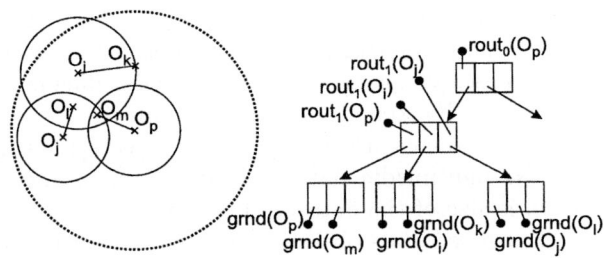

Fig. 1. Hierarchy of metric regions and the appropriate M-tree

2.1 Similarity Queries in M-Tree

The structure of M-tree was designed to support similarity queries (proximity queries actually). We distinguish two basic kinds of queries. The *range query* is specified as a hyper-spherical *query region* (Q, r_Q), defined by a query object Q and a covering query radius r_Q. The purpose of range query is to select all objects $O_i \in \mathbb{S}$ satisfying $d(Q, O_i) \leq r_Q$ (i.e. located inside the query region). The

k *nearest neighbours query* (k-NN query) is specified by a query object Q and a number k. A k-NN query selects the first k nearest (most similar) objects to Q. Technically, the k-NN query can be formulated as a range query $(Q, d(Q, O_k))$, where O_k is the k-th nearest neighbour. During query processing, the M-tree hierarchy is traversed down. Given a routing entry $rout(O_i)$, the subtree $T(O_i)$ is processed only if the region defined by $rout(O_i)$ overlaps the query region.

Range Search. The range query algorithm [5, 7] has to follow all M-tree paths leading to data objects O_j inside the query region, i.e. satisfying $d(Q, O_j) \leq r_Q$. In fact, the range query algorithm recursively accesses nodes the metric regions of which (described by the parent routing entries $rout(O_i)$) overlap the query region, i.e. such that $d(O_i, Q) \leq r_{O_i} + r_Q$ is satisfied.

2.2 Nearest Neighbours Search

In fact, the k-NN query algorithm for M-tree is a more complicated range query algorithm. Since the query radius r_Q is not known in advance, it must be determined dynamically (during the query processing). For this purpose a *branch-and-bound* heuristic algorithm has been introduced [5], quite similar to that one for R-trees [8]. The k-NN query algorithm utilizes a priority queue PR of pending requests, and a k-elements array NN used to store the k-NN candidates and which, at the end of the processing, contains the result. At the beginning, the *dynamic radius* r_Q is set to ∞, while during query processing r_Q is consecutively reduced down to the "true" distance between Q and the k-th nearest neighbour.

PR Queue. The priority queue PR of pending requests $[ptr(T(O_i)), d_{min}(T(O_i))]$ is used to keep (pointers to) such subtrees $T(O_i)$, which (still) cannot be excluded from the search, due to overlap of their metric regions (O_i, r_{O_i}) with the *dynamic query region* (Q, r_Q). The priority order of each such request is given by $d_{min}(T(O_i))$, which is the smallest possible distance between an object stored in $T(O_i)$ and the query object Q. The smallest distance is denoted as the lower-bound distance between Q and the metric region (O_i, r_{O_i}):

$$d_{min}(T(O_i)) = max\{0, d(O_i, Q) - r_{O_i}\}$$

During k-NN query execution, requests from PR are being processed in the priority order, i.e. the request with smallest lower-bound distance goes first.

NN Array. The NN array contains k entries of form either $[oid(O_i), d(Q, O_i)]$ or $[-, d_{max}(T(O_i))]$. The array is sorted according to ascending distance values. Entry of form $[oid(O_i), d(Q, O_i)]$ on the j-th position in NN represents a candidate object O_i for the j-th nearest neighbour. In the second case (i.e. entry of form $[-, d_{max}(T(O_i))]$), the value $d_{max}(T(O_i))$ represents upper-bound distance between Q and objects in subtree $T(O_i)$ (in which some k-NN candidates could be stored). The upper-bound distance $d_{max}(T(O_i))$ is defined as:

$$d_{max}(T(O_i)) = d(O_i, Q) + r_{O_i}$$

Since NN is a sorted array containing the k nearest neighbours candidates (or at least upper-bound distances of the still relevant subtrees), the dynamic query radius r_Q can be determined as the current distance stored in the last entry NN[k]. During the query processing, only the closer candidates (or smaller upper-bound distances) are inserted into NN array, i.e. such candidates, which are currently located inside the dynamic query region (Q, r_Q).

After insertion into NN, the query radius r_Q is decreased (because NN[k] entry was replaced). The priority queue PR must contain only the (still) relevant subtrees, i.e. such subtrees the regions of which overlap the dynamic query region (Q, r_Q). Hence, after the dynamic radius r_Q is decreased, all irrelevant requests (for which $d_{min}(T(O_i)) > r_Q$) must be deleted from PR.

At the beginning of k-NN search, the NN candidates are unknown, thus all entries in the NN array are set to $[-, \infty]$. The query processing starts at the root level, so that $[ptr(root), \infty]$ is the first and only request in PR. For a more detailed description of the k-NN query algorithm we refer to [7, 10].

Note: The k-NN query algorithm is optimal in I/O costs, since it only accesses nodes, the metric regions of which overlap the query region $(Q, d(Q, \text{NN}[k].d_{max}))$. In other words, the I/O costs of a k-NN query (Q, k) and I/O costs of the equivalent range query $(Q, d(Q, \text{NN}[k].d_{max}))$ are equal.

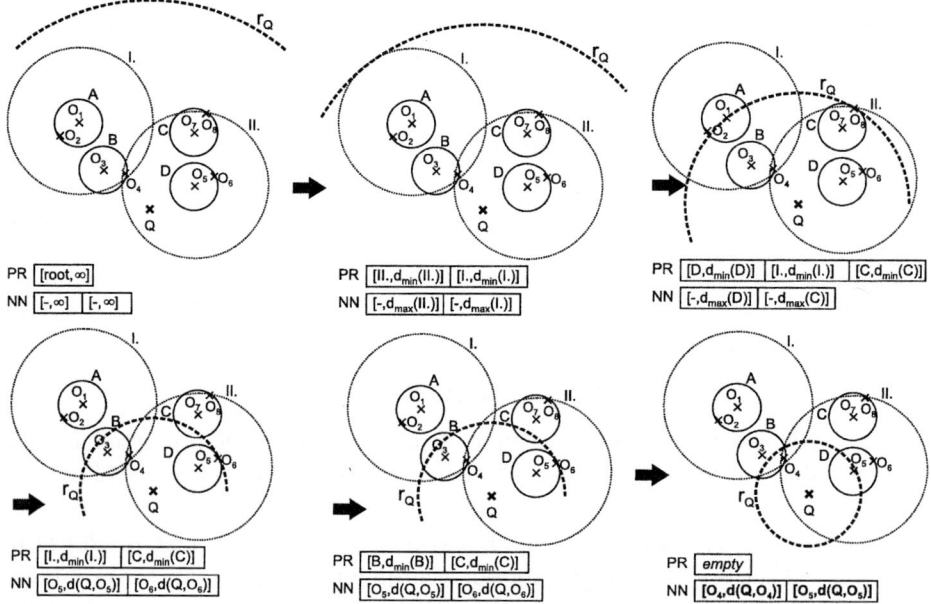

Fig. 2. An example of 2-NN search in M-tree

Example 1

In Figure 2 see an example of 2-NN query processing. Each of the depicted phases shows the content of PR queue and NN array, right before processing a request from PR. Due to the decreasing query radius r_Q, the dynamic query region (Q, r_Q) (represented by bold-dashed line) is reduced down to $(Q, d(Q, O_5))$. Note the algorithm accesses 5 nodes (processing of single request in PR involves a single node access), while the equivalent range query takes also 5 node accesses.

3 PM-Tree

Each metric region in M-tree is described by a bounding hyper-sphere. However, the shape of hyper-sphere is far from optimal, since it does not bound the data objects tightly together and the region "volume" is too large. Relatively to the hyper-sphere volume, there are only "few" objects spread inside the hyper-sphere – a huge proportion of dead space [1] is covered. Consequently, for hyper-spherical regions the probability of overlap with query region grows, thus query processing becomes less efficient. This observation was the major motivation for introduction of the *Pivoting M-tree* (PM-tree) [12, 10], an extension of M-tree.

3.1 Structure of PM-Tree

Some metric access methods (e.g. AESA, LAESA [4, 6]) exploit *global static pivots*, i.e. objects to which all objects of the dataset $\mathbb{S}$ (all parts of the index structure respectively) are related. The global pivots actually represent "anchors" or "viewpoints", due to which better filtering of irrelevant data objects is possible.

In PM-tree, the original M-tree hierarchy of hyper-spherical regions (driven by local pivots) is combined with so-called *hyper-ring regions*, centered in global pivots. Since PM-tree is a generalization of M-tree, we just describe the new facts instead of a comprehensive definition. First of all, a set of p global pivots $P_t \in \mathbb{S}$ must be chosen. This set is fixed for all the lifetime of a particular PM-tree index. A routing entry in PM-tree inner node is defined as:

$$rout_{PM}(O_i) = [O_i, ptr(T(O_i)), r_{O_i}, d(O_i, \text{Par}(O_i)), \text{HR}]$$

The new HR attribute is an array of p_{hr} intervals ($p_{hr} \leq p$), where the t-th interval HR[t] is the smallest interval covering distances between the pivot P_t and each of the objects stored in leaves of $T(O_i)$, i.e. HR[t] = $\langle$HR[t].min, HR[t].max$\rangle$, HR[t].min = $min\{d(O_j, P_t)\}$, HR[t].max = $max\{d(O_j, P_t)\}$, $\forall O_j \in T(O_i)$. The interval HR[t] together with pivot P_t define a hyper-ring region (P_t,HR[t]); a hyper-spherical region (P_t,HR[t].max) reduced by a "hole" (P_t,HR[t].min).

Since each hyper-ring region (P_t, HR[t]) defines a metric region bounding *all* the objects stored in $T(O_i)$, the intersection of all the hyper-rings and the hyper-sphere forms a metric region bounding *all* the objects in $T(O_i)$ as well. Due to the intersection with hyper-sphere, the PM-tree metric region is always smaller than the original hyper-spherical region. The probability of overlap between PM-tree region and query region is smaller, thus the search becomes more efficient (see Figure 3). A ground entry in PM-tree leaf is defined as:

$$grnd_{PM}(O_i) = [O_i, oid(O_i), d(O_i, \text{Par}(O_i)), \text{PD}]$$

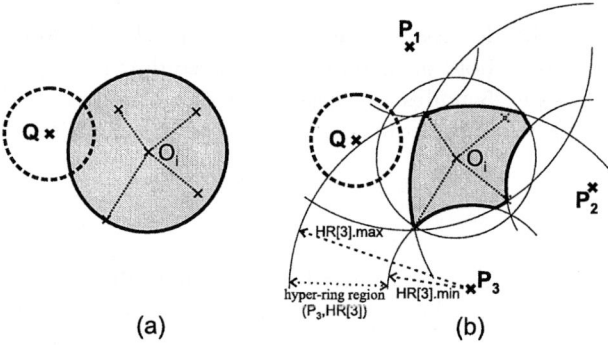

Fig. 3. (a) Region of M-tree. (b) Region of PM-tree (sphere reduced by 3 hyper-rings)

The new PD attribute stands for an array of p_{pd} pivot distances ($p_{pd} \leq p$) where the t-th distance PD[t] = $d(O_i, P_t)$. The distances PD[t] between data objects and the global pivots are used for simple sequential filtering in leaves, as it is accomplished in LAESA-like methods. For details concerning PM-tree construction as well as representation and storage of the hyper-ring intervals (HR and PD arrays) we refer to [12, 10].

3.2 Choosing the Global Pivots

Problems about choosing the global pivots have been intensively studied for a long time [9, 3, 2]. In general, we can say that pivots should be far from each other (close pivots give almost the same information) and outside data clusters. Distant pivots cause increased variance in distance distribution [4] (the dataset is "viewed" from different "sides"), which is reflected in better filtering properties.

We use a cheap but effective method of pivots choice, described as follows. First, m groups of p objects are randomly sampled from the dataset $\mathbb{S}$, each group representing a candidate set of pivots. Second, such group of pivots is chosen, for which the sum of distances between objects is maximal.

3.3 Similarity Queries in PM-Tree

The distances $d(Q, P_t), \forall t \leq max(p_{hr}, p_{pd})$ have to be computed before the query processing itself is started. The query is processed by accessing nodes, the regions of which are overlapped by the query region (similarly as M-tree is queried, see Section 2.1). A PM-tree node is accessed if the query region overlaps *all* the hyper-rings stored in the parent routing entry. Hence, prior to the standard hyper-sphere overlap check (used by M-tree), the overlap of hyper-rings HR[t] against the query region is tested as follows (no additional distance is computed):

$$\bigwedge_{t=1}^{p_{hr}} d(Q, P_t) - r_Q \leq \text{HR}[t].\text{max} \wedge d(Q, P_t) + r_Q \geq \text{HR}[t].\text{min} \qquad (1)$$

If the above condition is false, the subtree $T(O_i)$ is not relevant to the query, and can be excluded from further processing. At the leaf level, an irrelevant ground entry is determined such that the following condition is not satisfied:

$$\bigwedge_{t=1}^{p_{pd}} |d(Q, P_t) - \text{PD}[t]| \leq r_Q \tag{2}$$

In Figure 3 see that M-tree region cannot be filtered out, but PM-tree region can be excluded from the search, since the hyper-ring HR[2] is not overlapped.

4 Nearest Neighbours Search in PM-Tree

The hyper-ring overlap condition (1) can be integrated into the original M-tree's range query as well as into k-NN query algorithms. In case of range query the adjustment is straightforward – the hyper-ring overlap condition is combined with the original hyper-sphere overlap condition (we refer to [12]).

The M-tree's k-NN algorithm can be modified for the PM-tree, we only need to respect the changed region shape. As in the range query algorithm, the check for overlap between the query region and a PM-tree region is combined with the hyper-ring overlap condition (1). Furthermore, to obtain an *optimal* k-NN algorithm, there must be adjusted the lower-bound distance d_{min} (used by PR queue) and the upper-bound distance d_{max} (used by NN array), as follows.

The requests $[ptr(T(O_i)), d_{min}(T(O_i))]$ in PR represent the relevant subtrees $T(O_i)$ to be examined, i.e. such subtrees, the parent metric regions of which overlap the dynamic query region (Q, r_Q). Taking the hyper-rings HR[t] of a PM-tree region into account, the lower-bound distance is possibly increased, as:

$$d_{min}(T(O_i)) = max\{0, d(O_i, Q) - r_{O_i}, d^{low}_{HRmax}, d^{low}_{HRmin}\}$$

$$d^{low}_{HRmax} = max \bigcup_{t=1}^{p_{hr}} \{d(P_t, Q) - \text{HR}[t].max\} \quad d^{low}_{HRmin} = max \bigcup_{t=1}^{p_{hr}} \{\text{HR}[t].min - d(P_t, Q)\}$$

where $max\{d^{low}_{HRmax}, d^{low}_{HRmin}\}$ determines the lower-bound distance between the query object Q and objects located in the farthest hyper-ring. Comparing to M-tree's k-NN algorithm, the lower-bound distance $d_{min}(T(O_i))$ for a PM-tree region can be additionally increased, since the farthest hyper-ring contains all the objects stored in $T(O_i)$.

The entries $[oid(O_i), d(Q, O_i)]$ or $[-, d_{max}(T(O_i))]$ in NN represent the current k candidates for nearest neighbours (or at least the still relevant subtrees). Taking the hyper-rings HR[t] into account, the upper-bound distance $d_{max}(T(O_i))$ is possibly decreased, as:

$$d_{max}(T(O_i)) = min\{d(O_i, Q) + r_{O_i}, d^{up}_{HR}\} \quad d^{up}_{HR} = min \bigcup_{t=1}^{p_{hr}} \{d(P_t, Q) + \text{HR}[t].max\}$$

where d_{HR}^{up} determines the upper-bound distance between the query object Q and objects located in the nearest hyper-ring.

In summary, the modification of M-tree's k-NN algorithm for the PM-tree differs in the overlap condition, which has to be additionally combined with the hyper-ring overlap check (1) and (2), respectively. Another difference is in the construction of $d_{max}(T(O_i))$ and $d_{min}(T(O_i))$ bounds.

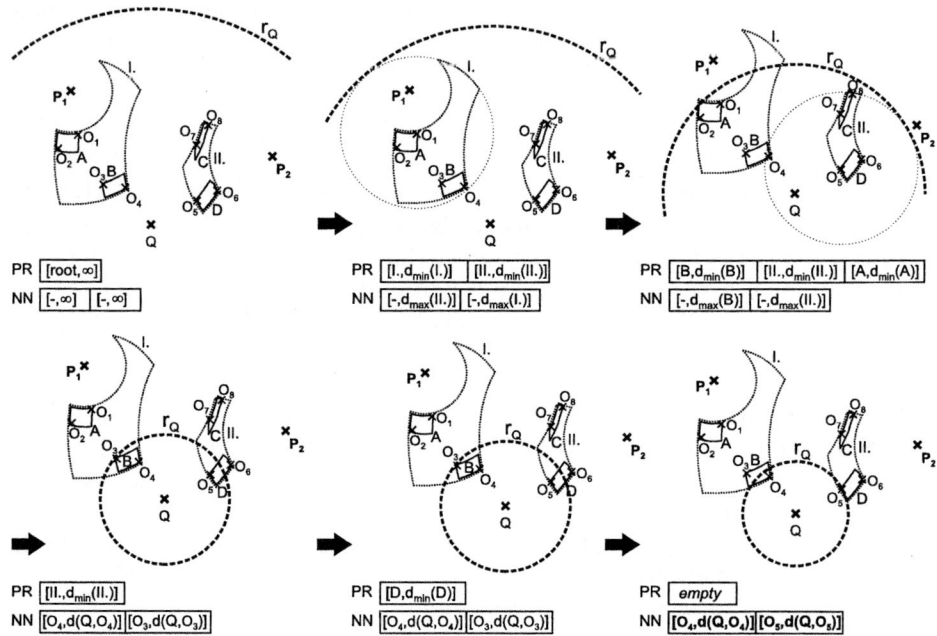

Fig. 4. An example of 2-NN search in PM-tree

Example 2

In Figure 4 see an example of 2-NN query processing. The PM-tree hierarchy is the same as the M-tree hierarchy presented in Example 1, but the query processing runs a bit differently. Although in this particular example both the M-tree's and the PM-tree's k-NN query algorithms access 4 nodes, searching the PM-tree saves one insertion into the PR queue.

Note: Like the M-tree's k-NN query algorithm, also the PM-tree's k-NN query algorithm is optimal in I/O costs, since it only accesses those PM-tree nodes, the metric regions of which overlap the query region $(Q, d(Q, \text{NN}[k].d_{max}))$. This is guaranteed (besides usage of the hyper-ring overlap check) by correct modification of lower/upper distance bounds stored in PR queue and NN array.

5 Experimental Results

In order to evaluate the performance of k-NN search, we present some experiments made on large synthetic as well as real-world vector datasets. The query objects were selected randomly from each respective dataset, while each particular test consisted of 1000 queries (the results were averaged). Euclidean (L_2) metric was used in all tests. The I/O costs were measured as the number of logic disk page retrievals. The experiments were aimed to compare PM-tree with M-tree – a comparison with other MAMs was out of scope of this paper.

Abbreviations in Figures. Each label of form "PM-tree(x,y)" stands for a PM-tree index where $p_{hr} = $ x and $p_{pd} = $ y. A label "<index> + SlimDown" denotes an index subsequently post-processed by the slim-down algorithm [11, 10].

5.1 Synthetic Datasets

For the first set of experiments, a collection of 8 synthetic vector datasets of increasing dimensionality (from $D = 4$ to $D = 60$) was generated. Each dataset (embedded inside unitary hyper-cube) consisted of 100,000 D-dimensional tuples

Table 1. PM-tree index statistics (synthetic datasets)

Construction methods: SingleWay + MinMax (+ SlimDown)	
Dimensionalities: 4,8,16,20,30,40,50,60	Inner node capacities: 10 – 28
Index file sizes: 4.5 MB – 55 MB	Leaf node capacities: 16 – 36
Pivot file sizes: 2 KB – 17 KB	Avg. node utilization: 66%
Node (disk page) sizes: 1 KB ($D = 4, 8$), 2 KB ($D = 16, 20$), 4 KB ($D \geq 30$)	

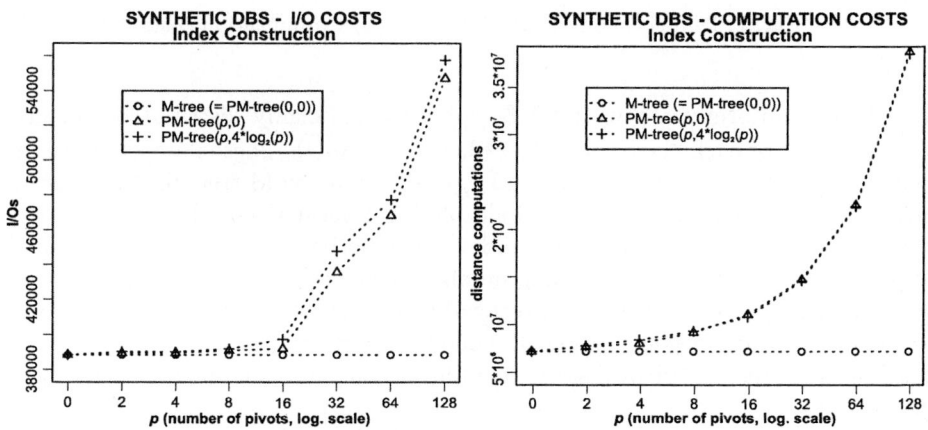

Fig. 5. Number of pivots: (a) I/O costs. (b) Computation costs

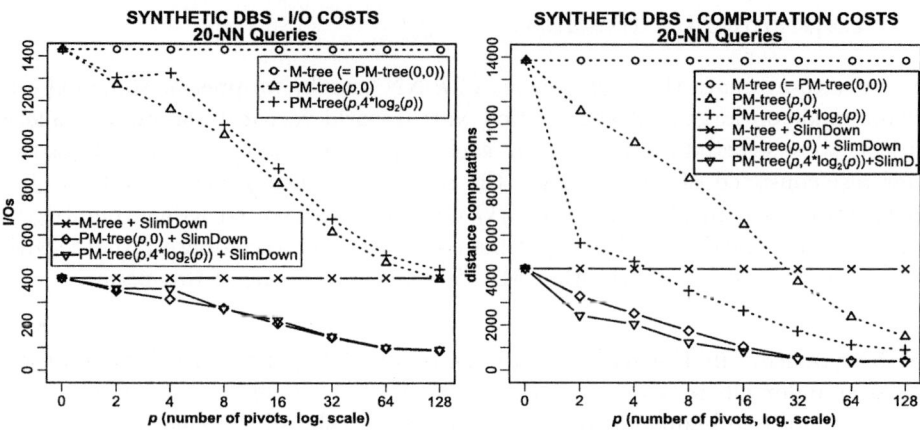

Fig. 6. Number of pivots: (a) I/O costs. (b) Computation costs

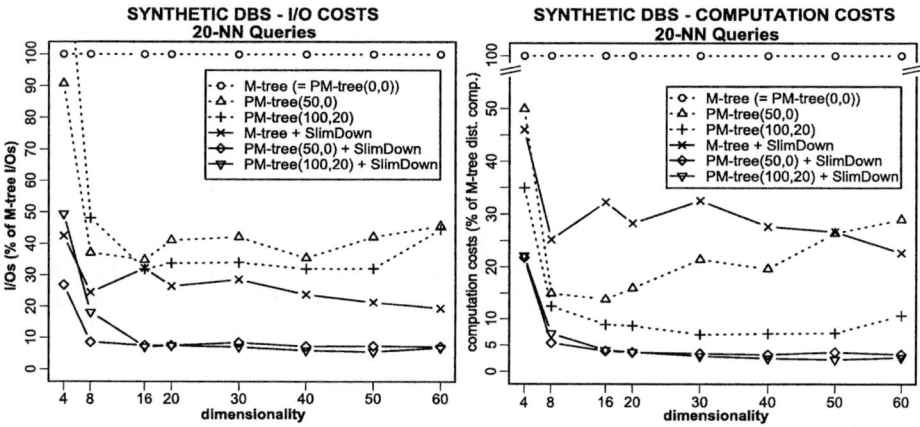

Fig. 7. Dimensionality: (a) I/O costs. (b) Computation costs

distributed uniformly among 1000 L_2-spherical uniformly distributed clusters. The diameter of each cluster was $\frac{d^+}{10}$ (where $d^+ = \sqrt{D}$). These datasets were indexed by PM-tree (for various p_{hr} and p_{pd}) as well as by M-tree. Some statistics about the created indices are shown in Table 1 (for details see [11]). Prior to k-NN experiments, in Figure 5 we present index construction costs (for 30-dimensional indices), according to the increasing number of pivots. The increasing I/O costs depend on the hyper-ring storage overhead (the storage ratio of PD or HR arrays to the data vectors becomes higher), while the increasing computation costs depend on the object-to-pivot distance computations performed before each object insertion.

In Figure 6 the 20-NN search costs (for 30-dimensional indices) according to the number of pivots are presented. The I/O costs rapidly decrease with the increasing number of pivots. Moreover, the PM-tree is superior even after postprocessing by the slim-down algorithm. The decreasing trend of computation costs is even quicker than of I/O costs, see Figure 6b.

The influence of increasing dimensionality D is depicted in Figure 7. Since the disk pages for different (P)M-tree indices were not of the same size, the I/O costs as well as the computation costs are related (in percent) to the I/O costs (CC resp.) of M-tree indices. For $8 \leq D \leq 40$ the I/O costs stay approximately fixed, for $D > 40$ they slightly increase. In case of $D = 4$, the higher PM-tree I/O costs are caused by higher hyper-ring storage overhead.

5.2 Image Database

For the second set of experiments, a collection of approx. 10,000 web-crawled images [13] was used. Each image was converted into 256-level gray scale and a frequency histogram was extracted. As indexed objects the histograms (256-dimensional vectors) were used. The index statistics are presented in Table 2.

Table 2. PM-tree index statistics (image database)

Construction methods: SingleWay + MinMax (+ SlimDown)	
Dimensionality: 256	Inner node capacities: 10 – 31
Index file sizes: 16 MB – 20 MB	Leaf node capacities: 29 – 31
Pivot file sizes: 4 KB – 1 MB	Avg. node utilization: 67%
Node (disk page) size: 32 KB	

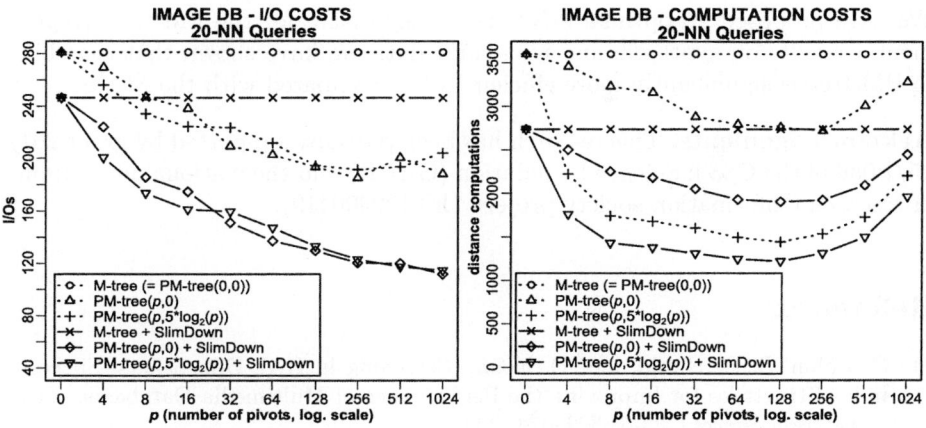

Fig. 8. Number of pivots: (a) I/O costs. (b) Computation costs

In Figure 8a the I/O search costs for increasing number of pivots are presented. The computation costs (see Figure 8b) for $p \leq 64$ decrease. However, for $p > 64$ the overall computation costs grow, since the number of necessarily computed query-to-pivot distances (i.e. p distance computations for each query) is proportionally too large. Nevertheless, this observation is dependent on the

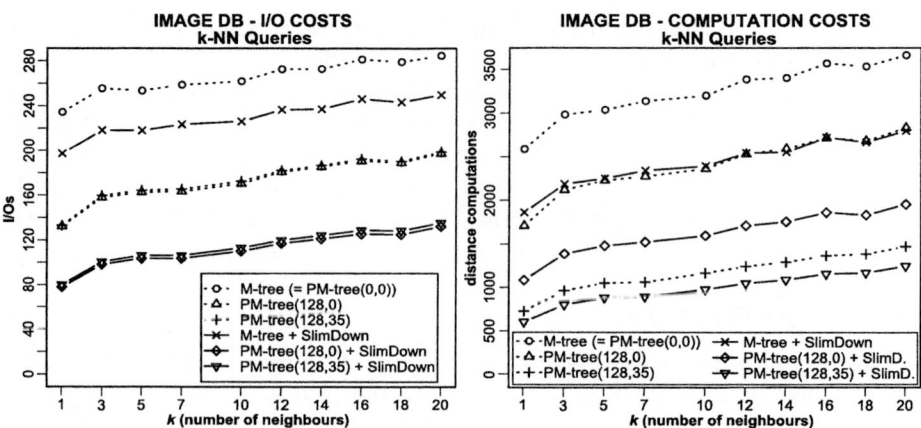

Fig. 9. Number of neighbours: (a) I/O costs. (b) Computation costs

database size – obviously, for million of images the proportion of p query-to-pivot distance computations would be smaller, when compared with the overall computation costs. Finally, the costs according to the increasing number of nearest neighbours are presented in Figure 9.

6 Conclusions

We have proposed an optimal k-NN search algorithm for the PM-tree. Experimental results on synthetic and real-world datasets have shown that searching in PM-tree is significantly more efficient, when compared with the M-tree.

Acknowledgements. This research has been partially supported by grant 201/05/P036 of the Czech Science Foundation (GAČR) and the National programme of research (Information society project 1ET100300419).

References

1. C. Böhm, S. Berchtold, and D. Keim. Searching in High-Dimensional Spaces – Index Structures for Improving the Performance of Multimedia Databases. *ACM Computing Surveys*, 33(3):322–373, 2001.
2. B. Bustos, G. Navarro, and E. Chávez. Pivot selection techniques for proximity searching in metric spaces. *Pattern Recognition Letters*, 24(14):2357–2366, 2003.
3. E. Chávez. Optimal discretization for pivot based algorithms. Manuscript. ftp://garota.fismat.umich.mx/pub/users/elchavez/minimax.ps.gz, 1999.
4. E. Chávez, G. Navarro, R. Baeza-Yates, and J. Marroquín. Searching in Metric Spaces. *ACM Computing Surveys*, 33(3):273–321, 2001.
5. P. Ciaccia, M. Patella, and P. Zezula. M-tree: An Efficient Access Method for Similarity Search in Metric Spaces. In *Proceedings of the 23rd Athens Intern. Conf. on VLDB*, pages 426–435. Morgan Kaufmann, 1997.

6. M. L. Micó, J. Oncina, and E. Vidal. A new version of the nearest-neighbour approximating and eliminating search algorithm (aesa) with linear preprocessing time and memory requirements. *Pattern Recognition Letters*, 15(1):9–17, 1994.
7. M. Patella. *Similarity Search in Multimedia Databases*. PhD thesis, University of Bologna, 1999.
8. N. Roussopoulos, S. Kelley, and F. Vincent. Nearest neighbor queries. In *Proceedings of the 1995 ACM SIGMOD International Conference on Management of Data, San Jose, CA*, pages 71–79, 1995.
9. M. Shapiro. The choice of reference points in best-match file searching. *Commun. ACM*, 20(5):339–343, 1977.
10. T. Skopal. *Metric Indexing in Information Retrieval*. PhD thesis, Technical University of Ostrava, http://urtax.ms.mff.cuni.cz/~skopal/phd/thesis.pdf, 2004.
11. T. Skopal, J. Pokorný, M. Krátký, and V. Snášel. Revisiting M-tree Building Principles. In *Proceedings of the 7th East-European Conference on Advances in Databases and Information Systems (ADBIS), Dresden, Germany, LNCS 2798, Springer-Verlag*, pages 148–162, 2003.
12. T. Skopal, J. Pokorný, and V. Snášel. PM-tree: Pivoting Metric Tree for Similarity Search in Multimedia Databases. In *Local proceedings of the 8th East-European Conference on Advances in Databases and Information Systems (ADBIS), Budapest, Hungary*, pages 99–114, 2004.
13. WBIIS project: Wavelet-based Image Indexing and Searching, Stanford University, http://wang.ist.psu.edu/.

Deputy Mechanism for Workflow Views*

Zhe Shan[1], Qing Li[1], Yi Luo[2], and Zhiyong Peng[2]

[1] Department of Computer Engineering and Information Technology,
City University of Hong Kong, Kowloon, Hong Kong
{zshan0, itqli}@cityu.edu.hk
[2] State Key Lab of Software Engineering, Wuhan University, Wuhan, China
luo_guo02@hotmail.com, zypeng@public.wh.hb.cn

Abstract. Adapted from the concept of views in databases, workflow views are derived from workflows as a fundamental support for workflow inter-operability and visibility by external parties in a e-service environment. However, until now there are few works focusing on its realization mechanism, i.e. the communication between views and their source entities. In this paper, we extend the object deputy model to the workflow deputy model supporting the interaction of workflow views in a systematic way. In this workflow deputy model, we formally specify the deputy class and the deputy algebra for workflow classes. According to the process meta-model of XPDL, deputy operations are defined for each kind of workflow component class specifically. Based on this deputy mechanism, workflow views are presented in forms of deputy classes. Lastly, several modeling issues are discussed.

1 Introduction

Workflow views [6] are derived from workflows as the fundamental support for workflow inter-operability and visibility by external parties [7][5]. The components of a workflow view include the process flow graph, input/output parameters, documents, and so on, which are also contained in a workflow. Hence, workflow view encloses the information about business process structure and contents. Based on specific business collaborations, a company may derive corresponding workflow views based on the local workflow system. Such a workflow view includes all the necessary information of the company for this business. It can be used as the interaction interface in a business transaction which is carried out with external parties. However, until now there is no formal modeling mechanism existing for defining and executing workflow views.

In our previous work [11], the object deputy model [8] was adopted to support the functions of workflow views. In a SmallTalk based environment, workflow components were added to support the workflow functions and the realization of workflow views. In

---

* This research is supported by the State Key Lab of Software Engineering (Wuhan University, China) under grant: SKLSE03-01, National Natural Science Foundation of China (60273072,60473076) and Hubei Natural Science Foundation for Distinguished Youth (2002AC003).

this paper we further extend the object deputy model and formally define the workflow deputy model as shown in Figure 1. In this model, we formally define workflow algebra classes based on general workflow classes. Then, workflow deputy algebra is designed, which includes four operations: Project, Extend, Union and Join. In XPDL, the underlying process model of our work, there are seven kinds of components. And, each kind of components has different properties. Hence, specific workflow component deputy class is defined for each of them. Lastly, workflow views are presented in forms of deputy classes.

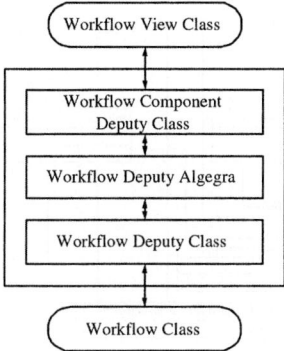

Fig. 1. Workflow View Model based on Deputy Mechanism

The remainder of the paper is organized as follows. Section 2 details the workflow deputy model, which includes workflow deputy class, workflow deputy algebra, workflow component deputy class and workflow view class. Section 3 discusses semantic constraints and structure conformance issues. Section 4 investigates the works related to this paper and Section 5 concludes the paper with future research issues.

2 Workflow Deputy Model

2.1 Underlying Process Model

XML Process Definition Language (XPDL) [12] is the language proposed by the Workflow Management Coalition (WfMC) to interchange process definitions between different workflow products. XPDL has been widely accepted in the workflow community and has been adopted by many commercial and open-source workflow products. In this work, we adopt XPDL as the process model of workflow views.

The Meta-model describes the top-level entities contained within a workflow definition, and their relationships and attributes. The top-level entities are shown in Figure 2. The *Workflow Process Definition* entity provides contextual information that applies to other entities within the process. A process definition consists of one or more *Workflow Process Activity*, each comprising a logical, self-contained unit of work within the process. Activities are related to one another via flow control conditions (*Transition*

Information). *Workflow Participant Declaration* provides descriptions of resources that can act as the performer of the various activities in the process definition. *Workflow Application Declaration* provides descriptions of the IT applications or interfaces which may be invoked by the workflow service to support, or to wholly automate, the processing associated with each activity and/or identified within the activity by an application assignment attribute (or attributes). *Workflow Relevant Data* defines the data that is created and used within each process instance during process execution.

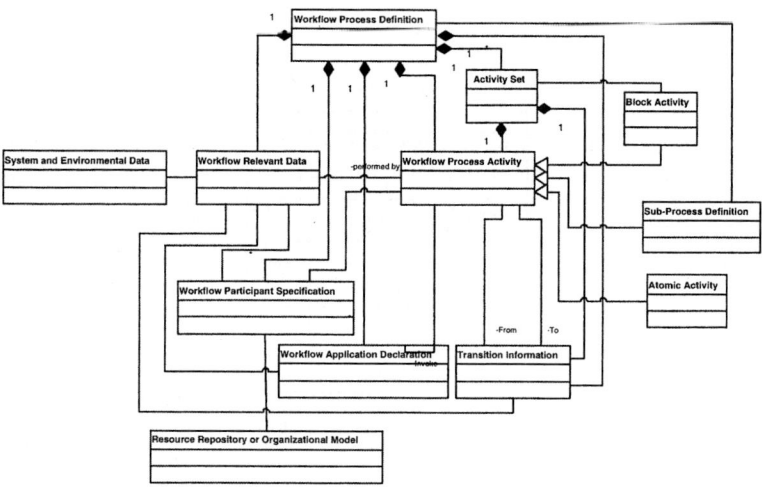

Fig. 2. XPDL Workflow Process Meta-model

2.2 Workflow Deputy Class

According to the meta-model in Figure 2, there are seven basic component classes for entities, which are *Process Class* ($\overset{p}{C}$), *Activity Class* ($\overset{a}{C}$), *Transition Class* ($\overset{t}{C}$), *Participant Class* ($\overset{r}{C}$), *Application Class* ($\overset{c}{C}$), *Relevant Data Class* ($\overset{d}{C}$), and *Activity Set Class* ($\overset{s}{C}$). A workflow definition W is defined as a set of these classes, namely $W = (\overset{p}{C}, \{\overset{a}{C}\}, \{\overset{t}{C}\}, \{\overset{r}{C}\}, \{\overset{c}{C}\}, \{\overset{d}{C}\}, \{\overset{s}{C}\})$. All these classes are called *Workflow Classes*, which are different from the general classes of the OO paradigm. Workflow classes have no method but they have two kinds of properties, one is called *attribute* which describes the class and the other is called *list* which shows the composition or some complicated properties of the class. The formal definition of Workflow Classes is given immediately below.

Definition 1. *Each workflow object has an identifier, attributes, and lists. Schema of objects with the same attributes and lists is defined by a workflow class which consists of a name, an extent and a type. The extent of a class is a set of objects belonging to it, called its instances. The type of a class consists definitions of its attributes and lists. A class named as C is represented as:*

$$C = \langle \{o\}, \{T_a : a\}, \{l : \{T_e : e\}\}\rangle$$

1. $\{o\}$ is the extent of C, where o is an instance of C.
2. $\{T_a : a\}$ is the set of attribute definitions of C, where a and T_a represent name and type of an attribute, respectively. The value of attribute a of object o is expressed by $o.a$. For each attribute $T_a : a$, there are two basic methods: $read(o, a)$ for reading $o.a$ and $write(o, a, v)$ for writing $o.a$ with the new value v, expressed as follows:

$$read(o, a) \Rightarrow \uparrow o.a$$

$$write(o, a, v) \Rightarrow o.a := v$$

Here, $\Rightarrow$, $\uparrow$ and $:=$ stand for operation invoking, result returning and assignment, respectively.

3. $\{l : \{T_e : e\}\}$ is a list of various properties, where l and $\{T_e : e\}$ are list name and a set of elements included in this list. For each element $T_e : e$, there are also two basic methods: $read(o, l.e)$ for reading $o.l.e$ and $write(o, l.e, v)$ for writing $o.l.e$ with the new value v, expressed as follows:

$$read(o, l.e) \Rightarrow \uparrow o.l.e$$

$$write(o, l.e, v) \Rightarrow o.l.e := v$$

Workflow deputy objects are defined as an extension and customization of workflow objects. An workflow object can have many deputy objects that are used to customize workflow objects for different applications or represent many facets of its nature (e.g. specialization, generalization, and aggregation). The schemas of deputy objects are defined by deputy classes that are derived by creating deputy objects as their instances, generating switching operations for inheritance of attributes and lists, and adding definitions for their additional attributes and lists. A formal definition of deputy objects and deputy classes is given as follows.

Definition 2. *A deputy object is defined based on object(s) or other deputy object(s). The latter is called source object(s) of the former. A deputy object must inherit some attributes from its source object. The schema of deputy objects with the same properties is defined by a deputy class, which includes a name, extent and type. Deputy classes are derived from classes of source objects called source classes. In general, let* $C^s = \langle \{o^s\}, \{T_{a^s} : a^s\}, \{l^s : \{T_{e^s} : e^s\}\}\rangle$ *be a source class. Its deputy class* C^d *is defined as:*

$$C^d = \langle \{o^d | (o^d \to o^s) \vee (o^d \to \cdots \times o^s \times \cdots) \vee (o^d \to \{o^s\}),$$

$$pp(o^s) \vee jp(\cdots \times o^s \times \cdots) \vee up(\{o^s\}) == true\},$$

$$\{T_{a^d} : a^d\} \cup \{T_{a^d_+} : a^d_+\}, \{l^d : \{T_{e^d} : e^d\}\} \cup \{l^d_+ : \{T_{e^d_+} : e^d_+\}\}\rangle$$

1. $\{o^d | (o^d \to o^s) \vee (o^d \to \cdots \times o^s \times \cdots) \vee (o^d \to \{o^s\}), pp(o^s) \vee jp(\cdots \times o^s \times \cdots) \vee up(\{o^s\}) == true\}$ is the extent of C^d, where $(o^d \to o^s) \vee (o^d \to \cdots \times o^s \times \cdots) \vee (o^d \to \{o^s\})$ representing the o^d is the deputy object of o^s, $\cdots \times o^s \times \cdots$ or $\{o^s\}$; pp, jp and up represent project, join and union predicate, respectively.

2. $\{T_{a^d} : a^d\} \cup \{T_{a^d_+} : a^d_+\}$ is the set of attribute definitions of C^d.
   (a) $\{T_{a^d} : a^d\}$ is the set of the attributes inherited from $\{T_{a^s} : a^s\}$ of C^s, of which switching operations are defined as:
   $$read(o^d, a^d) \Rightarrow\uparrow f_{T_{a^s} \mapsto T_{a^d}}(read(o^s, a^s)),$$
   $$write(o^d, a^d, v^d) \Rightarrow write(o^s, a^s, f_{T_{a^d} \mapsto T_{a^s}}(v^d))$$
   (b) $\{T_{a^d_+} : a^d_+\}$ is the set of the additional attributes of C^d, of which the basic methods are defined as:
   $$read(o^d, a^d_+) \Rightarrow\uparrow o^d.a^d_+,$$
   $$write(o^d, a^d_+, v^d_+) \Rightarrow o^d.a^d_+ := v^d_+$$
3. $\{l^d : \{T_{e^d} : e^d\}\} \cup \{l^d_+ : \{T_{e^d_+} : e^d_+\}\}$ is the set of list definitions of C^d.
   (a) $\{l^d : \{T_{e^d} : e^d\}\}$ is the set of the lists inherited from $\{l^s : \{T_{e^s} : e^s\}\}$ of C^s, of which switching operations are defined as:
   $$read(o^d, l^d.e^d) \Rightarrow\uparrow f_{T_{e^s} \mapsto T_{e^d}}(read(o^s, l^s.e^s)),$$
   $$write(o^d, l^d.e^d, v^d) \Rightarrow write(o^s, l^s.e^s, f_{T_{e^d} \mapsto T_{e^s}}(v^d))$$
   (b) $\{l^d_+ : \{T_{e^d_+} : e^d_+\}\}$ is the set of the additional lists of C^d, of which the basic methods are defined as:
   $$read(o^d, l^d_+.e^d_+) \Rightarrow\uparrow o^d.l^d_+.e^d_+,$$
   $$write(o^d, l^d_+.e^d_+, v^d_+) \Rightarrow o^d.l^d_+.e^d_+ := v^d_+$$

2.3 Workflow Deputy Algebra

A deputy class is derived by creating deputy objects as its instances, generating switching operations for inheritance of attributes and lists, and adding definitions for its additional attributes and lists. The object deputy model provides an object deputy algebra for deputy class derivation, which consists of the following four operations.

The **Project** operation is used to derive a deputy class which only inherits part of attributes and lists of a source class.

Definition 3. Let $C^s = \langle\{o^s\}, \{T_{a^s} : a^s\}, \{l^s : \{T_{e^s} : e^s\}\}\rangle$ be a source class, $\{T_{a^s_-} : a^s_-\}$ and $\{l^s_- : \{T_{e^s_-} : e^s_-\}\}$ be subsets of attributes and lists of C^s that can be inherited. A deputy class derived by the **Project** operation is represented as $C^d = \mathbf{Project}(C^s, \{T_{a^s_-} : a^s_-\}, \{l^s_- : \{T_{e^s_-} : e^s_-\}\})$, where

1. The extent of C^d is the set of deputy objects of instances of C^s, expressed as
$$\{o^d | o^d \to o^s\}$$

2. The set of attributes of C^d is defined as $\{T_{a^d_-} : a^d_-\}$, which are inherited from the attributes $\{T_{a^s_-} : a^s_-\}$ of C^s. The switching operations for inheriting $T_{a^s_-} : a^s_-$ in the form of $T_{a^d_-} : a^d_-$ are realized in the following way:
$$read(o^d, a^d_-) \Rightarrow\uparrow f_{T_{a^s_-} \mapsto T_{a^d_-}}(read(o^s, a^s_-)),$$
$$write(o^d, a^d_-, v^d_-) \Rightarrow write(o^s, a^s_-, f_{T_{a^d_-} \mapsto T_{a^s_-}}(v^d_-))$$

3. The set of lists of C^d is defined as $\{l_-^d : \{T_{e_-^d} : e_-^d\}\}$, which are inherited from the lists $\{l_-^s : \{T_{e_-^s} : e_-^s\}\}$ of C^s. The switching operations for inheriting $l_-^d : \{T_{e_-^d} : e_-^d\}$ in form of $l_-^s : \{T_{e_-^s} : e_-^s\}$ are realized in the following way:

$$read(o^d, l_-^d.e_-^d) \Rightarrow\uparrow f_{T_{e_-^s} \mapsto T_{e_-^d}}(read(o^s, l_-^s.e_-^s)),$$
$$write(o^d, l_-^d.e_-^d, v_-^d) \Rightarrow write(o^s, l_-^s.e_-^s, f_{T_{e_-^d} \mapsto T_{e_-^s}}(v_-^d))$$

The **Extend** operation is used to derive a deputy class of which instances are extended which additional attributes and lists that can not be derived from a source class.

Definition 4. *Let* $C^s = \langle\{o^s\}, \{T_{a^s} : a^s\}, \{l^s : \{T_{e^s} : e^s\}\}\rangle$ *be a source class,* $\{T_{a_+^d} : a_+^d\}$ *and* $\{l_+^d : \{T_{e_+^d} : e_+^d\}\}$ *be sets of additional attributes and lists. A deputy class derived by the* **Extend** *operation is represented as* $C^d = \textbf{Extend}(C^s, \{T_{a_+^d} : a_+^d\}, \{l_+^d : \{T_{e_+^d} : e_+^d\}\})$.

1. The extent of C^d is the set of deputy objects of instances of C^s, expressed as:

$$\{o^d | o^d \to o^s\}$$

2. The set of attributes of C^d is defined as union of attributes $\{T_{a^d} : a^d\}$ inherited from the attributes $\{T_{a^s} : a^s\}$ of C^s and its additional attributes $\{T_{a_+^d} : a_+^d\}$, expressed as $\{T_{a^d} : a^d\} \cup \{T_{a_+^d} : a_+^d\}$.

   (a) The switching operations for inheriting $T_{a^s} : a^s$ in form of $T_{a^d} : a^d$ are realized in the following way:

   $$read(o^d, a^d) \Rightarrow\uparrow f_{T_{a^s} \mapsto T_{a^d}}(read(o^s, a^s)),$$
   $$write(o^d, a^d, v^d) \Rightarrow write(o^s, a^s, f_{T_{a^d} \mapsto T_{a^s}}(v^d))$$

   (b) For each additional attribute $T_{a_+^d}$, the following two basic methods are realized, which are operated independently of the source object:

   $$read(o^d, a_+^d) \Rightarrow\uparrow o^d.a_+^d,$$
   $$write(o^d, a_+^d, v_+^d) \Rightarrow o^d.a_+^d := v_+^d$$

3. The set of lists of C^d is defined as the union of lists $\{l^d : \{T_{e^d} : e^d\}\}$ inherited from the lists $\{l^s : \{T_{e^s} : e^s\}\}$ of C^s and its additional lists $\{l_+^d : \{T_{e_+^d} : e_+^d\}\}$, expressed as $\{l^d : \{T_{e^d} : e^d\}\} \cup \{l_+^d : \{T_{e_+^d} : e_+^d\}\}$.

   (a) The switching operations for inheriting $l^s : \{T_{e^s} : e^s\}$ in the form of $l^d : \{T_{e^d} : e^d\}$ are realized in the following way:

   $$read(o^d, l^d.e^d) \Rightarrow\uparrow f_{T_{e^s} \mapsto T_{e^d}}(read(o^s, l^s.e^s)),$$
   $$write(o^d, l^d.e^d, v^d) \Rightarrow write(o^s, l^s.e^s, f_{T_{e^d} \mapsto T_{e^s}}(v^d))$$

   (b) For each additional list $l_+^d : \{T_{e_+^d} : e_+^d\}$, the following two basic methods are realized, which are operated independently of the source object:

   $$read(o^d, l_+^d.e_+^d) \Rightarrow\uparrow o^d.l_+^d.e_+^d,$$

$$write(o^d, l^d_+.e^d_+, v^d_+) \Rightarrow o^d.l^d_+.e^d_+ := v^d_+$$

The **Union** operation is used to derive a deputy class of which the extent consists of deputy objects of instances of more than one source class.

Definition 5. Let $C_1^s = \langle \{o_1^s\}, \{T_{a_1^s} : a_1^s\}, \{l_1^s : \{T_{e_1^s} : e_1^s\}\}\rangle, ..., C_m^s = \langle \{o_m^s\}, \{T_{a_m^s} : a_m^s\}, \{l_m^s : \{T_{e_m^s} : e_m^s\}\}\rangle$ be source classes, $\{T_{a^s} : a^s\} = \{T_{a_1^s} : a_1^s\} \cap ... \cap \{T_{a_m^s} : a_m^s\}$ and $\{l^s : \{T_{e^s} : e^s\}\} = \{l_1^s : \{T_{e_1^s} : e_1^s\}\} \cap ... \cap \{l_m^s : \{T_{e_m^s} : e_m^s\}\}$ be common sets of attributes and lists of $C_1^s,...,C_m^s$. A deputy class derived by the **Union** operation is represented as $C^d = \mathbf{Union}(C_1^s, ..., C_m^s)$, where

1. The extent of C^d is the union of sets of deputy objects of instances of $C_1^s,...,C_m^s$, expressed as:

$$\{o_1^d | o_1^d \to o_1^s\} \cup ... \cup \{o_m^d | o_m^d \to o_m^s\}$$

2. The set of attributes of C^d is defined as $\{T_{a^d} : a^d\}$, which are inherited from the common attributes $T_{a^s} : a^s$ of $C_1^s,...,C_m^s$. The switching operations for inheriting $T_{a^s} : a^s$ in form of $T_{a^d} : a^d$ are realized in the following way:

$$read(o_1^d, a^d) \Rightarrow \uparrow f_{T_{a^s} \mapsto T_{a^d}}(read(o_1^s, a^s)),$$
$$write(o_1^d, a^d, v^d) \Rightarrow write(o_1^s, a^s, f_{T_{a^d} \mapsto T_{a^s}}(v^d))$$
$$...$$
$$read(o_m^d, a^d) \Rightarrow \uparrow f_{T_{a^s} \mapsto T_{a^d}}(read(o_m^s, a^s)),$$
$$write(o_m^d, a^d, v^d) \Rightarrow write(o_m^s, a^s, f_{T_{a^d} \mapsto T_{a^s}}(v^d))$$

3. The set of lists of C^d is defined as $\{l^d : \{T_{e^d} : e^d\}\}$, which are inherited from the common lists $\{l^s : \{T_{e^s} : e^s\}\}$ of $C_1^s,...,C_m^s$. The switching operations for inheriting $l^s : \{T_{e^s} : e^s\}$ in the form of $l^d : \{T_{e^d} : e^d\}$ are realized in the following way:

$$read(o_1^d, l^d.e^d) \Rightarrow \uparrow f_{T_{e^s} \mapsto T_{e^d}}(read(o_1^s, l^s.e^s)),$$
$$write(o_1^d, l^d.e^d, v^d) \Rightarrow write(o_1^s, l^s.e^s, f_{T_{e^d} \mapsto T_{e^s}}(v^d))$$
$$...$$
$$read(o_m^d, l^d.e^d) \Rightarrow \uparrow f_{T_{e^s} \mapsto T_{e^d}}(read(o_m^s, l^s.e^s)),$$
$$write(o_m^d, l^d.e^d, v^d) \Rightarrow write(o_m^s, l^s.e^s, f_{T_{e^d} \mapsto T_{e^s}}(v^d))$$

The **Join** operation is used to derive a deputy class of which instances are deputy objects for aggregating instances of source classes according to a join predicate.

Definition 6. Let $C_1^s = \langle \{o_1^s\}, \{T_{a_1^s} : a_1^s\}, \{l_1^s : \{T_{e_1^s} : e_1^s\}\}\rangle, ..., C_n^s = \langle \{o_n^s\}, \{T_{a_n^s} : a_n^s\}, \{l_n^s : \{T_{e_n^s} : e_n^s\}\}\rangle$ be source classes. A deputy class derived by the **Join** operation is represented as $C^d = \mathbf{Join}(C_1^s, ..., C_n^s, jp)$, where

1. jp is a join predicate.
2. The extent of C^d is the set of deputy objects of aggregations of instances of $C_1^s, ..., C_n^s$, satisfying the join predicate jp, expressed as:

$$\{o^d | o^d \to o_1^s \times ... \times o_n^s, jp(o_1^s \times ... \times o_n^s) == true\}$$

3. The set of attributes of C^d is defined as the union of attribute sets $\{T_{a_1^d} : a_1^d\}, \ldots,$ $\{T_{a_n^d} : a_n^d\}$ inherited from $C_1^s, \ldots, C_n^s$ respectively, and is expressed as $\{T_{a_1^d} : a_1^d\} \cup \ldots \{T_{a_n^s} : a_n^d\}$. The switching operations for attributes $\{T_{a_1^d} : a_1^d\}$ of $C_1^s, \ldots, \{T_{a_n^s} : a_n^s\}$ of C_n^s are realized in the following way:

$$read(o^d, a_1^d) \Rightarrow \uparrow f_{T_{a_1^s} \mapsto T_{a_1^d}}(read(o_1^s, a_1^s)),$$
$$write(o^d, a_1^d, v_1^d) \Rightarrow write(o_1^s, a_1^s, f_{T_{a_1^d} \mapsto T_{a_1^s}}(v_1^d))$$
$$\ldots$$
$$read(o^d, a_n^d) \Rightarrow \uparrow f_{T_{a_n^s} \mapsto T_{a_n^d}}(read(o_n^s, a_n^s)),$$
$$write(o^d, a_n^d, v_n^d) \Rightarrow write(o_n^s, a_n^s, f_{T_{a_n^d} \mapsto T_{a_n^s}}(v_n^d))$$

4. The set of lists of C^d is defined as the union of list set $\{l_1^d : \{T_{e_1^d} : e_1^d\}\}, \ldots, \{l_n^d : \{T_{e_n^d} : e_n^d\}\}$ inherited from $C_1^s, \ldots, C_n^s$ respectively, and is expressed as $\{l_1^d : \{T_{e_1^d} : e_1^d\}\} \cup \cdots \cup \{l_n^d : \{T_{e_n^d} : e_n^d\}\}$. The switching operations for lists $\{l_1^d : \{T_{e_1^d} : e_1^d\}\}, \ldots, \{l_n^d : \{T_{e_n^d} : e_n^d\}\}$ respectively inherited from the lists $\{l_1^s : \{T_{e_1^s} : e_1^s\}\}$ of $C_1^s, \ldots, \{l_n^s : \{l_n^s : \{T_{e_n^s} : e_n^s\}\}$ of c_n^s are realized in the following way:

$$read(o^d, l_1^d.e_1^d) \Rightarrow \uparrow f_{T_{e_1^s} \mapsto T_{e_1^d}}(read(o_1^s, l_1^s.e_1^s)),$$
$$write(o^d, l_1^d.e_1^d, v_1^d) \Rightarrow write(o_1^s, l_1^s.e_1^s, f_{T_{e_1^d} \mapsto T_{e_1^s}}(v_1^d))$$
$$\ldots$$
$$read(o^d, l_n^d.e_n^d) \Rightarrow \uparrow f_{T_{e_n^s} \mapsto T_{e_n^d}}(read(o_n^s, l_n^s.e_n^s)),$$
$$write(o^d, l_n^d.e_n^d, v_n^d) \Rightarrow write(o_n^s, l_n^s.e_n^s, f_{T_{e_n^d} \mapsto T_{e_n^s}}(v_n^d))$$

The result of each of the above operations is a deputy class that can be manipulated by algebra operations(i.e. deputy classes have first-class citizen status and can be used as source classes for deriving new deputy classes); which achieves the same flexibility as the relational algebra. Specialization can be realized by the algebraic operations $Project$ and $Extend$, generalization can be realized by $Union$, and aggregation can be realized by $Join$.

2.4 Workflow Component Deputy Class

According to the introduction in Section 2.1, there are seven kinds of workflow component classes, which have different semantics. Each kind of component classes has different sets of attributes and lists. Therefore, considering workflow views, only specific operations are allowed on each of them.

1. **Process, Activity and Transition**

    For process, activity and transition, let $\overset{x}{C^s} = \langle \{o^s\}, \{T_{a^s} : a^s\}, \{l^s : \{T_{e^s} : e^s\}\}\rangle$ be a source process class. Some of its attributes and lists may be disclosed, but others may be protected, i.e., **Project**($\overset{x}{C^s}, \{T_{a_-^s} : a_-^s\}, \{l_-^s : \{T_{e_-^s} : e_-^s\}\}$). The deputy process class may have some additional attributes and lists, which are not included in the source class, i.e., **Extend**($\overset{x}{C^s}, \{T_{a_+^d} : a_+^d\}, \{l_+^d : \{T_{e_+^d} : e_+^d\}\}$). A deputy process class may also involve several source classes which are connected in some activities (as in the case of cross-organizational workflows), i.e., $\mathbf{Join}(\overset{x}{C_1^s}, ..., \overset{p}{C_n^s}, jp)$. Therefore, the deputy class of these component classes $\overset{x}{C^d}$ is defined as:

$$\overset{x}{C^d} = \{\overset{x}{C} \mid \overset{x}{C} = \mathbf{Project}(\overset{x}{C^s}, \{T_{a^s_-} : a^s_-\}, \{l^s_- : \{T_{e^s_-} : e^s_-\}\})$$
$$\vee \overset{x}{C} = \mathbf{Extend}(\overset{x}{C^s}, \{T_{a^d_+} : a^d_+\}, \{l^d_+ : \{T_{e^d_+} : e^d_+\}\})$$
$$\vee \overset{x}{C} = \mathbf{Join}(\overset{x}{C_1^s}, ..., \overset{x}{C_n^s}, jp)\}, where\ x = p,\ a\ or\ t.$$

2. **Participant and Application**

For participant and application, let $\overset{x}{C^s} = \langle \{o^s\}, \{T_{a^s} : a^s\}, \{l^s : \{T_{e^s} : e^s\}\} \rangle$ be a source participant class. The deputy class of these component classes $\overset{x}{C^d}$ can thus be defined as:

$$\overset{x}{C^d} = \{\overset{x}{C} \mid \overset{x}{C} = \mathbf{Project}(\overset{x}{C^s}, \{T_{a^s_-} : a^s_-\}, \{l^s_- : \{T_{e^s_-} : e^s_-\}\})$$
$$\vee \overset{x}{C} = \mathbf{Extend}(\overset{x}{C^s}, \{T_{a^d_+} : a^d_+\}, \{l^d_+ : \{T_{e^d_+} : e^d_+\}\})$$
$$\vee \overset{x}{C} = \mathbf{Union}(\overset{x}{C_1^s}, ..., \overset{x}{C_m^s})\}, where\ x = r\ or\ c.$$

3. **Relevant Data and Activity Set**

For relevant data and activity set, let $\overset{x}{C^s} = \langle \{o^s\}, \{T_{a^s} : a^s\}, \{l^s : \{T_{e^s} : e^s\}\} \rangle$ be a source relevant data class. The deputy class of these component classes $\overset{x}{C^d}$ is therefore defined as:

$$\overset{x}{C^d} = \{\overset{x}{C} \mid \overset{x}{C} = \mathbf{Project}(\overset{x}{C^s}, \{T_{a^s_-} : a^s_-\}, \{l^s_- : \{T_{e^s_-} : e^s_-\}\})$$
$$\vee \overset{x}{C} = \mathbf{Extend}(\overset{x}{C^s}, \{T_{a^d_+} : a^d_+\}, \{l^d_+ : \{T_{e^d_+} : e^d_+\}\}), where\ x = d\ or\ s.$$

2.5 Deputy Class for Workflow View

This section presents the definitions of restricted views and composition views, which are two fundamental categories in the taxonomy of workflow views. They provide a framework for the definition and development of further detailed categories of workflow views.

As introduced in Section 2.3, the result of each operation is a deputy class that can be manipulated by deputy algebra operations (i.e., deputy classes can be used as source classes for deriving new deputy classes). In order to simplify the descriptions in the following paragraphs, we define the iterative deputy operation of workflow classes. Let $\overset{w}{C^s}$ be a source workflow class, its iterative deputy operation $\overset{w}{C^{d^*}}$ is defined as:

$$\overset{w}{C^{d^*}} = \{\overset{w}{C} \mid \overset{w}{C} = \overset{w}{C^s} \vee \overset{w}{C} = \overset{w}{C^d} \vee \overset{w}{C} = (\overset{w}{C^d})^d \vee ... \vee \overset{w}{C} = ((\overset{w}{C^d})^{d...})^d\},$$

where

$$w = p, a, t, r, c, d\ or\ s.$$

As a workflow restriction view is a structurally correct subset of a workflow definition, it can be defined as the interface for such purposes as internal control, external interaction, etc.

Definition 7. Let $W = (\overset{p}{C}, \{\overset{a}{C}\}, \{\overset{t}{C}\}, \{\overset{r}{C}\}, \{\overset{c}{C}\}, \{\overset{d}{C}\}, \{\overset{s}{C}\})$ be a workflow definition. Its restriction workflow view W_r^v is defined as

$$W_r^v = (\overset{p}{C^{d^*}}, \{\overset{a}{C^{d^*}}\}, \{\overset{t}{C^{d^*}}\}, \{\overset{r}{C^{d^*}}\}, \{\overset{c}{C^{d^*}}\}, \{\overset{d}{C^{d^*}}\}, \{\overset{s}{C^{d^*}}\})$$

On the other hand, a workflow composition view is a virtual workflow composed of properties from different workflows, which may span across organizational boundaries.

Definition 8. Let $W_1 = (\overset{p}{C_1}, \{\overset{a}{C_1}\}, \{\overset{t}{C_1}\}, \{\overset{r}{C_1}\}, \{\overset{c}{C_1}\}, \{\overset{d}{C_1}\}, \{\overset{s}{C_1}\}),..., W_m = (\overset{p}{C_m}, \{\overset{a}{C_m}\}, \{\overset{t}{C_m}\}, \{\overset{r}{C_m}\}, \{\overset{c}{C_m}\}, \{\overset{d}{C_m}\}, \{\overset{s}{C_m}\})$ be a set of workflow definitions. Their composition workflow view W_c^v is defined as

$$W_c^v = (\overset{p}{C_J^d}, \{\overset{a}{C_1^{d^*}}, ..., \overset{a}{C_m^{d^*}}\}, \{\overset{t}{C_1^{d^*}}, ..., \overset{t}{C_m^{d^*}}\}, \{\overset{r}{C_1^{d^*}}, ..., \overset{r}{C_m^{d^*}}\}, \{\overset{c}{C_1^{d^*}}, ..., \overset{c}{C_m^{d^*}}\}, \{\overset{d}{C_1^{d^*}}, ..., \overset{d}{C_m^{d^*}}\}, \{\overset{s}{C_1^{d^*}}, ..., \overset{s}{C_m^{d^*}}\}),$$

where

$$\overset{p}{C_J^d} = \textbf{Join}(\overset{p}{C_1^{d^*}}, ..., \overset{p}{C_m^{d^*}}, jp)$$

3 Remarks on Modeling Related Issues

3.1 Semantic Constraints

There are several semantic constraints between objects and their deputy objects that are defined as predicates of deputy classes: 1) Existence Dependence (i.e. only when the source object satisfies some special condition, its deputy object can exist); 2) Key Equivalence (sometimes, the key equivalence between objects and their deputy objects is required in order to avoid generating deputy objects that have no relationships with their source objects); 3) Indirect Relativity (i.e. where there are semantic constraints between deputy objects of the same objects). In order to enforce these semantic constraints to maintain consistencies between deputy objects and their source objects, data update propagations between deputy objects and their source objects need to be supported. The following data update propagations are supported by the workflow deputy model: a) Updates on the source objects should be reflected in their deputy objects; b) Updates on the deputy objects should be propagated to their source objects. Hence, both directions of update propagation can follow automatically if updates do not cause dynamic classification, namely, addition and deletion of deputy objects of an object. There are three basic types of update operations which may cause dynamic classification, these being addition, deletion of an object and modification of attribute values of an object.

3.2 Structure Conformance

Same as workflows, workflow views should be structurally correct, which means activities and transitions are well connected and the activity-transition net satisfies some predefined requirements. For example, in the specification of XPDL, *loop-blocked* means that the activities and transitions of a workflow definition form an acyclic graph. Although we have provided the deputy mechanism for workflow views, it can not prevent workflow views from these structural problems. Additional tools similar to the verification tools provided for the design of workflows are needed to test the structural correctness of workflow view definitions. The details of such facilities and their implementations are out of the scope of this paper.

4 Related Work

There have been some earlier works in the area of workflow views. Liu and Shen [9] presented an algorithm to construct a process view from a given workflow, but did not discuss its correctness with respect to inter-organizational workflows. A preliminary approach of workflow views has been presented in [6]. From then, workflow views have been utilized as a beneficial approach to support the interactions of business processes in E-service environment [7][5]. However, most of these works focused on the conceptual level. The realization issues are largely neglected. Van der Aalst and Kumar [2] presented an approach to workflow schema exchange in an XML dialect called XRL but it does not include the support for workflow views. Besides, van der Aalst [1] modelled inter-organizational workflows and the inter-organizational communication structures by means of Petri Nets and message sequence charts (MSCs), respectively. The soundness and consistency of the inter-organizational workflow can be analyzed by checking the consistency of Petri Nets against target MSCs. Since the author abstracted from data and external triggers, the proposed communication protocol is not as complete as the inter-operation protocol presented in the workflow view approach [5]. To address the derivation of private workflows from inter-organizational workflows, Van der Aalst and Weske [3] used the concept of workflow projection inheritance introduced in [4]. A couple of derivation rules are proposed so that a derived workflow is behaviorally bisimilar to the original workflow based on branching semantics, in contrast to the trace semantics adopted in the workflow view model.

Until now, these is few work on the realization mechanism of workflow views. [10] considered communication aspects of workflow views in terms of state dependencies and control flow dependencies. They proposed to tightly couple private workflow and workflow view with state dependencies, whilst to loosely couple workflow views with control flow dependencies. A Petri-Net-based state transition method was proposed to bind states of private workflow tasks to their adjacent workflow view-task. This approach only consider the state aspect of workflow views. Moreover, it is difficult to accomplish the explicit modelling of state mapping. Against it, our workflow deputy model is a much more comprehensive and systematic solution.

5 Conclusion

Workflow views are derived from workflows as a fundamental support for workflow interoperability and visibility by external parties in a web services environment. However, until now there are no formal mechanisms existing for defining and executing workflow views. In this paper, we extended the object deputy model [8] to the workflow deputy model, supporting the realization of workflow views. After introducing the background of workflow views, we formally defined the deputy class and the deputy algebra (viz. Project, Extend, Union and Join) for workflow classes. Then, specific deputy operations were designed for each kind of workflow component classes. Based on these operations, we presented the realization workflow views through the deputy mechanism. Lastly, we discussed two modeling related issues.

Our future work will focus on the workflow view enactment with public E-services environments, such as ebXML and BPEL4WS. We are especially interested in the data management issues occurring in the B2B enactment interface.

References

1. W.M.P. van der Aalst. Interorganizational workflows: An approach based on message sequence charts and petri nets. *Systems Analysis - Modelling - Simulation*, 34(3):335–367, 1999.
2. W.M.P. van der Aalst and A. Kumar. Xml based schema definition for support of inter-organizational workflow. *Information Systems Research*, 14(1):23–46, 2003.
3. W.M.P. van der Aalst and M. Weske. The p2p approach to interorganizational workflows. In *13th International Conference Advanced Information Systems Engineering (CAiSE 2001)*, volume 2068 of *Springer LNCS*, pages 140–156, Interlaken, Switzerland, 2001.
4. T. Basten and W.M.P. van der Aalst. Inheritance of behavior. *Journal of Logic and Algebraic Programming*, 47:47–145, 2001.
5. Dickson K.W. Chiu, S.C. Cheung, Sven Till, Kamalakar Karlapalem, Qing Li, and Eleanna Kafeza. Workflow view driven cross-organizational interoperability in a web service environment. *Information Technology and Management*, to appear, 2005.
6. Dickson K.W. Chiu, Kamalakar Karlapalem, and Qing Li. Views for inter-organization workflow in an e-commerce environment. In *Semantic Issues in E-Commerce Systems, IFIP TC2/WG2.6 Ninth Working Conference on Database Semantics*, Hong Kong, 2001. Kluwer.
7. Dickson K.W. Chiu, Kamalakar Karlapalem, Qing Li, and Eleanna Kafeza. Workflow view based e-contracts in a cross-organizational e-services environment. *Distributed and Parallel Databases*, 12(2-3):193–216, 2002.
8. Yahiko Kambayashi and Zhiyong Peng. An object deputy model for realization of flexible and powerful objectbases. *Journal of Systems Integration*, 6:329–362, 1996.
9. Duen-Ren Liu and Minxin Shen. Modeling workflows with a process-view approach. In *Database Systems for Advanced Applications, 2001. Proceedings. Seventh International Conference on*, pages 260–267, 2001.
10. Karsten A. Schulz and Maria E. Orlowska. Facilitating cross-organisational workflows with a workflow view approach. *Data & Knowledge Engineering*, 51(1):109–147, 2004.
11. Zhe Shan, Zhiyi Long, Yi Luo, and Zhiyong Peng. Object-oriented realization of workflow views for web services - an object deputy model based approach. In *The Fifth International Conference on Web Age Information Management, WAIM 2004*, LNCS 3129. Springer-Verlag, 2004.
12. XPDL. Xml process definition language, http://www.wfmc.org/standards/xpdl.htm.

Automatic Data Extraction from Data-Rich Web Pages

Dongdong Hu and Xiaofeng Meng

School of Information
Renmin University of China
{hudd, xfmeng}@ruc.edu.cn

Abstract. Extracting data from web pages using wrappers is a fundamental problem arising in a large variety of applications of vast practical interests. In this paper, we propose a novel technique to the problem of differentiating roles of data items from Web pages, which is one of the key problems in our automatic extraction approach. The problem is resolved at various levels: semantic blocks, sections and data items, and several approaches are proposed to effectively identify the mapping between data items having the same role. Intensive experiments on real web sites show that the proposed technique can effectively help extracting desired data with high accuracies in most of the cases.

1 Introduction

The World Wide Web has become one of the most important connections of various information sources. A large proportion of data on the web is embedded in various HTML documents. The HTML language serves the visual presentation of data in Web browsers, while it is not suitable for automated, computer-assisted information management systems. This is not expected to change soon, even when XML is more and more popular today. Thus if data from different sources needs to be integrated, it is necessary to develop special and often complex programs to extract data from Web pages. To achieve this goal, people have developed *wrappers*, which are specialized programs that can automatically extract data from web pages and convert the information into a structured format.

There have been many works on semi-automatic and manual data extraction [1][2][3][4][5], in the past years. These approaches require human interactions to build sample mappings between the output results (or schemas) and items in the HTML pages, after that extraction rules will be induced for extracting pages having similar structures. Besides the flexibility of these approaches, there are still many challenges in constructing such wrappers. Firstly, the user should have good knowledge of contents in the web pages and should try to select more proper samples to cover more possible situations; also, another important problem is how to maintain existing wrappers if the corresponding web pages take changes on their layouts.

There still exists several other automatic approaches, Exalg [6] and Roadrunner [7], which can automatically extract data from *data-intensive* [7] web sites. Pages from data-intensive sites are created through encoding values, from the underground database, into web pages using templates [6]. In other words, such pages usually have the same schema and accordingly similar structures. Either Roadrunner or Exalg use the structure information of sample pages to induce HTML tags-based templates (see Section 5). A template covers the constant parts of the HTML sources' string sequence, and the left parts which are variant are viewed as the right data to be extracted.

```
5. Head First Java
Our Low Price: $26.56  ▶BUY NOW
Availability:  In Stock: Usually Ships in 1 to 2 business days
Authors: Bates, Bert & Allen, Robbie & Sierra, Kathy
Publish Date: 5/1/2003  Format: Paperback
```
(a) Sample 1

```
33. Java
Our Low Price: $8.05    ▶BUY NOW
Availability: Pre-Order Now: Get Yours First!
Author: Periplus  Publisher: Periplus Editions
Publish Date: 7/1/2004  Format: Calendar
```
(b) Sample 2

```
26. Oracle Database 10g XML & SQL: Design, Build, & Manage XML
Applications in Java, C, C++, & PL/SQL
Our Low Price: $39.89  ▶BUY NOW
Availability: Pre-Order Now: Get Yours First!
Authors: Mark Scardina & Jinyu Wang & Ben
Chang   Publisher: Osborne/McGraw-Hill
Publish Date: 6/1/2004  Format: Paperback
```
(c) Sample 3

Fig. 1. Sample HTML fragments from Buy

Unlike the previous work described above, we propose a novel automatic approach to generate wrappers without any user interactions. Firstly we break up the problem of automatically constructing a wrapper into four subproblems:

1. Discovering blocks (called *semantic block* in this paper, which corresponds to an instance of the schema) containing data to be extracted from sample pages;
2. Differentiating roles of data items in the semantic blocks;
3. Inducing schema describing the contents in the pages;
4. Computing extraction rule and generating wrappers.

Among these four steps, a simple way to tackle problem (1) is to use a technique of tree comparing for discovering data-rich sections [8]. For example, in Fig. 1 are three extracted blocks from sample pages from www.buy.com. Problem (3) is introduced in [9], and problem (4) is widely discussed in almost all the previous work of data extraction. In the previous work [3] we proposed an XQuery [10] based extraction rule system. Our work focuses on problem (2), which serves as the key step for the extraction problem. Once we have got a set of semantic blocks, which can be viewed as a set of instances of the schema, which describes the contents in the page, to be induced in the next step. To induce the schema from the instances, we firstly differentiate the roles of data items in them. In other words, for a data item in a sematic block, we want to find out the data items taking the same role, corresponding to the same schema element, in all other semantic blocks. For example, referring to Fig. 1, the items of "Head First Java" and "Thinking in Java with CDROM" are both corresponded to the schema element Title. The process of differentiating roles are named *Identification* in this paper. After all the data items are identified, each one is assigned a label indicating its role. Data items having the same roles have the same labels. Note that the label here does not provide any semantic information, but a symbol representing the role of a data item.

This paper is structured as follows. In the next section the challenges of we faces and some preliminary knowledge is described, in section 3 we introduce the technique of simple identification. Section 4 discusses the complex identification, and section 5 compares our work to the related work. In section 6 we report the experimental results. Finally in section 7 we highlight the conclusion and future research direction.

2 Challenges and Our Approach

The HTML pages are parsed into a tree representation in our work. Considering the DOM [11] model, a non-leaf node corresponds to a pair of HTML tags, such as "<tr>...</tr>". Nodes are ordered according to their occurrence sequence in the HTML page. Each leaf node is either of type PCDATA, or a single tag such as "<tr>". All the values are contained in the text nodes, and can be uniquely defined to be an element in the tree with an XPath [12] expression.

An important characteristic of pages belonging to the same site and encoding data of the same schema, is that the data encoding is done in a consistent manner across the pages. For example, in Fig. 1 each of the three fragments represents a record from database and is a *semantic block* conforming to the same schema {Book{Title, Price, Availability, Author|Authors{Person+}, Publisher?, PubTime?, Format}}. Intuitively a semantic block of a schema can be viewed as an instance of the corresponding schema in the web pages. In the semantic blocks are a set of data items without being identified their roles. For example, from Fig. 1(a) we get the following data items: "Head First Java", "Our Low Price:", "$26.56", "Availability:", ..., "Paperback". Here some text nodes are not included, e.g. text nodes containing the sequence number of the record, and text nodes containing only the symbol '&'.

As we saw in Fig. 1, the underlying schema for the contents of pages contains three kinds of special situations: iterations, optionals and disjunctions. To induce a schema which can precisely describe the data in the pages, we should be able to detect all these three situations when identifying data items.

Iterations means that the instances of these schema elements can iteratively appear in the page. Iterations are the most common cases in the real web pages, e.g. the element Person in the schema for Fig. 1.

Optionals indicate the cases that given a schema element, we cannot find corresponding data values in every semantic blocks. Optionals are represented by the cardinality "?". For instance, the element Publisher in in the schema describing Fig. 1 is optional.

Disjunctions can be represented by "|", e.g. "$a|b$", which means at the corresponding relative position can be "a" or "b", but only one of them. An example for disjunction is in Figure 1, which used Author for single author, while Authors for multi-authors. As to the corresponding schema, there can be a schema element of Author|Authors.

3 Simple Identification via HTML Path

The simple identification handles the situation that the pages have relatively regular layouts. From the point of tree structure, the pages that simple identification faces have the common feature that all the data items of the same role have the same HTML paths(in XPath [12] expressions), which start from the roots of the subtrees containing the semantic blocks and end at the nodes of the data items. Based on this characteristic, the following rule are used for identification data items in such pages.

Rule of HTML Path: Two data items with the same HTML path inside the semantic blocks have the same role.

Our experiments reveal that pages from most of web sites can be simply identified by this rule. For instance, pages from CDplus (http://www.cdplus.com, see Fig. 2) can be perfectly identified using this rule, each semantic block of which takes a row in the table and the data items having the same role locate in the same column, correspondingly with the same HTML path inside the semantic block.

Beach Boys	Today!/Summer Days (And Summer (CD)	3/20/2001	Cdn$18.49 (US$13.70)
Beatles	A Hard Days Night (CD)	1/1/1990	Cdn$18.99 (US$14.07)
Benet, Eric	A Day In The Life (CD)	4/27/1999	Cdn$17.49 (US$12.96)
Bet.E And Stef	Day By Day (CD)	10/1/2002	Cdn$18.49 (US$13.70)

Fig. 2. Fragment of sample pages from CDPlus.com

4 Complex Identification

Some situations that cannot be handled by simple identification, e.g. items with same role but different HTML paths, or different roles but with the same HTML path, are resolved in complex identification. The complex identification tries to divide the semantic blocks into smaller cells for improving the reliability of identification, thus the identification can be conducted inside matched cells without having to deal with the entire semantic blocks. This guarantees that the identification will not completely fail if the blocks can be divided.

Firstly we give the definition of *Occurrence Path*. An occurrence-path [6] of a data item is the path from the root to the certain node in the HTML tree. The only difference between an HTML path and a Occurrence path is that the former has predicates in the path expression. Our experiments show that data items having different occurrence paths usually have various roles in most of the complex pages. Two neighboring data items are divided into two *path-groups* if they do not have the same occurrence path. For instance, the three co-authors are assigned in one path-group for their common occurrence paths //table/tr/td/#text.

4.1 Block Segmentation Using Template Items

Based on the observation that web pages are designed to be consumed by human users, and therefore they usually contain text strings, i.e. annotations (labels) [14] [15], whose goal is to explicate to the final user the intentional meaning of the published data [13]. These kinds of strings are used to divide the semantic blocks into small cells in our approach.

Discovering Possible Template Items. The items in the semantic blocks can be classified into two categories: (*i*) Template items, which may be contents of the template of the pages, e.g. annotations, or some invariant strings; (*ii*) Data values, which are the exact values we want to extract from web pages.

The following features are used to find template items from the semantic blocks:

1. Template items of the same role have the same value in all the semantic blocks if occurring.
2. Template items of the same role have the same occurrence paths inside the semantic blocks.
3. The syntactic features, mainly the patterns of the template items in the semantic blocks are usually similar. For instance, all the annotations in 1 start with a capital letter and end with a colon.

The algorithm for searching possible template items starts from one of the blocks, and scans all other semantic blocks for discovering candidates by checking the above features. Meanwhile, all the discovered candidates are sorted by the order they occur in the semantic blocks. Turning to the example pages in Fig. 1, we get seven possible template items with their occurring order: "Our Low Price:", "Availability:", "Author:", "Authors:", "Publisher:", "Publish Date:", "Format:". We also get a list of template items from each semantic block. Note that in this step it is not necessary to precisely find out all the template items. The key purpose of the possible template items are used to divide semantic blocks into smaller sections for future operations.

Dividing Semantic Blocks into Sections Using Template Items. Since the discovered template items are expected to repeatedly occur in the semantic blocks. They can be used as markers to divide the semantic blocks to smaller sections. Furthermore, from the point of visual effect, sections between common template items' pair provide similar information.

Before dividing the real semantic blocks, we firstly build a *full-division* on all the possible template items. The full-division confirms that each template item may have a section containing data items on each of both sides. Fig. 3 shows the full-division of the example in Fig. 1, in which each section is assigned an ID using the sequence number.

Thus each semantic block is divided by comparing the list of discovered template items with the full-division (suppose the function $Id(section)$ gets the ID of a section).

1. For each pair of neighboring template items t_i and t_{i+1} in a semantic block, we first find out all the sections $\{s_j, ..., s_k\}$ contained between t_i and t_{i+1} in the full-

division. After that, the ID of the section s' between t_i and t_{i+1} is assigned to be $(Id(s_j)\text{-}Id(s_k))$;
2. As to the section s' just before the first template item t_0 in the semantic blocks, we first find the section s_j just before t_0 in the full-division, then the ID of s_0 is assigned to be $(0\text{-}Id(s_j))$; conversely the last section is handled.

Consequently the relation between a section s' in a semantic block and a section s in the full-division can be one of the follows: (i) If $Id(s) = Id(s')$, the two sections have the same role. (ii) $Id(s)$ is included by $Id(s')$, which means that $Id(s)$ locates at the range specified by the starting ID and ending ID of $Id(s')$, we know that there exists situation of optionals. In other words, at least one of sections included in the full division do not appear in the corresponding semantic block to be divided. Other, if the intersection of the ranges of two sections' ID is not empty, the two sections are called matched. And there exists at least one pair of data items having the same role in the two matched sections.

Considering our running example, the results of this step are shown in Fig. 4(a). For instance, the section between "Availability:" and "Authors:" is assigned to be 2-3 because the corresponding starting section's ID is 2 and the ending section's ID is 3 in the full-division. The ID containment here indicates that the semantic block does not contain one of the sections next to the template item "Author:" in the full-division.

```
{0} Our Low Price: {1} Availability: {2} Author: {3}
Authors: {4} Publisher: {5} Publish Date: {6} Format: {7}
```

Fig. 3. The full-division

```
{0} Our Low Price: {1} Availability: {2-3} Authors: {4-5}
Publish Date: {6} Format: {7}
```

(a) Buy sample 1

```
{0} Our Low Price: {1} Availability: {2} Author: {3-5}
Publish Date: {6} Format: {7}
```

(b) Buy sample 2

```
{0} Our Low Price: {1} Availability: {2-3} Authors: {4}
Publisher: {5} Publish Date: {6} Format: {7}
```

(c) Buy sample 3

Fig. 4. Semantic blocks divided into sections

4.2 Mapping Data Items in Matched Sections

Computing Similarities Between Data Items. To identify the data items in the matched sections, several additional rules are employed besides the rule of HTML path. All the rules are considered under the condition that the mappings to be verified are between matched sections.

Rule of Occurrence-Path: (*i*) Two items from *different semantic blocks* with different occurrence paths usually have different roles; (*ii*) Two items in the *same section* with different occurrence paths usually have different roles;

In practice, this rule is proved to be true in most of the situations. For example, the three co-authors in Fig. 1(a) have the same occurrence path //table/tr/td/#text and have the same role. An extension to this rule is that *consecutive* items with the same occurrence paths may possibly have the same role. In other words, there may be iterators, e.g. the example of three co-authors in Fig. 1(a). The rule may fail in several special cases, e.g. we report an exception in the sample pages of uefa(teams) in Section 7.2.

Rule of Visual Information: Two data items having the same role usually have the same visual information.

The visual information is also very important to the extraction problem. In real pages, data items having same role usually have the same appearances to keeping consistence on visual effects. In our work, we consider the following visual information: (i) Whether the data items use the same font and have the same font size; (ii) Whether the data items use the same color in the pages. (iii) Whether the data items have hyperlinks on them.

Rule of Context: Data items with incompatible contexts have different roles.

This rule captures the fact that the contents in the semantic blocks conforming to the same schema, which guarantees that data items of a role always occurs at the relatively same position comparing with other data items. The contexts of two items are said compatible if the contexts of one item can be contained by the other item's. For instance, items in unmatched sections always have different roles.

Rule of Syntactic Feature: Data items having the same role usually have same syntactic features.

This rule is based on the fact that items of the same role often have the same syntactic features [16] [14], e.g. the data items "In Stock: Usually Ships in 1 to 2 business days" and "Pre-Order Now: Get Yours First" in Fig. 1 can both be defined by the regular expression "[A-Z]([\\w]|[\\s])* (:)([\\w]|[\\s])*" indicating that each item starts with a capital letter and contains a colon inside the strings. More details about computing regular expressions of data items can refer to [16].

To judge if two data items, d_1 and d_2, matches, we compute an aggregate similarity of them, denoted as $Sim(d_1, d_2)$, based on all the four above rules.

$$\lambda_1 * RO(d_1, d_2) + \lambda_2 * RC(d_1, d_2) + \lambda_3 * RS(d_1, d_2) + \lambda_4 * RV(d_1, d_2). \quad (1)$$

Here the functions RO, RC, RS and RV correspond to the four rules presented above. For each of them, it takes value 1 if the two data items satisfy the certain rule, else its value is 0. $\lambda_i (i = 1, 2, 3, 4)$ is the weight of each rule which shows the importance of the rule in the process. For simplicity, the values of all of them are 0.25 (The values of them can be configured for better representing the real situations when extracting). Thus if the similarity are larger than a pre-given threshold, we know that the data items match most of the above rules and are considered to have the same role. Moreover, the aggregate similarity greatly decreases the chance that one of the rule's failure resulting an incorrect identification.

Detecting Iterations, Optionals and Disjunctions *Iterators* inside a path-group is detected by computing the similarity of all the data items in it. For example, suppose there're two matched path-groups $p = \{d_1, d_2, d_3\}$ and $p' = \{d'_1, d'_2\}$, with d_1 matches d'_1 and d_2 matches d'_2. Meanwhile, if the similarity $Sim(d_1, d_2, d_3)$ and similarity $Sim(d'_1, d'_2)$ are larger than the pre-given threshold, we say that there can be iterations inside p and p', and the two existing matchings are transformed into an extended matching that $\{d_1, d_2, d_3\}$ matches $\{d'_1, d'_2\}$. Note that we take into account here only the possible iterators inside path-groups. In fact, if a page contains more than one semantic blocks, it's also an iterator at the granularity of blocks. On other hand, separators are also used to discover possible internal iterations, e.g. the symbol '&' in Fig. 1 can be used as separator for discovering internal iterations.

The *optionals* can be naturally discovered. (*i*) At the granularity of sections in semantic blocks, optionals are detected by the ID containment judging (see Section 4.2). (*ii*) At the granularity of path groups and data items, the situation is that the data items having the same role do not appear in all the compatible sections.

The problem of detecting *disjunctions* can be transformed into the problem of discovering optionals under the environments of web pages. For instance, suppose we find a case of disjunction in a page, which can be expressed as $(a?|b?)$ or $(a|b)$. Since the page itself has determined that only one or zero of a and b can appear in a semantic block. The situation can also be described in $(a?, b?)$ without losing correctness.

Consequently, the complex identification problem is achieved through differentiating roles of sections, and then differentiating roles of path-groups and data items inside the set of matched path-groups. The results of this step are that each data item in the semantic blocks is assigned a label, may not have semantic meaning, which corresponds to a element in the schema describing the contents of the pages.

5 Related Work

There have been lots of work on data extraction [17]. These work can be classified by the degree of needs of human interaction (manual, semi-automatic and automatic approaches), sources of information targeted (human made v.s. machine generated), etc. In this paper, we mainly focus on the works on automatic approaches: Exalg [6] and Roadrunner [7].

Both Exalg and Roadrunner use the page creation model of encoding values into web pages using templates. The Roadrunner approach starts from the entire first input pages as the initial template. Then, for each subsequent sample page, it checks if the page can be generated by the current template, otherwise, it modifies the current template using *mismatch* technique to ensure that the updated template can generate all the pages seen so far. The Exalg approach works in two stages. In the first stage, it discovers "equivalence classes", sets of tokens associated with the same type constructor in the (unknown) template for creating the input sample pages. In the second stage, it uses the above sets to deduce the template by continuously growing the LFEQs (for Large and Frequently occurring EQuivalence classes) using several heuristic rules.

The key features differ our work from them are the followings:

1. Both Exalg and Roadrunner focus on inducing tag-based template from the input HTML tag sequences. While the problem of tag-based template is that too less template tokens may making it unable to precisely locate the data items encoded in them. For example, Exalg fails to extract the 4 attributes in the template "<{Name:*
,(Email:*
)?,(Organization:*
)?,(Update:*
)?>" for the reason that this template contains too less, just two template tokens, associated with each type constructors. This kinds of problems can be perfectly resolved by dividing semantic blocks into sections using template items in our approach.
2. Both Exalg and Roadrunner treat the input HTML document as a token sequence without considering the characteristic of tree structure of HTML document. They also ignore the following features, e.g. visual information, syntactic features, for assisting the extraction problem.
3. Roadrunner assumes that the "grammar" of the template used to generate the pages is union-free, which means that it cannot deal with pages with disjunctions in the page schema. Moreover, the complicated heuristic search involving "backtracking" for dealing the situation that the current template does not generate an input page makes Roadrunner difficult to low the complexity of the algorithm, since the search is exponential in the size of the schema of the pages.

On the other hand, some work related to wrapper maintenance [16] [14] [15] also take the step of locating data items in the changed web pages for repairing broken wrappers. While these were under the direction of pre-defined schema or pre-acquired features of data items, e.g. pre-computed syntactic features, pre-computed extraction rule, etc.

6 Experiments

Based on the techniques of item identification above, we have developed a prototype system. Several intensive experiments have been conducted on collections of real web

Table 1. Experimental results of our collections

No.	source	#n	#a	#c	#p	#i	#b	#t(ms)	extr.	#size(K)
1	amazon(hotel)	10	3	3	0	0	20	17.36	yes	86.5
2	buy(bag)	10	5	5	0	0	50	73.15	yes	241
3	buy(book)	10	8	8	0	0	50	86.16	yes	231
4	cdplus	10	5	5	0	0	40	12	yes	88.8
5	cnn(search)	10	3	3	0	0	30	28.93	yes	61.2
6	ebay(buy it now)	10	6	6	0	0	100	50	yes	241
7	ebay(auction)	10	6	5	0	1	100	58.29	yes	233
8	ecampus	10	8	8	0	0	20	28.89	yes	66.9
9	hotels	3	11	11	0	0	50	121.65	yes	476
10	yahoo(people)	10	3	3	0	0	20	19	yes	96.4
11	yahoo(shopping)	10	6	4	2	0	20	21.82	yes	130

pages. All the experiments have been conducted on a machine with an Intel Pentium IV processor working at 2GHz, with 256 MBytes of RAM, running Windows 2000 Server and Sun JDK 1.4. For each collection, the experiment contains the following steps:

1. Manually build a schema for presenting the data values to be extracted from the pages. The schema has nothing to do with the process of extraction, but only for verifying the extracted results.
2. Run the system to extract data values from the pages. Firstly the system automatically induces an wrapper from exactly *two* sample pages, and then the wrapper is applied on other pages in the collection.
3. Manually check the results.

The web pages for experiments were collected from two means: (*i*) Pages collected by ourselves from the various well-known site (see Table 1); (*ii*) Pages ever used in the related works (see Table 2). The pages collected by ourselves are universally larger in size and more complex structures than the pages from the related works.

6.1 Evaluation Metrics

Based on the manually built page schema, we evaluate the effectiveness of our approach using the three cases of *Correct, Partially-Correct* and *Incorrect* for each schema element. (i) *Correct*: All the data values corresponding to the schema element are correctly extracted and identified; (ii) *Partially Correct*: Only parts of the data values matching the schema element are extracted from the pages; (iii) *Incorrect*: Otherwise, the schema element is classified as incorrect.

6.2 Effectiveness Results

Table 1 shows the results on the pages collected by ourselves, and Table 2 provides the results on the pages from the related works. Both tables contain the following elements: (*i*) *source*: short description of each collection, *#n*: the number of sample pages; (*ii*) *#a*: the number of elements in the manually built schema; *#c*, *#p* and *#i* showing the cases of *correct, partially-correct* and *incorrect*; (*iii*) *#b* the number of semantic blocks in the two sample pages for creating wrapper; *#t* is the total time needed to inducing schema from the pages, starting from finding semantic blocks and ending after inducing the schema, and *#size* is the total size of the two sample pages used for inducing wrapper; (*iv*) finally *extr.* conclude that if the collection can be automatically extracted.

As it can be seen from the table, for most of the collections, the system was able to correctly induce a schema using only very short time. Let us describe some more details: Firstly, there're totally 2 reports of failing to induce a correct wrapper from the sampling. We conclude the reasons into two aspects: (*i*) The example of Barn.&Nob. (sw) fails because the system fails to discover the semantic blocks. Thus even the system can correctly extract one data items from each semantic block, it still fails to successfully built a correct wrapper. (*ii*) The failure on tennis can due to that the we can hardly get a good pair of sample pages for inducing wrapper. The pages in the collection do not have a consistent schema, making the system fail to induce a correct schema, and

Table 2. Experimental results of collections from related works

No.	source	#n	#a	#c	#p	#i	#b	#t(ms)	extr.	#size(K)
1	amazon(cars)	21	3	3	0	0	11	17.5	yes	53.1
2	Barn.&Nob.(sw)	10	3	1	2	0	39	33.55	no?	77
3	buy(prod)	10	8	8	0	0	2	5.33	yes	44.1
4	MLB(player)	10	4	4	0	0	141	65.5	yes	77.9
5	rpmfind(by dist.)	20	3	3	0	0	29	15.5	yes	8.93
6	rpmfind(by main.)	20	3	0	3	0	39	19	yes	15
7	tennis	10	-	-	-	-	-	-	no?	-
8	uefa(teams)	20	8	7	1	0	2	7.05	yes	11.8
9	uefa(play)	20	1	1	0	0	2	10.67	yes	22.1
10	wine(acc)	10	3	3	0	0	16	13	yes	68.2
11	wine(prod)	10	4	0	0	0	37	19.6	yes	120

accordingly a correct wrapper. Thus the induced wrapper can only extract randomly some data items. In fact, Exalg [6] also extract only parts of the data items.

There're still several examples that the system cannot build a perfect wrapper. On Yahoo Shopping in Table 1, there are two data items having different roles taking the same occurrence path (the only difference between the HTML path of them are the predicates on the text node, e.g. the difference between "//text[0]" and "//text[1]"), the system happened to identify them as a case of iteration. On eBay(auction), the selected sample pages for inducing wrapper contain only 5 data items of total 6 items, resulting the wrapper cannot extract the left one from several pages. The induced wrapper for another example uefa(teams) in Table 2 can only partially extract one of the data items since the data item takes different occurrence paths ("//#text" vs. "//span/#text") in the two sample page, making the system falsely identifying a case of disjunction. And rpmfind(by main.) extract only partial information for all the 3 data items because the system can not discover all the semantic blocks.

7 Conclusion

In this paper, we propose a novel technique to the problem of item identification, which is one of the key problems in our automatic extraction approach. The identification problem is distinguished into simple identification and complex identification based on the complexity of the pages we face. The problem is resolved at various levels: semantic blocks, sections, path-groups and data items, and several approaches are proposed to effectively identify the mapping between them. Experiments on real pages have proved the effectiveness of the approach of item identification.

Future work will focus on the following two aspects: (i) How to automatically annotate the extracted data items; (ii) How to automatically detect fails in the process of extraction, and how to adopt user interactions for satisfactory results.

Acknowledgements

This research was partially supported by the grants from 863 High Technology Foundation of China under grant number 2002AA116030, the Natural Science Foundation of China (NSFC) under grant number 60073014, 60273018, the Key Project of Chinese Ministry of Education (No.03044) and the Excellent Young Teachers Program of M0EP.R.C (EYTP).

References

1. Baumgartner, R., Flesca, S., Gottlob, G.: Visual web information extraction with lixto. In: Proceedings of VLDB. (2001) 119–128
2. Liu, L., Pu, C., Han, W.: Xwrap: An xml-enabled wrapper construction system for web information sources. In: Proceedings of ICDE. (2000) 611–621
3. Meng, X., Wang, H., Hu, D., Li, C.: A supervised visual wrapper generator for web-data extraction. In: Proceedings of COMPSAC. (2003) 657–662
4. Sahuguet, A., Azavant, F.: Building intelligent web applications using lightweight wrappers. Data Knowl. Eng. **36** (2001) 283–316
5. Muslea, I., Minton, S., Knoblock, C.A.: Hierarchical wrapper induction for semistructured information sources. Autonomous Agents and Multi-Agent Systems **4(1/2)** (2001) 93–114
6. Arasu, A., Garcia-Molina, H.: Extracting structure data from web pages. In: Proceedings of SIGMOD. (2003) 337–348
7. Crescenzi, V., Mecca, G., Merialdo, P.: Roadrunner: Towards automatic data extraction from large web sites. In: Proceedings of VLDB. (2001) 109–118
8. Wang, J., Lochovsky, F.H.: Data extraction and label assignment for web databases. In: Proceedings of WWW. (2003) 187–196
9. Grumbach, S., Mecca, G.: In search of the lost schema. In: Proceedings of ICDT. (1999) 314–331
10. : Xml query language (xquery). (http://www.w3.org/TR/xquery/)
11. : Xml path language (xpath) 2.0. (http://www.w3.org/TR/xpath20/)
12. : Document object model (dom) level 2 core specification. (http://www.w3.org/TR/DOM-Level-2-Core)
13. Arlotta, L., Crescenzi, V., Mecca, G., Merialdo, P.: Automatic annotation of data extracted from large web sites. In: Proceedings of WebDB. (2003) 7–12
14. Meng, X., Hu, D., Li, C.: Schema-guided wrapper maintenance for web-data extraction. In: Proceedings of ACM WIDM. (2003) 1–8
15. Meng, X., Wang, H., Hu, D., Gu, M.: Sg-wram: Schema guided wrapper maintenance. In: Proceedings of ICDE. (2003) 750–752
16. Lerman, K., Minton, S.: Learning the common structure of data. In: Proceedings of AAAI/IAAI. (2000) 609–614
17. Laender, A.H.F., Ribeiro-Neto, B.A., da Silva, A.S., Teixeira, J.S.: A brief survey of web data extraction tools. SIGMOD Record **31** (2002) 84–93

Customer Information Visualization via Customer Map

Ji Young Woo[1], Sung Min Bae[2], Chong Un Pyon[1], and Sang Chan Park[1]

[1] Department of Industrial Engineering, Korean Advanced
Institute of Science and Technology
Guseong-dong, Yusaong-gu, Daejeon, Republic of Korea
{jywoo,pcu,sangchanpark}@major.kaist.ac.kr
[2] Department of Industrial & Management Engineering, HANBAT National University,
DuckMyoung-dong, Yusaong-gu, Daejeon, Republic of Korea
loveiris@hanbat.ac.kr

Abstract. Many data mining techniques which are non-visual methods have been proved their virtues on various customer data. However, there have been hardly applications of visualization methods onto the customer information in spite of their ability of quick and easy knowledge discovery. In this paper, we propose a data visualization method for customer information using a customer map. To develop the customer map, we integrate numerous customer data from various data sources, perform data analyses using data mining techniques and finally visualize the information derived by the former analyses. The customer map makes it possible to mange diverse and complex data sets under the unified goal of value creation through customers. It also affords the ability to make quick observation of current state and the change of customer distribution based on their information without preconception. We applied the customer map to the credit card company, and suggested managerial implications from the customer maps obtained from its data.

1 Introduction

Many data mining techniques have been proved useful in revealing important patterns from large data sets. One of the best data mining technologies might be visualization because graphical display methods often offer superior results compared to other more conventional data mining techniques [3]. Visual tools have traditionally been used by high-end intelligence agencies, but have recently become accessible and useful as a practical, cost-effective approach for many businesses and corporate [3].

According to the recent customer-centric business environment, customer data became an emerging area of data mining techniques. Especially, the urgent importance of the customer in the company is demanding novel and improved methods for quick and explicit knowledge derivation from numerous data. Visualization offers new ways to slice, dice, and analyze huge amounts of customer data. Visualization is specialized in views, graphs, charts, and reports of customer data better than the conventional methods of textual, tabular presentation [9]. Especially to top managers, visualization tools are very useful for quick and easy knowledge discovery without preconception [3]. Furthermore, the combination of visualization technologies with traditional data mining and data warehousing will present the great value to customer-related marketing area. However, existing models and mining techniques related customer data are lack of ability of knowledge presentation to visualize and present the mined knowledge to decision-makers.

In association with customer-related marketing in management, customer targeting is one of major issues to create value through customers [5], [8]. Considering the importance of customer targeting, companies began to concentrate on the right customer not whole customers. Target market identification, evaluation, and selection are considered to be necessarily undertaken prior to determining specific strategies in the customer-centric environment. For target selection, customers have been examined and segmented in terms of their information. The exciting segmentation and targeting methods failed in integrating all kinds of customer data and deriving homogeneous target groups with all aspects. In respect of visualization, existing methods which is mostly based on self-organizing feature map is good at segmenting customers, but it is hardly to find visualization method for targeting itself.

When the dimensionality of the data is large like the customer data, it is more needed to synthesize and visualize the data. However, it is difficult to visualize the data with traditional visualization techniques because visualization on multi-dimensional data is incomprehensible. To overcome this multi-dimensional problem, dimensionality reduction techniques such as clustering and projection method, which focus on data structure, have been examined [7]. For better interpretability of the visualization, data reduction techniques should be combined with the domain knowledge of the customer data. We will consider the 3-dimensional visualization because of its comprehensibility, and suggest strategic building model for data reduction based on implicit knowledge of customer data. On the strategy-building model, customer data is categorized and analyzed following the suggested processes.

In this paper, we propose the data visualization method for customer targeting in terms of customer information using the customer map. To develop the customer map following visual mining steps, we integrate numerous customer data from various data sources, perform data analyses using data mining techniques and finally visualize the information derived by the former analyses. We will apply the customer map in a credit card company, and suggest managerial implications from the customer maps obtained from its data.

2 Visualization Techniques in Management

The application of advanced information visualization in management era has attracted a great deal of attention. One of the major applications of visualization techniques to management has been financial data. Many data mining techniques including visual methods have been proved their virtues on financial data [7]. One of the major methods is Self Organizing Map (SOM), which is the non-parametric neural network method with visualization ability. SOM has been deployed in segmenting companies in terms of their financial states [7]. The other outstanding method is link analysis, which is the process of building up networks of interconnected object through relationship in order to expose patterns and trends [3]. It contributes to detecting money laundering activities and fraud detection [3].

On the marketing era, visual mining has been used to achieve better customer satisfaction and retention. Visualization is useful in understanding the characteristics of discovered segments to determine the appropriate marketing approach. Network representation using SOM has been used for product segmentation and customer segmentation in terms of all possible data fields. Geopositional display has been used for geographical placement of customers, departments, product consumption and so on to expose abstract trends within complex data sets. The 3D cube method has been introduced to represent the customer buying patterns. Each axis of the cube was set according to decision makers' view such as the frequency of visits, the frequency of buying and the monetary amount of buying.

In today's e-business environment, e-CRM has been emerging. On-line transaction data such as click streams data and buying patterns are major applications of visualization [9]. The graphical depiction of web sites and their contents is originated for navigational purpose.

In recent, many data visualization applications are available in the commercial markets and some of them enhance their function combined with database mining techniques such as OLAP function. Some case studies which adapted commercial products such as Netmap [3], Visualmine [15], and Advizor [1] in visual analysis have proved the virtues of visualization in fraud detection, marketing data analysis, and other decision-making problems.

3 Customer Information Visualization for Customer Targeting

3.1 Prerequisite for Customer Map

To build customer-targeting strategy based on visual data mining, we propose a business strategy building model. The strategy building model is organized with three axes of goal, monitor, and control factor and is also organized with three-layers of basic processing, analysis, and strategic planning. When decision-makers build a strategy, they need a goal to achieve through the strategy, they should control any factors which will affects to the goal, and they monitor the affect of their actions. The goal factor is what they are pursuing, so should be achieved at the end. The control factor is the environmental factor which affects to the goal. The monitor factor means what they should do and also means the criteria which they can evaluate the performance of what they do with.

Turning to customer targeting issue, the goal component represents value creation through the customer that they are pursuing via the customer map. The control component indicates which customers they should target to achieve the goal and the monitor component is customer needs which corporate can do for the customer to achieve the goal and which can be monitored according to its actions.

Fig. 1 shows the business strategy building model. The proposed model emphasizes the three major axes to build the business strategy. Also, it says that there should be a process flow from basic processing, analysis to strategic planning. The basic processing includes data integration which combines the multiple data sources and data selection where relevant data to the analysis task are retrieved from databases.

The analysis is the process to mine the raw data and extract the useful information from the integrated data sources. Strategic planning is to build a business strategy based on the results of the above analyses.

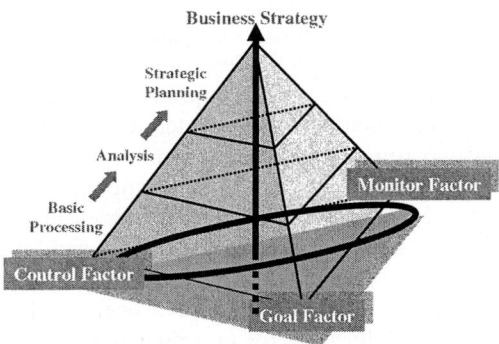

Fig. 1. Business strategy building model

Based on the business strategy building model, the proposed targeting model performs data sources integration, data selection, and data analysis.

3.2 Data Sources Integration

We apply the customer map to customer information for customer targeting. In order to facilitate the customer targeting, the data sources maintained by the separate business units should be integrated as a basic processing. Hence, customer information should be examined with respect to data sources and information characteristics.

It is for integrating customer information across distributed data sources so that the company can target the customers based on the integrated information. Decision-makers should check all customer related databases and derive critical information to describe their customers.

Customer information can be classified into three categories; customer profiles, customer needs, and customer value, based on information characteristics [2]. In terms of this classification, data integration is taken to incorporate customer profiles, customer needs, and customer value from various data sources.

The customer profile is all kinds of customer-related data that can define and describe the customer such as demographics, socioeconomics, psychographics, life styles, preferences or behaviors. Demographics and socioeconomics can be retrieved from the customer information database, psychographics, life styles or preferences from the survey database and the customer information database, and behaviors from the transaction database. Demographics and socioeconomics are contained within customer information databases which are obtained when the customer accesses the company such as customer name, age, income, gender, education and so on. The customer information databases, the transaction database and the survey database can be integrated by the customer identification.

Customer needs are retrieved from customer complaints which are occurred in the customer contact center and from the evaluation of customer satisfaction which is acquired from customer surveys. These data are stored in their own databases such as Voice of Customer (VOC) and Customer Satisfaction Index (CSI) databases. VOC has the advantage that it is monitored at all times, but VOC is possibly biased by active customers. CSI is an evaluator of company performance in term of customer satisfaction. It has the advantage that survey results can be a representative of whole customers when sampling is conducted appropriately. To supplement the shortages of VOC and CSI, two sources should be investigated together for derivation of customer needs. We integrate two sources by word mapping. Each names of the VOC code structure which defines VOC is matched to the questionnaire.

The customer value can be evaluated from histories of customers' transactions. Most of companies maintain the customer value as forms of profit, cost or loyalty value.

These three categories of customer data have been used for building customer-centric strategies and especially used for customer segmentation. They organize the three axes of the customer map. To build a strategy for customer targeting, we set the goal as customer value, the control factor as customer characteristics and the monitor factor as customer needs.

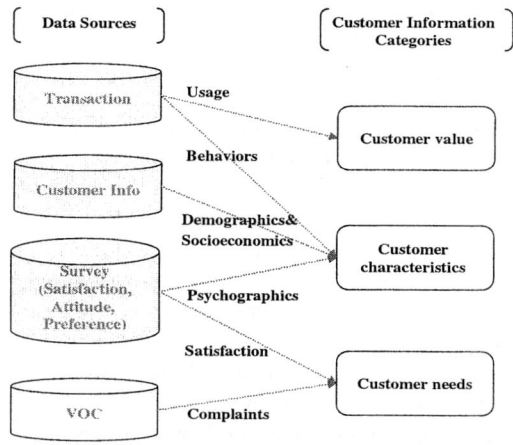

Fig. 2. Three categorized customer data from various sources

3.3 Data Selection and Formulation

To decide pivots of the customer map, data selection and formulation should be undertaken after the data source integration. The value components are formulated in a form of Frequency, Recency, Amount, and Type (FRAT). FRAT is an extended version of Recency, Frequency, and Monetary value (RFM) [11], which has been used to estimate the profitability associated with each customer. To overcome bias that is occurred by assuming value as mere profitability, we add Type attribute to the value component to reflect cost aspect too. When the type sets to current value, frequency, and recency will be calculated from the purchase date field, and the amount will be derived from the dollar amount field. When the type sets to cost, the occurrence date field should be selected from VOC table to estimate the frequency and the recency, and the dollar amount field which records how much the VOC costs should selected to estimate the amount.

The main idea of organizing customer profiles is to target very specific group of customers with controllable information. To access a target, the customer profile should be actionable rather than be just descriptive. Demographics, geographics, and socio-economics that were major sources of customer information in the past have been proved that it is not easy to extract discriminators between different customers using this information. Transaction behavior information is more actionable and differentiable. This information is the habitual behavior which can be recorded when the purchase occurs in the contract database, which is a sort of customer information databases. In the credit card company, transaction information includes payment method, billing method, the number of possessed cards, the kinds of possessed cards and so on. This information is useful for internal customers, but has a drawback that is not available for customers of other companies or latent customers. Instead, psychographic data such as lifestyle, preference, and attitudinal data is available for external customers. For an unbiased strategy for internal and external customers, the transaction behaviors and psychographics should be combined to identify characteristics of target customers and to access and control them.

Customer needs are formulated as a form of Family of Measurement (FOM) [10] for well-balanced measurement. FOM is organized with five measures: quantity, quality, timeliness, resource, and customer satisfaction. In the case of VOC, FOM defined quantity as the frequency of VOC occurrence, quality as importance onto customer satisfaction, timeliness as the average time for improvement, resource as the average dollar amount for improvement and customer satisfaction as the degree of contribution onto customer satisfaction. VOC code field, the dollar amount field and the time amount field should be selected from VOC table. For quality and customer satisfaction, the response value field of the questionnaire matched to specific VOC from CSI table.

3.4 Customer Data Analysis

In this phase, we derive key factors to build the customer map. We examine and integrate customer needs analysis, customer characteristics analysis, and customer value analysis on the targeting issue. Once the data selection has been done from the integrated data sources, key factor derivation is performed from the selected data. Customer data analysis derives key customer needs and customer characteristics which are critical to customer value. In this case, one of FRAT value which represents customer value is determined, and then customer needs analysis and customer characteristics analysis are performed.

As a first step, data reduction is undertaken to customer preference which has numerous continuous variables [6]. After checking the correlation matrix of the variables, we apply factor analysis, especially principal component analysis. In key driver analysis for customer characteristics, selected preference variables and all transaction behavior variables are analyzed together to check whether they affect to the goal factor or not. Upon the dependent variable of customer value, these variables are analyzed by the discriminant analysis.

For key driver analysis for customer needs, all measures in FOM are enumerated based on the selected raw data. The importance of a VOC is measured in terms of partial correlation of CS on the VOC onto customer satisfaction. It indicates the pure effect of a VOC to CS without interference of other VOC. The contribution on customer satisfaction of a VOC is enumerated following the formula (1). It indicates how much overall customer satisfaction will be increased as a result of improving customer satisfaction on a specific VOC.

$$Contribution = \lim_{\delta CSonVOC \to 0} \frac{\partial OverallCS}{\delta CSonVOC} \bigg|_{at\ current\ position} \quad (1)$$

3.5 Visual Representation via Customer Map

Once key factors have been derived from the three-categorized customer data, we visualize the key factors onto the customer map. The customer map evaluates the customer value distribution across customers based on customer profiles and customer needs. To implement the customer map, we organize a two-dimensional plane using a key customer profile and a key customer need. All customers are allocated in the space constituted with (x, y) coordinates geometrically. Then, the value component sets up the third dimension, z axis. The average value which is enumerated from the value component of customers in each grid conforms the third dimension value in the map. With the connection of all neighboring girds, the customer map exposes a 3D contour plot.

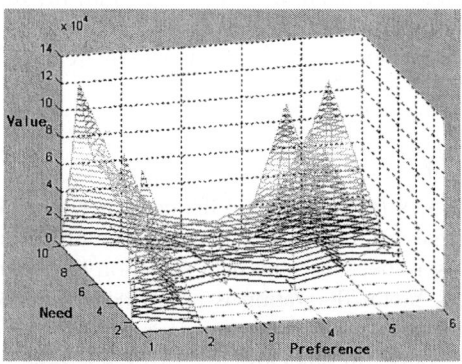

Fig. 3. Three dimensional customer map

We also reflect a cubic graph into a two-dimensional plane by expressing altitude as colors. The two dimensional contour map is easier to interpret than the three-dimensional map. The difference of customer value can be recognized through the difference of the color.

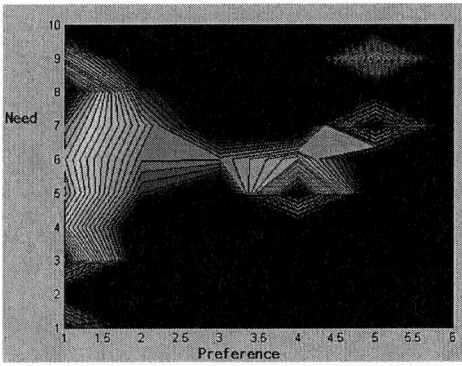

Fig. 4. Two dimensional customer map

3.6 Knowledge from Customer Map

The customer map indicates target customer segments which are homogenous in view point of three major axes of customer information: customer needs, customer characteristics, and customer value. Based on the customer map, marketers can derive various marketing strategies. From the value distribution on the customer map, we can diagnose portfolio of customers and determine what factors relate to value. Then, we can build strategies to increase customer satisfaction of the target based on their needs, and to eventually connect their satisfaction to value stream.

The target segment includes the most profitable or the most cost-consuming customers. Target identification ensures that better customers are separated from other customers to enable the company to focus the target and to maximize profits from them. We consider Pareto rule, which urges that top 20% of customers generate 80% of profits, when defining the target. Target customers are defined as the customers whose z dimensional value reaches to 80% of total altitude in the map. The highest area in a 3D map like Fig. 3 or the highlighted part in a 2D map like Fig. 4 indicates the target segment. There are three check points geometrically in the customer map. The height which represents the average of a value component in each position is a measure to evaluate the value of each target. The magnitude of the target indicates how big the base the target has, and the degree of homogeneousness within the target. The distance between targets on a map with same axes is a criterion which measures similarities in terms of the customer need and the customer characteristic between the targets.

Once we define a target group, differential profiles and needs of the target customer are identified. The profile and the need of the target are derived by just reading the (x,y) position of the target on the map. The identification of profiles and needs of the target provides a basis for developing efficient and effective marketing strategies for keeping and gaining profitable customers or avoiding cost-consuming customers.

4 Application to Credit Card Company

We applied the visualization mining tool for customer targeting to a service operation especially to a credit card company. The company deals numerous VOC in the call center and performs the CSI survey twice in a year. Also, it maintains numerous and various customer information in the enterprise data warehouse. From VOC and CSI, we could derive key customer needs to build the customer map. We collected the 235 thousand sampling VOC data and used 3200 data from the two customer surveys. Other surveys such as preference and attitude surveys supported the selection of customer characteristics. The company updates the customer value as forms of the current value and the life time value.

The results of the examination using FOM ranked "payback/receipt" and "limit/approval" as top key customer needs. As customer characteristics, we used the preference factor from CSI survey data. We derived "nobility" and "benefits pursing" propensities as the key preference factor based on their impacts onto customer value. We adapted current value which is calculated based on the amount of card usage as the customer value.

From the customer maps built based on the results of data analyses, we could derive retention and churn strategies. Retention strategy is for the customers who are profitable currently or have potentials, so should be retained. In Fig. 5, we can detect two targets. One target includes customers who show weak preference for the benefit and have low satisfaction on the "payback and receipt" service. The other target includes customers who show strong preference for the characteristic factor and have high satisfaction in the quality factor. We conclude that retention strategy should be built for customers who show medium above preference of the benefit. Especially for customers who pursue benefits strongly, the "payback/receipt" service should be satisfied.

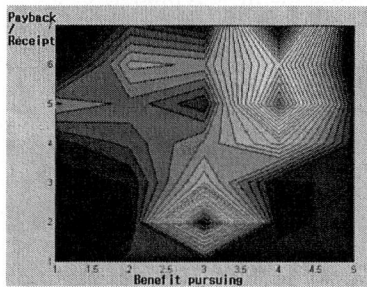

Fig. 5. Customer map for retention strategy

Churn strategy is designed to attract customers of other competitive, so we need to compare two customer maps with the same axes. In this case, we take the examination on the distance between two high-ends, and take comparison on the height difference of two segments. The closer the distance is, the easier it is to attract customers of the competitive. In Fig. 6, the high-end of company A is close to one of company C, so it is easy to attract the high-end customers of company C than those of company B for company A. When we target company C, it is required a little improvement of the service of the "payback/receipt" service because the target customers are a little more nobility pursuers and they are a little more sensitive to the quality of the payback/receipt. When we target company B, it is important to emphasize nobility which

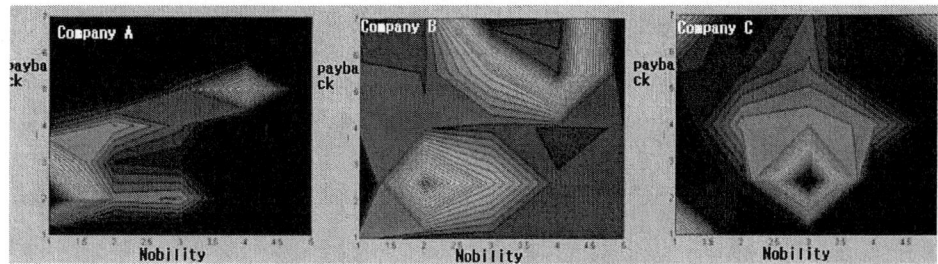

Fig. 6. Customer map for churn strategy

the credit card expresses and to provide additional services. Also, they should achieve a big improvement on the service of "payback and receipt".

5 Conclusion

We suggested the visualization method for customer targeting based on the customer three-categorical information. The visualization method was implemented as the customer map. To build the customer map, we suggest the business strategy building model which defines the required factors and the required processes for successful business strategy. Following the model, we integrated customer data from multiple sources and classified customer data into the customer profile, the customer need and the customer value. Then, we conducted data analyses on these data and derive key information to build the customer map. The customer map is a visualized tool that indicates the target which is homogeneous in terms of the need, the characteristic, and the value.

The customer map has three important meanings. First of all, it enables mangers to target right customers and to keep them. Secondly, the customer map helps marketers to mange diverse and complex data sets under the unified goal of value creation through customers and it also enables marketers to integrate the analytical process which have been conducted individually according to customer data sources. Thirdly, it affords them the ability to make quick observation of current state and its change of customer distribution based on their information without preconception due to the visualization ability of the customer map. We applied the customer map to a credit card company. We did research on interpretation and application onto deriving marketing strategies from the customer map that we got from the application.

References

1. Advizor Solution, Inc. URL: http://www.advizorsolutions.com
2. Chung-Hoon Park, Young-Gul Kim : A Framework of Dynamic CRM: Linking Marketing with Information Strategy. Business Process Management Journal, Vol. 9. No.5 (2003) 652-671
3. Christopher Westphal, Teresa Blaxton : Data Mining Solution. John Wiley & Sons, Inc. (1998) 123-147

4. David Adams : Data Visualization. URL: http://www.CFOProject.com
5. Jedid-Jah Jonker, Nanda Piersma, Dirk Van den Poel : Joint Optimization of Customer Segmentation and Marketing Policy to Maximize Long Term Profitability. Expert Systems with Applications, Vol. 27 (2004) 159-168
6. Jiawei Han, Micheline Kamber : Data Mining : Concepts and Techniques. Morgan Kaufmann Publishers (2001) 2-8
7. Kohonen, T. & Deboeck, G.: Visual Exploration in Finance with Self-Organizing Maps. Springer (1998)
8. Market Segmentation Revised Edition. Probus Publishing Company (1994)
9. Shobha Ganapathy, C. Ranganathan, Balaji Sankaranarayanan: Visualization Strategies and Tools for Enhancing Customer Relationship Management. Communication of ACM, Vol.47, No.11 (2004)
10. Thomas Teal : Service Comes First: An Interview with USAA's Robert F. McDermott. Harvard Business Review (1991)
11. Uzay Kaymak : Fuzzy Target Selection using RFM Variables. IEEE (2001)
12. VisualMine, URL: http://www.visualmine.com

Finding and Analyzing Database User Sessions

Qingsong Yao, Aijun An, and Xiangji Huang*

Department of Computer Science, York University, Toronto M3J 1P3 Canada
{qingsong, aan}@cs.yorku.ca, jhuang@yorku.ca

Abstract. A database user session is a sequence of queries issued by a user (or an application) to achieve a certain task. Analysis of task-oriented database user sessions provides useful insight into the query behavior of database users. In this paper, we describe novel algorithms for identifying sessions from database traces and for grouping the sessions different classes. We also present experimental results.

1 Introduction

A *database user session* is a sequence of queries issued by a user (or an application) to achieve a certain task. It consists of one or more database transactions, which are in turn a sequence of operations performed as a logical unit of work. Analysis of sessions allows us to discover high-level patterns that stem from the structure of the task the user is solving. The discovered patterns can be used to predict incoming user queries based on the queries that the user has already issued [1, 2, 3] and to redesign and rewrite the queries within a user session to achieve a better performance [4, 5].

In this paper, we are interested in identifying and clustering database user sessions from database workloads. We use a language modeling based algorithm to identify database sessions, and a distance-based clustering algorithm is proposed to group the user sessions into different session classes. Our contributions in this paper are summarized as follows. (1) We use a language statistical modeling based algorithm to identify database sessions. Three types of learning methods, namely, *supervised*, *semi-supervised* and *unsupervised learning*, are introduced to learn language models. These learning methods are designed to suit the different characteristics of real log data sets. (2) We propose a distance-based session clustering algorithm to cluster session instances. The distance between two session instances is measured according to three similarity scores: *coefficient score*, *alignment score* and *neighborhood score*. This approach considers not only the local similarity between sessions (coefficient score, alignment score), but also the global similarity (neighborhood score).

The rest of the paper is organized as follows. Related work is discussed in Section 2. We describe the language modeling based session identification algorithm in Section 3. In Section 4, a distance-based session clustering algorithm is proposed. We give experimental results in Section 5. Finally we conclude the paper in Section 6.

---

* This work is supported by research grants from Communications and Information Technology Ontario (CITO) and the Natural Sciences and Engineering Research Council of Canada (NSERC).

2 Related Work

Finding database user behaviors is a subject of workload characterization. There is a large variety of techniques used for workload characterization. Functionally, the workload characterization can be classified into two categories: static analysis and dynamic analysis. Static techniques explore the intrinsic characteristics of the workload, such as the static parameters related to hardware and software resource consumptions and the correlation between workload parameters, which do not change over time. On the other hand, dynamic techniques, such as *neural network based prediction, Markov models, user behavior graphs, customer behavior model graph* and *regression methods*, focus on analyzing the behavior of the workload and the way it fluctuates over time. These techniques usually analyze the historical data of the workload and aid to forecasting its behavior in the future. Surveys on workload characterization techniques on different computer systems, such as file servers and database systems, can be found in [6, 7]. In this paper, we focus on analyzing database user behaviors within the user session level, i.e, the queries submitted by a user within a user session.

The most commonly used session identification method is called *timeout*, in which a user session is defined as a sequence of requests from the same user such that no two consecutive requests are separated by an interval more than a predefined threshold. This session identification method suffers from the problem that it is difficult to set the time threshold. According to [8], timeout method is the only method provided by database vendors to keep track of sessions for electronic library database products. They reported that timeout values can vary widely between vendors, ranging from 7 to 30 minutes on average. Recently, an n-gram statistical language modeling based session detection method has been proposed in [9]. The method has been demonstrated to be more effective than the timeout and two other methods in discovering interesting association rules in a Web mining domain. However, some open issues, such as how to select parameters and how to measure the session identification results, are still unsolved. A review of N-gram modeling can be found in [10].

Data clustering is a subject of active research in several fields such as statistics analysis, pattern recognition, and machine learning. A review of clustering techniques is given in [11]. A survey on data clustering algorithms can be found in [12]. The session clustering algorithm presented in the paper is based on the idea of *Jaccard Coefficient* measurement [13], sequence alignment [14], and common neighbors between sessions [15]. Similar algorithms can be found in [15, 16, 17].

3 Database User Session Identification

First, we briefly discuss the procedure of finding and clustering user sessions from database workloads. The database workload contains many database connections, and each connection contains a sequence of queries. We assume that queries within a user session have the same connection id, and there is no interleave between two sessions of a connection. Thus, the query sequence of a connection corresponds to a sequence of user sessions. Language modeling provides a simple, natural approach to segmenting template sequences. Since the submitted SQL queries usually have certain format, they can be classified into different query templates (step 1). In particular, we replace each data value embedded in a SQL query with a wildcard character '%', and obtain a query template. The query template represents a set of queries that have the similar format. By replacing a submitted SQL statement with the corresponding query template, we obtain a set of query template sequences, referred to as *template sequences* (step 2 and 3), each for one database connection. The template sequences are the input of the session identification algorithm. For example, the session instance shown in Table 1 corresponds to a template sequence: *30-09-10-20-47-49*. Learning from session instances can help us to predict, prefetch and rewrite the queries in the session (see [2] for details).

Table 1. An instance of schedule display session procedure

Label	Statement
30	select authority from *employee* where employee_id ='**1025**'
09	select count(*) as num from *customer* where cust_num = '**1074**'
10	select card_name from *customer* t1,*member_card* t2 where 1.cust_num = '**1074**' and t1.card_id = t2.card_id
20	select contact_last,contact_first from *customer* where cust_num = '**1074**'
47	select t1.branch ,t2.* from *record* t1, *treatment* t2 where t1.contract_no = t2.contract_no and t1.cust_id ='**1074**' and check_in_date = '**2002/03/04**' and t1.branch ='**scar**'
49	select top **10** contract_no from *treatment_schedule* where cust_id = '**1074**' order by checkin_date desc

3.1 N-Gram Statistical Language Modeling

In this section, we present a session detection method based on language models. The method does not rely on any time intervals when identifying session boundaries. Instead, it uses an information theoretic approach to identifying session boundaries dynamically by measuring the change of information in the sequence of requests. The method was originally proposed for detecting session boundaries in Web logs [9].

Statistical language modeling was originally used in speech recognition, where the goal is to predict the probability of natural word sequences. The most successful statistical language model is the n-gram language model. In n-gram language modeling, it is assumed that the probability of a word only depends on its at most previous n-1 words. Thus, given a word sequence, $s = w_1w_2...w_N$, its probability can be written as:

$$P(s) = P(w_1)..P(w_N|w_1..w_{N-1}) = \prod_{i=1}^{N} P(w_i|w_1..w_{i-1}) = \prod_{i=1}^{N} P(w_i|w_{i-n+1}..w_{i-1})$$

A statistical language model, then, is a specific choice of conditional probabilities for all possible n-grams: $P(w_i|w_{i-n+1}...w_{i-1})$. The quality of a given statistical language model can be measured by its empirical *entropy* on a given word sequence s, where the empirical entropy is defined as

$$Entropy(s) = -\frac{1}{N}log_2 P(s)$$

That is, we would like the language model to place high probability on natural test sequences, and hence obtain a small value of empirical entropy.

In database applications, queries are issued sequentially in a particular order, similar to the word sequences that occur in a natural language. If we consider each query as a basic unit, like a word or character in natural language, we can then attempt to estimate the probability of query sequences using the same language modeling tools described above. Imagine a set of queries for a task/session that are frequently issued one after another. In this case, the entropy of the sequence is low. However, when a new query is observed in the sequence that is not relevant to the original task (but in fact indicates a shift to a new task), the introduction of this new query causes an increase in the entropy of the sequence because it is rarely issued after the preceding sequence of queries. If the change in entropy passes a threshold, a session boundary could be placed before the new query. In other words, the uncertainty (which is measured by entropy) within a session should be roughly constant, allowing for a fixed level of variability within a topic. However, whenever the entropy increases beyond a threshold, this presents a clear signal that the user's activity has changed to another topic. Thus, we should set a session boundary at the place where the entropy changes. The change in entropy is measured by the relative change in entropy values, defined as

$$\frac{Entropy(s_1) - Entropy(s_0)}{Entropy(s_0)}$$

where s_0 is a sequence of requests and s_1 contains s_0 plus the next request following s_0 in the test data sequence. Based on this definition, a threshold value of 0.20 means that if the change in entropy is over 20%, there is a boundary at the end of s_0.

Fig. 1 shows the entropy evolution of a query sequence within a database connection from our OLTP application, where the X-axis is the sequence represented by query template ids, Y-axis is the entropy of the sequence from the first query to the current query, and the threw curves are based on the n-gram models trained in the unsupervised, supervised and semi-supervised modes (explained in next section), respectively. As one can see, the entropy changes radically at some points, although it remains stable in other places. This figure gives an intuition how entropy could be used for session boundary detection.

3.2 Training Data and Learning Methods

The probabilities in an n-gram model come from the data it is trained on. The training data need to be carefully designed. If the training data is too specific to one task, the probabilities may be too narrow and do not generalize well to other tasks. If the training data is too general or too small, the probabilities may not reflect the task or the domain efficiently. A good training data should contain enough information about the observed application or user, i.e., the training data should reflect the dynamic behavior of the observed application or the users.

There are three kinds of training data, *separated training data*, *un-separated training data* and *partially separated training data*. In separated training data, sessions have been identified and thus the training data consists of a set of sessions. We refer to the n-gram learning method that is based on the separated training data as *supervised learning method.* In some situations, it is very difficult, if not impossible, to obtain a separated training data set. In this case, we can estimate request frequencies based on the unseparated data sequence, and the corresponding n-gram model contains both the inter-session and the intra-session request frequencies. The corresponding learning method is called the *unsupervised session detection method*. The unsupervised learning is more sensitive to the selection of parameters, such as the entropy threshold and the n-gram order (as shown in Fig. 1). In a third type of situation, the training data are partially separated by the boundary points such as use login/logout. In this case, we can build an n-gram model by estimating the probabilities based on the partially separated training data. We refer to this method as *semi-supervised learning method*.

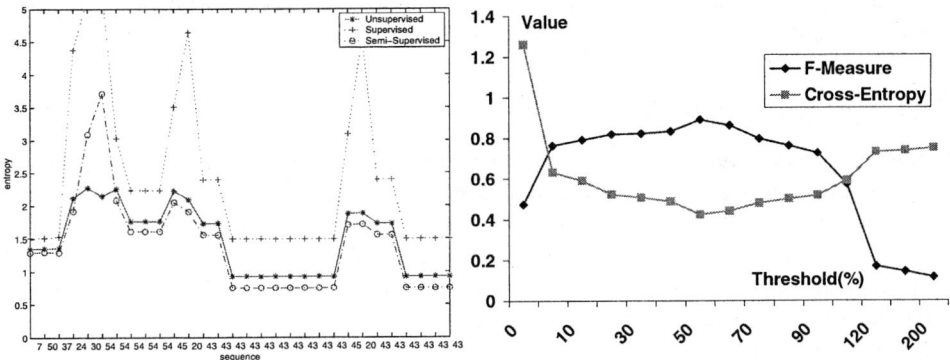

Fig. 1. Entropy evolution in one data set

Fig. 2. Correlation between F-measure and cross-entropy

3.3 Performance Measurement Metrics

After an n-gram model is built over the training data, it can be used to divide an unseparated template sequence into sessions. Performance measures are needed to evaluate the accuracy of the session detection. In this section, we propose to use two performance measures and discuss their correlations. The first measure is referred to as *F-measure*, which has been used in information retrieval to measure the retrieval performance. Suppose we know the true session boundaries in the test sequence, then *F-measure* is defined as

$$F\text{-}Measure = \frac{2 * precision * recall}{precision + recall},$$

where *precision* is defined as the ratio of the number of correctly detected session boundaries to the total estimated boundaries, and the *recall* is the hit-rate, that is, the ratio of the number of correctly detected true session boundaries to the total number of true boundaries, A higher F-measure value means a better overall performance.

The second measure is called *cross entropy*. Given a set of estimated sessions $T = \{t_1, ..., t_m\}$, detected by using a model $P(w_i|w_{i-n+1}...w_{i-1})$, the cross entropy of T is define as:

$$H_p(T) = \frac{\sum_i(|t_i| \times entropy(t_i))}{\sum_i |t_i|}$$

The cross-entropy value can be interpreted as the average number of bits needed to encode T by using the compression algorithm associated with model $P(w_i|w_{i-n+1}...w_{i-1})$. A smaller cross-entry value means a better compression algorithm, and a better session separating model as well. Fig. 2 shows the inverse correlation between F-measure and cross entropy. It depicts how the performance of the n-gram based session identification method, measured by both performance measures, changes with the value of the entropy threshold on a data set used in our application. An advantage of using cross entropy to measure the performance of an n-gram model for session detection is that we do not need to know the true session boundaries in test data to calculate the cross entropy. This feature makes it possible to make use of cross entropy as a performance measure on the test data set for adjusting the parameters of an n-gram model. However, the n-gram model should be trained in the supervised mode (i.e. on the separated data set) in order for cross entropy to be a reliable performance measure on test data.

3.4 Parameter Selection

There are two parameters in the language modeling based session detection method. One is the order of the n-gram model, which is n. The other is the entropy change threshold used in segmenting the test sequence. Threshold selection is a critical task of the language modeling based session boundary detection method. If the threshold is too large, many session boundaries are missed and the *recall* of the detection is low. On the other hand, a small threshold causes many non-boundary events to be mistreated as session boundaries, which results in low *precision*s. In both cases, the performance in term of *F-Measure* is low. To see how threshold selection is important, we compared the performances of the n-gram method based on different threshold values. The result is shown in Fig. 3. We can observe that the performance of an n-gram model greatly depends on the threshold value.

To achieve good performance, we propose an automatic method for choosing a threshold value for our language model session detection method. Suppose that the test data sequence has m sessions and N events. After we estimate the entropy value of each sequence in the test data, we can calculate and sort the relative entropy difference values in decreasing order. If our language model can find all m-1 session boundaries correctly, then the corresponding relative entropy difference values will occupy the first m-1 positions in the sorted list. Thus, the mth value in the sorted list is the estimated threshold value. In practice, we may not know the actual value of m. However, if we know the average session length $(avgLen)$, we can estimate m to be $N/avgLen$ and thus choose the $(N/avgLen)^{th}$ value in the sorted list as the threshold value. For supervised learning, we can estimate the average session length from the training data. For unsupervised or semi-supervised learning, we can use the development set to estimate the average session length. Also, for different n-gram orders, the estimated threshold values are different.

Fig. 4 illustrates how the performance of an n-gram method changes with the order of the model on one of our test data sets. Since different data sets may achieve the best performance at different order values, an automatic method for order selection is necessary. We propose the following method to select the best n-gram order for a data set. For supervised learning, we train a set of n-gram models with different n values,

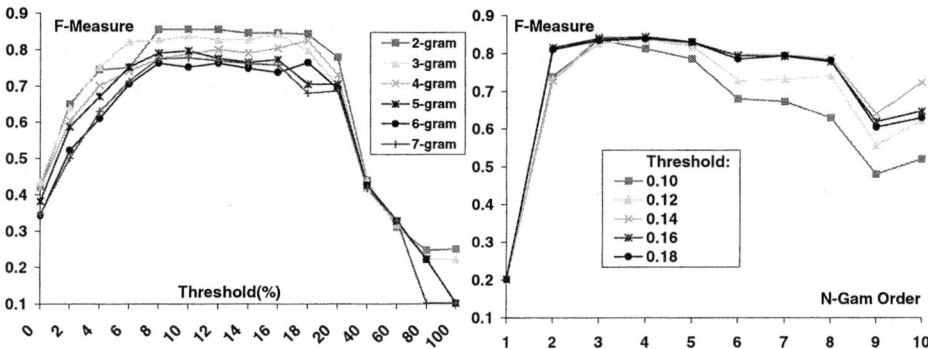

Fig. 3. Performance change with different threshold values

Fig. 4. Performance change with different n–gram orders

say from 2 to 8, on the training data set. We then test each model on the unseparated test data sequence with an entropy threshold selected using the automatic threshold selection method. The performance of each model on the test sequence is measured in terms of cross entropy. The model with the smallest cross entropy is selected. Cross entropy, instead of F-measure, is used as the performance measure in this process because it can be calculated without knowing the true boundaries in the test data sequence. For unsupervised or semi-supervised learning, a set of n-gram models with different n values is trained on the unseparated or partially separated training data. Then each model is tested on the development set. The performance of each model on the development set is measured by F-measure. The model with the highest F-measure is chosen. Note that we cannot use the test data sequence and cross entropy to test the models as in supervised learning because the models are trained on the unseparated data and thus the unseparated test data sequence will have the smallest cross entropy. Using F-measure on the development set is more reliable in this situation.

4 Database Session Clustering

4.1 Session Similarity Scores and Distance Function

Given a set of database session instances, $s = s_1, s_2, ..., s_n$, where each session instance contains a sequence of requests, i.e., $s_i = < r_{i_1} r_{i_2} .... r_{i_m} >$, our task is to group the session instances into meaningful session classes. The idea of our distance-based session clustering algorithm is described as follows. We first consider each session instance as a session class, and calculate the distance between them. Then, session groups are merged according to their intra-group distances, and group distances are updated correspondingly. The clustering procedure stops when all intra-group distances are more than a pre-defined distance threshold β_1. The distance between two session instances s_i and s_j is defined as:

$$1.0 - \alpha_1 \times csim(s_i, s_j) - \alpha_2 \times asim(s_i, s_j) - \alpha_3 \times nsim(s_i, s_j), \quad (1)$$

where *csim, asim, nsim* are the coefficient score, the alignment score, and the neighborhood score, respectively. α_1, α_2, and α_3 are the distance parameters, the sum of which is 1.0. The coefficient score $csim(s_i, s_j)$, for two session instances s_i and s_j, is defined as $\frac{|s_i \cap s_j|}{|s_i \cup s_j|}$, where $|s_i \cap s_j|$ is the number of the requests appearing in both s_i and s_j, and $|s_i \cup s_j|$ is the total number of requests appearing in s_i or s_j. The coefficient score is based on the Jaccard Coefficient measure [13] that treats sessions as un-ordered sets. The similarity between two sessions in this measure is defined as the fraction of common requests.

We observe that if two session instances belong to the same session class, they are very likely to have similar template sequence. Therefore, we propose another scoring schema based on the idea of *sequence alignment*. In sequence alignment, two or more strings are aligned together in order to get the highest number of matching characters. Gaps may be inserted into a string in order to shift the remaining characters into better matches. In this paper, we use the *Needleman-Wunsch* algorithm [14], a well-known sequence alignment algorithm, to align two sessions, and assign a score based on aligned session sequences, referred as *the alignment score*. We assume that the sessions are controlled by certain programming codes. The codes may contain branches (such as *if/else* and *switch-case* statements) or cycles (such as *for-loop* and *do-while* statements) that may cause the requests to be executed repeatedly. The branches and cycles can be observed from the aligned session instances. For example, given two session instances, *ABCDD* and *ABED*, the aligned sequences are $\frac{ABCDD}{ABED-}$. We observe that the sequences contain two matches (A and B), one branch (C/E) and one cycle (DD/D). We assign each match with a score of 2, each branch with a score of 1, and each cycle with a score of 1. To normalize the alignment score, we divide the assigned value by the length of the aligned sessions. The length is defined as *2 * (num. of matches + num. of branches + num. of cycles)*. Thus, the final alignment score of the two sequences is 6/8 = 0.75. The hidden logic/code in the real application may be complex than in the above example, but the principle is still applicable.

In some situations, two sessions are in the same session class but their distance is not so "near". Thus, simply applying the two similarity scores as the distance metric is not enough. It is necessary to take global similarity into consideration. We call two session instances s_i and s_j "neighbors" if the *local-distance* between them is within a pre-defined threshold β_2. The local-distance can be estimated by using the combination of the coefficient score and the alignment score by assuming that the neighborhood score is 0. Thus, each session has a set of neighbors. Each session pair, $< s_i, s_j >$, has a value, $nsim(s_i, s_j)$, which is the faction of common neighbors between them. This score is called the neighborhood score.

4.2 Distance-Based Session Clustering Algorithm

The step of session distance computing has a high space and time complexity. For example, given a data set that contains k session instances, k^2 scores need to be calculated. Meanwhile, to align two sequences with length m and n, the Needleman-Wunsch algorithm requires $O((m + 1) \times (n + 1))$ space to store the matrix, and $O(m \times n)$ time to compute the matrix and then $O(m + n)$ time to find an optimal path. In this section, several strategies are proposed to solve the problem.

First, we observe that there are some repeated session instances in the data set, which have the same template sequences. These session instances are in the same session class. Thus, we can represent repeated sessions by using a single session s_i associated with the occurrence frequency, $freq(s_i)$.

The next strategy is concerned with session class representation. It is implausible to use all session instances to represent a session class. Thus, we use two sets, the request set, $rset(g_j)$, and the session set, $sset(g_j)$ together, to represent a session class g_i. $rset(g_j)$ contains all distinct requests appeared in g_j, and $sset(g_j)$ contains a set of the representative session instances. We observe that if session group g_i and g_j are likely to be merged, they should have a large portion of common requests. Thus, we use formula $\frac{|rset(g_i) \cap rset(g_j)|}{|rset(g_i) \cup rset(g_j)|} > \beta_3$ to pre-eliminate un-related groups when merging them. The $sset$ is used to compute the distance between session groups. Frequent session instances are usually in $sset$. The distance between two session groups is then defined as:

$$\frac{\sum_{s_m \in sset(g_i)} \sum_{s_n \in sset(g_j)} distance(s_m, s_n) \times freq(s_m) \times freq(s_n)}{\sum_{s_m \in sset(g_i)} \sum_{s_n \in sset(g_j)} freq(s_m) \times freq(s_n)} \quad (2)$$

When two session groups are merged, the $sset$ and $rest$ are changed correspondingly.

Data sampling is used to reduce computing complexity and space requirement. Finally session classes with small number of session instances (the number is smaller than a predefined threshold) are treated as noise and are removed.

5 Experimental Results

To test our ideas in the project, we use a clinic OLTP application as a test bed. The clinic is a private physiotherapy clinic located in Toronto. It has five branches across the city. It provides services such as joint and spinal manipulation and mobilization, post-operative rehabilitation, personal exercise programs and exercise classes, massage and acupuncture. In each day, the client applications installed in the branches make connections to the center database server, which is Microsoft SQL Server 7.0. In each connection, a user may perform one or more tasks, such as checking in patients, making appointments, displaying treatment schedules, explaining treatment procedures and selling products. The database trace log (400M bytes) contains *81,417* events belonging to 9 different applications, such as front-end sales, daily report, monthly report, data backup, and system administration. Our target application is the front-end sales application. After preprocessing the trace log, we obtain 7,244 SQL queries, 18 database connection instances of the front-end sales application. The queries are classified into 190 query templates, and 18 template sequences are obtained.

5.1 Results for Session Identification Algorithm

We randomly selected four test data sets from the collected data set, referred to as D_1, D_2, D_3, and D_4. Each test data set corresponds to one database connection. For supervised learning, the four test data sets are taken out from the training data. For unsupervised or semi-supervised learning, we use the whole data set as the training data to calculate the probabilities in the n-gram model, and use D_1 as the development set to tune parameters. The learned model are tested on D_2, D_3, and D_4. For the semi-supervised method, some boundary "words" are used to partially separate the training data sequences. In our application, the boundary words are *user sign-in/sign-out* and *user authority checking*. However, in our data set, not all the sessions begin or end with a boundary word.

For the timeout method, we conducted experiments with a number of timeout thresholds, ranging from 0.2 second to 30 minutes. The results of these timeout methods in terms of *F-Measure* are shown in Fig. 5. The results show that the best performance in term of F-measure is around 70%. The performance of the timeout method obviously depends on the timeout threshold. Different applications may have different best timeout thresholds. In our particular application, a threshold value between 3 to 10 seconds leads to the best performance for the timeout method.

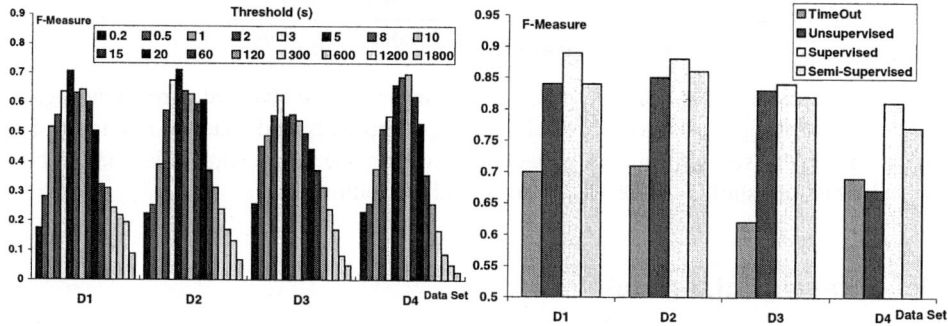

Fig. 5. Comparison of timeout thresholds   **Fig. 6.** Comparison of All the Methods

In Fig. 6, we compare all the methods in terms of F-measure. The results for the unsupervised, supervised and semi-supervised methods are the results from the automatic parameter selection method. The result for the timeout method on a data set is the best timeout result on that data set. We can observe from the figure that the supervised learning method achieves the best results on all the test data sets; semi-supervised learning method is comparable to the unsupervised method on the first three data sets but is significantly better than the unsupervised method on data set D_4; all the three n-gram methods are significantly better than the best timeout method (except on D_4 the performance of the unsupervised method is slightly worse than that of the best timeout method). In general, we can say that, using the automatic parameter selection method, the n-gram based session identification method is significantly better than the timeout method, which has been the only method for database session identification.

5.2 Results for Session Clustering Algorithm

We implement our session clustering algorithm in *Java*. The performance of the session clustering algorithm depends on the selection of distance thresholds and distance parameters. If the distance thresholds are too small, many session classes are generated. But if they are too large, sessions that belong to different classes may be merged. Among the three distance thresholds, β_1 is the most important since the two other values are related to it, and can be derived from it. The selection of threshold values depends on the application. Small threshold values can be used for applications in which the difference between session classes is significant, i.e., the distance between them is "far"; otherwise, large threshold values are used since they can discriminate the trivial difference between session classes. The selection of distance parameters is also important. The parameters can be viewed as the weight of the three similarity scores. Different applications may require different parameter values, and adjustment of these parameters accordingly is necessary.

In the experiments, we choose 721 session instances that belong to 4 template sequences as the input of clustering algorithm. We first test the number of clusters generated with different distance parameters in the sampling step. We set the neighborhood distance parameter as 0.3, and the coefficient parameter is dynamically changed from 0.0 to 0.7, and the alignment parameter is changed correspondingly. The result is shown in Fig. 7. The figure shows that more clusters are generated when the coefficient parameter is large, and fewer clusters are generated when the alignment parameter is large.

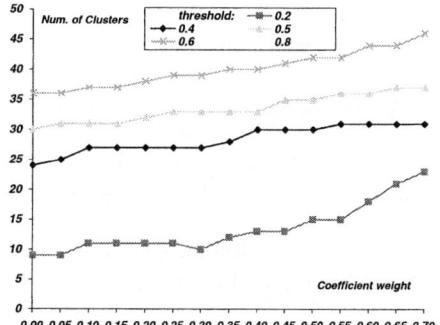

Fig. 7. Number of clusters vs. various distance parameter values

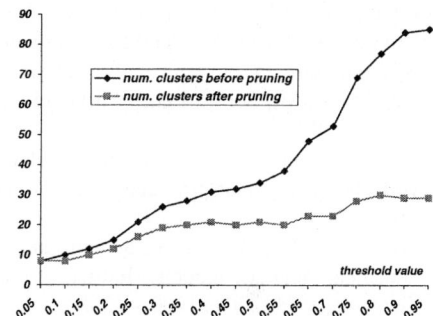

Fig. 8. Number of clusters vs. various threshold values (pruning threshold =10)

Next, we use *0.4,0.3,0.3* as distance parameters in the first step, and *0.5,0.5, 0.0* in the second step, and evaluate the performance under different threshold values. Since the values of β_2 and β_3 are correlated with β_1, we mainly change the value of β_1, and the other threshold values are changed correspondingly. The result is shown in Fig. 8. From the figure, we observe that the number of clusters increases when the threshold value increases. However, the increasing rate after pruning is lower than that before pruning.

6 Conclusion

In this paper, we have discussed our approach to identifying and grouping database user sessions. The results from our approach can be used to tune the database system and predict incoming queries based on the queries already submitted, which can be used to improve the database performance by effective query prefetching, query rewriting and cache replacement. The work presented in the paper has a broader impact on the database and data mining fields. Although the data set used in the paper is based on a clinic application, the idea presented in the paper can be used in other database-based applications, such as the *ERP/CRM* applications that may contain hundreds or even thousands different types of sessions. It can also be used on Web log analysis and DNA sequence analysis.

References

1. Sapia, C.: PROMISE: Predicting query behavior to enable predictive caching strategies for OLAP systems. In: DAWAK. (2000) 224–233
2. Yao, Q., An, A.: Using user access patterns for semantic query caching. In: Database and Expert Systems Applications (DEXA). (2003)
3. Bowman, I.T., Salem, K.: Optimization of query streams using semantic prefetching. In: Proceedings of the 2004 ACM SIGMOD, ACM Press (2004) 179–190
4. Yao, Q., An, A.: Characterizing database user's access patterns. In: DEXA. (2004) 528–538
5. Andreas Behm, Serge Rielau, R.S.: Returning modified rows - SELECT statements with side effects. In: VLDB 2004, Toronto, Canada. (2004)
6. Elnaffar, S., Martin, P.: Characterizing computer systems' workloads. Tr. 2002-461, School of Computing, Queen University. Ontario, Canada. (2002)
7. Calzarossa, M., Serazzi, G.: Workload characterization: A survey. Proc. IEEE **81** (1993) 1136–1150
8. Duy, J., Vaughan, L.: Usage data for electronic resources: A comparison between locally-collected and vendor-provided statistics. The Journal of Academic Librarianship **29** (2003) 16–22
9. Huang, X., Peng, F., An, A., Schuurmans, D.: Dynamic web log session identification with statistical language models. Journal of the American Society for Information Science and Technology **55** (2004) 1290 – 1303
10. Jurafsky, D., Martin, J.H.: Speech and Language Processing:An Introduction to Natural Language Processing,Computational Linguistics,and Speech Recognition. Prentice Hall (2000)
11. Jain, A.K., Murty, M.N., Flynn, P.J.: Data clustering: a review. ACM Computing Surveys **31** (1999) 264–323
12. Berkhin, P.: Survey of clustering data mining techniques. Technical report, Accrue Software, San Jose, CA (2002)
13. Jaccard, P.: The distribution of the flora in the alpine zone. New Phytologist **11** (1912) 37–50
14. Needleman, S.B., Wunsch, C.D.: A general method applicable to the search for similarities in the amino acid sequence of two proteins. Journal of Molecular Biology **58** (1970) 443–453
15. Guha, S., Rastogi, R., Shim, K.: ROCK: A robust clustering algorithm for categorical attributes. Information Systems **25** (2000) 345–366
16. Weinan Wang, O.R.Z.: Clustering web sessions by sequence alignment. In: 13th International Workshop on Database and Expert Systems Applications (DEXA'02). (2002)
17. Birgit Hay, G.W., Vanhoof, K.: Clustering navigation patterns on a website using a sequence alignment method. In: IJCAI Workshop on Intelligent Techniques for Web Personalization. (2001)

Time-Cognizant Recovery Processing for Embedded Real-Time Databases[1]

Guoqiong Liao, Yunsheng Liu, and Yingyuan Xiao

School of Computer Science and Technology, Huazhong University of Science, and Technology, Wuhan, Hubei, P. R. China, 430074
liaoguoqiong@163.com

Abstract. Recovery processing in embedded real-time databases (ERTDBs) is more complex than traditional databases. In this paper, the classifications and consistency constraints of data and transactions in embedded real-time databases are given first. Then time-cognizant recovery principles for different classes of data and transactions are discussed. In terms of these principles, a time-cognizant recovery scheme based on real-time logging is presented, which is suitable for a class of embedded real-time databases applications. Performance evaluations show that the suggested scheme has better performances than traditional recovery techniques in two aspects: the missing deadlines percent of transactions and the time of system denying services after crashes.

GLOSSARY OF NOTATION

X_i-a data object in databases
$avi_b(X_i)$-valid beginning instant of X_i
$avi_e(X_i)$-valid end instant of X_i
$avi(X_i)$-effective period of X_i
$d(X_i,X_j)$-time distance between X_i and X_j
R-deriving data set
R_{mvi}-threshold of time distance of R
TDO-temporal data object
INDO-invariant data object
OTDO-original temporal data object
DTDO-derived temporal data object
TDOS-set of temporal data objects
OTDOS-set of original temporal data objects
DTDOS-set of derived temporal data objects
INDOS-set of invariant data objects
x_i- current value of X_i
t_c-current time
LT-the last committed transaction
$UP(T, X_i)$- updated image of X_i by T
$COM(LT, X_i)$-committed image of X_i by LT

T-an embedded real-time transaction
RS(T)-read data set of T
WS(T)-write data set of T
DS(T)-access data set of T
TOS(T)- set of TDO accessed by T
D(T)-deadline of T
$D_f(T)$-final deadline of T
P(T)-execution period of T
AS(T)-actions set of T
OAS(T)-occurred actions set of T
EET(T)-estimate executing time of T
CT(T)-commit instant of T
T_s-sampling transaction
TSS-set of sampling transactions
T_p-processing transaction
TPS- set of processing transactions
T_m-manipulating transaction
TMS- set of manipulating transactions
$S_t(X_i)$-state of X_i at time t
$S_t(ERTDB)$-state of ERTDB at time t

[1] This work is supported by the National Postdoctor Foundation (No. 2003034482)

1 Introduction

With the advances of embedded hardware devices and the increasing amount of data processed in embedded systems, more and more applications of embedded databases are emerging[1]. One class of applications, such as data collections, air traffic controls, real-time monitoring and fault alarming, demand that embedded databases are able to process the timing constraints of data and transactions and provide timely and correct results[2]. The common characteristics of this kind of applications are that they all involve gathering data from external environment, processing the gathered data in time and providing timely responses. The embedded databases with these characteristics are called embedded real-time databases (ERTDBs).

In general, after being embedded into devices, ERTDBs should have the ability of high fault-tolerance, and can resume services again as quickly as possible after crashes. However, the probability of failures in embedded systems, especially in embedded mobile environment, is higher than that in desktop systems. Moreover, some unique recovery requirements of ERTDBs should be taken into consideration. The main recovery characteristics of ERTDBs can be generalized as following [3-7]:

(1) Besides internal or logical consistency, the time consistency of data is also required to recover in ERTDBs.

(2) In order to prevent "priority inversion", the fault transactions with higher priorities should be recovered earlier than other transactions with lower priorities.

(3) The recovery procedures of ERTDBs should be started as quick as possible and can be performed within a limited time.

(4) In order to reduce the time of system down, the recovery tasks of ERTDBs should be carried through in a parallel way. That is, the recovery processes can be executed alone with system services.

(5) The states of physical world changed by uncommitted transactions should also be restored though relative "compensate" or "alternation" transactions.

Therefore, the recovery processing of ERTDBs is more complex than traditional databases. Obviously, traditional recovery schemes based on REDO/UNDO operations, such as ARIES[8], which only aim to recover the internal consistency of databases, are not suitable for ERTDBs. It is necessary to develop new time-cognizant recovery principles and strategies to recover ERTDBs.

By now, embedded databases are attracting more and more attentions than ever and many software products of embedded databases have been developed[9]. However, fewer studies have been made on recovery processing of embedded databases. Through analyzing these products, almost all of them still adopt traditional UNDO/REDO recovery techniques, not taking embedded characteristics into account and without any consideration about the time constraints of data and transactions.

The researches on real-time databases have been over 20 years since 1980s', and many academic achievements on them have been acquired[10]. The recovery schemes of real-time databases can be classified into log-based and shadow-based. SPLIT is a parallel recovery method based on partitioned logging, which partitions logs into two parts: logs of hot and cold data according to data access frequency[11]. ARUN algorithms are partitioned logging methods with ephemeral logging facilitated by the presence of NVHSS, which can reduce the amount of logs processed at recovery time[12]. The recovery method suggested in [6] partitions logs across critical and non-critical data segments, which allows critical data to be recovered independently. In [13], a simple real-time logging method is presented. Although this approach is simple and easy to implement, as the invariant data objects and temporal data objects have different log record formats, extra overheads to check the formats will be incurred. To eliminate these overheads, multiple log buffers are designed to store the logs of invariant data objects and temporal data objects separately[14]. Shadow-based recovery methods are also studied to recover real-time databases[15-16]. But these methods can't be applied directly on embedded environment.

In this paper, a time-cognizant recovery scheme based on real-time logging is presented. The rest of the paper is organized as follows. Classifications and consistency constraints of real-time data and transactions in ERTDBs are described in Section 2 and Section 3, respectively. Time-cognizant recovery principles are given in Section 4. In section 5, a time-cognizant recovery scheme based on real-time logging is suggested. The performance evaluations of the suggested recovery approach are performed in Section 6. Section 7 concludes the paper.

2 A Classification and Consistency Constraints of Real-Time Data

In this section, a classification of data objects in ERTDBs is given first. Then the consistency constraints of data objects are discussed.

Definition 1. For a data object X, $avi(X)=[avi_b(X), avi_e(X)]$, $avi_b(X) < avi_e(X)$.

Definition 2. If $avi_e(X)$ is an appointed instant, then X is called a temporal data object (TDO); otherwise, X is called an invariant data object (INDO).

For a temporal data object, its value will become invalid once its $avi_e(X)$ is expired, even if it is still stored at databases. While for invariant data objects, their effective periods are deemed to be an arbitrary length. However, it is meaningless to discuss the future instants of invariant data objects. Hence, in following discussions, it is always considered that the valid end instants of all invariant data objects are equal to system current time (notated by t_c) at any time.

Definition 3. If X is derived from a set of data objects $R=\{X_1, X_2, \ldots, X_k\}(k \geq 1)$, then R is called a deriving data set on X, notated by $R \to X$.

Definition 4. If $R \to X$, then $avi(X)=avi(X_1) \cap avi(X_2) \cap \ldots \cap avi(X_k)$, $\forall X_i \in R$, i=1, 2, ..., k.

Definition 5. If X is a TDO and acquired from external environment through sensors (or devices), then X is called an original temporal data object (OTDO).

Definition 6. If X is a TDO and derived from a deriving data set R, then X is called a derived temporal data object (DTDO).

Definition 7. X is said to be externally consistent, iff $t_c \leq avi_e(X)$.

For any invariant data object $X \in INDOS$, it is assumed that their $avi_e(X)$ are always equal to t_c. Therefore, $\forall X \in INDOS$ are externally consistent forever.

Definition 8. If $\forall X \in TDOS$ ($t_c \leq avi_e(X)$), then ERTDB is said to be externally consistent.

Definition 9. For any two data objects X_i, X_j, $i \neq j$, $d(X_i, X_j)=|avi_b(X_i)-avi_b(X_j)|$.

Definition 10. If $\forall X_i, X_j \in R(d(x_i, x_j) \leq R_{mvi})$, $i \neq j$, then R is said to be a set with mutual consistency.

The mutual consistency is used to guarantee that all data objects in R can de produced at a common effective period. R_{mvi} is designed based on the minimal value of effective periods of all data objects in R.

Therefore, if all deriving data sets in an ERTDB are mutually consistent, then the ERTDB is said to be mutually consistent. And if an ERTDB is both externally consistent and mutually consistent, then the ERTDB is said to be time consistent.

3 A Classification and Consistency Constraints of Embedded Real-Time Transactions

In this section, a classification and consistency constraints of embedded real-time transactions are discussed.

Definition 11. For a transaction T, if $RS(T)=\Phi \wedge WS(T) \subseteq OTDOS$, then T is called a sampling transaction, notated by T_s. $TSS=\{T_{s1}, T_{s2}, \ldots, T_{sn}\}$ ($n \geq 1$) is the set of sampling transactions.

The sampling transactions are write-only transactions. They are responsible for sampling the states of physical objects in external environment periodically. In general, this kind of transactions should execute without waiting or blocking, thereby they are generally periodic real-time transactions with hard headlines.

Definition 12. For a transaction T, if $WS(T) \subseteq DTDOS \cup INDOS \wedge RS(T) \subseteq OTDOS \cup DTDOS \cup INDOS$, then T is called a processing transaction, notated by T_p. $TPS=\{T_{p1},T_{p2}, \ldots, T_{pv}\}$ ($v \geq 1$) is the set of processing transactions.

The processing transactions read all classes of data objects to make decisions and may write DTDOs and INDOs. Since they do not interact with physical world directly, they are commonly real-time transactions with soft deadlines.

Definition 13. For a transaction T, if $WS(T)=\Phi \wedge RS(T) \subseteq OTDOS \cup DTDOS \cup INDOS \wedge AS(T) \neq \Phi$, then T is called a manipulating transaction, notated by T_m. $TMS=\{T_{m1}, T_{m2}, \ldots, T_{mk}\}$ ($k \geq 1$) is the set of manipulating transactions.

The manipulating transactions read only all kinds of data to manipulate controlled subsystem through an actions set $AS(T)=\{a_1, a_2, \ldots, a_h\}$ ($h \geq 1$). This kind of transactions do not destroy the state of databases. However, they may change the states of physical world. They are generally hard real-time transactions.

The consistency constraints of embedded real-time transactions include the logical consistency and time consistency. Since the logical consistency of embedded real-time transactions is the same as the transactions in traditional databases, in this section we only discuss the time consistency constraints.

Definition 14. For a transaction T, T is said to be externally consistent, iff $t_c \leq D(T) \wedge \forall X_i \in DS(T)$ ($t_c \leq avi_e(X_i)$).

In terms of Definition 14, T is said to be externally consistent only if both its deadline is not expired and all data objects accessed by it are externally consistent.

Deduction 1. For a transaction T, $D_f(T)=MIN(D(T), MIN(avi_e(X_i)))$, $X_i \in RS(T)$

Proofs: Let $d(T)=MIN(avi_e(X_i))$. In the case of $D(T)>d(T)$: if $d(T)<t_c<D(T)$, then $\exists X \in TOS(T)$ $(t_c>avi_e(X_i))$, i.e., the external consistency of data objects X_i is violated. At this case, $D_f(T)=MIN(avi_e(X_i))$. In contrary, if $D(T)<d(T)$, as t_c is more than $D(T)$, the deadline of T is expired. At this case, $D_f(T)=D(T)$. Therefore, $D_f(T)= MIN(D(T), MIN(avi_e(X_i)))$. □

Definition 15. If $\forall R \in RS(T)$ (R is a set with mutual consistency), then T is said to be mutually consistent.

The mutual consistency of T is that all deriving data sets accessed by it must be mutually consistent. Therefore, differing from traditional transactions, whether an embedded real-time transaction can commit is not only determined by its internal consistency, but also by its external consistency and mutual consistency.

Definition 16. The commitment of T is said to be effective, iff
(1) $\forall X_i \in DS(T)(X_i$ is logical consistency)
(2) $CT(T) \leq D_f(T)$
(3) $\forall X_i \in RS(T)$ $(CT(T) \leq avi_e(X_i))$
(4) $\forall R_i \in RS(T)$ (R is a data set with mutual consistency)
are held at the same time.

Definition 16 can be used to determine whether to restart T or not after crashes. In other words, only if the logical consistency, external consistency and mutual consistency of T are still met at recover time, T should be scheduled to restart.

4 Time-Cognizant Recovery Principles of Embedded Real-Time Databases

In ERTDBs, to redo or undo the outdated values of temporal data objects is meaningless; and to undo a valid value of a temporal data object violates its external consistency. In addition, the recovery procedures of ERTDBs are required to restore the states of physical world influenced by uncommitted transactions. The recovery requirements for different classes of transactions are shown as Table 1.

Table 1. The recovery requirements of embedded real-time transactions

Transactions type / Recovery requirements	T_s	T_p	T_m
Undo TDO	No	No	No
Redo TDO	Yes	Yes	No
Redo INDO	No	Yes	No
Undo INDO	No	Yes	No
Restore the states of physical world	No	No	Yes
Restart transactions	No	Yes	Yes
Refresh OTDO	Yes	No	No

Definition 17. The current value x_i of X_i at time t is said to be the state of X_i at t, notated by $S_t(X_i)$, i.e., $S_t(X_i)=x_i$.

Definition 18. The set of values of all data objects in an ERTDB at time t is said to be the state of ERTDB at time t, i.e., $S_t(ERTDB)=\{S_t(X_i)|X_i \in ERTDB\}$.

Definition 19. The value of X_i updated by T is called the updated image of X_i by T, notated by $UP(T, X_i)$.

Definition 20. The value of X_i updated by the last committed transaction (LT) is called the committed image of X_i by LT, notated by $COM(LT, X_i)$.

Definition 21. At time t, if $\exists X_i \in ERTDB((S_t(X_i) \neq COM(LT, X_i)) \vee (X_i \in TDOS \wedge t > avi_e(X_i)))$, then ERTDB is said to be in an inconsistent state.

As an ERTDB is in an inconsistent state, it should be recovered in terms of following time-cognizant rules:

Criterion 1. (Undo criterion for TDO) As long as the value of a temporal data object $X_i \in TDOS$ is written into an ERTDB, the UNDO operation is not necessary even its updated transaction is aborted.

Criterion 2. (Redo criterion for TDO) For a transaction T, if $\exists X_i \in WS(T)(X_i \in TDOS \wedge t_c < avi_e(X_i) \wedge S_t(X_i) \neq UP(T, X_i))$, then redoing X_i with $UP(T, X_i)$.

Criterion 3. (Refresh criterion for OTDO) For a transaction T, if $\exists X_i \in WS(T)(X_i \in OTDOS \wedge t_c \geq avi_e(X_i))$, then starting a new sampling transaction to refresh X_i.

Theorem 1. The external and internal consistency of temporal data objects can be recovered by Criterion 1~3.

Proofs: As to a temporal data object X_i, whether it is needed to redo is determined by whether its $avi_e(X_i)$ is expired.

In the case of $t_c < avi_e(X_i)$: if $S_t(X_i) \neq UP(T, X_i)$, that is the state of X_i is not consistency with external environment, then X should be redone with $UP(T, X_i)$ regardless of the commitment of T(Criterion 2); if $S_t(X_i)=UP(T, X_i)$, that is the state of X_i is consistency with external environment, then no any recovery operation is necessary (Criterion 1).

In the case of $t_c \geq avi_e(X_i)$: if X_i is an original temporal data object, then starting a refreshing transaction to sample the up-to-date value of X_i (Criterion 3); if X_i is a derived temporal data object, then no any recovery operation is necessary. □

Criterion 4. (Undo criterion for INDO) For a transaction T, if $\exists X_i \in WS(T)(X_i \in INDOS \wedge S_t(X_i)=UP(T, X_i) \wedge$ T has not committed), then undoing X with $COM(LT, X_i)$.

Criterion 5. (Redo criterion for INDO) For a transaction T, if $\exists X_i \in WS(T)(X_i \in INDOS \wedge S_t(X_i) \neq UP(T, X_i) \wedge$ T has committed), then redoing X_i with $UP(T, X_i)$.

Theorem 2. The internal consistency of invariant data objects can be recovered by Criterion 4 and 5.

Proofs: As traditional databases, whether the values of invariant data objects are durative is determined by whether its updated transaction T has been committed. As T is not committed, if $S_t(X_i)=UP(T, X_i)$, that is the updated image of X_i by T has been written into database, then X_i should be undone with $COM(LT, X_i)$ (Criterion 4). As T has been committed, if $S_t(X_i) \neq UP(T, X_i)$, that is the updated image of X_i by T has not been written into database, then X_i should be redone with $UP(T, X_i)$) (Criterion 5).
□

Criterion 6. (Restore criterion of states of physical world) For a transaction T, if $\exists a_i \in AS(T)(a_i$ has not occurred), then $\forall a_j \in OAS(T)$(executing the compensating or alterative action of a_i).

Theorem 3. The states of physical world can be restored by Criterion 6.

Proofs: The states of physical world are only changed by the manipulating transactions, which are read only transactions and don't destroy the consistency of databases. The atomicity of the manipulating transactions is either all actions in AS(T) have been executed, or none has been executed. Therefore, as long as one action in AS(T) has not been executed as failures occur, the states of physical world must be restored.

In terms of Criterion 6, in the case of $OAS(T) \neq \Phi$ and $OAS(T) \neq AS(T)$, the compensating or alterative action of $\forall a_j \in OAS(T)$ should be executed; otherwise, no any recovery operation is necessary. □

Criterion 7. (Restart criterion of T_p and T_m transactions) For a transaction T, if
(1) $t_c + EET(T) \leq D_f(T)$
(2) $\forall X_i \in RS(T)(t_c < avi_e(X_i))$
(3) $\forall R \in RS(T)$(R is a data set with mutual consistency)
are met at the same time, then restarting T.

Criterion 7 is accordant with Definition 16.

5   Timing-Cognizant Recovery Scheme

In terms of above criteria, since UNDO operation never used to recover temporal data objects and whether to redo a temporal data object is determined by its effective period, we can leverage on this information to design proper logging strategies for different data types. In this section, a time-cognizant recovery scheme based on real-time logging is discussed.

For temporal data objects, before images (BFIM) are not necessary to write into logs, but the valid beginning and end instants should be written. Therefore, The log of a temporal data object consists of *a transactions identifier (TID), an object identifier (OID), an after image (AFIM), a valid beginning instant* and *a valid end instant*; while the log of an invariant data object consists of *TID, DID, BFIM* and *AFIM*.

Differing from traditional databases, the transactions with feasible deadlines should be restarted after crashes in ERTDBs. Therefore, besides *transactions operations type (BEGIN, COMMIT and ABORT)*, the timing information including *deadlines, execution periods, estimate executing time* and *begin time* of transactions should written into logs. If current time plus the estimate executing time is less than the deadline of the fault transaction, then it should be restarted.

Since ERTDBs will change the states of physical world through actions triggered by the manipulating transactions, the information of occurred actions should also be recorded into logs. Each action log consists of *a transaction identifier* and *an actions identifier(AID)*.

For supporting the sampling and manipulating transactions with hard deadlines to be recovered first, the logs of different classes of transactions are planned to place into different partitions. Thus, the system can restore services again once the sampling and manipulating transactions are recovered, and the recovery processing of the processing transactions can be made along with system services. The recovery algorithms of different transactions are described as Figure1, 2 and 3, respectively.

```
REV_SampleTrans( )
BEGIN
FOR ∀Tᵢ∈TSS
   get the BEGIN log of Tᵢ;
   IF t_c≥t_b+P(Tᵢ) /* Next period is expired; t_b is the last begin time of Tᵢ
      restart Tᵢ;
   ELSE
      scan logs of Tᵢ forward;
      IF update log of Xᵢ by T exists /* has sampled
         IF S_t(Xᵢ)≠AFIM(Xᵢ)
            S_t(Xᵢ):=AFIM(Xᵢ) /* Criterion 2
         ELSE /* has not sampled
            restart Tᵢ; // Criterion 3
END
```

Fig. 1. The recovery algorithm of T_s

```
REV_ProcTrans( )
BEGIN
FOR ∀Tᵢ∈TPS
   scan logs of Tᵢ forward;
   determine the write set of Tᵢ -WS(Tᵢ);
   IF T has committed
      FOR ∀Xᵢ∈WS(Tᵢ)( Xᵢ∈DTDOS)
         IF t_c<avi_e(Xᵢ) ∧ S_t(Xᵢ)≠AFIM(Xᵢ)
            S_t(Xᵢ) := AFIM(Xᵢ) /* Criterion 2
      FOR ∀Xᵢ ∈WS(Tᵢ)( Xᵢ ∈INDOS)
         IF S_t(Xᵢ)≠AFIM(Xᵢ)
            S_t(Xᵢ) := AFIM(Xᵢ) /* Criterion 5
   ELSE /* has not committed
      FOR ∀Xᵢ∈WS(Tᵢ)( Xᵢ∈INDOS)
         IF S_t(Xᵢ)=AFIM(Xᵢ)
            S_t(Xᵢ) := BFIM(Xᵢ); /* Criterion 4
      IF t_c+EET(Tᵢ)≤D_f(Tᵢ) ∧ ∀Xᵢ∈RS(Tᵢ)(t_c<avi_e(Xᵢ)) ∧ ∀R ∈RS(Tᵢ) (R is a set with
         mutual consistency)
         restart Tᵢ; /* Criterion 7
END
```

Fig. 2. The recovery algorithm of T_p

```
REV_ManiTrans( )
BEGIN
FOR ∀Tᵢ∈TMS
    scan logs of Tᵢ forward;
    determine the set of occurred actions-OAS(Tᵢ);
    IF OAS(Tᵢ)≠Φ ∧ OAS(T)≠AS(Tᵢ) /* Not all actions in AS(Tᵢ) have been executed
       FOR ∀aᵢ∈OAS(Tᵢ)
           execute the compensating or alterative action of aⱼ; // Criterion 6
       IF tc+EET(Tᵢ)≤Df(Tᵢ) ∧ ∀Xᵢ∈RS(Tᵢ)(tc<avie(Xᵢ)) ∧ ∀R∈RS(Tᵢ)(R is a set with
           mutual consistency)
           restart Tᵢ; // Criterion 7
END
```

Fig. 3. The recovery algorithm of T_m

6 Performance Evaluations

In this section, two performance measures have been selected to evaluate the performances of the suggested scheme: the missing deadlines percent (MDP) of transactions and time of denying services (TODS) after crashes. The selected comparison method is traditional recovery techniques which don't take any timing constraints into consideration.

6.1 Experimental Model and Parameters

The performance analysis is performed on an embedded real-time database prototype system ARTs-EDB, which is designed based on a main memory database(MMDB)[17].

In the system, there are three classes of transactions: the sampling transactions, processing transactions and manipulating transactions. The sampling transactions are periodic transactions invoked at the beginning time of each update periods, which response for updating the values of temporal data objects. One sampling transaction only updates the value of one temporal data object. Hence, the update period of a sampling transaction is defined to be half of the effective period of its corresponding temporal data object. The deadline of a sampling transaction is assumed to be the end of its update period. If a sampling transaction can't commit until its deadline, then it will be aborted and a new sampling transaction should be started.

The processing transactions are generated with an exponential distribution stream at a specified mean rate. Each processing transaction submitted to the system is associated with its creation time, transaction identifier, transaction size, operations, data objects on which operations are performed, deadline and execution priority. If a processing transaction is found to read any invalid value of temporal data objects, it will be aborted and releases all its locks. If the transaction still has a feasible deadline, it will be scheduled to restart later; otherwise, it is discarded.

The manipulating transactions are triggered by the sampling transactions or processing transactions as the internal states of temporal data objects are changed. When predefined conditions are held, one or more actions will triggered to change the states of physical world. The manipulating transactions are transactions with hard deadlines.

We model the database itself as a collection of data objects in main memory. The database consists of three classes of data objects: the original temporal data objects, derived temporal data objects and invariant data objects. Data and transactions characteristics are controlled by the parameters listed in Table 2.

Table 2. Simulation Parameters

Parameter	Meaning	Base value
NumOTDO	Number of original temporal data objects	200
NumDTDO	Number of derived temporal data objects	200
NumINDO	Number of invariant data objects	500
PercentTs	Percent of T_s	50%
PercentTp	Percent of T_p	30%
PercentTm	Percent of T_m	20%
PeriodTs	Period of T_s	5~15ms
NumUpTs	Number of update operations in each T_s	1
NumUpTp	Number of update operations in each T_p	3~5
NumUpTm	Number of update operations in each T_m	0
NumAtTm	Number of actions of each T_m	1~3

6.2 Simulation Results

Two sets of experiments are conducted to evaluate the behaviors of the suggested recovery scheme (SR) and traditional recovery techniques (TR).

Figure 4 shows a comparison of two recovery schemes on MDP with various transaction arrival rates. As we can see, the performance improvement obtained by the time-cognizant recovery scheme is significant. Since the sampling and manipulating transactions can be recovered individually in the suggested scheme, the transactions with hard deadlines can be restarted first, which finally leads to reducing the number of transactions missing deadlines.

Figure 5 shows the impact of transaction arrival rates on the time of denying services. When the transaction arrival rate is high, the time of system down will increases for more transactions are required to recover. The results also indicate that the time-cognizant recovery scheme consistently performs better than the traditional recovery scheme. This is because the time-cognizant recovery scheme can start system services earlier than traditional schemes. In traditional schemes, the system is up only after all data have been recovered. While in the time-cognizant recovery scheme, the system can be up as long as the data accessed by the sampling and manipulating transactions are recovered.

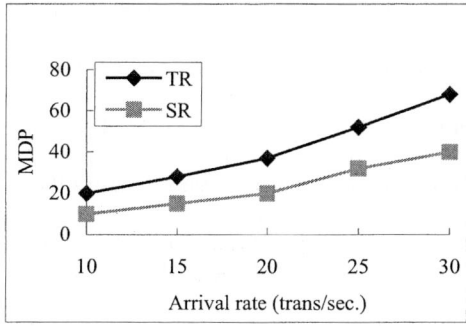 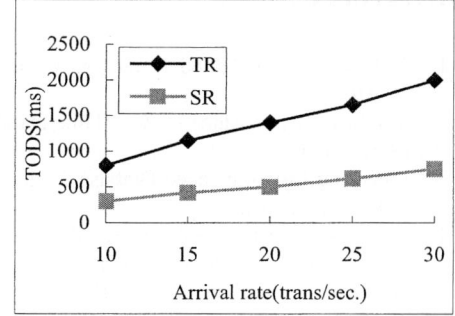

Fig. 4. The influence of arrival rate on MDP   **Fig. 5.** The influence of arrival rate on TODS

7   Conclusions

In this paper, a time-cognizant recovery scheme for embedded real-time databases is proposed. The simulation results show that the suggested scheme has better performances than traditional recovery techniques. The key features of the scheme can be summarized as follows.

(1) The data objects in embedded real-time databases are classified into temporal data objects and invariant data objects by external effective intervals. The temporal data objects can be further divided into both original and derived temporal data objects by the sources of data objects. For the temporal data objects, UNDO operation is not necessary and whether to redo a temporal data object is determined by whether its external effective interval is expired. For an original temporal data object, if its effective period is passed at recovery time, then a refreshing transaction should be started to sample its up-to-date value in physical world.

(2) The embedded real-time transactions can be classified into three classes: the sampling transactions, processing transactions and manipulating transactions, in terms of the access data sets of transactions. In order to support parallel recovery and reduce the time of system down, the logs produced by different classes of transactions are planned to store into different partitions. Thus the system can resume services again once the recovery processing to the sampling and manipulating transactions are performed; while the recovery processing to the processing transactions should be executed alone with system services.

(3) Apart from internal consistency, the suggested scheme can recover the external consistency of databases and the states of physical world influenced by embedded real-time transactions. The uncommitted transactions can be restarted automatically by the recovery procedures of ETRDBs if their internal consistency, external consistency and mutual consistency are still met after crashes.

References

1. Sixto Ortiz, Embedded Databases Come out of Hiding, IEEE Computers, 2000,33(3): 16~19.
2. A. Bestavros, Advance in Real-Time Database System Research. ACM SIGMOD Record, 1996, 25(1): 3~7.
3. Yunsheng Liu. Advanced Dtabase Technology. Beijing: National Defence Industry Press, 2001,3. (in Chinese)
4. J. Huang, L. Gruenwald. Impact of Timing Constraints on Real-time Database Recovery, in Proceedings of the Workshop on Databases: Active and Real-time Table of Contents, Maryland, United States, Nov. 1996: 54 ~58.
5. R. M. Sivasankaran, K. Ramamritham, J. A. Stankovic, System Failure and Recovery. Real-Time Database Systems, 2001: 109~124.
6. S. LihChyun, J. A. Stankovic., S. H. Son, Achieving Bounded and Predictable Recovery Using Real-time Logging, in IEEE Proceedings of Real-Time and Embedded Technology and Applications Symposium, Sept.2002: 286~297.
7. R. M. Sivasankaran, K. Ramamritham, and J. Stankovic, Logging and Recovery Algorithms for Real-time Databases, University of Massachusetts, Technical Report, 2000.
8. C. Mohan, D. Haderle, B. Lindsay et al. ARIES: A Transaction Recovery Method Supporting Fine-granularity Locking and Partial Rollbacks Using Write-ahead Logging. ACM Transactions on Database Systems, 1992, 17(1): 185~194.
9. MA Olson. Selecting and Implementing an Embedded Database System. IEEE Computers, 2000,33(9): 27~34.
10. J. R. Haritsa, K. Ramamritham. Real-time Database Systems in the New Millennium. Real-Time Systems, 2000,19: 205~208.
11. R. Sivasankaran, K. Ramamritham, JA Stankovic, et al. Data Placement, Logging and Recovery in Real-Time Active Databases, In International workshop on Active Real-Time Databases, June 1995, 226~241.
12. Kan-Yiu Lam, Tei-Wei Kuo, Real-time Database Systems Architecture and Techniques. Boston: Kluwer Academic Publishers, 2001.
13. L. Cabrere, J. A. Mcpherson, P. M. Schwarz, et al. Implementing Atomicity in Two Systems: Techniques, Tradeoffs and Experience, IEEE Transactions on Software Engineering, 1993, 19(10): 950~961.
14. J. Huang, L. Gruenwald, Logging Real-Time Main Memory Database, in Proceeding of International Computer Symposium, December 1994: 1291~1296.
15. Eun-Mi Song, Young-Keol Kim, Chanho Ryu. No-log Recovery Mechanism Using Stable Memory for Real-time Main Memory Database Systems. In Proceedings of the Sixth International Conference on Real-Time Computing Systems and Applications, 1999: 428~431.
16. LihChyun Shu, Huey-Min Sun, Tei-Wei Kuo, Shadowing-based Crash Recovery Schemes for Real-time Database Systems, in Proceedings of the 11th Euromicro Conference on Real-Time Systems, June 1999: 260~267.
17. GuoQiong Liao, YunSheng Liu, YingYuan Xiao, CPU Scheduling in an Embedded Active Real-Time Database System, In Proceedings of the 11th ISPE International Conference on Concurrent Engineering, June 2004: 903~908.

An Efficient Phantom Protection Method for Multi-dimensional Index Structures

Seok Il Song[1], Seok Jae Lee[2], Tae Ho Kang[2], and Jae Soo Yoo[2]

[1] Deparment of Computer Engineering, Chungju National University, 123 Iruymeon,
Gumdanli, Chungju, Chungbuk, 380-702, South Korea
sisong@chungju.ac.kr
[2] Department of Computer and Communication Engineering, Chungbuk National University,
8 Gaesindong Cheongju, Chungbuk, 361-763, South Korea
{cyberdb, thkang, yjs}@chungbuk.ac.kr

Abstract. In order for a multi-dimensional index structure to be integrated into a commercial database system, efficient concurrency control techniques are necessary. The techniques must support all degrees of isolation offered by the database system. Especially the degree 3 isolation, called no phantom read, protects search ranges from concurrent insertions and the rollbacks of deletions. In this paper, we propose a new phantom protection method for multi-dimensional index structures that uses multi-level grid technique. The proposed mechanism is independent of the types of multi-dimensional index structures, i.e., it can be applied to all types of index structures such as tree-based, file-based and hash-based index structures. Also, it achieves low development cost and high concurrency with low lock overhead. It is shown through various experiments that the proposed method outperforms existing phantom protection methods for multi-dimensional index structures.

1 Introduction

In the past couple of decades, modern database applications, such as geographic information systems (GIS), mobile location service (MLS), computer-aided design (CAD), medical image repositories and multimedia databases have emerged. The applications commonly are required to manipulate multi-dimensional data. For example, GISs store and retrieve two-dimensional geographic data about various types of objects such as a building, a river, a city and so on. Also, MLS systems provide clients with the current locations of moving objects such as mobile phones. The locations of moving objects are represented as points in the two-dimensional space.

To satisfy the requirements of the emerging database applications, various multi-dimensional index structures have been proposed. There are space partitioning methods like Grid-file[3] and K-D-B-tree[5] that divide the data space along predefined or predetermined lines regardless of data distributions. On the other hand, such as R-tree[1] and CIR-tree[4] are data partitioning index structures that divide the data space according to the distribution of data objects inserted or loaded into the tree. Besides,

Hybrid-tree[8] is a hybrid approach of data partitioning and space partitioning methods, VA-file[14] uses flat file structure, and [13] uses hashing techniques.

The multidimensional index structures are should be integrated into existing database systems to support the modern database applications. Even though the integration is an important and practical issue, not much previous work for it exists. To integrate an access method into a DBMS, we must consider two problems such as concurrency control and recovery. The concurrency control mechanism contains two independent problems. First, techniques must be developed to ensure the consistency of the data structure in presence of concurrent insertions, deletions and updates. Second, phantom protection methods that protect searchers' predicates from subsequent insertions, and the rollbacks of deletions before the searchers commit must be developed [6, 7]. On the first issue, which is the maintenance of physical consistency of index structures, several methods that use lock coupling techniques and link techniques have been proposed for multi-dimensional index structures [11, 12, 15]. However, on the second issue, which is a phantom protection technique, only a few methods have been proposed [6, 7, 12]. [6, 7] proposed a granular locking method for multi-dimensional index structures while [12] use predicate locking approach.

Those phantom protection methods have some problems. First, the lockable granules are the nodes of index trees. Therefore it is difficult to integrate them with existing concurrency control algorithms that use locks on the nodes of index trees. Second, they work efficiently in space partitioning methods that do not allow overlaps between lockable granules. However, in data partitioning methods which is more general index structures, they are less efficient due to the overlaps between the index nodes, and insert algorithms of the index structures must be modified. Finally, they are only applicable to the tree-based index structures. Even though most of existing multi-dimensional index structures are tree-based, there are several nontree-based index structures[13, 14]. They do not need complex concurrency control algorithms but proper phantom protection methods should be provided.

In this paper, we propose a new phantom protection method that uses a hybrid approach of predicate locking and granular locking. The basic idea of the proposed method is to partition the multi-dimensional data space into a fixed number of cells and to assign a unique number to each cell. Then, we use the cells as lockable units. A searcher's predicate is mapped to a set of a number of cells by selecting cells that are overlapped with the searcher's predicate. The searcher acquires locks on the cells to protect phantoms. An inserter(deleter) maps an object to be inserted(deleted) to a number of cells, and acquires locks on the cells.

The contributions of this paper can be summarized as follows. First, the proposed phantom protection method is easy to implement. Also, the integration of the proposed method into existing DBMSs is straightforward. Second, it can be used for all kinds of index structures regardless of their basic data structures, e.g., tree-based, file-based or hash-based. Finally, various experiments show that the performance of the proposed method outperforms the existing methods. This paper is organized as follows. Section 2 gives the description of existing phantom protection methods in detail, and presents the motives of our proposed algorithm. In section 3, we describe the proposed phantom protection method. In section 4, we show the performance results and finally, section 5 concludes this paper.

2 Related Works

To our knowledge, the initial phantom protection method for multi-dimensional index structures is proposed by Kornacker, Mohan and Hellerstein[11]. It addressed the problems of predicate locking mechanism and proposed hybrid approaches that synthesize two-phase locking of data record with predicate locking. In the hybrid mechanism, data records that are scanned, inserted or deleted are protected by the two-phase locking protocol. In addition, searchers set predicate locks to prevent phantoms. Furthermore, the predicate locks are not registered in a tree-global list before the searcher starts traversing the tree. Instead, it is directly attached to nodes. However, since the tree structure changes dynamically as nodes split and MBRs are expanded during key insertions, the attached predicates have to adapt to the structural changes. Also, each node of index trees has an additional space for a predicate table consisting of predicates of searchers, inserters and deleters. The size of the table is variable, and the contents of the table must be changed whenever the MBR updates or node splits are performed. These properties make the maintenance of predicate tables expensive.

To overcome the shortcomings of hybrid mechanism of [11], Chakrabarti and Mehrotra have proposed a granular locking approach in [6, 7]. The predicate locking offers potentially higher concurrency, typically the granular locking is preferred since the lock overhead of a predicate locking approach is much higher than that of a granular locking approach. [6, 7] define the lowest level MBRs as the lockable granules. Each lowest level MBR corresponds to a leaf node of the R-tree. The granules dynamically grow and shrink with insertions and deletions of entries to adapt data space to the distribution of the objects. The lowest level MBRs alone may not fully cover the embedded space, i.e., the set of granules may not be able to properly protect search predicates resulting in phantoms. Accordingly, they define additional granules called external granules for each non-leaf node in the tree, such that the lowest level MBRs together with the external granules fully cover the embedded space.

The granular locking mechanism is much more efficient than the predicate locking mechanism. The lockable granules are nodes of index trees so it uses the existing object locking mechanism of database systems. Also, unlike predicate locking mechanism, it does not need to maintain additional information at each node for storing predicates. However, when the granules are changed or overflow occurs, it must acquire ix-locks on all nodes overlapped with the object. This requires inserters to traverse the index tree from root to find overlapping nodes. Since it acquires locks on index nodes, it is difficult to integrate with existing concurrency control algorithms because of conflicts of purpose of locks.

3 The Proposed Phantom Protection Method

3.1 Basic Idea

The basic idea of the proposed phantom protection method is to partition the multi-dimensional data space into 2^b rectangular cells, where b denotes the user specified number of bits. Then, we allocate a unique bit-string of length b to each partitioned cell. Each unique bit string can be converted to a unique integer value, and the integer value is used as a lock identifier of database systems. A searcher's predicate is mapped to a number of cells, and use the bit-string of each cell as a lock identifier. Then, the searcher acquires s-locks on all of the cells that correspond to search predicates before starting search operations. On the other hand, inserters and deleters obtain x-locks on the cells corresponding to the objects to be deleted and inserted.

A small number of bits b_i is assigned for each dimension i, and 2^{b_i} slices along the dimension i are determined in such a way that all slices are equally full. Let b be the sum of all b_i, i.e., $b = \sum_{i=1}^{d} b_i$, where d is the number of dimension. Then, the data space is divided into 2^b hyper-rectangular cells, each of which can be represented by a unique bit-string of length b. Each cell covers the same size of region and the union of the cells covers the whole data space.

We use the partitioned cells as lockable units. A searcher's predicate can be converted to a number of cells. This is easily done by selecting cells that are overlapped with the predicate. Since we select all overlapped cells, the union of the selected cells covers the area of a search predicate. The searcher, then, acquires s-locks on all of the selected cells. Easy mapping of a given search predicate onto a set of lockable units is an important property for an efficient phantom protection method [6].

We should be able to easily map the cells to lock identifiers used by the standard lock managers of database systems to reduce the cost of lock management. Each cell has a unique bit-string of length b. The bit-string can be mapped to a unique integer. It will be done by casting the bit-string to integer type. It means that each cell is represented with a unique integer that is generally used as a lock identifier of the standard lock managers. With this mapping mechanism, the searcher can acquire s-locks on all of the selected cells by using the record locking mechanism of database systems. Similarly, an inserter(deleter) maps the MBR of an object to be inserted(deleted) to a number of cells, and acquires x-locks on the cells. This will protect phantom problems. Fig. 1 shows an example of the proposed algorithm. In this example, we assume that the data space is 2 dimension, the region is from (0, 0) to (15, 15), and b is 8. We divide the data space into 2^8 cells.

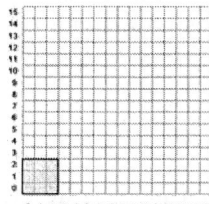

Fig. 1. Mapping of search region

The shaded area represents a searcher's predicate, which is from (0, 0) to (2, 2). The number of cells overlapped with the search predicate is 9. We map the cell that covers from (0, 0) to (1, 1) to 00000000(0). With the same method, the remained cells are mapped to 1, 2, 16, 17, 18, 32, 33 and 34. The searcher acquires s-locks on all of the cells by using a standard lock manager before starting its search operation. Subsequently, an inserter is trying to insert an object (0, 0) into the data space. Like the searcher, it maps the object to a cell 0, and requests commit duration x-lock on it before starting its insert operation. However, since the searcher already has an s-lock on the same cell, the inserter must wait until the searcher commits.

The number of locks of a searcher in the proposed method is totally dependant on the b and its query size, i.e., as the b and the query size increase, the number of locks increases. The number of locks of a searcher is calculated approximately by the following equation, $sn = \lceil 2^b \cdot querysize \rceil$, where sn is the number of cells of the searcher's predicate, and $querysize$ is the query size of the searcher, which is the ratio of the region size of the searcher's predicate to the total size of the data space.

When b is 10 and a $querysize$ is 0.05, the sn is 51. If b is 16 with the same $querysize$, the sn is 3237. As will be shown in the performance evaluation in Section 4, 6~10 is enough as the value of b. Also, we can fix the b as a reasonable value. However, the $querysize$ will be variable according to the users. Therefore, even though the b is fixed to 10, as the $querysize$ is increased, the sn is linearly increased.

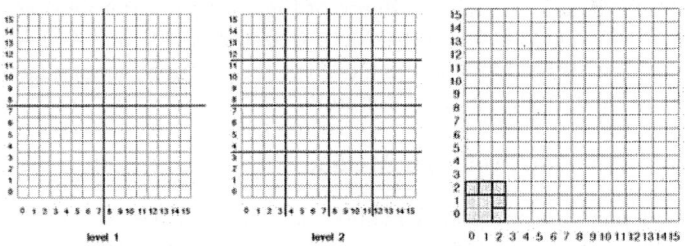

Fig. 2. Hierarchical organization & mapping

The shortcoming of the proposed algorithm is that the required number of locks for a searcher's predicate can be too large according to its query size. This lock overhead may degrade the overall performance. To overcome this problem, we hierarchically organize the partitioned cells like Multi-Level Grid-file[10]. On each level, we group cells to $2 \cdot l \cdot d$ clusters of cells, where l is the level. For example, as shown in first two figures of Fig. 2, on level 1, 4 clusters exist and each cluster contains 64 cells, and on level 2, there are 16 clusters, and each cluster contains 16 cells. On the highest level, level 0, only one cluster that covers all of the cells exists. The number of levels is determined by the equation, $\left\lceil \frac{b}{d} \right\rceil + 1$.

After clustering the cells on each level, we also assign a unique bit-string of length ($lb+b$) to each cluster, where lb denotes the number of bits for representing the level. A bit string for a cluster is composed of a bit string for a level of length lb and the bit string of the lower left cell in the cluster. In this hierarchical approach, lock identifiers are determined as the following. After obtaining overlapped cells with a searcher's predicate, for each level, clusters are selected from the selected cells. This is done in ascending order of level.

For example, in the third figures of Fig. 2, we map a searcher's predicate which is from (0, 0) to (2, 2) to lockable units. Overlapped cells with the search predicate are 0, 1, 2, 16, 17, 18, 32, 33 and 34. Then, we find clusters from the selected cells. There is one cluster on level 3, and 5 clusters on level 4. The cluster on level 3 is mapped to 011(level)+00000000(bit-string for the lower left cell in the cluster), which is 768 in decimal integer. The remained clusters can be also mapped by the same method to integers. The searcher acquires s-locks on all of the mapped clusters. The number of locks required for the searcher is reduced to 6 compared to that of Fig. 1. With this strategy, we can reduce the number of locks.

In this hierarchical approach, for an inserter(deleter), x-locks on the cells that are overlapped with the MBR of an entry to be inserted(deleted) are not sufficient. For example, in the third figure of Fig. 3, the searcher keeps an s-lock on a cluster on level 3 and s-locks on 5 clusters on level 4. Then, an inserter is trying to insert an object (0, 0). The inserter maps the entry to a cell 0, requests an x-lock on the cell, and acquires an x-lock on it since the searcher keeps s-locks not on the cell 0 but the cluster 768. The entry (0, 0) will be a phantom for the searcher. To avoid this situation, the inserter must acquire ix-locks on all clusters that overlapped with the MBR of the entry except the lowest level cluster. The x-lock must be acquired on the lowest level cluster. Again, in the third figure of Fig. 3, the inserter must acquire ix-locks on cluster 000+00000000, 001+00000000, 010+00000000 and 011+00000000, besides an x-lock on 100+00000000. In this case, the inserter cannot acquire the ix-lock on 011+00000000 until the searcher commits.

3.2 Dynamic Phantom Protection Method

The proposed phantom protection method described in the previous subsection assumes that the multi-dimensional data space is static. If the data space of an application is static and we can know the data space area preliminary, the proposed algorithm works well. However, when the entire data space is dynamically changed, we should estimate the maximum data space area to apply our proposed method. However, this will increase the dead space and the overall concurrency may be downgraded.

Consequently, we propose a dynamic phantom protection method. In order to efficiently protect phantoms in dynamically changing data space, 2^b rectangular cells must be adapted as the data space grows or shrinks. Fig. 3 (a) shows the original data space. Fig. 3 (b) shows the expanded data space by a number of insertions so the cells are resized to be adapted to the changed data space. Once the data space is changed and cells are resized, inserters, deleters and searchers must acquire locks on the resized cells

For example, in the right figure of Fig. 3, a searcher with a predicate, (6, 6) to (8, 8), which is initiated before the data space is changed, has been acquired an s-lock on cell 15 which is overlapped with the search predicate. Then, the data space grows, and the cells are resized to be adapted to the changed data space as in the right figure of Fig. 3. An inserter requests an x-lock on the cell 10' to insert a new point entry (7, 7) and it can acquire the x-lock on the cell since none keeps locks on the 10'. Subsequently, the searcher lost the s-lock on the area (6, 6) to (8, 8), and the new entry (7, 7) can be a phantom for the searcher if the searcher scans the area repeatedly.

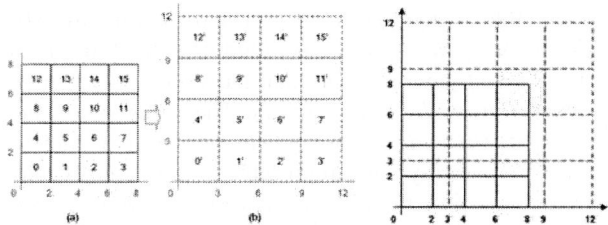

Fig. 3. The expansion of data space

In order to avoid this situation, the inserter must acquire x-locks on cells 15' which is 10 in the original data space as well as 10'. However, if transactions that are initiated before the data space is changed are not remained, the inserter does not need to acquire the x-lock on 15. From now on, a transaction that is initiated before the data space is changed and a transaction that is initiated after the data space is changed are called an old transaction and a new transaction, respectively. In the right figure of Fig. 5, we can easily know why cell 15 should be locked. The shaded cell, (6, 6) to (9, 9) is 10'. The cell 10' is overlapped with a cell 15, (6, 6) to (8, 8) on the old data space. From this fact, we can determine that the cell 15 of the original data space must be locked. Therefore, final cells to be locked are 10' and 15' on the changed data space. For another example, if a searcher tries to obtain an s-lock on the cell 5' in the right figure of Fig. 5, it must also acquire locks on 5, 6, 9 and 10 of the original data space that are overlapped with cell 5' of the changed data space.

Rule 1. *If the data space has been changed and old transactions are still being performed, new transactions must acquire locks on the cells of changed data space and, moreover, the cells of the original space that are overlapped with the locked cells of the changed data space.*

With the rule 1, we can protect phantoms from arising even when the data space is dynamically changed. However, we must solve the following two problems to apply the rule 1. First, who does determine the time to change the MBR of the data space and how does he or she inform other transactions of the changed MBR? Second, how can new transactions know that old transactions are remained?

In tree-based index structures, the MBR of the root node represents the MBR of the data space. When the index structure is nontree-based, we can easily maintain the MBR of data space by updating the MBR on every insertion. An inserter that updates the MBR of the root node can determine the time to change the MBR of the data space. If the MBR of the data space is changed whenever the MBR of the root node is updated, the overhead to handle the change may reduce the concurrency. Therefore, we fix the amount of the change to decide the time to change the MBR of the data space as $\left\lceil \dfrac{sidelength_i}{2^{b_i}} \right\rceil$, where $sidelength_i$ denotes the ith dimension's length of the data space and b_i denotes the number of bits for the ith dimension. That is, we change the MBR of the data space and inform others of the change when one of the $sidelength_i$ is increased or decreased by the side length of a cell along the dimension i.

In order to inform the change to others, we use data structures shown in Fig. 5. In the data structure, the array *dataspace_mbr[]* are used to store old and new MBRs of the data space. The *current_mbr* is a flag that has 0 or 1 as values, and they are used as the index number of array *dataspace_mbr[]*. The *current_mbr* indicates which one is the new MBR between *dataspace_mbr[current_mbr]* and *dataspace_mbr[1-current_mbr]*. Finally, the array *cnt[]* represents the number of old and new transactions that currently are being performed. *cnt[current_mbr]* means the number of transactions that are referring the new MBR, *dataspace_mbr[current_mbr]*.

Whenever an inserter changes the MBR of the root node, it checks the amount of the change by comparing the current MBR of the root or the whole data space with *dataspace_mbr[current_mbr]*. If one of the $sidelength_i$ is changed more than $\left\lceil \dfrac{sidelength_i}{2^{b_i}} \right\rceil$, it updates *current_mbr* as *1-current_mbr* so that *current_mbr* indicates the other *dataspace_mbr[]* which was the old MBR. Then, it updates *dataspace_mbr [current_mbr]*.

Inserters, deleters and searchers increase *cnt[current_mbr]* by 1 before starting their operations and decrease it by 1 when the initiating transactions commit or rollback. Also they generate locks according to the rule 1. At this time, they can decide whether old transactions still exist by reading the *cnt[current_mbr]*, i.e., new MBR and *cnt[1-current_mbr]*, i.e., old MBR. Inserters, deleters and searchers acquire s-latches on the Header data structure to maintain the consistency. They increase or decrease *cnt[]* without acquiring x-latches since we assume reading and writing of words are atomic. Only, inserters and deleters acquire x-latches on the Header when updating *dataspace_mbr[]*. The data structure can be added to an index table that is created when an index is opened. We can ignore the overhead to maintain the Header data structure because the data structure is small enough and most operations acquire s-latches on the Header for instant duration. X-latches are acquired only when the *dataspace_mbr[]* is updated. Usually, the update of *dataspace_mbr[]* is occurred very infrequently. Also, the data structure is not needed to be stored permanently.

Finally, we must consider a situation in Fig. 4. An inserter can insert an object (the point in the Fig. 4) to the outside of the data space. Also, a searcher's predicate (the circle in Fig. 4 (a)) can be placed on the outside of the data space in Fig. 4 (a). However, the inserter and the searcher only acquire locks on the cells that are overlapped with the search predicate or the MBR of an entry to be inserted. Therefore, the search predicate is not fully protected from arising phantoms. In this example, the inserter does not acquire any lock, and the searcher acquires s-locks on cells 14 and 15. Consequently, the inserter can insert the entry to the search predicate, and it will be a phantom for the searcher.

To solve this problem, we define additional lockable units. As shown in Fig. 4 (b), the shaded cells are the additional lockable units. The actual data space are covered by cells 0~15, and to cover the outside of the data space, we partition the outside of the data space into $2^{b_i} \cdot 2d + 2^d$ cells, i.e., additional 2^{b_i} cells are along the upper and lower sides of each dimension *i*, and 2^d cells are on corners of the data space. Then, we apply our mapping method, i.e., select all cells that are overlapped with the MBR of an entry to be inserted or a searcher's predicate.

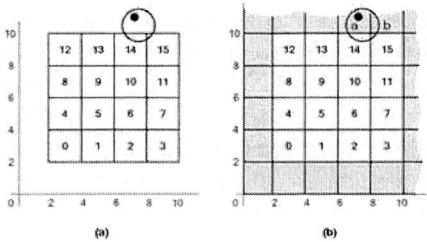

Fig. 4. Additional lock units

4 Performance Evaluation

4.1 Environments

To evaluate the performance of our phantom protection method, we compare it with the granular locking (GL) approach proposed in [6]. We integrate the GL and our proposed phantom protection method into the concurrency control algorithm of [15], which is called as RPLC. The RPLC is mainly focused on the physical consistency of index structure. We implemented both phantom protection methods based on a commercial storage system. Both of them are implemented with locks, latches and logging APIs of the storage system. In order to implement the GL, we modified the insertion algorithm of RPLC so as to perform correctly its granular locking algorithm. The modified insertion algorithm performs additional tree traversing whenever MBRs are changed by insertions or deletions of entries. In addition, we modified the locking strategy of RPLC to adapt the granular locking method.

Also, our phantom protection method was implemented on RPLC. The implementation was simple and easy. We did not need to modify original insert, search and delete algorithms of RPLC. We just add functions to generate locks for search predicates and objects to be inserted or deleted. Then, additional data structure is added into the index table of the storage system. We allocate the root node for lock identifiers of partitioned cells since the root node of RPLC is not changed unless the index structure is destroyed. The first and second records of the root node are reserved as a tree lock and a node lock so the available lock identifiers for phantom protection are $2 \sim 2^b+2$.

We use uniformly distributed 200000, 2~3 dimensional synthetic data set. One of the important parameters of an index tree is a node size. According to the node size, the performance of index trees is varied. We performed experiments with varying the node size ranging from 4Kbytes to 16Kbytes. In all experiments, our phantom protection method outperforms GL. Overall performance is improved as the node size becomes bigger. Also, the performance gap of the both algorithms increases about 10~15 % when the node size is 16Kbytes. The increase of performance gap may be from the growth of contention. We will discuss the results of experiments when the node size is 16Kbytes and the number of dimension is 2 for brevity.

Initially, a CIR-tree is constructed by bulk loading techniques. Subsequently, feature vectors are inserted concurrently by multiple processes under certain workload. Table 1 shows workload parameters. According to the input parameters, the workload generators decide the number of search and insert processes, the number of concurrent processes, the initial number of feature vectors to construct index trees and the selectivity of range queries. Subsequently, the workload generators pass the decided values to a driver program that is written with C and the APIs of the storage system. The driver executes search and insert processes. It randomly selects feature vectors from already inserted data set for queries and from data set to be inserted for insertions. Each process executes multiple transactions. We fix the number of buffer pools as 100 when initiating the storage system. The platform used in our experiments was dual Ultra Sparc processors, Solaris 2.7 with 128 Mbytes main memory.

Table 1. Paramenters and values

Parameters	Values
Number of feature vectors	200000
Insert probability	0% ~ 100 %
Range of queries	0.2 ~ 0.8 %
Number of concurrent processes(MPL)	10 ~ 50
Number of bits	6, 8, 10 (64, 256, 1024 cells)

4.2 Experimental Results

Table 2 compares the performance of the proposed phantom protection method and granular locking (GL) in terms of response time with varying the numbers of insert and search processes. Also, we varied the number of bits from 6 to 10. For brevity, we show the results when the number of bits is 1024 in Table 2.

Table 2 shows the response times of search operations when the insert process ratio is varied from 10 to 90 percent. The proposed algorithm outperforms GL regardless of the number of bits. However, when the insert process ratio is 0, all cases show almost same results. Since their basic search algorithms except the locking strategy are same, the results mean that the lock overheads of GL and the proposed method are similar. As the insert process ratio increases, the performance gap between GL and the proposed method becomes more and more large. The performance gap between GL and the proposed method of insert transactions is larger than that of search transactions. The insert algorithm of GL is more complex than that of the proposed method. It must traverse index tree to find nodes that are overlapped with the changed MBR by the insertion of a new entry.

Table 3 shows the response times of both methods when the selectivity is varying. As the selectivity increases, the overall response times of both methods increases, and the proposed method outperforms GL on all cases. The reason is that as the area of a searcher's predicate increases, the lock contention increases. A drawback of the proposed method is that the number of locks increases as the size of query increases. Consequently, this lock overhead may degrade the concurrency of the proposed method. However, as shown in Table 5, the average number of locks per a search is not so large, and this lock overhead is compensated by high concurrency as we showed in the previous figures. Table 4 shows the scalability of the proposed method. The performance of the proposed method is superior to that of GL. As the number of concurrent processes increases, the performance gap between both methods becomes larger. This result means that our proposed method is scalable for the number of concurrent processes.

Table 2. Response time of insert and search transactions with varying insertion ratios. IR : Insert Ratio, S : Search, I : Insert, DB : database, SEL = selectivity, MPL = multi-programming level, G :GL, P : proposed method

		IR	10	30	50	70	90
varying IR (SEL=0.02, DB size = 200K, MPL = 50)	S	G	0.107	0.128	0.149	0.149	0.149
		P	0.09	0.109	0.126	0.126	0.123
	I	G	0.042	0.044	0.045	0.055	0.072
		P	0.032	0.03	0.032	0.039	0.062

Table 3. Response time of search and insert transactions with varying selectivity

		SEL	0.2	0.4	0.8
varying SEL (MPL=40, IR=20%, DB size=200K)	S	G	0.065	0.071	0.099
		P	0.066	0.067	0.076
	I	G	0.039	0.049	0.062
		P	0.035	0.042	0.051

Table 4. Response time of search and insert transactions with varying MPL

		MPL	10	20	40
varying MPL (SEL=0.8%, IR=20%, DB size=200K)	S	G	0.026	0.054	0.099
		P	0.022	0.049	0.076
	I	G	0.014	0.031	0.062
		P	0.012	0.026	0.051

Table 5. Number of locks

Selectivity(%)	0.2	0.4	0.8
Number of locks	11.63	13.893	17.445

5 Conclusion

In this paper, we have proposed an efficient phantom protection method for multi-dimensional index structures. The proposed phantom protection method is a hybrid approach of predicate locking and granular locking. It does not require any modification of the original algorithm of index structures and acquire any locks on the nodes of index structures. Therefore it is easy to integrate the proposed method with existing concurrency control algorithms. Also, it supports all kinds of index structures regardless of tree-based or not. We performed experiments under the various conditions. The performance results show that our proposed algorithm outperforms GL. Our method is scalable for the number of concurrent processes and the size of query. The performance improvements are not so large, but the development cost of our method is much cheaper than that of GL.

In further research, we will perform more extensive experiments. We performed experiments with synthetic data in this paper. Even though the results are sufficient to show the superiority of our method, we need to perform experiments with real data set for the completeness of the verification. Also, we need to show that our method works well in high-dimensional data space.

Acknowledgement

This work was supported the Program for the Training of Graduate Students in Regional Innovation which was conducted by the Ministry of Commerce, Industry and Energy of the Korean Government. and grant No.R01-2003-000-10627-0 from the Basic Research Program of the Korea Science & Engineering Foundation.

References

1. A. Guttman., "R-Trees: A Dynamic Index Structure for Spatial Searching," Proceedings of ACM SIGMOD, 1984, pp. 47-57.
2. A. Silberschatz and P. B. Galvin, "Operating System Concepts," Addison-Wesley, 1995.
3. J. Nievergelt, H. Hinterberger, and K. C. Sevcik, "The Grid File: An Adaptable, Symmetric Multikey Structure," ACM Transactions on Database Systems, Vol. 9, No. 1, 1984, pp. 38-71.
4. J. S. Yoo, M. G. Shin, S. H. Lee, K. S. Choi, K. H. Cho and D. Y. Hur, "An Efficient Index Structure for High Dimensional Image Data," Proceedings of AMCP, 1998, pp. 134-147.
5. J. T. Robinson, "The K-D-B-Tree: A Search Structure for Large Multidimensional Dynamic Indexes," Proceedings of ACM SIGMOD, 1981, pp. 10-18.
6. K. Chakrabarti and S. Mehrotra, "Dynamic Granular Locking Approach to Phantom Protection in R-Trees," Proceedings of ICDE, 1998, pp. 446-454.
7. K. Chakrabarti and S. Mehrotra, "Efficient Concurrency Control in Multidimensional Access Methods," Proceedings of ACM SIGMOD, 1999, pp. 25-36.
8. K. Chakrabarti and S. Mehrotra, "The Hybrid Tree : An Index Structure for High-dimensional Feature Spaces," Proceedings of ICDE, 1999, pp. 440-447.
9. K. Eswaren, J. Gray, R. Lorie and I. Traiger, "On the Notions of Consistency and Predicate Locks in a Database System," Communication of ACM, November 1976, Vol. 19, No. 11, pp. 624-633.
10. K. Y. Whang, S. W. Kim, G. Wiederhold, "Dynamic Maintenance of Data Distribution for Selectivity Estimation," Journal of VLDB, Vol. 3, 1994, pp. 29-51.
11. M. Kornacker, C. Mohan and J. M. Hellerstein, "Concurrency and Recovery in Generalized Search Trees," Proceedings of ACM SIGMOD, 1997, pp. 62-72.

12. M. Kornacker and D. Banks, "High-Concurrency Locking in R-Trees," Proceedings of VLDB, 1995, pp. 134-145.
13. P. Indyk and R. Motwani "Approximate Nearest Neighbors: Towards Removing the Curse of Dimensionality," Proceedings of STOC, 1998, pp. 604-613.
14. R. Weber, H. Schek and S. Blott, "A Quantitative Analysis and Performance Study for Similarity-Search Methods in High-Dimensional Spaces," Proceedings of VLDB, 1998, pp 194-205.
15. S. I. Song, Y. H. Kim and J. S. Yoo, "An Enhanced Concurrency Control Algorithm for Multi-dimensional Index Structures," IEEE Transactions on Knowledge and Data Engineering, Vol. 16, No. 1, 2004, pp. 97-111.

CMC: Combining Multiple Schema-Matching Strategies Based on Credibility Prediction

KeWei Tu and Yong Yu

Department of Computer Science and Engineering,
Shanghai JiaoTong University, Shanghai, 200030, P.R.China
{tkw yyu}@apex.sjtu.edu.cn

Abstract. Schema matching is a key operation in data engineering. Combining multiple matching strategies is a very promising technique for schema matching. To overcome the limitations of existing combination systems and to achieve better performances, in this paper the CMC system is proposed, which combines multiple matchers based on credibility prediction. We first predict the accuracy of each matcher on the current matching task, and accordingly calculate each matcher's credibility. These credibilities are then used as weights in aggregating the matching results of different matchers into a combined one. Our experiments on real world schemas validate the merits of our system.

1 Introduction

Given two schemas, schema matching finds semantic correspondences between their elements. With the increasing request of knowledge sharing, numerous schema matching techniques have been developed [1, 2, 3, 4]. Combining multiple matching strategies in a single system could achieve better performance, because in this way every possible kind of information about the schemas to be matched can be utilized. Two representative such systems are LSD [2] and COMA [3].

LSD is used in schema integration, i.e. finding mappings between various local schemas to the same mediated schema. To combine individual matchers it performs meta-learning with the *stacking* technique. COMA employs quite straightforward methods such as average and maximization for combination, so that it could avoid the burden of learning. Apart from their merits, LSD and COMA still suffer from some limitations.

For the LSD system, (1) There is one meta-learner for each element of the target schema, thus each element must have a training set. To include enough positive training samples, LSD collects equivalent elements from other schemas which have already been mapped to the target schema. However, in applications other than schema integration, such existing mappings may be scarce. (2) Meta-learners are associated with particular schemas. For applications other than schema integration, matching is performed on arbitrary two schemas, so if the schemas are new to the system, then a set of meta-learners must be trained from scratch, which is very time-consuming. (However, it is possible to release such association at the cost of performance, i.e. to use one meta-learner for any schemas, as implemented for comparison purpose in Sect.3.) (3) Meta-learners must be re-trained if adding/removing base matcher(s). Unfortunately, adding or removing base matchers may be necessary in many scenarios. For example, if the matching task has a time limit, then matchers with iteration or training phase are undesirable and should be removed. (4) Meta-learners in LSD perform weighted sum of the results from base matchers. The weights are obtained by training, and then kept unchanged regardless of what source element is being matched. This, however, is improper because a matcher's effectiveness is always determined by both the target element and the source element.

For the COMA system, (1) The combination methods in COMA, e.g. average and maximization, may be inadequate for complex situations, because in fact each base matcher has very different performance in different conditions, and these simple methods couldn't capture such performance variation. (2) If better performance is needed, users of COMA have to manually choose and configure the combination methods, such as specifying weights for matchers.

In order to overcome these limitations as well as to further improve the performance of matcher combining, in this paper we propose the CMC (Credibility-based Matcher Combiner) system. The matcher combination procedure of CMC is based on the observation that every base matcher has quite different performance in different matching tasks. For example, a matcher exploiting schema structure information would perform well for elements from XML schemas with rich structures, but the same matcher would become unreliable when it comes to "flat" schemas. Therefore, CMC dynamically predicts the accuracy of each matcher based on the characteristics of the current matching task, and accordingly calculates the matcher's credibility. Then, the results from various base matchers are aggregated based on their credibilities.

2   The CMC System

As a matcher combining system, CMC contains a set of base matchers. Most schema-matching techniques developed so far can serve as base matchers. As in LSD and COMA, a base matcher takes two target schemas S_1 and S_2 as input, and outputs a similarity between 0 and 1 for each pairwise combination of S_1 elements and S_2 elements, constituting a $m \times n$ similarity matrix, where m and n are element numbers of S_1 and S_2 respectively. Based on whether an initial similarity matrix is needed or not, base matchers can be divided into two classes.

A key operation of CMC is base-matcher combination. Unlike LSD and COMA, a credibility-based approach is employed in CMC. The underlying rationale is that every base matcher performs very differently in matching different kinds of schema element pair, so the matcher combiner should take into account the anticipated performance of each base matcher for the current matching task and accordingly assign different credit on them. For instance, structure matchers are more credible if the schema elements being matched are embedded in

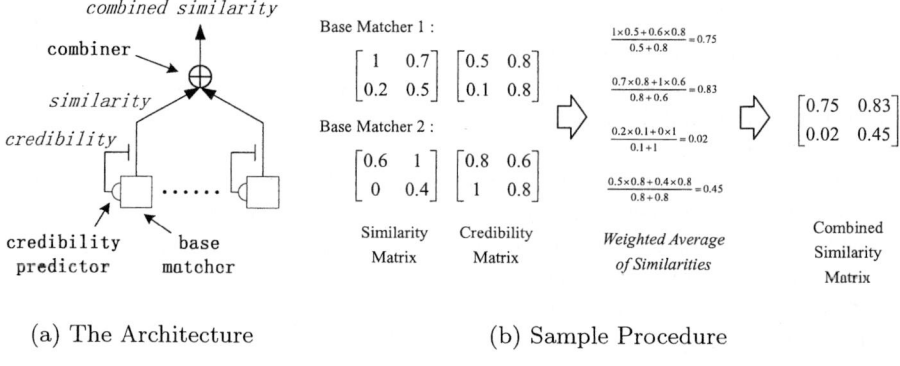

Fig. 1. Matcher Combiner

rich structures. To achieve this idea, in CMC each base matcher is attached with a credibility predictor, which dynamically predicts the matcher's credibility *for each pair of elements being matched*. In this way the combiner receives two matrices from each base matcher, i.e. the similarity matrix and the credibility matrix, then it aggregates all the similarity matrices into one matrix by weighted average, where the weights are determined by the credibility matrices. This procedure is illustrated in Fig.1. Notice that a matcher combiner itself could serve as a base matcher for another combiner.

With base matchers and combiners as modules, one could connect them freely. On the other hand, CMC also provides a default connection policy. There are two layers in this default structure. The bottom layer consists of base matchers that do not require initial similarity, and a combiner aggregates their outputs. Matchers requiring initial similarity constitute the upper layer, with the combined similarity of the first layer serving as their initial similarity. Finally a second combiner aggregates the results from the upper layer, as well as the result of the first combiner, and output the final similarity matrix.

To convert the final similarity matrix to the matching result, i.e. correspondences between schema elements, CMC adopts the method introduced in [3].

2.1 Credibility Prediction

In CMC, a matcher's credibility indicates how much the combiner should trust the matcher. There are two steps in predicting a base matcher's credibility: *accuracy predicting* and *converting accuracy to credibility*. An important feature of this mechanism is that the prediction procedure of one matcher is independent with the others, thus will not be affected by the addition, removal or relocation of the other matchers.

Accuracy Predicting. As the first step of credibility prediction, we predict a matcher's accuracy *for each inputted pair of schema elements*.

For a specific matcher, its matching accuracy in a matching task is correlated with several features of the task (here a *matching task* means the estimating of a pair of schema elements' similarity). For example, for some structure matchers, the number of edges connected to the element to be matched can serve as a feature, because more edges usually indicate more structural information, leading to higher matching accuracy. With this knowledge, we predict a matcher's accuracy in the current matching task as *the mean accuracy of the set of tasks bearing the same features as the current task*. Given that a matcher's output is a numeric similarity, the mean accuracy is defined in terms of the *mean square error (MSE)* of that set of tasks: $MSE = E_{\mathcal{F}}[(sim - sim_{actual})^2]$. Here $\mathcal{F}$ is that set of matching tasks bearing the same features as the current task, and $E_{\mathcal{F}}$ represents the mathematical expectation on the set $\mathcal{F}$. sim_{actual} is 1 for matched element pairs and 0 otherwise. Obviously the less MSE is, the higher the accuracy is.

Two different strategies are presented here to estimate MSE.

Manual Rule For some matchers, the MSE estimation is intuitive enough to be formulated manually.

Take for example the DataType matcher, which compares the data type of schema elements. Its outputted similarity is the only feature correlated to the matching accuracy, indicating the probability that the data types of the two elements are matched. If the data types are unmatched, then these two elements can't be matched at all. If the data types match, then the elements' being matched or not could be equally possible. Therefore, $MSE = (1-sim) \times (sim-0)^2 + sim \times \frac{(sim-1)^2 + (sim-0)^2}{2} = \frac{1}{2} sim$.

Notice that the matcher combiner of CMC could also be regarded as a base matcher, so its accuracy must be calculated as well. With the formulas from [5], we could formulate the MSE of a matcher combiner as follows, under the assumption that base matchers are uncorrelated: $MSE = \sum_{i,j} w_i w_j C_{ij} = \sum_i w_i^2 C_{ii} = \sum_i w_i^2 MSE_i$. Here w_i is the weight of the i-th matcher, and C_{ij} is the correlation between the i-th and the j-th matcher, which is zero under our assumption if $i \neq j$, and equals MSE_i otherwise.

Learning to Predict For most schema matchers, it is difficult, if not impossible, to manually formulate the MSE calculation. Therefore, we use machine-learning to predict MSE from the features of the current matching task.

It is important to select appropriate features of matching tasks for each matcher, and the feature set should include all the possible factors relevant to the matching accuracy. Take for example the Name matcher which compares the schema element labels: longer labels often convey more information, so the length of an element label is a feature; the outputted similarity is also a feature as matchers often have different reliability on different outputs.

With features selected, we train a learner which takes the values of the features as the input and outputs the estimated MSE. Any existing schema matches can be used to construct the training set: for each pair of elements $< e_1, e_2 >$ construct a training sample, where e_1 and e_2 come respectively from the two schemas of the existing match; let the input of the training sample be the feature values of $< e_1, e_2 >$, and the target output be the squared error of their estimated similarity by the base matcher. Since in actual schema matching the matched element pairs are far less than the unmatched ones, we duplicate those samples constructed by matched element pairs, so that their number is equivalent to the number of samples constructed by unmatched element pairs. This last step is to avoid producing a predictor with an overwhelming bias.

Notice that although machine learning is used here, for a particular matcher once the predictor is trained, it could be applied for any matching task and no retraining is mandatory. Moreover, while all kinds of supervised learning methods can be used here, the online learning techniques [6] are preferred as the learner could improve itself in operation, thus further eliminating the worry of having insufficient existing schema matchings for training.

From Accuracy to Credibility. With accuracy (i.e. MSE) estimated, the credibility of each outputted similarity can be calculated as $e^{-C \times MSE}$. Here C is a non-negative constant, determining how fast the credibility falls with the increase of MSE. If C is positive, higher credibility is assigned to matchers with higher accuracy (i.e. lower MSE); if C is zero, the results from matchers are simply averaged, as in COMA. The empirical value of C is 1.0.

3 Evaluation

The CMC system used in the experiments consists of four base matchers, i.e. the Name, DataType, PathName and Leaves matchers, which are introduced in detail in [3]. The default structure of CMC is used, and the machine learning technique used in credibility prediction is the multilayer perceptron [6].

For comparison, another two combination methods are also tested. The *average-combination* method, which is the default combination method of COMA, simply averages the results from base matchers. The *meta-learning* method uses *stacking* for combination, and it trains only one meta-learner for all elements so as to avoid LSD's limitations discussed in Sect.1. When testing these two methods, only the combiners in the system are substituted while all the others remain unchanged. In addition, all the three methods employ the same converter, which is discussed in [3], to convert the similarity matrix to matches. For each method the converter's parameters are tuned to achieve the best performance, and it happens that all the three sets of parameters are the same as in [3].

The test data are five real-world XML schemas on purchase order, which were first used in [3]. In the experiment, we tested the three methods on all the ten matches between the five testing schemas. Considering that machine learning is used in CMC and the meta-learning method, we adopted a cross-validation strategy [6]: the ten matches were divided into five groups, and each time two successive groups were used for testing and the rest were used for training. Thus the testing was conducted for five times altogether. Four measures are adopted to evaluate the matching results, i.e. Precision, Recall, Overall [3], and F-measure [4]. Comparisons between CMC and the other two methods are respectively illustrated in Fig.2 and Fig.3, where the data is computed by subtracting the results of the contrast method from the results of CMC.

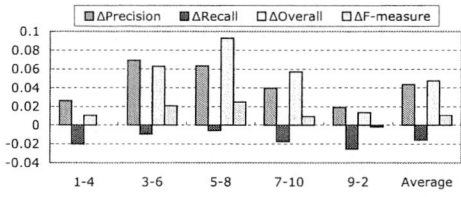 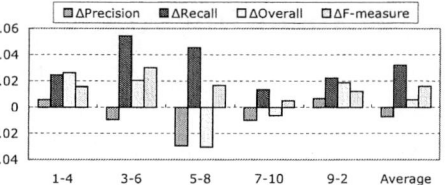

Fig. 2. Average-Combination vs. CMC   **Fig. 3.** Meta-Learning vs. CMC

On average the two integrated measures (Overall and F-measure) are increased significantly by CMC in both comparisons. For the two coupled measures (Precision and Recall), it is interesting to see that, CMC outperforms the average method by higher Precision while outperforms the meta-learning method mainly by higher Recall. We suppose this somewhat exposes the characteristic of the three methods, and CMC is more balanced between Precision and Recall.

4   Conclusion

CMC combines multiple schema-matchers based on their predicted credibility. It not only achieves better matching performance, but also overcomes the limitations of previous combination systems discussed in Sect.1: (1) When machine learning is used in accuracy prediction, arbitrary existing matches can be used for training, and online learning is also applicable, so collecting training set won't be a problem. Once trained, the predictor can work for arbitrary matching task and no retraining is obligatory, so the time for training is neglectable. Actually, as training can be accomplished by developers, the end users may even be unaware of it. (2) The credibility prediction for each base matcher is independent, so adding or removing matchers won't affect the combination. (3) Our combination method could take into account any available information of the current matching, which is specified as input features of credibility prediction. (4) The combination procedure is automatic, while permits users to do customization.

References

1. Rahm, E., Bernstein, P.A.: A survey of approaches to automatic schema matching. VLDB Journal: Very Large Data Bases **10** (2001) 334–350
2. Doan, A., Domingos P., Halevy, A.Y.: Reconciling schemas of disparate data sources: a machine-learning approach. SIGMOD Record **30** (2001) 509–520
3. Do H.H., Rahm, E.: COMA — A System for Flexible Combination of Schema Matching Approaches. In: VLDB 2002, Morgan Kaufmann Publishers (2002) 610–621
4. Berlin, J., Motro, A.: Database Schema Matching Using Machine Learning with Feature Selection. In: Proc. of 14th Intl. Conf. on Advanced Information Systems Engineering (CAiSE). (2002)
5. Perrone, M.P., Cooper, L.N.: When Networks Disagree: Ensemble Method for Neural Networks. In: Neural Networks for Speech and Image processing. (1993)
6. Mitchell, T.M.: Machine Learning. McGraw-Hill (1997)

Translating XQuery to SQL Based on Query Forests*

Ya-Hui Chang, Greg Liu, and Sue-Shain Wu

Department of Computer Science, National Taiwan Ocean University
yahui@mail.ntou.edu.tw

Abstract. It is a difficult task to transform an XQuery posed gainst an XML view into an SQL appropriate for the original relational schema to get data. The main reason lies in the difference of the schema modeling power and the query syntax. In this paper, we propose to represent an XQuery as a set of for trees and return trees, or called the query forests as a whole, based on the functionality of the path expressions specified in each clause. These trees show the structural constraint of the input query and serve as the vehicle to combine the mapping SQL fragments into a complete SQL statement. A prototype has been implemented to show the effectiveness of the transformation process.

1 Introduction

XML has emerged as the de facto standard for data representation and exchange on the World-Wide-Web, and XQuery is proposed as the standard query language for XML data. On the other hand, relational databases with mature techniques are still widely used in enterprises to support critical business operations. The interaction between XML and relational databases has therefore been widely discussed. Particularly, the XQuery posed against an XML view needs to be transformed into SQL appropriate for the relational schema, so that data could be retrieved [1, 2, 3, 4, 5, 6].

The transformation is a challenge due to the differences between the schema modeling power and the query expressive capability. As shown in Figure 1, we can see that a relational schema is *flat*, while the XML schema forms a tree-like structure. An XQuery posed against the sample XML schema is specified as follows to show the difference of the query languages, which intends to retrieve the information about the item whose description contains the word "bicycle" and its maximum bid:

```
XQuery 1:
L1: FOR $i in doc("auction.xml")//item_tuple
L2: LET $t := FOR $b in doc("auction.xml")//bid_tuple
```

---

* This work is partially supported by the Republic of China National Science Council under Contract No. NSC 93-2422-H-019-001.

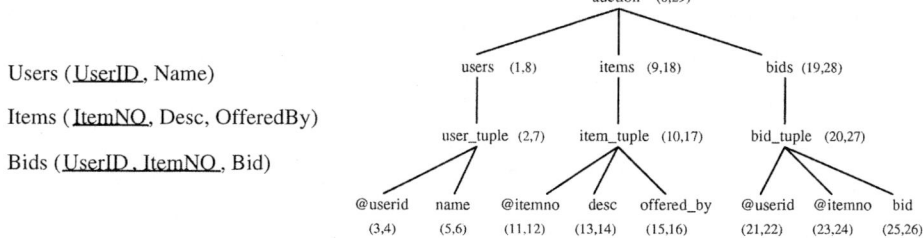

Users (<u>UserID</u>, Name)

Items (<u>ItemNO</u>, Desc, OfferedBy)

Bids (<u>UserID, ItemNO</u>, Bid)

Fig. 1. The sample relational schema and the XML schema

```
L3:            WHERE $b/@itemno = $i/@itemno
L4:            RETURN $b
L5: WHERE contains($i/desc, "Bicycle")
L6: ORDER BY $i/itemno
L7: RETURN    <item_tuple>
L8:              {$i/itemno} {$i/desc}
L9:              <high_bid> max($t/bid) </high_bid>
L10:          </item_tuple>
```

We can see that the compositional or nesting expressions of XQuery, is richer than what SQL could specify. We need to identify the most appropriate corresponding constructs. Moreover, there is no GROUP BY clause proposed for XQuery as in SQL, since XML data (elements) could define the *set* type, and the aggregation function could be directly applied.

This paper will address these issues. The main idea is to represent an XQuery as a set of *for trees* and *return trees*, which are called the *query forests* as a whole. The tree is used to illustrate the structural constraint imposed by each binding variable by collectively representing the path expressions associated with the particular binding variable. To distinguish the functionality presented by each path expression, those specified in the FOR, LET, and WHERE clauses will be used to construct the *for trees*, while the path expressions specified in the ORDER BY and RETURN clauses will be used to construct the *return trees*. By utilizing the tree structures, we propose a query translation system from XQuery to SQL. We have implemented a prototype, and experimental results show that the transformation process could be performed effectively and efficiently.

The rest of this paper is organized as follows. The definitions of query forests are given in Section 2. The procedure of producing the complete SQL statement is presented in Section 3. Future research directions are given in Section 4.

2 The Query Forests

Figure 2 shows the query forests for the sample XQuery, where the tree structures are shown on the left, the SQL fragments associated with each node are shown on the right, and the level sequence is listed in the bottom. They will be explained in this section.

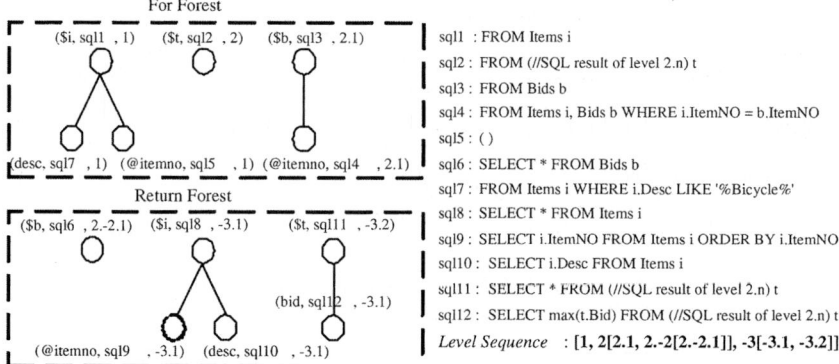

Fig. 2. The sample query forests

2.1 Level Number

Each tree is assigned a *level number* to reflect the nested structure corresponding to the original XQuery. A level number l is composed of one or more level component lc separated by the period, where each lc is an integer which might be positive or negative. In Figure 2, the outermost level has three level numbers: 1, 2, −3, which correspond to the statements in L1, L2, and L7 of XQuery 1, respectively. From L2 to L4, a nested FLOWR expression is represented by the LET clause. The level number 2.1 is assigned to its corresponding *for three*, and the level number $2.-2$ is assigned to its corresponding *return three*.

We briefly explain the rule of assigning the level number to the tree. The level number has the initial number 0. Whenever a new tree is created, the level number will be increased by one, and assigned to the tree. The level number corresponding to the *return tree* will become negative to distinguish from the *for tree*. When a nested structure is encountered, *e.g.*, a LET Clause assigns a new FLOWR expression to a binding variable, or a RETURN Clause consisting of a new FLOWR expression, the period will be added to the current level number to show the nesting structure. A special case is to treat the keyword "RETURN" as the start of a new nested structure. The reason is that many variables might be presented within the same RETURN clause, and we want to somehow represent them collectively.

When we assign the level number to each tree, we will also collect the level number into a level sequence, where the level number at the same level will be separated by comma, and the child level will be encompassed by a pair of square bracket to distinguish it from its parent level. By using the sequence, we know how to combine the SQL fragment produced by each tree into a query corresponding to the original nesting level.

2.2 Mapping Information

For each path possibly presented in the input XQuery, we represent the corresponding relational schema definition in the *mapping table*. Part of the mapping

Table 1. Part of the mapping table for the sample schemas

Path	Tag	Left	Right	Relation	Attribute
auction/items/item_tuple	item_tuple	10	17	Items	NULL
auction/items/item_tuple@itemno	@itemno	11	12	Items	ItemNO
auction/items/item_tuple/desc	desc	13	14	Items	Desc
auction/items/item_tuple/offered_by	offered_by	15	16	Items	OfferedBy
auction/bids/bid_tuple	bid_tuple	20	27	Bids	NULL
auction/bids/bid_tuple@userid	@userid	21	22	Bids	UserID
auction/bids/bid_tuple@itemno	@itemno	21	22	Bids	ItemNO
auction/bids/bid_tuple/bid	bid	21	22	Bids	Bid

Table 2. The join mapping table for the sample schemas

Path	PRelation	PK	FRelation	FK
auction/bids/bid_tuple@userid	Bids	UserID	Users	UserID
auction/bids/bid_tuple@itemno	Bids	ItemNO	Items	ItemNO

table for the two sample schemas is illustrated in Table 1. Consider the element *desc* with the complete path *auction/items/item_tuple/desc*. The corresponding information is represented by the attribute *Desc* of the relation *Items* in the sample relational schema. The interval encoding denoted by the *Left* and the *Right* field, *e.g.*, (13, 14), is used to determine the ancestor/descendent relationship between elements. For those paths with the descendent step, the complete paths with only the child step could be therefore produced. For example, the path "auction/users/user_tuple" will be identified for the path expression "auction//user_tuple".

The structural relationship is constructed by joining specific attributes from two relations in the relational schema, *e.g.*, the attribute *ItemNO* of the relation *Bids* and the attribute *ItemNO* of the relation *Items*. Such structural relationship might be implicitly represented by a path in XML, and the correspondence is represented in the *join mapping table*, as shown in Table 2. It will be used to create join statements in the WHERE clause if necessary.

2.3 FORET Nodes

A for tree or a return tree is a pair of (N, E), where each edge in E will be represented by a single line or a double line to represent the parent/child or ancestor/descendent relationship. Each node in N is a FORET node as defined in the following:

Definition 1. *A FORET Node N is a 3-tuple (label, SQLFrag, ln): (1) label corresponds to a binding variable if N is a root; and will be an XML element or attribute otherwise. (2) SQLFrag is an SQL fragment corresponding to the path from the root to N and the semantic of the tree. (3) ln is a level number.*

Basically, a *for tree* represents how a variable imposes *selection condition* in the query. It is rooted by a binding variable specified in the FOR clause or the LET clause. For this particular variable, all the related path expressions specified in the WHERE clause will be used to construct the remaining nodes of the tree. Consider the leftmost *for tree* in Figure 2. The root is labeled by $\$i$, which is a binding variable in the FOR clause. According to the path expression $\$i$/desc specified in the WHERE clause, the left child node is created, and labeled with *desc*. All the FORET nodes in the same tree have the same level number. On the other hand, the *return tree* represents how a variable is going to project data. It is constructed based on the path expressions specified in the RETURN clause and ORDER BY clause in a similar manner.

We now explain how to create the SQL fragment for each FORET node. Based on the path from the root to this particular node, we consult the mapping table to get the corresponding relation and attribute for this node. The relation will be used to produce the FROM clause, while the processing of the attribute will need to take the semantics into consideration. As to the *for tree*, since the node is created based on the WHERE clause of the XQuery, which poses constraints, the attribute will be represented in the WHERE clause of the SQL fragment, and completed based on the original predicates. For example, the node with the triple *(desc, sql_7, 1)*, is created based on the predicate `constains($i/desc, ''Bicycle'')`, as shown in L5 of XQuery 1. The corresponding SQL fragment sql_7 will be `FROM Items i WHERE i.Desc LIKE '%Bicycle%'`.

As to the *return tree*, the node is created based on the RETURN clause or ORDER BY clause of the XQuery for specifying outputs, so the attribute will be represented in the SELECT clause or the ORDER BY clause of the SQL fragment. Consider the node with the triple *(desc, sql_{10}, -3.1)*. It is created based on the expression {$\$i$/desc} in the RETURN clause of XQuery 1. Therefore, the corresponding SQL fragment will be `SELECT i.Desc FROM Items i`.

3 SQL Formulation

After the query forests are constructed, the SQL fragments will be collected and used to construct the SQL statement based on the *level sequence*. If the level numbers are separated by the comma, *i.e.*, the trees correspond to the expressions at the same nesting level of XQuery, the associated SQL fragments will be directly coerced into the appropriate clause of the primitive SQL statement constructed so far. If a square bracket is encountered, which stands for a nested clause, two situations will need to be distinguished. First, the last component of the level number in front of the square bracket is positive, which means that the SQL fragment associated with the inner level corresponds to a nested FLOWR expression specified in a LET clause of XQuery. The SQL fragment at the inner level will be represented by a derived relation in the FROM clause of SQL, as seen in L2-L4 of SQL1.

Second, if the last component of the level number in front of the square bracket is negative, which means that the SQL fragment associated with the inner level corresponds to the statement specified in the RETURN clause of the input XQuery. The clauses of the nested query will be coerced into the proper clauses of the query at the parent level, due to the constraint of the SQL syntax.

During the collecting process, if we encounter repeated SQL fragments from the same tree, we will only keep one copy. Also, for each *return tree*, if the leaf node represents more specific attributes in the SELECT clause, we will omit the fragment SELECT * associated with the root node. For queries with nested structures and aggregation functions, it will need to be processed further.

If a derived relation is represented in the FROM clause of the primitive SQL, we will identify the relation which is specified both at the outer level and at the inner level, and produce a joining statement by keys represented at the outer level. The queries with aggregation functions are more difficult to deal with. By heuristics, we adopt the attribute in the ORDER BY clause. The final output is as follows:

```
SQL 1:
L1: SELECT i.ItemNO, i.Desc, max(t.Bid)
L2: FROM Items i,(SELECT b., i.ItemNO
L3:              FROM Bids b, Items i
L4:              WHERE b.ItemNO = i.ItemNO) t
L5: WHERE i.Desc LIKE '%Bicycle%'
L6:              AND i.ItemNO = t.ItemNO
L7: GROUP BY i.ItemNO, i.Desc
L8: ORDER BY i.ItemNO
```

4 Conclusions and Future Research

Several issues require further study. Since the constructs in SQL and XQuery might not always have direct correspondence, we plan to study what can be translated and what can not. We also wish to conduct a comprehensive empirical evaluation by using more complicated schemas and queries on our prototype.

References

1. Krishnamurthy, R., Kaushik, R., Naughton, J.F.: Xml-to-sql query translation literature: The state of the art and open problems. In: Proceedings of the XML Symposium. (2003)
2. Benedikt, M., Chan, C.Y., Fan, W., Rastogi, R., Zheng, S., Zhou, A.: Dtd-directed publishing with attribute translation grammars. In: Proceedings of the 28th VLDB Conference. (2002) 814–825
3. Fernandez, M.F., Kadiyska, Y., Suciu, D., Morishima, A., Tan, W.C.: Silkroute: A framework for publishing relational data in xml. TODS **27** (2002)
4. DeHaan, D., Toman, D., Consens, M.P., Ozsu, M.T.: A comprehensive xquery to sql translation using dynamic interval encoding. In: Proceedings of the SIGMOD Conference. (2003) 623–634
5. Krishnamurthy, R., Chakaravarthy, V.T., Kaushik, R., Naughton, J.F.: Recursive xml schemas, recursive xml queries, and relational storage: Xml-to-sql query translation. In: Proceedings of the ICDE conference. (2004)
6. Shanmugasundaram, J., Tufte, K., Zhang, C., He, G., DeWitt, D.J., Naughton, J.F.: Relational databases for querying xml documents: limitations and opportunities. In: Proceedings of the VLDB conference. (1999)

A New Indexing Structure to Speed Up Processing XPath Queries*

Jeong Hee Hwang, Van Trang Nguyen, and Keun Ho Ryu

Database Laboratory, Chungbuk National University, Korea
{jhhwang, nvtrang, khryu}@dblab.chungbuk.ac.kr

Abstract. In this paper, the focus is on accelerating XPath location steps for evaluating regular path expression with predicate parameter in particular since it is a core component of many XML processing standards such as XSLT or XQuery. We present a new indexing structure, namely Xp-tree, which is used to speed-up the evaluation of XPath. Based on accelerating a node using planar combined with the numbering scheme, we devise efficiently derivative algorithms. Our experimental results demonstrate that the proposed method outperforms previous approaches using R-tree indexing mechanism in processing XML queries.

1 Introduction

Xpath[1] axes are used to describe path traversals about an XML document. Query languages for XML data rely on location paths such as XPath for selecting nodes in data items[2,3,4]. Therefore, it is essential to have the indexing structure for improving the performance of evaluating common XPath expression[5,6].

A typical node distribution in the pre/post plane for an XML instance is tightly packed with nodes of diagonal shape, while the upper left is only sparsely populated. The lower right is completely empty[7]. All previous methods[4,8,9,10] did not consider the phenomenon, but they only focused on processing the relationship between parent/child or ancestor/descendant and ignored the other axes that are considered important part on query processing, especially for stream processing of XPath queries with predicates. [7] proposed a R-tree[11] based indexing structure for XML, which supports all axes evaluated from arbitrary context nodes. However, it is not supported for eliminating redundant work in the predicate evaluation part of the XPath queries.

In this paper, we propose a new indexing structure based on the index technology for spatial data, to support the evaluation of XPath queries. It can easily support all XPath axes. Our main goal for this method is to enhance search performance using a spatial search tree, especially for searching the sibling relations from the given node.

The remainder of this paper is organized as follows. The main theme of this paper, Xp-tree, is presented in section 2. Experimental results are presented in section 3. Finally, we summarize our work in section 4.

---

* This work was supported by University IT Research Center Project in Korea.

2 Xp-Tree Index Structure and Operation Algorithms

We propose a new access method called Xp-tree, as the XPath accelerator. Xp-tree applies a different insertion/split strategy to achieve the sibling relationships of the XML data easily, while not compromising the space discrimination capabilities of the index too much. With the Xp-tree, we develop an access method that strictly preserves sibling trajectory. Hereafter, trajectory means the sibling nodes at the same level, having the same parent. As such, the structure of the Xp-tree is actually a set of leaf nodes, each containing a partial children of one parent, organized in a height–balanced tree hierarchy where internal nodes contain "directory" entries that point to nodes at the next level of the index.

Each node in XML document after parsing is represented as a node(E)={pre(E), post(E), par(E), att(E), level(E), and tag(E)} and considered as an entry in Xp-tree and inserted to leaf node. Non-leaf node entries are of the form (pointer, and MBR) where pointer points to a child node and MBR is the covering 2-dimensional interval. Leaf node is a set of pointer tuple(previouspointer, nextpointer, and parpointer). This means that we choose a doubly linked list that connects leaf nodes through previous sibling node and following-sibling node. In addition, we use one more pointer to connect from a node to its parent. This ensures that we can trace quickly its relationship from every node.

For example, Figure 1 depicts the element hierarchy of religion text, a real-world XML data set. After loading (for simplicity, here we only use preorder value), all of the nodes will be simply represented in the Xp-tree structure as in Figure 2, Data nodes (entries) that have the same parent will be stored in the same leaf node in the Xp-tree. In case the leaf node overflows, it will be split and be connected by pointers to each other to preserve siblings. The straight arrows imply the pointers from one node to its previous and next sibling nodes, and the curly narrow ones show the connection to its parent.

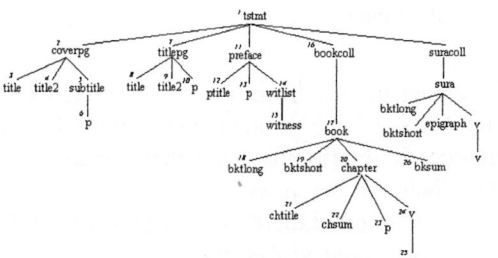
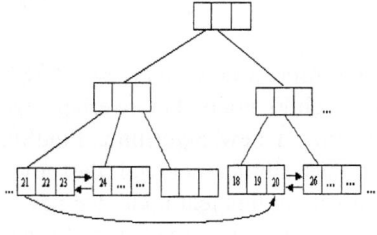

Fig. 1. Element hierarchy of religious text document instance

Fig. 2. Xp-tree in tree structure and it's data representation on leaf nodes

Our goal is to keep the sibling trajectory of the XML data. Figure 3 shows the insertion algorithm, in which a plain pseudo-code explains the insert process as well as the split strategy when leaf node is full.

Algorithm Insert(N, E)
1. Invoke **FindSiblingNode(N,E)** to find a leaf node N' containing the sibling precedecessor of the new context node entry E to be inserted.
2. if node N' is found
3.   if (N' has space) not full then
4.   insert new context node, E into N'
5.   else
6.   **CreateNewLeafNode(E)** to create new leaf node for new context node, E, insert newly created leaf node into tree
7.   endif
8. else
9.   **CreateNewLeafNode(E)** to create new leaf node for new context node, E, insert
10.   newly created leaf node into tree
11. endif

Algorithm FindSiblingNode(N, E)
1. if N is not a leaf
2.   for each entry E' of N whose MBR intersects with the MBR of E
3.   invoke **FindSiblingNode(N',E)** where N' is the child node of N pointed to by E'
4. else
5.   if N contains an entry that is previous sibling of E
6.   return N
7. endif

Algorithm CreateNewLeafNode(E)
Steps up to the tree until a non-full parent node, Q is found.
   Traverse the right-most path from this node, Q to reach the non-leaf parent node P at level 1
1.   if non-leaf node P is not full the newly created
2.   leaf node created is inserted into node P
3.   else
4.   split the non-leaf node P by creating a new non-leaf node R at level 1 and this new non-leaf node R has the new leaf node created previously as its first child,
5.   split of non-leaf nodes may propagate upwards the tree as the upper non-leaf nodes may become full
6.   endif

Fig. 3. Insert algorithms

To insert a new entry, we start by traversing the tree from the root and step into every child node that overlaps with the MBR of the context node (entry E) by invoking a new algorithm, FindSiblingNode. It returns the node that contains the previous sibling node of the new node. Then for the insertion, if there is space available in this leaf node, the new entry will be inserted there. If the leaf node is full, a split strategy is needed. Splitting a leaf node would violate our principle of total trajectory preservation, thus CreateNewLeafNode algorithm is required.

We demonstrate the framework of a set of basic algorithms for query processing that work on data encoded in Xp-tree. A typical search on sets of sibling nodes includes a selection with respect to a given range. Queries of the form "find all the children of the second node from the context node" remain very important. Figure 4 presents the algorithms for processing above queries. This class of algorithms is based on the major axes of XPath. The linked lists of the Xp-tree allow us to retrieve connected nodes without searching.

Algorithm SiblingQuery(N, E, RESULT)
1. **Invoke FindNode(N,E)** to find node N' which contains entry E
2. if N' is found
3. for each entry E' of N'
4. Add E' to **RESULT**
5. if following sibling pointer F is valid
   Invoke **FollowingSiblingQuery(NF,RESULT)** where NF is the child node of N pointed to by F
6. if preceding sibling pointer P is valid
   Invoke **PrecedingSiblingQuery(NP, RESULT)** where NP is the child node of N pointed to by P
7. else this node does not exist
8. endfor

Algorithm FollowingSiblingQuery(NF, RESULT)
1. for each entry E' of NF
2. Add E' to **RESULT**
3. if following sibling pointer F is valid
   Invoke **FollowingSiblingQuery(NF', RESULT)** where NF' is the child node of NF pointed to by F
4. endfor

Algorithm PrecedingSiblingQuery(NP, RESULT)
1. for each entry E' of NP
2. Add E' to **RESULT**
3. if preceding sibling pointer P is valid
   Invoke **PrecedingSiblingQuery(NP', RESULT)** where NP' is the child node of NP pointed to by P
4. endfor

Fig. 4. Algorithms for sibling queries

3 Experiments and Evaluation

We show the results of some experiment to verify the search performance of Xp-tree, by comparing with R-tree based methods.

3.1 Experimental Setup

The node capacity(fan-out) of both Xp-tree and R-tree was set to 1Kb. We have chosen a real-world application for our evaluation. The structures were constructed from 4 files with different size of religion 2.00 datasets. Specifically, bom (the Book of Mormon): 7.025Mb, nt (the New Testament): 0.99Mb, ot: (the Old Testament): 3.32Mb, and quran (the Quran): 897 Kb. The test dataset can be downloaded at [12].

Let us elaborate the details on descendant query. Here using level parameter we can cut down the window size of search space. For every node i in tree we have an equation: $post - pre + level = n$ (1) (in which: $post$, pre are postorder and preorder of i, and n is the number of descendant nodes). From equation (1), we have

$pre + n = post + level$, and $post - n = pre - level$. So, we can get a descendant window query for given node i as follows: $w = (pre, post+level, pre - level, post)$. This new window query helps shorten the size of search space and makes the result more preferable than compared method.

After loading the number of XML nodes for each dataset respectively are: quran: 6,710 nodes, nt: 8,577 nodes, ot: 25,317 nodes, and bom: 48,256 nodes. Nodes of each file were considered as entries and inserted into both an Xp-tree and an equivalent R-tree. The query windows were generated randomly.

3.2 Overall Evaluation

Figure 5 shows the average number of node accessed per 100 randomly queries obtained at different stages by varying the size for each of the four files described above. Here, we leave-off the parent axis because there exist a few nodes for parent due to the hierarchy of XML tree that is not high and all the subordinate axes (descendant-or-self, ancestor-or-self, etc.). The reason is that we only need to add context node to the result node set.

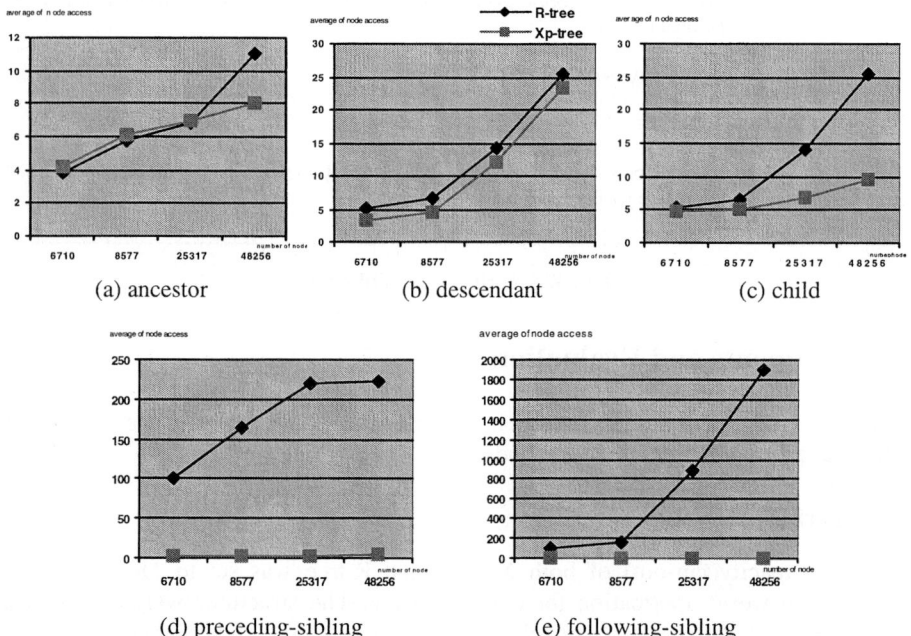

(a) ancestor   (b) descendant   (c) child

(d) preceding-sibling   (e) following-sibling

Fig. 5. Experiment results

Now we move on other interested group, which gets our strong interest of queries in Figure 5(d, e). It purely recognizes that preceding-sibling and following-sibling queries have the number of average node accessed similar with preceding and following queries in R-tree-based method. However, the answer for preceding-sibling query and following-sibling query in Xp-tree method are good as expected. The number of accessed nodes is remarkably small compared with that of the R-tree method. It is highly optimized for disk I/O.

In our experiments, the performance of Xp-tree is generally better than that of the original R-tree especially with preceding-sibling axis and following-sibling axis. The ancestor, descendant and child query also gave better results although the ancestor showed not good at three first datasets. But this is not significant because of using pointer. For large-scale datasets if we use purely R-tree based method, much more intersect will take place when searching the required nodes and it is one of the disadvantages for optimizing spatial-based index mechanism. Whereas, with Xp-tree, the set of required node would be tracked easily if one node has been found. Thus, the accessed nodes are reduced considerably than the R-tree based method. The graphs in Figure 5 (a)(b)(c) show superior results with high stability.

4 Conclusion

We proposed Xp-tree, which has been demonstrated to be superior to the previous works. The performance enhancement comes from the fact that the new algorithms are based on trajectory tracking by using pointers that are highly optimized for disk I/O. Our experimental studies showed that the proposed tree structure outperforms the naïve structure based on R-tree indexing method.

The XPath query could be processed by advanced index techniques to quickly determine the ancestor-descendant relationships between XML elements as well as fast accesses to XML values, such as spatial-based indexing method. This observation, together with the cost estimation procedures, could lead to a rather pragmatic cost model for XPath queries.

References

[1] Clark, J., Steven, D.: XML Path Language (XPath). Technical Report W3C Recommendation, Version 1.0, 1999. http://www.w3.org/TR/xpath
[2] Quanzhong, L., Bongki, M.: Indexing and Querying XML Data for Regular Path Expression. In Proc. of the 27th VLDB Conference, Roma, Italy (2001)
[3] Kha, D.D., Yoshikawa, M., Uemura. S.: An XML Indexing Structure with Relative Region Coordinate. In ICDE (2001)
[4] Milo, T., Sucio D.: Index Structure for Path Expressions. In Proc. of the Int'l Conf. on Database Theory (1999) 277-295
[5] Zhang, C., Naughton, J. DeWitt, D. et al.: on Supporting Containment Queries in Relational Databases Management Systems. In Proceedings of the 2001 ACM-SIGMOD Conference Santa Barbara, CA, May (2001)
[6] Cooper, B. et al.: A Fast Index for Semistructured Data. In Proc.of VLDB Conference (2001)
[7] Grust, T.,: Accelerating Xpath Location Steps. In SIGMOD Conference (2002)

[8] Kaushik, R., Naughton, J.F., Bohannon, P., Gudes, E.: Exploiting Local Similarity for Efficient Indexing of Paths in Graph Structured Data. In ICDE (2002)
[9] Goldman, J., Widom, J.: DataGuides: Enabling Query Formulation and Optimization in Semistructured Databases. In Proc. of 23rd VLDB Conference (1997)
[10] Kaushik, R., Naughton, J.F., Bohannon, P., Korth, H.F.: Covering Indexes for Branching Path Queries. In ACM SIGMOD (2002)
[11] Guttman, A.,: R-Trees: A Dynamic Index Structure for Spatial Searching. In Proc. of SIGMOD, Boston, Massachusetts (1984)
[12] Jon Bosak. Religious Texts in XML. http://www.ibiblio.org/xml/examples/religion (1998)

Translate Graphical XML Query Language to SQLX

Wei Ni and Tok Wang Ling

Department of Computer Science, National University of Singapore, Singapore
{niwei, lingtw}@comp.nus.edu.sg

Abstract: Semi-structured data has become more and more attention-getting with the emergence of XML, and it has aroused much enthusiasm for integrating XML and SQL in database community. Due to the complexity of XQuery, graphical XML query languages have been developed to help users query XML data. In this paper, we propose a new XML-to-SQL solution on the base of ORA-SS, a rich semantic model for semi-structured data. We model the data by ORA-SS schema and store them in an ORDB. Based on ORA-SS, we developed a graphical XML query language GLASS that not only expresses the query constraints and reconstruction structure in XML view but also the relational semantic in the XML view. This paper focuses on the translation algorithm from GLASS to SQLX, an XML extension on traditional SQL.

1 Introduction

XML has been accepted as a potential standard for data publishing, exchanging and integration on the web; and there is much enthusiasm for integrating XML and traditional object-relational data model, which will benefit from the fruit of over 30 years research on object-relational technology. Meanwhile, since XQuery[12] and other text-based functional languages are complex and difficult to common users, researchers have proposed graphical languages and graphical user interfaces (GUIs), such as Equix[3]/BBQ[7, 9], XML-GL[1, 2, 4], XMLApe [8], QURSED[11], etc, to make the XML query easier to use.

In this paper, we use ORA-SS (Object-Relational-Attribute model for Semi-Structured data) [5], a rich semantic data model for semi-structured data, to describe the XML schema; and the XML data are stored in an Object-Relational Database (ORDB). To query the data, we have designed a graphical language GLASS (Graphical query Language for Semi-Structured data) [10] with full consideration of relational semantic information in ORA-SS, which has stronger expressive power than other graphical XML query languages. And we translate the GLASS query into SQLX[6], an expansion of SQL which is often used as a publishing tool from relational table to XML file.

The rest of this paper is organized as follows. Section 2 is a brief presentation of ORA-SS model and the mappings from ORA-SS schema to ORDB schema. In Section 3, we introduce the GLASS query with an example. Section 4 discusses the translation from GLASS to SQLX based on the query example in Section 3. And before the end, we conclude this paper and highlight the future works in Section 5.

2 ORA-SS Model and the Storage of XML Data

Compared with DTD, XML Schema [14], OEM, Dataguide, XML Graph [1] and their equivalents, ORA-SS is a rich semantic data model for catching the relational information. The most significant feature of ORA-SS is that it not only represents the tree structure of the original schema in terms of object class, relationship types and attributes but also distinguishes relationship attributes from object attributes, etc. For example, the ORA-SS schema in Fig. 1(a) contains three object classes (*project*, *member* and *publication*) and two relationship types (binary relationship type *jm* between project and member; and ternary relationship type *jmp* among project, member and publication). The label "jm" on the arrow from member to job_title indicates that *job_title* is an attribute of the relationship type *jm*, i.e., the job_title attribute is determined by both *project and member* rather than member only. It should be emphasized that the object ID in ORA-SS (the attributes denoted as solid circles in the diagram such as *J#*) is different from the object identifier in OEM. In ORA-SS, the object ID identifies each unique object instance rather than each element instance (in OEM). For example, if one member attends two projects, the same member instance may appear as two element instances in the XML data. In ORA-SS, both use the same object ID (*M#*); but in OEM, they will have different object identifiers.

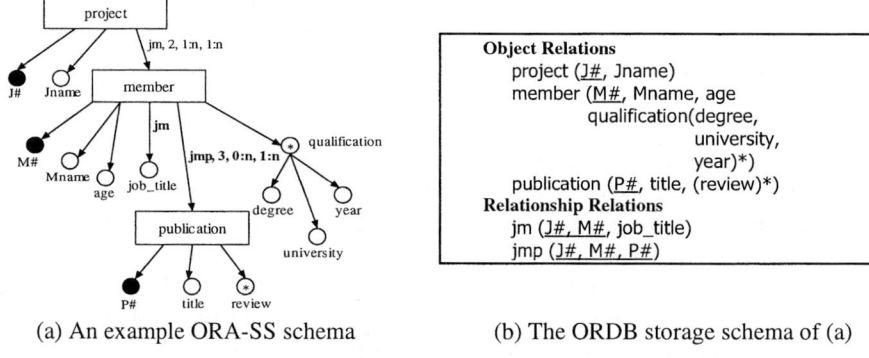

(a) An example ORA-SS schema   (b) The ORDB storage schema of (a)

Fig. 1. An example of ORA-SS schema and its ORDB storage schema

When we store the XML data in an ORDB, each object class will be stored in an *object relation* with its object attributes and each relationship type will be stored in a *relationship relation* with its relationship attributes. Composite attributes (e.g. the *qualification* in the example in Fig. 1.) will be stored as a *nested relation* inside an object relation or relationship relation according to the ORA-SS schema. Fig. 1(b) presents the ORDB schema when we store the XML data conforming to the ORA-SS schema in Fig. 1(a).

3 GLASS Query

GLASS is a graphical XML query language designed on the base of ORA-SS schema. The most significant features of GLASS from other graphical XML query languages (or GUIs) are:

(1) *GLASS separates the complex query logic from the query graph (the query graph is the graphical part of a GLASS query).* This feature makes the GLASS query clear and concise even if it contains complex query logic with quantifiers and negation.
(2) *GLASS considers relationship types in querying XML data.* The relationship types could be those either defined in ORA-SS schema or derived from the schema. This feature enables the GLASS to define the query semantic precisely.

A typical GLASS query consists of four parts:
(1) **Left Hand Side Graph** (LHS graph) – denotes the basic conditions of a query, which presents the fundamental features that users interest in.
(2) **Right Hand Side Graph** (RHS graph) – defines the output structure of the query result, which is a compulsory part in the GLASS query.
(3) **Link Set** – specifies the bindings between the RHS graph and LHS graph. When two graph entities are *linked*, they are visually connected by a line, which means the data type and value of the entity in the RHS graph are from the corresponding linked entity in the LHS graph.
(4) **Condition Logic Window** (CLW) – It is an optional part where users write conditions and constructions that are difficult to draw, which includes Logic expressions, Mathematic expressions, Comparison expressions and IF-THEN statements.

Most notations in GLASS are borrowed from those in ORA-SS schema diagram, yet some new notations are introduced to represent the query condition and result reconstruction such as *Box of group entities* and *Condition Identifier*. The box of group entities is used to specify multi-field aggregations such as the query in Example 1. The condition identifier is defined by user, quoted by a pair of ":"s, which specifies a connected sub-graph in the LHS graph (e.g. the condition identifier "A", appears to be ":A:" on the arrow from member to age).

Example 1. (For the schema in Fig. 1.)
*Find the member whose age is less than 35, and he **either** has taken part in less than 5 projects **or** written more than 6 publications in some of the projects he attended; display the member id and name.*

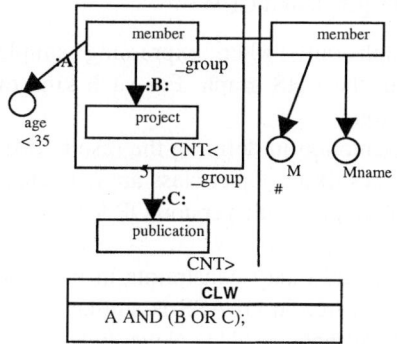
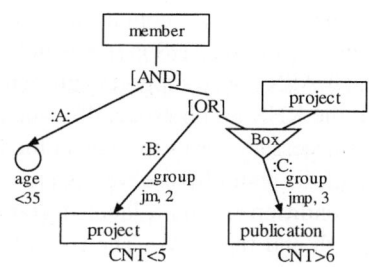

Fig. 2. The GLASS query of Example 1

Fig. 3. The condition tree of the GLASS query in Fig. 2 from its LHS graph and CLW

Fig. 2 shows the GLASS representation of Example 1. The result view structure is defined in the RHS graph. The object node with name "member" is linked with the object node with the same name in the LHS graph, which means the member in the RHS graph (the result view) is from the member in the LHS graph. In the LHS graph, there are three condition identifiers "A", "B" and "C" where "A" means *member* should have *age* attribute less than 35; "B" means to group *project* under *member* in the binary relationship type *jm* having count of *project* less than 5; and "C" means to group *publication* under each pair of *member* and *project* in the ternary relationship type *jmp* having count of *publication* more than 6. By default, the logic among the query conditions are "AND"; but it can be rewritten by the logic expressions specified in the CLW with the help of condition identifier. In the above example, the logic among the three conditions is defined as "A AND (B OR C)".

4 Translate GLASS into SQLX

In this section, we discuss the translation from GLASS to SQLX. SQLX (aka. SQL/XML) is an XML-related specification expanded on SQL. The syntax of SQLX combines the features in both XML document processing and the traditional SQL. Before introducing the translation algorithm, we shall preprocess the GLASS query as follows.

4.1 Preprocess

Observing the SQLX syntax [6], we find that, in translating from GLASS to SQLX query, the SELECT and FROM clauses can be easily generated by checking the GLASS query and the ORA-SS schema; and the major task in translation is *the generation of query conditions*. To generate the query conditions and the target SQLX expression, we need preprocess the GLASS query in the following 3 steps.

(1) Expansion of the simple projection;
(2) Expansion of the abbreviated RHS graph;
(3) Construction of the condition tree from LHS graph and CLW.

The GLASS query appears with RHS graph only when expressing simple projections that do not contain any constraints in the LHS graph. For such kind of query, we regard the LHS graph as null in translation.

The GLASS query supports abbreviated representation in defining the result XML view in the RHS graph especially when all attributes of an object class are extracted; and it is necessary for us to expand the RHS graph to get a full-version ORA-SS view schema of the result before we translate the query.

The condition tree is a labeled graph containing all query constraints in both the LHS graph and the CLW. The role of the condition tree in GLASS is similar to the condition tree in TQL (Tree Query Language) defined in [11]. Nevertheless, the condition tree in GLASS contains more features than TQL by including quantifiers, relationship type information and aggregation. The purpose of the condition tree is to combine the query constraints into one graph so that we can generate WHERE clauses by traversing the condition tree. The condition tree is initially a copy of the LHS graph in a given GLASS query, which can be a forest if the LHS contains multigraphs. When we copy the LHS graph, we record the aggregation information, add the relationship type information, mark the condition identifiers in the condition tree and insert the logic operators (and quantifiers) according to the expressions in CLW. Particularly, the box is represented as a composite node (a triangular node) in the condition tree. The condition tree of the GLASS query in Fig. 2 is shown in Fig. 3.

4.2 Translation Algorithm

The basic idea of the translation algorithm is to traverse the expanded RHS graph in depth-first order and generate the nested SQLX query blocks according to the tree structure. The XML construction functions in SQLX can be different due to different the data types (element or attribute) in the result XML view. Like the traditional XML-to-SQL method, parent-child/ancestor-descendant relations among different object classes are performed by a series of join operations, which can be obtained from the relationship type information in the ORA-SS schema. The query constraints in the LHS graph (and the CLW) are *only* for the nodes with links in the RHS graph. Checking the condition tree, we generate WHERE clauses (denoted as W(N)) in different forms by applying the following rule.

Rule (Generate WHERE clauses of Node N from the condition tree):

If N is an attribute node, then W(N) is the value comparison expressions on N.
If N is an object class, N has k child nodes (say C_1 to C_k); and it is associated in a relationship type of D degree where the D-1 ancestor nodes of N are P_1 ... P_{D-1}; then W(N) is

CASE 1. there is a (negated) existential quantifier in front of NL, then we generate

WHERE [NOT] EXIST (SELECT N FROM ...

$W(C_1)\theta^1 W(C_2)\theta^2...\theta^{k-1} W(C_k)\theta^k W(P_1)\theta^{k+1} W(P_2)\theta^{k+2}...\theta^{k+D-2} W(P_{D-1}))$

CASE 2. there is a "_group" label follows N, then we generate
WHERE N IN (SELECT DISTINCT N FROM...

$W(C_1)\theta^1 W(C_2)\theta^2...\theta^{k-1} W(C_k)\theta^k W(P_1)\theta^{k+1} W(P_2)\theta^{k+2}...\theta^{k+D-2} W(P_{D-1}))$

CASE 3. there is a "_group" label before N under object class M, then we generate
WHERE N IN (SELECT N, AGG(N) FROM ...

$W(C_1)\theta^1 W(C_2)\theta^2...\theta^{k-1} W(C_k)\theta^k W(P_1)\theta^{k+1} W(P_2)\theta^{k+2}...\theta^{k+D-2} W(P_{D-1}))$

GROUP BY M

HAVING value comparison on AGG(N))

CASE 4. for all other cases, we generate
WHERE N IN (SELECT N FROM ...

$W(C_1)\theta^1 W(C_2)\theta^2...\theta^{k-1} W(C_k)\theta^k W(P_1)\theta^{k+1} W(P_2)\theta^{k+2}...\theta^{k+D-2} W(P_{D-1}))$

where θ^m (m = 1, ..., k, k+1, ..., k+D-2) are the logic operators ("AND" or "OR"). To avoid repeating generation the where clauses of the same node, we exclude node N when we generate each $W(P_i)$ (i = 1, ..., D-1); and we ignore the parent nodes when generating each $W(C_j)$ (j = 1, ..., k).

```
SELECT XMLELEMENT(NAME "member",
         XMLATTRIBUTES (M1.M# AS "member_id")
         XMLELEMENT (NAME "Mname", M1.Mname)
)FROM member M1
   WHERE M1.age <35
   AND (M1.M# IN (SELECT DISTINCT M# FROM member
                    WHERE (SELECT COUNT(J#) FROM jm
                               WHERE M# = jm.M#)<5)
    OR   M1.M# IN (SELECT DISTINCT M# FROM member
                    WHERE (SELECT DISTINCT J# FROM project
                              WHERE(SELECT  COUNT(P#) FROM
jmp
                              WHERE jmp.J# = project.J#
```

Fig. 4. The translated SQLX expression of the Example in Fig. 2

It should be emphasized that $W(P_i)$ is indispensable when
(1) *N is not the root in the condition tree, and*
(2) *In the RHS graph, N does not have any parent/ancestor nodes that are linked with their counterparts in the LHS graph.*
Otherwise, $W(P_i)$ can be omitted.

Applying the above method and rules to the example in Fig. 2, we can get the SQLX expressions of the query as shown in Fig. 4.

5 Conclusion and Future Work

In this paper, we have introduced a new XML-to-SQL query solution based on ORA-SS and discussed the translation from GLASS, the graphical query language in our project, to SQLX. Compared with other graphical XML query languages (and GUIs), GLASS define both the structure and the relational semantic in the XML view; and the GLASS query is seamlessly cohered with the ORDB and SQL/SQLX on ORA-SS schema. Compared with traditional XML-to-SQL solutions that use XQuery or XPath [13], GLASS has stronger expressive power and provides an easy-to-use interface. So far, the case tool of GLASS query has been partially implemented. As to the future work, it may include the query optimization of GLASS queries and the translated SQLX expressions as well as the improvement of the case tool.

References

1. S. Ceri, S.Comai, E. Damiani, P.Fraternali, S. Paraboschi, and L.Tanca. XML-GL: a graphical language of querying and restructuring XML documents. In Proc. WWW8, Toronto, Canada, May 1999.
2. S. Ceri, S. Comai, E. Damiani, P. Fraternali, and L. Tanca. Complex Queries in XML-GL. SAC(2) 2000:888-893.
3. S. Cohen, Y. Kanza, Y. Kogan, W. Nutt, Y. Sagiv and A. Serebrenik. Equix – Easy Querying in XML Databases. In proceedings of Webdb'98 – The Web and Database Workshop, 1998.

4. S. Comai, E. Damiani, P. Fraternali. Computing Graphical Queries over XML Data. ACM Transactions on Information Systems, Vol. 19, No. 4, October 2001, Pages 371-430.
5. G. Dobbie, X. Y. Wu, T. W. Ling, M. L. Lee. ORA-SS: An Object-Relationship-Attribute Model for Semistructured Data. TR21/00, Technical Report, Department of Computer Science, National University of Singapore, December 2000.
6. Information technology -- Database languages -- SQL -- Part 14: XML-Related Specifications. ISO/IEC 9075-14:2003
7. B. Ludaescher, Y. Papakonstantinou, and P. Velikhov. Navigation-driven evaluation of virtual mediated views. In *Proceedings of the sixth International Conference on Extending Database Technology (EDBT)*(Konstanz, Germany, March), Lecture Notes in Computer Science, vol. 1777, Springer-Verlage, New York, 2000.
8. L. Mark, etc. XMLApe. College of Computing, Georgia Institue of Technology. http://www.cc.gatech.edu/projects/XMLApe/
9. K. D. Munroe, B. Ludaescher and Y. Papakonstantinou. Blended Browsing and Querying of XML in Lazy Mediator System. Konstanz, Germany, March 2000.
10. W. Ni, T. W. Ling. GLASS: A Graphical Query Language for Semi-Structured Data. DASFAA 2003.
11. Y. Papakonstantinou, M. Petropoulos and V.Vassalos. QURSED: Querying and Reporting Semistructured Data. ACM SIGMOD 2002, Jun 4-6, Madison, Wisconsin, USA.
12. XQuery 1.0: An XML Query Language. W3C Working Draft 22 August 2003 http://www.w3.org/TR/xquery/
13. XML Path Language (XPath) 2.0. W3C Working Draft 22 August 2003 http://www.w3.org/TR/xpath20/
14. XML Schema. http://www.w3.org/XML/Schema

GTree: An Efficient Grid-Based Index for Moving Objects

Xiaoyuan Wang, Qing Zhang, and Weiwei Sun

Department of Computing and Information Technology
Fudan University, Shanghai, China
{xy_wang, wwsun}@fudan.edu.cn, qzhang79@yahoo.com

Abstract. In mobile environments, tracking the changing positions of moving objects efficiently could substantially improve the quality of the Location Based Services. There arises the high demand for the indexes to support frequent updates. In this paper, we propose a novel grid-based index for moving objects, namely the GTree. Based on the recursive partition of the space and lazy maintenance, the GTree could maximize the stability of the index structure while minimizing the dynamic adjustment, and therefore significantly reduce the update overhead. Different from traditional top-down or bottom-up updates, we present a median-down approach, which could effectively reduce the number of disk access. As an alternative, a bulk-loading technique is introduced. The experiments show that the GTree has good update performance as well as query performance.

1 Introduction

With the rapid advances of wireless communications and electronic technologies, Location Based Services (LBS) is becoming a new and important application area. Tracking the changing positions of moving objects efficiently could substantially improve the quality of the services and there arises the need for storing and processing continuously moving data.

The continuous movement of moving objects poses new challenges to index technologies. Since most existing database systems assume that the data is fairly static and their values are not updated frequently, they are not suitable for processing continuously moving objects, whose positions are dynamically changing and need to be updated frequently.

Spatial indexing and its variants provide a basis for the extension for supporting moving objects. Two typical ones are R-tree [2] and Quadtree [4].

R-tree exhibits good query performance but poor update performance, because the MBR clusters the objects with close positions and it attempts to pick the subtree with the optimal bounding rectangle at each level, which in turn lead to the property of propagating upwards and the high cost for immediate maintenance of the index structure.

Quadtree does better than R-tree in updating, while its query performance is worse. It decomposes the k-dimensional space into 2^k subspaces, just like the binary tree in one-dimensional spaces. However, the concept of "binary" partition in hyperplanes, which performs well with a main memory structure, is not necessarily suitable for disk-based access methods. Furthermore, its fanout is too small, and thus subtrees corresponding to densely populated regions may be much deeper.

In this paper, based on the principle of recursive partition of the space and the concept of lazy maintenance, we propose a novel index for moving objects, which supports fast updates and efficient queries. It is grid-based, in which the space is equally divided into grids of the same size and each of them can be further divided into sub-grids recursively. The number of sub-grids is determined by the disk block size. It is a disk-resident tree with large fanout, and we call it GTree (the Grid-based Tree).

Different from the proposed top-down or bottom-up update approaches, the update in GTree is median-down, which could effectively reduce the number of disk access. As an alternative, the bulk-loading technique for updating is introduced. Meanwhile, as an elemental index structure, it is extensible.

The rest of this paper proceeds as follows. We describe the index structure of GTree in Section 2 and the update approaches in Section 3. Experimental evaluation is presented in Section 4 and we conclude the paper in Section 5.

2 Index Structures

2.1 Motivation

An update for moving objects leads to two kinds of changes: the change of the entries in the indexing nodes, and the change of the index structure itself. The former is unavoidable, since each update operation has to include deleting the entry of the old position, and adding the entry of the new position to another indexing node. So how to fast locating the old entry and the new entry becomes most important in this process.

As for the latter, the frequent modification of the index structure itself influences the performance on greater degree. An "industrious" structure, which appears sensitive to updates and tries to keep itself perfect each time the update is executed, is not suitable for indexing moving objects. For example, the property of propagating upwards in R-tree is not good for the updating of moving objects. To keep the balance of the tree, the splitting or merging of lower nodes will impact on the upper nodes immediately, which leads to the local or even the global modification of the index structure.

With the uniform partition of the space, the index structure of GTree is constructed based on the grids of the same size, which keep static during their lifetime. When an indexing node corresponds to a grid, its splitting and merging depend on the partition of the space, not directly on the distribution of moving data. Therefore we could maximize the stability of the index structure and minimize the dynamic adjustment to reduce the update overhead.

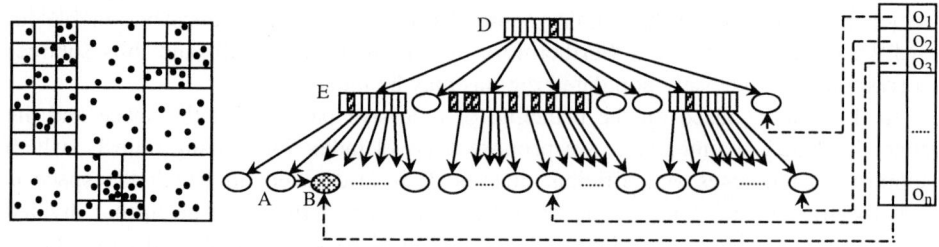

Fig. 1. The Structure of GTree

2.2 Index Structure

The two-dimensional space is equally divided into $k*k$ grids of the same size, where k is a regular parameter in GTree. A grid can be further divided into $k*k$ sub-grids if necessary and the partition is a recursive procedure. Each grid corresponds to a node in GTree and each node corresponds to a disk block. In the head of each node, the corresponding grid rectangle is kept. Assume a disk block can accommodate M entries, then $k = \max \{ t \mid t*t <= M, t \in \{1, 2, ...\} \}$. Thus the fanout of GTree is $k*k$, which is determined by the block size. Figure 1 shows the structure of GTree with $k = 3$, in which the position of the origin in the map is top-left, and sub-grids is row-major ordering.

We introduce the direct link and sibling node for GTree. The direct link is a kind of the secondary index [3]. Since an update request consists of the form (*oid, newPos*), the direct link is used as an additional path to find leaf nodes. The sibling node is a special leaf node concatenated after the normal leaf node, which is somewhat like the supernode in X-tree [1]. The basic goal of the sibling node is to avoid unnecessary partitions in the leaf grids. In some actual scenarios, objects may burst into an area and immediately leave after a short time. A partition has to be performed if the current leaf node has overflowed. With sibling nodes, this kind of partitions can be avoided.

The location relation between a grid and its sub-grids can be reckoned by simple computations. Assume the rectangle of Grid A is (x, y, w, h). Let xunit be w/k and yunit be h/k. Grid B is the sub-grid of Grid A, and it corresponds to the s-th entry in the node of Grid A. Let i be s/k and j be $s \% k$, then Grid B is a rectangle of (x + j * xunit, y + i * yunit, xunit, yunit). Further, if Point P(xp, yp) lies in Grid A, let u be (xp-x) / xunit, v be (yp-y) / yunit, and s be (v * xunit + u). Then in the node of Grid A, it is the s-th entry whose corresponding sub-grid contains P.

It should be noted that, to prevent unnecessary modification of the index structure, lazy maintenance is introduced. When deleting an entry, we simply remove it and an underflow is allowed if the node contains few entries after deletion. By periodical collecting, free space is regained.

For the sake of the median-down update, each leaf node stores the block IDs of its ancestor nodes. For example, in Figure 1, the block IDs of D, E are kept in the leaf node A as well as the sibling node B.

3 Updates of GTree

3.1 Median-Down Update

Motivated by the limitation of the traditional approaches and the character of the grid-based index, the median-down update is proposed. The Lowest Common Ancestor Node (LCAN in short), which is on the joint of the two paths from the leaf nodes with the old entry and with the new entry to the root node, can be found by the online calculation based on the grid information. Then according to the block IDs of the ancestor nodes stored in the leaf node, the LCAN can be located directly, skipping the access to intermediate nodes. From the LCAN, a top-down search is issued for finding another leaf node to insert the new entry. Algorithm 1 describes the median-down update, and Algorithm 2 describes how to find the LCAN without disk access.

Algorithm 1 Median-Down Update (oid, pos)

locate the leaf node N that contains the object by the direct link.
e = GetEntry(pos, N) .
if pos lies within the leaf grid
　set e.pos to pos.

else

　remove e from N.
　i = **GetLCAN** (N, pos) .
　Obtain LCAN according to the ancestor block IDs[i] in the head of N.
　　invoke **Insert** (oid, pos, LCAN).

Algorithm 2 GetLCAN (leaf node N, newPos)

i = 0.
r = N.gridRect.
while r != map_rectangle
　xunit = r.width $* k$.
　yunit = r.height $* k$.
　nx = newPos.x / xunit .
　ny = newPos.y / yunit .
　p.x = root.gridRect.x + (nx $*$ xunit) .
　p.y = root.gridRect.y + (ny $*$ yunit) .
　r = Rectangle (p.x, p.y, xunit, yunit) .
　if r contains newPos
　　return i .
　i = i + 1 .
newPos is beyond the map, return -1.

An example is illustrated in Figure 2. The dashed line shows the case in which the old entry is deleted in leaf node A and the new entry is inserted in leaf node B. The dotted line shows another case in which the new entry moves to the leaf node C. In two cases, the number of disk access in the top-down update is both 10 (Figure 2(a)), and that in the bottom-up update is 9 and 11 respectively (Figure 2(b)), including 2 accesses to the secondary index. As an alternative, the strategy combining the bottom deletion and top-down insertion is employed, whose cost is both 9 (Figure 2(c)).

Figure 2(d) illustrates the median-down update, whose cost is 8 and 9 respectively. It outperforms the former approaches in both cases.

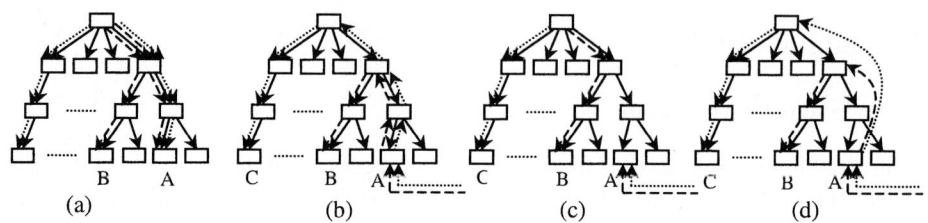

Fig. 2. The Examples of Updates

3.2 Bulk-Loading Update

In the bulk-loading update, first the objects are clustered in the buckets corresponding to the grids of a certain level, then from which a top-down insertion is issued respectively.

The starting level is an important parameter of the bulk-loading update. The lower the starting level reaches, the more buckets needed and the less disk I/O cost will be with a higher demand for memory. Inherently, it is a strategy utilizing memory for less disk access, regarding grids as the basic unit. Meanwhile, it utilizes the principle of locality, where the clustering of objects in one bucket can improve the cache hit rate.

4 Experimental Evaluation

We compare the following 4 approaches: i) the GTree with median-down update (GTree(MD)), ii) the GTree with bulk-loading update (GTree(BL)), iii) the R-tree with bottom-up update (R-tree(BU)), and iv) the R-tree with top-down update (R-tree(TD)). The performance metric is the number of disk access.

All experiments are performed on Pentium IV 2.2GHz with 512 MB RAM running on Windows Server 2003. The disk block size is set to 4KB. We use synthetic datasets generated by the "General_Spatio_Temporal_Data" (GSTD) [5]. The default number of moving objects is 100K. The starting level for bulk-loading updates is set to 2. By default, no memory buffer is used for all the approaches.

In Group 1, we vary the number of updates to examine the performance of GTree. In Figure 3(a), both alternatives for R-tree take more cost to update than GTree. Figure 3(b) shows that, with the default query size of 0.1, GTree performs not as well as R-tree in range queries, although it does not lag too far behind.

In Group 2, we vary the number of moving objects and the size of range rectangles to examine the update and query performance respectively. Figure3(c) shows that the costs increase as the number of objects increases from 100K to 1 million. Still the GTree with the median-down update performs best. Figure 3(d) shows an interesting result about the variable size of range queries. The GTree performs not as well as the R-tree at first. With the range size increases, the GTree outperforms the R-tree and does pretty well. This is because there are no overlapping regions in GTree and multiple paths selection for same objects will not occur.

From the experiments, we see that the GTree keeps the index structure stable in updates as well as queries. It does not fluctuate during the whole process and therefore has the stable performance.

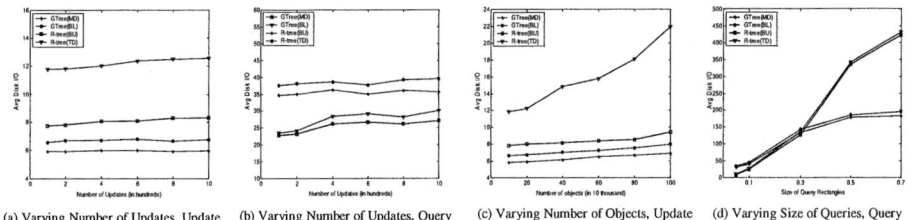

Fig. 3. Performance Results

5 Conclusion

In this paper, we propose a novel grid-based index for moving objects: GTree. Based on the recursive partition of the space, it keeps the index structure stable and minimizes the update overhead. The median-down update and bulk-loading update are introduced. Our experiments demonstrate that the GTree achieves significant improvement in update performance over the traditional approaches and keeps good query performance when faced with range queries of variable sizes.

References

1. S. Berchtold, D.A. Keim, and H.P. Kriegel. The X-tree: An Index Structure for High-Dimensional Data. In *Proc. of VLDB*, 1996.
2. A. Guttman. R-trees: A Dynamic Index Structure for Spatial Searching. In *Proc. of ACM SIGMOD*, 1984.
3. M.L. Lee, W. Hsu, C.S. Jensen, B. Cui, K. L. Teo. Supporting Frequent Updates in R-trees: A Bottom-Up Approach. In *Proc. of VLDB*, 2003.
4. H. Samet. The Quadtree and Related Hierarchical Data Structures. *ACM Computing Surveys*, Vol.16, No.2, pages 188–260, 1984.
5. Y. Theodoridis, J.R.O. Silva, and M.A. Nascimento. On the Generation of Spatiotemporal Datasets. In *Proc. of SSD*, 1999.

Adaptive Multi-level Hashing for Moving Objects*

Dongseop Kwon[1], Sangjun Lee[2], Wonik Choi[3], and Sukho Lee[1]

[1] School of Electrical Engineering and Computer Science,
Seoul National University, Seoul 151-742, Korea
dongseop@gmail.com, shlee@snu.ac.kr
[2] School of Computing, Soongsil University, Seoul 156-743, Korea
wisetank@gmail.com
[3] Thinkware Systems Corporation, Seoul 138-724, Korea
styxii@db.snu.ac.kr

Abstract. Although several sophisticated index structures for moving objects have been proposed, the hashing method based on a simple grid has been widely employed due to its simplicity. Since the performance of the hashing is largely affected by the size of a grid cell, it should be carefully decided with regard to the workload. In many real applications, however, the workload varies dynamically as time, for example the traffic in the commuting time vs. that in the night. The basic hashing cannot handle this dynamic workload because the cell size cannot be changed during the execution. In this paper, we propose the adaptive multi-level hashing to support the dynamic workload efficiently. The proposed technique maintains two levels of the hashes, one for fast moving objects and the other one for quasi-static objects. A moving object changes its level adaptively according to the degree of its movement.

1 Introduction

Traditional database systems have the problem in processing a large number of moving objects because the locations of moving objects are changed very rapidly and continuously. Moreover, traditional spatial index structures cannot support frequent updates well because they only focus on retrieving spatial data efficiently. To address this problem, several spatio-temporal index structures have been proposed for moving objects [1, 2, 3, 4, 5].

Among these, the hash-based approach [1] is one of the simplest ways to index the locations of moving objects. In this approach, the domain space is uniformly divided into grid cells of the same size. The hash value of an object is the cell number of a grid to which the object belongs. Because of using a grid cell, this is also called as the grid method [2]. Despite of the existence of other

---

* This work was supported in part by the Brain Korea 21 Project and in part by the Ministry of Information & Communications, Korea, under the Information Technology Research Center (ITRC) Support Program in 2004.

alternative index structures, the hashing method is widely adopted because it is simple, easy for implementation, and able to support a large number of frequent updates well [2, 6, 7]. Note that, from now on, the hashing in this paper represents the hash-based index structure using the uniform grid for moving objects.

The size of a grid cell is one of the most important factors that affect the performance of the hashing. If a large grid cell is used, which means that the number of grid cells is small, each hash bucket has to keep a lot of data items. Consequently, it suffers from the performance deterioration due to a long chain of overflow pages, which incurs a large number of disk accesses. On the contrary, in case of a small grid cell, the update performance becomes worse because a lot of hash buckets are required for the grid cells. Therefore, it is significantly critical to select the appropriate size of a grid cell with regard to the workload of queries and the distribution of data.

In many real applications, however, it is not easy to decide the appropriate size of a grid cell at the beginning because the workload or the distribution of data may change dynamically during the execution. For example, in the commuting time, the positions of most objects, e.g. people or cars, would move relatively fast and continuously. Therefore, the location management system might have to process large volumes of update operations in this period. On the other hand, most objects would be quasi-static in the night or in the office hours. Since the size of a cell cannot be changed during the execution, the hashing method cannot support this dynamic workload efficiently with the static size of a cell.

In this paper, to solve this problem, we propose the adaptive multi-level hashing for moving objects. The proposed method maintains two levels of hash structures. The upper level of the hashes, which is for the fast moving objects, uses a large grid cell to support update queries efficiently. The lower level of the hashes, which is for quasi-static objects, uses a small grid cell to support search queries efficiently. A moving object can change its level adaptively according to the degree of its agility. By adaptive escalating and de-escalating between two levels, the adaptive multi-level hashing can support the dynamic workload efficiently.

The rest of the paper is organized as follows. Section 2 explains the basic hashing method for moving objects. In Section 3, we propose the adaptive multi-level hashing to handle the dynamic workload. Related work is briefly discussed in Section 4. Finally, Section 5 concludes the paper.

2 Basic Hashing Algorithms for Moving Objects

The basic idea of hashing techniques for moving objects is introduced in [1]. Hash-based approaches for moving objects are principally identical with general hash-based file structures. An object is stored into the corresponding hash bucket to the hash value of its location. The algorithms for the basic hashing are as follows.

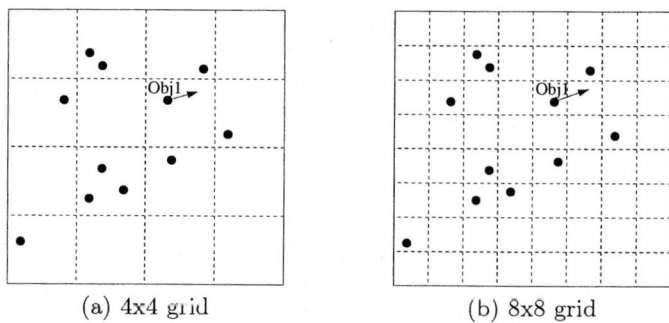

Fig. 1. Example of simple grids

Insert. Calculate the hash value of the given position of an object, then store the object into the corresponding disk bucket to the hash value.

Search. Examine all hash buckets that intersects the given query range.

Delete. Search the object, then delete it from the hash bucket.

Update. Search the object, then delete it from the old bucket and insert it into the new bucket again.

A simple grid is typically used as a hash function for moving objects. Figure 1 shows an example of a simple grid. The grid divides the domain space of the locations of moving objects into $i \times i$ equally-sized square. Figure 1 (a) uses a 4×4 grid and Figure 1 (b) uses an 8×8 grid. It is critical to decide the appropriate size of a grid cell for the performance of the hashing. In general, the small size of a grid cell, which means a fine grid, is good for search operations. A large size of a grid cell, which means a coarse grid, is good for update operations. For example, suppose that the Obj1 moves to a new position along the arrowed line in Figure 1. If a coarse grid like in Figure 1 (a) is used, the position of the Obj1 is updated only in the corresponding hash bucket. On the other hand, if a fine grid like in Figure 1 (b) is used, the Obj1 should be moved from the bucket for the original position to the bucket for the new position. Therefore, a coarse grid is generally better than a fine one for the update operations. However, since the coarse grid usually has to keep more data items in the bucket, it needs more disk pages. As a result, for the search operations, it needs to access more disk pages for retrieving one hash bucket. Therefore, the search performance of a coarse grid is worse than that of a fine one.

3 Adaptive Multilevel Hashing

3.1 Motivation

In many real applications, we have observed the following characteristics for moving objects.

1. **The workload of update operations changes dynamically as time.** For example, the traffic is generally heavy in the commuting time. On the contrary, it is relatively lighter in office hours, and only a few cars move in the night.
2. **The movement of an object maintains for a certain period.** A moving object generally has its destination. Until it reaches the destination, it moves continuously. Once arriving at the destination, it generally stops moving and stays in static state for a long time, e.g. a parked car.
3. **Most moving objects are in quasi-static state most of time.** The term "quasi-static" means that objects do not move or move slowly only within a small region of space such as an office or home. According to [8], most of objects, especially human beings, are in a quasi-static state most of the time.

The basic hashing cannot support the dynamic workload because the size of a grid cell is fixed at the initial time and cannot be changed during the execution. In addition, most objects are in quasi-static state and only a few objects move continuously for a certain period. However, the basic hashing stores these two types of objects into a hash structure together. Therefore, it is not efficient for update operations.

3.2 Adaptive Multi-level Hashing

To solve the problem of the basic hashing, we propose *the adaptive multi-level hashing*. The adaptive multi-level hashing consists of two levels of hash structures with different grid sizes. Figure 2 shows a basic concept of the adaptive multi-level hashing. The upper level of the hashes, named the *Coarse-Hash*, is for fast moving objects. It uses a large grid cell to support update queries efficiently. The lower level of the hashes, named the *Fine-Hash*, is for quasi-static objects. It uses a small grid cell for search operations.

In each hash structure in our approach, the basic algorithms of insert, search, and update operations are the same as the basic hashing. The difference is that the adaptive multi-level hashing has mechanisms for the *escalation* and the

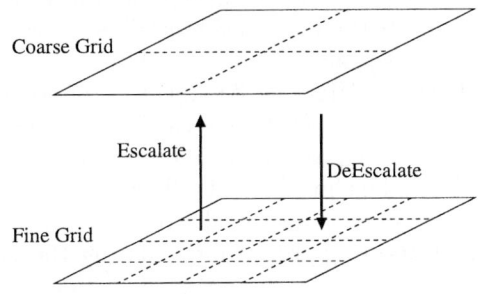

Fig. 2. Adaptive multi-level hashing

de-escalation. The escalation means the migration from the Fine-Hash to the Coarse-Hash, and the de-escalation means the opposite, the migration from the Coarse-Hash to the Fine-Hash.

3.3 Escalation

The escalation occurs during update operations. If a new position of an object is still in the grid cell which it belongs to, the same update algorithm as the basic hashing is used. However, if an object in the Fine-Hash moves out of the grid cell, it is recognized as a fast moving object. In this case, instead of updating in the Fine-Hash, the system escalates the object to the Coarse-Hash.

3.4 De-escalation

The de-escalation is the opposite operation of the escalation. It is not practical to perform the de-escalation in the update process because it is too expansive to examine all the objects in the Coarse-Hash in every update operation. For a search query, the system should examine both of the hashes. The de-escalation occurs with this search examination. Firstly, the system checks all the hash buckets which intersect a given query range in the Coarse-Hash. During this examination, it also finds expired objects for the de-escalation. Each object has a time-stamp for the last modification time, and an object that does not move for a given threshold time is expired. Among the expired objects, the system de-escalates the objects which can be stored in the corresponding grid cell to the query region in the Fine-Hash. For the de-escalate, the objects are deleted from the Coarse-Hash, and preserved in a temporary list. During the examination of the Fine-Hash, the expired objects in the temporary list are inserted again in the Fine-Hash.

4 Related Work

Several spatio-temporal index structures have been proposed for indexing moving objects. A detailed survey can be found in [9].

The Time-Parameterized R-tree (TPR-tree) [3] and its variants (e.g. TPR*-tree [4]) are the examples of this type of index structures. The main drawback of this approach is that it is hard to find an appropriate function for the movements in many real applications. If the movements of objects are complicated or not linear, this approach is not suitable.

The Lazy Update R-tree (LUR-tree) [5] aims to support frequent updates by reducing overhead in the update operation in the R-tree. It changes the structure of the index only when the new position of an object is out of the corresponding MBR. With adding a secondary index on the R-tree, it can perform the update operation in the bottom-up way. Lee et al. [10] extends the main idea of [5] and generalizes the bottom-up approach for updating the positions of moving objects.

The Q+Rtree [8] is a hybrid tree structure which consists of both the LUR-tree and the Quad-tree. It uses the LUR-tree for quasi-static objects and the

Quad-tree for fast moving objects. Since an object moves in two types of index structures adaptively, the Q+Rtree looks similar to our work. However, the Q+Rtree has pre-defined topological regions for the fast movements, and it recognizes all objects in the regions as fast moving objects. On the contrary, the adaptability of our work is based on the agility of an object itself. Therefore, our work does not need pre-defined regions.

5 Conclusion

Although several complicate index structures have been proposed, the hashing for moving object is widely used due to its simplicity and convenience for processing. However, the basic hashing cannot handle the dynamic workload of moving objects. In this paper, we have proposed the adaptive multi-level hashing method for the dynamic workload. Our proposed method maintains two levels of hashes, one for fast moving objects and the other for quasi-static objects. By escalating and de-escalating an object between two levels, the proposed method can support the dynamic workload adaptively.

References

1. Song, Z., Roussopoulos, N.: Hashing moving objects. In: Proceedings of the 2nd Int'l. Conf. on Mobile Data Management. (2001) 161–172
2. Chon, H.D., Agrawal, D., Abbadi, A.E.: Using space-time grid for efficient management of moving objects. In: Proceedings of the 2nd ACM international workshop on Data engineering for wireless and mobile access, ACM Press (2001) 59–65
3. Saltenis, S., Jensen, C.S., Leutenegger, S.T., Lopez, M.A.: Indexing the positions of continuously moving objects. In: Proceedings of the 2000 ACM SIGMOD Int'l. Conf. on Management of Data. (2000) 331–342
4. Tao, Y., Papadias, D., Sun, J.: The TPR*-Tree: An optimized spatio-temporal access method for predictive queries. In: Proceedings of 29nd Int'l. Conf. on Very Large Data Bases. (2003) 790–801
5. Kwon, D., Lee, S., Lee, S.: Indexing the current positions of moving objects using the Lazy Update R-tree. In: Proceedings of the 3nd Int'l. Conf. on Mobile Data Management. (2002) 113–120
6. Chon, H.D., Agrawal, D., Abbadi, A.E.: Storage and retrieval of moving objects. In: Proceedings of the 2nd Int'l. Conf. on Mobile Data Management. (2001) 173–184
7. Mokbel, M.F., Xiong, X., Aref, W.G.: SINA: scalable incremental processing of continuous queries in spatio-temporal databases. In: Proceedings of the 2004 ACM SIGMOD international conference on Management of data, ACM Press (2004) 623–634
8. Xia, Y., Prabhakar, S.: Q+Rtree: Efficient indexing for moving object databases. In: Proceedings of the Eighth International Conference on Database Systems for Advanced Applications, IEEE Computer Society (2003) 175
9. Mokbel, M.F., Ghanem, T.M., Aref, W.G.: Spatio-temporal access methods. IEEE Data Engineering Bulletin **26** (2003) 40–49
10. Lee, M.L., Hsu, W., Jensen, C.S., Cui, B., Teo, K.L.: Supporting frequent updates in R-Trees: A bottom-up approach. In: Proceedings of 29nd Int'l. Conf. on Very Large Data Bases. (2003) 608–619

Author Index

Afrati, Foto 548
Aghili, S. Alireza 17
Agrawal, Divyakant 17, 662
An, Aijun 851
An, Jiyuan 385

Bae, Sung Min 840
Bakiras, Spiridon 201
Balke, Wolf-Tilo 410
Bertino, Elisa 2
Bhowmick, Sourav S. 711, 724, 736

Cai, Zhihua 688
Cao, Xia 4
Chan, Chee-Yong 113
Chang, Ya-Hui 894
Chen, Arbee L.P. 163, 240
Chen, Ling 736
Chen, Tzung-Shi 561
Chen, Ya Bing 773
Chen, Yi-Ping Phoebe 385
Chen, Zhuo 311
Chia, Liang-Tien 736
Chirkova, Rada 548
Cho, Chung-Wen 163
Choi, Jin-Oh 625
Choi, Wonik 920
Chong, Zhihong 422
Chowdhary, Vishal 447
Cui, Bin 600

Dashti, Ali E. 461
Dobbie, Gillian 311
Dong, Guozhu 175

El Abbadi, Amr 17, 662

Feng, Jianhua 594
Feng, Ying 662
Fu, Kun 474
Furtado, Pedro 555

Ghodsi, Mohammad 588
Goh, Shen Tat 201
Grossmann, Matthias 779
Güntzer, Ulrich 410
Guo, Hang 594
Guo, Hong 226
Guo, Qi 594
Guo, Zhimao 372
Gupta, Himanshu 447
Gupta, Shalu 548

Hacıgümüş, Hakan 43
Han, Wook-Shin 95
Han, Zhongming 138
Hara, Takahiro 300
Haritsa, Jayant R. 214
Hassanzadeh, Oktie 588
Hou, Wen-Chi 226
Hsu, Shih-Chun 561
Hsu, Wynne 523, 649
Hu, Dongdong 828
Hu, Jianjun 576
Huang, Sheng 359
Huang, Xiangji 851
Hwang, Jeong Hee 900

Iyer, Bala 43

Jakob, Mihály 779
Jampani, Ravindranath 761
Jiang, Chunyu 175
Jiang, Daxin 188
Jiang, Liangxiao 688
Jiang, Yongguang 576
Jiao, Enhua 113
Jin, Xiaoming 56
Jung, Min-Ok 151

Kalnis, Panos 201
Kamali, Shahab 588
Kang, Ji-Hoon 151
Kang, Tae Ho 875
Kim, Byung-Kyu 151
Kim, Jin-Deog 625

Kim, Seon Ho   461
Kitsuregawa, Masaru   276, 487
Koh, Jia-Ling   568
Kriegel, Hans-Peter   511, 748
Kumaran, A.   214
Kunath, Peter   748
Kwon, Dongseop   920

Lai, Pohsan   30
Lau, Ho-Lam   68, 81
Le, Jiajin   138
Lee, Byung Suk   95
Lee, Ken C.K.   612
Lee, Min-Woo   151
Lee, Mong Li   523, 649, 773
Lee, Sangjun   920
Lee, Seok Jae   875
Lee, Sukho   920
Lee, Yong-Hee   151
Lei, Shan   637
Leonardi, Erwin   711
Leong, Hong Va   612
Leong, Tzeyun   30
Li, Changqing   125, 582
Li, Chuan   576
Li, Deyi   3, 56
Li, Hua-Gang   662
Li, Jinyan   175
Li, Qing   816
Li, Shuai Cheng   4
Li, Xiaoguang   536
Li, Zhao   347
Liao, Guoqiong   863
Lin, Dan   600
Lin, Li   30
Ling, Tok Wang   113, 125, 311, 582, 773, 907
Liu, Greg   894
Liu, Mengchi   323
Liu, Ning-Han   240
Liu, Yunsheng   863
Loftis, Charles   548
Lu, Hongjun   422
Lu, Qin   612
Luo, Yi   816

Madria, Sanjay   711
Meng, Xiaofeng   828
Mehrotra, Sharad   43
Mitschang, Bernhard   779

Monemizadeh, Morteza   588
Moon, Sang-Ho   625

Nagargadde, Aparna   675
Navathe, Shamkant B.   288
Ng, Wee Kong   347
Ng, Wilfred   68, 81
Ngu, Anne H.H   253
Nguyen, Van Trang   900
Ni, Wei   907
Nicklas, Daniela   779
Nishio, Shojiro   300
Nørvåg, Kjetil   791
Nybø, Albert Overskeid   791

Oguchi, Masato   487

Park, Jong-Hyun   151
Park, Sang Chan   840
Park, Young-Ho   95
Pei, Jian   175, 188
Peng, Dunlu   359
Peng, Jing   576
Peng, Zhiyong   816
Pfeifle, Martin   748
Pokorný, Jaroslav   803
Prabhakar, Sunil   637
Prasad, Sushil K.   288
Pryakhin, Alexey   511
Pudi, Vikram   761
Pyon, Chong Un   840

Qian, Weining   435, 498
Qin, Shouke   435

Ramamritham, Krithi   675
Renz, Matthias   748
Ryu, Keun Ho   900

Schubert, Matthias   511
Shan, Zhe   816
Shen, Jialie   253
Shepherd, John   253
Skopal, Tomáš   803
Snášel, Vášclav   803
Song, Seok Il   875
Su, Jiang   688
Sun, Jianzhong   637
Sun, Jing   594
Sun, Weiwei   914
Suyoto, Iman S.H.   265

Tan, Kian-Lee   201, 600
Tang, Changjie   576
Tang, Shiwei   699
Tu, KeWei   888
Tung, Anthony K.H.   4

Uchida, Wataru   300
Uitdenbogerd, Alexandra L.   265

Varadarajan, Sridhar   675

Wang, Botao   276
Wang, Daling   536
Wang, Guoren   323, 398
Wang, Haixun   239
Wang, Jianmin   56
Wang, Junhu   335
Wang, Junmei   649
Wang, Wei   239
Wang, Xiaoling   359, 372
Wang, Xiaoyuan   914
Whang, Kyu-Young   95
Wong, Limsoon   30, 175
Woo, Ji Young   840
Wu, Sue-Shain   894
Wu, Yi-Hung   163, 240

Xi, Congting   138
Xia, Yuni   637
Xiao, Yingyuan   863
Xie, Wanxia   288
Xie, Zhipeng   523

Xu, Linhao   498
Xu, Qinying   385

Yamaguchi, Saneyasu   487
Yan, Feng   226
Yang, Dongqing   699
Yao, Qingsong   851
Yo, Pei-Wy   568
Yong, Xiaojia   576
Yoo, Jae Soo   875
Yu, Ge   398, 536
Yu, Jeffrey Xu   422
Yu, Philip S.   1
Yu, Yong   888

Zhang, Aidong   188
Zhang, Harry   688
Zhang, Ming   699
Zhang, Qing   523, 914
Zhang, Wang   276
Zhang, Wei   311
Zhang, Zhengjie   422
Zhang, Zhihao   56
Zhang, Zhiqiang   594
Zhao, Peixiang   699
Zhao, Qiankun   724
Zheng, Jason Xin   410
Zhou, Aoying   359, 372, 422, 435, 498
Zhou, Jing   612
Zhou, Shuigeng   498
Zhou, Xiangmin   398
Zhou, Xiaofang   385, 398
Zhu, Qiang   226
Zimmermann, Roger   461, 474

Lecture Notes in Computer Science

For information about Vols. 1–3346

please contact your bookseller or Springer

Vol. 3453: L. Zhou, B.C. Ooi, X. Meng (Eds.), Database Systems for Advanced Applications. XXVII, 929 pages. 2005.

Vol. 3452: F. Baader, A. Voronkov (Eds.), Logic for Programming, Artificial Intelligence, and Reasoning. XI, 562 pages. 2005. (Subseries LNAI).

Vol. 3450: D. Hutter, M. Ullmann (Eds.), Security in Pervasive Computing. XI, 239 pages. 2005.

Vol. 3449: F. Rothlauf, J. Branke, S. Cagnoni, D.W. Corne, R. Drechsler, Y. Jin, P. Machado, E. Marchiori, J. Romero, G.D. Smith, G. Squillero (Eds.), Applications on Evolutionary Computing. XX, 631 pages. 2005.

Vol. 3448: G.R. Raidl, J. Gottlieb (Eds.), Evolutionary Computation in Combinatorial Optimization. XI, 271 pages. 2005.

Vol. 3447: M. Keijzer, A. Tettamanzi, P. Collet, J.v. Hemert, M. Tomassini (Eds.), Genetic Programming. XIII, 382 pages. 2005.

Vol. 3444: M. Sagiv (Ed.), Programming Languages and Systems. XIII, 439 pages. 2005.

Vol. 3443: R. Bodik (Ed.), Compiler Construction. XI, 305 pages. 2005.

Vol. 3442: M. Cerioli (Ed.), Fundamental Approaches to Software Engineering. XIII, 373 pages. 2005.

Vol. 3441: V. Sassone (Ed.), Foundations of Software Science and Computational Structures. XVIII, 521 pages. 2005.

Vol. 3440: N. Halbwachs, L.D. Zuck (Eds.), Tools and Algorithms for the Construction and Analysis of Systems. XVII, 588 pages. 2005.

Vol. 3436: B. Bouyssounouse, J. Sifakis (Eds.), Embedded Systems Design. XV, 492 pages. 2005.

Vol. 3434: L. Brun, M. Vento (Eds.), Graph-Based Representations in Pattern Recognition. XII, 384 pages. 2005.

Vol. 3433: S. Bhalla (Ed.), Databases in Networked Information Systems. VII, 319 pages. 2005.

Vol. 3432: M. Beigl, P. Lukowicz (Eds.), Systems Aspects in Organic and Pervasive Computing - ARCS 2005. X, 265 pages. 2005.

Vol. 3431: C. Dovrolis (Ed.), Passive and Active Network Measurement. XII, 374 pages. 2005.

Vol. 3427: G. Kotsis, O. Spaniol, Wireless Systems and Mobility in Next Generation Internet. VIII, 249 pages. 2005.

Vol. 3423: J.L. Fiadeiro, P.D. Mosses, F. Orejas (Eds.), Recent Trends in Algebraic Development Techniques. VIII, 271 pages. 2005.

Vol. 3422: R.T. Mittermeir (Ed.), From Computer Literacy to Informatics Fundamentals. X, 203 pages. 2005.

Vol. 3421: P. Lorenz, P. Dini (Eds.), Networking - ICN 2005, Part II. XXXV, 1153 pages. 2005.

Vol. 3420: P. Lorenz, P. Dini (Eds.), Networking - ICN 2005, Part I. XXXV, 933 pages. 2005.

Vol. 3419: B. Faltings, A. Petcu, F. Fages, F. Rossi (Eds.), Constraint Satisfaction and Constraint Logic Programming. X, 217 pages. 2005. (Subseries LNAI).

Vol. 3418: U. Brandes, T. Erlebach (Eds.), Network Analysis. XII, 471 pages. 2005.

Vol. 3416: M. Böhlen, J. Gamper, W. Polasek, M.A. Wimmer (Eds.), E-Government: Towards Electronic Democracy. XIII, 311 pages. 2005. (Subseries LNAI).

Vol. 3415: P. Davidsson, B. Logan, K. Takadama (Eds.), Multi-Agent and Multi-Agent-Based Simulation. X, 265 pages. 2005. (Subseries LNAI).

Vol. 3414: M. Morari, L. Thiele (Eds.), Hybrid Systems: Computation and Control. XII, 684 pages. 2005.

Vol. 3412: X. Franch, D. Port (Eds.), COTS-Based Software Systems. XVI, 312 pages. 2005.

Vol. 3411: S.H. Myaeng, M. Zhou, K.-F. Wong, H.-J. Zhang (Eds.), Information Retrieval Technology. XIII, 337 pages. 2005.

Vol. 3410: C.A. Coello Coello, A. Hernández Aguirre, E. Zitzler (Eds.), Evolutionary Multi-Criterion Optimization. XVI, 912 pages. 2005.

Vol. 3409: N. Guelfi, G. Reggio, A. Romanovsky (Eds.), Scientific Engineering of Distributed Java Applications. X, 127 pages. 2005.

Vol. 3408: D.E. Losada, J.M. Fernández-Luna (Eds.), Advances in Information Retrieval. XVII, 572 pages. 2005.

Vol. 3407: Z. Liu, K. Araki (Eds.), Theoretical Aspects of Computing - ICTAC 2004. XIV, 562 pages. 2005.

Vol. 3406: A. Gelbukh (Ed.), Computational Linguistics and Intelligent Text Processing. XVII, 829 pages. 2005.

Vol. 3404: V. Diekert, B. Durand (Eds.), STACS 2005. XVI, 706 pages. 2005.

Vol. 3403: B. Ganter, R. Godin (Eds.), Formal Concept Analysis. XI, 419 pages. 2005. (Subseries LNAI).

Vol. 3401: Z. Li, L.G. Vulkov, J. Waśniewski (Eds.), Numerical Analysis and Its Applications. XIII, 630 pages. 2005.

Vol. 3399: Y. Zhang, K. Tanaka, J.X. Yu, S. Wang, M. Li (Eds.), Web Technologies Research and Development - APWeb 2005. XXII, 1082 pages. 2005.

Vol. 3398: D.-K. Baik (Ed.), Systems Modeling and Simulation: Theory and Applications. XIV, 733 pages. 2005. (Subseries LNAI).

Vol. 3397: T.G. Kim (Ed.), Artificial Intelligence and Simulation. XV, 711 pages. 2005. (Subseries LNAI).

Vol. 3396: R.M. van Eijk, M.-P. Huget, F. Dignum (Eds.), Agent Communication. X, 261 pages. 2005. (Subseries LNAI).

Vol. 3395: J. Grabowski, B. Nielsen (Eds.), Formal Approaches to Software Testing. X, 225 pages. 2005.

Vol. 3394: D. Kudenko, D. Kazakov, E. Alonso (Eds.), Adaptive Agents and Multi-Agent Systems III. VIII, 313 pages. 2005. (Subseries LNAI).

Vol. 3393: H.-J. Kreowski, U. Montanari, F. Orejas, G. Rozenberg, G. Taentzer (Eds.), Formal Methods in Software and Systems Modeling. XXVII, 413 pages. 2005.

Vol. 3391: C. Kim (Ed.), Information Networking. XVII, 936 pages. 2005.

Vol. 3390: R. Choren, A. Garcia, C. Lucena, A. Romanovsky (Eds.), Software Engineering for Multi-Agent Systems III. XII, 291 pages. 2005.

Vol. 3389: P. Van Roy (Ed.), Multiparadigm Programming in Mozart/OZ. XV, 329 pages. 2005.

Vol. 3388: J. Lagergren (Ed.), Comparative Genomics. VII, 133 pages. 2005. (Subseries LNBI).

Vol. 3387: J. Cardoso, A. Sheth (Eds.), Semantic Web Services and Web Process Composition. VIII, 147 pages. 2005.

Vol. 3386: S. Vaudenay (Ed.), Public Key Cryptography - PKC 2005. IX, 436 pages. 2005.

Vol. 3385: R. Cousot (Ed.), Verification, Model Checking, and Abstract Interpretation. XII, 483 pages. 2005.

Vol. 3383: J. Pach (Ed.), Graph Drawing. XII, 536 pages. 2005.

Vol. 3382: J. Odell, P. Giorgini, J.P. Müller (Eds.), Agent-Oriented Software Engineering V. X, 239 pages. 2005.

Vol. 3381: P. Vojtáš, M. Bieliková, B. Charron-Bost, O. Sýkora (Eds.), SOFSEM 2005: Theory and Practice of Computer Science. XV, 448 pages. 2005.

Vol. 3380: C. Priami, Transactions on Computational Systems Biology I. IX, 111 pages. 2005. (Subseries LNBI).

Vol. 3379: M. Hemmje, C. Niederee, T. Risse (Eds.), From Integrated Publication and Information Systems to Information and Knowledge Environments. XXIV, 321 pages. 2005.

Vol. 3378: J. Kilian (Ed.), Theory of Cryptography. XII, 621 pages. 2005.

Vol. 3377: B. Goethals, A. Siebes (Eds.), Knowledge Discovery in Inductive Databases. VII, 190 pages. 2005.

Vol. 3376: A. Menezes (Ed.), Topics in Cryptology – CT-RSA 2005. X, 385 pages. 2005.

Vol. 3375: M.A. Marsan, G. Bianchi, M. Listanti, M. Meo (Eds.), Quality of Service in Multiservice IP Networks. XIII, 656 pages. 2005.

Vol. 3374: D. Weyns, H.V.D. Parunak, F. Michel (Eds.), Environments for Multi-Agent Systems. X, 279 pages. 2005. (Subseries LNAI).

Vol. 3372: C. Bussler, V. Tannen, I. Fundulaki (Eds.), Semantic Web and Databases. X, 227 pages. 2005.

Vol. 3371: M.W. Barley, N. Kasabov (Eds.), Intelligent Agents and Multi-Agent Systems. X, 329 pages. 2005. (Subseries LNAI).

Vol. 3370: A. Konagaya, K. Satou (Eds.), Grid Computing in Life Science. X, 188 pages. 2005. (Subseries LNBI).

Vol. 3369: V.R. Benjamins, P. Casanovas, J. Breuker, A. Gangemi (Eds.), Law and the Semantic Web. XII, 249 pages. 2005. (Subseries LNAI).

Vol. 3368: L. Paletta, J.K. Tsotsos, E. Rome, G.W. Humphreys (Eds.), Attention and Performance in Computational Vision. VIII, 231 pages. 2005.

Vol. 3367: W.S. Ng, B.C. Ooi, A. Ouksel, C. Sartori (Eds.), Databases, Information Systems, and Peer-to-Peer Computing. X, 231 pages. 2005.

Vol. 3366: I. Rahwan, P. Moraitis, C. Reed (Eds.), Argumentation in Multi-Agent Systems. XII, 263 pages. 2005. (Subseries LNAI).

Vol. 3365: G. Mauri, G. Păun, M.J. Pérez-Jiménez, G. Rozenberg, A. Salomaa (Eds.), Membrane Computing. IX, 415 pages. 2005.

Vol. 3363: T. Eiter, L. Libkin (Eds.), Database Theory - ICDT 2005. XI, 413 pages. 2004.

Vol. 3362: G. Barthe, L. Burdy, M. Huisman, J.-L. Lanet, T. Muntean (Eds.), Construction and Analysis of Safe, Secure, and Interoperable Smart Devices. IX, 257 pages. 2005.

Vol. 3361: S. Bengio, H. Bourlard (Eds.), Machine Learning for Multimodal Interaction. XII, 362 pages. 2005.

Vol. 3360: S. Spaccapietra, E. Bertino, S. Jajodia, R. King, D. McLeod, M.E. Orlowska, L. Strous (Eds.), Journal on Data Semantics II. XI, 223 pages. 2005.

Vol. 3359: G. Grieser, Y. Tanaka (Eds.), Intuitive Human Interfaces for Organizing and Accessing Intellectual Assets. XIV, 257 pages. 2005. (Subseries LNAI).

Vol. 3358: J. Cao, L.T. Yang, M. Guo, F. Lau (Eds.), Parallel and Distributed Processing and Applications. XXIV, 1058 pages. 2004.

Vol. 3357: H. Handschuh, M.A. Hasan (Eds.), Selected Areas in Cryptography. XI, 354 pages. 2004.

Vol. 3356: G. Das, V.P. Gulati (Eds.), Intelligent Information Technology. XII, 428 pages. 2004.

Vol. 3355: R. Murray-Smith, R. Shorten (Eds.), Switching and Learning in Feedback Systems. X, 343 pages. 2005.

Vol. 3354: M. Margenstern (Ed.), Machines, Computations, and Universality. VIII, 329 pages. 2005.

Vol. 3353: J. Hromkovič, M. Nagl, B. Westfechtel (Eds.), Graph-Theoretic Concepts in Computer Science. XI, 404 pages. 2004.

Vol. 3352: C. Blundo, S. Cimato (Eds.), Security in Communication Networks. XI, 381 pages. 2005.

Vol. 3351: G. Persiano, R. Solis-Oba (Eds.), Approximation and Online Algorithms. VIII, 295 pages. 2005.

Vol. 3350: M. Hermenegildo, D. Cabeza (Eds.), Practical Aspects of Declarative Languages. VIII, 269 pages. 2005.

Vol. 3349: B.M. Chapman (Ed.), Shared Memory Parallel Programming with Open MP. X, 149 pages. 2005.

Vol. 3348: A. Canteaut, K. Viswanathan (Eds.), Progress in Cryptology - INDOCRYPT 2004. XIV, 431 pages. 2004.

Vol. 3347: R.K. Ghosh, H. Mohanty (Eds.), Distributed Computing and Internet Technology. XX, 472 pages. 2004.